CASES IN
INTERNATIONAL FINANCE

ry

the last

D1585777

WILEY SERIES IN FINANCE

Edwin J. Elton   /   Martin J. Gruber
New York University
Series Editors

Elton/Gruber: *Modern Portfolio Theory and Investment Analysis 4/e*
Gup: *The Basics of Investing 5/e*
Hempel/Coleman/Simonson: *Bank Management: Text and Cases 4/e*
Jones: *Investments 3/e*
Poniachek: *Case Studies in International Finance*
Sulock/Dunkelberg: *Cases in Financial Management*

CASES IN INTERNATIONAL FINANCE

Harvey A. Poniachek

New York University
Stern School of Business

JOHN WILEY & SONS, INC.

New York • Chichester • Brisbane • Toronto • Singapore

ACQUISITIONS EDITOR	Whitney Blake
PRODUCTION SUPERVISOR	Micheline Frederick
DESIGNER	Ann Marie Renzi
MANUFACTURING MANAGER	Andrea Price
COPY EDITING SUPERVISOR	Marjorie Shustak

Recognizing the importance of preserving what has been written, it is a policy of John Wiley & Sons, Inc. to have books of enduring value published in the United States printed on acid-free paper, and we exert our best efforts to that end.

Library of Congress Cataloging in Publication Data:

Poniachek, Harvey A.
  Cases in international finance/Harvey A. Poniachek
    p. cm.—(Wiley series in finance)
  Published simultaneously in Canada.
    ISBN 0-471-53678-4 (pbk. : alk. paper)
    1. International finance—Case studies. I. Title. II. Series.
HG3851.P64 1993
658.15′99—dc20   92-34519
                                                      CIP

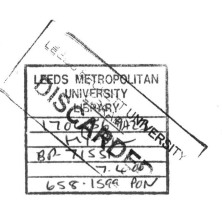

10 9 8 7 6 5 4 3 2 1

Dedicated to Shelley and Donna

Preface

In the past two decades, we have witnessed an accelerated progress toward the globalization of financial markets and a growing trend toward integration of the markets for goods and services. Through rapid technological advancement and other developments, financial products and services have proliferated throughout the world and across national borders, and the market for these products and services has become global.

Globalization of the financial markets has presented both multinational corporations, and corporations with extensive international business, with new challenges and opportunities, as well as considerable risk. In this environment, greater expertise and knowledge of international financial markets could enhance corporate management's effectiveness in positioning their corporation in an ever-competitive global marketplace.

This case book addresses financial management issues confronting multinational corporations and corporations with extensive international business. Through case studies that reflect the reality of functioning in the international marketplace, this book provides the student and executive reader an effective learning vehicle for the enhancement of international corporate financial management theory and application of analytical skills.

This book addresses a comprehensive set of issues that are commonly handled by the finance department of a multinational firm or a firm with extensive international business. Each case addresses specific issues that are typically encountered by corporate financial management and require decision making. Some cases are more complex and treat several issues, whereas other cases permit the narrow treatment of a select issue.

The case studies approach facilitates the reader's introduction to issues, information, and business circumstances that are commonly beyond the scope of standard textbooks on international corporate finance and international financial markets. An effort was made to develop case studies that contain attractive learning material—by selecting popular topics and providing interesting background information. Also, some cases contain extensive technical appendixes and references that introduce the reader to subject matter usually beyond the scope of standard texts.

The subjects addressed by the cases include the financial and capital markets, currency exposure and hedging, corporate funding and capital structure, international cash and working capital management, international portfolio management, international capital budgeting and direct foreign investment, international corporate taxation, and environmental analysis.

Many of the cases pertain to existing companies, and the problems described are actual business situations. However, the names and identities of some companies were disguised or changed for privacy. Most cases require point or range estimates, whereas a substantial number of cases are issue-oriented. Most cases require analysis and financial decision making for which sufficient information is provided in the case; in other cases, addressing the assignments requires additional data that can be obtained from outside sources.

The case book is divided into eight parts, each of which focuses on specific issues of international corporate financial management. Parts are organized as follows:

- Part I addresses the financial markets and financial transactions. Subjects addressed include the currency market, traditional and new financial instruments, and issues concerning pricing, cost, and risk.
- Part II deals with the subject of currency and price exposure and hedging.
- Part III addresses decision making concerning corporate funding and the capital structure of the firm.
- Part IV deals with international cash and working capital management.
- Part V addresses international portfolio investment.
- Part VI involves capital budgeting and direct foreign investment. International investment has assumed a significant role in international business and finance; direct foreign investment has been occurring through cross-border mergers and acquisitions.
- Part VII requires decisions concerning pricing of international intercompany transactions and international corporate taxation.
- Part VIII involves environmental analysis, including the assessment of risk and opportunities that are crucial to success in international business.

The entire case book is obviously beyond the scope of one semester. The cases lend themselves to homework assignments and classroom discussions in conjunction with the theoretical material covered in the course itself. Instructors can choose cases that correspond to the textbook material addressed in the classroom; alternatively, following a brief review of the theoretical issues, cases can be assigned and discussed in class. The cases in this book are powerful enough to require students to refer to their textbook for the principles and theory, and they require students to reach decisions on issues confronting the corporation.

The cases have benefited from the author's years of teaching and corporate experience, and from the contributing authors' diverse backgrounds and corporate and university affiliations.

Acknowledgments

A number of reviewers provided helpful suggestions as these cases were developed. I would like to thank the following for their insightful suggestions and comments: Azmi D. Mikhail, Ohio University; M. Anaam Hashmi, Mankato State University; Alfred Lubell, SUNY–Oneonta; James C. Baker, Kent State University; Andrea DeMaskey, University of Nevada Reno; Farhad F. Ghannadian, Mercer University; Ann M. Hackert, Idaho State University; Susan A. Block, University of California Santa Barbara.

Harvey A. Poniachek

Contents

Introduces an introductory discussion of the tax law related to foreign tax credit in the post-1986 Tax Reform Act. Requires a comparative analysis between Mobil and Ford Motor Corporation's international tax positions.

VIII ENVIRONMENTAL ISSUES AND ANALYSIS

CASES IN
INTERNATIONAL FINANCE

Atlantic Financial Services, Ltd.

Currency Rate Projections

HARVEY A. PONIACHEK

John Smith is a vice president and manager of the Atlantic Financial Services, Ltd. (AFS), international treasury advisory services at the company's Stamford, Connecticut office. In an effort to acquire new corporate business, Mr. Smith set out to assess the potential need for international treasury services of several *Fortune 100* companies, including General Electric Company (GE). As an expert on currency projection who formerly served at AFS's offices at Houston and who is often quoted in the financial press, he emphasized their possible need for reliable currency forecasts and advisory services. Mr. Smith reviewed several annual reports and trade associations literature for the prospective companies, including those of GE.

General Electric Company International Business

General Electric Company operates 13 businesses that include durable consumer goods, power systems, financial services, communications, and others.[1] GE's 1990 sales reached

[1]According to the company's 1990 Annual Report, GE's 13 businesses include aerospace, aircraft engines, appliances, financial services, industrial and power systems, lighting, medical systems, NBC, plastics, communications and services, electrical distribution and control, motors, and transportation systems.

$58.4 billion and net earnings were $4.3 billion.

GE's revenues from international transactions (through U.S. exports and from local operations abroad) reached $15.4 billion in 1990, or 26.4% of its total. Revenues from entities outside the United States were $9.2 billion in 1990 or approximately 60% of GE's total international revenues; and operating profit was approximately $0.9 billion or over 11% of its worldwide operating profit. Assets outside the United States were approximately $16.5 billion or over 10% of GE's total worldwide assets.

GE is emphasizing its leadership position in Western Europe, Asia-Pacific, and Canada. The company is laying the groundwork for participation in the emerging markets of India, the Soviet Union, Eastern Europe, and Mexico.

In 1990, GE exports from the U.S. totaled almost $6 billion, with Europe accounting for 41%, the Pacific Basin for 31%, the Americas for 13%, and other areas for 15% of total exports.

The Objective and the Methodology

Mr. Smith set the stage for the preparation of currency projections for several important currencies that could benefit his targeted clients, by applying one or several of the following

1

approaches:

1. Monetary/Assets Price Theories,
2. The PPP (bilateral and/or multilateral indexes),
3. Forward exchange rates, and
4. Ad hoc models.

Information and Sources of Data

Mr. Smith and his team reviewed several sources of data that were put together by their corporate librarian and economics department. The information included a survey on currency determination, available in Appendix 1-1, and a brief bibliography of available data sources.

Data Sources

1. International Monetary Fund (IMF), *International Financial Statistics* (IFS), economic and financial data for all member countries.
2. IMF/IFS foreign exchange rate data (spot, forward, effective exchange rates), and interest rates.

3. Morgan Guaranty, *"World Financial Markets,"* information on real and real effective exchange rates, and data on interest rates.

The Assignment

Mr. Smith instructed you, his new assistant, to prepare a five-year currency outlook from December 1985 through December 1990 for the sterling, mark, yen, Mexican peso, and Korean won exchange rates. You joined AFS several months ago following your graduation from the University of Chicago, where you earned an MBA in corporate finance and international business. You spent the past two summers as an intern in the currency trading rooms of two major money center banks in Chicago and New York. This assignment suited your interest and provided an excellent opportunity to distinguish yourself.

More specifically, you were asked to prepare long-term projections for year-end 1990 on the basis of information that was available at the end of 1985. Check the accuracy of the forecasts by examining several years later.

You were also asked to prepare quarterly projections for each currency during the 1985 through 1990 period.

APPENDIX 1-1

The Determination of Exchange Rates

Foreign currencies and currency rates play a significant role in international financial management, particularly for companies with foreign subsidiaries and foreign currency denominated transactions. Projecting currency rates is both a significant and difficult task because many factors affect the exchange rates. This appendix provides a framework for exchange rate assessment and forecasting.

The international monetary system has undergone profound changes in the past two decades. The fixed exchange rate regime of the Bretton Woods system was abolished and replaced by a heterogeneous system of fixed and flexible exchange rates. Since early 1973 the major currencies are floating, have no central par values, and are determined primarily by market forces. However, most currencies are pegged in terms of a major currency, or specially designed baskets of currencies or special drawing right (SDR). Under the present exchange rate system, exchange volatility of the major currencies increased dramatically. Experience to date with floating exchange rates reveals the following characteristics:[1]

1. Month-to-month variability in bilateral spot exchange rates is frequently large and unpredictable.

2. There is a strong positive correlation between spot and (contemporaneous) forward exchange rates. (However, during the early 1980s for many currencies the forward premium or discount on the dollar has tended to systematically mispredict the dollar exchange rate during the subsequent month, probably due to the existence of a risk premium.)

3. Short-term variability of nominal exchange rates has been significantly greater than the variability of relative national price levels.

4. The variability of nominal and real exchange rates differs across alternative national exchange rate systems.

Types of Currency Transaction and Exchange Rates

Spot foreign exchange transaction involves a contract for immediate delivery within 1 business day for exchange between North American currencies and 2 business days elsewhere. Forward exchange transaction involves contracts for delivery of currencies at a future date, where the standard maturities are available for 1, 2, 3, 6, and 12 months. For the major currencies, forward transactions are available for longer maturities, up to several years.

Exchange rates can be measured or expressed in several ways. The most common concept of currency rate is the bilateral exchange rate or the nominal exchange rate, which expresses the number of units of one currency per one unit of another currency (e.g., 135 yen per 1 dollar). Each country has as many bilateral foreign exchange rates or exchange rates as foreign currencies, and these exchange rates in turn imply cross-exchange rates between currencies. By using nominal bilateral exchange rates, one can translate foreign denominated financial transactions into the home currency or any other currency.

Real exchange rate is the nominal exchange rate adjusted for price level differences across countries. It measures the relative price of foreign goods in terms of domestic goods. Exchange rates are also expressed in terms of weighted baskets or composites, such as European Currency Unit (ECU) or the SDR.

The effective exchange rate measures the value of a currency on the basis of a weighted average of bilateral exchange rates. An effective or a weighted-average index involves the multiplication of index numbers by weights and a summation of these components. Several types of trade weighted averages are used, the most frequent being the bilateral and multilateral weighting schemes. Bilateral weights measure each country's share of the country's total exports plus imports. The multilateral weights measure the shares of each country in the aggregate trade of all foreign countries included in the effective exchange rate index.

The effective exchange rate is an index that shows the change in any currency against its major trading partners. It measures a currency's performance in relation to other currencies and reflects trends in international competiveness. Effective exchange rates have gained broad acceptance in formulation of official exchange rate policy.

[1]Jane Marrinan, "Exchange Rate Determination: Sorting out Theory and Evidence," *New England Economic Review*, Federal Reserve Bank of Boston, Nov.–Dec. 1989, pp. 39–51.

The real effective exchange rate is derived by adjusting the effective exchange rate by the effective inflation rate differentials (i.e., inflation differentials weighted by the same weights that are used in deriving the effective exchange rates). Several institutions issue effective and real effective exchange rates, including Morgan Guaranty Trust Company, the International Monetary Fund, the Federal Reserve Bank and others. However, these rates are based on different weighting schemes and often on different currencies. The effective exchange rate measures the value of a currency on a multilateral basis, its overall value in the market, and the overall competitiveness of a country's goods on the international markets.

The Framework of Exchange Rate Determination

Currency rate determination is a complex and interactive process that can be explained by the various factors that affect international transactions in goods, services, and financial assets, as well as by domestic monetary and financial conditions and expectations. Foreign exchange rate policy and intervention are widespread and play a significant role in exchange rate determination in the short run. There is no consensus in the literature and among practitioners on how exchange rates are determined. There is no one generally accepted theory or model of exchange rate determination; instead several main approaches or theories provide a general framework for analysis of exchange rates. These theories can be classified along the following features:

1. THE TRADITIONAL APPROACH. The traditional approach of exchange rate determination emphasizes developments in the goods market—the current account of the balance of payments, and the significance of relative prices and international competi-

tiveness, that is, purchasing power parity (PPP).

2. THE MONETARY AND ASSET MARKET THEORIES. The monetary and (financial) asset-market theories of exchange rate determination emphasize developments in the financial sector and include several versions: the monetary approach to (the balance of payments and) exchange rate determination; the quantity theory models; the (financial) asset-market theories of exchange rate determination; and the PPP theory.

3. THE GENERAL EQUILIBRIUM AND PORTFOLIO BALANCE THEORIES OF EXCHANGE RATES. This approach maintains that the exchange rate is determined within the general equilibrium of the economy, by the interaction of the real and monetary sectors.

4. ALTERNATIVE THEORIES. Additional or alternative theories or hypotheses of exchange rate determination are either derived from or based on the preceding approaches, or are formulated in reduced forms, usually based on single or multiple variables or factors, explaining exchange rate behavior.

The various theories of exchange rate determination, however, can be reconciled, for example, in terms of the time horizon that they are addressing (i.e., short, medium, and long). The short-term view of the exchange rate emphasizes the role of financial assets (or money), market equilibrium, expectations, the high degree of substitutability between assets denominated in different currencies, and a high degree of capital mobility. Some models view the exchange rate mainly in terms of its short-term effects on expectations and international capital flows, and its long-term effect on competitiveness. A long-term view of exchange rate determination is formulated in terms of monetary and real factors, in which the critical assumptions are that real as well as monetary factors are important in determining the behavior of exchange rates, and the purchasing power parity restores equilibrium in traded goods and the monetary sectors.

The Traditional Approach

The traditional approach of exchange rate determination is based on the Keynesian economic theory. This approach considers foreign exchange rates as prices that clear supply of and demand for goods in international transactions and, in turn, in foreign exchange markets, in a process that simultaneously determines many other variables in the economy. More specifically, this approach[2] maintains that:

1. The exchange rate is the relative price of national goods, rather than the relative price of national monies.
2. Changes in exchange rates modify relative prices and international competitiveness.
3. The current account of the balance payments is a major determinant of exchange rate variations.
4. Exchange rates adjust to balance receipts and payments arising from international transactions. Demand for foreign exchange is considered as a derived demand, representing the other side of the coin of demand and supply for international goods and services.

---

[2]M. Mussa, "The Theory of Flexible Exchange Rate Regimes and Macroeconomic Policy," in J. A. Frenkel and H. G. Johnson (eds.), *The Economics of Exchange Rates*, Addison-Wesley, Reading, MA, 1978. M. Mussa, "The Exchange Rate, the Balance of Payments and Monetary and Fiscal Policy under a Regime of Controlled Floating," in J. A. Frenkel and H. G. Johnson (eds.), *The Economics of Exchange Rates*, Addison-Wesley, Reading, MA, 1978. M. Mussa, *The Role of Official Intervention*, Occasional Papers 6, Group of Thirty, New York, 1981. A. Crockett, "Determinants of Exchange Rate Movements: A Review," *Finance and Development*, March 1982.

5. Deteriorating balance of trade (or current account) deficits (i.e., excess supplies of domestic exchange) are likely to lead to exchange rate depreciation; while improving conditions (excess demand for foreign exchange) have the opposite effect. In a sense, the exchange market is always in equilibrium, whereby supply and demand are always balanced at a going price.

The current account of the balance of payments does not explain exchange rate developments very satisfactorily.[3] Most of the short-term variations in exchange rates have little to do with balance of payments performance, and even over longer periods of time the relationship is loose.[4] Under the flexible exchange rate system, the flow of international capital funds assumed a greater role in exchange rate determination, thus reducing the appropriateness of the traditional theory of exchange rates.

An alternative interpretation of the traditional approach considers the exchange rate determination in the context of the entire balance of payments. According to this interpretation, the current account is affected by relative prices, whereas the capital account is influenced by interest rate differentials and currency expectations. The exchange rate equation can be expressed in the context of the entire balance of payments in the following manner:

$$S = a(Pd - Pf) + b(Yd - Yf) - c(Rd - Rf)$$

where S is the spot exchange rate, Pd and Pf are domestic and foreign inflation rates, Yd and Yf are domestic and foreign real GNP growth rates, Rd and Rf are domestic and foreign interest rates, and a, b, and c are coefficients. Higher domestic inflation than abroad causes a deterioration of the exchange

---

[3]Crockett, ibid.

[4]Ibid.

rate. A higher domestic growth rate than abroad leads to import expansion and a decline of the current account, which in turn leads to a depreciation of the exchange rate. A higher domestic interest rate than abroad leads to an appreciation of the exchange rate (i.e., the numerical value of S declines in a directly quoted currency rate, because it takes less of the local currency to acquire one foreign currency).

Purchasing Power Parity (PPP)

A critical feature of the PPP theory is that the exchange rate equates the price of traded goods in common currency in different countries and one price prevails everywhere. The purchasing power parity theory maintains that any divergence of the exchange rate from the equilibrium price levels in different countries will set in motion corrective forces to restore equilibrium over time. Alternatively, the PPP theory maintains that exchange rate changes would offset over time divergent movements in national price levels. Accordingly, a country that experiences higher inflation will experience a corresponding depreciation of its currency, while a country with a lower inflation rate will experience an appreciation.

If one assumes that the causal mechanism runs from prices to exchange rates, then exchange rate developments can be partly explained in terms of relative movements in price indexes. The PPP theory can be stated as follows:

Expected Exchange rate change

   = Rate of change in relative price levels

or

Expected exchange rate change

   = Expected inflation rate differential

The PPP theory has two versions. In its absolute version the theory states that the equilibrium exchange rate between domestic and foreign currencies would be that which equates prices everywhere (i.e., the law of one price is assumed perfect commodity market arbitrage).

The absolute PPP version contends that any change in the exchange rate between two currencies just equals the difference in their inflation rates. If eo is the current equilibrium exchange rate (domestic per foreign currency), Ph is the home currency price level, and Pf is the foreign price level, then $eo = Ph/Pf$ or $Pfeo = Ph$; that is, a unit of home currency should have the same purchasing power worldwide. Since PPP predicts that percentage changes in exchange rates are completely explained by differences in national inflation rates, an increase, for example, in the expected inflation in the United States will generate an expectation that the dollar will depreciate.[5] The exchange rate would tend to fall in exactly the same proportion as the price level rose. Thus if prices in Germany doubled while U.S prices remained unchanged, the value of the mark would be just half of what it was previously.

The relative version of the PPP theory relate equilibrium changes in exchange rates to changes in the ratio of domestic to foreign prices. The relative hypothesis state that the exchange rate between the currencies of any pair of countries should be a constant multiple of the ratio of general price indexes of the two countries, or equivalently, that percentage changes in the exchange rate should equal percentage changes in the ratio of the price index. Stated algebraically, if $Ph(t)$ and $Pf(t)$ are the home and foreign price levels at time t, and $Ph(o)$ and $Pf(o)$ are the home and foreign price levels at the initial period, and et and eo are the exchange rates (home currency per foreign currency) at time t and the

[5]Marrinan, op. cit.

base period,

$$\frac{et}{eo} = \frac{Ph(t)/Ph(o)}{Pf(t)/Pf(o)}$$

The above equation suggests that the spot rate at t is determined by the relative (domestic and foreign) price change over the two time periods and the initial spot exchange rate at time o. The above equation can be restated by substituting ih,t and if,t for expected home and foreign inflation as follows:[6]

$$\frac{Ph(t)}{Ph(o)} = 1 + ih,t$$

and

$$\frac{Pf(t)}{Pf(o)} = 1 + if,t$$

Then, by further substitution the relative PPP version can be stated as follows:

$$\frac{et}{eo} = \frac{ih,t - if,t}{1 + if,t}$$

The relative PPP version can be simplified and restated as follows:

$$\frac{et - eo}{eo} = ih,t - if,t$$

The real exchange rate is the nominal exchange rate adjusted for changes in relative purchasing power of each currency.

While high-inflation countries usually experience a depreciation in their exchange rates and the PPP theory holds over a long period of time, the PPP theory does not explain satisfactorily short-term movements in exchange rates.[7] Most observers of PPP conclude that the theory does not hold up except in a very loose and approximate fashion and the matching between inflation differentials and depreciation is not very close. The usefulness of the PPP model in estimating divergences between the actual exchange rate depends on the choice of a base period, the choice of the relevant price indexes, and the projection of the price indexes for the forecast period.[8]

The above shortcomings suggest that the PPP can be considered as a reduced form formulation of exchange rate determination that specifies a relationship between two endogenous variables—exchange rate and inflation—without providing the details of the process that brings about such a relationship.[9] Therefore, it should not be viewed as a theory of exchange rate determination.

The Monetary and Asset-Market Approach

The Monetary Approach

The monetary theory of exchange rate determination emphasizes the role of markets for money and securities in the currency rate determination process; views the exchange rate as a relative price of two national assets or monies rather than relative prices of different

[6]Alan C. Shapiro, *Multinational Financial Management*, Third Edition, Allyn & Bacon, Boston, MA, 1989, pp. 155–158. Richard M. Levich, "Evaluation of Exchange Rate Forecasting," in Robert Z. Aliber, ed., *The Handbook of International Financial Management*, Dow Jones-Irwin, Homewood, IL, 1989, Ch. 15. Alan C. Shapiro, *Foundations of Multinational Financial Management*, Allyn & Bacon, Boston, MA, 1991.

[7]Crockett, op. cit.

[8]J. R. Artus, "Methods of Assessing the Longer Run Equilibrium Value of an Exchange Rate," *Finance and Development*, June 1978.

[9]M. Michaely, "Analyses of Devaluation, Purchasing Power Parity, Elasticities, and Absorption," in D. Bigman and T. Taya (eds.), *The Functioning of Floating Exchange Rates; Theory, Evidence, and Policy Implications*, Ballinger, Cambridge, MA, 1980.

national output, determined primarily by the demand for and supply of the stocks of various national monies and expectations; considers the exchange rate as endogenously determined by stock equilibrium conditions in markets for national monies; and maintains that the equilibrium currency rate is attained when the existing stocks of the two national monies are willingly held.

The monetary approach of exchange rate determination—a subset of the broader, more general asset-market view of exchange rate determination—involves several assertions.

1. Exchange rate fluctuations are largely explained in terms of variation in the relative supplies of and demand for national money stocks, which, in turn, could be used to forecast exchange rates.

2. The exchange rate determination could be explained in the context of the quantity theory of money and the purchasing power parity theory. Each country's demand and supply for money determines its price level, and the prices in each country are linked by the exchange rate, assuming that goods prices are flexible and international arbitrage is efficient and assures one price of similar goods around the world.

3. In the short run the exchange rate is determined by the supply of and demand for financial assets, because they adjust more quickly to a monetary disturbance than the goods market. In the long run the domestic inflation rate is a monetary phenomenon, and the relative national price levels are a dominant factor in determining the exchange rate between two currencies (purchasing power parity theory).

In the monetary model the monetary authorities can affect the foreign exchange market by altering the relative money stock growth rates and relative rates of return on financial assets. (However, the exchange rate is not only a purely monetary phenomenon but is also affected by real factors that effect the demand for money.)

The monetary theory of exchange rate determination makes several significant assumptions about the market environment.

1. There are free capital markets and perfect capital mobility, which imply perfect substitutability between foreign and domestic assets denominated in different currencies.

2. Asset holders' expectations of future exchange rates strongly affect rates.

3. An efficient market prevails in which opportunities for profit are eliminated and market price expectations are unbiased predictors of actual future prices.

4. There are perfect arbitrage conditions.

Under free and efficient markets, future spot exchange rates, interest rates and inflation differentials, and forward discounts and premiums are simultaneously determined and their (theoretical) relationships are defined as follows:

1. Interest rate parity,
2. Purchasing power parity,
3. The Fisher effect,
4. The international Fisher effect, and
5. The forward rate as an unbiased predictor of future spot rate.

The monetary approach as a currency rate forecasting model (in logarithm form) can be expressed as follows:[10]

$$s = (m - m^*) + n(y^* - y)$$
$$+ (k^* - k) + a(i - i^*)$$

where m and m^* are the domestic and foreign money supply, y and y^* are the domestic and

[10]Richard M. Levich, "Exchange Rate and Currency Exposure," Part 2, Sec. 12, in Edward I. Altman (ed.), *Financial Handbook*, Fifth Edition, Wiley, New York, 1981, pp. 476–477.

foreign real GNP, k and k^* stand for structural economic changes at home and abroad, and i and i^* are the nominal domestic and foreign interest rates. The above equation states that relative changes (between two or more countries) in the money supply, GNP, structural characteristics and interest rate will affect their exchange rate.

Forward Exchange Rate as a Predictor of Future Spot

The forward exchange rate (e.g., $/sterling), F, is usually different from the spot exchange rate, S, with the difference being attributed to interest rate differentials between the two countries (e.g., the U.S. and the U.K.). The high interest rate country is usually at a forward discount and the lower interest country is at a forward premium.

The annualized forward premium or discount for directly quoted currencies (i.e., U.S. dollars per one foreign currency) can be expressed as follows:

Forward premium of discount

$$= \frac{F - S}{S} \times 100 \times \frac{12}{n}$$

or for indirectly quoted currencies (i.e., foreign currency per one U.S. dollar), the annualized forward premium or discount can be derived as follows:

Forward premium or discount

$$= \frac{S - F}{F} \times 100 \times \frac{12}{n}$$

where F is the forward rate, S is the spot rate, n is the maturity expressed in the number of months of the forward contract, and $12/n$ is the annualization of the forward premium or discount.

In the monetary models, the forward rate is the unbiased, efficient expectation of the future spot rate. According to the interest rate parity theory (IRPT) the interest rate differential must equal the expected change in the spot rate. The IRPT provides a link between interest rate differentials, the spot and forward exchange rates and the expectations of speculators.[11]

Interest Rate Parity Theory

The interest rate parity theory states that interest rate differential between two countries equals their forward discount or premium, as follows:[12]

$$\frac{Iu.s. - Iu.k.}{1 + Iu.k.} = \frac{F - S}{S}$$

where $Iu.s.$ and $Iu.k.$ are the interest rates in the United States and United Kingdom, F and S are the forward and spot exchange rates.

If rh,t and rf,t are the interest rates at home and abroad (e.g., the United States and the United Kingdom), then investing one dollar in New York will yield $1 + rh,t$ at the end of t periods. The same dollar invested in London will be worth $(1 + rf,t)ft/eo$ dollars at maturity.

One dollar will convert into $1/eo$ pounds that at rf,t will yield $(1 + rf,t)/eo$. By selling the proceeds forward today, this amount will be worth $(1 + rf,t)ft/eo$ dollars at maturity.

Funds will flow from New York to London if

$$(1 + rf,t)\frac{ft}{eo} > 1 + rh,t$$

[11]Richard Baillie and Patrick McMahon, *The Foreign Exchange Market: Theory and Econometric Evidence*, Cambridge University Press, Cambridge, 1989, pp. 151–152.

[12]Adrian Buckley, *Multinational Finance*, Philip Allan Publishers Limited, Oxford, 1986.

By subtracting $1 + rf, t$ from both sides of the equation and substituting D for the forward differential $(eo - ft)/eo$, the above inequality reduces to

$$rf, t - rh, t < D + rf, tD$$

Interest rate parity holds when there are no covered interest arbitrage opportunities, which holds under the following circumstances:

$$\frac{1 + rh, t}{1 + rf, t} = \frac{ft}{eo}$$

or

$$rf, t - rh, t = D + rf, tD$$

Interest rate parity can be approximated as follows:

$$rf, t - rh, t = \frac{eo - ft}{eo}$$

where

$$rf, t - rh, t = D$$

There are three arguments suggesting that the forward rate is a biased predictor. First, the forward rate may be influenced by official intervention; second, the forward rate may reflect a risk premium as well as exchange rate expectations (much the same as an interest rate can include a liquidity or risk premium); and third, expectations themselves may be weakly held or very imprecise. The forecasting accuracy of the forward rate is an extremely important question, but one that remains unsettled, given the empirical research to date.[13] The forward exchange rate as a forecaster of future spot can be examined in terms of its error term, et, where S_{t+n} is the future spot

rate and F_t is the forward rate:

$$et = S_{t+n} - F_t$$

When et is small or not statistically different from zero, the forward exchange rate is considered an unbiased predictor of the future spot.

The relationship between forward rate F_t and the future spot rate S_{t+n} suggests that the forward rate may offer reasonable prediction ability.[14]

1. The forward rate is an unbiased predictor of the future spot rate. The average forecast error is approximately zero, and in most cases the serial correlation of forecast errors is also zero. In a linear regression, variation in F_t generally explains more than 90 percent of the variation in S_{t+n}.

2. The forward premium $(F_t - S_{t+n})/S_{t+n}$ is an unbiased predictor of the future exchange rate change $(S_{t+1} - S_t)/S_t$; however, it is a poor predictor in the following sense: in a linear regression, variation in $(F - S)/S$ generally explains less than 10 percent of the variation in $(S_{t+1} - S_t)/S$. This suggests that the bulk of the short-run exchange rate changes are dominated by unanticipated events (i.e., news) and that the forward premium sits roughly in the middle of a wide distribution of exchange rate expectations.

3. Empirical studies do not support the existence of a positive risk premium in forward contracts. This may be because the premium actually is zero, the premium is too small to measure in the limited history of floating, or the premium changes signs and averages near zero.

4. Adding variables beyond the current forward rate may improve our ability to fit a regression equation explaining S_{t+1}. But in postsample comparisons, the forward rate

---

[13] Levich, 1981, op. cit.

[14] Ibid.

by itself generally has better predictive ability.

The exchange rate determination with interest rates can be expressed in the following formulary equations:

$$S = a(Md - Mf) - b(Yd - Yf) + c(Rd - Rf)$$

where S is the spot exchange rate (directly quoted), Md and Mf are the domestic and foreign money stocks, Yd and Yf are the domestic and foreign growth of real GNP, and Rd and Rf are domestic and foreign interest rates.

The Asset-Market Approach

The asset-market approach considers the exchange rate as the relative price of two national monies, or two assets, of which the price of a particular currency is determined mainly by the relative supplies of and demand for these monies or assets.[15] Alternatively, the exchange rate represents an equilibrium between the desire to hold assets denominated in that currency and the available supply of such assets.

Since the demands for the various assets denominated in national monies depend on expectations, incomes, rates of return thereof, as well as on other considerations, this approach is commonly referred to as "an asset-market approach" to the determination of exchange rates.[16] In this respect exchange rates are similar to stock prices, long-term bond prices and the prices of commodities traded on organized exchanges.[17]

The main principles of the asset-market approach suggest that the exchange rate can be best analyzed within a context that is appropriate for the analysis of asset prices, and the techniques for determining its price should be closely related to other financial assets. Like other asset prices, exchange rates are affected by an integrated process that includes[18] changes in supply of and demand for money and financial assets: economic and financial conditions and developments (e.g., interest rate, inflation, etc.), monetary and fiscal policy; market expectations; and efficient market behavior (where new information concerning the future is reflected immediately in current prices, thereby precluding unexploited profit opportunities from arbitrage).[19] Prices in the assets market are considered to adjust very quickly and (rational) expectations play a central role in the determination of equilibrium. Goods markets are important in varying degrees, although they are generally kept in the background.[20]

The theory implies that the exchange rate, like the prices of other assets, is much more sensitive to expectations concerning future events than the national price level. At times exchange rates demonstrate random fluctuations in response to new information that modifies the expectations of the markets about conditions that could influence exchange rates. Indeed, in periods that are dominated by news that alters expectations, exchange rates are likely to be much more volatile than national price indexes, and departures from PPP are likely.

The asset-market theory of exchange rate determination does not deny that there is a demand for currency for transactions for goods

[15]J. A. Frenkel, "A Monetary Approach to the Exchange Rate: Doctrinal Aspects and Empirical Evidence," in J. A. Frenkel and H. G. Johnson (eds.), *The Economics of Exchange Rules*, Addison-Wesley, Reading, MA, 1978.

[16]Ibid.

[17]Frenkel and Mussa, 1980, p. 375.

[18]Mussa, op. cit.

[19]Frenkel, "Monetary Approach," op. cit.

[20]Jeffrey R. Shafer and Bonnie E. Loopesko, "Floating Exchange Rates After Ten Years," *Brookings Papers on Economic Activity*, 1:1983.

and services. However, the stock of financial assets is large relative to the volume of money in circulation or transaction balances needed for current transactions. Furthermore, since assets can be exchanged relatively easily, while it takes time to benefit from improved international competitiveness in trade, it is likely that factors influencing the attractiveness of different assets to hold will, in the short run, play the greater role in determining exchange rate movements.[21]

Analysis of exchange rates must consider the factors affecting the demand for and supply of money. For instance, an increase in the expected inflation rate would decrease the attractiveness of holding domestic money relative to holding foreign money, implying a tendency for domestic money to depreciate in terms of foreign exchange.[22]

The exchange rate can be affected by monetary policy and the market's expectations of its future course. Modifications in policies or expectations thereof could induce shifts in the demand for assets denominated in different currencies. A significant factor that affects the relative attractiveness of currencies is interest rates. The relationship between exchange and interest rates is not tight.

The asset-market approach is mainly relevant for countries that have well-developed capital and money markets coupled with relatively free exchange markets where arbitrage between domestic and foreign assets is allowed. In countries where such arbitrage is limited or nonexistent, the exchange rate is determined by supply and demand in goods markets and official intervention.

There are several versions of the asset-market approach. The flexible-price asset-market model describes the exchange rate as the relative price of two monies. The model asserts that the money market determines the price levels in the two countries, and one world price prevails for goods, which implies purchasing power parity conditions. Under the assumptions of price inflexibility, exchange rate expectations would deviate from PPP equilibrium as long as it took goods prices to adjust fully to new monetary conditions and restore equilibrium in the goods market. The PPP becomes a long-run phenomenon.

If one country has a higher monetary growth and a higher expected inflation rate, its interest rate is expected to be higher but exactly offset by an expected depreciation of its exchange rate. Thus, uncovered interest rate parity implies that the expected rate of return on interest rate bearing assets denominated in different exchange rates be equal. In this model the exchange depreciation is equal to the difference in inflation rates between the two countries.

Expectations

In the monetary and asset-market framework of exchange rate determination, expectations play a crucial role. The market participants are assumed to have rational expectations, which means that they form expectations on the basis of all information, including any available information on the probable future actions of policy makers.[23] A rational expectation is a conditional average over a number of possible values that the variable can take. The rational expectations hypothesis became popular during the 1970s, evolving into the dominant hypothesis concerning expectation formulation.

There are two basic assumptions of the rational expectations theory—one is of continuous market-clearing equilibrium and the second is of the specification of imperfections and

[21] Frenkel, "Monetary Approach," op. cit.

[22] Mussa, "Official Intervention," op. cit.

[23] R. Gordon, *Macroeconomics*, 2nd ed.

asymmetries in the information on which market participants form expectations.[24]

The implications of rational expectations depend on the type of market. The rational expectations approach is particularly valid for auction markets (e.g., the New York Stock Exchange) but it does apply to other markets. In auction markets, where prices are free to fluctuate from day to day and hour to hour, all available information is already incorporated into these prices, including anticipation about likely government policy.

There is no consensus on the correct interpretation of rational expectations and the views associated with it are still in the process of evolution.[25] In the rational expectations framework, real variables should be viewed as being based on all information available to the market participants at a cost justified by the value of the information. This is a common element of all hypotheses involving rationality of expectations.[26]

Changes in current rates bring about an adjustment process that depends on the differential speeds of adjustment in the goods and money markets. The adjustment that occurs is in response to actual and anticipated events. Future spot exchange rates depend on the expected future values of the exogenous factors affecting it. Changes in expectations of future exogenous variables are brought by new information that, in turn, affects the exchange market. One of the critical variables influencing asset holders' expectations of future exchange rates is their outlook of the future growth of money supply of various countries.

Fiscal policy is also likely to influence the exchange rate and expectations about the exchange rate, since budget deficits are often financed by the central bank.[27]

The demand for domestic and foreign money and assets depends on the expected rates of return, which in turn could affect exchange rates. An important factor likely to induce fluctuations in asset prices is changes in the expectations of asset holders regarding likely returns (and capital gains) on particular assets. If a particular currency is expected to appreciate, the increased demand to hold it will appreciate it, unless the monetary authorities expand its supply.

The way in which exchange rate expectations are formed depends on the underlying economic structure, the characteristics of monetary and fixed policies, including the structure of disturbances to the demand and supply of money, as well as the type of expectations. Expectations are regressive if, for instance, a current depreciation of the exchange rate leads to the expectation that the exchange rate will return to its average level.

Efficient Market

The monetary and asset-market models of exchange rate determination hypothesize that the foreign exchange markets are efficient. A market is said to be efficient if its current prices appropriately reflect all currently available information and there are no opportunities for making extraordinary profits by further exploiting such information. This hypothesis suggests that market participants act on information available to them in such a way that the spot exchange rate always reflects all available information that could be potentially useful in earning excess profits.

[24]J. Tobin, "Are New Classical Models Plausible Enough to Guide Policy in Rational Expectation: A Seminar Sponsored by AEI," *Journal of Money, Credit and Banking* (November 1980).

[25]W. Felner, "Comments on Bennett T. McCallum, 'Rational Expectations and Macroeconomic Stabilization Policy,'" *Journal of Money, Credit and Banking* (November 1980).

[26]Ibid.

[27]Mussa, op. cit.

There are weak, semistrong, and strong forms of efficient market behavior.[28]

1. THE WEAK FORM. Where a current price is considered to incorporate all the information contained in past prices.

2. THE SEMI-STRONG FORM. Where a current price incorporates all publicly known information, including its own past prices.

3. THE STRONG FORM. Where prices reflect all information that can possibly be known. Therefore, the activities of investment analysts and other insiders make it impossible for any class of investor to consistently earn above average returns. The strong form of the hypothesis is probably unlikely to hold since secret non-random intervention by central bankers takes place in exchange markets.[29]

The weak efficient market hypothesis argues that the history of exchange rates conveys no information or future exchange rates that could help a market participant earn unusual profit by speculation. Unusual speculative profits or unusual return should not be earned by investors who use exchange rate forecasts based on publicly available information. Today's new information has its full impact on exchange rates today and provides no profitable information about how exchange rates will change tomorrow.[30]

Trader and speculator activity ensures that exchange rates fluctuate in anticipation of future demand and supply, rather than in reaction to present demand and supply. Exchange rates react to new information in an immediate and unbiased fashion, and since new information arrives randomly exchange rates fluctuate randomly. An analysis of future demand and supply is of no use in predicting exchange rate changes, unless a person is convinced of his or her ability to forecast change in future demand and supply faster or more accurate than the market can.[31]

The evidence is inconclusive as to whether or not the foreign exchange markets have been efficient during the present system of floating exchange rates. Empirical evidence for floating exchange rates shows conflicting results: (1) an increase in exchange market volatility and a corresponding decrease in the forecasting accuracy of the forward rate (i.e., the forward rate was found to be a poor but unbiased predictor of the future spot rate); and (2) large profit opportunities in forward speculation.[32] Because information is costly to collect market participants will never choose to be completely informed, market prices will never reflect all information, although they still may reflect available information.[33]

Recent findings on the market mechanism suggest that it is appropriate to consider market efficiency as a process rather than a hypothesis to accept or reject. In the short term, given that participants have diverse information, the foreign exchange market does not fully reflect all information, but as time passes, the market generally moves closer to a full reflection of all information. Hence, speculative markets will approach full efficiency in the long run but can never reflect all information in the short run.

---

[28]Richard M. Levich, "Further Results of the Efficiency of Markets for Foreign Exchange," in J. A. Frenkel and H. G. Johnson (eds.), *Managed Exchange Rate Flexibility: The Recent Experience*, Federal Reserve Bank of Boston, Conference Series No. 20, Boston, 1978. Richard M. Levich, "Tests of Forecasting Models and Market Efficiency in the International Money Market," in J. A. Frenkel and H. G. Johnson (eds.), *The Economics of Exchange Rates*, Addison-Wesley, Reading, MA, 1978. Richard M. Levich, "Overshooting," *Foreign Exchange Market*, The Group of Thirty, New York, 1982.

[29]Baillie and McMahon, op. cit.

[30]P. Isard, *Exchange Rate Determination: A Survey of Popular Views and Recent Models*, Princeton Studies in International Finance, No. 42, International Finance Section, Department of Economics, Princeton University, Princeton, NJ, 1978.

[31]G. Dufey and I. H. Giddy, *The International Money Market*, Prentice-Hall. Englewood Cliffs, NJ, 1978.

[32]Levich, "Efficiency of Markets," op. cit.

[33]Levich, 1981, op. cit.

Evidence of the possible existence of market inefficiencies, however, does not conflict with the general view that exchange rates behave much like the prices of other assets traded in organized markets, where price changes are frequently large and random, and occur primarily in response to new information received by market participants.[34]

The Portfolio and General Equilibrium Approaches

An integrated exchange rate model assumes relationships among exchange rates, interest rates, and relative prices. Accordingly, in equilibrium under perfect conditions, interest rates, prices, and forward and spot exchange rates are interdependent in a manner such that the purchasing power parity, interest rate parity, and the expectations of the forward exchange rate are maintained.

The exchange rate is determined as part of the general (real and monetary) equilibrium of the system by the interaction of all markets. Accordingly, the equilibrium exchange rate can change with an accompanying change in the money supply, or the real money demand, or both. The portfolio approach is a synthesis of both the traditional and monetary theories and considers exchange rate determination as a simultaneous process of adjustments and asset valuation induced by monetary and real factors.

Portfolio models treat domestic and foreign securities as imperfect substitutes and changes in the expected yields and risks associated with different securities lead to portfolio diversification, wealth

redistribution and hence affect the exchange rate. The stock of wealth also appears in the demand for money functions and allows a more flexible approach to modeling exchange rate fundamentals. For example, deficits in the current account lead to a redistribution of the world's wealth, while budgetary deficits lead to an increase in the stock of private wealth. Furthermore, sterilized central bank intervention, which leaves the money supply unaltered, still leads to a change in private wealth and hence to a change in the equilibrium exchange rate.[35]

Exchange rate movements could be explained in the context of a disequilibrium macroeconomic model. In this model, nominal prices of domestic output adjust slowly over time (primarily because of price inflexibility caused by long-term wage and price contracts), and asset markets adjust continuously in response to new information.[36] In the short run, the emphasis is shifted from the goods market and the current account to the asset market and capital account as the major determinants of the exchange rate. The exchange rate in the short run is determined in the asset market, since the asset market adjusts more quickly than the goods markets. The exchange rate can (in the short run) be inconsistent with both goods and bond market equilibrium, but in the long run, both markets must be in equilibrium at the same exchange rate.[37] For example, following an expansion in the U.S. money supply, nominal prices, including the dollar exchange rate, rise in proportion to the money supply increase. This could cause short-term deviation from the purchasing power parity, or an overshooting or an undershooting, which implies deviation from PPP equilibrium.

---

[34] Some techniques have been used to test spot market efficiency. One approach considers the time series properties of the spot rate, and tests the null hypothesis that changes in spot exchange rates are serially uncorrelated. The time series path of the spot rate depends on the time series path of the exogenous variables a well as the process that determines expectations.

[35] Marrinan, p. 62.

[36] Ibid.

[37] M. W. Keran, "The Value of the Yen," paper presented at American Enterprise Institute Conference on The International Monetary System Under Stress, Washington, D.C., February 1980.

Changes in the relative return and risk of foreign currency-denominated assets will affect their prices and the exchange rate. In addition, changes in wealth will affect the demand and supply of foreign assets over time and, in turn, the exchange rate. It is through growth of wealth via the current account of the balance of payments that the real sector affects foreign exchange rates.

Foreign Exchange Management and Intervention

Since March 1973 the exchange rate system has been floating, but managed to varying degrees by the monetary authorities through direct and indirect intervention. Different countries attach different degrees of importance to exchange rate stability and, in turn, exercise different exchange rate policies. There are four main objectives of foreign exchange market intervention.

- To prevent disorderly markets by resisting short-term currency rate changes.
- To lean against the wind by counteracting medium- and long-term variations in the exchange rate in order to affect trends in the currency rate.
- To establish either a moving or fixed exchange rate target; or to intervene if the exchange level is inconsistent with official monetary policy or if the exchange level does not appropriately reflect future trends because private market participants do not have sufficient information.
- To speed up real adjustments in the balance of payments and the economy, to affect domestic money supply, or to affect international reserves.

Intervention involves four major methods: central bank or monetary authority purchases or sales of foreign exchange in the market; official or quasi-official borrowing or lending

denominated in foreign currencies; various forms of controls on foreign transactions and payments; and indirect intervention through monetary and fiscal policy measures. The first intervention method is the most common, while the last exerts a major influence on the exchange market through effects on short-term capital flows.

Evidence shows that an active exchange rate management policy does not necessarily ensure exchange rate stability or a desired exchange level, but it becomes more effective if it is accompanied by fiscal and monetary measures. The experience since 1973 shows that intervention in the foreign currency market is an important feature of the exchange system. Some monetary authorities intervene in the market very actively and on a large scale to affect the behavior of exchange rates. Yet it is not clear whether this policy contributes to greater market stability.

For most countries, information on direct official intervention in foreign exchange markets is not made public. Therefore, the magnitude of intervention can generally be assessed only through an examination of changes in international reserves, although this measure of intervention has several limitations.

Alternative Theories of Exchange Rate Behavior

One approach to exchange rate forecasting is to specify the spot rate as a function of lagged endogenous variables and exogenous variables. The function is first estimated and then used to forecast rates. Alternatively, various indicators or indexes are utilized in assessing and forecasting exchange rates. These indicators (or factors) are subsets of and proxies for the various theories of exchange rate determination and, in a sense, are applied as reduced forms of these theories or models. Indicators are used by commercial banks, non-bank corporations, and various market participants.

The indexes can be classified in several groups.

1. Effective and real effective exchange rates,
2. Current account balance of the balance of payments,
3. Short-term interest rates,
4. Inflation (consumer price indexes, wholesale prices indexes),
5. Growth rate of the monetary aggregates,
6. Capital account balance of the balance of payments,
7. Economic and exchange rate policy and intervention, and
8. Forward exchange rates.

These indexes can be organized along the exchange rate theories (identified earlier) as follows:

- Indexes 1, 2, and 4 belong to the traditional approach of exchange rate determination.
- Indexes 1 and 4 are a reflection of the PPP theory, which could be classified in the context of the traditional and the monetary and asset-market theories.
- Indexes 3, 5, and 6 are derived from the monetary and asset-market framework of the exchange rate.
- Indexes 7 and 8 also operate through the channels outlined by the monetary theory and asset-market approach to the exchange rate.

In the present system of widespread floating of exchange rates, where many currencies undergo substantial changes, it is more appropriate to use effective exchange rates than bilateral rates. The effective exchange rate measures a currency's value in terms of a weighted average of the currencies of its major trading partners. The weights reflect the relative significance of the major trading partners in a country's trade. The weights are based on countries' bilateral and multilateral shares of trade in manufactures and they also take into account the relative size of countries' economies.

A more appropriate index of measuring exchange rate changes is in terms of real effective rates, where the trade-weighted exchange rate changes are adjusted for past inflation differentials. Real exchange rate indexes are particularly useful in assessments of the impact of past exchange rate changes and domestic price changes on a country's competitive position with its trading partners. A rise in one of these indexes denotes a loss of competitiveness; a decrease denotes an improvement.

Changes in current account balances affect exchange rates in two ways: through their direct impact on the derived demand and supply of the currencies concerned in the exchange market, and through the changes that they usually induce in the market's expectations about the equilibrium exchange rate of currencies. The resultant exchange rate movements themselves can temporarily amplify current payments imbalances. The initial increase in the surplus and the later swing into substantial deficit is due partly to the initially perverse J-curve effects of exchange rate changes.[38] Countries' current account balances do respond quite strongly, although usually with a considerable time lag, to changes in international competitive positions.

Changes in interest rate differentials influence exchange rates through their induced effects on international flows of funds. Usually an inflow of funds from one country to another will involve switching currencies from one denomination into another. This, in turn, will increase demand for the currency with the higher interest rate and appreciate its value. The reverse process occurs in the cur-

[38]Bank of International Settlements, *Annual Report*, 1981, BIS, 1981.

rency of the country with the lower interest rate.

Inflation differentials exert a significant impact on exchange rates, particularly over the medium or longer term. Exchange rates tend over time to reflect purchasing power parity relationships. The country that has the lowest rate of inflation (measured, for instance, by the consumer price indexes) has also the most steadily appreciating exchange rate. However, deviations from purchasing power parity can sometimes prove substantial,[39] because of, for instance, relatively substantial current account surplus or deficit and high inflation. Countries with a relatively better price performance that experience a serious deterioration of their current account balance of payments and much lower nominal interest rates are likely to experience substantial depreciation.

Different rates of monetary expansion affect exchange rates through a process that involves such factors as changes in the income velocity of money, interest rate differentials, and price expectations.

Governments' policies affect the environment of the foreign exchange markets. Exchange rates can be strongly influenced by the adoption of more vigorous anti-inflationary policies as well as by exchange rate intervention. These policies rely heavily on tighter domestic monetary conditions and they usually exert upward pressure on the level of domestic interest rates, thus widening interest rate differentials in favor of the countries pursuing them.[40]

Alternatively, forecasting can rely on forward exchange rates. However, the interest rate parity condition suggests that forward exchange rates are determined by interest rate differentials between countries. Therefore, the forward rate is not an efficient indicator of the future spot rate.

Reconciliation of the Various Exchange Rate Theories

There is no single theory of exchange rate determination. Different theories or factors explain alternative aspects of currency rate movements that can, however, be reconciled as explaining an interactive process that needs to be viewed as a whole.[41] While an interdependent and comprehensive approach to exchange rate determination is the most appropriate, various exchange rate theories could apply to different time horizons or involve different variables, reflecting different views or exchange rate determination and different economic theories.

One approach toward the reconciliation of the various theories of exchange rate determination is by applying them to various time horizons. For instance, elements of the traditional approach are implicitly integrated in the general equilibrium and portfolio models. This is in essence a long-term framework of currency rate determination. The asset-market framework and monetary theory relate primarily to the short term. An alternative method, however less effective, of reconciliation of the various exchange rate theories can classify the various theories along monetary and nonmonetary type models. Finally, statistical indicators can be derived from the various theories and applied in an ad hoc manner.

In summary, exchange rates are determined mainly by the monetary asset-market mechanism and expectations. In the long-term context, both monetary and real factors affect the exchange rate. The PPP does not provide a guide for day-to-day fluctuations of exchange rates, but can be valid in the long run if the economy does not experience structural changes that require adjustments of relative prices. However, it takes considerable time for

[39]"Exchange Rate Indications," *Finance and Development*, June, 1980.

[40]Bank of International Settlements, op. cit., note 38.

[41]Crockett, "Determinants," op. cit.

improved competitiveness in the goods markets to be fully reflected in trade flows.[42]

Currency Forecasting Services[43]

The increased volatility of exchange rates induced the emergence of a large number of commercial currency advisory and forecasting services, primarily at commercial banks. These forecasting services are based on econometric or judgmental methods.

The econometric based approaches are single equation model that are based on the PPP or the monetary-asset theories of exchange rate determination. This approach is simple and easy to apply, but may not always accurately describe the marketplace. More sophisticated models are large and often employ hundreds of equations that allow a better description of the marketplace and the determination of the exchange rate. The application of elaborate econometric models is expensive and requires ongoing updating and projection of the explanatory variables.

In addition, technical or momentum service provides currency rate projections, primarily

[42] Ibid.

[43] Levich, 1981, op. cit.

related to the short-term directions and trends. These forecasts are based on statistical analysis and on judgmental input. Evaluation of currency forecasting performance could include the forecasting error (i.e., predicted exchange rate − actual exchange rate) and the correctness of the forecasting trend. A small forecasting error might not necessarily be superior to a larger forecasting error, if the latter has correctly predicted the general trend of the future currency rate.

Summary and Conclusion

The currency exchange rates are determined in the marketplace by (the interaction of) several factors, but the exchange rates are not related to these factors in a simple manner. The exchange rates are also affected by new information and expectations about the future. In the long run, the PPP could explain substantial variation in the exchange rate, while in the short run the forward exchange rate could sometime predict the future spot rate. The monetary and asset theories of exchange rate determination maintain that national currencies are determined by supply and demand of financial assets, and the volatility of the exchange rates reflect the volatility of the underlying factors.

Societe Montage

Hedging International Transactions with Traditional Forward Exchange Transactions and Currency Options, and the Cost – benefit of Alternative Hedging Strategies

MARY ANN DOWLING

Part 1

You work for Societe Montage, a Swiss manufacturer of commercial furniture. Societe Montage buys some of its raw materials from a South American country and pays for them in U.S. Dollars. In June the firm ordered raw materials valued at USD 1,700,000. Delivery is due in the first week of October. Payment is due within 30 days of delivery.

When the raw materials were ordered in June, the USD/SFR rate was 1.7030. No cover was taken out because the Treasurer expected the dollar to weaken marginally.

There have been a number of unsettling developments recently: a military overthrow in the supplier's country, followed by a freeze on foreign assets, and stricter controls on trade. In fact, shortly after the coup, all except the most junior of your supplier's management were replaced by persons you consider to be ineffectual and inexperienced.

This morning, September 1, you received a reply to your requests for confirmation that the goods you ordered would be delivered in November. The reply stated that the exact delivery date could not be guaranteed, but delivery should take place as expected, in two months.

To add to these problems, you now believe that there is a strong possibility of the [U.S.] dollar strengthening dramatically. In order to maintain your market share of sales you must continue to manufacture, and there are no other sources of supply.

The Assignment

1. If you decided to use the traded options market, how many contracts would you buy? What would the total premium cost be? Base your analysis on the facts and the data in Exhibit 2-1. Please utilize Exhibit 2-2 to record your results.

2. How does the cost of using the traded option compare to the over-the-counter option?

3. How does the forward cover alternative compare to the cost of using options?

4. Taking into consideration the particular circumstances, which method would you choose to manage this exposure?

Part II

It is now 3 months later, December 1. The U.S. dollar has dramatically weakened and spot USD/SFR is 1.6910–20. The supplies you ordered arrived one month ago, and payment is due in two days. What would be the effective total cost (in SFR) of the raw materials if you had:

1. Bought dollars three months forward?
2. Left the position open?
3. Bought the over-the-counter SFR three month put option?
4. Bought the traded SFR December put option?

EXHIBIT 2-1

Foreign Exchange Rates

Spot	USD/SFR		1.7370–80
Forward Points	USD/SFR	1m	65–62
		2m	125–122
		3m	192–190
		6m	395–390
		12m	680–670

Interest Rates	3 Mos
US$	$5\frac{7}{8}$–6%
Swiss Franc	$2\frac{15}{16}$–3%

Over-the-counter Option

PUT SFR 3 month
Strike Price 1.7000
Premium 5 Centimes

Philadelphia Stock Exchange (PHLX) SFR Put Option

Strike Price: 59 cents
Expiry Month: December
Premium: 1.80 cents

EXHIBIT 2-2

Worksheet

Alternatives	Number of Contracts Premium cost per Contract Total Premium Cost	Effective Exchange Rate	Percentage Cost or Earning per Annum

Fidelity Trust Company

Forward Rate Agreement and Eurodollar Futures Designed to Hedge Interest Rate Risk on a Future Loan Commitment

HARVEY A. PONIACHEK

Fidelity Trust Company (FTC) is a U.S. subsidiary of a major Japanese commercial bank. FTC was acquired by the Japanese in the mid-1980s in a bail-out operation with the approval of the Federal Reserve, the Comptroller of the Currency, and the State Banking authorities. Following the acquisition, the U.S. operations have expanded tremendously in the 1980s and early 1990s through the growth of a large client base that consists of major U.S. and emerging Southeast Asian multinational companies (MNCs).

FTC is aggressively bidding for additional corporate lending business by often providing borrowers with future loan commitments at pre-agreed-upon interest rates. This policy in turn requires increased utilization of forward rate agreements, Eurodollar futures, and utilization of Treasury bill (TB) futures.

What Is an FRA?

A forward rate agreement (FRA) is a tailor-made, over-the-counter financial futures on

short-term deposits, such as Eurodollar contracts. An FRA transaction is a contract between two parties to exchange payments on a deposit, called the *notional amount*, to be determined on the basis of a short-term interest rate, referred to as the reference rate, over a predetermined time period at a future date.

An FRA transaction is entered as a hedge against interest rate changes. The buyer of the contract locks in the interest rate in an effort to protect against an interest rate increase, while the seller protects against a possible interest rate decline. At maturity, no funds exchange hands; rather, the difference between the contract interest rate and the market rate, commonly London Interbank Offered Rate (LIBOR), is multiplied by the notional deposit and the time period to determine the cash settlement. Since FRAs are priced off LIBOR, if LIBOR is higher than the contract rate, the buyer receives a cash payment from the seller, and vice versa if the interest rate is lower. An FRA is like a short-term interest rate swap.

A company that seeks to hedge against a possible increase in interest rates would purchase FRAs, whereas a company that seeks an interest hedge against a possible decline of the rates would sell FRAs. If the reference interest rate for a specific period on a specific date in the future is different from the one agreed upon, a settlement of the difference will be made.

The market for FRAs evolved in the latter half of the 1980s from the forward/forward deposit market where one party agrees to make a deposit with another one for a future date and set interest rate. The FRA market is composed primarily of sterling and dollars—some 80–90 percent of the market—as well as other currencies, such as the Deutsche mark, the yen, and Swiss franc. The market is dominated by interbank transactions, and transactions commonly range from $10 million, but they could sometimes be as large as $100 to $200 million. London is the financial center of FRA trading because it is the center of the Eurocurrency market. Non-banks in the U.S. prefer to use exchange-traded futures that are well established. The FRA market is rapidly growing, with an annual turnover of some $300–500 billion.

FRA quotations are described, for instance, in terms of "three against six" or "three against nine," which imply that a three-month LIBOR deposit to commence in three months (for a maturity of three months), or a six-month LIBOR deposit to commence in three months (and mature in six months).

While the principal amounts, or notional amounts, are stated in the contract, they are never exchanged since the transaction is settled in cash. The settlement amount between the contracting parties is the present value at the actual market interest rate of the notional principal multiplied by the difference between the contracted and market interest rate on the settlement date.

For example, Bank A purchases from Bank B on March 1 a $5 million FRA for "three months against six months" at 10 percent LIBOR. On June 1, three-month LIBOR is $10\frac{1}{4}$ percent. Bank A receives from Bank B a cash settlement that is determined according to the following formula:

$$\text{Cash settlement} = \frac{5{,}000{,}000 \times 0.25 \times 91}{360 \times 100} \times$$

$$= \$3159.70$$

Present value of cash settlement at $10\frac{1}{4}\%$ and 91 days

$$= \frac{3159.70}{1 + (0.1025 \times 91/360)}$$

$$= \$3{,}079.90$$

Why Hedge with an FRA?

FRAs are more flexible than financial futures in terms of maturity and amounts, they do not involve margins, they are usually not subject to marked-to-market and the consequent cash flows, and they eliminate the basis risk associated with futures. The FRAs credit risk is relatively small—unless interest rate volatility is significant. FRAs are also available in foreign currencies for which the organized exchanges do not trade. FRAs allow market participants to hedge their interest rate exposure without an impact on their liquidity position and/or balance sheet. FRAs cannot be traded unless both parties to the contract agree.

FRAs offer banks and non-bank corporations the ability to hedge their interest rate exposure without inflating their balance sheets, and they can be used to reduce interbank outstanding. While companies initially used the market for hedging purposes, many corporate participants are presently engaged in trading per se. Accounting treatment of FRA transactions varies among the major industrial countries, with some requiring that they be marked-to-market with the resulting gains/losses flowing through the Profit and Loss account.

EXHIBIT 3-1

Interest Rates

```
 TELERATE® MATRIX SM        08/24/92 14:25 EDT   ALERT        TERMINAL
                                                               PAGE 5
 FEDERAL FUNDS      14.23  T-BILLS     14.23  YIELD  EUROS/EP OPEN  GOV RP 14.00
 BID 3  5/16 OPEN 3  5/16  3M 3.14-12 +.06  3.187  3  5/16- 7/16 O/N 3.45-40
 ASK 3  3/8  HIGH 3  3/8   6M 3.25-23 +.07  3.328  3  7/16- 9/16 1WK 3.35-30
 LST 3  5/16 LOW  3  5/16  YR 3.41-39 +.08  3.528  3  9/16-11/16 2WK 3.35-30
 FUNDS SOURCE:G. GUYBUTLER                                       1MO 3.30-25
 TSY CPNS   N Y 1ST 14.23  YIELD
                           SECONDARY-CDS BID 14.20  BAS-BID         14.20
                             EARLY   LATE    EARLY    LATE
 04.250 07/94 100.03-04 -07 4.181
 04.625 08/95  99.20-22 -11 4.739 SEP 3.33 +03  3.33 +03  3.32 +03  3.32 +03
 06.375 06/97 102.29-31 -21 5.664 OCT 3.35 UNC  3.35 UNC  3.32 +03  3.32 +03
 05.500 07/97  99.09-11 -22 5.653 NOV 3.35 UNC  3.35 UNC  3.32 +03  3.32 +03
 06.375 07/99 100.29-01 -27 6.187 DEC 3.35 UNC  3.35 UNC  3.33 +04  3.33 +04
 06.375 08/02  97.30-02 -30 6.644 JAN 3.40 UNC  3.40 UNC  3.35 +04  3.35 +04
 09.375 02/06 120.02-06 -35 7.032 FEB 3.45 +05  3.45 +05  3.35 +04  3.35 +04
 08.125 08/21 107.12-16 -27 7.487 DEALER COMM PAPER INTER 12.11    BANK RATES
 08.000 11/21 106.03-07 -27 7.472 30  3.30   90  3.33  180  3.38 PRIME  6.00
 07.250 08/22  97.27-31 -26 7.420 60  3.33  120  3.33  240  3.43 BKR    5.25
```

```
 TELERATE® MATRIX SM        08/24/92 14:29 EDT   ALERT        TERMINAL
                                                               PAGE  261
 SPOT RATES                    GMT  SPOT RATES                    GMT
 STG  CITIBANK    N Y 1.9920 -30 18:26 CDN  CITIBANK    N Y 1.1891 -96 18:25
 DMK  U B S       N Y 1.4035 -45 18:14 ECU  CITIBANK    N Y 1.4400 -10 18:11
 YEN  CITIBANK    N Y 124.70 -80 18:28 HFL  CITIBANK    N Y 1.5824 -34 18:11
 SWF  RABOBANK    UTR 1.2429 -39 18:28 LIR  CITIBANK    N Y 1072   -74 18:06
 FFR  CITIBANK    N Y 4.7910 -40 18:11 AUS  MORGAN GTY  N Y 0.7138 -43 18:12
       USD        STG        DMK        YEN        SWF       IPE BRENT
 US$              1.9920 -30 0.7120 -25 0.8013 -19 0.8039 -46 16:13   GMT
 STG  0.5018 -20             0.3574 -76 0.4022 -24 0.4035 -37
 DMK  1.4035 -45 2.7965 -85            1.1251 -59 1.1208 -96 $1979-84
 YEN  124.70 -80 248.46 -66 88.82 -89             100.29 -37
 SWF  1.2429 -39 2.4765 -85 0.8853 -60 0.9963 -71            $1990-9541
 FED FUND   14.29 EUROS/DEPOSITS OPEN  GMT  US TREASURIES 14.29 EST   YIELD
 BID 3  5/16  O/N 3  5/16- 3  7/16  04.250 07/94 100.02-03    4.198
 ASK 3  3/8   1MO 3  1/4 - 3  3/8   06.375 08/02  97.28-00    6.652
 LAST 3 5/16  3MO 3  5/16- 3  7/16  09.375 02/06 120.01-05    7.035
 SOURCE:GUYBUTLER 6MO 3  7/16- 3  9/16  07.250 08/22  97.26-30    7.422
```

(*Continued*)

	EURO-DOLLAR 14:25 EDT	FED FUNDS 14:25 EDT	FRA'S 14:31 EDT	INT RATE SWAPS 14:31 EDT ACT/360
O/N	3 1/4 - 3 3/8	BID ASK	1X4	SXS
T/N	3 1/4 - 3 3/8	3 5/16 - 3 3/8	2X5	DXD
S/N	3 1/4 - 3 3/8	LAST OPEN	3X6	MXM
1WK	3 1/4 - 3 3/8	3 3/8 - 3 5/16	4X7	BSXS
2WK	3 1/4 - 3 3/8	TERM FED FUNDS	5X8	1YR
1MO	3 1/4 - 3 3/8	3 1/4 - 3 3/8	6X9	18MO
2MO	3 5/16 - 3 7/16	3 5/16 - 3 7/16	9X12	MEDIUM TERM
3MO	3 5/16 - 3 7/16	3 5/16 - 3 7/16	1X7	2 YRS T + 20 - 23
4MO	3 3/8 - 3 1/2	3 3/8 - 3 1/2	2X8	3 YRS T + 29 - 32
5MO	3 3/8 - 3 1/2	3 3/8 - 3 1/2	3X9	4 YRS T + 33 - 36
6MO	3 7/16 - 3 9/16	3 7/16 - 3 9/16	4X10	5 YRS T + 30 - 32
9MO	3 1/2 - 3 5/8	3 1/2 - 3 5/8	5X11	7 YRS T + 33 - 36
1YR	3 9/16 - 3 11/16	3 9/16 - 3 11/16	6X12	10YRS T + 35 - 38

Pricing and Using FRAs

Pricing reflects the market interest rates and the alternative cost of hedging. FRAs are commonly priced off the nearest futures contract. Bid–ask spreads are narrow, about 5–10 basis points or even less, and track futures prices very closely. The price of a "six against nine" FRA will be determined on the basis of interest rates on six and nine month deposits.

The FRAs interest rate reflects the forward/forward interest rates, because otherwise arbitrage would occur between the FRAs and the forward/forward interest transactions. The International Money Market (IMM) in Chicago introduced FRAs that are priced off the IMM's Eurodollar futures contracts and use IMM settlement dates.

The Assignment

FTC seeks to lock in an interest rate for $100 million six-month LIBOR-based funding that commences in three months. The hedge is needed so that FTC can make a loan commitment to a large MNC, a prime customer, now at a certain interest rate to be loaned in three months. The bank can make a commitment only if it can lock in the cost of funds through the FRA market or an alternative hedging method.

FTC seeks on August 24, 1992 to fund a $100 million six-month loan at LIBOR plus 25 basic points, which equals to nine month LIBOR of $3\frac{5}{8}$ percent plus $\frac{1}{4}$ of 1 percent or $3\frac{7}{8}$ percent. To hedge against the risk of higher interest rates, the bank could acquire an FRA for three against nine quoted at a bid/offer of 3.68–3.73. Alternatively, the bank could hedge its position in the Eurodollar IMM or LIFFE (London International Financial Futures Exchange) futures market at the rates shown in Exhibit 3-1.

Examine the cost and benefit (and the advantages and disadvantages) of interest rate hedging using FRA and Eurodollar futures. Based on your analysis and based on the characteristics of both instruments, which interest hedging approach do you recommend?

Interest and Liquidity Risks

Risks in treasury operations arise from credit risk, interest rate risk, exchange rate risk, and liquidity risk.

Credit Risk

Credit risk refers to the risk that a debtor will be unable to service its debt in a timely fashion due to lack of sufficient funds or other reasons.

Rate Risk

Rate risk, or interest rate risk, in the money market arises when assets and liabilities maturities are mismatched. For example, if we borrow funds for one month and lend them out for two months, the interest rate on the loan has been locked in, but the borrowed funds need to be rolled over two times. If the interest rate goes up, the fund manager will be funding the assets (i.e., raising funds) at a higher rate than the loan rate, thus incurring a loss on the transaction.

Exchange Rate Risk

Exchange rate risk is related to translations, transactions, and economic exposures that arise due to currency rate changes. Translation exposure arises from the need to report con-solidated global activities according to standard accounting rules in the parent's currency. Transaction exposure arises from the settlement of accounts denominated in foreign currency and the possible change in the exchange rate. Economic exposure refers to the likelihood that the net present value of the firm's cash flows will change due to changes in the exchange rates.

Liquidity Risk

The liquidity risk is closely associated with the rate risk. The risk arises because the cash inflows in a transaction are not matched. Liquidity risk in the money market occurs when there is a maturity mismatch between assets and liabilities. Liquidity risk in the foreign exchange market occurs due to the inability to secure funds in the desired currency denomination (and at a reasonable exchange rate).

Bibliography

1. KENNETH R. KAPNER AND JOHN F. MARSHALL, *The Swaps Handbook: Swaps and Related Risk Management Instruments*, New York Institute of Finance, New York, 1990, pp. 195–207.

2. RAYMOND, G. F. CONINX, *Foreign Exchange Dealer's Handbook*, Second Edition, Dow Jones-Irwin, Homewood, IL, 1986, Ch. 12.

Madesco Inc.

Hedging Export Receipts Through Forward Contracts and Currency Options

MARY ANN DOWLING

Part I

March 1, 199x

Madesco Inc. is a midwest American based manufacturer of microchips. International business for Madesco was brisk until 12 months ago when world economies went into a severe recession. Madesco was left with a large inventory of chips which is rapidly becoming outdated. The company has cut back substantially on production of new ones but is concerned about cash flows in the coming year if sales do not pick up.

The marketing department has recently completed a tentative agreement with a German distributor who will be purchasing roughly 75 percent of the current inventory at a discounted fixed price. Delivery will be on September 1, six months' time. Final agreement will be made June 1, to allow the cautious German distributor to better evaluate his sales and cash position. If the deal is consummated the payment of 30 million Deutsche mark (DM) will be paid on delivery.

The Madesco Treasury Group is contemplating their hedging strategy at this point. The sales department is confident that the deal will go through, but the treasury staff,

being of a more conservative nature, cannot be certain that the sale of inventory will occur.

Economic data from Germany has been very positive over the last year and consequently the Deutsche mark has appreciated against the currencies of its major trading partners. Most forecasters are predicting a continuation of this trend, with expectations for a 2–3 percent growth in GNP and a reduction in the already low inflation levels. Madesco's finance director agrees with these expectations; however some of his analysts feel the mark has peaked and will weaken over the next six months.

The Assignment

You are a member of Madesco's Treasury group and have been asked to look at options and forward cover. You are to give your recommendation on how to deal with this exposure. For options you do not have to be concerned with cost of carry. Please utilize the financial data in Exhibit 4-1 and record your results in Exhibit 4-2.

Part II

Three months later, June 1.

The marketing department held a meeting this morning to inform senior management that the Germans have confirmed their purchase order and request delivery by September 1.

Upon returning to your office you call your local banker for an update on the foreign exchange rates. Although the Deutsche mark has strengthened, the Finance Director now feels that it has peaked and will fall against the dollar over the next three months. The market forecasters are still predicting a further increase in the mark. Current rates are as shown in Exhibit 4-3.

The Assignment

1. In the light of the change in rates do you want to change your strategy? Please utilize the financial data in Exhibit 4-3.

2. List any action (if any) you decide to take.

EXHIBIT 4-1

Financial Data

Interbank Rates: March 1

DM/USD	Spot	1.8620	1.8625	(.5369)
	6 months	320	317	
	6 months outright	1.8300	1.8308	(.5462)

PHLX[a] Options: March 1

Currency	Strike Price	Calls			Puts		
62,500		Jun	Sep	Dec	Jun	Sep	Dec
DM	52	2.18	2.73	r[b]	0.55	0.84	r
Premium							
expressed in	53	1.51	2.08	r	0.99	1.27	r
cents per	54	1.04	1.61	r	1.45	1.90	r
unit	55	.65	1.17	r	2.11	2.30	r

[a] PHLX is Philadelphia Stock Exchange
[b] r: not traded

EXHIBIT 4-2

Worksheet

Alternatives	Currency Strike Price Month	No. of Contracts Premium in USD Terms	Premium (Paid) or Premium Received in Dollars	Effective Rate in USD Terms

EXHIBIT 4-3

PHLX

Currency	Strike Price	Calls			Puts		
		Jun	Sep	Dec	Jun	Sep	Dec
DM	52	4.55	5.02	r	0.00	0.10	r
Premium							
expressed in	53	3.51	4.09	r	0.00	0.20	r
cents per	54	2.58	3.30	s[a]	0.05	0.35	s
unit	55	1.62	2.48	r	0.13	0.57	r
	56	0.91	1.92	r	0.32	0.88	r
	57	0.35	1.32	s	0.87	1.41	r
	58	0.15	0.93	r	1.58	1.95	r

Interbank Rates

DM	Spot	1.7930	1.7840	(.5605)
	3 months points	158	156	
	3 months outright	1.7772	1.7684	(.5655)

[a] no option offered

Part III

September 1

Madesco sells the goods to the Germans, who pay on delivery. Rates are shown in Exhibit 4-4.

The Assignment

1. What is the effective rate at which you exchange German marks for dollars?
2. What is your percentage cost or earning in comparison to the spot rate on March 1?
3. How does this compare to the six-month forward outright taken out on March 1?

EXHIBIT 4-4

DM Exchange Rates

Interbank

DM	Spot	DM/USD	1.6815	1.6825	(.5944)

PHLX

Currency	Strike Price	Calls			Puts		
		Mar	Jun	Sep	Mar	Jun	Sep
DM	52	9.85	10.15	r	—	—	s
Premium							
expressed in	53	8.79	9.09	r	—	—	r
cents per	54	7.86	8.18	r	—	0.04	r
unit	55	6.81	7.17	r	—	0.07	s
	56	5.87	6.26	s	—	0.10	r
	57	4.82	5.28	s	—	0.15	r
	58	3.88	4.46	r	—	0.30	r

Chase Options, Inc.

Hedging Foreign Currency Exposure Through Currency Options

HARVEY A. PONIACHEK

This case study briefly reviews the foreign currency options market and hedging. It presents several international transactions that require currency options hedging strategies by the corporations involved.

The Currency Options Markets

Foreign currency options include options on spot exchange, options on foreign currency futures and futures-style option.[1] Foreign currency options can be transacted over-the-counter and on organized exchanges.

The market for currency options is comprised of an interbank market that consists of London, New York, and Tokyo. Markets for over-the-counter (OTC) currency options began to develop in the early 1980s. Transactions over-the-counter mainly involve the U.S. dollar against the major currencies, including the pound sterling, the German mark, the Japanese yen, and others. Over-the-counter options

[1]See for instance J. Orlin Grabbe, *International Financial Markets*, 2nd Ed., Elsevier, New York, 1991, Ch. 6, "Foreign Currency Options."

offer corporations tailor-made accommodation transactions in terms of size and maturity.

The main currency traded on the exchange-based markets include the DM, the yen, the Australian dollar, the Canadian dollar, the ECU, and the Swiss franc. Currency options in the United States are traded in standardized contracts that generally correspond to the features of the International Money Market (IMM) of the Chicago Mercantile Exchange currency futures contracts. Option prices are usually quoted in cents (or a fraction thereof) per unit of foreign currency. Currency options are listed on the Philadelphia Stock Exchange, the IMM, the CBOE (Chicago Board of Exchange), the LIFFE (London International Financial Futures Exchange), and several other exchanges.

American-style currency options on spot exchange are traded over-the-counter at the Philadelphia Stock Exchange (PHLX) in the amount of one-half the size of the IMM futures contracts. Options on currency futures—traded on the Chicago Mercantile Exchange (CME)—provide options on exchange traded currency futures contracts. All currency traded options on currency futures are American-type contracts.

Markets for foreign exchange options increased in breadth in recent years. International activity has expanded due to the high volatility of exchange rates, which has created a continuing need for hedging. The proliferation of market activity in currency options around the world led to the emergence of new centers and the establishment of links among different exchanges in different time zones. See Appendix 5-1 for information on where currency options are traded, contract size and volume of business.

Fundamentals of Options

A foreign currency option contract is an agreement between the buyer and the seller, where the seller grants the buyer the right to buy or sell a currency under certain conditions. The buyer of a call or put pays the seller a price, called the premium, for the right of buying or selling a specific amount of a currency at a pre-agreed upon price, known as the exercise price or strike price, during a specific period of time, or on a specific date, called the expiration date or maturity date. Foreign currency options limit the risk of the options buyer to the premium paid, but provide the buyer with unlimited potential gain. The option seller's gain is limited to its premium, but its loss is unlimited.

There are American and European options. Exchange traded currency options are all American style, whereas over-the-counter currency options are primarily European-style options. An American option affords the holder the right to exercise at any time before maturity, whereas a European option allows the holder the right to exercise only at maturity. In an option on a futures currency contract, the underlying asset is not a spot asset, but a futures contract on the currency. Acquiring an option on the futures implies that the holder obtains a long position in the currency futures.

In summary, currency options are characterized by several features: the currency option type (American or European), the expiration date, the strike price, premium, and the type of underlying instrument (spot or future).

Option valuation or pricing is determined by models that are based on the Black-Scholes principles, and by the application of several variables:

1. The spot price of the underlying currency (e.g., the price of dollar per yen),
2. The strike price of the option,
3. The maturity,
4. The volatility of the underlying currency, and
5. The interest rates in both countries (e.g., in the U.S. and Japan when the option price on yen is determined).

Hedging with Currency Options

The currency options market is rapidly becoming the preferred venue for corporations wishing to hedge their foreign currency exposure. The surge in demand for currency options has come from translation exposure—as defined according to Financial Accounting Standards Board (FASB) 52 requirements. In addition, the increased internationalization of the U.S. economy in the late 1980s has given rise to greater international involvement and currency exposure. These factors contributed to the growth of the over-the-counter options markets. Unlike organized exchange markets traded options, OTC options offer customized maturities, contract size and strike prices, do not involve the extra cost and inconvenience of posting and satisfying minimum margin requirements and have no brokerage fees.

Foreign currency forwards and options are imperfect substitutes for hedging of currency exposure. Forward currency hedging locks the firm into a rigid position, whereby the firm needs to perform the forward contract or else be in default. By entering into a forward contract the hedger could not enjoy favorable future developments in the currency market. Options are most suitable for hedging foreign currency denominated transactions that might not occur (e.g., competitive bidding for a construction project abroad that might not be awarded). In addition, hedging through options provides the potential for enjoying favorable market circumstances. Currency options have the advantage over forward exchange contracts because they allow corporations to benefit from favorable currency movements and limit the extent of currency losses. The option markets allow the trading of volatility; that is, taking a view on how volatile the underlying currency will be.

Currency options can be used to hedge foreign currency exposure under a variety of circumstances that involve transactions denominated in foreign currencies or attempts to enhance international competitiveness:

1. Anticipated currency transactions where the company seeks to take a view on the exchange rate trend (e.g., account payables or account receivables denominated in foreign exchange, dividend flows from foreign subsidiaries or investments). If the company doesn't have a view it should use forward exchange hedging.

2. Uncertain currency transactions (e.g., bids on international projects denominated in a foreign currency, portfolio hedges where the timing of the sale of securities due to interest rate conditions is difficult to determine ahead of time).

3. Economic exposure (e.g., circumstances where a company's market position stands to be hurt by foreign competition if its currency rises in value in relation to others).

The three most favored currency options strategies include:

1. BUYING AN OPTION. Allows unlimited upside potential and caps downside exposure.

2. SELLING AN OPTION. Caps upside potential but allows unlimited downside exposure.

Buying an option and selling a put provides the hedger with a comparable outcome. For instance, buying a dollar call against a yen implies that the buyers could exercise the option by buying dollars and paying yen. Alternatively, by buying a yen put against dollars, the hedger could exercise by delivering yen and getting paid dollars. Both options require that the hedger pays yen and obtains dollars.

3. BUY–SELL OPTIONS. Caps upside potential and downward exposure, and it is generally obtained at zero cost.

Devising Hedging Strategies

The Assignment

You are a member of Chase Options, Inc., who was asked to participate in designing hedging strategies for the following transactions:

ANTICIPATED CURRENCY TRANSACTIONS

1. A U.S. company expects DM 100 million in repatriated profits from its German subsidiary on March 20, 1991. The company believes that the dollar has reached a long-term low at the current level DM/$1.6700; however, it doesn't want to lock in a forward exchange contract because of uncertainty concerning the impact of the German reunification on the currency market. The company doesn't want to exchange at greater than DM/$1.7000 (e.g., 1.7200). Design a hedging strategy by using currency options and utilizing the rates available in Exhibit 5-1 (Row 1). Examine the implications of hedging instead with a forward contract. Consider whether strategy (III) B (3) listed below is applicable for this transaction. Utilize the data in Exhibit 5-1 (Row 2).

2. A U.S. firm has bought industrial equipment from a U.K. firm for £5 million payable in 60 days. The firm believes that UK's political and economic uncertainty might drive the pound sterling down signifi-

EXHIBIT 5-1

Currency Options Quotations

Row	Contract	Currency Exchange Rates		Interest Rate		Option Type	Strike Price
		Spot	Forward	U.S.	Foreign		
1	DM/$	1.67	1.6725	8.3	8.5106	PUT	1.7
2	DM/$	1.67	1.6725	8.3	8.5106	CALL	1.647
3	$/STG	1.7	1.6818	8.2	14.8657	CALL	1.7
4	A$/$	0.785	0.76	8.25	14.7892	PUT	0.72
5	A$/$	0.785	0.76	8.25	14.7892	CALL	0.8025
6	DM/STG	2.8921	2.8845	7.9091	14.8811	PUT	2.8845
7	YEN/$	120.0	116.5	8.7	7.1318	PUT	128.15

Row	Maturity	Premium per FC	Premium per Dollar	Hedging Ratio		
				Delta	Gamma	Theta
1	272	0.0164	0.0466	0.3387	0.039	0.00003
2	272	0.0164	0.0452	0.423	0.041	0.00003
3	60	0.0176	0.006105	0.388	0.098	0.00008
4	195	0.007211	0.0128	0.206	0.037	0.00007
5	195	0.007234	0.0115			
6	14	0.0161	0.001936	0.494	0.281	0.00085
7	731	0.000127	1.9595	0.188	0.019	N.A.

cantly. Design a hedging strategy for the corporation by employing either forward currency contracts or currency options and utilizing the date listed in Exhibits 5-1 (Row 3).

UNCERTAIN CURRENCY TRANSACTIONS

3. A U.S. fund manager who bought 100 million in Australian dollar (A$) bonds when the A$ was at US$/A$0.72 is worried that the A$ might depreciate because of disappointing Australian economic performance. He decides to set A$/$0.72 as the maximum downside loss that he wants to risk from the current level of A$/$0.7850 (spot). The fund manager doesn't mind foregoing profit opportunities from a further upward move in the A$ and is uncertain how long he will hold the bonds. He sets the year end as his time horizon. By utilizing Exhibit 5-1 (Rows 4 and 5) data, which hedging strategy should the fund manager adopt?

4. A German company is bidding on a contract in the U.K. The bid is estimated at £40 million and they anticipate a profit margin of 30 percent on the project. Hence, they will need to repatriate £12 million in profit, but they worry that the new U.K. economic trends could hurt the pound sterling exchange rate. Determine how the Germany company could hedge their potential exposure. Utilize Exhibit 5-1 (Row 6) for data.

ECONOMIC HEDGING

5. In late 1987 American Motors Corporation (AMC) believed that with the yen exchange rate at ¥/$120 the corporation was competitive vis-à-vis its Japanese rivals. However, if the dollar is to rise again, AMC believed that it could lose 5–10 percent of its sales for every 10 percent strengthening of the dollar. Propose a hedging policy for AMC

by utilizing the data in Exhibit 5-1 (Row 7). What is the cost of your recommendation and what is the company's break-even point?

CROSS HEDGING

6. Multinational corporation B has borrowed DM to finance expansion of its German subsidiary. The German subsidiary sells 89 percent of its products to an Italian cus-

tomer who pays in lira. Company B is exposed to the depreciation of the lira and the appreciation of the DM. Design a hedging strategy for the parent.

7. Multinational corporation B has lira sales, but because of high interest rates on lira denominated funds, hedging with lira options could be less favorable than hedging with DM options. Which hedging strategy would you consider as the most feasible?

APPENDIX 5-1

Currency Futures and Options

CURRENCY FUTURES AND OPTIONS: EXCHANGES, CONTRACTS, AND VOLUME OF TRADES, (1988–89)

Exchange/Type	Face Value of Contract	Volume of Contracts Traded	
		1988	1989 Jan.–Oct.
		(in thousands of contracts)	
United States			
Chicago Mercantile Exchange (CME)			
Currency			
Futures			
Eurodollar (three months)[a]	$1,000,000	21,705	35,862
Pound sterling[a]	£25,000	2,616	2,148
Canadian dollar	Can$100,000	1,409	1,108
Deutsche mark[a]	DM 125,000	5,662	6,729
Japanese yen[a]	¥12,500,000	6,433	6,762
Swiss franc	Sw F 125,000	5,283	5,194
French franc	F 250,000	4	2
Australian dollar	$A 100,000	76	104
Options			
Eurodollar	$1,000,000	2,600	5,181
Pound Sterling	£25,000	543	350
Deutsche mark	DM 125,000	2,734	3,164
Swiss franc	Sw F 125,000	1,070	1,305
Japanese yen	¥12,500,000	2,945	2,780
Canadian dollar	Can$100,000	314	246
Australian dollar	$A 100,000	7	21

(Continued)

Exchange/Type	Face Value of Contract	Volume of Contracts Traded	
		1988	1989 Jan.–Oct.
		(in thousands of contracts)	
Philadelphia Stock Exchange (PHLX)			
Currency[b]			
Options			
Australian dollar	$A 100,000	351	673
Canadian dollar	CAN$100,000	317	424
European currency unit	ECU 125,000	1	9
French franc	F 500,000	252	86
Japanese yen	¥12,500,000	2,921	2,876
Pound sterling	£62,500	1,283	409
Swiss franc	Sw F 125,000	1,067	919
United Kingdom			
London International Financial Futures Exchange (LIFFE)			
Currency			
Futures			
Eurodollar (three-month)	$1,000,000	1,662	1,850
Pound Sterling (three-month)	£500,000	3,555	6,049
Japanese Yen	¥12,500,000	3	3
Swiss franc	Sw F 125,000	3	1
Pound sterling	£25,000	7	5
Deutsche mark	DM 125,000	4	2
Euromark		n.t.	712
Options			
Eurodollar (three-month)	$1,000,000	77	71
Pound sterling (three-month)	£500,000	446	709
Pound/U.S. dollar		10	1
Pound sterling	£25,000	446	709
France			
March} © Terme d'Instruments Financiers (MATIF)			
Currency			
Futures			
Euro-deutsche mark		n.t.	481
The Netherlands			
European Options Exchange (EOE)			
Currency			
Options			
U.S. dollar/guilder and	$10,000		412
pound sterling/guilder	£10,000		

(*Continued*)

Exchange/Type	Face Value of Contract	Volume of Contracts Traded	
		1988	1989 Jan.–Oct.
		(in thousands of contracts)	
Australia			
Sydney Futures Exchange			
Currency			
Futures			
Australian dollar		22	5
Options			
Australian dollar		3	—
New Zealand			
New Zealand Futures Exchange			
Currency			
Futures			
U.S. Dollar	$50,000	19	4
N.Z. dollar	$NZ 100,000	n.t.	2
Singapore			
Singapore International Monetary Exchange (SIMEX)			
Currency			
Futures			
Deutsche mark	DM 125,000	98	23
Eurodollar	$1,000,000	1,881	3,406
Euro-yen		n.t.	58
Japanese yen	¥23,500,000	221	275
Pound sterling	£62,500	3	3
Options			
Deutsche mark	DM 125,000	12	1
Eurodollar	$1,000,000	11	10
Japanese yen	¥12,500,000	61	2

[a]CME Eurodollar, pound sterling, deutsche mark, and Japanese yen contracts are listed on a mutual offset link with SIMEX in Singapore.

[b]American volume.

n.t. = not traded; $A = Australian dollar; Can$ = Canadian dollar; DM = deutsche mark; ECU = European Currency Unit; F = French franc; HK$ = Hong Kong dollar; ¥ = Japanese yen; $NZ = New Zealand dollar; f. = Netherland guilder; £ = pound sterling; SKr = Swedish Krone; and $ = U.S. dollar. Options volume is puts and calls combined. 1989 covers January to October.

SOURCES: International Monetary Fund, International Capital Markets; Developments and Prospects, Washington, D.C., April 1990.

CASE **6**

Metro Corporation, Inc.

Investing Internationally with an Asset Swap

SUSAN M. MANGIERO

This case examines one means of investing internationally by buying a synthetic security. Metro Corporation, a large institutional investor, must decide whether to buy a fixed rate bond issued by a non-U.S. company or buy a floating rate bond issued by that same non-U.S. company and lock into a fixed rate of interest by entering into an interest rate swap.

Company Profile

Metro Corporation is a big life insurance company located in New York City. Its primary business is to provide a wide line of life insurance and investment products to its target market base comprised of individuals and small company owners. The types of life insurance policies offered to its clients include (1) term insurance; (2) whole life insurance; and (3) universal insurance.

Term insurance is a type of policy which pays a specified cash amount to a designated beneficiary in the event that the insured party dies during a defined time period. There are various restrictions imposed on the insured

party regarding the renewal of a term life insurance policy in the event that the policy matures before the insured's death.

Whole life insurance provides payments to a designated beneficiary whenever death of the insured party occurs. Moreover, a whole life insurance policy provides a cash value that fluctuates during the life of the policy. Initially, the insurer charges a premium which is significantly larger than what is perceived necessary to pay early death claims. (An insurance company's premium scale is based on complex actuarial estimates of the lifespan of individuals categorized by age, health, profession, lifestyle habits such as smoking, etc.) Over time, these relatively larger premiums and the compound interest earned on them add up to a substantial savings value. Part of this investment portion of the whole life insurance policy is payable to the insured party upon his request and subject to the terms and conditions of the policy.

Universal life insurance is a type of policy which combines the benefits of traditional term insurance with the opportunity to invest funds at a guaranteed interest rate as a minimum. A higher interest rate can be applied within certain parameters set by the insurance company. It was introduced by life insurance companies in the late 1970s to compete for investible funds with financial institutions such as banks and brokerage firms that were selling investment [along with] insurance products.

EXHIBIT 6-1

Analysis of Amount of Insurance Purchased
(data in percent)

	1978	1988
Term	44	38
Whole life	36	25
Universal	0	19
Other	20	18
Total	100%	100%

Source: 1989 Life Insurance Fact Book (Washington, D.C.: American Council on Life Insurance, annual), p. 7.

See Exhibit 6-1 for information about the popularity of these three types of life insurance policies.

Like most life insurance policies, Metro Corporation collects annual policy premiums and invests these funds until such time that policy-related claims must be paid out. The amount of premium charged for each insured party and subsequently reinvested is influenced by the type of life insurance product sold and the mortality statistics relative to its customer base.

As with any life insurance company, Metro Corporation expects to make a profit by collecting more in premia funds than is needed to pay out claims against early redemption of cash value or death. Because the cash flow timing between payment of policy-related claims and collection of premia is not a perfect match, life insurance companies spend a lot of time maximizing the use of collected funds by investing them prior to their dispersion for settling claims. In fact, the investment activity of a large insurance company is a key source of its annual revenue.

Metro Corporation, similar to other major life insurers, is subject to investment regulation which restricts what investments it can buy. The purpose of government regulation is to help maintain the insurers' solvency in order that all claimants' financial rights can be met.

In general, life insurers are not able to invest in risky investments. Specifically, life insurers can rarely invest more than 10 percent of their admitted assets in common stocks. The bulk of the investments therefore are fixed income in nature—e.g., U.S. treasury securities, corporate bonds, money market instruments, to name a few.

The Assignment

You are an investment officer in Metro Corporation's investment management department. Your job is to invest excess funds in fixed income securities with a term to maturity no longer than 5 years. Up until now, you have usually bought medium-term notes issued by large U.S. companies with ratings of Baa or better (or equivalent ratings). The bonds are seldom callable and can be traded in a liquid secondary market. Refer to Appendix 6-1 for background information on the asset swap market.

Because of the high credit quality and common features of the notes, Metro Corporation usually earns a per annum rate of return which is 30 to 50 basis points higher than the per annum rate of return offered on U.S. Treasury notes with similar maturities. The actual yield spread between a Medium Term Note (MTN) and a similar maturity U.S. Treasury Note will depend primarily on the credit rating of the MTN issuer.

Refer to Exhibit 6-2 for information on yield spreads between AA rated corporate bonds—a good proxy for medium-term note yields—and same maturity AAA rated corporate bonds.

Your boss has been visited by several Wall Street investment bankers from Taylor Brothers, Inc. during the spring of 1989. Their mission has been to educate the Investment Department at Metro Corporation about an alternative to direct fixed income investing,

EXHIBIT 6-2

AA Corporate Bond − AAA Corporate Bond
Spread (Five Year Maturity)

	AA Bond % Yield	AAA Bond % Yield	AA–AAA Spread
1985			
Jan.	12.43	12.08	0.35
Feb.	12.49	12.13	0.36
March	12.91	12.56	0.35
April	12.69	12.23	0.46
May	12.3	11.72	0.58
June	11.46	10.94	0.52
July	11.42	10.97	0.45
August	11.47	11.05	0.42
Sept.	11.46	11.07	0.39
Oct.	11.45	11.02	0.43
Nov.	11.07	10.55	0.52
Dec.	10.63	10.16	0.47
1986			
Jan.	10.46	10.05	0.41
Feb.	10.13	9.67	0.46
March	9.49	9	0.49
April	9.21	8.79	0.42
May	9.43	9.09	0.34
June	9.49	9.13	0.36
July	9.28	8.88	0.4
August	9.22	8.72	0.5
Sept.	9.36	8.89	0.47
Oct.	9.33	8.86	0.47
Nov.	9.2	8.68	0.52
Dec.	9.02	8.49	0.53
1987			
Jan.	8.86	8.36	0.5
Feb.	8.88	8.38	0.5
March	8.84	8.36	0.48
April	9.15	8.85	0.3
May	9.59	9.33	0.26
June	9.65	9.32	0.33
July	9.64	9.42	0.22
August	9.86	9.67	0.19
Sept.	10.35	10.18	0.17
Oct.	10.74	10.52	0.22
Nov.	10.27	10.01	0.26
Dec.	10.33	10.11	0.22

1988			
Jan.	10.09	9.88	0.21
Feb.	9.6	9.4	0.2
March	9.59	9.39	0.2
April	9.86	9.67	0.19
May	10.1	9.9	0.2
June	10.13	9.86	0.27
July	10.26	9.96	0.3
August	10.37	10.11	0.26
Sept.	10.06	9.82	0.24
Oct.	9.71	9.51	0.2
Nov.	9.72	9.45	0.27
Dec.	9.81	9.57	0.24

Source: Moody's Investor Services.

namely buying synthetic fixed income securities. A synthetic fixed income security is the result of buying a security such as a floating rate certificate of deposit or floating rate note with a variable interest stream and transforming this floating interest stream accruing to the investor to a fixed interest stream via an interest rate swap.

After a lengthy session, your boss has asked you to examine the specific investment opportunity offered to Metro Corporation. You have plenty of information to review, including the proposal from Taylor Brothers, Inc., shown in Exhibits 6-3 through 6-5 and Appendix 6-2. You also go to the library to retrieve some or all of the articles included in the bibliography.

Since it is Friday afternoon, you have the entire weekend to research synthetic securities generated via an asset linked interest rate swap (called an "asset swap"). The objective is to enter into an interest rate swap and floating rate note purchase if and only if the perceived rewards outweigh the perceived risks. By 9:00 AM Monday morning you must have answers for your boss to the following questions:

1. What are the economics associated with buying a floating rate certificate or note and entering into a simultaneous interest rate swap? In other words, what is the expected fixed rate return of the swap [along with

EXHIBIT 6-3

Taylor Brothers, Inc. Proposal for Metro Corporation

Taylor Brothers, Inc. proposes that Metro Corporation purchase a floating rate note and enter into an interest rate swap in order to exchange the floating rate investment income for a fixed rate cash inflow. This will provide Metro Corporation with an alternative source of fixed income and, at times, even offer a superior fixed income return to the five-year corporate bond (medium term note) now purchased by Metro Corporation.

TRANSACTION OPPORTUNITY. The Kingdom of Belgratia has issued a 10-year floating rate note which is currently selling at par. Its coupon of 6-month LIBOR plus 10 basis points resets every 6 months when 6-month LIBOR is recalculated. A basis point is 1/100 of 1%. One basis point equals 0.0001 or 0.01%. Specifically, if a 6-month LIBOR is reset at 8% for the next six months, the coupon the investor would receive would be equal to the dollar face value of the notes multiplied by one half of 8.10%. If the investor had purchased $5 million of notes, she would receive ($5.0 mm × 0.0810) or $202,500. Since 8.10% is a per annum rate but the reset period lasts for only six months, the investor receives only one half of the 8.10% annual rate. This issue is rated AA so the bond credit rating is similar to the credit quality of bonds currently purchased. The floating rate note has a final maturity in 10 years. Since Metro Corporation can only make 5-year investments, Metro Corporation will have to resell the floating rate note 5 years from now. Like any bond, the floating rate note could be sold at a different price than its original purchase price.

This is how it would work:

1. Metro Corporation buys $5 million of Kingdom of Belgratia FRN's (floating rate notes) priced at par and bearing interest equal to 6-month LIBOR plus 10 basis points. Metro Corporation currently prices its investible funds at a cost equal to 3-month Commercial Paper. The rationale for this is that if investible funds were not available for investing, Metro Corporation would raise funds by issuing 3-month Commercial Paper and reinvest the proceeds in anticipation of using the funds to meet insurance claims. Exhibit

6-4 provides information about 6-month LIBOR–3-month Commercial Paper spreads.

2. Metro Corporation enters into an interest rate swap with Fujimoto Bank which issues bonds currently rated as AAA. The interest rate swap is legally independent from Metro Corporation's purchase of a floating rate note. If Fujimoto Bank defaults on its contractual obligation with Metro Corporation to make interest payments as outlined in the swap agreement, the interest income payable to Metro Corporation from the floating rate note issued by the Kingdom of Belgratia still accrues to its investors.

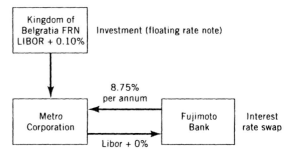

3. The interest exchange would be governed by an interest rate swap document in force for 5 years from the date of execution.

The annual return to Metro Corporation is provided below:

	Cash flows
Swap receipt of fixed rate from Fujimoto Bank	+8.75%
Payment of swap floating rate (payable every six months)	−6 month LIBOR
FRN Interest Income (payable every six months)	+6 month LIBOR +0.10%
Annual swap fee paid to Taylor Brothers, Inc. for the next five years	−0.05%
Net return to Metro Corporation	+8.80%

Currently, this compares favorably to a fixed income rate of return for a 5-year MTN which is yielding 8.70% per annum.

EXHIBIT 6-4

6-month LIBOR − 3-month CP Yield

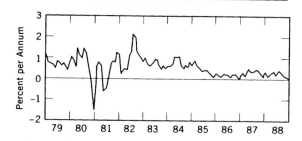

Date Range	Mean	Min.	Max.	Std. Dev.
1979–1988	88.779	61.125	117.095	14.989
1979	NC[1]	NC	NC	NC
1980	NC	NC	NC	NC
1981	NC	NC	NC	NC
1982	NC	NC	NC	NC
1983	NC	NC	NC	NC
1984	NC	NC	NC	NC
1985	72.361	61.125	80.842	5.841
1986	101.454	76.769	117.095	14.347
1987	96.759	89.136	116.450	7.937
1988	84.543	66.238	99.000	9.933

The pattern of swap spreads in longer maturities (4–10 years) reflects supply and demand pressures created by the absolute level of U.S. treasury rates, the shape of the treasury yield curve, credit perceptions, rate views, activity in the Eurobond and domestic markets, as well as speculation. For example, the stock market crash in October 1987 and the subsequent fall in interest rates brought many fixed rate payers to the swap market. This increased demand caused swap spreads to widen by 30 basis points almost overnight. Once the market stabilized, swap spreads began to fall back to more normal levels. The decline in swap spreads continued throughout 1988 as corporations used the swap market to achieve lower-cost floating rate funds by issuing fixed rate debt and swapping into floating. See Exhibit 6-5 for details.

Source: *Citicorp INTEREST RATE SPREADS ANALYSIS: Managing and Reducing Rate Exposure*, Probus Publishing Company, 1989, p. 34.

EXHIBIT 6-5

(5-year) Swap Spread (Offer)

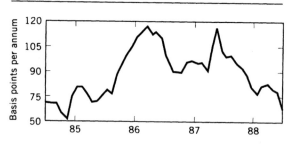

Date Range	Mean	Min.	Max.	Std. Dev.
1979–1988	0.529	−1.454	2.078	0.463
1979	0.699	0.398	1.202	0.199
1980	0.688	−1.454	1.430	0.789
1981	0.344	−0.671	1.220	0.623
1982	1.045	0.254	2.078	0.578
1983	0.705	0.479	0.929	0.161
1984	0.708	0.479	1.068	0.205
1985	0.442	0.112	0.831	0.224
1986	0.147	−0.024	0.212	0.065
1987	0.289	0.135	0.454	0.107
1988	0.221	−0.003	0.355	0.117

This spread is a function of (1) the shape of the yield curve; (2) the difference in investment quality between CP and LIBOR-based instruments; (3) the relative liquidity of CP versus LIBOR-based instruments.

Source: *Citicorp INTEREST RATE SPREADS ANALYSIS: Managing and Reducing Rate Exposure*, Probus Publishing Company, 1989, p. 61.

the] floating rate security purchase? How does this compare to the fixed rate return available to investors in the medium-term note market?

2. What is the liquidity for each of the two component elements of the synthetic security, namely the floating rate security and the interest rate swap?

3. What are the credit risks associated with the synthetic security?

4. What are the transaction dollar minimums for a synthetic security?

5. What other risk considerations are germane to this type of investment that don't exist with straight forward fixed income investing?

APPENDIX 6-1

The Asset Swap Market

In the past several years, international investing has offered investors a broad range of choices to minimize risk or enhance yield. According to *Pensions and Investments*,[1] U.S. assets invested abroad exceed $69 billion. This represents over a 20 percent increase in assets under management by U.S. tax-exempt institutions for the year ended March 31, 1991.[2] Myriad reasons exist for the phenomenal growth in international investing. The last decade was characterized by copious deregulation of various international financial markets. As a result, information flows and capital movement have become easier to effect.[3] Studies have shown that international capital markets have often outperformed U.S. stock and bond markets. For example, 1987–1990 average rates of return earned by U.S. investors holding British government bonds exceeded 17 percent per year.[4] Foreign currency appreciation as well as economic policies abroad which contribute to relatively stronger financial markets account for much of the return superiority over U.S. securities.

Moreover, empirical studies have shown that international investments are often statistically uncorrelated or have low positive correlation with their U.S. counterparts. As such, the investor who adds international investments to her current holdings can reduce the total risk of her portfolio. The extent of risk reduction can be measured quantitatively with the use of statistical measures of association between two classes of foreign securities.

International investing takes many forms. The nature of the issuer, currency of denomination, and/or the country of security placement characterize an investment as international. Often, one can invest internationally by buying securities issued in U.S. dollars and sold in the United States but issued by foreign companies. For example, Sony Corporation is-

---

[1]*Pensions and Investments*, May 20, 1991, p. 18.

[2]*Pensions and Investments*, June 24, 1991, p. 19.

[3]Susan M. Jarzombek, "Current Developments in the Capital Markets," *The Bankers Magazine*, January/February 1990, pp. 54–57.

[4]Michael R. Sesit, "Foreign Nations' Bonds May Lose Allure," *The Wall Street Journal*, July 2, 1991.

sues stock denominated in U.S. dollars and listed on the New York Stock Exchange. However, one could also be described as an international investor if she buys a bond issued by a non-U.S. company or government and denominated in U.S. dollars but placed outside the United States. For example, the Kingdom of Denmark is a frequent issuer of Eurodollar bonds which are bonds that are denominated in Eurodollars and sold outside the United States. Lastly, an investor could invest internationally by buying a security which is denominated in a currency other than U.S. dollars. For example, the Walt Disney Company has been a frequent issuer of bonds denominated in currencies such as Swiss francs or [Japanese] yen.

Suffice it to say that a plethora of securities exist today with one or several features that distinguish them as foreign investment vehicles. An investor can pick and choose according to her desire for diversity in currency, issuer, or trading market. The broad range of available international investments continues to grow in large part due to the development in the early 1980s of a new financial product known as an interest rate swap. An interest rate swap is defined as a contractual arrangement between two parties to exchange a defined stream of interest rate flows for a specified period of time.

In the swap contract, each party is referred to as either the floating rate payor or the fixed rate payor. Each party is also referred to as a counterparty to the swap contract. It is considered an off balance sheet financial instrument because participation in a swap is not directly reflected on the counterparty's balance sheet. The typical plain vanilla interest rate swap involves an agreement where one party pays a fixed rate such as 10 percent per annum in exchange for the receipt from the second party of a floating rate equal to 6-month LIBOR (London Interbank Offered Rate).

This type of interest rate swap is also referred to as a "coupon" interest rate swap. No principal is exchanged. Therefore, an interest rate swap is based on a "notional" principal amount. The market transaction size minimum is $5 million. Because no principal is exchanged, the credit risk of each is limited to the payments it will receive from its partner. There are endless variations on this theme of interest rate exchanges.

Interest rate swaps can be used to lower a company's cost of funding or increase the return of invested funds. Specifically, an interest rate swap facilitates the exchange of a funding advantage one participant enjoys in the fixed credit market for the relative advantage the second participant enjoys in the floating credit markets.

An asset swap is different from a liability driven interest rate swap since the investor is motivated by the asset side of the balance sheet. Moreover, the investor is taking on the credit risk of the floating rate note issuer when she buys a floating rate note plus the credit risk of the swap counterparty. Specifically, the investor is counting on receiving interest and principal from the floating rate note issuer as well as receiving interest payments from the swap counterparty. The nature of each risk is very different. The risk that the swap counterparty might default on the obligations under the swap is limited to the difference between prevailing market rates at the time of counterparty default and the rate she is obligated to pay under the swap contract. This is usually a fraction of the notional principal amount.

Bibliography

1. ANTL, BORIS (ed.), *Euromoney Special Financing Report: Swap Financing Techniques*, London, Euromoney Publications, Ltd., 1983.

2. ARNOLD, TANYA S., "How to Do Interest Rate Swaps," *Harvard Business Review*, September/October 1984, pp. 96–101.

3. BICKSLER, JAMES AND ANDREW H. CHEN, "An Economic Analysis of Interest Rate Swaps," *The Journal of Finance*, vol. XLI, No. 3, July 1986, pp. 645–655.

4. FLACK, STUART, "Swapping to Safety," *Corporate Finance*, January 1988, pp. 19–21.

5. FREEMAN, ANDREW, "Secondary Market Moves into First Place," *Financial Times*, June 7, 1990.

6. JARZOMBEK, SUSAN M., "Interest Rate Swaps Can Reduce Borrowing Costs," *The Financial Manager*, May/June 1989, pp. 70–74.

7. LEREAH, DAVID, "The Growth of Interest Rate Swaps," *The Bankers Magazine*, May/June 1986, pp. 36–41.

8. LOEYS, JAN G., "Interest Rate Swaps: A New Tool for Managing Risk," *Business Review*, Federal Reserve Bank of Philadelphia, May/June 1985, pp. 17–25.

9. PITMAN, JOANNA, "Swooping on Swaps," *Euromoney*, January 1988, pp. 68–80.

10. PRINGLE, JOHN J. AND LARRY D. WALL, "Alternative Explanations of Interest Rate Swaps," *Working Paper Series no. 87-2*, Federal Reserve Bank of Atlanta, April 15, 1987.

11. REIER, SHARON, "The Rise of Interest Rate Swaps," *Institutional Investor*, October 1982, pp. 95–100.

12. SHIRREFF, DAVID, "Not So Sexy," *RISK Magazine*, vol. 3, no. 6, June 1990.

13. "The Way to Any Market," *Euromoney*, November 1983, pp. 60–75.

14. WHITTAKER, J. GREGG, "Interest Rate Swaps: Risk and Regulation," *Economic Review*, Federal Reserve Bank of Kansas City, March 1987, pp. 3–13.

The American Electric Engine Corporation, Inc.

Foreign Currency Exposure Management and Eurocurrency Funding

HARVEY A. PONIACHEK

The Company and Its Business

The American Electric Engine Corporation, Inc. (AEE) was incorporated in 1945 in Delaware and is headquartered in Albany, Georgia. The corporation is engaged in designing, manufacturing, and servicing a wide range of electric engines and power transformation products for the industrial, commercial, and consumer markets. AEE corporation is among the largest companies in its field in the United States, but business is highly competitive, with numerous companies operating in the market. There is keen import price competition, primarily from the Asian Newly Industrialized Countries (NICs) and Brazil.

Worldwide sales in 1989 reached $385 million and net income was $18.5 million. The corporation employs a labor forces of 4000, of which 12000 work abroad. The company is listed on the American Stock Exchange under the symbol AEE, with approximately 8000 outstanding shares. Its stock and bond Standard & Poor's (S & P) ratings are AAB.

The corporation operates 70 facilities, including manufacturing plants, warehouses,

sales and services offices in 35 states, with the primary manufacturing facilities located in Georgia. AEE sells its products through sales offices and independent distributors throughout the United States.

International Operation

The company's products are marketed abroad through the International Sales Department personnel that are stationed overseas, local distributors and foreign affiliates. AEE corporation conducts business in 15 foreign countries, with the largest and most significant foreign operation being in Italy. The corporation has expanded its operations abroad in recent years through joint ventures in many countries. In 1988, AEE acquired all the outstanding common stock of its Italian Subsidiary (Angelica S.p.A.) for $20 million, paying $5 million in cash and the balance of $15 million was paid in 3-year notes yielding 11 percent.

AEE's exports sales from the United States were $50 million in 1989, up from $40 million in the previous year, about one-half of which was shipped to foreign affiliates. The weakness of the dollar in the past several years provided a competitive edge to AEE products. Sales by foreign affiliates reached $120 million in 1989, of which 64 percent were local sales, 24 percent were sales to other countries, including sister companies, and 12 percent went to the United States, including the parent company. Intercompany sales by foreign entities to the parent company and its domestic and foreign affiliates were 25 percent.

The Italian Affiliate

AEE operates in Italy through a wholly owned subsidiary—Angelica, S.p.A. Operations in Italy account for some 70 percent of international sales and 75 percent of foreign assets. Sales of Angelica S.p.A. in 1989 were approximately $85 million, earnings were $15 million, and assets were approximately $65 million. A recently instituted aggressive credit policy provided Angelica's clients with average terms of payments of 90–120 days, and possibly up to 120–150 days for selective clients, compared with 60–90 days at competing firms. The aggressive credit policy contributed to sharp sales expansion. Management assessed that Angelica's sales are expected to expand by 10–15 percent annually in the rest of the decade. Sufficient availability of funds, therefore, was crucial for the firm's competitive position in the marketplace. The firm has commonly followed a policy of raising working capital funds through the Eurocurrency market.

At the end of 1989, AEE corporation had an outstanding short-term revolving loan of $30 million equivalent denominated in Italian lire and priced at LIBOR plus 1 percent and rolled-over every three months from several foreign bank subsidiaries (Eurobanks) in Italy. At the end of 1989, Euro-lira interest rate were quoted at $12\frac{3}{8}$–$12\frac{7}{8}$, and the cost of this loan was $12\frac{7}{8}$ percent + 1 percent spread, which equaled $13\frac{7}{8}$. The loan was fully secured by an equal amount of Italian government medium term bonds that yielded 12 percent at the end of 1989. About one-third of the Italian government securities was maturing at the end of 1990, with the balance maturing on December 31, 1995.

Foreign Exchange

AEE follows FASB 52. Cumulative translation adjustments were $6 million in 1989 and $2.5 million in the previous year.

The Assignment

Mr. Joe Brown, Executive Vice President and Chief Financial Officer (CFO), has recently attended an executive conference at the Bank of America World Headquarters in San Francisco.

The conference addressed the global economic outlook, including the implications of the 1992 enhanced unification of the European Community (EC). The Bank's senior economist for Europe suggested the possibility of a major currency realignment in the EC by the middle of next year, as new member countries join the European Monetary System (EMS).

Expectations for a likely devaluation of the Italian currency within the EMS currency realignment was given a high probability. (The Italian lire was trading at lire/$1266.25–1272.50 at year end 1989, but an expected depreciation of some 7.5–10 percent was projected.) Furthermore, the near term maturing of Angelica's one-third of the Italian government securities, which were used as collaterals for its Euro-lira loan, prompted the CFO to request an assessment of the Italian operation and refinancing strategy.

The CFO requested you, the Assistant Treasurer for International Affairs, to undertake the following:

1. To submit an assessment of the foreign currency translation and transaction exposure

of Angelica and hedging recommendations. The analysis should include an evaluation of the most attractive and cost effective foreign currency hedging, either through the forward market, currency futures, the money market, swaps, the currency options market (if you can obtain quotations of currency options), or through balance sheet manipulation.

2. To consider the most cost effective method for refunding one-third of the Euro-lira loan of the Italian subsidiary, and provide it sufficient working capital in light of its anticipated sales growth and generous terms of payments. The proposed funding of Angelica should be considered in terms of the corporation's consolidated capital structure, cost of capital and foreign currency risk. (Recall that the Euro-lira loan is collateralized by government securities, of which one-third matures by year end 1990. Therefore, one-third of the Euro-loan or require a new form of collaterals.) The Executive Finance Committee has emphasized the need to refrain from unnecessary currency exposure, and/or to avoid provisions of collateral against new bank loans.

The corporation was receptive to various financing methods, including short- and long-term debt, and fixed and floating interest rate debt, an infusion of equity into its subsidiary, raising debt on behalf of its affiliates abroad and swaps.

Financial and Economic Data

The Assistant Treasurer was provided with AEE's consolidated financial statements and financial statements of its Italian subsidiary. The following data were gathered and/or reviewed in the business library by the Assistant Treasurer in preparation of the assignment:

1. A country study on Italy,
2. IMF, International Financial Statistics (the country pages related to Italy),

3. IMF, International Financial Statistics, currency, and interest rate data,
4. *The Wall Street Journal*, data on interest rates, exchange rates, options, and futures,
5. The *Financial Times*, data on interest rates, exchange rates, options, and futures,
6. IMF, Exchange Arrangements, and Exchange Restrictions,
7. U.S. Department of Commerce, Italy, Foreign Economic Trends, and
8. U.S. Department of Commerce, Investment Climates in Foreign Countries, vol. I. Italy.

CONSOLIDATED BALANCE SHEETS

The American Electric Engine Corporation, Inc.
(Dollars in thousands)

DECEMBER 31	1989	1988
ASSETS		
Current assets:		
Cash and short-term investments	$ 7,589	$ 4,564
Marketable securities	35,127	33,778
Trade receivables	79,793	72,734
Inventories	56,590	56,652
Other	5,301	5,875
Total current assets	184,000	173,603
Property		
Land and buildings	34,824	31,026
Machinery and equipment	189,311	172,393
Total	224,135	203,419
Less accumulated depreciation	104,870	86,658
Property—net	119,265	116,761
Investment in and advances to affiliates	34,380	14,285
Other assets	4,806	3,502
TOTAL	342,851	308,151

(Continued)

DECEMBER 31	1989	1988
LIABILITIES AND STOCKHOLDER' EQUITY		
Current liabilities:		
Current maturities of debt	32,674	41,414
Trade payables	28,948	30,998
Compensation and commissions	14,875	100,581
Federal, state, and foreign income taxes	2,053	135
Dividends payable	3,496	3,392
Other	15,908	12,423
Total Current liabilities	97,954	98,943
Long-term debt	62,716	42,044
Deferred taxes and other	26,643	25,896
Deferred common stock agreement	—	3,090
Stockholders' equity:		
Common stock and additional paid-in capital	29,922	28,128
Retained earnings	119,484	114,842
Cumulative translation adjustments	6,132	2,279
Treasury stock	—	(7,071)
Total stockholders' equity	155,538	138,178
TOTAL	342,851	308,151

STATEMENTS OF CONSOLIDATED INCOME

The American Electric Engine Corporation, Inc.

(Dollars in thousands except per share data)

FOR THE YEARS ENDED DECEMBER 31,	1989	1988
Net Sales	385,829	356,226
Cost of goods sold	276,867	257,297
Gross profit	108,962	98,929
Selling, general and administrative expenses	76,250	69,930
Loss of discontinued subsidiary in Brazil	—	1,991
Income from operations	32,712	27,008
Interest expense	9,032	10,059
Interest income	4,572	4,487
Income from affiliates	726	1,526
Other income (expense)—net	(517)	445
Income before income taxes	28,461	23,407
Federal, state and foreign income taxes	9,924	6,592
Net income	18,537	16,815
Net income per share	1.03	0.94

STATEMENT OF CONDITIONS

Angelica, S.p.A. (Italian Sub.)

Italian Lire, billions

DECEMBER 31	1989	1988
ASSETS		
Current assets:		
Cash and short-term investments	IL 1,684	1,176
Marketable securities[a]	40,926	47,534
Trade receivables	17,704	18,744
Inventories	12,556	14,599
Other	1,176	1,514
Total current sales	74,045	83,566
Property		
Land and buildings	7,727	7,995
Machinery and equipment	42,003	44,426
Total	49,730	52,421
Less accumulated depreciation	23,268	22,332

(Continued)

DECEMBER 31	1989	1988
Property—net	26,462	30,089
Other assets		902
TOTAL	100,507	114,558

LIABILITIES AND STOCKHOLDER'S EQUITY

	1989	1988
Current liabilities:		
Current maturities of debt	7,250	10,672
Trade payables[b]	6,423	7,988
Compensation and commissions	3,300	2,727
Federal, state and foreign income taxes	456	35
Dividends payable	776	874
Other	6,803	2,447
Total Current liabilities	25,007	24,743
Short-term liabilities	35,079	47,534
Deferred taxes and other	5,911	6,673
Stockholders' equity:	34,510	35,608
TOTAL[c]	IL 100,507	114,559

[a] 64% of the account receivables are denominated in Italian lire, 12% in dollars, 20% in DM, and 4% in French francs.

[b] Some 75% of the account payables are in dollars, 20% are in Italian lire, and 5% in DM.

[c] The Italian lire per dollars at the end of 1987, 1986, and 1985 were 1,169.3, 1,358.1, and 1,678.5, and the average rates for these years were 1296.1, 1490.8, and 1909.4.

STATEMENTS OF INCOME
Angelica, S.p.A. (Italian Sub.)

Italian Lire, billions   IL, billions

FOR THE YEARS ENDED DECEMBER 31,	1989	1988
Net Sales	110,401	117,242
Cost of goods sold	79,223	84,683
Gross profit	31,178	32,560
Selling, general and administrative expenses	21,818	23,016
Various expenses	0	655
Income from operations	9,360	8,889
Interest expense	2,584	3,311
Interest income	1,308	1,477
Various Income	208	502
Income before income taxes	8,144	7,704
Income taxes	2,840	2,170
Net income	5,304	5,534

Note: The exchange rates for translation are listed in footnote [c] of the Statement of Conditions.

The International Chemical Corporation, Inc.

Positioning of Global Activities, Currency Exposure, and Funding

HARVEY A. PONIACHEK

The Company and Its Business

The International Chemical Corporation, Inc. (ICC) was incorporated in 1917 in Delaware, and is headquartered in Elizabeth, New Jersey. ICC manufactures chemical products and pharmaceuticals that are sold throughout the United States and around the world. Sales were in excess of $1.1 billion in 1987 and net income was $52.4 million. The company employs 8000 people, with some 75 percent of them employed in the United States. The corporation is listed on the New York Stock Exchange under the symbol ICC and it has some 40,000 shares outstanding. ICC's bonds and stocks Standard & Poor's (S&P) credit ratings are AAA.

ICC has a significant market share in certain chemical and pharmaceutical products, but the company faces keen competition from many larger and smaller domestic and international corporations.

The company has rights to some natural resources, including oil and gas, which are

used in the production of certain chemical products. ICC owns some 900 U.S. and 1500 foreign patents, and some 800 U.S. and 2500 foreign registered trademarks.

ICC's major research and development (R&D) centers are located in New Jersey and Texas. About 900 employees are engaged in R&D activities, which cost $75 million in 1987 and $60 million in the year before.

International

ICC operates 75 plants and facilities in 20 countries outside the United States, of which 65 are chemicals and 10 pharmaceuticals. In 1987, international business accounted for 25 percent of worldwide sales, 32 percent of total earnings and 33 percent of consolidated assets. The bulk of the company's international operations (90% of sales, 80% of earnings and 80% of assets) is connected within the European Community (EC)—primarily the United Kingdom, France, Germany, the Netherlands, and Italy.

Operation in Canada has expanded sharply in recent years, while activities in Latin America, including Mexico, were adversely affected

EXHIBIT 8-1

The International Chemical Corporation
Geographic Position

| | Percent of Total | |
	Sales	Assets
United States	71.6	66.9
Europe	23.9	26.9
Other international	4.4	10.5
Total	100.0	100.0

Source: Annual Report and 10K.

by the region's external debt crisis that erupted since the early 1980s. See Exhibit 8-1 for information on the geographic operation of ICC. Operation in Asia is predominantly in the Southeast Asian Newly-Industrialized Countries (NICs) and Japan.

ICC's products are marketed abroad through several channels, including the International Sales Department overseas personnel that works closely with local distributors, and through affiliated and non-affiliated companies. Sales by foreign affiliates were 64 percent local, 24 percent to other countries (including sister companies), and 12 percent to the U.S. (including the parent company). Total sales to the parent and its affiliates were 25 percent.

ICC has a considerable amount of export business, mainly to its foreign affiliates that function as distributors. Exports from the U.S. were $150 million in 1987, up from $120 million in the previous year. The weakness of the dollar in the past several years provided a considerable competitive edge to the company.

International operations are subject to a number of potential risks and constraints, such as foreign currency volatility, country risk, foreign exchange controls, and the business climate in the various markets.

Performance

Consolidated financial statements, and data on affiliates in France and Mexico are shown on pp. 53–56. ICC's effective tax rate was 41.4 percent in 1987 and 36.9 percent in 1986.

Borrowing and Acquisitions

In 1987, ICC entered into a $50 million (equivalent) Euro-sterling Commercial Paper Program. The corporation also issued $75 million worth of Eurobonds denominated in D-mark (75%) and SF (25%).

In 1987 ICC acquired the assets of Chemex S. A., a French chemical company for $50 million in cash. The excess cost over the fair value of the net assets was approximately $10 million, which is being amortized on a straight-line basis over 40 years.

Currency Exposure Management

The corporation follows the Financial Accounting Standards Board (FASB) #52, but ICC hedges its translation exposure on a selective basis; that is, translation exposure hedging is done only in cases where there is expectations for an imminent depreciation of currency rates. Transaction exposure is always hedged by various instruments, including the forward markets, money markets, futures, currency options and swaps.

Cumulative translation loss was $26.7 million in 1986 and $40.7 million in the previous year.

Financial Statements of ICC

THE INTERNATIONAL CHEMICAL CORPORATION, INC (ICC)

Consolidated Balance Sheet

	1987	1986
	(Thousands of dollars)	

ASSETS

Current assets		
Cash	$ 4,858	$ 11,510
Short-term investments	48,544	49,053
Receivables, net allowance for doubtful accounts		
Trade	177,796	176,909
Other	28,728	16,794
Inventories	195,249	160,548
Prepaid expenses	11,915	13,266
Net assets of discontinued operations	39,119	42,451
Total current assets	506,209	470,531
Investments and other receivables		
Investments and advances		
Nonconsolidated subsidiaries	15,330	17,369
Affiliates	18,225	15,698
Long-term receivables	5,971	5,941
	39,526	39,008
Property, plant and equipment		
Land	36,343	33,812
Mineral, oil and gas properties	24,388	25,321
Buildings	148,130	133,888
Equipment	696,249	642,899
	905,110	835,920
Less accumulated depreciation, depletion, and amortization	473,081	410,009
	432,029	425,911
Goodwill and other intangible assets	48,037	34,433
Other assets	15,862	13,723
	1,041,663	$938,606

LIABILITIES AND SHAREHOLDERS' INVESTMENT

	1987	1986
Current Liabilities		
Notes Payable	$ 16,286	$ 31,161
Current maturities of long-term debt	32,326	17,553
Accounts payable		
Trade	81,927	55,420
Other	11,285	9,274
Federal and other income taxes	17,802	6,665
Accrued salaries and wages	22,754	20,292
Other current liabilities	73,546	70,828
Total current liabilities	255,926	211,193
Long-term debt	218,941	188,457
Deferred income taxes	70,416	63,303
Deferred credits	21,233	24,851
Redeemable preference stock	—	125,339
Shareholders' investment		
Voting preference stock	1,904	1,999
Common stock	13,076	12,946
Additional paid-in capital	239,434	215,300
Earnings retained for use in the business	294,490	287,057
Cumulative translation adjustment	(3,346)	(26,762)
	545,558	490,540
Less common stock in Treasury	(70,411)	(116,077)
Total shareholders' investment	475,147	374,463
	$1,041,663	$983,606

THE INTERNATIONAL CHEMICAL CORPORATION, INC. (ICC)

Consolidated Statement of Operations

	1987	1986
	(Thousands of dollars except per share amounts)	
Income		
Sales and operating revenues	$ 1,142,750	$ 1,050,451
Other net	7,139	11,601
	1,149,889	1,062,022

(Continued)

	1987	1986
	(Thousands of dollars except per share amounts)	
Cost and expenses		
Cost of goods sold	739,444	677,637
Selling and administrative	247,276	237,591
Research and development	45,067	43,994
Interest	26,332	22,114
	1,058,119	981,336
Earnings from continued operations before income taxes	91,770	80,686
Income taxes	37,967	29,805
Earnings from continuing operations	53,803	50,881
Discontinued operations, net of income taxes Earnings (loss) from discontinued operations	(1,365)	1,066
(Loss) from disposal	—	—
	(1,365)	1,066
Net earnings (loss)	$ 52,438	$ 51,947
Earnings per common and common equivalent share earnings from continuing operations	$ 4.12	$ 3.57
Net earnings (loss)	$ 4.02	$ 3.64

	1987	1986
Other	15,187	10,732
Inventories	103,220	102,597
Prepaid expenses	6,299	8,478
Net assets of discontinued operations	20,681	27,128
Total current assets	267,612	300,690
Investments and other receivables		
Investments and advances		
Nonconsolidated subsidiaries	8,104	11,100
Affiliates	9,635	10,032
Long-term receivables	3,157	3,797
	20,896	24,928
Property, plant and equipment		
Land	19,213	21,607
Mineral, oil and gas properties	12,893	16,181
Buildings	78,310	85,560
Equipment	368,079	410,841
	478,495	534,190
Less accumulated depreciation, depletion, and amortization	250,099	262,014
	228,396	272,176
Goodwill and other intangible assets	25,395	22,004
Other assets	8,386	8,770
	550,686	628,568

ICC, FRANCE

Balance Sheet

	1987	1986
	(Thousands of French francs)	
ASSETS		
Current assets		
Cash	2,568	7,355
Short-term investments	25,663	31,347
Receivables, net of doubtful accounts		
Trade	93,994	113,053

LIABILITIES AND SHAREHOLDERS' INVESTMENT

	1987	1986
Current Liabilities		
Notes Payable	8,610	19,913
Current maturities of long-term debt	17,089	11,217
Accounts payable		
Trade	43,312	35,416
Other	5,966	5,927
Federal and other income taxes	9,411	4,259
Accrued salaries and wages	12,029	12,968
Other current liabilities	38,881	45,262
Total current liabilities	135,298	134,962
Long-term debt	115,745	120,433

(Continued)

Deferred income taxes	37,226	40,453
Deferred credits	11,225	15,881
Redeemable preference stock		80,097
Total shareholders' investment	251,191	239,299
	550,686	628,568

ICC, FRANCE
Statement of Operations

	1987	1986
Income		
Sales and operating revenues	2,060,618	2,182,594
Other net earnings	4,248	24,105
Cost and expenses		
Cost of goods sold	440,013	464,645
Selling and administrative	147,144	162,912
Research and development	26,818	30,166
Interest	15,669	15,163
Restructuring program charges		
	629,644	672,886
Earnings from continued operations before income taxes	54,609	55,325
Income taxes	22,593	20,437
Earnings from continuing operations	32,016	34,888
Discontinued operations, net of income taxes: Earnings (loss) from discontinued operations (Loss) from disposal	(812)	731
	(812)	731
Net earnings (loss)	31,204	35,619

ICC, MEXICO
Balance Sheet

	1987	1986
	(Mexican Pesos, Millions)	
ASSETS		
Current assets		
Cash	429	425
Short-term investments	4,291	1,812
Receivables, net allowance for doubtful accounts		
Trade	15,715	6,535
Other	2,539	620
Inventories	17,258	5,931
Prepaid expenses	1,053	490
Net assets of discontinued operations	3,458	1,568
Total current assets	44,743	17,381
Investments and other receivables		
Investments and advances		
Affiliates	2,966	1,222
Long-term receivables	528	219
	3,494	1,441
Property, plant and equipment		
Land	3,212	1,249
Mineral, oil and gas properties	2,156	935
Buildings	13,093	4,946
Equipment	61,540	23,749
	80,001	30,879
Less accumulated depreciation, depletion and amortization	0 41,815	0 15,146
	38,186	15,733
Goodwill and other intangible assets	4,246	1,272
Other assets	1,402	507
	92,071	34,672

LIABILITIES AND SHAREHOLDERS' INVESTMENT

Current Liabilities		
Notes Payable	1,439	1,151

(Continued)

	1987	1986
	(Mexican Pesos, Millions)	
Current maturities		
of long-term debt	2,857	648
Accounts payable	0	0
Trade	7,241	2,047
Other	997	343
Income taxes	1,573	246
Accrued salaries and wages	2,011	750
Other current liabilities	6,501	2,616
Total current liabilities	22,621	7,801
	0	0
Long-term debt	19,352	6,962
Deferred income taxes	6,224	2,338
	0	0
Deferred credits	1,877	918
Redeemable stock	—	4,630
Total shareholders'		
investment	41,997	13,833
Total	92,071	34,672

ICC, MEXICO

Statement of Operations

(Mexican Pesos, Millions)

Income		
Sales and operating revenues	62,998	25,707
Other net earnings	394	284
	135,377	114,468
Cost and expenses		
Cost of goods sold	40,764	16,583
Selling and administrative	13,632	5,814
Research and development	2,484	1,077
Interest	1,452	541
	58,332	24,015

Earnings from continued operations	0	0
before income taxes	5,059	1,975
Income taxes	2,093	729
Earnings from continuing operations	2,966	1,245
Discontinued operations,		
net of income taxes	0	0
Earnings (loss) from		
discontinued operations	−75	26
(Loss) from disposal	0	0
	−75	26
Net earnings (loss)	2,891	1,271

The Assignment

The planned expansion of the European Community by 1992 and the signing of the Free Trade Agreement with Canada (and possibly further liberalization of trade relations with Mexico in the near future), induced many U.S. corporations to evaluate their international position particularly in Europe and Canada. James M. Robinson, Executive Vice President and Chief Financial Officer, has undertaken a strategic assessment of ICC's international position with special emphasis on the following objectives and issues:

1. Assessment of the international geographic operations of ICC. The objective is to determine whether ICC is properly positioned in the EC, Canada and Mexico, in comparison with other U.S. multinational companies. (Appendix 8-1 on direct foreign investment position and performance by U.S. MNCs should provide you with a benchmark on U.S. positioning abroad. You may, however, use alternative data.)

2. In light of the expected expansion of the European Monetary System (EMS) membership and the subsequent currency realignment that could occur, the CFO instructed his assistant for international affairs to assess ICC's currency translation

and transaction exposure in the French franc, as their European operation is headquartered in France, and examine several hedging programs in light of a possible French franc to dollar (FF/$) depreciation by 5–10 percent over the next year.

3. Determine the translation and transaction exposure of the Mexican subsidiary, and propose a suitable hedging policy.

4. The corporation has considered for some time expansion of its Mexican operation by $25 million. However, the type and source of funding are to be determined in light of Mexico's precarious macroeconomic and financial conditions, and the availability and cost of capital. Given that ICC seeks to maintain its capital structure (within plus/minus 5 percentage points) and weighted average cost of funds (within plus/minus 1 to 2 percentage points), what funding methods do you recommend for the Mexican operation? (Keep in mind Mexico's

international financial position, the scarcity of foreign exchange, the direct foreign investment law, and requirements for funding of foreign investment.)

Economic and Financial Data

The research assistant gathered, or reviewed in the library, the following information:

1. U.S. Department of Commerce, Survey of Current Business, U.S. Investment Abroad,
2. Country Reports on France and Mexico,
3. IMF, International Financial Statistics (country pages on), France and Mexico,
4. IMF, International Financial Statistics, Interest and Currency Rates,
5. IMF, Exchange Arrangements and Exchange Restrictions, and
6. U.S. Department of Commerce, Investment Climates in Foreign Countries, vol. IV.

APPENDIX 8-1

U.S. Direct Investment Abroad

Detail for Position and Balance of Payments Flows, 1988

The following tables[1] contain BEA's country-by-industry estimates and estimates by detailed account of the position and related capital and income flows for U.S. direct investment abroad. They also contain estimates of the position, capital flows, and income for all

countries and for all industries in which there was investment.

Summary position and flow estimates and analyses of the estimates were published in the June 1989 Survey of Current Business[2]

Source: U.S. Department of Commerce, Survey of Current Business, August 1989.

[1]Tables from Survey of Current Business, August 1989.

[2]The quarterly survey from which the annual estimates of U.S. direct investment abroad were derived was conducted by Mark New, under the supervision of Patricia C. Walker, Chief, U.S. Direct Investment Abroad Branch. Marie Laddomada, Richard J. McDermott, Steve Schorr, and Dwayne Torney assisted in preparing the estimates. Smith W. Allnutt III, Chief, Data Retrieval and Analysis Branch, designed the computer programs for data retrieval and tabular presentation.

in the articles "The International Investment Position of the United States in 1988" and "U.S. International Transactions, First Quarter 1989." Two other articles on U.S. direct investment abroad—"Capital Expenditures by Majority-Owned Foreign Affiliates of U.S. Companies, 1989" and "U.S. Multinational Companies: Operations in 1987"—appeared in the March 1989 and June 1989 *Surveys*, respectively.

Table A8-1   U.S. DIRECT INVESTMENT POSITION ABROAD

	Direct Investment Position			Change			
	Millions of Dollars			Millions of dollars		Percent	
	1986	1987	1988	1987	1988	1987	1988
All areas	**259,800**	**307,983**	**326,900**	**48,182**	**18,917**	**18.5**	**6.1**
Petroleum	58,497	61,800	59,658	3,303	−2,142	5.6	−3.5
Manufacturing	105,101	127,074	133,819	21,973	6,745	20.9	5.3
Other	96,202	119,109	133,424	22,907	14,315	23.8	12.0
Developed countries	**194,280**	**232,690**	**245,498**	**38,410**	**12,808**	**19.8**	**5.5**
Petroleum	36,502	40,312	40,299	3,810	−13	10.4	0.0
Manufacturing	85,392	105,605	108,850	20,212	3,245	23.7	3.1
Other	72,386	86,773	96,349	14,387	9,576	19.9	11.0
Canada	50,629	58,377	61,244	7,748	2,868	15.3	4.9
Petroleum	10,684	12,098	11,711	1,414	−388	13.2	−3.2
Manufacturing	23,564	26,782	28,141	3,219	1,359	13.7	5.1
Other	16,380	19,496	21,393	3,115	1,897	19.0	9.7
Europe	120,724	146,243	152,232	25,519	5,989	21.1	4.1
Petroleum	20,749	21,828	21,323	1,079	−505	5.2	−2.3
Manufacturing	52,231	67,424	67,930	15,193	506	29.1	.7
Other	47,744	56,991	62,978	9,246	5,988	19.4	10.5
Other	22,928	28,070	32,022	5,142	3,952	22.4	14.1
Petroleum	5,069	6,386	7,265	1,317	879	26.0	13.8
Manufacturing	9,598	11,398	12,779	1,800	1,381	18.8	12.1
Other	8,261	10,287	11,978	2,025	1,691	24.5	16.4
Developing countries	**61,072**	**70,676**	**76,837**	**9,604**	**6,161**	**15.7**	**8.7**
Petroleum	18,334	18,060	16,007	−274	−2,053	−1.5	−11.4
Manufacturing	19,709	21,469	24,969	1,761	3,499	8.9	16.3
Other	23,030	31,147	35,861	8,117	4,715	35.2	15.1
Latin American and Other							
Western Hemisphere	36,851	44,905	49,283	8,054	4,378	21.9	9.7
Petroleum	6,947	6,354	4,974	−593	−1,380	−8.5	−21.7
Manufacturing	14,805	15,768	17,850	963	2,082	6.5	13.2
Other	15,099	22,783	26,459	7,684	3,676	50.9	16.1
Other	24,221	25,771	27,553	1,550	1,783	6.4	6.9
Petroleum	11,386	11,706	11,033	319	−673	2.8	−5.8
Manufacturing	4,904	5,701	7,119	797	1,418	16.3	24.9
Other	7,931	8,363	9,402	433	1,038	5.5	12.4
International	**4,448**	**4,617**	**4,565**	**169**	**−52**	**3.8**	**−1.1**

*Less than 0.05 percent (±).

Table A8-2   U.S. DIRECT INVESTMENT POSITION ABROAD BY ACCOUNT (in millions of dollars)

| | 1987 | | | | | 1988 | | | | |
| | | | | Intercompany Debt | | | | | Intercompany Debt | |
	Total	Equity[1]	Net	U.S. Parents' Receivables	U.S. Parents' Payables	Total	Equity[1]	Net	U.S. Parents' Receivables	U.S. Parents' Payables
All areas	307,983	311,623	−3,641	60,665	64,306	326,900	322,559	4,341	63,023	58,682
Petroleum	61,800	57,434	4,366	14,255	9,889	59,658	53,557	6,100	14,580	8,480
Manufacturing	127,074	117,123	9,951	20,750	10,799	133,819	125,030	8,788	19,351	10,563
Other	119,109	137,067	−17,958	25,660	43,618	133,424	143,971	−10,547	29,092	39,639
Developed countries	232,690	208,427	24,263	41,901	17,638	245,498	218,898	26,601	44,221	17,621
Petroleum	40,312	34,611	5,701	7,827	2,126	40,299	33,639	6,660	8,436	1,775
Manufacturing	105,605	96,683	8,921	16,520	7,599	108,850	101,337	7,513	15,169	7,656
Other	86,773	77,132	9,641	17,555	7,914	96,349	83,922	12,427	20,616	8,189
Canada	58,377	51,798	6,579	10,599	4,020	61,244	54,699	6,545	10,878	4,333
Petroleum	12,098	11,194	904	1,161	257	11,711	10,165	1,545	1,755	210
Manufacturing	26,782	24,343	2,440	5,490	3,050	28,141	26,546	1,595	4,958	3,363
Other	19,496	16,260	3,235	3,948	713	21,393	17,988	3,405	4,165	760
Europe	146,243	132,631	13,612	25,651	12,039	152,232	137,011	15,221	27,246	12,025
Petroleum	21,828	17,741	4,087	5,736	1,649	21,323	16,910	4,413	5,862	1,449
Manufacturing	67,424	61,997	5,428	9,589	4,162	67,930	63,360	4,570	8,530	3,960
Other	56,991	52,894	4,097	10,325	6,228	62,978	56,741	6,238	12,854	6,616
Other	28,070	23,998	4,072	5,652	1,579	32,022	27,188	4,834	6,098	1,263
Petroleum	6,386	5,676	709	929	220	7,265	6,564	702	819	117
Manufacturing	11,398	10,344	1,054	1,441	387	12,779	11,431	1,348	1,681	334
Other	10,287	7,978	2,309	3,281	973	11,978	9,193	2,785	3,597	812
Developing countries	70,676	98,307	−27,632	18,022	45,654	76,837	98,717	−21,881	18,233	40,114
Petroleum	18,060	19,174	−1,114	5,814	6,928	16,007	16,374	−367	5,710	6,077
Manufacturing	21,469	20,440	1,029	4,230	3,201	24,969	23,694	1,275	4,182	2,907
Other	31,147	58,693	−27,547	7,978	35,525	35,861	58,650	−22,789	8,342	31,130
Latin American and Other Western Hemisphere	44,905	71,373	−26,468	9,718	36,186	49,283	71,034	−21,751	9,745	31,495
Petroleum	6,354	6,203	152	1,212	1,060	4,974	4,744	230	1,023	793
Manufacturing	15,768	13,855	1,913	2,816	903	17,850	15,987	1,863	2,876	1,013
Other	22,783	51,316	−28,533	5,690	34,222	26,459	50,303	−23,844	5,846	29,690
Other	25,771	26,934	−1,164	8,304	9,468	27,553	27,683	−130	8,489	8,619
Petroleum	11,706	12,972	−1,266	4,602	5,868	11,033	11,630	−597	4,687	5,284
Manufacturing	5,701	6,585	−884	1,414	2,298	7,119	7,707	−588	1,306	1,894
Other	8,363	7,378	986	2,288	1,302	9,402	8,347	1,055	2,496	1,441
International	4,617	4,889	−272	742	1,014	4,565	4,944	−379	568	947

[1]Includes capital stock, additional paid-in capital, and retained earnings.

Table A8-3   CHANGE IN THE U.S. DIRECT INVESTMENT POSITION ABROAD BY ACCOUNT (millions of dollars)

		Capital Outflows								
		Equity Capital				Rein-vested Earnings	Intercompany Debt			Valuation Adjust-ments
	Total	Total	Net	Increases	Decreases		Net	Increases in U.S. Parents' Receivables	Increases in U.S. Parents' Payables[1]	
1987										
All areas	**48,182**	**44,194**	**3,677**	**14,831**	**11,154**	**34,264**	**6,252**	**4,173**	**−2,079**	**3,988**
Petroleum	3,303	3,346	2,217	3,508	1,381	1,822	−604	−577	27	−43
Manufacturing	21,973	20,861	744	2,692	1,948	19,903	213	1,987	1,774	1,112
Other	22,907	19,988	806	8,631	7,825	12,539	6,642	2,763	−3,879	2,919
Developed countries	**38,410**	**33,954**	**1,746**	**8,748**	**7,003**	**29,296**	**2,912**	**3,980**	**1,068**	**4,455**
Petroleum	3,810	3,345	1,304	2,269	966	1,788	253	−549	−803	465
Manufacturing	20,212	19,181	626	2,159	1,533	17,683	872	2,296	1,424	1,031
Other	14,387	11,428	−184	4,320	4,504	9,825	1,787	2,234	446	2,959
Canada	7,748	7,450	1,610	2,529	919	4,393	1,447	1,730	283	298
Petroleum	1,414	1,154	71	D	D	906	176	123	−54	260
Manufacturing	3,219	3,139	668	841	173	2,337	133	546	413	80
Other	3,115	3,157	871	D	D	1,149	1,137	1,061	−76	−42
Europe	25,519	22,376	502	5,085	4,583	21,140	734	1,439	705	3,143
Petroleum	1,079	914	D	1,429	D	575	D	−724	D	165
Manufacturing	15,193	14,298	136	1,240	1,104	13,402	761	1,699	939	895
Other	9,246	7,163	D	2,416	D	7,163	D	465	D	2,083
Other	5,142	4,128	−366	1,134	1,501	3,763	731	811	80	1,014
Petroleum	1,317	1,277	D	D	22	307	D	52	D	39
Manufacturing	1,800	1,744	−178	78	256	1,944	−22	50	73	56
Other	2,025	1,107	D	D	1,223	1,513	D	708	D	918
Developing countries	**9,604**	**10,057**	**1,632**	**5,736**	**4,103**	**5,124**	**3,301**	**149**	**−3,151**	**−454**
Petroleum	−274	116	D	1,227	D	209	D	−99	D	−389
Manufacturing	1,761	1,680	118	533	415	2,220	−658	−309	350	81
Other	8,117	8,262	D	3,976	D	2,695	D	557	D	−1,435
Latin America and Other Western Hemisphere	8,054	8,042	914	3,287	2,373	3,258	3,870	271	−3,599	12
Petroleum	−593	−327	−20	46	66	−18	−288	−125	163	−266
Manufacturing	963	978	138	435	297	1,201	−360	−194	166	−15
Other	7,684	7,391	797	2,807	2,010	2,076	4,519	590	−3,929	293
Other	1,550	2,015	718	2,448	1,730	1,866	−570	−122	448	−465
Petroleum	319	443	D	1,181	D	227	D	27	D	−123
Manufacturing	797	701	−20	98	118	1,019	−298	−115	183	96
Other	433	871	D	1,169	D	619	D	−33	D	−438
International	**169**	**183**	**300**	**347**	**48**	**−156**	**39**	**44**	**5**	**−13**
1988										
All areas	**18,917**	**17,533**	**−5,469**	**8,655**	**14,124**	**15,170**	**7,831**	**2,357**	**−5,474**	**1,385**
Petroleum	−2,142	−1,753	−3,381	1,167	4,549	45	1,584	325	−1,259	−390
Manufacturing	6,745	5,306	−797	1,992	2,789	7,266	−1,163	−1,399	−237	1,439
Other	14,315	13,979	−1,290	5,495	6,786	7,859	7,410	3,432	−3,979	336
Developed countries	**12,808**	**10,812**	**−1,890**	**6,643**	**8,532**	**10,361**	**2,341**	**2,320**	**−21**	**1,997**
Petroleum	−13	−146	−1,688	877	2,565	583	959	609	−350	133
Manufacturing	3,245	1,906	−812	1,614	2,426	4,126	−1,408	−1,350	58	1,339
Other	9,576	9,052	610	4,151	3,541	5,652	2,790	3,062	272	524

(Continued)

		Capital Outflows							
	Equity Capital				Rein-vested Earnings	Intercompany Debt			Valuation Adjust-ments
Total	Total	Net	Increases	Decreases		Net	Increases in U.S. Parents' Receivables	Increases in U.S. Parents' Payables[1]	

	Total	Total	Net	Increases	Decreases	Reinvested Earnings	Net	Incr. Receivables	Incr. Payables[1]	Valuation Adjustments
1988 (Continued)										
Canada	2,868	4,101	−89	754	843	4,224	−34	279	313	−1,233
Petroleum	−388	501	121	D	D	−262	641	594	−47	−889
Manufacturing	1,359	1,116	−99	188	287	2,060	−845	−532	313	242
Other	1,897	2,484	−111	D	D	2,426	169	217	47	−587
Europe	5,989	3,335	−877	5,100	5,977	2,599	1,613	1,595	−18	2,654
Petroleum	−505	−1,497	−1,842	D	D	20	326	125	−201	992
Manufacturing	506	−242	−116	1,183	1,299	731	−857	−1,059	−202	747
Other	5,988	5,073	1,081	D	D	1,848	2,144	2,529	385	915
Other	3,952	3,376	−923	789	1,712	3,537	762	446	−316	576
Petroleum	879	850	33	48	14	824	−8	−111	−103	30
Manufacturing	1,381	1,031	−597	243	840	1,335	293	240	−53	350
Other	1,691	1,495	−359	498	857	1,377	477	316	−161	196
Developing countries	**6,161**	**6,897**	**−3,494**	**2,012**	**5,506**	**4,794**	**5,598**	**211**	**−5,386**	**−736**
Petroleum	−2,053	−1,419	D	D	1,911	−395	D	D	−701	−635
Manufacturing	3,499	3,400	15	378	363	3,139	246	−49	−294	99
Other	4,715	4,916	D	D	3,233	2,049	D	D	−4,391	−201
Latin America and Other Western Hemisphere	4,378	4,579	−2,864	1,512	4,376	2,729	4,714	27	−4,687	−201
Petroleum	−1,380	−1,150	−1,079	D	D	−149	79	−189	−267	−230
Manufacturing	2,082	1,916	72	329	256	1,894	−50	59	110	166
Other	3,676	3,813	−1,857	D	D	984	4,686	156	−4,530	−137
Other	1,783	2,318	−630	501	1,131	2,065	884	185	−699	−535
Petroleum	−673	−269	D	150	D	−246	D	D	−434	−404
Manufacturing	1,418	1,484	−57	50	107	1,245	296	−108	−404	−67
Other	1,038	1,103	D	301	D	1,065	D	D	138	−64
International	**−52**	**−176**	**−85**	*	**85**	**15**	**−107**	**−174**	**−67**	**124**

D Suppressed to avoid disclosure to data of individual companies.

[1] An increase in U.S. parents' payables is a decrease in intercompany debt and, thus, a capital inflow.

Table A8-4 U.S. DIRECT INVESTMENT ABROAD: EARNINGS AND REINVESTMENT RATIOS (millions of dollars or ratio)

	1987				1988				1987–88 Change in Earnings		
	Earnings			Reinvestment Ratio[1]	Earnings			Reinvestment Ratio[1]			
	Total	Distributed	Reinvested		Total	Distributed	Reinvested		Total	Distributed	Reinvested
All areas	58,527	24,262	34,264	.59	52,335	37,165	15,170	.29	−6,192	12,903	−19,095
Petroleum	8,657	6,835	1,822	.21	7,949	7,904	45	.01	−709	1,068	−1,777
Manufacturing	28,105	8,202	19,903	.71	24,655	17,389	7,266	.29	−3,450	9,188	−12,638
Other	21,765	9,225	12,539	.58	19,731	11,872	7,859	.40	−2,033	2,647	−4,680

(Continued)

	1987 Earnings			1987 Reinvestment Ratio[1]	1988 Earnings			1988 Reinvestment Ratio[1]	1987–88 Change in Earnings		
	Total	Distributed	Reinvested		Total	Distributed	Reinvested		Total	Distributed	Reinvested
Developed countries	**45,925**	**16,628**	**29,296**	**.64**	**38,166**	**27,806**	**10,361**	**.27**	**−7,758**	**11,178**	**−18,936**
Petroleum	6,226	4,438	1,788	.29	5,566	4,983	583	.10	−661	545	−1,206
Manufacturing	24,531	6,847	17,683	.72	19,336	15,210	4,126	.21	−5,194	8,362	−13,557
Other	15,168	5,343	9,825	.65	13,265	7,613	5,652	.43	−1,903	2,270	−4,173
Canada	6,967	2,574	4,393	.63	8,996	4,772	4,224	.47	2,029	2,197	−168
Petroleum	1,480	574	906	.61	822	1,083	−262	2	−658	510	−1,168
Manufacturing	3,562	1,225	2,337	.66	4,986	2,926	2,060	.41	1,424	1,701	−278
Other	1,925	776	1,149	.60	3,189	763	2,426	.76	1,264	−13	1,277
Europe	33,307	12,167	21,140	.63	22,884	20,284	2,599	.11	−10,424	8,117	−18,541
Petroleum	3,821	3,246	575	.15	2,997	2,977	20	.01	−824	−269	−555
Manufacturing	18,283	4,881	13,402	.73	11,818	11,087	731	.06	−6,465	6,206	−12,671
Other	11,203	4,040	7,163	.64	8,068	6,220	1,848	.23	−3,135	2,180	−5,315
Other	5,650	1,887	3,763	.67	6,287	2,750	3,537	.56	637	863	−226
Petroleum	926	619	307	.33	1,747	923	824	.47	822	304	518
Manufacturing	2,685	742	1,944	.72	2,532	1,197	1,335	.53	−153	455	−608
Other	2,039	526	1,513	.74	2,007	630	1,377	.69	−32	104	−135
Developing countries	**12,492**	**7,368**	**5,124**	**.41**	**13,915**	**9,121**	**4,794**	**.34**	**1,423**	**1,753**	**−330**
Petroleum	2,446	2,237	209	.09	2,328	2,723	−395	2	−118	486	−604
Manufacturing	3,574	1,354	2,220	.62	5,319	2,180	3,139	.59	1,744	825	919
Other	6,472	3,777	2,695	.42	6,268	4,219	2,049	.33	−204	442	−646
Latin American and Other Western Hemisphere	7,218	3,960	3,258	.45	7,700	4,971	2,729	.35	482	1,011	−529
Petroleum	317	335	−18	2	370	519	−149	2	53	184	−131
Manufacturing	2,081	880	1,201	.58	3,251	1,357	1,894	.58	1,170	476	693
Other	4,820	2,744	2,076	.43	4,079	3,095	984	.24	−741	351	−1,092
Other	5,275	3,409	1,866	.35	6,216	4,151	2,065	.33	941	742	199
Petroleum	2,129	1,901	227	.11	1,958	2,204	−246	2	−171	302	−473
Manufacturing	1,493	474	1,019	.68	2,068	823	1,245	.60	575	349	226
Other	1,653	1,033	619	.37	2,189	1,124	1,065	.49	537	91	446
International	**110**	**266**	**−156**	**2**	**253**	**238**	**15**	**.06**	**143**	**−28**	**171**

[1]Reinvested earnings divided by earnings.

[2]Reinvestment ratio is not defined because reinvested earnings are negative.

Note: Earnings and reinvested earnings include all increases (gains) and decreases (losses) in affiliate book value resulting from changes in the exchange rate at which foreign currency-denominated assets or liabilities are translated into U.S. dollars. Most of these gains and losses are excluded from the affiliate's calculation of its own earnings and reinvested earnings. An alternative measure of reinvestment ratios—one that more closely approximates the reinvestment ratio from the affiliate's, not from the U.S. balance of payments, perspective —excludes such amounts from earnings and reinvested earnings. For 1987 and 1988, this alternative measure results in reinvestment ratios of approximately 0.43 and 0.29, respectively.

Table A8-5   SELECTED TRANSACTIONS WITH, AND POSITION IN, NETHERLAND ANTILLEAN FINANCE AFFILIATES (millions of dollars)

Line		1982	1983	1984	1985	1986	1987	1988
1	Direct investment position	−20,089	−23,300	−25,078	−20,784	−17,230	−14,519	−12,055
2	Equity[1]	12,485	14,996	16,911	16,684	16,425	15,320	12,743
3	Intercompany debt, net	−32,574	−38,296	−41,989	−37,468	−33,655	−29,838	−24,798
4	U.S. parents' receivables	562	398	539	1,172	512	579	761
5	U.S. parents' payables	33,136	38,695	42,527	38,640	34,168	30,417	25,560

(Continued)

Line		1982	1983	1984	1985	1986	1987	1988
6	Capital outflows	−8,655	−3,136	−1,977	4,245	4,867	2,992	2,728
7	Equity capital	4,173	1,411	982	−864	745	−1,342	−2,524
8	Reinvested earnings	796	994	895	902	−400	535	212
9	Intercompany debt, net	−13,623	−5,542	−3,855	4,208	4,523	3,799	5,040
10	Increases in U.S. parents' receivables	187	−164	−40	695	120	66	182
11	Increases in U.S. parents' payables[2]	13,810	5,378	3,814	−3,513	−4,403	−3,732	−4,858
12	Income (13 − 14 + 15)	−1,997	−3,246	−3,430	−3,132	−2,734	−2,205	−2,120
13	Earnings	1,067	1,358	1,769	1,643	1,198	1,129	750
14	Withholding taxes on distributed earnings	*	14	2	3	*	*	*
15	Interest (net of withholding taxes)	−3,064	−4,591	−5,196	−4,772	−3,931	−3,334	−2,870

*Less than $500,000.

[1]Includes the additional paid-in capital and retained earnings.

[2]An increase in U.S. parents' payables is a decrease in intercompany debt and, thus, a capital inflow.

Note: This table shows only transactions with, and positions in, affiliates established to borrow funds abroad and relend them to their U.S. parents.

Table A8-6 U.S. DIRECT INVESTMENT ABROAD: INCOME

	Income			Change			
	Millions of Dollars			Millions of Dollars		Percent	
	1986	1987	1988	1987	1988	1987	1988
All areas	38,533	54,754	48,264	16,221	−6,490	42.1	−11.9
Petroleum	8,477	8.667	7,932	190	−735	2.2	−8.5
Manufacturing	18,061	27,616	23,319	9,555	−4,297	52.9	−15.6
Other	11,995	18,471	17,013	6,476	−1,458	54.0	−7.9
Developed countries	32,323	45,527	37,183	13,205	−8,345	40.9	−18.3
Petroleum	6,607	6,201	5,548	−406	−654	−6.1	−10.5
Manufacturing	15,733	24,190	18,302	8,458	−5,889	53.8	−24.3
Other	9,983	15,135	13,333	5,153	−1,802	51.6	−11.9
Canada	5,063	6,990	8,954	1,927	1,964	38.1	28.1
Petroleum	843	1,491	813	648	−678	76.9	−45.5
Manufacturing	2,675	3,528	4,821	853	1,293	31.9	36.6
Other	1,545	1,971	3,320	426	1,349	27.6	68.4
Europe	22,971	32,975	22,033	10,004	−10,942	43.6	−33.2
Petroleum	4,544	3,823	3,009	−721	−814	−15.9	−21.3
Manufacturing	11,163	18,037	11,026	6,874	−7,011	61.6	−38.9
Other	7,264	11,114	7,998	3,851	−3,116	53.0	−28.0
Other	4,289	5,563	6,196	1,274	633	29.7	11.4
Petroleum	1,220	888	1,726	−333	838	−27.3	94.5
Manufacturing	1,894	2,625	2,455	731	−171	38.6	−6.5
Other	1,174	2,050	2,015	876	−35	74.6	−1.7

(Continued)

| | Income | | | Change | | | |
| | Millions of Dollars | | | Millions of Dollars | | Percent | |
	1986	1987	1988	1987	1988	1987	1988
Developing countries	**6,726**	**9,100**	**10,823**	**2,374**	**1,723**	**35.3**	**18.9**
Petroleum	2,364	2,472	2,314	108	−159	4.6	−6.4
Manufacturing	2,328	3,425	5,017	1,097	1,592	47.1	46.5
Other	2,034	3,202	3,492	1,169	290	57.5	9.0
Latin America and Other Western Hemisphere	3,516	3,812	4,617	296	805	8.4	21.1
Petroleum	929	311	338	−618	27	−66.5	8.6
Manufacturing	1,529	1,964	2,988	434	1,024	28.4	52.1
Other	1,058	1,537	1,292	480	−245	45.3	−16.0
Other	3,210	5,288	6,206	2,078	918	64.8	17.4
Petroleum	1,435	2,161	1,976	726	−185	50.6	−8.6
Manufacturing	799	1,462	2,030	663	568	83.0	38.9
Other	976	1,665	2,200	689	535	70.6	32.1
International	**−516**	**127**	**258**	**642**	**131**	**−124.6**	**103.5**

[1]The percent change is not calculated because income is negative in one or both years.

Table A8-7   SOURCE AND RELATIONSHIP OF INCOME AND ITS COMPONENTS (millions of dollars)

Line		1988 Amount	Source and Relationship
1	Earnings	52,335	2 + 3
2	Capital gains/losses	−144	Reported[1]
3	Earnings before capital gains/losses	52,479	Extrapolated[2]
4	Distributed earnings	37,165	6 + 11
5	Reinvested earnings	15,170	1 − 4
6	Withholding taxes on distributed earnings	2,475	Extrapolated[2]
7	Interest (net of withholding taxes)	−1,596	Extrapolated[2]
8	Income	48,264	1 − 6 + 7
9	Income before capital gains/losses	48,408	8 − 2
10	Earnings (net of withholding taxes)	49,860	1 − 6
11	Distributed earnings (net of withholding taxes)	34,690	Extrapolated[2]

[1]Data are as reported by the sample; no estimate for nonreporting affiliates is made.

[2]Universe estimates are calculated by extrapolating forward data from the 1982 benchmark survey, based on the movement of reported sample data in subsequent years.

Table A8-8 U.S. DIRECT INVESTMENT ABROAD: INCOME AND RATE OF RETURN (millions of dollars or percent)

	1987 Income									1988 Income								
	Total (=col. 2 less Col. 5 plus Col 6)	Earnings Total	Earnings Before Capital Gains/ Losses	Capital Gains/ Losses	Withholding Taxes on Distributed Earnings	Interest (Net of Withholding Taxes) Net	U.S. Parents' Receipts	U.S. Parents' Payments	Rate of Return[1]	Total (=col. 11 less Col. 14 Plus Col. 15)	Earnings Total	Earnings Before Capital Gains/ Losses	Capital Gains/ Losses	Withholding Taxes on Distributed Earnings	Interest (Net of Withholding Taxes) Net	U.S. Parents' Receipts	U.S. Parents' Payments	Rate of Return[1]
	(1)	(2)	(3)	(4)	(5)	(6)	(7)	(8)		(10)	(11)	(12)	(13)	(14)	(15)	(16)	(17)	(18)
All areas	54,754	58,527	42,353	16,174	1,281	-2,492	1,615	4,107	19.3	48,264	52,335	52,479	-144	2,475	-1,596	2,052	3,648	15.2
Petroleum	8,667	8,657	7,610	1,047	213	223	362	139	14.4	7,932	7,949	7,492	456	344	328	441	113	13.1
Manufacturing	27,616	28,105	19,026	9,079	720	231	379	148	23.8	23,319	24,665	26,784	-2,129	1,687	351	433	82	17.9
Other	18,471	21,765	15,717	6,084	348	-2,946	874	3,819	17.2	17,013	19,731	18,203	1,582	444	-2,275	1,178	3,453	13.5
Developed countries	45,527	45,925	30,139	15,785	995	598	1,158	560	21.3	37,183	38,166	37,618	548	1,995	1,011	1,512	501	15.6
Petroleum	6,201	6,226	5,213	1,014	196	170	254	83	16.1	5,548	5,556	4,931	634	300	282	306	24	13.8
Manufacturing	24,190	24,531	15,266	9,264	514	174	312	138	25.3	18,302	19,336	20,849	-1,513	1,332	297	364	66	17.1
Other	15,135	15,168	9,660	5,507	286	254	592	339	19.0	13,333	13,265	11,838	1,427	363	432	842	410	14.6
Canada	6,990	6,967	5,634	1,333	187	210	272	61	12.8	8,954	8,996	7,306	1,690	416	374	422	47	15.0
Petroleum	1,491	1,480	1,181	298	45	56	64	8	13.1	813	822	925	-103	104	95	96	1	6.8
Manufacturing	3,528	3,562	2,824	738	106	72	99	27	14.0	4,821	4,986	4,035	950	248	83	102	19	17.6
Other	1,971	1,925	1,629	296	36	82	108	26	11.0	3,320	3,189	2,346	843	65	196	224	28	16.2
Europe	32,975	33,307	20,982	12,325	634	301	781	480	24.7	22,033	22,884	25,392	-2,508	1,402	551	967	415	14.8
Petroleum	3,823	3,821	3,260	560	110	112	187	75	18.0	3,009	2,997	2,964	33	174	186	209	23	13.9
Manufacturing	18,037	18,283	10,773	7,510	315	69	174	106	30.1	11,026	11,818	14,375	-2,557	976	184	230	46	16.3
Other	11,114	11,203	6,949	4,225	209	120	420	300	21.2	7,998	8,068	8,053	15	252	182	528	346	13.3
Other	5,563	5,650	3,523	2,127	174	87	105	18	21.8	6,196	6,287	4,921	1,366	177	86	124	38	20.6
Petroleum	888	926	771	155	41	3	3	*	15.5	1,726	1,747	1,043	704	23	2	2	*	25.3
Manufacturing	2,685	2,685	1,670	1,016	93	33	38	5	25.0	2,455	2,532	2,439	93	108	31	32	1	20.3
Other	2,050	2,039	1,083	956	40	51	64	13	22.1	2,015	2,007	1,438	569	46	53	90	37	18.1
Developing countries	9,100	12,492	12,219	273	285	-3,107	435	3,543	13.8	10,823	13,915	14,630	-715	479	-2,613	516	3,129	14.7
Petroleum	2,472	2,446	2,529	-83	17	43	97	54	13.6	2,314	2,328	2,530	-202	43	29	116	87	13.6
Manufacturing	3,425	3,574	3,760	-186	206	57	68	11	16.6	5,017	5,319	5,934	-615	355	54	69	15	21.6
Other	3,202	6,472	5,930	542	62	-3,207	271	3,478	11.8	3,492	6,268	6,166	102	81	-2,695	331	3,026	10.4
Latin America and Other Western Hemisphere	3,812	7,218	7,331	-113	229	-3,177	304	3,481	9.3	4,617	7,700	9,170	-1,471	414	-2,669	351	3,019	9.8
Petroleum	311	317	492	-175	8	2	10	8	4.7	338	370	632	-262	38	6	9	4	6.0
Manufacturing	1,964	2,081	2,325	-244	173	55	60	5	12.8	2,988	3,251	3,943	-692	315	52	57	5	17.8
Other	1,537	4,820	4,514	306	48	-3,234	234	3,468	8.1	1,292	4,079	4,595	-516	60	-2,727	284	3,011	5.2
Other	5,288	5,275	4,889	386	57	70	131	61	21.2	6,206	6,216	5,460	755	66	56	165	109	23.3
Petroleum	2,161	2,129	2,037	92	9	42	87	46	18.7	1,976	1,958	1,897	61	5	23	106	83	17.4
Manufacturing	1,462	1,493	1,435	58	34	2	8	6	27.6	2,030	2,068	1,992	76	40	1	12	10	31.7
Other	1,665	1,653	1,417	236	14	27	36	10	20.4	2,200	2,189	1,571	618	21	32	47	15	24.8
International	127	110	-6	116	*	17	22	5	2.8	258	253	230	23	1	5	24	19	5.6

*Less than $500,000 (±).

D Suppressed to avoid disclosure of data of individual companies.

[1] Income divided by the average of the beginning- and end-of-year direct investment position.

Table A8-9 U.S. DIRECT INVESTMENT ABROAD: ROYALTIES AND LICENSE FEES AND CHARGES FOR OTHER SERVICES

(millions of dollars)

	1987						1988					
	Royalties and License Fees			Charges for Other Services[1]			Royalties and License Fees			Charges for Other Services[1]		
	Net	U.S. Parents' Receipts	U.S. Parents' Payments	Net	U.S. Parents' Receipts	U.S. Parents' Payments	Net	U.S. Parents' Receipts	U.S. Parents' Payments	Net	U.S. Parents' Receipts	U.S. Parents' Payments
All areas	6,900	7,049	150	2,196	5,106	2,910	8,319	8,431	112	2,858	6,168	3,310
Petroleum	5	5	0	509	669	160	5	5	*	491	663	173
Manufacturing	5,445	5,521	76	906	2,021	1,115	6,454	6,526	72	1,027	2,359	1,332
Other	1,449	1,523	74	781	2,416	1,635	1,860	1,900	40	1,341	3,146	1,805
Developed countries	6,573	6,706	133	1,488	3,962	2,474	7,846	7,952	107	1,968	4,781	2,813
Petroleum	4	4	0	264	332	69	4	5	*	310	375	65
Manufacturing	5,248	5,318	70	667	1,732	1,065	6,179	6,249	70	624	1,904	1,280
Other	1,321	1,383	62	558	1,898	1,340	1,662	1,699	36	1,033	2,502	1,468
Canada	584	610	26	954	1,127	174	683	702	19	1,030	1,204	174
Petroleum	*	*	0	41	89	48	*	*	0	54	113	60
Manufacturing	481	503	23	605	621	17	566	584	18	D	639	D
Other	103	107	3	308	417	109	117	118	1	D	451	D
Europe	4,678	4,766	88	784	2,444	1,660	5,440	5,519	78	1,256	3,135	1,878
Petroleum	4	4	0	186	205	19	4	5	*	229	234	5
Manufacturing	3,716	3,760	44	D	993	D	4,241	4,288	46	D	1,148	D
Other	958	1,002	44	D	1,246	D	1,195	1,227	32	D	1,753	D
Other	1,311	1,329	18	-249	391	640	1,722	1,731	9	-319	443	761
Petroleum	*	*	0	37	38	1	*	*	0	27	28	1
Manufacturing	1,052	1,055	3	D	118	D	1,372	1,377	5	-396	117	514
Other	259	275	15	D	235	D	350	354	3	51	298	247
Developing countries	327	344	17	663	1,021	358	473	479	6	890	1,299	409
Petroleum	1	1	0	214	238	25	1	1	0	D	D	33
Manufacturing	197	203	6	239	289	50	275	278	2	402	454	52
Other	129	140	12	210	494	284	197	201	3	D	D	325
Latin America and Other												
Western Hemisphere	166	172	7	159	433	273	200	205	5	270	523	253
Petroleum	1	1	0	D	74	D	1	1	0	52	69	18
Manufacturing	92	96	4	80	104	24	116	118	2	118	138	20
Other	73	75	3	D	254	D	84	87	3	100	315	215
Other	161	172	11	504	588	85	273	274	1	620	776	156
Petroleum	*	*	0	D	164	D	*	*	0	D	D	15
Manufacturing	105	106	2	159	185	26	159	160	1	284	316	32
Other	56	65	9	D	240	D	114	114	*	D	D	109
International	0	0	0	45	122	78	0	0	0	1	88	87

*Less than $500,000 (±).

D Suppressed to avoid disclosure of data of individual companies.

[1] Consists of service charges, rentals for the use of tangible property, and film and television tape rentals. In 1988, U.S. parents' receipts of service charges were $5,644 million, receipts of rentals for the use of tangible property were $204 million, and receipts of film and television tape rentals were $320 million; U.S. parents' payments were $3,257 million, $50 million, and $3 million, respectively.

Table A8-10 U.S. DIRECT INVESTMENT ABROAD: POSITION
AND BALANCE OF PAYMENTS FLOWS, 1977–88 (millions of dollars)

	1977	1978	1979	1980	1981	1982[1]	1983	1984	1985	1986	1987	1988
Direct investment position	145,990	162,727	187,858	215,375	228,348	207,752	207,203	211,480	230,250	259,800	307,983	326,900
Capital outflows (inflows(-))	11,893	16,056	25,222	19,222	9,624	-2,369	373	2,821	18,068	26,311	44,194	17,533
Equity capital	[2]	[2]	[2]	[2]	[2]	9,708	4,903	1,347	-2,210	551	3,677	-5,469
Reinvested earnings	[2]	[2]	[2]	[2]	[2]	1,359	7,139	8,447	19,009	17,654	34,264	15,170
Intercompany debt	[2]	[2]	[2]	[2]	[2]	-13,436	-11,669	-6,973	1,269	8,106	6,252	7,831
Income	19,673	25,458	38,183	37,146	32,549	21,380	20,499	21,217	33,202	38,533	54,754	48,264
Royalties and license fees, net receipts	2,173	2,697	3,002	3,693	3,658	3,507	3,597	3,921	4,096	5,412	6,900	8,319
Charges for other services, net receipts[3]	1,710	2,008	1,978	2,087	2,136	1,816	2,532	2,483	2,490	3,024	2,196	2,858

[1]There is a break in series between 1981 and 1982 because, beginning with 1982, the estimates of all items have been revised to incorporate the results of the 1982 benchmark survey of U.S. direct investment abroad. Previous estimates for these years were, and current estimates for 1977–81 continue to be, linked to the 1977 benchmark survey.

[2]For years prior to 1982, capital outflows cannot be disaggregated by component because data for the components were not reported separately for unincorporated foreign affiliates.

[3]Consists of service charges, rentals for the use of tangible property, and film and television tape rentals.

Table A8-11 U.S. DIRECT INVESTMENT POSITION ABROAD, 1988
(millions of dollars)

	All Industries	Petroleum	Manufacturing								Wholesale Trade	Banking	Finance (Except Banking), Insurance, and real Estate	Services	Other Industries
			Total	Food and Kindred Products	Chemicals and Allied Products	Primary and Fabricated Metals	Machinery, Except Electrical	Electric and Electronic Equipment	Transportation Equipment	Other Manufacturing					
All countries	**326,900**	**59,658**	**133,819**	**13,121**	**30,467**	**7,825**	**25,608**	**10,580**	**17,614**	**28,604**	**34,401**	**16,120**	**60,604**	**7,130**	**15,168**
Developed countries	**245,498**	**40,299**	**108,850**	**10,907**	**24,583**	**6,226**	**22,703**	**6,414**	**14,634**	**23,384**	**28,427**	**9,337**	**43,240**	**5,608**	**9,736**
Canada	61,244	11,711	28,141	2,178	5,393	3,312	3,160	2,176	6,408	5,514	3,819	781	10,377	1,286	5,130
Europe	152,232	21,323	67,930	7,812	14,691	2,464	16,373	3,283	7,306	16,002	19,574	7,470	29,810	3,819	2,304
European Communities (12)	126,502	15,695	65,431	7,364	14,409	2,408	15,798	3,079	7,431 D	14,943 D	12,774	5,829	21,634	2,922	2,216
Belgium	7,224	551 D	3,897	286	2,181 D	109	203	231	D	D	1,477	412	780	73	34
Denmark	1,191	D	265	164	D	D	2	7	*	41	513	41	174	D	-1
France	12,495	926	8,047	293	1,753	155	3,025	250	456	2,114	2,377	235	446	176	287
Germany, Federal Republic of	21,673	2,043	14,200	854 D	1,377	523	4,074	601	3,927	2,843 D	1,114	1,678	1,921 D	-21 D	739
Greece	194	45	107	D	65	*	0	9	0	D	33	-24	D	D	5
Ireland	5,743	-9	4,138	659	1,010	139	750	412	8	1,161	16	9	1,662	-66	-7
Italy	9,075	401	6,561	476	1,657	124	2,980	335	135	854	1,153	253	481	170	56
Luxembourg	756	3	456	0	D	30	D	D	*	381 D	5	199	93	D	D
Netherlands	15,367	2,212	6,073	1,371 D	2,220	403 D	767 D	95 D	D	37 D	2,419	173	3,178 D	887 D	427
Portugal	425	D	194	D	3	D	D	D	D	D	105	104	D	D	8
Spain	4,368	96	2,626	488	571	161	D	29	237	D	757	477	26	274	111
United Kingdom	47,991	9,327	18,867	2,715	3,546	731	3,347	997	2,469	5,061	2,805	2,271	12,850	1,312	558
Other Europe	25,730	5,628	2,499	448	283	56	574	203 D	-125	1,059	6,800	1,641	8,177	897	88
Austria	1,167	127 D	95	23	D	3	37 D	D	5	12	836	47 D	30	15	17
Finland	413	D	29	0	4	*	D	0	0	D	331	D	0	1	*
Norway	3,834	3,276 D	36	2	-12	-1	8 D	0	0	40	350	21	119	26	6 D
Sweden	1,089	D	627	42 D	34	13	8 D	0 D	0 D	49	222	50	50	-7 D	D
Switzerland	18,672	D	1,734	D	241	37	68	172	0	D	4,944	1,512	7,718	D	41
Turkey	193	41	62	D	D	*	*	10	2 D	D	33	24 D	0	D	D
Other	362	73	-85	0	0	3	D	0	2 D	D	83	D	260	11	D
Japan	16,868	3,468	7,876	382	2,430	197	2,630	852	630	753	3,473	262	1,258	206	325
Australia, New Zealand, and South Africa	15,154	3,798	4,903	535	2,068	253	540	103	290	1,114	1,560	824	1,795	297	1,977
Australia	13,058	3,089 D	4,178	519	1,853	140	414	97	257	898	1,322	D	1,685	255 D	D
New Zealand	826	D	217	-4	93	D	14	10	D	77	158	0	41	D	40
South Africa	1,270	D	508	20	122	D	113	-5	D	139	80	0	69	D	D
Developing countries	**76,837**	**16,007**	**24,969**	**2,214**	**5,884**	**1,599**	**2,905**	**4,166**	**2,980**	**5,220**	**5,975**	**6,782**	**17,364**	**1,522**	**4,219**
Latin America and Other Western Hemisphere	49,283	4,974	17,850	1,796	4,107	1,277	2,081	1,057	2,828	4,704	2,812	4,800	14,535	1,079	3,234
South America	21,687	2,421	12,378	1,225	2,576	991	1,990	651	1,646	3,299	681	1,323	1,741	701	2,443
Argentina	2,390	405 D	1,215	170	258	110	257	41	95	283	99	377	176	65	52
Brazil	11,810	244	9,004	506	1,739	977 D	1,733	477 D	1,308 D	2,265 D	55	661	1,272	470	104
Chile	731	71	9	37	138	D	0	D	D	D	32	247	220	34	117

Colombia	2,429	399	176	186	4	4	6	D	D	D	7	D	2	D
Ecuador	448	189	33	16	16	0	D	11	D	41	3	D	*	D
Peru	1,064	348	7	19	D	0	*	0	362	67	-6	D	D	D
Venezuela	2,273	634	231	205	95	-8	94	161	362	285	4	6	116	88
Other	543	130	64	14	2	4	*	-2	2	D	29	D	D	D
Central America	12,441	1,593	526	1,434	266	92	397	1,182	1,327	1,290	266	3,227	215	627
Mexico	5,516	60	257	1,197	234	92	382	1,182	1,243	376	D	-20	138	D
Panama	6,140	1,419	78	148	5	0	0	0	17	847	217	3,221	47	141
Other	785	114	191	89	27	0	16	0	67	66	D	26	31	D
Other Western Hemisphere	15,155	960	44	97	21	*	8	0	77	841	3,211	9,567	163	165
Bahamas	2,244	206	D	D	0	0	0	0	*	268	860	882	-35	29
Bermuda	19,880	114	0	0	0	0	0	0	0	406	D	19,265	58	58
Jamaica	156	D	15	44	0	0	0	0	11	22	7	D	33	*
Netherlands Antilles	-11,796	D	D	D	D	0	0	0	0	-28	D	-12,055	*	D
Trinidad and Tobago	429	D	8	-5	0	*	0	0	8	24	D	4	D	-5
United Kingdom Islands, Caribbean	3,577	D	1	0	0	0	D	0	0	64	2,147	1,242	63	40
Other	664	199	5	20	1	1	D	58	58	86	16	D	D	D
Other Africa	4,603	3,548	43	110	115	1	29	11	2	75	155	365	95	54
Saharan	2,097	1,752	25	D	9	1	4	10	D	44	66	3	78	79
Egypt	1,705	1,405	D	D	6	1	4	8	-4	D	65	-2	74	D
Libya	312	299	0	0	0	0	0	0	0	6	0	0	4	D
Other	79	48	D	*	3	0	2	2	D	31	*	5	*	-5
Sub-Saharan	2,506	1,796	18	D	106	0	25	*	D	31	89	362	17	-25
Liberia	132	53	0	0	0	0	0	0	0	D	2	44	D	49
Nigeria	1,342	1,214	0	0	-2	0	D	0	0	21	39	0	7	4
Other	1,032	528	18	48	109	0	D	*	-11	D	48	318	D	-77
Middle East	4,090	2,317	*	216	31	27	175	0	73	366	-238	779	110	234
Israel	722	58	0	24	2	D	172	0	D	D	4	133	34	D
Saudi Arabia	2,047	731	0	159	D	*	3	0	D	D	D	575	182	D
United Arab Emirates	680	562	0	D	0	D	0	0	-3	47	-9	D	-22	D
Other	641	965	*	D	0	1	0	0	-5	30	D	D	-84	-2
Other Asia and Pacific	18,860	5,168	375	1,451	176	796	2,905	142	441	2,721	2,065	1,685	237	697
Hong Kong	5,028	237	13	208	34	105	100	D	134	2,008	654	1,253	85	196
India	457	5	1	176	69	100	D	0	48	-1	35	2	*	*
Indonesia	3,006	2,638	7	59	8	4	-3	0	17	63	-3	46	-4	26
Malaysia	1,363	735	5	20	-1	16	429	0	52	101	-10	29	0	-21
Philippines	1,305	127	238	236	17	-3	96	-2	29	114	268	145	73	37
Singapore	3,005	559	21	192	-4	306	1,434	33	17	49	218	35	42	30
South Korea	1,302	10	58	104	D	D	224	2	74	172	567	137	12	28
Taiwan	1,546	497	23	392	24	239	382	63	39	64	99	D	-2	D
Thailand	1,126	596	9	47	0	D	215	0	29	D	57	3	11	21
Other	721	68	0	15	0	0	D	D	2	30	D	D	D	D
International	4,565	3,351	271	500	145	8	116	173	509	478	101	728	209	1,213
Addendum—OPEC[1]	10,229	6,383	1,721										188	608

*Less than $500,000 (±).

D Suppressed to avoid disclosure of data of individual companies.

[1] OPEC is the Organization of Petroleum Exporting Countries. Its members are Algeria, Ecuador, Gabon, Indonesia, Iran, Iraq, Kuwait, Libya, Nigeria, Qatar, Saudi Arabia, United Arab Emirates, and Venezuela.

Table A8-12 U.S. DIRECT INVESTMENT ABROAD: CAPITAL OUTFLOWS, 1988 (millions of dollars; inflows (−))

	All Industries	Petroleum	Manufacturing — Total	Food and Kindred Products	Chemicals and Allied Products	Primary and Fabricated Metals	Machinery, Except Electrical	Electric and Electronic Equipment	Transportation Equipment	Other Manufacturing	Wholesale Trade	Banking	Finance (Except Banking), Insurance, and Real Estate	Services	Other Industries
All countries	**17,533**	−1,753	5,306	85	3,342	1,271	−1,539	886	565	697	3,026	624	8,407	406	1,51
Developed countries	**10,812**	−146	1,906	205	2,472	886	−1,784	−267	102	291	2,409	−90	5,283	327	1,12
Canada	4,101	501	1,116	4	433	578	57	−11	−424	480	688	153	862	260	52
Europe	3,335	−1,497	−242	316	1,679	258	−2,028	−486	354	−335	1,024	−413	4,275	−32	21
European Communities (12)	4,439	−639	82	226	1,657	258	−2,027	−536	399	104	1,617	59	3,136	−38	22
Belgium	263	107	383	−33	513	−10	6	−19	D	D	−51	−65	−35	−77	D
Denmark	130	D	8	9	D	D	D	−19	0	3	−78	D	158	D	D
France	754	−12	−27	−274	334	−24	−95	−47	5	72	547	−44	162	68	61
Germany, Federal Republic of	−3,521	−1,246	−1,813	215	126	39	−1,016	−538	−377	−263	−52	−107	−275	−32	D
Greece	54	1	14	D	13	0	0	1	0	D	D	D	D	D	
Ireland	593	14	381	35	104	16	90	18	−1	118	7	31	197	3	D
Italy	−12	−108	66	28	284	16	−215	−49	15	−14	79	−40	52	•	−61
Luxembourg	152	D	202	0	D	8	D	D	•	206	D	−8	−45	0	0
Netherlands	882	−111	−135	11	−235	72	−104	63	•	D	541	−4	469	19	104
Portugal	32	D	5	D	11	D	D	D	D	1	20	1	D	D	1
Spain	485	−13	254	104	51	9	D	−47	D	D	102	84	5	−46	99
United Kingdom	4,627	689	744	129	481	122	−659	98	682	−110	497	214	2,458	9	16
Other Europe	−1,104	−858	−323	90	22	•	−2	50	−45	−438	−594	−472	1,139	7	−4
Austria	27	10	−21	0	−1	•	−10	0	0	−5	83	−1	8	−46	−6
Finland	24	D	2	•	D	−1	D	0	0	D	28	D	D	−6	0
Norway	−74	−113	15	D	3	−7	5	0	0	D	17	−1	D	0	D
Sweden	−20	D	6	D	11	6	D	D	0	D	11	D	3	−5	D
Switzerland	−983	−47	−290	D	3	•	−9	43	0	D	−753	−454	1,119	−4	1
Turkey	−26	−6	3	0	D	2	•	1	−2	D	D	−8	0	D	D
Other	−52	−6	−38	D	0	D	D	0	D	D	D	D	D	D	D
Japan	1,976	806	551	12	144	23	D	219	15	D	524	−82	74	49	53
Australia, New Zealand, and South Africa	1,400	43	480	−127	216	27	D	11	157	D	174	252	72	49	330
Australia	1,681	−22	765	83	223	31	142	12	159	115	181	D	81	63	D
New Zealand	46	D	−37	−24	9	D	D	2	D	−13	22	0	−13	D	D
South Africa	−327	D	−247	−186	−15	D	−36	−3	D	D	−29	D	3	D	D
Developing countries	**6,897**	−1,419	3,400	−120	870	384	245	1,152	462	406	617	713	3,124	79	381
Latin America and Other Western Hemisphere	4,579	−1,150	1,916	−138	564	342	128	172	445	402	358	307	2,852	179	117
South America	308	−1,237	1,131	−242	268	315	113	140	316	221	23	247	107	39	−2
Argentina	−224	41	−271	−119	−20	5	−48	5	D	−13	−37	20	18	8	−2
Brazil	1,403	21	1,044	−88	202	163	143	130	317	176	−4	226	78	32	6
Chile	291	12	168	5	33	D	0	D	D	D	15	16	73	−5	12

Table (values in millions of dollars; D = suppressed, * = less than $500,000):

Area / Country														
Colombia	-1,369	-1,334	57	-4	21	1	1	-1	D	D	D	D	D	1	D
Ecuador	-19	7	-1	3	-1	0	0	D	D	-6	-6	D	-1	D	D
Peru	-39	-5	-6	-35	2	16	0	*	*	-15	-12	-15	D	5	D
Venezuela	256	81	129	D	28	1	16	3	36	46	63	-2	-42	5	21
Other	9	-62	10	-1	2	15	1	-1	D	*	D	0	D	13	D
Central America	809	52	754	98	275	-1	15	28	130	130	207	-130	-143	13	56
Mexico	607	-5	651	46	244	D	15	24	130	130	114	-215	-215	15	D
Panama	52	71	24	-1	21	3	16	-1	5	5	54	-141	65	-4	-17
Other	150	-14	79	52	9	0	0	0	0	0	39	39	7	2	D
Other Western Hemisphere	3,462	36	32	7	21	*	4	D	0	0	128	191	2,888	127	62
Bahamas	152	52	8	D	D	0	0	0	0	0	90	24	-17	-24	20
Bermuda	857	-9	0	0	0	0	0	0	0	0	39	D	718	135	D
Jamaica	28	D	11	2	8	0	0	0	1	1	-1	1	D	1	12
Netherlands Antilles	2,722	D	3	D	D	0	0	0	0	0	-30	D	2,728	-1	D
Trinidad and Tobago	9	D	3	1	2	*	0	0	0	*	D	D	*	D	D
United Kingdom Islands, Caribbean	-415	D	D	1	0	0	D	D	D	D	-2	199	-637	17	*
Other	109	D	D	1	2	0	0	0	0	0	D	-5	D	-5	D
Other Africa	-8	-161	52	6	19	*	9	18	-10	10	-4	-28	127	14	-8
Saharan	-75	-124	7	7	D	*	-1	D	D	1	15	*	-1	13	15
Egypt	31	-6	9	0	1	0	-1	1	D	1	D	0	-1	10	D
Libya	5	-2	0	0	D	0	0	0	D	0	D	0	0	3	D
Other	-111	-116	-3	D	D	0	0	D	D	0	D	1	1	0	D
Sub-Saharan	68	-36	46	-1	0	0	10	D	-20	9	-29	128	-23	1	-23
Liberia	21	1	0	0	16	0	D	-1	D	0	1	32	9	D	9
Nigeria	125	143	15	0	D	0	D	D	-4	0	-30	0	*	1	*
Other	-78	-180	31	-1	-1	0	D	D	D	9	D	96	-32	-30	-32
Middle East	-25	-65	129	0	131	1	25	-14	-13	0	133	-225	D	-117	120
Israel	99	D	18	0	-12	-1	28	-1	D	0	D	-24	9	9	D
Saudi Arabia	-111	-121	114	0	D	D	-3	D	D	0	D	-101	-186	-101	D
United Arab Emirates	-23	5	1	0	D	D	0	0	0	0	7	-6	D	-17	D
Other	11	D	-4	0	D	D	0	D	D	0	-5	-8	D	-8	D
Other Asia and Pacific	2,351	-44	1,303	12	156	116	947	37	7	27	130	435	370	3	154
Hong Kong	729	10	29	D	-3	-56	71	15	0	D	117	67	382	21	104
India	23	-2	33	*	2	12	D	9	9	9	D	-5	D	*	*
Indonesia	61	25	6	*	9	-5	-1	1	2	2	8	-2	7	-3	D
Malaysia	316	114	190	-7	*	D	182	-1	-38	0	24	41	4	0	2
Philippines	77	14	26	16	30	1	14	3	26	1	-47	77	9	7	-44
Singapore	629	-19	608	-6	27	92	516	-1	26	1	192	192	-4	11	4
South Korea	293	2	145	17	72	95	95	D	6	-2	45	45	-18	-26	D
Taiwan	230	D	181	-7	D	23	23	5	3	21	12	12	D	*	6
Thailand	-154	-261	65	3	10	45	45	D	D	D	17	14	D	2	D
Other	147	D	20	D	D	0	D	0	*	D	14	14	D	-8	D
International	-176	-188	265	-32	197	12	-1	24	108	21	108	-41	-261	-116	12
Addendum—OPEC[1]	132	-44	-32	24		12	-1	21	44	108	-41	-261	-116		221

*Less than $500,000 (±).

[D]Suppressed to avoid disclosure of data of individual companies.

[1]See footnote 1, Table A8-11.

71

Table A8-13 U.S. DIRECT INVESTMENT ABROAD: EQUITY CAPITAL OUTFLOWS, 1988 (millions of dollars; inflows (−))

	All Industries	Petroleum	Manufacturing								Wholesale Trade	Banking	Finance (Except Banking), Insurance, and Real Estate	Services	Other Industries
			Total	Food and Kindred Products	Chemicals and Allied Products	Primary and Fabricated Metals	Machinery, Except Electrical	Electric and Electronic Equipment	Transportation Equipment	Other Manufacturing					
All countries	-5,469	-3,381	-797	-194	-170	-38	-117	-342	333	-269	294	338	-1,575	-211	-136
Developed countries	-1,890	-1,688	-812	-127	-167	-19	-139	-379	309	-289	192	-155	786	-176	-37
Canada	-89	121	-99	D	-124	-1	D	D	2	39	23	D	-125	D	-102
Europe	-877	-1,842	-116	-120	208	-7	-122	-188	329	-216	330	-243	1,217	-221	-2
European Communities (12)	-1,093	D	-110	-124	211	D	-122	-188	329	D	332	-81	671	D	-2
Belgium	-32	0	-45	D	-7	D	0	0	0	0	2	D	D	0	0
Denmark	D	0	0	0	0	0	0	0	0	0	0	9	D	0	0
France	12	0	-210	D	44	-1	59	D	D	-14	D	29	D	*	0
Germany, Federal Republic of	-1,320	D	D	*	D	D	-26	D	D	-14	13	-2	5	D	*
Greece	4	0	-2	0	0	0	0	0	0	-2	0	6	0	0	0
Ireland	-80	0	D	0	-1	0	0	0	0	D	0	*	0	0	D
Italy	D	0	3	D	D	0	D	0	0	D	D	5	6	0	D
Luxembourg	-48	0	D	0	0	0	D	0	0	0	0	-4	D	0	0
Netherlands	-198	D	-28	4	25	D	D	0	D	D	8	6	D	0	-1
Portugal	-39	0	-1	0	0	0	0	0	0	-1	0	D	D	0	0
Spain	72	0	-4	1	0	0	0	0	0	4	-5	-9	1	0	D
United Kingdom	392	-506	426	D	-37	-9	1	D	0	-57	122	D	624	D	D
Other Europe	215	D	-6	3	-2	D	D	D	*	D	-2	-162	546	-141	D
Austria	0	0	-2	0	-2	0	0	0	*	0	1	4	*	D	0
Finland	D	0	0	0	0	0	0	0	0	0	0	0	0	0	0
Norway	0	D	0	0	0	0	0	0	0	0	3	0	*	0	0
Sweden	-8	0	0	0	0	0	0	0	0	0	-8	0	-1	0	0
Switzerland	375	0	3	3	0	0	0	0	0	0	3	-168	548	0	0
Turkey	11	2	D	0	0	0	0	0	0	0	0	D	0	0	0
Other	-2	0	0	D	0	0	0	0	0	0	0	-2	0	0	0
Japan	-609	0	-428	D	-138	-7	0	D	D	-69	-78	-2	-159	D	12
Australia, New Zealand, and South Africa	-314	33	-169	-39	-114	-5	D	D	D	-43	-81	D	-146	D	55
Australia	-78	D	D	D	D	D	D	D	D	D	D	1	-158	-2	D
New Zealand	51	D	D	0	0	0	0	0	0	D	3	D	D	0	D
South Africa	-287	0	-131	0	0	D	0	0	*	0	D	0	D	0	D
Developing countries	-3,494	15	20	-66	-3	-19	22	37	23	20	101	493	-2,361	-35	D
Latin America and Other Western Hemisphere	-2,864	-1,079	72	-55	6	-19	25	D	23	D	102	367	-2,343	D	21
South America	-697	D	111	-58	6	-19	25	D	43	-1	D	D	D	-5	D
Argentina	17	0	6	0	*	D	0	0	0	1	0	D	D	D	0
Brazil	318	0	D	1	13	D	25	0	43	3	0	103	64	D	0
Chile	82	146	D	-2	D	0	0	0	0	-1	0	13	D	D	-1
Colombia	D	D	-11	D	5	D	0	0	0	0	*	0	0	*	0

Ecuador	2
Peru	−5 D
Venezuela	D
Other	1
Central America	98
Mexico	8
Panama	87
Other	3
Other Western Hemisphere	−2,265
Bahamas	321
Bermuda	−60
Jamaica	−2
Netherlands Antilles	−2,525
Trinidad and Tobago	D
United Kingdom Islands, Caribbean	−9 D
Other	−184 D
Other Africa	D
Saharan	2
Egypt	D
Libya	D
Other	D
Sub-Saharan	*
Liberia	D
Nigeria	D
Other	D
Middle East	−418
Israel	−14 D
Saudi Arabia	D
United Arab Emirates	D
Other	−6
Other Asia and Pacific	−28
Hong Kong	−42
India	−8
Indonesia	−16
Malaysia	−12
Philippines	−62
Singapore	−10
South Korea	74
Taiwan	−28
Thailand	5
Other	70
International	−85
Addendum—OPEC[1]	−627

*Less than $500,000 (±).

D Suppressed to avoid disclosure of data of individual companies.

[1] See footnote 1, Table A8-11.

Table 8-14 U.S. DIRECT INVESTMENT ABROAD REINVESTED EARNINGS, 1988 (millions of dollars)

Columns 4–10 ("Total" through "Other Manufacturing") fall under the **Manufacturing** grouping.

	All Industries	Petroleum	Manufacturing — Total	Food and Kindred Products	Chemicals and Allied Products	Primary and Fabricated Metals	Machinery, Except Electrical	Electric and Electronic Equipment	Transportation Equipment	Other Manufacturing	Wholesale Trade	Banking	Finance (Except Banking), Insurance, and Real Estate	Services	Other Industries
All countries	**15,170**	**45**	**7,266**	**673**	**3,307**	**1,145**	**-760**	**672**	**1,229**	**1,000**	**2,407**	**275**	**3,314**	**600**	**1,263**
Developed countries	**10,361**	**583**	**4,126**	**531**	**2,493**	**749**	**-1,009**	**-26**	**775**	**613**	**1,843**	**68**	**2,324**	**601**	**815**
Canada	4,224	-262	2,060	111	634	385	427	18	176	309	668	114	951	192	500
Europe	2,599	20	731	377	1,296	239	-1,601	-85	439	66	469	-180	1,103	342	114
European Communities (12)	3,446	834	1,012	274	1,297	234	-1,607	-120	465	470	743	130	341	267	119
Belgium	464	3	403	18	383	-16	0	-6	D	D	82	-77	47	4	1
Denmark	-30	D	7	-8	3	9	*	1	0	2	-65	-3	-16	D	-1
France	236	-82	262	-15	254	-20	-152	-12	27	181	-9	-71	103	24	9
Germany, Federal Republic of	-1,394	-198	-980	43	17	42	-820	-40	-151	-70	-136	-104	91	-54	-13
Greece	36	1	12	2	9	0	0	1	0	1	-4	25	*	2	-1
Ireland	588	-7	353	30	121	16	52	1	2	132	2	-9	D	D	-1
Italy	85	D	89	22	228	16	-184	-53	5	55	41	-44	49	D	10
Luxembourg	16	3	2	0	D	-4	-4	D	*	D	1	-4	14	0	0
Netherlands	900	49	73	-39	-78	52	-87	66	*	160	547	-10	14	184	55
Portugal	27	*	-8	1	D	1	2	D	D	2	-5	25	D	D	1
Spain	613	-11	443	96	62	19	2	-29	D	89	52	93	6	30	*
United Kingdom	1,904	1,102	356	126	316	118	-399	-25	D	D	236	309	-204	48	58
Other Europe	-847	-814	-281	103	-1	5	6	35	-26	-403	-274	-310	762	75	-5
Austria	-19	D	D	7	-1	*	D	3	D	D	-23	-5	5	4	D
Finland	6	D	-3	0	D	0	-4	0	0	1	16	D	0	*	0
Norway	23	-19	16	*	D	-1	6	0	0	D	13	-1	D	-1	D
Sweden	30	D	13	D	D	1	-4	1	3	-14	20	-3	5	1	D
Switzerland	-809	D	-276	D	-10	6	*	30	0	D	-312	D	737	69	D
Turkey	-46	D	-1	2	*	-3	D	1	-2	1	10	-12	D	2	1
Other	-33	-5	-31	0	0	2	D	0	D	2	2	D	D	1	*
Japan	1,818	695	630	52	229	27	D	24	85	D	473	-103	76	8	39
Australia, New Zealand, and South Africa	1,719	129	706	-8	334	99	D	17	76	D	231	237	194	60	162
Australia	1,835	98	817	86	331	92	82	18	78	131	259	239	217	56	150
New Zealand	-31	D	-9	D	8	2	D	2	-5	D	-11	-2	-31	2	D
South Africa	-84	D	-103	D	-4	5	-28	-3	3	D	-16	0	8	2	D
Developing countries	**4,794**	**-395**	**3,139**	**142**	**814**	**396**	**249**	**698**	**454**	**387**	**565**	**207**	**989**	**-1**	**290**
Latin America and Other Western Hemisphere	2,729	-149	1,894	96	465	338	108	48	471	368	268	-70	590	88	108
South America	988	-286	1,088	22	190	274	109	33	292	169	8	122	37	66	-48
Argentina	-95	1	-111	7	-28	6	D	D	D	-36	-23	16	14	9	-1
Brazil	1,019	-1	828	-23	167	128	119	26	279	132	-6	123	25	46	3
Chile	172	D	146	7	15	D	0	3	D	3	-4	2	16	5	D
Colombia	-274	-260	88	13	12	D	D	-1	D	34	-5	D	D	*	D

Table (rotated); column headers not present on this portion of the page.

Area/Country													
Ecuador	-4	-1	4	3	-2	2	0	*	-2	2	*	*	*	-1
Peru	-78	D	-9	-13	*	2	D	*	0	2	-6	*	*	1
Venezuela	198	29	132	20	23	D	1	2	36	32	52	-3	6	2
Other	49	-12	12	8	2	-1	0	0	*	0	*	-1	*	D
Central America	993	74	769	68	254	62	*	10	179	196	155	-225	8	90
Mexico	811	-1	703	39	235	51	*	8	179	191	67	2	8	36
Panama	83	92	19	-1	D	D	0	0	0	*	57	-229	-3	22
Other	99	-17	47	29	D	D	0	2	0	5	31	2	2	31
Other Western Hemisphere	749	64	37	7	21	2	*	4	0	3	105	32	13	67
Bahamas	-99	D	D	7	D	0	0	0	0	0	22	-178	2	1
Bermuda	949	25	0	0	0	0	0	0	0	0	23	D	-2	D
Jamaica	82	1	11	2	8	0	0	0	0	1	D	1	5	D
Netherlands Antilles	235	6	3	2	1	*	0	0	0	0	D	D	-1	*
Trinidad and Tobago	-14	D	3	1	2	0	*	0	0	*	*	D	1	D
United Kingdom Islands, Caribbean	-445	*	2	1	0	0	0	1	0	0	D	194	D	*
Other	40	4	D	2	D	2	*	3	0	2	D	D	D	5
Other Africa	-290	-481	68	7	D	D	0	1	10	-3	-8	-33	18	32
Saharan	-144	-188	9	7	*	*	*	1	1	1	5	-2	17	D
Egypt	-124	-150	7	D	*	D	0	-1	1	*	5	-2	14	4
Libya	1	-7	0	0	0	0	0	-1	-1	0	1	0	3	4
Other	-21	-32	3	D	0	0	0	0	0	1	*	D	0	D
Sub-Saharan	-146	-293	59	*	D	D	0	0	0	-4	-13	-31	2	D
Liberia	12	1	0	0	0	0	0	2	9	0	-22	*	1	D
Nigeria	-232	-217	13	0	14	-1	0	0	0	0	1	-30	-1	*
Other	75	-77	45	*	D	D	0	2	9	-4	8	-1	*	D
Middle East	351	255	187	0	D	-1	1	45	0	*	33	-55	-107	-28
Israel	62	7	D	0	D	D	*	47	0	1	D	D	D	-2
Saudi Arabia	219	110	D	0	D	D	-1	-2	0	*	D	D	-103	-18
United Arab Emirates	22	34	1	0	*	0	1	0	0	0	6	-4	-3	3
Other	49	104	*	0	*	0	*	0	0	-1	25	*	D	-10
Other Asia and Pacific	2,003	-19	990	39	176	36	141	603	-27	22	271	365	220	176
Hong Kong	684	17	6	5	3	D	D	38	1	5	244	109	208	98
India	32	*	39	*	6	9	13	1	1	10	-1	-4	-1	*
Indonesia	65	24	13	*	9	1	*	-1	0	4	3	-4	7	23
Malaysia	327	D	143	*	*	-1	*	127	0	16	D	D	0	2
Philippines	115	5	36	20	31	2	0	20	1	-39	9	31	7	26
Singapore	476	47	384	9	D	*	126	241	D	3	-9	46	11	4
South Korea	221	98	98	4	D	D	-1	66	D	21	10	135	-23	4
Taiwan	270	*	208	-3	74	D	D	67	5	-1	10	42	5	5
Thailand	-180	D	59	3	5	2	2	42	0	3	D	5	2	5
Other	-7	-19	6	0	-1	0	0	2	6	*	-13	4	4	10
International	15	-143	298	23	197	19	-11	-1	34	38	81	39	-3	158
Addendum—OPEC[1]	233	-83											-101	37

*Less than $500,000 (±).

D Suppressed to avoid disclosure of data of individual companies.

[1] See footnote 1, Table A8-11.

Table A8-15 U.S. DIRECT INVESTMENT ABROAD: INTERCOMPANY DEBT OUTFLOWS, 1988 (millions of dollars; inflows (−))

	All Industries	Petroleum	Manufacturing								Wholesale Trade	Banking	Finance (Except Banking), Insurance, and Real Estate	Services	Other Industries
			Total	Food and Kindred Products	Chemicals and Allied Products	Primary and Fabricated Metals	Machinery, Except Electrical	Electric and Electronic Equipment	Transportation Equipment	Other Manufacturing					
All countries	**7,831**	**1,584**	**−1,163**	**−394**	**205**	**164**	**−662**	**556**	**−997**	**−34**	**325**	**10**	**6,669**	**17**	**389**
Developed countries	**2,341**	**959**	**−1,408**	**−199**	**147**	**157**	**−636**	**138**	**−983**	**−33**	**374**	**−3**	**2,173**	**−98**	**344**
Canada	−34	641	−845	D	−77	194	D	D	−602	131	−3	D	36	D	122
Europe	1,613	326	−857	59	175	27	−306	−213	−414	−185	224	9	1,955	−152	107
European Communities (12)	2,086	D	−820	76	150	D	−298	−228	−395	−75	542	9	2,124	D	106
Belgium	−169	104	25	D	136	D	D	−13	−12	−75	−135	D	D	−81	*
Denmark	D	−15	2	17	D	D	D	−20	D	1	−14	D	D	4	D
France	506	70	−79	D	36	−3	−1	D	D	−95	D	−2	D	44	51
Germany, Federal Republic of	−807	D	D	172	D	D	−169	D	D	−178	71	−1	−372	D	17
Greece	14	*	3	D	4	0	D	*	0	D	D	0	D	D	0
Ireland	84	21	D	6	−16	*	D	17	−3	D	5	−1	−11	D	0
Italy	D	D	−27	D	D	*	D	D	10	D	D	D	−4	D	D
Luxembourg	185	D	D	0	−4	*	D	16	*	D	5	−1	D	D	0
Netherlands	181	D	−180	46	−182	20	D	−3	D	−75	−15	0	D	−165	50
Portugal	43	D	14	D	D	D	D	9	*	*	25	0	0	−3	0
Spain	−200	−2	−186	8	−11	−1	D	−18	−146	D	56	0	−2	D	D
United Kingdom	2,331	93	−38	8	203	D	D	D	−34	D	139	D	2,039	102	D
Other Europe	−473	D	−37	−17	25	D	−8	15	−19	D	−318	0	−169	D	1
Austria	D	D	−18	D	D	*	D	D	−19	D	105	0	4	D	D
Finland	18	1	5	0	−1	*	D	0	0	D	12	0	0	0	0
Norway	D	D	−2	0	2	*	*	0	0	−4	1	0	*	−5	*
Sweden	−42	D	−18	0	D	*	4	0	0	D	−9	0	−1	−5	0
Switzerland	−550	72	−18	−18	21	0	−5	13	0	−29	−433	0	−166	−5	*
Turkey	9	D	D	D	D	3	0	0	0	D	D	D	0	D	2
Other	−17	−1	−7	0	0	0	D	D	0	D	D	D	−5	D	D
Japan	767	111	350	D	53	3	D	D	D	14	129	0	158	D	3
Australia, New Zealand, and South Africa	−5	−119	−57	−79	−4	−67	50	D	D	7	24	D	23	D	113
Australia	−76	D	D	D	D	D	D	D	D	D	D	D	22	9	78
New Zealand	27	D	D	1	1	1	−8	0	D	1	29	0	D	9	3
South Africa	44	D	−14	−12	D	7	D	0	D	D	D	0	D	−2	32
Developing countries	**5,598**	**D**	**246**	**−195**	**59**	**7**	**−27**	**418**	**−15**	**−1**	**−49**	**13**	**4,496**	**116**	**D**
Latin America and Other Western Hemisphere	4,714	79	−50	−179	93	23	−5	D	−49	D	−12	10	4,605	96	D
South America	17	D	−68	−206	D	D	−21	D	−19	53	D	D	D	D	−13
Argentina	−146	40	−166	−130	8	*	D	2	−3	D	−14	0	D	−2	D
Brazil	66	D	70	−66	22	1	−1	D	−5	42	19	0	−10	D	3
Chile	37	D	*	*	D	0	0	D	*	D	D	0	D	D	D
Colombia	D	D	−20	D	5	−2	D	*	−22	D	D	0	2	*	2

Ecuador	−16	8	−4	0	*	D	0	D	0	D	−1	0	D	−1	D
Peru	44	D	3	D	2	D	0	0	0	D	−6	D	D	D	D
Venezuela	D	50	D	D	5	D	D	1	10	6	11	0	−20	−1	20
Other	−42	D	2	D	*	0	0	D	0	D	D	0	0	D	−4
Central America	−282	−22	17	27	D	−26	16	17	−30	D	D	D	D	D	−33
Mexico	−212	−4	−18	4	D	D	16	17	−30	D	D	0	D	D	D
Panama	−118	−21	5	*	D	0	0	0	0	D	−3	0	−59	−1	−38
Other	48	4	30	23	D	D	0	0	0	−1	8	D	3	−1	D
Other Western Hemisphere	4,979	D	1	*	2	D	0	0	0	D	D	10	4,945	114	D
Bahamas	−70	D	D	D	*	0	0	0	0	0	D	0	D	−26	D
Bermuda	−33	−35	0	0	0	0	0	0	0	0	16	D	D	138	D
Jamaica	−52	D	3	*	2	0	0	0	0	*	D	0	D	−4	D
Netherlands Antilles	5,013	D	0	D	D	D	0	0	0	0	D	0	5,040	0	D
Trinidad and Tobago	D	34	*	0	*	0	0	0	0	0	D	D	0	D	D
United Kingdom Islands, Caribbean	38	D	D	0	0	0	0	D	0	0	D	10	22	D	0
Other	D	−9	−2	*	D	D	0	D	0	D	3	D	57	0	D
Other Africa	467	466	−13	−1	D	D	0	8	*	−5	4	D	14	−4	D
Saharan	D	D	*	0	D	D	0	0	*	D	10	D	D	−4	D
Egypt	152	D	3	D	D	D	0	0	*	D	D	D	0	−4	D
Libya	4	4	0	0	0	0	0	0	0	0	D	0	0	*	D
Other	D	D	−3	D	*	D	0	0	0	D	D	0	D	0	0
Sub-Saharan	D	D	−13	−1	D	−18	0	8	0	D	−6	0	D	*	*
Liberia	9	*	0	0	0	0	0	0	0	0	D	0	D	D	D
Nigeria	D	D	2	0	2	0	0	D	0	D	−5	0	0	0	0
Other	D	D	−15	−1	D	−18	0	D	0	D	D	0	D	D	D
Middle East	41	124	−53	0	D	D	*	−22	0	−15	100	D	−292	D	D
Israel	50	D	−23	0	−1	0	D	−22	0	D	111	0	D	D	−2
Saudi Arabia	D	D	−26	0	−11	D	*	−1	0	D	17	0	D	D	D
United Arab Emirates	D	D	0	0	D	0	D	0	0	0	1	0	D	−13	D
Other	−33	2	−3	0	D	D	0	0	0	D	−30	D	D	D	D
Other Asia and Pacific	376	D	362	−15	−21	2	−21	D	34	D	−140	4	169	D	D
Hong Kong	86	−7	30	D	−6	D	D	D	0	−2	D	−6	180	20	D
India	−1	0	−1	0	*	*	*	D	D	*	D	0	D	0	*
Indonesia	12	D	−6	*	*	0	−5	*	0	−1	D	D	0	−1	D
Malaysia	*	D	D	D	*	0	D	54	0	D	D	0	*	0	*
Philippines	24	8	−9	−4	−1	*	1	−6	0	1	14	D	8	0	D
Singapore	163	−67	267	D	−17	−1	−33	D	D	D	−39	−2	3	*	1
South Korea	−2	2	31	D	D	*	D	26	*	D	D	D	D	−3	D
Taiwan	−13	D	D	D	D	D	D	−44	15	7	2	4	0	*	*
Thailand	21	D	7	0	D	D	D	4	0	*	D	D	D	0	D
Other	84	27	D	0	D	0	0	D	D	0	25	D	D	D	D
International	−107	D													D
Addendum—OPEC[1]	525	602	D	D	−4	6	23	*	10	−15	27	0	−299	D	182

*Less than $500,000 (±).

[D]Suppressed to avoid disclosure of data of individual companies.

[1]See footnote 1, Table A8-11.

Table A8-16 U.S. DIRECT INVESTMENT ABROAD: INCOME, 1988 (millions of dollars)

	All Industries	Petroleum	Total	Food and Kindred Products	Chemicals and Allied Products	Primary and Fabricated Metals	Machinery, Except Electrical	Electric and Electronic Equipment	Transportation Equipment	Other Manufacturing	Wholesale Trade	Banking	Finance (Except Banking), Insurance, and Real Estate	Services	Other Industries
			Manufacturing												
All countries	48,264	7,932	23,319	2,219	5,996	1,503	3,346	1,788	4,113	4,355	6,360	2,560	5,299	926	1,868
Developed countries	37,183	5,548	18,302	1,855	4,742	1,034	2,872	856	3,331	3,612	5,255	1,288	4,708	824	1,258
Canada	8,954	813	4,821	419	1,238	461	573	304	822	1,005	953	114	1,290	219	744
Europe	22,033	3,009	11,026	1,248	2,704	432	1,668	364	2,325	2,286	3,202	933	3,076	524	263
European Communities (12)	18,957	2,517	10,665	1,115	2,630	425	1,603	314	2,352	2,225	2,085	976	2,018	432	264
Belgium	959	34	647	32	512	-4	D	4	D	D	143	51	69	13	2
Denmark	80	D	23	4	3	9	*	1	0	5	18	*	-14	D	-1
France	1,321	-25	871	35	356	-11	148	-2	43	302	240	10	171	36	18
Germany, Federal Republic of	1,683	-42	1,277	142	213	99	154	99	282	288	123	9	291	-37	63
Greece	56	3	15	2	10	0	0	2	0	1	-2	38	1	D	-1
Ireland	1,127	-7	735	46	282	27	116	32	3	228	37	3	D	D	-1
Italy	1,120	D	915	128	327	19	323	-42	10	150	169	-39	119	D	11
Luxembourg	57	3	40	0	D	-4	-3	D	*	D	*	-1	14	0	0
Netherlands	2,388	502	762	164	219	73	14	81	*	212	763	1	70	232	58
Portugal	138	4	52	1	D	1	2	D	D	6	33	28	D	D	1
Spain	1,393	-6	1,137	120	113	52	D	-20	D	115	114	93	6	39	9
United Kingdom	8,636	2,069	4,191	439	598	164	693	135	D	D	446	783	930	111	105
Other Europe	3,076	492	361	132	74	7	64	50	-26	60	1,117	-43	1,058	92	-1
Austria	271	D	24	16	6	*	D	3	D	D	196	4	21	4	D
Finland	104	D	1	0	*	0	-4	0	0	4	84	D	0	*	0
Norway	421	348	25	*	D	-1	6	0	0	D	33	-1	D	1	0
Sweden	145	D	99	D	D	1	D	1	3	-2	50	-3	6	1	D
Switzerland	2,153	D	243	D	48	8	-4	44	0	D	736	D	1,000	83	2
Turkey	-18	D	1	2	*	-3	*	2	-2	3	10	4	0	2	2
Other	*	-3	-31	0	0	2	D	0	D	2	8	D	D	2	*
Japan	3,270	871	1,490	179	355	35	D	162	91	D	746	1	105	15	42
Australia, New Zealand, and South Africa	2,926	855	965	9	445	107	D	26	92	D	354	240	237	66	209
Australia	2,862	759	1,015	101	425	97	107	25	92	167	347	241	256	61	183
New Zealand	19	D	*	D	8	2	D	3	-3	D	11	-1	-30	2	D
South Africa	45	D	-50	D	12	7	-19	-1	3	D	-4	0	11	2	D
Developing countries	10,823	2,314	5,017	364	1,254	469	474	932	782	743	1,105	1,272	591	101	423
Latin America and Other Western Hemisphere	4,617	338	2,988	265	740	358	241	97	615	672	469	643	-72	130	122
South America	2,277	29	1,806	137	346	289	231	75	359	369	71	200	131	81	-42
Argentina	173	148	-44	22	-10	6	D	3	-3	-25	-19	56	15	17	*
Brazil	1,641	52	1,304	25	259	135	220	50	342	272	*	137	95	50	4
Chile	220	D	159	8	21	D	0	3	D	7	4	16	26	5	D
Colombia	-117	-168	141	37	27	D	D	1	D	43	6	D	D	*	D

Ecuador	8	4	7	3	–1	3	0	1	–2	2	3	–6	*	*	1
Peru	–66	D	–4	–9	*	2	D	*	0	–1	3	D	D	D	1
Venezuela	351	44	227	40	47	*	1	17	38	74	64	2	–8	8	3
Other	67	–8	15	11	2	*	10	0	*	4	1	4	D	1	D
Central America	1,868	156	1,132	121	365	67	10	18	256	194	295	–16	283	24	95
Mexico	1,190	*	1,024	91	311	55	10	16	256	90	284	2	16	18	40
Panama	542	155	45	–1	D	D	0	0	0	72	*	–20	263	3	24
Other	136	1	63	30	D	D	0	3	0	32	10	2	3	3	31
Other Western Hemisphere	473	153	50	8	29	2	4	4	0	203	7	459	–485	25	69
Bahamas	259	D	D	D	D	0	0	0	0	24	0	113	56	2	2
Bermuda	1,518	23	0	0	0	0	0	0	0	49	0	D	1,413	5	D
Jamaica	155	2	13	3	9	0	0	0	0	D	1	1	–	6	D
Netherlands Antilles	–2,090	6	3	2	1	*	0	0	0	D	0	D	–2,120	–1	1
Trinidad and Tobago	72	D	5	1	3	0	0	0	0	1	1	D	*	1	D
United Kingdom Islands, Caribbean	460	1	2	1	0	0	1	0	0	D	0	310	149	D	*
Other	78	9	D	2	D	2	3	0	0	D	6	D	16	D	5
Other Africa	808	369	113	11	1	1	4	3	10	26	3	–18	224	19	74
Saharan	210	150	16	9	1	D	2	4	1	7	2	4	D	17	D
Egypt	226	186	12	D	1	1	2	2	1	5	*	4	*	14	5
Libya	2	–7	0	D	0	D	0	0	0	1	0	0	0	3	4
Other	–18	–29	4	D	0	D	0	0	0	*	0	0	0	0	D
Sub-Saharan	597	220	97	2	0	0	2	0	9	19	1	–22	D	2	D
Liberia	40	1	0	0	0	0	0	0	0	3	0	1	D	1	D
Nigeria	185	196	14	0	15	–1	0	0	0	3	*	–29	0	*	*
Other	373	23	83	2	D	D	0	2	9	14	1	6	0	1	D
Middle East	792	420	295	0	D	D	1	46	0	62	2	–20	151	–92	–24
Israel	88	8	D	0	D	*	D	48	0	D	1	*	D	D	–1
Saudi Arabia	470	175	D	0	D	D	–1	–2	0	D	1	D	D	–93	–16
United Arab Emirates	90	81	2	0	1	0	0	0	0	8	0	1	–2	–3	3
Other	145	157	*	0	*	0	0	0	0	32	*	D	*	D	–10
Other Asia and Pacific	4,606	1,186	1,622	88	245	49	231	785	157	549	66	666	288	44	251
Hong Kong	1,168	37	159	5	27	D	D	51	0	422	29	189	247	17	97
India	56	*	50	*	11	9	15	1	1	–1	12	7	–1	*	*
Indonesia	848	719	20	2	14	1	*	–1	0	7	5	4	9	–1	91
Malaysia	404	D	148	*	3	–1	*	128	0	D	17	D	4	0	3
Philippines	182	5	83	41	50	3	0	22	1	12	–34	44	1	7	29
Singapore	940	48	700	9	D	*	131	369	D	37	4	143	–2	11	4
South Korea	345	*	126	14	D	D	–1	81	D	17	22	178	17	3	4
Taiwan	365	D	263	10	82	D	D	90	7	28	6	61	6	*	7
Thailand	276	D	65	6	7	3	2	42	0	D	4	D	5	2	5
Other	21	–16	8	0	*	0	0	2	6	–10	*	22	1	4	12
International	258	71	509	45	320	31	–11	14	37	118	74	–17	133	–87	187
Addendum—OPEC[1]	1,935	1,168													111

*Less than $500,000 (±).

D Suppressed to avoid disclosure of data of individual companies.

[1]See footnote 1, Table A8-11.

79

Table A8-17 U.S. DIRECT INVESTMENT ABROAD: COUNTRY DETAIL FOR SELECTED ITEMS
(millions of dollars)

Line		Direct Investment Position					Capital Outflows (Inflows (−))					Income				
		1984	1985	1986	1987	1988	1984	1985	1986	1987	1988	1984	1985	1986	1987	1988
1	All countries	211,480	230,250	259,800	307,983	326,900	2,821	18,068	26,311	44,194	17,533	21,217	33,202	38,533	54,754	48,264
2	Developed countries	157,123	172,058	194,280	232,690	245,498	1,101	13,669	18,589	33,954	10,812	13,436	26,098	32,323	45,527	37,183
3	Canada	46,730	46,909	50,629	58,377	61,244	2,259	-705	2,565	7,450	4,101	4,910	4,307	5,063	6,990	8,954
4	Europe	91,589	105,171	120,724	146,243	152,232	47	13,622	14,054	22,376	3,335	7,399	19,800	22,971	32,975	22,033
5	European Communities (10)	69,500	81,380	95,629	115,865	121,709	-65	11,849	12,354	17,793	3,922	5,010	16,317	19,121	26,932	17,427
6	Belgium	4,584	5,038	5,006	6,757	7,224	142	485	237	1,735	263	251	944	1,479	1,744	959
7	Denmark	1,144	1,281	1,085	1,091	1,191	7	149	-157	-149	130	123	235	276	254	80
8	France	6,406	7,643	8,952	11,771	12,495	-404	1,504	1,236	2,222	754	357	1,447	2,043	2,759	1,321
9	Germany, Federal Republic of	14,823	16,764	20,932	24,792	21,673	-520	1,920	3,542	3,568	-3,521	272	3,401	4,826	6,056	1,683
10	Greece	265	210	87	132	194	-73	-36	-34	22	54	-15	-20	-122	33	56
11	Ireland	2,869	3,693	4,308	5,135	5,743	394	721	665	1,007	593	514	785	840	1,156	1,127
12	Italy	4,594	5,906	7,426	9,008	9,075	138	985	459	1,446	-12	348	1,025	2,650	2,127	1,120
13	Luxembourg	424	690	802	787	756	40	48	41	-20	152	59	79	148	147	57
14	Netherlands	5,839	7,129	11,643	14,361	15,367	-679	1,241	4,515	2,593	882	696	2,197	3,523	3,228	2,388
15	United Kingdom	28,553	33,024	35,389	42,031	47,991	891	4,831	1,850	5,370	4,627	2,405	6,224	3,456	9,428	8,636
16	Other Europe	22,089	23,791	25,095	30,378	30,523	112	1,773	1,700	4,583	-588	2,389	3,483	3,850	6,043	4,606
17	Austria	530	493	715	714	1,167	-15	-16	-103	-62	27	18	36	142	130	271
18	Finland	191	258	292	389	413	-7	71	27	94	24	38	85	94	169	104
19	Norway	2,841	3,215	3,216	3,844	3,834	-253	376	424	540	-74	760	601	481	502	421
20	Portugal	205	237	288	412	425	-22	15	35	118	32	-7	49	85	94	138
21	Spain	2,139	2,281	2,707	3,789	4,368	-146	197	389	1,005	485	32	312	432	1,294	1,393
22	Sweden	844	933	918	1,111	1,089	-42	71	49	145	-20	102	190	189	182	145
23	Switzerland	14,725	15,766	16,441	19,518	18,672	580	1,049	979	2,666	-983	1,394	2,119	2,371	3,668	2,153
24	Turkey	228	234	215	207	193	101	6	-22	-14	-26	52	49	27	33	-18
25	Other	385	375	302	394	362	-84	3	-79	92	-52	1	42	28	-21	*
26	Cyprus	17	16	13	10	6	-4	-1	-4	-3	-4	9	12	5	5	4
27	Greenland	0	0	-39	D	D	0	0	-36	D	D	0	0	D	D	-4
28	Hungary	0	0	D	D	D	0	0	D	D	D	0	0	1	-4	D
29	Iceland	7	8	8	8	9	1	1	*	*	*	2	1	1	1	1
30	Liechtenstein	327	350	339	411	377	7	37	-11	72	-14	20	61	62	*	18
31	Malta	D	D	D	D	D	D	D	D	D	D	3	*	*	2	2
32	Romania	D	D	5	1	3	D	D	D	-5	2	3	3	2	-6	2
33	Yugoslavia	D	D	D	D	D	D	D	D	D	D	-33	-35	D	D	D
34	Japan	7,936	9,235	11,472	14,671	16,868	-361	1,160	1,987	2,908	1,976	729	1,617	3,387	3,873	3,270
35	Australia, New Zealand, and South Africa	10,868	10,743	11,455	13,399	15,154	-844	-408	-17	1,220	1,400	398	373	902	1,689	2,926
36	Australia	8,918	8,772	9,340	11,143	13,058	-237	-271	-37	1,062	1,681	748	278	548	1,182	2,862
37	New Zealand	510	576	598	732	826	-60	42	21	121	46	17	61	69	141	19
38	South Africa	1,440	1,394	1,517	1,524	1,270	-548	-180	-1	37	-327	-367	35	285	367	45
39	Developing countries	49,153	52,764	61,072	70,676	76,837	2,382	4,226	8,610	10,057	6,897	7,223	6,845	6,726	9,100	10,823
40	Latin America and Other Western Hemisphere	24,627	28,261	36,851	44,905	49,283	-171	4,083	7,441	8,042	4,579	1,495	2,338	3,516	3,812	4,617
41	South America	18,714	17,623	19,813	20,690	21,687	103	-1,057	1,243	382	308	1,198	908	1,697	1,718	2,277
42	Argentina	2,753	2,705	2,913	2,673	2,390	104	10	210	-129	-224	60	115	367	222	173
43	Brazil	9,237	8,893	9,268	10,288	11,810	239	-251	123	572	1,403	544	524	833	988	1,641
44	Chile	47	88	265	343	731	-68	43	87	71	291	33	52	94	119	220
45	Colombia	2,111	2,148	3,291	3,241	2,429	-11	-466	198	-68	-1,369	201	164	153	180	-117

No.	Country/area															
46	Ecuador	371	361	413	466	448	-75	-11	126	55	-19	81	93	79	20	8
47	Peru	1,902	1,243	1,103	1,084	1,064	-143	-218	-104	-42	-39	113	-37	-3	-56	-66
48	Venezuela	1,761	1,588	1,987	2,036	2,273	78	-218	545	-58	256	153	22	162	223	351
49	Other	534	597	572	560	543	-21	53	57	-19	9	14	-25	12	21	67
50	Bolivia	168	216	203	172	101	8	39	-2	-31	-72	19	-4	3	-12	-15
51	French Guiana	D	D	D	D	D	D	D	D	D	D	D	D	D	D	D
52	Guyana	3	2	2	4	5	-4	-1	*	1	1	*	-1	*	*	*
53	Paraguay	26	29	21	14	9	-10	3	-8	-7	-5	-8	-2	-8	-18	-5
54	Surinam	D	D	D	D	D	D	D	D	D	D	D	D	D	D	D
55	Uruguay	88	96	117	133	124	-12	6	21	11	17	-8	*	21	8	22
56	Central America	9,853	9,658	10,698	11,657	12,441	-75	69	395	889	809	739	1,128	1,285	1,529	1,868
57	Mexico	4,597	5,088	4,623	4,898	5,516	190	436	-132	275	607	347	642	217	707	1,190
58	Panama	4,474	3,959	5,525	6,131	6,140	-373	-140	581	547	52	350	490	1,007	688	542
59	Other	782	611	549	629	785	108	-227	-54	67	150	41	-4	61	134	136
60	Belize	-35	2	D	-15	-16	11	-21	D	D	-1	D	-1	-2	D	D
61	Costa Rica	158	113	113	141	174	-9	-46	-1	28	33	12	-8	12	25	29
62	El Salvador	94	73	51	51	57	-6	-15	28	10	6	10	3	10	10	8
63	Guatemala	240	213	181	174	203	37	-27	-7	21	21	20	-10	20	7	32
64	Honduras	288	171	167	185	231	72	-111	4	-6	46	-6	13	21	49	32
65	Nicaragua	39	39	51	93	137	3	-6	43	45	45	6	-2	11	43	36
66	Other Western Hemisphere	-3,941	980	6,341	12,558	15,155	-199	5,071	5,803	6,771	3,462	-442	302	534	565	473
67	Bahamas	3,331	3,795	2,991	2,706	2,244	-131	61	-929	-388	152	617	1,097	733	-15	259
68	Bermuda	13,019	13,116	15,373	19,100	19,880	1,068	599	1,552	4,085	857	1,265	1,415	1,740	2,261	1,518
69	Jamaica	257	122	106	102	156	-53	-116	-16	-16	28	29	30	53	96	155
70	Netherlands Antilles	-24,664	-20,499	-16,969	-14,257	-11,796	-1,908	4,092	4,852	3,020	2,722	-3,322	-3,220	-2,700	-2,197	-2,090
71	Trinidad and Tobago	667	484	424	388	429	-195	-172	-105	-28	9	64	156	56	54	72
72	United Kingdom Islands, Caribbean	2,992	3,490	3,794	3,953	3,577	1,042	543	341	182	-415	872	774	609	315	480
73	Other	458	472	620	566	664	-21	64	106	-84	109	33	50	44	50	78
74	Antigua and Barbuda	4	7	7	D	11	D	D	D	*	D	7	1	1	1	1
75	Barbados	47	81	212	179	304	-11	49	94	*	125	7	18	17	19	49
76	Cuba	*	*	1	9	D	*	*	D	*	D	D	D	D	D	5
77	Dominica	*	1	*	1	*	*	*	*	1	*	*	*	*	*	*
78	Dominican Republic	239	212	199	156	141	-10	11	-10	-106	-8	17	22	10	4	7
79	French Islands, Caribbean	11	9	12	26	22	-2	-2	3	14	-4	*	*	3	9	7
80	Grenada	*	*	*	1	1	5	3	*	*	*	0	0	0	0	0
81	Haiti	22	26	29	34	27	D	3	3	6	-4	6	8	6	6	6
82	St. Christopher and Nevis	0	0	0	1	*	0	0	0	1	-1	0	0	0	0	0
83	St. Lucia	0	0	*	D	D	0	0	0	D	D	D	D	D	D	2
84	St. Vincent	1	1	D	D	2	1	1	*	2	*	*	*	*	4	*
85	Other Africa	4,456	4,497	3,999	4,488	4,603	276	32	-417	409	-8	1,016	941	22	832	808
86	Saharan	2,037	2,423	2,115	2,103	2,097	183	386	-218	-101	-75	636	554	10	199	210
87	Egypt	1,538	1,926	1,807	1,680	1,705	117	369	-118	-159	31	579	485	80	209	226
88	Libya	348	325	241	310	312	109	-7	14	56	5	109	96	-24	-1	2
89	Other	152	172	67	113	79	-43	24	-113	2	-111	-52	-28	-45	-9	-18
90	Algeria	40	103	60	56	11	2	63	-42	-4	-19	10	D	11	11	D
91	Morocco	35	35	24	30	26	2	*	-19	6	-2	-3	5	6	6	4
92	Tunisia	77	35	-18	27	42	-47	-39	-52	1	-89	-58	-10	-27	-27	D
93	Sub-Saharan	2,420	2,074	1,884	2,385	2,506	92	-354	-199	510	68	380	388	11	633	597
94	Liberia	133	123	130	112	132	18	-10	-16	-3	21	-17	-53	9	23	40
95	Nigeria	327	44	781	1,159	1,342	85	-281	509	349	125	303	391	467	315	185
96	Other	1,959	1,907	973	1,114	1,032	-11	-62	-691	164	-78	95	50	-465	295	373
97	Angola	52	51	187	396	406	38	22	144	220	11	94	80	47	D	D

(Continued)

Line	Country	Direct investment position					Capital outflows (inflows (−))					Income				
		1984	1985	1986	1987	1988	1984	1985	1986	1987	1988	1984	1985	1986	1987	1988
98	Botswana	D	D	D	D	D	D	D	D	D	D	D	-28	D	D	D
99	Burkina	4	D	D	D	D	1	D	D	D	D	1	2	1	2	1
100	Burundi	1	*	0	0	0	1	-1	*	0	0	0	0	0	0	0
101	Cameroon	D	472	D	D	236	1	D	D	0	0	D	30	D	D	D
102	Central African Republic	*	D	*	*	*	D	D	-2	*	*	*	*	-3	*	*
103	Chad	1	2	37	37	36	*	2	6	*	*	*	-9	D	1	-2
104	Congo	19	31	14	13	36	3	12	D	-3	-1	*	1	D	*	-9
105	Djibouti	-1	-1	6	3	4	-19	*	*	*	23	D	1	*	-2	1
106	Ethiopia	2	2	2	2	2	*	*	*	*	1	1	1	-2	*	*
107	Gabon	179	212	197	245	178	70	21	-12	57	-116	*	13	*	10	3
108	Gambia	1	1	0	0	0	-1	D	-1	0	0	2	0	0	0	0
109	Ghana	131	118	102	63	84	-22	-14	-31	-39	21	0	-2	5	24	D
110	Guinea	D	D	39	7	D	D	D	D	-26	0	-7	D	D	D	D
111	Ivory Coast	153	134	51	73	104	-69	-19	-103	20	47	-34	-5	-87	30	44
112	Kenya	119	97	106	90	98	-37	-22	11	-16	11	6	-1	10	10	16
113	Lesotho	-3	-5	-7	-8	-9	-1	-1	-2	D	D	-1	D	-2	-1	-1
114	Madagascar	7	30	D	D	1	10	23	D	D	*	D	-1	D	-6	-3
115	Malawi	3	4	5	5	2	-7	1	1	D	D	1	2	2	2	1
116	Mali	2	5	D	D	D	1	3	D	-1	D	-7	-1	1	1	*
117	Mauritania	3	D	1	*	-1	*	*	D	*	*	*	-2	-1	-1	-1
118	Mauritius	8	3	4	3	4	D	D	-1	-3	D	-6	1	2	2	*
119	Mozambique	D	1	*	-2	-5	-7	1	-2	-5	-3	-7	1	-1	-3	-3
120	Namibia	11	D	5	1	0	-1	2	-2	1	-21	1	-2	-8	-5	-1
121	Niger	54	54	36	36	34	3	7	12	-33	-1	5	1	-1	1	-3
122	Rwanda	3	4	2	3	2	D	-7	1	-2	-1	7	6	4	D	1
123	Senegal	25	27	29	29	29	-7	5	-2	1	60	-12	9	4	5	5
124	Sierra Leone	-2	5	17	-16	44	3	5	12	-33	-2	28	-12	D	-2	5
125	Somalia	5	-2	10	8	6	D	-7	1	-2	-30	*	-21	-3	-2	-2
126	Sudan	343	361	-179	-204	-234	99	5	-474	-25	D	28	-21	-381	-26	-25
127	Swaziland	*	*	-1	D	1	*	*	D	D	-3	*	*	*	D	*
128	Tanzania	20	4	-7	-10	-14	-11	-16	-11	-4	-3	-20	-20	-6	-3	-2
129	Togo	6	9	D	D	-1	D	3	D	D	D	*	3	3	4	*
130	Uganda	D	D	D	D	D	D	D	D	D	D	4	4	3	1	1
131	Zaire	121	135	123	94	99	-12	14	-35	-23	6	29	38	-25	12	18
132	Zambia	65	46	36	41	47	-3	-19	-10	6	5	-3	-16	-5	8	7
133	Zimbabwe	58	52	49	46	36	-6	-5	-5	-1	-7	*	8	10	13	7
134	**Middle East**	5,025	4,606	4,891	4,589	4,090	607	-76	507	240	-25	906	402	586	491	792
135	Israel	733	717	427	653	722	119	116	-110	198	99	120	58	97	77	88
136	Saudi Arabia	2,352	2,442	2,460	2,140	2,047	224	73	43	194	-111	535	269	336	353	470
137	United Arab Emirates	981	792	840	703	680	280	-183	68	-111	-23	202	150	79	145	90
138	Other	959	655	1,163	1,092	641	-15	-82	506	-41	11	50	-74	74	-84	145
139	Bahrain	790	440	320	91	-324	6	-120	-120	-229	27	102	-45	-193	-119	-10
140	Iran	-23	-8	-25	-38	-41	-39	15	-8	-8	-2	-22	15	-14	-8	-6
141	Iraq	2	2	2	2	-1	*	D	D	*	4	-3	*	*	*	*
142	Jordan	D	D	D	D	D	12	-4	13	-44	D	13	-1	3	2	2
143	Kuwait	45	41	54	10	-31	-3	-1	*	1	-27	4	6	17	8	1
144	Lebanon	37	37	49	25	18	-3	-1	*	1	-7	*	D	6	4	*

No.	Country / Area	C1	C2	C3	C4	C5	C6	C7	C8	C9	C10	C11	C12	C13	C14	C15
145	Neutral Zone	0	0	0	0	0	0	0	0	0	0	0	0	0	0	0
146	Oman	51	60	27	23	38	6	*	-33	-4	15	-44	-39	-27	*	11
147	Qatar	6	6	6	5	4	1	1	D	-1	-1	5	4	3	2	3
148	Syria	2	2	2	2	2	-2	D	D	D	D	-4	D	D	2	D
149	Yemen (Aden)	D	2	2	2	2	0	0	0	0	0	1	0	0	0	0
150	Yemen (Sana)	D	D	D	D	D	-2	D	D	D	D	-1	-1	D	D	D
151	**Other Asia and Pacific**	15,045	15,400	15,332	16,694	18,860	1,670	186	1,079	1,366	2,351	3,805	3,163	2,602	3,965	4,606
152	Hong Kong	3,253	3,295	3,912	4,390	5,028	196	44	740	381	729	451	515	666	1,043	1,168
153	India	329	383	421	439	457	-20	52	65	50	23	38	64	88	70	56
154	Indonesia	4,093	4,475	3,217	3,050	3,006	930	176	35	-288	61	1,985	1,385	667	953	848
155	Malaysia	1,101	1,140	1,021	1,019	1,363	-113	42	-61	20	316	393	332	157	228	404
156	Philippines	1,263	1,032	1,299	1,220	1,305	-69	-244	64	-89	77	84	116	203	180	182
157	Singapore	1,932	1,874	2,256	2,462	3,005	220	-45	205	275	629	511	397	480	746	940
158	South Korea	716	743	782	1,003	1,302	127	37	64	215	293	171	170	109	184	345
159	Taiwan	736	750	869	1,280	1,546	107	1	99	432	230	191	90	109	395	365
160	Thailand	1,081	1,074	1,078	1,274	1,126	186	-43	2	194	-154	51	140	146	172	276
161	Other	541	635	476	556	721	106	166	-134	175	147	-69	-46	-24	-6	21
162	Afghanistan	*	*	*	*	*	*	0	0	0	0	0	0	0	0	0
163	Bangladesh	12	10	10	12	13	1	-2	1	1	1	2	1	1	3	2
164	Brunei	1	*	-29	-18	-18	D	-1	-1	D	*	8	3	2	3	D
165	Fiji	D	D	D	D	D	D	D	D	D	D	-1	2	2	1	*
166	French Islands, Indian Ocean	2	2	2	3	3	*	*	1	1	*	*	*	*	*	1
167	French Islands, Pacific	2	3	3	4	4	*	*	1	1	*	*	1	1	1	4
168	Macau	*	*	*	*	*	*	*	*	*	*	*	*	*	*	*
169	Pakistan	113	104	109	161	190	8	-6	5	75	29	14	35	21	43	24
170	Papua New Guinea	147	140	144	151	181	44	-7	4	15	29	1	-5	10	12	15
171	People's Republic of China	209	311	167	207	310	100	172	-119	102	99	-98	-91	-69	-76	-44
172	Sri Lanka	11	11	12	11	13	-1	1	1	-1	1	1	*	2	3	D
173	Tonga	2	2	2	3	3	D	D	D	1	*	*	*	*	1	1
174	Vanuatu	D	D	D	D	D	D	D	D	D	D	5	5	5	3	*
175	Vietnam	*	*	*	*	1	0	0	0	0	0	0	0	0	0	4
176	Western Samoa	*	*	*	*	1	0	0	*	0	0	0	0	0	0	0
177	**International**	5,204	5,428	4,448	4,617	4,565	-662	173	-887	183	-176	558	258	-516	127	258
	Addenda:															
178	OPEC[1]	10,481	10,383	10,235	10,143	10,229	1,677	-355	1,289	196	132	3,373	2,463	1,743	2,032	1,935
179	European Communities (12)[2]	98,624	120,066	126,502					12,778	18,916	4,439			19,638	28,321	18,957

*Less than $500,000 (±).

[D] Suppressed to avoid disclosure of data of individual companies.

[1] See footnote 1, Table A8-11.

[2] European Communities (12) comprises European Communities (10), Portugal, and Spain.

Table A8-18 U.S. DIRECT INVESTMENT ABROAD: INDUSTRY DETAIL FOR SELECTED ITEMS (millions of dollars)

Line		Direct Investment Position					Capital Outflows (Inflows (−))					Income				
		1984	1985	1986	1987	1988	1984	1985	1986	1987	1988	1984	1985	1986	1987	1988
1	All industries	211,480	230,250	259,800	307,983	326,900	2,821	18,068	26,311	44,194	17,533	21,217	33,202	38,533	54,754	48,264
2	Petroleum	58,051	57,695	58,497	61,800	59,658	−565	−1,433	3,357	3,346	−1,753	9,269	9,306	8,477	8,667	7,932
3	Oil and gas extraction	30,222	31,366	30,681	33,680	32,556	1,709	1,249	1,558	2,466	−1,440	7,335	6,840	3,692	5,552	4,760
4	Crude petroleum extraction (no refining) and natural gas	24,310	25,546	25,677	28,915	28,133	1,896	1,134	2,090	2,601	−1,147	6,605	6,387	4,252	5,501	4,700
5	Oil and gas field services	5,912	5,820	5,004	4,765	4,423	−187	115	−532	−135	−293	730	453	−560	52	60
6	Petroleum and coal products	17,221	16,465	16,383	17,053	17,190	−581	−2,189	760	651	−254	1,664	1,669	3,060	2,246	1,697
7	Integrated petroleum refining and extraction	9,871	8,625	9,608	10,057	9,633	−40	−2,616	990	493	−834	1,234	1,096	1,736	1,625	922
8	Petroleum refining without extraction	7,209	7,546	6,612	6,807	7,360	−547	450	−247	132	582	410	571	1,294	592	738
9	Petroleum and coal products, nec	142	194	163	189	197	7	−22	18	26	−2	19	1	30	29	37
10	Petroleum wholesale trade	8,801	8,048	9,554	9,369	8,107	−1,411	−523	1,251	189	−101	232	747	1,541	735	1,274
11	Other	1,807	1,816	1,879	1,699	1,805	−282	30	−212	40	43	38	51	184	134	201
12	Petroleum tanker operations	1,101	1,262	1,108	938	961	−403	10	−193	−28	−40	−97	−35	68	38	55
13	Petroleum and natural gas pipelines	197	257	313	318	350	18	21	17	29	31	67	58	66	61	45
14	Petroleum storage for hire	64	83	D	243	247	6	7	D	D	4	D	13	D	23	18
15	Gasoline service stations	445	215	D	200	247	97	−7	D	D	48	D	15	D	12	83
16	Manufacturing	85,865	94,700	105,101	127,074	133,819	1,862	9,043	10,084	20,861	5,306	5,839	14,677	18,061	27,616	23,319
17	Food and kindred products	8,156	9,252	11,366	12,995	13,121	478	1,196	1,607	1,614	85	683	1,619	2,202	2,865	2,219
18	Grain mill and bakery products	2,087	2,626	3,095	3,495	4,138	−30	461	487	447	610	61	378	452	793	621
19	Grain mill products	1,703	1,978	2,257	2,583	3,188	−45	314	302	364	584	58	254	286	640	505
20	Bakery products	384	647	838	912	950	15	147	185	83	26	3	124	166	153	116
21	Beverages	1,754	1,852	2,582	2,940	2,467	211	170	557	247	−512	224	447	722	857	509
22	Other	4,315	4,774	5,689	6,560	6,515	296	565	563	921	−13	398	793	1,029	1,216	1,089
23	Meat products	189	287	337	338	240	−19	80	34	57	−98	11	72	46	49	54
24	Dairy products	760	686	732	909	1,008	23	59	79	156	83	115	156	164	201	157
25	Preserved fruit and vegetables	459	545	768	561	693	52	96	80	116	147	27	49	133	119	95
26	Other food and kindred products	2,906	3,256	3,853	4,752	4,575	240	329	370	591	−145	244	516	686	847	782
27	Chemicals and allied products	19,200	20,273	22,653	27,071	30,467	242	782	2,249	4,779	3,342	1,206	2,320	4,226	5,825	5,996
28	Industrial chemicals and synthetics	9,217	9,104	10,242	12,166	14,128	364	79	1,118	1,984	1,882	728	870	1,626	2,258	2,752
29	Drugs	4,438	4,940	6,227	7,640	8,423	−64	566	1,078	1,352	935	295	787	1,418	1,822	1,751
30	Soap, cleaners, and toilet goods	2,316	2,440	2,262	3,051	3,429	−158	65	−65	758	342	21	82	476	772	736
31	Agricultural chemicals	821	1,096	1,102	752	813	40	−64	18	86	32	72	12	96	111	131
32	Other	2,407	2,692	2,819	3,463	3,674	60	136	101	598	151	90	568	610	863	625
33	Paints and allied products	426	620	642	566	608	−29	36	33	−90	9	1	55	88	147	104
34	Chemical products, nec	1,982	2,073	2,177	2,897	3,067	89	100	68	689	142	90	514	523	716	521

No.	Category															
35	Primary and fabricated metals	5,256	5,012	5,542	6,426	7,825	33	62	719	586	1,271	292	453	735	1,201	1,503
36	Primary metal industries	1,509	1,417	1,749	2,153	2,818	127	72	399	260	519	103	157	253	402	657
37	Ferrous	614	716	749	1,316	1,416	4	110	54	409	-25	24	86	126	133	70
38	Nonferrous	894	701	1,000	837	1,402	123	-38	346	-149	544	79	71	128	269	588
39	Fabricated metal products	3,747	3,595	3,793	4,273	5,007	-94	-11	320	325	752	190	296	482	799	846
40	Metal cans and shipping containers	744	481	557	639	854	-19	-37	59	83	212	29	32	82	137	93
41	Cutlery, hand tools, and hardware	510	673	636	634	707	-3	51	43	-179	72	65	136	146	154	237
42	Plumbing fixtures and heating equipment, ex. electric	126	152	180	228	198	-57	-6	54	46	-43	-7	30	46	48	-25
43	Fabricated structural metal products	452	366	276	296	352	-17	-70	-32	-7	56	47	5	31	57	50
44	Screw machine products, bolts, etc.	155	182	199	214	254	1	23	34	38	53	11	29	31	45	46
45	Metal stampings and forgings	444	427	538	690	730	-36	30	120	152	66	13	50	69	148	71
46	Fabricated metal products, nec, ordinance, and services	1,315	1,314	1,408	1,572	1,913	35	-2	42	192	335	32	13	76	211	375
47	Machinery, except electrical	14,816	18,987	22,090	26,887	25,608	216	3,996	3,481	4,755	-1,539	1,389	4,738	4,988	6,461	3,346
48	Farm and garden machinery	285	406	351	6	140	-88	15	19	-184	-47	-15	D	-150	-107	-43
49	Construction, mining, and materials handling machinery	2,237	2,257	2,323	2,935	3,033	-28	109	-38	279	91	-72	D	33	163	302
50	Office and computing machines	9,079	12,747	15,649	19,843	18,130	625	3,569	3,305	3,992	-1,768	1,476	D	4,694	5,803	2,627
51	Other	3,215	3,577	4,767	4,104	4,305	-293	303	195	668	186	1	379	411	603	459
52	Engines and turbines	428	497	529	721	736	-230	31	28	219	11	-59	68	-2	57	48
53	Metalworking machinery	565	538	504	480	468	-26	4	15	30	-7	5	22	22	48	3
54	Special industry machinery	495	636	700	732	736	9	60	86	119	-36	24	89	110	105	82
55	General industry machinery and equipment	997	986	1,109	1,130	1,147	-93	71	10	121	40	-15	88	142	218	147
56	Refrigeration and service industry machinery	445	524	522	5,771	758	63	71	41	110	182	41	71	74	92	134
57	Machinery, except, electrical, nec	284	396	402	465	460	-16	66	15	69	-5	6	41	64	83	45
58	Electric and electronic equipment	8,193	8,515	7,049	9,372	10,580	760	275	-1,306	1,345	886	862	1,042	1,370	1,641	1,788
59	Household appliances	1,103	1,080	1,372	1,643	1,173	3	-5	189	276	-599	36	116	118	231	50
60	Radio, television, and communication equipment	2,073	2,283	76	882	1,071	188	88	-2,215	-94	207	169	274	343	195	251
61	Electronic components and accessories	2,893	3,170	3,867	4,708	6,095	587	169	638	814	1,162	598	446	691	843	1,214
62	Other	2,124	1,982	1,734	2,139	2,242	-17	22	83	349	115	59	207	218	373	272
63	Electric lighting and wiring equipment	508	408	322	566	624	-95	-56	-19	206	127	-1	52	65	141	123
64	Electrical machinery, nec	1,617	1,574	1,412	1,572	1,617	78	79	102	142	-11	61	155	153	232	150
65	Transportation equipment	10,664	11,719	13,985	16,760	17,614	29	1,065	1,599	2,023	565	495	2,005	1,088	3,815	4,113
66	Motor vehicles and equipment	9,754	10,865	12,910	15,486	16,533	37	1,116	1,366	2,905	758	320	1,762	906	3,562	4,165
67	Other	910	854	1,075	1,274	1,081	-8	-51	233	118	-193	174	243	181	253	-52

(Continued)

Line		Direct Investment Position					Capital Outflows (Inflows (−))					Income				
		1984	1985	1986	1987	1988	1984	1985	1986	1987	1988	1984	1985	1986	1987	1988
68	Other manufacturing	19,581	20,942	22,416	27,563	28,604	104	1,666	1,735	4,759	697	913	2,501	3,452	5,806	4,355
69	Tobacco manufacturers	1,674	1,938	2,653	3,711	2,864	−46	265	389	905	−849	−21	325	444	884	302
70	Textile products and apparel	1,169	1,249	1,131	1,450	1,429	−139	112	18	251	−16	86	140	162	274	240
71	Textile mill products	738	788	772	986	965	−4	51	17	144	−24	94	73	95	151	149
72	Apparel and other textile products	431	461	359	463	464	−135	61	1	107	8	−8	66	68	122	92
73	Lumber, wood, furniture, and fixtures	587	660	480	519	670	−14	−32	47	46	26	−9	48	44	75	97
74	Lumber and wood products	354	445	300	320	434	−37	−19	38	20	−13	−30	11	32	51	59
75	Furniture and fixtures	233	215	180	198	237	23	−13	9	26	38	21	37	12	24	39
76	Paper and allied products	4,351	4,822	4,779	5,604	6,022	271	439	265	773	382	343	623	732	1,121	962
77	Pulp, paper, and board mills	1,810	1,633	1,591	1,772	2,052	160	156	−71	60	280	182	261	212	379	479
78	Miscellaneous converted paper products	1,983	2,432	2,778	3,088	3,207	71	184	319	413	81	109	252	441	670	448
79	Paperboard containers and boxes	558	757	410	744	763	39	99	17	300	21	52	109	80	72	36
80	Printing and publishing	579	612	696	879	993	34	68	−54	229	170	48	108	107	202	208
81	Rubber products	2,028	2,203	2,255	2,743	3,124	1	155	−37	486	369	76	272	345	628	452
82	Miscellaneous plastics products	1,197	1,343	1,664	2,216	2,856	89	164	261	577	514	137	207	433	684	448
83	Glass products	693	729	896	1,211	1,081	−46	66	172	142	−126	26	113	208	307	246
84	Stone, clay, and other nonmetallic mineral products	942	1,012	1,098	1,196	1,342	−80	70	136	134	137	35	104	195	258	233
85	Instruments and related products	5,512	5,493	5,918	7,130	7,393	−33	303	481	1,175	176	190	471	682	1,231	1,111
86	Scientific and measuring instruments	1,103	1,191	1,199	1,836	1,839	70	78	139	384	−33	102	154	224	230	229
87	Optical and opthalmic goods	D	D	155	−47	19	D	D	D	−53	34	D	31	20	D	4
88	Medical instruments and supplies	739	777	986	1,185	1,523	33	36	136	204	322	75	80	180	257	338
89	Photographic equipment and supplies	3,533	3,330	3,538	4,147	3,997	−163	159	204	644	−150	−25	209	267	730	538
90	Watches, clocks, and watchcases	D	D	40	9	15	D	D	D	−4	3	D	−3	−7	D	2
91	Other	851	881	847	905	830	67	56	56	41	−84	2	90	98	142	55
92	Leather and leather products	79	86	83	93	103	5	7	−3	10	10	5	10	7	10	10
93	Miscellaneous manufacturing industries	771	795	764	812	726	62	50	59	31	−94	−4	80	91	132	45
94	Wholesale trade	21,117	22,790	26,214	31,379	34,401	455	1,834	2,279	5,133	3,026	2,210	3,161	4,522	6,713	6,360
95	Durable trade	14,651	16,450	18,697	22,162	24,677	554	1,392	1,521	3,433	2,472	1,424	2,373	3,163	4,558	3,833
96	Motor vehicles and equipment	466	844	1,267	1,411	1,814	−37	198	136	86	69	13	163	315	363	449
97	Lumber and other construction materials	82	67	53	58	69	−21	−23	−13	6	8	17	4	5	4	1
98	Metals and minerals	668	533	374	494	574	57	−27	−77	119	76	58	66	45	60	112
99	Electrical goods	1,710	1,744	2,209	2,337	3,071	291	114	157	149	803	210	232	287	349	457
100	Hardware, plumbing, and heating equipment and supplies	141	151	311	373	437	−3	10	44	39	58	6	10	28	46	85
101	Farm and garden machinery and equipment	415	464	749	1,411	1,993	−80	−22	156	407	446	−25	−10	63	265	416

(Continued)

Line	Industry	1	2	3	4	5	6	7	8	9	10	11	12	13	14	15
102	Machinery, equipment and supplies, nec	9,741	10,876	11,884	13,793	14,076	419	1,065	972	2,175	687	1,106	1,822	2,187	3,111	1,857
103	Durable goods, nec	1,428	1,771	1,850	2,286	2,642	−73	77	146	452	326	39	86	233	360	446
104	Nondurable goods	6,466	6,340	7,518	9,216	9,724	−99	442	759	1,700	554	786	788	1,359	2,156	2,528
105	Paper and paper products	240	229	257	407	581	32	23	47	153	168	23	35	62	92	80
106	Drugs, proprietaries, and sundries	1,517	1,343	1,458	1,577	1,516	−85	19	146	75	−26	53	129	255	326	306
107	Apparel, piece goods, and notions	214	195	289	508	395	−46	−25	5	182	−113	3	32	94	195	114
108	Groceries and related products	871	954	1,146	1,333	1,527	19	247	199	262	146	182	202	289	317	371
109	Farm product raw materials	802	671	798	943	959	92	−84	6	123	−6	66	52	154	48	100
110	Nondurable goods, nec	2,821	2,947	3,570	4,450	4,746	−111	263	356	904	385	458	339	506	1,177	1,556
111	**Banking**	13,516	14,461	14,510	15,161	16,120	1,246	1,094	−602	338	624	2,630	2,886	2,494	2,106	2,560
112	**Finance (except banking), insurance, and real estate**	15,683	22,501	36,414	52,032	60,604	394	7,246	10,883	14,396	8,407	64	1,464	3,112	6,953	5,299
113	Finance, except banking	−13,575	−8,980	−2,555	5,005	10,372	−328	4,899	6,881	6,972	5,537	−2,355	−1,866	−1,019	−138	−931
114	Franchising, business	−7	10	D	155	121	D	17	D	D	−34	4	3	8	4	D
115	Other	−13,568	−8,990	D	4,850	10,252	D	4,882	D	D	5,571	−2,358	−1,869	−1,026	−142	D
116	Insurance	8,039	8,322	9,589	11,297	12,677	103	537	305	1,639	1,381	858	1,167	1,039	1,834	1,439
117	Life insurance	1,432	1,482	1,420	1,579	1,776	226	150	−203	75	71	214	310	195	188	324
118	Accident and health insurance	532	632	792	928	1,092	100	153	135	160	*	84	128	190	110	110
119	Other	6,075	6,208	7,377	8,790	9,809	−90	287	354	1,430	1,150	644	772	717	1,457	1,005
120	Real estate	445	384	348	1,868	2,148	−45	4	−7	1,513	278	15	26	11	102	267
121	Lessors of agricultural and forestry land real estate	0	0	0	0	0	0	0	0	0	0	0	0	0	0	0
122	Real estate, nec	445	384	348	1,868	2,148	−45	4	−7	1,513	278	15	26	11	102	267
123	Holding companies	20,774	22,775	29,033	33,861	35,407	664	1,806	3,705	4,272	1,211	1,545	2,137	3,080	5,154	4,524
124	Nonbusiness entities, except Government	0	0	0	0	0	0	0	0	0	0	0	0	0	0	0
125	**Services**	4,447	4,683	5,128	6,408	7,130	37	278	220	1,644	406	645	720	688	1,163	926
126	Hotels and other lodging places	462	548	593	744	799	−31	56	18	167	64	26	68	100	173	179
127	Business services	1,903	1,882	2,228	2,615	3,068	−80	25	428	336	247	277	277	270	565	340
128	Advertising	374	361	377	456	482	17	3	−52	77	71	56	64	62	99	60
129	Management, consulting, and public relations services	666	683	716	618	686	45	−75	−125	83	109	82	89	67	121	78
130	Equipment rental (ex. automotive land computers)	127	152	379	616	714	−15	−53	194	57	86	24	44	8	34	27
131	Computer and data processing services	141	138	193	161	122	−27	−13	33	17	−197	−6	5	2	83	30
132	Other	594	548	564	764	1,064	105	58	−24	194	267	91	74	131	228	145
133	Research and development and testing laboratories	D	D	D	D	D	D	D	D	D	D	3	D	D	D	D
134	Employment agencies and temporary help supply services	D	D	D	D	D	D	D	D	D	D	D	D	D	D	D
135	Other	484	429	416	594	883	94	50	−54	175	257	84	53	95	191	114
136	Motion pictures, including television tape and film	590	664	823	835	971	−63	74	95	41	43	81	69	81	66	121
137	Engineering, architectural, and surveying services	673	587	505	598	789	37	−65	63	54	126	85	44	24	80	67
138	Health services	203	398	258	695	647	−23	183	65	700	−63	103	101	75	64	38
139	Other services	617	603	720	922	855	−9	109	−45	252	−100	102	161	138	216	182
140	Automotive rental and leasing	225	275	242	386	430	−65	65	−13	98	28	−12	87	62	69	63
141	Accounting, auditing, and bookkeeping services	14	49	95	53	−21	*	39	−1	11	−89	6	9	2	8	−5
142	Legal services	D	D	D	D	D	D	D	D	D	D	D	D	9	9	D
143	Educational services	D	D	D	D	D	D	D	D	D	D	D	D	6	6	D

Line		Direct investment position					Capital outflows (inflows (−))					Income				
		1984	1985	1986	1987	1988	1984	1985	1986	1987	1988	1984	1985	1986	1987	1988
144	Other services provided on a commercial bias	345	242	344	441	396	51	10	−33	140	−48	90	49	59	124	107
145	Other industries	12,779	13,421	13,935	14,129	15,169	−608	7	89	−1,573	1,516	559	988	1,179	1,537	1,868
146	Agriculture, forestry, and fishing	729	497	378	551	548	143	−244	−120	53	−12	−4	12	44	86	87
147	Agricultural production—crops	510	271	215	358	370	122	−245	−89	24	13	−16	D	27	49	52
148	Agricultural production—livestock	136	141	101	107	75	19	5	−14	6	−41	8	D	9	9	*
149	Agricultural production—beef cattle feedlots	0	0	0	0	0	0	0	0	0	0	0	0	0	0	0
150	Agricultural services	3	12	D	1	1	−5	4	D	D	1	−1	3	*	*	−1
151	Forestry	77	70	57	63	D	7	−7	−16	5	D	D	D	8	D	D
152	Fishing, hunting, and trapping	3	3	D	22	D	−1	−1	D	D	D	D	D	*	D	D
153	Mining	4,902	4,916	5,076	4,786	5,286	−666	−97	−532	−1,011	311	158	102	160	191	286
154	Metal mining	3,826	3,612	3,919	2,763	3,268	−123	−239	−485	−1,124	302	58	95	145	196	332
155	Iron ores	922	937	909	769	889	−95	54	−154	−140	120	37	122	123	−3	77
156	Copper, lead, zinc, gold, and silver ores	2,277	2,201	2,024	1,723	1,999	−6	−58	−201	−727	95	−20	−18	−11	90	116
157	Bauxite and other aluminum ores	D	D	238	D	230	D	D	D	D	D	65	31	73	92	110
159	Other metallic ores	D	D	19	D	135	D	D	D	1	2	−26	−41	−39	15	27
159	Metal mining services	28	29	19	6	15	3	1	−1	1	3	3	2	−1	2	3
160	Nonmetallic minerals	1,076	1,304	1,885	2,023	2,019	−542	142	−47	113	8	100	7	15	−4	−46
161	Coal	494	755	1,574	1,665	1,615	−495	168	132	77	−50	65	7	12	−47	−96
162	Nonmetallic minerals, except fuels	582	550	311	358	404	−47	−26	−179	36	58	35	6	3	43	50
163	Construction	1,069	1,331	1,341	1,062	1,095	67	231	−61	−153	111	117	250	96	68	82
164	Transportation, communication, seating and public utilities	2,373	2,679	2,586	2,902	2,599	−178	12	317	74	318	166	289	310	409	503
165	Transportation	1,702	1,679	1,542	1,955	2,079	−178	126	200	202	131	200	119	93	233	280
166	Railroads	D	D	D	D	D	D	D	D	D	D	−2	−1	−4	−3	−3
167	Water transportation	1,171	1,040	985	1,347	1,391	−119	38	−3	290	32	85	8	−18	140	199
168	Transportation by air	137	195	61	61	50	72	58	10	1	−12	52	68	37	17	D
169	Pipelines, except petroleum and natural gas	0	0	0	0	0	0	0	0	0	0	0	0	0	0	0
170	Travel agents	D	D	D	D	W0	D	D	D	D	D	2	*	*	−1	D
171	Transportation and related services, nec	441	478	569	615	676	−95	37	216	−93	79	64	44	78	80	45
172	Communication and public utilities	669	1,000	1,044	947	520	*	−114	117	−128	186	−34	170	218	176	223
173	Communication	154	618	660	656	72	15	26	64	−25	30	28	58	75	65	15
174	Electric, gas, and sanitary services	516	383	385	291	447	−14	−140	53	−103	156	−62	112	143	112	208
175	Retail trade	3,727	3,997	4,554	4,827	5,640	27	105	485	−536	789	122	335	569	782	910
176	Food stores and eating and drinking places	1,408	1,427	1,855	1,907	2,480	11	−56	236	−529	574	98	184	262	347	473
177	Retail trade, nec	2,319	2,570	2,699	2,920	3,160	15	160	249	−7	215	25	151	307	435	438

*Less than $500,000 (±).

D Suppressed to avoid disclosure of data of individual companies.

The Manhattan Trading Corporation, Inc.

Hedging Through the Futures Commodity Market

HARVEY A. PONIACHEK

This case study involves price exposure of an international trading corporation and the need to formulate a hedging program designed to improve corporate profitability performance. The reader is introduced to commodity hedging through the futures commodity market.

The Corporation

The Manhattan Trading Corporation, Inc. (MTC) is an international trading corporation primarily engaged in international trading of commodities, such as rice, sugar, and sugar by-products. In addition, through several wholly-owned subsidiaries, MTC markets, and processes/cans a wide range of vegetables and fruits. Sales in 1990 reached $300 million and net income was $15 million. The profitability performance of the corporation was adversely affected in the past several years by the poor performances of the Yankee Rice Corporation, Inc. (YRC) and Caribbean Molasses, Inc. (CMI)

—the rice and molasses wholly-owned subsidiaries.

The Yankee Rice Corporation, Inc. and Caribbean Molasses, Inc. enjoyed considerable sales growth in the late 1980s and early 1990, but their profitability performance was highly volatile and often in the red. The Chief Financial Officer appointed John Smith, a newly recruited financial analyst (MBA Finance and International Business, New York University, Stern School of Business, class of 1988), to determine the cause(s) for these entities' unsatisfactory performances and to propose a policy on how to improve it.

Smith was provided with facts related to YRC and CMI transactions, including highlights of their financial statements shown in Exhibit 9-1. He first reviewed the facts and then arranged to interview several executives from each corporation.

The facts revealed that YRC purchases of unpolished rice from growers abroad (35% of total) and in the United States (65% of total) reached approximately $21.5 million in 1990 and were expected to reach $25 million in 1991. These purchases, in turn, were sold to wholesale distributors and/or large food processors. YRC imports of rice from abroad usually involved a 3-month time lag between

EXHIBIT 9-1

Yankee Rice Corporation, Inc.

	1991	1990
Assets ($,000)		
Cash	28	25
Marketable securities	53	47
Receivables	2,278	2,051
Inventories	7,021	6,319
Total current assets	9,380	8,442
Property, plant & equipment	10,234	9,210
Accumulated depreciation	2,874	2,586
Net property & equipment	7,360	6,624
Other assets	345	310
Intangibles	541	487
Total assets	17,626	15,863
Liabilities ($,000)		
Notes payable	3,845	3,460
Account payable	880	792
Current long-term debt	644	580
Other current liabilities	3,418	3,076
Total current liabilities	8,787	7,908
Deferred charges	31	28
Long-term debt	5,599	5,040
Total liabilities	14,417	12,976
Total equity	3,209	2,888
Total liabilities and networth	17,626	15,863
Annual Income ($,000)		
Net sales	25,000	22,500
Cost of goods sold	23,750	21,375
Gross profit	1,250	1,125
R & D expenditures	N.A.	N.A.
Selling, general & admin. exp.	2,767	2,490
Income before dep & amor.	(1,517)	(1,365)
Depreciation & amort.	485	437
Non-operating income	96	87
Interest expense	964	868
Income before tax	(3,063)	(2,757)
Provision for income tax	(1,041)	(937)
Net income	(2,022)	(1,819)

EXHIBIT 9-2

Caribbean Molasses, Inc.

	1991	1990
Assets ($,000)		
Cash	17	16
Marketable securities	32	30
Receivables	1,367	1,299
Inventories	4,213	4,002
Total current assets	5,628	5,347
Property, plant & equipment	6,140	5,833
Accumulated depreciation	1,724	1,638
Net property & equipment	4,416	4,195
Other assets	207	196
Intangibles	325	308
Total assets	10,575	10,047
Liabilities ($,000)		
Notes payable	2,307	2,191
Account payable	528	502
Current long-term debt	386	367
Other current liabilities	2,051	1,948
Total current liabilities	5,272	5,008
Deferred charges	19	18
Long-term debt	3,360	3,192
Total liabilities	8,650	8,218
Total equity	1,925	1,829
Total liabilities and networth	10,575	10,047
Annual Income ($,000)		
Net sales	15,000	13,500
Cost of goods sold	13,500	12,150
Gross profit	1,500	1,350
R & D expenditures	ERR	ERR
Selling, general & admin. exp.	1,660	1,494
Income before dep & amor.	842	758
Depreciation & amort.	291	262
Non-operating income	58	52
Interest expense	578	521
Income before tax	(1,814)	(1,633)
Provision for income tax	(544)	(490)
Net income	(1,270)	(1,143)

purchasing, shipping, and receiving. Often following YRC receipt of shipments the rice was stored in public warehouses in the United States for several additional months before it could be sold.

In 1990 CMI purchased approximately $12.2 million worth of molasses from abroad (60% of total, particularly from the EC) and from U.S. sources (40% of total), and was expected to purchase $13.5 million in 1991. Molasses, in turn, was sold through wholesale distributors and directly to sugar manufacturers and other end users. The transaction cycle between CMI purchases, delivery, and sales usually took three months. Smith interviewed several executives from YRC and CMI relating to the functioning of their companies and to the possible cause of the poor profitability performances.

During the interviews, many executives expressed the common hypothesis that price volatility is contributing to narrow gross profit margins that erode the viability of both corporations.

The Assignment

As a summer intern at MTC who was working under Mr. Smith's supervision, you are requested to review the facts related to YRC and CMI business, including their financial statements, and to address the assignment listed below within the next couple of weeks. You are also provided with technical data, Appendix 9-1, "Hedging through the Futures Commodity Market," which could introduce you to the subject of futures commodity hedging and provide you with additional references on the subject matter.

1. Define the commodity and price volatility exposure of YRC and CMI in 1990 and 1991.

2. Propose a hedging policy for YRC and CMI for 1991 that could eliminate the price risk and improve their performance. Consider the implications of your proposal on cost and benefit of both companies.

APPENDIX 9-1

Hedging Through the Futures Commodity Market

Introduction

This Appendix provides a preliminary introduction to the principles of hedging through the futures commodity market. The purpose is to introduce the reader to some basic concepts on how to hedge, particularly when the commodity or product is not listed on the futures exchanges. The approach outlined here is primarily suitable for trading companies and wholesale distributors who are engaged in international trade of import and export.

Merchants, dealers, processors, and warehousers who seek to enhance their profitability performance by reducing the business risk associated with their inventory, could hedge in the commodity futures markets. Hedging reduces risk or exposure to risk by establishing an opposite position in the futures market from that held, or anticipated to be held, in the spot or cash market. Hedging is accomplished through the purchase or sale of commodity futures contracts and/or options on futures contracts—opposite from that held, or anticipated to be held, in the cash or spot market.

Hedging of commodities or products that are not traded on the commodity futures markets is more complex than the hedging of commodities for which futures contracts are readily available. Commodities for which no futures contracts are available could be hedged through cross hedging or synthetic hedging.

Hedging, similar to acquiring an insurance policy, involves several costs, which include brokerage commissions for purchasing and selling contracts, allocation of working capital for trading margins, and management time. Trading positions cause daily cash flows because positions are marked-to-market daily (i.e., trading positions are valued at the end of each trading day to determine whether gains or losses occurred). A well-constructed hedge should always lessen the hedger's risk exposure, but few if any hedges are able to totally eliminate all risks, due to other risks that are still inherent in every hedge, namely the basis risks. The basis risk is caused by the changing spread between spot and futures prices during the life of the contract.

Hedging is a reasonable policy for companies that are excessively exposed to commodity price fluctuations that can result in severe volatility in profitability performance. Hedging could remove some or all of the risk in carrying inventory, but it could also eliminate or reduce the windfall gains that companies may enjoy in favorable market conditions. In fact, hedging could fix the gross profit margins on commercial transactions.

The Futures Commodity Market

Principal Features

In the futures commodity market, commodities (and financial instruments) are bought and sold for future delivery. The market is highly standardized in terms of contract sizes and maturities. Commodity futures are transacted through brokers vis-à-vis various commodity exchanges. Transacting futures requires maintenance of approximately 5 to 10 percent mar-

gin of the contract value and payment of brokerage fees. Many commodities have also established options on futures.

Trading in most commodities is for delivery in specified months. These trading months usually cover a period as far ahead as one year, or up to 18 months in the future, varying with each commodity. For example, a contract of May soybeans will expire in May, but it must be liquidated before that time. Trading stops sometime before the end of the delivery month. The final trading day within the delivery month varies with the commodity and is determined by the rules of each exchange.

The initial margin needed to guarantee performance of the contract of commodity trading normally averages 5 to 10 percent of the value of the contract. Each commodity exchange establishes its own minimum margin requirement, which varies from time to time. A brokerage firm cannot request less than the exchange required minimum. Because the value of the contract is marked-to-market daily, this margin must be restored when the total current market values of all future contracts in an account have declined by an amount specified in the particular rules for each Exchange. The additional margin required to keep an account liquid because of variation in the value of the contracts held is called the "variation margin." Clients of most commodity brokerages are allowed to give the brokerage either cash or an interest-bearing U.S. Treasury bill or some combination of both to meet their margin requirement.

Customers pay a commission to their broker to execute a round-trip transaction, for which a single price is quoted. Commissions are charged only after the entire commodity transaction has been completed; for example, after a purchase of futures is subsequently liquidated. All orders in excess of a certain number of contracts are subject to negotiated rates. All contracts are agreements between the client and the exchange clearing house, rather than between the two clients involved.

Price Relations

The physical commodities are traded in what are synonymously called the cash, spot, physicals, or actuals markets. The commodity futures contracts are traded at markets for financial instruments called futures exchanges. Appendix 9-2 provides commodity futures prices.

Commodity futures prices vary for each trading month. In a normal market, the more distant months are selling at premiums over the nearer months. On a rare occasion, an inverted market prevails, with discounts on the more distant maturities. The size of the premium and discounts depends primarily on the level of the commodity stock, supply and demand conditions, expectations about prices, and the cost of carrying the commodity in storage.

Futures prices cannot diverge excessively from the spot market prices, because of the possibility of arbitrage. Arbitrage involves making delivery of spot commodities against the sales of futures, or of demanding spot commodity delivery against purchases of futures when the contract matures. The maximum premium above distant months normally equals the cost of carrying commodities, which varies from one commodity to another and from one period to the next, depending primarily on interest rates.

By storing commodities, for example, it is possible to convert a commodity received in September into a commodity that can be delivered in December. The difference in price between the September commodity and the December commodity futures is, therefore, related to the carrying cost. Inventory carrying charges include storage, transportation and financial costs. For example, assume that the carrying cost per contract of wheat is 4 cents per month and that the December premium was 20 cents above September. One can then buy September wheat, store it at the cost of 12 cents, and sell December wheat at 20 cents premium and make a sure 8 cents profit per contract. Arbitrage will ultimately reduce the price of the December futures and restore equilibrium in the marketplace where the carrying cost will just correspond to the premium.

While maximum premium exists for the more distant month over the nearer month (in non-perishable commodities), there is no limit to the possible premium of a near month over a more distant month.

All commodity futures prices are interconnected—where the basis points (i.e., the difference between the spot price and futures price of the nearby maturity contract), the time spreads (i.e., the difference in the price for two futures delivery months), and the premium and discounts on future prices constitute a coherent price system. At delivery, the futures prices and the cash prices should be equal (i.e., prices converge), except for minor discrepancies that result from transportation and other transaction costs.

Commodity futures prices have both minimum and maximum price limit fluctuations imposed by the commodity exchanges. The minimum price limit fluctuations are designed to prevent bids involving price changes that are not significantly different from zero. Maximum price fluctuations are permitted on most commodities. The purpose of these maximum limits is to prohibit large and potentially destabilizing price changes. Thus, if a commodity's price rises to the day's limit, trading in that commodity for the remainder of the day cannot exceed that day's maximum price.

The Principles of Hedging

Hedging is defined as the establishment of a position in the futures market—through the purchase or sale of commodity futures contracts and/or options on futures contracts—opposite from that held, or anticipated to be held, in the spot market. For example, a company that owns, acquires, or anticipates to acquire commodities in the spot market could protect the value of its inventory against a possible price decline by selling an equivalent amount of futures as a hedge. The company is said to be long cash and short futures. This form of hedging is defined as a *selling hedge* (i.e., selling futures). The selling hedge is used by merchants, processors, and manufacturers who own commodities.

Hedging works in the following manner. If the commodity price should decline after its purchase, there would be an inventory loss. However, if a position is hedged by selling futures contracts, the price of the futures declines too, and the loss on the cash position would be offset by the profit on the futures position. If prices rose after the commodity was acquired and the hedge had been placed, then there would be a loss on the short position in the futures, which would be compensated for by the rise in the value of the inventory. In either case, there would be a loss on one side of the transaction (spot or futures) compensated for by a profit on the other side.

The impact of hedging can be illustrated by the following example. Suppose a grain elevator operator buys on October 23, 19xx, 10,000 bushels of corn at $2.50 per bushel from a farmer, but he cannot immediately sell the grain. The grain elevator might then incur an inventory loss if the price of corn declines. To prevent a possible loss, he hedges by selling 10,000 bushels December futures at $2.50 per bushel. Two weeks later, the elevator operator is able to sell the corn at $2.35 per bushel to a manufacturer, and he lifts the futures contracts. Hence, he suffered a 15 cents per bushel loss on 10,000 bushels, or a total loss of $1500. However, at the same time that he sells the spot corn, he lifts the future hedge by repurchasing other December futures contracts (i.e., similar as could be to the one which was originally sold) at $2.35 per bushel. Because he

EXHIBIT A9-1

Hedging in the Commodity Futures Market

Cash Market	Futures Market
Buys 10,000 bushels at $2.50	Sells 10,000 bushels December at $2.50
Sells 10,000 bushels at $2.35	Buys 10,000 bushels December at $2.35
Loss $0.15 per bushel	Gain $0.15 per bushel

EXHIBIT A9-2

Hedging in the Commodity Futures Market

Cash Market	Futures Market
Buys 10,000 bushels at $2.50	Sells 10,000 bushels December at $2.50
Sells 10,000 bushels at $2.35	Buys 10,000 bushels December at $2.40
Loss $0.15 per bushel	Gain $0.10 per bushel

sold futures at $2.50 per bushel and purchased them at $2.35, he realizes a gain of 15 cents per bushel on 10,000 bushels, or a total gain of $1500. Thus, the loss on the cash or spot position is exactly offset by the gain on the futures. Exhibit A9-1 illustrates the transaction.

If the futures price declined to $2.40 per bushel, then the elevator operator's commodity futures hedging would be modified, as illustrated in Exhibit A9-2.

Because of the basis risk (i.e. , the difference between the cash market price and the futures contract price), the commodity futures hedge did not provide sufficient protection, with the elevator operator losing 5 cents per bushel. If, however, futures prices decline to $2.30 per bushel, then the commodity futures' profit outweighs the loss on the spot market, as shown in Exhibit A9-3.

EXHIBIT A9-3

Hedging in the Commodity Futures Market

Cash Market	Futures Market
Buys 10,000 bushels at $2.50	Sells 10,000 bushels December at $2.50
Sells 10,000 bushels at $2.35	Buys 10,000 bushels December at $2.30
Loss $0.15 per bushel	Gain $0.20 per bushel

In the corn examples, the hedger's needs were perfectly matched in the commodity futures corn market in terms of the type of contract, size of contract and maturity. Often, however, the hedging needs will differ in terms of (1) the type of goods to be hedged, (2) the amount of the commodity, and (3) the time span covered. In such cases, when the characteristics of the position to be hedged do not perfectly match the characteristics of the futures contract used in the hedge, the hedge is defined as a *cross hedge*, or a synthetic hedge. A cross hedge is less effective in reducing risk than a direct hedge. More sophisticated techniques are also required to conduct cross hedging.

Hedging Commodity X in the Commodity Futures Market

Commodity X price patterns could be explained by reference to soybean meal (SBM), because both commodities are used as feed for poultry, hogs, and cattle. We have performed a monthly regression analysis for the three most recent years to determine the correlation between the price movement of commodity X and SBM, and to derive the hedging ratio. The hedge ratio indicates the number of contracts of SBM that need to be sold in the futures market in order to hedge a cash or spot position of commodity X.

Our regression model and the estimates are as follows:

Cash prices of commodity X

$$= a + b \text{ SBM futures prices} + e \quad (1)$$

The variables in Equation 1 are defined as follows:

Where a = constant, b measures the effect of a change in the SBM price on the price of commodity X, and e is a random factor that affects commodity X prices. Regression analysis of Equation 1 for monthly data for the three most recent years provided Equation 2 as follows:

Cash prices of commodity X

$$= 889.95 + 11.43 \text{ SBM futures prices}$$

$$\text{R-square} = 0.31 \quad (2)$$

The b coefficient provides the hedge ratio that minimizes the variability of commodity X prices by hedging in the futures through SBM. The beta coefficient states that the price of commodity X moves up or down by $11.43 for every one dollar variation in the price of SBM futures. This relationship occurs quite often as is reflected by the R-square statistics. The R-square reflects the variance in the commodity X price that can be eliminated by hedging in the futures market.

Cross Hedging of Commodity X: A Hypothetical Example

Assume that in the beginning of September, ABC Inc. seeks to hedge $3 million worth of commodity X inventory (i.e., $3,000,000/$3389 per metric ton based on September's 1989 price level, or 885.22 metric tons) by selling SBM futures contracts. The hedge ratio indicates that ABC Inc. needs to sell 11.43 × 885.22 or 10,118.07 metric tons of SBM for December, which is equivalent to 101 SBM contracts on the Chicago Board of Trade and valued at 101 × 100 × $216.73 = $2,188,973. Exhibit A9-4

EXHIBIT A9-4

Cross Hedging in the Commodity Futures
Market: Hedging Commodity X Inventory

Cash Market	Futures Market
Buys 885 MT of commodity X at $3389 on September 1	Sells 10,118 MT of SBM at $216.73 on September 1
Sells 885 MT of commodity X at $2998 on December 1	Buys 10,118 MT of SBM at $179.75 on December 1
Loss $391 per MT and $346,035 on the position	Gain $36.98 per MT and $373,488 on the position

presents the commodity X futures hedging transaction.

The performance of the hedge was not perfect because the loss on the long spot/cash position was not exactly offset by the gain on the futures short position. ABC Inc. could have lost $391 per metric ton or $391,000 on its 885 metric tons of commodity X if the spot price would have declined (i.e., $(3,389 - 2,998) \times 885 = \$346,035$), but it would have made a profit of $373,488 on it futures position (i.e., $(216.73 - 179.75) \times 101 \times 100 = \$373,498$). Due to its hedging in the SBM futures, ABC Inc. loss in the cash market was more than offset by the gain in the futures, with the profit amounting to $27,463. The profit on the futures, however, is pre-brokerage commission on the purchase and sale of SBM futures (i.e., approximately $25 to $50 for roundtrip per contract or $2525 to $5050), and prior to determining the cost of required margins (i.e., approximately, 5% of the contract value, or $109,448, which has an implied cost of $2736 on the basis of 10% interest rate).

While the hedging is imperfect, the hedging efficiency is 107.93 percent. The imperfection in the hedge is due primarily to basis risk (i.e., the changing relations between the price of commodity X and SBM during the hedging period from 15.63 to 1 to 16.67 to 1). We should also recognize that we applied hypothetical data in this example.

Hedging Commodity X by Commodity Futures Options Market

The futures options market is similar to the options market in other financial products. A put on a commodity futures gives the holder the right to sell the underlying commodity futures at a certain price (i.e., the strike price) during a given period of time, until the expiration period. For this right, the buyer of the put options pays a fee, called a premium.

For example, assume that ABC Inc. U.S.A. brought 885 MT of commodity X at $3389 per ton on September 1. The hedge ratio indicates that we need 101 SBM contracts to hedge the approximately 885 MT of commodity X. ABC Inc. could hedge in the futures options market by purchasing 101 SBM put options on December strike price of $190 per ton at a premium of $4.40 per ton. Assume that by December, when ABC Inc. sells the commodity X, the price of commodity X has declined to $2998 per MT. Also, the price of SBM futures price declines to $153 per ton and ABC Inc. executes its option to purchase at $150 per ton. ABC Inc. realizes a loss of $346,035 on the sale of the X commodity but realizes a profit of $404,000 on the SBM position. The gain on the SBM position results because ABC Inc. purchases the right to sell SBM at $190, and executed that right when the price of SBM futures was $150. Therefore it realizes a profit of $40 per ton.

Exhibit A9-5 illustrates the profit and loss that are incurred in the cash and options market.

The put options cost $4.4 per ton × 101 contracts × 100 ton per contract = $44,440. We need to deduct the premium cost of $44,440

EXHIBIT A9-5

Cross Hedging in the Futures Options
Market: Hedging Commodity X Inventory

Cash Market	Futures Market
Buys 885 MT of commodity X at $3389 on Sept. 1	Purchases 101 put option $190 strike price on Sept. 1
Sells 885 MT of commodity X at $2998 on Dec. 1	Executes put option at $150 in December
Loss $391 per MT or $346,035 on the position	Profit $40 per ton at $404,000 for the position

from the gain on the options of $404,000, which yields a net profit of $359,560. This net gain on the options of $359,560 exceeds the $346,035 loss from the sale of commodity X by $13,525. Hence, the hedging efficiency is 103.90 percent. Were ABC Inc. not hedged, their loss would have been $346,035, which is equivalent to $1.38 million on an annualized basis (i.e., 346,035 × 4 quarters).

Hedging through options on futures provides the hedges with the opportunity to benefit from favorable market trends. For example, if in the case presented in Exhibit A9-5 prices in December go up to $3500 per ton, ABC Inc. could benefit from a windfall gain of $111 per ton, without the need to execute the put option. However, if ABC Inc. doesn't exercise the option it still has to pay $44,440 in premium. In this case ABC Inc.'s profit would be $98,235 ($111 profit per MT × 885 MT) less the $44,440 in premiums, for a net profit of $53,795.

Conclusion

In examining the possibilities of hedging, we need to consider the consequences of brokerage commission expenses, minimum margins and the cash flow effects of marked-to-market. These costs will reduce the benefit of hedging and they need to be considered explicitly. If ABC Inc. would seek to hedge its approximately three months worth of commodity X inventory, it would need to assume sizable positions in the commodity futures and/or options market. These positions require careful management and considerable allocation of capital for funding margins and transaction fees.

Bibliography

1. R. W. ANDERSON, *The Industrial Organization of Futures Markets*. D.C. Heath and Company, Lexington, MA, 1984.

2. ROBERT W. KOLB, *Understanding Futures Markets*, Third Edition. Kolb Publishing Company, Miami, FL, 1991.

3. M. J. PRING, *The McGraw-Hill Handbook of Commodities*. McGraw-Hill, New York, 1985.

Commodity Futures Prices

APPENDIX 9-2

FUTURES PRICES

Thursday, July 9, 1992

Open Interest Reflects Previous Trading Day.

GRAINS AND OILSEEDS

CORN (CBT) 5,000 bu.; cents per bu.

	Open	High	Low	Settle	Change	Lifetime High	Lifetime Low	Open Interest
July	243¾	243¾	241¾	242¼	- 1¼	285	239½	5,021
Sept	241¾	242	240¾	241¼	- ¾	279½	236½	56,112
Dec	242½	243¾	242¼	243	- ½	275¾	236½	124,042
Mr93	250½	251½	250	251	- ¼	281¼	252½	17,778
May	255½	256	255	255¾	- ¼	284¾	256¼	4,568
July	258½	260	258½	259¾	....	286	258½	3,777
Sept	256½	256½	255½	255½	- 1½	271½	254	357
Dec	255½	256	254	254½	- 1½	268½	251	2,574

Est vol 39,000; vol Wed 53,972; open int 214,229, +2,077.

OATS (CBT) 5,000 bu.; cents per bu.

	Open	High	Low	Settle	Change	Lifetime High	Lifetime Low	Open Interest
July	127½	131	126¾	131	+ 3¾	191½	122¼	61
Sept	129¼	131½	129	131¼	+ 1½	194	127¼	7,226
Dec	136½	137¼	135¾	137¼	+ ½	198½	135	5,351
Mr93	141¾	141¾	141	141¾	- ½	195¼	140½	479

Est vol 2,000; vol Wed 595; open int 13,198, -59.

SOYBEANS (CBT) 5,000 bu.; cents per bu.

	Open	High	Low	Settle	Change	Lifetime High	Lifetime Low	Open Interest
July	575	575¼	569½	569¾	- 5	668	554	3,543
Aug	578	579¾	573	573½	- 5¼	660	565	27,738
Sept	581	583	575	575½	- 5¾	645	557	14,922
Nov	587½	589¾	581	581½	- 6	651	552	55,575
Ja93	596	597	589¼	589½	- 6	659	578½	7,551
Mar	605	606	598	598½	- 6	664	590½	5,250
May	612½	612½	606	606	- 5¼	668½	606	2,591
July	615	615	609½	609¾	- 5½	671	609½	2,582
Nov	604	604½	599	600	- 3¼	620	589½	1,333

Est vol 44,000; vol Wed 38,716; open int 121,108, -1,269.

SOYBEAN MEAL (CBT) 100 tons; $ per ton.

	Open	High	Low	Settle	Change	Lifetime High	Lifetime Low	Open Interest
July	175.80	176.00	174.80	175.40	- .10	196.00	166.00	3,292
Aug	176.20	176.60	175.30	175.80	- .30	190.00	170.90	21,680
Sept	177.20	177.50	176.00	176.40	- .50	190.60	171.30	12,425
Oct	193.40	193.70	192.20	193.10	- .10	208.80	182.30	10,681
Dec	193.70	193.70	192.00	192.80	- .50	209.00	183.50	13,150
Ja93	194.00	194.00	192.50	193.00	- .60	209.00	190.80	747
Mar	195.00	195.00	193.60	194.30	- .30	210.00	192.80	1,124
May	195.50	195.50	194.20	194.30	- 1.20	210.00	194.20	452

Est vol 17,000; vol Wed 18,479; open int 63,572, +745.

SOYBEAN OIL (CBT) 60,000 lbs.; cents per lb.

	Open	High	Low	Settle	Change	Lifetime High	Lifetime Low	Open Interest
July	19.87	19.87	19.71	19.74	- .11	24.30	19.25	3,322
Aug	19.98	20.01	19.81	19.84	- .12	22.46	19.42	19,029
Sept	20.14	20.14	19.95	20.00	- .12	22.60	19.57	18,495
Oct	20.28	20.28	20.11	20.14	- .12	22.65	19.66	5,911
Dec	20.58	20.60	20.40	20.45	- .13	22.99	19.93	14,176
Ja93	20.61	20.65	20.56	20.56	- .15	23.00	20.05	1,182
Mar	21.00	21.00	20.84	20.86	- .11	23.20	20.50	1,098
May	21.15	21.20	21.07	21.11	- .09	23.50	21.00	205

Est vol 19,500; vol Wed 19,411; open int 63,464, -1,213.

WHEAT (CBT) 5,000 bu.; cents per bu.

	Open	High	Low	Settle	Change	Lifetime High	Lifetime Low	Open Interest
July	340	340½	335½	355¾	- 4¾	429½	279	4,823
Sept	342½	343	337½	338	- 4¾	432	292	24,645
Dec	351¾	352¼	348	348¼	- 4	440	329½	20,616
Mr93	354½	354½	350¼	350¼	- 4	440	349½	5,288
May	346¼	346½	343	343	- 2½	375	340¼	391
July	329½	330	326	327	- 1½	373	326	1,158

Est vol 13,000; vol Wed 13,718; open int 56,930, +66.

WHEAT (KC) 5,000 bu.; cents per bu.

	Open	High	Low	Settle	Change	Lifetime High	Lifetime Low	Open Interest
July	340½	341	335	335	- 5	430½	272	1,006
Sept	341	341½	336	336¼	- 4¾	431½	314	15,641
Dec	350	350	345½	345¾	- 4½	440	345½	10,210
Mr93	352½	352½	348½	348½	- 4	410	346	720

Est vol 4,683; vol Wed 6,903; open int 27,659, +231.

WHEAT (MPLS) 5,000 bu.; cents per bu.

	Open	High	Low	Settle	Change	Lifetime High	Lifetime Low	Open Interest
July	368½	368½	362½	362½	- 6	436	308	464
Sept	338	338	332¼	332½	- 5½	422	315	6,972
Dec	346½	346½	341½	342	- 4	429	341½	1,561
Mr93	352	352	349½	351	- 3½	384	349½	342

Est vol 2,394; vol Wed 3,204; open int 9,349, +319.

BARLEY (WPG) 20 metric tons; Can. $ per ton

	Open	High	Low	Settle	Change	Lifetime High	Lifetime Low	Open Interest
July		....	....	89.40	- 1.40	100.30	84.10	83
Oct	93.60	93.60	92.90	93.40	- .20	102.50	74.70	3,119
Dec	95.50	95.50	94.60	94.60	- .90	103.50	90.90	1,539
Mr93	98.00	98.00	97.90	97.90	- .60	101.10	95.50	410

Est vol 1,375; vol Wed 973; open int 25,552, +25.

FLAXSEED (WPG) 20 metric tons; Can. $ per ton

	Open	High	Low	Settle	Change	Lifetime High	Lifetime Low	Open Interest
July	217.50	217.70	217.50	217.70	+ .40	223.00	194.80	88
Oct	226.20	227.00	224.70	225.00	- 1.20	232.00	202.20	4,231
Dec	230.00	230.30	229.10	229.10	- 1.60	237.00	219.00	1,866
Mr93		....	....	237.10	- 1.20	245.30	227.80	160

Est vol 355; vol Wed 204; open int 6,355, -105.

CANOLA (WPG) 20 metric tons; Can. $ per ton

	Open	High	Low	Settle	Change	Lifetime High	Lifetime Low	Open Interest
Sept	288.30	288.50	287.40	287.50	- .60	310.70	274.80	10,646
Nov	291.30	291.50	290.40	290.50	- .50	314.50	278.20	8,324
Ja93	296.50	296.50	295.40	295.70	- .50	319.90	291.80	4,439
Mar	299.50	300.10	299.40	299.50	- .30	322.70	298.00	2,133

Est vol 1,375; vol Wed 973; open int 25,552, +25.

WHEAT (WPG) 20 metric tons; Can. $ per ton

	Open	High	Low	Settle	Change	Lifetime High	Lifetime Low	Open Interest
July	101.50	101.50	101.50	101.50	+ .50	119.80	96.70	386
Oct	102.50	102.50	101.70	102.00	+ .50	120.00	100.50	4,646
Dec	103.80	103.80	103.60	103.60	- .60	120.00	102.80	2,914
Mr93		....	....	108.00	....	115.00	106.80	621

Est vol 300; vol Wed 293; open int 8,642, +12.

LIVESTOCK AND MEAT

CATTLE–FEEDER (CME) 44,000 lbs.; cents per lb.

	Open	High	Low	Settle	Change	Lifetime High	Lifetime Low	Open Interest
Aug	80.25	81.40	80.22	81.32	+ 1.10	83.00	72.65	5,537
Sept	78.70	80.02	78.70	79.97	+ 1.15	82.40	72.15	1,186
Oct	78.10	79.30	78.10	79.15	+ .97	79.50	72.10	1,798
Nov	78.35	79.60	78.35	79.37	+ 1.02	79.60	72.30	1,443
Ja93	78.30	79.15	78.25	79.00	+ .95	79.15	75.50	242

Est vol 1,971; vol Wed 1,021; open int 10,332, -34.

CATTLE–LIVE (CME) 40,000 lbs.; cents per lb.

	Open	High	Low	Settle	Change	Lifetime High	Lifetime Low	Open Interest
Aug	72.20	73.45	72.20	73.37	+ 1.25	73.45	65.90	31,131
Oct	72.22	73.22	72.20	73.10	+ .87	73.25	66.25	15,002
Dec	70.40	71.47	70.40	71.20	+ .67	71.80	67.10	13,351
Fb93	69.95	70.80	69.90	70.50	+ .57	70.80	68.10	4,256
Apr	71.40	72.20	71.40	72.05	+ .57	72.20	69.25	2,820
June		....	....	69.07	+ .42	69.35	66.80	768
Aug	67.85	68.00	67.85	67.87	+ .20	68.75	66.10	465

Est vol 18,960; vol Wed 9,523; open int 67,793, +397.

HOGS (CME) 40,000 lbs.; cents per lb.

	Open	High	Low	Settle	Change	Lifetime High	Lifetime Low	Open Interest
Jly	46.20	46.52	46.00	46.30	+ .10	48.20	43.05	4,130
Aug	42.70	43.70	42.70	43.32	+ .32	46.85	41.80	9,527
Oct	38.55	39.20	38.50	38.90	+ .05	42.25	38.35	4,332
Dec	39.75	40.10	39.60	39.60	+ .10	45.15	39.40	4,341
Fb92	41.10	41.25	40.90	41.05	+ .15	45.95	40.90	995
Apr	40.50	40.70	40.40	40.45	+ .10	43.50	40.35	987
June	45.87	46.15	45.87	45.95	+ .07	48.05	45.87	338

Est vol 9,339; vol Wed 10,214; open int 24,748, -877.

PORK BELLIES (CME) 40,000 lbs.; cents per lb.

	Open	High	Low	Settle	Change	Lifetime High	Lifetime Low	Open Interest
July	30.45	31.10	30.30	30.97	+ .87	59.00	29.50	1,559
Aug	27.30	28.05	27.30	27.75	+ .62	51.00	27.02	8,842
Fb93	37.00	37.40	36.97	37.32	+ .65	49.30	35.90	3,132
Mar	36.70	37.10	36.70	36.85	+ .35	49.00	35.55	286

Est vol 2,226; vol Wed 3,656; open int 14,209, +154.

FOOD AND FIBER

COCOA (CSCE)–10 metric tons; $ per ton.

	Open	High	Low	Settle	Change	Lifetime High	Lifetime Low	Open Interest
July	980	980	953	965	- 25	1,410	785	16
Sept	1,021	1,031	1,003	1,015	- 21	1,427	830	20,387
Dec	1,078	1,088	1,063	1,075	- 19	1,460	885	13,664
Mr93	1,119	1,125	1,110	1,120	- 13	1,495	929	5,431
May	1,155	1,155	1,150	1,150	- 11	1,518	960	1,942
July	1,175	1,178	1,161	1,178	- 8	1,530	990	2,695
Sept		....	....	1,207	- 8	1,536	1,029	2,301
Dec	1,232	1,236	1,228	1,248	- 7	1,506	1,064	1,714
Mr94		....	....	1,286	- 9	1,220	1,108	1,670
May		....	....	1,315	- 8	1,270	1,198	352

Est vol 7,055; vol Wed 10,564; open int 50,172, +824.

COFFEE (CSCE)–37,500 lbs.; cents per lb.

	Open	High	Low	Settle	Change	Lifetime High	Lifetime Low	Open Interest
July	59.50	59.50	58.80	59.05	- .35	106.40	54.50	252
Sept	60.65	61.90	60.50	60.95	- .20	108.00	56.80	29,495
Dec	63.40	64.30	63.10	63.60	- .30	107.25	59.75	10,913
Mr93	66.00	66.80	65.80	66.25	- .15	94.75	62.50	6,642
May	70.00	70.50	69.75	70.10	- .30	96.50	67.50	8,099
July	72.50	72.50	72.50	72.20	- .20	87.05	69.30	409
Sept		....	....	74.25	- .20	84.00	71.75	222

Est vol 9,176; vol Wed 6,998; open int 56,033, -122.

SUGAR–WORLD (CSCE)–112,000 lbs.; cents per lb.

	Open	High	Low	Settle	Change	Lifetime High	Lifetime Low	Open Interest
Oct	9.48	9.54	9.22	9.30	- .22	10.18	7.93	54,868
Mr93	9.30	9.35	9.10	9.23	- .10	9.98	8.20	31,259
May	9.25	9.28	9.07	9.20	- .07	9.88	8.30	4,404
July	9.25	9.25	9.07	9.13	- .09	9.78	8.40	2,792
Oct	9.05	9.05	9.00	9.08	- .02	9.60	8.69	1,094

Est vol 12,656; vol Wed 7,325; open int 94,414, -417.

SUGAR–DOMESTIC (CSCE)–112,000 lbs.; cents per lb.

	Open	High	Low	Settle	Change	Lifetime High	Lifetime Low	Open Interest
Sept	20.90	20.91	20.90	20.91	+ .05	22.30	20.83	1,564
Nov	21.30	21.30	21.25	21.27	- .03	22.10	21.17	2,359
Ja93	21.40	21.40	21.40	21.39	+ .02	22.00	21.33	445
Mar		....	....	21.42	- .01	22.05	21.33	1,121
May		....	....	21.58	....	21.86	21.45	908
July		....	....	21.67	- .02	21.85	21.58	764
Sept	21.70	21.70	21.70	21.70	- .02	21.85	21.58	202

Est vol 86; vol Wed 662; open int 7,389, +9.

COTTON (CTN)–50,000 lbs.; cents per lb.

	Open	High	Low	Settle	Change	Lifetime High	Lifetime Low	Open Interest
July	65.40	65.40	63.25	64.14	- 1.76	77.70	54.80	502
Oct	63.55	64.05	63.30	63.75	+ .12	70.60	57.65	8,444
Dec	62.10	62.75	62.08	62.52	+ .24	69.00	58.45	17,012
Mr93	63.12	63.70	63.10	63.55	+ .32	67.30	59.90	5,183
May	63.60	64.20	63.60	64.20	+ .35	66.25	60.40	1,838
July	64.00	64.75	64.00	64.45	+ .45	66.28	61.00	588
Dec	63.42	63.75	63.40	63.40	- .10	64.25	63.40	779

Est vol 7,500; vol Wed 5,860; open int 34,415, +772.

ORANGE JUICE (CTN)–15,000 lbs.; cents per lb.

	Open	High	Low	Settle	Change	Lifetime High	Lifetime Low	Open Interest
July	127.00	127.60	126.50	126.80	- .20	175.50	115.25	701
Sept	123.90	124.00	122.80	123.05	- 1.25	175.00	116.00	3,432
Nov	116.95	117.10	116.10	116.90	- .30	165.50	112.00	1,889
Ja93	114.90	115.00	114.00	114.75	- .25	178.00	111.40	2,520
Mar	114.60	115.25	114.40	114.65	- .20	164.00	111.25	1,139
May	115.25	115.25	114.50	114.65	- .20	122.75	111.75	178

Est vol 1,200; vol Wed 1,846; open int 10,004, +269.

METALS AND PETROLEUM

COPPER-HIGH (CMX)–25,000 lbs.; cents per lb.

	Open	High	Low	Settle	Change	Lifetime High	Lifetime Low	Open Interest
July	113.80	113.95	111.00	111.60	- 1.10	113.95	92.80	3,036
Aug	113.40	114.20	111.30	111.65	- 1.40	114.20	95.70	926
Sept	113.90	114.25	110.90	111.55	- 1.50	114.25	92.80	27,942
Oct		....	....	111.00	- 1.30	105.90	95.90	456
Nov		....	....	110.80	- 1.20	104.80	96.00	375
Dec	112.70	112.75	109.95	110.55	- 1.10	112.75	91.60	10,359
Ja93		....	....	110.05	- .90	112.00	93.30	129
Mar	110.40	110.60	108.50	109.05	- .70	110.60	92.80	2,387
May	109.30	109.60	108.40	108.05	- .50	109.60	93.70	822
July	108.00	108.00	108.00	107.15	- .40	108.20	95.80	861
Sept	107.00	107.00	107.00	106.25	- .30	107.00	95.80	562
Dec		....	....	105.15	- .30	106.70	97.00	507

Est vol 17,500; vol Wed 3,645; open int 48,468, -724.

GOLD (CMX)–100 troy oz.; $ per troy oz.

	Open	High	Low	Settle	Change	Lifetime High	Lifetime Low	Open Interest
July		....	....	348.70	+ 1.10	347.30	347.30	16
Aug	348.20	349.50	347.80	349.40	+ 1.00	426.50	336.60	46,066
Oct	349.80	351.10	349.70	351.10	+ 1.00	410.00	338.50	4,117
Dec	352.00	353.20	351.40	343.00	+ 1.00	431.00	340.40	17,558
Fb93	353.90	355.00	353.40	354.90	+ 1.00	404.20	343.00	9,929
Apr	355.80	356.30	355.80	356.80	+ 1.00	410.00	346.00	8,458
June	358.60	358.80	358.50	358.80	+ 1.00	418.50	347.70	5,810
Aug		....	....	361.00	+ 1.00	395.50	353.00	2,338
Oct		....	....	363.30	+ 1.00	395.00	365.60	746
Dec		....	....	365.60	+ 1.00	402.80	356.40	4,135
Fb94		....	....	368.10	+ 1.00	367.30	364.50	442
June		....	....	373.50	+ 1.00	379.00	367.00	220
Dec		....	....	384.00	+ 1.00	383.00	383.00	206
Ju95		....	....	394.40	+ 1.00	....	....	102
Dec		....	....	404.70	+ 1.00	....	....	100

Est vol 20,000; vol Wed 22,356; open int 100,373, +443.

PLATINUM (NYM)–50 troy oz.; $ per troy oz.

	Open	High	Low	Settle	Change	Lifetime High	Lifetime Low	Open Interest
July	389.00	389.00	389.00	388.00	+ 5.20	427.50	331.00	382
Oct	385.50	390.50	385.50	389.50	+ 4.70	404.00	336.00	15,466
Ja93	385.00	388.00	384.50	387.90	+ 5.10	391.50	339.00	3,723
Apr		....	....	387.90	+ 5.10	390.50	339.00	1,134

Est vol 1,387; vol Wed 1,645; open int 20,705, +246.

PALLADIUM (NYM) 100 troy oz.; $ per troy oz.

	Open	High	Low	Settle	Change	Lifetime High	Lifetime Low	Open Interest
Sept	85.50	85.50	84.55	84.90	+ .90	89.30	79.50	2,550
Dec	85.00	85.00	84.50	84.90	+ 1.15	90.65	79.75	1,130

Est vol 141; vol Wed 266; open int 3,732, -41.

SILVER (CMX)–5,000 troy oz.; cents per troy oz.

	Open	High	Low	Settle	Change	Lifetime High	Lifetime Low	Open Interest
July	390.0	393.0	389.5	392.6	+ 4.3	557.0	382.0	203
Sept	391.0	395.0	390.5	394.7	+ 4.2	483.0	383.5	37,130
Dec	395.5	399.0	395.0	398.7	+ 4.2	507.0	387.0	27,307
Mr93	401.0	402.0	401.0	403.2	+ 4.2	513.0	394.0	5,597
May	402.0	405.5	402.0	406.2	+ 4.2	473.0	399.0	3,215
July	406.5	407.5	406.5	409.2	+ 4.2	470.5	400.0	5,541
Sept	410.0	410.0	409.5	412.2	+ 4.2	469.0	404.0	1,228
Dec	414.0	415.5	414.0	417.3	+ 4.2	462.0	408.0	2,551

Est vol 7,000; vol Wed 13,436; open int 82,822, +380.

SILVER (CBT)–1,000 troy oz.; cents per troy oz.

	Open	High	Low	Settle	Change	Lifetime High	Lifetime Low	Open Interest
July	389.0	393.0	388.0	393.0	+ 5.0	414.0	385.0	6
Aug	389.0	391.5	389.0	393.0	+ 5.0	495.0	383.0	180
Dec	395.0	399.0	395.0	399.0	+ 5.0	460.0	387.5	3,262
Fb93	399.0	399.0	399.0	402.0	+ 5.5	448.0	394.0	675
Apr	403.0	403.0	403.0	405.0	+ 6.0	454.0	398.0	446
June	405.0	407.0	405.0	408.0	+ 5.5	435.0	401.0	744

Est vol 200; vol Wed 160; open int 5,413, +41.

CRUDE OIL, Light Sweet (NYM) 1,000 bbls.; $ per bbl.

	Open	High	Low	Settle	Change	Lifetime High	Lifetime Low	Open Interest
Aug	21.29	21.45	21.26	21.40	- .01	22.95	17.75	67,071
Sept	21.26	21.45	21.26	21.39	+ .01	24.00	17.78	59,277
Oct	21.25	21.43	21.24	21.38	+ .03	22.75	18.42	32,952
Nov	21.29	21.42	21.26	21.37	+ .04	22.60	18.50	22,825
Dec	21.21	21.41	21.21	21.35	+ .04	24.00	18.25	29,943
Ja93	21.22	21.32	21.20	21.29	+ .06	22.30	18.62	26,660
Feb	21.08	21.21	21.08	21.21	+ .07	22.10	18.67	13,279
Mar		....	....	21.11	+ .07	21.91	18.51	8,951
Apr	21.00	21.00	20.95	21.02	+ .08	21.75	18.75	4,093
May		....	....	20.93	+ .08	21.59	18.93	3,419
June	20.80	20.80	20.80	20.84	+ .04	23.00	18.63	12,026
July	20.66	20.73	20.66	20.70	+ .03	22.58	18.97	8,783
Aug		....	....	20.69	+ .10	21.22	18.99	3,573
Sept	20.55	20.55	20.55	20.65	+ .11	21.18	18.90	9,596
Oct	20.60	20.65	20.55	20.63	+ .11	21.15	19.05	1,827
Nov		....	....	20.62	+ .11	21.15	20.24	607
Dec	20.50	20.50	20.50	20.61	+ .11	23.00	18.70	11,177
Ja94	20.60	20.60	20.54	20.61	+ .12	21.15	20.66	482
Mar		....	....	20.62	+ .13	21.10	19.14	990
June		....	....	20.63	+ .13	21.35	19.25	11,842
Dec		....	....	20.64	+ .13	21.26	19.40	6,107
Ju95		....	....	20.73	+ .13	21.21	20.62	7,671

Est vol 92,072; vol Wed 111,373; open int 343,151, +2,069.

HEATING OIL NO. 2 (NYM) 42,000 gal.; $ per gal.

	Open	High	Low	Settle	Change	Lifetime High	Lifetime Low	Open Interest
Aug	.5870	.5980	.5870	.5925	+ .0019	.6475	.4950	27,785
Sept	.5980	.6070	.5980	.6031	+ .0016	.6530	.5220	18,301
Oct	.6100	.6180	.6100	.6136	+ .0016	.6605	.5315	12,079
Nov	.6230	.6275	.6225	.6236	+ .0016	.6675	.5430	8,125
Dec	.6290	.6360	.6290	.6321	+ .0011	.6745	.5525	14,860
Ja93	.6360	.6385	.6340	.6361	+ .0016	.6740	.5550	7,467
Feb	.6280	.6305	.6275	.6276	+ .0016	.6590	.5435	5,627
Mar	.6050	.6075	.6040	.6046	+ .0016	.6350	.5310	1,373
Apr	.5870	.5870	.5830	.5831	+ .0016	.6070	.5525	853
May	.5670	.5670	.5670	.5676	+ .0016	.5910	.4950	196
June	.5590	.5590	.5590	.5606	+ .0016	.5825	.5525	407
July	.5570	.5570	.5570	.5596	+ .0016	.5820	.5095	2,702
Aug	.5670	.5670	.5640	.5646	+ .0016	.5800	.5600	321
Sept		....	....	.5761	+ .0016	.6200	.6160	123
Oct		....	....	.5861	+ .0016	.5950	.5950	210

Est vol 22,445; vol Wed 43,773; open int 100,548, +1,336.

GASOLINE, Unleaded (NYM) 42,000 gal.; $ per gal.

	Open	High	Low	Settle	Change	Lifetime High	Lifetime Low	Open Interest
Aug	.5820	.5925	.5820	.5876	+ .0023	.6735	.5070	30,061
Sept	.5890	.6000	.5890	.5947	+ .0023	.6580	.5465	14,931
Oct	.5865	.5930	.5835	.5892	+ .0043	.6330	.5310	12,166
Nov	.5775	.5850	.5775	.5822	+ .0048	.6185	.5300	7,089
Dec	.5760	.5800	.5755	.5787	+ .0058	.6105	.5350	12,889
Ja93	.5770	.5790	.5770	.5793	+ .0058	.6100	.5465	5,455
Feb		....	....	.5850	+ .0060	.6040	.5700	699
Mar		....	....	.5965	+ .0060	.6120	.5895	514

Est vol 24,686; vol Wed 39,372; open int 83,872, +235.

NATURAL GAS, (NYM) 10,000 MMBtu.; $ per MMBtu's

	Open	High	Low	Settle	Change	Lifetime High	Lifetime Low	Open Interest
Aug	1.638	1.657	1.625	1.639	+ .009	1.657	1.180	7,531
Sept	1.640	1.650	1.625	1.632	....	1.660	1.230	5,398
Oct	1.725	1.735	1.715	1.715	- .005	1.780	1.360	4,509
Nov	1.890	1.900	1.880	1.880	- .015	1.985	1.560	4,423
Dec	2.100	2.105	2.080	2.090	- .015	2.185	1.745	5,658
Ja93	2.160	2.165	2.150	2.150	- .015	2.230	1.825	6,754
Feb	1.840	1.840	1.830	1.830	- .005	1.865	1.520	3,392
Mar	1.563	1.570	1.558	1.570	+ .008	1.620	1.150	2,658
Apr	1.515	1.520	1.505	1.520	+ .010	1.550	1.200	1,550
May	1.525	1.530	1.520	1.530	+ .010	1.555	1.200	1,031
June	1.538	1.540	1.528	1.540	+ .010	1.570	1.215	959
July	1.545	1.555	1.545	1.555	+ .015	1.610	1.180	1,110
Aug	1.560	1.580	1.555	1.580	+ .025	1.605	1.250	835
Sept	1.610	1.620	1.610	1.620	+ .020	1.660	1.470	416
Oct	1.685	1.725	1.685	1.720	+ .030	1.745	1.630	311
Nov		....	....	1.895	+ .015	1.960	1.765	386
Dec		....	....	2.105	+ .015	2.180	2.000	344
Ja94	2.170	2.178	2.170	2.170	+ .030	2.178	2.100	199

Est vol 5,819; vol Wed 7,978; open int 47,464, -414.

BRENT CRUDE (IPE) 1,000 net bbls.; $ per bbl.

	Open	High	Low	Settle	Change	Lifetime High	Lifetime Low	Open Interest
Aug	19.90	20.07	19.87	19.98	- .02	21.61	17.11	30,137
Sept	19.95	20.16	19.90	20.08	+ .01	21.50	17.15	23,523
Oct	20.00	20.18	19.97	20.13	+ .07	21.38	27.15	11,540
Nov	20.02	20.14	19.97	20.11	+ .01	21.24	17.30	5,507
Dec	20.00	20.12	20.00	20.09	+ .03	21.19	17.22	9,192
Ja93	19.97	20.07	19.94	19.93	- .02	20.97	17.80	1,442
Feb		....	....	19.85	+ .20	20.77	19.14	2,356
Mar		....	....	19.75	+ .12	20.65	18.82	1,060
Apr		....	....	19.65	+ .15	20.50	19.81	1,060

Est vol 32,360; vol Wed 34,564; open int 85,817, +2,202.

GAS OIL (IPE) 100 metric tons; $ per ton

	Open	High	Low	Settle	Change	Lifetime High	Lifetime Low	Open Interest
July	181.50	182.50	179.75	182.25	- .25	196.50	155.00	12,715
Aug	183.75	184.25	181.75	184.25	....	196.00	158.00	23,841
Sept	184.00	186.00	183.75	186.00	- .25	197.50	159.00	10,706
Oct	187.25	188.50	186.75	188.50	- .50	199.50	166.00	11,107
Nov	189.25	190.50	189.00	190.00	- 1.00	201.50	169.00	13,582
Dec	190.00	191.75	189.50	191.50	- .50	202.50	174.00	6,306
Ja93	189.00	190.75	189.00	190.75	- .25	201.00	179.25	2,196
Feb	186.50	186.50	186.00	186.00	- 2.00	196.00	177.00	769
Mar	182.50	183.00	182.00	183.00	- .50	190.50	182.00	536

Est vol 28,299; vol Wed 22,879; open int 81,758, +2,363.

EXCHANGE ABBREVIATIONS
(for commodity futures and futures options)

CBT-Chicago Board of Trade; CME-Chicago Mercantile Exchange; CMX-Commodity Exchange, New York; CRCE-Chicago Rice & Cotton Exchange; CTN-New York Cotton Exchange; CSCE-Coffee, Sugar & Cocoa Exchange, New York; FOX-London Futures and Options Exchange; IPE-International Petroleum Exchange; KC-Kansas City Board of Trade; MCE-MidAmerica Commodity Exchange; MPLS-Minneapolis Grain Exchange; NYM-New York Mercantile Exchange; PBOT-Philadelphia Board of Trade; WPG-Winnipeg Commodity Exchange.

SOURCE: *The Wall Street Journal*, July 10, 1992.

ABC Airlines

Managing Strategic Risks

VIPUL K. BANSAL

M. E. ELLIS

JOHN F. MARSHALL

Introduction

Every business is exposed to various types of risks. These risks may be divided into two broad groups known as core business risks and environmental risks. *Core business risks* are risks over which the firm has at least some direct control. Successful firms are generally good at managing core business risks. *Environmental risks* are risks over which the firm has little or no direct control. These would include such things as general market softness as a consequence of a recession and various price risks. Price risks include the financial impact on the firm from changes in such things as interest rates, exchange rates and commodity prices.

Price risks are also known as strategic risks. The term strategic risks, however, is meant to capture the notion that business entities are exposed to more than just inventory and transactional price risks. They are also exposed to translational price risks, competitive price risks, and anticipatory price risks. Many of the most operationally efficient producers have gone from solid financial health to total demise as a

consequence of their exposure to strategic risks. This transition may occur in a remarkably short period of time. In many cases, producers do not realize that they have such risks; in other cases, they fail to accurately measure the risks; and, in still other cases, they fail to adequately manage the risks.

In this case study we are taking a look at strategic risks, the measurement of strategic risks, and the management of strategic risks. To illustrate the concepts, we will examine one specific, although hypothetical, airline. For purposes of the case, we will assume that today is August 1, 1991.

Strategic Risks

Strategic risks include a variety of price risks. Specifically, there is inventory price risk, transactional price risk, translational price risk, competitive price risk, and anticipatory price risk. Let's consider some of these in the context of the airline industry.

An airline that purchases jet fuel each day and which pays the spot price for fuel is exposed to an ongoing transactional price risk for fuel. The same would be true of an airline that sells tickets in a currency other than its functional currency. In the former case, the airline's profit is made volatile by volatility in the price of jet fuel. In the latter case, the airline's profit is made volatile by volatility in the exchange rate between its functional currency and the currency of its ticket sales. These are obvious price risks. Now consider some of the less obvious forms.

Fluctuations in exchange rates make travel to other countries either more or less expensive, exclusive of air fares. Thus, when the dollar weakens vis-à-vis other currencies, travel to the United States by foreigners tends to increase because travel to the United States becomes relatively cheaper in the traveler's domestic currency. Simultaneously, travel by Americans to other parts of the world will decline because international travel becomes relatively more expensive for Americans. These shifts in tourism patterns will increase or decrease airline ticket sales revenue for airlines depending on how they have positioned themselves. For example, an international carrier that has marketed itself heavily to American travelers but not to Japanese travelers will suffer a decline in ticket sales revenue if the yen strengthens vis-à-vis the dollar. A carrier, on the other hand, that has marketed itself heavily to Japanese travelers will enjoy an increase in ticket revenues from a stronger yen. The point then is that, irrespective of the transactional consequences of a stronger or weaker yen, there is also a competitive price risk associated with fluctuations in an exchange rate.

The same is true for fluctuations in interest rates. Consider an airline that has financed its aircraft and other capital purchases with fixed-rate debt. The fixed-rate would seem, on the surface, to suggest that the airline is not exposed to interest-rate risk. After all, if interest rates rise, the airline's borrowing costs do not change very much. But, all other things being equal, rising interest rates tend to occur during periods of economic expansion. During such periods, air travel—both business and personal—also increases. Thus, the airline's

revenues increase when interest rates rise and decline when interest rates fall. The point is that an airline's revenues can be shown to fluctuate with interest rates. This is not a cause-and-effect relationship. Rather, it is merely a reflection of the fact that interest rates and airline revenues are both positively correlated, allowing for lags, with the strength of the economy. This correlation between revenues and interest rates constitutes a strategic risk.

Consider now a U.S.-based airline that does not routinely convert its foreign sales revenues to dollars. Instead, the airline operates a series of foreign subsidiaries. Each subsidiary earns revenue and incurs expenses in a foreign currency. All profits are funneled back into the subsidiary to finance growth. If net revenues are not to be repatriated, then there would appear not to be a price risk. But, again, this conclusion is premature. At the end of each fiscal year, the U.S. airline is required to consolidate its financial statements and restate all values in dollars (its function currency). Fluctuations in the exchange rate will impact the translational values and result in translation profits or losses. In addition to making consolidated profit more volatile, exchange-rate fluctuations will also have a very real impact on the airline's tax liabilities.

Finally, consider an airline that has made a decision to purchase foreign built aircraft, such as the French-built Airbus. Suppose that the aircraft are priced in French francs and orders must be placed several years in advance. Suppose further that the terms of the contract require a 20 percent down payment with the remainder due on delivery. The forward commitment to pay a specific number of francs upon the delivery of the aircraft exposes the airline to a sizable price risk. A strengthening of the French franc, vis-à-vis the airline's functional currency will make the aircraft more expensive.

Many operationally efficient airlines have been put out of business over the years because they failed to take into consideration and to properly manage the various strategic risks to which they were exposed. Laker Airlines and Braniff Airlines are two examples from a decade ago. More recently, fuel price shocks and weak markets have contributed to the bankruptcies of Eastern Airlines and Pan Am, and to the sorry state of TWA and Continental.

Risk Management Techniques

Strategic risks can be managed in a variety of ways. Which is appropriate will depend on the nature of the risk, the costs of various risk-management alternatives, the tax and legal implications of different risk-management methods, and the efficiency and flexibility of the various risk-management instruments.

The simplest way to manage strategic risks is to pass the risks along to customers and/or vendors. For example, in some businesses, any increase in input prices can be immediately passed along to customers in the form of higher prices for output. This can be described as passing risks forward. This form of risk management is typical of the home heating oil industry. In that industry, each dealer posts a price each day that is equal to that day's wholesale price plus a fixed mark-up. At other times, fluctuations in the market price of the firm's output can be passed along to the firm's vendors. This is called passing risks backward.

Passing risks to others is only viable when the nature of the firm's business is such that the customer or vendor, as the case may be, has no choice but to accept the risk. For most businesses, the ability to pass strategic risks along to others is quite limited and often impossible. In the case of passing risks forward to customers, it works best when the firm is a regulated monopoly. In the case of passing risks backward to vendors, it works best when the firm is a monopsony. Even in these cases, however, the method is limited.

The second way to manage strategic risks is by way of asset/liability management. In this approach, the firm attempts to match the strategic risks associated with its asset portfolio with the strategic risks associated with its liability portfolio. When the risks on one side of the balance sheet precisely offset the risks on the other side of the balance sheet, the risks are self-cancelling. In practical terms, this approach requires that the value change in the firm's assets is precisely offset by the value change in the firm's liabilities from each and every price change to which the firm is exposed. When the value changes are offsetting, the balance sheet is said to be immunized. Immunization strategies are most highly developed for managing interest-rate risk and exchange-rate risk, particularly when the firm is a financial institution.

Immunization works well for the management of inventory risks—that is, we can match the value changes of our "inventory" of assets and our "inventory" of liabilities. It is much more difficult to manage other forms of strategic risks with asset/liability management techniques.

The third important way to manage strategic risks is to hedge. Hedging may be described as the art and science of creating offsetting risks. We must distinguish, however, between hedging and natural hedges.

Often, a firm is exposed to multiple strategic risks, some of which are partially or wholly offsetting. Such positions are said to be natural hedges for one another. Natural hedges should not be confused with asset/liability management. First, natural hedges can occur on the same side of the balance sheet. Second, natural hedges are ordinarily the result of happenstance and need not be the consequence of careful planning. Nevertheless, asset/liability risk offsets can be viewed as a special case of natural hedges.

As useful as natural hedges are at offsetting risks, they are rarely complete hedges and even more rarely perfectly effective. Hedging, as distinct from natural hedges, is a conscious effort to take positions solely for the purpose of risk management. The most widely used hedging instruments today are futures contracts, forward contracts, swap contracts, and options contracts. It is also possible, however, to structure hedges with other forms of derivative securities.

Quantifying Strategic Risks

The first step in the management of strategic risks is the identification of the risks—that is, we cannot begin to measure and manage strategic risks if we are unaware of their existence. It might seem silly to even point this out, but failure to recognize the existence of strategic risks has been one of the explanations given for the failure to manage these risks.[1]

Once a strategic risk has been identified, the next step is to quantify it. This may seem rather straightforward, but in fact it often isn't. As already noted, a firm may have many similar exposures—some of which may be offsetting.

Consider a simple scenario. Imagine a corporate bond trader that trades on relative value (i.e., the bond trader sells bonds that are overvalued and buys bonds that are undervalued). At any given point in time, the trader is long some bonds and short some bonds. Each bond position the trader holds exposes her to interest-rate risk (i.e., the values of the bonds will vary as interest rates fluctuate). The interest-rate risks associated with the short positions are natural hedges for the interest-rate risks associated with the long positions. Since each bond is different with respect to maturity, coupon payments, and so on, the firm's interest-rate exposure is also different for each bond. How do we determinne the net expo-

sure from the overall portfolio? The answer is, we convert each bond to some baseline or benchmark equivalent in order to make all the bonds directly comparable. For example, perhaps we select a 10-year Treasury note (T-note) as the baseline security. We then determine the risk equivalence of each individual bond in terms of this baseline security.

Let's make this example a little more concrete by adding a few numbers. Suppose that the trader is long $3 million dollars of a General Motors note and short $4 million of a Shell Oil Company note. Suppose further that the General Motors' position is risk equivalent to a $1.8 million long position in 10-year T-notes and that the Shell Oil position is risk equivalent to a $1.4 million short position in 10-year T-notes. The net exposure is then risk equivalent to a $0.4 million long position in T-notes. We would hedge this net exposure by going short an equivalent amount of T-notes or T-note futures. If we use futures, we would sell four T-note futures with a face value $0.1 million each.

When we conduct a thorough risk analysis, we must take all of the exposures into consideration. Electronic spreadsheets and risk management software can greatly aid in such an endeavor. The process, which employs *what if* or *sensitivity analysis* (sometimes called scenario analysis) requires us to build a financial model of the income statement. In the model, we explicitly incorporate the financial prices that have been identified as sources of strategic risks for the firm. The current values of the financial prices are entered into a separate section of the spreadsheet called an *assumptions block*. The rest of the statement is then tied to the assumptions block in a fashion that represents the actual structural relationships between the firm's cost and revenue entries. In this modeling exercise, we must also take care to include the value changes in the firm's assets and liabilities because it is the *real* value change we want to hedge—not just the accounting values.

---

[1]For a more thorough discussion of the identification of strategic risks, see Chan, et al. (1992).

After all income and value change influencing factors have been built into the model, we can begin the process of examining how a change in a financial price affects the firm's value (or income, if we are limiting ourselves to that variable). For example, after beginning with the current values of interest rates, exchange rates, and commodity prices, we can change each of these prices (one at a time) and examine how the firm's income is affected. Through this analysis, we can determine the firm's precise risk profile with respect to each of the financial prices.

Converting Price Risk to Performance Risk

A price risk, measured as the volatility (standard deviation) of a price or, sometimes, as the volatility of the rate of change in the price, is a risk that exists independently of a given firm's exposure to that risk. For example, jet fuel prices and diesel fuel prices are determined, largely, by world oil prices, and these fuel prices are volatile largely because oil prices are volatile. This volatility exists irrespective of whether or not a particular user of these fuels exists and irrespective of the extent of the user's fuel consumption.

Again, let's add reality to the example by working with some numbers. Suppose that oil prices are expected to average $20 per barrel over the coming year. Suppose further that the standard deviation of the forecast is $1.80 per barrel and that oil prices are apprpoximately normally distributed.[2] The distribution of the market place is depicted in Exhibit 10-1.

---

[2] In reality, prices tend to be distributed lognormally rather than normally. The treatment of price here as a normally distributed variate is for expositional convenience only. In any practical application of the principles discussed here the true nature of the underlying distribution of price must be taken into consideration. For more thorough discussion of these points see Marshall and Bansal (1992), Kapner and Marshall (1990), and Marshall (1989).

EXHIBIT 10-1

The Distribution of Oil Prices

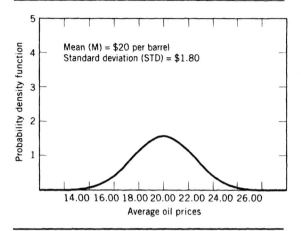

We can compute and plot a confidence interval around the mean forecast. For example, the 95 percent confidence interval for the average price of oil over the coming year is given by the mean plus and minus 1.96 standard deviations and is depicted in Exhibit 10-2.

Now consider two firms in the transportation industry that employ oil derivatives in

EXHIBIT 10-2

95% Confidence Interval

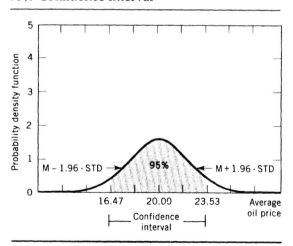

their business. One is an airline and the other is a long-haul trucking line. These two firms are both publicly owned, the stock of both is currently priced at about $24 a share, and both expect earnings of about $1 a share for the coming year. Both firms have an oil price exposure because both use oil derivatives in their inputs to their operations: the airline uses jet fuel, and the trucking line uses diesel fuel. The management of each firm has considered what the impact on profit, measured in terms of earnings per share, would be from a change in oil prices (i.e., we are using EPS as our definition of performance). Thes exposures are depicted graphically in the form of risk profiles in Exhibit 10-3, panels A and B.

Risk profiles depict a specific firm's exposure to a price risk—that is, the financial consequences to the firm of a change in the price. Such profiles, however, do not tell us the *likelihood* of any given departure from the expected outcome. We will call the latter performance risk. To get a more precise measure of the firm's performance risk, we can combine the market measure of price volatility, depicted in Exhibit 10-2, with risk profiles, depicted in Exhibit 10-3. The result, which is depicted in Exhibit 10-4, measures performance risk.

Notice that we have now quantified both the extent and the likelihood of financial injury from a change in financial prices. Notice also that the airline is considerably more susceptible to financial damage from a rise in the price of oil than the trucking line. For example, the worst case scenario for the airline, at a 95 percent level of confidence, is a drop in EPS from the expected $1 a share to about $0.30 a

EXHIBIT 10-3

Risk Profiles

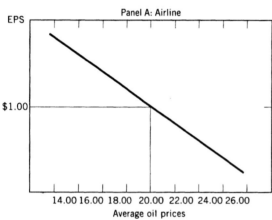

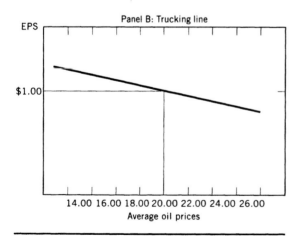

EXHIBIT 10-4

Comparative Performance Risk

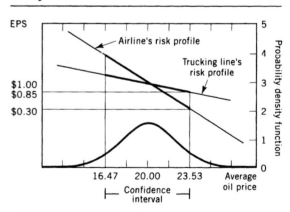

share. For the trucking line, the worst case scenario is a drop from $1 a share to about $0.85 a share. Of course, if the risk profile is perfectly flat, then the firm is immune to changes in price, or equivalently, has no exposure. The goal of risk management, barring other considerations, is, therefore, to make the firm's risk profile as close to perfectly flat as possible.

The Tools of Hedging

Today, a firm with an exposure to strategic risks has many hedging vehicles available to it. The most widely used are futures, forwards, options, and swaps. A futures contract is a standardized contract for the deferred, or later, delivery of a given quantity of some underlying asset. Delivery is scheduled during some specific period of time for a price agreed to at the time of initial contracting. A forward contract is essentially the same thing but the contracts are less standardized and trade in dealer-type markets—as opposed to futures which trade on futures exchanges. Futures and forwards are very good at eliminating price risks that are of a single-period nature. Swaps involve a series of exchanges between two parties, called counterparties. The first counterparty pays the second counterparty a fixed price, or rate, on a given quantity of some underlying asset. In exchange for these payments, the second counterparty pays the first counterparty a floating price, or rate, on the same underlying assets. The underlying assets are called notionals. For practical purposes, swaps may be viewed as a series of successive futures contracts, sometimes called a futures strip. Swaps are very good at eliminating price risks that are of a multi-period nature. In all three cases, these instruments are used to eliminate *any* deviation from the *expected* or *targeted* outcome.

An option is a right but not an obligation to do something or to receive something. Single-period options are of two types—calls and puts. A call option grants its holder the right, but not the obligation, to buy the underlying asset at the option's strike price. If the call is cash settled, then it entitles the holder to receive a cash settlement if the price of the underlying asset is above the option's strike price. A put option grants its holder the right, but not the obligation, to sell the underlying asset at the option's strike price. If the put is cash settled, then it entitles its holder to receive a cash settlement if the price of the underlying asset is below the strike price of the option. The multi-period counterpart of a call option is called a cap, and the multi-period counterpart of a put option is a called a floor. A cap entitles its holder to receive a payment at the end of each settlement period *if* the price of the underlying asset is above the strike price of the cap. The cap has a series of successive settlement periods before its final termination. For this reaon, a cap is related to a call in the same way that a swap is related to a futures; that is, a cap is a strip of calls. Similarly, a floor may be regarded as a strip of puts.

Options are used to eliminate only negative deviation from an expected outcome. When we wish to confine our discussion to the elimination of negative outcomes only, the risk is referred to as downside risk. Of course, there are no free lunches and we cannot expect to eliminate downside risk while preserving upside potential without paying a price for this more attractive alternative. The price comes in the form of an up-front premium that is paid for the option. If markets price assets efficiently, then the premium paid for the option should be equal to the present value of the benefits afforded by the option (relative to other hedging alternatives).

Just as strategic exposures give rise to risk profiles, hedge positions give rise to payoff profiles. The payoff profiles for a long position in a futures, a long position in a forward, and one-period of a swap for the fixed-price payer

EXHIBIT 10-5

Payoff Profiles: Long Positions in Futures and Forwards or Fixed-Price Payer Swap

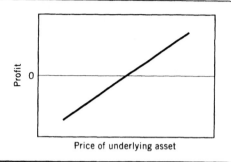

all look the same and are depicted in Exhibit 10-5. The payoff profile for a long call option is depicted in Exhibit 10-6. The payoff profiles for short positions in futures and forwards and one-period of a swap for the fixed-rate receiver are the mirror images of those depicted in Exhibit 10-5. The payoff profile for a short call option is the mirror image of the payoff profile for a long call option. These mirror image relationships are a consequence of the *zero sum game* nature of futures, forwards, swaps, and options trading.

EXHIBIT 10-6

Payoff Profiles: Long Call Options

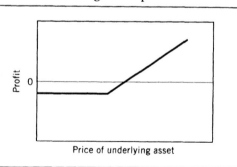

With this background, we are now ready to examine the airline industry.

The Airline Industry In the Early 1990s

The first two years of the 1990s represented a period of considerable uncertainty for the airline industry in the United States. The decade opened with declining consumer confidence and an economic recession, both of which cut into ticket sales and hurt revenues. The dip in air travel was further aggravated by the Iraqi invasion of Kuwait and the strong U.S. military response. Personal and business air travel were further curtailed as hostilities approached, largely out of fear of terrorism—the memory of Pan Am Flight 103 still fresh in the public's mind.

The precipitous decline in airline revenues was only one of several bombshells for the industry. Another was a dramatic rise in the price of fuel as a consequence of a more than doubling of oil prices in the wake of the Iraqi conquest of Kuwait. For example, jet fuel averaged $0.58 per gallon during the second quarter of 1990 and represented 16.5 percent of the industry's operating costs. By mid-October 1990, jet fuel had risen to $1.40 per gallon. For 1990 as a whole, expenditures on jet fuel were 70 percent higher for the airline industry than they were in 1989. The consequences for the industry were devastating.

A third problem for the airline industry is the age of the fleets. Many U.S. airlines fly fleets that are old by any measure—an average age of 15 years is not uncommon. A series of accidents in the late 1980s and 1990 involving older aircraft led authorities in the United State to insist on more frequent inspections of aircraft, more frequent maintenance checks, and more frequent parts replacements. In addition, older aircraft are as much as 30 to

35 percent less fuel efficient than newer aircraft.

Deregulation of the airline industry during the 1980s led to more intensive price competition. Fare wars cut heavily into profits. So too did the advent of technology that allowed first the traveling public and later business travelers to "shop around" and compare different airlines' fares. Frequent fliers programs, introduced in the early 1980s to build customer loyalty, came back to haunt some carriers as customers increasingly claimed "free seats."

The decline in revenue and the increase in costs occurred at precisely-the wrong time for the airline industry. As a result of the deregulation of the airline industry in 1978, the industry had passed through an extended period of restructuring. Leveraged buyouts, expensive battles for corporate control, and aggressive efforts to expand in a belief that only the largest carrier would survive had resulted in an increase in already heavy debt burdens.[3] Survival depended on keeping revenues up, keeping costs down, and replacing aging fleets. For some of the heavily leveraged firms, asset sales were imperative to pay down the heavy debt loads taken on in the corporate restructurings.

---

[3]Even before deregulation, airlines were highly leveraged (with few exceptions). Routes and prices, however, were regulated which assured each airline a "reasonable" return despite the leverage. More specifically, regulations insulated the industry from potential adverse consequences of a high degree of operating leverage. This allowed the airline industry to employ higher degrees of financial leverage than other industries with similar operating leverage and no greater overall risk. After deregulation, airlines suffered the full impact of leverage—both operational and financial. The combined burdens of higher fuel costs, labor strife, and safety and maintenance issues, proved too much for some airlines. Delta Airlines was an interesting exception. Delta's degree of financial leverage was significantly lower than that for the industry as a whole before deregulation. This was a key factor in Delta's survival.

The globalization of business and the dramatic rise of the Japanese economy, the German economy, and others led to an increase in international travel throughout the 1960s, 1970s, and 1980s. As a consequence, airlines with international routes were forced to conduct an increaing portion of their business in currencies other than their functional currency. The demise of fixed exchange rate, following the collapse of the Bretton Woods Agreement in the early 1970s, led to a sharp increase in exchange-rate volatilities; thereby exposing international carriers to another form of risk.

By the middle of 1991, the bones of defunct airlines littered the landscape. Some of the oldest and most staid carrier, including Eastern, Pan Am, and Continental had gone bankrupt, as had some of the niche carriers like Midway. If nothing else, the opening two years of the 1990s had demonstrated the true extent of the strategic risks faced by the airline industry. It has become clear that, while necessary, it is not sufficient to operate an airline efficiently to survive. Survival requires a mastering of the art and science of strategic risk management.

ABC Airlines

ABC airlines was launched by a small group of pilots and investors in 1980. In that year, the group bought several planes from a failed carrier and carved a niche for itself by servicing out-of-the-way locations that were neglected by larger carriers. From the beginning, management concentrated on keeping fares low, operating costs down, and debt down. Pilots, baggage handlers, flight attendants, and other employees received a significant part of their compensation in the form of profit sharing, in lieu of salary. Average salaries at ABC have long been 25 percent below those of other airlines, but total compensation, after profit sharing, is about the same. Profit sharing compensation is paid with additional shares of stock—to preserve equity capital for the expansion of the airline.

The 1981–82 recession made ABC's start-up difficult, but its below market salaries and further, although temporary, concessions from workers, got the airline through the crunch. By the middle of 1983, ABC was in good stead and positioned nicely for the boom of the 1980s. The remainder of the 1980s were a phenomenal growth period for the airline. Between 1983 and 1987, a new city was added to the airline's service base on average once every two months. The airline continued its strategy of purchasing the older planes of other airlines to service these cities. By 1986, ABC's annual revenues from its U.S. operations had reached $2 billion, placing ABC in the ranks of the mid-size carriers. At this point, ABC's management decided it was time to enter the international arena.

By 1990, ABC's operating revenues had reached $3.8 billion of which 15 percent was from transatlantic routes. The airline provided regular service to London, Paris, and Frankfurt.

Despite a bumpy start, the 1980s were good to ABC's owners, managers, and employees. As the decade closed, however, problems were looming for the industry. For a time, ABC's management, consisting largely of former pilots and other "hearts in the sky" personnel, failed to see the dangers. The airline's method of aircraft acquisitions had resulted in one of the oldest, most fuel inefficient fleets in the industry. Also, its low-budget operating strategy had led to a reputation for cheap no-frills flights—making it difficult to sell upscale service. On the other hand, the airline had stayed relatively debt free—much of its aircraft acquisitions had been made out of profits and additional sales of equity. Indeed, at the close of 1990, ABC's capital structure was 82 percent equity—of which almost half was owned by employees. The remaining 18 percent of capital was debt. Of this, 94 percent was fixed rate and 6 percent was floating rate.

In July 1990, after two years of general economic stagnation and little growth, ABC flew straight into an economic recession, which only now seems to be coming to an end. As with the industry as a whole, both domestic and international ticket sales declined significantly during the recession; however, ABC suffered a smaller ridership loss on its domestic routes than most of its competitors. The dramatic rise in oil prices, following the Iraqi invasion of Kuwait, cut deeply into profits. For 1990 as a whole, the firm suffered a sizable loss that shocked management and cast a pall over the future of the airline. The fourth quarter of 1990 was the worst. With oil prices at their peak and with no relief in sight, management began counting the days to insolvency. As the financial situation grew ever bleaker, management began plotting asset sales and route sales to generate cash to buy time. Layoffs were scheduled for the first time in the firm's history and management salaries were slashed. It had become very clear just how serious ABC's strategic risk exposures really were.

Fortunately, for ABC, the U.S. military success in the war with Iraq brought oil prices down even faster than they had risen. Indeed, on January 17, 1991, alone, the price of West Texas crude fell by more than $10 a barrel. By late January 1991, oil prices approached their pre-war levels.

While revenues were still off significantly from their peak, the first two quarters of 1991 showed considerable improvement. Nevertheles, the firm still suffered a loss for both quarters. The third quarter, however, looks very promising. The firm's earnings per share history is depicted in Exhibit 10-7. The data start with the first quarter in which the airline was operational and ends with the projected earnings for the third quarter of 1991.

ABC's dismal performance over the past 18 months has focused management's attention on the long-neglected need for strategic risk

EXHIBIT 10-7

ABC Airline's Earnings History

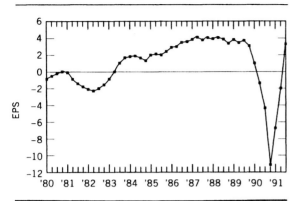

management, the age of its fleet, and its long-term growth strategy. In May 1991, ABC's Board of Directors decided to revamp its strategic plan. To assist in the process, management hired Judy Waters, an experienced financial engineer.

Judy, who was thoroughly versed in financial risk management, joined the airline in early June 1991. She spent her first two months analyzing the nature of the airline's business, its historic cash flows, its future funding requirements, its strategic risk exposures, and various economic forecasts. Not surprisingly, she determined that the airline had a significant exposure to oil prices, interest rate, several different exchange rates and general market softness. She set out to draft a plan to deal with these risks. Her plan is as yet incomplete, but it is beginning to take form, and she wants to impress management with the need to implement some risk-management strategies as quickly as possible.

Judy recognized that ABC does not operate in a vacuum. It must function within the context of the macroeconomic environment. For this reason, Judy began her report to her superiors with a discourse on the current economic environment and then focused on her prelimi-

nary examination of the firm's strategic risk exposures. Judy's report concludes this case study.

Strategic Planning Committee Preliminary Risk Management Report (August 1, 1991)

The Economy

At this time (Summer 1991) the economy appears to be nearing the bottom of the recession that began in July 1990. The prior two years were a period of relative stagnation.

Part of the stagnation was caused by the reluctance of the Federal Reserve (Fed) to stimulate the economy through lower interest rates out of a fear of igniting inflation. The recession and the relatively low rate of inflation during 1990, 5.4 percent, however, seems to have inspired the Fed to work toward lower interest rates. The discount rate has been lowered to 5.5 percent, the prime rate has declined to 8.5 percent, the three-month T-bill rate has declined to 5.7 percent, and the 30-year T-bond rate has leveled off at about 8.3 percent.

Despite the weaker U.S. economy, relative to Europe and Japan, the dollar has recently been gaining strength. (The U.S. government's efforts to encourage a weaker dollar to stimulate U.S. exports not withstanding.) The Deutschemark/dollar exchange rate has, over the last year, been in the 1.45–1.84 range. Over the last three years, this exchange rate has been in the 1.35–2.10 range.

Economic forecasts vary widely concerning the direction of the economy. Some economists are forecasting a double-dip recession with the worst yet to come. They support their position by pointing to the current banking crisis, the

Federal and states budget crises, high unemployment, and low consumer confidence. Since two thirds of the growth in GNP is due to consumer spending, the low level of consumer confidence is particularly troublesome.

These same economists argue that interest rates have already hit bottom and that the Fed will not lower rates again due to concerns over inflation. They cite as evidence the upward spike in the inflation rate during the first quarter of 1991. They also argue that the downturn they foresee for the U.S. economy is a prelude to international economic problems. They are particularly concerned about the burden on Germany to finance the reunification of that country, the pressure to finance Eastern Europe's move to a market economy, the economic chaos in the Soviet Union, and serious trade imbalances with Japan. In times of economic troubles, there tends to be a flight to dollars and, they conclude, the dollar will strengthen vis-à-vis other currencies.

At the other end of the spectrum are some very optimistic economists who point to the underlying strength of the U.S. economy. They argue that the recent increase in the inflation rate is a short-term phenomenon attributable to the Desert Storm operation and not indicative of a long-term structural problem. They stress that new home sales have begun to increase, that the unemployment rate has stopped increasing, that retail sales have stopped decreasing, and that the index of leading economic indicators has increased for five consecutive months. They conclude that interest rates will continue to decline, or, at the very least, will not rise significantly for some time. However, they accept that a strengthening economy will, eventually, lead to higher interest rates as the demand for funds increases.

These same economists feel that the international economy is not at all bleak and that the current uncertainties merely represent a natural apprehension associated with significant structural change. They argue that the

opening of Eastern European markets is an unambiguously positive economic development that will foster demand for U.S. capital goods and encourage both business and personal travel to Eastern Europe. They stress that the economic union of the European Community scheduled for 1992 will position Europe for a major expansion during the remainder of the decade. This scenario argues for a weaker dollar.

Other economic opinion falls between the two extremes. As usual, the only consensus opinion is that the economic future is anything but certain.

Risk Management Strategies

ABC airlines is exposed to a number of strategic risks that have been shown to significantly impact earnings per share. What follows is a summary of my preliminary analysis of those risks, the implications for the firm, and some possible strategies for dealing with the risks. It should be stressed that I have isolated the individual risks and I have examined the financial consequences of various manifestations of the risks individually. Ideally, we need to develop a more complete model of the firm's exposure that considers the interrelationships among the risks. For example, I have considered the financial impact on the firm from a rise in the price of oil, and I have considered the financial impact from an increase in interest rates. We need to consider the joint impact from a rise in the price of oil and a rise in interest rates. My estimate is that it will take about a year to develop a fully integrated financial model of the firm. In the interim, we should begin managing the risks individually. I have highlighted the key considerations below.

Oil Price Risk

ABC spends approximately 36–40 percent of its operating budget on fuel. This is considerably more than the average airline, which spends 10–20 percent of its operating budget on fuel. This discrepancy is explained in part by the age of our fleet and in part by our ability to keep our other costs, notably employee compensation, down. As the past year has unequivocally demonstrated, any increase in fuel prices impacts our earnings directly and quickly. Such costs cannot be passed along to customers until profit pressure on the industry has driven other carriers' fares higher. In general, this takes about 16 months. We are currently consuming approximately 1.5 billion gallons of fuel a year or, approximately, 125 million gallons a month. The impact on quarterly EPS (annualized) from unexpected fluctuations in the price of jet fuel are depicted in Exhibit 10-8.

Now that oil prices have returned, approximately, to their pre-war levels, it is my opinion that it is time to hedge our future cost of fuel. Since increases in fuel costs cannot be passed on to our customers for about 16 months, it follows that our fuel needs should be hedged out to 16 months. We have several hedging alternatives available. We could eliminate uncertainty almost entirely, and almost costlessly, by hedging our future fuel requirements in a series of oil futures contracts. For example, the price of jet fuel and heating oil futures prices have a 96 percent correlation. These futures contracts are traded on the New York Mercantile Exchange (NYMEX). There are no jet fuel contracts currently traded. While the hedge will not be perfect, the risk that remains, called basis risk, will be small.

The advantage of hedging by futures is that the size of our hedges can easily be adjusted to address changes in anticipated fuel usage. For example, expansion or contraction of service, cancelled or added flights, new, more fuel-efficient equipment, and so on, will all impact our fuel consumption. Further, each month we can add additional back months to our futures hedge to keep the firm hedged for a full 16 months. With this type of hedge, we must be prepared to deal with daily variation margin which will require transfers from, or to, a margin account. This will necessitate some additional liquidity on our part to meet these exchange requirements. While a futures hedge will effectively eliminate most of the oil price risk, importantly, it will also eliminate our opportunity to benefit from any unexpected decline in the price of oil.

The second alternative is to hedge by commodity swaps. In this structure, we would enter a multi-period swap agreement with a commodity swap dealer. We would continue to purchase our fuel in the spot market, just as we have always done. Each month, the swap dealer would pay us the average spot price for jet fuel, based on a notional quantity of 125 million gallons, and we would pay the swap dealer a fixed price. At present, the dealer would be willing to enter the swap at a fixed price of $0.608 per gallon. For comparative purposes, the current spot price of jet fuel is $0.60 a gallon and the average forward price for the next 16 months is approximately $0.606 per gallon. We would pay the swap dealer the same fixed price for the life of the swap. This is depicted in Exhibit 10-9.

There are two advantages to this structure. The swap dealer is prepared to enter a swap

EXHIBIT 10-8

ABC's Risk Profile with Respect to Fuel Prices

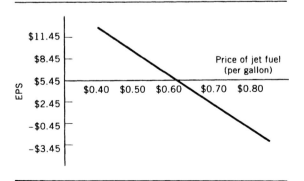

EXHIBIT 10-9

Fixing the Price of Jet Fuel
with a Commodity Swap

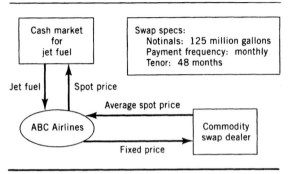

tied specifically to jet fuel rather than to oil. This will result in less basis risk than an oil futures hedge. Second, there will be no variation margin and, hence, no need to maintain extra liquidity. The downside is that the swap structure is not easily adjusted for changes in our expected fuel needs and would probably prove a bit more costly. The extension of the swap beyond 16 months could also be a problem, but I have obtained a commitment from a swap dealer to write a 48-month swap with the fixed price initially set for the first 16 months only. As each month elapses, a fixed-price will be set for the 16th month out. Thus, we are always hedged 16 months into the future. The dealer has agreed to this special structure in exchange for a one-time up-front fee of $0.01 per gallon of fuel on the notionals (this represents a one-time fee of $1,250,000).

The final strategy we should consider is a multi-period option on jet fuel. The same swap dealer I consulted for the commodity swap has offered a 48-month jet fuel cap for a one-time up-front premium of $2.25 a gallon with a strike price (cap price) of $0.60 a gallon, which is the current spot price. That is, we would pay the dealer $2.25 per gallon for each

notional gallon covered by the contract as a one-time up-front option premium. This would require the payment of $281.25 million if we cover our entire 125 million gallon anticipated monthly usage. After that, the dealer will pay us the difference, each month, between the average spot price of jet fuel and the strike price whenever the average price of jet fuel for the month is above the strike price. We would neither receive from, nor make payments to, the cap dealer when the price of jet fuel is at or below the strike price. The dealer is also prepared, for the same option premium, to modify the terms of the cap so that the $0.60 cap price would apply to the first 16 months only. As each month elapses, the strike price for the 16th month out would be set equal to the current market price. This specially engineered structure would keep our option hedge current with market conditions.

While the option strategy (commodity cap) involves a substantial up-front premium, it has the unique advantage of allowing us to benefit from any unexpected declines in the price of jet fuel. I have depicted the payoff profile for this option for one month of the 48 months in Exhibit 10-10. In Exhibit 10-10, the up-front premium has been amortized to more accu-

EXHIBIT 10-10

Payoff Profile for one-period of a Jet Fuel Cap
(Profit expressed in terms of impact on EPS)

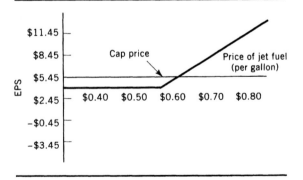

EXHIBIT 10-11

ABC's Residual Risk Profile with Jet Fuel Cap

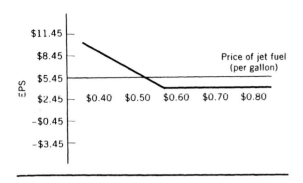

rately reflect its per-period cost. The per-period cost of the cap is $0.057 a gallon (at a 10 percent discount rate). When the cap's payoff profile is combined with the firm's jet fuel risk profile, we can get a good picture of the risk mitigating effect of the cap. The residual risk profile (i.e., the risk profile after the hedge is in place) is depicted in Exhibit 10-11.

I realize that the up-front option premium that we would have to pay to acquire the jet fuel cap would represent a sizable outlay for the firm. There are a number of variations on the basic cap approach, however, which could be employed to reduce the impact. First, we could purchase a cap with a strike price above the current market price instead of the one I have described in which the strike price would be set at the current market price. For example, the same cap dealer is willing to provide a 48-month cap with a strike price of $0.65 for the first 16 months, with subsequent months set at the spot price plus $0.05, for an up-front premium of $1.65 per gallon. With a strike price of $0.70 for the first 16 months, and future strike resets at the spot price plus $0.10, the premium would decline to $1.15. We could also employ a mix involving different strike prices. Of course, the downside of employing caps with higher strike prices is that we give

up some of our protection against higher fuel prices.

Another way to reduce the cost of the cap is to employ a participating cap. In this case, the dealer would pay us the full difference between the spot price and the strike price when the spot price is above the strike price. We, on the other hand, would pay the dealer a fixed percentage of the difference between the spot price and the strike price whenever the spot price is below the strike price. There is no up-front premium on this option. For example, if we selected a participating cap with an initial strike price of $0.70 a gallon, and subsequent strike are resets at spot plus $0.10, the participation rate would be 30 percent. Thus, whenever the spot price is below $0.70 a gallon, we would pay the dealer 30 percent of the difference. This strategy affords us protection against fuel price increases with no up-front cash outlay but with some sacrifice of the benefits which would otherwise accrue from a fuel price decrease.

A final variant that I would like the board to consider, which can be used to keep the cost of the cap down, is to write (sell) a floor at the same time that we buy the cap. For example, the cap dealer, which is also a floor dealer, would be willing to pay us an up-front premium of $1.45 for a jet fuel floor having a strike price of $0.50 per gallon, with subsequent strike resets at spot less $0.10. On this option, we would pay the floor dealer the difference between the spot price and the strike price whenever the spot price is below the strike price. The premium we would receive would partially offset the premium we would pay for the cap. This combination, in which we purchase a cap and write a floor, is often called a collar as it places both an upper limit and a lower limit on the cost of our fuel. If we purchase a cap and write a floor with appropriate strike prices on each, we can actually acquire some protection against higher fuel prices with no cash outlay at all. We do, however, give up some of our potential gain from a decline in fuel prices. A collar written with strike prices such that there is no up-front cost to us is called a zero cost collar.

While all of the hedging options are viable, I would like to suggest that we consider employing a combination of all three. I would suggest that we hedge 60 percent of our anticipated fuel needs in the commodity swap because that alternative removes the bulk of the basis risk. Further, I would suggest that we hedge 15 percent of our needs in the futures market because that market affords us the flexibility of adjusting the size of our hedge as our requirements change over time. Finally, I would suggest that we hedge the remaining 25 percent of our needs in a jet fuel cap or one of the cap variants. My reasoning is simple. There is a very good chance that the price of oil, and, consequently, jet fuel, will ease over an extended period of time as Kuwait's oil fields are gradually brought back into production. The cap would allow us to benefit from the decline at a time when our unhedged competitors enjoy windfall profits. This will prevent us from finding ourselves at too much of a cash flow disadvantage. On the other hand, the cap, like the swap and futures, will protect us from any increases in fuel prices and leaving us in a good position to "pick the bones" of our competitors if fuel prices rise.

This brings me to my final point on fuel costs. The age of our fleet is hurting us badly. While our strategy of buying relics from other carriers served us well in our early years, it has now come back to haunt us. Our fuel costs, our inspection and maintenance costs, and our down-time are cutting deeply into our operating profits. It is time to modernize the fleet. I know that I do not have to persuade you of the importance of this since the decision has already been made. What I would like to do, however, is discuss the financial risks involved and how we might manage those risks.

Interest Rate Risk

At present, we are carrying $320 million of intermediate to long-term debt with a fixed rate of interest. This debt has an average maturity of eight years and carries an average coupon of 10.25 percent. We also have $21 million of floating-rate debt with an average maturity of about three years. Most of our floating-rate debt is pegged to LIBOR with an average rate of LIBOR plus 150 basis points. The remainder is pegged to prime rate with an average rate of prime plus 75 basis points.

While floating-rate debt has the advantage, in a stable, upward-sloping yield curve environment, of keeping borrowing costs down, it can also add significantly to our financial costs should interest rates move higher as some economists are predicting. This would seem, on the face of it, to mitigate against the issuance of additional floating-rate debt. Indeed, a careful reading of the minutes of past board meetings makes clear that this was the counter argument presented whenever the treasurer suggested the issuance of floating-rate debt.

My studies of this airline's financial history lead me to conclude that our ticket revenues are positively correlated with interest rates. A statistical decomposition suggests that the correlation is highest when we allow for a three-month interest rate lag. That is, our revenues begin to rise, on average, about three months before interest rates begin to rise, and our revenues begin to fall about three months before interest rates begin to fall, which means our revenues lead interest rates by about three months. The interest-rate effect on our revenues is quite pronounced.

The analysis suggests that, allowing for the three-month lag, floating-rate debt is a natural hedge for our revenue sensitivity to interest rates—that is, we are in the strongest position to pay interest when interest rates are high, and we are in the weakest position to pay interest when interest rates are low. This point has been completely neglected in our past financing decisions. I am convinced that we could greatly reduce the firm's overall interest-rate sensitivity if we revamp our financing strategy to incorporate the offsetting natures of these risks.

Despite the treasurer's occasional protestations, the interest-rate character of our debt has never been a major issue for this airline because the firm has, from its beginning, employed very little debt in its capital structure. This, however, will soon change. Our recent decision to replace 70 percent of our planes over the next four years will require a net cash outlay of almost $2 billion. Projected cash flows are such that internally generated financing will only be able to cover about 30 percent of our needs. Thus, we must tap the capital markets for $1.4 billion over the next four years. My suggestion is that we raise $0.4 billion by selling additional equity and that we raise the remaining $1 billion by the sale of debt. I have arrived at these numbers with two thoughts in mind. First, after adding debt and equity in

the proportions suggested, our capital structure will be approximately 34 percent debt and 66 percent equity. While our leverage will increase, and I know management is loath to leverage up, the other risk-management measures I am suggesting should more than offset the additional risk from the increase in financial leverage. I would also point out that this debt ratio is still low by current industry standards. (In June 1991, our industry, on average, employed a capital structure consisting of 50 percent debt.) Second, this amount of debt, if all our debt is converted to a floating-rate character, will be just sufficient to eliminate the effect of interest rates on sales revenue. I should point out, however, that the correlation between conventional floating rate interest rates and ticket revenues is only about 0.58 and thus the residual basis risk will be considerable.

We can either sell the debt as floating-rate debt directly or we can sell it as fixed-rate debt and then employ an interest-rate swap to convert it to floating-rate debt. I have illustrated the latter approach in Exhibit 10-12. In either case, we can maximize the interest-rate risk offset by advancing the reset date by three months. For example, suppose that we issue floating-rate debt with quarterly payments tied to three-month LIBOR. For purposes of illustration, suppose that the payment dates are March 15, June 15, September 15, and December 15 of each year. If the debt is conventional, then on June 15 we would pay our debt holders the three-month LIBOR rate that prevailed on March 15. Similarly, on September 15, we would pay our debt holders the three-month LIBOR rate that prevailed on June 15. What I am suggesting is that instead of this usual payment scheme, we advance the time frame for rate resets by three months. Thus, on June 15, we would pay the three-month LIBOR rate prevailing on June 15. On September 15, we would pay the three-month LIBOR rate prevailing on September 15. This is a relatively

EXHIBIT 10-12

Using an Interest-rate swap to convert the Interest-character of debt

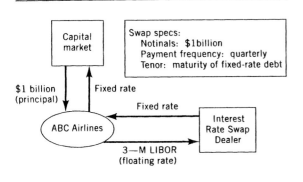

EXHIBIT 10-13

EPS with floating-rate debt used to offset interest-rate risk

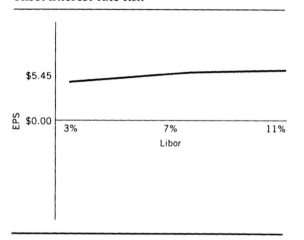

EXHIBIT 10-14

EPS with all fixed-rate debt financing

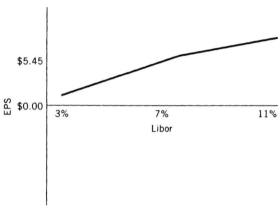

minor twist on conventional floating-rate debt. If we advance the remaining dates as I am suggesting, the correlation between the floating rate of interest and our revenues rises to 0.67 from 0.58 and, therefore, there is less basis risk.

The choice of selling debt directly as floating-rate debt or as fixed-rate debt swapped into floating-rate debt depends on the all-in cost of these financing alternatives.[4] Under current market conditions, a fixed-rate issuance with swap into floating rate is more cost effective by about 60 basis points. This situation may change and we should remain flexible. Our existing fixed-rate debt can also be swapped into floating-rate debt.

---

[4]All-in cost is a more accurate way to measure the true cost of a debt financing than is the coupon rate. The coupon rate measures the interest cost of the debt, but it ignores the flotation costs, the cost of any credit enhancements employed, administrative costs, and other incidental costs associated with issuing and servicing debt. The all-in cost takes all costs into consideration and expresses the cost as a percentage annual rate. For a fuller discussion of all-in cost and its calculation, see Marshall and Bansal (1992) or Kapner and Marshall (1990).

To help you visualize my thinking on this, I have examined the EPS performance of the firm with respect to fluctuations in six-month LIBOR, assuming that we issue floating-rate debt. My calculations take into consideration the interest cost of the debt but also the impact on sales revenue of fluctuations in interest rates. For comparison, I have also examined this same relationship if we fund the equipment purchases with fixed-rate debt (our past method). The risk profiles associated with these two approaches are contrasted in Exhibits 10-13 and 10-14, respectively.

Exchange Rate Risk

Our transatlantic routes to London, Paris, and Frankfurt have only proven marginally profitable, and some members of management have suggested retrenching by selling off our international routes. I disagree. The future of air travel is increasingly international in scope. In addition, many of our domestic passengers fly our domestic routes on the way to connecting with one of our international flights. For example, a customer that flies our New Orleans to Atlanta route in order to connect to our Atlanta to London flight will have less incentive to fly our airline to Atlanta if we cannot deliver the European connection. In addition, the sale of our transatlantic routes will surely shake the confidence of some domestic travellers who may be reluctant to book their travel with us. Remember, as Eastern discovered, in this business perceptions can sometimes be more important than reality.[5]

I have examined the cash flow history of our international routes, and I have concluded that we have two problems. First, it is even more difficult to adjust international airfares than it is to adjust domestic airfares in response to changing market prices. The market prices to which I refer, in this case, are exchange rates. Second, we have marketed our international service almost exclusively to Americans. When the dollar weakens, our ticket sales to Americans traveling to Europe decline precipitously. While for the industry as a whole, this is offset by an increase in the number of Europeans travelling to the United States, we have not positioned ourselves to capture this market. Finally, on our transatlantic routes, a relatively large portion of our expenses are paid in currencies other than the dollar. Specifically, over the last three years, 28 percent of our transatlantic ticket sales were made in currencies other than the dollar, but 40 percent of our expenses on our transatlantic operation were paid in currencies other than the dollar. Thus, we have a significant currency mismatch between our revenues and our expenses. While our non-dollar revenues and expenses currently represent a rather small portion of our overall business, this component can be expected to grow significantly in the years to come.

I have several suggestions. First, we need to assess the impact of exchange rates on the firm's revenues in dollars, after adjusting for expenses, by way of a formal model of the firm's sensitivity to exchange-rate fluctuations. Second, we need to develop hedges that could be used to offset the exchange-rate risk—including the transactional, the translation, and the competitive risks. The net exposure can then be hedged in currency futures, currency options, forward contracts, or currency swaps. Finally, we should consider a focused marketing effort to capture a larger share of the European travel market. As Freddie Laker proved long ago, Europeans are at least as cost conscious as Americans.[6] I should think that our low-cost image would appeal to Europeans. Building this business would create a natural hedge for some of our exchange-rate risk.

---

[5] In 1986, Eastern Airlines was taken over by Texas Air. Management subsequently sought significant concessions from employees, which led to a serious and prolonged labor strike. Eastern attempted to replace striking employees but could not stem the rupture in its cash flow. Travelers shunned Eastern out of fear that the airline would declare bankruptcy—disrupting their travel plans and, possibly, resulting in the forfeiture of their airfares. The labor strife ended after a transfer of control and management undertook a forceful advertising campaign to persuade travelers to return. Travelers, however, were reluctant to take the risk and the airline failed to attract them back. The sharp rise in oil prices shortly thereafter finished the airline off.

[6] Laker Airlines was the first carrier to exclusively and aggressively market cut-rate transatlantic airfares. Travellers flocked to Laker's inexpensive, no-frills, low-margin airline. In response to this very rapid growth, Laker placed orders for a large number of U.S. built aircraft. Unfortunately for Laker, the aircraft purchases were made in dollars while the airline's revenues were mostly in Sterling and other European currencies. The long lead time between placing an order for aircraft and taking delivery exposed Laker to sizable exchange rate risk which the firm did not hedge. A dramatic strengthening of the dollar after the orders were placed was a major contributing factor to the subsequent demise of Laker Airlines. This is another illustration that efficiency in operation is not enough to assure survival.

Ancillary Benefits of Hedging

Because risk management is new to most of you, I would like to offer some insights on ancillary benefits of hedging. A 1985 survey by Smith and Stulz of managers of widely held, value-maximizing corporations revealed some important but often overlooked benefits of hedging.[7] These benefits may also apply to our firm. According to those respected researchers, managers engage in hedging for three basic reasons. The first explanation is tax related. On average, a firm with less variable before-tax profits will pay less total taxes over time than will a firm with the same average, but more volatile, before-tax profits. This is a direct consequence of the progressive tax structure applicable to U.S. corporations. Thus, less volatile profits imply a higher after-tax corporate value.

Second, Smith and Stulz argue that hedging lowers the probability that the firm will go bankrupt and thus incur bankruptcy costs. Hedging will, therefore, add value by reducing the expected future costs of bankruptcy. On a related point, corporate debt, including our own, often contains protective covenants that limit our maneuverability should we find ourselves in financial distress. Hedging reduces the likelihood of financial distress and, therefore, preserves management flexibility.

The final reason for management hedging is that when management compensation is tied to the market value of the firm, as it surely is at ABC, management has a natural tendency to be more risk averse and, therefore, derive greater personal value from hedging.

I would like to close my report by adding a few, rather obvious, observations. A well-hedged firm can safely operate on a larger scale than an unhedged firm with the same capital base. In addition to the greater potential profits associated with a larger operation, there are, as we all well know, significant economies of scale associated with a larger operation. Finally, lenders, quite rightly, perceive hedged firms as more creditworthy than unhedged firms. Thus, hedged firms often have greater access to debt capital and at lower cost than unhedged firms. All of these benefits accrue to our bottom line and make us more competitive.

The Assignment

1. Develop a payoff for a short position in futures (equivalent to the payoff profile for a short position in forwards and for a one-period payoff profile for a swap for the fixed-rate receiver). Develop a payoff profile for a short call option. What do the authors mean when they say that futures, forwards, swaps, and options trading are zero sum games?

2. Review the individual hedging strategies for hedging oil prices. What are the advantages and disadvantages of each from the airline's perspective?

3. How can the up-front cost of an option-based hedging strategy be reduced? Provide a specific numeric example to illustrate your arguments. If the derivative securities (i.e., futures, swaps, and options) markets are "efficient" then what can we say about the market's assessment of the "present value" of each of these alternatives. Does that necessarily mean that they are equally good for ABC? Why or why not?

4. Explain clearly why Judy Waters concluded that ABC Airlines has an interest-rate risk exposure. What are the sources of this exposure and how does Judy propose to deal with it? Does her strategy seem reasonable? What opportunities does the firm surrender if it adopts Judy's plan?

5. Evaluate Judy's suggestions for dealing with the firm's exchange-rate risk. Can you think

---

[7]See Smith and Stulz (1985).

of any alternative ways of dealing with this risk. If so, what are they?

6. In general, discuss the advantages, both direct and ancillary, of a hedging program. Can you think of any disadvantages of having a hedging program? What are they? Where within the firm do you think that the strategic risk management function belongs? Why?

References

1. CHAN, J., ET AL. "The Corporate Treasurer's Perspective: Reading Between the Lines," in *The Financial Engineering Handbook*, by J. F. Marshall and V. K. Bansal, New York: New York Institute of Finance, 1992.

2. MARSHALL, J. F. AND V. K. BANSAL. *The Financial Engineering Handbook*, New York: New York Institute of Finance, 1992.

3. KAPNER, K. R. AND J. F. MARSHALL. *The Swaps Handbook*, New York: New York Institute of Finance, 1990.

4. MARSHALL, J. F. *Futures and Option Contracting*, Cincinnati, OH: South-Western Publishing, 1989.

5. SMITH, C. W. AND R. M. STULZ. The Determinants of Firms' Hedging Policies," Journal of Financial and Quantitative Analysis, 20 (4), pp. 391–406.

Intel Overseas Corporation

Notes Funding, Cost, and the Capital Structure of the Parent and the Subsidiary

HARVEY A. PONIACHEK

Introduction

This case involves notes issuing in 1987 by Intel Overseas Corporation for $110 million at 8.125 percent and a maximum maturity of 10 years. The notes contained an early redemption feature starting on or after March 1994.

The case study seeks to introduce the student to issues concerning notes funding, capital structure, cost of funding, and currency exposure issues. The case study is based on the Intel Corporation and Intel Overseas Corporation prospectus (Form S-3, Registration Statement) that was filed with the SEC. This prospectus was edited here to address information particularly relevant to the issues that are examined in this case study. Appendix 11-1 contains select excerpts from the corporate prospectus.

The Assignment

1. Examine the advantages and disadvantages of borrowing through notes issuing.
2. Assess Intel Overseas Corporation's funding policy (as reflected in its statement of outstanding debt), particularly in terms of the cost and currency exposure. What alternative sources of funds could they have used to yield a greater advantage?
3. Does Intel Overseas Corporation have an independent funding policy, or is its funding dictated by Intel Corporation?
4. Compare and contrast the capital structure of Intel Corporation, Intel Overseas Corporation, and an average company in Standard Industrial Classification (SIC) Code 3674 as shown in Appendix 11-2. (Intel Corporation is classified under SIC Codes 3674 and 3573. However, financial information for comparable firms in the industry was available only for SIC Code 3674.)

APPENDIX 11-1

Intel Corporation and Intel Overseas Corporation[1]

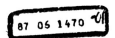
87 06 1470

SIGNED COPY

TOTAL OF SEQUENTIALLY NUMBERED PAGES 117
EXHIBIT INDEX ON SEQUENTIALLY NUMBERED PAGE 66

Registration No. 33-11902

SECURITIES AND EXCHANGE COMMISSION
Washington, D.C. 20549

RECEIVED
MAR 27 1987
Bechtel Information Services
33 - Gaithersburg, Maryland

Amendment No. 2
to
Form S-3(a)
REGISTRATION STATEMENT
Under
THE SECURITIES ACT OF 1933

33-11902

INTEL CORPORATION	★ INTEL OVERSEAS CORPORATION
(Exact name of Guarantor of the Notes and Issuer of the Warrants and Capital Stock as specified in its charter)	(Exact name of Issuer of the Notes as specified in its charter)
California	California
(State or other jurisdiction of incorporation or organization)	(State or other jurisdiction of incorporation or organization)
94-1672743	77-0053722
(I.R.S. Employer Identification No.)	(I.R.S. Employer Identification No.)

3065 Bowers Avenue, Santa Clara, California 95051 (408) 987-8080
(Address and telephone number of Registrants' principal executive offices)

F. THOMAS DUNLAP, JR., ESQ.
3065 Bowers Avenue, Santa Clara, California 95051 (408) 987-8080
(Name, address and telephone number of Registrants' agent for service)

Copies to:

WILLIAM D. SHERMAN, ESQ.	ALAN K. AUSTIN, ESQ.
TODD H. BAKER, ESQ.	DANA M. KETCHAM, ESQ.
WILLIAM I. SCHWARTZ, ESQ.	ELIZABETH BARTH, ESQ.
MORRISON & FOERSTER	ORRICK, HERRINGTON & SUTCLIFFE
345 California Street	600 Montgomery Street
San Francisco, CA 94104-2105	San Francisco, California 94111
(415) 434-7000	(415) 392-1122

Approximate date of commencement of proposed sale to the public:
As soon as practicable after the effective date of this Registration Statement.

If the only securities being registered on this Form are being offered pursuant to dividend or interest reinvestment plans, please check the following box. ☐

If any of the securities being registered on this Form are to be offered on a delayed or continuous basis pursuant to Rule 415 under the Securities Act of 1933, other than securities offered only in connection with dividend or interest reinvestment plans, check the following box. ☒*

* Only the Capital Stock is being offered pursuant to Rule 415.

This Registration Statement shall hereafter become effective in accordance with Section 8(a) of the Securities Act of 1933 on such date as the Commission, acting pursuant to said Section 8(a), may determine.

PROSPECTUS

$110,000,000

INTEL OVERSEAS CORPORATION

8⅛% Notes Due March 15, 1997

Payment of principal of and interest on the Notes
is unconditionally guaranteed by

 **CORPORATION**

Interest on the Notes (the "Notes") of Intel Overseas Corporation ("Intel Overseas") will be payable semiannually on March 15 and September 15 of each year beginning September 15, 1987. The payment of the principal of and interest on the Notes will be fully and unconditionally guaranteed by Intel Corporation ("Intel"). Intel's guarantees of the Notes will rank equally with other unsecured and unsubordinated indebtedness of Intel. The Notes are redeemable on or after March 15, 1994, in whole or in part, at the option of Intel Overseas, at 100% of the principal amount plus accrued interest to the date of redemption. See "Description of Notes."

Concurrently with this offering, Intel is offering by a separate prospectus Warrants to purchase an aggregate of 3,500,000 shares of its Capital Stock at a price of $45 per share. See "Concurrent Offering."

THESE SECURITIES HAVE NOT BEEN APPROVED OR DISAPPROVED BY THE SECURITIES AND EXCHANGE COMMISSION NOR HAS THE COMMISSION PASSED UPON THE ACCURACY OR ADEQUACY OF THIS PROSPECTUS. ANY REPRESENTATION TO THE CONTRARY IS A CRIMINAL OFFENSE.

	Price to Public(1)	Underwriting Discounts and Commissions(2)	Proceeds to Intel Overseas(1)(3)
Per Note	99.63%	.65%	98.98%
Total..........................	$110,000,000	$715,000	$109,285,000

(1) Plus accrued interest, if any, on the Notes from April 1, 1987 to the date of delivery.

(2) See "Underwriting."

(3) Before deducting expenses estimated to be approximately $376,500.

The Notes offered by this Prospectus are offered by the Underwriters subject to prior sale, to withdrawal, cancellation or modification of the offer without notice, to delivery to and acceptance by the Underwriters and to certain other conditions. It is anticipated that delivery of the Notes will be made at the offices of Shearson Lehman Brothers Inc., New York, New York on or about April 1, 1987.

Shearson Lehman Brothers Inc.

L.F. Rothschild, Unterberg, Towbin. Inc.

Salomon Brothers Inc

March 25, 1987

SOURCE: Adopted from Intel Corporation and Intel Overseas Corporation Form S-3 Registration Statement, dated March 1987.

[1]Intel's Form S-3 Registration Statement was edited by the author of this case due to space limitations, and to focus the information on the issues of concern in this case. Selected excerpts are hereby available.

This summary is qualified in its entirety by the more detailed information appearing elsewhere in this Prospectus.

SUMMARY OF THE OFFERING

Terms of the Notes

Notes $110,000,000 $8\frac{1}{8}$% Notes Due March 13, 1997 of Intel Overseas (the "Notes").

Interest $6\frac{1}{4}$% per annum payable semiannually on March 15 and September 15, beginning September 15, 1987.

Guarantee The Notes are fully and unconditionally guaranteed by Intel. The guarantees will rank equally with other unsecured and unsubordinated indebtedness of Intel.

Redemption The Notes are redeemable on or after March 15, 1994, in whole or in part, at the option of Intel Overseas, at 100% of the principal amount, plus accrued interest to the date of redemption.

Trustee Wachovia Bank and Trust Company, N.A.

Use of Proceeds

The net proceeds from the sale of the Notes will be used by Intel and Intel Overseas for working capital purposes.

Concurrent Offering

Warrants of Intel to purchase 3,500,000 shares of its Capital Stock at an exercise price of $45 per share.

Intel

Intel Corporation (together with its subsidiaries, unless the context otherwise requires "Intel" or the "Company") designs, develops, manufactures and markets advanced semiconductor very large-scale integrated (VLSI) circuit components, and computer systems incorporating these components. Intel conducts worldwide operations principally in the United States, Israel, Western Europe, the Pacific Basin and Japan. At December 27, 1986, Intel employed approximately 15,200 persons.

Intel's products include complex electronic circuits constructed within a "chip" of silicon by a series of chemical and physical processing steps. Intel's VLSI products are primarily (1) microprocessors, which control the flow of information into and out of memory storage and process the information according to the program being executed, (2) microcomputer peripheral circuits used with a microprocessor to assemble microcomputer systems, (3) memory circuits used in data processing applications, including erasable programmable read only memories (EPROMs) and (4) microcontrollers, which include a central processing unit (CPU), random access memory (RAM), programmable memory and input–output devices on the same chip. In 1986, Intel entered the application specific integrated circuit ("ASIC") market to design, develop, manufacture and market VLSI products utilizing Intel technology for custom and semi-custom product applications.

Intel also engages in several VLSI-related activities such as the development, manufacture and sale of board-level products incorporating a wide variety of VLSI components. Other products include microcomputer design aids, microcommunications products, personal computer add-on boards, fully integrated microcomputer systems, and related software.

Intel's products are used in many electronic applications, including computers, terminals, computer peripheral equipment, industrial controls, and a wide variety of miscellaneous electronic equipment. Most of Intel's products are of its own design.

In early 1983, International Business Machines Corporation ("IBM") bought $250 million of newly issued Intel Capital Stock, constituting approximately 12 percent of Intel's then outstanding Capital Stock. In 1983 and 1984, IBM purchased, principally on the open market, approximately an additional 8 percent of Intel's outstanding Capital Stock, thus bringing its total ownership to approximately 20 percent. IBM has agreed to a 30 percent maximum limitation on its ownership of Intel's Capital Stock and to other limitations designed to assure Intel's independence; however, such agreement permits IBM to purchase shares at market value from Intel to maintain its percentage ownership interest. IBM will be permitted, subject to certain exceptions, to purchase shares of Intel Capital Stock at market value concurrently with Intel's issuance of shares of Capital Stock upon exercise of the Warrants being offered concurrently herewith. Intel is unable to determine, however, whether IBM will seek to exercise its right to purchase any such shares. In February 1986, IBM issued and sold $300,000,000 principal amount of its $6\frac{3}{8}$ percent Exchangeable Subordinated Debentures Due 1996 (the "IBM Debentures"), which are exchangeable for an aggregate of 7,792,208 shares of Intel's Capital Stock owned by IBM at an exchange price of $38.50 for each share of Intel Capital Stock. The IBM Debentures may be redeemed at the option of IBM at any time on or after March 1, 1989 at declining premiums. The IBM Debentures may also be redeemed prior to March 1, 1989 at 105 percent of their principal amount, in the event the market price of Intel Capital Stock has been at least 130 percent of the exchange price for a specified period.

Intel was incorporated in California on July 18, 1968. Its principal executive offices are located at 3065 Bowers Avenue, Santa Clara, California 95051 and its telephone number is (408) 987-8080.

Intel Overseas

Intel Overseas Corporation ("Intel Overseas"), a wholly-owned subsidiary of Intel, was incorporated in California on December 31, 1984. In January 1985, Intel Overseas issued ¥12.5 billion (approximate U.S. dollar equivalent of $49 million) principal amount of $6\frac{3}{8}$% Yen Guaranteed Bonds Due 1992, of which a U.S. dollar equivalent of approximately $32 million remained outstanding at December 27, 1986. In May 1985, Intel Overseas issued $236,500,000 principal amount of Zero Coupon Notes Due 1995 (the "Zero Coupon Notes"). The Zero Coupon Notes were issued as units (the "Units") with warrants to purchase 5,912,500 shares of Capital Stock of Intel at $40 per share (the "1995 $40 Warrants"). In June 1986, Intel Overseas issued $16,270,000 of Yen Promissory Notes Due 1992. In addition to the offering of Notes described in this Prospectus, Intel Overseas engages in domestic sales financings and other special financings and investments. Its principal executive offices are located at 3065 Bowers Avenue, Santa Clara,

California 95051 and its telephone number is (408) 987-8080.

Concurrent Offering

Concurrently with this offering, Intel is by a separate prospectus offering warrants (the "Warrants" or the "1992 $45 Warrants") to purchase an aggregate of 3,500,000 shares of its Capital Stock at an exercise price of $45 per share, subject to adjustment in certain events. The Warrants may be exercised at any time prior to their expiration at the close of business on March 15, 1992, unless previously accelerated by Intel. The expiration of the Warrants may be accelerated by Intel on or after March 15, 1989 in the event the market price

of Intel's Capital Stock has been at least 140% of the then effective exercise price on any 20 trading days within a period of 30 consecutive trading days.

Use of Proceeds

The net proceeds from the offering of the Notes and the concurrent offering of the Warrants will be used by Intel and Intel Overseas for working capital purposes. Pending use, the proceeds will be invested in short-term, interest-bearing securities. See "Concurrent Offering" and "Management's Discussion and Analysis of Financial Condition and Results of Operations of Intel."

CAPITALIZATION OF INTEL

The consolidated capitalization of Intel at December 27, 1986, and as adjusted to give effect to the offering of the Notes made hereby and the concurrent offering by Intel of the Warrants, is set forth below:

	Outstanding	As Adjusted
	(thousands)	
Long Term Debt[a]:		
8% Industrial Revenue Bonds Due 2013[b]	$ 80,000	$ 80,000
7.95% Industrial Revenue Bonds Due 2013[b]	30,000	30,000
$6\frac{3}{8}$% Yen Guaranteed Bonds Due 1992	32,279	32,279
Zero Coupon Notes Due May 15, 1995	90,840	90,840
$8\frac{1}{8}$% Notes Due March 15, 1997	—	110,000
Yen Promissory Notes Due 1992	16,270	16.270
Yen Japanese Government Bonds Due 1992	20,211	20,211
Other	17,000	17,000
Total long term debt	286,600	396,600
Shareholders' Equity:		
Capital Stock, without par value: 20,000,000 shares authorized; 117,772,906 shares issued and outstanding	743,100	743,100
1995 $40 Warrants to purchase 5,912,500 shares of Capital Stock	27,136	27,136

(Continued)

	Outstanding	As Adjusted
	(thousands)	
1992 $45 Warrants to purchase 3,500,000 shares of Capital Stock[c]	—	33,250
Retained earnings	504,991	504,991
Total shareholders' equity	1,275,227	1,308,477
Total capitalization	$1,561,827	$1,705,077

[a]See Notes to Consolidated Financial Statements (Borrowings).

[b]Adjustable and redeemable (at the option of either Intel or the bondholder) every five years beginning 1988 through 2008.

[c]See "Concurrent Offering."

CAPITALIZATION OF INTEL OVERSEAS

The capitalization of Intel Overseas at December 27, 1986, and as adjusted to give effect to the offering made hereby, is set forth below:

	Outstanding	As Adjusted
	(thousands)	
Long Term Debt:		
$6\frac{5}{8}$ Yen Guaranteed Bonds Due 1992	$ 32,279	$ 32,279
Zero Coupon Notes Due May 15, 1995	90,840	90,840
$8\frac{1}{8}$% Notes Due March 15, 1997	—	110,000
Yen Promissory Notes Due 1992	16,270	16,270
Total long term debt	139,389	249,389
Shareholder's Equity:		
Capital Stock, without par value: 1,000 shares authorized, issued and outstanding	28,500	28,500
Retained earnings (deficit)	(5,621)	(5,621)
Total shareholder's equity	22,879	22,879
Total capitalization	$162,268	$272,268

SELECTED FINANCIAL DATA

The selected financial information of Intel presented in the table below is qualified in its entirety by and should be read in conjunction with the consolidated financial statements and related notes incorporated by reference in Intel's Annual Report on Form 10-K for the year ended December 28, 1985 and the consolidated financial statements and related notes for the year ended December 27, 1986 included elsewhere herein. The reports of Arthur Young & Company with respect to the financial statements for the years ended December 28, 1985 and December 27, 1986 are incorporated by reference or included elsewhere herein. The selected financial information for each of the five years in the period ended December 27, 1986 (except for the ratios of earnings to fixed charges) has been derived from audited consolidated financial statements which have been examined by Arthur Young & Company.

	Years Ended				
	Dec. 31, 1982	Dec. 31, 1983	Dec. 31, 1984	Dec. 28, 1985	Dec. 27, 1986
	(thousands except share, per share and ratio data)				
Net revenues	$899,812	$1,121,943	$1,629,332	$1,364,982	$1,265,011
Cost of sales	541,928	624,296	882,738	943,435	860,680
Research and development	130,801	142,295	180,168	195,171	228,250
Marketing, general and administrative	198,640	216,635	315,976	286,545	311,340
Restructuring of operations	—	—	—	—	60,000
Operating costs and expenses	871,369	983,226	1,378,882	1,425,151	1,460,270
Operating income (loss)	28,443	138,717	250,450	(60,169)	(195,259)
Interest and other	1,903	39,738	47,699	54,721	20,625
Income (loss) before taxes and extraordinary item	30,346	178,455	298,149	(5.448)	(174,634)
Provision (benefit) for taxes	300	62,344	99,960[a]	(7,018)	8,630
Income (loss) before extraordinary item	30,046	116,111	198,189	1,570	(183,284)
Extraordinary item	—	—	—	—	10,119
Net income (loss)	$ 30,046	$ 116,111	$ 198,189	$ 1,570	$ (173,165)
Earnings (loss) per capital and capital equivalent share					
Income (loss) before extraordinary item	$.32	$1.05	$1.70	$.01	$(1.57)
Extraordinary item	—	—	—	—	.09
Net income (loss) per share	$ .32	$1.05	$1.70	$.01	$(1.48)
Capital shares and equivalents	92,542	110,544	116,765	117,850	117,025
Ratio of earnings to fixed charges[b]	2.2 ×	8.3 ×	12.6 ×	—	—

[a]The provision for income taxes for the year ended December 31, 1984 includes the reversal of $19.3 million of deferred tax on prior years' Domestic International Sales Corporation income. The Tax Reform Act of 1984 provided for the forgiveness of such deferred tax for the years 1972 through 1984.

[b]The ratio of earnings to fixed charges is computed by dividing earnings before taxes and extraordinary item and fixed charges by fixed charges. Fixed charges consist of interest expense, including amortization of related underwriting fees, capitalized interest and the estimated interest component of rent expense. Results were inadequate to cover fixed charges by $11.7 million and $177.1 million for the years ended December 28, 1985 and December 27, 1986, respectively. Intel believes that its anticipated cash flows together with its existing cash balances will be sufficient to service its fixed charges in the future.

Management's Discussion and Analysis of Financial Condition and Results of Operations of Intel

Overview

Intel's large operating loss for 1986 is the result of continuing weakness in the semiconductor marketplace, restructuring actions taken by management to improve manufacturing efficiency, and continued high investments in strategic programs. Although unit demand improved over 1985, continued industry overcapacity resulted in pressure on selling prices and a decline in revenue from the previous year. In response to these conditions, manufacturing plants were closed and several others downsized, worldwide employment was reduced by 15 percent from 1985 levels and a decision was made to sell the Company's bubble memory business. These actions resulted in a $60 million charge to operations and accounted for about one third of the year's operating loss.

Results of Operations

1986 revenues of $1.3 billion were 7 percent below 1985's $1.4 billion level and 22% below 1984's record $1.6 billion. A recovery from the severe semiconductor industry downturn began in 1986 as revenues increased in each of the last three quarters from the immediately preceding quarter, but was not strong enough to produce year-to-year growth. The downturn began in late 1984 as a slowdown in the growth of the small-computer market allowed semiconductor supply to surpass demand and led to steep price declines in 1985. The pricing pressure was intensified by the "dumping" of certain memory devices (including EPROMs competitive with the Company's products) on the market by Japanese suppliers. The price declines of 1985 moderated in 1986, and 1986 unit shipments were up from the prior year.

However, the combination of industry excess capacity and a still-weak computer market continued to have a depressing effect on 1986 revenue performance as evidenced by a $200 million decrease in sales to IBM from 1985 to 1986. The Company delivered more units to IBM in 1985 pursuant to a contract entered into in the more demand-driven 1984 period. That portion of 1985 deliveries was left in inventory carried by IBM through some of 1986. Purchases by IBM have recovered somewhat in late 1986.

Gross margin was 32 percent in 1986 up 1 percent from 1985 but down 14 percent from 1984. The continuing gross margin weakness is the result of the persistently low selling prices and the high cost of excess capacity. In a move to reduce excess production capacity and decrease operating costs, the Company closed its Barbados component assembly plant, phased out its Puerto Rico test plant and reduced the workforce at its other Puerto Rico facilities. Even if unit volumes grow, new equipment with greater utilization rates should enable the Company to meet such unit volumes with the remaining plants and thereby improve gross margin performance.

The 1986 operating loss of $195 million represents the Company's second consecutive year of operating losses. The 1986 operating results were $135 million worse than 1985 and $445 million worse than 1984's profit of $250 million. The 1986 operation loss increased over 1985 due mainly to the $60 million charge for restructuring of operations, continuing weakness in the semiconductor industry, and increased spending levels for research and development, marketing and administration described below. The dramatic change from 1984 reflects the industry-wide semiconductor slump which began in late 1984 and was characterized by weak demand, falling prices and industry-wide excess capacity. Marketing and administrative expenses of $311 million in 1986 were up 9 percent from 1985, back to about 1984 levels, and research and development expenses of $228 million were 18 percent of revenue in 1986, up from 14 percent in 1985 and 11 percent in 1984 as investments in strategic programs (such as ASIC and Intel Development Organization) continued at high levels. The Company expects investments in emerging growth areas of the industry to be important additions to the Company's portfolio and play a significant role in its future.

Interest and other income of $21 million is down $34 million from 1985, which was up $7 million from 1984. The decline from 1985 is due to a combination of higher average borrowing balances, lower interest rates on investments and a decrease in gains on sales of investments. The increase in 1985 over 1984 was due primarily to $15 million in gains on the sale of long-term marketable securities and income from other investments in 1985.

Despite the pretax loss for 1986, the provision for foreign income taxes exceeded the benefits provided by tax credits and resulted in a worldwide tax provision in 1986 of $9 million, versus a benefit of $7 million in 1985. In 1984, a year of significant profits, the effective tax rate was 34 percent which reflects a normal tax provision reduced by the one-time reversal of $19 million of deferred tax on prior years income of the Company's Domestic International Sales Corporations (DISCs). Without the DISC impact, the effective tax rate in 1984 would have been 40 percent.

The extraordinary gain in 1986 was a result of the repayment of approximately $39 million of short-term and long-term debt owed to an agency of a foreign government.

Financial Condition

Although the semiconductor industry weakness continued throughout 1986 and the Company's results of operations have been severely impacted by the economic environment, the Company's financial condition remains strong. The Company has working capital, cash and investments sufficient to maintain its operations in the current uncertain business climate and management believes that the Company is in a solid financial position.

Working capital of $649 million represents a decrease of $68 million from the prior year. The decrease is due primarily to continued operational losses and capital additions, offset by depreciation and asset retirements. Capital additions to property, plant and equipment, while still substantial at $155 million, were cut significantly from 1985's $236 million and 1984's $388 million levels as the slowdown has reduced the need for capital expansion. As of December 27, 1986, cash and short-term and long-term investments of $582 million remain substantial. Intel also has established foreign and domestic lines of credit totaling approximately $600 million and a commercial paper program under which it was authorized to borrow up to $300 million at the end of 1986. This ceiling was subsequently raised to $400 million. As of December 27, 1986, Intel had short-term borrowings outstanding of $94.7 million under the lines of credit, and had no obligations outstanding under the commercial paper program. The balance of cash and investments, together with the lines of credit and commercial paper program will allow the Company to continue supporting strategic investments as it enters 1987. As of December 27, 1986, the Company's long-term debt-to-equity ratio was approximately 0.2, virtually unchanged from the prior year. During 1986 the Company repaid approximately $39 million of short-term and long-term debt owed to an agency of a foreign government. In addition, the Company entered into several borrowing agreements involving Japanese Yen Promissory Notes and Japanese Government Bonds.

Description of Notes

General

Intel Overseas will pay interest on the Notes on March 15 and September 15 of each year, beginning September 15, 1987, at the rate per annum shown on the cover page of this Prospectus to persons who are registered holders ("Holders") of the Notes on the March 1 or September 1 next preceding the interest payment date. Intel Overseas may pay principal and interest by check and may mail an interest check to the Holder's registered address. There will be no sinking fund for payment of the Notes.

The Notes will be unsecured obligations of Intel Overseas. The guarantees of the Notes (the "Guarantees") will rank equally with other unsecured and unsubordinated indebtedness of Intel. The Notes are to be issued under an Indenture (the "Indenture"), dated as of May 1, 1963 among Intel Overseas, Intel and Wachovia Bank and Trust Company, N.A., as trustee (the "Trustee"). The Indenture does not limit the amount of indebtedness that may be incurred by Intel Overseas or Intel, whether secured or unsecured. In addition to the Notes, Intel Overseas may issue from time to time other series of debt securities which are guaranteed by Intel consisting of notes, bonds, debentures or other evidences of indebtedness, but such other series will be separate and independent from the Notes. Some of Intel's assets are owned by subsidiaries, and therefore, Intel's rights and the rights of creditors of Intel, including the Holders, to participate in the distribution of assets of any subsidiary upon its liquidation or recapitalization would be subject to prior claims of the subsidiaries' creditors.

Intel will take such steps as are necessary to ensure that at all times it will own, directly or indirectly, all the outstanding voting stock of Intel Overseas.

Principal will be payable at the Corporate Trust Office of the Trustee in Winston-Salem, North Carolina, or at the office or agency of Intel Overseas maintained for such purpose in New York City. The Notes are to be issued only in registered form without coupons in denominations of $1,000 and any integral multiple of $1,000.

A copy of the indenture has been filed as an exhibit to the Registration Statement of which this Prospectus is a part. The statements herein relating to the Notes and the Indenture are summaries and are subject to the detailed provisions of the Indenture, to which reference is hereby made for a complete statement of those provisions. Whenever particular provisions of the Indenture or terms defined therein are referred to herein, those provisions or definitions are incorporated by reference as a part of the statements made, and the statements are qualified in their entirety by that reference. Persons desiring to obtain copies of the Indenture may do so by contacting F. Thomas Donlap, Jr., Secretary, Intel Corporation, 3065 Bowers Avenue, Santa Clara, California 95051 (telephone (408) 987-8080).

Guarantees

Intel will fully and unconditionally guarantee the due and punctual payment of the principal of and interest on the Notes when and as the same shall become due and payable whether at maturity, upon acceleration or otherwise.

Redemption

The Notes may be redeemed on or after March 15, 1994, in whole or in part, at the option of Intel Overseas, at 100 percent of the principal amount, plus accrued and unpaid interest to the date of redemption.

The Trustee

The Indenture will contain certain limitations on the right of the Trustee, as a creditor of Intel, to obtain payment of claims in certain cases, or to realize on certain property received in respect of any such claim as security or otherwise. (Section 613)

Events of Default and Notice Thereof

The following events are defined in the Indenture as "Events of Default" with respect to the Notes: (a) failure to pay principal of any Note when due; (b) failure to pay interest on any Note for a period of 30 days or more; (c) failure to perform any other covenant of Intel Overseas or Intel in the Indenture (other than a covenant included in the Indenture solely for the benefit of a series of debt securities other than the Notes), continued for 60 days after written notice given to Intel Overseas and Intel by the Trustee or the Holders of at least 25 percent in principal amount of the Notes outstanding and affected thereby; (d) any default by Intel under any Public Debt (as defined below) which default constitutes default in payment of principal or results in acceleration of any indebtedness for Public Debt, if such Public Debt has not been discharged or becomes no longer due and payable or such acceleration has not been rescinded or annulled within 10 days after written notice given to Intel by the Trustee or the Holders of at least 25 percent in principal amount of the outstanding Notes; and (e) certain events in bankruptcy, insolvency or reorganization. (Section 501) If an Event of Default with respect to Notes at the time outstanding shall occur and be continuing, then either the Trustee or the Holders of at least 25 percent in principal amount of the outstanding Notes may declare the Notes to be due and payable immediately; provided, however, that under certain circumstances the Holders of a majority in aggregate principal amount of outstanding Notes may rescind and annul such declaration and its consequences. (Section 502)

"Public Debt" means any indebtedness for money borrowed pursuant to debt securities which are or were offered to the public (1) pursuant to a registration statement filed under the Securities Act of 1933, (2) outside the United States or (3) in connection with a tax exempt financing.

The Indenture provides that the Trustee, within 90 days after the occurrence of a default with respect to the Notes, shall give to the Holders of the Notes notice of all uncured defaults known to it (the term default to mean the events specified above without grace periods); provided that, except in the case of default in the payment of principal of any Note, the Trustee shall be protected in withholding such notice if it in good faith determines that the withholding of such notice is in the interest of the Holders of Notes. (Section 602)

Intel Overseas and Intel are required to furnish to the Trustee annually a statement by certain officers of Intel Overseas or Intel, as the case may be, to the effect that to the best of their knowledge neither Intel Overseas nor Intel, as the case may be, is in violation of any of its covenants under the Indenture, or, if so, specifying each such default. (Section 1007)

The Holders of a majority in principal amount of outstanding Notes affected (voting as one class) will have the right, subject to certain limitations, to direct the time, method and place of conducting any proceeding for any remedy available to the Trustee or exercising any trust or power conferred on the Trustee with respect to the Notes, and to waive certain defaults. (Sections 512 and 513)

The Indenture provides that in case an Event of Default shall occur and be continuing, the Trustee shall exercise such of its rights and powers under the Indenture and use the same degree of care and skill in their exercise, as a prudent man would exercise or use under the circumstances in the conduct of his own affairs. (Section 601) Subject to such provisions, the Trustee will be under no obligation to exercise any of its rights or powers under the Indenture at the request of any of the Holders of the Notes unless they shall have offered to the Trustee reasonable security or indemnity against the costs, expenses and liabilities which might be incurred by it in compliance with such request. (Section 603)

Modification of the Indenture

Modification and amendments of the Indenture may be made by Intel Overseas, Intel and the Trustee, with the consent of the Holders of not less than 66-2/3 percent in aggregate principal amount of the outstanding Notes if they are affected by the modification or amendment, provided that no such modification or amendment may without the consent of each Holder of the Notes affected thereby: (1) change the stated maturity date of the principal of any such Note; (2) reduce the principal amount of any Note; (3) change the place or currency of payment of principal or interest, if any, on any such Note; (4) impair the right to institute suit for the enforcement of any such payment on or with respect to any Note; (5) modify or affect in any manner adverse to the holders of the Notes the terms and conditions of the Guarantees; (6) reduce the above-stated percentage of holders of Notes necessary to modify or amend the Indenture; or (7) modify the foregoing requirements or reduce the percentage of outstanding Notes necessary to waive compliance with certain provisions of the Indenture or for waiver of certain defaults. (Section 902)

Defeasance of Certain Covenants

The Notes provide Intel Overseas and Intel with the option to omit to comply with certain restrictive covenants described in Sections 1004 through 1006 of the Indenture. Intel Overseas, in order to exercise such option, will be required to deposit with the Trustee money and/or U.S. Government Obligations (as defined) which through the payment of principal and interest thereof in accordance with their terms will provide money in an amount sufficient to pay the principal of the Notes on their stated maturity in accordance with the terms of the Indenture and the Notes. Intel

Overseas will also be required to deliver to the Trustee an opinion of counsel to the effect that the deposit and related covenant defeasance will not cause the holders of the Notes to recognize income gain or loss for Federal income tax purposes. (Section 1008)

Recent Development

On February 6, 1987, Moody's Investors Service lowered the senior debt rating of Intel from A1 to A2. Intel's senior debt is rated A by Standard & Poor's Corporation. Intel's commercial paper is rated Prime-I and A1 by Moody's and Standard & Poor's, respectively.

Underwriting

The Underwriters, for whom Shearson Lehman Brothers Inc., L. F. Rothschild, Unterberg, Towbin, Inc. and Salomon Brothers Inc. are acting as representatives (the "Representatives"), have severally agreed, subject to the terms and conditions contained in, the Underwriting Agreement, a copy of which is filed as an exhibit to the Registration Statement to purchase from Intel Overseas the Notes offered hereby. The principal amount of Notes to be purchased by each of the Underwriters is as follows:

Underwriter	Principal Amount
Shearson Lehman Brothers Inc.	$ 28,000,000
L. F. Rothschild, Unterberg, Towbin, Inc.	28,000,000
Salomon Brothers Inc.	28,000,000
The First Boston Corporation	6,500,000
Goldman, Sachs & Co.	6,500,000
Merrill Lynch, Pierce, Fenner & Smith Incorporated	6,500,000
Morgan Stanley & Co. Incorporated	6,500,000
Total	$110,000,000

The Underwriting Agreement provides that the obligations of the Underwriters are subject to certain conditions precedent, and that the Underwriters will be obligated to purchase all of the Notes to be purchased by them pursuant to such Underwriting Agreement if any such Notes are purchased.

Intel Overseas has been advised by the Representatives that the Underwriters propose to offer the Notes to the public initially at the offering price set forth on the cover page of this Prospectus and to certain selected dealers (who may include the Underwriters) at such price less a concession not to exceed 0.4 percent of the principal amount of the Notes. The Underwriters and such selected dealers may reallow a concession to certain other deals not to exceed 0.25 percent of the principal amount of the Notes. After the initial public offering, the public offering price, the concession to selected dealers and the reallowance to other dealers may be changed by the Representatives.

Shearson Lehman Brothers Inc., L. F. Rothschild, Unterberg, Towbin, Inc. and Salomon Brothers Inc. have also agreed to the concurrent purchase from Intel of Warrants to purchase 3,500,000 shares of Intel's Capital Stock and to offer such Warrants to the public. All such Warrants will be purchased by such underwriters if any are purchased. See "Concurrent Offering."

Certain of the Underwriters may, from time to time, be customers of, engage in transactions with, and perform services for Intel and Intel Overseas in the ordinary course of business.

In the Underwriting Agreement, Intel and Intel Overseas have agreed to indemnify the Underwriters with respect to certain liabilities, including liabilities under the Securities Act of 1933, as amended.

The Underwriters have severally advised the Company that they initially intend to make a market in the Notes, but there can be no assurance that all or any of them will continue to do so.

Experts

The consolidated financial statements and related schedules of Intel Corporation incorporated by reference or included in Intel's Annual Report on Form 10-K for the year ended December 28, 1985 and the consolidated financial statements of Intel Corporation for the year ended December 27, 1986 are included elsewhere herein.

CONSOLIDATED BALANCE SHEETS

December 23, 1985 and December 27, 1986

(thousands)

	1985	1986
ASSETS		
Current assets:		
Cash and temporary cash investments	$ 187,911	$ 74,528
Short-term investments (at cost, which approximates market)	173,233	298,696
Accounts receivable, net of allowance for doubtful accounts of $4,498 ($4,656 in 1985)	305,102	298,378

(Continued)

	1985	1986
Inventories	170,758	197,931
Prepaid taxes on income	88,849	105,298
Refundable income taxes	58,655	—
Other current assets	39,402	48,826
Total current assets	1,023,910	1,023,657
Property, plant and equipment:		
Land and buildings	431,183	529,964
Machinery and equipment	725,573	748,020
Construction in progress	181,621	86,081
	1,338,382	1,364,065
Less accumulated depreciation	490,136	384,744
Property, plant and equipment, net	848,246	779,321
Long-term investments		
(at cost, which approximates market)	216,340	209,195
Investment in unconsolidated subsidiary	31,058	54,604
Other non-current assets	12,311	13,289
TOTAL ASSETS	$2,151,865	$2,080,066

LIABILITIES AND SHAREHOLDERS' EQUITY

Current liabilities:		
Short-term debt	$ 88,898	$ 112,055
Accounts payable	36,988	61,987
Deferred income on shipments		
to distributors	72,421	67,367
Accrued compensation and benefits	38,336	45,849
Other accrued liabilities	47,155	72,210
Income taxes payable	2,893	14,814
Total current liabilities	306,691	374,282
Long-term debt	270,831	286,600
Deferred taxes on income	133,956	132,441
Unamortized investment tax credits	18,906	11,516
Commitments and contingencies		
Shareholders' equity:		
Capital stock, no par value,		
200,000 shares authorized,		
117,773 issued		
and outstanding		
in 1986 (116,078 in 1985)	743,325	770,236
Retained earnings	678,156	504,991
Total shareholders' equity	1,421,481	1,275,227
TOTAL LIABILITIES		
AND SHAREHOLDERS' EQUITY	$2,151,865	$2,080,066

Certain 1985 amounts have been reclassified to conform to the 1986 presentation. See accompanying notes.

CONSOLIDATED STATEMENTS OF OPERATIONS

Three Years Ended December 27, 1986

(thousands—except per share amounts)

	1984	1985	1986
Net Revenues	$1,629,332	$1,364,982	$1,265,011
Cost of sales	882,738	943,435	860,580
Research and development	180,168	195,171	228,250
Marketing, general and administrative	315,976	286,545	311,340
Restructuring of operations	—	—	60,000
Operating costs and expenses	1,378,882	1,425,151	1,460,270
Operating income (loss)	250,450	(60,169)	(195,259)
Interest and other	47,699	54,721	20,625
Income (loss) before taxes and extraordinary item	298,149	(5,448)	(174,634)
Provision (benefit) for taxes	99,960	(7,018)	8,650
Income (loss) before extraordinary item	198,189	1,570	(183,284)
Extraordinary gain on debt repayment	—	—	$ 10,119
Net Income (Loss)	$ 198,189	$ 1,570	$(173,165)
Earnings (loss) per capital and capital equivalent share			
Income (loss) before extraordinary item	$ 1.70	$ .01	$ (1.57)
Extraordinary item	—	—	.09
Net income (loss) per share	$ 1.70	$ .01	$ (1.48)
Capital shares and equivalents	116,765	117,550	117,025

See accompanying notes.

CONSOLIDATED STATEMENTS OF SHAREHOLDERS' EQUITY

Three Years Ended December 27, 1986

(thousands)

	CAPITAL STOCK		RETAINED EARNINGS	TOTAL
	NUMBER OF SHARES	AMOUNT		
Balance at December 31, 1983	111,701	$643,343	$478,397	$1,121,740
Proceeds from sales of shares through employee stock plans, tax benefit of $3,678 and other	2,044	37,236	—	37,236
Proceeds from sale of shares	87	2,998	—	2,998
Net Income	—	—	198,189	198,189
Balance at December 31, 1984	113,832	683,577	676,586	1,360,163

(Continued)

| | CAPITAL STOCK | | | |
	NUMBER OF SHARES	AMOUNT	RETAINED EARNINGS	TOTAL
Proceeds from sales of shares through employee stock plans, tax benefit of $1,448 and other	2,246	32,612	—	32,612
Proceeds from issuance of warrants	—	27,136	—	27,136
Net Income	—	—	1,570	1,570
Balance at December 28, 1985	116,078	743,325	678,156	1,421,481
Proceeds from sales of shares through employee stock plans	1,695	26,911	—	26,811
Net (Loss)	—	—	(173,165)	(173,165)
Balance at December 27, 1986	117,773	$770,236	$504,991	$1,275,227

See accompanying notes.

Notes to Consolidated Financial Statements (December 31, 1984, December 28, 1985 and December 27, 1986)

Borrowings

SHORT-TERM DEBT

Short-term debt at December 27, 1986 consists of $17.4 million of notes payable and $94.7 million borrowed under foreign and domestic lines of credit. At December 27, 1986 Intel and its subsidiaries had established foreign and domestic lines of credit of approximately $600 million. These lines are generally renegotiated on an annual basis. Intel complies with compensating balance requirements related to certain of these lines of credit: however, such requirements are immaterial and do not legally restrict the use of cash. The weighted average interest rate on short-term debt outstanding at December 27, 1986 approximated 5.0 percent.

On July 7, 1986 the Company began borrowing under a commercial paper program in the U.S. under which aggregate outstanding maturities reached $300 million. This debt is rated A1 by Standard and Poor's and P1 by Moody's Investor Service. The proceeds are used to fund short-term working capital needs of the Company. There were no commercial paper obligations outstanding as of December 27, 1986.

LONG-TERM DEBT

Long-term debt at fiscal year-ends is as follows:

	1985	1986
	(thousands)	
Payable in U.S. dollars:		
1983 Series A Industrial, Medical and Environmental Pollution Control Revenue Bonds	$ 80,000	$ 80,000
1983 Series B Industrial, Medical and Environmental Pollution Control Revenue Bonds	30,000	30,000

(Continued)

	1985	1986
1983 Series B Industrial, Medical and Environmental Pollution Control Revenue Bonds	30,000	30,000
Zero Coupon Notes, net of unamortized discount $145,660 ($155,420 in 1985)	1,080	90,840
Other U.S. dollar debt	4,500	4,500
Payable in other currencies:		
Yen Guaranteed Bonds	41,571	32,279
Yen Promissory Notes	—	16,270
Yen Japanese Government Bonds	—	20,211
Other foreign currency debt	38,212	12,580
(Less current portion of long-term debt)	(4,532)	(80)
Total long-term debt	$270,831	$286,600

Proceeds of $80 million from the Adjustable Rate Industrial Revenue Bonds issued in September, 1983 (the 1983 Series A Bonds) and $30 million issued in December, 1983 (the 1983 Series B Bonds) by the Puerto Rico Industrial, Medical and Environmental Pollution Control Facilities Financing Authority (the Authority) have been loaned to the Company. In accordance with loan agreements between the Company and the Authority, the Company has guaranteed repayment of principal and interest on these Bonds, which are subject to redemption prior to maturity upon the occurrence of certain events. The 1983 Series A Bonds are due September 1, 2013, bear interest at 8 percent through August 1988 and are adjustable and redeemable (at the option of either the Company or the bondholder) every five years beginning September 1988 through September 2008 in accordance with certain formulas. The 1983 Series B Bonds are due December 1, 2013, bear interest at 7.95 percent through November 1988 and are adjustable and redeemable (at the option of either the Company or the bondholder) every five years beginning December 1988 through December 2008 in accordance with certain formulas. As a result of the redemption options, this debt has

been included in the 1988 debt maturities noted below.

In connection with these agreements, the Company is obligated to spend a total of $110 million to finance expansion in Puerto Rico. As of December 27, 1986, the Company had spent $86.1 million. The remainder of the Company's commitment is restricted, invested in short-term and long-term interest-bearing instruments and included in long-term investments. (See Investments.)

On May 20, 1985 the Company issued $236.5 million aggregate principal amount of zero coupon notes with detachable warrants. The warrants entitle the holders to purchase 5,912,000 shares of Capital Stock reserved for issuance at an exercise price of $40 per share through May 15, 1995. These warrants are subject to acceleration by Intel upon the occurrence of certain events. $27.1 million, representing the original value of the warrants net of related offering expenses, is included in paid-in capital. The notes are due May 15, 1995 and have an effective yield to maturity of 11.75 percent, compounded semiannually, with interest paid at maturity. As of December 27, 1986, $90.5 million of notes were outstanding, net of unamortized discount.

On January 29, 1985 the Company issued Yen 12.5 billion $6\frac{3}{4}$ percent Yen Guaranteed Bonds due January 29, 1992. As of December 27, 1986 Yen 5.3 billion (approximate U.S. dollar equivalent of $32 million) were outstanding and invested in short-term and long-term interest-bearing instruments. The loan has been hedged for currency fluctuations, resulting in an effective dollar interest rate of 11.38 percent.

On June 27, 1986 the Company borrowed Yen 2.7 billion (approximate U.S. dollar equivalent of $16 million) under promissory note agreements maturing February 10, 1992. Proceeds of the borrowings have been used to repurchase a portion of the $6\frac{5}{8}$ Yen Guaranteed Bonds described above. The notes have been hedged for currency fluctuations, resulting in an affective dollar interest rate of 10.25 percent.

On July 21, 1986 the Company borrowed Yen 3 billion (approximate U.S. dollar equivalent of $20 million) 7.7 percent Japanese Government Bonds maturing February 20, 1992 under a securities borrowing arrangement. In connection with this transaction, the Company sold these bonds at a premium and invested the proceeds from the sale in short-term and long-term Yen denominated interest-bearing instruments. The premium will be amortized over the term of the borrowing, yielding an effective Yen interest rate of 5.7 percent. Under this arrangement the Company is obligated to return the bonds or their equivalent Yen denominated face value at maturity.

Approximately $39 million of short-term and long-term debt owed to an agency of a foreign government as of December 28, 1985 was repaid in 1986 as a result of an agreement between Intel and the foreign government. Under that agreement, the foreign government assumed the full indebtedness of Intel to the agency in consideration for a cash payment from Intel to the foreign government. An extraordinary gain amounting to $19.x million was realized as a consequence of the debt repayment.

As of December 27, 1986, aggregate debt maturities are as follows: 1987—$.1 million; 1988—$116.1 million; 1989—$6.1 million; 1990—$0; 1991–$0; and thereafter—$310.0 million.

Investments

Investments consist of marketable securities, Eurodollar deposits, precious metals which are hedged by forward contracts, unrealized gains on long-term currency swaps, and investments under repurchase agreements. Investments denominated in foreign currencies are hedged by forward contracts. Investments with maturities of greater than one fiscal year and restricted investments are classified as

long-term. In addition, the Company has entered into contractual agreements (interest rate swaps) to hedge certain investment positions against fluctuations in interest rates. The company records net interest expense or net interest income related to these transactions on a monthly basis.

Investment in Unconsolidated Subsidiary

During 1985 the Company formed a wholly-owned offshore banking subsidiary which is accounted for under the equity method. Assets of this subsidiary of $57 million as of December 27, 1986 consist primarily of loans to third-party financial institutions. Earnings of the subsidiary in 1986 were $3.5 million.

INTEREST AND OTHER

	1984	1985	1986
	(Thousands)		
Interest income	$57,063	$53,345	$41,566
Interest expense	(11,336)	(19,408)	(36,325)
Foreign currency gains	4,300	3,449	3,007
Other income (expense)	(2,328)	15,335	12,377
Total	$47,699	$54,721	$20,625

Interest expense for 1986, 1985, and 1984 excludes $2,429,000, $6,273,000, and $3,642,000, respectively, which was capitalized as a component of construction costs. Other income for 1986 includes income from equity investments hedged with market index futures contracts, income from hedged precious metal investments, equity income from its banking subsidiary and income from other investments. Other income in 1985 includes gains from the sale of long-term marketable securities and income from other investments.

Provision (Benefit) for Taxes

Income (loss) before taxes and extraordinary item and the provision (benefit) for taxes consist of the following:

	1984	1985	1986
	(thousands)		
Income (loss) before taxes and extraordinary item: U.S.	$159,535	$(56,949)	$(222,713)
Foreign	138,614	51,501	48,079
Total income (loss) before taxes and extraordinary item	$298,149	$ (5,448)	$(174,634)
Provision (benefit) for taxes:			
Federal:			
Current	$ 34,756	$(62,639)	$ 20,514
Deferred (prepaid)	5,865	31,650	(28,673)
	40,621	(30,989)	(7,859)
State:			
Current	20,713	—	—
Deferred (prepaid)	(2,829)	—	—
	17,839	—	—
Foreign:			
Current	38,962	25,640	13,190
Deferred (prepaid)	2,488	(1,669)	3,319
	41,450	23,971	16,509
Total taxes on income	$ 99,960	$ (7,018)	$ (8,650)
Effective tax rate	34%	—	—

The provision (benefit) for taxes reconciles to the amount computed by applying the statutory Federal rate to income (loss) before taxes and extraordinary item as follows:

	1984	1985	1986
	(thousands)		
Computed expected tax	$137,149	$(2,506)	$(80,332)
U.S. operating loss carryforward	—	—	86,454
State taxes, net of Federal benefits	9,660	—	—
Amortization of investment tax credits	(9,177)	(9,470)	(6,700)
Research and experimental credit	(9,796)	(7,900)	(2,902)
Reversal of deferred tax on prior years' DISC income	(19,300)	—	—
Provision for combined foreign and U.S. taxes on certain foreign income at rates in excess of U.S. rate	—	11,181	7,157
Other	(8,576)	1,677	4,973
Provision (benefit) for taxes	$99,960	$(7,018)	$8,650

The 1984 reversal of deferred tax on prior years' DISC income is due to the Tax Reform Act of 1984 which provided for the forgiveness of such deferred tax for the years 1972 through 1984.

Industry Segment Reporting

Intel and its subsidiaries operate in one dominant industry segment. The company is engaged principally in the design, development, manufacture, and sale of semiconductor components and related products. In 1986, 1985 and 1984, approximately 5.7 percent, 19.9 percent and 11.9 percent, respectively, of Intel's revenues were derived from sales to one significant customer. (See Related Party Transactions.)

Major operations outside the United States include manufacturing facilities in Israel, Malaysia, the Philippines, and Singapore, and sales subsidiaries throughout Europe and other parts of the world. Summary balance sheet information for operations outside of the United States at fiscal year-ends is as follows:

Geographic information for the three years ended December 27, 1986 is presented in the tables below. Transfers between geographic

	1985	1966
	(thousands)	
Total assets	$496,780	$513,544
Total liabilities	$192,547	$202,634
Net property, plant and equipment	$174,857	$156,641

areas are accounted for at amounts which are generally above cost and consistent with rules and regulations of governing tax authorities. Such transfers are eliminated in the consolidated financial statements. Operating income by geographic segment does not include an allocation of general corporate expenses. Identifiable assets are those assets that can be directly associated with a particular geographic area. Corporate assets include principally cash, short-term investments, prepaid taxes on income and refundable income taxes.

	U.S	Europe	Other	Eliminations	Corporate	Consolidated
			(thousands)			
1986						
Sales to unaffiliated customers	$ 760,895	$358, 79	$165,337	$ —	$ —	$1,263,011
Transfers between geographic areas	365,99	6	132,101	(503,338)	—	—
Net revenues	$1,128,889	$344,3	$297,438	$(503,858)	—	$1,263,011
Operating income (loss)	(145,667)	$ 33,943	$(20,364)	$ 8,596	$(71,767)	$ (195,239)
Identifiable assets	$1,237,780	$155,534	$358,010	$(103,017)	$431,759	$2,060,066
1985						
Sales to unaffiliated customers	$ 892,410	$361,323	$110,049	$ —	$ —	$1,364,982
Transfers between geographic areas	313,386	—	113,134	(428,720)	—	—
Net revenues	$1,208,996	$361,523	$223,183	$(428,720)		$1,364,962
Operating income (loss)	$ (49,334)	$ 43,691	$ 202	$ 14,673	$(99,391)	$ (60,469)
Identifiable assets	$1,313,396	$139,554	$337,226	$ (120,139)	$439,928	$2,131,863
1984						
Sales to unaffiliated customers	$1,159,392	$317,947	$131,993	$ —	$ —	$1,629,332
Transfers between geographic areas	310,349	—	107,856	(418,405)	—	—
Net revenues	$1,469,941	$317,947	$259,849	$(418,405)	$ —	$1,629,332
Operating income	$ 259,722	$ 45,477	$ 49,381	$ (12,742)	$(91,388)	$ 240,450
Identifiable assets	$1,429,541	$143,463	$254,286	$ (97,868)	$299,977	$2,029,399

Related Party Transactions

In February 1983 International Business Machines Corporation (IBM) became a related party due to its purchase of Intel stock. In 1984 the Company sold an additional 86,309 shares of previously authorized but unissued capital stock to IBM in accordance with an agreement reached in December 1982. As of December 27, 1986 and December 28, 1985,

IBM owned less than 20% of Intel's outstanding capital stock. In 1986 approximately 5.7 percent of Intel's revenues were derived from sales to IBM (19.9 percent in 1985 and 11.9 percent in 1984). In addition, Intel had purchases from IBM (including lease obligations) of approximately $5 million in 1986 ($7 million in 1985 and $24 million in 1984). Amounts receivable from and payable to IBM are immaterial at December 27, 1986 and December 28, 1985.

APPENDIX 11-2

Financial Statements of SIC Code 3674

	SIC 3669 Communicatn Equip Nec (No breakdown)		SCI 3672 Print Circuit Boards (No Breakdown)		SIC 3674 &RLTD DVCS SMCNDCTRS (No Breakdown)		SIC 3675 Electronic Capacitors (No Breakdown)	
	1988 (127 Estab)		1988 (247 Estab)		1988 (257 Estab)		1988 (14 Estab)	
	$	%	$	%	$	%	$	%
Cash	139,526	11.7	76,726	10.2	319,909	16.2	269,179	11.0
Accounts receivable	367,300	30.8	239,206	31,8	456,166	23.1	591,399	25.1
Notes receivable	9,540	0.8	8,274	1.1	5,924	0.3	2,356	0.1
Inventory	306,481	25.7	111,328	14.8	420,621	21.3	617,317	26.2
Other current	60,819	5.1	36,107	4.8	102,687	5.2	70,685	3.0
Total current	883,666	74.1	471,641	62.7	1,305,306	66.1	1,540,936	65.4
Fixed assets	151,452	12.7	191,064	25.4	416,671	21.1	600,824	25.5
Other Non-current	157,414	13.2	89,514	11.9	252,767	12.8	214,412	9.1
Total assets	1,192,532	100.0	752,219	100.0	1,974,745	100.0	2,356,171	100.0
Accounts payable	155,029	13.0	112,081	14.9	242,894	12.3	228,549	9.7
Bank Loans	25,043	2.1	6,770	0.9	37,520	1.9	21,206	0.9
Notes payable	50,086	4.2	31.593	4.2	75,040	3.8	139,014	5.9
Other current	158,607	13.3	100,797	13.4	272,515	13.8	235,617	10.0
Total current	388,765	32.6	251,241	33.4	627,969	31.8	624,385	26.5
Other long term	174,110	14.6	153,453	20.4	282,389	14.3	407,618	17,3
Deferred credits	5,963	0.5	4,513	0.6	7.899	0.4	28,274	1.2
Net worth	623,694	52.3	343,012	45.6	1,056,489	53.5	1,295,894	55.0
Total liab. & net worth	1,192,532	100.0	752,219	100.0	1,974,745	100.0	2,356,171	100.0
Net sales	3,010,494	100.0	1,500,000	100.0	3,402,780	100.0	4,687,224	100.0
Gross profit	1,098,830	36.5	498,000	33.2	1,150,140	33.8	1,171,806	25.0
Net profit after tax	96,336	3.2	96,000	6.4	173,542	5.1	117,181	2.5
Working capital	494,901	—	220,400	—	677,337	—	916,551	—

(Continued)

Ratios	UQ	MED	LQ	UQ	MED	LQ	UQ	MED	LQ	UQ	MED	LQ
Solvency												
Quick ratio (times)	2.3	1.4	0.9	2.4	1.3	0.8	2.3	1.2	0.7	1.9	1.2	1.0
Current ratio (times)	4.6	2.5	1.7	3.4	2.0	1.3	3.7	2.4	1.4	3.6	2.5	2.0
Curr. liab to NW (%)	23.8	53.3	104.2	30.0	60.4	137.1	21.8	47.4	115.5	30.1	44.0	69.0
Curr. liab. to INV (%)	63.0	122.3	172.5	91.8	187.1	276.0	67.0	122.0	229.9	79.6	108.5	129.1
Total liab. to NW (%)	27.8	86.6	199.9	43.6	101.8	231.0	35.4	81.4	166.2	42.8	96.4	131.5
Fixed assets to NW (%)	11.7	23.8	65.9	24.3	62.7	120.6	19.4	46.0	80.3	31.7	58.6	71.3
Efficiency												
Coll. period (days)	44.1	60.2	84.0	38.9	52.8	67.2	36.9	53.1	72.0	50.4	56.6	78.6
Sales to inv. (times)	12.9	7.9	4.9	32.1	15.8	9.1	13.3	7.6	4.5	9.8	8.4	4.5
Assets to sales (%)	36.5	56.3	86.5	31.4	45.0	62.8	39.9	68.0	108.6	42.6	61.1	93.6
Sales to nw (times)	6.8	4.3	3.0	14.5	7.7	4.6	8.8	3.6	2.3	6.3	4.0	2.7
Acct. pay to sales (%)	3.0	5.8	9.1	3.3	6.2	11.4	3.0	6.3	10.9	3.1	4.7	7.5
Profitability												
Return on sales (%)	8.0	4.0	0.2	11.7	5.3	2.1	13.0	4.9	0.6	5.7	4.0	0.8
Return on assets (%)	13.6	4.7	0.1	16.3	6.7	2.4	10.4	4.7	(0.5)	6.4	6.3	3.8
Return on NW (%)	26.6	11.2	0.1	44.5	16.2	4.5	23.1	10.4	(0.6)	8.5	8.2	7.6

Note: UQ is upper quartile, MED is median, LQ is lower quartile, NW is net worth, coll. is collection, inv. is inventories, acct. pay. is account payables.

SOURCE: Dun & Bradstreet Credit Services, *Industry Norms & Key Business Ratios, Desk-Top Edition 1988–89*. Robert Morris Associates (RMA), Annual Statement Studies, 6/30/88 through 3/31/89. (SIC 0100-8999), p. 120.

RMA 1989 ANNUAL STATEMENT STUDIES[1]
MANUFACTURERS—ELECTRONIC COMPONENTS & ACCESSORIES
[SIC# 3671(72, 74–79)]

Current Data: 191 6/30–9/30/88 ; 268 10/1/88–3/31/89

	Current Data					Comparative Historical Data				
	0-1MM	1-10MM	10-50MM	50-100MM	All	6/30/84–3/31/85 All	6/30/85–3/31/86 All	6/30/86–3/31/87 All	6/30/87–3/31/88 All	6/30/88–3/31/89 All
Type of Statement										
Unqualified	12	108	48	21	189	253	229	205	196	189
Qualified	2	11	4		17	15	19	15	17	17
Reviewed	23	68	3		94	109	79	100	77	94
Compiled	47	23			70	71	57	68	67	70
Other	18	55	14	2	89	71	74	67	72	89
Number of Statements	102	265	69	23	459	519	458	455	429	459
Assets	%	%	%	%	%	%	%	%	%	%
Cash & Equivalents	10.5	6.9	9.7	18.4	8.7	8.1	8.7	9.2	9.3	8.7
Trade Receivables (net)	34.3	29.8	24.5	23.4	29.7	29.0	26.3	27.6	28.4	29.7
Inventory	26.8	28.3	27.3	18.7	27.3	28.1	27.8	25.3	26.1	27.3
All Other Current	3.8	1.9	1.8	2.3	2.3	2.3	2.7	2.3	1.9	2.3
Total Current	75.4	66.9	63.3	62.9	68.0	67.5	65.5	64.4	65.7	68.0
Fixed Assets (net)	19.4	26.6	28.6	28.8	25.4	26.0	27.5	28.1	27.5	25.4
Intangibles (net)	.4	1.1	2.3	2.8	1.2	1.0	1.3	1.4	1.4	1.2
All Other Non-current	4.8	5.4	5.8	5.5	5.3	5.5	5.7	6.1	5.4	5.3
Total	100.0	100.0	100.0	100.0	100.0	100.0	100.0	100.0	100.0	100.0
Liabilities										
Notes Payable–Short Term	10.1	11.1	8.8	2.7	10.1	9.0	10.0	9.8	10.3	10.1
Cur. Mat-L/T/D	5.4	4.3	3.1	1.8	4.3	3.4	3.5	4.6	4.0	4.3
Trade Payables	15.7	14.8	10.0	7.9	14.0	14.3	12.6	12.7	14.0	14.0
Income Taxes Payable	1.6	1.6	1.1	1.1	1.5	2.0	1.3	1.3	1.4	1.5
All Other Current	9.4	10.0	9.7	9.8	9.8	10.4	9.1	8.5	8.7	9.8
Total Current	42.3	41.9	32.8	23.4	39.7	39.1	36.4	36.9	38.4	39.7
Long Term Debt	10.3	15.6	15.1	12.6	14.2	14.4	15.5	16.3	16.4	14.2
Deferred Taxes	.4	1.2	1.2	2.2	1.1	.9	1.0	.8	1.1	1.1
All Other Non-current	3.8	2.5	3.9	2.5	3.0	2.7	2.4	3.1	1.8	3.0
Net Worth	43.2	38.9	47.1	59.2	42.1	42.9	44.7	43.0	42.4	42.1
Total Liabilities & Net Worth	100.0	100.0	100.0	100.0	100.0	100.0	100.0	100.0	100.0	100.0
Income Data										
Net Sales	100.0	100.0	100.0	100.0	100.0	100.0	100.0	100.0	100.0	100.0
Gross Profit	36.8	33.5	31.7	35.4	34.0	34.0	34.2	33.6	33.2	34.0
Operating Expenses	31.7	27.5	26.0	29.5	28.3	26.6	28.9	30.0	28.5	28.3
Operating Profit	5.2	6.0	5.7	5.9	5.7	7.8	5.3	3.6	4.7	5.7
All Other Expenses (net)	1.4	1.5	1.8	.0	1.5	1.1	1.3	1.3	1.4	1.5
Profit Before Taxes	3.8	4.4	3.9	5.9	4.3	6.6	4.0	2.3	3.2	4.3
Ratios										
Current	2.7	2.4	3.3	3.7	2.7	2.7	3.1	2.9	2.7	2.7
	2.0	1.7	2.0	2.8	1.8	2.8	1.9	1.8	1.8	1.8
	1.3	1.3	1.4	1.8	1.3	1.3	1.3	1.3	1.3	1.3
Quick	1.6	1.4	1.8	2.4	1.5	1.5	1.6	1.6	1.6	1.5
	1.1	.9	1.0	2.0	1.0	1.0	1.0	1.0	1.0	1.0
	.8	.6	.7	1.1	.7	.7	.6	.7	.7	.7
							(454)			
Sales/Receivables	39 9.4	44 8.3	51 7.5	43 7.2	43 8.4	44 8.3	42 8.6	43 8.5	44 8.3	43 8.4
	47 7.8	54 6.8	63 6.2	54 5.8	54 6.7	56 6.5	51 7.1	54 6.7	55 6.6	54 6.7
	66 5.5	63 5.8	96 5.1	66 3.8	66 5.5	70 5.2	68 5.4	68 5.4	69 5.3	66 5.5

(Continued)

[1]Fiscal year ends 6/30/88 through 3/31/89. Published by Robert Morris Associates, Philadelphia, PA, p. 100.

Comparative Historical Data / Current Data / Type of Statement table

Note: In the table below, each ratio cell shows three values (upper quartile / median / lower quartile) where applicable. Columns 1–5 are "Current Data" (columns 1–4 broken out by "Type of Statement"; column 5 is the current total). Columns 6–10 are "Comparative Historical Data."

	Current Data (Type of Statement) 1	2	3	4	5	Comparative Historical Data 6	7	8	9	10
(count set 1)	29 / 53 / 104	44 / 78 / 126	64 / 104 / 140	25 / 96 / 159	43 / 79 / 126	47 / 85 / 130	47 / 85 / 140	45 / 76 / 130	43 / 78 / 126	43 / 79 / 126
(count set 2)	20 / 32 / 55	22 / 35 / 55	25 / 33 / 51	25 / 35 / 44	22 / 34 / 54	23 / 38 / 56	21 / 34 / 50	20 / 35 / 55	22 / 38 / 56	22 / 34 / 54
Cost of Sales/Inventory	12.6 / 6.9 / 3.5	8.3 / 4.7 / 2.9	5.7 / 3.5 / 2.6	7.5 / 3.8 / 2.3	8.4 / 4.6 / 2.9	7.7 / 4.3 / 2.8	7.7 / 4.3 / 2.6	8.1 / 4.8 / 2.8	8.5 / 4.7 / 2.9	8.5 / 4.6 / 2.9
Cost of Sales/Payables	17.9 / 11.5 / 6.6	16.6 / 10.4 / 6.6	14.8 / 10.9 / 7.2	14.4 / 10.4 / 8.3	16.4 / 10.6 / 6.7	15.9 / 9.7 / 6.5	17.3 / 10.8 / 7.3	18.2 / 10.4 / 6.6	16.5 / 9.7 / 6.5	16.4 / 10.6 / 6.7
Sales/Working Capital	5.0 / 7.4 / 15.0	4.7 / 7.8 / 15.5	2.8 / 5.1 / 8.9	1.9 / 2.5 / 7.1	4.1 / 7.1 / 14.0	3.9 / 7.0 / 14.8	3.4 / 5.9 / 14.7	3.6 / 6.8 / 16.3	4.0 / 6.8 / 15.7	4.1 / 7.1 / 14.0
EBIT/Interest	12.5 / 5.4 / 1.3	9.1 / 3.3 / 1.4	7.2 / 3.6 / 1.0	22.1 / 7.1 / 2.9	9.5 / 3.8 / 1.4	11.0 / 4.6 / 2.0	8.3 / 3.1 / .8	7.1 / 2.6 / .6	7.5 / 3.1 / 1.0	9.5 / 3.8 / 1.4
(count)	(81)	(226)	(61)	(16)	(384)	(447)	(409)	(392)	(377)	(384)
Net Profit + Depr., Dep., Amort./Cur. Mat. L/T/D	6.0 / 2.0 / .7	5.9 / 3.0 / 1.6	7.5 / 3.5 / 1.6	20.5 / 14.9 / 4.4	6.4 / 3.0 / 1.4	9.0 / 4.0 / 2.1	8.8 / 2.8 / 1.1	7.1 / 2.2 / 1.0	5.3 / 2.4 / 1.0	6.4 / 3.0 / 1.4
(count)	(46)	(162)	(56)	(14)	(278)	(354)	(322)	(306)	(278)	(278)
Fixed/Worth	.2 / .4 / 1.0	.4 / .7 / 1.2	.3 / .7 / 1.2	.3 / .5 / .9	.3 / .6 / 1.1	.3 / .6 / 1.1	.3 / .6 / 1.1	.3 / .6 / 1.3	.3 / .6 / 1.4	.3 / .6 / 1.1
Debt/Worth	.6 / 1.3 / 3.1	.8 / 1.5 / 3.5	.7 / 1.2 / 2.3	.4 / .7 / 1.3	.7 / 1.4 / 3.1	.7 / 1.4 / 2.7	.6 / 1.3 / 2.4	.7 / 1.4 / 2.8	.7 / 1.5 / 3.2	.7 / 1.4 / 3.1
% Profit Before Taxes/Tangible Net Worth	56.3 / 21.4 / 4.7	45.7 / 24.3 / 6.0	32.9 / 16.4 / 5.3	22.4 / 15.9 / 3.5	42.4 / 20.7 / 5.5	52.8 / 28.5 / 10.0	35.0 / 16.8 / .6	33.0 / 14.2 / .5	38.5 / 17.1 / 2.2	42.4 / 20.7 / 5.5
(count)	(97)	(248)	(67)	(18)	(435)	(507)	(438)	(433)	(409)	(435)
% Profit Before Taxes/Total Assets	18.4 / 9.0 / 1.1	17.4 / 7.8 / 1.5	13.5 / 6.1 / 1.8	14.6 / 9.5 / 1.7	16.8 / 8.5 / 1.5	20.7 / 11.5 / 3.9	16.2 / 7.5 / -.4	13.7 / 5.3 / -1.1	13.5 / 6.5 / .2	16.8 / 8.5 / 1.5
Sales/Net Fixed Assets	27.4 / 16.9 / 8.7	15.1 / 8.4 / 5.0	8.7 / 5.4 / 3.4	6.4 / 4.3 / 2.8	17.1 / 8.5 / 4.7	14.4 / 7.6 / 4.4	13.4 / 7.3 / 4.2	14.5 / 6.8 / 3.5	14.4 / 7.3 / 3.7	17.1 / 8.5 / 4.7
Sales/Total Assets	3.2 / 2.5 / 1.8	2.5 / 1.9 / 1.6	1.7 / 1.5 / 1.1	1.5 / 1.2 / .9	2.5 / 1.9 / 1.5	2.4 / 1.9 / 1.4	2.3 / 1.7 / 1.3	2.4 / 1.7 / 1.2	2.4 / 1.8 / 1.3	2.5 / 1.9 / 1.5
% Depr., Dep., Amort./Sales	2.4 / 3.7	2.7 / 4.4	3.8 / 6.7	4.9 / 7.1	3.0 / 4.8	2.8 / 3.9	3.0 / 4.9	3.4 / 5.4	3.4 / 5.3	3.0 / 4.8
(count)	(92)	(224)	(64)	(18)	(398)	(462)	(415)	(402)	(381)	(398)
% Officers' Comp./Sales	3.8 / 6.7 / 12.1	2.9 / 4.9 / 6.9			3.0 / 5.3 / 9.2	3.2 / 5.7 / 9.4	3.6 / 5.6 / 8.1	3.4 / 5.7 / 9.7	3.5 / 6.5 / 10.3	3.0 / 5.3 / 9.2
(count)	(47)	(60)			(111)	(138)	(110)	(94)	(113)	(111)
Net Sales ($)	136280M[b]	1926011M	2273362M	1941328M	6276981M	8548212M	6508945M	5513493M	5490941M	6276981M
Total Assets ($)	55792M	1013949M	1647430M	1639347M	4356518M	5885645M	5034487M	4609137M	4368750M	4355618M

[a] MM = $million
[b] M = $thousand

Standard Industrial Classification Manual, 1987[2]

Industry Group No. 366

Industry
No.

COMMUNICATIONS EQUIPMENT

3669   Communications Equipment, Not Elsewhere Classified

Fire detection systems, electric
Highway signals, electric
Intercommunications equipment, electronic
Marine horns, electric
Pedestrian traffic control equipment
Railroad signaling devices, electric
Signaling apparatus, electric
Signals: railway, highway, and traffic—electric
Sirens, electric: vehicle, marine, industrial, and air raid
Smoke detectors
Traffic signals, electric

Industry Group No. 367

Industry
No.

ELECTRONIC COMPONENTS AND ACCESSORIES

3671   Electron Tubes

Establishments primarily engaged in manufacturing electron tubes and tube parts. Establishments primarily engaged in manufacturing X-ray tubes and parts are classified in Industry 3844.

Cathode ray tubes
Electron beam (beta ray) generator tubes
Electron tube parts, except glass blanks: bases, getter, and guns
Electron tubes
Gas and vapor tubes
Geiger Mueller tubes
Klystron tubes
Light sensing and emitting tubes
Magnetron tubes
Photomultiplier tubes

[2]Executive Office of the President, Office of Management and Budget, *Standard Industrial Classification Manual*, 1987, p. 230–31.

Picture tube reprocessing
Planar triode tubes
Receiving type electron tubes
Television tubes
Transmitting electron tubes
Traveling wave tubes
Tubes for operating above the X-ray spectrum (with shorter wavelength)
Vacuum tubes

3672   Printed Circuit Boards

Establishments primarily engaged in manufacturing printed circuit boards.

Circuit boards, television and radio: printed
Printed circuit boards
Printed circuits
Wiring boards

3674   Semiconductors and Related Devices

Establishments primarily engaged in manufacturing semiconductors and related solid-state devices. Important products of this industry are semiconductor diodes and stacks, including rectifiers, integrated microcircuits (semiconductor networks), transistors, solar cells, and light sensing and emitting semiconductor (solid-state) devices.

Computer logic modules
Controlled rectifiers, solid-state
Diodes, solid-state (germanium, silicon; etc.)
Fuel cells, solid-state
Gunn effect devices
Hall effect devices
Hybrid integrated circuits
Infrared sensors, solid-state
Laser diodes
Light emitting diodes
Light sensitive devices, solid-state
Magnetic bubble memory device
Magnetohydrodynamic (MHD) devices
Memories, solid-state
Metal oxide silicon (MOS) devices
Microcircuits, integrated (semiconductor)
Microprocessors
Modules, solid-state
Molecular devices, solid-state
Monolithic integrated circuits (solid-state)
Optical isolators
Parametric diodes
Photoconductive cells
Photoelectric cells, solid-state (electronic eye)
Photoelectric magnetic devices

(Continued)

Photovoltaic devices, solid-state
Random access memories (RAMS)
Read only memories (ROMS)
Rectifiers, solid-state
Schottky diodes
Semiconductor circuit networks
  solid-state integrated circuits)
Semiconductor devices
Silicon wafers, chemically doped
Solar cells
Solid-state electronic devices
Strain gages, solid-state
Stud bases or mounts
  for semiconductor devices
Switches, silicon control
Thermionic devices, solid-state
Thermoelectric devices, solid-state
Thin film circuits
Thyristors
Transistors
Tunnel diodes
Ultraviolet sensors, solid-state
Variable capacitance diodes
Wafers (semiconductor devices)
Zener diodes

3675   Electronic Capacitors

Establishments primarily engaged in manufacturing electronic capacitors. Establishments primarily engaged in manufacturing electrical capacitors are classified in Industry 3629.

Capacitors, electronic: fixed and variable
Condensers, electronic

3676   Electronic Resistors

Establishments primarily engaged in manufacturing electronic resistors. Establishments primarily engaged in manufacturing resistors for telephone and telegraph apparatus are classified in Industry 3661.

Resistor networks
Resistors, electronic
Thermistors, except temperature sensors
Varistors

3677   Electronic Coils, Transformers, and Other Inductors

Establishments primarily engaged in manufacturing electronic coils, transformers, and inductors. Establishments primarily engaged in manufacturing electri-

cal transformers are classified in Industry 3612; those manufacturing transformers and inductors for telephone and telegraph apparatus are classified in Industry 3661, and those manufacturing semiconductors and related devices are classified in Industry 3674.

Baluns
Coil windings, electronic
Coils, chokes and other inductors,
  electronic
Constant impedance transformers
Coupling transformers
Flyback transformers
Transformers, electronic types
Transformers: power supply
  electronic type

3678   Electronic Connectors

Establishments primarily engaged in manufacturing electronic connectors. Establishments primarily engaged in manufacturing electrical connectors are classified in Industry 3643; those manufacturing electronic capacitors are classified in Industry 3675; and those manufacturing electronic coils, transformers, and other inductors are classified in Industry 3677.

Connectors, electronic: e.g., coaxial,
  cylindrical, rack and panel,
  printed circuit

3679   Electronic Components, Not Elsewhere Classified

Establishments primarily engaged in manufacturing electronic components, not elsewhere classified, such as receiving antennas, switches, and waveguides. Establishments primarily engaged in manufacturing radio and television transmitting antennas are classified in Industry 3663.

Antennas, receiving: automobile, home,
  and portable
Antennas, satellite: home type
Attenuators
Commutators, electronic
Cores, magnetic
Cyrogenic cooling devices (e.g., cryostats)
  for infrared detectors)

Hydro-Québec

The Evolution of the International Financial Policy of Canada's Major Public Utility Corporation

GUY STANLEY

CHRISTINE DESHAYES

This case addresses Hydro-Québec's financial policies and approach to financial management over an extended period of time. This case introduces the reader to financial decision making in a major Canadian corporation whose viability depends on continuous excess to financial markets and funding sources. In many respects, the financial history of Hydro-Québec tracks the evolution of the international financial markets. The concerns of Hydro-Québec—where to borrow, the cost of borrowing, the currency denomination of the debt, and how to minimize the cost of funds and currency exposure while at the same time maintain acceptable liquidity conditions and maintain the corporation's financial structure—reflect the universal concerns of

most international and multinational corporations around the world.

The Company and Its Business

The first hydro-electric station in Quebec came on stream in 1894 with the opening of a power station at Montmorency Falls, near Quebec City. Gradually, as small, privately-owned stations were established, a grid was put together. However, owing to lack of standardization and coordination, it could only offer service close to larger settlements and at relatively expensive rates. Public dissatisfaction led, in 1944, to the creation of the Quebec Hydro-Electric Commission.

The Commission was chiefly concerned with the supply of electricity to Montreal. It oversaw the takeover of the two private companies then undertaking this responsibility—Montreal Light, Heat and Power Consolidated and Montreal Island Power Company were nationalized, reorganized and renamed Hydro-Québec under the Hydro-Québec Act of that year. The new company also acquired ownership of Beauharnois Light, Heat and Power Company and was entrusted with the

©1990 by Dr. Guy Stanley, Director, and Christine Deshayes, Research Associate, Institute of U.S.—Canada Business Studies, Lubin School of Business, Pace University.

The case was written to serve as the basis for classroom discussion rather than to illustrate either effective or ineffective financial management at Hydro-Québec. The authors acknowledge the kind assistance of M. Paul Lacoursiere, financial coordinator, Hydro-Québec, Montreal, M. Denis Chaput, L'École des haute études commercials, Montreal, and officials at the Hydro-Québec office in New York.

management of the provincially-owned hydro-electric power development at Rapid VII on the Upper Ottawa River.

Between 1944 and 1963, the company grew by acquiring most of the private power companies around Montreal and smoothing out the imperfections in the grid. This was in accordance with its legislative mandate, namely the provision of low-cost electricity to the region.

Today, Hydro-Québec has three subsidiaries: the James Bay Company, set up in 1971, Hydro-Québec International, set up in 1978 and Cedar Rapids Transmissions Company Limited. Hydro-Québec also owns 34.2 percent in the Churchill Falls (Labrador) Corporation Limited, 100 percent of Nouveler Inc., which markets technology developed by Hydro-Québec. In 1985, Hydro-Québec also acquired 50 percent in Electrolyser Inc., HydrogenAl Inc. and ArgonAl Inc.

Hydro-Québec is a joint stock company whose sole shareholder is the government of Quebec. It has 2.8 million customers and operates 80 generators of which 90 percent are hydro-electric. In addition, the company has developed an extensive transmission system in order to serve communities at a long distance from its generators and sells surplus energy outside Quebec and Canada itself.

In terms of assets, it is the largest non-financial corporation in Canada and in terms of net income it ranks only slightly behind the top U.S. utilities. From its beginnings as a technical, construction/expansion oriented company, it is now a giant entity of some 18,900 employees geared to the "marketing" of power. (See Exhibit 12-1.)

The Business Economics of an Electric Company

The unique feature of a power company is that its capacity cannot be adjusted in the short term to fluctuations in demand: it must always be sufficient to cover demand at peak periods (although this can be mitigated through power sharing). The hazards involved in having to maintain essentially excess capacity for most of its operating hours are offset to a degree by a monopoly position as sole supplier. But the monopoly extends only to electricity—it doesn't cover hydrocarbon sources such as gas and oil. Nor does it cover private sources such as woodburning and sunlight, or for that matter, private generation.

This limits the ability of the monopoly to set its own prices. So too does its position as a state-owned (as in Canada) or even state-regulated (as in the United States) monopoly.

The pricing practices of public utilities with monopolistic positions are usually subject to political considerations. In the case of Hydro-Québec, the company's position on prices is subject to review by a Committee of the National Assembly and approval by the Government of Quebec.

EXHIBIT 12-1

Hydro-Québec Operating Statistics
(in thousands)

	1983	1984	1985	1986	1987
Energy sold (GWh)					
Quebec	88.1	100.9	109.7	117.2	124.1
Export	19.5	22.9	24.2	26.9	20.8
	107.6	123.8	133.9	144.1	152.9
Installed capacity at end of period (MW)	25.6	27.7	27.8	28.7	29.6
Peak winter requirements beginning Dec. (MW)	22.0	25.5	25.7	26.0	28.3
Customer accounts	2644	2697	2784	2862	2947
Permanent employees	19.0	18.6	18.2	18.5	18.9

Source: Annual Reports.

For Hydro-Québec, the pricing issue also involves export considerations. Here the matter becomes more complicated, because the federal government in Ottawa, not the provincial government in Quebec City, regulates exports.

In the period covered by the case, exports required a permit from the National Energy Board that were based on at least two principal considerations: (1) an estimate of national requirements and a demonstration by the applicant that the amounts to be exported would be surplus to domestic requirements and (2) a "least cost alternative" constraint, which meant that the price offered for export could not be significantly less than the least cost alternative available to the U.S. customer.

The least cost alternative rule arguably created a trade barrier that prevented energy exports that would lower input costs to Quebec's major trading partners in the northeastern United States. Given the importance of energy in an industrial economy, it can reasonably be concluded that higher than necessary energy costs would ultimately distort factor prices in both economies, with a retarding effect on growth and competitiveness.

The energy provisions of the Free Trade Agreement recently signed by Canada and the United States eliminate the least cost rule but maintain other price criteria of cost recovery and whether the export price is less than the domestic price (Canadian energy prices are considerably lower than those in the northeastern United States). Cost recovery, however, raises other complexities—essentially whether one should be recovering marginal costs attributable to extensions of existing infrastructure, or average costs applied across the whole system.

Evolution of the Financial Strategy

The spectacular expansion of Hydro-Québec required the setting up of a comprehensive financial strategy tailored to the business objectives of the company at each stage of its evolution.

Under its 1944 mandate, the company had to maintain accumulated reserves of 20 percent or more of total capitalization and maintain rates sufficient to pay the provincial government $20 million in profits from gross revenues. These funds would flow into the provincial consolidated revenue fund. The early expropriations were not trouble-free. Controversy remained lively and the financial rules were not actually implemented until 1947 when Hydro-Québec conducted its first major borrowing: C$112.5 at 2 percent interest placed through Canadian banks.

From its first bond issue on the U.S. market in 1953 to its acquisition of rival power companies in 1963, Hydro-Québec borrowed capital at the rate of approximately C$100 million a year. During this period, the company worked out the fundamentally conservative principles that would govern its future financial strategy:

- Maximize long-term debt at fixed rates,
- Obtain the longest possible maturities, and
- Keep intermediaries' commissions to a minimum.

The U.S. market was particularly attractive because of its lower long-term interest rates than were available in Québec, and the longer available maturities in the United States—30 years vs. 25 in Canada—so that the company was able to borrow under attractive conditions. However, from 1960 to 1962, Hydro-Québec abstained from borrowing in U.S. markets, however attractive the terms available, because of a 15 percent withholding tax imposed by the Canadian federal government on all interest payments to foreigners. This restriction was imposed in order to maintain the value of the Canadian dollar.

In 1963, taking advantage of a favorable spread between short- and long-term rates, the company decided to use short-term notes to complete the acquisition of subsidiaries not acquired in previous buy-outs. By that time, Hydro-Québec's debt securities equalled about half those issued by all of Canada's non-financial enterprises.

In 1966, Hydro-Québec issued short-term notes on the New York market. The under-writing and market-maker responsibilities were undertaken by Lehman Brothers. It was the first issue in the United States by a foreign entity. In the same year, the Quebec govern-ment established the Caisse de depots et placements, provincial portfolio management organization that managed the Quebec provincial pension fund among others. It be-came the largest buyers of Hydro-Québec obli-gations issued in Canada.

Internationalization of Financial Activities

Throughout the 1950s and 1960s Hydro-Québec chiefly thought of itself as a provider of low-cost electricity. During this period, Quebec underwent a profound social transfor-mation, known as the Quiet Revolution. In essence, French-speaking Quebecers of the Pierre Trudeau–René Levesque generation mounted a political and legislative assault on the managerial and technological power cen-ters of the province (and the federal govern-ment of Canada).

From the mid-1950s onwards, they trans-formed a province in which English was the language of social power into a province in which French became the language of busi-ness and official affairs, and French speaking professionals increasingly formed the core of the province's technocracy. Hydro-Québec en-joyed symbolic importance as a demonstration of the capability of this new class.

Globally, too, the decade of the 1970s was one of furious change. In particular, it was the decade of quadrupling oil prices and the scramble for new energy sources of every sort —chiefly fossil fuel to be sure, but hydroelec-tric as well.

Reflecting these changes, the company em-barked on a massive construction program to ensure adequate energy sources for a new urbanized and technology-driven society, cul-minating in the James Bay project.

Financially, until 1969, Hydro-Québec was limited to financial markets in Canada and the United States. But in the late 1970s, the com-pany began to borrow increasingly on the Eurodollar market. This ultimately developed into a new financial strategy designed to uti-lize the international markets to diversify the sources of funds. This was partly the result of necessity rather than choice as credit markets tightened in North America, forcing the com-pany to look offshore where, however, the terms of the loans tended to be shorter. The diversification of financial borrowing also re-duced Hydro-Québec's dependence on the United States.

- From 1969 to 1973, five significant issues were launched on the German market with the participation of two German banks, the Westdeutsche Landesbank and the Com-merzbank.

- After a disappointing attempt at a European Canadian dollar issue in 1972, the company succeeded in 1975, with some difficulty, in a Canadian dollar placement in Europe as-sisted by a financial syndicate led by Union Banques Suisses (UBS).

- From 1972 to 1976, the company successfully issued eight Swiss franc placements, with the assistance of the three major Swiss banks, UBS, Credit Suisse and the Swiss Bank Corp.

- From 1973 to 1983, Hydro-Québec began to reach out to other markets, such as the Mid-dle East in 1973–74, a private placement in Japan in 1977, in London in 1981 and in the European market denominated in ECUs a year later.

See Appendix 12-1 for a discussion by a senior financial officer of Hydro-Québec on debt issuing activities by the company.

New and Sophisticated Borrowing Techniques

The autumn of 1976 marked another turning point in Hydro-Québec's financial strategy. At the beginning of this period, the Canadian dollar traded slightly higher than the U.S. dollar. By the end of the 1970s, the Canadian dollar had dropped to U.S. $0.89 and was still falling. This exchange rate meant a considerable rise in the cost of servicing U.S. dollar denominated debt. Clearly U.S. capital mar-

kets could not be avoided, but henceforth the company would try harder to diversify its borrowings. Additionally, to cover its foreign exchange risk with the United States, it would seek to expand energy sales in U.S. markets and use the receipts from these sales to cover its U.S. dollar denominated debt. See Exhibit 12-2 and 12-3 on the company's financial data.

A major accomplishment of Hydro-Québec's financial strategy was a private placement of $1 billion in 1976. Canadian markets were used to the maximum but putting together a sum of

EXHIBIT 12-2

Hydro-Québec Financial Information

	1983	1984	1985	1986	1987
Electricity Sales Revenue					
(dollar amounts in millions)					
Quebec	$3,065	$3,455	$3,750	$4,024	$4,327
Export	$ 528	$ 646	$ 673	$ 649	$ 713
Total Sales	$3,593	$4,101	$4,423	$4,673	$5,040
Net income	$ 707	$ 301	$ 209	$ 303	$ 508
Funds from operations before interest	$1,984	$2,309	$2,542	$2,751	$2,950
Capital expenditure	$2,248	$1,681	$1,615	$1,566	$1,688
Dividends declared by the Government	$ 60	$ 156	—	—	—
General rate increase	7.3%	3.4	2.5	5.4%	4.6%
Interest coverage before dividends[a]	1.04 ×	1.01 ×	1.12 ×	1.15 ×	1.24 ×
(billions of dollars at end of period)					
Assets	$25.2	$27.1	$29.2	$30.6	$31.7
Long-term and perpetual debt	$16.5	$18.3	$20.1	$20.4	$21.2
Shareholder equity	$6.4	$6.5	$6.7	$7.0	$7.5

[a]Income before interest and exchange loss plus net investment income divided by gross interest charges.

Source: Annual Reports.

EXHIBIT 12-3

Hydro-Québec Funds from External Financing
(millions of dollars)

	1983	1984	1985	1986	1987
Net Issues					
Long-term debt	1,841	1,164	1,952	1,259	1,842
Perpetual debt	—	—	—	550	—
Redemption of long-term debt	(436)	(759)	(1,228)	(1,050)	(1,541)
	1,402	405	724	759	301

Source: Annual Reports.

that size required access to U.S. markets as well. This was undertaken in the form of an exceptional borrowing with the cooperation of First Boston, Prudential, Metropolitan and four other investment bankers. The placement facilitated the financing of the James Bay project.

Beginning in 1978, Hydro-Québec negotiated a series of standby credit lines in Euromarkets. Unlike previous borrowings, these were at variable rates of London Interbank Offered Rate (LIBOR) plus a spread that was renegotiated downwards at various times over subsequent years. This marked an opening towards floating rates, which henceforth played a major role in the company's financial strategy.

Starting in 1983, Hydro-Québec sought to reduce exchange risks by entering into swap arrangements. To date the company has completed 53 swap transactions—both interest rate and foreign currency swaps—mainly between U.S. dollar and Canadian dollar, or U.S. dollar and Swiss francs. Swap techniques play a part in company financing insofar as they serve to reduce borrowing costs and exchange rate risk. The company also limits its exposure in floating rates to 12 percent of total debt.

A New Financial Policy

In 1981, the legislation founding Hydro-Québec was amended (under Bill 16 of the Quebec National Assembly). One aim of the bill was to guarantee greater security to company bondholders. Hydro-Québec redefined its capitalization in terms of 50 million common shares at a par value of C$100, of which 43,741,000 shares were allocated to the Provincial Government of Quebec. Financial management guidelines were explicitly stated, setting out ratios that must be maintained if dividends were to be paid to its owner, the Quebec Government. The guidelines were as follows:

- First, interest charges had to be covered by net operating revenues.
- Second, the capitalization was calculated on a more conservative basis than that of its competitors, with equity to remain at least 25 percent of total capitalization.
- Third, the return on capital had to exceed the cost of debt.
- Fourth, the company sought to achieve self-financing equal to or greater than 30 percent.

One of the priorities of Hydro-Québec at the beginning of 1987 was to improve its position vis-à-vis the guidelines which it had technically breached since 1985. Against the backdrop of any increasingly unpredictable economic and energy environment, the company took steps to reduce its commercial risk and to minimize the costs and risks of meeting its capital requirements. This led to increasing borrowings in floating-rate instruments for which, it was hoped, the average interest rate would be less than that for fixed rate instruments.

In the short term, the company had to restore compliance with the financial guidelines, in particular those dealing with covering interest charges, the company's self-financing capability and its rate of capitalization. This could be achieved by taking steps to reduce operating costs, developing new, profitable export markets and establishing an energy price that reflected costs of production (including the financing of enlarged capacity). The aim was to achieve a superior capital ratio and liquidity.

At the same time, the company sought to lower its finance costs, exercise greater effort to control and reduce risk by the following measures:

- Enhancing the credit of some partners as a way of participating in their expansion and thus expanding sales of power.
- Increasing Canadian dollar denominated debt to minimize foreign exchange risk.
- Accepting maturities of 10 years or longer.
- Refinancing loans subject to recall whenever it would be advantageous in order to lower debt costs.
- Gradually reducing the volatility of debt costs by using the futures or options markets in the short term. Gradually expanding the proportion of floating rate debt insofar as that would increase the company's financial margin for manoeuvre.

With respect to minimizing exchange risk with the United States, Hydro-Québec sought to: (1) increase sale of electricity to the United States and repay its loans in the foreign ex-change earned by these sales and (2) reduce financial dependence on the United States.

In this connection, Hydro-Québec forecast a reduction of U.S. dollar debt, at the same time expanding Canadian dollar denominated debt. The financial policy described herein is of cardinal importance to Hydro-Québec whose expenditures as well as long-term sinking fund requirements of $6.3 billion (from 1987 to 1991) represent cash requirements of some $20.1 billion. Capital requirements are forecast to rise from $1.9 billion in 1987 to $2.7 billion in 1988. In addition to this, an annual refinancing of $1 billion for the foreseeable future requires regular access to world capital markets. See Appendix 12-2, Hydro-Québec Prospectus, for debt issuing data and Appendix 12-3, Company Profile and Financial Data.

The Assignment

1. Evaluate Hydro-Québec's refunding opportunities based on the swap market for swapping fixed for floating debt.
2. Formulate a funding deal with which to go to market from the standpoint of the utility, or a deal from the perspective of a would-be underwriter.
3. Recommend a short- and long-term foreign exchange hedging program for the corporation.

How to Borrow a Billion Dollars

The first stage in international borrowing is to put together all the available information about the costs of borrowing on the various markets. This is not as difficult as it sounds, because bankers will be happy to provide this kind of information, hoping to become the leading underwriter in a syndicate handling your account.

Why International?

The second step is to understand why large firms in general turn to international markets to meet their borrowing requirements. The reasons are the following:

1. MARKET SIZE. The market in which the company is primarily active may be too small to provide all the funds the company needs because a too significant presence in a market generally implies higher costs. This was the case for Hydro-Québec when financing the James Bay project at a cost of $14 billion.

2. FOREIGN CURRENCY NEEDS. If your company operates in different markets, it is likely that its capital needs to finance expansion will cover several currencies. Borrowing exclusively in Canadian or American dollars means accepting an exchange risk exposure if your revenues are in other currencies. The most logical thing to do is to borrow in the currencies in which you have revenues.

Excerpts from a presentation by M. Claude Germain, financial officer of Hydro-Québec, to a seminar on financial services in New York.

3. ARBITRAGE. Big borrowers often try to take advantage of the arbitrage possibilities between different markets, trading off interest rate against exchange rate risk, which explains why they keep an eye on exchange rates. For example, an issue for a company like Hydro-Québec for 10 years would cost, say (assuming AA + ratings):

9 3/4% in Canadian dollars
8 7/8% in U.S. dollars
4 3/4% in Swiss francs

Clearly, if I am ready to accept an exchange rate risk, I will choose the 4 3/4 percent in the Swiss market.

4. SWAPS. Finally—and very widespread in the last few years—are swap transactions which, generally speaking, are more economical and virtually eliminate foreign exchange risk. For example, Hydro-Québec wants to borrow C$100 million. Rather than make a public issue on the Canadian or Euro-Canadian markets, we can make a Euro-yen issue for 9.1 billion yen and exchange it for Canadian dollars. Depending on market conditions, it is sometimes possible to realize substantial savings compared to the costs of a domestic issue (sometimes as much as 25 to 30 basis points).

Where do these savings come from? Some borrowers have a competitive advantage on certain markets. For example, Hydro-Québec can get costs the same as AAA in the Swiss and German market and the yen market, despite the fact that the company is only rated AA and pays more or less the price of an AA rated obligation in the United States and Canada. On the other hand, another borrower who wants Swiss francs could have to pay more, whatever the rating.

Borrowing on Wall Street

Let us discuss the procedures for an issue in particular markets. The procedure varies according to the regulations affecting companies and stock market authorities such as the Securities and Exchange Commission in the United States or the provincial securities commissions in Canada. The U.S. market (see Exhibit A12-1) is the most sophisticated and the most stringent in its formal requirements (except perhaps for the Samurai market in Japan).

1. RATINGS. Before borrowing on Wall Street, your company has to be known and has to have received at least one rating by one of the big rating agencies, such as Standard and Poor, Moody's or Duff & Phelps.

2. RELATIONSHIPS. You should have developed links with one or more investment banks. It's easy. All you have to do is to accept their invitations to lunch. If your company is highly rated, you won't have to pay for lunch for weeks. If it is less highly rated, you have to do the asking for lunch for weeks before the links are established. Then you have to bring together a syndicate of banks whose number will de-

pend on the size of your needs and the relations your company enjoys with the banking community. Hydro-Québec's syndicate is composed of 36 institutions. Five institutions make up the guarantee commission.

3. SEC APPROVAL. Then you have to get SEC approval. For this, you need to prepare an issuing prospectus. The prospectus has to provide all financial information about the company and the risks associated with the investment.

It's ultimately easier and quicker to get approval for an issue if the SEC has already reviewed the prospectus by means of a basic prospectus filed previously with the agency. Then, when the time comes for an issue, you provide the prospectus already reviewed or the basic prospectus with a supplementary section updating the basic prospectus. Before final approval is received, the issue prospectus, along with the registration declaration, must be sent to the SEC.

4. GUARANTEE CONTRACT. At the same time as you deposit a prospectus with the SEC, you have to negotiate a guarantee contract with your syndicate members. This agreement has to clearly set out the conditions under which your syndicate will buy your company's issue. In other words, it's a normal loan agreement. The particular conditions of the loan are fixed by the terms of the contract.

5. SPECIAL CLAUSES. Particular clauses (showing the amount, interest rate, term of the loan) will be set out in the contract, which sets the terms as of the date of issue.

6. TIMING. Whenever the market looks favorable, the interest rate is at an acceptable level, and there is firm demand for long-term obligations, you decide to make an issue. You will negotiate the exact amount, the interest rate and the term of

EXHIBIT A12-1

How to Borrow a Billion on Wall Street

1. Company rating by a major agency
2. Syndication
3. Prospectus
4. Guarantee contract with syndicate
5. Consent of the board of directors
6. Letters of attestation
7. "Blue Sky" (U.S. municipals only)
8. Printing
9. Pre-closure
10. Closure
11. Payment and delivery

payment and of course get the approval of your board of directors.

7. OTHER FORMALITIES.   A series of declarations that the legal steps have been respected and that the borrower is legally entitled to make such issues must also be put together.

8. AUDITOR'S LETTER.   A letter from your auditor stating that he has reviewed the finances and found that no significant changes had occurred since the last quarterly or annual report.

9. BLUE SKY.   The "Blue Sky memorandum" is a certificate signed by bankers' lawyers saying that they have verified the relevant legislation in different states and have no objections to the selling of the issue in those states. (Only for municipal bonds in the United States.)

10. RESPONSIBILITY.   The agreement with the fiscal agent for payment is a convention signed between the borrower and a company mandated to look after interest and capital payments to the lenders. This agreement should be negotiated directly between the borrower and the mandated company. In certain countries like Germany or Switzerland, a choice is not available. The banker responsible for the issue will insist on being your payment agent.

11. PRINTING.   You then have to negotiate with a printer to have the obligations printed.

12. PRE-CLOSURE.   A ceremony in the course of which the lawyers for the two parties verify that the whole document is satisfactory.

13. CLOSURE.   A signing ceremony.

14. DELIVERY AND PAYMENT.

Euro-markets

Procedures for borrowing on other markets are, with the exception of Japan, rather similar but in general easier. In Europe, central bankers are less demanding regarding declarations and legal procedures than is the case in the United States. In London, the prospectus has been replaced by a so-called "Extel Card." Generally speaking, one or two pages is enough to describe the issue and the company whereas in the United States, it can take between 60 to 100 pages.

Borrowing approval is virtually automatic if you are a regular borrower. The same thing is true in Switzerland where the prospectus takes the form of a summary prospectus of a few pages. In Germany, a complete prospectus is required, but it is less stringent. In both countries approval is straightforward if you have indicated your intention to borrow to the central bank, generally a few weeks in advance. The other stages are almost the same as in the United States.

Conditions in Canada

In Canada, a complete prospectus has to be provided by most companies unless they are the property of the government, which are exempt from this requirement. It is therefore much easier for Hydro-Québec to borrow on the Canadian market. The guarantee contract consists of only a few pages. Generally, we prepare a circular of offer of about a page giving the essential details of the issue (although this is not required by law).

We get the approval of the Board of Directors and of the Government of Quebec, which guarantees our issues. For companies subject to the Canadian Security Commissions, the steps are virtually the same as those in the United States.

Hydro-Québec 1990 Prospectus

Prospectus

Hydro-Québec
Debt Securities

Guaranteed unconditionally as to principal, premium, if any, and interest by

Province de Québec (Canada)

Hydro-Québec may from time to time offer Debt Securities, guaranteed by Province de Québec, and, together with such Debt Securities or separately, Warrants to purchase such Debt Securities (collectively, the "Securities") in an aggregate principal amount of not more than U.S. $1,200,000,000 (or the equivalent thereof in one or more other currencies or currency units) on terms to be determined at the time of sale. Prospectus Supplements hereto will contain (i) the terms of the Securities, including, where applicable, the designation, currency or currencies of denomination and payment (which may include the European Currency Unit), aggregate principal amount, maturity, rate or rates of interest, or any formula for the determination thereof, interest payment dates, purchase price, denominations and any terms for redemption or sinking funds, (ii) the names of and principal amounts to be purchased by any underwriters, any underwriting discounts and commissions and other terms of the plan of distribution and, if appropriate, (iii) information relating to developments subsequent to the date of this Prospectus.

THESE SECURITIES HAVE NOT BEEN APPROVED OR DISAPPROVED BY THE SECURITIES AND EXCHANGE COMMISSION OR ANY STATE SECURITIES COMMISSION NOR HAS THE SECURITIES AND EXCHANGE COMMISSION OR ANY STATE SECURITIES COMMISSION PASSED UPON THE ACCURACY OR ADEQUACY OF THIS PROSPECTUS. ANY REPRESENTATION TO THE CONTRARY IS A CRIMINAL OFFENSE.

The date of this Prospectus is April 3, 1990.

CONSOLIDATED FINANCIAL STATEMENTS, HYDRO-QUÉBEC

Consolidated Statements of Operations

	Year Ended December 31				
	1985	1986	1987	1988	1989
	(in millions of dollars)				
Revenue:					
Sales of electricity (Note 3)	$4,423	$4,673	$5,040	$5,223	$5,503
Other operating income	46	39	28	55	56
	4,469	4,712	5,068	5,278	5,559
Expenditure:					
Operations	1,140	1,107	1,219	1,391	1,597
Electricity purchased	122	118	110	136	253
Depreciation of fixed assets	419	464	500	538	585
Taxes (Note 4)	246	272	289	295	324
	1,927	1,961	2,118	2,360	2,759

(*Continued*)

| | YEAR ENDED DECEMBER 31 | | | | |
	1985	1986	1987	1988	1989
Income before Interest and Exchange Loss	2,542	2,751	2,950	2,918	2,800
Interest (Note 5)	2,077	2,259	2,170	2,050	2,165
Exchange loss	256[a]	189[a]	272[a]	249[a]	70[a]
	2,333	2,448	2,442	2,299	2,235
Net Income	$ 209	$ 303	$ 508	$ 619	$ 565

[a]Including amortization of unrealized exchange loss of $252 million in 1985, $171 million in 1986, $208 million in 1987, $93 million in 1988 and $48 million in 1989. Since 1986, these amounts reflect the effective hedge by Hydro-Québec against the exchange rate risk on its long-term debt denominated in U.S. dollars.

HYDRO-QUÉBEC

Consolidated Balance Sheets

| | As AT DECEMBER 31 | |
	1988	1989
	(in millions of dollars)	
ASSETS		
Fixed Assets:		
Property and plant (Note 6):		
In service	$29,990	$31,415
Less accumulated depreciation	4,402	4,898
	25,588	26,517
Construction in progress	3,402	4,293
	28,990	30,810
Current Assets:		
Cash and temporary investments	145	571
Accounts receivable	1,051	1,251
Materials, fuel, and supplies	242	289
	1,438	2,111
Other Assets:		
Investments (Note 7)	127	153
Deferred expenses (Note 8)	1,207	878
	1,334	1,031
	$31,762	$33,952

LIABILITIES AND SHAREHOLDER'S EQUITY		
Long-term Debt (Note 9):	$20,576	$21,957
Current Liabilities:		
Accounts payable	723	1,090
Dividends payable	300	182
Notes payable	16	18
Accrued interest	756	865
Long-term debt payable within one year (Note 9)	989	1,045
	2,784	3,200
Other Liability:		
Decommissioning of the nuclear generating station (Note 10)	—	10
Perpetual Debt (Note 11):	552	552
Shareholder's Equity:		
Share capital		
Authorized		
50,000,000 shares, par value of $100 each		
Issued and fully paid		
43,741,090 shares	4,374	4,374
Retained earnings	3,476	3,859
	7,850	8,233
	$31,762	$33,952

HYDRO-QUÉBEC

Consolidated Statements of Shareholder's Equity

	YEAR ENDED DECEMBER 31				
	1985	1986	1987	1988	1989
	(in millions of dollars)				
Retained Earnings:					
Balance at beginning of period	$2,137	$2,346	$2,649	$3,157	$3,476
Plus: Net income	209	303	508	619	565
Less: Dividends (Note 12)	—	—	—	300	182
Balance at end of period	2,346	2,649	3,157	3,476	3,859
Capital Stock:	4,374	4,374	4,374	4,374	4,374
Shareholders' Equity at end of period:	$6,720	$7,023	$7,531	$7,850	$8,233

Consolidated Statements of Changes in Financial Position

	YEAR ENDED DECEMBER 31				
	1985	1986	1987	1988	1989
	(in millions of dollars)				
Funds Provided by Operations:					
Net income	$ 209	$ 303	$ 508	$ 619	$ 565
Depreciation of fixed assets	419	464	500	538	585
Amortization of deferred expenses	397	364	383	358	181
Difference between pension expense and contributions	—	(75)	(75)	(77)	(66)
Other	(10)	5	5	3	24
	1,015	1,061	1,323	1,441	1,289
Declared dividends	—	—	—	(300)	(182)
	1,015	1,061	1,323	1,141	1,107
Changes in working capital[a] (Note 13)	(35)	(254)	64	355	(313)
	980	807	1,387	1,496	794
Funds Provided by External Financing:					
Issue of long-term and perpetual debt	1,952	1,809	1,842	1,860	2,894
Redemption of long-term debt	(1,228)	(1,050)	(1,541)	(1,249)	(1,223)
	724	759	301	611	1,671
Funds Available for Investment:	$1,704	$1,566	$1,688	$2,107	$2,465
Investment:					
Fixed assets	$1,528	$1,470	$1,581	$2,033	$2,412
Grants under sales programs	87	67	88	62	32
Other	89	29	19	12	21
	$1,704	$1,566	$1,688	$2,107	$2,465

[a]Excluding long-term debt payable within one year.

Note 8: Deferred Expenses

Deferred expenses comprise the unamortized balances of the following items:

	1988	1989
	(in millions of dollars)	
Unrealized exchange loss	$ 469	$120
Grants under sales programs	226	170
Debt-security discount and expenses	197	229
Pension expense	225	291
Other	80	68
	$1,207	$878

Note 9: Long-Term Debt

Hydro-Québec's long-term debt is guaranteed by the Province de Québec, except for an amount of $169 million ($177 million in 1988).

Debenture and other long-term maturities and sinking fund requirements, translated into Canadian dollars, are shown in the following table:

	DECEMBER 31, 1988		DECEMBER 31, 1989	
YEARS OF MATURITY	(IN MILLIONS OF DOLLARS)	WEIGHTED AVERAGE INTEREST RATE	(IN MILLIONS OF DOLLARS)	WEIGHTED AVERAGE INTEREST RATE
1989	$ 989		$ —	
1990	1,068		1,045	
1991	1,517		1,531	
1992	1,801		1,698	
1993	863		1,050	
1994	—		1,044	
1–5 years	6,238	12.31%	6,368	13.08%
6–10 years	6,089	10.44%	6,282	10.09%
11–15 years	3,046	9.75%	3,138	9.93%
16–20 years	3,319	10.67%	2,824	10.74%
21–25 years	1,682	11.36%	2,268	10.94%
26–30 years	434	10.25%	509	10.16%
31–35 years	—	—	—	—
36–40 years	757	8.25%	1,613	8.50%
	21,565	10.92%	23,002	10.97%
Less: Portion payable within one year	989		1,045	
	$20,576		$21,957	

See "Long-term Debt by Issue" for a breakdown by specific issuances of Hydro-Québec's long-term debt.

Repayments to be made in Canadian dollars and in foreign currencies, with their Canadian dollar equivalent, are shown in the following table:

	1988	1989			
	TOTAL (IN MILLIONS OF DOLLARS)	(IN MILLIONS OF UNITS)			TOTAL (IN MILLIONS OF DOLLARS)
	1989 TO 2027	1990 TO 1994	1995 TO 2029	TOTAL	1990 TO 2029
Canadian dollars	$ 9,608	2,275	8,863	11,138	$11,138
At rates established according to conditions of monetary agreement:					
United States dollars	2,934	1,986	316	2,302	2,983
Deutsche marks	179	470	301	771	447
Swiss francs	195	575	100	675	439
Yen	412	25,000	20,450	45,450	412
Pounds sterling	174	—	75	75	174
ECUs	—	—	125	125	157
	13,502				15,750
At rates in effect at balance sheet date:					
United States dollars	6,058	316	4,886	5,202[a]	6,027
Deutsche marks	700	373	385	758	518
Swiss francs	639	21	450	471	354
Yen	191	—	—	—	—
Pounds sterling	324	—	150	150	280
ECUs	70	—	—	—	—
Guilders	81	75	45	120	73
	8,063				7,252
	$21,565				$23,002

[a]A proportion of 91% (80% in 1988) is hedged by future revenue streams in United States dollars.

Hydro-Québec has two undrawn revolving standby credits for U.S. $400 million and U.S. $750 million which expire in 1993 and 1994, respectively. Any borrowing under these lines of credit will bear interest at a rate based on the London Interbank Offered Rate (LIBOR).

Subsequent to December 31, 1989, Hydro-Québec has issued or agreed to issue the following long-term debt:

CURRENCY	RATES	YEAR OF MATURITY	PRINCIPAL AMOUNT (IN MILLIONS OF UNITS)
United States dollars (medium-term notes)	9.00–9.41%	2000	70
Swiss francs	7.25%	2000	200
Deutsche marks	LIBOR	2000	500
Swiss francs	7.50%	2000	100
United States dollars	LIBOR	2000	200
Canadian dollars	10.25%	2012	100
Pounds Sterling	$12\frac{5}{8}$%	2015	150

Note 10: Decommissioning of the Nuclear Generating Station

With a view to the decommissioning of the Gentilly 2 nuclear generating station, Hydro-Québec has this year begun to constitute a provision for its dismantlement and final disposal of the irradiated fuel. For 1989, this provision amounts to $1 million and $9 million respectively.

Note 11: Perpetual Debt

Perpetual notes in the amount of U.S. $400 million bear interest at a rate based on the London Interbank Offered Rate (LIBOR) established twice yearly. They are guaranteed by the Province de Québec and are redeemable, at Hydro-Québec's option only, beginning in 1991. These notes are shown in Canadian dollars at the exchange rate in effect at date of issue ($463 million at exchange rate in effect at December 31, 1989).

Note 12: Restrictions on Dividends

Under the Hydro-Québec Act, the dividends to be paid by Hydro-Québec are declared once a year by the Gouvernement du Québec, which also determines the terms and conditions of payment. For a given financial year,

they cannot exceed the distributable surplus, which is established as follows: 75% of income before interest and exchange loss and the year's net investment income, less interest on debt securities and amortization of debt-security discount and expenses. This calculation is made on the basis of the consolidated financial statements.

However, in respect of a given financial year no dividend may be declared in an amount that would have the effect of reducing the rate of capitalization to less than 25% at the end of the year concerned. This rate corresponds to the ratio between shareholder's equity (less dividends declared for the year) and the total of long-term debt, notes payable, perpetual debt and shareholder's equity (less dividends declared for the year).

The government declares the dividends for a given year within 30 days after the transmission by Hydro-Québec to the government of the financial data relative to the distributable surplus. On expiry of the time prescribed, any distributable surplus or part thereof which has not been subject to a dividend declaration may no longer be distributed to the shareholder as a dividend. In accordance with the above, dividends of $238 million could have been declared for the 1989 financial year. However, the Gouvernement du Québec declared dividends of $182 million.

Note 13: Changes in Working Capital

	YEAR ENDED DECEMBER 31				
	1985	1986	1987	1988	1989
	(in millions of dollars)				
(Increase) decrease in current assets:					
Cash and temporary investments	$ 146	$ (58)	$ (88)	$ 17	$(426)
Accounts receivable	(132)	(106)	(40)	36	(200)
Materials, fuel and supplies	(46)	12	(9)	(19)	(47)
	(32)	(152)	(137)	34	(673)

(Continued)

	YEAR ENDED DECEMBER 31				
	1985	1986	1987	1988	1989
Increase (decrease) in current liabilities:					
Accounts payable	11	(80)	119	129	367
Dividends payable	(156)	—	—	300	(118)
Notes payable	66	(59)	85	(78)	2
Accrued interest	76	37	(3)	(30)	109
	(3)	(102)	201	321	360
	$ (35)	$ (254)	$ 64	$355	$(313)

Note 14: Retirement Plan

The Hydro-Québec Retirement Plan is a contributory, defined benefit pension plan based on final pay, under which benefits payable are guaranteed by Hydro-Québec. At December 31, 1989, 19,073 employees were contributing to the plan. An actuarial valuation was made in 1989 in order to determine the present value of accrued benefits based on employees' expected basic salary until retirement. The retirement fund assets are valued at market-related value.

At December 31, 1989, the date of the most recent valuation, the retirement plan showed a surplus as follows:

	(IN MILLIONS OF DOLLARS)
Retirement fund assets	$ 3,178
Present value of accrued benefits	(2,573)
Excess special contributions made by Hydro-Québec	(21)
Surplus	$ 584

For the year ended December 31, 1989, pension expense amounted to $27 million ($14 million in 1988).

Note 15: Commitments and Projected Capital Expenditures

CHURCHILL FALLS

On May 12, 1969, Hydro-Québec signed a contract with Churchill Falls (Labrador) Corporation Limited (CFLCo) whereby Hydro-Québec undertook to purchase virtually all the power generated at the Churchill Falls generating station for a period of 40 years from September 1, 1976, except for an amount not to exceed 300,000 kilowatts of such power which may be recaptured by CFLCo. This contract will be automatically renewed for a further period of 25 years upon already agreed terms.

By this contract, Hydro-Québec undertook to make payment for energy whether or not taken, subject to certain limitations and compensations, and to pay CFLCo an amount equal to a portion of the interest charges on the debt incurred by CFLCo to finance the construction of the plant as well as an amount equal to a portion of the losses on foreign exchange incurred to service the debt issued in U.S. dollars. Hydro-Québec can also be required to make additional advances, against the issue of units of Subordinated Debentures and shares of Common Stock, to service the debt of CFLCo and to cover its expenses if funds are not otherwise available.

PROJECTED CAPITAL EXPENDITURES

Hydro-Québec plans call for capital expenditures in the amount of $3,480 million for the year 1990.

Note 16: Reclassification

Some of the comparative figures for years 1985 to 1988 were reclassified in order to conform to the presentation adopted in 1989.

Long-term Debt by Issue

The following table sets forth the long-term debt of Hydro-Québec outstanding as of December 31, 1989 expressed in Canadian dollars and in currency of issue:

Series	Interest Rate per Cent	Years of Issue	Years of Maturity	December 31, 1989 Canadian Dollars	References
				(in thousands)	
Payable in Canadian Dollars					
BM[a]	9.50	1970	1990	$ 5,072	2
AZ[a]	6.50	1967	1990	22,793	2
FT1	11.00	1985	1990	117,000	1
FT3	11.00	1985	1990	55,000	1
GK	9.00	1986	1990	100,000	1
BH[a]	7.75	1969	1990	199	2
DV1	14.00	1980	1990	154,711	1
AW[a]	6.00	1966	1990	25,267	2
ED	13.25	1980	1990	80,000	1, 11
BO[a]	9.50	1970	1990	22,675	2
FS	12.375	1985	1991	50,000	1
AU[a]	6.00	1966	1991	27,935	2
EF1	13.50	1981	1991	52,118	1
EN1	17.50	1981	1991	129,778	1
GR	8.25	1987	1992	250,000	1
DW1	14.00	1980	1992	198,115	1
BK[a]	8.50	1969	1992	21,915	2
FE	9.50	1982	1992	45,855	1
FFA	12.00	1983	1993	50,000	1
FF1	12.00	1983	1993	98,000	1
EX	16.90	1982	1993	100,000	1
FJ	12.75	1983	1993	79,772	10
FI2	12.50	1983	1993	67,000	1
FIA	12.50	1984	1993	50,000	1
BZ[a]	8.25	1972	1993	50,925	2
AN2[a]	5.50	1964	1994	923	2
FO	13.00	1984	1994	75,000	1
FQ2	14.25	1984	1994	115,000	1
BE[a]	7.00	1968	1994	21,826	2

(Continued)

Series	Interest Rate per Cent	Years of Issue	Years of Maturity	December 31, 1989 Canadian Dollars	References
BC1[a]	6.00	1967	1994	21,153	2
BC2[a]	7.00	1967	1994	10,400	2
FR	13.00	1984	1994	110,000	1
GM	9.50	1986	1994	65,000	1
AR2[a]	5.00	1965	1995	24,837	2
FZ	8.00	1985	1995	53,242	1
FX	12.25	1985	1995	100,000	10
GX	10.25	1988	1995	125,000	1
GA	11.00	1985	1995	100,000	10
GC1	10.75	1985	1995	220,000	1
BT[a]	7.75	1971	1996	36,690	2
CY[a]	10.75	1976	1996	13,627	7
CLA	9.875	1974	1996	25,000	2
CL	9.875	1974	1996	55,000	2
EH1	15.75	1981	1996	158,446	1
BU[a]	8.75	1971	1996	41,189	2
GI	9.25	1986	1996	150,000	1
EL1	17.50	1981	1996	127,762	1
CB	8.25	1972	1996	50,000	2
GP	9.25	1986	1996	565,000	1
GN[a]	9.50	1987	1997	28,000	6
GS	9.00	1987	1997	150,000	1
BY[a]	8.25	1972	1997	39,764	2
DD	10.00	1977	1997	100,000	2
DD1	10.00	1984	1997	90,984	2
GU1	9.75	1987	1997	278,000	1
CU	10.25	1975	1997	65,000	2
CA[a]	8.375	1972	1997	45,539	2
CD	8.00	1973	1998	50,000	2
CE	8.25	1973	1998	55,000	2
CG	8.75	1973	1998	50,000	2
CH	8.50	1975	1998	50,000	2
HA	10.75	1988/1989	1999	600,000	1
HC	11.00	1989	1999	500,000	1
CK	9.00	1974	1999	60,000	2
CRA	9.75	1977	2000	125,000	2
CR2	9.75	1975	2000	100,000	2
CS	10.00	1975	2000	80,000	2
ED1	13.25	1980	2000	5,000	1
GG	9.50	1986	2001	150,000	1
DA	10.00	1976	2001	120,000	2
EZ2	15.75	1982	2002	46,000	2
FF2	13.00	1983	2003	67,000	2

(Continued)

Series	Interest Rate per Cent	Years of Issue	Years of Maturity	December 31, 1989 Canadian Dollars	References
DG	10.25	1978	2003	120,000	2
DGA	10.25	1979	2003	140,000	2
DGB	10.25	1979	2003	150,000	2
DH	10.00	1978	2003	125,000	2
DHA	10.00	1978	2003	125,000	2
DM2	10.75	1979	2004	135,000	2
DMA	10.75	1979	2004	135,000	2
DRA	11.00	1979	2004	200,000	2
DR	11.00	1979	2004	150,000	2
DZ	11.75	1980	2005	200,000	2
EA	13.25	1980	2005	185,000	2
EA1	13.25	1983	2005	125,000	2
EA2	13.25	1984	2005	50,000	2
EA3	13.25	1984	2005	50,000	2
EA4	13.25	1984	2005	50,000	2
FT2	12.25	1985/1988	2006	203,000	1
GO[a]	9.75	1987	2007	54,000	6
GZ	11.25	1988	2008	100,000	1
GC2	11.25	1985	2008	100,000	2
HF	10.00	1989	2011	450,000	1
GU2	10.25	1987/1989	2012	1,017,000	1
HG	10.00	1989	2019	100,000	1

Government of Quebec 1990–1994   359

Government of Canada 1990–2008   12,619

Atomic Energy of Canada Limited 1990–1999   138,214

Present value of lease obligations for regional offices
    and service facilities for a period not exceeding
    25 years ending in 2007   156,976

Churchill Falls (Labrador) Corporation Limited
    (CFLCo), 1990–1992   11,759

Notes payable   125,000

Less Sinking Fund Investments   (245,822)

    11,137,617

Adjustments relating to swaps and
    forward exchange contracts   4,612,323

    $15,749,940

Series	Interest Rate per Cent	Years of Issue	Years of Maturity	December 31, 1989 Canadian Dollars	Currency of Issue		References
				(in thousands)			
(Payable in U.S. Dollars)							
EI	16.25	1981	1991	$ 231,700	U.S. $	200,000	[1]
EK	17.375	1981	1991	289,625		250,000	[1]
AX[a]	6.25	1966	1991	27,950		24,126	[4]
EM	17.25	1981	1991	173,775		150,000	[1]
BG[a]	7.25	1968	1991	39,069		33,724	[4]
EQ	16.625	1982	1992	231,700		200,000	[1]
AV[a]	5.375	1966	1992	45,082		38,914	[4]
DE[a]	9.00	1977	1992	93,835		80,997	[9]
EY	14.625	1982	1992	173,775		150,000	[1]
BB[a]	6.50	1967	1992	37,619		32,472	[4]
FD[a]	11.50	1982	1992	99,428		85,825	[9]
AY[a]	6.25	1967	1993	43,706		37,726	[4]
BA[a]	6.25	1967	1993	38,460		33,198	[4]
FL1	12.375	1983	1993	115,850		100,000	[1]
AO[a]	4.50	1964	1994	57,925		50,000	[4]
GBU	8.00	1985	1995	127,059		109,675	[1, 12]
CX[a]	10.25	1976	1996	448,193		386,874	[7]
GJ	8.175	1986	1996	83,412		72,000	[1]
DC[a]	8.75	1976	1996	22,562		19,475	[7]
DF[a]	9.25	1977	1997	144,954		125,122	[3]
HB	9.75	1988	1998	173,775		150,000	[1]
BR[a]	8.75	1971	1999	56,500		48,770	[4]
BI[a]	8.75	1969	1999	38,899		33,577	[4]
BV[a]	8.50	1971	2001	61,463		53,054	[4]
BX[a]	7.875	1972	2002	88,615		76,491	[4]
FY	Floating	1985	2002	231,700		200,000	[8]
CC[a]	7.50	1973	2003	111,882		96,575	[4]
CF[a]	8.50	1973	2003	82,877		71,538	[4]
CI[a]	8.25	1974	2004	115,299		99,524	[4]
FV	Floating	1985	2005	231,700		200,000	[8]
CT[a]	9.75	1975	2005	195,695		168,921	[4]
CW[a]	10.00	1975	2005	229,297		197,926	[4]
CZ[a]	8.60	1976	2006	234,125		202,093	[4]
GV	10.70	1987	2007	289,625		250,000	[5]
DJ[a]	10.00	1978	2008	108,690		93,820	[4]
DL[a]	10.00	1979	2009	223,901		193,268	[4]
DQ[a]	10.125	1979	2009	211,548		182,605	[4]
DS[a]	11.25	1979	2009	229,367		197,986	[4]
DY[a]	10.75	1980	2010	272,479		235,200	[4]
EC2[a]	13.25	1980	2010	148,756		128,404	[4]
FU[a]	11.75	1985	2012	231,700		200,000	[1]
FG2[a]	13.375	1983	2013	103,570		89,400	[4]

(Continued)

Series	Interest Rate per Cent	Years of Issue	Years of Maturity	December 31, 1989		References
				Canadian Dollars	Currency of Issue	
FL2[a]	13.25	1983	2013	158,743	137,025	4
GW	9.75	1988	2018	289,625	250,000	5
GF[a]	8.875	1986	2026	289,625	250,000	1
GH[a]	8.25	1986	2026	289,625	250,000	1
GQ	8.25	1987	2027	289,625	250,000	1
HE	8.625	1989	2029	289,625	250,000	1
HH	8.50	1989	2029	579,250	500,000	1
Medium-term notes payable at rates ranging from 9.23% to 9.82% ending in 1998				184,873	159,580	
Notes payable				179,568	155,000	
Less Sinking Fund Investments				(9,455)	(8,161)	
				8,738,246	7,542,724	
Adjustments relating to swaps and forward exchange contracts				271,380	(38,400)	
Long-term debt at rates established according to conditions of monetary agreement				(2,983,146)	(2,302,356)	
				$ 6,026,480	U.S.$5,201,968	
(payable in Deutsche Marks)						
D8[a]	10.25	1981	1991	$ 102,704	DM150,000	1
D9	10.50	1982	1992	102,704	150,000	1
D10	10.25	1982	1992	123,245	180,000	1
D11[a]	8.00	1983	1993	136,938	200,000	9
D12B[a]	7.75	1984	1994	67,476	98,550	1
D13[a]	7.125	1985	1995	136,254	199,000	1
D15A[a]	5.50	1986	1996	77,370	113,000	1
D16[a]	6.75	1989	1999	205,408	300,000	1
D15B[a]	6.00	1986	2016	94,488	138,000	1
Less Sinking Fund Investments				(10)	(14)	
				1,046,577	1,528,536	
Adjustments relating to swaps and forward exchange contracts				(81,161)		
Long-term debt at rates established according to conditions of monetary agreement				(446,514)	(770,675)	
				$ 518,902	DM 757,861	
(payable in Japanese Yen)						
GE	6.625	1986	1994	$ 80,479	¥ 10,000,000	1
GT	4.625	1987	1994	120,718	15,000,000	1
J4	5.20	1987	1997	84,101	10,450,000	1
J5	5.50	1988	1998	80,479	10,000,000	
				365,777	45,450,000	

(Continued)

Series	Interest Rate per Cent	Years of Issue	Years of Maturity	December 31, 1989 Canadian Dollars	Currency of Issue	References
Adjustments relating to swaps and forward exchange contracts				46,423		
Long-term debt at rates established according to conditions of monetary agreement				(412,200)	(45,450,000)	
				$ 0	¥ 0	
(payable in Swiss Francs)						
F25	6.00	1983	1990	$ 75,081	SF 100,000	1
F27	5.50	1984	1990	112,622	150,000	1
F13[a]	3.75	1978	1993	58,563	78,000	3
F26[a]	5.875	1984	1994	112,021	149,200	9
F29	4.75	1986	1994	56,311	75,000	10
F31	5.125	1987	1997	75,081	100,000	3
F32A[a]	4.625	1988	1998	75,081	100,000	3
F30[a]	5.00	1987	2002	150,162	200,000	3
F32B[a]	5.00	1988	2008	75,081	100,000	3
Less Sinking Fund Investments				(4,336)	(5,775)	
				785,667	1,046,425	
Adjustments relating to swaps and forward exchange contracts				7,497	100,000	
Long-term debt at rates established according to conditions of monetary agreement				(439,213)	(675,000)	
				$ 353,951	SF 471,425	
(payable in Pounds Sterling)						
GY	9.625	1988	1995	$ 139,932	£ 75,000	1
FH	13.24	1983	2003	111,946	60,000	1
EG	15.00	1981	2011	74,631	40,000	1
FA	12.75	1982	2015	93,288	50,000	1
				419,797	225,000	
Adjustments relating to swaps and forward exchange contracts				34,421		
Long-term debt at rates established according to conditions of monetary agreement				(174,353)	(75,000)	
				$ 279,865	£150,000	
(payable in European Currency Units)						
HD	9.25	1989	1999	$ 173,456	ECU 125,000	1
Adjustments relating to swaps and forward exchange contracts				(16,559)		

(Continued)

| | | | | December 31, 1989 | | |
Series	Interest Rate per Cent	Years of Issue	Years of Maturity	Canadian Dollars	Currency of Issue	References
Long-term debt at rates established according to conditions of monetary agreement				(156,897)	(125,000)	
				$ 0	ECU 0	
(payable in Dutch Guilders)						
EW	11.125	1982	1997	$3,0 72,766	DG 120,000	*1*
Total Long-term Debt				$23,001,094*b*		

*a*Sinking-fund debentures.

*b*See Note 9 of the Notes of Consolidated Financial Statements.

[1]Noncallable.

[2]Redeemable at par 1 to 6 years prior to maturity.

[3]Redeemable at a premium within 10 years after the date of issue and thereafter at various declining premiums.

[4]Redeemable 15 years after the date of issue and thereafter at various declining premiums or discounts.

[5]Redeemable at par 5 to 15 years after the date of issue.

[6]Redeemable at par in annual installments for sinking fund purposes 1 year after the date of issue.

[7]Redeemable at par in annual installments for sinking fund purposes 3 years after the date of issue.

[8]Redeemable at par in semiannual installments 3 years after the date of issue.

[9]Redeemable at par or less in quarterly, in semiannual or in annual instalments for purchase fund purposes.

[10]Redeemable at a premium 3 to 5 years prior to maturity.

[11]Exchangeable at the holder's option into debentures maturing in 2000.

[12]This represents a dual currency Japanese Yen U.S. dollar issue, the principal of which is payable in U.S. dollars.

Hydro-Québec: Company Profile and Financial Data

Company Profiles: Hydro-Québec

75 Boulevard René-Levesque Ouest
Montreal Quebec H2Z 1A4
Canada

Telephone: (514) 289-2211

SEDOL no	445143
ISIN no	CA448814BX09
Ticker symbol	NA
Exchange	NA
Indices	NA
Current exchange rate	0.88183 U.S. Dollars per Canadian Dollars
SIC codes	4911 Electric services
Industry class	Utility
Major industry group	Utilities
Minor industry group	Electric power companies
Industry average category	Utilities—Canada
Description of business	Residential & farm use accounted for 37% of 1990 revenues; industrial, 37%; general, 22% & other, 4%
Product lines	Consumer services
Current outstanding shares	43,741,090
Shareholders	NA
Number of employees	20,067
Market value	NA
Fiscal year end	12/31

Latest annual financial date	12/31/90
Auditor	Deloitte & Touche
Auditor's report	Unqualified
Date of acquisition/ status	NA
Security identifier	NA

All Annual Financial Information: Hydro-Québec

	Five-Year Summary		
Date	Sales (000's)	Net Income (000's)	EPS
1990	5,885,000	404,000	9.24
1989	5,559,000	565,000	12.92
1988	5,306,000	619,000	14.15
1987	5,040,000	508,000	11.61
1986	4,673,000	303,000	6.93
Growth rate	5.88	14.09	14.0

BALANCE SHEET

FISCAL YEAR ENDING	12/31/90	12/31/89	12/31/88
ASSETS (000's)			
Cash & equivalents	760,000	571,000	145,000
Net receivables[a]	1,236,000	1,251,000	1,051,000
Raw materials	NA	NA	NA
Work in process	NA	NA	NA
Finished goods	NA	NA	NA
Other inventories	NA	NA	NA
Inventories	312,000	289,000	242,000

Source: Disclosure, 1991.

(*Continued*)

FISCAL YEAR ENDING	12/31/90	12/31/89	12/31/88
Prepaid expenses	0	NA	NA
Other current assets	0	0	0
Total current assets	2,308,000	2,111,000	1,438,000
Invest in assoc comp	0	153,000	127,000
Long-term receivables	0	NA	NA
Gross PP&E	38,764,000	35,708,000	33,392,000
Accum depreciation	5,509,000	4,898,000	4,402,000
Net PP&E	33,255,000	30,810,000	28,990,000
Tangible oth assets	NA	0	NA
Intangible oth assets	NA	878,000	NA
Other assets	929,000	878,000	1,207,000
Total assets	36,684,000	33,952,000	31,762,000

FISCAL YEAR ENDING	12/31/90	12/31/89	12/31/88

LIABILITIES (000's)

	12/31/90	12/31/89	12/31/88
Accounts payable	914,000	1,090,000	NA
St debt & cur ltd	1,576,000	1,063,000	1,005,000
Accrued payroll	NA	NA	NA
Dividend payable	0	182,000	NA
Income taxes payable	NA	NA	NA
Oth cur liabilities	920,000	865,000	1,779,000
Tot cur liabilities	3,410,000	3,200,000	2,784,000
Long-term debt	24,624,000	22,509,000	21,128,000
Risk & charge prov	NA	NA	NA
Deferred taxes	0	NA	NA
Other liabilities	13,000	10,000	0
Unreal sec gain / loss	0	NA	NA
Total liabilities	28,047,000	25,719,000	23,912,000
Non-equity reserves	0	NA	NA
Minority interest	0	0	0
Preferred stock	0	0	0
Common stock / ord cap	4,374,000	4,374,000	NA
Capital surplus	NA	NA	NA
Revaluation reserves	0	NA	NA
Oth approp reserves	NA	NA	NA
Unapp reserves	NA	NA	NA
Retained earnings	4,263,000	3,859,000	NA
Esop guarantees	0	NA	NA
Foreign currency	0	NA	NA
Treasury stock	0	NA	NA
Common shldrs equity	8,637,000	8,233,000	7,850,000
Tot liab & shldrs eq	36,684,000	33,952,000	31,762,000

FISCAL YEAR ENDING	12/31/90	12/31/89	12/31/88

INCOME STATEMENT (000's)

	12/31/90	12/31/89	12/31/88
Net sales	5,885,000	5,559,000	5,306,000
Cost of goods sold	2,009,000	NA	NA
Gross income	NA	NA	NA
Depreciation & amort	677,000	585,000	538,000

	12/31/90	12/31/89	12/31/88
Sell gen & admin exp	NA	NA	NA
Other oper expenses	0	1,850,000	1,555,000
Total oper expenses	2,686,000	2,435,000	2,093,000
Operating income	3,199,000	3,124,000	3,213,000
Interest expense	2,339,000	2,165,000	2,307,000
Interest capitalized	0	0	257,000
Extra credit—pretax	0	NA	NA
Extra charge—pretax	0	NA	NA
Net oth inc / exp	−95,000	−70,000	−415,000
Inc / dec in reserves	0	NA	NA
Pretax income	765,000	889,000	748,000
Income taxes[b]	361,000	324,000	129,000
Minority interest	0	0	0
Equity in earnings	0	0	0
After tax inc / exp	0	NA	NA
Disc operations	0	0	0
Net inc bef ex items	404,000	565,000	619,000
Extraordinary items	0	0	0
Net inc bef pref div	404,000	565,000	619,000
Pref div requirement	0	0	0
Net income	404,000	565,000	619,000

FISCAL YEAR ENDING	12/31/90	12/31/89	12/31/88

KEY FINANCIAL ITEMS (000's US$)

	12/31/90	12/31/89	12/31/88
Market capital (US$)	NA	NA	NA
Common equity (US$)	7,445,699	7,109,196	6,579,870
Total assets (US$)	31,624,176	29,317,552	26,622,908
Sales (US$)	5,073,282	4,800,197	4,447,489
Net income (US$)	348,276	487,878	518,846

Sources of Funds

FISCAL YEAR ENDING	12/31/90	12/31/89	12/31/88

FUNDS FLOW STATEMENT (000's)

	12/31/90	12/31/89	12/31/88
Net income	404,000	565,000	619,000
Depre, deple & amort	881,000	766,000	NA
Defer tax & itc	0	0	0
Other cash flow	−11,000	−355,000	639,000
Funds from operation	1,274,000	976,000	1,796,000
Extraordinary items	0	0	0
Funds—oth oper act	−311,000	NA	NA
Proceed sale / iss stk	0	0	0
Stockoption proceeds	0	0	0
Other stock sales	0	0	0
Disposal fix assets	0	0	0
Net assets—acquisitn	0	0	NA
Incr / decr in st debt	0	0	NA
Long-term borrowing	3,378,000	2,894,000	1,860,000
Decr in investments	0	0	NA
Other sources	0	NA	−1,549,000
Total sources	4,652,000	3,870,000	2,107,000

(Continued)

Uses of funds

FISCAL YEAR ENDING	12/31/90	12/31/89	12/31/88
Total dividends paid	0	182,000	300,000
Capital expenditure	3,133,000	2,412,000	2,033,000
Addits to oth assets	0	0	0
Reduction in lt debt	972,000	1,223,000	2,107,000
Com/pfd purch rtrd	0	0	0
Incr in investments	0	NA	NA
Other uses	45,000	NA	-2,333,000
Total uses	4,150,000	3,817,000	2,107,000

Reconciliation of sources

FISCAL YEAR ENDING	12/31/90	12/31/89	12/31/88
Effect—exch on cash	NA	NA	NA
Inc/dec cash & st invs	NA	NA	NA
Inc/dec work capital	-13,000	257,000	-440,000
Nt cash fl—oper-actv	NA	NA	NA
Net csh flow—investg	NA	NA	NA
Net csh flow—fincing	NA	NA	NA

FISCAL YEAR ENDING	12/31/90	12/31/89	12/31/88

SUPPLEMENTARY DATA (000's)[c]

	12/31/90	12/31/89	12/31/88
Working capital	-1,102,000	-1,089,000	-1,346,000
Total capital	33,261,000	30,732,000	28,978,000
Goodwill written off	0	NA	NA
R & D expense	NA	NA	NA
For cur trans g/l	-95,000	-70,000	-249,000
External financing	2,406,000	1,671,000	-247,000
Interest exp on debt	2,339,000	2,165,000	2,307,000
Interest capitalized	0	0	257,000
Total debt	26,200,000	23,572,000	22,133,000
Market value	NA	NA	NA

[a]1989, 1988, 1987, 1986, 1985, 1984, 1983, 1982, 1981: includes other current non-trade receivables and/or other current assets.

[b]1986, 1985, 1984, 1983, 1982, 1981: includes other taxes.

[c]All the financial data are denominated in Canadian dollars, except when otherwise shown.

Guinness Peat Aviation

Going Public, International Funding and Currency Exposure

FINBARR BRADLEY

On August 20, 1989 in Galbally, County Limerick, Ireland, Sheila Farrell, Harvard MBA, Class of 1980 and President of the New York-based financial consulting company, Rockaway Associates, is putting the final touches to her presentation. Next morning, she is due at the corporate headquarters of Guinness Peat Aviation (GPA) in Shannon, Ireland. Her analysis will center on whether this closely-held private company should go public. She will also assess GPA's international borrowing strategy and its foreign currency exposure and hedging policies. She is scheduled to meet Tony Ryan, the founder and Chairman and Maurice Foley, President and CEO to present her recommendations. These two are tough characters so she knows she had better be prepared.

Sheila first met Mr. Ryan at the GPA Game and Country Fair in the village of Adare in May that year. GPA took over sponsorship of the fair some years before, renaming it to include the word GPA, a tad pretentious in the opinion of many. Sheila, a racehorse owner and member of the famed Scarteen Hunt, had been visiting Ireland for years. Receiving an invitation to the GPA Marquee and not known to miss an opportunity, she broached the subject of a study with Mr. Ryan. Shortly after submitting a proposal in early June, she was given the consulting contract.

The Evolution of GPA

GPA was formed in 1975 by Tony Ryan, at the time a middle level manager at Aer Lingus, the Irish national airline. The idea for the company can be traced to 1972, when Mr. Ryan was instructed by Aer Lingus to lease a recently purchased Boeing 747 then sitting idle at Shannon Airport. Because of the strife in Northern Ireland, the bottom had just fallen out of the Irish tourist market. Mr. Ryan successfully leased the jet to Air Siam at a considerable profit to Aer Lingus. Know-how gained from this deal was not lost on the shrewd Mr. Ryan. A short while later, he started GPA with $5,000 of his own money and $45,000 from two partners, his former employer Aer Lingus and Guinness Peat, the U.K. merchant bank. While the ownership base of GPA broadened and its capitalization grew enormously in subsequent years, Mr. Ryan's equity in the company never exceeded his original 10 percent share.

Today, GPA dominates the world aircraft leasing market, perhaps leasing up to twice as

©Finbarr Bradley, New York University, 1990.

This case was prepared as a basis for class discussion. My thanks to Mr. Anthony Buckley of Córas Tráchtála (Irish Export Board) in New York for helpful information.

many airlines as its nearest rival, the International Lease Finance Corporation. In addition, it buys, sells and trades new and used aircraft, in its capacity as either principal or agent. It has more new planes on order than any other airline in the world. Between January 1986 and May 1989, it committed itself to about 600 new jetliners and 100 turboprops. When the current aircraft it has on order are delivered, its fleet will more than triple from the present level of 172 aircraft. It is estimated that by the year 1991, GPA will own 3 percent of the world's Western manufactured jet fleet. The company controls about 40 percent of the world market for short-term leases of new planes. It employs 177 people, it made $152 million after tax in fiscal year 1989, and analysts expect this figure to rise to $191 million on revenue of $1.2 billion in the fiscal year ending March 1990. Its net profits grew at a dizzying 64 percent compound annual growth rate for the five years up to 1989. While it remains a private company, its market value is estimated to top the $2 billion mark. For the

EXHIBIT 13-1

Consolidated Balance Sheet of Guinness Peat Aviation

	($000s), Year Ending March					
	1985	1986	1987	1988	1989	1990(e)[a]
Cash & Mkt. Secs.	20,636	91,972	61,169	84,719	123,046	167,832
Receivables	70,352	19,582	51,393	71,180	103,379	141,010
Aircraft for sale	73,747	82,431	216,134	246,131	293,923	329,637
Current Assets:	164,735	193,985	328,696	402,030	520,348	638,479
Aircraft for lease	105,871	200,691	526,212	701,817	981,552	1,287,782
Aircraft lease recs.[b]	0	18,562	48,670	59,918	77,354	93,787
Investments	2,064	10,654	27,935	34,965	45,892	56,568
Deferred expenses	3,743	9,926	26,026	30,439	37,333	43,000
Other fixed assets	2,954	4,455	9,109	11,526	16,872	21,901
Fixed Assets:	114,632	244,288	637,952	838,665	1,158,993	1,503,038
Assets:	279,367	438,273	966,648	1,240,695	1,679,341	2,141,517
Payables	31,834	32,116	59,087	81,835	118,855	162,118
Short-term loans	120,074	80,705	116,385	131,343	155,434	172,750
Proposed dividend	4,421	6,700	16,736	23,180	33,666	45,918
Current Liabilities:	156,329	119,521	192,208	236,358	307,955	380,786
Deposit for aircraft	3759	5,106	8,032	9,897	12,767	15,480
Prov. for maintenance	2,705	5,490	14,395	19,199	26,851	35,268
Medium/LT. loans	64,349	133,271	488,298	623,828	851,445	1,093,443
Total liabilities:	227,142	263,388	693,933	889,282	1,199,018	1,524,977
Share capital	5,473	6,973	9,142	11,723	15,765	17,911
Share premium	34,365	141,711	190,402	193,947	205,281	219,688
Revenue reserves	12,387	26,201	73,171	145,743	259,277	396,941
Total Equity:	52,225	174,885	272,715	351,413	480,323	616,540
Liabilities + Equity:	279,367	438,273	966,648	1,240,695	1,679,341	2,141,517

[a](e) = estimate. [b] = receivables

Source: Adapted from A. Buckley, et al., *Guinness Peat Aviation*, MBS Term Paper, UCD, Dublin, 1987.

EXHIBIT 13-2

Consolidated Profit and Loss Account of Guinness Peat Aviation

	($000s), Year Ending March					
	1985	1986	1987	1988	1989	1990(e)[a]
Gross Revenues	202,349	155,527	448,989	666,418	1,002,042	1,246,878
Trading profit	16,032	24,739	66,001	97,964	147,301	183,857
Deposit interest	376	551	1,696	2,384	3,431	4,134
Profit/noncon. co.	956	71	935	1,389	2,088	2,604
Profit Before Tax	17,364	25,371	68,632	101,737	152,820	190,595
Taxes	289	259	386	442	510	584
Profit After Tax	17,075	25,112	68,246	101,295	152,310	190,011
Reserves, start—year	2,439	12,387	26,201	73,171	145,743	259,277
Total reserves	19,514	37,499	94,447	174,466	298,053	449,288
Dividends	7,127	11,298	21,276	28,723	38,776	52,347
Reserves, end—year	12,387	26,301	73,171	145,743	259,277	396,941
EPS	N/A	$5.3	$7.4	$10.5	$13.4	$40.0

[a](e) = estimate.

Source: Adapted from A. Buckley, et al., *Guinness Peat Aviation*, MPS Term Paper, UCD, Dublin, 1987.

first half of 1989, GPA's earnings per share (EPS) rose 51 percent to $20.25 over the same period in 1988. It is estimated that its EPS could reach around $40 for the year ending March 1990 and as high as $50 the following year. The enormous growth in GPA's earnings in recent years is illustrated in the consolidated balance sheet and income statements presented in Exhibits 13-1 and 13-2, respectively.

GPA achieved its present status through a combination of smart investment planning and old-fashioned good luck. A fruitful strategy was its reliance on joint ventures, with GPA usually taking a 50 percent share or thereabouts in each venture it entered. In 1981, for example, it teamed up with Midland Bank of the U.K. to form GPA Midland Ltd. to provide long-term aircraft financial leases.[1] In 1984,

[1]See the following section for definitions of the various forms of aircraft leases.

GPA formed a partnership with McDonnell Douglas Corporation to acquire 24 of the latter's MD-83 aircraft valued at about $800 million. GPA and McDonnell Douglas each controlled 50 percent of the new company, Irish Aerospace Ltd. This operation concentrated its marketing efforts on selling operating leases to airlines in Europe and Africa. In June 1986, GPA placed an order for 96 McDonnell Douglas and Boeing aircraft with options for a further 10 aircraft. This order, worth $2.75 billion, doubled the company's portfolio of aircraft available for lease to 187. In November 1986, GPA formed a joint venture with Fokker of Holland and Mitsubishi Trust & Banking Corporation of Japan to set up a company called GPA Fokker 100. The venture bought 40 and options on a further 60 Fokker F-100 twin-jet airlines for leasing.

In January 1987, GPA formed a joint venture with Airbus Industrie, the European aircraft-building consortium, called GPA Airbus

320 with GPA owning 50.5 percent, Airbus 17.5 percent, Pacific Western Airlines of Canada 24.5 percent and Banque Paribas of France 7.5 percent. The company immediately ordered 25 Airbus A320s with options to buy 25 more, a deal worth $2 billion should the options be exercised. In January 1988, GPA ordered 22 Boeing 737s worth $594 million with delivery scheduled to begin April 1990. In May 1988, GPA formed a joint venture with British Airways and McDonnell Douglas with GPA holding 50 percent and the other companies holding 25 percent each. The objective of this venture was to specialize in the leasing of McDonnell Douglas MD-11 airliners.

In July 1988, GPA took its diversification strategy a step further by going into airline ownership. It acquired an option to buy 10 percent of Braniff, the U.S. carrier. Under the deal, GPA Fokker 100 agreed to sell 12 new F-100s to Braniff. Payment was to be partly in cash and partly in the form of 12 BAC-111 aircraft owned by Braniff. GPA Fokker 100 then leased the BAC-111s back to Braniff for use until the new medium-haul F-100s were built by Fokker and delivered between September 1989 and December 1989. The value of the entire transaction was estimated at $300 million. Also in July 1988, GPA arranged with Rolls Royce to set up a joint company, GPA Rolls, to buy a fleet of 757s using Rolls Royce engines.[2] This deal was similar to one GPA also made with another engine manufacturer, CFM International, to sell engines. GPA also formed two other joint ventures with financial institutions and airlines to buy and lease commuter aircraft.

GPA has also ventured into the smaller turboprop aircraft business. The single-turboprop is used by regional carriers for short distances since they are more economical than jet-airliners. In 1986, GPA formed a partnership, named GPA Jetprop, with Pacific Western Airlines of Canada. This affiliate specializes in the leasing and trading of aircraft for commuter and regional airlines. In March 1989, 88 new-technology turboprops, worth $850 million were ordered from European and Canadian manufacturers for delivery between 1990 and 1996. GPA also formed another affiliate, called GPA ATR Ltd., which was a joint venture owned 50 percent by GPA Jetprop, 25 percent by the Avions de Transport Regional consortium, 12.5 percent by the Italian bank Instituto Bancario San Paulo di Torino and 12.5 percent by France's Banque Indosuez.

In February 1989, the company expanded into painting and refurbishing aircraft by buying a 50 percent interest in Expressair Aviation Services, a company based in Shannon. One of Expressair's largest contracts was a five-year deal to repaint 285 aircraft owned by Aeroflot, the Soviet national airline.

GPA received enormous press coverage in April 1989, when it ordered 308 airliners worth $16.8 billion, at the time the largest single aircraft order in aviation history. Of this total, Boeing received an order for 182, worth $9.4 billion, the largest in the company's history.[3] The breakdown of Boeing's order was 92 of 737s, 50 of 757s, and 40 of 767s. McDonnell Douglas received orders for 72 planes valued at $3.1 billion and Airbus Industrie received orders for 54 planes valued at $4.3 billion.

The dynamism of GPA's activity is reflected in activity during the first half of 1988. In that period, GPA leased 108 aircraft to 41 airlines in 21 countries. In addition, it purchased 89 used aircraft and sold 29 from its portfolio. GPA currently (i.e., August 1989) owns a total of

---

[2] In January 1989, GPA agreed to buy 26 Airbus A320s and lease them to Braniff. This deal later fell through because of Braniff's bankruptcy proceedings.

[3] Interestingly, just eight days later, this deal was topped when United Airlines made another record-setting order from Boeing. A total of 370 aircraft worth $15.74 billion were ordered.

EXHIBIT 13-3

Number and Characteristics of Main Aircraft in GPA Fleet

Model	Manufacturer	Passenger Capacity	Owned	Ordered	Total
Jets					
MD-83	McDonnell Douglas	155	10	21	31
MD-11	McDonnell Douglas	321–405	36	14	50
A320	Airbus Industrie	140–179	9	52	51
B737	Boeing	141–159	20	104	124
B747	Boeing	360–500	15	16	31
B757	Boeing	186–220	3	48	51
B767	Boeing	174–290	9	56	65
Turboprops					
F-100	Fokker	100 +	21	13	34
ATR42	Aeritalia/Aerospatiale	42–50	14	7	21
ATR72	Aeritalia/Aerospatiale	64–74	5	5	10
Others	N/A		30	14	44
Total			172	350	522

Sources: *Aviation Week & Space Technology,* March 20, 1989; and various company and press reports.

172 aircraft worth $3.2 billion. In addition, it has firm orders for another 289 worth $7.6 billion from manufacturers. Through 1995 GPA will take delivery on average of one new plane per week.[4]

Exhibit 13-3 presents the number and key characteristics of the main aircraft GPA either owned or had on order in August 1989.

Exhibit 13-4 illustrates the substantial growth in GPA's fleet numbers over the past five years.

The company also owns a substantial number of options to buy aircraft. These options total 150, are exercisable from 1991 through 1996, and have a value of approximately $5.6 billion if exercised.

[4]*The New York Times,* September 17, 1988.

EXHIBIT 13-4

GPA Group's Fleet

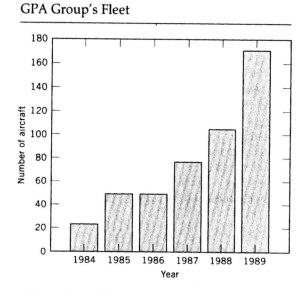

Source: *The Wall Street Journal,* May 11, 1989.

Tony Ryan and GPA

The stuff of legend, Tony Ryan is both an admired and perhaps feared figure at GPA.[5] He likes to describe himself as "just a Tipperary farmer" although his business acumen has made him a millionaire several times over. Fifty-three years of age, he was born into the transport business. His grandfather was a stationmaster and his father a train-driver for Córas Iompar Éireann, the former Irish national transport agency. Mr. Ryan started as a 19-year-old dispatcher with Aer Lingus. While assigned to Chicago in the 1960s, he obtained a degree in business administration at night. Ryan owns a 300-acre farm in County Tipperary where he relaxes by farming a prize head of cattle. He owns a valuable collection of 19th- and 20th-century Irish art. Recently, he became in money-terms Ireland's top patron of the arts, announcing plans to finance a wide range of prizes for artists, authors and musicians. Ryan has a reputation as a tough taskmaster but stories are also told about generous corporate perks such as clothing allowances for secretaries and free flights to spouses in order to spend weekends with partners away on out-of-town assignments.[6]

Mr. Ryan provided financial backing for his sons in an airline called Ryanair, which now gives Aer Lingus a run for its money on a number of Ireland-U.K. routes. Not all Mr. Ryan's ventures have had the Midas touch. A public house, "Matt, The Thrasher" was a much publicized failure as was an ill-fated investment in the *Sunday Tribune*, an Irish newspaper. Whether through fear or respect, Mr. Ryan has been successful in embuing GPA with a distinct corporate culture. Employees form a close-knit group, work almost slavish hours and are continually tied to the office even by home facsimile machine and car telephone. One GPA brochure, for instance, boasts that senior executives typically spend about 140 days travelling and visiting clients each year.[7] Employee ownership in the company and generous wages, by Irish standards, have helped developed a strong *esprit de corps*. Aside from Mr. Ryan, 100 workers own 6.3 percent of the company. Many of the senior staff borrowed heavily to buy equity, hence their futures are closely linked with that of the company's.

The Aircraft Leasing Business

Aircraft leases are contractual agreements between a lessee (e.g., an airline carrier) and a lessor (e.g., GPA), where the former has the right to use the asset but must make periodic payments to the lessor who retains ownership.[8] There are basically three types of aircraft leases: financial, operating and wet. A financial lease is usually long-term, often stretching up to 20 years, whereas an operating lease is short-term, usually ranging up to 6 years. In wet leases, the lessor supplies not only the aircraft, but all the necessary operational support, including the operating crews. This is not true for either the financial or operating leases, which are also called dry leases.

Financial leases can be distinguished from operating leases in the following principal ways:

1. Financial leases include maintenance or service by the lessor whereas operating leases do not.

---

[5] Because of their enormous financial success, Ryan, along with Irish-born Tony O'Reilly, CEO of Heinz Corporation and Michael Smurfit, CEO of Ireland's only major multinational Jefferson Smurfit Ltd., are portrayed in almost mythic terms by the Irish media.

[6] "Is Ryan of GPA Flying Too High?" *Euromoney*, April 1989.

[7] "The World of GPA," GPA Corporate Brochure, 1987.

[8] For a good analysis of the financial aspects of leasing, see the following text: Stephen A. Ross and Randolph W. Westerfield, *Corporate Finance*, Times Mirror/Mosby College Publishing, St. Louis, Missouri, 1988.

2. Financial leases are usually fully or almost fully amortized. Thus after the lease expires the aircraft becomes the property of the lessee. Operating leases are usually set up for a period of time less than the useful life of the asset. As a result, monthly payments for a long-term financial lease are substantially lower than those for a short-term operating lease.

3. Generally, financial leases cannot be cancelled, whereas operating lessees have the right to cancel the lease contract before the expiration date. Thus, if its passenger numbers do not grow as expected or it wishes to substitute to a more technologically advanced aircraft, an airline can cancel the lease. In a sense, the extra cost is like an insurance premium.

4. Operating leases are not listed on the airline's balance sheet as debt, thereby giving it more borrowing capacity and added financial flexibility.

The forces stimulating the growth in aircraft leasing stem from developments in the airline industry itself. This industry has undergone a fundamental structural change in the past few years. Airlines are no longer as eager or as financially able to purchase aircraft outright and are focusing more on operating rather than owning planes. Leasing allows them to acquire newer technology planes at lower cost. This is where the leasing companies discovered a niche, purchasing and leasing planes either on a short-term or long-term basis. It allows the carriers to operate planes on flexible schedules without assuming more debt. It is particularly attractive to new airlines, exemplified by the many discount-fare lines set up in the U.K. in the 1980s, since it reduces start-up costs. Yet leasing is also attractive to the established carriers giving them flexibility to react to market conditions as well as reduce their costs in today's competitive environment.

Leasing does have some disadvantages. It tends to blur the lines of communication between manufacturers and users. It can be costly and in some cases lessors and aircraft manufacturers have incurred the wrath of some airlines by taking up so much of the aircraft order queue. In fact, until recently manfacturers tended to shun the lessors and still try to allocate less than 20 percent of all sales in each year to lessors. However, as Exhibit 13-5 shows, the importance of lessors in the industry continues to increase. In fact, the aircraft manufacturers themselves have entered the leasing business with joint ventures like the Irish Aerspace venture cited earlier.

Leasing has recently become popular with U.S. carriers. American Airlines leased $2.5 billion worth of Airbus A300s and 15 Boeing 767s in March 1987 from aircraft manufacturers. At present, American Airlines leases 50 percent,

EXHIBIT 13-5

World Aircraft Deliveries Going to Leasing Companies

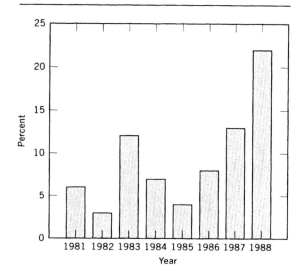

Source: The Wall Street Journal, May 20, 1988.

Delta leases 40 percent and Northwest leases 19 percent of their total fleet. Estimates put the percentage of all U.S. commercial aircraft leased at 30 percent, and this level is expected to rise to 60–70 percent in the 1990s. Analysts estimate that lessors of GPA's size receive discounts ranging anywhere from 5 percent to 25 percent depending on the size of their orders.

Provisions in the 1986 U.S. Tax Reform Act eliminated some of the incentives, based on the Investment Tax Credit and Accelerated Depreciation, for U.S. airlines to purchase new aircraft. The act also increased the after-tax cost of financial leases. The net effect appears to be that it encouraged a trend toward short-term operating leases. While the short-term leases are generally more expensive than financial leases, the act eroded the after-tax advantage of longer-term financial leases.

While GPA today tends to concentrate on operating leases, it has not shunned entirely the other forms of lease arrangement. As part of a broad-based aviation strategy, GPA formed specialized companies that focus on a different form of lease. For example, GPA Midland was set up to provide finance leases, whereas Air Tara was structured to provide wet leases.

The Market

The world jet and turbo-prop market is enjoying a decidedly upbeat outlook at present. In 1988, high demand resulted in record orders for more than 1000 new jet airliners worth $47.47 billion. This growth continued into the first half of 1989 and shows no sign of abating in the foreseeable future. The Boeing Company estimates that between 1990 and 2005, a total of 8,417 new jets will be added to the world fleet. Of this total worth about $516 billion, $96 billion is already on the order books, and a further $420 billion in new sales is anticipated over the next 15 years. The latter is composed of $295 billion, measuring new

aircraft to be bought to meet growth in traffic and $125 billion, coming from the replacement market. Exhibit 13-6 provides more details on these orders.

This optimism regarding aircraft sales is being generated from a number of directions. First, worldwide travel is expected to grow at an annual rate of about 6 percent from now through the end of the century. This figure is slightly lower than the grow rate over the past few years, but world air passenger numbers are expected to double from 1.1 billion in 1988 to 2 billion by the year 2000. These projections are built on the assumption of continued growth in discretionary personal income, a decrease in the real cost of travel after allowing for inflation, continued stability in fuel prices, and no economic recession in the foreseeable future, all of which are by no means certain to occur.

Another reason for the continued high growth rate in jet aircraft sales is the need to replace older models. About 36.6 percent of all aircraft are 15 years old or older. Public safety about aircraft aging is providing further stimulus to the order-books. Other reasons are due to the rising costs of maintenance and stricter environmental regulations against aircraft noise. An additional factor that accounts for the rising demand is the desire of many airlines to obtain larger aircraft to alleviate some of the severe congestion problems at both airports and along the air routes.

The Competition

While GPA is today the principal player in international aircraft leasing, the leasing business is quite competitive. An early pioneer of operating leases, International Lease Finance Corporation (ILFC), formed in 1973 in Beverly Hills, California, is the number two player in the market. ILFC differs from GPA in a number of important ways. With a far different

EXHIBIT 13-6

The World Commercial Jet Aircraft Market

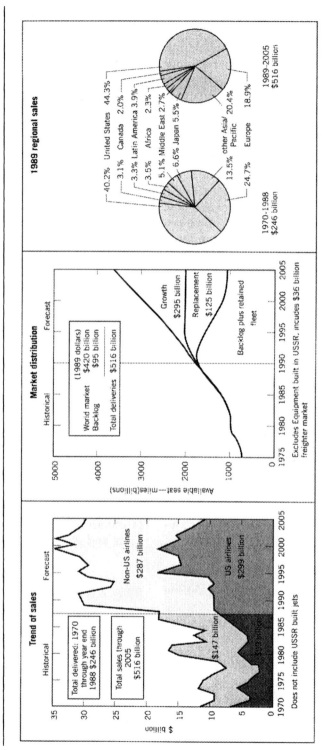

Source: The Financial Times, June 7, 1989.

and leaner organizational structure, it went public in 1983. It is much smaller than GPA with just 18 employees compared to GPA's 177. Its revenues and assets are approximately half those of GPA.

Competition is also getting tougher from other directions. While in the 1970s, there were only three or four firms involved in aircraft leasing, today there are over 30 firms. These range from subsidiaries of giant multinationals to the aircraft manufacturers themselves. GATX Corporation, Polaris Aircraft Leasing Corporation (80 percent owned by General Electric) and Ansett Aviation Worldwide Services of Australia are some of the other important players. A major difference in approach between GPA and its rivals is that the former has largely concentrated on leasing new state-of-the-art aircraft, whereas its competitors have tended to focus on the sale and lease of older aircraft.

Perhaps, the great competitive uncertainty facing GPA lies in the intentions of the Japanese. Financial giants like Mitsubishi own shares in GPA, but there is the possibility that they or other Japanese companies will enter the business as independent entities. Prior to taking a stake in GPA in 1986, Japanese groups had been trying to break into the international aviation leasing market for some time. With the GPA shareholding they gained access to the company's expertise while GPA in turn reduced the threat that the Japanese would set up a rival operation.[9]

The GPA Organizational Structure

GPA has divided its activities into three main sections. First, the company is organized geographically, second it has divisions that mar-

ket leases on particular types of aircraft (e.g., the B737 division), and third it has divisions that provide services in related airline businesses. The principal operating and holding company is GPA Group Ltd., which has responsibility for determining the policies and direction of the group and for financing, asset acquisition and marketing in areas not covered by subsidiaries.

Three marketing subsidiaries around the world report to corporate headquarters at Shannon. GPA Europe Ltd., based in London, markets in Europe, the Middle East and North Africa. GPA Corporation, based in Stamford, Connecticut, markets group services in the Americas. The Stamford office is also the base of Transportation Analysis International, the group's consulting service. GPA Asia Ltd., based in Hong Kong, markets services in Southern and Eastern Asia and Australasia. While GPA has decentralized marketing and customer services to these subsidiaries, key strategy formulation is retained at headquarters.

Business Strategies

The historical development of GPA can be linked to a number of key strategic decisions by management. The company began mainly as a provider of wet leases, then it shifted to dry operating leases. It concentrated on leasing surplus used planes from established carriers to start-up and small airlines such as Air Lanka and Nigeria Airways. Owning just eight planes in 1984, the company then shifted its focus in a very short period into buying and then leasing new aircraft to major carriers. This radical change in strategy occurred in 1986 when it ordered 100 new planes from manufacturers, even though at the time it had not landed any firm orders for the planes. Moreover, the airline industry at that time was facing an uncertain future caused by deregulation, privatization and the declining prof-

---

[9]As part of a Japanese equity investment in GPA, personnel from Japan are trained in the mechanics of aircraft leasing at Shannon.

itability of some of major carriers. In retrospect, deliveries of these planes were timed perfectly to meet the extremely tight supply situation which developed in the late 1980s.

The heart of GPAs global information system is a computerized "trading floor" at Shannon. Here, aircraft market information is collected and analyzed. The 10-foot high screens display details such as the rental hours and engine maintenance of every one of the world's airlines. GPA has one or two employees assigned exclusively to track the whereabouts at any point in time of all the western world's 8,000 aircraft.

Many analysts believe that GPA is more vulnerable to the effect of a recession than ILFC because of its strategic posture. GPA faces particular risks for a number of reasons. First, it would be severely hurt by another oil-based recession since many of the airlines it now has on order would be cancelled with little or no penalty to the carriers. Second, GPA's commitments to the aircraft manufacturers involve enormous non-refundable deposits. One analyst estimates that if a full-blown recession occurred in the next five years, all of GPA's net worth would be wiped out in a year. Others, including in particular GPA executives, are more optimistic. They assert that since GPA has diversified its operations geographically and operationally, it is largely immune to a recession. Suffice to say, that given the company's enormous expansion in the past few years, the next economic downturn will prove a critical test of GPA's ability to survive into the next century.

GPA's wide and diverse client base does appear to be a good hedge against recession. Its clients cover the whole world. It has customers from 63 different airlines, with no single customer leasing more than eight planes at any point in time. The company prides itself on its ability to react quickly and effectively to potential deals—not surprising given its broad scope of interlocking services, the scale of its financial resources and its dominant position in the aircraft marketplace. An example of this ability was a recent transaction that required GPA to provide eight Boeing 727s at short notice for a specialist freight operation. To assemble that package, GPA arranged a total of 42 separate contracts involving 21 aircraft and 10 airlines on four continents. Some aircraft were purchased outright and others were returned from lease in exchange for different aircraft.[10]

With leasing as its core business, the company is now attempting to broaden its product base from pure aircraft leasing into other activities such as aircraft portfolio sales, trading, as well as financial, legal and technical services. The company has already made a start in financial services, including arranging lease financing, conducting underwriting, doing credit-risk studies, procuring, re-marketing planes for customers, providing fleet planning and operations consulting. For instance, GPA provides a consulting service which includes engineering advice, technical and financial appraisal of specific aircraft, the forecasting of residual values and airline economic modelling. These activities already provide 25 percent of pretax profit. Moreover, these activities are more profitable than leasing. For instance, while operating leases provide GPA with a return on equity (ROE) of 20 percent, its ROE on fee-generating activities in recent years has topped the 35 percent mark.

Another GPA proposal is to sell packages of planes to individuals. Other companies such as Polaris already serve this market. GPA is taking its first step by forming a joint venture with the credit subsidiary of Pacific Corporation, a Portland Oregon utility. The two companies have set up a $300 million fund based

---

[10]Another example was a deal for a British charter carrier that wanted to replace its GPA-owned Boeing 737-200 twin-jets with new 737-300s, which have a larger seating capacity. GPA placed the 737-200s with a Canadian carrier, shipped off the Canadian airline's planes to Brazil, and placed the Brazilian airlines' planes in Mexico (*The Wall Street Journal*, May 20, 1988).

on 17 leased planes, to be marketed to U.S. institutional investors by Merrill Lynch & Company. A more ambitious plan is what GPA calls its Fund Avia. Based in Dublin's recently set-up tax-free International Financial Services Centre, the fund is slated to attract up to $13 billion in private capital to buy airplanes that have already been leased. GPA would manage the fund, collecting fees for buying the planes and marketing them.

GPA also has ambitious plans to build a division that will team up with a major European airline to handle the heavy-duty maintenance for both its own jets and those of others. It is presently scouting for sites in Europe to house centers to train pilots and engineers, facilities to maintain and overhaul aircraft and an airplane paint shop. The new company would eventually employ 5,000 workers, almost 30 times GPA's present workforce.[11]

[11] *Business Week*, May 1, 1989.

Financing GPA's Expansion

A major problem now facing GPA is how to finance its current ambitious expansion program. As Exhibit 13-7 shows, both GPA itself and its joint ventures have borrowed heavily in recent years on the international capital markets. In 1986, Irish Aerospace arranged a $225 million 12-year credit for the purchase of 12 MD-83s. Cash was provided by 10 major banks in North America, Europe and Japan. In August 1986, GPA obtained a $65 million multicurrency revolving loan and guarantee facility provided by 10 banks in Europe, America and Asia. The company's most complex and most difficult financing to-date occurred in September 1987. Given GPA's rapid expansion at that time, the company found itself restricted by the covenants in its existing $750 million credit facility. It ran into initial problems in attempting to finance using a new $1.5 billion revolving credit facility. According to

EXHIBIT 13-7

Principal GPA Borrowings Since 1984

Date	Borrowing Entity	Description
January 1984	Guinness Peat Group	*Amount*: $55 million *Maturity*: 7 years *Cost*: 87.5 bp over LIBOR
March 1985	GPA	*Amount*: $135 million *Maturity*: 6 years *Cost*: 1.125% over LIBOR

April 1986	Irish Aerospace	*Amount*: $225 million
		Maturity: 12 years
		Cost: Rising from 125–175 bp
		    for 75% of each drawdown; 1.75% over LIBOR
		    for balance

May 1986	GPA	*Amount*: $65 million *Maturity*: 5.5 years *Cost*: 87.5 bp over LIBOR
September 1987	GPA	*Amount*: $1.5 billion *Maturity*: Up to 7 years with possible extension to 12 years *Cost*: Revolving facility with tender panels

Source: Euromoney, November 1987. bp = basis point

Patrick Blaney, Managing Director of GPA's financial services group, this was due to the banks' lack of sophistication in aircraft leasing:

At first, GPA put on a road show for different lenders, trying to explain its position from a podium in a 45-minute presentation. Later when they sat down with banks across the table selling became easier.[12]

A major advantage of the $1.5 billion financing was that it increased GPA's flexibility and speed in moving planes between customers. Prior to this, every time a plane was returned from one customer it had to be re-registered before being put out to another customer. Under the new package, the lending banks' have what is referred to as a "floating charge security" based on GPA's aircraft assets as a pool, not on individual aircraft.

GPA has also financed its expansion in part by issuing equity in private placements on a number of occasions. In April 1986, it completed a $125 million private share placement in Japan, the United States and United Kingdom. This deal tripled GPA's equity by 1987 to $190 million. The placement consisted of 9.5 percent convertible preferred shares. The largest investor in the private placement was The Long Term Credit Bank of Japan, which in association with Japan Leasing Corporation and Kawasaki Enterprises contributed $55 million. The other investors were Prudential Insurance Company of America with $35 million, General Electric Capital Corporation with $15 million, Morgan Grenfell with $5 million, First Boston with $2 million and GPA employees with $3 million. A group of other small investors took up a further $10 million. At the same time, two of GPA's existing shareholders reduced their holdings to bring in the Mitsubishi group as a shareholder with a 22 percent stake.

In April 1988, GPA issued 330,000 ordinary shares at $250 each worth $82.5 million. The principal investors were J. Rothschild Holdings, Allied Irish Banks, The Bank of Nova Scotia, Irish Life Assurance, The Mitsubishi Trust & Banking Corporation, Aer Lingus, PacifiCorp Credit, The Toronto-Dominion Bank, Mitsubishi Corporation, and the Foreign & Colonial Investment Trust.

In December 1988, GPA made another large share issue. Shares were sold at $285 each. Guinness Peat Group's 14 percent share was sold for $240 million, which brought in Irish Life Assurance and Prudential Insurance Corporation of America. In January 1989, Northwestern Mutual Life Insurance, the 10th-largest life insurance company in the United States bought 1.4 percent of GPA. It paid $22.4 million for the stake, putting the total value of the company at $1.6 billion.

In May 1989, ownership of the company consisted of:[13]

Air Canada	22.4%
Mitsubishi Group	19.1%
Aer Lingus	15.3%
Tony Ryan	8.0%
Irish Life Assurance	6.9%
Long Term Credit Bank of Japan	4.2%
GPA Employees	3.3%
Prudential Insurance Company	1.0%
Others	19.8%

In June 1989, GPA raised $192 million in a new share issue. Shares were priced at $425 per share, putting a value of $2.45 billion on the group as a whole. Hanson, the U.K.-based industrial conglomerate took up part of the issue along with Chiyoda Finance of Japan, Gamlestaden and Nyckeln Holding of Sweden and The Bank of Ireland. Brokers estimate that GPA shares are currently worth between $525 and $575 each. In other words, investors doubled their money in just 12 months.

---

[12]*Euromoney*, April 1989, pp. 35–40.

[13]*The Wall Street Journal*, May 11, 1989.

A key pressure on GPA is cash-outflow for aircraft. At any time GPA has $100 million to $600 outstanding in aircraft deposit payments. Such deposits owed to the airline manufacturers are not refundable so that if a recession occurs between 1991 and 1996, GPA could find itself in serious trouble.

In order to get better terms, GPA places its planes only 18 months into the future. Yet it must pay a cumulative total of 30 percent of the aircraft price a year prior to delivery. If there is a slump in air travel, leasing rates could then fall and force GPA to sell off planes at substantial losses. Its lease contracts include a three-month security deposit so that if an airline ends a lease earlier, GPA has only three months to find a new lessee before it stops receiving money. Apparently, it has never failed to re-lease any of its aircraft, a testimony to its marketing prowess.[14]

Having raised so much capital by borrowing has resulted in a rapidly expanded indebtedness. GPA is now very highly leveraged, at least compared to other businesses. Its average debt to net worth ratio has averaged 180 percent recently, admittedly down substantially from 750 percent in 1983, 222 percent in 1984 and 423 percent in 1985, but it raises the spectre of disaster should the airline travel business slump in the foreseeable future.

Going Public

The syndication of its 1987 $1.5 billion revolving credit facility highlights the problems that GPA could face raising capital. GPA has become so large and requires so much capital that it must now disclose extensive information to banks. Thus, the company is losing some of the advantages of being a private company. By going public, GPA could lose

[14]Ibid.

some of its prized ability to react quickly to business situations. Shareholder approval might be necessary before it could commit easily to a fast-moving deal.

There will undoubtedly be tax disadvantages to some people if it does go public. The Irish Government granted GPA tax-free status for a decade to locate in Shannon. Both corporate taxes and dividends to private shareholders who are Irish citizens are tax free. This corporate tax-free status ended in April 1990, and the tax rate raised to 10 percent. From GPA's perspective, ending its tax holiday made little difference since it had enough tax-loss carry forwards to reduce its effective tax rate to zero for the next few years. It is a big concern, nevertheless, to its Irish shareholders who might have welcomed an opportunity to disinvest before their tax-free status ended.

Another issue is the question of employee loyalty to Mr. Ryan and the top executive team. The new ownership is unlikely to be as loyal to Mr. Ryan. Some of the shareholders, Aer Lingus and Air Canada for example, would like to see GPA go public since this would provide them a means of unloading their shares. This pressure for a proper market for GPA shares will undoubtedly grow in future years. For instance, employees who now own over 6 percent would like to turn their holdings into cash. Yet many managers feel that by going public they would be selling out too cheaply.

The Assignment

1. Do you think Sheila should recommend that GPA go public? Why or why not? What are the risks and benefits of either going or not going public?

2. What are the other alternatives available to the company? For instance, do you think a leveraged buy-out (LBO) or management

buy-out (MBO) might be a more satisfactory arrangement for Mr. Ryan to sell his shares?

3. If the company does go public, where do you think they should list GPA stock? List the advantages and disadvantages of listing on some of the important global stock exchanges.

4. Examine GPA's 1986–1987 cost of international borrowing. Has the cost of borrowing been affected by the growing debt of GPA? Has GPA been subject to the going market borrowing rate?

5. Is GPA assuming an excessive currency risk given that its headquarters is located in Ireland? How could an effective currency hedging of transaction exposure be accomplished?

Genentech, Inc. and Royal Gist-brocades nv

Capital Structure and the Cost of Capital in Biotechnology Corporations Across Countries

HARVEY A. PONIACHEK

This case study addresses issues concerning corporate capitalization and the cost of capital, and the cost of capital across international borders. Two biotechnology corporations in the United States and the Netherlands are examined.

The Biotechnology Industry

Biotechnology utilizes scientifically engineered biological methods (through the recombination of DNA and RNA techniques) to create products for a number of applications, including the health-care pharmaceuticals, agriculture, chemicals, and energy sectors. The world biotechnology market sales could reach $50 billion by the year 2000.

Nearly 500 biotech companies have been established in the United States since the mid-1970s, with more than 75 percent being privately held. There are about 1,100 companies in the industry, of which nearly 200 are publicly traded—and the number of firms has remained approximately the same in the past three years.[1] The difficulty of raising funds in the stock market in recent years led many companies to either merge, to be acquired, or to form alliances with foreign firms.

Some firms are engaged in creative financing such as selling off certain R&D product lines, and R&D partnerships. Biotech companies raised some $2 billion during the first half of 1990.

A growing share of new investment is now flowing into manufacturing and marketing rather than into research and development of new products—which reflects a growing level of maturity. Biotechnology's most significant contribution is expected in the area of health care. By the early 1990s some 89 biotechnology driven drugs and vaccines could be approved by the FDA.

[1] Martin Chase, "Biotechnology Starts to Fulfill Promise with New Products and Jump in Capital," *The Wall Street Journal*, September 24, 1991. Barnaby J. Feder, "A Chronicler of Growth in Biotechnology Area," *The New York Times*, September 25, 1991.

Major developments are expected in the area of agriculture, specifically in animal agriculture concerning vaccines, growth promoters, and improved animal feeds. Also, genetically engineered plants with improved resistance to diseases or pests, and agriculturally useful microorganisms could be commercially available by the mid-1990s.[2]

The U.S. biotechnology industry has experienced a 75 percent growth in its capitalization to $35 billion during mid-1991. Companies raised a record $1.8 billion in initial public offerings. With the advent of new products, the industry's sales and revenues have increased. However, the industry still lost money in the fiscal year ended in mid-1991.[3] See Appendix 14-1 for a comprehensive survey of the biotechnology industry in the United States.

Genentech, Inc. and Royal Gist-brocades nv

Genentech, Inc.

Genentech, Inc. is a biotechnology company that discovers, develops, manufactures and markets human pharmaceuticals. Sales in 1990 reached over $476 million, assets were over $1.2 billion, stockholders' equity was over $893 million, and the company employed over 1900 people.

The company was organized in 1976 as a California corporation and in 1988 changed its state of incorporation to Delaware. Genentech merged in 1990 with a wholly owned subsidiary of Roche Holdings, Inc—a Swiss corporation—where Roche acquired approximately 60 percent of the outstanding equity of Genentech, and Roche has the right to in-

crease its holdings to 75 percent by open market purchases.

Genentech has three main products: Protropin human growth hormone, Activase tissue plasminogen activator, and Actimmune gamma interferon.

Genentech shares were trading at the end of 1990 at a low of 21 3/4 and a high of 27 1/2.

Royal Gist-brocades nv

Royal Gist-brocades nv is a multinational corporation whose core business is biotechnology based on fermentation processes. The corporation is one of the world's largest producers of bakers' yeast, penicillin, and enzymes. Sales in 1990 reached over 1.6 billion Dutch guilders, net profit after tax was 67.7 million Dutch guilders, total assets were 1.4 billion Dutch guilders, and capital and reserves were over 992 million Dutch guilders. The corporation employs 5833 people, of whom 2746 are in the Netherlands.

The corporation principal establishment is in Delft, Holland and has production facilities and sales operations in almost all EC countries, in the United States and other major countries.

In 1990, net income per share was 1.87 guilders and the dividend per share was 1.30 guilders. Appendix 14-2 provides financial statements and additional background information about these two corporations.

Financial Structure and the Cost of Capital

Following the identification of the most feasible investment projects and the determination of the funding requirements, the corporation needs to select its sources of financing. The most important funding decision concerns the relative share of debt and equity. Debt is considerably less expensive than equity because of the deductibility of interest payments for

---

[2] U.S. Department of Commerce, *U.S. Industrial Outlook 1991*, Chapter 18, "Advanced Materials," Washington D.C., January 1991. See Appendix 14-1 for a reprint of this chapter.

[3] *WSJ*, op. cit.

tax purposes. The debt and equity financing mix affects the company's capital structure, the weighted average cost of capital (WACC) and risk, and it is addressed by the capital structure theory.

An increase in the corporate business risk (i.e., the probability of financial distress) occurs as its indebtedness expands in relation to its equity. The relationship between the debt to asset ratio, the cost of debt, cost of equity, and the weighted average cost of capital indicate that the debt to asset ratios have significant effect on the cost of debt and equity. Initially, the firm's WACC declines as the debt to assets ratio increases. However, as debt financing continues to expand the financial risk rises significantly and the cost of equity goes up because of the higher risk associated with the firm. Different leverage levels (i.e., debt to assets ratios or debt to equity ratios) are associated with varying cost of capital. Firms with higher operating leverage are subject to higher business risk, as measured by the standard deviation of the expected rate of return on equity (ROE).

The optimum financial structure of debt and equity mix minimizes the firm's cost of capital for a given level of business risk. The firm's lowest average weighted cost of capital is commonly found within the debt to asset ratio range of 30 percent and 60 percent. The firm's WACC is significantly affected by the availability of capital. Therefore, companies that can access funds from a variety of sources and are able to reduce the investing public's and/or suppliers' of funds risk by providing investors portfolio diversification opportunities can reduce the cost of capital.

The firm reaches a minimum WACC at a level of debt where the value of the firm is maximized.[4] In practice, it is difficult to establish precisely a firm's capital structure. Wide variations in the use of financial leverage occur among industries and firms in the same industry. The main task of financial management is to determine whether the firm is over leveraged or underleveraged in comparison with other firms in the industry.

International Differences in Capital Structure

The WACC is affected by several factors[5] of which the most significant are the following: the availability of capital, segmented national capital markets, portfolio diversification motives, foreign exchange, and political risk and disclosure.

Important differences prevail between the capital structure of U.S. companies and companies in other major countries. For example, Japanese firms' average debt to asset ratio is 85 percent, German firms' ratio is 64 percent, whereas the U.S. firms' ratio is 55 percent. After adjusting for accounting differences among these countries, Japanese and German firms use substantially more financial leverage than U.S. corporations.[6]

The differences in financial leverage could be explained by differences in financial distress costs—that is, a given level of debt causes a lower threat of financial distress for a German or a Japanese firm than for a U.S. firm with the same financial leverage. Legal and institutional differences could also account for differences in the capital structure of firms across national borders.[7]

In 1990 the Federal Reserve Bank of New York published a comprehensive research report entitled "Understanding International Differences in Leverage Trends," which sur-

[4]Eugene F. Brigham and Louis C. Gapenski, *Financial Management, Theory and Practice*, 6th ed., The Dryden Press, Chicago, 1991, p. 470.

[5]David K. Eiteman, Arthur I. Stonehill, and Michael H. Moffett, *Multinational Business Finance*, 6th ed., Addison-Wesley, Reading, MA, 1992, pp. 399–400.

[6]Brigham and Gapensky, op. cit., pp. 516–517.

[7]Ibid.

veys the phenomenon in the major industrial countries during the 1980s and advances several theoretical interpretations of these differences. Appendix 14-3 reprints this report.

As U.S. MNCs become more involved in global operations, they are likely to adopt similar capital structures that prevail abroad in order to remain competitive. MNCs that also fund internationally are able to reduce their cost of funds in comparison with strictly domestic corporations. The trend toward financial integration around the world enhanced the accessibility of corporations to a broad variety of financial resources and lowered the cost of capital. Remaining domestic market imperfections result in cost of capital differentials between domestic and international capital markets.[8]

The Assignment

Review the financial information of Genentech, Inc. and Royal Gist-brocades nv, for which financial statements are enclosed in Ap-

[8]Eiteman et al., op. cit., pp. 411–416.

pendix 14-2. Additional information can be found in *Value Line*, *Worldscope*, and other sources.

1. Calculate the WACC of each corporation.
2. Estimate the target capital structure of each firm (i.e., the capital structure which maximizes the value of the firm and minimizes its weighted average cost of capital).
3. Determine whether any one corporation could be recapitalized.

Bibliography

1. Eugene F. Brigham and Louis C. Gapenski, *Financial Management, Theory and Practice*, 6th ed., The Dryden Press, Chicago, 1991.
2. Richard A. Brealey and Stewart C. Myers, *Principles of Corporate Finance*, 3rd ed., McGraw-Hill, New York, 1988.
3. David K. Eiteman, Arthur I. Stonehill, and Michael H. Moffett, *Multinational Business Finance*, 6th ed., Addison-Wesley, Reading, MA, 1992.
4. James C. Van Horne, *Financial Management and Policy*, 6th ed., Prentice Hall, Englewood Cliffs, NJ, 1983.

APPENDIX 14-1

U.S. Industrial Outlook (Advanced Materials: Biotechnology)

Many advanced materials manufacturers are still in the embryonic stage, and produce low-volume, high value-added products for market niches. Many rely on military contracts for R&D funding and for end users. Advanced

Source: U.S. Department of Commerce, International Trade Administration, U.S. Industrial Outlook 1991, Advanced Materials, 18, Washington, D.C., January 1991.

materials include fiber composites, metal matrix composites, and advanced ceramics. Growth in these industries should remain strong for the next 5 to 10 years, although there may be a slowdown in R&D if the defense budget is cut. Any decrease in military procurement that includes the materials discussed in these sections will adversely affect demand.

There are no SIC codes for these industries, except powder metallurgy, so there are no data from the Bureau of the Census. Industry sources supply some data, but companies dependent on government funding for developing and/or manufacturing products with military applications often keep data secret for strategic reasons.

Exports of high technology products are often covered under the export control program, which restricts sales of strategic importance.

As biotechnology gains in health care and agricultural applications, it could account for $5 billion in sales by the mid-1990s. Engineering plastics should also exhibit strong growth, based on increased use in the automotive sector. The powder metal industry, which also relies principally on the automotive sector, is expecting a slight decrease in shipments for 1991; but over the next 10 years, the weight of powder metal parts in cars should double.

Biotechnology

Biotechnology is a set of scientific disciplines and technologies that use biological processes or organisms to produce goods and services.

It encompasses such diverse disciplines as molecular and cellular manipulation (including recombinant DNA and monoclonal antibody technologies); enzymology; protein engineering; X-ray crystallography; biomolecular instrumentation; industrial microbiology; bioprocess engineering (fermentation, cell culturing, and separation and purification technologies); and embryo sexing, manipulation, and transfer. Biotechnology also encompasses traditional plant and animal breeding; use of microorganisms to make fermented beverages and foods, antibiotics, enzymes, vitamins, amino acids, etc.

The development of new biotechnology tools, particularly recombinant DNA (or genetic engineering) and monoclonal antibody (MAbs) production technologies in the mid-1970s, spawned hundreds of new companies and significant investment to develop new substances, increase the production of rare substances, and improve manufacturing processes.

Recombinant DNA technology makes it possible to transfer specific genetic messages from one organism to another, and stimulate the second organism to produce large quantities of substances such as interferon, growth hormone, and other rare proteins. The same technique has enabled plants to produce their own pesticides. Also, the development of hybridoma cells through the artificial merging of two cells into one has made possible the production of large quantities of chemically identical antibodies, or MAbs, which are valuable tools in medicine, research, and industry because of their ability to recognize and bind to a wide variety of molecules. They are most commonly used in *in vitro* diagnostic tests to identify the presence of specific antigens associated with diseases or conditions. MAbs are also used in treating organ transplant rejection, and in extracting and purifying valuable proteins from mixtures and vaccines. They are soon to be used inside the body to produce X-ray-like pictures of damaged or cancerous tissue that could not be detected before, and as a therapy for septic shock infections.

DNA probe diagnostics make use of genetic information in cells and thus offer even greater accuracy than other diagnostic technologies. DNA probes are finding use in forensic testing to solve crimes and paternity cases, and in testing for genetic diseases and food contaminants.

Gene therapy may enable doctors to treat hereditary diseases and cancer by replacing defective genetic material with normal DNA. The first trials of human gene therapy for patients with advanced melanoma and a severe immune deficiency disorder were set to begin in late 1990.

Since biotechnology is not an industry in itself, but processes integrated into industrial research and production, the Government does not collect or tabulate biotech production, employment, or trade statistics. The statistics that follow are from a variety of sources.

Industrial Structure

Estimates of the number of biotechnology companies vary, depending on definition and criteria (e.g. level of total R&D or activity devoted to biotechnology). In the United States, about 1150 companies, including subsidiaries of foreign firms, are applying biotechnology. These include about 550 mostly small, new companies founded to exploit recombinant DNA and monoclonal antibody technologies; 200 manufacturing firms, predominantly pharmaceutical, chemical, and agribusiness; and 400 firms that supply the raw materials, instruments, equipment, and services needed in research and production.

These companies are often linked as an industry because they share business alliances and concerns regarding regulations, patent protection, and research and development. Difficulties in raising capital to fund product development have slowed the formation of new companies since the peak years of 1980–84. These difficulties are leading to industry consolidation through acquisitions, mergers, and equity investments. Although there are alliances between U.S. and foreign firms, these are far outnumbered by partnerships between U.S. firms. Estimates of total biotech-related employment are hard to come by, but in 400 firms about 42,000 people are employed.

Industrial Production

Products developed through biotechnology are not sufficiently identified in company reports or in Government data to assess produc-

tion. According to unofficial estimates, shipments by U.S. firms of products developed through recombinant DNA and monoclonal antibody technologies—mostly pharmaceuticals and diagnostics—were about $2 billion in 1990 (see Exhibit A14-1). Revised estimates for previous years are: $1.5 billion for 1989, $1 billion for 1988, $600 million for 1987, and $350 million for 1986.

Although sales have grown dramatically over the past five years, most biotechnology R&D is in human therapeutics and agriculture, and these products require long lead times for development and regulatory review (7–10 years and $100 million for new drugs). As a result, many potentially profitable substances have yet to reach the market. In contrast, due to shorter development and approval times, the FDA has approved more than 450 diagnostic kits using MAbs and DNA probes since 1981.

Biotechnology has been responsible for some major medical milestones: a safe version of human growth hormone to replace the natural hormone withdrawn from the market because of possible contamination with a deadly virus; alpha interferon, the only effective treatment for a rare cancer; and a MAb that rids an important blood-clotting factor of the AIDS virus. Biotechnology has also been indispensable in research on AIDS: not only discovery of the virus, but development of diagnostic tests, deciphering the virus' structure, and as a tool in designing new drugs and vaccines. Development of screening tests for the AIDS virus in 1985 and for the hepatitis-C virus in 1990 have helped ensure the safety of the nation's blood supply.

Other biotech pharmaceutical products currently in use include erythropoietin, which treats life-threatening anemia; a therapeutic MAb which prevents rejection of kidney transplants; human insulin; hepatitis-B vaccine; and tissue plasminogen activator, a blood clot dissolver. Genetically engineered mouse models are beginning to be used to study specific

EXHIBIT A14-1

Products Developed Through Biotechnology[a] on the Market in the U.S.

Product	Treatment or Use (year first approved)
Human Healthcare	
Alpha interferon	Hairy cell leukemia (1986), Kaposi's sarcoma (1988), non-A non-B hepatitis (1990[b])
Erythropoeitin	Anemia associated with kidney disease (1989)
Gamma interferon	Chronic granulomatous disease (1990[b])
Human growth hormone	Dwarfism (1986)
Insulin	Diabetes (1982)
Tissue plasminogen activator	Dissolve blood clots (1987)
Vaccines	Hepatitis-B (1986)
Monoclonal antibodies (MAbs)	Treat kidney transplant rejection (1986), purify blood clotting agents (1987)
Diagnostic tests (MAbs and DNA probes)	Diagnose pregnancy and fertility; bacterial and viral infections; cancer; genetic diseases; DNA fingerprinting; forensic and paternity testing, etc.
Agriculture	
Animals:	
Vaccines	Colibacillosis or scours (1984), pseudorabies (1987)
Diagnostic tests	Bacterial and viral infections, pregnancy, presence of antibiotic residues
Plants:	
Diagnostic tests	Diagnose plant diseases (e.g. turfgrass fungi)
Food Processing	
Diagnostic tests	Diagnose food and feed contaminants (e.g. salmonella, aflatoxin, listeria)
Chymosin or rennin	Enzyme used in cheesemaking (1990)
Other	
Transgenic mice	Cancer research
Luciferase TM	Detection agent used in food and medical diagnostic tests

[a] Defined as recombinant DNA and monoclonal antibody technologies.

[b] Recommended for approval by the FDA Biological Response Modifiers Advisory Committee; final FDA approval was expected in 1990.

human diseases and test experimental drugs. And DNA probes, which can locate specific genetic characteristics, are used to diagnose pathogenic and genetic diseases and to help resolve criminal cases.

Biotech veterinary products include vaccines for pseudorabies and scours. Food industry products include faster, more accurate tests for such food contaminants as salmonella, aflatoxin, and listeria. In 1990, chymosin, or rennin, became the first genetically engineered food product approved in the United States. It offers cheese producers a less costly alternative to the natural version, taken from calf's stomach, which is expensive and of uncertain purity.

Breakthroughs are also occurring elsewhere. A Japanese firm is manufacturing an amino acid called tryptophan, used in feed additives. A Danish firm has developed a detergent containing a lipase enzyme that breaks down protein-based stains. The U.K. approved a genetically engineered yeast in 1990 developed by a Dutch firm that decreases bread-making time.

International Trade

Since U.S. biotech companies are leaders in commercializing biotechnology, sales of products and services and royalties from licenses have contributed to a positive trade balance. Preliminary data from a National Science Foundation (NSF) survey indicate foreign sales by 48 biotech companies in 1989 were worth $180 million, a quarter of their total sales. The major markets are Western Europe and Japan.

Industrial R&D

According to the NSF, industry spent about $2.3 billion on biotechnology R&D in 1990, an increase of 19 percent a year over the $1.4 billion spent in 1987. Seventy-seven percent of industrial research funds is now spent on hu-

man health care, the fastest growing field (therapeutics 63%, diagnostics 14%). The remainder goes to plant agriculture (10%), animal agriculture (5%), chemicals and food additives (4%), biosensors and bioinstruments (3%), and other (1%).

Human Health Care

Most commercial applications of biotechnology are occurring in health care because the U.S. government has supported biomedical research over the past several decades—it now allocates most of its $3.5 billion biotech budget to biomedical research—and because of the high value-added nature of medical products. Over 100 biotech-derived drugs and vaccines are in research and testing, according to the Pharmaceutical Manufacturers Association. The major categories are treatments for cancer, AIDS, and cardiovascular diseases; and vaccines for diseases such as AIDS and malaria. Products nearing the market in the United States include beta and gamma interferons; colony stimulating factors to treat depressed white cell counts associated with AIDS, chemotherapy, burns, or cancers; and blood clotting factors to treat hemophilia.

Diagnostics are one of the fastest growing applications of biotechnology. Recent breakthroughs in amplifying minute amounts of genetic material into larger quantities that can be analyzed is revolutionizing the speed and accuracy of testing. A new technique for producing monoclonal antibodies will make more varieties available for research at lower cost, and provide MAbs more compatible with the human immune system. Most MAbs are used in *in vitro* (test tube) diagnostic tests, but industry is also developing MAbs for *in vivo* (inside the body) imaging to detect cancers, and therapeutic MAbs linked to toxins as drug delivery agents. Researchers are also trying to determine whether MAbs can predict the remission, relapse, and outcome of drug therapies in cancer patients.

Animals

The same biomedical techniques are also being applied to animal heath care. Veterinary products now being developed include diagnostic tests, vaccines (rabies, mastitis, and rinderpest), drugs (alpha interferon for treating shipping fever in cattle), and drug delivery systems.

Biotechnology is being used to identify genes in livestock animals for such desired traits as improved disease resistance, faster growth, and better quality meat (lower fat, lower cholesterol) for selective breeding. Efforts to transplant such genes into livestock are in the early stages. But biotechnology is providing a faster route to developing improved livestock over traditional breeding methods. Animal breeding techniques such as embryo multiplication and transfer will speed production of high-quality animals. One of the most promising developments is transgenic chickens that possess an inheritable resistance to avian leukosis virus, a disease that costs U.S. egg producers $50–100 million a year. Companies are developing transgenic animals to mass produce milk out of which proteins are extracted for use in drugs.

In aquaculture, work is underway to enhance the size and growth rate of fish, and to transfer genes among fish species to promote resistance to diseases, pollution, and temperature changes.

Plants

In plant agriculture, biotechnology is providing tools to develop crops with better resistance to pests, diseases, herbicides, pesticides, and environmental stresses, and to improve their nutritional content. New varieties of fruits and vegetables will offer enhanced flavors and such improved commercial characteristics as higher solids content and controlled ripening. Plants have been engineered to mass produce such commercially valuable substances as drugs and melanin for use in sunscreens. Other commercial targets are diag-

nostics for plant diseases, new varieties of ornamental flowers, and more nutritous oilseeds.

Although small-scale field tests have been successful on agriculturally useful microorganisms to increase nitrogen intake by plants, inhibit frost damage in crops, and kill pests, and although there is increasing pressure to substitute biological fertilizers and pesticides for chemical ones, an uncertain regulatory environment and limited market prospects have dampened investment in genetically engineered microorganisms. Killed genetically engineered microorganisms or those used in containers are having an easier time getting approval.

Food Processing

In food processing, genetic and protein engineering are expected to yield many improved enzymes, amino acids, starter cultures for fermented foods, vitamins, flavoring and food coloring agents, thickeners, emulsifiers, and vegetable oils. Products nearing the market are thaumatin (a sweetener), vitamin C, glucose isomerase (an enzyme used to make high fructose corn syrup), alpha-amylase (an enzyme used in wet corn milling), low-calorie beer, and various food flavors. Faster, more accurate diagnostic tests to detect bacterial contamination and pesticide residues are another important area of research.

New Materials

In materials science, research has already yielded a superadhesive derived from a mussel that will be tested in medical and dental surgery. Other important research areas include biodegradable plastics, high-tensile strength fibers, anticorrosive coatings for marine vessels, and cellulosic fibers for a variety of industrial processes.

Biosensors

Biosensors—devices that combine biological and electrical components—are in the early development stages. Because they can provide highly specific detection, real-time feedback, and control of targeted substances, biosensors show promise for medical diagnostic testing: for *in situ* drug delivery; and for monitoring industrial processes, toxins, and pollutants in air, water, and soil.

Bioremediation and Natural Resources

One of the most important potential applications of biotechnology is the use of microorganisms to clean up hazardous wastes. With recent successes in using microorganisms to clean toxic waste dumps and oil spills, and with the high cost of conventional incineration and landfill methods, funding in bioremediation is growing rapidly. Use is limited to selectively-bred natural organisms, however. The uncertain regulatory environment and concerns about adverse public reaction are major deterrents to developing recombinant organisms, which will be needed to attack less easily-degradable contaminants such as PCBs. Genetically-engineered enzymes capable of degrading lignin without using chlorine are being developed, which will reduce pollution in the pulp and paper industry.

In energy, promising developments include a microbial strain which provides an economic method of removing sulphur from coal, and improved microbial strains for enhanced oil recovery and metal and mineral mining. Research on biomass conversion to produce commodity chemicals and fuels may pick up if high energy prices are sustained.

Commercialization

Commercial application of biotechnology depends on public and private funding of basic and applied research. More research is needed on the genetic makeup, structure, and metabolism of industrially useful microorganisms, plants, and animals, including those from marine environments. The potential of protein engineering, for example, is limited by the lack of predictive models that can show the relationship between the structure and function of proteins. Although researchers have identified and produced genes of interest, more work is needed in large-scale production, monitoring, separation, and purification technology; in bioreactor design; in biosensors; in enzymology; and in drug delivery. These activities will determine product cost, quality, and competitiveness. The most significant problem for biotech companies is access to affordable capital to fund final development and regulatory approval for the many worthwhile products.

Both large and small companies have shied away from applications involving release of genetically engineered organisms out of doors because of public concerns and an uncertain regulatory environment. Future regulations will depend upon Government's gaining more experience and knowledge about the risks posed by genetically engineered organisms. Some states are passing laws which add new layers of regulations to the complex Federal system.

Other factors that influence the commercial use of biotechnology are the political and socio-economic impact of a new product on employment and price levels (e.g., the impact of bovine growth hormone on the dairy industry). The public's concerns about the safeness of genetically engineered foods and products used in the environment will continue to influence government regulatory attitudes and sales.

The ability to obtain prompt patent protection to enforce intellectual property rights is especially important to small companies that rely on revenues from technology licensing. The United States offers the most comprehensive patent protection in the world for biotechnology inventions; microorganisms, plants, and animals are patentable, provided they meet the criteria for novelty, inventiveness and practical application, and disclosure. The Government is attempting to gain greater international protection for biotechnology inventions, to harmonize patenting procedures with Europe and Japan, and to reduce the backlog of patent applications.

Lack of affordable product liability insurance will create obstacles to commercialization as biotech firms develop such products as drugs, vaccines, and chemicals that traditionally have been subject to greater product liability risks. Insurers are uncertain as well about the risks and liability of insuring genetically engineered organisms used in the environment.

Outlook for 1991

The market value of products developed through genetic engineering and monoclonal antibody techniques could reach $2.5 billion in 1991. Most of that will be derived from health care products. Several new human health care products could be approved this year, including the first MAbs for *in vivo* imaging to detect damaged heart muscle and various cancers, therapeutic MAbs with toxins attached to treat septic shock or prevent transplant rejections, and granulocyte colony stimulating factor to alleviate the effects of cancer chemotherapy. Previously approved products may be cleared for new uses, such as alpha interferon to treat AIDS and erythropoeitin to treat anemic conditions.

Bovine somatotrophin (BST), a growth hormone that increases milk production, is expected to be approved by the FDA in 1991. Although the FDA has determined that milk from herds treated with BST is safe for human consumption, negative consumer perceptions may affect sales. Another growth hormone, porcine somatotrophin (PST), which promotes

faster growth in animals with lower fat content, could be approved in 1992. In aminal health care, a safer recombinant DNA-derived feline leukemia vaccine should soon be on the market.

Long-term Prospects

The large number of industries involved in biotechnology, the lack of data, competitive factors, and technical hurdles to new product development make it difficult to predict long-term market values. Based on the large number of promising products in the R & D pipeline, however, market values could be in the $4 to $5 billion range by 1995 and several tens of billions of dollars by the early 21st century. Human health care products will dominate the market, followed by products for animal and plant agriculture. Other industry categories are not likely to be significant for the next 5 to 10 years. Biotechnology will also contribute directly to a greater understanding of the molecular biology of cells and the origin and biochemical pathways of diseases. Research to dicipher the human genetic doe will play an important role in increasing our knowledge of the biochemistry of life. This knowledge will stimulate the design of new drugs to prevent or intervene in disease progression, the development of new drug delivery devices, and the discovery of new therapeutic substances.

Of the dozen drugs in the late approval stage, several will have a multiplicity of uses and could eventually reach $1 billion in worldwide sales. Market values will depend on effectiveness, safety, competition, price reimbursement limits set by Medicare, and the number and timing of approved uses. Diagnostic tests using monoclonal antibodies and DNA probes will gain an increasing share of the medical testing market.

Market values outside human health care will be much lower because industry is investing less and the economic constraints are more severe. In animal healthcare and agriculture, sales of vaccines, growth promoters, and improved animal feeds may account for several hundred million dollars in sales by the mid-1990s. Genetically engineered plants with improved resistance to herbicides or pests, fruits and vegetables engineered to ripen on the vine and stay fresh longer, and agriculturally useful microorganisms should be on the market within the five years if they demonstrate price-performance advantages. Public acceptance and the regulatory environment will influence investment in genetically engineered plants, microorganisms, animals, and foods. (*Emily Arakaki, Basic Industries, (202) 377-3888, August 1990.*)

Additional References

"Biotechnology at Work" (series) and "Biotechnology in Perspective" (1990), David B. Sattelle, Industrial Biotechnology Association, 1625 K. St. N.W., Washington, D.C. 20005. Tel.: (202) 857-0244.

"Biotechnology for All" (1990), Association of Biotechnology Companies, 1666 Connecticut Avenue NW, Washington, D.C. 20009-1039. Tel.: (202) 234-3330.

"Biotechnology: Implications for Agribusiness in the 1990s" (1988), Marvin Hayenga, Technology and Social Change Program, Iowa State University, Ames, IA 50011. Tel.: (515) 294-0938.

Biotechnology in Japan (1988); *Biotechnology in Singapore, South Korea, and Taiwan* (1989); *Biotechnology in the PRC and Hong Kong* (1989); *and Biotechnology in Western Europe* (1987). National

Technical Information Service, U.S. Department of Commerce, 5285 Port Royal Road, Springfield, VA 22161. Tel.: (703) 487-4650.

BIO/TECHNOLOGY (monthly), Nature Publishing, 65 Bleecker St., New York, NY 10012. Tel.: (800) 524-0328.

"Biotechnology Products in the Pipeline" and "AIDS Medicines in Development" (1990), Pharmaceutical Manufacturers Association, 1100 15th St. NW, Washington, D.C. 20005. Tel.: (202) 835-3400.

Field Testing Genetically Modified Organisms (1989), National Academy Press, Washington, D.C. 20418. Tel.: (202) 334-2665.

Genetic Engineering News (monthly), Mary Ann Liebert Inc., 157 East 86th St., New York, NY 10028. Tel.: (212) 289-2300.

"Industrial Biotechnology R&D Performance," *Science Resource Studies HIGHLIGHTS* (March 18, 1988, update in progress), National Science Foundation, Washington, D.C., 20550. Tel.: (202) 634-4634.

New Developments in Biotechnology (series, 1987–9), Biological Applications Program, Office of Technology Assessment, U.S. Congress. See esp. vol. 4, *U.S. Investment in Biotechnology* (1988). Government Printing Office, Washington, D.C. Tel.: (202) 783-3238.

"Solving Agricultural Problems with Biotechnology" (1990), Agricultural Research Service, U.S. Department of Agriculture, Beltsville, MD 20705. Tel.: (301) 344-1918.

State-by-State Biotechnology Directory: Centers, Companies and Contacts (1990), prepared by North Carolina Biotechnology Center, Research Triangle Park, NC 27709-3547 and available from Bureau of National Affairs, 9435 Key West Avenue, Rockville, MD 20850. Tel.: (800) 372-1033.

Financial Data: Genentech, Inc. and Royal Gist-brocades nv

FINANCIAL HIGHLIGHTS

(thousands, except per share amounts)

	1990	1989	1988
Income Statement			
Total revenues	$ 476,136	$400,455	$334,840
Product sales	367,170	319,067	262,476
Costs and expenses	572,692[a]	352,929	311,732[b]
Net income (loss)	(98,031)[a]	43,961	20,565[b]
Net income (loss) per share	$ (1.05)[a]	$ 0.51	$ 0.24[b]
Shares outstanding (weighted average)	93,040	85,967	84,459
Balance Sheet			
Cash and investments	$ 691,274	$204,951	$152,489
Property, plant and equipment (net)	300,236	299,111	289,425
Total assets	1,157,670	711,191	662,895
Long-term debt	153,534	154,409	155,269
Stockholders' equity	$ 893,182	$468,952	$399,295
Employees	1,923	1,790	1,744

[a]Costs and expenses in 1990 include a special charge which was primarily merger related of $167.7 million, which amounted to $1.74 per share net of the applicable income tax benefit.

[b]Costs and expenses in 1988 include a special charge which was primarily a reserve against inventory of $23.3 million, which amounted to $.26 per share net of the applicable income tax benefit.

Source: Company Annual Reports and 10-K.

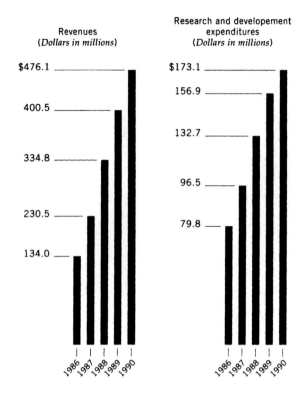

Revenues
(*Dollars in millions*)

Research and developement expenditures
(*Dollars in millions*)

CONSOLIDATED STATEMENTS OF OPERATIONS

(thousands, except per share amounts)

YEAR ENDED DECEMBER 31	1990	1989	1988
Revenues:			
Product sales	$367,170	$319,067	$262,476
Contract and other (including amounts from related parties: 1990—$17,045; 1989—$13,868; 1988—$2,394)	79,526	64,143	60,283
Interest	29,440	17,245	12,081
Total revenues	476,136	400,455	334,840
Costs and expenses:			
Cost of sales	68,305	60,556	46,897
Special charge (primarily merger related in 1990 and inventory related in 1988)	167,735	—	23,349
Research and development (including contract related: 1990—$16,719; 1989—$11,080; 1988—$21,001)	173,090	156,883	132,682

(*Continued*)

YEAR ENDED DECEMBER 31	1990	1989	1988
Marketing, general and administrative	158,058	127,922	101,989
Interest	5,504	7,568	6,906
Total costs and expenses	572,692	352,926	311,732
Income (loss) before taxes	(96,556)	47,526	23,108
Income tax provision	1,475	3,565	2,543
Net income (loss)	$ (98,031)	$ 43,961	$ 20,565
Net income (loss) per share	$ (1.05)	$ 0.51	$ 0.24
Weighted average number of shares used in computing per share amounts	93,040	85,967	84,459

CONSOLIDATED STATEMENTS OF CASH FLOWS

(dollars in thousands)

YEAR ENDED DECEMBER 31	1990	1989	1988
Cash flows from operating activities:			
Net income (loss)	$(98,031)	$ 43,961	$ 20,565
Adjustments to reconcile net income (loss) to net cash provided (used) by operating activities:			
Depreciation and amortization	47,629	44,605	38,325
Gain on sale of Genencor investment	(11,874)	—	—
Net loss on fixed asset write-downs and dispositions	664	—	118
Non-cash portion of special charge (primarily merger related in 1990 and inventory related in 1988)	8,058	—	23,349
Changes in assets and liabilities, net of the effects from the special charge:			
Decrease (Increase) in receivables and other assets	8,034	(4,131)	28,989
Decrease (Increase) in inventories	9,685	14,241	(26,244)
Increase in accounts payable and accrued liabilities	22,577	875	12,399
Net cash provided (used) by operating activities	(13,258)	99,551	97,501
Cash flows from investing activities:			
Purchases of short-term investments	(538,046)	(223,685)	(145,154)
Dispositions of short-term investments	223,261	188,060	201,440
Capital expenditures	(35,980)	(37,160)	(110,858)
Net proceeds from sale of Genencor investment	19,101	—	—
Acquisition of Genentech Canada	—	(3,300)	—
Proceeds from sale of fixed assets	—	1,000	—
Increase in other assets	(3,883)	(1,274)	(1,315)
Net cash used in investing activities	(335,547)	(76,359)	(55,887)

(*Continued*)

YEAR ENDED DECEMBER 31	1990	1989	1988
Cash flows from financing activities:			
Stock issuance to Roche Holdings, Inc.	487,340	—	—
Stock issuances, net of notes receivable and redemption of preferred share purchase rights	34,921	17,197	21,735
Reduction in long-term debt including current portion	(1,918)	(23,552)	(12,885)
Net cash provided (used) by financing activities	520,343	(6,355)	8,850
Increase (Decrease) in cash and cash equivalents	171,538	16,837	50,464
Cash and cash equivalents at beginning of year	113,189	96,352	45,888
Cash and cash equivalents at end of year	$284,727	$113,189	$ 96,352
Supplemental schedule of noncash investing and financing activities:			
Issuance of warrants related to contract arrangements	$ —	$ 8,499	$ 1,583
Investment financed by debt	—	620	—
Supplemental cash flow data:			
Cash paid during the year for:			
Interest, net of portion capitalized	$ 5,552	$ 7,540	$ 6,996
Income taxes	324	—	1,222

CONSOLIDATED BALANCE SHEETS

(dollars in thousands)

DECEMBER 31	1990	1989
ASSETS		
Current assets:		
Cash and cash equivalents	$ 284,727	$113,189
Short-term investments, at cost which approximates market	406,547	91,762
Accounts receivable (less allowances of: 1990—$3,800; 1989—$2,144)	58,751	66,764
Inventories	39,573	49,258
Prepaid expenses and other current assets	6,108	6,129
Total current assets	795,706	327,102
Property, plant and equipment, at cost:		
Land	38,260	38,207
Buildings	76,299	72,844
Equipment	154,074	135,279
Leasehold improvements	73,060	72,872
Construction-in-progress	59,479	55,090
	401,172	374,292
Less: accumulated depreciation	100,936	75,181
Net property, plant and equipment	300,236	299,111

(Continued)

DECEMBER 31	1990	1989
Purchased product technology, net	40,319	56,114
Other assets	21,409	28,864
Total assets	$1,157,670	$711,191

LIABILITIES AND STOCKHOLDERS' EQUITY

	1990	1989
Current liabilities:		
Accounts payable	$ 10,215	$ 7,229
Accrued compensation	19,238	15,369
Accrued interest	5,708	5,708
Accrued royalties	20,830	14,471
Other accrued liabilities	44,359	31,071
Current portion of long-term debt	1,062	2,085
Total current liabilities	101,392	75,933
Long-term debt	153,534	154,409
Other long-term liabilities	9,562	11,897
Total liabilities	264,488	242,239
Commitments and contingencies		
Stockholders' equity:		
Preferred Stock, $.02 par value; authorized 100,000,000 shares; none issued	—	—
Redeemable Common Stock, $.02 par value; authorized 100,000,000 shares, outstanding: 1990—43,476,851; 1989—none	870	—
Common Stock, $.02 par value; authorized 200,000,000 shares; outstanding: 1990—67,133,409; 1989—84,269,481	1,343	1,685
Additional paid-in capital	927,940	406,207
Retained earnings (deficit) (since October 1, 1987 quasi-reorganization in which a deficit of $329,457 was eliminated)	(36,971)	61,060
Total stockholders' equity	893,182	468,952
Total liabilities and stockholders' equity	$1,157,670	$711,191

CONSOLIDATED STATEMENTS OF STOCKHOLDERS' EQUITY

(dollars in thousands)

YEAR ENDED DECEMBER 31	1990	1989	1988
Redeemable Common Stock—Beginning of Year	$ —	$ —	$ —
Conversion of Common Stock to Redeemable Common Stock during the merger with Roche Holdings, Inc. (42,699,458 shares)	854	—	—
Issuance of Redeemable Common Stock (777,393 shares)	16	—	—
End of Year (43,476,851 shares)	$ 870	$ —	$ —

(*Continued*)

YEAR ENDED DECEMBER 31	1990	1989	1988
Common Stock—Beginning of Year	$ 1,685	$ 1,658	$ 1,575
Conversion of Common Stock to Redeemable Common Stock during the merger with Roche Holdings, Inc. (42,699,458 shares)	(854)	—	—
Issuance of Common Stock to Roche Holdings, Inc. (24,433,951 shares)	489	—	—
Other issuances of Common Stock (1990—1,129,435 shares; 1989—1,345,042 shares; 1988—4,184,543 shares)	23	27	83
End of Year, after conversion and issuance of Common Stock (67,133,409 shares)	$ 1,343	$ 1,685	$ 1,658
Restricted Stock—Beginning of Year	$ —	$ —	$ 59
End of Year, after issuance of Common Stock	$ —	$ —	$ —
Additional Paid-in Capital—Beginning of Year	$406,207	$366,518	$336,267
Issuance of Common Stock to Roche Holdings, Inc.	486,851	—	—
Other issuances of Common Stock	15,974	17,170	21,391
Issuance of Redeemable Common Stock	19,762	—	—
Redemption of preferred share purchase rights	(854)	—	—
Issuance of warrants	—	8,499	1,583
Tax benefits arising prior to quasi-reorganization	—	14,020	7,277
End of Year	$927,940	$406,207	$366,518
Notes Receivable from sale of stock—Beginning of Year	$ —	$ —	$ (320)
End of Year, after payments on notes receivable	$ —	$ —	$ —
Retained Earnings—Beginning of Year	$ 61,060	$ 31,119	$ 17,831
Net income (loss)	(98,031)	43,961	20,565
Tax benefits arising prior to quasi-reorganization	—	(14,020)	(7,277)
End of Year	$(36,971)	$ 61,060	$ 31,119
Total stockholders' equity	$893,182	$468,952	$399,295

Notes to Consolidated Financial Statements

PRINCIPLES OF CONSOLIDATION

The consolidated financial statements include the accounts of the Company and its wholly-owned and majority owned subsidiaries. All significant intercompany balances and transactions have been eliminated.

CASH AND CASH EQUIVALENTS

The Company considers all highly liquid debt instruments purchased with a maturity of three months or less to be cash equivalents.

INVENTORIES

Inventories are stated at the lower of cost or market. Cost is determined using a weighted-average approach, which approximates the first-in, first-out method.

PROPERTY, PLANT AND EQUIPMENT

The costs of buildings and equipment are depreciated for financial reporting purposes using the straight-line method over the estimated useful lives of the assets. Accelerated methods of depreciation are used for income tax purposes. Leasehold improvements are generally amortized over the length of the

applicable lease. Expenditures for maintenance and repairs are expensed as incurred.
Interest on construction-in-progress is capitalized. Interest of $2.4 million in 1990, $2.4 million in 1989 and $4.1 million in 1988 has been
capitalized and included in property, plant
and equipment.

PURCHASED PRODUCT TECHNOLOGY

Approved product rights and technology (related to Protropin) acquired from a research
and development partnership are amortized
on a straight-line basis over their estimated
useful lives of six years. At December 31, 1990,
1989 and 1988 accumulated amortization related to these assets was $58.9 million, $42.7
million and $26.5 million, respectively.

PATENTS

As a result of its research and development
programs, the Company owns and is in the
process of applying for patents in the United
States and other countries which relate to
products and processes of significant importance to the Company. Costs of patents and
patent applications are amortized on a
straight-line basis over their estimated useful
lives of approximately 12 years.

CONTRACT REVENUE

Contract revenue for research and development is recorded as earned based on the performance requirements of the contract. In return for contract payments, contract partners
may receive certain marketing and manufacturing rights (including rights to future product royalties), products for clinical use and
testing or research and development services.

INCOME TAXES

Income taxes are accounted for in accordance
with Statement of Financial Accounting Standards No. 96, "Accounting for Income Taxes."
For financial statement purposes, investment
tax credits are accounted for on the flow-
through method as a reduction of federal income tax expense.

EARNINGS PER SHARE

Earnings per share are computed based on the
weighted average number of shares of Redeemable Common Stock, Common Stock and
equivalents, if dilutive, (options and warrants
in 1990, 1989 and 1988). The Company's convertible subordinate debentures are common
stock equivalents but have been antidilutive to
date and, therefore, have not been included in
earnings per share calculations.

CONCENTRATION OF CREDIT AND MARKET RISK

The Company sells primarily to hospitals and
distributors throughout the United States and
Canada, performs ongoing credit evaluations
of its customers' financial condition and generally requires no collateral. In fiscal years
1990, 1989 and 1988 the Company did not
record any material additions to its provision
for doubtful accounts.

The Company invests its excess cash principally in marketable securities from a diversified portfolio of institutions with strong credit
ratings and, by policy, limits the amount of
credit exposure to any one institution. These
investments are generally not collateralized
and primarily mature within one year. The
Company has not experienced any material
losses in fiscal years 1990, 1989 and 1988.

Note 1: Merger with Roche Holdings, Inc.

Genentech's merger ("Merger") with a
wholly-owned subsidiary of Roche Holdings,
Inc. ("Roche") was consummated on September 7, 1990. Genentech stockholders of record
on September 7, 1990 received, for each share
of Common Stock that they owned, $18 in
cash from Roche and one half share of newly
issued Redeemable Common Stock from the
Company. In the Merger, Roche acquired one
half of the Company's outstanding Common
Stock for $1,537.2 million. Stockholders also
received $0.01 per share from the Company
for redemption of their Preferred Share Pur-

chase Rights, as allowed for under the Preferred Share Purchase Rights Plan (which was terminated concurrently with the Merger consummation). The new Genentech Redeemable Common Stock is substantially identical to the Genentech Common Stock, previously held by stockholders, except that it is redeemable by the Company at the election of Roche, provided that Roche first deposits in trust sufficient funds to pay the aggregate redemption price of all outstanding shares of Redeemable Common Stock. Roche will have the right to require the Company to exercise its redemption right, providing it does so for all shares of Genentech's outstanding Redeemable Common Stock at $39 per share in the first calendar quarter of 1991, to $40 per share in the second calendar quarter and increasing by $1.25 per share every quarter to $60 per share on April 1, 1995. The redemption right expires on June 30, 1995.

In connection with the Merger the Company issued 24,433,951 shares of Common Stock to Roche for $487.3 million in cash. The Common Stock issued to Roche, combined with the Common Stock Roche acquired in the Merger, represented approximately 60 percent of the outstanding equity of the Company at the effective date of the Merger (See also Note 8).

Independent of its right to have the Company redeem the Redeemable Common Stock, Roche is permitted by the terms of its agreements with the Company to acquire additional shares of Genentech stock through open market of privately negotiated purchases, provided that Roche's aggregate holdings do not exceed 75 percent of the Company's stock outstanding on a fully diluted basis.

The Company incurred a special charge in 1990 of $167.7 million which consists primarily of Merger-related expenses. The majority of the Merger-related expenses included in the special charge were associated with the cashout of employee options (approximately $125 million). The total Merger-related expenses were $153.3 million and included investment banking fees, and legal, printing and filing fees. The balance of the special charge was for litigation, facility and other corporate charges.

Note 2: Operating Revenues

One major customer in 1990, 1989 and 1988 contributed 10% or more of the Company's total revenues. The portions of revenues attributable to this customer were 27% in 1990, 21% in 1989 and 21% in 1988. Revenues from foreign customers were as follows: Europe— approximately $17.6 million in 1990; $17.6 million in 1989, and $24.9 million in 1988; Asia—approximately $5.6 million in 1990; $3.2 million in 1989, and $4.9 million in 1988; Canada—approximately $9.2 million in 1990, $4.7 million in 1989 and $1.7 million in 1988.

In the first quarter of 1990 Genentech sold its interest in Genencor, Inc., an industrial enzyme joint venture which Genentech helped found in 1982. The sales resulted in a pre-tax gain of approximately $11.9 million which is included in contract and other revenues.

Note 3: Income Taxes

The income tax provision consists of the following (in thousands):

	1990	1989	1988
Current:			
State	$ 450	$ 200	$ 200
Foreign	—	200	—
	450	400	200
Deferred:			
Federal	1,025	2,139	575
State	—	1,026	1,768
	1,025	3,165	2,343
Income tax provision	$1,475	$3,565	$2,543

A reconciliation between the Company's effective tax rate and the U.S. statutory rate follows:

	1990 Amount (in thousands)	Tax Rate		
		1990	1989	1988
Tax at U.S. statutory rate	$(32,828)	(34.0)%	34.0%	34.0%
Operating losses not utilized/(utilized)	32,828	34.0%	(29.5)	(31.5)
Other, including state taxes	1,475	1.5%	3.0	8.5
Income tax provision	$ 1,475	1.5%	7.5%	11.0%

Deferred taxes are provided on temporary differences between the timing of income and deductions for tax return and financial statement purposes. The principal differences relate to the amortization of purchased technology and to accelerated depreciation.

At December 31, 1990 the Company had operating loss carryforwards for Federal tax purposes of approximately $356 million. For financial reporting purposes, such carryforwards approximate $264 million. The difference between the amounts for tax and financial statement purposes is attributable to the temporary differences described above and to approximately $50 million of deductions related to stock option exercises, the tax benefit of which will be credited to paid-in capital when realized. Such losses expire from 2000 through 2005.

In addition, at December 31, 1990 the Company had available general business credit carryforwards for financial reporting purposes of $29 million which expire in 1996 through 2005.

Note 4: Research and Development Arrangements

The Company entered into contracts to perform research and development (R&D) with Genentech Clinical Partners III (GCP III) in 1984 and Genentech Clinical Partners IV(GCP IV) in 1989, both limited partnerships (See also Note 9). The Company also entered into licensing agreements with these contract partners wherein they were granted exclusive territorial rights to practice under the Company's patents and to use the Company's know-how for certain projects. GCP III acquired the Company's United States rights for tumor necrosis factor-alpha (TNF) and GCP IV acquired the Company's United States and European rights for recombinant CD4 and recombinant CD4-IgG. As discussed below, the technology owned by GCP III was acquired by the Company in October 1989 and the related research and development contracts were terminated.

Under these R&D arrangements, the Company recognized revenue from the partnerships for the costs of the work performed on the respective project's development on a cost reimbursement basis. The Company recorded approximately $13.2 million, $10.1 million, and $2.2 million as revenue under these research and development partnerships in 1990, 1989 and 1988, respectively.

Under the GCP IV contracts with the Company, if development cannot be successfully completed the Company's obligation is terminated and the Company has no further obligations, except for a supply agreement, under the agreements or rights or interests in the products within the involved territory. If development is successfully completed and regulatory approval is received, the Company has options to first manufacture and market the products in a joint venture with GCP IV and then to purchase the Partnership interests including all the rights to the respective products. If the Company exercises the purchase option, the Limited Partners will receive a fixed initial payment plus future cash payments based on a percentage of product revenues. In January 1991, the Board of Directors of the general partner of GCP IV announced that it will concentrate the clinical research program for CD_4-IgG on studies aimed at preventing the spread of disease from HIV-infected pregnant women to their fetuses; and that it has no current plans to continue the clinical trials of CD_4-IgG as a stand-alone therapy for HIV-infected adults.

During the third quarter of 1988 the Company discontinued revenue recognition under the development agreement with GCP III. In November 1988, the Company accrued $2.5 million for its obligations under a guarantee for GCP III's outstanding loan which was repaid by the Company in 1989. In October 1989, upon the purchase of GCP III's technology assets, the Company recorded a net expense of $1.6 million associated with the purchase. The purchase agreement requires the Company to pay royalties for a specified period on net sales by Genentech of human pharmaceutical products containing TNF if such sales commence in the United States prior to December 31, 2005.

In the second half of 1990, the Company began co-sponsorship of a major comparative mortality trial known as GUSTO. The GUSTO trial will focus on three thrombolytic treatment study groups: an accelerated dose of the Company's t-PA; the use of streptokinase; and the combined therapy of t-PA and streptokinase. All these groups will also receive aspirin and heparin The GUSTO trial is expected to enroll about 33,000 patients and take several years to complete at an estimated cost of more than $40 million.

In December 1990, the Company entered into an agreement with Glycomed, Inc. for a $15 millions research collaboration to develop carbohydrate-based therapeutics in the field of cell adhesion molecules. The agreement includes partial research support for an initial three-year period and a two-stage, $7 million equity investment by Genentech in Glycomed, Inc. The research will be funded by Genentech through a combination of sponsored research funding and milestone payments over a three

year period with a potential two year extension.

In January 1991, the Company entered into an agreement with Telios Pharmaceuticals, Inc. ("Telios") for a $15 million research collaboration to develop and commercialize an injectable drug to help prevent the formation of blood clots. Under the agreement, the companies will co-develop a drug based on Telios' proprietary matrix-peptide technology and Genentech's expertise in peptide design and recombinant-receptor assay screening. Genentech will provide Telios with milestone-based payments and will pay the company royalties on sales. In return, Genentech will have the right to market the drug worldwide, except in Japan and the Far East.

Note 5: Inventories

Inventories at December 31, 1990 and 1989 are summarized in the following table (in thousands):

	1990	1989
Raw materials and supplies	$ 7,632	$ 9,159
Work in process	18,302	27,728
Finished goods	13,639	12,371
Total	$39,573	$49,258

During the fourth quarter of 1988 the Company recorded a special charge of $23.3 million which was primarily a write down of certain quantities of Activase inventory.

Note 6: Long-Term Debt and Credit Arrangements

Long-term debt consists of the following (in thousands):

	1990	1989
Convertible subordinated debentures, interest at 5%, due in 2002	$150,000	$150,000
Mortgage note payable on buildings and land, interest at 9.5%, due 1990 to 1996	3,997	4,540
Obligations under capital leases	—	729
Non-interest bearing notes payable as capital contributions to GCP IV, due 1990 to 1992	389	620
Other	190	605
	154,576	156,494
Less current maturities	1,042	2,085
Total long-term debt	$153,534	$154,409

Maturities of long-term debt in 1991 and in the four subsequent years are $1.0 million, $0.8 million, $0.7 million, $0.8 million and $0.9 million, respectively.

Convertible subordinated debentures are convertible at the option of the holder into shares of the Company's Redeemable Common Stock at a conversion price of $74 per debenture. Upon conversion, the holder receives, for each debenture converted, one-half share of Redeemable Common Stock and $18 in cash. Under the terms of the Merger Agreement, the $18 in cash per debenture converted is reimbursed by Roche to the Company. The Company may redeem the debentures at 103% of par with the redemption price decreasing by 1% each year until 1993 when the debentures become redeemable at par.

Note 7: Leases and Commitments

The Company has leased equipment under leasing arrangements. Certain of these arrangements require that the Company maintain $10 million of working capital (as defined), place limits on certain types of debt and require certain approvals for the payment of dividends. The Company is responsible for taxes, insurance and maintenance under its leasing arrangements.

Included in the equipment caption of the consolidated balance sheets are capitalized leases of $5.2 million in 1989. They account for

accumulated depreciation of $4.6 million for 1989. Capitalized leases for equipment in 1990 are fully depreciated.

Future minimum lease payments under noncancelable operating leases at December 31, 1990 are as follows (in thousands):

1991	$ 8,602
1992	7,806
1993	3,790
1994	1,778
1995	1,494
Thereafter	2,575
Total minimum lease payments	$26,045

Rent expense under operating leases was approximately $9.6 million, $12.7 million and $12.4 million for 1990, 1989 and 1988, respectively. Income from subleases was immaterial.

The Company has arranged a $2 million unsecured line of credit to provide guarantees for employees in connection with short-term residential bridge loan financing resulting from relocation. At December 31, 1990 the Company was contingently liable for approximately $0.8 million as guarantor of such loans.

Note 8: Capital Stock

STOCK OPTION PLANS

1984 Plans The Merger agreement with Roche ("Merger Agreement") provided that as of

September 7, 1990 (the "Effective Date"), each outstanding stock option granted under the Company's 1984 Option Plans ("Employee Stock Options") was to be cancelled, and the holder to receive, in exchange, a substitute option (an "Adjusted Option") to purchase a number of shares of Redeemable Common Stock equal to the number of shares of Common Stock subject to such cancelled option multiplied by a defined adjustment factor ("Adjustment Factor") at a per share exercise price equal to the per share exercise price of such canceled option multiplied by a fraction equal to one divided by the Adjustment Factor. Any Adjusted Option issued is subject to the same terms and conditions (other than number of shares and exercise price) as the option for which it is exchanged, including the terms related to vesting and the conditions relating to exercise. As defined in the Merger Agreement, the Adjustment Factor equals 1.11.

The Merger Agreement further provided that notwithstanding the provision described above relating to conversion of Employee Stock Options, prior to the Effective Date, each holder of an Employee Stock Option (other than any director of Genentech who was not an employee of Genentech) had an opportunity to make a cash-out election ("Cash-Out Election") with respect to all Employee Stock Options held. At the Effective Date, each outstanding Employee Stock Option that was subject to a Cash-Out Election and was not then fully vested became vested with respect to 25% of the unvested portion in addition to the portion that already was vested. The additional vesting is credited against the next regularly scheduled vestings of the Employee Stock Options. At the Effective Date, the vested portion of each Employee Stock Option that was subject to a Cash-Out Election and that was not yet exercised was cancelled and promptly after the Effective Date, the Company paid the holder an amount in cash of $36.00 less the applicable exercise price for each option. Immediately following the Effective Date, the

unvested portion of these options was cancelled and exchanged for substitute options to purchase, at a per share exercise price equal to the per share exercise price of the cancelled options, an equal number of shares of Redeemable Common Stock. The substitute options are subject to the same terms and conditions as the option for which it is exchanged, including the terms related to vesting (treating such substitute options as if they were granted at the same time as the options for which they were exchanged) and the conditions relating to exercise.

Directors of Genentech who are not also employees of Genentech were not entitled to receive Adjusted Options or make a Cash-Out Election. Instead, each Employee Stock Option held by such non-employee directors of Genentech was, at the Effective Date, cancelled, and the holder received, in exchange, a substitute option to purchase, at a per share exercise price equal to the per share exercise price of such cancelled options and on the identical terms and conditions to such cancelled options, the number of shares of Redeemable Common Stock equal to the number of shares of Common Stock subject to such cancelled option.

The number of shares of Redeemable Common Stock subject to the 1984 Option Plans was increased by 94,397 shares as a result of the application of the Adjustment Factor.

At December 31, 1990, 5,427,105 shares of Redeemable Common Stock were reserved for issuance under either the 1984 Incentive Stock Option Plan or the 1984 Non-Qualified Stock Option Plan. Options may be granted under the 1984 Incentive Stock Option Plan only to employees (including officers) of the Company. Options may be granted under the 1984 Non-Qualified Stock Option Plan to employees (including officers), directors and consultants to the Company. Options granted under the 1984 Incentive Stock Option Plan and the 1984 Non-Qualified Stock Option Plan expire in five and ten years, respectively, from the date of grant. The options generally become exercisable in increments over a period of four years from the date of grant, with the first increment vesting after one year. Options may be granted with different vesting terms from time to time. In 1988 the price of the Company's stock declined sharply resulting in the exercise prices of many of the outstanding stock options greatly exceeding the then current fair market value of the Company's Common Stock. During 1988 the Company granted option holders the right to cancel certain existing stock options in exchange for options on an equal number of shares at the fair market value on the date of grant. In general, exchanged options were immediately exercisable with respect to one fourth of the shares subject to each option and were subject to prospective vesting during the four year period following the grant date for three-fourths of the shares subject to each option.

Under the 1984 Incentive Stock Option Plan and the 1984 Non-Qualified Stock Option Plan collectively, 4,898,641 shares of Redeemable Common Stock and 11,432,037 shares of the Company's Common Stock were subject to options outstanding at December 31, 1990 and 1989, respectively. As of December 31, 1990 and 1989 the weighted average per share exercise price of outstanding options was $17.72 and $16.59, respectively, and 197,023 and 3,747,811 shares, respectively, were exercisable under outstanding options. At December 31, 1990 and 1989, options for 528,464 and 348,216 shares, respectively, were reserved for future grants under the two plans. During 1990, 435,821 shares of Common Stock and 5,574 shares of Redeemable Common Stock were issued upon the exercise of options at prices ranging from $7.28 to $20.13 per share. During 1989 and 1988, 982,905 and 1,144,397 shares, respectively, were issued upon the exercise of options under both 1984 Plans at prices of $7.28 to $18.88 per share in 1989 and $7.28 to $40.69 per share in 1988. During 1990, option-holders with options for 6,006,151 shares re-

ceived cash in lieu of exercise under the Cash-Out Election noted above, options for 498,550 shares were granted and options for 635,944 shares were cancelled. Options to purchase 888 shares expired in 1990.

1990 Plan In February, 1990, the 1990 Stock Option/Stock Incentive Plan ("1990 Plan") was adopted. At December 31, 1990, 4,000,000 shares of Redeemable Common Stock were reserved for issuance under the 1990 Plan. The 1990 Plan permits the granting of options intended to qualify as incentive stock options and the granting of options that do not so qualify. In addition, the 1990 Plan permits the granting of stock appreciation rights in connection with non-qualified options or incentive options and the issuance of shares of Redeemable Common Stock, either fully vested at the time of issuance or vesting according to a pre-determined schedule. Incentive options may only be granted to employees (including officers and employee-directors). The non-qualified options and other non-option stock incentives may only be granted under the 1990 Plan to employees (including officers and employee-directors) and consultants of Genentech. All non-qualified options have a maximum term of 20 years and all incentive options have a maximum term of 10 years. Shares may be issued under the 1990 Plan at the discretion of the Compensation Committee of the Board of Directors, and may be fully vested or may be subject to a vesting schedule. In addition, the 1990 Plan contains a special provision whereby Genentech's former Chairman of the Board was granted a special Non-statutory Option for 170,000 shares of Redeemable Common Stock with a per share exercise price of $25.70 in cancellation of outstanding options for the same number of shares with an exercise price of $44.25.

In 1990, options to purchase 3,036,100 shares of Redeemable Common Stock were issued at prices ranging from $25.50 to $25.75 per share.

Options to purchase 750 shares of Redeemable Common Stock were exercisable at December 31, 1990 and options to purchase 22,550 shares were cancelled during 1990.

Three types of stock appreciation rights may also be granted under the 1990 Plan: tandem stock appreciation rights, concurrent stock appreciation rights and limited stock appreciation rights. At December 31, 1990 no stock appreciation rights had been granted under the 1990 Plan.

At December 31, 1990, 1,738 out of 1,923 employees held options granted under the 1984 and 1990 Plans. Options for the issuance of 807,939 shares were held by consultants and directors of the Company at December 31, 1990.

EMPLOYEE STOCK PLANS

The 1987 Employee Stock Plan was adopted on July 1, 1987. Under the provisions of the Merger Agreement, the 1,500,000 shares of Common Stock originally reserved for issuance under the 1987 plan were changed to 1,539,916 shares of Redeemable Common Stock at the Effective Date. As of December 31, 1990, 1,281,165 shares have been issued. The 1987 plan may be terminated at the Company's option subject to any rights then outstanding. No new rights may be granted under the 1987 plan after December 31, 1990. As of December 31, 1990, 1,584 of the 1,881 eligible employees participated in the 1987 plan.

The 1991 Employee Stock Plan was adopted on December 4, 1990. Of the 1,500,000 shares of Redeemable Common Stock reserved for issuance under the 1991 plan, no shares had been issued as of December 31, 1990.

WARRANTS

In consideration of the grant to the Company by each Limited Partner of GCP IV admitted from June to August of 1989 of an option to purchase all of such Limited Partners' interest in GCP IV, the Company issued warrants with each partnership interest, to purchase an aggregate of 2,639,250 shares of Genentech Common Stock (subsequently converted to 1,319,625 shares of Redeemable Common Stock under the terms of the Merger Agreement). The warrants are exercisable at prices ranging from $22.57 to $23.26 at various dates from July 28, 1989 until July 31, 1994. Warrants to purchase approximately 462,828 shares of Redeemable Common Stock are exercisable at December 31, 1990 at prices ranging from $22.57 to $22.88. Beginning on August 1, 1994, the warrants are exercisable at prices ranging from $27.57 to $28.26 until July 31, 1996, at which time the warrants expire. During 1990, 48,040 shares of Common Stock and 30,592 shares of Redeemable Common Stock were issued upon the exercise of these warrants at prices ranging from $22.57 to $22.88 per share. None of these warrants had been exercised as of December 31, 1989. The warrants are not detachable from the partnership interests until after certain events occur. The Company has the right to accelerate the date of expiration under certain circumstances.

In addition to the above, as part of financing and contract arrangements, the Company has, at certain times, issued warrants to purchase the Company's Common Stock. These warrants are exercisable at various dates through 1993. At December 31, 1990 and 1989, 257,270 and 1,922,740 shares, respectively, of the Company's Redeemable Common Stock and Common Stock, respectively, were reserved for issuance under warrant agreements and the weighted average per share exercise price was $21.58 and $15.58 on those respective dates. At December 31, 1990, 245,270 shares of Redeemable Common Stock were issuable under currently exercisable warrants. During 1990, 218,400 shares of Common Stock and 616,650 shares of Redeemable Common Stock were issued upon the exercise of warrants at prices of $11.30 to $18.75 per share. During 1989, 57,056 shares of Common Stock were issued upon the exercise of warrants at prices of $11.28 to $11.70 per share. Warrant holders exercising warrants after the Effective Date receive, for each warrant exercised, $18 in cash and one half share of Redeemable Common Stock. Under the terms of the Merger Agreement, the $18 in cash per warrant exercised after the Effective Date is reimbursed by Roche to the Company.

Note 9: Related Party Transactions

The Company has transactions with related parties in the ordinary course of business. Pursuant to contracts, principally to perform research and development on specific projects and product licensing agreements, the Company recorded as revenue approximately $17.0 million in 1990, $13.9 million in 1989 and $2.4 million in 1988 from the following related parties: two independently funded limited partnerships for which the Company has performed research services under cost reimbursement development agreements, GCP III and GCP IV; Hoffman-LaRoche, Inc. (a wholly-owned subsidiary of Roche; two officers of Roche's parent company serve on the Company's Board of Directors—see also Note 1): GLC Associates (a partnership between a subsidiary of The Lubrizol Corporation and the Company; a former officer of The Lubrizol Corporation serves on the Company's Board of Directors); and Genencor (a corporation formally owned by Corning Glass Works, Tate and Lyle plc Group, Eastman Kodak Company and the Company—see also Note 2). Through a private placement, GCP IV raised approximately $72.5 million in 1989. The Company's arrangement with GCP III was effectively terminated in October 1989 when that partnership agreed to sell substantially all of its assets to the Company. See Note 4 to the consolidated financial statements for additional information related to the GCP III asset acquisition. The officers and directors of the Company, as a group, have owned immaterial amounts of limited partnership interests in GCP III and

GCP IV. Genentech Research Corporation, a wholly-owned subsidiary of the Company, owns a one percent interest in GCP IV and serves as its general partner. Genentech Development Corporation, a wholly-owned subsidiary of the Company, owned a one percent interest in GCP III and served as its general partner. As part of ongoing facilities expansion projects, the Company has paid a subsidiary of the Fluor Corporation (a director of Fluor Corporation serves on the Company's Board of Directors) an immaterial amount in 1990, $3.0 million in 1989 and $11.4 million in 1988 for engineering, design and construction management.

Note 10: Legal Proceedings

The Company is a party to various legal proceedings including patent infringement cases involving Protropin and Activase, product liability cases involving Activase and a breach of contract case involving Humulin.® In addition, the Company has been named as a defendant in a consolidated class action lawsuit alleging, among other things, violations of the Securities Exchange Act of 1934; a settlement has been reached in this case. The settlement totals $29 million, a substantial portion of which is covered by insurance. The Company has established adequate reserves to cover its portion of the settlement. The Company and its directors are defendants in several suits filed in Delaware and California challenging their actions in connection with the Merger.

Based upon the nature of the claims made and the investigation completed to date by the Company and its counsel, the Company believes the outcome of the described actions will not have a material adverse effect on the financial position or results of operations of the Company.

Note 11: Quasi-reorganization

On February 18, 1988 the Company's Board of Directors approved the elimination of the

Company's accumulated deficit through an accounting reorganization of its stockholders' equity accounts (a quasi-reorganization) effective October 1, 1987. The quasi-reorganization did not involve any revaluation of assets or liabilities because for similar classes of assets their fair values were no less than their book values and for similar classes of liabilities their book values were no less than their fair values. The effective date of the quasi-reorganization (October 1, 1987) reflected the beginning of the quarter in which the Company received approval for and commenced marketing of its second major product, and as such, marked a turning point in the Company's operations. The accumulated deficit of $329,457 was eliminated by a transfer from additional paid-in capital in an amount equal to the accumulated deficit.

Simultaneously with the quasi-reorganization the Company adopted Financial Accounting Standards Board Statement No. 96 (FAS 96), providing for recognition of the tax benefits of operating loss and tax credit carryforward items which arose prior to a quasi-reorganization involving only the elimination of a deficit in retained earnings being reported in the income statement and then reclassified from retained earnings to additional paid-in capital.

Subsequently in September 1989 the staff of the Securities and Exchange Commission issued Staff Accounting Bulletin No. 86 (SAB 86). This bulletin outlines the SEC staff's view that a quasi-reorganization that meets the SEC staff's guidance cannot involve only an elimination of a deficit in retained earnings and therefore the tax benefits of prior operating loss and tax credit carryforwards must be reported as a direct addition to additional paid-in capital rather than being recorded in the income statement.

The Company will continue to report in income the recognition of operating loss and tax credit carryforward items arising prior to the quasi-reorganization due to the Company's adoption of its quasi-reorganization in the context of its interpretation of FAS 96 and the quasi-reorganization literature existing at the date the quasi-reorganization was effected. The SEC staff has indicated that under the circumstances they would not object to the Company's accounting for such tax benefits. If the provisions of SAB 86 had been applied, the net loss for the year ended December 31, 1990 would have been unaffected. Net income for each of the years ended December 31, 1989 and 1988 would have been reduced by $14,020,000 and $7,227,000, respectively.

Price Range of Common Stock (Unaudited)

The Common Stock of the Company was traded on the New York Stock Exchange under the symbol GNE from March 2, 1988 and until September 7, 1990, and on the Pacific Stock Exchange under the symbol GNE from April 12, 1988 until September 7, 1990. The Company's Common Stock was previously traded in the NASDAQ National Market System under the symbol GENE. The Company's Redeemable Common Stock has been traded on the New York Stock Exchange and the Pacific Stock Exchange under the symbol GNE since September 10, 1990. No dividends have been paid on the Common Stock. For a description of conditions precedent on the Company's ability to pay dividends see Note 6 to the consolidated financial statements. Genentech's merger with a wholly-owned subsidiary of Roche Holdings, Inc. ("Roche") was consummated on September 7, 1990. Genentech stockholders of record on September 7, 1990 received, for each share of Common Stock owned, $18 in cash from Roche and one half share of newly issued Redeemable Common Stock from the Company. See Note 1 to the consolidated financial statements for a further description of the merger transaction.

	Redeemable Common Stock from September 10, 1990 to December 31, 1990		Common Stock from January 1, 1990 to September 7, 1990		Common Stock 1989	
	High	Low	High	Low	High	Low
4th Quarter	27\frac{1}{2}$	21\frac{3}{4}$	$ 0	$ 0	23\frac{3}{8}$	18\frac{1}{8}$
3rd Quarter	27$\frac{1}{8}$	23$\frac{3}{4}$	30	25	23$\frac{1}{4}$	16$\frac{3}{4}$
2nd Quarter	0	0	28$\frac{3}{8}$	24$\frac{5}{8}$	20$\frac{1}{4}$	16$\frac{3}{4}$
1st Quarter	0	0	30$\frac{7}{8}$	20$\frac{1}{8}$	21$\frac{7}{8}$	16

Number of Holders of Common Stock

As of January 31, 1991 there were approximately 24,700 stockholders of record of the Company's Redeemable Common Stock.

QUARTERLY FINANCIAL DATA (unaudited)

(In thousands except per share amounts)	1990 Quarter Ended			
	December 31	September 30	June 30	March 31
Total revenues	$131,250	$112,094	$112,545	$120,247
Product sales	99,365	88,420	89,509	89,876
Gross margin from product sales	81,244	71,709	72,615	73,297
Net income (loss)	17,143	(133,740)	5,295	13,271
Per share	0.15	(1.45)	0.06	0.15

	1989 Quarter Ended			
	December 31	September 30	June 30	March 31
Total revenues	$111,418	$100,047	$97,888	$91,102
Product sales	90,985	76,011	79,098	72,973
Gross margin from product sales	73,599	61,420	64,456	59,036
Net income	15,520	11,415	9,596	7,430
Per share	0.18	0.13	0.11	0.09

Report of Management

The consolidated financial statements presented in this report have been prepared by Company management in conformity with generally accepted accounting principles from the Company's financial records. Management is responsible for all information and representations made in the financial statements and the other sections of this annual report. In those cases where judgment and best estimates are necessary, appropriate consideration is given to materiality in the preparation of the financial statements.

Systems of internal accounting controls, applied by operating and financial management, are designed to provide reasonable assurance as to the integrity and reliability of the financial statements, reasonable, but not absolute, assurance that assets are safeguarded from unauthorized use or disposition, and that transactions are recorded according to management's policies and procedures. These systems are continually reviewed and modified, where appropriate, to maintain such assurance. Management believes that, as of December 31, 1990, the Company's system of internal control is adequate to accomplish the objectives discussed herein.

The selection of the Company's independent auditors, Ernst & Young, has been approved by the Company's Board of Directors and ratified by the stockholders. An Audit Committee of the Board of Directors, composed of four non-management directors, meets regularly with, and reviews the activities of, corporate financial management and the independent auditors to ascertain that each is properly discharging its responsibilities. The independent auditors separately meet with the Audit Committee, with and without management present, to discuss the results of their work, the adequacy of internal accounting controls and the quality of financial reporting.

Report of Ernest & Young, Independent Auditors

The Board of Directors and Stockholders of Genentech, Inc.

We have audited the accompanying consolidated balance sheets of Genentech, Inc. as of December 31, 1990 and 1989, and the related consolidated statements of operations, stockholders' equity and cash flows for each of the three years in the period ended December 31, 1990. These financial statements are the responsibility of the Company's management Our responsibility is to express an opinion on these financial statements based on our audits.

We conducted our audits in accordance with generally accepted auditing standards. Those standards require that we plan and perform the audit to obtain reasonable assurance about whether the financial statements are free of material misstatement. An audit includes examining, on a test basis, evidence supporting the amounts and disclosures in the financial statements. An audit also includes assessing the accounting principles used and significant estimates made by management, as well as evaluating the overall financial statement presentation. We believe that our audits provide a reasonable basis for our opinion.

In our opinion, the financial statements referred to above present fairly, in all material respects, the consolidated financial position of Genentech, Inc. at December 31, 1990 and 1989, and the consolidated results of its operations and its cash flows for each of the three years in the period ended December 31, 1990, in conformity with generally accepted accounting principles.

Ernst & Young

San Jose, California
January 14, 1991

SECURITIES AND EXCHANGE COMMISSION
Washington, D.C. 20549
Form 10-K

(Mark one)

× ANNUAL REPORT PURSUANT TO SECTION 13 OR 15(d) OF THE SECURITIES EXCHANGE ACT OF 1934

For the year ended: December 31, 1990

‒ TRANSITION REPORT PURSUANT TO SECTION 13 OR 15(d) OF THE SECURITIES EXCHANGE ACT OF 1934

For the transition period from _____ to _____ .

Commission file number: 1-9813

GENENTECH, INC.

A Delaware Corporation

460 Point San Bruno Boulevard
South San Francisco, California 94080

94-2347624
(I.R.S. employer identification number)
(415) 266-1000
(telephone number)

Securities registered pursuant to Section 12(b) of the Act:

TITLE OF EACH CLASS	NAME OF EACH EXCHANGE ON WHICH REGISTERED
REDEEMABLE COMMON STOCK, $.02 PAR VALUE	NEW YORK STOCK EXCHANGE Pacific Stock Exchange

Indicate by check mark whether the registrant (1) has filed all reports required to be filled by Section 13 or 15(d) of the Securities Exchange Act of 1934 during the preceding 12 months (or for such shorter period that the registrant was required to file such reports), and (2) has been subject to such filling requirements for the past 90 days.

Yes ×   No ___

The approximate aggregate market value of voting stock held by nonaffiliates of the registrant is $873,725,130 as of February 15, 1991. (A)

Number of shares of Common Stock outstanding as of February 15, 1991: 67,133,409

Number of shares of Redeemable Common Stock outstanding as of February 15, 1991: 43,667,953

Documents Incorporated by reference:

DOCUMENT	PARTS INCORPORATED BY REFERENCE
(1) Definitive Proxy Statement with respect to the 1991 Annual Meeting of Stockholders filed by Genentech, Inc. (SEC file No. 1-9813) with the Securities and Exchange Commission (hereinafter referred to as "Proxy Statement")	III

(A) Excludes 79,173,303 shares of Common Stock and Redeemable Common Stock held by Directors, Officers and stockholders whose ownership exceeds five percent of either the Common Stock of Redeemable Common Stock outstanding at February 15, 1991. Exclusion of shares held by any person should not be construed to Indicate that such person possesses the power, direct or indirect, to direct or cause the direction of the management or policies of the registrant, or that such person is controlled by or under common control with the registrant.

Item 1: Business

Genentech, Inc. is a biotechnology company that discovers, develops, manufactures and markets human pharmaceuticals for significant medical needs. Genentech was organized in April 1976 as a California corporation. On January 28, 1988 the stockholders approved a change in the state of Genentech's incorporation from California to Delaware. As used in this report, except where the context otherwise indicates, the "Company" means Genentech, Inc. and its subsidiaries, including subsidiary operations in Canada and Japan.

Genentech's merger ("Merger") with a wholly-owned subsidiary of Roche Holdings, Inc. ("Roche") was consummated on September 7, 1990. Genentech stockholders of record on September 7, 1990 received, for each share of common stock owned, $18 in cash and one half share of newly issued redeemable common stock. In the Merger, Roche acquired approximately 60 percent of the outstanding equity of the Company. Roche has the right to purchase additional shares on the open market at any time to raise its common equity holding to up to 75 percent on a fully diluted basis. Until June 30, 1995, Roche has the right to require the Company to redeem the outstanding redeemable common stock, at escalating prices each calendar quarter ranging from $38 per share for the fourth quarter 1990 to $60 per share during the quarter ended June 30, 1995, provided that Roche first deposits in trust sufficient funds to pay the aggregate redemption price of all outstanding shares of redeemable common stock. The Company expects to use the net proceeds from the Merger for development of new products and markets which may include acquisitions or in-licensing of products, facilities expansion and general corporate purposes.

Genentech and Roche entered into an agreement (the Governance Agreement) at the time of the Merger. The Governance Agreement contains terms relating to the corporate governace of the Company after the Merger and the acquisition and disposition of securities of the Company by Roche and its affiliates. The Governance Agreement specifies that the approval of the directors of the Company designated by Roche under the Governance Agreement is required for the acquisition, sale, lease, license or transfer of all or a substantial portion of the business or assets of the Company and certain issuances and redemptions of capital stock of the Company. In addition, the Governance Agreement provides that the Company will not enter into any material licensing or marketing agreement for any products, processes, inventions or developments made by the Company or its subsidiaries unless the Company has first negotiated in good faith with Roche for at least three months with a view towards reaching a mutually beneficial licensing or marketing agreement. The Governance Agreement also states that Roche and the Company will negotiate in good faith with respect to the establishment of a marketing arrangement under which the Company would market, on agreed terms, one or more of Roche's products.

Products

Genentech has three products that it has developed and markets: Protropin® human growth hormone and Activase® tissue plasminogen activator. A third human pharmaceutical, Actimmune® gamma interferon, was approved by the United States Food and Drug Administration ("FDA") in December 1990 for use in the treatment of chronic granulomatous disease (a rare immunodeficiency disorder). The Company began marketing Actimmune in the United States in March 1991.

PROTROPIN

Human growth hormone is a naturally occurring human protein produced in the pituitary gland, which regulates metabolism and is responsible for growth in children. A recombinant human growth hormone product developed by Genentech, Protropin, was approved for marketing in the United States by the United States FDA in October 1985 for the treatment of growth hormone inadequacy in children.

Genentech manufactures Protropin in the United States and markets it in the United States and Canada. Genentech has licensed rights to recombinant human growth hormone products outside of the United States and Canada to KabiVitrum AB. KabiVitrum AB markets recombinant human growth hormone under the trademarks Somatonorm® and Genotropin® in certain countries. Genentech receives a royalty on KabiVitrum's sales of this product.

Protropin or a related recombinant human growth hormone product, somatropin, are currently being evaluated by the Company through clinical trials for use in treating impaired growth in children with chronic renal insufficiency, stature-related symptoms of Turner's Syndrome, children with idiopathic short stature due to possible growth hormone inadequacy and pediatric burns.

ACTIVASE

Tissue plasminogen activator, or t-PA, is an enzyme that is produced naturally by the body to dissolve blood clots. However, when a blood clot obstructs blood flow in the coronary artery and causes a heart attack, the body is unable to produce enough t-PA to dissolve the clot rapidly enough to prevent damage to the heart. Through recombinant DNA technology Genentech can produce Activase, a form of t-PA, in sufficient quantity for therapeutic use. In November 1988, the FDA approved Activase in the United States for the treatment of heart attacks. Activase is used to dissolve blood clots in coronary arteries that cause heart attacks. In February 1989, the FDA approved adding the claim that Activase reduces mortality to the labeling for the product. In 1990,

Activase was licensed by the FDA for use in the treatment of pulmonary embolism (blood clots in the lungs). In December 1990 the Company filed with the FDA an amendment to its Product License Application ("PLA") for Activase, for use of the product in the management of limb ischemia due to peripheral arterial occlusive disease (PAO). PAO is most often caused by a blood clot blocking flow in the arteries of the extremities. Other indications under study in clinical trials include deep vein thrombosis, retinal vein occlusion, unstable angina and certain forms of stroke.

Genentech manufactures Activase in the United States and markets it in the United States and Canada. Genentech has licensed marketing rights to recombinant t-PA in Japan to Kyowa Hakko Kogyo Co., Ltd. and Mitsubishi Kasei Corporation, and in Europe and certain other international markets to Boehringer Ingelheim International GmbH ("BI"). BI has received approval to market a form of recombinant t-PA, sold under BI's trademark Actilyse®, and has launched sales of the product in various countries outside North America and Japan. Genentech receives a royalty on BI's sales of Actilyse.

ACTIMMUNE

In December 1990, the Company received approval from the FDA to market Actimmune for the management of chronic granulomatous disease. Actimmune has received designation as an orphan drug by the FDA. Chronic granulomatous disease is a rare, inherited disorder of the immune system which affects an estimated 250 to 400 Americans. Actimmune is currently being studied for use in both allergic disease indications (such as atopic dermatitis) and infectious disease indications (such as trauma-related infections).

The Company also receives royalties on product sales of Humulin® recombinant human insulin (manufactured by and a trademark of Eli Lilly and Company), Roferon-A® recombinant alpha interferon (manufactured by and a trademark of Hoffman-LaRoche, Inc.) and a hepatitis B vaccine manufactured by Merck and Co., Inc.

PRODUCTS IN DEVELOPMENT

As part of Genentech's program of research and development, a number of other products are in various stages of development. Product development is focused primarily in the areas of growth and endocrinology, genetic disorders, cardio-pulmonary disease, and immunology, oncology and infectious disease.

Products in clinical development include: DNase, a mucus-dissolving enzyme, which may be useful in the management of cystic fibrosis and chronic bronchitis; relaxin, a naturally-occurring hormone that appears to have a role in childbirth by softening the cervix and birth canal, being studied as an aid in circumstances where natural childbirth may be complicated by certain medical problems; insulin-like growth factor (IGF-1), being studied for nutritional support and wound healing indications; argatroban, an anticoagulant, being studied as an additional cardiovascular product potentially useful in speeding clot dissolution and preventing reclotting; gp120, a recombinant form of the envelope protein of human immunodeficiency virus (HIV-1), which may serve as the basis for the development of a vaccine for HIV infection; and a HER-2 monoclonal antibody, an antibody targeted against a cell-surface protein that may be useful in the treatment of breast and ovarian tumors. In January 1991, the Company received an official notification of designation from the FDA granting orphan drug status for DNase for the management of cystic fibrosis.

Another product in development is CD4-IgG, which has been licensed to an affiliated research and development partnership, Genentech Clinical Partners IV (GCP IV). In January 1991, the Board of Directors of the general partner of GCP IV announced that it will concentrate the clinical research program for CD4-IgG on studies aimed at preventing the spread of disease from HIV-infected pregnant women to their fetuses; and that it has no current plans to continue the clinical trials of CD4-IgG as a stand-alone therapy for HIV-infected adults. GCP IV has contracted with Genentech for the development of recombinant CD4 products as potential therapeutic agents for HIV infection.

In cases where a product does not fit with Genentech's marketing strategy, the Company may license the product to another firm. These contract partners are chosen for their ability to both fund and perform advanced product development and to facilitate effective entry into major markets. In the past Genentech has licensed the foreign rights to some of its products to major foreign pharmaceutical companies and actively coordinated development and clinical programs with these partners. In some cases Genentech has retained manufacturing rights to the licensed products. The Company has retained United States and European marketing rights for most of its products currently under development.

Distribution

Genentech has a marketing department and a North American-based pharmaceutical sales and distribution organization for human therapeutics. Genentech's sales efforts are directed primarily at specialist physicians based at major medical centers in the United States and Canada. Products are sold to distributors or directly to pharmacies or medical centers. Genentech's sales organization numbered 345 at year end 1990 and is the fourth largest hospital-based pharmaceutical sales force in the United States. Genentech utilizes common pharmaceutical company marketing techniques, including professional conventions and symposia, advertisements, direct mail, and medical cable television.

During 1990, Genentech provided certain marketing programs relating to Activase. The Activase Stocking Assistance Program provided extended payment terms, up to 195 days, to wholesalers on certain orders, subject to certain restrictions on the timing and quantities of the orders. Additionally, a comprehensive wastage replacement program exists for Activase which, subject to specific conditions, provides customers the right to return Activase to Genentech for replacement related to both patient related product wastage and product related wastage. Genentech maintains the right to renew, modify or discontinue the above programs. Both Activase and Protropin are available at no charge to selected patients under Genentech's Uninsured Patient Program.

One major customer in 1990, 1989 and 1988 contributed 10% or more of Genentech's total revenues. Revenues from foreign customers were as follows: Europe—approximately $17.6 million in 1990, $17.6 million in 1989 and $24.9 million in 1988; Asia—approximately $5.6 million in 1990, $3.2 million in 1989 and $4.9 million in 1988; Canada—approximately $9.2 million in 1990, $4.7 million in 1989, and $1.7 million in 1988.

Raw Materials

Raw materials and supplies required for the production of Genentech's principal products are generally available in quantities adequate to meet the Company's needs.

Proprietary Technology—Patents and Trade Secrets

Genentech has a policy of seeking patents on inventions arising from its ongoing research and development activities. Patents issued or applied for cover inventions ranging from basic recombinant DNA techniques, processes relating to specific products and to the products themselves. The Company has either been granted patents or has patent applications pending which relate to a number of current and potential products, including Protropin and Activase and products licensed to others. Genentech considers that in the aggregate its patent applications, patents and licenses under patents owned by third parties are of material importance to its operations. Issued United States patents will expire during the period from 1999 to 2008. Important legal issues remain to be resolved as to the extent and scope of available patent protection for biotechnology products and processes in the United States and other important markets outside of the United States. Genentech expects that litigation will likely be necessary to determine the validity and scope of certain of its proprietary rights. Genentech is currently involved in a number of patent lawsuits, as either a plaintiff or defendant, and administrative proceedings relating to the scope of protection of its patents and those of others. These proceedings and lawsuits may result in a significant commitment of Company resources in the future. There can be no assurance that the patents Genentech obtains or the unpatented proprietary technology it holds will afford Genentech significant commercial protection.

The Company's trademarks GENENTECH, PROTROPIN, ACTIVASE and ACTIMMUNE in the aggregate are considered to be of material importance and are registered in the United States Patent and Trademark Office and in other countries throughout the world.

In 1980, a patent purporting to cover many of the fundamental gene splicing techniques of recombinant DNA technology was granted to Stanford University as a result of research by Herbert Boyer, Ph.D., a co-founder of Genentech, and Stanley Cohen, Ph.D. Genentech is one of the many companies that has signed a license agreement with Stanford University under which Genentech has been granted a non-exclusive license under the Boyer–Cohen patent, in return for a royalty obligation on product sales (subject to certain exclusions). Genentech has also been granted a royalty-bearing, non-exclusive license by Columbia University under patents relating to the production of products in mammalian cells. In addition, Genentech has obtained other licenses which it deems to be necessary or desirable for the manufacture, use or sale of its products.

Royalty income recognized by the Company during 1990 for patent licenses, know-how and other related rights amounted to approximately $47.6 million. In 1990 the Company incurred royalty expenses amounting to approximately $39.7 million under licenses from others relating to its operations.

Competition

Genentech faces competition, and believes significant long-term competition can be expected, from large pharmaceutical and chemical companies as well as biotechnology companies. This competition can be expected to become more intense as commercial applications for biotechnology products increase. Some competitors, primarily large pharmaceutical companies, have greater clinical, regulatory and marketing resources and experience than Genentech. Many of these companies have commercial arrangements with other companies in the biotechnology industry to supplement their own basic research capabilities. The introduction of new products and the development of new processes by competitors may result in price reductions or product replacements, even for products protected by patents. However, the Company believes its competitive position is enhanced by its commitment to research leading to the discovery and development of new products and manu-

facturing methods. Additionally, other factors which should help the Company meet competition include ancillary services provided to support is products, customer service and dissemination of technical information to prescribers of its products and the health care community generally.

Item 5: Market for the Registrant's Common Stock and Related Security Holder Matters

Price Range of Common Stock and Redeemable Common Stock

The Common Stock of the Company was traded on the New York Stock Exchange under the symbol GNE from March 2, 1988 until September 7, 1990, and on the Pacific Stock Exchange under the symbol GNE from April 12, 1988 until September 7, 1990. The Company's Common Stock was previously traded in the NASDAQ National Market System under the symbol GENE. The Company's Redeemable Common Stock has been traded on the New York Stock Exchange and the Pacific Stock Exchange under the symbol GNE since September 10, 1990. No dividends have been paid on the Common Stock. For a description of conditions precedent on the Company's ability to pay dividends see Note 6 to the consolidated financial statements. Genentech's merger with a wholly-owned subsidiary of Roche Holdings, Inc. ("Roche") was consummated on September 7, 1990. Genentech stockholders of record on September 7, 1990 received, for each share of common stock owned, $18 in cash from Roche and one half share of newly issued redeemable common stock from the Company. See Note [a] to the consolidated financial statements for a further description of the merger transaction.

	Redeemable Common Stock from September 10, 1990 to December 31, 1990		Common Stock from January 1, 1990 to September 7, 1990		Common Stock 1989	
	High	Low	High	Low	High	Low
4th Quarter	$27\frac{1}{2}$	$21\frac{3}{4}$	$—	$—	$23\frac{3}{8}$	$18\frac{1}{8}$
3rd Quarter	$27\frac{1}{8}$	$23\frac{3}{4}$	30	25	$23\frac{1}{4}$	$16\frac{3}{4}$
2nd Quarter	—	—	$28\frac{3}{8}$	$24\frac{5}{8}$	$20\frac{1}{4}$	$16\frac{3}{4}$
1st Quarter	—	—	$30\frac{7}{8}$	$20\frac{1}{8}$	$21\frac{7}{8}$	16

Number of Holders of Redeemable Common Stock

As of January 31, 1991 there were approximately 24,700 stockholders of record of the Company's Redeemable Common Stock.

Item 6: Selected Financial Data

(In thousands except per share amounts)

	1990	1989	1988	1987	1986
Total revenues	$ 476,136	$400,455	$334,840	$230,543	$133,954
Product sales	367,170	319,067	262,476	141,416	43,563
Costs and expenses	572,692[a]	352,929	311,732[b]	186,606	484,562[c]
Net income (loss)	(98,031)[a]	43,961	20,565[b]	42,230	(352,983)[c]
Net income (loss) per share	(1.05)[a]	0.51	0.24[b]	0.50	(5.10)[c]
Total assets	1,157,670	711,191	662,895	617,734	375,233
Long-term debt	153,534	154,409	155,269	168,078	31,577
Stockholders' equity	893,182	468,952	399,295	355,412	292,616
Average shares outstanding	93,040	85,967	84,459	84,418	69,268

The Company has paid no dividends.

[a]Costs and expenses in 1990 include a special charge which was primarily merger related of $167.7 million, which amounted to $1.74 per share net of the applicable income tax benefit.

[b]Costs and expenses in 1988 include a special charge which was primarily a reserve against inventory of $23.3 million, which amounted to $0.26 per share net of the applicable income tax benefit.

[c]Costs and expenses in 1986 include a charge for the purchase of in-process research and development of $366.6 million, or $361.6 million after taxes. Income after taxes and exclusive of the charge for the purchase of in-process research and development in 1986 was $8.7 million and $0.12 per share.

Item 7: Management's Discussion and Analysis of Financial Condition and Results of Operations

Overview

Genentech, Inc. (the Company) is a biotechnology company that discovers, develops, manufactures and markets human pharmaceuticals for significant medical needs. The Company manufactures and markets two human pharmaceuticals in the United States and Canada, Activase® tissue plasminogen activator (t-PA), a thrombolytic (blood clot dissolving) agent, and Protropin® human growth hormone. A third human pharmaceutical, Actimmune® gamma interferon, was approved by the United States Food and Drug Administration (FDA) in December 1990 for use in the treatment of chronic granulomatous disease (a rare immunodeficiency disorder). The Company began marketing Actimmune in the United States in March 1991.

Activase was approved in 1987 by the FDA for use in the treatment of myocardial infarction (heart attack) and in 1990 was licensed by the FDA for use in the treatment of pulmonary embolism (blood clots in the lungs). Studies are currently underway to evaluate Activase for several other important indications including unstable angina (chest pain caused by lack of oxygen to the heart) and stroke. In December 1990 the Company filed with the FDA an amendment to its Product License Application for Activase, for use in the management of limb ischemia due to peripheral arterial occlusive disease (PAO). PAO is most often caused by a blood clot blocking blood flow in the arteries of the extremities.

Protropin was approved by the FDA in 1985 for marketing in the United States for the treatment of growth hormone inadequacy in children. Protropin or a related recombinant human growth hormone product, somatropin, are currently being evaluated by the Company through clinical trials for their potential use in treating impaired growth in children with chronic renal insufficiency, stature-related symptoms of Turner's Syndrome, children with idiopathic short stature due to possible growth hormone inadequacy and pediatric burns.

Actimmune is currently being studied for use in both allergic disease indications (such as atopic dermatitis) and infectious disease indications (such as trauma-related infections).

Other products in clinical development include: DNase, mucus-dissolving enzyme, which may be useful in the management of cystic fibrosis and chronic bronchitis; relaxin, a naturally-occurring hormone that appears to have a role in childbirth by softening the cervix and birth canal, being studied as an aid in circumstances where natural childbirth may be complicated by certain medical problems; insulin-like growth factor (IGF-1), being studied for nutritional support and wound healing indications; argatroban, an anticoagulant, being studied as an additional cardiovascular product potentially useful in speeding clot dissolution and preventing reclotting; gp120, a recombinant form of the envelope protein of human immunodeficiency virus (HIV-1), which may serve as the basis for the development of a vaccine as well as an immunotherapeutic for HIV infection; and a HER-2 monoclonal antibody, an antibody targeted against a cell-surface protein, that may be useful in the treatment of breast and ovarian tumors. In January 1991, the Company received notification from the FDA granting Orphan Drug status for DNase for the management of cystic fibrosis. The Company owns the European marketing rights on most of its products under development.

Another product in development is CD4-IgG, which has been licensed to an affiliated research and development partnership, Genentech Clinical Partners IV (GCP IV). In January 1991, the Board of Directors of the general partner of GCP IV announced that it will concentrate the clinical research program for CD4-IgG on studies aimed at preventing the spread of disease from HIV-infected pregnant women to their fetuses; and that it has no current plans to continue the clinical trials of CD4-IgG as a stand-alone therapy for HIV-infected adults. GCP IV has contracted with Genentech for the development of recombinant CD4 products as potential therapeutic agents for HIV.

For its currently marketed products, the Company's international presence has been established primarily through the use of licensing arrangements with corporate partners. The Company has licensed marketing rights to recombinant t-PA in Japan to Kyowa Hakko Kogyo, Ltd., and Mitsubishi Chemical Industries, Limited, and rights in Europe and certain other markets to Boehringer Ingelheim International GmbH (Boehringer). Boehringer has received approval to market a form of recombinant t-PA, sold under the trademark Actilyse®, in a number of countries outside North America and Japan. The Company has licensed rights to recombinant human growth hormone outside of the United States and Canada to Kabivitrum AB (Kabivitrum). Kabivitrum markets recombinant human growth hormone under the trademarks Somatonorm® and Genotropin® in certain countries. The Company receives royalties on product sales of Actilyse, Somatonorm and Genotropin. In addition, the Company receives the majority of the remainder of its royalties on product sales of Humulin® (recombinant human insulin) and Roferon-A® (recombinant alpha interferon), manufactured by and registered trademarks of Eli Lilly and Company and Hoffmann-LaRoche, Inc., respectively.

Genentech's merger ("Merger") with a wholly-owned subsidiary of Roche Holdings, Inc. ("Roche") was consummated on September 7, 1990. Genentech stockholders of record on September 7, 1990 received, for each share of common stock owned, $18 in cash from Roche and one half share of newly issued redeemable common stock from the Company. In the Merger, Roche acquired one half of the Company's outstanding common stock for $1,537.2 million. In addition, the Company issued 24,433,951 shares of common stock to Roche, upon consummation of the Merger, for $487.3 million in cash. The common stock issued to Roche, combined with the common stock Roche acquired in the Merger, represented approximately 60 percent of the outstanding equity of the Company on the effective date of the Merger. Roche has the right to purchase additional shares on the open market at any time to raise its common equity holding to up to 75 percent on a fully diluted basis. Roche has the right to require the Company to redeem the outstanding redeemable common stock, at escalating prices each calendar quarter ranging from $38 per share for the fourth quarter of 1990 to $60 per share during the quarter ended June 30, 1995, when the redemption right expires, provided that Roche first deposits in trust sufficient funds to pay the aggregate redemption price of all outstanding shares of redeemable common stock. The Company expects to use the net proceeds from the Merger for development of new products and markets, which may include acquisitions or in-licensing of products, facilities expansion and general corporate purposes.

In December 1990, the Company entered into an agreement with Glycomed, Inc., a privately held company, for a $15 million research collaboration to develop carbohydrate-based therapeutics in the field of cell adhesion molecules. The agreement includes partial research support for an initial three-year period and a two-stage, $7 million equity investment by Genentech in Glycomed, Inc. The research will be funded by Genentech through a combination of sponsored research funding and milestone payments over a three year period with a potential two year extension.

In January 1991, the Company entered into an agreement with Telios Pharmaceuticals, Inc. ("Telios"), a privately held company, for a $15 million research collaboration to develop and commercialize an injectable drug to help prevent the formation of blood clots. Under the agreement, the companies will co-develop a drug based on Telios' proprietary matrix-peptide technology and Genentech's expertise in peptide design and recombinant-receptor assay screening. Genentech will provide Telios with milestone-based payments and will pay the company royalties on sales. In return, Genentech will have the right to market the drug worldwide, except in Japan and the Far East.

Results of Operations

REVENUES

Revenues have increased in each year since the Company's inception. Total revenues reached $476.1 million in 1990, up 19% from 1989. In 1989 total revenues were $400.5 million, an increase of 20% from 1988 revenues of $334.8 million. The increase in 1990 and 1989 revenues resulted principally from increased product sales.

Product sales increased to $367.1 million, a 15% increase over 1989 product sales of $319.1 million. In 1989, product sales increased 22% over 1988 product sales of $262.5 million.

Net sales of Activase increased to $210 million in 1990, up from $196.4 million in 1989 and $151.4 million in 1988. The increase in Activase net sales in 1990 as compared to 1989, as well as 1989 compared to 1988, is believed to be due principally to an increase in the number of patients treated. Factors which may influence future sales of Activase include the number, effectiveness, safety and relative price of competing products, the effectiveness of the Company's marketing programs, physicians' personal experiences in the administration of thrombolytic therapy, the further acceptance of thrombolytic therapy in the treatment of heart attacks, third party reimbursement for the costs of thrombolytic therapies and the results of additional thrombolytic clinical stud-

ies, including studies comparing Activase with its competitors.

In January 1990 a competitor in the thrombolytic marketplace began marketing a clot-dissolving agent, Eminase® (a trademark of SmithKline Beecham), a modified form of streptokinase. While Eminase has not achieved a significant share of the thrombolytic market to date, this product may potentially pose substantial competition in 1991. Data from a major European clinical trial (GISSI-2) directly comparing Actilyse, an alteplase t-PA equivalent to Activase marketed by Genentech's licensee, Boehringer, with streptokinase were released in March 1990. The results indicated that both agents were equally effective in saving lives of heart attack victims, but that there was a significantly greater overall stroke rate with Actilyse. However, the European study did not use the treatment regimen of anticoagulant therapy (intravenous heparin) that is recommended by the American Heart Association and favored by cardiologists in the United States using thrombolytic therapy, a fact which apparently affected the applicability of the study's results to prevalent medical practice in the United States. The GISSI-2 clinical trial has had minimal impact on Activase sales to date and is not expected to have a material impact on sales in 1991. Market share for t-PA was approximately two-thirds during the course of 1990.

The results of a second major mortality study, ISIS-3 (comparing duteplase t-PA manufactured by Burroughs Wellcome [Wellcome], streptokinase and Eminase), were released in March 1991. This study used Wellcome's duteplase t-PA rather than Genentech's alteplase t-PA. The ISIS-3 study failed to utilize anticoagulant therapy (intravenous heparin) in a manner recommended by the American Heart Association and favored by United States cardiologists, a fact which may influence the applicability of the ISIS-3 results to United States medical practice. It is too early to determine what the impact of this study will be on

Activase sales. However, the results of the ISIS-3 study are expected to lead to a decrease in Activase's share of the thrombolytic market and could have a negative impact on Activase sales, although it is not currently known if that impact will be material.

In the second half of 1990, the Company began co-sponsorship of a major comparative mortality trial known as GUSTO. The GUSTO trial will focus on three thrombolytic treatment study groups: an accelerated dose of the Company's t-PA; the use of streptokinase; and the combined therapy of t-PA and streptokinase. All three groups will also receive aspirin and heparin. The Company expects that the method of use of heparin in the GUSTO trial will provide the opportunity for trial results to be analyzed within the context of the acute myocardial infarction treatment therapy used predominantly in the United States. The GUSTO trial is expected to enroll about 33,000 patients and take several years to complete at an estimated cost to Genentech of over $40 million. Additionally, a number of patients participating in GUSTO might otherwise have received commercially available Activase and this will have an impact on Activase sales during the course of the GUSTO trial.

Protropin had net sales in 1990 of $157.1 million, compared with 1989 net sales of $122.7 million, and net sales of $111.1 million in 1988. The increase in Protropin sales from 1989 to 1990, and from 1988 to 1989, is believed to be due to higher revenues per existing patient, due to the larger average size of patients being treated at a correspondingly larger dose, and more growth hormone inadequate patients starting treatment. Protropin is currently protected from some possible additional competition by virtue of its designation as an Orphan Drug. In the past, several proposals to amend the Orphan Drug Act have been considered by Congress, including some which would have eliminated Protropin's market exclusivity. Legislation enacted by the Congress in 1990 but vetoed by the President would not have affected Protropin's exclusivity. Efforts to amend the Orphan Drug Act are expected to continue in 1991. Protropin sales are expected to increase in 1991, assuming the Orphan Drug Act is not adversely amended.

In December 1990, the Company received approval from the FDA to market Actimmune for the management of chronic granulomatous disease. Actimmune has received designation as an Orphan Drug by the FDA. Chronic granulomatous disease is a rare, inherited disorder of the immune system which affects an estimated 250 to 400 Americans. Due to the small size of the patient population, sales are expected to be immaterial in 1991. The Company hopes to expand the market potential of Actimmune over time through obtaining new approvals in additional indications with larger patient populations.

Over the longer term, the Company's (and its partners') ability to successfully market current products, expand their usage and bring new products to the marketplace will depend on many factors, including the effectiveness and safety of such products, FDA and foreign regulatory agencies' approvals of new indications, the degree of patent protection afforded to particular products, Orphan Drug Act legislation, and the possible future enactments of biotechnology product protection in the United States as well as Europe and Japan. The Company believes it has strong patent protection or the potential for strong patent protection for Activase and for certain other products which generate royalty revenue or which it is developing; however, the ultimate strength of the patent protection of the Company's products and that of others will likely be decided by the courts.

Royalties, which are included in contract and other revenue, have increased in each of the last three years due primarily to increases in product sales by the Company's licensees (royalty income in 1990—$47.6 million, 1989—$36.7 million and 1988—$26.7 million). The largest dollar increases in royalty income from the Company's licensees were from Lilly (recombinant human insulin) and Kabivitrum (recombinant human growth hormone). Royalty obligations associated with these revenues are included in marketing, general and administrative expenses.

Contract revenues, which are included under the contract and other revenues caption, were higher in 1990 than 1989. Contract revenues were lower in 1989 than 1988. The Company had fewer revenue contract-related activities in each succeeding year in the three year period. The primary reason for the increase in contract revenues in 1990 was the Company's sale of its interest in Genencor, Inc., an industrial enzyme joint venture established in 1982. The sale resulted in a pre-tax gain of approximately $11.9 million. The Company may, from time to time, enter into new contractual arrangements, which would provide additional revenue. As in the past, contract revenues will continue to fluctuate due to variations in the timing of contract benchmark achievements, varying payment amounts and the presence of new arrangements and the conclusion of existing arrangements. In June 1989, GCP IV was formed to fund the research, development and clinical trials relating to the development of CD4 and CD4-IgG as potential therapeutics for HIV-infected individuals. GCP IV raised approximately $72.5 million, a substantial portion of which is expected to be available to fund the development costs of CD4-based products through 1992 under a cost reimbursement development agreement between the Company and GCP IV. Amounts received as reimbursements are classified as contract revenues. Due to the revised development plans for CD4-based products announced by GCP IV in January 1991, it is expected that the amount recognized as revenue under the cost reimbursement arrangement in 1991 will be less than the $13.2 million recognized in 1990.

One major customer in 1990, 1989 and 1988 contributed 10% or more of the Company's total revenues in each period.

In 1990 interest income was $29.4 million, compared with $17.2 million in 1989 and $12.1 million in 1988. Interest income was higher in 1990 than 1989 due to higher average portfolio balances during the current period resulting from the September 1990 sale of stock to Roche for $487.3 million (which was partially offset by cash payments for Merger-related charges). Interest income was higher in 1989 than in 1988 due to higher average portfolio balances and higher average interest rates. The Company expects that interest income will be significantly increased in 1991 primarily due to the relatively higher average portfolio balance outstanding during the entire year. However, the average portfolio balance in 1991 will be dependent upon, among other things, the amount of the actual cash outflows for capital expenditures and product in-licensing and acquisitions, if any.

Costs and Expenses

Excluding the special charge (primarily Merger-related) of $167.7 million, total costs and expenses increased 15% to $405 million for 1990 from $352.9 million in 1989. Total costs and expenses in 1989 reflected an increase of $64.5 million over 1988 (excluding a special charge in 1988 of $23.3 million). The special charge in 1988 related primarily to a write-down of certain quantities of Activase inventory.

Cost of sales for 1990 increased by $7.7 million or 13% over 1989. Cost of sales for 1990 increased over 1989 primarily due to the higher level of product sales for both Activase and Protropin, and higher cost inventory layers for Activase. Cost of sales for 1989 and 1988 were $60.6 million and $46.9 million, respectively. The increase from 1988 to 1989 was primarily caused by the increase in product sales combined with higher additional costs, which include the amortization of the costs of product technology purchased from a research and development partnership in 1986.

The increase of $44.3 million in costs and expenses from 1989 to 1990, excluding cost of sales and the special charge in 1990, resulted primarily from higher marketing and promotional expenses, increased pre-clinical, clinical and other outside scientific expenditures and royalty expenses.

The increase of $50.9 million in costs and expenses from 1988 to 1989, excluding cost of sales and the special charge in 1988, resulted principally from the absence of Activase production throughout 1989 and the associated reallocation of the Company's production facility primarily to research and development efforts, the increase in the size of the Company's sales force and marketing and sales related expenses, increased pre-clinical, clinical and other outside scientific expenditures and royalty expenses.

The increase in research and development expenses between the years 1990, 1989 and 1988 reflects the Company's continued commitment to the development of new products and new indications for existing products. During 1990, three new products entered clinical trials: relaxin, DNase, and gp120. A monoclonal antibody against HER-2 has been scheduled to begin clinical trials during the first quarter of 1991. The Company then will have 10 products in the clinic for more than 15 indications. In addition, a number of new candidate molecules have been identified for pre-clinical development and others are nearing clinical trials. The Company restarted production of Activase in 1990. In 1991, research and development expense is expected to increase primarily because of the greater number of products in the clinic and an increased pre-clinical effort. The Company's co-sponsorship of the GUSTO trial is expected to contribute significantly to the expected increase in research and development expense.

Marketing, general and administrative expenses have increased in each successive year beginning in 1988 due primarily to growth in the Company's marketing and promotional programs, and its sales and marketing organi-zation. Royalty expenses have increased primarily due to higher income on which royalties are owed in each year. Increases in marketing programs in 1990, in response to the release of the GISSI-2 study and the launch of Eminase, have been the major factors in the growth in this area. Marketing, general and administrative expenses are expected to increase in 1991 due to growth in existing expenses and increased marketing programs for Activase and Protropin, and the launch of Actimmune.

During the third quarter of 1990, a special charge of $167.7 million was incurred which consisted primarily of Merger-related expenses. Total Merger-related expenses were $153.3 million. The majority of the Merger-related expenses included in the special charge were associated with the cash-out of stock options (approximately $125 million). Other Merger-related expenses included investment banking fees and legal, printing and filing fees. The balance of the special charge was for litigation, facility and other corporate charges.

Interest expense in 1990, 1989 and 1988, net of amounts capitalized, relates primarily to interest on the Company's 5% convertible subordinated debentures which were issued in March 1987.

INCOME TAXES

The 1990 tax provision reflects losses with no current tax benefits available. The effective tax rates of 7.5% in 1989 and 11% in 1988 reflect the benefit of loss carryforwards. At December 31, 1990 there were $264 million and $29 million, respectively, in loss carryforwards and credit carryforwards available for financial statement purposes to reduce income taxes in future years. The 1989 rate was lower than the 1988 tax rate primarily because of increased state research tax credits. The income tax provision for 1991 is expected to approximate the 1990 provision as a result of the utilization of some of the Company's loss carryforwards.

EARNINGS

In 1990 the Company recorded a net loss of $98 million and a loss per share of $1.05. In 1989 the Company recorded net income of $44 million and $.51 per share compared with $20.6 million and $.24 per share in 1988. The 1990 results include a special charge of $167.7 million (discussed above under "Costs and Expenses"), which amounted to $1.74 per share net of applicable income tax benefit. The 1988 results also include a special charge of $23.3 million (also discussed under "Costs and Expenses"), which amounted to $.26 per share net of applicable income tax benefit.

Liquidity and Capital Resources

Genentech had cash, cash equivalents and short-term investments of $691.3 million at December 31, 1990 compared with $205.0 million at year end 1989. Cash required by operations in 1990 was $13.3 million, after taking into account the special charge of $167.7 million. In 1989 operations provided $99.6 million in cash. In 1990, the Company also received cash proceeds of $487.3 million from the investment in the Company by Roche. During 1990, the Company also raised $34.9 million through the issuance of stock under its employee stock plans and from the exercise of warrants, compared with $17.2 million in 1989.

Capital expenditures totaled $36 million in 1990, compared with $37.2 million in 1989. The Company believes it has the necessary facilities to maintain its current level of operations and has the ability to selectively invest in new facility projects as the need arises. Capital expenditures for 1991 are expected to approach $90 million. The major reason for this expected increase is construction of the Genentech Research Center, a new 3-building state-of-the-art facility to house the Company's research activities. Construction commenced in 1990 and is expected to be complete in 1992, at an estimated total cost of $75 million.

Working capital totaled $694.3 million at December 31, 1990, compared to $251.2 million at year end 1989. With working capital, revenues from product sales, contracts and royalties and other sources of financing, the Company believes that its capital resources are sufficient to meet its anticipated operating requirements as well as provide the opportunity for the development of new products and markets through vehicles such as acquisitions, product in-licensing and geographic diversification.

Item 8: Consolidated Financial Statements and Supplementary Data

GENENTECH, INC.

Consolidated Statements of Operations

(thousands except per share amounts)

	YEAR ENDED DECEMBER 31		
	1990	1989	1988
Revenues:			
Product sales	$367,170	$319,067	$262,476
Contract and other (including amounts from related parties: 1990—$17,045; 1989—$13,868; 1988—$2,394)	79,526	64,143	60,283
Interest	29,440	17,245	12,081
Total revenues	476,136	400,455	334,840
Costs and expenses:			
Cost of sales	68,305	60,556	46,897
Special charge (primarily merger related in 1990 and inventory related in 1988)	167,735	—	23,349
Research and development (including contract related: 1990—$16,719; 1989—$11,080; 1988—$21,001)	173,090	156,883	132,682
Marketing, general and administrative	158,058	127,922	101,898
Interest	5,504	7,568	6,906
Total costs and expenses	572,692	352,929	311,732
Income (loss) before taxes	(96,556)	47,526	23,108
Income tax provision	1,475	3,565	2,543
Net income (loss)	$(98,031)	$ 43,961	$ 20,565
Net income (loss) per share	$ (1.05)	$ 0.51	$ 0.24
Weighted average number of shares used in computing per share amounts	93,040	85,967	284,459

See notes to consolidated financial statements.

GENENTECH, INC.

Consolidated Statements of Cash Flows

(dollars in thousands)

	YEAR ENDED DECEMBER 31		
	1990	1989	1988
Cash flows from operating activities:			
Net income (loss)	$(98,031)	$ 43,961	$ 20,565
Adjustments to reconcile net income (loss) to net cash provided (used) by operating activities:			
Depreciation and amortization	47,629	44,605	38,325
Gain on sale of Genencor investment	(11,874)	—	—
Net loss on fixed asset write-downs and dispositions	664	—	118
Non-cash portion of special charge (primarily merger related in 1990 and inventory related in 1988)	8,058	—	23,349
Changes in assets and liabilities, net of the effects from the special charge:			
Decrease (Increase) in receivables and other current assets	8,034	(4,131)	28,989
Decrease (Increase) in inventories	9,685	14,241	(26,244)
Increase in accounts payable and accrued liabilities	22,577	875	12,399
Net cash provided (used) by operating activities	(13,258)	99,551	97,501
Cash flows from investing activities:			
Purchases of short-term investments	(538,046)	(223,685)	(145,154)
Dispositions of short-term investments	223,261	188,060	201,440
Capital expenditures	(35,980)	(37,160)	(110,858)
Net proceeds from sale of Genencor investment	19,101	—	—
Acquisition of Genentech Canada	—	(3,300)	—
Proceeds from sale of fixed assets	—	1,000	—
Increase in other assets	(3,883)	(1,274)	(1,315)
Net cash used in investing activities	(335,547)	(76,359)	(55,887)
Cash flows from financing activities:			
Stock issuance to Roche Holdings, Inc.	487,340	—	—
Stock issuances, net of notes receivable and redemption of preferred share purchase rights	34,921	17,197	21,735
Reduction in long-term debt including current portion	(1,918)	(23,552)	(12,885)
Net cash provided (used) by financing activities	520,343	(6,355)	8,850
Increase (Decrease) in cash and cash equivalents	171,538	16,837	50,464
Cash and cash equivalents at beginning of year	113,189	96,352	45,888
Cash and cash equivalents at end of year	$284,727	$113,189	$ 96,352

(Continued)

	YEAR ENDED DECEMBER 31		
	1990	1989	1988
Supplemental schedule of noncash investing and financing activities:			
Issuance of warrants related to contract arrangements	$ —	$ 8,499	$ 1,583
Investment financed by debt	—	620	—
Supplemental cash flow data:			
Cash paid during the year for:			
Interest, net of portion capitalized	$ 5,552	$ 7,540	$ 6,996
Income taxes	324	—	1,222

See notes to consolidated financial statements.

GENENTECH, INC.

Consolidated Balance Sheets

(dollars in thousands)

	DECEMBER 31	
	1990	1989
ASSETS		
Current assets:		
Cash and cash equivalents	$ 284,727	$113,189
Short-term investments, at cost which approximates market	406,547	91,762
Accounts receivable (less allowances of: 1990—$3,800; 1989—$2,144)	58,751	66,764
Inventories	39,573	49,258
Prepaid expenses and other current assets	6,108	6,129
Total current assets	795,706	327,102
Property, plant and equipment, at cost:		
Land	38,260	38,207
Buildings	76,299	72,844
Equipment	154,074	135,279
Leasehold improvements	73,060	72,872
Construction-in-progress	59,479	55,090
	401,172	374,292
Less: accumulated depreciation	100,936	75,181
Net property, plant and equipment	300,236	299,111
Purchased product technology, net	40,319	56,114
Other assets	21,409	28,864
Total assets	$1,157,670	$711,191

See notes to consolidated financial statements.

GENENTECH, INC.

Consolidated Balance Sheets, Continued

(dollars in thousands)

	DECEMBER 31	
	1990	1989
LIABILITIES AND STOCKHOLDERS' EQUITY		
Current liabilities:		
Accounts payable	$ 10,215	$ 7,229
Accrued compensation	19,238	15,369
Accrued interest	5,708	5,708
Accrued royalties	20,830	14,471
Other accrued liabilities	44,359	31,071
Current portion of long-term debt	1,042	2,085
Total current liabilities	101,392	75,933
Long-term debt	153,534	154,409
Other long-term liabilities	9,562	11,897
Total liabilities	264,488	242,239
COMMITMENTS AND CONTINGENCIES		
Stockholders' equity:		
Preferred Stock, $0.02 par value; authorized 100,000,000 shares; none issued	—	—
Redeemable Common Stock, $0.02 par value; authorized 100,000,000 shares, outstanding: 1990—43,476,851; 1989—none	870	—
Common Stock, $0.02 par value; authorized 200,000,000 shares; outstanding: 1990—67,133,409; 1989—84,269,481	1,343	1,685
Additional paid-in capital	927,940	406,207
Retained earnings (deficit) (since October 1, 1987 quasi-reorganization in which a deficit of $329,457 was eliminated)	(36,971)	61,060
Total stockholders' equity	893,182	468,952
Total liabilities and stockholders' equity	$1,157,670	$711,191

See notes to consolidated financial statements.

GENENTECH, INC.

Consolidated Statements of Stockholders' Equity

(dollars in thousands)

	YEAR ENDED DECEMBER 31		
	1990	1989	1988
Redeemable Common Stock—Beginning of Year	$ —	$ —	$ —
Conversion of Common Stock to Redeemable Common Stock during the merger with Roche Holdings, Inc. (42,699,458 shares)	854	—	—
Issuance of Redeemable Common Stock (777,393 shares)	16	$ —	—
End of year (43,476,851 shares)	$ 870	$ —	$ —
Common Stock—Beginning of Year	$ 1,685	$ 1,658	$ 1,575
Conversion of Common Stock to Redeemable Common Stock during the merger with Roche Holdings, Inc. (42,699,458 shares)	(854)	—	—
Issuance of Common Stock to Roche Holdings, Inc. (24,433,951 shares)	489	—	—
Other issuances of Common Stock (1990–1,129,435 shares; 1989–1,345,042 shares; 1988—4,184,543 shares)	23	27	83
End of year, after conversion and issuance of Common Stock (67,133,409 shares)	$ 1,343	$ 1,685	$ 1,658
Restricted Stock—Beginning of Year	$ —	$ —	$ 59
End of year, after issuance of Common Stock	$ —	$ —	$ —
Additional Paid-in Capital—Beginning of Year	$406,207	$366,518	$336,267
Issuance of Common Stock to Roche Holdings, Inc.	486,851	—	—
Other issuances of Common Stock	15,974	17,170	21,391
Issuance of Redeemable Common Stock	19,762	—	—
Redemption of preferred share purchase rights	(854)	—	—
Issuance of warrants	—	8,499	1,583
Tax benefits arising prior to quasi-reorganization	—	14,020	$ 7,277
End of year	$927,940	$406,207	$366,518
Notes Receivable from sale of stock—Beginning of Year	$ —	$ —	$ (320)
End of Year, after payments on notes receivable	$ —	$ —	$ —
Retained Earnings—Beginning of Year	$ 61,060	$ 31,119	$ 17,831
Net income (loss)	(98,031)	43,961	20,565
Tax benefits arising prior to quasi-reorganization	—	$ (14,020)	(7,277)
End of Year	$ (36,971)	$ 61,060	$ 31,119
Total stockholders' equity	$893,182	$468,952	$399,295

See notes to consolidated financial statements.

Notes to Consolidated Financial Statements

Summary of Significant Accounting Policies

PRINCIPLES OF CONSOLIDATION

The consolidated financial statements include the accounts of the Company and its wholly-owned and majority owned subsidiaries. All significant intercompany balances and transactions have been eliminated.

CASH AND CASH EQUIVALENTS

The Company considers all highly liquid debt instruments purchased with a maturity of three months or less to be cash equivalents.

INVENTORIES

Inventories are stated at the lower of cost or market. Cost is determined using a weighted-average approach which approximates the first-in, first-out method.

PROPERTY, PLANT AND EQUIPMENT

The costs of buildings and equipment are depreciated for financial reporting purposes using the straight-line method over the estimated useful lives of the assets. Accelerated methods of depreciation are used for income tax purposes. Leasehold improvements are generally amortized over the length of the applicable lease. Expenditures for maintenance and repairs are expensed as incurred. Interest on construction-in-progress is capitalized. Interest of $2.4 million in 1990, $2.4 million in 1989 and $4.1 million in 1988 has been capitalized and included in property, plant and equipment.

PURCHASED PRODUCT TECHNOLOGY

Approved product rights and technology (related to Protropin) acquired from a research and development partnership are amortized on a straight-line basis over their estimated useful lives of six years. At December 31, 1990, 1989 and 1988 accumulated amortization related to these assets was $58.9 million, $42.7 million and $26.5 million, respectively.

PATENTS

As a result of its research and development programs, the Company owns and is in the process of applying for patents in the United States and other countries which relate to products and processes of significant importance to the Company. Costs of patents and patent applications are amortized on a straight-line basis over their estimated useful lives of approximately 12 years.

CONTRACT REVENUE

Contract revenue for research and development is recorded as earned based on the performance requirements of the contract. In return for contract payments, contract partners may receive certain marketing and manufacturing rights (including rights to future product royalties), products for clinical use and testing or research and development services.

INCOME TAXES

Income taxes are accounted for in accordance with Statement of Financial Accounting Standards No. 96, "Accounting for Income Taxes." For financial statement purposes, investment tax credits are accounted for on the flow-through method as a reduction of federal income tax expense.

EARNINGS PER SHARE

Earnings per share are computed based on the weighted average number of shares of Redeemable Common Stock, Common Stock and equivalents, if dilutive, (options and warrants in 1990, 1989 and 1988). The Company's convertible subordinated debentures are common stock equivalents but have been antidilutive to date and, therefore, have not been included in earnings per share calculations.

CONCENTRATION OF CREDIT AND MARKET RISK

The Company sells primarily to hospitals and distributors throughout the United States and Canada, performs ongoing credit evaluations of its customers' financial condition and generally requires no collateral. In fiscal years 1990, 1989 and 1988 the Company did not record any material additions to its provision for doubtful accounts.

The Company invests its excess cash principally in marketable securities from a diversified portfolio of institutions with strong credit ratings and, by policy, limits the amount of credit exposure to any one institution. These investments are generally not collateralized and primarily mature within one year. The Company has not experienced any material losses in fiscal years 1990, 1989 and 1988.

Notes to Consolidated Financial Statements

Note 1: Merger with Roche Holdings, Inc.

Genentech's merger ("Merger") with a wholly-owned subsidiary of Roche Holdings, Inc. ("Roche") was consummated on September 7, 1990. Genentech stockholders of record on September 7, 1990 received, for each share of Common Stock that they owned, $18 in cash from Roche and one half share of newly issued Redeemable Common Stock from the Company. In the Merger, Roche acquired one half of the Company's outstanding Common Stock for $1,537.2 million. Stockholders also received $.01 per share from the Company for redemption of their Preferred Share Purchase Rights, as allowed for under the Preferred Share Purchase Rights Plan (which was terminated concurrently with the Merger consummation). The new Genentech Redeemable

Common Stock is substantially identical to the Genentech Common Stock previously held by stockholders, except that it is redeemable by the Company at the election of Roche, provided that Roche first deposits in trust sufficient funds to pay the aggregate redemption price of all outstanding shares of Redeemable Common Stock. Roche will have the right to require the Company to exercise its redemption right, providing it does so for all shares of Genentech's outstanding Redeemable Common Stock at $39 per share in the first calendar quarter of 1991, to $40 per share in the second calendar quarter and increasing by $1.25 per share every quarter to $60 per share on April 1, 1995. The redemption right expires on June 30, 1995.

In connection with the Merger the Company issued 24,433,951 shares of Common Stock to Roche for $487.3 million in cash. The Common Stock issued to Roche, combined with the Common Stock Roche acquired in the Merger, represented approximately 60 percent of the outstanding equity of the Company on the effective date of the Merger (see also Note 8).

Independent of its right to have the Company redeem the Redeemable Common Stock, Roche is permitted by the terms of its agreements with the Company to acquire additional shares of Genentech stock through open market or privately negotiated purchases, provided that Roche's aggregate holdings do not exceed 75 percent of the Company's stock outstanding on a fully diluted basis.

The Company incurred a special charge in 1990 of $167.7 million which consists primarily of Merger-related expenses. The majority of the Merger-related expenses included in the special charge were associated with the cashout of stock options (approximately $125 million). The total Merger-related expenses were $153.3 million and included investment banking fees, and legal, printing and filing fees. The balance of the special charge was for litigation, facility and other corporate charges.

Note 2: Operating Revenues

One major customer in 1990, 1989 and 1988 contributed 10% or more of the Company's total revenues. The portions of revenues attributable to this customer were 27% in 1990, 21% in 1989 and 21% in 1988. Revenues from foreign customers were as follows: Europe—approximately $17.6 million in 1990; $17.6 million in 1989, and $24.9 million in 1988; Asia—approximately $5.6 million in 1990; $3.2 million in 1989, and $4.9 million in 1988; Canada—approximately $9.2 million in 1990, $4.7 million in 1989 and $1.7 million in 1988.

In the first quarter of 1990 Genentech sold its interest in Genencor, Inc., an industrial enzyme joint venture which Genentech helped found in 1982. The sale resulted in a pre-tax gain of approximately $11.9 million which is included in contract and other revenues.

Note 3: Income Taxes

The income tax provision consists of the following (in thousands):

	1990	1989	1988
Current			
State	$ 450	$ 200	$ 200
Foreign	—	200	—
	450	400	200
Deferred			
Federal	1,025	2,139	575
State	—	1,026	1,768
	1,025	3,165	2,343
Income tax provision	$1,475	$3,565	$2,543

A reconciliation between the Company's effective tax rate and the U.S. statutory rate follows:

	1990 Amount	Tax Rate 1990	Tax Rate 1989	Tax Rate 1988
	(in thousands)			
Tax at U.S. statutory rate	$(32,828)	(34.0)%	34.0%	34.0%
Operating losses not utilized/ (utilized)	32,828	34.0%	(29.5)	(31.5)
Other, including state taxes	1,475	1.5%	3.0	8.5
Income tax provision	$ 1,475	1.5%	7.5%	11.0%

Deferred taxes are provided on temporary differences between the timing of income and deductions for tax return and financial statement purposes. The principal differences relate to the amortization of purchased technology and to accelerated depreciation.

At December 31, 1990 the Company had operating loss carryforwards for Federal tax purposes of approximately $356 million. For financial reporting purposes, such carryforwards approximate $264 million. The difference between the amounts for tax and financial statement purposes is attributable to the temporary differences described above and to approximately $50 million of deductions related to stock option exercises, the tax benefit of which will be credited to paid-in capital when realized. Such losses expire from 2000 through 2005.

In addition, at December 31, 1990 the Company had available general business credit carryforwards for financial reporting purposes of $29 million which expire in 1996 through 2005.

Note 4: Research and Development Arrangements

The Company entered into contracts to perform research and development (R & D) with Genentech Clinical Partners III (GCP III) in s1984 and Genentech Clinical Partners IV (GCP IV) in 1989, both limited partnerships (See also Note 9). The Company also entered into licensing agreements with these contract partners wherein they were granted exclusive territorial rights to practice under the Company's patents and to use the Company's know-how for certain projects. GCP III acquired the Company's United States rights for tumor necrosis factor-alpha (TNF) and GCP IV acquired the Company's United States and European rights for recombinant CD4-based products. As discussed below, the technology owned by GCP III was acquired by the Company in October 1989 and the related research and development contracts were terminated.

Under these R & D arrangements, the Company recognized revenue from the partnerships for the costs of the work performed on the respective project's development on a cost reimbursement basis. The Company recorded approximately $13.2 million, $10.1 million, and $2.2 million as revenue under these research and development partnerships in 1990, 1989 and 1988, respectively.

Under the GCP IV contracts with the Company, if development cannot be successfully completed the Company's obligation is terminated and the Company has no further obligations, except for a supply agreement, under the agreements or rights or interests in the products within the involved territory. If development is successfully completed and regulatory approval is received, the Company has options to first manufacture and market the products in a joint venture with GCP IV and then to purchase the Partnership interests including all the rights to the respective products. If the Company exercises the purchase option, the Limited Partners will receive a fixed initial payment plus future cash payments based on a percentage of product revenues. In January 1991, the Board of Directors of the general partner of GCP IV announced that it will concentrate the clinical research

program for CD4-IgG on studies aimed at preventing the spread of disease from HIV-infected pregnant women to their fetuses; and that it has no current plans to continue the clinical trials of CD4-IgG as a stand-alone therapy for HIV-infected adults.

During the third quarter of 1988 the Company discontinued revenue recognition under the development agreement with GCP III. In November 1988, the Company accrued $2.5 million for its obligations under a guarantee for GCP III's outstanding loan which was repaid by the Company in 1989. In October 1989, upon the purchase of GCP III's technology assets, the Company recorded a net expense of $1.6 million associated with the purchase. The purchase agreement requires the Company to pay royalties for a specified period on net sales by Genentech of human pharmaceutical products containing TNF if such sales commence in the United States prior to December 31, 2005.

In the second half of 1990, the Company began co-sponsorship of a major comparative mortality trial known as GUSTO. The GUSTO trial will focus on three thrombolytic treatment study groups: an accelerated dose of the Company's t-PA; the use of streptokinase; and the combined therapy of t-PA and streptokinase. All three groups will also receive aspirin and heparin. The GUSTO trial is expected to enroll about 33,000 patients and take several years to complete at an estimated cost to Genentech of over $40 million.

In December 1990, the Company entered into an agreement with Glycomed, Inc. for a $15 million research collaboration to develop carbohydrate-based therapeutics in the field of cell adhesion molecules. The agreement includes partial research support for an initial three-year period and a two-stage, $7 million equity investment by Genentech in Glycomed, Inc. The research will be funded by Genentech through a combination of sponsored research funding and milestone payments over a three year period with a potential two year extension.

In January 1991, the Company entered into an agreement with Telios Pharmaceuticals, Inc. ("Telios") for a $15 million research collaboration to develop and commercialize an injectable drug to help prevent the formation of blood clots. Under the agreement, the companies will co-develop a drug based on Telios' proprietary matrix-peptide technology and Genentech's expertise in peptide design and recombinant-receptor assay screening. Genentech will provide Telios with milestone-based payments and will pay the company royalties on sales. In return, Genentech will have the right to market the drug worldwide, except in Japan and the Far East.

Note 5: Inventories

Inventories at December 31, 1990 and 1989 are summarized in the following table (in thousands):

	1990	1989
Raw materials and supplies	$ 7,632	$ 9,159
Work in process	18,302	27,728
Finished goods	13,639	12,371
Total	$39,573	$49,258

During the fourth quarter of 1988 the Company recorded a special charge of $23.3 million which was primarily a write down of certain quantities of Activase inventory.

Note 6: Long-term Debt and Credit Arrangements

Long-term debt consists of the following (in thousands):

	1990	1989
Convertible subordinated debèntures, interest at 5% due in 2002	$150,000	$150,000
Mortgage note payable on buildings and land, interest at 9.5%, due 1990 to 1996	3,997	4,540
Obligations under capital leases	—	729
Non-interest bearing notes payable as capital contributions to GCP IV, due 1990 to 1992	389	620
Other	190	605
	154,576	156,494
Less current maturities	1,042	2,085
Total long-term debt	$153,534	$154,409

Maturities of long-term debt in 1991 and in the four subsequent years are $1.0 million, $0.8 million, $0.7 million, $0.8 million and $0.9 million, respectively.

Convertible subordinated debentures are convertible at the option of the holder into shares of the Company's Redeemable Common Stock at a conversion price of $74 per debenture. Upon conversion, the holder receives, for each debenture converted, one-half share of Redeemable Common Stock and $18 in cash. Under the terms of the Merger Agreement, the $18 in cash per debenture converted is reimbursed by Roche to the Company. The Company may redeem the debentures at 103% of par with the redemption price decreasing by 1% each year until 1993 when the debentures become redeemable at par.

Note 7: Leases and Commitments

The Company has leased equipment under leasing arrangements. Certain of these arrangements require that the Company maintain $10 million of working capital (as defined), place limits on certain types of debt and require certain approvals for the payment of dividends. The Company is responsible for taxes, insurance and maintenance under its leasing arrangements.

Included in the equipment caption of the consolidated balance sheets are capitalized leases of $5.2 million in 1989. They account for accumulated depreciation of $4.6 million for

1989. Capitalized leases for equipment in 1990 are fully depreciated.

Future minimum lease payments under noncancelable operating leases at December 31, 1990 are as follows (in thousands):

1991	$ 8,602
1992	7,806
1993	3,790
1994	1,778
1995	1,494
Thereafter	2,575
Total minimum lease payments	$26,045

Rent expense under operating leases was approximately $9.6 million, $12.7 million and $12.4 million for 1990, 1989 and 1988, respectively. Income from subleases was immaterial.

The Company has arranged a $2 million unsecured line of credit to provide guarantees for employees in connection with short-term residential bridge loan financing resulting from relocation. At December 31, 1990 the Company was contingently liable for approximately $0.8 million as guarantor of such loans.

Note 8: Capital Stock

STOCK OPTION PLANS

1984 Plans The Merger agreement with Roche ("Merger Agreement") provided that as of September 7, 1990 (the "Effective Date"), each outstanding stock option granted under the Company's 1984 Stock Option Plans ("Employee Stock Options") was to be cancelled, and the holder to receive, in exchange, a substitute option (an "Adjusted Option") to purchase a number of shares of Redeemable Common Stock equal to the number of shares of Common Stock subject to such cancelled option multiplied by a defined adjustment factor ("Adjustment Factor") at a per share exercise price equal to the per share exercise price of such cancelled option multiplied by a fraction

equal to one divided by the Adjustment Factor. Any Adjusted Option issued is subject to the same terms and conditions (other than number of shares and exercise price) as the option for which it is exchanged, including the terms related to vesting and the conditions relating to exercise. As defined in the Merger Agreement, the Adjustment Factor equals 1.11.

The Merger Agreement further provided that notwithstanding the provision described above relating to conversion of Employee Stock Options, prior to the Effective Date, each holder of an Employee Stock Option (other than any director of Genentech who was not an employee of Genentech) had an opportunity to make a cash-out election ("Cash-Out Election") with respect to all Employee Stock Options held. At the Effective Date, each outstanding Employee Stock Option that was subject to a Cash-Out Election and was not then fully vested became vested with respect to 25% of the unvested portion in addition to the portion that already was vested. The additional vesting is credited against the next regularly scheduled vestings of the Employee Stock Options. At the Effective Date, the vested portion of each Employee Stock Option that was subject to a Cash-Out Election and that was not yet exercised was cancelled and promptly after the Effective Date, the Company paid the holder an amount in cash of $36.00 less the applicable exercise price for each option. Immediately following the Effective Date, the unvested portion of these options was cancelled and exchanged for substitute options to purchase, at a per share exercise price equal to the per share exercise price of the cancelled options, an equal number of shares of Redeemable Common Stock. The substitute options are subject to the same terms and conditions as the option for which it is exchanged, including the terms related to vesting (treating such substitute options as if they were granted at the same time as the options for which they were exchanged) and the conditions relating to exercise.

Directors of Genentech who are not also employees of Genentech were not entitled to receive Adjusted Options or make a Cash-Out Election. Instead, each Employee Stock Option held by such non-employee directors of Genentech was, at the Effective Date, cancelled, and the holder received, in exchange, a substitute option to purchase, at a per share exercise price equal to the per share exercise price of such cancelled options and on the identical terms and conditions to such cancelled options, the number of shares of Redeemable Common Stock equal to the number of shares of Common Stock subject to such cancelled option.

The number of shares of Redeemable Common Stock subject to the 1984 Option Plans was increased by 94,397 shares as a result of the application of the Adjustment Factor.

At December 31, 1990, 5,427,105 shares of Redeemable Common Stock were reserved for issuance under either the 1984 Incentive Stock Option Plan or the 1984 Non-Qualified Stock Option Plan. Options may be granted under the 1984 Incentive Stock Option Plan only to employees (including officers) of the Company. Options may be granted under the 1984 Non-Qualified Stock Option Plan to employees (including officers), directors and consultants to the Company. Options granted under the 1984 Incentive Stock Option Plan and the 1984 Non-Qualified Stock Option Plan expire in five and ten years, respectively, from the date of grant. The options generally become exercisable in increments over a period of four years from the date of grant, with the first increment vesting after one year. Options may be granted with different vesting terms from time to time. In 1988 the price of the Company's stock declined sharply resulting in the exercise prices of many of the outstanding stock options greatly exceeding the then current fair market value of the Company's Common Stock. During 1988 the Company granted option holders the right to cancel certain existing stock options in exchange for options on

an equal number of shares at the fair market value on the date of grant. In general, exchanged options were immediately exercisable with respect to one fourth of the shares subject to each option and were subject to prospective vesting during the four year period following the grant date for three-fourths of the shares subject to each option.

Under the 1984 Incentive Stock Option Plan and the 1984 Non-Qualified Stock Option Plan collectively, 4,898,641 shares of Redeemable Common Stock and 11,432,037 shares of the Company's Common Stock were subject to options outstanding at December 31, 1990 and 1989, respectively. As of December 31, 1990 and 1989 the weighted average per share exercise price of outstanding options was $17.72 and $16.59, respectively, and 197,023 and 3,747,811 shares, respectively, were exercisable under outstanding options. At December 31, 1990 and 1989, options for 528,464 and 348,216 shares, respectively, were reserved for future grants under the two plans. During 1990, 435,821 shares of Common Stock and 5,574 shares of Redeemable Common Stock were issued upon the exercise of options at prices ranging from $7.28 to $20.13 per share. During 1989 and 1988, 982,905 and 1,144,397 shares, respectively, were issued upon the exercise of options under both 1984 Plans at prices of $7.28 to $18.88 per share in 1989 and $7.28 to $40.69 per share in 1988. During 1990, optionholders with options for 6,006,151 shares received cash in lieu of exercise under the Cash-Out Election noted above, options for 498,550 shares were granted and options for 635,944 shares were cancelled. Options to purchase 888 shares expired in 1990.

1990 Plan In February, 1990, the 1990 Stock Option/Stock Incentive Plan ("1990 Plan") was adopted. At December 31, 1990, 4,000,000 shares of Redeemable Common Stock were reserved for issuance under the 1990 Plan. The 1990 Plan permits the granting of options intended to qualify as incentive stock options and the granting of options that do not so qualify. In addition, the 1990 Plan permits the granting of stock appreciation rights in connection with non-qualified options or incentive options and the issuance of shares of Redeemable Common Stock, either fully vested at the time of issuance or vesting according to a pre-determined schedule. Incentive options may only be granted to employees (including officers and employee-directors). The non-qualified options and other non-option stock incentives may only be granted under the 1990 Plan to employees (including officers and employee-directors) and consultants of Genentech. All non-qualified options have a maximum term of 20 years and all incentive options have a maximum term of 10 years. Shares may be issued under the 1990 Plan at the discretion of the Compensation Committee of the Board of Directors, and may be fully vested or may be subject to a vesting schedule. In addition, the 1990 Plan contains a special provision whereby Genentech's former Chairman of the Board was granted a special Non-statutory Option for 170,000 shares of Redeemable Common Stock with a per share exercise price of $25.70 in cancellation of outstanding options for the same number of shares with an exercise price of $44.25.

In 1990, options to purchase 3,036,100 shares of Redeemable Common Stock were issued at prices ranging from $25.50 to $25.75 per share. Options to purchase 750 shares of Redeemable Common Stock were exercisable at December 31, 1990 and options to purchase 22,550 shares were cancelled during 1990.

Three types of stock appreciation rights may also be granted under the 1990 Plan: tandem stock appreciation rights, concurrent stock appreciation rights and limited stock appreciation rights. At December 31, 1990 no stock appreciation rights had been granted under the 1990 Plan.

At December 31, 1990, 1,738 out of 1,923 employees held options granted under the 1984 and 1990 Plans. Options for the issuance of 807,939 shares were held by consultants and directors of the Company at December 31, 1990.

EMPLOYEE STOCK PLANS

The 1987 Employee Stock Plan was adopted on July 1, 1987. Under the provisions of the Merger Agreement, the 1,500,000 shares of Common Stock originally reserved for issuance under the 1987 plan were changed to 1,539,916 shares of Redeemable Common Stock at the Effective Date. As of December 31, 1990, 1,281,165 shares have been issued. The 1987 plan may be terminated at the Company's option subject to any rights then outstanding. No new rights may be granted under the 1987 plan after December 31, 1990. As of December 31, 1990, 1,584 of the 1,881 eligible employees participated in the 1987 plan.

The 1991 Employee Stock Plan was adopted on December 4, 1990. One of the 1,500,000 shares of Redeemable Common Stock reserved for issuance under the 1991 plan, no shares had been issued as of December 31, 1990.

WARRANTS

In consideration of the grant to the Company by each Limited Partner of GCP IV admitted from June to August of 1989 of an option to purchase all of such Limited Partners' interests in GCP IV, the Company issued warrants with each partnership interest, to purchase an aggregate of 2,639,250 shares of Genentech Common Stock (subsequently converted to 1,319,625 shares of Redeemable Common Stock under the terms of the Merger Agreement). The warrants are exercisable at prices ranging from $22.57 to $23.26 at various dates from July 28, 1989 until July 31, 1994. Warrants to purchase approximately 462,828 shares of Redeemable Common Stock are exercisable at December 31, 1990 at prices ranging from $22.57 to $22.88 . Beginning on August 1, 1994, the warrants are exercisable at prices ranging from $27.57 to $28.26 until July 31, 1996, at which time the warrants expire. During 1990, 48,040 shares of Common Stock and 30,592 shares of Redeemable Common Stock were issued upon the exercise of these warrants at prices ranging from $22.57 to $22.88 per share. None of these warrants had been exercised as of December 31, 1989. The warrants are not detachable from the partnership interests until after certain events occur. The Company has the right to accelerate the date of expiration under certain circumstances.

In addition to the above, as part of financing and contract arrangements, the Company has, at certain times, issued warrants to purchase the Company's Common Stock. These warrants are exercisable at various dates through 1993. At December 31, 1990 and 1989, 257,270 and 1,922,740 shares, respectively, of the Company's Redeemable Common Stock and Common Stock, respectively, were reserved for issuance under warrant agreements and the weighted average per share exercise price was $21.58 and $15.58 on those respective dates. At December 31, 1990, 245,270 shares of Redeemable Common Stock were issuable under currently exercisable warrants. During 1990, 218,400 shares of Common Stock and 616,650 shares of Redeemable Common Stock were issued upon the exercise of warrants at prices of $11.30 to $18.75. During 1989, 57,056 shares of Common Stock were issued upon the exercise of warrants at prices of $11.28 to $11.70 per share. Warrant holders exercising warrants after the Effective Date receive, for each warrant exercised, $18 in cash and one half share of Redeemable Common Stock. Under the terms of the Merger Agreement, the $18 in cash per warrant exercised after the Effective Date is reimbursed by Roche to the Company.

Note 9: Related Party Transactions

The Company has transactions with related parties in the ordinary course of business. Pur-suant to contracts, principally to perform research and development on specific projects and product licensing agreements, the Company recorded as revenue approximately $17.0 million in 1990, $13.9 million in 1989 and $2.4 million in 1988 from the following related parties: two independently funded limited partnerships for which the Company has performed research services under cost reimbursement development agreements, GCP III and GCP IV; Hoffmann-LaRoche, Inc. (a wholly-owned subsidiary of Roche; two officers of Roche's parent company serve on the Company's Board of Directors—see also Note 1); GLC Associates (a partnership between a subsidiary of The Lubrizol Corporation and the Company; a former officer of The Lubrizol Corporation serves on the Company's Board of Directors); and Genencor (a corporation formally owned by Corning Glass works, Tate and Lyle plc Group, Eastman Kodak Company and the Company—see also Note 2). Through a private placement, GCP IV raised approximately $72.5 million in 1989. The Company's arrangement with GCP III was effectively terminated in October 1989 when that partnership agreed to sell substantially all of its assets to the Company. See Note 4 to the consolidated financial statements for additional information related to the GCP III asset acquisition. The officers and directors of the Company, as a group, have owned immaterial amounts of limited partnership interests in GCP III and GCP IV. Genentech Research Corporation, a wholly-owned subsidiary of the Company, owns a one percent interest in GCP IV and serves as its general partner. Genentech Development Corporation, a wholly-owned subsidiary of the Company, owned a one percent interest in GCP III and served as its general partner. As part of ongoing facilities expansion projects, the Company has paid a subsidiary of the Fluor Corporation (a director of Fluor Corporation serves on the Company's Board of Directors) an immaterial amount in 1990, $3.0 million in 1989 and $11.4 million in 1988 for engineering, design and construction management.

Note 10: Legal Proceedings

The Company is a party to various legal proceedings including patent infringement cases involving Protropin and Activase, product liability cases involving Activase and a breach of contract case involving Humulin®. In addition, the Company has been named as a defendant in a consolidated class action lawsuit alleging, among other things, violations of the Securities Exchange Act of 1934; a settlement has been reached in this case. The settlement totals $29 million, a substantial portion of which is covered by insurance. The Company has established adequate reserves to cover its portion of the settlement. The Company and its directors are defendants in several suits filed in Delaware and California challenging their actions in connection with the Merger.

Based upon the nature of the claims made and the investigation completed to date by the Company and its counsel, the Company believes the outcome of the described actions will not have a material adverse effect on the financial position or results of operations of the Company.

Note 11: Quasi-reorganization

On February 18, 1988 the Company's Board of Directors approved the elimination of the Company's accumulated deficit through an accounting reorganization of its stockholders' equity accounts (a quasi-reorganization) effective October 1, 1987. The quasi-reorganization did not involve any revaluation of assets or liabilities because for similar classes of assets their fair values were no less than their book values and for similar classes of liabilities their book values were no less than their fair values. The effective date of the quasi-reorganization (October 1, 1987) reflected the beginning of the quarter in which the Company received approval for and commenced marketing of its second major product, and as such, marked a turning point in the Company's operations. The accumulated deficit of $329,457 was eliminated by a transfer from additional paid-in capital in an amount equal to the accumulated deficit.

Simultaneously with the quasi-reorganization the Company adopted Financial Accounting Standards Board Statement No. 96(FAS 96), providing for recognition of the tax benefits of operating loss and tax credit carryforward items which arose prior to a quasi-reorganization involving only the elimination of a deficit in retained earnings being reported in the income statement and then reclassified from retained earnings to additional paid-in capital.

Subsequently in September 1989, the staff of the Securities and Exchange Commission issued Staff Accounting Bulletin No. 86 (SAB 86). This bulletin outlines the SEC staff's view that a quasi-reorganization that meets the SEC staff's guidance cannot involve only an elimination of a deficit in retained earnings and therefore the tax benefits of prior operating loss and tax credit carryforwards must be reported as a direct addition to additional paid-in capital rather than being recorded in the income statement.

The Company will continue to report in income the recognition of operating loss and tax credit carryfoward items arising prior to the quasi-reorganization due to the Company's adoption of its quasi-reorganization in the context of its interpretation of FAS 96 and the quasi-reorganization literature existing at the date the quasi-reorganization was effected. The SEC staff has indicated that under the circumstances they would not object to the Company's accounting for such tax benefits. If the provisions of SAB 86 had been applied, the net loss for the year ended December 31, 1990 would have been unaffected. Net income for each of the years ended December 31, 1989 and 1988 would have been reduced by $14,020,000 and $7,227,000, respectively.

Corporate Profile[1]

Royal Gist-brocades nv is a group with international operations whose core business is biotechnology based on fermentation processes. The group is one of the largest producers in the world of bakers' yeast, of penicillin and intermediates, and of enzymes.

Gist-brocades' principal establishment is in Delft. In addition, the group has production facilities and/or sales organisations in almost all EC countries, the United States of America and on other continents.

The group has three autonomous divisions:

1. The Food Ingredients (FID) Division's main products are yeast, yeast extracts and enzyme derivatives. While bakers' yeast is an important product in the bakery market, Gist-brocades is also a leading producer of bread improvers and confectioners' ingredients. Ingredients for the production of cheese, wine, beer and fruit juices, as well

as a growing range of natural flavourings are finding their way to the international foodstuffs industry.

2. The Industrial Pharmaceutical Products (IPPD) Division supplies raw materials and (bulk) intermediates to the pharmaceutical industry. The IPPD is the world's largest producer of penicillin and has a prominent position in the market for penicillin derivatives for traditional antibiotics. This division's strong position in biotechnology and its position in the industrial pharmaceutical market constitute the basis for the development of new innovative products.

3. The International Bio-Synthetics (IBIS) Division supplies industrial enzymes to the detergents, starch processing, textile and leather industries. A well-known application is the use of enzymes in washing powders. A multitude of highly specific enzymes are used in the textile industry for depasting fabrics and for special effects such as the stonewashed effect in jeans.

Scientific research as an integral part of commercial operations is one of the mainstays of Gist-brocades.

Turnover amounted to Dfl. 1,620 million in 1990. Gist-brocades has a workforce of 5,024 as of March 1 1991.

---

[1]The rest of the material in this Appendix is from Gist-brocades' *Annual Report 1990*.

GROUP FIGURES (in thousands of guilders, unless stated otherwise)

	1990	1989
Net turnover	1,619,571	1,849,503
Percentage decrease	12.4	1.9
Net turnover excl. Brocacef	1,619,571	1,588,867
Percentage increase	1.9	14.9
Operating profit	99,339	105,728
Percentage decrease	6.0	4.8
As a percentage of net turnover	6.1	5.7
Operating profit excl. Brocacef	99,339	96,136
Percentage increase	3.3	4.4
As a percentage of net turnover	6.1	6.1

(Continued)

	1990	1989
Interest, net	(21,449)	(21,134)
Taxation on profit on ordinary activities	13,082	17,706
Extraordinary income and expenditure after taxation	(1,074)	24,571
Profit after taxation	63,734	91,459
Percentage decrease	30.3	4.9
As a percentage of net turnover	3.9	4.9
As a percentage of average capital and reserves	6.6	9.3
Per share of Dfl. 2	Dfl. 1.87	Dfl. 2.68

Profit Appropriation

	1990		1989	
Dividend and Supervisory Directors' emoluments	69.7%	44,434	48.6%	44,429
General reserve	30.3%	19,300	51.4%	47,030
Dividend per share of Dfl. 2		Dfl. 1.30		Dfl. 1.30
Share capital		68,255		68,194
Depreciation of tangible fixed assets		98,211		98,723
Cash flow		161,876		190,079
Per share of Dfl. 2		Dfl. 4.74		Dfl. 5.57
Expenditure on tangible fixed assets		149,981		134,084
Wages, salaries and social security		493,469		504,298
Average number of employees		5,833		6,122
In the Netherlands		2,746		3,218

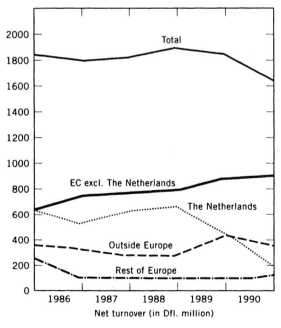

Net turnover (in Dfl. million)

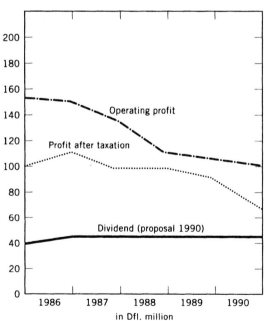

in Dfl. million

(*Continued*)

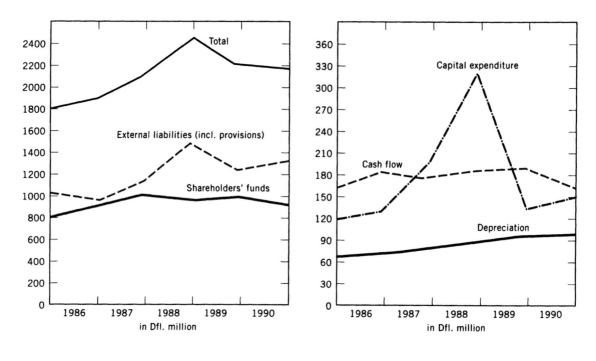

KEY FIGURES (in thousands of guilders, unless stated otherwise)

	1990	1989	1988	1987	1986
Profit and Cash Flow					
Operating profit	99,339	105,728	111,065	137,174	149,278
Interest, net	(21,449)	(21,134)	(14,617)	(5,374)	(3,809)
Extraordinary income and expenditure	(1,074)	24,571	27,531	(47)	5,023
Profit before taxation	76,816	109,165	123,979	131,753	150,492
Corporate income tax	13,082	17,706	27,855	35,586	39,392
Profit after taxation	63,734	91,459	96,124	96,167	111,100
Less: Profit added to the reserves	19,300	47,030	51,695	51,870	66,839
Profit available for distribution	44,434	44,429	44,429	44,297	44,261
Profit after taxation	63,734	91,459	96,124	96,167	111,100
Add: Depreciation of tangible fixed assets	98,211	98,723	91,012	80,233	72,389
Less: Supervisory Directors' emoluments	69	103	103	115	119
Cash flow	161,876	190,079	187,033	176,285	183,370
Per share of Dfl. 2					
Cash flow	4.74	5.57	5.49	5.19	5.40
Profit after taxation	1.87	2.68	2.82	2.83	3.27
Dividend	1.30	1.30	1.30	1.30	1.30
Profit reserved as a percentage of profit after taxation	30.3	51.4	53.8	53.9	60.2

(Continued)

	1990	1989	1988	1987	1986
General Information					
Net turnover	1,619,571	1,849,503	1,885,210	1,837,357	1,803,456
Indices	90	103	105	102	100
Percentage increase on previous year	12	2	(3)	(2)	2
Profit after taxation	63,734	91,459	96,124	96,167	111,100
Percentage increase on previous year	30.3	4.9	—	13.4	(10.9)
As a percentage of net turnover	3.9	4.9	5.1	5.2	6.2
Expenditure on tangible fixed assets	149,981	134,084	326,490	195,996	134,865
Depreciation of tangible fixed assets	98,211	98,723	91,012	80,233	72,389
Capital expenditure: depreciation	1.5	1.4	3.6	2.4	1.9
Stocks as a percentage of net turnover	22.2	18.7	20.9	18.8	19.9
Average number of employees	5,833	6,122	6,459	6,380	6,295
Employees in the Netherlands	2,746	3,218	3,702	3,754	3,747
Wages, salaries and social security	493,469	504,298	490,602	466,672	466,476
Funding					
Share capital issued and paid up	68,255	68,194	68,194	67,972	67,910
Share premium account	191,364	190,525	190,525	189,048	188,638
Reserves	673,366	731,971	726,774	745,400	694,637
Capital and reserves	932,985	990,690	985,493	1,002,420	951,185
Provisions	328,627	345,104	331,887	319,498	373,767
Long-term liabilities	92,434	166,896	175,582	68,109	42,333
Current liabilities	900,108	752,615	964,650	754,790	580,407
Liabilities	992,542	919,511	1,140,232	822,899	622,740
Loan capital	1,321,169	1,264,615	1,472,119	1,142,397	996,507
Total capital employed	2,254,154	2,255,305	2,457,612	2,144,817	1,947,692
Debt/equity ratio	0.71	0.78	0.67	0.88	0.95
Capital and reserves per ordinary share of Dfl. 2	27.34	29.06	28.90	29.49	28.01
Capital Employed					
Fixed assets	1,354,328	1,375,174	1,443,391	1,190,335	1,097,549
Stocks	359,143	346,030	393,160	346,341	359,732
Debtors	409,136	375,788	453,775	431,421	374,601
Cash	131,547	158,313	167,286	176,720	115,810
Current assets	899,826	880,131	1,014,221	954,482	850,143
Total assets	2,254,154	2,255,305	2,457,612	2,144,817	1,947,692

1986 dividend: Dfl. 1.30 in cash
1987 dividend: Dfl. 1.30 in cash
1988 dividend: Dfl. 1.30 in cash
1989 dividend: Dfl. 1.30 in cash
1990 dividend: Dfl. 1.30 in cash

Foreword by the Board of Management

The most important objective that the Board of Management set itself in 1989 was to achieve a significant improvement in the company's profits. To achieve this, a highly radical process of change is being implemented. A process which is not only directed at strategic and operational elements, but also affects the way in which Gist-brocades as a whole intends to and has to achieve specific results. Clearly, this process cannot be completed from one day to the next. Both during discussions within the company and in commentary on the company, expressions such as uncertainty, turbulence and change will continue to be heard regularly for a number of years.

In the second half of 1989 we initiated an in-depth reassessment of our operations. An important element of this is an investigation of where we can generate significant added value and how we can use our know-how and skills to hold our own with, and distinguish ourselves from, our competitors. By defining the core activities, we are also able to indicate which activities do not belong or no longer belong within our business. The disposal of Brocacef in 1989 and that of the Pharma Division in 1991, for example, must be seen in this light.

Another important element was an investigation into the reasons for the low profitability of a substantial part of the core activities.

The main conclusions were:

There is not an acceptable balance between existing and new activities, so that we are too dependent on a number of existing products which are already at an advanced stage in their life cycles.

A substantial part of our existing product range consists of 'commodity' products, the success of which is determined to a large extent by the degree to which the supplier is able to market such items at the lowest cost.

To be successful with existing products, but also in particular with new products, it is necessary to improve our knowledge of the market and our skill in tackling that market.

One of our major strengths, the Research & Development department, is insufficiently market-driven.

Further elaboration of this reassessment produced a stream of projects, a number of which already generated results during 1990. Examples are production improvements, efficiency measures and organisational changes, particularly with regard to marketing and the control of Research and Development.

In continuation of this strategic and operational reorientation, aimed at improving profits in the short term, a plan was drawn up, outlining the company's envisaged growth in the medium term.

Successful implementation of all these changes will only be possible if projects are tackled in an effective, result-oriented manner. New patterns of cooperation are being developed for this purpose. We have every confidence that this satisfies an essential precondition for attainment of the ultimate goal.

This process rests on two important cornerstones, namely our experience in the field of biotechnology and the knowledge and loyalty of our employees. These cornerstones form a solid foundation for the improvements that we seek in the short term and for the development of our business in the years ahead.

In view of the radical nature of all strategic and organisational changes, a word of thanks is due more than ever to our employees for their efforts. This also applies to the various works councils, whose contributions have made it possible to carry out the many changes rapidly and effectively.

Despite the adverse impact of a number of political and currency developments, we can report that the expectations expressed for 1990 have been fulfilled.

We are convinced that, provided we pursue with maximum effort the course on which we have embarked, we will achieve our objectives.

H. C. Scheffer
P. J. Strijkert

Review of Operations

Economic Developments

A number of major global developments left a clear mark on Gist-brocades' results in the year under review.

The world economy in 1990 was influenced on the one hand by events in the Middle East and on the other hand by differing economic developments in both the United States and Europe. This affected in particular energy costs, the U.S. dollar, and capital market interest rates.

The Gulf crisis contributed to a strong increase in energy costs in the second half of 1990. In addition, a large proportion of sales to the Middle East were interrupted.

The decline in confidence in the American economy, which was severely tested by the low level of economic activity, was one of the major causes of a downward trend in the dollar exchange rate in 1990.

At the same time, capital market interest rates increased steadily as a result of economic developments in Western Europe, together with German unification.

Developments at Gist-brocades

Analysis of Gist-brocades' product range revealed clearly that it was unbalanced. A few commodity-type products formed a disproportionately large part of turnover, whilst Gist-brocades had an inadequate presence in areas in which, on the basis of its specialisation, the company could be expected to have a very significant presence indeed. Moreover, a number of products had little in common with Gist-brocades' core activities.

During the year, with the start of implementation of the Strategic Business Plan, a large number of measures were set in motion in order to bring about changes in this situation.

A programme was set up to produce and market the commodities, mentioned earlier, as efficiently as possible and at the lowest possible cost. In addition, high priority was given to the development of specialties, which, though produced in relatively small quantities, nevertheless enjoy high margins. Close interaction with the market also provided the impetus for new products.

To the extent strategically possible, products less in keeping with or entirely unsuited to the remainder of the range, were discarded. The development of new activities well suited to the business was accelerated, where appropriate in cooperation with third parties.

A good example of the latter type of activity is the development of the new 3-BMC™ cephalosporin intermediate.

Two events left a special mark on 1990: the proposed transfer of the Pharma Division (pharmaceutical end products) to the Japanese company Yamanouchi Pharmaceutical Co., Ltd. and the winding-up of the IBIS joint venture. Major events which are a direct result of the strategic choices made and which make it clear that the company is willing to accept the consequences of those choices.

The decision to dispose of the Pharma Division was based on two considerations. Firstly this division had insufficient critical mass to achieve independently a position of significance in the pharmaceutical world. The innovative research required to achieve such a position would greatly exceed the reasonably available budgets. Secondly there was also insufficient synergy with Gist-brocades' other divisions, with respect both to the nature of the activities and to the technology.

A careful search was therefore made for a party capable of guaranteeing the division's continuity and hence also the jobs of the employees. Within a relatively short space of time, agreement was reached with Yamanouchi, which took over the whole of the Pharma Division. The final transfer took place on 28 February 1991.

When the IBIS joint venture was started with Shell in 1987, the expectation was that, after a certain introductory period and a quantifiable amount of capital investment, the business would be able to develop sufficient strength to be capable of operating successfully in the Biofine® chemicals market.

However, the development of this market proved to be slower than expected. It also emerged that the necessary development costs were higher than estimated. It was therefore decided by mutual agreement with Shell that the joint venture would be wound up. The enzyme activities will be continued within Gist-brocades in a division bearing the name IBIS. The actual winding-up took place at the end of 1990.

It was also decided to seek a future outside the company for the activities of Gb Biothane International, which pulls together expertise in the area of biological waste water purification.

The attitude of many governments, including that of the Netherlands, to biotechnology, remains an uncertain factor. Their position on this subject is ambivalent. On the one hand they sing the praises of biotechnology as a spearhead industry and source of innovation. On the other hand the approvals policy in numerous countries, including the Netherlands, is characterised by caution and hesita-tion. It is right to demand of the industry that the effectiveness and safety of the products it wishes to market must be fully documented. But this involves the industry in substantial effort and expenditure and should be matched by clear ground rules, consultation opportunities and decision-making procedures.

Financial Information

Net Turnover

Net turnover in 1990 increased by 1.9% in relation to 1989 (after deducting Brocacef from the 1989 figure).

Operating Expenses

Personnel costs amounted to Dfl. 493 million in 1990. The figure for the previous year was Dfl. 504 million. The decrease resulted primarily from the reduction in the number of employees. As a result of the 'Oort' tax changes, the ratio of wages and salaries to social security contributions changed substantially in comparison with 1989. Depreciation remained at the 1989 level.

Operating Profit

Despite a weak dollar and rising energy prices, operating profit was Dfl. 3 million higher than the figure (excluding Brocacef) for 1989. Operating profit in 1990 was in excess of Dfl. 99 million.

The growth of the Food Ingredients product group continued in 1990. Gist-brocades was able to maintain its position in the yeast market, which is still struggling with overcapacity. The other market sectors covered by this product group contributed to a small increase in operating profit.

The product group Industrial Products was severely hampered in 1990 by the lower dollar exchange rate. As a result of better positioning of the products, the decline in operating profit was limited to Dfl. 2 million.

The product group Pharmaceutical Products maintained the level of 1989 (excluding Brocacef).

Progress in New Business Development was in line with expectations.

Financial Expenses

Financial expenses were unchanged in 1989. Total interest-bearing liabilities declined as a result of the release of funds. The resulting reduction in interest expense was cancelled out by higher market interest rates.

Taxation

The average tax burden, expressed as a percentage of profit on ordinary activities, decreased from 20.9% to 16.8%. A number of exempt amounts included in profit on ordinary activities were the major cause of this.

Extraordinary Items

The extraordinary loss after taxation, amounting to Dfl. 1 million, consisted mainly of reorganisation costs.

Net Profit

As a result of the virtual absence of an extraordinary result, net profit was Dfl. 64 million.

Capital Expenditure

Total expenditure on tangible fixed assets amounted to Dfl. 150 million. A significant part of this was spent on efficiency improvement. Of the expenditure on tangible fixed assets, Dfl. 9 million resulted from acquisitions.

Share Capital

Share capital increased by Dfl. 0.1 million to Dfl. 68.3 million in connection with the issue of shares to management in the context of a share purchase plan.

Dividend Proposal

Despite the lower net profit, the proposal to the General Meeting of Shareholders is, as for 1989, to appropriate Dfl. 44.4 million for distribution to shareholders in cash and for Supervisory Directors' emoluments. Dfl. 19.3 million can then be added to the general reserve (1989: Dfl. 47 million). Upon adoption of this proposal, which is based on the expectation that net profit will increase as a result of the initiated restructuring programme, the dividend per Dfl. 2 share will remain unchanged at Dfl. 1.30.

Prospects

General

The prospects for 1991 are determined to a large extent by the development of the dollar exchange rate, interest rates and energy prices. Any forecast made must therefore be subject to serious reservations.

We expect turnover to increase in 1991, after deduction of the turnover of the Pharma Division. Operating profit will decline in 1991. However, as a result of improvement in the financial position, net profit will increase. These forecasts do not take account of extraordinary income and expense.

A number of important activities, commenced in 1990, will reach completion during 1992. The results of such activities will start to become noticeable in the figures from that year.

A Corporate Development Plan, aimed at the medium term, will be completed during 1991. The basis for this plan is formed by the Strategic Business Plan (Stratbus), which is aimed more at the short term and was drawn up in 1990. The Corporate Development Plan will indicate the growth options and areas of expansion for our company for the medium term. It is already clear that growth will take place primarily within the product groups which currently account for Gist-brocades' core activities. This growth will be achieved both organically and by means of acquisitions.

Food Ingredients

The markets for food ingredients, and in particular natural food ingredients, are again expected to develop favourably in 1991. With appropriately geared strategies and a modified, market-oriented organisation, it will therefore be possible for the Food Ingredients Division to increase both turnover and profits in 1991.

The starting premise for this is maintenance of the position of market leadership in bakers' yeast and strengthening of the market position in the growth sectors of the bakery ingredients market in Europe.

Developments in the instant yeast market outside Europe offer opportunities for significant sales growth.

A further increase in turnover is expected, not only for Maxiren®, but also for the existing range of dairy ingredients.

Launches of new natural flavourings are planned for 1991. Further strengthening of our application know-how will make it possible to achieve an increase in turnover and profits in this sector.

Industrial Products

In 1991 this group's traditional products will again have to be sold in a market which is threatened by over-capacity and is sensitive to the dollar. Turnover and profits will therefore remain under pressure. This implies a need for tight control of costs and expenditure. New activities in the area of industrial products require expenditure on know-how, markets and hardware. These activities are not expected to contribute to the product group's profits until 1992.

New Business Development

Prospects for 1991 are favourable. The Agro Business Group, for instance, will be able to launch the enzyme phytase under the name Natuphos® and the pigment Astaxanthin under the name Natupink®. It should also be possible to complete the discussions on Gb Biothane International. The new activity under the name Technology Application Services will start to generate income in 1991.

Finance

There is no need for any call on the capital market.

Personnel

The number of employees will decline as a result of the transfer of the Pharma Division.

CONSOLIDATED PROFIT AND LOSS ACCOUNT FOR 1990

(In thousands of guilders, unless stated otherwise)

	1990		1989	
Net turnover[a]		1,619,571		1,849,503
Change in stocks of finished and semi-manufactured goods	(7,180)		(49,170)	
Other operating income	9,863		7,372	
		2,683		(41,798)
Total operating income		1,622,254		1,807,705
Raw materials and consumables	585,191		773,974	
Wages and salaries	384,924		375,490	
Social security	108,545		128,808	
Depreciation of tangible fixed assets	98,211		98,723	
Other operating expenses	346,044		324,982	
Total operating expenses		1,522,915		1,701,977
Operating profit[a]		99,339		105,728
Interest income	27,605		26,887	
Interest expense	49,054		48,021	
Balance of financial income and expense		(21,449)		(21,134)
Profit on ordinary activities before taxation		77,890		84,594
Tax on profit on ordinary activities		13,082		17,706
Profit on ordinary activities after taxation		64,808		66,888
Extraordinary profit (loss) after taxation		(1,074)		24,571
Net profit for the year		63,734		91,459

[a] The company's 50% share in Brocacef was transferred to ACF on 1 July 1989. Taking this transfer into account, the comparative figures are as follows:

Net turnover	1,619,571	1,588,867
Operating profit	99,339	96,136

CONSOLIDATED BALANCE SHEET AT 31 DECEMBER 1990
AFTER PROFIT APPLICATION

(In thousands of guilders, unless stated otherwise)

ASSETS	1990			1989		
FIXED ASSETS						
Tangible fixed assets						
Land	73,870			73,323		
Buildings including service pipes	399,343			378,359		
Plant and machinery	625,880			635,066		
Other operating fixed assets	46,259			43,614		
Under construction and on order	200,667			198,609		
Not used in the production process	4,477			43,410		
		1,350,496			1,372,381	
Financial fixed assets						
Loans		3,832			2,793	
			1,354,328			1,375,174
CURRENT ASSETS						
Stocks						
Raw materials and consumables	87,437			72,255		
Packaging and technical stores	33,917			28,806		
Finished and semi-manufactured						
goods	237,789			244,969		
		359,143			346,030	
Debtors						
Trade debtors	351,966			330,469		
Other	55,171			41,844		
Prepayments and accrued income	1,999			3,475		
		409,136			375,788	
Securities		5,843			53,389	
Cash		125,704			104,924	
			899,826			880,131
			2,254,154			2,255,305

LIABILITIES	1990		1989	
Capital and reserves		932,985		990,690
PROVISIONS				
Pension commitments	12,037		10,574	
Deferred taxation	192,970		181,044	
Other provisions	123,620		153,486	
		328,627		345,104

(Continued)

LIABILITIES	1990		1989	

LIABILITIES

Long-term liabilities

Private loans	4,137		10,820	
Other creditors	88,297		156,076	
		92,434		166,896

Current liabilities

Banks	78,982		45,912	
Tangible fixed assets on order	49,858		86,260	
Trade creditors	174,780		166,706	
Taxation and social security	6,641		3,348	
Pension liabilities	2,060		3,253	
Other creditors	517,990		383,396	
Accrued liabilities and deferred				
income	822		183	
Repayment of long-term liabilities	24,541		19,128	
Dividend and Supervisory				
Directors' emoluments	44,434		44,429	
		900,108		752,615
			992,542	919,511
			2,254,154	2,255,305

SOURCE OF FUNDS

Net profit for the year	63,734	
Tangible fixed assets:		
Depreciation	98,211	
		161,945

Decrease in current assets:		
Stocks	(13,113)	
Debtors	(33,348)	
Securities	47,546	
		1,085

Increase (decrease) in liabilities:		
Long-term liabilities (decrease)	(74,462)	
Current liabilities (increase)	147,493	
		73,031
		236,061

(Continued)

LIABILITIES	1990	1989

APPLICATION OF FUNDS

Tangible fixed assets:		
Expenditure, net	74,542	
Decrease in provisions		
(Excluding movements on account of		
revaluation of tangible fixed assets)	14,176	
Goodwill	62,570	
Distribution previous year's profit	44,429	
		195,717
Other movements		19,564
		215,281
Increase in cash		20,780

Notes to the Annual Accounts

Accounting Policies

CONSOLIDATION

The consolidated annual accounts include the accounts of group companies, being subsidiaries and joint ventures, with which the Company forms a permanent entity on account of the nature of their operations.

1. Group companies in which the Company has a majority interest are consolidated in full.

2. Joint ventures are those interests in which the Company holds 50% of the share capital; these are consolidated pro rata.

GENERAL

Balance sheet items in foreign currencies are translated into guilders at the rates ruling at the balance sheet date. Capital gains and losses on subsidiaries arising from exchange differences are taken direct to Reserves after allowing for taxation.

The profit and loss accounts of participating interest in foreign currencies are translated at average annual rates. Other exchange differences are taken to profit and loss account.

Intercompany profits included in stocks are eliminated in the consolidation.

Goodwill paid on acquisitions (i.e. the difference between cost and net asset value) is taken to General reserve, net of taxation, if any.

VALUATION

Assets and liabilities are carried at face value, unless stated otherwise.

FIXED ASSETS

Tangible Fixed Assets   Land, buildings (including service pipes) and plant and machinery are carried at current value, allowing for the technical and estimated economic useful lives of the assets concerned. This value is based on regular appraisals by external experts. Other operating fixed assets, including equipment and vehicles, and tangible fixed assets not used in the production process, are carried at cost less depreciation based on the technical and estimated useful lives of the assets concerned.

Tangible fixed assets under construction and on order are stated at cost to balance sheet date plus commitments.

Financial Fixed Assets Participating interests in group companies. Participating interests in group companies are included at net asset value based on the accounting policies in use by the Group.

Loans Loans are stated at face value allowing for bad and doubtful debts. The proportion due within one year is included under Other debtors.

CURRENT ASSETS

Stocks Raw materials and consumables, packaging and technical stores are carried at the lower of cost and market value.

Finished and semi-manufactured goods are carried at the lower of cost and market value, net of a provision for obsolescence.

Receivables Trade debtors are carried at face value, net of a provision for doubtful debts.

Securities Securities are stated at the lower of cost and market value.

CAPITAL AND RESERVES

Revaluation Reserve This reserve forms part of capital and reserves and is adjusted annually for the revaluation of tangible fixed assets, including those of participating interests, after allowing for deferred taxation. Tax owing on the difference between depreciation based on cost and on current value is not expressed in the results but charged to the Provision for deferred taxation annually.

PROVISIONS

The provision for deferred taxation relates to future tax liabilities arising mainly from timing differences on assets and liabilities. It is based on the various countries' current tax rates, except for the provision for Dutch taxes, which

is calculated at a rate of 42%. The provision is included at face value.

The provision for pension commitments, which is included at present value, relates to back service and to commitments not insured with third parties.

Other provisions relate to risks and commitments the amounts of which are uncertain but can be estimated fairly accurately. They include conditional government grants and the provision for reorganisation and restructuring.

Conditional government grants on tangible fixed assets, such as grants under the Investment Account Act (WIR), are credited to operating profit in proportion to the terms of depreciation of the assets concerned.

The provision for reorganisation and restructuring is to cover the cost of measures for improving Group structure and the earning capacity of units requiring improvement in so far as steps have been taken to implement the measures or in so far as they have in principle been decided upon.

LIABILITIES

Long-term liabilities due within one year are included separately under current liabilities.

INCOME AND EXPENSE RECOGNITION

Income and expenses are accounted for at the time the goods or services are supplied.

Net turnover represents goods invoiced and delivered to third parties, net of value added tax and excise duties.

Other operating income consists of royalties from licensing contracts.

Depreciation of land, buildings (including service pipes) and plant and machinery is calculated on current cost at fixed rates based on the expected economic life of the category of asset concerned. Depreciation of equipment and vehicles and of tangible fixed assets not used in the production process is based on historical cost.

Extraordinary income and expenditure consists of items not arising from ordinary activities.

Taxation is calculated on the profit as shown in the annual accounts at the various countries' tax rates allowing for specific corporate income tax relief facilities.

GENERAL

For the accounting policies, we refer to the notes to the company annual accounts.

As the Company's financial data are included in the consolidated accounts, the Company profit and loss account has been prepared in conformity with Art 402, Book 2, of the Dutch Civil Code.

FIXED ASSETS	BOOK VALUE 1 JAN. 1990	EXPENDITURE	DISPOSALS	REVALUATIONS EXCHANGE RATE DIFFERENCES	DEPRECIATION IN FINANCIAL YEAR	BOOK VALUE AT 31 DEC. 1990
TANGIBLE FIXED ASSETS						
Land	73,323	2,000	523	(867)	63	73,870
Buildings including service pipes	378,359	43,362	4,270	(3,123)	14,985	399,343
Plant and machinery	635,066	74,888	23,099	6,921	67,896	625,880
Other fixed assets	43,614	23,053	5,204	41	15,245	46,259
Under construction and on order	198,609	6,327	3,140	(1,129)	—	200,667
Not used in the production process	43,410	351	39,203	(59)	22	4,477
Total	1,372,381	149,981	75,439	1,784	98,211	1,350,496

Gains on the disposal of real estate in 1990 amounted to Dfl. 19,000,000 (1989: Dfl. 5,200,000).

	31-12-1990	31-12-1989
Book value based on current value	1,350,496	1,372,381
Less: revaluation included in book value	270,947	276,426
Book value based on historical cost	1,079,549	1,095,955
Add: accumulated depreciation based on historical cost	658,986	587,469
Historical cost	1,738,535	1,683,424
Current value	2,101,842	2,101,841

The depreciation rates applied to the various categories are:

Buildings including service pipes	2.5%
Plant and machinery	7%
Other operating fixed assets	20–25%
Not used in the production process	0–2.5%

Trends in the valuation of tangible fixed assets indicate that there is a shift towards applying historical cost.

The company is currently investigating whether it would be advisable to follow this trend.

CAPITAL EXPENDITURE	1990	1989
The Netherlands	65,579	45,473
EC excluding		
the Netherlands	58,862	57,534
Total EC	124,441	103,007
Outside Europe	16,721	18,780
	141,162	121,787
Additions of tangible fixed		
assets through		
acquisitions	8,819	12,297
	149,981	134,084

FINANCIAL FIXED ASSETS

These relate solely to loans
to customers
and employees.

LOANS

Loans	4,188	3,052
Repayable within one year	356	259
	3,832	2,793

CURRENT ASSETS

Securities The value of listed securities at 31 December 1990 was Dfl. 2,143,000 (31 December 1989: Dfl. 52,000,000).

Cash Cash at 31 December 1990 includes Dfl. 1,921,003 (31 December 1989: Dfl. 35,435,000) in cash resources of participating interests in which the company has a stake of 50%.

PROVISIONS

All provisions are of a long-term nature. An amount of Dfl. 21,233,000 was charged to the provision for reorganisation and restructuring, which amounted to Dfl. 83,000,000 at 31 December 1989.

LIABILITIES	1990	1989
LONG-TERM LIABILITIES		
PRIVATE LOANS		
(Interest-bearing		
at an average rate		
of 8% payable		
on average by 1994)	4,817	13,236
Repayable within one year	680	2,416
	4,137	10,820
Repayable after five years	4,817	6,721
OTHER CREDITORS		
(Interest-bearing		
at an average rate		
of 9%, repayable		
on average by 1993)	112,158	172,788
Repayable within one year	23,861	16,712
	88,297	156,076
Repayable after five years	11,229	132,484

Other long-term creditors include the following mortgage loans secured by tangible fixed assets:

	1990	1989
	25,279	24,806
Repayable within one year	1,560	1,118
	23,719	23,688
Repayable after five years	—	336

OTHER CREDITORS

These include Dfl. 196,000,000 in commercial paper at 31 December 1990 (31 December 1989: Dfl. 116,000,000). Cash loans at 31 December 1990 amounted to Dfl. 134,000,000 (31 December 1989: nil).

CONDITIONAL COMMITMENTS ARISING FROM GUARANTEES

In addition to the commitments included in the balance sheet, guarantees have been given to an amount of Dfl. 188,975,000 for commitments entered into by third parties.

Notes to the Consolidated Profit and Loss Account

(in thousands of guilders, unless stated otherwise)

TURNOVER BREAKDOWN	1990	1989
TURNOVER BY GEOGRAPHICAL AREAS		
The Netherlands	195,703	453,001
EC excluding the Netherlands	919,616	870,844
Total EC	1,115,319	1,323,845
Rest of Europe	135,718	115,003
Outside Europe	368,534	410,655
	1,619,571	1,849,503
TURNOVER BY PRODUCT GROUP		
Food ingredients	916,636	840,788
Industrial products	463,422	489,319
Pharmaceuticals and Animal Health	233,610	510,847
New Business Development	5,903	6,930
Other products	—	1,619
	1,619,571	1,849,503
OPERATING PROFIT BY PRODUCT GROUP (In millions of guilders)		
Food ingredients	47	45
Industrial products	48	50
Pharmaceuticals and Animal Health	23	30
New Business Development	(19)	(19)
	99	106
PAYROLL COSTS		
This item represents the total of wages, salaries and social security.		
Wages and salaries	384,924	375,490
Pension costs	20,476	23,779
Other social security	88,069	105,029
	493,469	504,298
EMPLOYEES		
The average number of employees is based on the policies used for consolidation.		
Average number of employees	5,833	6,122
In the Netherlands	2,746	3,218

(Continued)

TURNOVER BREAKDOWN	1990	1989
AVERAGE NUMBER OF EMPLOYEES BY PRODUCT GROUP		
Food ingredients	2,794	2,677
Industrial products	1,729	1,834
Pharmaceuticals and Animal Health	1,133	1,452
New Business Development	177	150
Other products	—	9
	5,833	6,122
EXTRAORDINARY INCOME AND EXPENDITURE AFTER TAXES		
Extraordinary income		
Sale of investments and		
participating interests	208	128,361
Taxation	65	560
	143	127,801
Extraordinary expenditure		
Diminution in value of tangible fixed assets		
on account of termination of operations	—	60,000
Reorganisation costs and addition		
to provision for reorganisation		
and restructuring	1,879	95,530
	1,879	155,530
Taxation	(662)	(52,300)
	(1,217)	103,230
Net income (expenditure)	(1,074)	24,571

STATEMENT OF GROUP VALUE ADDED AND ITS ALLOCATION	1990	1989
GROUP VALUE ADDED		
Sources of income		
Net turnover	1,619,571	1,849,503
Other operating income	9,863	7,372
Interest receivable	27,605	26,887
Extraordinary income and expenditure		
before taxation	(1,671)	(27,169)
	1,655,368	1,856,593
Less: raw materials and purchased services	938,415	1,148,126
	716,953	708,467

(Continued)

STATEMENT OF GROUP VALUE ADDED
AND ITS ALLOCATION

	1990		1989	
ALLOCATION OF GROUP VALUE ADDED				
Payroll costs				
Wages, salaries and social security	493,469	69%	504,298	71%
Government				
Taxation	12,485	2%	(34,034)	(5%)
Borrowed funds				
Interest payable	49,054	7%	48,021	7%
Dividend (incl. Supervisory Directors' emoluments)	44,434	6%	44,429	6%
Not distributed				
Depreciation	98,211	14%	98,723	14%
Taken to the reserves	19,300	2%	47,030	7%
	716,953	100%	708,467	100%

CONSOLIDATED BALANCE SHEET AT 31 DECEMBER 1990

Based on Historical Cost and After Profit Appropriation

(In millions of guilders, unless stated otherwise)

ASSETS	1990	1989	LIABILITIES	1990	1989
FIXED ASSETS			*CAPITAL AND RESERVES*	776	830
Tangible fixed assets	1,080	1,096	Provisions	215	229
Financial fixed assets	4	3	*LIABILITIES*		
			Long-term liabilities	93	167
	1,084	1,099	Current liabilities	900	753
				993	920
CURRENT ASSETS					
Stocks	359	346			
Debtors	409	376			
Securities	6	53			
Cash	126	105			
	900	880			
	1,984	1,979		1,984	1,979

COMPANY BALANCE SHEET AT 31 DECEMBER 1990

After Profit Appropriation

(In thousands of guilders, unless stated otherwise)

ASSETS	1990			1989		
FIXED ASSETS						
Tangible fixed assets						
Land	52,120			52,510		
Buildings including service pipes	271,003			263,489		
Plant and machinery	346,178			360,668		
Other operating fixed assets	25,899			23,579		
Under construction and on order	159,483			159,189		
Not used in the production process	33			1,014		
		854,716			860,449	
Financial fixed assets						
Group companies	581,531			564,204		
Loans	3,263			1,379		
		584,794			565,583	
			1,439,510			1,426,032
CURRENT ASSETS						
Stocks						
Raw materials and consumables	17,804			22,489		
Packaging and technical stores	13,541			15,494		
Finished and semi-manufactured goods	109,351			145,898		
	140,696			183,881		
Debtors						
Trade debtors	134,719			143,552		
Group companies	151,587			81,355		
Other debtors	40,129			22,988		
Prepayments and accrued income	—			1,270		
		326,435			249,165	
Securities		3,935			52,150	
Cash		25,887			17,415	
			496,953			502,611
			1,936,463			1,928,643

(*Continued*)

LIABILITIES	1990			1989		
CAPITAL AND RESERVES						
Ordinary shares		90,000			90,000	
Preference shares		90,000			90,000	
Authorised capital unissued:		180,000			180,000	
Ordinary shares	21,745			21,806		
Preference shares	90,000			90,000		
		111,745			111,806	
Share capital issued and paid up		68,255			68,194	
Share premium account (free of Dutch corporate income tax)		191,364			190,525	
Revaluation reserve		202,012			199,025	
General reserve		471,354			532,946	
			932,985			990,690
PROVISIONS						
Pension commitments		7,646			8,012	
Deferred taxation		144,536			147,690	
Other provisions		120,932			151,584	
			273,114			307,286
LIABILITIES						
Long-term liabilities						
Private loans	4,137			10,820		
Other creditors	22,564			22,590		
Group companies	16,666			16,666		
		43,367			50,076	
Current liabilities						
Group companies	80,939			81,724		
Tangible fixed assets on order	34,534			69,968		
Trade creditors	61,941			57,741		
Taxation and social security	9,649			7,854		
Pensions	—			1,689		
Other creditors	454,820			314,770		
Repayment of long-term liabilities	680			2,416		
Dividend and Supervisory Directors' emoluments	44,434			44,429		
		686,997			580,591	
			730,364			630,667

COMPANY PROFIT AND LOSS ACCOUNT FOR 1990

(In thousands of guilders, unless stated otherwise)

	1990	1989
Profit from participating interests	38,600	40,065
Other profit after tax	25,134	51,394
Profit after taxation	63,734	91,459

Notes to the Company Balance Sheet

(In thousands of guilders, unless stated otherwise)

General

For the accounting policies, we refer to the notes to the consolidated annual accounts.

FIXED ASSETS	BOOK VALUE 1 JAN. 1990	EXPENDITURE	DISPOSALS	REVALUATION	DEPRECIATION IN FINANCIAL YEAR	BOOK VALUE AT 31 DEC. 1990
TANGIBLE FIXED ASSETS						
Land	52,510	128	518	—	—	52,120
Buildings including service pipes	263,489	25,880	3,973	(6,297)	8,096	271,003
Plant and machinery	360,668	21,178	8,833	11,123	37,958	346,178
Other operating fixed assets	23,579	11,962	591	—	9,051	25,899
Under construction and on order	159,189	3,434	3,140	—	—	159,483
Not used in the production process	1,014	—	979	—	2	33
Total	860,449	62,582	18,034	4,826	55,107	854,716

	31-12-1990	31-12-1989
Book value based on current value	854,716	860,449
Less: revaluation included in book value	200,581	210,349
Book value based on historical cost	654,135	650,100
Add: accumulated depreciation based on historical cost	387,451	358,385
Historical cost	1,041,586	1,008,485
Current value	1,313,317	1,331,521

(Continued)

The depreciation rates applied to the various categories are:

Buildings including service pipes	2.5%	Other operating fixed assets	20–25%
Plant and machinery	7%	Not used in the production	0–2.5%

FINANCIAL FIXED ASSETS

GROUP COMPANIES

Book value 1 January 1990		564,204
Add: 1990 profit	38,600	
Less: Dividend distribution	5,533	
	33,067	
Capital payments less book value of participating interests sold	7,509	
Change in value owing to exchange rate differences	(15,168)	
Revaluation of tangible fixed assets	4,193	
Goodwill	(12,274)	
		17,327
Book value 31 December 1990		581,531

LOANS

These are loans to customers and employees.

	1990	1989
	3,332	1,511
Repayable within one year	69	132
	3,263	1,379

SECURITIES

The market value of securities at 31 December 1990
was Dfl. 2,143,000.
(31 December 1989: Dfl. 52,000,000).

CAPITAL AND RESERVES	SHARE CAPITAL ISSUED AND PAID-UP	SHARE PREMIUM ACCOUNT	REVALUATION RESERVE	GENERAL RESERVE	CAPITAL AND RESERVES
1 January 1990	68,194	190,525	199,025	532,946	990,690
Undistributed 1990 profit	—	—	—	19,300	19,300
Increase in share capital	61	—	—	—	61
Share premium on capital increase	—	839	—	—	839
Goodwill	—	—	—	(62,570)	(62,570)
Addition to revaluation reserve	—	—	2,987	—	2,987
Movements in value of participating interests owing to exchange rate differences (net)	—	—	—	(18,322)	(18,322)
31 December 1990	68,255	191,364	202,012	471,354	932,985

In the context of a share purchase plan for the management, the company, by means of a private placement, issued 30,456 shares of Dfl. 2 nominal value each at a price of Dfl. 29.55 per share. Payment was effected in cash.

The share premium was added to the share premium account. The depositary receipts meanwhile issued for these shares may not be sold by the holders for a period of five years.

Provisions

All provisions are of a long-term nature.

Liabilities

LONG-TERM LIABILITIES

For more detailed information about the private loans and other liabilities we refer to the notes to the consolidated balance sheet.

CURRENT LIABILITIES

For more detailed information we refer to the notes to the consolidated balance sheet.

Supervisory Directors' Emoluments

Supervisory Directors' emoluments for 1990 totalled Dfl. 206,000 (1989: Dfl. 241,000), consisting of fixed remunerations of Dfl. 137,000 and a share in the profit of Dfl. 69,000.

Managing Directors' and Former Managing Directors' Emoluments

Emoluments to managing directors and former managing directors amounted to Dfl. 1,283,000 in 1990 (1989: Dfl. 2,626,000).

Loans and Guarantees to Managing Directors

In the context of a share purchase plan, the company issued loans and guarantees to man-

aging directors to a total amount of Dfl. 400,000. The loans bear no interest and are to be repaid in 1996 at the latest.

Commitments Not Disclosed in the Balance Sheet

In addition to the commitments disclosed in the balance sheet, guarantees totalling Dfl. 105,254,000 have been provided to third parties and group companies for commitments entered into.

Principal Group Companies and Joint Ventures

THE NETHERLANDS

B.V. Pharmaceutische Fabrieken v/h
  Brocades-Stheeman & Pharmacia, Meppel
Brocachemie B.V., Meppel
Exter Holding B.V., Zaandam (50%)
Gist-brocades B.V., Dordrecht
Gist-brocades Farma B.V., Rijswijk
Nederlandse Gist-en Spiritusfabriek B.V., Delft
International Bio-Synthetics B.V., Rijswijk

BELGIUM

Gist-brocades N.V., Bruges
International Bio-Synthetics N.V., Bruges

CURAÇAO

Gist-brocades International N.V., Willemstad

DENMARK

Gist-brocades Pharmaceuticals A/S, Glostrup

FRANCE

Gist-brocades France S.A., Prouvy
Gist-brocades Pharma S.A., Paris
Littorale Oenologie S.A., Béziers

GERMANY

Rheinische Presshefe- und Spritwerke
  G.m.b.H.,
Monheim

Uniferm G.m.b.H.& Co., Hefefabrik, Werne (50%)

Gist-brocades Pharma G.m.b.H., Heidelberg

ITALY

Gist-brocades Farma S.p.A., Milan

Gist-brocades S.p.A., Milan

PORTUGAL

Gist-brocades Lda., Matosinhos

SPAIN

Gist-brocades S.A., Barcelona

SWITZERLAND

Gist-brocades A.G., Zurich

UNITED KINGDOM

British Fermentation Products Ltd., Brentwood

Brocades (Great Britain) Ltd., West Byfleet

Paines & Byrne Ltd., Greenford

UNITED STATES

Gist-brocades Food Ingredients, Inc., King of Prussia (PA)

International Bio-Synthetics Inc., Charlotte (NC)

Unless stated otherwise, the list gives the legal entities and companies for which Royal Gist-brocades nv provides, either direct or indirect, 100% of the capital.

The complete list with the information referred to in Article 379, Book 2, of the Dutch Civil Code has been filed at the Company Registry in Delft and is available for inspection.

APPENDIX 14-3

Understanding International Differences in Leverage Trends

After a remarkable period of stability in the ratio of aggregate debt to economic activity in the United States, this ratio and various other measures of leverage rose in the 1980s. In earlier decades, trends in public and private sector debt had tended to offset each other; over the past several years, however, both forms of debt have increased.[1] Observers have responded to these developments with apprehension. Some worry that high leverage in the corporate sector would restrict the ability of firms to adjust to adverse developments and thus would heighten macroeconomic instability.[2] Others suggest that in a sharp downturn the higher levels of debt could lead first to a wave of bankruptcies and then to a general liquidity crisis.[3]

Source: Eli Remolona, "Understanding International Differences in Leverage Trends," *FRBNY Quarterly Review,* Spring 1990.

[1] Benjamin M. Friedman, "Increasing Indebtedness and Financial Stability in the United States," in *Debt, Financial Stability and Public Policy,* Federal Reserve Bank of Kansas City, 1986; E.P. Davis, *Rising Sectoral Debt/Income Ratios: A Cause for Concern?* BIS Economic Papers, no. 20, June 1987.

[2] See, for example, Henry Kaufman, "Debt: The Threat to Economic and Financial Stability," in *Debt, Financial Stability and Public Policy.*

[3] See, for example, Ben S. Bernanke and John Y. Campbell, "Is There a Corporate Debt Crisis?" *Brookings Papers on Economic Activity,* 1: 1988.

Researchers who follow international developments have noted that other major market economies have not experienced a similar rise in leverage.[4] Yet these economies have been riding the current business cycle roughly in tandem with the United States. Moreover, other factors that might influence leverage, such as interest rates and stock prices, have also been correlated across countries.

This article investigates why leverage trends in the United States have differed from those in other countries. Distinguishing the developments underlying the U.S. experience from developments abroad may help clarify the extent to which high leverage is a problem. If leverage has risen in the United States only because investment has so exceeded internal funds that much debt financing has been required, then the situation might not be cause for concern. As long as the funds have been invested well and no adverse shocks arise, the investment should generate cash flows in the future to bring leverage back down.

The data presented here show that declines in leverage abroad have tended to be associated with reductions of short-term debt. An analysis of firm-level data suggests that this pattern is consistent with the so-called pecking-order hypothesis, which links a decline in leverage to strong internal cash flows relative to investment. In Germany and France, leverage among large firms has fallen sharply, precisely because they have had very favorable cash flows. In Japan, aggregate leverage has declined because cash-rich firms have been scrupulously retiring debt. The puzzle is why leverage has risen for large U.S. firms, which have had reasonably strong cash flows relative to investment.

This article stresses the finding that much of the rise in U.S. leverage has been due to a buildup of long-term debt, particularly by firms that have been borrowing heavily in order to buy back their own common stock. Reacting, perhaps, to perceived threats of takeover, some firms have been raising their leverage sharply through stock buybacks.

The article begins with a fuller description of recent international trends in leverage. The next section provides a brief discussion of existing theories of leverage. The third section presents estimates of leverage-target behavior to assess the degree to which taxes, interest rates, or stock prices can explain the recent trends. A direct test of the pecking-order hypothesis follows; the object of this section is to evaluate whether strength of cash flows can account for the differences in leverage trends. The article concludes with a brief interpretation of the results.

Global Patterns of Leverage

The Familiar Ratios

Table 1 reports book-value debt-to-asset ratios familiar to researchers who have tried to compare leverage in different countries.[5] The ratios reported here are based on data from the Banque de Comptes Harmonisées (BACH) database maintained by the European Commission in Brussels, but they tend to be very close to ratios based on the usual OECD financial statistics and the various official flow-

---

[4]See Claudio E.V. Borio, "Leverage and Financing of Nonfinancial Companies: An International Perspective," Paper presented at the Eighteenth MSG Conference on Financial Markets and Policy, Brasenose College, Oxford, September 19–21, 1989.

[5]The analysis here explains leverage in terms of the book values of debt and assets instead of market values. This approach is justified on two counts. First, survey evidence shows that most corporate financial executives use book values for setting leverage targets: see A. Stonehill and others, "Financial Goals and Debt Ratio Determinants: A Survey of Practice in Five Countries," *Financial Management*, Autumn 1977, pp. 27–41. Second, other researchers have found that it makes little difference whether market or book values are used: see Paul Marsh, "The Choice Between Equity and Debt: An Empirical Study," *Journal of Finance*, March 1982, pp. 121–44; and Robert A. Taggart, "A Model of Corporate Financing Decisions," *Journal of Finance*, December 1977, pp. 1467–84.

Table 1 BOOK-VALUE DEBT–ASSET RATIOS OF NONFINANCIAL FIRMS (Percent)

	1982	1983	1984	1985	1986	1987
France	69.2	70.7	76.6	73.3	71.0	70.2
Germany	62.0	60.9	59.7	58.6	57.1	
Italy	70.4	68.2	67.5	67.0	67.3	66.9
Japan	73.4	73.2	72.6	71.5	70.5	70.1
Netherlands	55.4	55.2	53.9	54.3	52.4	52.3
United Kingdom	47.9	47.6	48.1	47.6	46.6	
United States		39.4	40.6	42.2	43.3	44.3

SOURCE: Banque de Comptes Harmonisées (data collected by the European Commission from official sources and "harmonized" to correct for differences in data collection and to make comparisons possible).

Note: The composition of each country's sample is as follows:

France—Firms with 500 or more employees, unconsolidated.

Germany—Over 70,000 corporations, sole proprietorships, and partnerships; unconsolidated.

Italy—Mostly industrial firms and a few construction firms, unconsolidated.

Japan—All nonfinancial firms, unconsolidated.

Netherlands—Nonfinancial firms, consolidated.

United Kingdom—Large firms, consolidated.

United States—All nonfinancial firms, excluding construction and services, consolidated.

of-funds statistics.[6] The computation of these ratios follows OECD convention in including accounts payable in the definition of debt, along with short-term and long-term debt. The argument for this inclusion is the importance of accounts payable on balance sheets in such countries as France, Italy, and Japan.[7]

The ratios confirm the common distinction between low-leverage and high-leverage countries. France, Germany, Italy, and Japan have higher leverage, while the United Kingdom and the United States have lower leverage. The Netherlands seems to belong in the middle. These differences appear to be due to differences in financial practices, not to differences in the mix of industries within a country.[8]

[6]See, for example, Janette Rutterford, "An International Perspective on the Capital Structure Puzzle," in J.M. Stern and D.H. Chew, eds., *New Developments in Corporate Finance* (Oxford: Basil Blackwell, 1988), pp. 194–207.

[7]For this sample of companies, accounts payable are on the order of 30 percent of assets for France, Italy, and Japan. In the sample of larger companies represented in Chart 1, accounts payable on average amount to 15 percent of assets for France and 20 percent for Japan.

[8]For a discussion of differences in financial systems, see Robert N. McCauley and Steven Zimmer, "Explaining International Differences in the Cost of Capital," Federal Reserve Bank of New York *Quarterly Review*, Summer 1989, pp. 7–28. For a study showing that differences in leverage are not due to differences in industrial mix, see Joëlle Laudy and Daniel Szpiro, "Des Entreprises Industrielles Plus Endettées en France que dans les Autres Pays Européens," *Economie et Statistique*, no. 217/218 (1989).

Of greater interest, however, are the trends in leverage and, in particular, the emergence of the United States as the only country with consistently rising leverage. Leverage in France was initially rising but has been declining since 1984. Leverage in the United Kingdom has stayed within a fairly narrow range. In Germany, Italy, Japan and the Netherlands, leverage has clearly been falling. The trends indicate some convergence between high-leverage and low-leverage countries. However, while Japan, Italy, and France have had the highest leverage ratios, Germany's ratio has declined the fastest.

Publicly Traded Industrial Companies

The representation of leverage trends in Chart 1 is based on Global Vantage data on publicly traded industrial companies.[9] The analyses below rely on these data for information at the firm level. Use of these data, instead of the official flow-of-funds statistics, makes it possible to focus on larger firms, which can be more readily compared across countries because of their similar degree of access to capital markets. The leverage ratios shown in the chart are computed with accounts payable included in the definition of debt, as in Table 1, but also with provisions for pension liabilities subtracted from assets, because these provisions are not reported on balance sheets in the United States.[10] The firms selected for analysis are limited to those for which a complete set of observations is available to construct the cash flow estimates used later, although use of larger samples from Global Vantage will produce the same leverage patterns.

[9]Global Vantage (Standard and Poor's international version of Compustat) draws data from financial statements of publicly traded industrial companies.

[10]Provisions for pension liabilities are most significant for German firms: the item amounts to an average of 15 percent of firm assets.

Chart 1

Ratios of Debt to Assets for Publicly Traded Industrial Companies

Short-term debt has accounted for much of the decline in leverage in some countries ...

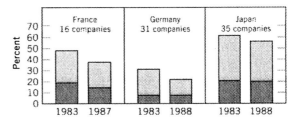

... while long-term debt has accounted for much of the rise in leverage in Australia and the United States.

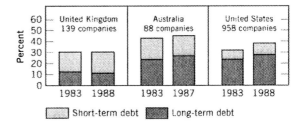

Source: Basic data are drawn from Standard and Poor's Global Vantage.

A comparison of the figures in Table 1 with those in Chart 1 shows substantial differences in leverage levels between samples, but the trends in leverage remain basically the same. The generally lower leverage ratios in Chart 1 suggest that large firms are much less leveraged than small firms in a given country. Indeed, the Global Vantage data now show large German firms to have lower leverage ratios than large U.S. firms. The chart includes leverage ratios for Australia, and these show higher leverage than the ratios for France or Germany. In spite of the differences between the two data sets, the trends persist and in fact become more striking with the Global Vantage data. The United Kingdom and Australia both show a slight rise in leverage, but the United States still stands apart because of the marked rise in its leverage. Note that this rise in U.S. leverage cannot be attributed directly to leveraged buyouts (LBOs), since Global Vantage data include only firms that have remained public. France and Germany show sharper declines in leverage than before.

Short-term and Long-term Debt

Chart 1 also divides the leverage ratios into short-term debt and long-term debt components. In France and Germany, large firms have achieved a sharp decline in total leverage mainly by reducing short-term debt as a ratio to assets. In Japan, the decline in total leverage has been more modest, but the reduction in short-term debt has been just as apparent. In the United Kingdom, total leverage has remained essentially unchanged, while the ratio of short-term debt to assets has risen slightly. In Australia and the United States, a rise in leverage has been associated with a rise in long-term debt.

The broad pattern appears to be that in countries with falling leverage, the decline can be attributed to short-term debt, while in countries with rising leverage the increase can be traced to long-term debt.

Theories of Capital Structure

Can existing theories of capital structure explain differences in leverage behavior across countries? Can the theories explain the association of falling leverage with short-term debt and rising leverage with long-term debt? It is useful to distinguish two approaches to analyzing how firms determine leverage. One approach sees firms as trying to achieve a leverage target or an optimal capital structure. The other approach sees a firm's capital structure as a by-product of a history of financing decisions, in which the firm has in every period matched its uses of funds with the cheapest sources it could find. The two approaches are discussed in greater detail below.

The Leverage-target Approach

Under the first approach, the optimal capital structure or leverage target depends on such factors as conditions in capital and credit markets, the tax treatment of returns on different assets, the riskiness of the firms' earnings, the costs of financial distress, and various agency problems associated with debt and equity.[11] The costs of financial distress include the loss of flexibility experienced by a firm having difficulty servicing its debt, as well as the trustee and legal fees and reorganization costs incurred if the situation deteriorates into bankruptcy. Agency problems with debt arise when firms have an incentive to choose riskier projects against the interest of creditors, while agency problems with equity occur when firms have an incentive to spend on managerial prerequisites against the interest of shareholders.

Indirect evidence for the existence of leverage targets is provided by the finding that average leverage ratios for broad industry groups tend to be consistent over time.[12] Direct evidence for particular models remains hard to find, however, perhaps because unobservable agency costs are critical explanatory variables.[13] For example, efforts to explain differences in leverage across countries in terms of tax differences alone have largely failed. In general, there is little correlation between the ranking of countries according to the relative tax advantage of debt over equity and their ranking according to leverage.[14] Hence expla-

[11]For a summary of this literature, see Colin Mayer, "New Issues in Corporate Finance," *European Economic Review*, vol. 32 (1988), pp. 1167–89.

[12]Ezra Solomon, *The Theory of Financial Management* (New York: Columbia University Press, 1963), pp. 91–106.

[13]This lack of evidence led Stewart Myers to the subject of his presidential address to the American Finance Association, "The Capital Structure Puzzle," *Journal of Finance*, vol. 39 (July 1984), pp. 575–92.

[14]See Mayer, "New Issues"; Rutterford, "An International Perspective"; and Borio, "Leverage and Financing."

nations often turn to special institutional factors—for example, the system of universal banking in Germany or the organization of *keiretsus* (groups of companies with cross-holding of shares) in Japan—which somehow provide more effective ways of dealing with financial distress or agency problems of debt.

The Pecking-order Approach

Under the second approach, the determination of leverage hinges on the strength of cash flows. The formal statement of this approach is the so-called pecking-order hypothesis developed by Myers and Majluf.[15] The theory assumes that managers know more about the firm than do outside investors. Since managers are less likely to issue new stock if they regard existing shares as undervalued than if they regard the shares as overpriced, investors will regard a decision to issue stock as a sign of possible "bad" news. Thus, firms can only issue equity at a discount, and cash flows will normally be a cheaper source of funds than external equity. The asymmetry of information will also make debt financing cheaper than external equity, simply because debt contracts are safer in that they limit the possible ways by which holders could lose. Hence, to finance investment, firms will first use cash flows as the cheapest source, then debt financing, and finally outside equity financing (see Box 1 for an illustration). In short, the stronger the cash flows relative to investment, the less likely the firms will turn to debt and the more likely leverage will fall.

Thus far the evidence for the pecking-order theory, like the evidence for leverage targets, has been indirect only. For example, the finding that cash flow is a significant determinant of investment indicates that there is indeed an

[15]Stewart C. Myers and Nicholas S. Majluf, "Corporate Financing and Investment Decisions When Firms Have Information Investors Do Not Have," *Journal of Financial Economics*, vol. 13 (1984), pp. 187–221.

Box 1:

A Graphical Exposition

The chart below illustrates pecking-order behavior for different levels of investment demand. Abstracting from dividend payments, a firm with the weak investment demand I_1 would finance investment entirely with internal funds and use the remaining cash flow to retire debt. With the stronger investment demand I_2, the firm would invest all its cash flow and then turn to debt financing. With the still stronger investment demand I_3, the firm would use internal funds, debt financing, and outside equity, although the cases in which firms actually turn to outside equity are considered relatively uncommon. The interesting case occurs when investment demand happens to be I_4, falling in the gap between the costs of internal and external finance. In this case investment would be constrained by cash flow. While the return to investment would be high enough to justify further cash flow financing, it would fall short of the hurdle rate for any borrowing.

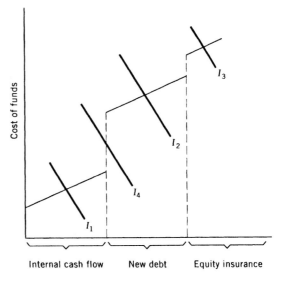

Pecking-order behavior.
The cost of funds for varying investment demands

important distinction between internal and external finance.[16] Another form of indirect evidence is the strong inverse correlation between profitability and leverage.[17] If profitability is correlated with cash flow, then this result indicates that firms with strong cash flow avoid borrowing, consistent with pecking-order behavior.

The Two Approaches Together

In practice, firms must decide on capital structure and financing at the same time. One can imagine firms to be constantly seeking their optimal capital structure but often finding themselves bumped away by shocks to cash flow. Unexpectedly good earnings would put a firm below its leverage target, and the firm would then try to raise its debt ratio over time, perhaps by making investment plans that would require much debt financing. An adverse shock to cash flow would put the firm above its target; to reduce leverage, the firm might then postpone large investments.

The empirical results reported in the next two sections suggest somewhat more subtle behavior. Analysis of Global Vantage data for four major countries in the 1980s indicates that leverage-target considerations determine the ratio of long-term debt to assets, while pecking-order considerations determine the ratio of total debt to assets.[18] Together, these results mean that firms manage their long-term debt to achieve an optimal capital structure while they adjust short-term debt to accommodate cash-flow shocks. The link between cash flows and short-term debt makes sense to the extent that shocks to cash flow are transitory, since the transactions costs for both issuing and retiring debt are much lower for short-term debt than for long-term debt.

This pattern of behavior implies that in France, Germany, and Japan, where major firms have been reducing primarily short-term debt, strong cash flows would explain the decline in leverage. In Australia and the United States, where corporations have been taking on largely long-term debt, something other than weak cash flows would be needed to explain the rise in leverage.

Leverage-target Behavior

To evaluate the extent to which interest rates and stock prices can explain recent trends in leverage, this section presents estimates of leverage-target behavior. Leverage is specified in terms of both total debt and long-term debt. The leverage target is specified to depend on the observable costs of debt and equity and on a proxy for the costs of financial distress. Overall, the empirical results for leverage-target behavior are less than impressive for explaining the trends in leverage. To the extent that observable cost factors can explain such behavior in the 1980s, however, they appear to work better when leverage is measured in terms of long-term debt than when leverage is measured in terms of total debt.[19]

The estimating equations assume gradual adjustment by firms to the leverage target. Formally, the adjustment is described by $\Delta d =$

[16]See Steven M. Fazzari, R. Glenn Hubbard, and Bruce C. Petersen, "Financing Constraints and Corporate Investment," *Brookings Papers on Economic Activity*, 1: 1988, pp. 141–206. See also Richard Cantor, "A Panel Study of the Effects of Leverage on Investment and Employment," in *Studies on Financial Changes and the Transmission of Monetary Policy*, Federal Reserve Bank of New York, May 1990.

[17]W. Carl Kester, "Capital and Ownership Structure: A Comparison of United States and Japanese Corporations," *Financial Management*, Spring 1986, pp. 5–16; and John Baskin, "An Empirical Investigation of the Pecking Order Hypothesis," *Financial Management*, Spring 1989, pp. 26–35.

[18]Firms may have leverage targets for total debt as well, but the adjustment may happen too slowly to be detected.

[19]This result is consistent with Donaldson's finding that the most common measure of debt capacity used by U.S. corporations is the ratio of long-term debt to capitalization. See Gordon Donaldson, *Corporate Debt Capacity*, Harvard Business School Division of Research, 1961.

$\lambda(d^* - d_{-1})$, where d is the ratio of debt to assets, d^* is the desired ratio, d_{-1} is the previous period's debt-asset ratio, and λ is the adjustment coefficient, with $\lambda = 1$ implying complete adjustment in a fiscal year. Here the amount of adjustment is proportional to the difference between desired and actual leverage. The desired ratio is then specified as a function, $d^* = f(c^D, c^E, c^{FD})$, where c^D, c^E, and c^{FD} are the costs of debt, equity, and financial distress, respectively. Since Δd is $d - d_{-1}$, the estimating equation can be written as $d = \lambda f(c^D, c^E, c^{FD}) + (1 - \lambda)d_{-1}$. The cost of debt would have a negative effect on leverage, the cost of equity a positive effect, and the costs of financial distress a negative effect.

The equations are estimated for Germany, Japan, the United Kingdom, and the United States for the period covering the fiscal years from 1983 to 1988. The estimates are based on panel data from Global Vantage and use the same sample of firms used for the leverage ratios in Chart 1. The cost of debt is measured as the real interest rate on corporate bonds minus the product of the corporate tax rate and the nominal interest rate.[20] The cost of equity is measured as the ratio of cash flow per share to the stock price for each firm. The results tend not to be sensitive to the way in which the costs of debt and equity are measured. For the costs of financial distress, the equations use the ratio of fixed assets to total assets as a proxy negatively related to these costs.[21]

[20] For a fuller explanation of the variables, see Eli M. Remolona, "Why International Trends in Leverage Have Been So Different," Federal Reserve Bank of New York, Working Paper no. 9002, February 1990.

[21] In justifying this proxy as a measure of the value of tangible assets available for liquidation in case of bankruptcy, Long and Malitz argue that the costs of financial distress are associated largely with the loss of intangible assets. See Michael S. Long and Ileen B. Malitz, "Investment Patterns and Financial Leverage," in Benjamin Friedman, ed., *Corporate Capital Structure in the United States* (Chicago: University of Chicago Press, 1985), pp. 325–48.

Total Debt

Table 2*a* reports the leverage-target equations for total debt. The costs of debt and equity for Germany, Japan, and the United Kingdom show signs contrary to those predicted by theory. Given that the cost of equity is measured as the ratio of cash flow to stock price, the minus sign on this variable may in fact be picking up pecking-order behavior, with strong cash flows tending to reduce leverage. The equation for the United States gives the theoretically correct signs, but the coefficient is significant only for the cost of equity. In all cases, the equations show the wrong sign for the ratio of fixed assets to total assets, a variable which should have a positive effect on leverage if it is an inverse proxy for the costs of financial distress. The final disappointment is that the coefficients on the lagged debt–asset ratio for German, Japanese, and U.K. firms are not significantly different from one, implying to discernible adjustment towards a leverage target.

Long-term Debt

On the whole, estimates of leverage-target behavior in terms of long-term debt yield modestly more favorable results than estimates in terms of total debt. For the United States, however, it seems to make a difference whether firms buying back their stock are included in the sample. Table 2*b* reports a second set of estimates for the United States that excludes cash-rich U.S. firms using long-term debt to finance stock buybacks.[22] Stock buybacks have become an important U.S. phenomenon, and it would be of interest to know whether they represent a separate kind of leveraging behavior. When even cash-rich firms go deeper into debt to finance buybacks,

[22] This study defines "cash-rich" firms as those whose measured cash flows exceed predicted investment and dividends, with the prediction based on sales and lagged dividends.

Table 2a LEVERAGE-TARGET EQUATIONS FOR TOTAL DEBT
(Dependent Variable Is the Ratio of Total Debt to Assets)

Explanatory Variable	Germany	Japan	United Kingdom	United States
Constant	0.0254	0.0658	0.1045	0.1993
	(1.6076)[a]	(2.0184)	(3.2453)	(12.7756)
Cost of debt	1.3425	0.4784	1.4295	−0.2964
	(1.6388)	(0.3489)	(1.9813)	(−0.4984)
Cost of equity	−0.0021	−0.1183	−0.1308	0.0371[b]
	(−0.8750)	(−3.4794)	(−6.5729)	(3.0917)
Lagged fixed	−0.0323	−0.1448	−0.522	−0.0377
to total assets	(−0.7341)	(−2.5134)	(−1.2429)	(−1.7700)
Lagged long-term	0.9524	1.0517	0.9712	0.6458[b]
debt to assets	(−1.4783)	(1.5029)	(−0.5125)	(−16.6291)
F	1.547	4.874	13.622	79.579
Adjusted R2	0.012	0.082	0.022	0.052
n	185	173	2,291	5,777

[a]The t-values for the null hypotheses are in parentheses.
[b]Correct sign and significance at the 5 percent level.

Table 2b LEVERAGE-TARGET EQUATIONS FOR LONG-TERM DEBT
(Dependent Variable Is the Ratio of Long-Term Debt to Assets)

Explanatory Variable	Germany	Japan	United Kingdom	United States Full Sample	United States Without Buyback Firms
Constant	0.0072	0.0287	0.0127	0.0548	0.0297
	(1.2632)[a]	(2.0648)	(4.2333)	(10.1481)	(6.1875)
Cost of debt	0.1677	−0.2196	−0.0830	−0.2188	−0.1899
	(0.4712)	(−0.3402)	(−0.8755)	(−1.0069)	(−1.0544)
Cost of equity	−0.0004	0.0078	−0.0003	0.0103[b]	−0.0178
	(−0.4000)	(0.4937)	(−0.1154)	(2.3409)	(−4.3415)
Lagged fixed	0.0060	−0.0267	0.0184[b]	0.1481[b]	0.0564[b]
to total assets	(0.2985)	(−0.9744)	(3.4074)	(18.5125)	(7.7260)
Lagged long-term	0.8806[a]	0.8836[b]	0.7912[b]	0.4436[b]	0.7943[b]
debt to assets	(−2.9337)	(−3.1290)	(16.5714)	(−65.4588)	(−21.2062)
F	2.382	3.200	69.044	1,061.232	124.294
Adjusted R2	0.029	0.048	0.106	0.423	0.101
n	185	173	2,291	5,777	5,485

[a]The t-values for the null hypotheses are in parentheses.
[b]Correct sign and significance at the 5 percent level.

such behavior may reflect an effort to leverage up and not just to substitute for dividends.[23] The exclusion of these buyback firms from the U.S. sample reduces the explanatory power of the costs of debt and equity in the leverage-target equations.

With leverage measured in terms of long-term debt, the estimated effects of the cost of debt for Japan, the United Kingdom, and both U.S. samples now have the correct sign, although in no case is the effect statistically significant. The estimated effects of the cost of equity have the right sign for Japan and the U.S. full sample (with statistical significance in the case of the latter), but the sign is reversed when the buyback firms are excluded for the United States. This time the ratio of fixed assets to total assets works as a negative proxy for the costs of financial distress for the United Kingdom and both U.S. samples.[24] The coefficients on the lagged debt-asset ratio now indicate significant adjustment towards a leverage target, whether or not the sample shows rising leverage over the period. The coefficients suggest that German and Japanese firms adjust their capital structures about 12 percent a year towards their leverage targets, British firms adjust 21 percent a year, and American firms adjust about 56 percent a year.

The sample period may have been too short to allow enough variation in interest rates and stock prices to show marked effects on leverage trends.[25] Nonetheless, the fact that the long-term debt equations work better than the total debt equations suggests that long-term debt is probably what is determined by leverage-target behavior.

Pecking-order Behavior

The pecking-order hypothesis explains why firms might rationally let cash flows determine leverage. If managers are seen as having an informational advantage, outside investors will demand a return premium that will make internal cash flows a cheaper source of financing than external funds. Thus firms will use up their cash flow before they turn to debt, so that strong cash flows relative to investment will tend to lead to a decline in leverage.

Aggregate Data on Cash Flows and Financing

Table 3 shows how large corporations in six countries actually matched their sources and uses of funds in the 1980s. The sources are internal cash flow and external finance. The uses are investment and dividends. A negative residual suggests that total identified financing is short of total known uses.[26] The negative residuals indicate that it is easier to underestimate cash flow than to overestimate it (see Box 2 for the measurement of cash flow).

In most cases, relatively strong cash flows in the aggregate seem to accompany declines in leverage, a finding which is consistent with the pecking-order hypothesis. In the case of Australian firms, even counting the large negative residual as unidentified additional cash flow would result in cash flows weak enough to be somewhat consistent with the modest rise in their total leverage during the period.

---

[23] Bagwell and Shoven view stock buybacks as a substitute for dividend payments. See Laurie S. Bagwell and John B. Shoven, "Cash Distributions to Shareholders," *Journal of Economic Perspectives*, vol. 3 (Summer 1989), pp. 129–40.

[24] In *Corporate Debt Capacity*, Donaldson finds that debt contracts often limit new long-term borrowing to a percentage of tangible assets.

[25] To reduce multicollinearity, the costs of debt and equity were combined in a single ratio, but the results were not substantially better. Logarithmic transformations also failed to improve results.

[26] Sources and uses do not always balance because most of the figures are constructed from income statements and balance sheets, not from flow of funds statements.

Table 3 SOURCES AND USES OF FUNDS IN SIX COUNTRIES[a]
(Averages over the Period, Percent of Total Sources)

	Australia 1984–87	France 1983–87	Germany 1983–87	Japan 1984–88	United Kingdom 1983–88	United States 1983–88
Sources						
Internal cash flow	34.6	88.7	104.6	63.2	82.5	77.7
External finance	65.4	11.3	−4.6	36.8	17.5	22.4
Short-term debt[b]	16.5	6.6	−9.4	22.2	−9.3	5.3
Long-term debt	39.0	1.4	2.3	10.7	9.4	15.4
Equity	9.8	3.3	2.6	3.9	17.4	1.9
Uses						
Investment[c]	121.4	105.2	92.6	99.3	83.3	73.8
Dividends	13.1	9.1	9.5	6.2	15.3	23.5
Residual	−34.4	−14.2	−2.1	−5.5	1.4	2.7

[a] The sample of companies corresponds to that in Chart 1.

[b] Short-term debt includes accounts payable.

[c] Investment includes fixed capital, inventory stocks, acquisitions, and financial assets.

See Box 2 for the components of cash flow.

SOURCE OF BASIC DATA: Standard and Poor's Global Vantage.

Box 2

Measurement of Cash Flows

Financial statement data from Global Vantage allow the estimation of cash flows by a procedure suggested by Cottle, Murray, and Block.[1] This procedure adds back to reported after-tax earnings those reported expenses that drain no cash—expenses such as depreciation of fixed assets, amortization of intangibles, increases in deferred taxes, and additions to provisions and reserves. The reason for this adjustment is that reported earnings alone are not always an adequate measure of cash flow. As the table below shows, for most of the countries, and especially for France and Germany, charges to depreciation of fixed assets and amortization of intangibles are a more important source of cash flow than earnings. In the case of Germany, additions to provisions and reserves represent nearly twice as much cash flow as earnings. Moreover, increases in deferred taxes, although not nearly as important as earnings, can also be a significant component of cash flow.

COMPONENTS OF MEASURED CASH FLOW (Percent of Measured Cash Flow)

	Australia 1984–87	France 1983–87	Germany 1983–87	Japan 1984–88	United Kingdom 1983–88	United States 1983–88
Earnings after taxes[a]	79.2	37.8	16.6	48.7	80.8	47.6
Depreciation and amortization	51.2	59.5	59.8	62.3	32.5	52.5
Provisions and reserves	2.3	9.7	31.0	4.0	0.6	—
Deferred taxes	9.8	7.9	0.8	0.8	1.0	7.2
Accounts receivable	−42.5	−14.9	−8.3	−15.8	−15.0	−7.3

[a] Earnings include extraordinary items.

[1] Sidney Cottle, Roger F. Murray, and Frank E. Block, *Security Analysis*, 5th ed. (New York: McGraw-Hill, 1988), pp. 237–62.

By contrast, cash flows were so strong among French and German firms that it is easy to see why they had a sharp decline in leverage.[27] Significantly, much of this cash flow went into reducing short-term debt. One seeming inconsistency is that Japanese firms apparently suffered weaker cash flows than U.S. firms without seeing the rise in leverage that characterized U.S. firms during the period.[28] But Japanese firms also paid much smaller dividends than American firms.

Although these aggregate ex post financing patterns are suggestive, they do not provide a convincing test of pecking-order behavior. The patterns do not reveal whether the firms reducing debt were also the ones with excess cash flow or whether the firms borrowing heavily were also the ones with strong investment demands. Moreover, if firms with strong cash flows were investing the excess cash instead of retiring debt, then investment would appear strong ex post and it would be difficult to verify pecking-order behavior.

Testing for Pecking-order Behavior

Estimates of cash flow and investment demand at the firm level allow a more direct test of the pecking-order hypothesis. The test compares borrowing behavior of firms with different strengths of cash flow relative to investment demand to determine whether differences in such behavior seem to reflect the existence of a gap between the costs of internal and external finance.

The strength of investment demand relative to cash flow is measured in terms of the *predicted* external financing need (PEF), which in turn is specified as the difference between *predicted* investment and dividends (PID) and *actual* measured cash flow (CF), that is, PEF = PID − CF.[29] For PID, an ex ante concept of investment is obtained by taking fitted values from a regression of the sum of investment and dividends on the change in sales and the first lag in dividends (all variables normalized by firm asset size), since accelerator models of investment tend to work well and dividends tend to adjust slowly.

Subtracting actual cash flow from PID yields the PEF for each firm in a given year. The observations are then divided into three groups:

1. cash-rich firms with negative PEFs (corresponding to firms with investment demands such as I_1 in Box 1);
2. a middle group with positive but relatively small PEFs (corresponding to cash-constrained firms with investment demands such as I_4, as well as firms with demands such as I_2 in Box 1); and
3. cash-poor firms with relatively large PEFs (corresponding mainly to firms with investment demands such as I_2 in Box 1).

The precise separation of firms into the middle and cash-poor groups is determined through an iterative maximum-likelihood procedure, which finds the division that produces

---

[27] In France, the large societies apparently enjoyed strong cash flows in part because of government policies to restrain wages in the early 1980s.

[28] If the figures are accurate, financing patterns would necessarily be consistent with leverage trends. When the ratio of new debt to net investment is lower than the initial leverage ratio, leverage must decline. In the case of Japan, for example, investment net of depreciation and amortization was 61 percent of funds from all sources. Given that new debt was 33 percent of all funding, leveraging at the margin was 54 percent (33 divided by 61). With an initial leverage ratio of 60 percent at end-1983, the 54 percent debt financing over the period reduced the leverage ratio to 56 percent at end-1988.

[29] Clearly, it will not do to use *actual* external financing or *actual* investment and dividends. Given the amount of cash flow, the accounting balance between sources and uses of funds will ensure that changes in debt and equity always match actual investment and dividends. Such data will preclude detection of any gap between the costs of internal and external financing.

the best combined fit for regression estimates.[30] The idea of the test is to try to detect in the middle group borrowing behavior that reflects a cash constraint.

For each group, we estimate the equation $\Delta D/A = a + b$ (PEF/A), where ΔD is net borrowing in terms of the change in total debt, A is total firm assets, a is the constant term, and b is the pecking-order coefficient. The variables are divided by assets to avoid problems of heteroskedasticity related to firm size. Under the pecking-order hypothesis, the pecking-order coefficient for the cash-rich group would be close to one. This result would reflect the use of excess cash flow to retire debt, with the amount retired varying one-to-one with investment demand across firms. Within the middle group, the coefficient would be less than one, reflecting the presence in the group of at least some cash-constrained firms for which debt would be unaffected by the strength of investment demand. Finally, within the cash-poor group, the coefficient would again be close to one, reflecting amounts of borrowing that varied one-to-one with investment demand. (The presumption is that relatively few firms actually resort to external equity financing.)

Test Results

Table 4 reports the regression estimates for Germany, Japan, the United Kingdom, and the United States for the same large firms as before. The change in total debt is used for the dependent variable.[31] For the cash-rich groups in the United States, two sets of estimates are reported, one for the full sample and one for the sample excluding firms that were buying back stock and engaging in net long-term borrowing at the same time.

The results are broadly in accord with pecking-order behavior. Nine of the thirteen estimated pecking-order coefficients are consistent with the hypothesis. The most telling result in favor of the pecking-order hypothesis is the difference between the estimated coefficients for the cash-poor and the middle groups, particularly in the case of German and British firms. The much lower propensity for debt financing by firms in the middle groups suggests the presence among them of cash-constrained firms with investment demands caught in a gap between the costs of internal and external finance.[32] In the case of the full sample of U.S. firms, only the coefficient for the middle group is consistent, but when the buyback firms are excluded, the coefficient for the cash-rich group becomes consistent with pecking-order behavior.

Aberrant Behavior

The deviations from pecking-order behavior are noteworthy. It is the cash-rich firms that tend to depart from pecking-order behavior. In theory, these firms should have been using all their excess cash flow to retire debt in order to create slack for possible future borrowing needs. It appears, however, that only the cash-rich firms in Japan were behaving according to the pecking-order hypothesis, conscientiously using excess cash flow to retire debt. In Germany and the United Kingdom, the firms

---

[30]Steve Peristiani wrote an algorithm for seeking a maximum for the concentrated log-likelihood of a bivariate switching regression model. The log-likelihood is from Stephen M. Goldfeld and Richard E. Quandt, "The Estimation of Structural Shifts by Switching Regression," *Annals of Economic and Social Measurement*, vol. 2 (1973), pp. 475–85.

[31]Similar equations were estimated for long-term debt by combining net short-term borrowing with cash flow, but the results were not nearly as favorable.

[32]The large relative sizes of the middle groups, especially for the United Kingdom and the United States, indicate that these groups probably include many firms that were not cash-constrained. The algorithm for dividing the sample between the middle and cash-poor groups tended not to be very effective because the shape of the concentrated log-likelihood function was quite flat for wide ranges.

Table 4 PECKING-ORDER EQUATIONS (Dependent Variable Is $\Delta D/A$)

Explanatory Variable	Germany	Japan	United Kingdom	United States Full Sample	United States Without Buyback Firms
Cash-rich group	$n = 74$	$n = 11$	$n = 229$	$n = 918$	$n = 626$
Constant	−0.0166	0.0285	−0.0109	0.0577	−0.0209
PEF/A	0.2252	1.0657^c	−0.0382	0.7855	0.9238^b
	$(−9.3462)^a$	(0.0674)	(−15.2006)	(−3.8718)	(−1.6710)
Middle group	$n = 54$	$n = 66$	$n = 1,190$	$n = 3,375$	
Constant	0.0028	−0.0062	0.0030	0.0082	
PEF/A	0.1384^c	0.6132^c	0.4149^c	0.4472^c	
	(0.4878)	(1.4819)	(−8.9877)	(−11.7617)	
Cash-poor group	$n = 27$	$n = 68$	$n = 491$	$n = 522$	
Constant	−0.0424	−0.0267	−0.1897	−0.2306	
PEF/A	0.8515^c	0.8204^c	1.0461^c	1.2776	
	(−0.4914)	(−0.5390)	(1.3599)	(4.7130)	

[a] The t-values under the null hypotheses are in parentheses.

[b] Failure to reject the pecking-order hypotheses at the 5 percent level.

[c] Failure to reject at the 10 percent level. The null hypotheses are $b = 1$ for the cash-rich and cash-poor groups and $b = 0$ for the middle group, where b is the coefficient on PEF/A. In the case of the middle groups for the United Kingdom and the United States, however, [c] indicates rejection of the null hypothesis that $b = 1$.

were putting their excess cash flow into financial assets, including stock to acquire other firms; a few British firms were even borrowing for this purpose. The German firms may have been averse to retiring debt because of their close relationship to their banks. In spite of this reluctance to retire debt, many German firms were so cash-rich that aggregate debt retirement was sufficient to cause leverage to fall sharply. The British firms appear to have been simply taking advantage of unusually favorable credit conditions in the United Kingdom at a time of government budget surpluses. Indeed some large British firms were also providing trade credit liberally to other firms while paying off their own trade debt. In effect, these British and German industrial firms were engaging in some financial intermediation of their own.

U.S. Stock Buybacks

Unlike firms in other countries, firms in the United States may buy back their stock with little restriction.[33] Indeed, while many cash-rich U.S. firms were exhibiting good pecking-order behavior by retiring debt, nearly a third of their number at a given time were returning cash to their stockholders not only by paying generous dividends but also by borrowing heavily to buy back their own common stock. For the sample used here, 292 of 918 observations on cash-rich U.S. firms were on firms engaged in stock buybacks financed with long-term debt. Table 5 shows the

[33] In the United Kingdom, the power of a company to buy back its own stock must be granted by a shareholder vote, but even the firms already granted the power have rarely exercised it.

Table 5   STOCK BUYBACKS AND LONG-TERM BORROWING BY CASH-RICH U.S. FIRMS[a] (Millions of Dollars)

Year	Number of Firms	Amount of Buyback (Net)	Long-Term Borrowing (Net)
1983	20	628.2	557.4
1984	37	2,462.8	2,019.6
1985	64	11,491.2	14,474.8
1986	51	3,275.2	6,907.4
1987	62	4,791.0	5,542.4
1988	58	5,638.3	9,028.8
Total	292	28,286.7	38,530.4

[a]Cash-rich firms are selected on the basis of the difference between predicted investment and dividends, on the one hand, and on the other, actual measured cash flow.

SOURCE: Global Vantage.

amounts of buybacks and long-term borrowing by these firms. In the 1980s, stock repurchases were the difference between rising leverage and falling leverage in terms of long-term debt in the United States. Chart 2 shows that in the absence of the repurchases, the ratio of long-term debt to assets for the sample would have been about 18 percent in 1988 instead of 27 percent.

Significantly, nearly all the new debt used to finance the U.S. buybacks was long term, and in some cases short-term debt was reduced. If the firms were seeking merely to put cash in the hands of stockholders through some method other than dividends, then they could have accomplished their goal using more modest amounts drawn from the available cash flow or financed with short-term debt that could be promptly repaid. The fact that cash-rich firms resorted to long-term debt suggests that a lasting change in leverage was an important motive. Some firms may have raised their leverage ratios to defend themselves against perceived takeover threats, others to

Chart 2

Effect of Stock Repurchases on the Ratio of Long-Term Debt to Assets in the United States

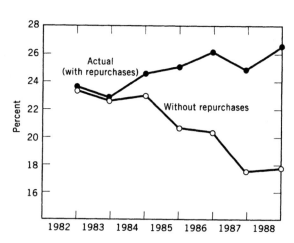

Note: Interest expense due to cumulative stock repurchases since 1982 is calculated using LIBOR.

SOURCE: Standard and Poor's Global Vantage.

support the market value of their shares.[34] But whatever the motive, it appears that the capital restructuring in the form it took would be difficult to reverse in the short run.[35]

Conclusion

The international evidence examined here suggests that two distinct types of company behavior have accounted for the differences in leverage trends across countries. For the most part, declines in leverage abroad and among many U.S. corporations have resulted from a type of behavior in which firms enjoying strong cash flows have retired debt or reduced their use of debt for financing investment. In contrast, much of the rise in leverage in the United States has been a consequence of a strikingly different type of behavior, in which some cash-rich U.S. firms have actually borrowed heavily, not to invest, but to repurchase their stocks.

Although both types of behavior can be found among U.S. firms, the U.S. trend in the aggregate differs from trends elsewhere because of the large number of firms buying back their stock. The precise reasons for the buybacks are not well understood, but the use of long-term debt to finance the buybacks suggests a lasting change in attitudes towards leverage.

Where aggregate trends show that declining leverage accompanied strong cash flows, disaggregate data reveal the firm-level behavior underlying the trends: companies were acting as if external funds were substantially more costly than internal funds, a behavior consistent with the so-called pecking-order hypothesis. Moreover, the finding that the declines in leverage were achieved largely through reductions in short-term debt indicates that firms were treating favorable cash flows as transitory shocks and that the declines in leverage were a cyclical phenomenon.

Some countries, of course, have had stronger cash flows than others. The large German companies and French societies appear to have enjoyed the strongest cash flows and thus have seen the sharpest declines in leverage. British firms have also had impressive cash flows, but their investment in financial assets and acquisitions has kept their leverage from falling. Japanese corporations as a group have had relatively modest cash flows, but those firms with excess funds have been scrupulously retiring their debt, so that leverage on the whole has declined. American corporations have actually had somewhat strong cash flows, but the debt-financed stock buybacks have caused aggregate leverage to rise.

---

[34] Financial innovations such as junk bonds, strip financing, and blind-pool buyout funds may have made takeover threats more credible in the 1980s than before. Bagwell finds that share repurchases make a potential target more expensive to acquire. See Laurie S. Bagwell, "Share Repurchase and Takeover Deterrence," Northwestern University Department of Finance, Working Paper no. 53, 1989.

[35] In Australia, where leverage in terms of long-term debt has also risen, developments similar to those in the United States may be taking place.

CASE 15

World Tours, Inc.

Cash Management Swaps

JOHN F. MARSHALL

VIPUL K. BANSAL

ALAN L. TUCKER

Swaps as a Cash Management Tool

This case study details how fixed-for-fixed interest rate swaps may be employed as a cash management tool for a firm with a seasonal component to its cash flows. Such an approach to cash management may be more cost effective than traditional borrow/lend techniques. In keeping with the global dimension of the swaps markets and their uses, we have avoided making the case currency specific.

I: Introduction

Interest rate swaps, currency swaps, commodity swaps and equity swaps have revolutionized modern risk management, allowing investors, firms, and governments to hedge preexisting positions against unanticipated changes in interests rates, foreign exchange rates, commodity prices, and equity values. For analyses relating to these swaps as hedging tools, see Arak et al. [1], Aspel et al. [2],

Bicksler and Chen [3], Felgran [4], Grabbe [5], Hull [6], Kapner and Marshall [7], Marshall and Bansal [8], Marshall and Kapner [9], Marshall and Tucker [10], Park [11], Smith et al. [12, 13], Tucker [14], Turnbull [15], Wall [16], Wall and Pringle [17], and others.[1]

While principally used as a hedging tool, the swaps product is a remarkably versatile instrument, new uses for which are still being discovered. In this chapter we detail a new and potentially valuable use for swaps, namely as a cash management tool. Specifically, we describe how fixed-for-fixed interest rate swaps may be employed to deseason a firm's cash flows. In such a swap, each counterparty pays the other a fixed rate of interest on notional principals denominated in the same currency. On the surface, such a swap would not seem to make any sense. However, by mismatching the payment's dates, it can be shown that such a swap is useful as a cash management tool. Although an empirical issue, there is considerable likelihood that such an approach to cash management may be more cost effective than traditionally employed borrow/lend techniques.

---

[1]Numbers in brackets refer to Bibliography at end of case.

This case is organized as follows: In Section II we provide a brief tutorial on swaps. In Section III we describe, in general terms, the fixed-for-fixed swap as a cash management tool. A specific application of the approach is provided in Section IV. Here we examine a firm with a profit history described by three distinct components: A secular trend, a seasonal pattern, and a foreign exchange exposure. The firm's objective is to remove the seasonal component while preserving the secular trend. Also, management seeks to hedge the exchange rate risk, but doing so requires the seasonal component and secular trend to be isolated. This is the task before you. The specific assignment is presented in Section V. You are also asked to consider certain adjustments to the dealer's spread to equate the present values of the two legs of the swap.

II: Swaps Tutorial[2]

All swaps are founded on the same basic structure. First, there is some notional amount specified at the time the swap is written. This notional amount is notional principal in the case of interest rate, currency, and equity swaps, and notional commodities in the case of commodity swaps. The notionals may or may not be exchanged, depending on the nature and purpose of the swap, and, if exchanged, may be exchanged more than once. In addition, the counterparties to a swap also exchange usage payments, which are made at designated intervals over the life of the swap, called its tenor.

Typically, one party pays a fixed price and the other party pays a floating price determined by some index to which the floating price is pegged. Except for commodity swaps, the "prices" take the form of rates. The two

sides of the swap are called the fixed and floating legs of the swap and the fixed rate is called the swap coupon.

Most swaps are effected between an end user and a swap dealer, as opposed to directly between two end users. Investment and commercial banks acting as swap dealers add liquidity to the market by eliminating the need to precisely match all provisions of swaps between end users and by minimizing their search costs. For their services, swap dealers earn a bid–ask spread, sometimes called a pay–receive spread, and often collect a front-end fee if complex financial engineering is involved.[3]

With the exception of currency swaps, notionals are usually not exchanged and only exist for purposes of calculating the size of the usage payments. Ignoring the initial and terminal exchanges of notionals, which are optional in the sense that most swaps do not require them, the basic swap structure is easily described by a boxed cash flow form of illustration. For example, two basic swaps with the swap dealer standing between the end users are illustrated in Exhibit 15-1 together with the accompanying cash market transactions. As this exhibit shows, the swap converts Counterparty A's fixed price obligation to a floating price obligation and converts Counterparty B's floating price obligation to a fixed price obligation. This can allow each party to hedge a preexisting cash market risk. For instance, if B had issued floating-rate dollar-denominated debt, then by using this swap form it could immunize against interest rate risk.

If the cash markets of the two end users are the same, then the swap can fix the price for

---

[2]A similar swaps tutorial is presented in Marshall and Tucker [10]. For a more thorough treatment of the subject see Kapner and Marshall [7] and Marshall and Kapner [9].

[3]Financial engineering involves the creative and innovative application of financial technology to the solution of problems in finance. Financial technology includes both the body of financial theory and technique and the collection of financial instruments and processes as they exist at any given point in time. For a thorough discussion of the many dimensions of financial engineering, see Marshall and Bansal [8].

EXHIBIT 15-1

Basic Swap Structure

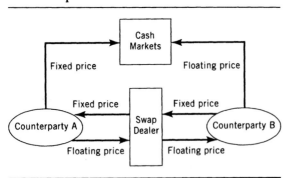

EXHIBIT 15-2

Commodity Swap Structure

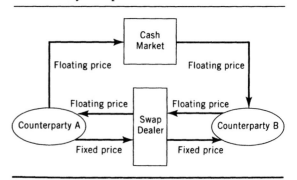

both end users. A common scenario is depicted in Exhibit 15-2. This is typically the objective of commodity swaps. As principally used, such swaps allow both parties to hedge commodity price risk. For instance, if A is an oil producer while B requires oil as an input factor of production, then by using this swap both parties can fix the price of oil received/paid for the tenor of the commodity swap.

III: Cash Management with Swaps

Swaps have been defined as contracts that entail the transfer of cash flows at recurrent intervals. Indeed, Grabbe [5] and others have argued that forward and futures contracts represent particular forms of swap contracts. Because swaps entail the periodic transfer of cash flows, they should be useful as a cash flow management tool. In this section, we provide a simple framework for using swaps to deseason an end user's cash flows.

Define CF_p as a periodic cash flow. For instance, CF_p may represent a corporation's annual profit. Also, define CF_i, $i + 1, 2, 3, \ldots, n$ as intraperiod cash flows. For instance, CF_i may represent quarterly profits ($n = 4$) or

monthly profits ($n = 12$). Thus, $CF_1 + CF_2 + CF_3 + \cdots + CF_n = CF_p$. Finally, let $CF_i \neq CF_j$, $i \neq j$, $j = 1, 2, 3, \ldots, n$. In other words, intraperiod cash flows are uneven or seasonal. The end user's goal is to deseason these intraperiod cash flows; that is, the end user desires that $CF_i = CF_j = CF_p/n$.

To achieve equivalent intraperiod cash flows, the end user can engage in a swap in which it pays the swap dealer the amount $CF_i - CF_p/n$ each intraperiod i. Exhibit 15-3 illustrates this swap. Recognize that for any intraperiod i in which $CF_i < CF_p/n$, the end user would "pay" the swap dealer a negative amount; that is, the end user would receive net cash flow.

As a simple example, suppose that a firm experiences annual profit of $CF_p = \$1,200,000$

EXHIBIT 15-3

Fixed-for-Fixed Interest Rate Swaps with Mismatched Payment Dates

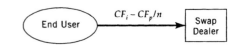

with seasonal quarterly profits of $CF_1 = \$400,000$, $CF_2 = \$100,000$, $CF_3 = \$600,000$, and $CF_4 = \$100,000$. By engaging in a swap in which the firm pays $CF_i - \$300,000$ for each quarter i, it achieves a constant quarterly profit of \$300,000.

It is important to recognize that the swap arrangement described above and illustrated in Exhibit 12-3 is equivalent to a fixed-for-fixed interest rate swap with mismatched payment dates. The firm pays the dealer fixed sums during the first and third quarters of the year, while the swap dealer pays the firm fixed sums during the second and fourth quarters. A more detailed and realistic application is presented in the next section.

IV: An Application: The Case of World Tours, Inc.[4]

Consider the following situation. World Tours, Incorporated (WTI), a travel agent that books overseas, primarily European, tours, aggressively markets its product. Company policy requires that tours be booked and paid for at least 90 days prior to departure. Tour payments are nonrefundable after the payment due date unless a cancellation is dictated by a demonstrable medical condition. Revenue is recorded, for reporting purposes, on the tour departure date. The firm receives 15 percent of tour revenue for its booking services. The remainder is paid to the tour organizers. The firm has a fixed overhead of 160,000 domestic currency units (DCU) per calendar quarter. Its variable costs amount to 7 percent of tour revenue. Of this, 4 percent represents commissions to its salespeople and 2 percent represents advertising expenditures. The remaining 1 percent covers miscellaneous variable costs.

[4] This application stems from a specific consulting case. The name of the firm, which is intended to be fictitious, and the context of the case have been changed to protect proprietary materials provided by the client.

EXHIBIT 15-4
WORLD TOURS, INCORPORATED
(all values in thousands)

Calendar Quarter	Period	Revenue	Quarterly Profit
185	1	1,700.93	−23.93
285	2	1,354.72	−51.62
385	3	2,250.09	20.01
485	4	1,622.80	−30.18
186	5	2,629.77	50.38
286	6	1,941.60	−4.67
386	7	3,143.01	91.44
486	8	2,077.74	6.22
187	9	3,397.65	111.81
287	10	2,464.48	37.16
387	11	3,735.75	138.86
487	12	2,060.46	4.84
188	13	3,817.29	145.38
288	14	2,379.80	30.38
388	15	3,895.08	151.61
488	16	2,335.96	26.88
189	17	4,360.80	188.86
289	18	2,506.56	40.52
389	19	4,726.50	218.12
489	20	2,507.70	40.62
190	21	5,002.83	240.23
290	22	2,950.92	76.07
390	23	5,129.23	250.34
490	24	3,176.10	94.09

The firm's quarterly revenue can be converted to before-tax profit as follows:

Before Tax Profit

$$= [(15\% - 7\%) \times \text{Revenue}] - 160,000 \text{ DCU}$$

WTI's bookings and profits have been growing over time. However, profit is highly variable from quarter to quarter. The historic quarterly revenue and profit for the 24 calendar quarters from the first quarter of 1985 to the last quarter of 1990 are reported in Exhibit 15.4. Historic profit is also depicted graphically in Exhibit 15-5.

Until early 1991, WTI was entirely equity financed and had no outstanding debt. In late

EXHIBIT 15-5

World Tours Inc.: Raw Historical Profit—
No Hedge

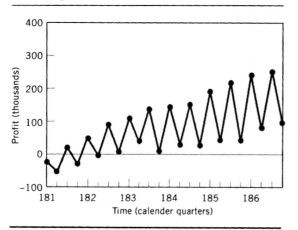

**EXHIBIT 15-6
ECI / DOMESTIC EXCHANGE RATE**

Quarter	Rate	Quarter	Rate	Quarter	Rate
185	2.040	187	1.874	189	1.605
285	2.111	287	1.924	289	1.518
385	2.103	387	1.856	389	1.586
485	1.989	487	1.614	489	1.504
186	2.022	188	1.663	190	1.528
286	2.026	288	1.671	290	1.497
386	2.033	388	1.568	390	1.463
486	1.899	488	1.570	490	1.558

1990, the firm's management began to consider issuing debt in an effort to increase leverage. Its underwriters suggested that WTI could sell its debt at a lower coupon if it reduced its quarterly profit volatility. Management believed that shareholders would also prefer greater profit stability. In order to remove some of the volatility from profit, management sought to identify the sources of the firm's profit volatility and then to reduce the volatility by properly structured swaps.

Since sales had been growing over the years, management believed that there was a secular trend to sales which was explained by its increasing expenditures on advertising and customers word-of-mouth endorsements. Management also noted that recorded revenues tended to rise in the first quarter (explained by the popularity of its winter ski tours) and in the third quarter (explained by the popularity of its summer tours). Management suspected that sales may also be a function of the strength of its domestic currency, vis-à-vis European currencies. Management decided to measure the strength of its domestic currency relative to an index of European

currencies that we will call the European Currency Index (ECI). The ECI values for the same 24 quarters are reported in Exhibit 15-6. Management also believed that sales revenue exhibits a significant random component.

A statistical decomposition of the revenue history confirmed the trend and seasonal components of WTI's business. It also revealed the link between WTI's revenue and the strength of its domestic currency. There was a random component to revenue but this proved considerably less important than originally believed. Specifically, the decomposition revealed the following relation between revenue and the various revenue components:

$$\text{Revenue} = \text{Trend} + \text{Seasonal} + \text{ECI Factor} + \text{Random}$$

$$\text{Trend} = 1200 + (200 \times \text{Period})$$

$$\text{Seasonal} = 0.2 \times D \times \text{Trend}$$

$$\text{ECI Factor} = 0.6 \times (\text{ER} - 2.000) \times \text{Trend}$$

where

Period: Quarter number
(1 through 24)

D: Seasonal dummy
= +1 for quarters 1 and 3
= −1 for quarters 2 and 4

ER: Exchange rate of ECI
for domestic currency

V: The Assignment

As already noted, management has concluded that it would like to deseason the firm's cash flows and remove the exchange rate risk associated with its operations. Based on the description of swaps provided in the tutorial and the specific decomposition of the firm's profit history provided above, answer the following questions. (Note: an electronic spreadsheet will be of considerable aid in designing your solutions and graphing your results.)

1. Based on the analysis of the firm's profit history described above, design a fixed-for-fixed interest rate swap with mismatched payment dates that would deseason WTI's cash flows. Be sure to take account of growth in the firm's profits when structuring the notional principals. Assume that the fixed rate on both sides of the swap is 10 percent semiannual (sa).

2. Assuming that this swap could be retroactively applied, generate the quarterly cash flows on the swap for WTI. Use a spreadsheet for this part of the analysis.

3. Now, combine the quarterly cash flows on the swap with WTI's quarterly profits, and graph the combined outcomes using the same graphical form as that depicted in Exhibit 15-4. Comment on the effect of the swap on quarterly profit volatility.

4. Why could this swap be accurately described as an "accreting fixed-for-fixed interest rate swap"?

5. Again assuming that a swap could be retroactively applied, design a currency swap, based on the ECI and the firm's domestic currency unit (DCU), that would allow the firm to hedge its exchange rate exposure. Be sure to take account of the growth in profits over time. Assume that the swap would employ an ECI/DCU exchange rate of 2:1.

6. Using a spreadsheet, generate the quarterly cash flows associated with the currency swap that you have designed. Combine these cash flows with the combined profits from the firm's operations and the cash management swap obtained in item 3 and graph the newly combined cash flows. Comment on the effect of the currency swap on the firm's profit volatility and performance.

7. Consider one last time the fixed-for-fixed accreting interest rate swap you developed in item 1. If both legs of the swap pay 10 percent, as we assumed, do the two sides of the swap necessarily have the same present value? If not, how can the swap be adjusted to equate the present values of the two sides of the swap? Assuming that you equate the present values by adjusting the dealer-pays-fixed rate (holding the WTI-pays-fixed rate constant at 10 percent), what rate must the dealer pay to equate the present values?

8. The fixed-for-fixed accreting interest rate swap that you developed in item 1, and which you adjusted in item 8, does not afford any profit for the swap dealer since the present values of both legs are the same. What additional adjustment needs to be made to compensate the dealer? Briefly discuss.

Bibliography

1. M. Arak, A. Estrella, L. Goodman, and A. Silver, "Interest Rate Swaps: An Alternative Explanation, " *Financial Management* (Summer 1988), pp. 12–18.

2. D. Aspel, J. Cogen, and M. Rabin, "Hedging Long Term Commodity Swaps with Futures," *Global Finance Journal* (Fall 1989), pp. 77–93.

3. J. Bicksler and A. Chen, "An Economic Analysis of Interest Rate Swaps," *Journal of Finance* (July 1986), pp. 645–655.

4. S. Felgren, "Interest Rate Swaps: Use, Risk, and Prices," *New England Economic Review*, Federal

Reserve Bank of Boston (November 1987), pp. 22–32.

5. J. Grabbe, *International Financial Markets*, New York: Elsevier Science Publishing Co., 1986.

6. J. Hull, *Options, Futures and Other Derivative Securities*, Englewood Cliffs, NJ: Prentice Hall, 1989.

7. K. Kapner and J. Marshall, *The Swaps Handbook*, New York: New York Institute of Finance, 1990.

8. J. Marshall and V. Bansal, *The Financial Engineering Handbook*, New York: New York Institute of Finance, 1991.

9. J. Marshall and K. Kapner, *Understanding Swaps Finance*, Cincinnati: South Western, 1990.

10. J. Marshall and A. Tucker, "Equity Derivatives: The Plain Vanilla Equity Swap and Its Variants," working paper, St. John's University, February 1991.

11. Y. Park, "Currency Swaps as a Long-Term International Financing Technique, *Journal of International Business Studies* (Winter 1984), pp. 47–54.

12. C. Smith, C. Smithson, and L. Wakeman, "The Evolving Market for Swaps," *Midland Corporate Finance Journal* (Winter 1986), pp. 20–32.

13. C. Smith, C. Smithson, and L. Wakeman, "The Market for Interest Rates Swaps," *Financial Management* (Winter 1988), pp. 34–44.

14. A. Tucker, *Financial Futures, Options, and Swaps*, St. Paul: West Publishing, 1991.

15. S. Turnbull, "Swaps: A Zero Sum Game," *Financial Management* (Spring 1987), pp. 15–22.

16. L. Wall, "Interest Rate Swaps in an Agency Theoretic Model with Uncertain Interest Rates," Working paper No. 86-6, Federal Reserve Bank of Atlanta, July 1986.

17. L. Wall and J. Pringle, "Alternative Explanations of Interest Rate Swaps," Working paper No. 87-2, Federal Reserve Bank of Atlanta, April 1987.

The Computerized Numerical Control Corporation, Inc.

Projecting the Yen / Dollar Exchange Rate, Hedging Dividedend Remittances from Japan, and Positioning of Funds in the MNC

HARVEY A. PONIACHEK

The Company and Its Business

The Computerized Numerical Control (CNC) Corporation, Inc. was founded and incorporated in Boston, Massachusetts in 1962. The corporation had expanded rapidly in the mid-1970s through a series of mergers and acquisitions of small- and medium-size machine tool and computer software companies. CNC went public in 1978, and it is currently listed on the NYSE—under the symbol CNC—and on several regional exchanges in the United States. Its shares are also traded on the London and Tokyo stock exchange markets.

The company specializes in research, design, and manufacturing of computerized numerical control systems, and one of its divisions is an original-equipment-manufacturer (OEM) for the computer industry. Some of CNC's two dozen systems for various industrial applications are marketed worldwide. In the past decade, CNC has undertaken an expansion program in the areas of computer-aided designed (CAD), computer-aided engineering (CAE), and computer-aided manufac-

turing (CAM). Appendix 16-1 provides some background information on the computerized machine tool industry in the United States.

With nearly 4,250 employees in the United States and around the world, CNC corporation sales are rapidly approaching the $1 billion level. The company operates several divisions, of which the most significant are the Lexington Electronics (30% of sales), the Machinery Configuration (25%), and the Computer Engineering Systems (25%).

The company is recognized for its innovations and industrial application, quality control, cost competitiveness, and after-sales services of clients. CNC's market niches are in the automotive and electronics industries, as well as in textile and shoe manufacturing.

Financial Performance

Sales in 1989 reached $950 million, net income was $57 million, and the rate of return on equity was 84 percent. The company has experienced a steady growth in sales and income over the past decade. Exhibit 16-1 contains CNC's balance sheet and income statements.

EXHIBIT 16-1

Computerized Numerical Control (CNC) Corporation, Inc.

Consolidated Balance Sheet

(end of year, thousands of U.S. dollars)

	1989	1988
ASSETS		
Cash	16,624	14,581
Marketable securities	5,031	3,553
Trade receivables	143,276	138,758
Inventories	109,641	112,010
Other current assets	17,993	16,741
Total current assets	292,564	285,642
Total property & equipment	283,383	273,044
Less accumulated		
depreciation	147,612	139,310
Net property & equipment	135,772	139,335
Investment & other assets	75,466	70,640
Foreign currency		
translation adjustment	8,825	12,271
TOTAL ASSETS	512,627	502,287
LIABILITIES		
Short-term loans	163,358	163,496
Debt due	11,307	1,022
Notes & account		
payables	98,040	99,859
Accrued expenses	17,174	16,489
Accrued taxes	3,742	3,615
Other current		
liabilities	7,056	5,728
Total current		
liabilities	300,677	290,210
Long-term debt	114,027	107,608
Retirement benefits	17,381	17,665
Other long-term liabilities	9,129	6,741
Minority interest	3,546	3,423
Common stock	18,782	22,414
Capital surplus	31,957	34,180
Legal reserve	1,937	1,874
Retained earnings	15,190	18,173
Shareholders' equity	67,866	76,640
TOTAL LIABILITIES AND		
STOCKHOLDERS' EQUITY	512,627	502,287

Consolidated Income Statement

(end of year, thousands of dollars)

Net sales	950,016	890,342
Cost of sales	628,681	590,750
Selling, general, and		
administrative expenses	205,192	191,980
Operating income	116,143	107,612
Interest & dividend income	10,649	8,950
Interest expenses	26,224	24,829
Other expenses, net	3,939	3,666
Extraord. charge	1,790	2,300
Income before taxes	84,190	76,817
Income taxes	29,467	26,886
Minority interest	308	444
Foreign currency		
adjustment	1,850	1,250
Net income	56,882	51,626

Notes:

Return on sales	5.99 percent
Return on assets	11.10 percent
Return on equity	83.82 percent

International Operation

CNC is engaged in worldwide manufacturing and marketing of computerized numerical control products through wholly-owned subsidiaries, branches, and commissioned agents. Approximately 30 percent of CNC's sales is generated by its subsidiaries abroad. The U.S. operation is engaged in considerable export and import activities that contribute about 10 percent of total sales.

CNC operates subsidiaries and branches in 10 countries, including the European Community (EC), with the United Kingdom accounting for 10 percent of international sales, Germany (10%), Belgium (10%), and Spain (5%); Asia, with Japan (25%) and Hong Kong (15%) being the most significant markets; Latin America, including Mexico (3%) and Brazil (2%); Canada (5%), and Australia (5%).

CNC operates engineering and marketing personnel around the world, with major R&D

centers located in Boston, Tokyo, London, and Frankfurt.

CNC in Japan

Activities in Japan, through CNC Uno, Ltd., were commenced with an acquisition in the early 1980s of 75 percent of the controlling equity of a small electronic tool maker, Uno, Ltd. of Yokohama. Operations in Japan are highly successful in terms of growth and profitability. The financial statements of CNC Uno, Ltd. are provided in Exhibit 16-2.

EXHIBIT 16-2

CNC Uno, Ltd.

Consolidated Balance Sheet

(end of year, thousands of U.S. dollars)

	1989	1988
ASSETS		
Cash	1,781	1,696
Marketable securities	539	513
Trade receivables	15,351	14,620
Inventories	11,747	11,188
Other current assets	1,928	1,836
TOTAL CURRENT ASSETS	31,346	29,853
Total property & equipment	30,362	28,917
Less accumulated deprec.	15,816	15,062
Net property & equipment	14,547	13,854
Investment & other assets	8,086	7,701
Foreign currency translation adjustment	946	900
TOTAL ASSETS	54,924	52,309
LIABILITIES		
Short-term loans	17,503	16,669
Debt due	1,211	1,154
Notes & account payables	10,504	10,004
Accrued expenses	1,840	1,752
Accrued taxes	401	382
Other current liabilities	756	720
Total Current Liabilities	32,215	30,681
Long-term debt	12,217	11,635
Retirement benefits	1,862	1,774
Other long-term liabilities	978	932
Minority interest	380	362
Common stock	2,012	1,917
Capital surplus	3,424	3,261
Legal reserve	208	198
Retained earnings	1,628	1,550
Shareholders' equity	7,271	6,925
TOTAL LIABILITY & STOCKHOLDERS' EQUITY	54,924	52,309

Consolidated Income Statement

(Year ended March 31, thousands of dollars)

	1989	1988
Net sales	75,020	71,448
Cost of sales	51,080	48,648
Selling, general and administrative expense	15,267	14,540
Operating income	8,672	8,259
Interest expense	2,071	1,972
Other expenses, net	311	296
Extraord. charge	0	0
Income before taxes	6,291	5,991
Income taxes	3,397	3,235
Foreign currency adjustment	1,161	1,105
Net income	2,894	2,756

Notes:

Return on sales	3.86 percent
Return on assets	5.27 percent
Return on equity	39.80 percent

As shown in Exhibit 16-2, Japanese sales reached $75 million in 1989, the return on sales was 3.9 percent, return on assets was 5.2 percent, and the return on equity was approximately 40 percent. The subsidiary services primarily the Japanese market, but some of its output is now marketed to the EC through the Belgian subsidiary of CNC. The expansion of the existing Japanese facilities and the creation of new ones are presently being considered.

The Assignment

CNC needs to remit dividends from its foreign subsidiary in Japan, CNC Uno, Ltd. The corporation dividend payout ratio was commonly 33 percent. The yen/dollar outlook remains uncertain for the foreseeable future. CNC management seeks to expand the activities in Japan, but withholding tax and best opportunities for the employment of these funds need to be considered. More specifically, the finance department, of which you are a junior member that is responsible for Japan, needs to undertake the following tasks:

1. Prepare a yen/dollar exchange rate outlook based on the purchasing power parity (PPP) approach. Verify the results against publicly available data on the basis of effective and real effective exchange rate indexes that are provided by Morgan Guaranty, *World Financial Markets*; or IMF, International Financial Statistics. The yen/dollar exchange rate outlook obtained should be examined in light of the balance of payments performance, interest rates, and financial conditions.

2. Determine the most appropriate dividends repatriation approach.

3. Examine foreign currency hedging strategies for remittances of profit. Consider the forward exchange market, money market, currency futures and currency options. Which strategy is most effective in terms of cost, availability, flexibility, and the effect on the corporate debt?

4. Given the relatively high profitability of the Japanese operation, will it be more suitable for CNC to retain earnings in Japan? That is, in positioning of funds within the CNC Corporation, consider whether a reinvestment of earnings in the Japanese subsidiary is more lucrative in terms of various taxes and rates of return. Please bear in mind that CNC Uno, Ltd. is jointly owned by the United States (75%) and Japan (25%). Under the U.S.–Japan Tax Treaty there is a 10% withholding tax on the remittances of dividends abroad, corporate income tax is 37.5 percent, and local taxes range from 17.3 to 20.7 percent of the corporation's national income tax payable for the same accounting period, with larger companies in the Tokyo area being taxed at the maximum rate of 20.7 percent.

5. Explain whether and how CNC could reduce its effective tax rate in Japan. What is its foreign tax credit position in Japan?

The Computerized Machine Tool Industry in the United States

Computer-Numerically Controlled (CNC) machine tools have proliferated in the United States and abroad in the 1980s in an effort to achieve greater productivity through automation.[1] U.S. purchase of CNC tools was $1.2 billion in 1986. Foreign suppliers, primarily the Japanese, dominate the U.S. market, with the joint venture Fanuc and General Electric accounting for the lion's share of 66 percent.

Computer-aided design and manufacturing (CAD/CAM) systems—which combine computers and software systems—have expanded tremendously in recent years. It reached over $4.3 billion in 1986, and is expected to be $12 billion in 1990. U.S. companies control the market with very slight foreign competition.

For several years the industry experienced a contraction due to the state of the business cycle and primarily because of formidable foreign competition. Internationalization of the industry is well under way. In the long run, U.S. companies are expected to derive a growing share of their income from abroad.

In the past decade, the machine tools industry in the United States was adversely affected by foreign competition, primarily from Japan and Southeast Asian newly industrialized countries (NICs). The result has been a shrinking share of domestic productive capacity and market share, an ever growing share of imports, consolidation through mergers and acquisitions, and an increased production abroad by U.S. companies. According to the National Machine Tool Builders Association,

new orders for machine tools remain in 1988 at less than half their peak. Employment in the industry has declined to 64,300 in 1987, down from the peak of 101,700 in 1981. Plant closing has slowed, but foreign ownership in U.S. machine tool companies has increased. Various production and supply arrangements with off-shore manufacturers have proliferated for U.S. producers in an effort to lower cost and improve productivity.

Exports declined to $590 million in 1986, compared with over $1 billion in 1981, while imports reached 2.3 billion compared with $1.5 billion in the prior period. The U.S. Voluntary Restraint Agreement, which began in 1986, gives the industry a 5-year period to establish its competitiveness. In the long term, the process of internationalization throughout the industry will continue. U.S. companies are expected to enhance their international sourcing and are expected to manufacture a larger portion of their final products abroad through joint ventures and wholly-owned affiliates.

Power-driven hand tool sales reached $2 billion in 1987. The U.S. imposed retaliatory tariffs on certain Japanese imports, yet imports remained vigorous—over $800 million in 1987. U.S. exports reached over $300 million expanding 15 percent over the previous year. Foreign competition in the long run will remain formidable, particularly from Japan and Germany, who have already established manufacturing facilities in the United States. The lower U.S. dollar and the need for producers to supply parts quickly to service dealers has induced foreign companies to establish manufacturing facilities in the United States.

[1] See for instance U.S. Department of Commerce, *U.S. Industrial Outlook*, 1989.

Templeton Growth Fund, Inc.

International Portfolio Investment Management

HARVEY A. PONIACHEK

This case study addresses some of the theories and practices of international portfolio investment management. The reader is required to assess the international fund management performance of Templeton Growth Fund, Inc. (Templeton), one of the nation's most successful funds, by applying the main principles of international portfolio investment management, particularly concerning assets selection, portfolio construction and performance assessment criteria.

The Scope of International Investment

The global stock markets and international portfolio investments expanded considerably in the past decade. The world's stock market capitalization was $4,949 billion at the end of October 1990, of which the U.S. stock markets accounted for 32.2 percent, Western Europe for 26.7 percent and Japan for 34 percent.[1] Exhibit 17-1 illustrates the world stock market capitalization. International portfolio investment has expanded in magnitude and scope among investors around the world.

[1] Morgan Stanley, Morgan Stanley, *Capital International Perspective*, Monthly Issue 11/90.

EXHIBIT 17-1

World Stock Markets' Capitalization
(billions of dollars and percentages)

	Billions	Percent
Austria	15.6	0.3
Belgium	37.2	0.8
Denmark	25.9	0.5
Finland	7.9	0.2
France	176.4	3.6
Germany	209.6	4.2
Italy	83.1	1.7
Netherlands	85.2	1.7
Norway	16.4	0.3
Spain	56.5	1.1
Sweden	51.2	1.0
Switzerland	98.0	2.0
United Kingdom	515.7	10.4
Europe (13 countries)	1,378.6	27.9
Australia	70.4	1.4
Hong Kong	43.3	0.9
Japan	1,681.1	34.0
New Zealand	6.8	0.1
Singapore/Malaysia	33.4	0.7
Pacific	1,834.9	37.1
EAFA	3,213.5	64.9
Canada	129.8	2.6
USA	1,595.1	32.2
South Africa (gold mines)	10.2	0.2
The World Index	4,948.7	100.0

Source: Morgan Stanley, *Morgan Stanley Capital International Perspective*, Monthly Issue 11/90, p. 5.

Diversification through international investment could enhance the rate of return and diminish the risk of the investment portfolio. The sheer size and composition of the world stock market could justify significant investment in it. Because two-thirds of the world stock market capitalization is composed of non-U.S. corporations, foreign securities could afford U.S. investors diversification. International diversification could yield a better risk–return trade off than investing solely in domestic securities; that is, investors could obtain a higher level of return for a given level of risk.

Portfolio Investment Management Principles

Portfolio investment management involves several decision-making procedures[2] as shown in Exhibit 17-2, including:

1. Establishing investment objectives and formulation of necessary policies to attain them. Investment objectives set the expected rates of return on investment, define the maximum level of risk to be undertaken by the investment, and articulate the desired growth rate of the assets under management. Whereas investment policies specify the companies, industries, and/or countries in which to invest.

2. Performing security analysis to identify under - and over-valued securities in which to invest or divest.

3. Constructing a portfolio by selecting securities in which to invest and determining the amount of funds to be allocated to each security.

4. Evaluating the performance of the portfolio in terms of the rate of return (over time)

[2]William F. Sharpe and Gordon J. Alexander, *Investments*, 4th ed., Prentice Hall, Englewood Cliffs, NJ, 1990.

EXHIBIT 17-2

Portfolio Investment Management Principles

1. Investment objectives and policies
   Define the rate of return and risk
   Expected growth rate
   Where to invest
2. Securities analysis
3. Portfolio construction
   Assets allocation among various securities
4. Performance Evaluation

Source: Based on William F. Sharpe and Gordon J. Alexander, *Investments*, 4th ed., Prentice Hall, Englewood Cliffs, NJ, 1990.

and risk, and in comparison to the market's performance as reflected by a specific market index.

Security Analysis, Assets Selection and Portfolio Construction

Security Analysis

The rate of return on a common stock (Re) is determined by its dividend (D) and capital gain ($P2 - P1$), where capital gain is defined by the change in the stock's price between period 1 and 2. The rate of return can be expressed algebraically in the following form:

$$Re = (D1 + (P2 - P1))/P1$$

$$Re = (D1 + P2 - P1)/P1$$

Where $P1$ is the stock price at the beginning, at time 1, $P2$ is the stock price at the end of the second period, at time 2, (e.g., year end), and $D1$ is the dividend paid during the first period (e.g., year).

The rate of return (in dollars) on foreign held securities could be determined by the following formula:[3]

$$1 + Rs = (1 + (R2 - R1 + D)/P1)(1 + g)$$

$$Rs = (1 + (P2 - P1 + D)/P1)(1 + g) - 1$$

Rs is the total one period rate of return in dollars on a foreign security, $P1$ is the initial stock price, $P2$ is the end of period stock price, D is the dividend received, and g is the percent change in the dollar value of the foreign currency.

Assets Selection and Portfolio Construction

ASSETS SELECTION

The selection of assets/securities for an efficient investment portfolio could be based on their ratio of excess return to risk or variability. An alternative approach could involve the selection of assets/securities based on their relatively low correlation coefficient with other assets/securities or with the market, which in turn yields low betas.

Individual securities can be combined into a portfolio that yields the maximum rate of return for a given level of risk. One method of constructing an optimum investment portfolio is by applying the Markowitz model.[4] The Markowitz model derives an optimum or efficient portfolio by determining the percent share of each security in the investment portfolio. An efficient portfolio has the maximum

expected rate of return for its risk level, or the minimum risk for its expected rate of return. Alternatively stated, an efficient portfolio minimizes the portfolio variance, or the portfolio standard deviation, for a given expected rate of return. The expected rate of return of the portfolio could be defined as follows:[5]

$$E(Rp) = \sum_{i=1}^{N} X_i E(R_i) \qquad (1)$$

where $E(Rp)$ is the expected return on the portfolio, Xi is the percent share of assets i in the portfolio, and $E(Ri)$ is the expected rate of return on the ith security.

The portfolio standard deviation could be defined as follows:

$$\sigma_p = \left[\sum_{i=1}^{N} X_i^2 \sigma_i^2 + \sum_{i=1}^{N} \sum_{j=1}^{N} X_i X_j \sigma_i \sigma_j p_{ij} \right]^{1/2} \qquad (2)$$

where i is the variance of the ith risky asset and ij is the covariance of the rates of return of two risky assets, i and j. The standard deviation (STD) of the portfolio is defined in terms of the variance of each security, and the correlation coefficient (i.e., the covariance) between each pair of securities.

Assessment of the optimum portfolio according to the Markowitz model requires a large number of computations of correlation coefficients. This computation can be approximated with a fair degree of accuracy by the application of the Single Index Model (SIM). The SIM facilitates the estimation of the optimal investment portfolio[6] by describing the stock price as a linear function of a market index, in the following manner:

$$R_{it} = \alpha_{it} + \beta_{it} R_{mt} + e_{it} \qquad (3)$$

[3]Alan C. Shapiro, *Foundations of Multinational Financial Management*, Allyn & Bacon, Boston, MA, 1991, Chapter 16, "International Portfolio Investment".

[4]Edwin J. Elton and Martin J. Gruber, *Modern Portfolio Theory and Investment Analysis*, 3rd ed., Wiley, New York, 1987. Haim Levy and Marshall Sarnat, *Portfolio Investment Selection: Theory and Practice*, Prentice Hall International, Englewood Cliffs, NJ, 1984. Robert A. Haugen, *Modern Investment Theory*, 2nd Ed., Prentice Hall, Englewood Cliffs, NJ, 1990.

[5]Elton and Gruber, Chapter 5.

[6]Elton and Gruber, op. cit. Levy and Sarnat, op. cit. Haugen, op. cit.

where R_{it} is the rate of return on stock i in period t. The t subscript in all the other variables indicates observation in period t. The SIM defines the rate of return on a stock in terms of three variables: One is a constant which is independent of the market (i.e., α_i). The second variable is determined by beta (i.e., β_i), which measures the average change in R_{it} as a result of a given change in the market index, R_{mt}. The beta measures the systematic risk, or the sensitivity of the stock's rate of return to the market's rate of return index. The market index in the model is usually the rate of return on the market portfolio, such as the Standard and Poor's (S&P) index, the Dow Jones Industrial Average (DJIA), or other market indexes. The third factor in the rate of return model is a random factor (i.e., e_{it}).

The parameters in the SIM are estimated by using historic (monthly, quarterly or annual) rates of return on stocks and the market index data and by the application of time series regression analysis.

The beta coefficient is determined by the covariance of the common stock and the market variance. The covariance, in turn, is determined by the standard deviations of the return on the stock and the entire portfolio and the correlation coefficient between them. The beta can be expressed as follows:

$$\beta = \text{Cov}(X_i, X_m)/\sigma^2(Rm)$$

The covariance between two stocks in the SIM can be described in the following manner:[7]

$$\text{Cov}(r_j, r_k) = \beta_j \beta_k \sigma^2(Rm)$$

In the context of the SIM, the variance of the return on a security and/or portfolio could be defined as follows:

$$\sigma_i^2 = \beta_i^2 \sigma^2(Rm) + \sigma_{ei}^2$$

[7]Elton and Gruber, op. cit. p. 100.

The first term on the right side of the above equation is called the systematic risk, whereas the second term is attributed to the residual variance and is called unsystematic risk.

The portfolio risk can be described in the following manner:

$$\sigma^2(Rp) = \beta_p^2 \sigma^2(Rm) + \sum_{i=1}^{N} x_i^2 \sigma_{ei}^2$$

The beta factor of a portfolio is a weighted average of all the betas of the stocks in the portfolio, where the weights are the relative share of each security in the portfolio or the fraction of funds invested in each security. The portfolio beta could be described as follows:

$$\beta_p = \sum_{i=1}^{N} x_i \beta_i$$

PORTFOLIO CONSTRUCTION

Under the excess return to risk approach,[8] the optimal portfolio consists of securities for which the excess return to risk—i.e., $(R_i - R_f)/B_i$—is greater than a particular cutoff point C^*, where R_i is the mean rate of return, R_f is the rate of return on a riskless asset, and β_i is the securities beta.

The cut-off rate C^* could be derived by the application of the following formula:[9]

$$C_i = \frac{\sigma_m^2 \sum_{j=1}^{i} \frac{(\overline{R}_j - R_f)\beta_j}{\sigma_{ej}^2}}{1 + \sigma_m^2 \sum_{j=1}^{i} \left(\frac{\beta_j^2}{\sigma_{ej}^2}\right)}$$

where σ_m^2 is the variance of the market index, and σ_{ej}^2 is the securities unsystematic risk (i.e., the variance of the security that is not associ-

[8]Elton and Gruber, op. cit., Levy and Sarnat, p. 149.

[9]Elton and Gruber, op. cit., p. 151.

ated with the movement of the market index). (In prior notations, we used $\sigma^2(Rm)$ instead of σ_m^2 to denote the variance of the market rate of return, or the rate of return on the market index.)

The selection criterion requires that securities be added to the portfolio whenever the following conditions are maintained:

$$(R_i - R_f)/B_i > C_i$$

Once the securities to be included in an optimum portfolio are selected, we need to determine the share of each security in the portfolio. The share of funds to be invested in each security, X_i, could be determined as follows:[10]

$$X_i = \frac{Z_i}{\displaystyle\sum_{j=1}^{N} Z_j}$$

where

$$Z_i = \frac{\beta_i}{\sigma_{ei}^2}\left(\frac{\overline{R}_i - R_F}{\beta_i} - C^*\right)$$

Diversification Through International Investment

Domestic security prices usually move in tandem because they are influenced by similar (domestic) macroeconomic and industry conditions. However, foreign securities, which may have different price trends than domestic securities, may provide domestic investors reasonable opportunities for diversification of yields and risk. Securities' and stock markets'

[10]Elton and Gruber, op. cit., p. 154.

EXHIBIT 17-3

Portfolio Diversification and the Rate of Return and Risk

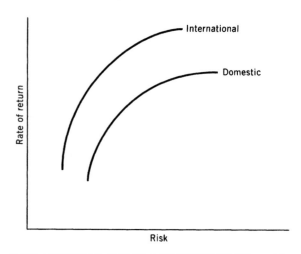

relative independent trends across national borders are commonly reflected by their low correlation coefficients.

Generally, securities within a national market have a higher correlation than securities in different national markets. While much of the risk in a foreign country is unsystematic, it is, however, systematic from a U.S. perspective and it could be diversified away.[11] Through international diversification investors could reduce the variability of their portfolios. As shown in Exhibit 17-3, in the context of the risk (on the x axis) and expected return (on the y axis), international portfolio diversification shift the efficient frontiers upward, so that higher returns correspond to a given level of risk. The efficient frontier is defined as the set of portfolios with the maximum expected rate

[11]Alan C. Shapiro, *Foundations of Multinational Financial Management*, Allyn & Bacon, Boston, 1991, Ch. 16, "International Portfolio Investment."

of return for a given level of risk. Foreign market betas can be calculated in the following manner:[12]

$$\beta_i = \rho_{im} \times \frac{\sigma_i}{\sigma_m}$$

β_i stands for the foreign market beta, ρ_{im} denotes the correlation coefficient between the foreign and the U.S. markets, σ_i is the standard deviation of the foreign market, and σ_m is the standard deviation of the U.S. market. Given the STDs of the foreign and U.S. markets, the lower the foreign markets' correlation with the U.S. market, the lower is the beta or risk of the foreign market.

As discussed in the previous section, the portfolio risk is determined by the percent share of each asset in the portfolio, by the standard deviation of each asset's rate of return, and by the correlation coefficient, or covariance, of the various assets' rates of return. Hence, the smaller the correlation coefficient between the assets' rates of return, the lower the portfolio risk. By constructing international investment portfolios, the correlation coefficient of the securities could be reduced and total risk diminished.

In a well-diversified portfolio, company or unsystematic risk is diversified away and only the market or systematic risk remains. Diversification implies spreading the risk—for example, diversification implies that a portfolio with 100 securities is 10 times more diversified than a portfolio with 10 securities. Since international diversification reduces risk, it is justified even if expected rate of return is less than domestic return. International diversification is profitable for investors, unless the rate of return is substantially reduced by taxes or currency fluctuation.

D. R. Lessard assessed the significance of international diversification relative to domestic diversification.[13] He examined the correlation between the market indexes in different countries and a common world market index. He has shown that there is less to be gained by diversifying across industries than diversifying internationally, because only a small proportion of the variance of the national portfolios is common in an international context, which gives rise to considerable risk reduction through international diversification.

Investing in foreign securities involves the risk associated with investing in a domestic security plus political risk and currency risk. In translating the rate of return from foreign held securities into dollars, we need to consider the exchange rate changes that have occurred during the investment period and its effects on dividends and capital gains or losses.

Foreign securities may be more volatile than domestic securities due to political risk and currency fluctuation. However, the addition of foreign securities to domestic investment portfolios reduces the total portfolio risk thanks to the less than perfect correlation between foreign and domestic securities.[14] Currency fluctuation can be hedged at reasonable cost, or diversified away through selection of securities from different countries. Hence, investors that diversify by acquiring foreign securities enhance the yield and reduces the risk performance.

[13] D. R. Lessard, "World, Country and Industry Relationship in Equity Returns," *Financial Analyst Journal*, January/February 1976. D. R. Lessard, "International Portfolio Diversification: A Multivariate Analysis for a Group of Latin American Countries," *Journal of Finance*, June 1973. T. Agmon and D. Lessard, "Investor Recognition of Corporate International Diversification," *Journal of Finance*, September 1977. B. Solnik, "The International Pricing of Risk: An Empirical Investigation of the World Capital Structure," *Journal of Finance*, May 1984.

[14] Elton and Gruber, op. cit.

[12] Ibid.

Portfolio Performance Assessment

The Sharpe Ratio of an investment portfolio (or asset or security) measures the reward to risk or risk premium or reward to volatility or reward to variability.[15] The reward to volatility ratio (RVOL) is defined in terms of the excess risk or risk premium to risk as follows:

$$RVOL = \frac{(R - TB)}{\beta}$$

where the rate of return, R, minus the riskless rate of return on Treasury bills, TB, equals excess return or risk premium, $R - TB$, and β is the beta.

The reward to variability ratio (RVAR) assesses excess return relative to the total risk of the portfolio, where the risk is measured in terms of the standard deviation (STD) of the portfolio's rate of return. The reward to variability can be expressed as follows:

$$RVAR = \frac{(R - TB)}{STD}$$

The Sharpe Ratios provide a comparable index by which various securities and portfolios can be assessed and ranked. The higher the Sharpe Ratio the better off is the security or portfolio performance and the more likely is its inclusion in an investment portfolio.

Templeton Group of Funds

The Company and Its Management Approach

The Templeton Group of Funds have over 700,000 investors and institutional accounts

[15]Jack Clark Francis, *Investments: Analysis and Management*, 4th ed., McGraw-Hill, New York, 1986. Elton and Gruber, op. cit.

with a total assets under management (AUM) in excess of $17 billion. The company has been in the fund management business for 50 years. Templeton always attempted to remain ahead of the funds management industry by devising and applying five or more assets selection methods.

Templeton pioneered quantitative security analysis in worldwide investment. In the firm's marketing brochure, *Templeton Growth Fund, 35 Good Years* 1990, management suggests that the Templeton growth fund is essentially a long-term investment and they do not believe it pays to try to play the market. The fund has one of the lowest rates of portfolio turnover in the mutual fund industry.

The Templeton management seeks to continuously improve their analytical methods because they believe that existing methods become obsolete, especially if they become too popular. Some of the methods used by Templeton include bargain hunting (i.e., a stock selling below its assessed value by the firm), worldwide diversification, and flexibility.

Information and Data Sources

The Templeton Growth Fund, Inc. ("the Fund") was incorporated in 1986 and in May 1990 its net AUM was over $2.6 billion. The Fund's investment objectives and policies, risk, and investment subscription procedures are discussed in Templeton Growth Fund, Inc.'s prospectus, dated January 1, 1990. The prospectus is shown in Appendix 17-1.

The investment policies and performance of the Fund are provided in Templeton Growth Fund, Inc., *Portfolio & Performance*, May 31, 1990. This information is found in Appendix 17-2. Select excerpts from Morgan Stanley, Morgan Stanley Capital International Perspective, Monthly Issue 11/90 are given in Appendix 17-3.

The Assignment

Assess Templeton's international portfolio management and performance by applying standard portfolio investment management theory. More specifically, please address the following questions:

1. Determine whether Templeton has provided U.S. investors with an optimal portfolio in terms of international diversification, rates of return, and risk. More specifically, review Templeton's portfolio composition by country on the basis of the data provided in Appendix 17-2, Templeton Growth Fund, Inc., *Portfolio & Performance*, May 31, 1990. Utilize the data on risk and return per country as reflected by Morgan Stanley, Morgan Stanley Capital Investment Perspective. Assume that Morgan Stanley's data was available to you prior to the investment.

2. Construct an internationally diversified portfolio by identifying countries to be invested in, and determine the amount of funds to be allocated to each country. Utilize Morgan Stanley, Morgan Stanley Capital International Perspective (that is available in Appendix 17-3) data on the rate of return and risk on country-market indexes.

3. Evaluate the performance of your constructed portfolio in terms of risk and the rate of return and compare its performance to Templeton's performance, the DJIA, and the Morgan Stanley World Index.

APPENDIX 17-1

Templeton Growth Fund, Inc.: Selected Excerpts from the Prospectus

SELECTED PER SHARE DATA AND RATIOS FOR A SHARE OUTSTANDING THROUGHOUT THE PERIOD

The following statement of Per Share Data and Ratios has been audited by McGladrey & Pullen, independent certified public accountants, for the periods indicated in their report which is incorporated by reference and which appears in the Fund's 1989 Annual Report to Shareholders. This statement should be read in conjunction with the other financial statements and notes thereto included in the Fund's 1989 Annual Report to Shareholders.

	Year Ended August 31, 1989	Year Ended August 31, 1988	Eight Months Ended August 31, 1987	Eight Months Ended December 31, 1986	Pro Forma[b] Year Ended April 30						
					1986	1985	1984	1983	1982	1981	1980
Investment income	$ .67	$ .54	$ .35	$ .31	$ .42	$ .50	$ .43	$ .31	$ .43	$ .27	$ .23
Operating expenses (excluding taxes on income)	.09	.09	.06	.05	.07	.07	.07	.05	.06	.04	.04
Income taxes	—	—	—	.12	.16	.20	.16	.11	.16	.10	.08
Total expenses	.09	.09	.06	.17	.23	.27	.23	.16	.22	.14	.12
Net investment income	.58	.45	.29	.14	.19	.23	.20	.15	.21	.13	.11
Dividends from net investment income[a]	(.48)	(.44)	—	(.40)	(.24)	(.19)	(.18)	(.20)	(.15)	(.12)	(.08)
Net realized gain and increase (decrease) in unrealized appreciation	3.12	(2.41)	3.97	.28	3.72	.83	.50	2.56	(1.22)	2.18	.46
Distributions from net realized capital gains[a]	(.25)	(1.08)	—	(.48)	(.48)	(.29)	—	(.35)	—	(.38)	(.09)
Net increase (decrease) in net asset value	2.97	(3.48)	4.26	(.46)	3.19	.58	.52	2.16	(1.16)	1.81	.40
Net asset value at beginning of period	13.65	17.13	12.87	13.33	10.14	9.56	9.04	6.88	8.04	6.23	5.83
Net asset value at end of period	$16.62	$13.65	$17.13	$12.87	$13.33	$10.14	$9.56	$9.04	$6.88	$8.04	$6.23
Ratios to average net assets of:											
Operating expense (excluding taxes on income)	0.66%	0.69%	0.66%[c]	0.83%[c]	0.73%	0.77%	0.78%	0.87%	0.78%	0.75%	0.78%
Total expenses (including taxes on income)	0.66%	0.69%	0.66%[c]	2.40%[c]	2.50%	2.97%	2.48%	2.62%	3.04%	2.69%	2.55%
Net investment income	4.20%	3.50%	2.99%[c]	1.76%[c]	2.11%	2.66%	2.10%	2.45%	2.96%	2.54%	2.58%
Portfolio turnover rate	11.55%	11.44%	17.55%	9.50%	23.00%	20.41%	3.35%	10.07%	22.62%	6.83%	21.19%
Number of shares outstanding at end of year (000)	141,682	115,192	95,376	88,022	75,742	58,724	52,504	51,154	46,707	45,236	32,981

[a]Dividends per share paid from net investment income and distributions paid from net realized capital gains have been calculated on the basis of shares outstanding at date of dividend and distribution.

[b]Templeton Growth Fund, Inc. (the Fund), commenced operations on December 31, 1986 as successor in interest to 58% of Templeton Growth Fund, Ltd. (the Canadian Fund) which reorganized into two funds on that date. In accordance with the terms of the reorganization, the Canadian shareholders, representing 42% of the shares outstanding, remained shareholders of the Canadian Fund and the non-Canadian shareholders, representing 58% of the shares outstanding, became shareholders of the Fund. The per share table is presented as if the reorganization took place as of the inception of the Canadian Fund, 58% of the net assets and shares outstanding were allocated to the Fund and the Fund continued to operate in Canada subject to Canadian federal and provincial taxes until December 31, 1986. No other pro forma adjustments have been made for any changes in operating costs had the reorganization taken place at that date. Since the table is on the basis of a single share outstanding throughout the period, the results illustrated, except for the number of shares outstanding at the end of each year, are the same as those shown for the Canadian Fund.

EXPENSE TABLE

Shareholder Transaction Expenses

Maximum Sales Load Imposed on Purchases (as a percentage of Offering Price)		8.50%

Annual Fund Operating Expenses
(as a percentage of average net assets)

Management Fees		0.43%
Other Expenses		0.23%
Transfer Agent Fees	0.07%	
Other	0.16%	
Total Fund Operating Expenses		0.66%

You would pay the following expenses on a $1,000 investment, assuming (1) 5% annual return and (2) redemption at the end of each time period:

	1 Year	3 Years	5 Years	10 Years
	$91	$104	$119	$160

The information in the above table is an estimate based on the Fund's expenses as of the end of the most recent fiscal year and is provided for purposes of assisting current and prospective Shareholders in understanding the various costs and expenses that an investor in the Fund will bear, directly or indirectly. The information in the table does not reflect the charge of $15 per transaction if a Shareholder requests that redemption proceeds be sent by express mail or wired to a commercial bank account. The 5% annual return and annual expenses should not be considered a representation of actual or expected Fund performance or expenses, both of which may vary. For a more detailed discussion of the Fund's fees and expenses, see "Management of the Fund."

The Fund

Templeton Growth Fund, Inc. (the "Fund") was incorporated under the laws of Maryland on November 10, 1986 and is a successor to Templeton Growth Fund, Ltd. The Fund is registered under the Investment Company Act of 1940 (the "1940 Act") as an open-end, diversified management investment company.

Investment Objective and Policies

The Fund's investment objective is long-term capital growth, which it seeks to achieve through a flexible policy of investing in stocks and debt obligations of companies and governments of any nation. Any income realized will be incidental.

Although the Fund generally invests in common stock, it may also invest in preferred stocks and certain debt securities, rated or unrated, such as convertible bonds and bonds selling at a discount. Whenever, in the judgment of the Investment Manager, market or economic conditions warrant, the Fund may, for temporary defensive purposes, invest without limit in U.S. Government securities, bank time deposits in the currency of any major nation and commercial paper meeting the quality ratings set forth under "Investment Objective Policies" in the SAI, and purchase from banks or broker-dealers Canadian or U.S. Government securities with a simultaneous agreement by the seller to repurchase them within no more than 7 days at the original purchase price plus accrued interest.

The Fund may invest no more than 5% of its total assets in securities issued by any one company or government, exclusive of U.S.

Government securities. Although the Fund may invest up to 25% of its assets in a single industry, it has no present intention of doing so. The Fund may not invest more than 5% of its assets in warrants (exclusive of warrants acquired in units or attached to securities) nor more than 10% of its assets in securities with a limited trading market. The Investment Objective and Policies described above, as well as most of the Investment Restrictions described in the SAI, cannot be changed without Shareholder approval. The Fund invests for long-term growth of capital and does not intend to place emphasis upon short-term trading profits. Accordingly, the Fund expects to have a portfolio turnover rate of less than 50%.

The Fund may purchase and sell stock index futures contracts up to an aggregate amount not exceeding 20% of its total net assets. A stock index futures contract is an agreement under which two parties agree to take or make delivery of an amount of cash based on the difference between the value of a stock index at the beginning and at the end of the contract period. When the Fund enters into a stock index futures contract, it must make an initial deposit, known as "initial margin," as a partial guarantee of its performance under the contract. As the value of the stock index fluctuates, either party to the contract is required to make additional margin deposits, known as "variation margin," to cover any additional obligation it may have under the contract. In addition, when the Fund enters into a futures contract, it will segregate assets or "cover" its position in accordance with the 1940 Act. See "Investment Objectives and Policies—Stock Index Futures Contracts" in the SAI. The Fund may not at any time commit more than 5% of its total assets to initial margin deposits on futures contracts.

In order to increase its return or to hedge all or a portion of its portfolio investments, the Fund also may purchase and sell put and call options on securities indices in standardized contracts traded on national securities exchanges, boards of trade, or similar entities, or quoted on NASDAQ. An option on a securities index gives the purchaser of the option, in return for the premium paid, the right to receive from the seller cash equal to the difference between the closing price of the index and the exercise price of the option. The Fund sells only "covered" options, which means that the Fund must maintain with its custodian cash or cash equivalents equal to the contract value (in the case of call options) or exercise price (in the case of put options). The Fund will not purchase put or call options if the appropriate premium paid for such options would exceed 5% of its total assets at the time of purchase.

Risk Considerations

Shareholders should understand that all investments involve risk and there can be no guarantee against loss resulting from an investment in the Fund, nor can there be any assurance that the Fund's investment objective will be attained. The Fund is designed for investors seeking international diversification, and is not intended as a complete investment program.

Successful use of stock index futures contracts and options on securities indices by the Fund is subject to certain special risk considerations. A liquid stock index option or futures market may not be available when the Fund seeks to offset adverse market movements. In addition, there may be an imperfect correlation between movements in the securities included in the index and movements in the securities in the Fund's portfolio. Successful use of stock index futures contracts and options on securities indices is further dependent on the Investment Manager's ability to predict correctly movements in the direction of the stock markets and no assurance can be given that its judgment in this respect will be correct. Risks in the purchase and sale of stock index futures and options are further referred to in the SAI.

The Fund has the right to purchase securities in any foreign country, developed or underdeveloped. Investors should consider carefully the substantial risks involved in investing in securities issued by companies and governments of foreign nations, which are in addition to the usual risks inherent in domestic investments. Although the Fund invests only in nations which it considers to have relatively stable and friendly governments, there is the possibility of expropriation, nationalization or confiscatory taxation, foreign exchange controls (which may include suspension of the ability to transfer currency from a given country), default in foreign government securities, political or social instability or diplomatic developments which could affect investment in securities of issuers in those nations. In addition, in many countries there is less publicly available information about issuers than is available in reports about companies in the United States. Foreign companies are not generally subject to uniform accounting, auditing and financial reporting standards, and auditing practices and requirements may not be comparable to those applicable to United States companies. In many foreign countries, there is less government supervision and regulation of business and industry practices, stock exchanges, brokers and listed companies than in the United States. Foreign securities transactions may be subject to higher brokerage costs than domestic securities transactions. In addition, the foreign securities markets of many of the countries in which the Fund may invest may also be smaller, less liquid, and subject to greater price volatility than those in the United States.

The Fund does not conduct business in, and does not conduct business with any person or group located in, South Africa. This information is accurate only as of the date of this prospectus. For further information, investors may contact the Office of the Secretary of State of California, 1230 J Street, Room 100, Sacramento, California 95814—telephone (916) 327-6427.

The Fund usually effects currency exchange transactions on a spot (i.e., cash) basis at the spot rate prevailing in the foreign exchange market. However, some price spread on currency exchange (to cover service charges) will be incurred when the Fund converts assets from one currency to another. Further, the Fund may be affected either unfavorably or favorably by fluctuations in the relative rates of exchange between the currencies of different nations. Also, some countries may withhold portions of interest and dividends at the source. There are further risk considerations, including possible losses through the holding of securities in domestic and foreign custodian banks and depositories, described in the SAI.

Purchase of Shares

Shares of the Fund may be purchased at the Offering Price through any broker which has a dealer agreement with Templeton Funds Distributor, Inc. ("TFD"), the Principal Underwriter for the Shares of the Fund, or directly from TFD, whose toll free telephone number is (800) 237-0378.

Net Asset Value

The net asset value of the Shares is computed as of the close of trading on each day the New York Stock Exchange is open for trading, by dividing the value of the Fund's securities plus any cash and other assets (including accrued interest and dividends receivable) less all liabilities (including accrued expenses) by the number of Shares outstanding, adjusted to the nearest whole cent. A security listed or traded on a recognized stock exchange or NASDAQ is valued at its last sale price on the principal exchange on which the security is traded. The value of a foreign security is determined in its national currency as of the close of trading on the foreign exchange on which it is traded, or as of 4:00 p.m., New York time, if that is earlier, and that value is then converted into its U.S. dollar equivalent at the foreign exchange rate in effect at noon New York time on the day the value of the foreign security is determined. If no sale is reported at that time, the mean between the current bid and asked price is used. All other securities for which over-the-counter market quotations are readily available are valued at the mean between the current bid and asked price. Short term securities having a maturity of 60 days or less are valued at their amortized cost. Securities for which market quotations are not readily available and other assets are valued at fair value as determined by the management and approved in good faith by the Board of Directors.

Offering Price

The price to the public on purchases of Shares made at one time by a single purchaser, by an individual, his spouse and their children under the age of 21, or by a single trust or fiduciary account other than employee plans, is the net asset value per Share plus a sales commission not exceeding 8.50% of the Offering Price (equivalent to 9.29% of the net asset value), which is reduced on larger sales as shown below.

This schedule applies to purchase of Shares made at one time for each participant account under an employee pension, profit sharing or other trust, including a 403(b) Plan account sponsored by an organized religion (the custodian of which is Templeton Funds Trust Company). A sales commission of 4% of the Offering Price (4.17% of the net asset value) is applicable to all purchases of Shares regardless of amount, made for any qualified or non-qualified employee benefit plan that (1) has ten or more separate employee accounts in the Fund or certain other Templeton Funds; or (2) is a 403(b) Plan account (the custodian of which is Templeton Funds Trust Company); and (3) continues to meet conditions (1) or (2) as determined once each year by TFD. Any purchases qualifying for the 4% sales commission described above must be made by direct investment only and may not be included as purchases under a current Letter of Intent or for purposes of qualifying for the Cumulative Quantity Discount (see "Cumulative Quantity Discount" and "Letter of Intent," below). The entire sales commission will be reallowed to selected dealers who establish that Shares sold to 403(b) (7) Plan accounts exceed $10 million per annum.

From time to time, TFD may reallow the entire sales commission to selected dealers who sell or are expected to sell significant amounts of Shares during specified time periods. Dur-

Total Sales Commission

Amount of Single Sale at Offering Price	As a Percentage of Offering Price of the Shares Purchased	As a Percentage of Net Asset Value of the Shares Purchased	Portion of Total Offering Price Retained by Dealers
Less than $10,000	8.50%	9.29%	7.00%
$10,000 but less than $25,000	7.75%	8.40%	6.25%
$25,000 but less than $50,000	6.25%	6.67%	5.00%
$50,000 but less than $100,000	4.50%	4.71%	3.60%
$100,000 but less than $250,000	2.75%	2.83%	2.20%
$250,000 but less than $1,000,000	1.50%	1.52%	1.20%
$1,000,000 but less than $2,000,000	0.75%	0.76%	0.60%
$2,000,000 or more	0.50%	0.50%	0.40%

ing periods when 90% or more of the sales commission is reallowed, such dealers may be deemed to be underwriters as that term is defined in the Securities Act of 1933.

As to telephone orders placed with TFD by dealers (see "Principal Underwriter" in the SAI), the dealer must receive the investor's order before the close of the New York Stock Exchange and transmit it to TFD by 5:00 p.m., New York time, for the investor to receive that day's Offering Price. Payment for such orders must be made by check in U.S. currency and must be promptly submitted to TFD. Orders mailed to TFD by dealers or individual investors are effected at the Offering Price next computed after the purchase order accompanied by payment has been received by TFD. Such payment must be by check in U.S. currency drawn on a commercial bank in the U.S. and, if over $100,000, may not be deemed to have been received until the proceeds have been collected unless the check is certified or issued by such bank. Any subscription may be rejected by TFD or by the Fund.

Investors should promptly check the confirmation advice that is mailed after each purchase (or redemption) in order to insure that it has been accurately recorded in the investor's account.

The minimum initial purchase order is $500 (other than in monthly investment plans, such as sponsored payroll deduction, pre-authorized check, split-funding or comparable plans), with subsequent investments of $25 or more.

The Fund may involuntarily redeem an investor's Shares if the net asset value of such Shares is less than $250; provided that involuntary redemptions will not result from fluctuations in the value of an investor's Shares. In addition, the Fund may involuntarily redeem the Shares of any investor who has failed to provide the Fund with a certified taxpayer identification number or such other tax-related certifications as the Fund may require. A notice of redemption, sent by first class mail to the investor's address of record,

will fix a date not less than 30 days after the mailing date, and Shares will be redeemed at net asset value at the close of business on that date, unless sufficient additional Shares are purchased to bring the aggregate account value up to $250 or more, or unless a certified taxpayer identification number (or such other information as the Fund has requested) has been provided, as the case may be. A check for the redemption proceeds will be mailed to the investor at the address of record.

Shares may be sold at net asset value in any amount to certain unit investment trusts and to unit holders of such trusts reinvesting their distributions from the trusts in the Fund.

In order for the Fund to avoid the additional expense and burden of withholding taxes required under regulations of the Internal Revenue Service, the Fund will not accept applications without certified Social Security (taxpayer identification) numbers.

Issuance of Shares for Securities

The Fund may accept securities which are consistent with the Fund's investment objective and policies (as described in the Prospectus) in lieu of cash in connection with sales of Fund Shares to certain persons. This alternative is available only with respect to sales of Shares in excess of $50 million. These sales will be effected at the Fund's Offering Price per Share based on the total amount of the sale. Any securities acquired by the Fund in this manner will be valued in accordance with the valuation procedures as described in "Purchase of Shares—Net Asset Value" above. The Fund reserves the right to amend or terminate this practice at any time.

Cumulative Quantity Discount

The schedule of reduced sales commissions also may be applied to qualifying sales on a cumulative basis. For this purpose, the dollar amount of the sale is added to the higher of (1) the value (calculated at the current Offering Price), or (2) the purchase price of any other Shares of the Fund and/or any other eligible Templeton Fund (except Shares of Templeton Money Fund or Templeton Tax Free Money Fund acquired by direct purchase) owned at that time by the investor. For example, if the investor held Shares valued at $9,000 (or, if valued at less than $9,000, had been purchased for $9,000) and purchased an additional $6,000 of the Fund's Shares, the sales commission for the $6,000 purchase would be at the rate of 7.75%. It is TFD's policy to give investors the best sales commission rate possible; however, there can be no assurance that an investor will receive the appropriate discount unless, at the time of placing the purchase order, the investor or the dealer makes a request for the discount and gives TFD sufficient information to determine whether the purchase will qualify for the discount. On telephone orders from dealers for the purchase of Shares to be registered in "street name," TFD will accept the dealer's instructions with respect to the applicable sales commission rate. The cumulative quantity discount may be amended or terminated at any time. Shares held in the name of a nominee or custodian under pension, profit sharing, or other employee plans may not be combined with other Shares to qualify for the cumulative quantity discount.

Letter of Intent

The reduced sales charges set forth above apply immediately to all purchases where the purchaser has executed a Letter of Intent calling for the purchase within a 13-month period of an amount qualifying for a reduced sales charge. For a description of the Letter of Intent, see the Application and "Letting of Intent" in the SAI.

Exchange Privilege

Shares of any eligible Templeton Fund may be exchanged for Shares of any other eligible Templeton Fund, without sales charge, on the basis of their relative net asset values per Share

at the time of exchange. However, if a Shareholder's original investment was in a Fund with a lower sales charge, or no sales charge, the Shareholder must pay the difference.

All exchanges must be for a minimum of $1,000. Exchanges are permitted only after at least 15 days have elapsed from the date of a previous exchange or the purchase of the Shares to be exchanged. Exchanges are limited to one exchange of the same Shares from the Fund and back to the Fund from which the previous exchange was made once each calendar quarter, provided that at least 15 days have elapsed between the transactions.

Exchange instructions may be given in writing or by telephone. Telephone exchange privileges automatically apply to each Shareholder of record unless and until the Transfer Agent receives written instructions from the Shareholder(s) of record cancelling such privileges. No telephone exchange by a single investor will be accepted for amounts in excess of $500,000 on any given business day.

Telephonic exchanges can involve only Shares in non-certificated form. Shares held in certificate forms are not eligible, but may be returned and qualify for these services. All accounts involved in a telephonic exchange must have the same registration and dividend option as the account from which the Shares are being exchanged. If all telephone exchange lines are busy (which might occur, for example, during periods of substantial market fluctuations), Shareholders might not be able to request telephone exchanges and would have to submit written exchange requests.

Unless a Shareholder elects to decline the telephone exchange privilege, the Shareholder constitutes and appoints the Transfer Agent as the true and lawful attorney to surrender for redemption or exchange any and all unissued Shares held by it in an account with any eligible Templeton Fund, and authorizes and directs the Transfer Agent to act upon any instruction from any person. The Transfer Agent will accept instructions by telephone to exchange Shares held in any account for

Shares of any other eligible Templeton Fund, provided the registration and mailing address of the Shares to be purchased are identical to those of the Shares to be redeemed. Further, a Shareholder(s) agrees that neither the Transfer Agent, any of its affiliates nor the Fund(s) will be liable for any loss, damages, expense or cost arising out of any requests effected in accordance with an authorization, including requests effected by imposters or persons otherwise unauthorized to act on behalf of the account. If the Shareholder is an entity other than an individual, such entity may be required to certify the persons that have been duly elected and are now legally holding the titles given and that the said entity is duly organized and existing and has the power to take action called for by this continuing authorization.

Neither the Fund nor the Transfer Agent will be responsible for acting upon any instructions believed by them to be genuine. Forms for declining the telephone exchange privilege and prospectuses of the other Templeton Funds may be obtained from TFD. A gain or loss for tax purposes will be realized upon the exchange, depending on the cost basis of the Shares redeemed.

This exchange privilege is available only in states where Shares of the Fund being acquired may legally be sold and may be modified, limited or terminated at any time by the Fund upon sixty (60) days written notice. A shareholder who wishes to make an exchange should first obtain and review a current prospectus of the Fund into which he or she wishes to exchange. Broker–dealers who process exchange orders on behalf of their customers may charge a fee for their services. Such fee may be avoided by making requests for exchange directly to the Transfer Agent.

Other Special Purchase Plans

Other special purchase plans are described in the SAI under the heading "Purchase, Redemption and Pricing of Shares," including Pre-Authorized Check, Tax Deferred Retirement Plans and Cash Withdrawal Program.

Redemption and Repurchase of Shares

Shares will be redeemed, without charge, on request of the Shareholder in "Proper Order" to the Fund's Transfer Agent, Templeton Funds Trust Company. "Proper Order" means that the request to redeem must meet all the following requirements:

1. It must be in writing, signed by the Shareholder(s) *exactly in the manner as the Shares are registered*, and must specify either the number of Shares, or the dollar amount of Shares, to be redeemed and sent to Templeton Funds Trust Company, P.O. Box 33030, St. Petersburg, Florida 33733-8030;

2. The signature(s) of the redeeming Shareholder(s) must be guaranteed by a commercial bank located in the United States (or having a correspondent relation with a commercial bank in the United States), by a trust company located in New York City or Colorado (or having a correspondent relation with a trust company located in either jurisdiction), or by a member firm of the New York, Boston, Philadelphia, Midwest or Pacific Stock Exchanges, which are participants in the signature guarantee program, and if the Shares are registered in more than one name, the signature of each of the redeeming Shareholders must be guaranteed separately;

3. Any outstanding certificates must accompany the request together with a stock power signed by the Shareholder(s), with signature(s) guaranteed as described in Item 2 above;

4. If the Shares being redeemed are registered in the name of an estate, trust, custodian, guardian, retirement plan or the like, or in the name of a corporation or partnership,

documents also must be included which, in the judgment of the Transfer Agent, are sufficient to establish the authority of the person(s) signing the request, and/or as may be required by applicable laws or regulations, with signature(s) guaranteed as described in Item 2 above; and

5. Redemption of Shares held in a Templeton Tax Deferred Retirement Plan must conform to the requirements of the Plan and the Fund's redemption requirements above. Distributions from such plans are subject to additional requirements under the Internal Revenue Code (the "Code") and certain documents (available from the Transfer Agent) must be completed before the distribution may be made. Distributions from retirement plans are subject to withholding requirements under Code, and the IRS Form W-4P (available from the Transfer Agent) must be submitted to the Transfer Agent with the distribution request, or the distribution will be delayed. Templeton Funds Trust Company and its affiliates assume no responsibility to determine whether a distribution satisfies the conditions of applicable tax law and will not be responsible for any penalties assessed.

A signature guarantee also is required in connection with a request for proceeds to be mailed other than to the registered owner of the Shares or to an address different from the address of record or a request for transfer of Shares to another person. Guarantee of the signature(s) on a request to redeem *less than $5,000 may be waived*, if approved by the Transfer Agent. Shareholders with questions as to redemption of their Shares may obtain further information by writing to Templeton Funds Trust Company at the above address or calling (800) 237-0738.

Neither the Fund nor the Transfer Agent will be responsible for acting upon instructions believed by them to be genuine. The redemption price will be the net asset value of the Shares next computed after the redemption request in Proper Order is received by the Transfer Agent. Payment of the redemption price ordinarily will be made by check (or by wire at the sole discretion of the Transfer Agent if wire transfer is requested including name and address of the bank and the Shareholder's account number to which payment of the redemption proceeds is to be wired) within seven days after receipt of the redemption request in Proper Order. However, if Shares have been purchased by check, the Fund will make redemption proceeds available when a Shareholder's check received for the Shares purchased has been cleared for payment by the Shareholder's bank, which, depending upon the location of the Shareholder's bank, could take up to 15 days or more. The check will be mailed by first class mail to the Shareholder's registered address (or as otherwise directed). Remittance by wire (to a commercial bank account in the same name(s) as the Shares are registered that has been in existence for more than six (6) months) or express mail, if requested, *will be at a charge of $15* which will be deducted from the redemption proceeds.

The Fund, through TFD, also repurchases through securities dealers Shares for which certificates have been issued. The Fund normally will accept orders to repurchase such Shares by wire or telephone from dealers for their customers at the net asset value next computed after the dealer has received the certificate holder's request for repurchase, if the dealer received such request before closing time of the New York Stock Exchange on that day. Dealers have the responsibility of submitting such repurchase requests by calling not later than 5:00 p.m., New York time, on such day in order to obtain that day's applicable redemption price. Repurchase of Shares is for the convenience of Shareholders and does not involve a charge by the Fund; however, securities dealers may impose a charge on the Shareholder for transmitting the notice of repurchase to the Fund. The Fund reserves the right to reject any order for repurchase, which right of rejection might adversely affect Shareholders seeking redemption through the repurchase procedure. For Shareholders redeeming through their securities dealer, ordinarily payment will be made as requested, either to the securities dealer or directly to the redeeming Shareholder, within seven days after tender of the certificates for the Shares properly endorsed and with signatures guaranteed as described above. The Fund will also accept, from member firms of the New York Stock Exchange, orders to repurchase Shares for which no certificates have been issued by wire or telephone without a redemption request signed by the shareholder, provided the member firm indemnifies the Fund and TFD from any liability resulting from the absence of the Shareholder's signature. Forms for such indemnity agreement can be obtained from TFD.

Upon any redemption or repurchase of a portion of a Shareholder's Shares leaving a balance of unredeemed Shares of less than $250 at net asset value as of the time of the redemption, the Fund may also redeem such balance of Shares and add the proceeds thereof to the proceeds of the redemption or repurchase which the Shareholder requested. As to the Fund's right to redeem the Shares of an investor the net asset value of whose holding is less than $250, see "Purchase of Shares."

The value of the Fund's Shares on redemption or repurchase may be more or less than the investor's cost, depending on the market value of the portfolio securities at the time of redemption or repurchase. A former Shareholder of any eligible Templeton Fund may, within 90 days from the date of redeeming his Shares, apply the proceeds thereof to purchase new Shares of any eligible Templeton Fund without sales commission at the net asset value in effect on the date such proceeds are received by the Transfer Agent. However, if a Shareholder's original investment was in a Fund with a lower sales charge, or no sales charge, the Shareholder must pay the difference. This privilege is available only once to each Shareholder.

Management of the Fund

The Fund is managed by its Board of Directors and all powers are exercised by or under authority of the Board. Information relating to the Directors and Executive Officers is set forth under the heading "Management of the Fund" in the SAI.

Investment Manager

The Investment Manager of the Fund is Templeton, Galbraith & Hansberger Ltd., Nassau, Bahamas ("TG & H"), a corporation in which Mr. John M. Templeton owns the controlling stock interest. On December 31, 1989, TG & H assumed the investment management functions previously performed by Templeton Investment Counsel Limited ("TICL"), a wholly owned subsidiary of TG & H.

The Investment Manager furnishes the Fund with investment research, advice and supervision. The Investment Manager does not furnish any overhead items or facilities for the Fund, although such expenses are paid by some investment advisers of other investment companies. As compensation for its services, the Fund pays the Investment Manager a fee which, during the most recent fiscal year, was paid to TICL, and which represented 0.43% of the Fund's average daily net assets. Further information concerning the Investment Manager is included under the heading "Investment Advisory and Other Services" in the SAI.

Transfer Agent

Templeton Funds Trust Company serves as transfer agent and dividend disbursing agent for the Fund.

Expenses

For the fiscal year ended August 31, 1989, expenses amounted to 0.66% of the Fund's average net assets.

Brokerage Commissions

The Fund may allocate some portfolio transactions to RBC Dominion Securities Inc. and to Raymond James & Associates, Inc., officers of which are Directors of the Fund. The prices and execution of all securities transactions by these firms for the Fund will be, in the good faith judgment of the Fund's management, equal to the best available within the scope of the Fund's brokerage policies, which are described under the heading "Brokerage Allocation" in the SAI. The Fund's brokerage policies provide that the sale of Shares by a broker is one factor among others to be taken into account in allocation securities transactions to that broker, provided that the prices and execution provided by such broker equal the best available within the scope of the Fund's brokerage policies.

Description of Shares

The Fund's authorized capital consists of 300,000,000 Common Shares of $0.01 par value per Share. Each Share entitles the holder to one vote and to participate equally in dividends, distributions of capital and net assets of the Fund on liquidation.

The Fund will not ordinarily issue certificates for Shares purchased. Share certificates representing whole (not fractional) Shares are issued only upon the specific request of the Shareholder made in writing to the Transfer Agent. No charge is made for the issuance of one certificate for all or some of the Shares purchased in a single order. If multiple certificates are requested for Shares purchased in a single order, there will be a charge of $1.00 for each additional certificate. Securities deal-

ers can exercise the wire order repurchase procedure on behalf of investors holding certificates. (See "Redemption and Repurchase of Shares.")

Dividends and Distributions

The Fund intends normally to pay a dividend at least once annually representing substantially all of its net investment income and any net realized capital gains. Income dividends and capital gain distributions paid by the Fund, other than on those Shares whose owners keep them registered in the name of a broker–dealer, are automatically reinvested on the payable date in whole or fractional Shares of the Fund at net asset value as of the record date, unless a Shareholder makes a written request for payments in cash. Income dividends and capital gains distributions will be paid in cash on Shares during the time that their owners keep them registered in the name of a broker–dealer.

Prior to purchasing Shares of the Fund, the impact of dividends or capital gains distributions which have been declared but not yet paid should be carefully considered. Any dividend or capital gains distribution paid shortly after a purchase by a Shareholder prior to the record date will have the effect of reducing the per share net asset value of the Shares by the amount of the dividend or distribution. All or a portion of such dividend or distribution, although in effect a return of capital, generally will be subject to tax.

Checks are forwarded by first class mail to the address of record. The proceeds of any such checks which are not accepted by the addressee and returned to the Fund will be reinvested for the Shareholder's account in whole or fractional Shares at net asset value next computed after the check has been received by the Transfer Agent. Subsequent distributions will be reinvested automatically at net asset value as of the record date in additional whole or fractional Shares.

Federal Tax Information

The Fund intends to elect to be treated and to qualify each year as a regulated investment company. See the SAI for a summary of the requirements that must be satisfied to so qualify. A regulated investment company is not subject to Federal income tax on income and gains distributed in a timely manner to its Shareholders. The Fund intends to distribute substantially all of its net investment income and realized capital gains to Shareholders, which generally will be taxable income or capital gains in their hands. Distributions declared in October, November or December to Shareholders of record on a date in such month and paid during the following January will be treated as having been received by Shareholders on December 31 in the year such distributions were declared. The Fund will inform Shareholders each year of the amount and nature of such income or gains. A more detailed description of tax consequences to Shareholders is contained in the SAI under the heading "Tax Status."

Inquiries

Shareholders' inquiries will be answered promptly. They should be addressed to Templeton Funds Trust Company, 700 Central Avenue, P.O. Box 33030, St. Petersburg, Florida 33733-8030—telephone (800) 237-0738. Transcripts of Shareholder accounts less than three years old are provided on request without charge; a fee of $15 per account is charged for transcripts going back more than three years from the date the request is received by the Transfer Agent.

Performance Information

The Fund may include its total return in advertisements or reports to Shareholders or prospective investors. Quotations of average annual total return will be expressed in terms of the average annual compounded rate of return on a hypothetical investment in the Fund over a period of 1, 5 and 10 years (or up to the life of the Fund), will reflect the deduction of the maximum initial sales charge and deduction of a proportional share of Fund expenses (on an annual basis), and will assume that all dividends and distributions are reinvested when paid. Total return may be expressed in terms of the cumulative value of an investment in the Fund at the end of a defined period of time. For a description of the methods used to determine total return for the Fund, see the SAI.

VALUE OF SHARES

Year Ended April 30,	Initially Acquired	Accepted as Capital Gains Distributions (cumulative)	Received Through Reinvestment of Dividends (cumulative)	Total Value
1955	$ 9,516	$ —	$ —	$ 9,516
1956	11,072	—	—	11,072
1957	10,889	—	—	10,889
1958	9,699	—	—	9,699
1959	14,457	—	—	14,457
1960	14,650	—	—	14,640

(*Continued*)

Year Ended April 30,	Initially Acquired	Accepted as Capital Gains Distributions (cumulative)	Received Through Reinvestment of Dividends (cumulative)	Total Value
1961	19,398	—	—	19,398
1962	19,124	—	—	19,124
1963	17,477	—	—	17,477
1964	19,856	—	251	20,107
1965	25,712	—	325	26,037
1966	28,182	—	757	28,939
1967	28,365	—	1,123	29,488
1968	32,391	—	1,840	34,231
1969	42,548	—	3,019	45,567
1970	43,920	—	3,868	47,788
1971	48,312	—	5,116	53,428
1972	65,423	1,286	8,025	74,734
1973	85,095	3,667	11,376	100,138
1974	71,370	12,685	11,515	95,570
1975	73,383	13,043	12,492	98,918
1976	91,134	16,656	16,889	124,679
1977	112,271	22,238	22,681	157,190
1978	138,531	39,321	30,664	208,516
1979	160,034	46,371	37,476	243,881
1980	171,014	53,697	43,731	268,442
1981	220,698	90,293	63,066	374,057
1982	188,856	77,266	60,076	326,198
1983	248,148	126,197	93,036	467,381
1984	262,422	133,456	108,153	504,031
1985	278,317	159,242	126,295	563,854
1986	365,874	244,919	183,817	794,610
12/31/86	353,248	265,624	202,110	820,982
8/31/87	470,174	353,546	269,009	1,092,729
8/31/88	374,657	362,931	247,444	985,032
8/31/89	456,176	464,011	344,406	1,264,593

This chart illustrates the cumulative total return of an initial $10,000 investment in the Fund from November 29, 1954 (inception) to August 31, 1989. The results shown should not be considered as a representation of the dividend income or capital gain or loss which may be realized from an investment made in the Fund today.

Templeton Growth Fund, Inc. was incorporated in Maryland in November 10, 1986 and commenced operations on December 31, 1986. The Fund is the successor in interest to approximately 58% of Templeton Growth Fund Ltd., a Canadian corporation organized on September 1, 1954 (the "Canadian Fund"), which was reorganized on December 31, 1986 into two mutual funds. Under the reorganization, 58% of the portfolio and other assets of the Canadian Fund were transferred to the Fund and the non-Canadian Shareholders of the Canadian Fund, representing 58% of the Shares outstanding, became Shareholders of the Fund.

(Continued)

Dividends from investment income were paid commencing in 1964 and distributions of capital gains were paid commencing in 1972. Prior to those years net income and realized capital gains were retained by the Canadian Fund. Income dividends and capital gains distributions are shown in the chart as reinvested at net asset value in accordance with the reinvestment policy described in the current prospectus.

Initial net asset value is the amount received by the Fund after deducting the maximum sales commission of $8\frac{1}{2}\%$. The actual sales commission on an investment of $10,000 is $7\frac{3}{4}\%$ as described in the prospectus. No adjustment has been made for any income taxes payable by shareholders. The results reflect the deduction of all fees and expenses. The total amount of capital gains distributions accepted in shares was $218,766, the total amount of dividends reinvested was $159,311.

Illustration of an Assumed Investment of $10,000

with Income Dividends Reinvested
and Capital Gains Distributions Accepted
in Shares
(states in U.S. dollars)

This chart covers the period from November 29, 1954 (inception) to August 31, 1989. The Fund's results shown should not be considered as a representation of the dividend income or capital gain or loss which may be realized from an investment made in the Fund today.

The cost of living as set out in the chart represents the annual change in the Consumer Price Index, applied to an initial value in November 1954 of $10,000. (The Consumer Price Index is prepared by the U.S. Bureau of Labor Statistics based on prevailing economic factors.) This presentation has been made so as to compare the increase in value of a $10,000 investment in Templeton Growth Fund, Inc. with the increase in the cost of living over the same time period.

The investment return and principal value of an investment will fluctuate so that an investor's shares, when redeemed, may be worth more or less than their initial cost. The performance information shown represents past historical performance and is not an indication of the Fund's future performance.

The average annual total return for the 1-, 5- and 10-year periods ended august 31, 1989 was

+17.5%, +16.9% and +15.2%, respectively. Total return quotations reflect the deduction of the maximum initial sales charge, deduction of a proportional share of Fund expenses on an annual basis and assume that all dividends and distributions are reinvested when paid.

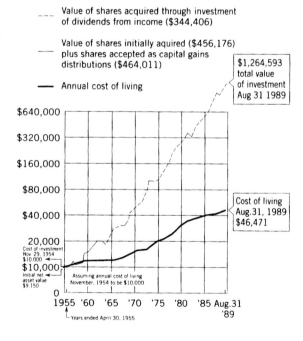

Templeton Growth Fund, Inc.: Selected Excerpts from Portfolio & Performance, May 31, 1990

SUMMARY OF PORTFOLIO

Common Stocks & Convertible Issues

United States	36.0%
Canada	9.2
Australia	8.8
United Kingdom	6.6
Hong Kong	5.1
France	4.5
Mexico	4.2
Germany	3.8
Switzerland	3.6
Netherlands	2.0
Spain	1.7
Norway	1.7
Sweden	1.5
Italy	0.7
Turkey	0.5
Singapore	0.5
New Zealand	0.2
Malaysia	0.2
Chile	0.1
	90.9

Fixed Income

Bonds & preferred stocks	0.9
Short-term securities and all other assets, net	8.2
Total net assets	100.0%

INVESTMENT PORTFOLIO
May 31, 1990 (unaudited)

	Number of Shares	Value

COMMON STOCKS: 90.8%

Energy Sources: 7.9%

British Gas PLC	4,000,000	$ 14,627,364
Hong Kong & China Ga Co. Ltd.	7,812,000	11,148,521
Norsk Hydro AS	1,400,000	44,136,870
Nova Corp.	3,000,000	21,385,710
Repsol SA	250,000	6,017,391
Shell Transport & Trading Co. PLC	2,500,000	19,626,163
Societe Nationale Elf Aquitiane	200,000	24,648,195
Total Campagnie Francaise Des Petroles	536,325	66,472,236
Wainoco Oil Corp.	119,900	1,049,125
		209,111,575

Utilities: 2.0%

Centerior Energy Corp.	200,000	3,700,000
Empresa Nacional De Electricidad SA ADR	300,000	6,825,000
Endesa	700,000	15,783,165
General Public Utilities Corp.	207,900	9,173,587
Hong Kong Electric Holdings, Ltd.	5,500,000	5,656,981
Potomac Electric Power Corp.	420,000	8,925,000
Sevillana de Electric	500,000	2,801,774
		52,865,507

Building Materials & Components: 0.7%

Cementia Holding AG	18,000	$ 14,490,725
Owens Corning Fiberglass Corp.	100,000	2,350,000
Pioneer International Ltd.	500,000	841,374
		17,682,099

Chemicals: 5.6%

Akzo NV	278,000	17,218,985
Akzo NV, ADR	96,600	3,006,675
ARCO Chemical Co.	700,000	29,662,500
Bayer A.G.	152,300	26,824,191
Dow Chemical Co.	200,000	12,450,000
Hoechst A.G.	191,900	33,131,453
Monsanto Co.	247,800	25,399,500
		147,693,304

(*Continued*)

	Number of Shares	Value
Forest Products & Paper: 5.2%		
Canadian Pacific Forest products Ltd.	232,400	6,428,906
Canfor Corp.	520,000	12,005,788
Carter Holt Harvey Ltd.	2,000,000	3,280,350
Champion International Corp.	681,000	20,770,500
Elders Resources Ltd.	453,200	490,335
Empresa Nacional de Celulosa	110,000	4,206,941
Fletcher Challenge Ltd., Aus.	857,142	2,137,066
Fletcher Challenge Ltd., N.Z.	1,850,000	4,631,338
Georgia-Pacific Corp.	87,100	3,952,163
International Paper Co.	350,000	18,375,000
James River Corp.	700,000	17,675,000
Louisiana Pacific	500,000	22,312,500
Pentair Corp. Inc.	58,980	1,754,655
Weyerhaeuser Co.	720,000	19,710,000
		137,730,542
Mining & Metals: 4.8%		
Alcan Aluminium Ltd.	1,356,850	30,749,570
Alcan Australia Ltd.	200,000	378,232
Aluminum Co. of America	250,000	16,500,000
Comalco, Ltd.	400,000	1,296,797
Reynolds Metals Co.	737,808	43,346,220
Sandvik AB, B	715,564	34,774,636
		127,045,455
Aerospace & Military Technology: 2.0%		
Boeing Co. (The)	632,150	52,152,375
Construction & Housing: 1.6%		
Boral Ltd.	483,925	1,322,342
Holderbank Financier Glarus AG	8,000	38,221,911
Hovnanian Enterprises, Inc.	144,200	757,050
MDC Holdings, Inc.	287,500	251,563
PHM Corp.	200,000	1,750,000
		42,302,866
Electrical & Electronics: 2.6%		
Compagnie Generale D'Electricite	240,114	26,737,631
Siemens A.G.	95,300	40,659,086
		67,396,717

	Number of Shares	Value
Energy Equipment & Services: 0.3%		
Burlington Resources	200,000	8,475,000
Industrial Components: 0.5%		
Goodyear	300,000	$ 10,725,000
SKF, B	79,400	2,136,497
		12,861,497
Machinery & Engineering: 0.2%		
Schindler Holdings AG, Ptg	5,973	5,686,580
Appliances & Household Durables: 0.5%		
Leggett & Platt, Inc.	105,400	3,636,300
Whirlpool Corp.	300,000	8,925,000
		12,561,300
Automobiles: 1.1%		
Ford Motor Co.	550,000	25,368,750
Volvo AB, B	40,000	2,341,813
		27,710,563
Food & Household Products: 2.7%		
Dairy Farm International Holdings Ltd.	11,368,340	15,492,978
Goodman Fielder Wattie Ltd.	3,439,857	4,248,375
Hillsdown Holdings	1,250,000	5,535,585
Nestle, D	2,000	12,600,630
Unilever NV	400,000	32,335,925
		70,213,493
Health & Personal Care: 0.3%		
Marion Laboratories Inc.	56,872	1,386,255
Pfizer Inc.	100,000	6,562,500
		7,948,755
Recreation, Other Consumer Goods: 1.5%		
Eastman Kodak Co.	800,000	32,200,000
Russ Berrie & Co., Inc.	503,300	7,864,063
		40,064,063
Textiles & Apparel: 0.1%		
Winsor Industrial Corp. Ltd.	2,934,125	3,017,871
Broadcasting & Publishing: 1.2%		
News Corp. Ltd.	3,114,500	24,161,117
News Corp. Ltd., ADR	72,900	1,129,950
News International Ltd.	1,632,400	7,256,413
		32,547,480

(Continued)

	Number of Shares	Value
Business & Public Service: 2.4%		
Brunswick Corp.	890,000	12,348,750
Enstar Inc.	142,271	284,542
Humana, Inc.	963,513	43,228,088
Kinder-Care, Inc.	305,513	954,728
ManPower PLC	2,600,000	3,380,062
National Medical Enterprises	80,000	2,880,000
		63,076,170
Merchandising: 4.5%		
American Stores Co.	698,636	$ 48,555,202
Burton Group PLC	1,170,000	3,611,214
Cifra SA, B	34,869,621	36,698,358
CUC International, Inc.	400,000	7,850,000
Hechinger Co., A	451,000	7,033,000
K-Mart Corp.	450,000	15,806,250
		119,554,024
Telecommunications: 4.3%		
BCE, Inc.	265,542	8,956,124
Blockbuster Entertainment Corp.	100,000	2,387,500
Setemer SpA	33,200	1,270,938
SIP (NEW)	1,787,500	2,333,202
STET	3,000,000	15,576,924
Telefonica Nacional De Espana	1,140,000	8,893,371
Telefonos de Mexico SA, 90	40,547,647	74,356,518
		113,774,577
Transportation: 4.3%		
Air Canada Inc.	200,000	1,744,904
British Airways PLC	5,100,000	17,537,737
Burlington Northern Inc.	500,000	18,687,500
Jurong Shipyward Ltd.	150,000	686,620
Keppel Corp. Ltd.	500,000	2,166,847
Laidlaw Inc., A	47,100	1,052,368
Laidlaw Inc., B	792,900	17,715,985
Malaysian International Shipping Corp.	1,055,000	4,857,800
Singapore Airlines	900,000	9,848,321
Stolt Tankers & Terminal Holdings SA	243,500	5,204,812
Swissair, Br	28,350	21,334,442
TNT Ltd.	5,507,520	10,840,738
TNT Ltd., Warrants	556,600	580,016
		112,258,090

	Number of Shares	Value
Wholesale & International Trade: 0.1%		
Sime Darby Hong Kong Ltd.	3,564,000	1,569,390
Banking: 14.6%		
ANZ Banking Group Ltd.	13,357,578	52,172,402
Bank of Montreal	1,126,351	25,645,733
Bank of New Zealand	287,000	150,303
Bank of Nova Scotia	2,957,313	35,240,569
Barclays Bank PLC	5,229,700	35,353,415
Barclays Bank PLC. ADR	140,300	5,278,788
CS Holdings	1,440	2,479,804
First of America Bank Corp.	130,000	6,175,000
Hong Kong & Shanghai Banking	6,870,967	5,211,972
National Australia Bank Ltd.	13,232,712	65,984,812
National Bank of Canada	300,000	2,330,085
National Westminster Bank Ltd.	3,929,600	23,400,560
Republic New York Corp.	238,600	11,601,925
The Royal Bank of Canada	574,920	11,438,699
Royal Bank of Scotland Group	1,135,555	3,390,609
The Toronto-Dominion Bank	1,862,486	28,535,344
Wells Fargo & Co.	100,000	7,950,000
Westpac Banking Corp.	16,547,898	63,355,911
		385,695,931
Financial Services: 6.0%		
American Capital Mgt & Research	550,000	$ 5,568,750
American Express Co.	516,200	15,098,850
Calfed, Inc.	634,000	12,431,250
Coast Savings Financial Inc.	64,800	494,100
Core States Financial	25,000	1,068,750
Dime Savings Bank of New York	500,000	3,500,000
Dreyfus Corp.	652,300	22,259,737
Federal National Mortgage Assn.	350,000	13,912,500
First Capital Holdings Corp.	1,175,860	5,585,335
First Chattanooga Financial Corp.	10,000	190,000
Franklin Resources, Inc.	648,300	22,528,425
Homestead Financial Corp.	380,600	856,350
M & G Group PLC	650,000	4,852,024
Merrill Lynch & Company, Inc.	1,546,400	36,727,000
Monarch Capital Corp.	45,900	625,387

(Continued)

	Number of Shares	Value
Peoples Heritage Financial Group	290,000	2,791,250
Pioneer Group Inc.	75,000	1,912,500
Primerica Corp.	205,000	6,688,125
		157,090,333

Insurance: 7.0%

Aetna Life & Casualty Co.	182,700	9,591,750
AMBase Corp.	230,000	1,408,750
American International Group, Inc.	300,000	30,450,000
Chubb Corp.	240,000	11,520,000
Cigna Corp.	720,272	37,454,144
FAI Insurances Ltd.	629,548	753,222
First Executive Corp.	375,821	892,575
Kemper Corp.	1,088,397	44,352,178
NWNL Companies, Inc.	331,100	10,181,325
Progressive Corp, Ohio	867,700	35,792,625
Travelers Corp.	100,000	3,037,500
		185,434,069

Real Estate: 0.7%

Cheung Kong (Holdings) Ltd	10,000,000	15,813,830
Hong Kong Realty & Trust Co. Ltd., A	1,500,000	887,118
Marathon Realty	100,000	659,659
Patten Corp.	472,700	709,050
		18,069,657

Multi-Industries: 6.1%

ADT Ltd.	5,074,099	16,171,940
Canadian Pacific Ltd.	2,062,500	38,621,952
Hanson Trust PLC	3,000,000	12,027,315
Hanson Trust PLC, Warrants	87,100	522,600
Hutchison Whampoa Ltd.	8,981,000	12,816,803
Jardine Matheson Holdings Ltd.	5,499,499	24,216,747
Jardine Strategic Holdings Ltd.	7,000,000	16,559,529
Pacific Dunlop, Ltd.	1,142,500	4,277,209
Polly Peck International PLC	1,983,258	14,072,431
Swire Pacific, Ltd.	8,070,500	20,129,554
		159,416,080
Total common stocks		2,391,005,363

Preferred Stocks: 0.5%

Jardine Strategic Holdings Ltd., 6.50% conv., pfd.	900,000	$ 1,154,250
Mesa LP, pfd. A	500,000	2,500,000
NCNB Corp., pfd. B	187,000	11,126,500
Total preferred stocks		14,780,750

	Principal Amount[a]	

BONDS: 0.4%

Compagnie Generate D'Electricite, 6%, 1/1/99 ECU.	1,452,000	356,800
Deutsche Bank, 7.20%, 10/9/91 H.K.	3,000,000	372,165
Metro Airlines, Inc., 8.50%, conv., 10/12/01 U.S.	67,000	41,038
Ontario Hydro, 9.25%, 4/1/06 Can.	5,810,000	4,228,242
Quebec Hydro Electric Commission, 9.75%, 8/1/05 U.S.	1,162,000	1,141,595
Robert Half Int'l., Inc., 7.25%, conv., 8/12/01 U.S.	1,300,000	1,163,500
Supermarkets General Corp., 13,125%, 10/5/03 U.S.	958,000	401,163
U.S. Treasurey Bond, 7.25%, 5/15/16 U.S.	5,000,000	$4,269,000
Total bonds		11,973,503

Short-Term Obligations: 7.4%

Dai-ichi Kang Yo Bank, 7.1875%, 2/26/91 H.K.	7,000,000	881,975
Morgan Guaranty Trust, 6.95%, 11/12/90 H.K.	15,000,000	1,902,481
Security Pacific Credit Ltd., 7.50%, 1/28/91 H.K.	8,000,000	1,011,057
Sumitomo Bank, 6.90%, 2/4/91 H.K.	7,000,000	881,795
U.S. Treasurey Bills, with maturities to 7/26/90 U.S.	191,500,000	189,518,365
Total short-term obligations		194,195,673
Total Investments		2,611,955,289
Other Assets, less liabilities: 0.9%		22,769,257
Total Net Assets: 100%		$2,634,724,546

Net asset value per share, May 31, 1990–$15.99

[a]Principal amounts are in currency of countries indicated.

HISTORICAL RECORD

Period Ended	Net Asset Value	Capital Gains Distributions	Adjusted Net Asset Value[a]	Percentage Change From Previous Period	From Inception
Inception— Nov. 29, 1954	$ .33⅓				
4/30/55	.35	$ —	$ .35	+ 4%	+ 4%
4/30/56	.40	—	.40	+16	+ 21
4/30/57	.40	—	.40	− 2	+ 19
4/30/58	.35	—	.35	−11	+ 6
4/30/59	.53	—	.53	+49	+ 58
4/30/60	.53	—	.53	+ 1	+ 60
4/30/61	.71	—	.71	+33	+ 112
4/30/62	.70	—	.70	− 1	+ 109
4/30/63	.64	—	.64	− 9	+ 91
4/30/64	.72	—	.72	+14	+ 117
4/30/65	.94	—	.94	+29	+ 181
4/30/66	1.03	—	1.03	+10	+ 208
4/30/67	1.03	—	1.03	+ 1	+ 210
4/30/68	1.18	—	1.18	+14	+ 254
4/30/69	1.55	—	1.55	+31	+ 365
4/30/70	1.60	—	1.60	+ 3	+ 380
4/30/71	1.76	—	1.76	+10	+ 429
4/30/72	2.38	.03	2.41	+37	+ 624
4/30/73	3.10	.05	3.18	+32	+ 854
4/30/74	2.60	.31	2.99	− 6	+ 798
4/30/75	2.67	—	3.06	+ 3	+ 820
4/30/76	3.32	.01	3.72	+25	+1,017
4/30/77	4.09	.04	4.53	+24	+1,259
4/30/78	5.05	.24	5.73	+29	+1,617
4/30/79	5.83	.02	6.53	+16	+1,859
4/30/80	6.23	.09	7.02	+ 8	+2,006
4/30/81	8.04	.38	9.21	+35	+2,666
4/30/82	6.88	—	8.05	−14	+2,317
4/30/83	9.04	.35	10.56	+36	+3,068
4/30/84	9.56	—	11.08	+ 6	+3,224
4/30/85	10.14	.29	11.95	+ 9	+3,485
4/30/86	13.33	.48	15.62	+36	+4,586
12/31/86	12.87	.48	15.64	—	+4,592
8/31/87	17.13	—	19.90	+33	+5,870
8/31/88	13.65	1.08	17.50	−14	+5,151
8/31/89	16.62	.25	20.72	+24	+6,117
5/31/90	15.99	.47	20.56	− 1	+6,068

[a] Does not reflect an adjustment for income distributions; however, it is the total of net asset value per share plus the cumulative amount of capital gains distributions.

(Continued)

The above data give effect to a four-for-one stock split effective August 24, 1959, a five-for-one split effective October 25, 1971, and a three-for-one split effective March 2, 1979. Dividends per share paid from investment income were as follows: 1964—$.01; 1965—None; 1966—$.01; 1967—$.01; 1968—$.02; 1969—$.02; 1970—$.03; 1971—$.03; 1972—$.02; 1973—$.02; 1974—$.06; 1975—$.02; 1976—$.03; 1977—$.04; 1978—$.05; 1979—$.04; 1980—$.08; 1981—$.12; 1982—$.15; 1983—$.20; 1984—$.18; 1985—$.19; 1986—$.24; 12/31/86—$.40; 1987—$.44; 1988—$.48; 1989—$.62; total—$3.51.

The above table gives the historical record per Share during the period from November 29, 1954 (inception) to February 28, 1990. No adjustment has been made for income taxes payable by shareholders. The results shown should not be considered as a representation of the dividend income or capital gain or loss which may be realized from an investment made in the Fund today.

Morgan Stanley Capital International Perspective: Selected Excerpts

INTERNATIONAL STOCK MARKET TRENDS — 30 November 1990

P/BV	P/CE	P/E	Yield			this month	since 1.1.90	from high[1]
				INTERNATIONAL INDICES (in US dollars)				
1.78	6.8	15.0	3.2	THE WORLD INDEX (20)		-1.9	-20.1	-20.7
1.81	7.2	13.9	3.8	NORTH AMERICA (2)		6.0	-8.7	-12.3
1.77	6.4	15.8	2.8	EAFE (18)		-5.1	-25.8	-26.2
				EUROPE 17 (17)		0.6	-4.8	-14.1
1.45	5.1	10.8	4.6	EUROPE 13 (13)		0.7	-4.8	-13.9
				EC (12)		1.2	-3.7	-12.3
1.55	5.5	10.2	2.9	NORDIC COUNTRIES (4)		-5.0	-15.2	-26.4
2.16	9.7	25.6	1.2	PACIFIC (5)		-11.2	-37.6	-39.2
2.26	10.1	27.0	1.0	FAR EAST (3)		-11.6	-38.2	-40.0
				INTERNATIONAL FREE INDICES (in US dollars)				
1.79	6.8	15.1	3.2	THE WORLD INDEX FREE (20)		-1.8	-20.2	-20.7
1.78	6.5	16.0	2.8	EAFE FREE (18)		-6.5	-25.9	-26.4
				EUROPE 17 FREE (17)		0.8	-4.1	-13.4
1.47	5.1	10.9	4.6	EUROPE 13 FREE (13)		1.0	-4.1	-13.1
1.40	4.4	10.9	3.9	EUROPE 13 FREE ex THE UK (12)		-1.7	-10.4	-18.9
1.86	5.9	12.0	2.3	NORDIC COUNTRIES FREE (4)		-5.4	-6.5	-23.1
				SPECIAL AREAS (in US dollars)				
1.74	6.5	15.8	2.8	THE WORLD INDEX ex USA (19)		-5.7	-25.5	-26.0
1.74	6.5	15.8	2.8	EAFE + CANADA (19)		-5.7	-25.5	-26.0
1.61	6.3	12.3	4.2	KOKUSAI INDEX (WORLD ex JAPAN) (19)		3.4	-7.6	-12.9
1.42	5.3	10.9	4.6	EASEA INDEX (EAFE ex JAPAN) (17)		0.5	-5.8	-14.4
1.19	7.9	11.9	5.3	PACIFIC ex JAPAN (4)		-1.3	-14.0	-27.2
1.81	6.8	15.8	2.9	THE WORLD INDEX ex THE UK (19)		-2.7	-22.6	-23.0
1.82	6.4	17.6	2.1	EAFE ex THE UK (17)		-8.2	-30.5	-30.9
1.39	4.4	10.7	3.9	EUROPE 13 ex THE UK (12)		-1.8	-11.2	-19.6
				NATIONAL INDICES (in US dollars)				
1.18	7.7	13.9	6.5	AUSTRALIA	10	-0.2	-18.6	-33.3
2.23	5.2	33.4	1.7	AUSTRIA	8	0.0	5.8	-30.5
1.28	4.3	9.0	5.7	BELGIUM	18	-3.1	-14.4	-17.1
1.30	6.9	16.2	3.9	CANADA	5	2.4	-18.6	-19.4
2.11	7.4	14.8	1.8	DENMARK	20	-4.6	1.4	-11.9
0.70	4.3	10.4	3.8	FINLAND	4	-4.1	-29.3	-45.4
0.75	4.0	11.6	3.4	FINLAND (FREE)	1	1.4	-26.5	-35.9
1.45	4.8	9.8	3.8	FRANCE	13	-1.2	-10.8	-17.9
1.82	4.1	13.0	3.8	GERMANY	6	1.8	-7.3	-19.8
				* GREECE	26	-10.3	79.3	-44.0
1.08	8.4	9.5	5.9	HONGKONG	12	-0.7	2.9	-23.0
1.39	7.4	12.4	2.0	** IRELAND	24	-9.2	-17.6	-25.3
1.10	2.3	9.3	4.0	ITALY	27	-10.3	-23.1	-31.2
2.35	10.2	29.0	0.8	JAPAN	28	-12.1	-39.3	-41.2
				* LUXEMBURG	9	-0.1	-11.8	-22.8
1.22	5.1	11.9	4.9	NETHERLANDS	7	0.6	-6.3	-9.2
0.86	4.3	6.2	7.6	NEW ZEALAND	21	-5.5	-33.5	-70.6
2.49	5.7	11.0	2.3	NORWAY	11	-0.6	7.3	-20.3
2.67	5.9	13.3	1.9	NORWAY (FREE)	15	-2.2	7.8	-20.7
				* PORTUGAL	25	-9.4	-31.5	-45.2
1.95	10.1	14.8	2.0	SINGAPORE/MALAYSIA	19	-3.8	-17.5	-26.2
0.92	3.6	8.7	5.4	SPAIN	17	-2.2	-15.0	-38.9
1.51	5.3	8.8	3.4	SWEDEN	22	-7.9	-24.3	-34.7
1.56	5.5	9.7	3.2	SWEDEN (FREE)	23	-9.0	-19.0	-34.8
1.26	6.2	11.2	3.0	SWITZERLAND	16	-2.2	-7.8	-21.0
1.29	6.3	11.2	3.0	SWITZERLAND (FREE)	14	-1.8	-7.9	-19.9
1.57	6.6	10.8	5.6	UNITED KINGDOM	3	5.1	7.1	-4.0
1.87	7.2	13.6	3.8	USA	2	6.2	-7.9	-12.3
				GDP WEIGHTED INDICES (in US dollars)				
--	--	--	3.5	WORLD GDP WEIGHTED (20)		-0.6	-15.3	-16.3
--	--	--	3.3	EAFE GDP WEIGHTED (18)		-4.6	-19.1	-20.3
--	--	--	4.2	EUROPE 13 GDP WEIGHTED (13)		-1.1	-8.9	-18.2
				HEDGED INDICES (in US dollars)				
				EAFE (HEDGED) (18)		-4.9	-33.2	

Valuation: P/BV: price to book value ratio; P/CE: price to cash earnings (earnings + depreciation) ratio; P/E: price to earnings ratio; Yield: gross dividend yield.
Performance: % changes are calculated on the Morgan Stanley Capital International stock market indices-adjusted for foreign exchange fluctuations relative to the US$; change from high is from highest index level reached since the base date (except Finland and New Zealand since 1.1.82).
Base dates: Europe 17, EC, Free and Hedged indices. Finland, Greece, Ireland, Luxembourg, New Zealand and Portugal: 1.1.88 = 100; all others 1.1.70 = 100.
The indices "World" include South African Gold Mines quoted in London (except World GDP weighted).
Europe 17 includes all European countries on this page; Europe 13 (formerly called Europe) includes the European countries currently in EAFE.
Figures in parenthesis indicate the number of countries included. For detailed constituents of the international indices, see the matrix on the inside back cover.
* Not a component of EAFE and World Indices.
** Inclusion in EAFE and World Indices forthcoming.

INTERNATIONAL MARKET TRENDS — 30 November 1990

EMERGING MARKET TRENDS

INDEX LEVEL		PERFORMANCE		

% change in stock market indices

1990 Range high	low	month and index		this month	since 1.1.90	from high[1]
			EMERGING MARKETS (in US dollars)			
256.6	177.9	177.9	ENF (EMERGING MARKETS FREE) (12)	-5.6	-16.7	-30.7
306.7	158.2	175.3	EMG (EMERGING MARKETS GLOBAL) (14)	2.7	-34.5	-42.8
			FAR EAST EMERGING MARKETS			
247.9	156.8	156.8	EMF FAR EAST (4)	-7.4	-26.1	-36.7
332.1	135.9	166.1	EMG FAR EAST (6)	6.1	-42.3	-50.0
912.7	535.9	535.9	* INDONESIA	-9.9	-9.9	-41.3
207.1	114.4	146.5	KOREA	1.4	-27.7	-33.8
216.5	156.9	161.3	* MALAYSIA	-3.9	-15.1	-25.5
232.7	103.9	111.5	* PHILIPPINES (FREE)	-2.7	-51.3	-61.4
537.8	110.9	176.5	TAIWAN	24.8	-56.5	-67.2
365.9	181.5	181.5	* THAILAND	-13.6	-37.4	-50.4
			LATIN AMERICA EMERGING MARKETS			
294.0	183.1	220.5	EMF LATIN AMERICA (4)	3.0	-11.7	-25.0
295.2	201.6	233.9	EMG LATIN AMERICA (4)	2.5	-8.1	-20.8
448.2	132.0	291.7	* ARGENTINA	4.7	-0.1	-53.4
341.8	90.8	105.0	* BRAZIL	3.5	-59.8	-73.5
221.0	177.2	190.6	* CHILE	0.9	7.6	-13.7
503.0	304.1	486.8	* MEXICO (FREE)	3.3	58.9	-3.2
443.9	287.2	414.8	MEXICO (TOTAL)	2.4	43.4	-6.6
			OTHER EMERGING MARKETS			
539.1	167.5	301.9	* GREECE	-10.3	79.3	-44.0
67.3	52.3	53.7	* JORDAN	0.2	-15.5	-48.4
98.5	67.2	67.2	* PORTUGAL	-9.4	-31.5	-45.2
403.3	220.1	220.1	* TURKEY	-30.4	-9.0	-45.4
			COMBINED DEVELOPED & EMERGING MARKETS (in US dollars)			
137.5	76.9	85.0	COMBINED FAR EAST FREE (7)	-11.6	-38.2	-39.8
256.0	130.2	151.6	COMBINED FAR EAST ex JAPAN (8)	3.6	-33.5	-40.8
193.0	136.7	139.3	COMBINED FAR EAST FREE ex JAPAN (6)	-3.9	-13.6	-27.8
142.8	104.8	112.3	**ALL COUNTRY WORLD INDEX (36)**	-1.7	-20.8	-21.4

* Included in EMF; other countries are not normally open to foreign investors. EMG includes the 14 countries listed above, using the "total" version of the index for Mexico. All Country World Index is composed of the countries included in the World Index, in the EMG index and Ireland, Luxembourg. In order to avoid double counting Singapore / Malaysia is replaced by Singapore only.
Base date: 1.1.88 = 100.
[1] from highest index level reached since the base date.
Figures in parenthesis indicate the number of countries included. For detailed constituents of the international indices, see the matrix on the inside back cover.

EXCHANGE RATES, INTEREST SPREADS, BOND YIELDS

country	exchange rate	% change this month	covering cost * %	bond definition	yield to maturity	change in basis points this month	since 1.1.90	from high
AUSTRALIA	1.29224	-1.4	-3.81	10-YEAR COMMONWEALTH	12.3	-112	-66	-425
AUSTRIA	10.57250	1.0	-0.74	10-YEAR BUNDESANLEIHE	8.3	-15	68	NA
BELGIUM	31.02000	0.7	-0.68	8-YEAR DETTE DE L'ETAT	10.1	5	29	-443
CANADA	1.16505	0.2	-3.67	10-YEAR GOVERNMENT BOND	10.5	-71	86	-738
DENMARK	5.76500	0.6	-1.91	6-YEAR GOVERNMENT BULLET	10.5	-3	-25	NA
FINLAND	3.60050	0.3	-5.72	7-YEAR BULLET	13.8	-15	95	NA
FRANCE	5.06750	0.4	-1.69	10-YEAR GOVERNMENT BOND	10.0	-19	64	-739
GERMANY	1.50060	1.2	-0.88	10-YEAR BUNDESANLEIHE	8.9	-16	153	-218
HONGKONG	7.79950	-0.1	0.18					
ITALY	1127.000	0.9	-3.85	5-YEAR GOVERNMENT BOND	13.8	1	-4	-770
JAPAN	133.3000	-2.7	0.08	9-YEAR GOVERNMENT BOND	6.9	-28	136	-322
NETHERLANDS	1.69250	1.1	-0.74	10-YEAR GOVERNMENT BOND	9.1	-6	136	-320
NEW ZEALAND	1.63934	-0.7	-4.71	5-YEAR GOVERNMENT BOND	12.8	-108	0	NA
NORWAY	5.86750	0.7	-3.07	6-YEAR GOVERNMENT BOND	10.1	8	-27	NA
SINGAPORE/MALAYSIA	1.72100	-0.8	1.51					
SPAIN	95.4700	-0.3	-5.93	9-YEAR GOVERNMENT BOND	12.0	-52	3	-753
SWEDEN	5.62100	0.4	-6.64	10-YEAR GOVERNMENT BOND	15.1	-107	28	NA
SWITZERLAND	1.28000	0.6	-0.56	5-YEAR E.I.B.	7.5	2	57	NA
UNITED KINGDOM	0.51492	-0.1	-4.86	10-YEAR EXCHEQUER	10.7	-62	17	-507
USA				10-YEAR U.S. TREASURY	8.3	-43	34	-720

* against US$, based on three months forward rates, annualized. The sign — indicates a cost.

INDICES WITH DIVIDENDS REINVESTED MONTHLY — 30 November 1990

TOTAL RETURNS

WITH GROSS DIVIDENDS (1)
% change in index

WITH NET DIVIDENDS (1) (2)
% change in index

1 month	3 months	12 months	since 1.1.90		1 month	3 months	12 months	since 1.1.90
				INTERNATIONAL INDICES (in US dollars)				
-1.6	-3.7	-15.6	-18.2	THE WORLD INDEX	-1.7	-3.9	-16.1	-18.7
6.3	0.9	-3.5	-5.6	NORTH AMERICA	6.2	0.6	-4.6	-6.6
-5.9	-6.3	-21.6	-24.4	EAFE	-5.9	-6.4	-21.9	-24.7
1.0	-3.2	8.6	-2.0	EUROPE 13	1.0	-3.4	8.1	-2.4
-4.7	-17.2	-4.2	-13.4	NORDIC COUNTRIES	-4.8	-17.3	-4.8	-13.9
-11.1	-8.8	-36.9	-37.0	PACIFIC	-11.1	-8.8	-37.0	-37.1
-11.6	-8.5	-37.8	-37.8	FAR EAST	-11.6	-8.5	-37.9	-37.8
				SPECIAL AREAS (in US dollars)				
-5.5	-6.3	-21.4	-24.1	THE WORLD INDEX ex USA	-5.6	-6.4	-21.6	-24.4
-5.5	-6.2	-21.3	-24.1	EAFE + CANADA	-5.6	-6.3	-21.6	-24.4
3.7	-1.5	0.8	-4.5	KOKUSAI INDEX (WORLD EX JAPAN)	3.6	-1.7	0.0	-5.3
0.9	-4.1	6.9	-2.9	EASEA INDEX (EAFE ex JAPAN)	0.8	-4.2	6.4	-3.3
-0.9	-11.1	-6.2	-10.2	PACIFIC ex JAPAN	-1.0	-11.3	-7.0	-10.9
-2.4	-4.6	-18.8	-20.9	THE WORLD INDEX ex THE UK	-2.5	-4.8	-19.3	-21.4
-8.0	-8.3	-27.5	-29.5	EAFE ex THE UK	-8.1	-8.4	-27.7	-29.7
-1.6	-7.3	1.3	-8.9	EUROPE 13 ex THE UK	-1.7	-7.5	0.5	-9.5
				NATIONAL INDICES (in US dollars)				
0.3	-13.8	-9.3	-13.9	AUSTRALIA	0.2	-14.3	-10.9	-15.4
0.2	-14.4	34.3	7.1	AUSTRIA	0.1	-14.5	33.8	6.7
-2.6	-4.6	-5.8	-10.4	BELGIUM	-2.8	-4.9	-7.0	-11.4
2.8	-4.7	-14.2	-15.9	CANADA	2.7	-5.0	-14.9	-16.6
-4.4	-4.8	9.6	2.9	DENMARK	-4.5	-4.9	9.1	2.4
4.4	-15.4	-20.1	-27.3	FINLAND	4.4	-15.6	-20.7	-27.8
-1.0	-1.6	1.9	-9.0	FRANCE	-1.1	-1.8	1.3	-9.4
2.0	-5.1	13.6	-5.5	GERMANY	2.0	-5.2	13.0	-6.0
-0.2	-3.4	9.5	7.9	HONGKONG	-0.2	-3.4	9.5	7.9
-10.0	-17.0	-14.8	-21.0	ITALY	-10.1	-17.2	-15.6	-21.6
-12.0	-8.5	-39.0	-38.9	JAPAN	-12.0	-8.6	-39.1	-39.0
1.0	0.4	7.2	-2.1	NETHERLANDS	0.9	0.1	6.0	-3.2
-4.9	-24.0	-32.0	-29.7	NEW ZEALAND	-5.1	-24.4	-33.2	-30.9
-0.4	-13.1	22.5	9.1	NORWAY	-0.4	-13.3	21.9	8.7
-3.5	-12.3	-9.7	-16.3	SINGAPORE/MALAYSIA	-3.5	-12.3	-9.7	-16.3
-1.8	-8.3	-7.6	-11.0	SPAIN	-1.9	-8.6	-8.8	-12.0
-7.7	-23.8	-13.2	-22.5	SWEDEN	-7.8	-24.0	-13.9	-23.0
-1.9	-8.1	-2.6	-5.6	SWITZERLAND	-2.0	-8.3	-3.5	-6.4
5.4	3.8	22.3	11.1	UNITED KINGDOM	5.4	3.8	22.3	11.1
6.6	1.3	-2.6	-4.7	USA	6.5	1.0	-3.6	-5.7
				NATIONAL INDICES (in local currencies)				
1.7	-9.5	-8.3	-12.2	AUSTRALIA	1.5	-9.9	-9.9	-13.6
-0.9	-17.9	12.8	-4.9	AUSTRIA	-0.9	-18.0	12.4	-5.2
-3.3	-8.4	-22.2	-21.9	BELGIUM	-3.4	-8.8	-23.1	-22.8
2.6	-4.0	-14.0	-15.4	CANADA	2.5	-4.2	-14.8	-16.1
-5.0	-8.4	-8.8	-9.9	DENMARK	-5.0	-8.5	-9.3	-10.3
4.1	-17.4	-31.5	-35.2	FINLAND	4.0	-17.6	-32.0	-35.7
-1.4	-5.6	-15.3	-20.2	FRANCE	-1.4	-5.7	-15.7	-20.6
0.8	-9.5	-4.6	-16.2	GERMANY	0.8	-9.7	-5.1	-16.6
-0.2	-2.9	9.3	7.8	HONGKONG	-0.2	-2.9	9.3	7.8
-10.8	-19.8	-27.1	-29.7	ITALY	-10.9	-20.1	-27.8	-30.3
-9.5	-15.0	-43.0	-43.4	JAPAN	-9.5	-15.1	-43.1	-43.4
-0.1	-4.2	-9.9	-13.2	NETHERLANDS	-0.2	-4.5	-11.0	-14.1
-4.2	-23.4	-34.2	-31.5	NEW ZEALAND	-4.4	-23.8	-35.4	-32.6
-1.1	-16.0	5.5	-2.9	NORWAY	-1.1	-16.1	5.0	-3.3
-2.7	-14.5	-20.1	-24.2	SINGAPORE/MALAYSIA	-2.7	-14.5	-20.1	-24.2
-1.5	-10.8	-23.4	-22.4	SPAIN	-1.6	-11.1	-24.3	-23.2
-8.0	-25.8	-23.6	-29.7	SWEDEN	-8.1	-26.0	-24.1	-30.1
-2.5	-9.8	-21.8	-21.6	SWITZERLAND	-2.6	-10.1	-22.5	-22.2
5.5	1.1	-1.3	-7.7	UNITED KINGDOM	5.5	1.1	-1.3	-7.7
6.6	1.3	-2.6	-4.7	USA	6.5	1.0	-3.6	-5.7

(1) With dividends reinvested monthly (2) net, after withholding taxes for foreigners not benefitting from any double taxation treaty (such as Luxembourg investment companies).

RECENT AND LONG TERM PERFORMANCES UP TO 30 November 1990

% change		% change	compound annual growth rates in %		% change
3 months		12 months	2 years	5 years	10 years
	THE WORLD INDEX				
-4.4	THE WORLD INDEX	-17.7	-3.9	13.0	10.7
-7.4	THE WORLD INDEX IN LOCAL CURRENCIES	-23.2	-3.2	8.3	9.4
-3.7	THE WORLD INDEX WITH GROSS DIVIDENDS (1)	-15.6	-1.7	15.7	14.5
-3.9	THE WORLD INDEX WITH NET DIVIDENDS (1)(2)	-16.1	-2.2	15.1	13.5
-4.2	THE WORLD INDEX FREE (3)	-17.8	-4.0	NA	NA
-4.9	WORLD GDP WEIGHTED	-10.8	1.8	14.1	11.7
	EAFE				
-6.9	EAFE	-23.1	-9.8	17.1	14.1
-11.4	EAFE IN LOCAL CURRENCIES	-31.0	-8.9	8.5	11.9
-6.3	EAFE WITH GROSS DIVIDENDS (1)	-21.6	-8.2	19.1	16.9
-6.4	EAFE WITH NET DIVIDENDS (1) (2)	-21.9	-8.5	18.8	16.2
-6.6	EAFE FREE (3)	-23.3	-9.9	NA	NA
-7.9	EAFE GDP WEIGHTED	-13.1	-1.5	18.2	15.0
	NORTH AMERICA				
-0.1	NORTH AMERICA	-7.0	8.2	9.1	7.9
-0.1	NORTH AMERICA IN LOCAL CURRENCIES	-6.9	8.1	9.0	7.9
0.9	NORTH AMERICA WITH GROSS DIVIDENDS (1)	-3.5	12.1	13.0	12.6
0.6	NORTH AMERICA WITH NET DIVIDENDS (1) (2)	-4.6	10.9	11.8	11.2
	PACIFIC				
-9.1	PACIFIC	-37.5	-20.0	19.0	16.0
-14.8	PACIFIC IN LOCAL CURRENCIES	-41.3	-16.5	10.2	11.6
-8.8	PACIFIC WITH GROSS DIVIDENDS (1)	-36.9	-19.3	20.0	17.6
-8.8	PACIFIC WITH NET DIVIDENDS (1) (2)	-37.0	-19.5	19.8	17.3
	EUROPE 13				
-4.1	EUROPE 13	5.2	9.4	14.8	11.8
-7.3	EUROPE 13 IN LOCAL CURRENCIES	-13.0	3.7	5.9	11.9
-3.2	EUROPE 13 WITH GROSS DIVIDENDS (1)	8.6	12.8	18.2	16.2
-3.4	EUROPE 13 WITH NET DIVIDENDS (1) (2)	8.1	12.3	17.7	15.2
-3.3	EUROPE 13 FREE (3)	6.2	10.0	NA	NA
	EUROPE 13 EX THE UK				
-8.1	EUROPE 13 EX THE UK	-1.5	8.3	14.8	12.4
-11.5	EUROPE 13 EX THE UK IN LOCAL CURRENCIES	-17.4	1.0	4.6	11.4
-7.3	EUROPE 13 EX THE UK WITH GROSS DIVIDENDS (1)	1.3	11.3	17.9	16.4
-7.5	EUROPE 13 EX THE UK WITH NET DIVIDENDS (1)(2)	0.5	10.5	17.1	15.3
-19.5	**EMERGING MARKETS FREE INDEX**	-7.3	16.1	NA	NA

(1)With dividends reinvested monthly(2) net, after withholding taxes for foreigners not benefitting from any double taxation treaty (such as Luxembourg investment companies) (3) excludes non free shares in Finland, Norway, Sweden and registered shares, when not available to foreigners, in Switzerland.
Based on the Morgan Stanley Capital International $ denominated indices except when otherwise specified.

WEIGHTS IN MSCI INDICES — 30 November 1990
GDP WEIGHT (1)
relative weights

MARKET CAPITALIZATION INDICES
weight as a percentage of index

EAFE	World		US $ billion	Europe 13 Ex-UK	Europe 13 free	Europe 13	EAFE free	EAFE	Kokusai	World
1.6	0.9	AUSTRIA	15.6	1.8	1.2	1.1	0.5	0.5	0.5	0.3
2.0	1.2	BELGIUM	36.0	4.2	2.7	2.6	1.2	1.2	1.1	0.7
1.4	0.9	DENMARK	24.7	2.9	1.8	1.8	0.8	0.8	0.7	0.5
1.3	0.8	FINLAND	8.2	1.0	--	0.5	--	0.3	0.2	0.2
--	--	FINLAND (FREE)	1.5	0.2	0.1	0.1	0.1	0.1	0.0	0.0
12.2	7.2	FRANCE	177.1	20.8	13.3	12.7	6.0	5.9	5.2	3.6
15.3	9.1	GERMANY	213.8	25.1	16.0	15.4	7.2	7.1	6.3	4.4
8.8	5.2	ITALY	74.5	8.8	5.6	5.4	2.5	2.5	2.2	1.5
3.1	1.9	NETHERLANDS	85.8	10.1	6.4	6.2	2.9	2.8	2.5	1.8
1.2	0.7	NORWAY	16.3	1.9	--	1.2	--	0.5	0.5	0.3
--	--	NORWAY (FREE)	12.1	1.4	0.9	0.9	0.4	0.4	0.4	0.2
4.6	2.7	SPAIN	55.4	6.5	4.1	4.0	1.9	1.8	1.6	1.1
1.8	1.1	SWEDEN	47.1	5.5	--	3.4	--	1.6	1.4	1.0
--	--	SWEDEN (FREE)	20.6	2.4	1.5	1.5	0.7	0.7	0.6	0.4
2.0	1.2	SWITZERLAND	95.9	11.3	--	6.9	--	3.2	2.8	2.0
--	--	SWITZERLAND (FREE)	77.1	9.1	5.8	5.5	2.6	2.5	2.3	1.6
10.9	6.5	UNITED KINGDOM	541.8	--	40.6	38.9	18.3	17.9	16.0	11.1
--	--	EUROPE 13 (FREE)	1336.1	--	100.0	96.0	45.0	44.2	39.5	27.5
66.2	39.4	EUROPE 13	1392.3	--	--	100.0	--	46.0	41.1	28.6
3.3	1.9	AUSTRALIA	70.3	--	--	--	2.4	2.3	2.1	1.4
0.7	0.4	HONGKONG	43.0	--	--	--	1.4	1.4	1.3	0.9
29.1	17.3	JAPAN	1479.6	--	--	--	49.9	48.9	--	30.4
0.4	0.2	NEW ZEALAND	6.0	--	--	--	0.2	0.2	0.2	0.1
0.3	0.2	SINGAPORE/MALAYSIA	32.2	--	--	--	1.1	1.1	1.0	0.7
33.8	20.1	PACIFIC	1631.2	--	--	--	55.0	54.0	--	33.5
--	--	EAFE (FREE)	2967.3	--	--	--	100.0	98.1	61.0	
100.0	59.4	EAFE	3023.5	--	--	--	--	100.0	--	62.2
--	4.0	CANADA	133.2	--	--	--	--	--	3.9	2.7
--	36.6	USA	1696.5	--	--	--	--	--	50.1	34.9
--	--	STH AFRICAN GOLD MINES	10.0	--	--	--	--	--	0.3	0.2
--	--	THE WORLD INDEX (FREE)	4806.9	--	--	--	--	--	--	98.8
--	100.0	THE WORLD INDEX	4863.2	--	--	--	--	--	--	100.0
--	--	NORDIC COUNTRIES (FREE)	58.8	6.9	4.4	4.2	2.0	1.9	1.7	1.2
5.7	3.4	NORDIC COUNTRIES	96.3	11.3	--	6.9	--	3.2	2.8	2.0
55.3	32.9	EUROPE 13 EX THE UK	850.5	100.0	--	61.1	--	28.1	25.1	17.5
30.1	17.9	FAR EAST	1554.8	--	--	--	52.4	51.4	--	32.0
70.9	42.1	EASEA (EAFE EX JAPAN)	1543.9	--	--	--	--	51.1	45.6	31.7
--	40.6	NORTH AMERICA	1829.6	--	--	--	--	--	54.1	37.6
--	82.7	KOKUSAI (WORLD EX JAPAN)	3383.5	--	--	--	--	--	100.0	69.6

(1) GDP weight figures represent the initial weights applicable for the next month. They are used exclusively in MSCI "GDP weighted" indices.

MORGAN STANLEY CAPITAL INTERNATIONAL INDICES LEVELS – 30 Nov. 1990

WITH DIVIDENDS REINVESTED (1) (2)					WITHOUT DIVIDENDS REINVESTED			
GROSS		NET						
month end	29.12.89	month end	29.12.89		month end	1990 Range		29.12.89
INTERNATIONAL INDICES (in US dollars)								
985.7	1205.7	789.8	971.3	THE WORLD INDEX	453.1	571.0	423.1	567.3
795.1	842.7	614.6	657.8	NORTH AMERICA	330.3	376.6	303.4	361.9
1537.0	2034.3	1277.8	1696.3	EAFE	777.6	1054.3	717.2	1047.9
				EUROPE 17	134.6	156.7	123.9	141.4
1216.2	1241.0	934.8	958.1	EUROPE 13	487.0	565.3	447.0	511.7
				EC	135.2	154.2	123.0	140.3
1954.0	2256.1	1551.6	1802.2	NORDIC COUNTRIES	888.1	1207.5	870.2	1046.9
2616.7	4152.3	2382.1	3786.9	PACIFIC	1665.7	2667.7	1518.8	2667.7
3665.0	5890.2	3388.3	5451.7	FAR EAST	2404.8	3892.3	2168.7	3892.3
INTERNATIONAL FREE INDICES (in US dollars)								
				THE WORLD INDEX (FREE)	110.9	139.8	103.5	138.9
				EAFE (FREE)	102.3	139.0	94.2	138.1
				EUROPE 17 (FREE)	135.2	156.1	123.9	140.9
				EUROPE 13 FREE	135.1	155.5	123.4	140.8
				EUROPE 13 (FREE) ex THE UK	129.4	159.4	120.8	144.4
				NORDIC COUNTRIES (FREE)	189.4	246.5	185.8	202.6
SPECIAL AREAS (in US dollars)								
1497.4	1974.0	1241.0	1641.2	THE WORLD INDEX ex USA	745.8	1007.6	691.1	1001.6
1452.6	1914.2	1215.0	1606.2	EAFE + CANADA	731.1	987.5	677.1	981.5
855.4	896.2	662.0	698.8	KOKUSAI INDEX (WORLD EX JAPAN)	352.9	405.1	331.7	381.9
1077.2	1108.9	840.4	869.4	EASEA INDEX (EAFE ex JAPAN)	439.1	513.1	407.9	466.2
737.1	820.3	618.2	693.9	PACIFIC ex JAPAN	326.5	413.7	322.9	379.8
939.6	1187.7	756.1	961.5	THE WORLD INDEX ex THE UK	440.5	572.1	414.2	569.2
1604.0	2274.2	1369.5	1948.4	EAFE ex THE UK	871.5	1258.5	811.2	1253.9
1107.9	1216.1	856.8	947.0	EUROPE 13 ex THE UK	467.1	580.9	438.9	526.0
NATIONAL INDICES (in US dollars)								
476.0	553.1	361.6	427.2	AUSTRALIA	190.2	244.8	184.3	233.6
1918.6	1792.1	1782.8	1670.3	AUSTRIA	1057.1	1520.8	946.4	999.6
2166.2	2418.5	1693.1	1911.6	BELGIUM	567.1	684.2	534.7	662.2
722.7	859.1	624.0	748.0	CANADA	328.6	407.7	315.7	403.9
2137.6	2077.9	1649.3	1610.2	DENMARK	897.6	1018.8	859.8	885.4
75.6	103.9	74.2	102.8	FINLAND	70.2	110.0	65.1	99.3
				FINLAND (FREE)	94.4	141.1	85.0	128.4
1221.8	1342.3	945.4	1043.7	FRANCE	485.4	591.5	439.0	543.9
1172.6	1240.9	948.4	1008.4	GERMANY	572.3	713.5	498.5	617.2
				* GREECE	301.9	539.1	167.5	168.3
3652.7	3386.1	3412.6	3163.6	HONGKONG	1535.5	1903.5	1427.6	1492.0
				** IRELAND	139.7	187.0	134.4	169.7
356.0	450.4	297.2	379.3	ITALY	199.4	283.7	198.9	259.3
3768.1	6166.9	3478.1	5698.9	JAPAN	2520.5	4149.2	2266.5	4149.2
				* LUXEMBURG	158.1	190.9	149.0	179.3
1986.9	2029.7	1476.0	1524.5	NETHERLANDS	595.7	656.2	569.5	636.0
69.8	99.4	66.4	96.1	NEW ZEALAND	59.0	92.9	58.7	88.8
1985.6	1819.5	1660.5	1528.1	NORWAY	968.7	1216.1	891.6	902.8
				NORWAY (FREE)	216.9	273.7	201.1	201.2
				* PORTUGAL	67.2	98.5	67.2	98.2
1817.9	2171.1	1733.1	2069.8	SINGAPORE/MALAYSIA	1106.7	1499.2	1065.9	1341.7
575.3	646.7	443.0	503.7	SPAIN	135.2	175.1	121.4	159.2
1998.0	2577.3	1569.1	2038.2	SWEDEN	893.7	1368.2	868.7	1179.8
				SWEDEN (FREE)	168.9	259.1	163.1	208.5
990.8	1049.6	821.5	877.4	SWITZERLAND	567.3	717.7	547.9	615.1
				SWITZERLAND (FREE)	110.7	138.2	105.7	120.2
1438.5	1294.7	1075.1	967.6	UNITED KINGDOM	519.3	541.0	425.9	484.6
726.5	762.6	557.0	590.5	USA	299.5	341.4	273.7	325.0
GDP WEIGHTED INDICES (in US dollars)								
				WORLD GDP WEIGHTED	534.9	639.4	503.7	631.6
				EAFE GDP WEIGHTED	818.5	1026.7	764.0	1011.4
				EUROPE 13 GDP WEIGHTED	574.7	702.4	535.0	631.1

(1) With dividends reinvested monthly (2) net, after withholding taxes for foreigners not benefitting from any double taxation treaty (such as Luxembourg investment companies).
Base dates: Europe 17, EC, Free and Hedged indices, Finland, Greece, Ireland, Luxembourg, New Zealand and Portugal: 1.1.88 = 100; all others 1.1.70 = 100.
The indices "World" include South African Gold Mines quoted in London (except World GDP weighted).
Europe 17 includes all European countries on this page; Europe 13 (formerly called Europe) includes the European countries currently in EAFE.
For detailed constituents of the international indices, see the matrix on the inside back cover.
  * Not a component of EAFE and World Indices.
  ** Inclusion in EAFE and World Indices forthcoming.

MORGAN STANLEY CAPITAL INTERNATIONAL INDICES LEVELS – 30 Nov. 1990

GROSS month end	GROSS 29.12.89	NET month end	NET 29.12.89		month end	1990 Range		29.12.89
				INTERNATIONAL INDICES (in local currencies)				
759.5	988.3	608.2	795.8	THE WORLD INDEX	349.0	469.8	332.2	464.9
815.6	863.9	630.4	674.4	NORTH AMERICA	338.8	386.1	311.0	371.0
905.9	1323.4	754.7	1105.7	EAFE	458.0	686.6	435.6	681.1
				EUROPE 17	128.6	160.8	122.6	156.7
923.0	1092.9	709.2	843.5	EUROPE 13	369.6	460.7	351.3	450.7
				EC	128.6	157.7	121.4	154.8
1835.9	2365.2	1457.8	1889.4	NORDIC COUNTRIES	834.4	1183.1	808.7	1097.4
1159.1	1971.0	1158.9	1970.8	PACIFIC	737.9	1268.2	687.9	1266.3
1458.5	2523.8	1348.4	2335.9	FAR EAST	957.0	1668.7	886.5	1667.7
				INTERNATIONAL FREE INDICES (in local currencies)				
				THE WORLD INDEX (FREE)	113.7	152.9	108.1	151.3
				EAFE (FREE)	106.3	159.5	100.9	158.3
				EUROPE 17 (FREE)	129.0	160.0	122.4	156.0
				EUROPE 13 FREE	128.8	159.3	121.9	155.9
				EUROPE 13 FREE ex THE UK	124.0	163.9	119.9	157.5
				NORDIC COUNTRIES (FREE)	179.6	244.4	174.3	215.4
				SPECIAL AREAS (in local currencies)				
902.5	1307.9	748.0	1087.4	THE WORLD INDEX ex USA	449.5	669.0	428.8	663.6
892.8	1292.9	746.8	1084.9	EAFE + CANADA	449.4	668.4	428.4	663.0
754.7	841.4	584.1	656.2	KOKUSAI INDEX (WORLD EX JAPAN)	311.4	369.9	296.6	358.6
778.7	917.2	607.5	719.1	EASEA INDEX (EAFE ex JAPAN)	317.4	396.4	303.4	385.6
894.3	1007.7	750.1	852.4	PACIFIC ex JAPAN	389.9	494.8	383.6	459.2
697.2	925.9	561.1	749.6	THE WORLD INDEX ex THE UK	326.8	448.0	312.6	443.8
776.8	1199.4	663.2	1027.6	EAFE ex THE UK	422.1	665.5	403.4	661.3
660.3	824.6	510.7	642.2	EUROPE 13 ex THE UK	278.4	371.1	270.5	356.7
				NATIONAL INDICES (in local currencies)				
683.9	778.7	523.2	605.6	AUSTRALIA	275.3	345.3	265.5	331.2
807.1	848.3	725.0	764.4	AUSTRIA	429.9	692.4	399.4	457.4
1343.8	1720.5	1050.3	1359.9	BELGIUM	351.9	483.2	344.4	471.2
778.7	920.0	672.5	801.2	CANADA	354.1	437.9	338.3	432.5
1642.2	1821.9	1267.7	1412.7	DENMARK	689.9	831.2	681.2	776.8
69.0	106.5	67.8	105.3	FINLAND	64.1	109.2	59.3	101.8
				FINLAND (FREE)	86.1	141.0	77.6	131.6
1116.7	1399.1	862.6	1086.0	FRANCE	443.6	595.0	415.9	566.9
463.0	552.3	388.9	466.1	GERMANY	234.7	316.2	213.2	285.3
				* GREECE	370.1	689.4	209.2	209.2
5129.9	4758.9	4391.6	4074.0	HONGKONG	2156.5	2660.9	1995.5	2096.9
				** IRELAND	131.0	199.1	130.4	181.6
642.0	913.1	535.8	768.8	ITALY	359.6	559.5	354.9	525.6
1392.9	2460.1	1287.8	2277.1	JAPAN	931.7	1655.3	861.5	1655.3
				* LUXEMBURG	147.7	204.6	141.4	192.2
933.4	1075.3	690.1	803.9	NETHERLANDS	278.4	341.9	270.7	335.2
75.4	110.0	71.7	106.4	NEW ZEALAND	63.7	102.8	63.4	98.3
1631.7	1680.5	1364.0	1410.8	NORWAY	795.7	1056.4	721.2	833.6
				NORWAY (FREE)	204.0	272.2	186.3	212.7
				* PORTUGAL	67.7	111.9	67.7	111.7
1017.3	1341.3	974.3	1284.6	SINGAPORE/MALAYSIA	619.3	885.5	604.8	828.9
769.4	991.0	604.2	787.2	SPAIN	184.5	253.0	169.9	248.8
2169.8	3084.7	1705.1	2440.9	SWEDEN	971.1	1561.7	934.1	1413.0
				SWEDEN (FREE)	163.8	266.7	156.4	222.8
295.3	376.6	243.4	312.9	SWITZERLAND	169.1	233.0	165.1	220.7
				SWITZERLAND (FREE)	110.9	150.9	107.4	145.1
1771.9	1920.0	1327.7	1438.7	UNITED KINGDOM	641.6	734.6	585.4	721.0
726.5	762.6	557.0	590.5	USA	299.5	341.4	273.7	325.0

(1) With dividends reinvested monthly (2) net, after withholding taxes for foreigners not benefitting from any double taxation treaty (such as Luxembourg investment companies).
Base dates: Europe 17, EC, Free indices, Finland, Greece, Ireland, Luxembourg, New Zealand and Portugal: 1.1.88 = 100; all others 1.1.70 = 100.
The indices "World" include South African Gold Mines quoted in London (except World GDP weighted).
Europe 17 includes all European countries on this page; Europe 13 (formerly called Europe) includes the European countries currently in EAFE.
For detailed constituents of the international indices, see the matrix on the inside back cover.
* Not a component of EAFE and World Indices.
** Inclusion in EAFE and World Indices forthcoming.

MORGAN STANLEY CAPITAL INTERNATIONAL INDICES LEVELS – 30 Nov. 1990

PERFORMANCE — **INDEX LEVEL**

% change in stock market indices

1 month	3 months	12 months		month end	1990 Range		29.12.89
			EMERGING MARKETS (in US dollars)				
-5.6	-19.5	-7.3	EMF (EMERGING MARKETS FREE)	177.9	256.6	177.9	213.4
2.7	-4.3	-30.8	EMG (EMERGING MARKETS GLOBAL)	175.3	306.7	158.2	267.8
			FAR EAST EMERGING MARKETS				
-7.4	-23.3	-20.4	EMF FAR EAST	156.8	247.9	156.8	212.2
6.1	1.9	-40.1	EMG FAR EAST	168.1	332.1	135.9	287.9
-9.9	-31.3	-11.4	* INDONESIA	535.9	912.7	535.9	594.7
1.4	17.8	-28.4	KOREA	146.5	207.1	114.4	202.8
-3.9	-13.7	-6.7	* MALAYSIA	161.3	218.5	156.9	190.0
-2.7	-16.2	-58.7	* PHILIPPINES (FREE)	111.5	232.7	103.9	229.0
24.8	14.3	-54.2	TAIWAN	176.5	537.8	110.9	405.4
-13.6	-35.5	-31.0	* THAILAND	181.5	365.9	181.5	289.9
			LATIN AMERICA EMERGING MARKETS				
3.0	-8.3	2.1	EMF LATIN AMERICA	220.5	294.0	183.1	249.7
2.5	-8.1	5.3	EMG LATIN AMERICA	233.9	295.2	201.6	254.4
4.7	1.6	-7.3	* ARGENTINA	291.7	448.2	132.0	292.0
3.5	-37.5	-48.9	* BRAZIL	105.0	341.8	90.8	260.9
0.9	-0.4	20.4	* CHILE	190.6	221.0	177.2	177.2
3.3	9.3	73.2	* MEXICO (FREE)	486.8	503.0	304.1	306.5
2.4	5.9	56.4	* MEXICO (TOTAL)	414.8	443.9	287.2	289.4
			OTHER EMERGING MARKETS				
-10.3	-32.0	82.4	* GREECE	301.9	539.1	167.5	168.3
0.2	0.2	-11.4	* JORDAN	53.7	67.3	52.3	63.6
-9.4	-20.7	-32.0	* PORTUGAL	67.2	98.5	67.2	98.2
-30.4	-34.3	37.5	* TURKEY	220.1	403.3	220.1	241.8
			COMBINED DEVELOPED & EMERGING MARKETS (in US dollars)				
-11.6	-9.1	-38.2	COMBINED FAR EAST FREE	85.0	137.5	76.9	137.5
-3.6	-1.1	-31.1	COMBINED FAR EAST ex JAPAN	151.6	256.0	130.2	227.8
-3.9	-13.9	-9.7	COMBINED FAR EAST FREE ex JAPAN	139.3	193.0	136.7	161.2
-1.7	-4.4	-18.3	**ALL COUNTRY WORLD INDEX**	112.3	142.8	104.8	141.7
			HEDGED INDICES (in US dollars)				
-4.9	-11.7	-31.4	EAFE (HEDGED)	110.4			165.3
0.7	-11.6	-19.3	AUSTRALIA	89.1			114.0
-1.1	-18.2	12.7	AUSTRIA	211.1			225.4
-3.9	-9.8	-27.0	BELGIUM	134.0			181.8
1.8	-6.0	-20.9	CANADA	93.1			118.9
-5.3	-9.2	-12.7	DENMARK	198.2			228.8
3.3	-19.2	-36.8	FINLAND	59.0			98.2
-1.7	-6.5	-18.6	FRANCE	150.5			196.4
0.6	-10.0	-5.8	GERMANY	160.4			194.9
-0.6	-4.3	3.6	HONGKONG	133.3			130.0
-11.5	-21.0	-31.6	ITALY	87.6			132.2
-9.3	-15.0	-42.0	JAPAN	100.7			175.1
-0.8	-5.4	-14.3	NETHERLANDS	133.7			161.7
-5.2	-25.9	-41.6	NEW ZEALAND	53.5			87.1
-1.5	-17.2	0.6	NORWAY	183.3			197.6
-2.8	-14.6	-21.0	SINGAPORE/MALAYSIA	140.0			186.9
-2.4	-13.2	-30.8	SPAIN	77.5			110.0
-9.0	-27.6	-29.0	SWEDEN	127.0			194.1
-2.8	-10.6	-24.7	SWITZERLAND	127.1			188.2
4.6	-1.4	-10.9	UNITED KINGDOM	109.5			130.7

* Included in EMF; other countries are not normally open to foreign investors. EMG includes the 14 countries listed above, using the "total" version of the index for Mexico. All Country World Index is composed of the countries included in the World Index, in the EMG index and Ireland, Luxembourg. In order to avoid double counting Singapore / Malaysia is replaced by Singapore only.
Base date: 1.1.88 = 100. For detailed constituents of the international indices, see the matrix on the inside back cover.

IBM and Thailand

Factors Considered in a Decision-making Process of Investing Abroad

THOMAS A. PUGEL

JANG RO LEE

Introduction

This case asks the reader to consider the following, presumably hypothetical, situation in late 1984:

IBM increasingly has recognized Asia as a major area of sales for its product, since its sales in this region expanded above the average growth rate for the rest of the world. In late 1984, IBM had a major manufacturing operation in Japan, but it considered establishing a manufacturing operation in another country in the area to perform some local production of components and parts, as well as assembly of final products such as personal computers. The Thai Government has by 1984 become more interested in hosting more foreign direct investors in the Thai manufacturing sector, but on terms that attempt to maximize the net benefits to Thailand. Thailand was among the strongest contenders as a site for this new IBM operation.

The case materials provided are:

1. A short description of the Thai economic and political situation, of the general business climate in Thailand, and of Thai policy and regulations toward inward foreign di-

rect investment (FDI). Included are several exhibits of data and information.
2. Several newspaper articles on IBM, focusing on its general business strategy, its international strategy, and its general policy toward relations with host country governments. Included here are several exhibits providing information on IBM's corporate performance and international operations.

The Economic and Business Environment

Economic Overview

With a population of 50 million, Thailand's GDP has grown at an average annual rate of about 5 to 6 percent in real terms for the five years 1979–1983. The outlook for the next few years is for continued growth at 5 to 6 percent per annum in real terms. At current market prices, gross domestic product (GDP) was $40.4 billion in 1983.

Growth in official external debt, estimated at $6.8 billion at the end of 1983, slowed substantially, and annual debt service costs, at $1.7 billion, remained sustainable. Frost & Sullivan reported Thailand's economic perfor-

EXHIBIT 18-1

Thailand: Economic Performance Profile

Economic Indicator	Value	Ranking[a]
GDP per capita (US $)	723	Worst quarter
Real GDP growth (percentage annual rate)	5.6	Best quarter
Inflation (percentage annual rate)	10.2	Upper middle quarter
Unemployment (percentage)	1.5	Best quarter
Real investment (percentage of GDP)	23.8	Upper middle quarter
Government surplus/deficit (percentage of GDP)	−3.3	Upper middle quarter
Current account balance (percentage of GDP)	−6.2	Worst quarter
Debt service/exports (percentage)	16.2	Lower middle quarter
Currency change (percentage annual rate)	2.0	Best quarter

[a]Relative to other countries examined by Frost & Sullivan, Inc., based on five-year averages.

Source: Adapted from Frost & Sullivan, Inc., *World Political Risk Forecasts* (Thailand), December 1984.

mance ranking relative to other WPRF (World Political Risk Forecasts) countries as shown in Exhibit 18-1.

Thailand's Fifth National Economic and Social Development Plan (1982–86) stresses the expansion of rural income and employment, expanding agro-based and export-oriented industries utilizing local resources to create employment, and reduction of the disparity between urban and rural incomes.

Agriculture accounts for about 25 percent of output but 75 percent of employment. Thailand's manufacturing sector increased its share of GDP from 13.1 percent in 1960 to 22 percent in 1982. The sector employs approximately 10 percent of the labor force. Manufacturing production is centered in Bangkok and its five surrounding provinces. Manufacturing is expected to grow by 5.5 percent, and agriculture by 3 percent annum.

Government policy on manufacturing has concentrated on promotional activities, while investment decisions were left largely to the private sector. Price controls were imposed on about 40 manufactured commodities consumed primarily by the working class.

Throughout the 1960s and early 1970s, the Government influenced the structure of the manufacturing sector primarily through policies designed to encourage import substitution. Tariff protection on finished goods and reduction of tariffs on raw materials and capital goods imports were the principal instruments. The dominant industries in the sector were those producing food, beverages, tobacco, non-durable consumer goods and construction materials.

External Sector

Balance of payments problems in the mid-1970s led to the encouragement of industries which were export-oriented, labor-intensive industries, and industries which were built on Thailand's resource base. Thailand has been suffering from chronic balance of trade deficits, but foreign capital inflows were usually large enough to finance these trade deficits.

Eight major items account for 60 percent of Thailand's exports: rice, tapioca, tin, sugar, maize, textiles, rubber, and shrimp. The import picture was dominated by petroleum, while other major imports included dairy products, household and electrical appliances, raw materials (wood and textile), base metals, fertilizers, and electrical machinery and parts.

Thailand's principal export markets are Japan, the United States, the Netherlands, Germany, other members of the European Economic Community, and Thailand's ASEAN partners. The largest sources of imports are Japan, the United States, the EEC, and the Middle East.

The Business Climate

Although the economy's basic orientation is toward a free-enterprise system, the government controls such areas as public services, tobacco, and pharmaceuticals. Transportation, water, electricity, telecommunications, and financial services are provided by state enterprises.

Most of Thailand's revenue is obtained from indirect taxes such as customs duties on imports and exports. Import duties are levied on nearly all goods. The rate can be as high as 60 percent for luxury goods or goods which are produced by local industries and have been placed under government protection. However, it is normal for statutory rates to be markedly lower on agricultural and industrial equipment and supplies for industries that have received promoted industry status from the Board of Investment.

Export duties are imposed on a limited number of products including rice, scrap iron and steel, hides, skins, leather, and rubber.

All companies and partnerships registered under Thai law, or incorporated under foreign laws and conducting business in Thailand (e.g., branches), are subject to company income tax.

The tax rate is 30 percent for companies listed on the stock exchange and 40 percent for others.

Dividends, interest, royalties, and fees transmitted to persons overseas are taxed at 25 percent of the sums transmitted. In the case of remittances of interest and fees by Thai companies to foreign corporate shareholders, the amounts are tax deductible. This is not the case for similar remittances by a branch to its head office.

The Thai labor force is overwhelmingly rural with 63 percent of the total classified as farmers and 84 percent living in non-urban areas. Unskilled labor, prepared to work for wages at or below the legal minimum of $2.66 per day in 1983, is plentiful, while Thai universities and technical schools produce more graduates than there are jobs available. Salaries for experienced, qualified engineers range from U.S. $8400 to $16,000 per year with other professional level employees receiving similar wages. Skilled production workers are relatively more difficult to find but are available. The labor turnover rate for multinational corporations is among the lowest in Asia.

Thai labor law and practice present few impediments to the management of work forces. The normal work week is 54 hours in commercial operations, 48 hours in industrial operations, and 42 hours for hazardous work, with overtime payable for work in excess of these limits.

Investment Promotion

The government, through the Board of Investment (BOI), has actively sought to promote both domestic and foreign investment in the priority areas of the economy. The Board defines priority areas for investment, provides services to investors, and decides which investments will qualify for promoted status and privileges.

In 1983, the BOI announced a policy of giving special consideration to investment projects which: (1) significantly strengthen the balance of payments position, especially through production for export; (2) support the development of resources in the country; (3) substantially increase employment; (4) locate operations in the provinces; (5) conserve energy or replace imported energy supplies; (6) establish or develop basic industries which form the bases for further stages of industrial development; or (7) are considered important and necessary by the government.

Under this policy, the most generous BOI incentives are available for projects which are export-oriented, labor-intensive, resource-based and located outside of Bangkok. Companies which locate in investment promotion zones in upcountry locations qualify for additional incentives.

Incentives for export-oriented projects include: (1) exemption of import duties and business taxes on imported raw materials and components; (2) exemption of imported duties and business taxes on re-export items; (3) allowance to deduct from corporate taxable income an amount equivalent to 5 percent of any increase in income derived from export, excluding costs of insurance and transportation.

Projects located in Investment Promotion Zones may qualify for further discretionary benefits as follows:

1. Reductions, not exceeding 90 percent, of business taxes on sales of products for a maximum of 5 years.

2. Reduction by 50 percent of company income taxes for a further 5 years after any period of total tax exemption.

3. Additional deductions in computing company income taxes equal to:

   a. Double the actual cost of transport, water, and electricity.

   b. Up to 25 percent of the capital investment on installation and construction of facilities. This may be carried forward for a maximum of 10 years. Normal depreciation allowance may also be claimed.

In order to achieve greater efficiency, the Thai cabinet, in 1982, established two Investment Service Centers (ISC). The centers aid investors by helping them make appropriate applications. Permits must be processed and completed with 90 days. In the past, the procedure could take up to 15 months.

Intra-ASEAN Trade

The Association of South East Asian Nations (ASEAN) includes Thailand, Malaysia, Indonesia, Singapore, the Philippines, and Brunei. Although intra-ASEAN trade has expanded 14-fold since 1967, it still only accounted for 16 percent of Thai exports and 12 percent of imports in 1983. Thailand has been hoping for a considerable expansion of trade with its ASEAN partners, but has been disappointed by the slow progress in recent years.

In the early 1980s, the BOI approved a joint-venture to produce 20,000 sets of truck cab parts and 6000 sets of rear body parts a year. The Thai investors hold 60 percent and a Japanese firm 40 percent. The plant is expected to benefit from the ASEAN Automotive Complementation Scheme, under which Thailand is to produce body parts with preferential tariff privileges throughout the ASEAN countries.

Computers and Business Machines

Thailand is entirely dependent on imports for computers, peripherals, and other business machines and computer-related equipment. The total apparent market for these products in 1982 was approximately $70 million.

In Thailand the computerization trend is toward smaller and less expensive computers that render higher efficiency. The need for computerization has persistently increased as the advantages become more apparent, especially for expanding enterprises. For that reason and in spite of conservative spending patterns, many large businesses, not only in Bangkok but also in the provinces, have been computerized.

About 50 to 60 new computer systems are sold each year. Principal customers are banks, finance companies, large business firms, manufacturing companies, and government agencies.

Historically, U.S. computers and business machines have dominated the Thai market, but in recent years the U.S. market share has been diminishing. Japanese suppliers have made concerted efforts to promote the sales of their equipment and their initiatives appear to have been successful. While U.S. firms still dominate the computer market, their percentage share of the business machine market is declining.

The number of computer and advanced business machine users is low considering the increasing sophistication of industry and commerce in Thailand, leaving room for impressive growth. A large untapped market lies with smaller companies that can use (and afford) a computer priced at $50,000 or less. Microcomputers appear to have a bright future and positive market potential. Automatic typewriters, typewriters with memory, word processors, automatic banking equipment, personal computers, blueprint machines, and paper shredders also have a receptive and growing market in Thailand.

Foreign Direct Investment Policy and Regulations

Thailand is committed to international trade and welcomes foreign private investment. Foreign investors in Thailand generally have the same basic rights as Thai nationals unless those rights are specifically reserved for nationals or denied to or restricted to aliens. The important

Thai laws governing the rights of aliens are the Alien Business Law of 1966, the Alien Occupation Law of 1973, the Immigration Act of 1979, and the Investment Promotion Act of 1977.

Previous Foreign Investment

The Thai government does not maintain statistics on foreign investment by nationality. The only available data on investments from abroad apply solely to those investors seeking promotional privileges from the Board of Investment. Exhibit 18-2 covers only the incoming promoted investment over the period 1960–81.

In 1983, the BOI received 341 applications of B56.1 billion, a considerable increase over 1982's B21.5 billion. The BOI approved 235 applications, totaling B33.8 billion. Foreign investors accounted for 24 percent of the applications, 41 percent of approvals and 15 percent of the firms operating. From 1960 to June 1984, 16 percent of all investment in Thailand came from overseas.

EXHIBIT 18-2

Cumulative Amount of Foreign Direct Investment in Thailand, 1960–81 (values in baht)

Nationality of Ownership	100% Owned	Joint Venture	Total Amount
Japan	204,194	1,390,121	1,594,315
Taiwan	3,000	685,124	688,124
United States	60,740	507,689	568,429
Hong Kong	—	289,692	289,692
United Kingdom	11,000	279,164	290,164
Malaysia	—	172,852	172,852
India	8,000	126,967	134,967
West Germany	19,750	91,213	110,963
Switzerland	—	95,385	95,385
Netherlands	—	94,750	94,750

Source: U.S. Department of Commerce, International Trade Administration, *Investment Climate in Foreign Countries. Volume III, Asia.* August 1983, p. 291.

EXHIBIT 18-3

U.S. Investment in Manufacturing
by Industrial Sector, 1983

Sector	Investment (US$ millions)	Percent of Total
Chemicals/pharmaceuticals	195.4	28.5
Consumer products	156.0	22.8
Agriculture/food processing	144.4	21.1
Rubber processing/tires	72.0	10.5
Electronics	64.7	9.4
Metals processing	52.2	7.6
Total	684.7	100.0

Source: Office of the Board of Investment, Royal Thai Government, *Make It in Thailand*, 1984.

From a survey of U.S. firms in Thailand undertaken in the third-quarter of 1983, the US Embassy estimated the value of American investments in Thailand at over US $3 billion. American equity holdings in these firms averaged 77.5 percent of the total. In 1982, US firms generated revenues in excess of US $2.6 billion, and provided employment to 33,910 persons. In 1984 and 1985, U.S. firms in Thailand planned to invest an additional US $794 million in expansion. In the manufacturing sector, the Embassy survey estimated U.S. investments in Thailand at US $684.7 million, as shown in Exhibit 18-3.

Investment Incentives

Foreign investors have the option of setting up operations in Thailand with or without the BOI approval. The advantages of the BOI approval are the protection provided by the Investment Act of 1977 and the possible provision of promotional incentives, which are summarized as follows:

GUARANTEES
• Against nationalization
• Against competition of new state enterprises
• Against state monopolization of the sale of products similar to those produced by promoted firms
• Against imports by government agencies or state enterprises

PROTECTION MEASURES
• Imposition of surcharge on foreign products
• Import ban on competing products

PERMISSIONS
• To bring in foreign nationals to undertake investment feasibility studies
• To bring in foreign technicians and experts to work on promoted projects
• To own land for carrying out promoted activities
• To take or remit abroad foreign currency

TAX INCENTIVES
• Exemption or reductions of import duties and business tax on imported machinery
• Reduction of import duties and business taxes on imported raw materials and components
• Exemption of corporate income taxes from 3 to 8 years with permission to carry forward losses and deduct them as expenses for up to 5 years
• Exemption of up to 5 years on withholding tax on royalties or fees remitted abroad
• Exclusion from taxable income of dividends derived from promoted enterprises during the income tax holiday

Additional incentives are gained for export-oriented industries and those located in the Investment Promotion Zones.

Ownership Limitations

Late in 1972, the Government enacted the Alien Business Decree (ABD), designed to promote the development of domestic enterprise and to reserve some fields of business to Thai nationals. The ABD sets forth three groups of businesses, Categories A, B, and C, in which all foreign firms must apply for licenses to operate. Moreover, under the Alien Business Law, certain activities are not open to foreign investors. Exhibit 18-4 shows the restricted activities under the Alien Business Law.

In considering the approval of any foreign investment in a wholly foreign-owned project or of foreign equity participation in a joint-venture project, to which investment promotion is granted, the Board of Investment utilities the following criteria:

1. For an investment project for manufacturing products mainly for domestic distribution, Thai nationals are required to own shares totalling not less than 51 percent of the registered capital.

2. For an investment project in agriculture, animal husbandry, fishery, mineral exploration and mining, or the services sector, Thai nationals must hold shares totalling not less than 60 percent of the registered capital.

3. For an investment project which exports at least 50 percent of its output, the foreign investors may hold shares comprising the majority of the registered capital, and comprising all registered capital if the production is totally for export.

4. When there are justified reasons, the Board may consider waiving the above criteria by taking into account: (a) the necessary amount of project investment; (b) the level of technology; (c) local employment; (d) site of the plant; (e) social and economic benefits of the project; (f) other considerations that the Board deems appropriate. To consider waiving any of the above criteria, the Board may stipulate conditions as appropriate.

Registration

With the exception of some restrictions on aliens (e.g., the Alien Business Law), foreign companies in Thailand generally operate un-

EXHIBIT 18-4

Restricted Business Activities
Under the 1972 Alien Business Law

CATEGORY A (requires majority Thai ownership)

Section 1—Agricultural Businesses

1. Rice farming
2. Salt farming including salt mining, except rock salt

Section 2—Commercial Businesses

1. Internal trade of local agricultural products
2. Trade in real estate

Section 3—Service Businesses

1. Accounting
2. Law
3. Architecture
4. Advertising
5. Brokerage or agency
6. Auctioning
7. Barbering, hairdressing and beauty salons

Section 4—Other Businesses

1. Building construction
2. Mining

CATEGORY B (new investments require majority Thai ownership: established foreign firms may continue under restrictions)

Section 1—Agricultural Businesses

1. Farming except those in category A
2. Orchard farming
3. Animal husbandry including silkworm raising
4. Timbering
5. Fishing

Section 2—Industrial and Handicraft Businesses

1. Rice milling
2. Flour milling from rice or other crops
3. Sugar milling
4. Production of beverages with or without alcohol
5. Ice making
6. Manufacturing of pharmaceuticals
7. Cold storage

(Continued)

8. Lumber milling or processing
9. Manufacturing of gold, silver, neilloware and stone inlaid products
10. Manufacturing or casting of Buddha images and alms bowls
11. Wood carving
12. Production of lacquerware
13. Manufacturing of matches
14. Manufacturing of white cement, portland cement and cement products
15. Stone quarrying
16. Manufacturing of plywood, veneer wood or chipboard
17. Manufacturing of garments or footwear except for exports
18. Silk spinning, weaving or silk fabric printing, manufacturing of finished products from silk

Section 3—Commercial Businesses

1. Retail trade except as listed in category C
2. Trading in mineral ores except as listed in category C
3. Sale of foods and beverages except as listed in category C
4. Trade in antiques, old objects or works of art

Section 4—Service Businesses

1. Tourist agencies
2. Hotels except hotel management
3. Businesses governed by the laws on entertainment places
4. Photographic studio, photographic processing and printing
5. Laundry
6. Tailoring or dressmaking

Section 5—Other Businesses

1. Domestic land, water and air transport
2. Operation of printing establishments
3. Newspaper publishing

CATEGORY C (majority foreign ownership allowed with restrictions)

Section 1—Commercial Businesses

1. All kinds of wholesale trade except those listed in category A
2. All kinds of export trade
3. Retail trade in machinery, engines and tools
4. Sale of foods and beverages to promote tourism

Section 2—Industrial and Handicraft Businesses

1. Manufacturing of animal feed
2. Extraction of vegetable oils
3. Production of textile and knitted products including yarn spinning and dyeing and fabric printing
4. Manufacturing of glassware including light bulbs
5. Manufacturing of food cups, bowls and plates
6. Manufacturing of stationery and printing paper
7. Rock salt mining

Section 3—Service Businesses

1. Any business not listed under categories A or B

Section 4—Other Businesses

1. Construction except that listed under category A

Source: Business International Corp., *IL & T THAILAND*, December 1984.

der the same laws, rules and regulations as do Thai companies. Foreign businesses must, however, obtain a license from the Alien Businesses Registration Section, Department of Commercial Registration, Ministry of Commerce, before commencing business. U.S. firms which claim an exemption from the provisions of the Alien Business Law under the provision of the 1966 Treaty of Amity and Economic Relations between Thailand and the United States must obtain a written confirmation from the Director-General of the Department of Commercial Registration. This procedure is quite straightforward.

The principal forms of business organization under Thai law are sole proprietorships, partnerships, limited companies and public limited companies. It is a prerequisite for most applicants for BOI "promoted investor" status that they set up a limited liability company equivalent to the Western type.

Performance Requirements

The Thai government maintains two types of investment performance requirements: local content requirements and export requirements. Of these only the former (local content requirements) is mandatory and then only in the case of certain motor vehicles assembled for the domestic market. In other cases, the granting of investment incentives may be conditioned on meeting either local content or export performance targets, but firms which do not meet those goals are not prevented or hindered from making the investments. However, in judging eligibility for promotional status, the BOI gives very favorable consideration to projects using local raw materials and products. Consequently, many promoted projects have pledged to achieve a certain degree of local content within a specified period of time. The Factories Act also empowers the Minister of Industry, with the approval of the Thai cabinet, to prescribe the source, type, quality and amount of raw materials to be used in factories under consideration for establishment or expansion.

Exchange Controls

Thailand has a comprehensive Exchange Control Act that is administered by the Foreign Exchange Control Division in the Bank of Thailand on behalf of the Ministry of Finance. In practice, restrictions are minimal on payments and transfers for current international transactions, provided that requisite formalities are complied with.

In the fields that have not been specifically closed to foreigners, entry of capital for investment purposes is unrestricted. However, foreign exchange created as the result of investment in Thailand must be sold to an authorized agent within seven days.

The Bank of Thailand maintains a Special Register, in which all amounts of foreign exchange remitted or brought to Thailand by investors, either as capital or as a loan for use in the establishment or expansion of industrial enterprises, are recorded.

To obtain permission to remit foreign exchange for purposes other than in payment for imports, Form E.C. 31 must be filed with the Bank of Thailand. Documentary evidence indicating the nature of the repatriation is required. In addition, for example, evidence must be presented to assist the Bank in determining whether or not the investor has sufficient remaining funds to operate his business.

The Exchange Control authorities usually grant approval for the following types of remittances:

1. Profits and dividends, after all taxes have been paid and reserve requirements under the company law have been satisfied.
2. Fifty percent of the anticipated net profit for the first six months of the fiscal year.
3. Principal and interest on loans, and fees and royalties.
4. Proceeds of the liquidation of a business or other sums which are surplus to the requirements of a business venture. In the case of transfers of large amounts, approval may be granted for remittances in installments.

A promoted person or an investor in a promoted business whose domicile is outside Thailand is permitted by the Investment Promotion Act of 1977 to take out or remit abroad capital in foreign currency if:

1. It represents investment capital which the promoted person brought into Thailand or dividends or other forms of returns derived from such investment capital;
2. It represents a foreign loan and interest charged on such loan which the promoted person invested in the promoted activity under a contract approved by the Board; or
3. it represents foreign obligations by the promoted person under a contract for the use of rights and services relating to the pro-

moted activity, provided that such contract was approved by the Board.

The Bank of Thailand, however, is authorized temporarily to restrict the remittance abroad of monies in order to preserve foreign exchange at a reasonable level.

IBM's General Business Strategy

The following materials provide insights into IBM's strategy for competing in the world's computer markets[1].

IBM depends heavily on its non-American operations. Foreign business accounts for roughly 50 percent of IBM's total revenues and earnings. Last year, largely because of the strength of the dollar, foreign operations accounted for only 48 percent of revenues of $29.1 billion and 37.5 percent net income of $3.3 billion.

Government actions can help or hurt IBM as much as, if not more than, actions of other computer companies. Over the years, IBM has developed an elaborate system for managing its dealings with national governments. It generally behaves ethically—no bribery scandals mar its past—yet it is not above playing one government against another, using the law to its fullest advantage or bringing into play its own considerable power and resources, which stem from its size and its dominance of the market for a vital product.

IBM has clearly benefited from the United States Government's concern over technology. The company, has changed from antitrust target to national flag-bearer in an international battle for technological supremacy. IBM has taken care recently to build up this image by publicizing its technological accomplishments. To the extent that the national interest is perceived to coincide with that of IBM, IBM stands to benefit.

The European Economic Community, in its antitrust case, wants to compel IBM to release specifications of its new computers in time to let other computer companies get to market with machines that can attach to IBM computers or compete with them. The United States Government said it has argued on IBM's behalf because such early disclosure in Europe would, in effect, be disclosure elsewhere, helping the Japanese and hurting American technology.

But at the same time as IBM is portraying itself in America as red, white and blue, it is trying to convince France that it is a French company, Britain that it is a British company and Japan that it is a Japanese company. Being perceived as too American can thus hurt IBM abroad.

Governments have three reasons to be wary of IBM. First, it is a multinational corporation, meaning its interests might not coincide with those of the nations in which it operates. Second, it is an American company. Third, it is a computer company.

Computers are considered vital for national economic growth and national defense, much as is oil. There has even been some expression that control of computers and related telecommunications should be the province of government itself.

European nations and Japan began major efforts in the late 1960s and early 1970s to foster their own computer companies to take on IBM. The Governments provided subsidies and favored the local companies in procurements.

But with the exception of Japan, the efforts failed. IBM still controls more than half the world market for large computers. In terms of yearly computer revenues, it is the leader in all major non-Communist countries except Britain and Japan, where it is No. 2. European competitors like Britain's ICL, West Germany's Siemens and Italy's Olivetti are now selling Japanese computers to compete with IBM in the mainframe business.

To cope with economic nationalism, IBM's main tactic is protective coloring. IBM hires local citizens wherever it operates. Less than 1 percent of IBM's 150,000 overseas employees in 125 nations are Americans. It tries to buy from local suppliers, where possible, and contribute to the tax base and the balance of trade.

"We should be considered a local company," said Dean P. Phypers, IBM senior vice president who has responsibility for foreign operations.

IBM also reminds the local populace of its good citizenship. In Europe, IBM's frequent corporate

[1]Excerpts from Andrew Pollack, "The Far-Flung Wars of IBM," *The New York Times*, September 19, 1982.

image advertising portrays it as a friendly local company that employs 100,000 Europeans.

IBM also carefully distributes manufacturing and research responsibility among different nations. Plants in each nation do not make all the products used in that nation. Rather, each plant makes enough of one or a few products to supply the world or the region, so that IBM is exporting and importing to each nation, hopefully achieving a balance in major countries.

By having each plant produce large amounts of a single product, IBM helps maintain economies of scale while distributing production. Such a strategy also helps fend off attempts at nationalization. A Government trying to nationalize IBM's operations in its nation will end up with a unit that is part of a complex worldwide web and cannot easily stand on its own.

Another part of IBM strategy is to try to steer clear of partisan politics, government regulation and political controversy. IBM does not even have a political action committee to make contributions. Nevertheless, its influence in Washington is felt.

IBM also takes care to employ prominent people in each nation, both to help it in political circles and for the practical reason that in many less developed nations, the government is IBM's prime customer.

On occasion, however, IBM has had to give ground. It pulled out of Nigeria and India in the late 1970s, rather than give up 100 percent ownership in its subsidiaries in those countries. In Indonesia, IBM markets through an Indonesia-owned company. Brazil has prevented IBM and other American companies from manufacturing and selling smaller computers in that country.

Mr. Phypers of IBM said the company has no specific strategy for dealing with governments, other than trying to be a good citizen in each area in which it operates. In locating facilities, "the political realities are a factor in the equation but the fundamental driver is what makes economic sense," he said.

On one hand, European nations seem less upset with IBM now than they were several years ago and the General Agreement on Tariffs and Trade has reduced governmental procurement practices favorable to home industries. With the United States antitrust suit over, IBM is in its strongest position in years.

IBM'S SUPREMACY IN MAINFRAMES

	IBM	Other U.S. Makers	Non-U.S. Makers
United States[a]	$39,403	$18,762	$0
Japan	4,515	1,457	9,664
West Germany	6,287	1,799	1,916
Russia	29	81	9,079
France	4,685	2,527	1,105
Britain	2,972	1,705	2,238
Canada	2,230	1,673	15
Italy	2,478	1,153	143
Other Eastern Europe	158	143	1,784
Australia	644	886	257
Other	9,884	4,291	1,727
Total	73,546	35,206	27,928

[a]Dollar value of mainframe computers installed by IBM and other manufacturers, in millions of dollars at end 1980. Countries ranked by total size of market.

The Reshaping of IBM[2]

With nearly 300,000 employees worldwide, and consolidated sales in 1976 of $16.3 billion (half outside America), IBM is not just a giant but immensely profitable: its $2.4 billion of net earnings gave it a 14.7 percent return on turnover exceeded by only seven significant American industrial companies and by none anywhere near IBM's size. Yet problems it has, and they could lead to dramatic changes in its corporate behavior.

THE THIRD WORLD

Four major countries—India, Indonesia, Nigeria and Brazil—are challenging IBM's insistence on 100 percent control of its subsidiaries. IBM's worldwide integration of its research and manufacturing is highly sophisticated, and—perhaps rightly—the company reckons that foreign bodies in the mechanism would wreck it. There are not very many multinationals that really benefit hugely from being such, and could suffer correspondingly from the world's zeal for decentralization. IBM is one.

[2]Excerpts from "Reshaping IBM," *Economist* October 29, 1977, pp. 92–93.

It bought out the 38 percent British interest in its British subsidiary 20 years ago, at an enormous price. It gave a rude reply to Japan's rude attempt to ensure partial local ownership there.

But Indian law requires foreign companies to divest 60 percent of their equity to local shareholders unless they manufacture solely for export. IBM's counterproposal was to do that for its computer service bureaus, but retain full ownership not only of an export-only manufacturing plant but of marketing and service operations inside India. The government said no.

Nigeria too wants an equity stake for locals, and Indonesia says that marketing must be done by Indonesian-controlled companies. In both countries' negotiations, better-tempered than in India, continue.

In Brazil, the problem is over the right to manufacture small computers. Sixteen bids have been put in; three will be selected by the government within the next few weeks. Among the criteria for suitability are local sourcing and the local equity stake. Other foreign competitors such as Philips, Honeywell-CII, Fujitsu, Nixdorf and (Japan's) NEC have got together with Brazilian interests to make joint proposals. Not IBM.

Back at Armonk there is a vigorous argument at this moment. Should IBM give way, knowing that would make it harder to fend off similar demands that will arise elsewhere? (In Malaysia, for instance, by 1990, 70 percent of equity must be locally owned —but everyone knows this is, in fact, a bargaining figure.) Or should IBM simply wash its hands of these markets, if need be? They are indeed significant and growing—but still unimportant compared with the industrial world where it makes a very handsome living.

EUROPE

The problem here is a conflict between IBM's manufacturing integration and its "good citizen" philosophy on plant location.

The company's manufacturing is (by and large) integrated region-wide rather than world-wide: the United States; Europe/Middle East/Africa; and Americas/Far East. In practice, the three-way split is more of a two-way one—but not the one suggested by the fact that the two last named regions were carved out of a single entity, IBM World Trade, in 1974. These have not reunited. Instead,

Americas/Far East has never been really independent of the United States operation. Its headquarters is in New York state, and much of its manufacture is done in America.

Europe/Middle East/Africa (head office in Paris), has greater freedom (though capital investment above a very low figure requires American approval). And Europe is the market where IBM has best been able to carry out its stated philosophy that plants should be so located that value added in a given country is in fair proportion to IBM sales there. It has 14 plants, four each in France and Germany, two in Britain, one each in Holland, Sweden, Italy and, quite recently, Spain. Some effort is made also to ensure that bought-in parts come from countries where there is no direct manufacturing.

This is good citizenry. It is not particularly efficient. Nor—given IBM's wide product range, and the international nature of many customers—is the country-by-country marketing set-up.

On marketing, there is talk now of sub-regional integration, for example, Europe's French-speakers, German-speakers and English-speakers (including Dutch-speakers and the Scandinavians) could be treated as single markets.

Plant location would be a harder nut. One road to profit would be to shift European production to low-wage countries like Britain and Spain—and then what would the West Germans, Swedish and Dutch governments and unions say? Another would be neither to shift nor centralize within Europe but integration between Europe and America. Company policy is to manufacture every item in both continents (and sometimes a third). If this policy were reversed there would be sore governments on both sides of the Atlantic (mostly in Europe, since labor there is by now mostly costlier than in America). There would also be ruffled feathers at the 1300-strong Paris headquarters since integration would tend to mean integration under Armonk.

AMERICA

While the economic pressure is for reintegration, the political pressure at home is for the opposite. IBM faces a 8-year-old antitrust suit, one of whose aims is to split the company up. The government is nearing the end of its evidence in this suit. IBM could drag it on for years yet. But there would be a price for doing so.

Although it no longer dominates the American market entirely as it did in 1969, IBM is still reckoned to hold over half of it. But competitors are cutting into that share with cheaper, advanced technology sold to customers prepared to put it together themselves rather than, as they used to, pay a premium for IBM's skill at providing the complete package. IBM's justly famed organization needs reshaping for the new conditions. But every move it makes is fiercely scrutinized by its own lawyers, and the government's, while the suit drags on.

So IBM now would like to see the government's suit thrown out, or to settle.

PROFITABLE GIANT. IBM 1976

	Turnover $m	Post-tax profits $m	Return on turnover %
Worldwide[a]	16,304	2,398	14.7
IBM (Deutschland)	2,523	327	12.9
IBM (France)	1,766	131	7.4
IBM (UK)	841	70	8.3
IBM (Italia)	704	59	8.4
IBM (Nederland)	422	58	13.7
IBM (Svenska)	334	27	8.1

[a]Worldwide figures consolidated. European ones not comparable, since they include intra-group sales.

International Business Machines Corporation[3]

SUMMARY

IBM is the world's largest computer company with substantial activities in office products. Approximately half of the sales, profits and assets are outside the USA.

STRUCTURE

The organization is a complex structure of product divisions and functional responsibilities. The main units are: DP Marketing Group

[3]From John M. Stopford, John H. Dunning, and Klaus O. Haberich, *World Directory of Multinational Enterprises*, vol. 1. New York: Facts on File, Inc., 1980, pp. 540–542.

(U.S. marketing and service, information systems, federal systems etc.), DP Products Group (global development responsibilities and U.S. manufacturing for information systems), General Business Group (global development responsibilities and U.S. manufacturing for low to moderate price information systems and includes global management of office products), together with two area divisions (Americas/ Far East and Europe/Middle East/Africa) and IBM World Trade Corp. (designated support services to area divisions).

PRODUCTS

DP Marketing Group: Products and services include information handling systems, equipment, computer programming, systems engineering, education and other related services to customers who require larger centralized systems as well as distributed processing systems. The Federal Systems division provides information handling and control systems to the Federal government for seaborne, space-borne, airborne and ground based environment. Also participates in applied research and exploratory development. Field Engineering division provides maintenance and related services for the information handling systems and equipment and support for programming systems developed and manufactured by or for the DP Product Group and marketed by the Data Processing Division, and central programming service for assigned products.

DP Products Group: Worldwide development responsibility for large complex systems with primary emphasis on high performance products and associated programming, plus U.S. manufacturing responsibility for those products. Supplies computer components, including logic and selected memory technologies. General products division products include tape units, disk products, and mass storage systems, as well as system printers, program products, programming languages and related programming. System communications division produces systems that prepare and process information for communication such as distributed systems, industry systems, display terminals, line switching and related technologies and programming. Systems products division produces intermediate range processors and related programming and impact printer products and semiconductor packaging.

General Business Group: Includes electric and electronic typewriters, copiers and related supplies, magnetic media typewriters, information processors, dictation equipment and direct impression composing products; component technology requirements of the low-to-moderate price computers made by the General Systems Division, and supplies components of other IBM operating units. Information records division manufactures data processing cards, business forms, ribbons, and other consumable products used in information handling systems; also manufactures biomedical supplies and devices.

Other divisions: Real Estate and Construction division manages the selection and acquisition of sites, design and construction of buildings, purchase or lease of facilities for all IBM operations in U.S. Has responsibility for world wide energy and environmental programmes and provides facility services to some headquarters locations. Research division deals with areas of company interest and technology developments for company.

Subsidiaries: Science Research Associates Inc. produces a wide range of educational materials for schools and health science industry, as well as testing and training materials for industry. *IBM World Trade Americas/Far East Corporation* is responsible for operations in 44 countries. *IBM World Trade Europe/Middle East/Africa Corporation* is responsible for operations in 77 countries. *IBM World Trade Corporation* provides support to IBM World Trade organizational units.

Product Sales %	1979	1978	1977	1976	1975
Data Processing	80	81	81	82	82
Equipment Sales	27	28	25	23	18
Equipment Rentals & Services	39	41	45	49	54
Services, Programs, Supplies	14	12	11	10	10
Office Products	17	16	16	15	15
Sales	9	9	8	8	8
Rentals & Services	8	7	8	7	7
Other	3	3	3	3	3
Total Net Sales ($ million)	22,863	21,076	18,133	16,304	14,437

Product Profits %	1979	1978	1977
Data Processing	89	92	93
Office Products	11	7	6
Federal Systems	1	1	1
Other	0	0	0
Total Operating Profits ($ million)	5,344	5,530	4,734

INTERNATIONAL BUSINESS MACHINES CORPORATION FIVE-YEAR SUMMARY

Financial year: 31 December

($ million)

Currency: US$

	1979	%	1978	%	1977	%	1976	%	1975	%
Total Net Sales	22,863		21,076		18,133		16,304		14,437	
By Foreign Subs		53		52		50		50		50
Europe		36		35		33				
Middle East, Africa		2		2		2				
Other		15		15		15				
Net Profit	3,011		3,111		2,719		2,398		1,990	
Foreign		47		50		45		44		56
Europe, Middle East, Africa		35		33		30				
Other		12		15		13				
Earnings per Share ($)[a]	5.16		5.32		4.58		3.99		3.34	
Foreign Exchange Gains/(Losses) (after tax)	(52.0)		113.0		28.0					
Total Assets	24,530		20,771		18,978		17,723		15,530	
Foreign Assets[b]		49		48		48		44		43
Europe, Middle East, Africa		36		37		35				
Other		13		11		13				
Shareholders' Equity	14,961		13,494		12,618		12,749		11,416	
Foreign Net Assets		46		46		42		37		35
Long-Term Debt	1,589		286		256		275		295	
Capital Expenditure[c]	5,991		4,046		3,395		2,518		2,439	
Abroad		47		53		55		50		60
R&D Expenditure	1,360		1,255		1,142		1,012		946	
Total Employees	337,100		325,500		310,200		292,000		288,600	
Domestic		56		56		55		54		54
Abroad		44		44		45		46		46
Europe, Middle East, Africa		30		31						
Other		14		13						

Consolidation: Includes all subsidiaries.

[a]Adjusted for 1979 stock split.

[b]Percentages based on figures before eliminations.

[c]Includes investment in rental machines (1979: $4,212 million).

BACKGROUND

IBM was first incorporated in 1911 as the Computing-Tabulating Recording Company by the merger of three companies: Tabulating Machine Co. (est. 1896), Computing Scale Co. (est. 1891), International Time Recording (est. 1889). The first products were commercial scales, tabulating and time-recording equipment. First move abroad was to Canada in 1917 under International Business Machines Co. Ltd. (the name adopted by the parent in 1924) and an office in Brazil established. Early acquisitions included Ticketograph Co. (1921), Pierce Accounting Machine Co. (1922) and the counting and weighing machine division of National Scale Corp. (1932), though the Dayton Scale Division was sold to Hobart in 1935, using assets acquired from Electromatic Typewriter two years earlier. In 1944 IBM's first large-scale computer (the automatic sequence controlled calculator) was presented to Harvard, the 603 commercial electronic calculator was announced, and in 1948 company's first large-scale digital calculator was announced, four years before the first production computer. During this period IBM turned down the offer of UNIVAC which was later bought by Sperry-Rand. During the 1950s, developments in computing and office machinery followed rapidly, and sales passed the $1 billion level in 1957. Time Equipment Division was sold off in 1958. Apart from the acquisition of Science Research Associates in 1964, growth has been by means of introducing new generations of machines and by establishing companies abroad. A wholly owned policy has dominated the overseas expansion, leading to a withdrawal in India in 1977 when this policy irreconcilably conflicted with local ownership regulations. Research efforts have been established in many countries and are coordinated centrally.

CURRENT SITUATION

IBM's massive research investments create a stream of new hardware and software products which in turn create demand for more capacity. This expansion, coinciding with a consumer shift towards leasing rather than purchasing computers, led to company's first major borrowing of $1 billion from the debt market followed in December 1979 by a $300 million placement of notes with the Saudi Arabian Monetary Agency. Increasing competition from the Japanese is likely to erode some of company's dominant market share position (currently leader in all major markets except UK). In September 1979 company formed a 50–50 venture with MCA, DiscoVision Associates, to enter the video disc and disc player markets. This move may herald a major expansion into the consumer market.

IBM: 1983

Operations by Geographic Areas	U.S. $million	As % of Consolidated
United States		
Sales	$23,127	58
Profits	3,296	60
Margins (%)	14.3	
Assets at December 31	23,083	62
Europe/Middle East/Africa		
Sales	11,324	28
Profits	1,580	29
Margins (%)	14.0	
Assets at December 31	10,011	27
Americas/Far East		
Sales	5,729	14
Profits	562	10
Margins (%)	9.8	
Assets at December 31	5,110	14
Consolidated		
Sales	40,180	100
Profits	5,485	100
Margins (%)	13.7	
Assets at December 31	37,243	100

(Continued)

Research and Development Expenditures: $2,514 million (6.3% of sales).

Principal Plants and Properties: IBM's manufacturing and development facilities in the United States had an aggregate floor space of approximately 53.3 million square feet. Similar facilities in other countries totaled approximately 20.6 million square feet. In the United States, company has plants and laboratories in 23 cities. In addition IBM World Trade Corp. has 23 major manufacturing plants in 14 countries outside the U.S. as follows:

Argentina Australia Brazil Canada Columbia
France Germany (W) Italy Japan Mexico
Netherlands Spain Sweden United Kingdom

Source: *IBM Annual Report*, 1983.

The Assignment

1. A firm attempting to operate a production facility in a foreign country faces inherent disadvantages (relative to local firms). What are these inherent disadvantages? Given these inherent disadvantages, why is IBM able to succeed in operating substantial facilities in foreign countries? That is, what are the sources of strength that give IBM offsetting advantages in operating facilities in foreign countries? Instead of direct foreign investment, why does IBM not use licensing of foreign firms for production in foreign countries, or exporting from the United States, in order to earn profits from foreign markets?

2. If IBM might be interested in establishing a facility in Thailand, IBM and the Thai government (probably the Board of Investment) are likely to negotiate about the conditions of IBM's entry and operations in Thailand. Many items might be covered in these conditions. What should IBM seek from the Thai government? What should IBM offer to the Thai government? What should IBM consider non-negotiable?

3. As indicated above, the Thai government will negotiate with IBM over the conditions of IBM's entry and operations. What should the Thai government seek from IBM? What should the Thai government offer to IBM? What should the Thai government view as non-negotiable?

4. The goals and objectives of a multinational enterprise differ from those of a national government. Given these differing goals, the outcome of the negotiations is likely to depend on relative bargaining power and bargaining skills. It is not easy to analyze skill differences, but we can examine relative bargaining power. What are the strengths and weaknesses of each side in terms of bargaining power? Which side appears stronger? What outcome do you expect from the negotiations? How would your assessment change if the Thai government attempts to renegotiate the agreement several years after IBM has built a factory in Thailand?

The Dallas Energy Corporation, Inc.

The Feasibility, Funding, Currency Hedging, and Debt Conversion Option of Direct Foreign Investment in Southern Europe

HARVEY A. PONIACHEK

International Energy Business

The Dallas Energy Corporation, Inc. (DEC) is headquartered in Dallas, Texas and is engaged in petroleum production, supply of energy related equipment, furnishing services and transportation services, including construction, to integrated energy and petroleum companies in the United States and abroad. In 1990, DEC's sales reached about $4 billion, of which energy, including oil and coal production, accounted for 60 percent of worldwide sales, equipment and supplies accounted for 15 percent, and energy related services such as construction and transportation accounted for 25 percent of sales. DEC's performance ratios show that rate of return on shareholders' investment averaged 10.4 percent in 1990, the rate of return on sales was approximately 4 percent, and the total debt to shareholders' equity ratio was 15.9 percent.

The company has engaged in recent years in several large port construction and transportation projects in Southern Europe and Southeast Asia. These projects were promoted and financed primarily by multilateral and regional economic and financial institutions, including the World Bank, in conjunction with leading international construction, transportation and energy corporations.

DEC was approached at a recent international energy conference in London by the energy minister of Portugal, a rapidly developing country in Southwest Europe, offering DEC the opportunity to participate in an international consortium to construct a coal handling port (CHP) in Portugal. DEC was expected to put up some $5 to $10 million for construction costs for 5 to 7 years, but would be given the option of converting its credit to equity (i.e., foreign debt conversion) after the fifth year of operation by acquiring CHP's common shares at a discount of 25 percent from the price, which would be determined on the basis of a comparable P/E multiplier (i.e., the price per common share to earnings per share that prevail for comparable private or public companies), or capitalized over 5 years at CHP's weighted average cost of capital, or at the long-term U.S. government bonds yield rate plus 2 percent, whichever is lower or more readily available.

During preliminary discussions between the chief financial officer (CFO) and Portuguese government officials, and according to the investment prospectus that was issued by a

British investment bank, it was estimated that the construction of the coal project could cost $150–175 million equivalent, of which $100–125 million was expected to be in local currency.

The project is expected to be financed by several multilateral financial institutions at concessionary terms, including the World Bank and European Community (EC) institutions, several West European governments, credit suppliers, the government of Portugal, and private sources.

The CHP company will be operated by a public company with foreign stockholders' ownership holding up to 49 percent of the controlling equity. Conservative projections suggested a profitable operation immediately after inauguration of the facility in 1990.

Investment Opportunity

DEC's Board of Directors was briefed on several preliminary details of the coal facility and the request to participate in the project. A board member—an energy expert and a former chief economist for a major Fortune 100 company—recently visited Portugal and was impressed by their development programs, the vast opportunities inherent in their membership in the EC, their prospects from the enlargement of the EC by 1992, and their positive attitude toward American investment.

Subsequently, the board recommended a thorough review of the proposed project, with the objective of (1) determining under which terms and conditions should DEC join the international construction consortium and what share of the project should they assume, and (2) whether an investment in the proposed project is viable, given the alternative opportunities that are being considered by DEC.

The deputy Chief Financial Officer, senior vice president Don White, was instructed to travel to Portugal and obtain all relevant infor-

mation concerning the proposed investment, including:

1. A country study,
2. Portugal's energy sector review and analysis,
3. The consulting firm's project analysis, including investment and cash flow analysis for 1990–96, and
4. The investment banks' financing memorandum.

Mr. White was requested to present the board of directors with preliminary findings during DEC's board meeting next month.

Following intense scheduling of some dozen appointments, Mr. White and a senior treasury analyst, Barbara Miller, left for Portugal on Saturday evening, with a stopover in London. In London they planned a late lunch on Monday with the senior partner of the energy consulting firm, and dinner with several investment bankers. The deputy CFO and the senior analyst planned to fly to Lisbon on Tuesday morning for a host of meetings with government officials in the energy ministry, commercial bankers, the national development bank, and inspect the proposed investment site.

The Assignment

During their flight to Lisbon, Mr. White and Ms. Miller further reviewed some of the analytical issues which they planned on discussing with government officials and investment bankers in Portugal, and for which they sought additional data and clarification. These issues, listed below, which will constitute part of their write up and scheduled presentation to the board of directors, were faxed to you upon their arrival in Lisbon.

1. Determine the country risk by applying either the country risk rating approach

known as the "Check-List" methodology as discussed in Harvey A. Poniachek, (ed.), *International Corporate Finance*, Allen & Unwin, London and Boston, 1989; or as discussed in Case 30 in this book. You may, however, apply an alternative empirical country risk rating approach. (Use economic and financial data about Portugal from the Organization of Economic Cooperation and Development (OECD), *OECD Economic Survey, Portugal*, 1990/1991, Paris, 1991. OECD, *Main Economic Indicators*, January–March 1991, Paris, 1991. OECD, *Financial Statistics Monthly* (Sections 1 and 2), December 1991, Paris, 1991. International Monetary Fund (IMF), *International Financial Statistics*, December 1991. IMF, *International Financial Statistics, Yearbook* 1991. U.S. Department of Commerce, International Trade Administration, *Foreign Economic Trends and Their Implications for the United States*: *Portugal*, Washington, D.C., July 1991, prepared by the American Embassy in Lisbon. If you are unable to obtain these issues, you may be equally assisted by older or more recent issues, or by other references that generally address the subject matter.)

2. Determine the project's risk by calculating the "Beta" and/or the standard deviation of earnings (of comparable firms if necessary) to assess the systematic and unsystematic risk.

3. Determine the feasibility of the coal handling project, on the basis of the data in Exhibit 19-1 on the expected performance of the project, and the advisability for DEC to participate with an investment of $5–10 million in construction costs. [In applying either a Net Present Value (NPV) or Internal Rate of Return (IRR) approach to assess the investment viability, you need to determine the outlook of the Escudo/dollar exchange rate according to the Purchasing Power Parity (PPP) approach, or rely on the real effective exchange rates published by Morgan Guaranty or any other comparable index available publicly, and utilize CHP's Weighted Average Cost of Capital (WACC), or the yield on long-term government securities plus 2% as the discount rate.]

4. Propose a funding policy for DEC with the objective of utilizing a variety of sources that will minimize funding cost.

5. Formulate a foreign currency hedging policy for DEC. (Be aware that DEC foreign exchange exposure consists of two parts: (a) The initial international bidding process requires a 5% deposit of the proposed investment, and (b) in case DEC's bid is accepted it needs to make a substantial investment in Escudo-denominated assets abroad).

6. Evaluate the options exercise price that is offered to DEC and assess the reasonableness of converting credit to equity.

EXHIBIT 19-1

Energy Project Abroad: Projected Income Statement, 1990–96
(millions of escudos)

	1990	1991	1992	1993	1994	1995	1996
Operating revenue	5,000	7,000	10,500	14,700	16,250	22,250	25,000
Operating expenses	650	845	1,100	1,375	1,700	2,500	3,125
Depreciation	125	175	200	1750	2000	5000	6500
Operating income	4,225	5,980	9,200	11,575	12,550	14,750	15,375
Interest cost	4,000	5,750	8,500	10,000	10,000	12,750	13,000
Interest income	100	100	100	100	100	100	100
Net interest cost	3,900	5,650	8,400	9,900	10,900	12,650	12,900
Net income	325	330	800	1,675	1,650	2,100	2,475

Select Economic and Financial Data

LC/$	175.5						
CPI index							
U.S.A.	158.1	166.0	174.3	183.0	190.3	198.0	205.9
Portugal	432.1	484.0	542.0	607.1	704.2	816.9	947.6
GNP growth	2.0						

Cost Estimates (millions of $)

Total	163
Local currency	53
Dollars	110

Financial Resources

World Bank	53 (Debt)
Government	40 (Equity)
Suppliers	50 (Debt)
Investors	10–15 (Equity)

The FMC Corporation

Investment Bankers Assess the Feasibility of Foreign Direct Investment, Risk and Funding Methods

HARVEY A. PONIACHEK

Introduction

Ted P. Harris received a B.A. degree with honors in economics and mathematics from the University of California at Los Angeles in 1981. Following graduation he worked for two years as a junior analyst at a small merchant banking company in Chicago that specializes in international joint ventures. In 1983, Ted enrolled at New York University's (NYU) MBA program, specializing in corporate finance and international business. While at NYU, he spent two summers as an intern at First Boston corporate finance department, where he worked on several corporate restructuring and acquisition projects.

Upon graduation from NYU, Ted accepted an attractive offer from Morgan Stanley, where within two years he was elected to be a partner in the corporate finance division. While at Morgan, he was instrumental in developing empirical procedures designed to identify undervalued companies, and companies that were not optimizing their full potential.

In 1988, Ted and several of his former colleagues established their own investment firm, Harris, Coleman, Ltd. (HCL). The firm en-

gaged in merger and acquisition financing, corporate finance and strategic planning for Fortune 500 firms. During their first year of operation, HCL sold 25 percent of their firm to a Japanese investment company for $25 million.

HCL pursued a unique and innovative marketing approach in developing client assignments. They conducted intensive research on corporations and then approached the senior management of these companies for discussion, thereby attempting to be hired and bidding for jobs. For HCL, this "fishing" strategy involved considerable risk of wasted time and resources. However, in the keenly competitive market for investment banking deals, this strategy had considerable upside potential.

Ted's main approach to corporate finance is guided by his macroeconomic view of the world economy. According to this view, the U.S. corporate sector needs to restructure and reposition itself in light of the major new trends and developments that occurred in the world economy during the late 1980s and early 1990s. Some of the most significant trends and developments include the EC 1992 enhanced integration plans, the demise of communism and the democratization of Eastern Europe, the implementation of the U.S.–Canada free-trade agreement, the emergence of Japan as a dominant global economic and financial power, and the accelerated shift in the global competitive advantage in manufacturing toward the Newly Industrialized Countries (NICs) and less-developed countries (LDCs).

Ted and his assistant, Julie Ford, have set out to conduct a strategic review of the FMC Corporation in order to identify its strengths, weaknesses, and opportunities. FMC management is continuously reviewing its operation with the purpose of divesting under-performing entities, while at the same time identifying and pursuing new business opportunities and adding and expanding in high performing markets. Ted and Julie ultimately intend to prepare a proposal to several board members and senior corporate executives on how to improve FMC's performance in the 1990s.

To prepare their strategic review they, first, thoroughly reviewed FMC's Annual Report and 10K; second, requested the corporate librarian for a computer search and print out (based on several data bases, including Dialog Information Services, Inc., Lexis-Nexis and other on-line data bases) on FMC for the past 12 months; and third, prepared an examination of several selected issues (listed under the section of this case entitled "The Assignment"). The completion of this review will set the stage for their meeting with the board members and top executives of FMC.

The Company and Its Strategy[1]

FMC Corporation—a Fortune 500 company with $3.4 billion in sales, 24,000 employees worldwide and 89 manufacturing facilities and mines in 24 states and 14 countries abroad—is one of the world's leading producers of chemicals and machinery for industry, agriculture and government. FMC is heavily involved in

[1]FMC Corporation, *Annual Report*, 1989.

international business, deriving 37 percent of total revenues from international sales.

FMC is engaged on a global basis in selected segments of five broad markets, including industrial chemicals, with 29 percent of sales, performance chemicals (17%), precious metals (6%), defense systems (26%), and machinery and equipment (23%). Sales in 1989 reached $3.4 billion, net income was $218 million, earnings per common share, on a fully diluted basis and before extraordinary charges, were $4.34. In 1989, the firm's revenue, and net income, respectively, expanded by 3.4 percent and approximately by 5.7 percent from the previous year.

The corporation went through a recapitalization in 1986 which involved divestiture of businesses that generated about 25 percent of sales, cost-cutting measures and productivity improvements. Cash generated by divestitures were employed in internal investment and expansion, repurchase of common shares and acquisitions. The corporate goal is to achieve a 15 percent post-tax return on capital employed.

To achieve this goal, FMC strategy is to identify the most attractive segments of their markets in which they have a competitive advantage that meet their profitability requirements and in which they could become the most valued supplier to their customers. FMC seeks new opportunities where it can leverage its low-cost position, technological leadership, customer-driven research and development, and a growing global presence.

New opportunities receive necessary capital investment and R&D support. Capital appropriation for 1989 was established at approximately $280 million. FMC maintains a strong and highly focused R&D program and the corporation is constantly introducing new products into the marketplace. Planned R&D was budgeted at $150 million or 4.4 percent of sales.

FMC enhanced its worldwide presence with new plants in western Canada, Thailand, and

Turkey, and expanded facilities in Spain, Ireland, Mexico, and Japan. See Appendix 20-1 for excerpts and data from FMC's 1989 Annual Report.

Financial Performance

The company's rate of return on investment or capital funds (defined as net income before interest expenses and taxes as a percent of the average of stockholders' equity plus long term debt) was 19.1 percent in 1989, compared with 18.8 percent in the previous year. In 1989, for the sixth consecutive year, FMC recorded a rate of return on investment in excess of 15 percent, at or above the target set in 1980. This performance ranks FMC among the top 25 percent of the U.S. industrial companies. This performance reflects the corporation management capabilities, and business composition.

International Operation

FMC strengths in the international market is derived by their ability to tailor products to meet foreign markets requirements, and their experience with establishing and managing overseas joint ventures. Over the past decade, the corporation expanded its international activities considerably. FMC's international business—of some $1.25 billion or 37 percent of total sales—continues to grow faster than the domestic business. The corporation operates in over 40 foreign countries, but international sales are concentrated in western Europe, with 78.1 percent of the total international sales, followed by Latin America and Canada (17.4%) and Africa and Asia (4.5%). The corporation anticipates that the events in eastern Europe should provide growing business opportunities in the years ahead. Also, the unification of

the EC market in 1992 is expected to stimulate FMC's business opportunities there.

FMC is expanding its presence in western Canada, Thailand, Turkey, Spain, Ireland and Mexico. The corporation is enhancing its hydrogen peroxide capacity with new plants in western Canada and Thailand, and a major expansion of an existing plant in Spain, and an anticipated buyout of their partner in the hydrogen peroxide Mexican joint venture.

The corporation operates three affiliates in Spain with highly impressive results. No operation exists in Portugal, while activities in Italy through two wholly-owned affiliates yielded to date attractive returns. Operation in Canada has been relatively small compared with other U.S. corporations presence in that country and the volume of business between the two countries, and in light of the promising prospects of the free-trade agreement.

Analysis

For the purpose of this task, Ted assembled a team of four members, including his assistant, Julie Ford, HCL's industry expert, a vice president for corporate finance, and a junior analyst with good skills in empirical research methods and computer applications.

During the research team's brainstorming, a member of the international finance department commented that expansion in the EC, particularly in southern Europe, eastern Europe, and Canada have recently been considered by several large U.S. corporations in light of the expansion of the European Community, the democratization of eastern Europe, and the gradual implementation of the U.S.–Canada Free-Trade Agreement, which commenced in 1989.

The industry specialist assumed that FMC's board of directors is likely to endorse the corporate plan for expansion abroad through investment in existing entities and acquisition of attractive opportunities. Although joint ventures were identified as the least attractive strategy because of the unsatisfactory past experiences of major U.S. corporations, FMC's experience has been quite satisfactory. Also, the business conditions in eastern Europe are likely to modify this attitude.

The corporate finance specialist maintained that there is a common financial trend among large U.S. companies—that is, in funding international operations the chief financial officer (CFO) often follows uniform guidelines throughout the corporation. Accordingly, the companies seek to minimize the cost of funding, maintain maximum possible debt leverage, attract long-term debt through the international bond market (i.e., the Eurobond and the foreign bond markets), minimize the country risk by tapping the local market to the largest possible extent, and, finally, minimize the currency exposure, particularly where there is an imminent possibility of a currency appreciation. Some or all of the features inherent in this corporate funding policy could probably be observed at FMC as well.

The Assignment

You are a member of HCL's study team. The team tried to assess how a company such as FMC would address/assess several investment opportunities that have arisen around the world; and how these investment projects would be funded. More specifically, the research team attempted to address the following issues/assignments:

1. Ted and Julie attempted to prepare an analysis whether (and why) the FMC board of directors should endorse expansion abroad through investment in existing entities, acquisition of attractive opportunities, or joint ventures. They were aware, however, that joint ventures were the least attractive strategy to many large companies they reviewed in the past several years because of divergent objectives with foreign partners and unsatisfactory past performance. The company's annual report suggested that the FMC board could approve an investment budget of $300 million for each year during 1990 through 1995, and it is likely to earmark a budget of approximately 25 to 35 percent, depending on the relative merit of the opportunities, for expansion abroad if qualified projects are to be found.

2. HCL was recently approached with a long list of industrial chemical and food processing machinery and equipment projects abroad which could fit into FMC's strategy. These projects' expected earnings outlook is listed in Exhibit 20-1. Ted instructed the research team to assess and rank the feasibility of these projects on the basis of their Internal Rate of Return (IRR) and the Net Present Value (NPV) methods.

3. Ted requested that the research team (of which you are a member) assess the risk associated with each project in terms of probability distribution. (The team was given a reprint of an article by David B. Hertz, "Risk Analysis in Capital Investment," *Harvard Business Review*, September–October 1979, pp. 169–181). A team member has recently acquired a new computer simulation package "Risk Analysis & Modeling, @Risk," Risk Analysis and Simulation Add-In for Lotus 1-2-3, Palisade Corporation, Newfield, NY, 1991.

4. The research team, together with the assistance of several top managers of HCL, formulated a funding policy for the two most attractive projects in light of the "standard" Fortune 500 corporate funding guidelines and philosophy as discussed earlier, and with due regard to FMC's capital structure and the cost of capital.

EXHIBIT 20-1

Initial Investment and Expected Cash Flows
(Initial investment in millions of local currency, pre-tax cash flows in millions of dollars)

| | | | Expected Cash Flows[a] | | | | | | | | | | |
Country	Investment	FC/$[b]	1990	1991	1992	1993	1994	1995	1996	1997	1998	1999	2000
Canada	30	1.2045	3	8	9	12	14	18	22	27	33	40	49
Italy	26,090	1,304.5	3	7	8	10	12	15	19	23	28	35	43
Spain	1,710	114	3	8	10	12	14	18	22	27	33	41	50
Portugal	733	146.5	5	11	13	16	20	25	31	38	46	57	70
United States[c]	50	1	2	5	6	8	9	12	14	18	22	26	33
Japan	4,275	142.5	2	5	6	7	9	11	14	17	21	26	31
Mexico	300	100	4	9	11	13	16	20	25	30	37	46	56
Brazil	1,000	500	0	1	1	1	1	2	2	2	3	4	5

[a]Cash flows are earnings before taxes.

[b]FC/$ is the foreign currency per dollar exchange rate.

[c]For information on U.S. MNCs performance in these countries see, for instance, U.S. Department of Commerce, Survey of Current Business, U.S. Direct Investment Abroad.

APPENDIX 20-1

FMC Corporation: Excerpts and Data from FMC's *Annual Report 1989*

FINANCIAL SUMMARY

(In millions, except per share, employee and stockholder data)

	1989	1988	CHANGE
Sales			
In the United States	$ 2,164.0	$ 2,067.8	+ 5%
Outside the United States	1,250.5	1,219.1	+ 3%
Total sales	3,414.5	3,286.9	+ 4%
Other revenue	16.8	25.5	−34%
Total revenue	$ 3,431.3	$ 3,312.4	+ 4%

(Continued)

	1989	1988	CHANGE
Operating earnings before unusual items	$ 310.8	$ 298.2	+ 4%
Earnings before interest, taxes, and extraordinary items	$ 346.7	$ 337.9	+ 3%
Income before extraordinary items	$ 156.8	$ 129.2	+21%
Net income	$ 136.4	$ 129.2	+ 6%
Earnings per common share–primary			
Income before extraordinary items	$ 4.35	$ 3.60	
Extraordinary items	(0.56)	—	
Net income	$ 3.79	$ 3.60	
Earnings per common share—fully diluted			
Income before extraordinary items	$ 4.34	$ 3.60	
Extraordinary items	(0.56)	—	
Net income	$ 3.78	$ 3.60	
Common stock price range	$49–31$\frac{5}{8}$	39\frac{1}{8}$–24$\frac{3}{8}$	
Capital expenditures	$ 280.8	$ 186.5	+51%
Research and development expenditures	$ 149.7	$ 143.6	+ 4%
At December 31 Operating working capital[a]	$ 34.9	$ 67.0	
Number of employees	24,110	24,342	
Number of stockholders	18,151	19,155	
Return on investment[b]	19.1%	18.8%	

[a]Composed of inventories and trade receivables less payables and accrued liabilities.

[b]Return on investment

$$= \frac{\text{Net income before extraordinary items plus after-tax interest expense on debt}}{\text{Average of stockholders' equity plus total debt}}$$

[c]Extraordinary items of $20.4 million, or $0.56 per share, in 1989, and the gain on the sale of FMC Gold Company stock and a partially offsetting extraordinary item totaling $84 million, or $2.00 per share, in 1987 have been excluded from the return on investment and earnings per share charts below:

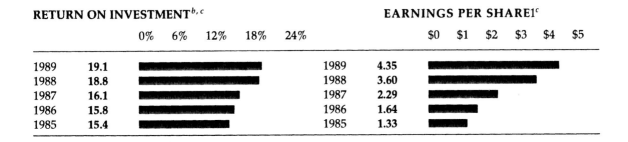

RETURN ON INVESTMENT[b, c]

		0%	6%	12%	18%	24%
1989	19.1					
1988	18.8					
1987	16.1					
1986	15.8					
1985	15.4					

EARNINGS PER SHARE1[c]

		$0	$1	$2	$3	$4	$5
1989	4.35						
1988	3.60						
1987	2.29						
1986	1.64						
1985	1.33						

INDUSTRY SEGMENT DATA
(In millions)

	Year Ended December 31				
	1989	1988	1987	1986	1985
Sales					
Industrial Chemicals	$ **975.9**	$ 914.0	$ 876.8	$ 835.1	$ 766.2
Performance Chemicals	**565.6**	521.0	478.1	477.9	494.4
Precious Metals	**190.2**	175.7	133.3	86.3	—
Defense Systems	**900.3**	945.7	1,020.3	971.1	1,300.5
Machinery and Equipment	**783.0**	734.1	634.1	645.4	715.5
Eliminations	**(0.5)**	(3.6)	(3.5)	(13.1)	(15.8)
Total	**$3,414.5**	$3,286.9	$3,139.1	$3,002.7	$3,260.8
Income (Loss) Before Income Taxes					
Industrial Chemicals	**$137.7**	$146.9	$141.9	$138.6	$127.0
Performance Chemicals	**82.7**	76.8	44.2	39.8	25.8
Precious Metals[a]	**100.9**	93.3	55.3	29.7	—
Defense Systems	**47.3**	54.2	88.9	123.5	189.6
Machinery and Equipment	**28.3**	11.7	13.0	(3.2)	(4.6)
Eliminations	**—**	—	—	—	—
Operating profit	**396.9**	382.9	343.3	328.4	337.8
Net interest expense	**(128.4)**	(148.4)	(184.9)	(130.8)	(3.4)
Gain on FMC Gold Company sale of stock	**—**	—	94.7	—	—
Corporate and other	**(86.2)**	(84.7)	(94.7)	(76.6)	(75.0)
Unusual items[b]	**36.0**	39.7	43.0	71.6	9.7
Total	**$218.3**	$189.5	$201.4	$192.6	$269.1
Identifiable Assets					
Industrial Chemicals	$ **931.5**	$ 842.3	$ 846.4	$ 830.9	$ 881.0
Performance Chemicals	**397.4**	391.2	392.0	420.2	385.6
Precious Metals	**99.3**	102.5	96.8	93.0	—
Defense Systems	**502.9**	492.4	478.9	535.4	490.4
Machinery and Equipment	**459.3**	450.8	462.2	423.0	490.4
Eliminations	**—**	(0.1)	(0.1)	(0.3)	(0.6)
Subtotal	**2,390.4**	2,279.1	2,276.2	2,302.2	2,246.8
Corporate and other	**428.6**	469.7	318.9	383.6	559.9
Total	**$2,819.0**	$2,748.8	$2,595.1	$2,685.8	$2,806.7

[a] Includes 100 percent of FMC Gold Company's income before income taxes of $60.7 million in 1989, $82.7 million in 1988, $65.1 million in 1987 and $26.8 million in 1986 and the effects of the FMC Corporation hedging program. Minority shareholder interests since the initial public offering in June 1987 are included in Corporate and other.

[b] See Financial Review for discussion of unusual items.

CONSOLIDATED STATEMENTS OF INCOME

(In thousands, except per share data)

	YEAR ENDED DECEMBER 31		
	1989	1988	1987
Revenue			
Sales	**$3,414,521**	$3,286,907	$3,139,133
Equity in net earnings of affiliates (Notes 1 and 6)[1]	**3,784**	6,525	4,667
Other income	**12,966**	18,950	15,433
Total revenue	**3,431,271**	3,312,382	3,159,233
Costs and expenses			
Cost of sales	**2,517,544**	2,433,532	2,353,113
Selling, general and administrative expenses	**446,337**	428,677	420,735
Research and development	**149,651**	143,624	132,049
Minority interests	**6,938**	8,319	4,738
Total costs and expenses	**3,120,470**	3,014,152	2,910,635
Operating earnings before unusual items	**310,801**	298,230	248,598
Unusual items (Note 1)	**35,968**	39,699	42,982
Earnings before interest, gain on FMC Gold Company sale of stock, taxes and extraordinary items	**346,769**	337,929	291,580
Interest income	**33,490**	40,278	33,821
Interest expense (Note 1)	**161,920**	188,678	218,761
Gain on FMC Gold Company sale of stock (Note 2)	**—**	—	94,747
Income before income taxes and extraordinary items	**218,339**	189,529	201,387
Provision for income taxes (Note 10)	**61,590**	60,296	10,190
Income before extraordinary items	**156,749**	129,233	191,197
Extraordinary items, net of taxes (Note 1)	**(20,356)**	—	(10,660)
Net income	**$ 136,393**	$ 129,233	$ 180,537

Earnings per common share (Note 1)

Primary:			
Income before extraordinary items	**$4.35**	$3.60	$4.54
Extraordinary items	**(0.56)**	—	(0.25)
Net income	**3.79**	3.60	4.29
Assuming full dilution:			
Income before extraordinary items	**4.34**	113.60	4.52
Extraordinary items	**(0.56)**	—	(0.25)
Net income	**3.78**	3.60	4.27

[1]Notes referred to in this portion and succeeding portions of FMC's *Annual Report* are not included in this appendix. Readers can find these notes in the 1989 *Annual Report*.

CONSOLIDATED BALANCE SHEETS

(In thousands, except per share data)

	DECEMBER 31	
	1989	1988
ASSETS		
Current assets		
Cash	$ **6,516**	$ 9,741
Marketable securities	**88,005**	121,069
Trade receivables, net (Note 3)	**587,426**	582,780
Inventories (Note 4)	**443,727**	424,691
Other current assets	**77,741**	67,110
Deferred income taxes (Note 10)	**108,580**	111,210
Total current assets	**1,311,995**	1,316,601
Investments (Note 6)	**111,479**	90,009
Property, plant and equipment, net (Note 7)	**1,334,918**	1,268,060
Patents and deferred charges	**40,676**	52,956
Intangibles of acquired companies	**19,899**	21,125
Total assets	**$2,818,967**	$2,748,751
LIABILITIES AND STOCKHOLDERS' EQUITY (DEFICIT)		
Current liabilities		
Short-term debt (Note 8)	$ **73,238**	$ 68,989
Accounts payable, trade and other	**623,046**	541,946
Accrued payroll	**78,952**	80,672
Accrued and other liabilities	**294,207**	317,844
Current portion of long-term debt (Note 9)	**27,835**	5,337
Current portion of accrued pension cost, net (Note 13)	**11,325**	24,757
Income taxes payable (Note 10)	**85,747**	49,199
Total current liabilities	**1,194,350**	1,088,744
Long-term debt, less current portion (Note 9)	**1,325,639**	1,468,013
Accrued pension cost, net, less current portion (Note 13)	**175,450**	198,428
Deferred income taxes (Note 10)	**88,023**	125,676
Reserve for discontinued operations (Note 2)	**79,985**	71,789
Minority interests in consolidated companies	**26,153**	19,748
Stockholders' equity (deficit) (Note 11)		
Common stock, $0.10 par value, authorized 60,000,000 shares; issued 34,513,264 shares in 1989 and 34,265,619 shares in 1988	**3,451**	3,427
Capital in excess of par value of capital stock	**19,983**	16,328
Retained earnings (deficit)	**(72,570)**	(208,963)
Foreign currency translation adjustment (Note 5)	**(21,005)**	(20,219)
Investment valuation allowance (Note 6)	**—**	(13,838)

(Continued)

	DECEMBER 31	
	1989	1988
Treasury stock, common, at cost; 14,183 shares in 1989 and 11,235 shares in 1988	**(492)**	(382)
Total stockholders' equity (deficit)	**(70,633)**	(223,647)
Total liabilities and stockholders' equity (deficit)	**$2,818,967**	$2,748,751
Commitments and contingent liabilities (Note 16)		

Income Taxes

Domestic and foreign components of pre-tax income are shown below:

	Year Ended December 31		
(In thousands)	**1989**	1988	1987
Domestic	**$141,729**	$110,660	$129,591
Foreign	**76,610**	78,869	71,796
Total	**$218,339**	$189,529	$201,387

The provision for income taxes consists of:

	Year Ended December 31		
(In thousands)	**1989**	1988	1987
Current:			
Federal	**$75,939**	$13,299	$ 116,941
Foreign	**13,079**	19,765	16,820
State and local	**12,955**	6,168	19,762
Total current	**101,973**	39,232	153,523
Deferred	**(40,383)**	21,064	(143,333)
Total income taxes	**$61,590**	$60,296	$ 10,190

The source and tax effect of the deferred income tax provision (benefit) is as follows:

	Year Ended December 31		
(In thousands)	**1989**	1988	1987
Tax depreciation greater (less) than book	**$ (5,286)**	$ 5,981	$ 3,288
Change in employee benefit reserves	**(2,635)**	18,157	(11,648)
Prepaid pension costs	**10,090**	15,698	(110,585)
Change in inventory and receivable reserves due to 1986 tax act	**(359)**	(68)	(5,895)
Profit on long-term contracts	**(3,928)**	1,763	(5,007)
Change in general reserves	**3,036**	(11,622)	(9,899)
Research, intangible drilling, exploration and development	**(38,292)**	(3,632)	(3,541)
Alternative minimum tax	**(1,280)**	(5,256)	—
Other timing differences	**(1,729)**	43	(46)
Continuing operations	**(40,383)**	21,064	(143,333)
Discontinued operations	**5,360**	2,314	12,606
Total deferred income tax provision (benefit)	**$(35,023)**	$23,378	$(130,727)

The effective income tax rate applicable to pre-tax income is less than the statutory U.S. federal income tax rate for the following reasons:

PERCENT OF PRE-TAX INCOME

	Year Ended December 31		
	1989	**1988**	**1987**
Statutory U.S. tax rate	**34%**	**34%**	40%
Net increase (decrease):			
Effect of income not expected to be subject to U.S. tax:			
Changes in FMC Gold Company equity due to sale of stock	—	—	(21)
Foreign sales corporation income	(3)	(4)	(4)
Percentage depletion	(9)	(10)	(11)
State and local income taxes, less federal income tax benefit	6	3	1
Foreign earnings subject to lower tax rate	(5)	(4)	(5)
Tax on intercompany dividends	2	12	2
Alternative minimum tax	—	2	—
Other	3	(1)	3
Total decrease	(6)	(2)	(35)
Effective tax rate	**28%**	**32%**	5%

FMC's federal income tax returns for years through 1973 have been examined by the U.S. Treasury Department and settled. Management believes that adequate provision for income taxes has been made for all open years. Income taxes have not been provided for the equity in undistributed earnings of foreign consolidated subsidiaries ($252.8 million at December 31, 1989). Restrictions on the distribution of these earnings are not significant. Foreign earnings received in the United States and taxable as dividends were $25.8 million, $159.1 million and $20.1 million in 1989, 1988 and 1987, respectively.

Segment Information

Sales to various agencies of the U.S. government aggregated $804.9 million, $860.2 million and $883.4 million in 1989, 1988 and 1987, respectively. These sales were made primarily by the Defense Systems segment.

Summarized financial information for the geographic areas in which the company operates (including export sales) is shown in the following tables. Unusual items are included in the profits below.

U.S. EXPORT SALES TO UNAFFILIATED CUSTOMERS BY DESTINATION OF SALE

	Year Ended December 31		
(In thousands)	**1989**	**1988**	**1987**
Latin America and Canada	**$161,021**	**$145,904**	$139,557
Western and Eastern Europe	**245,485**	249,017	233,156
Asia, Africa and others	**224,870**	252,401	240,170
Total	**$631,376**	**$647,322**	$612,883

OPERATIONS BY GEOGRAPHIC AREA

(In thousands)	Sales			Income (Loss) Before Income Taxes			Identifiable Assets		
	Year Ended December 31			Year Ended December 31			December 31		
	1989	1988	1987	1989	1988	1987	1989	1988	1987
United States	$2,874,727	$2,776,751	$2,671,616	$347,642	$326,362	$287,718	$1,771,748	$1,771,574	$1,750,905
Latin America and Canada	112,032	94,807	86,210	1,543	12,314	(1,710)	116,719	63,954	59,856
Western Europe	503,011	477,891	411,944	65,614	59,610	62,384	480,619	419,911	433,253
Asia, Africa, and others	29,139	26,999	26,456	870	(1,820)	(2,431)	32,978	31,114	43,773
Eliminations	(104,388)	(89,541)	(57,093)	(3,819)	(1,605)	(396)	(11,681)	(7,447)	(11,560)
Subtotal	3,414,521	3,286,907	3,139,133	411,850	394,861	345,565	2,390,383	2,279,106	2,276,227
Net interest expense	—	—	—	(128,430)	(148,400)	(184,940)	—	—	—
Gain on FMC Gold Company sale of stock	—	—	—	—	—	94,747	—	—	—
Corporate and other	—	—	—	(65,081)	(56,932)	(53,985)	428,584	469,645	318,833
Total	$3,414,521	$3,286,907	$3,139,133	$218,339	$189,529	$201,387	$2,818,967	$2,748,751	$2,595,060

367

TEN-YEAR FINANCIAL SUMMARY

(In millions, except per share, employee and stockholder data)

Summary of Earnings

	1989	1988	1987	1986	1985	1984	1983	1982	1981	1980
Sales	$3,414.5	3,286.9	3,139.1	3,002.7	3,260.8	3,337.8	3,246.8	3,187.3	2,855.2	2,599.9
Equity in earnings of affiliates	3.8	6.5	4.7	4.4	15.4	16.6	17.0	16.2	9.7	10.2
Other income	18.8	30.7	22.7	71.8	20.1	6.0	8.9	16.1	13.2	3.3
Total revenue	3,437.1	3,324.1	3,166.5	3,078.9	3,296.3	3,360.4	3,272.7	3,219.6	2,878.1	2,613.4
Cost of sales	2,502.5	2,419.4	2,344.5	2,237.0	2,448.5	2,521.6	2,520.1	2,444.6	2,094.5	1,975.7
Selling, general and administrative expenses	438.2	423.2	398.4	372.7	425.9	396.9	389.1	421.7	383.0	325.6
Research and development	149.7	143.6	132.0	145.8	149.4	120.6	102.4	105.1	93.7	81.0
Total costs and expenses	3,090.4	2,986.2	2,874.9	2,755.5	3,023.8	3,039.1	3,011.6	2,971.4	2,571.2	2,382.3
Earnings before interest, gain on FMC Gold Company sale of stock, taxes and extraordinary items	346.7	337.9	291.6	323.4	272.5	321.3	261.1	248.2	306.9	231.1
Interest income	33.5	40.3	33.8	28.6	32.1	69.4	48.1	38.9	39.3	20.5
Interest expense	161.9	188.7	218.7	159.4	35.5	42.0	49.0	45.3	66.2	54.1
Gain on FMC Gold Company sale of stock	—	—	94.7	—	—	—	—	—	—	—
Income before income taxes and extraordinary items	218.3	189.5	201.4	192.6	269.1	348.7	260.2	241.8	280.0	197.5
Provision for income taxes	61.5	60.3	10.2	40.1	72.5	122.8	71.8	56.6	89.2	44.8
Income from continuing operations before extraordinary items	156.8	129.2	191.2	152.5	196.6	225.9	188.4	185.2	190.8	152.7
Loss from discontinued operations, net of taxes	—	—	—	—	—	(187.9)	(19.6)	(32.8)	(51.3)	(10.0)
Extraordinary items, net of taxes	(20.4)	—	(10.7)	—	—	—	—	—	—	—
Net income	$ 136.4	129.2	180.5	152.5	196.6	38.0	168.8	152.4	139.5	142.7
Total dividends	—	—	—	14.4	57.6	56.9	62.0	56.9	55.8	50.8

(Continued)

	1989	1988	1987	1986	1985	1984	1983	1982	1981	1980
Share Data										
Average number of shares used in earnings per share computations (thousands):										
Primary	36,006	35,860	42,108	92,746	146,889	168,690	187,238	184,977	185,181	184,149
Fully diluted	36,106	35,884	42,257	94,257	151,785	178,811	203,899	206,143	207,135	208,160
Primary earnings (loss) per share:										
Continuing operations	$ 4.35	3.60	4.54	1.64	1.33	1.32	0.99	0.98	1.01	0.80
Discontinued operations	(0.56)	—	—	—	—	(1.11)	(0.10)	(0.18)	(0.28)	(0.05)
Extraordinary items	—	—	(0.25)	—	—	—	—	—	—	—
Net income	$ 3.79	3.60	4.29	1.64	1.33	0.21	0.89	0.80	0.73	0.75
Earnings (loss) per share assuming full dilution:										
Continuing operations	$ 4.34	3.60	4.52	1.62	1.30	1.27	0.93	0.91	0.93	0.74
Discontinued operations	(0.56)	—	—	—	—	(1.05)	(0.10)	(0.16)	(0.25)	(0.05)
Extraordinary items	—	—	(0.25)	—	—	—	—	—	—	—
Net income	$ 3.78	3.60	4.27	1.62	1.30	0.22	0.83	0.75	0.68	0.69
Financial Position at Year-end										
Working capital	$ 117.6	227.9	(93.7)	(37.7)	90.5	143.8	495.8	394.5	384.3	317.1
Property, plant and equipment, at cost	$2,908.0	2,750.2	2,628.1	2,490.9	2,347.4	2,022.3	1,916.1	1,834.3	1,672.1	1,513.9
Accumulated depreciation	$1,573.1	1,482.1	1,325.9	1,145.8	1,019.7	913.9	822.8	729.0	652.9	592.2
Total assets	$2,819.0	2,748.8	2,595.1	2,685.8	2,806.7	2,539.7	3,093.7	3,084.8	2,960.8	2,680.8
Long-term debt	$1,325.6	1,468.0	1,380.2	1,787.3	303.2	292.2	345.8	384.1	394.6	416.7
Stockholders' equity (deficit)	$ (70.6)	(223.6)	(343.2)	(506.6)	1,123.1	959.8	1,460.4	1,351.0	1,302.3	1,245.9
Other Data										
Income from continuing operations as a return on investment	19.1%	18.8	16.1	15.8	15.4	15.6	11.6	11.5	12.6	10.5
Capital expenditures	$ 280.8	186.5	157.2	232.8	319.0	182.6	169.2	274.3	263.7	244.5
Provision for depreciation	$ 197.8	199.3	200.5	192.1	161.2	140.2	143.4	131.6	120.6	96.1
Employees at year-end	24,110	24,342	24,797	24,966	28,064	27,096	27,641	30,490	33,528	32,709
Stockholders of record at year-end, common and preferred	18,151	19,155	20,231	21,203	24,619	26,471	32,713	36,320	39,961	40,177

Major Operating Units

INDUSTRIAL CHEMICALS

Chemical Products Group
- Alkali Chemicals Division
- Foret, S.A.
- Lithium Division
- Peroxygen Chemicals Division
- Phosphorus Chemicals Division

PERFORMANCE CHEMICALS

Agricultural Chemical Group
Chemical Products Group
- Food and Pharmaceutical Products Division
- Marine Colloids Division

PRECIOUS METALS

FMC Gold

DEFENSE SYSTEMS

Defense Systems Group
- Defense Systems International Division
- Ground Systems Division
- Naval Systems Division
- Steel Products Division

MACHINERY AND EQUIPMENT

Food Machinery Group
- Agricultural Machinery Division
- Food Processing Systems
  Citrus Machinery & Services Division
  Citrus Machinery & Services—
  South America
  Food Machinery Europe Division
  Food Processing Machinery Division
- Packaging Systems Division

Petroleum Equipment Group
Specialized Machinery Group
- Airline Equipment Division
- Automotive Service Equipment Division
- Conveyor Equipment Division
- Material Handling Equipment Division
- Material Handling Systems Division
- Sweeper Division

Executive Offices

FMC Corporation
200 East Randolph Drive
Chicago, Illinois 60601

Subsidiaries and Affiliates in Other Nations

ABU DHABI
- FMC International, S.A.

ARGENTINA
- FMC Argentina, S.A.

AUSTRALIA
- FMC (Australia), Ltd.

AUSTRIA
- FMC Chemikalien Handelsgesellschaft m.b.H.

BELGIUM
- FMC Europe, S.A.
- FMC Food Machinery Europe, N.V.
- FMC Packaging Machinery Europe, N.V.
- Food Machinery Coordination Center, S.A.

BRAZIL
- CBV Industria Mecanica, S.A.
- FMC do Brasil, Ltda.
- FMC-Kramer, S.A.

CANADA
- FMC of Canada, Ltd.
- Marine Colloids, Ltd.
- Mid-Atlantic Investments, Ltd.

CHINA
- FMC Far East Ltd

COLOMBIA
- Asociacion Experimental Agricola, AEA

DENMARK
- Litex, A/S

DUBAI
- FMC International, A.G.

EGYPT
- FMC International, A.G.

FRANCE
- FMC Europe, S.A.
- FMC Food Machinery, S.A.
- FMC Food Machinery France, S.A.
- Gelagar, S.A.R.L.

GABON
- FMC Gabon, S.A.R.L.

GERMANY
- FMC Machinery (Germany), G.m.b.H.
- Gelagar (Litex), G.m.b.H.

GREECE
- FMC Hellas, EPE
- FMC International, A.G.

GUATEMALA
- FMC Guatemala, S.A.

HONG KONG
- FMC Far East, Ltd.

INDONESIA
- P.T. FMC Santana Petroleum Equipment Indonesia

IRELAND
- FMC International, A.G.

ITALY
- FMC Food Machinery Italy, S.p.A.
- FMC Packaging Machinery, S.p.A.

IVORY COAST
- FMC International, A.G.

JAPAN
- Asia Lithium Corporation
- FMC Far East, Ltd.
- Tokai Denka Kogyo, K.K.

KENYA
- FMC International, A.G.

KOREA
- FMC International, A.G.

MEXICO
- Electro Quimica Mexicana, S.A. de C.V.
- Fabricacion, Maquinaria y Ceras, S.A. de C.V.
- FMC de Mexico, S.A. de C.V.
- FMC Agroquimica de Mexico S. de R.L. de C.V.

NETHERLANDS
- FMC Nederland, B.V.

NORWAY
- FMC Norway, A/S

PAKISTAN
- FMC International, S.A.

PHILIPPINES
- FMC International, S.A.
- Marine Colloids (Philippines) Inc.

SINGAPORE
- FMC Southeast Asia Pte., Ltd.

SPAIN
- FMC Airline Equipment Europe, S.A.
- FMC Spain, S.A.
- Foret, S.A.

SWITZERLAND
- FMC International, A.G.

THAILAND
- Thai Peroxide Co., Ltd.
- FMC (Thailand), Ltd.

TURKEY
- FMC Nurol Savunma Sanayii A.S.

UNITED KINGDOM
- FMC Corporation (UK), Ltd.
- Litex, Ltd.

U.S.S.R.
- FMC Corporation

VENEZUELA
- Tripoliven, C.A.
- FMC Wellhead de Venezuela, S.A.

VIRGIN ISLANDS
- FMC International Sales Corporation
- Freeport/FMC Foreign Sales Corporation

Ford Motor Company

Direct Foreign Investment in Mexico

HARVEY A. PONIACHEK

This case reviews Ford Motor Company and its international operations, examines major trends in the automobile industry, and addresses some features of Ford de Mexico and the foreign direct investment climate in Mexico's auto industry. The case is accompanied by appendices that provide information on the auto industry in Mexico and on the financial performance of Ford and several of its subsidiaries, and financial data on the performance of publicly traded automobile corporations around the world.

The reader is then requested to address several issues related to Ford's international investment and financial management of its operations in Mexico.

Ford Motor Company and Its International Operations

Scope of Operations

Ford is the fourth-largest industrial corporation in the world, in terms of sales, and is the world's second-largest producer of cars and trucks.[1] With 332,700 employees in 26 countries, of which 157,000 are in the United States, sales of cars, trucks and tractors in 1991 reached approximately 5.4 million, and sales and revenues of automotive and financial services exceeded $88 billion.

The company's vehicles are sold under the Ford, Mercury, and Lincoln brand names. In 1990 Ford acquired Jaguar, a British luxury car manufacturer. Worldwide automobile sales in 1991 accounted for over $70 billion, of which some 68 percent were in North America and 22 percent in Europe.[2] Sales in the United States accounted for approximately 2.9 million cars and trucks, Canada for 390,899, Mexico for 111,849, and Japan for 96,298. Ford's share of the U.S. vehicle market in 1991 was 23.1 percent.[3]

The U.S. Marketplace

The U.S. auto industry has evolved into a global network of manufacturing plants, suppliers, and distribution channels that span the world. The principal car and truck manufacturers in the United States market include General Motors, Ford Motor Company and Chrysler. In recent years competition from foreign manufacturers, particularly Japanese, has increased substantially. Several Japanese companies operate, in addition to distribution net-

[1] Ford Motor Company, *Annual Report*, 1991, p. 1.

[2] J. V. Kirnan, Ford Motor Company, *Company Report*, Kidder, Peabody, Inc., March 12, 1992.

[3] Ford, *Annual Report*, op. cit., p. 5.

works, manufacturing and assembly facilities in the United States that are often referred to as "transplants."

U.S. car market share of the three U.S. carmakers declined from 67.6 percent in 1987 to 64.3 percent in 1991, whereas the share of the Japanese companies, including their transplants and exports to the United States, expanded from 23.2 percent to 30.4 percent during this period, and the share of all other suppliers declined from 9.2 percent to 5.3 percent. The share of Ford remained virtually unchanged throughout the five-year period. The performance of the U.S. truck market share displayed a somewhat different performance, with the share of the major U.S. companies expanding from 80.6 percent in 1987 to 82.2 percent in 1991 and the Japanese share declining from 18.1 percent to 16.5 percent.[4] The market share of Ford remained stable over the entire period, whereas GM expanded its share and Chrysler's share remained unchanged.

Competition in the automotive markets in the United States and Canada and around the world reflects excess manufacturing capacity. Assembly plants in the United States and Canada had productive capacity in 1991 of 11.2 million cars and 6.6 million trucks a year operating at normal capacity, compared with an output of 6.7 million cars and 4.2 million trucks, or a capacity utilization of 61.8 percent. The overall capacity utilization in the United States and Canada during 1987–1991 ranged from 61.8 percent to 77.9 percent.[5] Some industry executives maintain that the world auto industry faces a massive overcapacity of some 8 million units, compared with global sales of about 50 million units.[6]

[4]Chrysler Corporation Annual Report on Form 10-K, for the year ended December 31, 1991, p. 5.

[5]Ibid., p. 6.

[6]James P. Womack, Daniel T. Jones and Daniel Roos, *The Machine that Changed the World*, (New York: Macmillan, 1990) p. 6.

EXHIBIT 21-1

Ford Motor Company:
Annual Factory Sales by Geographic Areas

	Thousands of Units	
	1991	1992
North America	3,114	3,500
Overseas	2,232	2,325
Mexican Imports	117	200
Worldwide	5,346	5,825

Source: H. E. Heinbach, *Industry Report*, Merrill Lynch Capital Markets, March 23, 1992.

Business Segments and Investment Information

Ford's segment information shows that automotive sales to unaffiliated customers in the United States and Canada were $44.4 billion, or approximately 61.7 percent of total, Europe accounted for $22.2 billion, or 30.8 percent, and all other geographic areas for $5.4 billion, or 7.5 percent. Of the corporation's total assets, $29.5 billion, or 56.3 percent, are located in the United States and Canada, $19.8 billion, or 39.7 percent, in Europe and $11.2 billion, or 21.5 percent, in all other areas (before elimination of intercompany receivables).[7] Exhibit 21-1 shows the geographic distribution of Ford's car sales. (See Appendix 21-1 for segment information on geographic distribution of Ford's activities.)

Ford's financial services division includes Ford Motor Credit Company, which is the world's second largest savings and loan network, and the Associates. The company's other divisions consist of Ford Aerospace and others.

Ford operates an enormous global network of supply sourcing. Efficient supplier relations is a significant determinant in the competitive-

[7]Ford *Annual Report*, op cit, p. 5.

ness of a company in the marketplace. In 1991, Ford procured from outside suppliers $32 billion of production parts, raw materials and supplies for its North American facilities. Of this total, $24 billion came from 1700 supplier companies at 3000 locations in 40 states and Canada. In Europe, purchases from suppliers totaled $11 billion.[8]

Capital expenditures of the automotive business were $5.7 billion, or 7.9 percent of sales. During the five years 1987–1991, Ford's total capital spending was $28 billion, and over the following several years the pace of investment for product change will continue at high levels.[9] The heavy investments—for facilities, machinery, and equipment, and tooling—are designed to meet the challenges of the 1990s by striving for ever-enhanced cost efficiency, improved and innovative products and global competitiveness. Capital expenditure during 1989 through 1991 was directed almost entirely to the United States, 53.1 percent of total, Canada, 7.8 percent, Europe, including Jaguar, 35.9 percent, and all other areas 3.1 percent. Ford has been the quality leader among U.S. automakers for 11 consecutive years, and in 1991 five out of the 10 best-selling U.S. vehicles were Fords.[10]

Major Trends in the World Auto Industry

Four Major Phases

The world auto industry entered a period of major competitive imbalance among producing regions during the 1970s. There is intense competition throughout the world among multinational auto producers. Competition in the marketplace is driven by styling, price, image, performance, and reliability.

The MIT study on the future of the automobile industry identified four industrial transformation phases in the world auto industry since the turn of the century,[11] as follows:

1. Phase I occurred between 1902 through the 1920s and involved standardized products and mass production. The industry was dominated by U.S. companies.

2. Phase II lasted from the 1950s through the 1960s. This stage was characterized by product differentiation and proliferated in Europe.

3. Phase III occurred in the 1960s through the 1970s and was dominated by the Japanese. The phase was characterized by just-in-time, total equality, and the emergence of new corporate groupings for production organization.

4. Phase IV began in the late 1980s and is still in effect. This phase is characterized by expanding auto production capacity in low-cost areas in Less-Developed Countries (LDCs), including Korea, Mexico, and Brazil; and the introduction of flexible manufacturing techniques, also referred to as "lean production." Lean production combines the advantages of craft (i.e., tailor-made) and mass production, while avoiding the high cost of the former and the rigidity of the latter.[12] Lean production seeks to obtain ever-declining costs, zero defects, and zero inventory. This phase also reflects the emergence of new forms of cooperative competitiveness that may reduce the incentive to locate in LDCs.

---

[8] Ibid., p. 2.

[9] Ibid., p. 3.

[10] Ibid., p. 4.

[11] Allan Altshuler, Martin Anderson, Daniel Jones, Daniel Roos and James Womack, "The Future of the Automobile," *The Report of MIT's International Automobile Program*, (MIT Press: Cambridge, MA, 1984), p. 12.

[12] Womack, op cit, p. 13.

The Japanese stressed integrated high-volume output, high quality and low labor content. The Japanese have a cost advantage vis-à-vis the United States of $1000 to $1500 per small car.[13] Perhaps the key competitive advantage of the U.S. automakers lies in the marketplace—namely, the vast size of the North American market for large size cars.[14]

Product cycle theories suggest that because the auto industry is now mature and subject to keen price competition, auto production ought to shift to LDCs where the wages are low.[15] The need to achieve acceptable economies of scale in the LDCs with high local content requirements, coupled with the feasibility of building highly automated plants in those countries, provided the impetus for transferring some manufacturing activities to Mexico, Korea, and Brazil.[16] By manufacturing in the LDCs, auto companies gain access to local markets and could supply their own markets. Technological advancements could give rise to declining minimum efficient scale in manufacturing.[17]

In determining the degree of the auto industry migration to the LDCs, several factors need to be considered, including the technological complexities, investment requirements, labor and shipping costs, and country risk.

The automobile is one of the most complex consumer goods. Cars and trucks are constructed from thousands of parts and incorporate many technologies. The parts must be manufactured and assembled at a competitive cost and acceptable quality. Auto production is a complex process that involves the final assembler and thousands of suppliers, distrib-utors, and enormous financial resources.[18] The final assembler functions as the coordinator of the entire process of manufacturing the car or truck. Because of these auto industry complexities and a host of additional reasons, only moderate manufacturing has occurred in LDCs to date.

The automotive industry is capital intensive. Developing an entirely new model with a new engine and other mechanical components may cost $3 billion. It takes some five years between the first spending and its introduction to the market.[19]

There are advantages in manufacturing and sourcing in low-wage LDCs, but as the industrial countries enhance their automation, the cheap labor cost advantage could diminish considerably. The assembly plants in the LDCs, notably Brazil, Korea, Mexico, and Taiwan, show an extraordinary range of performance. The best plant in terms of quality is Ford at Hermosillo, Mexico.[20] The assembly plant at Hermosillo is based on a lean manufacturing variant of Mazda.[21] In general, LDCs are most suitable for manufacturing of components, which can be classified in three groups:[22]

1. Major mechanical components, such as engines and transmissions. These require heavy capital investment, are highly automated, and contain relatively low labor content.

2. Finished parts such as exterior body stamping, seats and others that must fit precisely.

3. Minor mechanical components, including starters, radiators, springs, and wiring harnesses, which require relatively simple production methods.

---

[13]Altshuler, p. 155.

[14]Ibid., p. 171.

[15]Ibid., p. 175.

[16]Ibid., p. 177.

[17]Ibid., p. 183.

[18]Ibid., p. 189.

[19]Ibid., p. 143–144.

[20]Womack, op. cit., p. 87.

[21]Ibid., p. 87.

[22]Altshuler, op. cit., p. 176.

The Role of LDCs

LDCs that enjoy rapid domestic growth, have good prospects for car and truck demand, and legislate high local content requirements, constitute good candidates for manufacturing locally by the major auto companies. For these reasons, Mexico attracted several major auto manufacturing companies since 1980. Over the long run the potential car and truck demand of the LDCs exceeds that of the industrial countries.

The internationalization of the automobile industry combined with fierce Japanese competitiveness, particularly in the small car segment in the United States, induced U.S. companies to reposition themselves through foreign wholly-owned subsidiaries (e.g., in Mexico) and joint ventures (e.g., in Japan). Against this background, Mexico emerged from the mid-1980s as a significant offshore automobile manufacturing site for the U.S. Big Three automakers.

Mexico offers U.S. automakers an opportunity to regain their price and cost competitiveness in some segments of the market vis-à-vis the Japanese. Mexico's abundant and relatively cheap labor cost, its favorable treatment of foreign direct investment, its close proximity to the United States markets, and the prospects of the forthcoming North American Free Trade Association (NAFTA) could enhance the price competitiveness of the U.S. auto industry in certain segments and help restore its position in the marketplace.

Ford Operations in Mexico

Sixty-five Years of Activities

Ford has operated in Mexico for over 65 years. In 1925 it established the first automotive assembly plant ever opened in the country. Ford de Mexico operates assembly and manufacturing facilities that produce vehicles, engines, and components for the Mexican, U.S. and Canadian markets. The company also distributes in Mexico vehicles imported from the United States. Ford's operations in Mexico expanded sharply during the 1980s, and toward the end of the decade it was the biggest U.S. car exporter from Mexico, with some 64,929 cars, including the Mercury Tracer that was produced jointly with Mazda.

Historically, the U.S. auto industry's interest in Mexico began in the 1960s, when the auto companies opened low wage in-bond assembly plants, known as *maquiladoras*, on the U.S.–Mexican border. These plants were initially engaged in simple labor-intensive manufacturing and assembling of goods that were shipped to the United States. In the 1980s, as the U.S. auto industry came under intense Japanese competitive pressure, the *maquiladoras* were enhanced, with more work transferred there by U.S. automakers. With the liberalization of the Mexican auto industry in 1981 and in the late 1980s, foreign companies expanded their activities to supply the domestic market and export to North America. Today, some 100,000 Mexicans are employed by U.S. automakers in *maquiladoras* and are involved in ever-increasingly sophisticated manufacturing activities.

There are approximately 1700 *maquiladora* facilities in Mexico. Ford established its first *maquiladora*, Favesa, in late 1981, to make seat covers and armrests. Favesa has since expanded to five plants making a wide variety of products and employing nearly 4500 people. Exhibits 21-2 and 21-3 provide data on Ford's *maquiladora* facilities and plants in Mexico.

In the mid-1980s, Ford established a plant in Hermosillo, Mexico equipped with state-of-the-art technology. The plant is one of the most productive automobile stamping and assembly plants in North America. It is equipped with Japanese robots and stamping machines

EXHIBIT 21-2

Ford's Maquiladora Facilities in Mexico and Their Functions

Altec Electronica (Chihuahua)	Employs 2500 people. Produces radios.
Autovidrio (Chihuahua)	Employs 500 people. Glass plant.
Coclisa (Chihuahua)	Employs 1000 people. Manufactures radiators, heaters, air conditioning components, and wiring harnesses.
Favesa	Employs 5000 people. Makes seat covers and soft trim products.
Lamosa (Nuevo Larado)	Employs 1000 people. Makes catalytic converters, stabilizers, wheels, and coil springs.

Source: Ford Motor Company, *Ford Motor Company's Maquiladora Facilities in Mexico*, March 19, 1991.

EXHIBIT 21-3

Ford's Plants in Mexico and Their Description

Cauautitlan I	Involved in engine manufacturing. Has a capacity of 180,000 per year.
Cauautitlan II	Established in 1980. Has the capacity of assembling 60,000 autos per year.
Chihuahua	Established in 1983. Manufactures engines. Has a capacity of 400,00 per year.
Guadalajara	A foundry and parts manufacturer.
Hermosillo	Established in 1986. Produces the Mercury Tracer with a capacity of 130,000 per year.

Source: Chambre Syndicate des Constructeurs d'automobiles, *Repertoire mondial des activities d'assemblage et de production de vehicules automobiles*, Paris, December 1987, p. 173.

and applies Japanese flexible manufacturing methods that were adopted from Mazda Motor Company. The plant has a complete management team and a productive and quality-oriented work force.

Ford's plants in Hermosillo produced 108,000 autos in 1991 (Ford Escorts and Mercury Tracers), which were exported to the United States and Canada.[23]

Ford completed an investment of $30 million in its Cauautitlan auto plant, which expanded its capacity to 520 vehicles per day, designed for the Mexican market.[24] The plant in Chihuahua manufactures motors.[25] Ford's project in Chihuahua involves a $750 million investment in an engine manufacturing plant, which will produce 40 percent of North America's Z-engines.

Ford operates a facility in Guadalajara, which has 6000 employees and is engaged in auto assembly and parts manufacturing.[26]

According to the Mexican Automobile Industry Association (AMIA), the largest share of cars exported from Mexico in the first quarter of 1992 was held by Ford, with 32.9 percent of total, Chrysler, 28.2 percent, General Motors, 17.3 percent, Volkswagen, 12.9 percent, and Nissan with 8.7 percent.[27] The U.S. Big Three auto companies' share of exports surpassed VW to become the Mexican industry's biggest producer in 1991. Car and truck output increased 30.5 percent to 222,523 units. About half were Escorts and Tracers built in Hermosillo and sold in the United States. Ford also posted the industry's largest gain in Mexican sales.[28] Some market analysts in Mexico anticipate that by 1997, General Motors, Ford and Chrysler will see their share of the Mexican market decline to 50 percent, as the share of Nissan expands to 25 percent—up from

[23]*Mexican Business Monthly*, January 1992.

[24]*Mexico: Company Monitor*, January 31, 1991.

[25]*Mexican Business Monthly*, January 1992.

[26]*Dun's Latin America's Top 25,000*, 1991, p. 478.

[27]*Latin America News Wire*, June 2, 1992.

[28]*Automotive News*, March 9, 1992.

approximately 15 percent in 1991. Ford's share is expected to decline to 20.5 percent from 23.1 percent in 1991.

The Auto Industry in Mexico

The Mexican auto industry could double by the turn of the century to 2 million vehicles manufactured per year, up from 1 million vehicles in 1991, accounting for one out of six vehicles made in North America.[29]

The Mexicans are emerging as a low-cost high-quality work force that could help transform the North American auto industry.[30] Mexican workers earn $10 to $30 a day. Cheap labor costs could permit U.S. companies to substitute labor for expensive capital investment; that is, U.S. companies could continue to economize on robots and machinery. The Big Three U.S. automakers are expected to manufacture small cars in Mexico that are suitable for the local marketplace. One half of them will be shipped to the United States, up from one-third that were imported in the early 1990s.[31]

Some U.S. MNCs are considering Mexico as an integral part of their North American plants. The full adoption and application of the North American Free Trade Agreement (NAFTA) could integrate Mexico into the United States and afford companies increased operating flexibility in the movement of capital and goods. This flexibility could save U.S. automakers approximately $1000 per car and render them competitive with the Japanese. Ultimately, the Mexican auto industry could

be integrated into the U.S.–Canadian industry to form a North American auto industry.[32]

The *Maquiladora*

Significant amounts of foreign direct investment occurred in the *maquiladora* sector, or in-bond facilities. The *maquiladora* program was initiated in the mid-1960s and during the 1980s the number of *maquiladora* plants increased dramatically. U.S.-owned *maquiladoras* represent over half of the approximately 1700 plants in Mexico, and account for 95 percent of the work force and output.[33] Most *maquiladoras* are affiliated with either Mexican or U.S. companies, and third country operations represent only about 4 percent of the total.

The *maquiladora* allows foreign companies to set up in-bond assembly plants along the United States–Mexican border. U.S. companies were attracted to the *maquiladora* because of low wage rates, exemption from Mexican taxes on material and equipment, and exemption from U.S. tariff on goods imported from the *maquiladora* that were manufactured or assembled with U.S.-made components. Foreign firms located in the *maquiladora* region were not allowed to sell their goods in the domestic Mexican markets. (See Appendix 21-2 for additional information on the *maquiladoras*).

NAFTA

The NAFTA is designed to reduce the trade and investment barriers in North America among the United States, Canada and Mexico. The negotiation between the United States and Mexico are structured along the U.S.–Canadian agreement that was signed in

[29]"Detroit South: Mexico's Boom: Who Wins, Who Loses," *Business Week*, March 16, 1992, p. 89–103.

[30]Ibid.

[31]Ibid.

[32]Womack, op. cit., p. 266.

[33]*Business Latin America*, "Mexico's Maquilas Foresee Limited Effect of FTA," January 7, 1991, p. 6.

the late 1980s. The agreement would have significant implications for the auto industry, albeit gradual.

A shift in tariff classification has been adopted for most goods as the standard to determine preferential treatment under the NAFTA. For most industries, an item produced from foreign inputs will be considered North American and therefore be subject to preferential tariff treatment if the good undergoes sufficient transformation to warrant a change on tariff classification. The automotive industry will have a special rule-of-origin test based on value-added—by the North American corporation—to determine if cars and trucks are deemed to be North American. The value-added requirements were set at 60 percent, compared with 50 percent requirement in the U.S.–Canadian treaty. The United States is concerned that third country companies will gain access to the U.S. market through Mexico.[34] (See Appendix 21-3 for additional information on NAFTA.)

Foreign Investment in Mexico

As market conditions in Mexico improve, a growing number of U.S. corporations are investing there or expanding their local presence. Mexico's competitive labor cost, the prospects of the NAFTA and the enormous potential of the domestic market are inducing renewed interest in investing there. (See Appendix 21-4 for information and regulation on investing in Mexico. See Appendix 21-5 for data on the Mexican economy.)

Financial Performance

Appendix 21-6 provides financial data on Ford Motor Company, Ford Motor Ltd. (a U.K. company), and Ford Motor Company of Canada,

[34] Ibid.

Ltd. Appendix 21-7 provides financial data on two Mexican automotive companies.

The Assignment

After a brief summer vacation at Club Med following your completion of the first year at a highly regarded MBA program, where you specialized in corporate finance and international business, you were offered a summer internship at Ford Motor Company, Finance Department. You were asked to familiarize yourself with the company's international operations, particularly in Mexico. Your immediate supervisor requested that you and another graduate intern address the issues listed below —qualitatively and/or analytically depending on data availability.

You were given several weeks to perform the task and were asked to file a memorandum at its completion. You were advised that your findings might be utilized in the corporation's long-term strategic review that commences in the fall. Excited about the warm reception and the prospects of getting familiarized with the operations of a world-class company, you set out to address the following issues:

1. The NAFTA could offer many opportunities as well as challenges. Evaluate Ford's position in Mexico in light of the forthcoming NAFTA, and map out a long-term corporate financial strategy for the 1990s. Specifically, determine whether new investment is necessary for expansion and/or new plants.

2. Examine Ford's funding approach in Mexico in terms of sources, cost and alternative methods. Assume that Ford's overall funding principles in Mexico are generally similar to those practiced in the United States, U.K. and Canada, but these principles are modified to accommodate the local regulations and conditions in Mexico. Base your

analysis on the financial data in Appendix 21-6 and 21-7 related to Ford Motor Ltd., Ford Motor Company of Canada, Ltd., Grupo Industria Saltillo SA (Mexico), and Transmisiones Y Equipos S.A. (Mexico).

3. Define the currency and country risks that Ford de Mexico is facing and devise policies to reduce these risks.

4. Examine the feasibility of Ford Motor company's investment in Mexico as compared with investment in South Korea, Brazil, the United States and Canada. Utilize the financial data available in Appendix 21-8.

Bibliography

1. K. FATEMI (ed.), *The Maquiladora Industry*, Praeger, New York, 1990.

Ford Motor Company: Segment Information on Geographic Distribution of Activities

Note 15: Segment Information

Industry

The company operates in two principal business segments—Automotive and Financial Services. The Automotive segment consists of the manufacture, assembly and sale of cars, trucks and related parts and accessories. The Financial Services segment consists primarily of savings and loan operations, financing operations, insurance operations and vehicle and equipment leasing principally through First Nationwide Financial Corporation ("First Nationwide"), The Associates, Ford Motor Credit Company, The American Road Insurance Company and United States Leasing International, Inc. Entities in the Automotive and Financial Services segments are parties to various financing arrangements in the normal course of business. These financing arrangements are reflected in the respective business segment.

Reference should be made to the consolidated financial statements for industry segment information required to be included under Statement of Financial Accounting Standards No. 14. In the statements, the captions identifying intersegment transactions represent principally: (a) transactions occurring in the ordinary course of business, (b) borrowings and related interest between entities in the Financial Services and Automotive segments and (c) interest on special financing programs.

Source: Excerpted from Ford Motor Company, Annual Report 1991.

GEOGRAPHIC AREA—AUTOMOTIVE

(in millions)	1991	1990	1989
Sales to Unaffiliated Customers			
United States	$40,627	$48,761	$52,850
Canada	3,809	3,716	4,332
Europe[a]	22,228	23,736	19,848
All other	5,387	5,631	5,849
Total outside sales	$72,051	$81,844	$82,879
Intercompany Sales Among Geographic Areas			
United States	$ 7,340	$ 8,141	$ 8,602
Canada	5,543	6,919	7,617
Europe[a]	1,852	1,999	1,384
All other	2,622	2,509	1,453
Total intercompany sales	$17,357	$19,568	$19,056
Total Sales			
United States	$47,967	$56,902	$61,452
Canada	9,352	10,635	11,949
Europe[a]	24,080	25,735	21,232
All other	8,009	8,140	7,302
Elimination			
of intercompany sales	(17,357)	(19,568)	(19,056)
Total sales	$72,051	$81,844	$82,879
Operating (Loss)/Income			
United States	$(3,238)	$ (230)	$ 1,667
Canada	(80)	78	364
Europe[a]	(711)	460	1,755
All other	260	8	2466
Total operating (loss)/income	$(3,769)	$316	$ 4,252
Net (Loss)/Income			
United States	$(2,215)	$ (17)	$ 1,099
Canada	(69)	67	186
Europe[a]	(1,079)	145	1,190
All other	178	(96)	700
Total net (loss)/income	$(3,185)	$ 99	$ 3,175
Assets at December 31			
United States	$26,865	$23,207	$25,245
Canada	2,635	2,872	2,534

(Continued)

(in millions)	1991	1990	1989
Europe[a]	19,860	19,553	15,401
All other	11,256	10,585	5,287
Net receivables			
from Financial Services	156	577	706
Elimination of intercompany			
receivables	(8,375)	(5,971)	(3,354)
Total assets	$52,397	$50,823	$45,819

Capital Expenditures (Facilities, Machinery and Equipment and Tooling)

United States	$ 3,042	$ 3,787	$ 4,121
Canada	449	390	290
Europe[a]	2,055	2,713	1,915
All other	177	273	369
Total capital expenditures	$ 5,723	$ 7,163	$ 6,695

[a]Includes Jaguar for 1991 and 1990.

GEOGRAPHIC AREA—FINANCIAL SERVICES

(in millions)	1991	1990	1989
Total Revenue			
United States	$ 13,182	$ 13,010	$ 11,332
Europe	1,847	1,662	1,123
All other	1,206	1,134	812
Total revenue	$ 16,235	$ 15,806	$ 13,267
Income before Income Taxes[a]			
United States	$ 1,163	$ 955	$ 637
Europe	184	195	169
All other	118	70	68
Total income			
before income taxes	$ 1,465	$ 1,220	$ 874
Net Income			
United States	$ 768	$ 645	$ 528
Europe	118	118	99
All other	41	(2)	33
Total net income	$ 927	$ 761	$ 660

(Continued)

(in millions)	1991	1990	1989
Assets at December 31			
United States	$100,730	$102,591	$ 97,906
Europe	13,662	12,667	10,058
All other	7,640	7,590	7,120
Elimination of intercompany receivables	—	(9)	(10)
Total assets	$122,032	$122,839	$115,074

[a]Financial Services activities do not report operating income; income before income taxes is representative of operating income for these operations.

Intercompany sales among geographic areas consist primarily of vehicles, parts and components manufactured by consolidated subsidiaries and sold to other consolidated subsidiaries. Transfer prices between these companies are established through negotiations between the affected parties.

Financial Services total revenue includes revenue of $310 million in 1991, $239 million in 1990 and $221 million in 1989 from the Federal Savings and Loan Insurance Corporation Resolution Fund in connection with the acquisition by First Nationwide of certain savings and loan institutions.

APPENDIX 21-2

The *Maquiladoras*

The *Maquiladora* Industry[1]

The *maquiladora* program was initiated in the mid-1960s. It allows foreign capital to set up in-bond assembly plants, primarily along the United States–Mexican border. An important incentive for United States firms to locate assembly plants in Mexico is the permission to export products to the United States without tariff if they are assembled abroad with United States-made components. Tariffs are only paid on the value-added which is incorporated abroad. In this manner, United States firms can take advantage of the comparatively low Mexican wages and the country's proximity to the United States.

During the 1980s the number of *maquiladora* plants increased dramatically. From 1986 to 1988, *maquiladora* exports nearly doubled from $5.6 billion to $10.1 billion, and their value-added increased from $1.3 billion to $2.3 billion. Jobs in the industry rose to more than 400,000 in 1989.[2] The value-added represents foreign exchange generation. Thus, after petroleum, the *maquiladoras* have become Mexico's single largest foreign exchange earner.

The *maquiladora* plants moved to more skilled-labor assembly activities during the

[1]*Source*: United Nations, "Foreign Direct Investment and Industrial Restructuring in Mexico," *UNCTC Current Studies*, Series A, No. 18, New York, 1992.

[2]Banco de Mexico, *Indicadores Economicos*, February 1991, tables IV-7, IV-3, and IV-10a.

1980s, and most of the production now consists of automotive assembly, machinery and equipment, televisions, and other electronic assembly.[3] The shift in sectoral composition of *maquiladora* output towards more high-tech production represents an important source of technology transfer through job training. *Maquiladoras* use only about 2–3 percent Mexican-produced input, which partly can be explained by the large distance of the border region from potential Mexican suppliers which are located in other areas.[4] The boom of the *maquiladora* sector is another indication of the corporate strategy of United States-based TNCs towards including Mexico in regional core network.

Ford's Maquiladora Facilities in Mexico[5]

Background on Ford's *Maquiladora* Operations

Ford Motor Company has been a part of Mexico for over 65 years; we have actively participated in Mexican economic, social and cultural growth in many ways. In 1925 Ford established a subsidiary in Mexico and began local production in the first automotive assembly plant ever opened in Mexico. As elsewhere at that time, Ford workers in Mexico were paid more than the "going rate" for similar work. Our active cultural and community participation is a matter of public record of which we

---

[3]See also Joseph Grundwald, "Opportunity Missed: Mexico and Maquiladoras." *The Brookings Review*, 9 (Winter 1990/91), p. 45; and Perez Nuñez, *From Globalization*, p. 38.

[4]Grundwald, op. cit.

[5]Excerpts from "Environmental Practices, Health and Safety Standards and Employee Welfare at Ford Motor Company's *Maquiladora* Facilities in Mexico," Ford Motor Company, March 19, 1991.

are proud. Today, Ford of Mexico operates three major plants and employs 8950 nationals. The Ford of Mexico facilities are located in Mexico City, Hermosillo, and Chihuahua.

WHAT IS A MAQUILADORA?

In the final months of 1965, the Mexican Government authorized a program for the industrial development of Mexico's Northern Border Zone. The program permitted the establishment of plants for the assembly, processing and/or finishing of foreign materials and components and was intended to address the serious unemployment problem of northern Mexico.

The Border Industrialization Program, as it was called in 1966 when initiated, was more formally implemented by a specific law in March 1971. This law expressly authorized the establishment of industrial plants which would be permitted to import, duty free, all equipment and machinery, materials and component parts, necessary for production. This was under the condition that all finished products be exported and none be kept or sold in Mexico. Originally this was construed as a border operation only. In November 1972, however, the authorized zone for such operations was expanded, and U.S. businesses were encouraged to establish plants in economically depressed areas of the interior of Mexico.

In October 1977, the new Regulations of Article 321 of the Customs Code were issued in a further effort to clarify, stabilize and expedite operating procedures and afford greater protection to in-bond industries. This program has made Mexico highly competitive in production costs with the world market. This is due to its proximity to the United States, especially its northern border zone, faster and safer delivery, lower wages, and lower freight, handling and other expenses (such as warehousing, travel, etc.)

On the U.S. side of the border, the program is to some extent facilitated by sections 906.30 and 807.000 of the U.S. Customs Tariff, which permit U.S. products processed or assembled abroad, to return to the United States with duty paid only on the value of the foreign processing (value added). With respect to *maquiladoras*, this normally is the cost of Mexican labor and overhead.

FORD MAQUILADORA OPERATIONS

Within the context of Mexico's Border Industrialization Program, Ford Motor Company established its first *maquiladora*, Favesa, in September 1981. Since that time Favesa has expanded from one plant making seat covers and armrests to five plants making a wide range of soft trim products and employing 4372 hourly and 272 salaried nationals. The expanded Favesa facilities include a medical service center, extensive training rooms and equipment, "COMPA" (employee involvement) meeting rooms, along with a separately located employee recreational park with playgrounds, two swimming pools and a gymnasium. Following Favesa, Ford established four more *maquiladoras*, currently employing 5247 hourly personnel and 629 salaried personnel.

In 1986, Ford began production of automotive radiators at its Coclisa Plant in Cd. Juarez, Chihuahua, Mexico (adjacent to El Paso, Texas). Since then, automotive heaters, air conditioning components, and wiring harnesses have been added to the product line-up at Coclisa, and employment has grown from 150 nationals to 1100 nationals. Also in 1986, the Ford Lamosa Plant was built at Nuevo Laredo, Tamaulipas, Mexico, just south of Laredo, Texas. The Lamosa Plant has grown from its original 160,000 square foot size to 320,000 square feet, and today employs 1141 nationals. Its product line-up includes catalytic converters, stabilizer bars, wheels, and coil springs.

In June, 1987 Ford began production of radios at its new Altec Electronics Plant located in Chihuahua, Chihuahua, Mexico. Since then, the plant has expanded from a single building to a complex of four major facilities. Employment has grown from 80 salaried and 300 hourly employees in 1987 to 365 salaried and nearly 2400 hourly employees today. Concurrent with this expansion, Ford added an employee training center, a medical services center, and an employee recreational center including basketball courts, baseball and soccer fields and a playground.

A recent Ford *maquiladora* is the Autovidrio Glass Plant which began production in September, 1988 and is located in Cd. Juarez, Chihuahua, Mexico. Autovidrio's complex glass tempering systems are among the most advanced glass forming technologies in the world. Its facilities include offices, cafeteria, gymnasium, and employee facilities for about 60 salaried and 315 hourly employees.

The following table summarizes the present number of male and female, hourly and salary, personnel at each of the Ford Maquiladoras in Mexico.

| | Number of Employees | | | | | |
| | Hourly | | Salary | | Total | |
Facility	Male	Female	Male	Female	Male	Female
Altec Electronica	520	1,744	255	110	775	1,854
Autovidrio	301	11	48	9	349	20
Coclisa	706	302	85	15	791	317
Favesa	2,255	1,845	202	70	2,457	1,915
Lamosa	1,034	0	94	13	1,128	13
Total	4,816	3,902	684	217	5,500	4,119

The North American Free Trade Association (NAFTA)

The North American Free Trade Agreement

By the end of the 1980s it seemed that Mexico was pursuing a global outward-oriented strategy, aiming at expanding trade and attracting foreign direct investment multilaterally. However, in 1989 there were signs that this strategy was too ambitious. The free trade agreement between the United States and Canada could be a potential threat to Mexican exports to the United States. The Europe 1992 initiative and the opening up of the Central and Eastern European countries could redirect European FDI destined for Mexico. And, finally, the anticipated expansion of FDI from Japan to create production facilities to serve the North American market did not materialize because Japanese TNCs invested directly in the United States or pursued a strategy of creating regional core networks of affiliates in South-East Asia.[1]

These factors led the Government of Mexico to redirect its global orientation towards closer formalized regional integration with the United States. It considered that a free trade agreement with the United States would carry several benefits. Most importantly, it would be a very clear signal to the national and international business communities that the economic liberalization of the Mexico economy was a long-run, irreversible process, and that goods produced in Mexico would be assured future access to the United States market. One of the main benefits from a free trade agreement is that it would attract investment flows from non-United States based transnational corporations.[2]

In mid-1989, the President of Mexico approached the Government of the United States to initiate negotiations on a free trade agreement. In September 1990, President Bush gave formal notification to Congress of his intention to begin free trade negotiations with Mexico. On 14 May 1990, the Congress of the United States decided to grant authority for using "fast-track procedures" to negotiate a free trade agreement with Mexico, and many observers expect that a free trade agreement will materialize during 1992.[3] The free trade negotiations will also include Canada, as Canada already has a free trade agreement with the United States. However, the parties have yet to agree on an agenda for the negotiations. Speaking in London, Serra Puche, the Mexican Trade Minister, noted that the negotiations will probably take place under six headings: market access, trade rules, services, investment, intellectual property rights and dispute settlement.[4] But no matter what the

Source: United Nations, "Foreign Direct Investment and Industrial Restructuring in Mexico," *UNCTC Current Studies*, Series A, No. 18, New York 1992, p. 19.

[1]See United Nations Centre on Transnational Corporations, *World Investment Report 1991: The Triad in Foreign Direct Investment* (United Nations publication, Sales No. E.91.II.A.12).

[2]See Nora Lustig, *Bordering on Partnership: The United States–Mexico Free Trade Agreement* (Washington D.C., The Brookings Institution, 1991), and Peres Nuñez, op. cit.

[3]*Business Week* (27 May 1991). Under "fast-track procedures," Congress can only vote "yes" or "no" on the final agreement. This gives the Administration wider authority during the negotiations.

[4]See "Mexican Minister Expects U.S. Free Trade Deal Soon," *Financial Times*, 12 July 1991.

agenda is, the negotiations and an eventual agreement will make it very difficult for future policy makers in Mexico to reverse the present open economy strategy. In fact, they will probably result in even further liberalization of the Mexican economy.

APPENDIX 21-4

Regulations Related to Foreign Direct Investment in Mexico's Auto Industry

Sectoral Programmes

The sectoral programmes for specific manufacturing industries constitute an important component of the Government's policy to restructure Mexico's manufacturing industry. The aim of the programmes is to extend the import-substitution policy to goods that either have a more complex technological content or are considered strategically important to Mexico. However, protection from foreign competition is strongly linked to the fulfillment of certain performance requirements, especially regarding exports. The following is a presentation of the specific content of the sectoral programmes for the automotive, computer and pharmaceutical industries, which, as mentioned, are all strongly dominated by affiliates of TNCs.

The Automotive Industry

The automotive industry has been a central concern to the industrialization efforts of Mexico. In 1980, the automotive industry represented the largest manufacturing activity, with a share of 8 percent of total manufacturing production. In 1981 the Mexican automotive sector was almost exclusively oriented towards the internal market, causing a trade deficit of more than $2 billion that year (equivalent to nearly 15 percent of Mexico's total trade deficit). The industry consists of five large terminal car producers, all of which are affiliates of TNCs: General Motors (United States), Chrysler (United States), Ford (United States), Volkswagen (Germany) and Nissan (Japan). Further, a large number of firms produce autoparts for the five terminal car producers.[1] The local autoparts industry has been promoted by the Government by requiring the five terminal car producers to achieve a certain level of local content in their final products, and by restricting FDI to a 40 percent share of total equity of each firm producing autoparts.

In light of Mexico's serious economic deficiencies at the beginning of the 1980s, the Administration introduced new regulations for the automotive sector in September 1983. A decree was issued with the intention of improving the efficiency of the industry, standardizing components, promoting research and development and making the industry "balance-of-payments neutral" (by either in-

Source: United Nations, "Foreign Direct Investment and Industrial Restructuring in Mexico," *UNCTC Current Studies*, Series A, No. 18, pp. 9–14, 20. New York 1992.

[1] The autoparts industry consists of firms whose sale of components destined for motor vehicles is more than 50 percent of their total sales. It does not include the production of components and engines by terminal car producers.

creasing exports or the local content of final products).[2] The novelty of the 1983 decree, compared with previous decrees, is that it intended to promote the integration of the Mexican automotive sector with the globalization of the world car industry. The most important elements of the decree were:

- Automotive producers were required to reduce the number of possible car lines and models. This would permit the firms to use economies of scale, thus making them more efficient and competitive. However, the assembly plants could earn the right to produce additional car lines if a car line was "balance-of-payment neutral." The intention of the policy makers was that this mechanism would integrate production for the domestic market with export production, and thereby ensure more competitive production overall.

- The local content requirement for finished vehicles was increased from 50 to 60 percent.[3] If this objective could not be fulfilled, the automotive firm had to compensate by way of increasing exports. For example, if national integration fell below 30 percent, the entire production would have to be exported.

- Vehicle assemblers were required to balance foreign exchange transactions on a yearly basis. This meant that, if an enterprise did not succeed in being "balance-of-payments neutral", it had to make additional exports or reduce imports in spite of fulfilling the national integration requirements.

[2] Published in *El Diario Oficial de la Federación*, 15 September 1983.

[3] The degree of national integration (DNI) was calculated in the following way: DNI (1-*VIM*) VAP 100 where VIM is the value of imports and VAP is the value of all parts. Methodological problems exist in calculating the value of all parts. See "Acuerdo que establece las reglas de aplicación del decreto para la racionalización de la industrial automotriz", *El Mercado de Valores*, No. 38 (17 September 1984), p. 948.

In return, the automotive industry was granted full protection against foreign competition in the domestic market through import licenses. Furthermore, the industry reaped the benefits of trade liberalization through reduction of costs of imported parts. The export requirements may also have resulted in higher vehicle prices on the domestic market, because the assemblers may have been exporting at a loss and increased domestic prices to recuperate global profits. If this has, in fact, been the case, local consumers have in effect been subsidizing sales on export markets.

A new automotive decree was issued in December 1989, with the specific aim of strengthening the domestic auto industry's position on the international market.[4] The most important elements were:

- A gradual trade liberalization allowing terminal car producers already operating in Mexico to import passenger cars according to specific ratios derived from the firms' trade surplus. This affects Chrysler, General Motors, Ford, Nissan and Volkswagen.

- Local content requirements were reduced from 60 to 35 percent. Furthermore, export requirements were to be relaxed over the next three years from the 1990 level of $2.50 in exports for every dollar of imports to $1.75 in 1992.

- There would be no national integration requirements for exported vehicles.

The new decree is more favourable towards the terminal car producers by relaxing national integration requirements and allowing them to import finished vehicles in quantities determined by their export performance. With this decree, the terminal car producers indeed have a strong incentive to increase exports, as they will maintain effective trade protection and furthermore profit from the gradual trade liberalization on finished passenger cars. The

[4] See *Diario Oficial de la Federación*, 11 December 1989.

Administration also downgraded the previous priority aim of developing the national autoparts industry (which is restricted to mixed firms). The Government either concluded that the global integration of the terminal car producers had been restrained by the requirement of using high priced and low quality local inputs, or that the autoparts industry had reached levels of international competitiveness and the terminal car producers would subcontract voluntarily.

Foreign Direct Investment Policy

As mentioned earlier, FDI has been assigned a key role in the industrial restructuring of the Mexican manufacturing sector, because TNCs possess such assets as modern state-of-the-art technology, access to foreign markets and new management methods. Also, since the beginning of the debt crisis, Mexico has been in great need of foreign direct investment to compensate for the drop in both national investment and foreign reserves. In what follows, the Mexican regulation of foreign direct investment, including the recent liberalization of policy, will be outlined.

The centerpiece of FDI legislation is the 1973 "Law to Promote Mexican Investment and Regulate Foreign Investment."[5] The law restricts FDI in product groups that are reserved exclusively for Mexican public sector investment, which include petroleum and other hydrocarbons, basic petroleum products, radioactive and strategic minerals, nuclear en-

ergy, electricity, railroads, telegraphic and radio communications and banking (article 4). FDI is also restricted in product groups reserved exclusively for Mexican public or private investments which include radio and television, agricultural activities, road, air and maritime transportation, forestry, gas distribution and financial intermediation (article 4). In addition, there are product groups in which FDI is allowed only a specific proportion of the firm's capital: mining (49 percent), secondary petrochemicals (40 percent) and fabrication of automobile components (40 percent).

The law states that, in cases in which it, or other regulations have not established a specific limit, foreign equity participation should not exceed 49 percent of total capital (article 5). However, this is only a general principle, and exceptions are allowed, subject to a case-by-case review. If majority foreign ownership complements national investments; it does not displace national companies; if it has a positive balance-of-payments effect, particularly by expanding exports; if it increases local employment; and if it utilizes local inputs and components in final products or contributes to the technological modernization of Mexico. Firms with up to 49 percent foreign capital outside the restricted product groups can operate without prior approval.

Prior to the 1982 debt crisis the law was applied in a restrictive way. The regulatory approach could be characterized as defensive, with the fundamental aim to limit FDI to certain industries of the economy and as a general principle to only allow foreign majority-owned enterprises in exceptional cases.[6]

The regulation of FDI was gradually modified after the 1982 debt crisis. The Administration of President de la Madrid maintained the

---

[5] "Ley para promover la inversión mexicana y regular la inversión extranjera", published by the National Commission of Foreign Investment, *Inversiones Extranjeras: Marco Jurídico y su Applicación* (Mexico City, 1984). The other laws concerning FDI are the 1973 technology transfer law and the 1976 law on inventions and trademarks. They will be covered in the section on technology transfer.

[6] The principal exception to this policy was the *maquiladora* programme which was initiated in the 1960s and allows 100 percent foreign ownership for in-bond assembly plants operating along the Mexican-United States border.

1973 "Law to Promote Mexican Investment and Regulate Foreign Investment" as the basic legal framework for FDI, but there was a change of approach as to how the law and the regulations were interpreted and applied. New regulations were issued in 1984 in the form of "Guidelines for Foreign Investment and Objectives for its Promotion," released by the National Commission for Foreign Investment. The Guidelines specified that foreign ownership would be particularly encouraged in such high-priority industries as heavy machinery, electronic equipment, high-technology products and tourism.[7] Thus, the Administration actively aimed at promoting FDI in selective complex industries with high investment requirements per person-hour; activities with dynamic technology; and activities primarily oriented towards exports.

The Administration of Salinas de Gortari has been determined to continue the more favourable treatment of foreign capital. As outlined in the development plan mentioned in the previous section, FDI is expected to assist in converting the Mexican industrial sector into a major international competitor. The Administration basically intends to attract new FDI by stepping up the liberalization process and making regulations more transparent. So far, the most important measure taken by this Administration to liberalize FDI policy has been the May 1989 regulation in respect to the regulation of the 1973 "Law to Promote Mexican Investment and Regulate Foreign Investment." (Again, the basic law has not been changed, but rather the way the law is to be administered.[8]) According to the new regulation, automatic authorization for up to 100 percent foreign ownership is given in the newly-classified product groups, if the invest-

ment fulfills the following somewhat binding conditions:

- A maximum of $100 million dollars is invested in fixed assets.
- Direct funding is obtained from abroad.
- Investment in industrial establishments is located outside the three largest metropolitan areas.
- The accumulated foreign net exchange flows are positive over the first three years of operation.

An investment project still requires approval by the National Commission for Foreign Investment if it does not comply with these criteria, or in cases in which the foreign stockholders' position is changed from a minority to a majority share. But the intention is to limit case-by-case authorizations to exceptional instances and to minimize administrative delays.

It should be noted that there are no criteria concerning the displacement of Mexican investment or the content level of Mexican input in final products. The new regulation reflects the obvious interest of the Administration in attracting new investment and boosting exports. Accordingly, no authorization is needed for foreign investors to acquire stocks for an in-bond processing company (*maquiladora* plant) or other export-oriented enterprises (article 6). Certain industries that were previously excluded from majority foreign ownership—such as glass, cement, iron, steel and cellulose—are now open. There has been no change in the 40 percent limit on foreign ownership in secondary petrochemicals and automotive parts. However, several products previously considered basic petrochemicals, and therefore restricted to state production, have been reclassified as secondary petrochemicals.[9] Another new element in the regu-

[7]See Peres Nuñez, *Foreign Direct Investment*, p. 41.

[8]"Reglamento de la ley para promover la inversión Mexicana y regular la inversión extranjera", *Diario Oficial de la Federación*, 16 May 1989.

[9]See, "Medidas para la modernización y el fomento de la Industria Petroquímica", *El Mercado de Valores*, No. 17 (1 September 1989), pp. 36–38.

lation is that foreign capital can participate with a majority interest in activities reserved for Mexicans if the investment is done through trusts (*Fideicomisos*). The activities include national air and maritime transportation, mining, secondary petrochemicals and automotive parts.

In sum, the Government of Mexico has gradually stepped up the liberalization of its FDI regulatory framework during the 1980s. The central aim has been to attract new foreign direct investment that could advance the industrial restructuring process. In this respect, FDI is expected to create new employment, provide the country with fresh financial resources (both for new investment and the restructuring of indebted enterprises), provide modern technology and advance the country's efforts to increase manufactured exports.

A crucial element of the Mexican industrial restructuring policy is to redirect industrial development towards technologically more complex production, and increase production efficiency in order to make better use of inputs and expand exports. In this sense, the technology transfer policy establishes the scope for foreign and domestic firms in Mexico to make use of foreign technology to bring about their industrial restructuring. This makes the technology transfer policy another central element of the Government's efforts to promote industrial restructuring in Mexico. Accordingly, the Mexican technology transfer policy has undergone fundamental changes during the 1980s.

Conclusion

Foreign direct investment has been assigned a major role in the restructuring of Mexico's manufacturing sector. The Government has aimed at promoting FDI in selective complex industries with high investment requirements

per person-hour, activities with dynamic technology and activities primarily oriented towards exports. During the 1980s, the regulation of FDI has gradually been liberalized within the framework of the (restrictive) 1973 Law to Promote Mexican Investment and Regulate Foreign Investment. Thus, with the May 1989 regulation, foreign investors receive automatic authorization of 100 percent foreign ownership if the investment in fixed assets does not exceed $100 million. However, there are still important industries in the manufacturing sector in which the activities of foreign investors are restricted (basic petrochemicals, petroleum refining), and others in which foreigners are permitted to have only a minority share of the fixed assets (secondary petrochemicals and autoparts).

The technology transfer regulation is a second policy area that directly affects FDI. In this area crucial for Mexico's advance towards modernization, policy has completely changed in recent years from a restrictive and regulatory approach to one of actively promoting the acquisition of foreign technology. There is no longer a limit on royalties or confidentiality provisions; official discretionary powers have been reduced; and, finally registration and approval procedures have been streamlined. Most recently, the Government has provided TNCs with more extensive protection for intellectual property.

The policy changes in Mexico during the 1980s indicate a firm political determination to restructure the manufacturing sector through the internationalization of the economy, especially by liberalizing policies on foreign trade and FDI. However, the important sectoral programmes and the remaining restrictive measures on FDI suggest that the opening of the Mexican economy to foreign trade and FDI has been undertaken in a selective and pragmatic manner.

The Mexican Economy: Basic Data

Table A21-1   MANUFACTURED EXPORTS FROM MEXICO, 1981–1990
(millions of dollars)

	1981	1982	1983	1984	1985	1986	1987	1988	1989	1990
All manufactured goods	3427.3	3386.0	5447.9	6985.7	6720.6	7782.1	10588.1	12381.3	13014.1	14783.7
Food and beverages	679.2	707.4	724.6	821.9	747.1	937.4	1313.4	1369.3	1268.1	1095.3
Textiles and clothing	150.1	128.5	171.5	246.3	182.7	301.8	480.1	510.2	505.7	498.9
Leather and skin products	31.2	21.7	19.8	29.0	24.4	31.0	86.1	116.2	117.1	133.3
Wood and wood products	59.3	52.0	81.9	98.1	91.4	100.5	134.5	181.8	197.5	168.2
Paper and printing	81.4	78.4	75.1	96.9	99.1	137.7	222.3	323.9	268.9	202.9
Oil derivates	610.9	260.8	737.8	1244.2	1351.1	639.6	632.0	617.8	423.7	892.2
Basic petrochemicals, excl. PVC	132.7	108.0	101.4	95.8	53.3	17.7	17.0	70.4	59.5	220.7
Chemicals	471.9	467.0	687.0	846.3	766.5	954.9	1254.8	1606.5	1734.5	1832.9
Plastic materials/fibers, including PVC	31.8	54.4	107.7	170.7	154.1	213.6	338.8	431.5	416.5	404.3
Pharmaceuticals	51.7	35.1	29.8	27.8	22.0	35.9	30.9	36.5	29.9	39.9
Other chemicals	388.4	377.5	549.5	647.8	590.4	705.4	885.1	1138.5	1288.1	1388.7
Tires and other rubber products	8.0	8.4	19.6	39.3	13.8	22.4	54.4	84.7	82.2	44.1
Nonmetallic minerals	124.7	139.6	210.2	288.5	315.3	375.0	446.8	526.8	566.7	524.6
Cement	0.0	0.0	45.0	79.3	88.8	116.1	134.5	146.2	155.5	81.7
Other nonmetallic minerals	124.7	139.6	165.3	209.2	226.5	258.9	312.3	380.6	411.2	442.9
Steel and steel products	64.0	112.4	318.6	377.7	246.0	443.1	629.6	759.0	866.7	973.6
Basic metals	70.3	377.7	562.3	510.3	403.2	474.2	630.2	818.0	1033.1	962.9
Transport equipment and its parts	462.1	533.5	1118.4	1580.4	1616.3	2326.8	3353.1	3559.5	3810.5	4659.8
Automobiles	70.1	66.9	109.7	119.1	116.6	516.4	1306.3	1397.6	1534.1	2614.3
Engines	83.3	241.6	643.4	1029.6	1089.3	1233.6	1384.4	1464.3	1473.9	1356.2
Autoparts	183.5	159.9	213.6	317.5	288.4	384.6	490.2	492.8	450.0	439.0
Other transport equipment	125.2	65.1	151.7	114.3	121.9	192.2	172.6	204.8	352.5	250.3
Metal products, machinery and equipment	481.6	390.5	619.6	710.9	810.6	1020.0	1333.7	1837.2	2079.9	2574.3
Electric and electronic equipment	109.7	91.3	180.2	227.4	284.9	363.4	435.0	588.5	670.3	888.2
Computers	0.0	0.0	16.1	50.6	69.7	93.8	218.1	339.7	376.9	368.4
Machinery equipment, excl. computers	332.2	260.9	358.6	383.4	394.1	478.6	557.6	749.6	908.5	1152.5
Other metal products	39.7	38.3	64.7	49.5	61.9	84.3	122.9	159.3	124.2	165.2

SOURCE: Comercio Exterior, various years.

Source: United Nations, "Foreign Direct Investment and Industrial Restructuring in Mexico," *UNCTC Current Studies*, Series A No. 18, New York 1992, pp. 93 and 95.

Table A21-2 AGGREGATE INDICATORS OF THE MEXICAN ECONOMY

	1980	1981	1982	1983	1984	1985	1986	1987	1988	1989
GDP (Real growth in %)[a]	8.3	8.8	−0.6	−4.2	3.5	2.5	−3.7	1.5	1.1	1.5
Consumer price index										
(growth rate in %) yearly average[b]	26.3	27.9	56.6	104.8	65.5	37.8	86.2	131.9	114.2	20.0
Public financial deficit (at % of GDP)[a]	7.5	14.1	16.9	8.6	8.5	9.6	16.0	16.1	12.3	6.4
Stock of total foreign debt (U.S. billion)[c]	50.8	74.9	87.6	93.8	96.7	97.8	100.5	125.8	107.0	—
Foreign debt (as % of GDP)[c]	27.7	33.5	54.4	66.6	55.4	53.8	74.3	75.8	77.0	—
Net foreign resource transfer (as % of GDP)[c]	−2.5	−7.4	2.8	5.3	6.6	6.1	6.5	5.5	6.4	—
Real average wages yearly growth rate[a]	−0.8	4.2	−2.4	−26.5	−4.9	1.0	−9.9	5.5	—	—
Gross fixed investment (as % of GDP)[a]	24.8	26.4	23.0	17.5	17.9	19.1	19.4	18.9	—	—
Private investment yearly growth rate[c]	13.9	−17.3	−24.2	9.0	13.4	−8.8	2.1	10.1	—	—
FDI yearly growth rate[d]	57.9	31.0	−41.5	−72.2	−15.1	25.4	210.2	113.4	−20.1	−71.9

[a]Bank of Mexico: Indicadores economicos, February 1991.

[b]IMF, *International Financial Statistics*, 1988 Yearbook.

[c]Nora Lustig, *The Mexican Economy in the Eighties: An Overview*, Washington, D.C., Brookings Institution, 1989.

[d]UNCTC, *The World Investment Directory: Foreign Direct Investment, Legal Framework and Corporate Data*, forthcoming.

APPENDIX 21-6

Financial Data: Ford Motor Company, Ford Motor Ltd., and Ford Motor Company of Canada Ltd.

Ford Motor Company: United States

Description of Business

Provider of automotive products, electronics, communications, space technology, steel, financial services & insurance.

PRODUCT LINES

Consumer durables & services. Number of employees: 370,383. (as of 12/31/90)
Market value: 16,467,739,533 (as of 02/28/92)
Fiscal year end: 12/31
Latest annual financial date: 12/31/90

BALANCE SHEET

FISCAL YEAR ENDING	12/31/90	12/31/89	12/31/88
ASSETS (000's)			
Net receivables	41,319,500	45,202,400	4,395,700
Raw materials	3,025,700	2,983,900	NA
Work in process	NA	NA	NA

(Continued)

Source: Disclosure, June 1992.

Fiscal Year Ending	12/31/90	12/31/89	12/31/88
Finished goods	3,628,200	3,832,900	NA
Other inventories	461,500	NA	NA
Inventories	7,115,400	6,816,800	6,638,200
Prepaid expenses	NA	NA	NA
Other current assets	2,448,800	6,749,700	31,539,400
Total current assets	59,130,200	65,870,400	57,343,300
Invest in assoc comp	2,180,000	4,178,500	0
Long-term receivables	68,309,900	62,286,000	NA
Gross PP & E	40,694,600	34,969,700	27,504,900
Accum. depreciation	18,486,800	16,364,500	15,675,400
Net PP & E	22,207,800	18,605,200	11,829,500
Tangible other assets	NA	9,953,200	NA
Intangible other assets	NA	705,600	NA
Other assets	14,198,200	9,953,200	74,193,700
Total assets	173,662,700	160,893,300	143,366,500

LIABILITIES (000's)

Accounts payable	9,332,800	11,381,900	NA
St. debt & cur ltd.	51,596,100	46,486,900	37,835,500
Accrued payroll	644,200	196,100	NA
Dividend payable	NA	0	NA
Income taxes payable	155,800	803,000	NA
Other current liabilities	7,881,800	19,115,500	18,841,000
Total current liabilities	69,610,700	77,983,400	56,676,500
Long-term debt	45,331,800	38,921,300	32,112,800
Risk & charge prov	NA	NA	NA
Deferred taxes	3,103,200	3,392,800	NA
Other liabilities	31,578,900	16,901,200	32,884,100
Unreal sec gain/loss	0	NA	NA
Total liabilities	149,624,600	137,198,700	121,673,400
Non-equity reserves	NA	0	NA
Minority interest	0	166,800	164,100
Preferred stock	800,000	800,000	0
Common stock/ord cap	473,100	472,800	NA
Capital surplus	766,200	574,200	NA
Revaluation reserves	NA	0	NA
Other approp reserves	NA	0	NA
Unapp reserves	NA	0	NA
Retained earnings	21,175,500	21,704,000	NA
ESOP guarantees	0	0	NA
Foreign currency	823,300	−23,200	NA
Treasury stock	0	0	NA
Common shareholders' equity	23,238,100	22,727,800	21,529,000
Total liability & shareholders equity	173,662,700	160,893,300	143,366,500

(Continued)

FISCAL YEAR ENDING	12/31/90	12/31/89	12/31/88

INCOME STATEMENT (000's)

Net sales	97,650,000	96,145,900	92,445,600
Cost of goods sold	73,593,000	70,748,700	69,858,700
Gross income	19,177,400	21,168,500	18,794,600
Depreciation & amortization	4,879,600	4,228,700	3,792,300
Selling, general & administrative (SG & A) expenses	4,000,000	3,752,400	3,452,000
Other operating expenses	4,637,300	3,436,000	7,032,900
Total operating expenses	87,109,900	82,165,800	84,135,900
Operating income	10,540,100	13,980,100	8,309,700
Interest expense	9,572,900	8,598,500	354,000
Interest capitalized	0	0	0
Extraordinary credit—pretax	0	NA	NA
Extraordinary charge—pretax	0	561,300	NA
Net other income/expenses	624,700	786,700	386,800
Increase/decrease in reserves	NA	NA	NA
Pretax income	1,591,900	5,607,000	8,342,500
Income taxes	530,400	2,112,400	2,998,700
Minority interest	104,500	82,200	43,600
Equity in earnings	−96,900	422,600	0
After tax income/expenses	0	NA	NA
Discontinued operations	0	0	0
Net income before extraordinary items	860,100	3,835,000	5,300,200
Extraordinary items	0	0	0
Net income before preferred dividend	860,100	3,835,000	5,300,200
Preferred dividend requirement	0	0	0
Net income	860,100	3,835,000	5,300,200

GROWTH RATES—ANNUAL

FISCAL YEAR ENDING	12/31/90	12/31/89	12/31/88	12/31/87	12/31/86	12/31/85
Net sales growth	1.56	4.00	29.04	14.24	18.84	0.78
Operating income growth	−24.61	68.24	34.00	52.87	48.61	−20.24
Net income growth	−77.57	−27.64	14.59	40.79	30.60	−13.46
Total assets growth	7.94	12.23	218.91	18.51	20.03	15.14
Equity growth	2.25	5.57	16.42	24.45	21.12	24.71
Total employee growth	1.03	2.13	2.47	−8.37	3.52	−3.75
Earnings per share (EPS) growth	−77.37	−25.00	21.10	46.92	35.58	−13.68
Dividend/share growth	0.00	30.43	46.03	42.11	38.54	20.00
Book value/share growth	2.18	9.59	20.38	31.64	25.97	24.71
Net margin growth	−77.92	−30.43	−11.19	23.25	9.90	−14.13
Reinvestment rate/share	−2.37	11.90	23.77	27.00	22.99	21.24
Reinvestment rate/total	−2.33	11.29	22.21	25.71	21.96	21.07

(Continued)

FISCAL YEAR ENDING	12/31/90	12/31/89	12/31/88	12/31/87	12/31/86	12/31/85
PROFITABILITY RATIOS—ANNUAL						
Cash flow/sales	6.26	7.98	10.12	12.09	10.52	9.8
Cost of goods (COG)/sales	75.36	73.58	75.57	81.65	83.83	85.51
Gross profit margin	19.64	22.02	20.33	13.93	11.45	9.96
SG & A/sales	0.45	0.61	0.56	1.07	1.30	0.96
R & D/sales	3.64	3.29	3.17	3.51	3.68	3.82
Pretax margin (%)	1.63	5.83	9.02	9.25	6.78	5.75
Effective tax rate (%)	33.32	37.67	35.94	41.14	41.72	36.38
Net margin (%)	0.88	3.99	5.73	6.46	5.24	4.77
Sales/employee (mil)	0.2636	0.2623	0.2576	0.2045	0.1640	0.1429
Effective interest rate	9.88	10.07	0.51	12.12	14.03	13.01
Operating income/total capital	16.83	25.98	40.77	36.26	27.90	22.58
Return on investment capital	6.58	10.38	24.86	26.71	22.42	21.56
Return on equity per share	3.87	18.74	30.08	32.69	28.03	25.78
Return on equity	3.78	17.81	28.66	31.13	26.78	25.57
Return on assets	4.46	6.63	12.31	12.96	11.22	10.04
Operating profit margin	10.79	14.54	8.99	8.66	6.47	5.17
Cash earnings return on equity (ROE)	26.88	35.65	50.59	58.29	53.80	52.97
LEVERAGE RATIOS—ANNUAL						
Total debt/common equity	417.11	375.79	324.90	19.65	23.16	27.97
Long-term debt/ common equity	195.08	171.25	149.16	9.47	14.38	17.58
Total debt/total capital	80.13	78.28	76.33	16.33	18.70	21.70
Preferred stock/total capital	1.15	1.28	0.00	0.00	0.00	0.00
Total debt/total assets	55.81	53.08	48.79	8.08	9.07	10.86
Cash dividend cover ratio	4.40	5.47	7.84	10.76	11.16	11.77
Dividend payout	161.45	36.60	22.52	17.40	18.00	17.60
Fixed assets/total capital	95.57	81.86	54.95	56.84	88.84	101.25
Working capital/total capital	−15.11	−19.34	1.24	20.55	16.56	8.51
Long-term debt/total capital	65.35	62.16	59.68	8.60	12.50	14.84
Equity/total capital	33.50	36.30	40.01	90.73	86.89	84.38
Common equity/total assets	13.38	14.13	15.02	41.14	39.17	38.82
Total capital/total assets	39.95	38.92	37.53	45.34	45.09	46.01
Fixed charges coverage ratio	1.17	1.65	24.57	16.04	9.81	7.79

Ford Motor Ltd: United Kingdom

Description of Business

Engaged in the manufacture and sale of motor vehicles, together with associated and other finance operations.

PRODUCT LINES

Consumer durables. Number of employees: 60,300 (as of 12/31/90)
Fiscal year end: 12/31
Latest annual financial date: 12/31/90
Data stated in Sterling

BALANCE SHEET

FISCAL YEAR ENDING	12/31/90	12/31/89	12/31/88
ASSETS (000's)			
Net receivables	1,660,000	1,466,000	1,426,000
Raw materials	45,000	59,000	NA
Work in process	279,000	274,000	NA
Finished goods	1,268,000	1,093,000	NA
Other inventories	261,000	167,000	NA
Inventories	1,853,000	1,593,000	1,204,000
Prepaid expenses	NA	NA	NA
Other current assets	36,000	25,000	618,000
Total current assets	3,834,000	3,372,000	3,350,000
Investment in associate companies	39,000	91,000	21,000
Long-term receivables	1,111,000	1,142,000	NA
Gross PP & E	4,223,000	3,539,000	2,407,000
Accumulated depreciation	1,657,000	1,553,000	1,336,000
Net PP & E	2,566,000	1,986,000	1,071,000
Tangible other assets	0	0	NA
Intangible other assets	1,383,000	1,221,000	NA
Other assets	1,383,000	1,221,000	115,000
Total assets	8,933,000	7,812,000	4,557,000
LIABILITIES (000's)			
Accounts payable	581,000	632,000	NA
Short-term debt & current liabilities	2,245,000	1,771,000	424,000
Accrued payroll	NA	88,000	NA
Dividend payable	0	NA	NA
Income taxes payable	3,000	156,000	NA
Other current liabilities	2,745,000	2,931,000	2,215,000
Total current liabilities	5,574,000	5,578,000	2,639,000
Long-term debt	2,438,000	837,000	535,000
Risk & charge provision	NA	NA	8,000
Deferred taxes	33,000	28,000	112,000
Other liabilities	190,000	397,000	274,000
Unrelated securities gain/loss	0	0	NA
Total liabilities	8,235,000	6,840,000	3,568,000
Non-equity reserves	0	0	0
Minority interest	0	33,000	10,000
Preferred stock	0	0	0
Common stock/ordinary capital	39,000	39,000	NA
Capital surplus	NA	NA	NA
Revaluation reserves	0	0	NA
Other appropriated reserves	14,000	14,000	NA
Unappropriated reserves	NA	NA	NA
Retained earnings	645,000	886,000	NA

(Continued)

FISCAL YEAR ENDING	12/31/90	12/31/89	12/31/88
ESOP guarantees	0	0	NA
Foreign currency	0	0	NA
Treasury stock	0	0	NA
Common shareholders equity	698,000	939,000	979,000
Total liabilities & shareholders' equity	8,933,000	7,812,000	4,557,000

INCOME STATEMENT (000's)

	12/31/90	12/31/89	12/31/88
Net sales	7,509,000	6,732,000	5,936,000
Cost of goods sold	6,542,000	5,566,000	4,767,000
Gross income	624,000	915,000	968,000
Depreciation & amortization	343,000	251,000	201,000
SG & A expenses	576,000	523,000	430,000
Other operating expenses	0	0	0
Total operating expenses	7,461,000	6,340,000	5,398,000
Operating income	48,000	392,000	538,000
Interest expense	462,000	54,000	33,000
Interest capitalized	0	0	0
Extraordinary credit—pretax	19,000	29,000	0
Extraordinary charge—pretax	0	0	0
Net other income/expenses	121,000	106,000	168,000
Increase/decrease in reserves	0	0	0
Pretax income	−274,000	473,000	673,000
Income taxes	−32,000	76,000	236,000
Minority interest	−7,000	−4,000	1,000
Equity in earnings	0	10,000	0
After tax income/expenses	0	0	0
Discontinued operations	0	0	0
Net income before extraordinary items	235,000	411,000	436,000
Extraordinary items	0	0	0
Net income before preferred dividend	235,000	411,000	436,000
Preferred dividend requirement	0	0	0
Net income	235,000	411,000	436,000

FISCAL YEAR ENDING	12/31/90	12/31/89	12/31/88	12/31/87	12/31/86	12/31/85
GROWTH RATES—ANNUAL						
Net sales growth	11.54	13.41	13.91	19.14	8.13	7.81
Operating income growth	−87.76	−27.14	128.94	389.58	−51.52	NA
Net income growth	NA	−5.73	100.92	174.68	−31.30	210.81
Total assets growth	14.35	71.43	3.78	15.43	3.82	13.23
Equity growth	−25.67	−4.09	−10.18	−0.37	−17.12	1.46
Total employee growth	25.10	0.42	2.13	−4.08	−8.07	−9.66
Earnings per share (EPS) growth	NA	−5.73	100.92	174.68	−31.30	210.81
Dividend/share growth	−100.00	−17.43	161.19	−31.72	206.64	NA

(*Continued*)

FISCAL YEAR ENDING			12/31/90		12/31/89		12/31/88
Book value/share growth	−25.67	−4.09	−10.18	−0.37	−17.12	1.46	
Net margin growth	NA	−16.88	76.38	130.56	−36.47	188.30	
Reinvestment rate/share	−25.24	−4.07	−10.09	0.73	−17.21	1.17	
Reinvestment rate/total	−25.03	−4.09	−19.63	10.24	−17.20	1.15	

PROFITABILITY RATIOS—ANNUAL

Cash flow/sales	−1.04	7.20	12.16	7.46	4.60	8.08	
Cost of goods (COG)/sales	87.12	82.68	80.31	83.34	87.08	86.13	
Gross profit margin	8.31	13.59	16.31	12.97	8.76	9.81	
SG & A/sales	4.81	5.12	4.85	5.68	5.92	5.83	
R & D/sales	2.86	2.64	2.39	2.78	2.83	2.74	
Pretax margin (%)	−3.65	7.03	11.34	6.08	2.49	3.96	
Effective tax rate (%)	NA	16.07	35.07	31.55	27.52	28.13	
Net margin (%)	−3.13	6.11	7.35	4.16	1.81	2.84	
Sales/employee (mil)	0.1245	0.1397	0.1237	0.1109	0.0893	0.0759	
Effective interest rate	9.87	2.07	3.44	7.34	10.55	11.24	
Operating income/total capital	2.65	25.72	33.37	15.17	2.73	5.97	
Return on investment capital	1.95	22.93	25.18	16.27	5.97	8.53	
Return on equity per share	−25.24	41.98	40.00	19.84	5.98	8.84	
Return on equity	−25.03	41.98	40.00	19.84	5.98	8.84	
Return on assets	0.90	9.80	10.43	6.62	2.86	4.37	
Operating profit margin	0.64	5.82	9.06	4.51	1.10	2.45	
Cash earnings return on equity (ROE)	−8.31	49.54	66.24	35.56	15.23	25.13	

LEVERAGE RATIOS—ANNUAL

Total debt/common equity	670.92	277.74	97.96	66.24	41.59	33.03	
Long-term debt/common equity	349.28	89.14	54.65	47.34	41.59	33.03	
Total debt/total capital	87.03	72.85	49.23	39.71	29.37	24.83	
Preferred stock/total capital	0.00	0.00	0.00	0.00	0.00	0.00	
Total debt/total assets	52.42	33.38	21.04	16.44	11.96	11.90	
Cash dividend cover ratio	NA	1.08	1.11	3.70	0.66	3.27	
Dividend payout	0.00	109.73	149.08	48.39	387.34	86.96	
Fixed assets/total capital	367.62	211.50	109.40	96.15	87.75	68.64	
Working capital/total capital	−55.48	−121.95	46.65	22.58	17.69	45.16	
Long-term debt/total capital	77.74	46.27	35.10	32.01	29.37	24.83	
Equity/total capital	22.26	51.91	64.24	67.62	70.63	75.17	
Common equity/total assets	7.81	12.02	21.48	24.82	28.76	36.03	
Total capital/total assets	35.11	23.16	33.44	36.71	40.72	47.93	
Fixed charges coverage ratio	0.41	9.76	21.39	6.98	3.27	4.27	

Ford Motor Company of Canada Ltd.

Description of Business

Manufactures, assembles and markets cars, trucks, related parts and accessories.

PRODUCT LINES

Consumer durables. Number of employees: 28,000 (as of 12/31/90)
Market value: 72,132,860 (as of 02/28/92)
Fiscal year end: 12/31
Latest annual financial date: 12/31/90
Data stated in Canadian dollars

BALANCE SHEET

FISCAL YEAR ENDING	12/31/90	12/31/89	12/31/88
ASSETS (000's)			
Net receivables	374,400	685,200	287,400
Raw materials	NA	NA	NA
Work in process	330,000	337,000	NA
Finished goods	538,800	457,200	NA
Other inventories	0	0	NA
Inventories	868,800	794,200	774,600
Prepaid expenses	NA	NA	NA
Other current assets	150,000	163,600	121,100
Total current assets	1,655,000	1,824,700	1,910,100
Investment in associate companies	32,700	28,600	27,300
Long-term receivables	22,900	22,000	NA
Gross PP & E	3,032,600	2,266,200	2,635,900
Accumulated depreciation	1,244,000	1,118,000	1,014,000
Net PP & E	1,788,600	1,148,200	1,621,900
Tangible other assets	65,000	NA	NA
Intangible other assets	0	NA	NA
Other assets	65,000	505,500	48,900
Total assets	3,564,200	3,529,000	3,608,200
LIABILITIES (000's)			
Accounts payable	1,174,500	NA	NA
Short-term debt & current liabilities	448,400	112,800	83,700
Accrued payroll	NA	NA	NA
Dividend payable	0	NA	NA
Income taxes payable	38,100	145,900	NA
Other current liabilities	0	1,147,700	1,619,700
Total current liabilities	1,661,000	1,406,400	1,703,400
Long-term debt	13,800	31,000	34,300
Risk & charge provision	NA	NA	NA
Deferred taxes	156,400	192,100	165,400
Other liabilities	300,900	313,200	288,500
Unrelated securities gain/loss	0	0	NA
Total liabilities	2,132,100	1,942,700	2,191,600

(Continued)

FISCAL YEAR ENDING	12/31/90	12/31/89	12/31/88
Non-equity reserves	0	NA	NA
Minority interest	0	0	0
Preferred stock	0	0	0
Common stock/ordinary capital	13,400	13,400	NA
Capital surplus	NA	NA	NA
Revaluation reserves	0	0	NA
Other appropriated reserves	NA	NA	NA
Unappropriated reserves	NA	NA	NA
Retained earnings	1,527,700	1,676,000	NA
ESOP guarantees	0	NA	NA
Foreign currency	−109,000	−103,100	NA
Treasury stock	0	0	NA
Common shareholders equity	1,432,100	1,586,300	1,416,600
Total liabilities & shareholders' equity	3,564,200	3,529,000	3,608,200

INCOME STATEMENT (000's)

	12/31/90	12/31/89	12/31/88
Net sales	13,706,200	15,311,800	15,943,300
Cost of goods sold	13,145,700	14,129,600	14,884,400
Gross income	268,700	872,800	767,200
Depreciation & amortization	291,800	309,400	291,700
SG & A expenses	384,600	386,900	354,200
Other operating expenses	0	3,000	0
Total operating expenses	13,822,100	14,828,900	15,530,300
Operating income	−115,900	482,900	413,000
Interest expense	48,000	21,000	40,000
Interest capitalized	0	0	0
Extraordinary credit—pretax	0	0	NA
Extraordinary charge—pretax	0	0	NA
Net other income/expenses	80,200	59,100	77,300
Increase/decrease in reserves	0	0	0
Pretax income	−83,700	521,000	450,300
Income taxes	−27,300	210,000	183,900
Minority interest	0	0	0
Equity in earnings	−700	3,000	3,400
After tax income/expenses	0	NA	NA
Discontinued operations	0	0	0
Net income before extraordinary items	−57,100	314,000	269,800
Extraordinary items	0	0	0
Net income before preferred dividend	−57,100	314,000	269,800
Preferred dividend requirement	0	0	0
Net income	−57,100	314,000	269,800

(*Continued*)

FISCAL YEAR ENDING	12/31/90	12/31/89	12/31/88	12/31/87	12/31/86	12/31/85
GROWTH RATES—ANNUAL						
Net sales growth	−10.49	−3.96	14.07	−2.44	7.30	10.15
Operating income growth	NA	16.29	171.71	2.56	−59.64	−24.85
Net income growth	NA	16.38	222.73	−17.31	−49.20	−54.09
Total assets growth	1.00	−2.20	−0.39	16.29	4.79	7.61
Equity growth	−9.72	11.98	23.76	6.63	−0.11	3.93
Total employee growth	−1.06	3.66	0.37	−1.09	−7.41	−16.57
Earnings per share (EPS) growth	NA	16.38	117.95	22.48	−49.21	−54.07
Dividend/share growth	−38.89	350.00	−33.33	−50.00	−14.29	100.00
Book value/share growth	−9.72	11.98	23.76	6.63	−0.11	3.97
Net margin growth	NA	21.18	182.92	−15.24	−52.65	−58.33
Reinvestment rate/share	−9.35	11.63	20.67	6.90	0.15	8.02
Reinvestment rate/total	−9.35	15.73	20.67	3.16	0.20	8.02
PROFITABILITY RATIOS—ANNUAL						
Cash flow/sales	1.43	4.60	4.08	3.01	2.72	4.16
Cost of goods (COG)/sales	95.91	92.28	93.36	94.64	97.52	95.91
Gross profit margin	1.96	5.70	4.81	4.23	1.04	2.75
SG & A/sales	2.81	2.53	2.22	2.32	2.14	NA
R & D/sales	NA	NA	NA	NA	NA	NA
Pretax margin (%)	−0.61	3.40	2.82	1.50	1.50	2.96
Effective tax rate (%)	NA	40.31	40.84	44.31	48.04	49.62
Net margin (%)	−0.42	2.05	1.69	0.60	0.71	1.49
Sales/employee (mil)	0.4895	0.5411	0.5840	0.5139	0.5210	0.4496
Effective interest rate	10.39	14.60	33.90	8.99	10.89	120.00
Operating income/total capital	−7.17	33.28	30.10	12.89	13.70	29.19
Return on investment capital	−1.47	21.36	19.74	8.39	10.29	16.21
Return on equity per share	−3.60	22.17	23.57	11.53	9.41	19.25
Return on equity	−3.60	22.17	23.57	7.79	9.41	19.25
Return on assets	−0.72	9.09	8.18	3.36	3.75	7.38
Operating profit margin	−0.85	3.15	2.59	1.09	1.03	2.75
Cash earnings return on equity (ROE)	12.38	49.71	56.82	39.22	36.24	53.67
ASSET UTILIZATION RATIOS—ANNUAL						
Assets/employee (mil)	0.127	0.1247	0.1322	0.1332	0.1133	0.1001
Sales/fixed assets	4.52	6.76	6.05	5.85	7.51	8.19
Capital expenditure/fixed assets	14.32	17.54	12.17	20.68	22.34	18.15
Capital expenditure/total assets	12.19	11.26	8.89	13.64	13.68	9.95
Capital expenditure/sales	3.17	2.60	2.01	3.54	2.97	2.22
Accumulated depreciation/ fixed asset	41.02	49.33	38.47	36.87	40.28	42.27
Asset turnover	3.85	4.34	4.42	3.86	4.60	4.49

(Continued)

FISCAL YEAR ENDING	12/31/90	12/31/89	12/31/88	12/31/87	12/31/86	12/31/85
LEVERAGE RATIOS—ANNUAL						
Total debt/common equity	32.27	9.07	8.33	31.10	16.26	0.70
Long-term debt/common equity	0.96	1.95	2.42	19.86	9.87	0.70
Total debt/total capital	24.40	8.31	7.69	23.72	13.98	0.69
Preferred stock/total capital	0.00	0.00	0.00	0.00	0.00	0.00
Total debt/total assets	12.97	4.07	3.27	9.83	5.60	0.25
Cash dividend cover ratio	2.15	7.72	19.59	8.47	3.93	4.78
Dividend payout	−159.72	29.04	12.31	59.45	97.92	58.34
Fixed assets/total capital	124.89	72.38	114.49	131.81	106.09	87.57
Working capital/total capital	−0.41	25.86	14.25	7.73	26.08	37.39
Long-term debt/total capital	0.95	1.92	2.36	16.57	8.98	0.69
Equity/total capital	99.05	98.08	97.64	83.43	91.02	99.31
Common equity/total assets	40.18	44.95	39.26	31.60	34.46	36.15
Total capital/total assets	40.57	45.83	40.21	37.87	37.86	36.40
Fixed charges coverage ratio	−0.74	25.81	12.26	7.57	12.27	44.89

Financial Data: Two Publicly Listed Mexican Automotive Companies

Transmisiones y Equipos Mecanicos S.A.: Mexico

Description of Business

Engaged in the manufacture of speed boxes for cars and trucks, car transmissions and construction equipment.

Fiscal year end: 12/31

Latest annual financial date: 12/31/90. Data stated in pesos.

BALANCE SHEET

FISCAL YEAR ENDING	12/31/90	12/31/89	12/31/88
ASSETS (000's)			
Net receivables	54,184,000	66,379,000	43,607,000
Raw materials	13,441,000	23,261,000	NA

Source: Disclosure/*Worldscope*, March 1992.

(Continued)

FISCAL YEAR ENDING	12/31/90	12/31/89	12/31/88
Work in process	11,324,000	20,484,000	NA
Finished goods	13,277,000	24,373,000	NA
Other inventories	10,995,000	11,661,000	NA
Inventories	49,037,000	79,779,000	47,187,000
Prepaid expenses	379,000	747,000	NA
Other current assets	0	0	0
Total current assets	115,903,000	159,097,000	103,391,000
Investment in associate companies	NA	0	NA
Long-term receivables	0	NA	NA
Gross PP & E	232,430,000	210,515,000	164,086,000
Accumulated depreciation	60,865,000	44,183,000	27,081,000
Net PP & E	171,565,000	166,332,000	137,005,000
Tangible other assets	0	0	NA
Intangible other assets	0	0	NA
Other assets	0	0	403,000
Total assets	287,468,000	325,429,000	240,799,000

LIABILITIES (000's)

Accounts payable	34,163,000	0	NA
Short-term debt & current liabilities	50,562,000	111,308,000	1,507,000
Accrued payroll	NA	NA	NA
Dividend payable	NA	NA	NA
Income taxes payable	3,644,000	NA	NA
Other current liabilities	18,049,000	39,341,000	78,720,000
Total current liabilities	106,418,000	150,649,000	80,227,000
Long-term debt	5,145,000	9,559,000	10,730,000
Risk & charge provision	977,000	871,000	NA
Deferred taxes	0	NA	NA
Other liabilities	5,267,000	0	553,000
Unrelated securities gain/loss	0	NA	NA
Total liabilities	117,807,000	161,079,000	91,510,000
Non-equity reserves	0	NA	0
Minority interest	0	0	4,458,000
Preferred stock	0	0	0
Common stock/ordinary capital	376,416,000	3,225,000	NA
Capital surplus	0	NA	NA
Revaluation reserves	−317,764,000	NA	NA
Other appropriated reserves	9,175,000	161,125,000	NA
Unappropriated reserves	NA	NA	NA
Retained earnings	101,834,000	NA	NA
ESOP guarantees	NA	NA	NA
Foreign currency	0	NA	NA
Treasury stock	0	NA	NA
Common shareholders equity	169,661,000	164,350,000	144,831,000
Total liabilities & shareholders' equity	287,468,000	325,429,000	240,799,000

(Continued)

FISCAL YEAR ENDING	12/31/90	12/31/89	12/31/88
INCOME STATEMENT (000's)			
Net sales[b]	454,118,000	396,755,000	227,054,000
Cost of goods sold	373,581,000	345,019,000	182,988,000
Gross income	61,262,000	37,340,000	32,772,000
Depreciation & amortization	19,275,000	14,396,000	11,294,000
Selling, general & administrative (SG & A) expenses	34,515,000	22,297,000	14,752,000
Other operating expenses	0	0	6,540,000
Total operating expenses	427,371,000	381,712,000	215,574,000
Operating income	26,747,000	15,043,000	11,480,000
Interest expense	31,069,000	19,451,000	9,255,000
Interest capitalized	0	0	0
Extraordinary credit—pretax	2,117,000	0	NA
Extraordinary charge—pretax	0	0	NA
Net other income/expenses	18,334,000	10,712,000	6,431,000
Increase/decrease in reserves	NA	NA	0
Pretax income	16,129,000	6,304,000	8,656,000
Income taxes	17,011,000	5,567,000	2,583,000
Minority interest	0	0	0
Equity in earnings	NA	0	0
After tax income/expenses	0	NA	NA
Discontinued operations	0	0	0
Net income before extraordinary items	−882,000	737,000	6,073,000
Extraordinary items	16,539,000	0	585,000
Net income before preferred dividend	15,657,000	737,000	6,658,000
Preferred dividend requirement	0	0	0
Net income	−882,000	737,000	6,658,000

FISCAL YEAR ENDING	12/31/90	12/31/89	12/31/88	12/31/87	12/31/86	12/31/85
GROWTH RATES—ANNUAL						
Net sales growth	14.46	74.74	NA	NA	NA	NA
Operating income growth	77.80	31.04	NA	NA	NA	NA
Net income growth	2,024.42	−88.93	NA	NA	NA	NA
Total assets growth	−11.66	35.15	NA	NA	NA	NA
Equity growth	3.23	13.48	11.82	NA	NA	NA
Earnings per share (EPS) growth	NA	−88.95	67.37	NA	NA	NA
Dividend/share growth	0.00	−100.00	NA	NA	NA	NA
Book value/share growth	3.23	13.28	11.82	NA	NA	NA
Net margin growth	1,756.04	−93.67	NA	NA	NA	NA
Reinvestment rate/share	−0.54	0.51	3.98	NA	NA	NA
Reinvestment rate/total	9.53	0.51	3.98	NA	NA	NA

(Continued)

FISCAL YEAR ENDING	12/31/90	12/31/89	12/31/88	12/31/87	12/31/86	12/31/85
PROFITABILITY RATIOS—ANNUAL						
Cash flow/sales	4.05	4.10	8.75	NA	NA	NA
Cost of goods (COG)/sales	82.27	86.96	80.59	NA	NA	NA
Gross profit margin	13.49	9.41	14.43	NA	NA	NA
SG & A/sales	7.60	5.62	6.50	NA	NA	NA
R & D/sales	NA	NA	NA	NA	NA	NA
Pretax margin (%)	3.55	1.59	3.81	NA	NA	NA
Effective tax rate (%)	105.47	88.31	29.84	NA	NA	NA
Net margin (%)	3.45	0.19	2.93	NA	NA	NA
Sales/employee (mil)	NA	NA	NA	NA	NA	NA
Effective interest rate	55.77	16.09	75.63	NA	NA	NA
Operating income/total capital	15.38	9.40	NA	NA	NA	NA
Return on investment capital	12.68	8.40	NA	NA	NA	NA
Return on equity per share	−0.54	0.51	5.14	NA	NA	NA
Return on equity	9.53	0.51	5.14	NA	NA	NA
Return on assets	11.11	5.64	NA	NA	NA	NA
Operating profit margin	5.89	3.79	5.06	NA	NA	NA
Cash earnings return on equity (ROE)	11.19	11.23	15.34	NA	NA	NA
LIQUIDITY RATIOS—ANNUAL						
Cash & equivalent/current assets	10.61	7.66	12.18	NA	NA	NA
Receivables/current assets	46.75	41.72	42.18	NA	NA	NA
Inventory/total current assets	42.31	50.14	45.64	NA	NA	NA
Accounts receivable days	47.79	49.90	NA	NA	NA	NA
Days inventory held	62.07	66.24	NA	NA	NA	NA
Net sales/working capital	47.88	46.96	9.80	NA	NA	NA
Current ratio	1.09	1.06	1.29	NA	NA	NA
Quick ratio	0.62	0.52	0.70	NA	NA	NA

EXCHANGE RATES (MEXICAN PESOS TO U.S. DOLLAR)

	1992	1991	1990	1989	1988	1987	1986	1985
Jan	0.00033	0.00034	0.00037	0.00043	0.00045	0.00103	0.00225	0.00441
Feb	0.00033	0.00034	0.00036	0.00043	0.00044	0.00096	0.00211	0.00420
Mar	NA	0.00034	0.00037	0.00042	0.00044	0.00090	0.00206	0.00412
Apr	NA	0.00033	0.00036	0.00041	0.00044	0.00085	0.00193	0.00465
May	NA	0.00033	0.00035	0.00041	0.00044	0.00079	0.00181	0.00362
Jun	NA	0.00033	0.00035	0.00040	0.00044	0.00074	0.00156	0.00316
Jul	NA	0.00033	0.00035	0.00040	0.00044	0.00071	0.00158	0.00290
Aug	NA	0.00033	0.00035	0.00039	0.00044	0.00068	0.00148	0.00298
Sep	NA	0.00033	0.00035	0.00039	0.00043	0.00065	0.00137	0.00270
Oct	NA	0.00033	0.00034	0.00038	0.00043	0.00061	0.00123	0.00209
Nov	NA	0.00032	0.00034	0.00038	0.00043	0.00043	0.00115	0.00211
Dec	NA	0.00032	0.00034	0.00037	0.00043	0.00045	0.00110	0.00222

Grupo Industrial Saltillo SA: Mexico

Description of Business

Engaged in the manufacture of auto parts, home products and construction materials. No sales breakdown available.

PRODUCT LINES

Industrial materials. Number of employees: 9,602 (as of 06/30/89)
Fiscal year end: 06/30
Latest annual financial date: 06/30/89
Data stated in pesos

BALANCE SHEET

FISCAL YEAR ENDING	06/30/89	06/30/88	06/30/87
ASSETS (000's)			
Net receivables	171,393,000	272,071,000	41,688,992
Raw materials	36,216,000	NA	NA
Work in process	10,638,000	NA	NA
Finished goods	12,351,000	NA	NA
Other inventories	7,442,000	NA	NA
Inventories	66,647,000	73,122,000	31,333,207
Prepaid expenses	NA	NA	NA
Other current assets	325,000	0	0
Total current assets	428,109,000	532,509,000	179,657,133
Investment in associate companies	0	NA	NA
Long-term receivables	NA	NA	NA
Gross PP & E	659,672,000	749,221,000	419,996,492
Accumulated depreciation	296,356,000	348,739,000	205,787,861
Net PP & E	363,316,000	400,482,000	214,208,631
Tangible other assets	NA	NA	NA
Intangible other assets	NA	NA	NA
Other assets	4,202,000	11,025,000	15,259,394
Total assets	795,627,000	944,016,000	409,125,158
LIABILITIES (000's)			
Accounts payable	NA	NA	NA
Short-term debt & current liabilities	13,027,000	155,868,000	9,519,564
Accrued payroll	NA	NA	NA
Dividend payroll	NA	NA	NA
Income taxes payable	10,629,000	NA	NA
Other current liabilities	86,592,000	151,414,000	43,755,286
Total current liabilities	110,248,000	307,282,000	53,274,850
Long-term debt	88,345,000	105,934,000	147,336,464
Risk & charge provision	4,676,000	NA	NA
Deferred taxes	NA	NA	NA

(Continued)

FISCAL YEAR ENDING	06/30/89	06/30/88	06/30/87
Other liabilities	11,179,000	25,547,000	6,433,627
Unrelated securities gain/loss	NA	NA	NA
Total liabilities	214,448,000	438,763,000	207,044,941
Non-equity reserves	0	0	0
Minority interest	3,687,000	76,393,000	33,659,613
Preferred stock	0	0	0
Common stock/ordinary capital	2,008,000	NA	NA
Capital surplus	13,803,000	NA	NA
Revaluation reserves	NA	NA	NA
Other appropriated reserves	1,476,000	NA	NA
Unappropriated reserves	441,686,000	NA	NA
Retained earnings	118,519,000	NA	NA
ESOP guarantees	NA	NA	NA
Foreign currency	NA	NA	NA
Treasury stock	NA	NA	NA
Common shareholders equity	577,492,000	428,860,000	168,420,604
Total liabilities & shareholders' equity	795,627,000	944,016,000	409,125,158

INCOME STATEMENT (000's)

Net sales	913,537,000	662,074,000	262,856,253
Cost of goods sold	604,173,000	385,197,000	162,763,599
Gross income	273,372,000	241,414,000	87,646,277
Depreciation & amortization	35,992,000	35,463,000	12,446,377
SG & A expenses	124,609,000	77,026,000	31,806,203
Other operating expenses	0	0	0
Total operating expenses	764,774,000	497,686,000	207,016,179
Operating income	148,763,000	164,388,000	55,840,074
Interest expense	13,312,000	126,006,000	80,716,527
Interest capitalized	0	0	0
Extraordinary credit—pretax	0	NA	NA
Extraordinary charge—pretax	0	NA	NA
Net other income/expenses	3,457,000	124,386,000	62,797,801
Increase/decrease in reserves	0	0	0
Pretax income	138,908,000	162,768,000	37,921,348
Income taxes	56,587,000	34,802,000	7,068,059
Minority interest	8,847,000	11,172,000	964,112
Equity in earnings	0	155,000	0
After tax income/expenses	38,916,000	NA	NA
Discontinued operations	0	0	0
Net income before extraordinary items	112,390,000	116,949,000	22,429,956
Extraordinary items	0	0	0
Net income before preferred dividend	112,390,000	116,949,000	22,429,956
Preferred dividend requirement	0	0	0
Net income	112,390,000	116,949,000	22,429,956

(Continued)

FISCAL YEAR ENDING	06/30/89	06/30/88	06/30/87	06/30/86	06/30/85	06/30/84
GROWTH RATES—ANNUAL						
Net sales growth	37.98	151.88	111.49	80.01	78.45	99.72
Operating income growth	−9.50	194.39	135.87	137.88	159.78	−20.99
Net income growth	−3.90	421.40	182.21	175.21	325.96	−44.20
Total assets growth	−15.72	130.74	116.37	76.76	50.67	58.82
Equity growth	34.66	154.64	144.13	108.16	71.15	34.48
Total employee growth	−21.38	−4.29	−7.45	−6.96	13.08	12.89
Earnings per share (EPS) growth	−4.07	421.48	197.73	175.21	325.96	−44.20
Dividend/share growth	178.23	NA	0.00	0.00	0.00	0.00
Book value/share growth	34.43	154.64	157.60	108.16	71.15	34.48
Net margin growth	−30.35	107.00	33.44	52.89	138.69	−72.06
Reinvestment rate/share	22.90	66.46	34.30	23.98	14.91	4.71
Reinvestment rate/total	22.95	66.46	32.51	23.98	14.91	4.71
PROFITABILITY RATIOS—ANNUAL						
Cash flow/sales	20.08	35.12	23.02	26.02	25.95	7.97
Cost of goods (COG)/sales	66.14	58.18	61.92	63.05	67.06	71.64
Gross profit margin	29.92	36.46	33.34	30.95	26.66	22.17
SG & A/sales	13.64	11.63	12.10	13.70	12.25	12.71
R & D/sales	NA	NA	NA	NA	NA	NA
Pretax margin (%)	15.21	24.58	14.43	6.98	2.38	−10.78
Effective tax rate (%)	40.74	21.38	18.64	86.51	109.00	NA
Net margin (%)	12.30	17.66	8.53	6.39	4.18	1.75
Sales/employee (mil)	95.14	54.21	20.60	9.01	4.66	2.95
Effective interest rate	13.13	48.13	51.46	50.97	41.74	24.46
Operating income/total capital	24.34	47.05	34.48	27.57	16.99	12.04
Return on investment capital	15.80	55.75	46.74	34.47	22.29	16.81
Return on equity per share	26.16	69.44	34.30	23.98	14.91	4.71
Return on equity	26.21	69.44	32.51	23.98	14.91	4.71
Return on assets	12.84	48.91	40.04	27.66	18.39	11.96
Operating profit margin	16.28	24.83	21.24	19.05	14.41	9.90
Cash earnings return on equity (ROE)	42.78	138.06	87.72	97.58	92.46	21.42
LEVERAGE RATIOS—ANNUAL						
Total debt/common equity	17.55	61.05	93.13	113.98	136.16	182.60
Long-term debt/common equity	15.30	24.70	87.48	113.98	136.16	182.60
Total debt/total capital	14.85	34.13	43.70	48.55	52.56	60.36
Preferred stock/total capital	0.00	0.00	0.00	0.00	0.00	0.00
Total debt/total assets	12.74	27.73	38.34	41.59	42.18	49.80
Cash dividend cover ratio	13.12	46.33	NA	NA	NA	NA
Dividend payout	12.45	4.29	0.00	0.00	0.00	0.00
Fixed assets/total capital	62.91	93.38	127.19	141.17	170.99	194.09
Working capital/total capital	47.48	36.85	36.17	24.31	17.40	17.21
Long-term debt/total capital	13.20	17.33	42.17	48.55	52.56	60.36
Equity/total capital	86.25	70.17	48.20	42.60	38.60	33.05

(Continued)

FISCAL YEAR ENDING	06/30/89	06/30/88	06/30/87	06/30/86	06/30/85	06/30/84
Common equity/total assets	72.58	45.43	41.17	36.48	30.98	27.27
Total capital/total assets	84.15	64.74	85.41	85.65	80.26	82.51
Fixed charges coverage ratio	11.43	2.29	1.47	1.22	1.09	0.52

LEVERAGE RATIOS—FIVE-YEAR AVERAGES

Total debt/common equity	84.38	117.38	127.75	133.31	121.21	100.53
Long-term debt/common equity	75.52	108.98	126.62	133.31	121.21	100.53
Total debt/total capital	38.76	47.86	51.25	53.17	50.26	44.61
Preferred stock/total capital	0.00	0.00	0.00	0.00	0.00	0.00
Total debt/total assets	32.52	39.93	41.65	41.07	37.65	32.64
Cash dividend cover ratio	NA	NA	NA	NA	NA	NA
Dividend payout	7.24	3.33	0.00	0.61	NA	NA
Fixed assets/total capital	119.13	145.36	165.02	179.81	179.31	166.74
Working capital/total capital	32.44	26.39	17.64	10.03	8.06	9.04
Long-term debt/total capital	34.76	44.19	50.94	53.17	50.26	44.61
Equity/total capital	57.16	46.52	41.54	40.71	44.91	52.05
Common equity/total assets	45.33	36.27	33.62	31.25	33.09	37.36
Total capital/total assets	80.04	79.71	81.00	77.22	74.47	72.50
Fixed charges coverage ratio	3.50	1.32	1.18	1.20	1.43	1.73

Financial Performance: Publicly Listed Automotive Companies around the World (1990–1991)

COMPANY NAME	COUNTRY	DATE OF LATEST ANNL DATA	TOTAL ASSETS (000s)	NET SALES (000s)	NET SALES GROWTH 5YA[a]	OPER INC[b] GROWTH 5YA	RETURN ON EQUITY 5YA	RETURN ON ASSETS 5YA
AMI Toyota Ltd.	Australia	06/30/87	316,673	681,354	10.14	NA	−14.88	0.21
General Motors-Holden Ltd.	Australia	12/31/85	843,935	1,642,619	10.63		−31.60	−7.79
Mitsubishi Motors Australia Lt	Australia	12/31/90	650,820	1,289,565	6.46	18.35	18.24	8.59
Repco Corporation Ltd.	Australia	06/30/86	713,491	1,032,390	13.22	3.16	8.43	6.67
York Motors Holding Ltd.	Australia	06/30/87	95,488	338,474	14.60	8.67	10.12	7.55
Miba AG	Austria	01/31/91	2,058,089	1,505,000	8.80	8.96	18.86	7.85
Steyr-Daimler-Puch AG	Austria	12/31/90	12,187,900	14,826,000	−0.66		8.42	3.24
Budd Canada Inc.	Canada	09/30/90	151,031	238,248	−1.48	−14.18	24.48	16.59
Ford Motor Co. of Canada Ltd.	Canada	12/31/90	3,564,200	13,706,200	0.52	NA	11.87	4.73
Hayes-Dana Inc.	Canada	12/31/90	204,195	438,496	−0.28	−6.76	13.84	9.13
Magna International Inc.	Canada	07/31/91	1,469,000	2,017,200	14.44	5.31	−3.52	2.10
TCG International Inc.	Canada	12/31/90	336,940	518,938				
UAP Inc.	Canada	12/31/90	242,721	412,761	10.64	15.30	11.25	6.86
Industry Average Record[c]	Canada	12/31/89	1,198,487	3,685,242	6.56	1.44	16.00	7.02
Bertrand Faure SA	France	12/31/90	4,711,616	6,567,142	20.53	15.24	14.81	6.63
Chausson (SA Des Usines Chauss.	France	12/31/90	2,621,103	4,245,050	−7.71	NA	−0.71	2.17
Peugeot S.A.	France	12/31/90	115,265,000	159,976,000	9.79	56.07	44.04	10.16
Renault (Regie Nationale Des U	France	12/31/90	119,451,000	163,620,000	8.00	NA		6.44
Soc. Pour L'Equipement de Vehic	France	12/31/86	3,185,492	5,219,508	13.12	13.06	−21.46	2.49
Adam Opel AG	Germany	12/31/90	9,933,391	23,707,569	9.89	NA	47.50	9.50
Bayerische Motoren Werke AG	Germany	12/31/90	22,578,054	27,177,615	13.01	−18.76	14.06	5.32
Daimler-Benz AG	Germany	12/31/90	73,005,000	85,500,000	10.28	−39.08	24.88	6.12
Ford-Werke AG	Germany	12/31/90	8,110,700	20,753,900	7.52	NA	50.80	9.21
Iveco-Magirus AG	Germany	12/31/90	1,742,904	2,455,312	6.33	−3.90	26.43	8.83
Kolbenschmidt AG	Germany	09/30/91	1,336,539	1,445,619	7.51	NA	7.27	5.10
Moto Meter	Germany	12/31/90	111,604	225,422	9.56	18.42	13.13	6.16
Porsche AG	Germany	07/31/91	2,290,597	3,102,207	−2.76	NA	7.37	2.66
Robert Bosch GMBH	Germany	12/31/90	24,110,700	31,823,700	8.44	−33.79	10.11	3.70
Volkswagen AG	Germany	12/31/90	62,707,500	68,061,100	5.33	NA	8.29	3.66
YMOS AG	Germany	06/30/90	609,745	671,281	6.54	−2.37	3.27	3.53
Industry Average Record[c]	Germany	12/31/89	17,420,289	22,421,721	10.18	−20.65	17.13	5.27
Jardine International Motor Ho	Hong Kong	12/31/90	2,031,963	3,358,788	45.98	16.10	41.94	25.75
Fiat Spa	Italy	12/31/90	74,445,000,000	57,209,000,000	16.12	16.87	22.90	9.00
Gilardini Spa	Italy	12/31/90	2,282,246,000	2,006,675,000	37.39	41.42	9.78	4.69
Magneti Marelli Spa	Italy	12/31/90	3,235,558,000	3,808,740,000	44.50	−3.02	NA	NA
Pininfarina Spa	Italy	12/31/90	326,057,000	479,491,000				
Valeo Spa	Italy	12/31/90	330,457,000	415,824,000				
Aichi Machine Industry Co., Lt	Japan	03/31/91	134,096,000	265,012,000	5.49	−0.95	7.21	2.86
Aisin Seiki Co., Ltd.	Japan	03/31/91	497,673,000	768,618,000	17.00	7.69	8.18	4.30
Akebono Brake Industry Co., Lt	Japan	03/31/91	94,573,469	115,344,006				
Ashimori Industry Co., Ltd.	Japan	03/31/91	33,171,234	22,098,432	6.72	6.81	5.94	3.99

(*Continued*)

Source: Disclosure/*Worldscope*, March 1992.

COMPANY NAME	COUNTRY	DATE OF LATEST ANNL DATA	TOTAL ASSETS (000s)	NET SALES (000s)	NET SALES GROWTH 5YA[a]	OPER INC[b] GROWTH 5YA	RETURN ON EQUITY 5YA	RETURN ON ASSETS 5YA
Atsugi Unisia Corporation	Japan	02/28/91	135,660,925	170,281,756	4.86	−12.13	3.72	2.37
Calsonic Corporation	Japan	03/31/91	155,393,000	257,483,000	6.99	−7.06	2.60	2.44
Daihatsu Motor Co., Ltd.	Japan	03/31/91	587,867,000	872,319,000	8.13	10.15	4.93	1.93
Fuji Heavy Industries, Ltd.	Japan	03/31/91	809,474,000	819,306,000	0.93	NA	−3.22	−0.21
Futaba Industrial Co., Ltd.	Japan	03/31/91	78,818,489	124,778,811	7.76	13.40	9.30	5.25
Hino Motors, Ltd.	Japan	03/31/91	365,550,000	657,057,000	6.90	15.72	8.02	3.27
Honda Motor Co., Ltd.	Japan	03/31/91	2,953,328,000	4,301,518,000	8.13	−13.63	10.77	5.56
Ichikoh Industries Ltd.	Japan	03/31/91	86,227,000	119,645,000	3.94	−29.63	5.16	1.93
Isuzu Motors Ltd.	Japan	10/31/90	1,141,378,000	1,520,006,000	8.38	−7.53	3.22	2.50
Kanto Auto Works Ltd.	Japan	03/31/91	120,999,000	411,139,000	5.77	−8.47	11.09	3.26
Kinugawa Rubber Industrial Co	Japan	03/31/91	53,440,808	74,101,795	5.02	13.30	4.42	2.66
Koito Manufacturing Co., Ltd.	Japan	03/31/91	157,870,000	203,667,000	10.39	5.36	7.52	3.61
Mazda Motor Corporation	Japan	03/31/91	1,535,297,000	2,714,352,000	9.46	25.70	4.47	2.56
Mitsubishi Motors Corporation	Japan	03/31/91	2,036,493,000	2,797,770,000				
Morita Fire Pump Mfg. Co., Ltd	Japan	03/31/91	50,045,458	37,432,695	8.50	19.09	6.30	3.89
NGK Spark Plug Co., Ltd.	Japan	03/31/91	144,099,000	110,564,000	7.27	6.53	7.71	5.24
Nippon Air Brake Co., Ltd.	Japan	03/31/91	83,056,140	73,309,889	12.58	25.83	6.47	3.08
Nippon Piston Ring Co., Ltd.	Japan	03/31/91	53,410,000	48,699,000	6.15	9.91	10.15	3.13
Nippondenso Co., Ltd.	Japan	12/31/90	1,393,066,000	1,511,641,000	9.63	4.20	8.69	4.85
Nissan Diesel Motor Co., Ltd.	Japan	03/31/91	365,675,000	393,762,000	8.53	31.00	5.89	2.66
Nissan Motor Co., Ltd.	Japan	03/31/91	6,287,682,000	5,964,912,000	5.21	7.42	4.85	3.36
Nissan Shatai Co., Ltd.	Japan	03/31/91	211,353,000	530,965,000	−0.57	−21.24	3.93	1.91
Pacific Industrial Co., Ltd.	Japan	03/31/91	48,958,214	44,920,027	7.16	−2.99	8.18	4.81
Press Kogyo Co., Ltd.	Japan	03/31/91	110,807,000	161,679,000	5.10	−27.56	5.70	2.50
Riken Corporation	Japan	03/31/91	84,043,317	78,093,222	5.04	20.73	7.99	3.63
Sanden Corp.	Japan	03/31/91	161,133,000	158,319,000	9.24	−7.57	3.43	3.22
Shin Meiwa Industry Co., Ltd.	Japan	03/31/91	150,290,000	163,636,000	19.99	75.09	7.47	4.33
Shiroki Corporation	Japan	03/31/91	68,225,324	94,133,117	9.30	−2.78	5.70	3.02
Showa Manufacturing Co., Ltd.	Japan	03/31/91	42,560,000	64,338,000	5.30	−8.58	4.54	2.57
Suzuki Motor Corporation	Japan	03/31/91	731,238,000	1,210,271,000	8.05	14.44	7.23	2.81
Tokai Rika Co. Ltd.	Japan	03/31/91	114,813,733	196,045,071	12.60	−1.37	6.38	2.82
Tokico, Ltd.	Japan	03/31/91	96,998,000	135,903,000	8.94	7.28	7.22	4.24
Tokyu Car Corp.	Japan	03/31/91	110,721,000	93,446,000	2.35	0.19	1.76	1.64
Topre Corporation	Japan	03/31/91	49,199,460	42,821,777	1.83	4.05	6.54	4.21
Topy Industries, Limited	Japan	03/31/91	275,454,000	261,801,000	6.16	10.23	9.17	3.22
Toyo Radiator Co., Ltd.	Japan	03/31/91	52,648,576	52,687,007	6.83	3.72	4.13	2.73
Toyoda Boshoku Corporation	Japan	04/30/91	25,092,233	47,587,220	1.71	−4.27	15.19	8.33
Toyoda Gosei Co., Ltd.	Japan	04/30/91	164,941,000	245,374,000	11.20	4.52	6.14	2.88
Toyoda Machine Works, Ltd.	Japan	03/31/91	204,406,000	210,580,000	9.36	0.93	3.29	2.47
Toyota Auto Body Co., Ltd.	Japan	03/31/91	145,450,000	487,103,000	10.51	6.63	8.92	3.08
Toyota Motor Corp.	Japan	06/30/91	8,978,922,000	9,855,132,000	8.20	−10.46	10.39	6.63
Yamaha Motor Co., Ltd.	Japan	03/31/91	550,291,000	692,715,000	6.35	9.26	19.20	4.52
Zexel Corporation	Japan	03/31/91	303,607,000	286,486,000	7.94	12.71	5.42	2.55
Industry Average Record[c]	Japan	12/31/89	1,097,908,676	1,314,566,284	5.94	−0.11	9.94	5.23
Tan Chong Motor Holdings Berha	Malaysia	12/31/90	1,230,974	2,018,745	14.06	42.75	10.55	7.03
UMW Holdings Berhad	Malaysia	12/31/90	920,112	1,931,408	14.84	100.04	−8.44	3.19
Grupo Industrial Saltillo SA	Mexico	06/30/89	795,627,000	913,537,000	88.20	107.89	33.41	29.57
Transmisiones y Equipos Mecani	Mexico	12/31/90	287,468,000	454,118,000				
Daf N.V.	Netherlands	12/31/90	5,821,171	5,202,172	18.76	NA	6.44	3.88

(Continued)

Company Name	Country	Date of Latest Annl Data	Total Assets (000s)	Net Sales (000s)	Net Sales Growth 5YA[a]	Oper Inc[b] Growth 5YA	Return on Equity 5YA	Return on Assets 5YA
Emco Group Ltd.	New Zealand	03/31/85	245,474	452,065	16.84	24.34	14.54	8.80
Salvador Caetano Ind Met Veic	Portugal	12/31/90	31,136,044	52,921,186	28.28	25.93	40.03	19.83
Cycle & Carriage Ltd.	Singapore	09/30/90	627,180	573,482	23.40	47.64	9.28	8.02
Inchcape Berhad	Singapore	12/31/90	678,638	829,462	5.97	NA	20.58	12.87
Toyota South Africa Limited	South Africa	12/31/90	1,349,200	3,117,937				
Hyundai Motor Co.	South Korea	12/31/89	3,556,443,174	3,806,509,546	41.58	25.47	16.22	5.89
Kia Motors Corporation	South Korea	12/31/90	2,455,432,000	2,540,389,000	38.38	22.21	9.52	5.30
Citroen Hispania, S.A.	Spain	12/31/90	110,470,481	234,400,476	16.23		46.10	14.45
Construc. y Auxiliar de Ferroc	Spain	12/31/90	20,540,792	22,558,534				
Santana Motor SA	Spain	12/31/90	30,349,000	35,493,300	5.93	NA	−10.10	−0.08
Sociedad Esp. de Automoviles TU	Spain	12/31/90	409,514,000	503,297,000	19.29			2.24
Saab-Scania AB	Sweden	12/31/90	43,146,000	29,035,000	−1.83	−3.66	15.42	5.17
Volvo AB	Sweden	12/31/90	102,097,000	83,185,000	−0.71	−38.56	15.32	5.49
Adwest Group Plc	United Kingdom	06/30/91	126,111	122,359	5.46	−14.83	12.00	8.24
Associated Engineering	United Kingdom	12/31/86	339,100	485,600	1.94	29.72	6.04	4.69
Automotive Products Plc	United Kingdom	11/30/89	283,237	114,711	−13.41	25.29	NA	NA
BBA Group Plc	United Kingdom	12/31/90	902,800	1,229,200	39.88	46.10	17.58	8.96
BSG International Plc	United Kingdom	12/31/90	251,583	648,997	12.76	14.01	23.33	10.53
Chloride Group Plc	United Kingdom	03/31/91	138,600	215,600	−6.99	1.86	8.84	5.18
First Technology Plc	United Kingdom	04/30/91	24,099	37,293				
Ford Motor Ltd.	United Kingdom	12/31/90	8,933,000	7,509,000	13.17	−13.48	16.56	6.12
Kenning Motor Group Plc	United Kingdom	09/30/85	174,828	419,423	11.55	10.65	6.36	4.40
Kwik-Fit (Tyres & Exhausts) Ho	United Kingdom	02/28/91	172,406	229,381	23.25	42.17	25.88	13.08
Lucas Industries Plc	United Kingdom	07/31/91	2,070,600	2,365,000	7.87	−0.36	14.20	7.51
Renold Ltd.	United Kingdom	03/30/91	117,000	128,900	−0.15	−17.51	4.80	3.57
Rover Group	United Kingdom	12/31/87	1,745,000	3,096,400	0.16		NA	−11.46
T & N Plc	United Kingdom	12/31/90	1,193,000	1,253,500	18.56	17.09	15.91	8.81
Vauxhall Motors Ltd.	United Kingdom	12/31/90	1,029,500	2,620,200	10.86	64.19		14.70
Industry Average Record[c]	United Kingdom	12/31/89	1,460,068	1,680,092	13.65	66.09	20.36	6.96
Allen Group Inc. (The)	United States	12/31/90	330,427	352,281	−2.47	2.73	−1.87	1.91
American Motors Corporation	United States	12/31/86	2,225,342	3,462,504	5.99	NA	−63.57	−4.09
Arrow Automotive Industries, I	United States	06/28/91	64,827	91,238				
Arvin Industries, Inc.	United States	12/30/90	1,192,669	1,687,068	15.49	8.30	8.93	6.55
Athey Products Corp.	United States	12/31/90	34,048	30,614	−0.23	−42.14	14.21	11.38
Buell Industries, Inc.	United States	10/31/89	55,992	86,836	3.44	−30.87	8.24	6.27
Champion Spark Plug Company	United States	12/31/88	575,600	738,000	−0.70	−7.47	3.84	3.24
Chrysler Corporation	United States	12/31/90	46,374,000	30,620,000	7.57	9.33	15.85	8.88
Collins Industries, Inc.	United States	10/31/90	52,278	140,045	10.42	48.67	7.27	6.27
Dana Corporation	United States	12/31/90	4,513,193	5,185,148	6.67	2.22	12.31	7.06
Defiance, Inc.	United States	06/30/91	49,558	59,132	34.51	2.81	−5.25	1.02
Douglas & Lomason Co.	United States	12/31/90	148,820	418,118	9.42	2.83	3.91	3.75
Durakon Industries, Inc.	United States	12/31/90	48,149	112,402				
Eaton Corporation	United States	12/31/90	3,013,000	3,639,000	−0.19	−4.20	16.85	8.17
Echlin Inc.	United States	08/31/91	1,191,793	1,685,876	13.33	−2.70	8.35	6.51
ESI Industries, Inc.	United States	12/31/90	47,903	96,234	14.61	NA	7.28	5.06
Excel Industries, Inc.	United States	12/31/90	155,724	281,369	25.01	18.71	18.48	10.07
Facet Enterprises, Inc.	United States	09/30/87	222,859	280,542	16.89	21.68	0.12	2.80
Ford Motor Company	United States	12/31/90	173,662,700	97,650,000	13.10	31.02	21.63	9.52
General Motors Corporation	United States	12/31/90	180,236,500	122,020,800	4.83	14.99	8.51	6.24
Hastings Manufacturing Company	United States	12/31/90	44,230	67,294	1.46	7.71	7.66	5.61
Hayes-Albion Corporation	United States	07/31/86	97,772	212,687	3.71	NA	−0.71	0.45
International Controls Corp.	United States	12/31/86	538,535	736,829	39.90	23.62	12.38	9.23
K-H Corp.	United States	12/31/88	1,583,703	2,053,508	−0.72	−5.39	NA	3.23

(Continued)

COMPANY NAME	COUNTRY	DATE OF LATEST ANNL DATA	TOTAL ASSETS (000s)	NET SALES (000s)	NET SALES GROWTH 5YA[a]	OPER INC[b] GROWTH 5YA	RETURN ON EQUITY 5YA	RETURN ON ASSETS 5YA
Larizza Industries, Inc.	United States	12/31/90	78,386	96,739				
Mack Trucks, Incorporated	United States	12/31/89	1,616,219	1,750,734	−3.62		−8.99	−1.24
Mr. Gasket Company	United States	12/31/90	106,389	102,386	−2.83	NA	−20.14	−2.30
Myers Industries, Inc.	United States	12/31/90	116,373	202,104	18.84	26.15	18.12	10.86
Navistar International Corpora	United States	10/31/90	3,795,000	3,854,000	1.90	−11.11		5.22
Oshkosh Truck Corp.	United States	09/30/91	219,587	419,616	0.97	−46.70	11.68	7.15
Paccar Inc.	United States	12/31/90	2,906,220	2,791,448	8.08	19.78	15.62	10.12
Ragan (Brad), Inc.	United States	12/31/90	114,959	209,688				
Raytech Corporation	United States	12/30/90	72,471	120,291	1.36	NA	NA	−2.93
Schwitzer, Inc.	United States	12/31/90	89,371	114,384				
Sheller Globe	United States	09/30/85	494,418	917,702	15.29	64.64	16.16	7.90
Simpson Industries, Inc.	United States	12/31/90	122,899	193,064	6.82	0.73	14.21	8.71
SPX Corporation	United States	12/31/90	624,141	708,195	2.55	−5.82	14.04	8.39
Standard Motor Products, Inc.	United States	12/31/90	422,099	507,820	15.90	9.13	9.55	7.52
Standard Product Company (The	United States	06/30/91	367,814	592,090	6.45	NA	10.19	7.87
Steego Corporation	United States	04/30/91	33,676	0	−100.00	NA	−9.17	−0.91
Superior Industries Internatio	United States	12/31/91	271,356	273,490	12.98	18.43	21.36	10.27
TBC Corporation	United States	12/31/91	135,284	499,469	4.91	15.70	25.39	13.05
Trico Products Corporation	United States	12/31/90	151,448	243,105				
Venturian Corporation	United States	12/31/90	22,118	32,245	−4.91		−2.24	−0.62
Voplex Corporation	United States	12/31/90	31,506	56,546	−6.59	NA	−9.16	−3.68
Walbro Corp.	United States	12/31/90	143,026	166,678	17.95	8.05	13.52	9.35
Wynn's International, Inc.	United States	12/31/90	187,765	285,123	3.81	NA	6.68	4.79
Industry Average Record	United States	12/31/89	15,080,668	10,377,721	9.63	21.99	17.28	8.71

[a] 5YA = 5-year average.

[b] oper inc = operating income.

[c] industry average record for Canadian companies.

The Anglo–French War for the Irish Distillers Group

An International Acquisition of an Industrial Company in the European Community

FINBARR BRADLEY

It is 3:30 PM on Sunday afternoon, September 4, 1988 in Dublin, Ireland. Mr. Nihal Sirisena, assistant to the chairman of the U.K. multinational Grand Metropolitan PLC (Grand Met) must act within the half-hour. Nihal, a graduate in Hotel Management from Surrey University, England with an MBA from New York University, joined Grand Met in 1986 through its subsidiary Inter-Continental Hotels. During 1988, when Grand Met sold the hotel chain to The Saison Group of Japan, Nihal was offered a high-visibility position at corporate headquarters in London. He is spending this weekend in Dublin to negotiate details on Grand Met's behalf in their battle with the French outfit, Pernod-Ricard (Pernod) for control of the Irish Distillers Group (IDG).

Nihal has just completed two telephone conversations. The first was with Grand Met's London bankers. He was informed that permission had been received from the executive board of the U.K. Takeover Panel to increase Grand Met's I400p[1] per share bid for IDG. Nihal is aware that the Pernod chairman, Mr. Thierry Jacquillat, has been in Dublin all weekend for talks with IDG shareholders. On Saturday, Jacquillat got a handshake agreement from the single largest shareholder in IDG, the Irish fruit company FII Fyffes, verbally committing to sell its 20 percent share in IDG to Pernod at I450p per share.

His second phone conversation was with Mr. Jim Flavin, a director of FII Fyffes. Mr. Flavin indicated that his company was willing to entertain a substantially increased bid from Grand Met for its stake in IDG. Flavin told him that while he and his co-directors had indeed given Pernod a verbal agreement the previous afternoon, nothing had yet been signed. However, the two parties were scheduled to sign the papers at 4:30 PM that afternoon. Nihal knows this is the last window of opportunity to act. He must phone Flavin at home by 4:00 PM if Grand Met is prepared to make a higher bid. Otherwise, Grand Met

©Finbarr Bradley, New York University, 1990. This case was prepared as a basis for class discussion.

[1]The letter 'I' preceding a price denotes Irish currency, the punt. The Irish punt is divided into 100 pence. At the time of this case study, one British pound (or £1) was approximately equal to 1.19 Irish punts (or I£1.19).

must fold its hand, ending the long and contentious bidding war for IDG.

Nihal must first phone his boss, the Grand Met chairman, Mr. Allen Sheppard at his country home with a recommendation. Obviously, it is the chairman who must ultimately make the go, no-go decision. Nevertheless, Nihal must have a recommendation of his own to present. This is Nihal's first major decision since he became Mr. Sheppard's assistant, thus his judgement in this instance will be under close scrutiny. The key issue facing Nihal is whether or not he should recommend that Grand Met increase its bid for IDG, and if so by how much. He has not yet fully clarified in his own mind the business and legal ramifications of recent events but he regards it of critical importance that he decide whether Grand Met really needs IDG as part of its business operations. Moreover, should the IDG shareholders accept an increased bid, the courts in either Ireland, the United Kingdom or the European Community (EC) may rule against the Grand Met takeover. His company could conceivably find itself with a large block of shares which it then would have to unload at probably a substantial loss—not a terribly auspicious start to his career at Grand Met, he surmises.

Nihal knows he has to move fast. But first, he decides to review what he knows about the participants and events leading to the present situation. He feels like a character in one of those fast-paced thrillers. Little did he imagine, growing up in Sri Lanka, that he would one day find himself on a lovely fall afternoon in Dublin playing a poker game for the world's only producer of Irish whiskey.

The Principal Players

Irish Distillers Group

Whiskey was invented by the ancient Celts. In fact, the word whiskey comes from the Gaelic, *uisce beatha* which translated means, water of life. The Irish Distillers Group was formed in 1966 when three Irish distillers, the Cork Distilleries Company Ltd., John Jameson & Son Ltd. and John Power & Son Ltd., all established in the 18th century, merged. The acquisition in the early 1970s of the oldest whiskey distillery in the world, Old Bushmills Distillery Co. Ltd. consolidated the group's position, making it the only producer of Irish whiskey worldwide. IDG is a holding company whose principal subsidiaries engage in the businesses of whiskey distilling and blending, in addition to the distribution of spirits, wines and food. It also owns a minority share in a number of small Irish pharmaceutical companies.

By 1988, IDG employed some 1100 people throughout Ireland. Its main subsidiary, Irish Distillers Ltd. had a payroll of 530, down 200 from two years before due to ambitious rationalization and cost reduction plans by the company. IDG's shares are quoted on both the Dublin and London Stock Exchanges. While the company has 5000 shareholders, 80 percent of which reside in Ireland, the biggest block of shares is held by FII Fyffes with 20 percent. Next comes Irish Life, an Irish insurance company, with 9.7 percent. No other shareholder holds more than 5 percent of the issued share capital. The directors as a whole own about 3 percent of the shares.

IDG's consolidated balance sheet and income statements are given in Exhibit 22-1 and Exhibit 22-2, respectively. The cost of rationalization throughout the Group led to an extraordinary charge against income of I£10.4 million in 1987 reducing the profit before tax to I£2.7 million, from an all-time high of I£12.9 million the year before. Because IDG sold a 71 percent shareholding in United Drug in 1986, its sales revenue decreased from I£239.5 million to I£227.6 million between 1986 and 1987.

A breakdown of activities by sector is presented in Exhibit 22-3 which shows that about 48 percent of the Group's sales comes from

EXHIBIT 22-1

Consolidated Balance Sheet of Irish Distillers Group

	(I£000), Year Ending September	
	1987	1986
Cash	9,582	12,276
Debtors and prepayments	30,391	28,552
Loans to directors	33	34
Inventory	88,647	84,319
CURRENT ASSETS	128,653	128,181
Investment in associated companies	1,480	1,386
Unquoted investments	813	825
Deferred taxation	1,671	—
Fixed assets	59,891	58,787
TOTAL ASSETS	192,508	184,179
Creditors and accruals	42,159	38,581
Bank advances	18,982	12,319
Current taxation	1,341	1,690
Proposed dividend	3,569	3,560
CURRENT LIABILITIES	66,411	56,150
Bank advances repayable after 1 year	28,750	32,784
Taxation payable after 1 year	1,816	681
TOTAL LIABILITIES	96,977	89,615
Share capital	15,756	15,647
Capital reserve	23,666	19,967
Revenue reserve	55,708	58,580
Minority interest in companies	401	370
EQUITY	95,531	94,564
LIABILITIES and EQUITY	192,508	184,179

Source: Irish Distillers Group, 1987 Annual Report.

distilling, but a sizeable 43 percent comes from its food division.

Tradition, quality and innovation are the hallmarks of IDG's reputation. Its slogan "The Spirit of Ireland: Tradition and Quality" is an attempt to capture this image. Northern Ireland and the Irish Republic constitute IDG's biggest market. In the Republic of Ireland, IDG accounts for 80 percent of whiskey sales,

over 90 percent of gin sales and over 30 percent of vodka sales. At the same time, IDG exports to over 100 countries, with the United States, Britain, West Germany, Holland, France and duty free outlets constituting the principal export markets. A total of 61 percent of the sales of Irish whiskey take place outside the Republic of Ireland. Worldwide, Irish whiskey brands command 4 percent of the premium,

EXHIBIT 22-2

Consolidated Profit and Loss Account of Irish Distillers Group

	(I£000), Year Ending September		
	1988	1987	1986
Turnover	244,110	227,580	239,496
Trading profit before interest & depreciation	N/A	20,094	19,881
Interest	N/A	(3,733)	(3,994)
Depreciation	N/A	(3,584)	(3,228)
Trading profit	N/A	12,777	12,659
Share of profits of associated companies	N/A	349	269
Profit before exceptional item	18,502	13,126	12,928
Exceptional item	—	(10,391)	—
Profit before taxation	18,502	2,735	12,928
Taxation	(3,474)	(1,012)	(2,686)
Profit after taxation	15,028	1,723	10,242
Profit attributable to minority interest	(45)	(45)	(72)
Net profit after taxation	14,983	1,678	10,170
Retained profits, beginning of year	55,708	58,580	53,724
Dividends	N/A	(4,828)	(4,811)
Foreign currency transition adjustments	N/A	278	(503)
Retained profits, end of year	N/A	55,708	58,580
Earnings per 125p ordinary share:			
Before exceptional item	l23.70p	l17.42p	l16.28p
After exceptional item	l23.70p	l2.67p	l16.28p

Source: Irish Distillers Group, *1987 Annual Report* plus Supplementary Note (March 1989).

EXHIBIT 22-3

A Breakdown of IDG's Sales Revenue

	1987		1986	
	I£000	%	I£000	%
Distilling divisions	112,587	47	110,621	48
Agency companies	18,322	7	19,632	9
Food division	99,924	1	99,513	43
Sub-total	230,833	96	229,766	100
United drug	8,663	4	—	—
Total	239,496	100	229,766	100

Source: Irish Distillers Group, *1987 Annual Report*.

deluxe and malt market sectors. Fortunately, it is these sectors of the whiskey market which are growing while overall whiskey consumption is falling. In Britain, Irish whiskey holds 6.6 percent of the premium segment and is the fastest growing whiskey category in Britain. In West Germany and Holland, Irish whiskey commands 15.6 percent and 38.7 percent, respectively, of the premium segment.

The company's product list is presented in Exhibit 22-4. The leading brands of Irish whiskey are Jameson, Bushmills, Power's Gold Label, Paddy, Black Bush, Crested Ten and Tullamore Dew. The company recently intro-

EXHIBIT 22-4

IDG's Product List

GROUP BRANDS

Whiskeys

Power's Gold Label
Jameson
Jameson Crested Ten
Jameson 1780
Paddy
Midleton Very Rare
Bushmills
Black Bush
Bushmills Malt
Coleraine
Tullamore Dew
Dunphy's
Hewitts
Three Stills

Gins

Cork Dry
Power's Special
    Dry

Vodkas

Huzzar
Imperial Huzzar
Nordoff
Sarotov

White Rum

Kiskadee

Schnapps

Hundhaar

Liqueurs

Gallwey's Coffee
    Liqueur
Waterford Cream
Ryan's Cream

Specialty Spirits

Mulligan

Rosc

Pre-mixed Products

Snug-Hot Irish Whiskey
Irish Velvet-Irish Coffee

Wine-based Products

West Coast Cooler
Unislim Spritzer
Buck's Fizz

AGENCY PRODUCTS

These include a broad range of well-known products such as Hennessy Cognac, Dewar's Scotch Whiskey, Gordon's Gin, Sandeman Sherry, Paul Masson Wine, Grahams Port, and so forth.

Source: Irish Distillers *Annual Report, 1987.*

duced three new deluxe brands with great success, namely Jameson 1780, Bushmills Malt and Midleton Very Rare. It also launched Hundhaar schnapps, Imperial Huzzar vodka and Rosc Irish Spirit. In 1984 the company launched a wine cooler, West Coast Cooler, which became the market leader in Australia, New Zealand, Papua New Guinea and Hong Kong. It also introduced recently a number of soft drinks such as Unislim Spritzer and Buck's Fizz with the objective of broadening the base of the company's activities to reflect movements towards lifestyles which emphasize diet and fitness. The company extended its range of wine and spirits in 1969 by purchasing the Irish import house Edward Dillon & Co. and in 1984 it bought BWG Ltd., a large distributor of food and drink in Ireland.

In recent years, the company's export strategy had been to concentrate its efforts and investment behind a selected brand or at most two brands in the growth premium sector of these markets. In Britain, for example, Jameson was chosen as the premium brand based on market research and since 1985 Black Bush has been promoted in the clearly defined deluxe segment. The U.S. market, which traditionally had been the largest export market for the company, declined from 1984 onward. However, Irish whiskey sales slowed at a much slower rate than the industry in general and domestic whiskey in particular. IDG's strategy in the United States has recently been to concentrate behind its premium brands, Jameson and Bushmills and to phase out lower priced brands such as Murphy and Paddy. A geographical analysis of IDG turnover is given in Exhibit 22-5. It shows the importance of the Irish and U.K. markets to the Group as well as the dominant role of excise duty in whiskey revenue.

Grand Metropolitan Plc

Grand Met is a leading U.K.-based multinational consumer goods company that concen-

EXHIBIT 22-5

Geographical Composition
of IDG's Sales Revenue

	1987		1986	
	I£000	%	I£000	%
Sales (Excluding Excise Duty)				
Republic of Ireland & United Kingdom	148,285	64	143,978	60
Continental Europe	8,248	4	5,934	3
North America	6,396	3	8,139	3
Other	3,520	1	7,191	3
Sub-total	166,449	72	165,242	69
Excise Duty				
Republic of Ireland & United Kingdom	63,317	28	65,591	27
Subtotal	229,766	100	230,833	96
Pharmaceutical Division				
to January 1986	—	—	8,663	4
Grand Total	229,766	100	239,496	100

Source: Irish Distillers Group, *1987 Annual Report.*

EXHIBIT 22-6

Consolidated Balance Sheet
of Grand Metropolitan

	(£ MILLION), YEAR ENDING SEPTEMBER	
	1988	1987
Cash	137.8	113.4
Debtors	873.5	827.5
Inventory	761.1	733.7
Current assets	1,772.4	1,674.6
Investments	206.1	177.2
Tangible assets	3,279.4	2,725.2
Intangible assets-brands	588.3	608.0
Fixed assets	4,073.8	3,510.4
Total assets	5,846.2	5,185.0
Short-term borrowings	186.7	329.7
Other short-term creditors	1,301.3	1,166.3
Current liabilities	1,488.0	1,496.0
Long-term borrowings	702.4	1,141.9
Other long-term creditors	162.6	103.3
Other long-term liabilities/charges	55.1	70.4
Long-term liabilities	920.1	1,315.6
Total Liabilities	2,408.1	2,811.6
Share capital	442.5	440.9
Retained earnings & reserves	2,964.2	1,904.2
Minority interest	31.4	28.3
Equity	3,438.1	2,373.4
Total Liabilities + Equity	5,846.2	5,185.0

Source: Grand Metropolitan, *1988 Annual Report.*

trates on the food, drinks and retailing business. Grand Met's consolidated balance sheet and income statements are presented in Exhibit 22-6 and Exhibit 22-7, respectively.

In recent years, Grand Met has narrowed considerably its range of operations. Its stated objective, as articulated in its recent annual reports, is to become one of the top half-dozen international companies in each of its strategic sectors of operations: namely food, drinks and retailing. As part of this strategy, it sold in September 1988 its Inter-Continental Hotels chain, while at the same time it purchased Pillsbury in the United States. A further objective of the company is to strike a geographical balance between its operations in western Europe, North America and Japan/Far East. As Exhibit 22-8 shows, this objective is still far from target, since 56 percent of its trading

profit in 1988 came from operations in the United Kingdom and Ireland, and 35 percent from North America.

The key ingredients for a successful pursuit of Grand Met's strategy are illustrated in the following statement by the chairman, Mr. Allen Sheppard:

Brand building and distribution are key success factors in most areas of Grand Metropolitan's business. The evidence of Grand Metropolitan's brand

EXHIBIT 22-7

Consolidated Profit and Loss Account of Grand Metropolitan

	(£ MILLION), YEAR ENDING SEPTEMBER	
	1988	1987
Turnover	6,028.8	5,705.5
Operating Costs	(5,386.7)	(5,111.8)
Share of Profits of Related Companies	(11.5)	(7.9)
Trading Profit	653.6	571.6
Reorganization Costs	(24.6)	(9.3)
Profits on Sale of Property	39.1	14.0
Interest	(93.0)	(120.2)
Profit Before Taxation	575.1	456.1
Taxation	(154.8)	(120.1)
Profit After Taxation	420.3	336.0
Minority Shareholders & Preferred Dividends	(8.3)	(2.8)
Profit Attributable to Ordinary Shareholders	412.0	333.2
Extraordinary Items	289.7	127.8
Ordinary Dividends	(129.1)	(103.1)
Transferred to Reserves	572.6	357.9
Reserves, Beginning of Year	1,296.4	1,606.5
Capitalization of Brands	608.0	119.3
Reserves, Beginning of Year (Restated)	1,904.2	1,725.8
Retained Profit for the Year	572.6	357.9
Adjustments (Property, Currency, Goodwill)	487.4	(179.5)
Reserves, End of Year	2964.2	1,904.2
EPS	48.0p	38.9p

Source: Grand Metropolitan, *1988 Annual Report*.

EXHIBIT 22-8

Grand Metropolitan Trading Profit, 1988

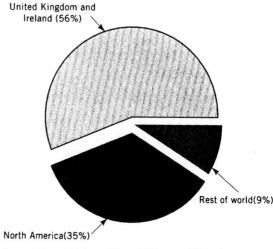

Source: Grand Metropolitan, *1988 Annual Report*.

particularly in the increasingly important markets of the Far East and, in preparation for 1992, in all countries of the EEC. The smooth integration of Heublein, Almaden, and Saccone and Speed illustrates our ability to work on an amicable basis with acquired companies and quickly get benefits therefrom.[2]

In the first six months of 1988 Grand Met made the following significant acquisitions and divestitures:

March 1988	Disposal of 701 tenanted pubs
April/May 1988	Acquisitions of Vision Express and Eye + Tech
June 1988	Disposal of U.S. soft drink operations

A summary of Grand Met highlights during the first nine months of 1988 is presented in Exhibit 22-9.

A key corporate strategy is that, instead of spending a great deal of money promoting

led strategy is excellently illustrated in our wines and spirits operations, where worldwide leadership is constantly being strengthened by the addition and development of new brands, while distribution and sales for well established brands continues to be reinforced. Widening distribution of our brands is of major importance and this is being successfully addressed, both with partners and independently,

[2]Grand Metropolitan, *1988 Annual Report*.

EXHIBIT 22-9

Highlights of the Year 1988,
Grand Metropolitan

January	Long-term agreement signed with Holstein Brauerei.
	ADR facility established in New York.
	£500 million commercial paper program established.
February	£150 million pension surplus established.
March	Sale of 701 smaller tenanted properties for £80 million.
	Intrepreneur 20-year assignable lease scheme announced.
	Meurice Hotel in Paris sold for £35 million.
April	J. Thayer & Sons acquired by Express.
	Pearle acquired by Vision Express Superstores for $40 million.
	Healthworks specialty snack chain acquired by Grand Met Retailing.
	Eden Vale launched Ski Cool yogurt-based drink nationally.
May	Eye + Tech Superstores acquired for $32 million by Pearle.
	Listing on Swiss stock exchanges.
June	U.S. soft drink interests sold to PepsiCo for $705 million.
	First Greenfield site Berni restaurant opened in Stratford-Avon.
	Kaysens acquired by Express.
July	£5.8 million expansion in Northern Ireland by Express Foods Group.
	First Berni franchise deal signed with Mansfield Inns.
August	Marketing and distribution agreement signed with Seagrams.
	Mecca Bookmakers gets exclusive rights for off-course betting in Malaysia.
September	Agreement to sell Inter-Continental Hotels to The Saison Group of Japan for around $2 billion.

Source: Grand Metropolitan, *1988 Annual Report*.

Grand Met itself, resources are spent on promoting individual brands. In drinks, unlike Guinness and Seagram which rely on prestige brands like Johnnie Walker and Chivas Regal, Grand Met figures out what consumers like and then creates a product to fit that demand. Examples of this are Bailey's Irish Cream, Piat d'Or and Malibu. The company also has a reputation for running a lean operation, disdaining the pomp and waste of most big corporations.[3] When it acquired Pillsbury in the United States, for example, 1200 staff were dismissed at Pillsbury and at subsidiary Burger King's Miami office.

The approximate breakdown in sales of Grand Met's operations are drinks (38%), food (18%), retailing and property (26%) and other activities (18%). In recent years, the company has carried out a comprehensive restructuring of its operations, getting rid of businesses that did not fit in with its consumer-marketing focus. Its Pillsbury acquisition, for example, added names like Poppin' Fresh dough, Green Giant vegetables and Häagen-Dazs ice cream. The company has had particular success in its drinks operations and is now trying to replicate this in food and retailing.

The following is a brief summary of Grand Met's four major operations:

1. The drinks sector, its biggest profit source, is composed of its international wines and spirits operations and its U.K. brewing operations. This sector operates under the overall title, International Distillers and Vintners (IDV). The wines and spirits side of IDV is an international organization of

[3]"We've Got a Serious Problem," *Forbes*, December 25, 1989.

wine and spirit producers, distillers, importers, exporters and distributors. It markets and develops leading brands in over 200 markets worldwide. As one of the world's largest wines and spirits operations, IDV's annual sales are in excess of 90 million cases—the world leader in liquor case sales. Grand Metropolitan Brewing operates five regional companies, five breweries, 3650 pubs, and has a portfolio of 28 draught and 38 packaged beers, including four international brands brewed under license. IDV has developed its business by building brands. It now owns 15 wine and spirits brands, each of which sells over 1 million cases a year, and it acts as importer to three additional brands. Its own brands include Smirnoff, Gilbey's Gin, Bailey's Irish Cream and J&B Scotch Whiskey. It owns a host of California wines such as Christian Brothers, Almaden, Inglenook and Beaulieu.

2. As the eighth-largest world food products producer, Grand Met's food sector is composed of branded dairy-based and other food products in the United Kingdom and Ireland and branded petfoods in the United States. Express Foods Group (International) operates through seven divisions in the United Kingdom and Ireland which manufacture and market dairy and non-dairy products. It produces many well-known brands and is a major supplier of private-label products to U.K. retail chains. Its ALPO Petfoods is a major manufacturer and supplier of petfoods and the market leader in canned dog food in the United States. In acquiring Pillsbury Company and its Burger King chain, Grand Met now has more restaurant outlets worldwide than any company except PepsiCo.

3. Grand Met's retailing and property activities sector consists of companies which manage multiple unit branded retail operations and associated property interests. Pearle in the United States is the world's largest retailer of eyecare products and services. It operates 1300 outlets, which are mainly located in the United States. Grand Metropolitan Retailing operates 1500 pubs, over 450 branded restaurants and 1400 hotel rooms primarily in the United Kingdom. Grand Met also operates a specialist drinks retailer, bookmakers and property service.

4. In the other areas of activities, Grand Met's main interests are casinos, such as London Clubs, Golden Nugget and the Cannes Casino, hotels and account card services. The sale of Inter-Continental Hotels for $2 billion is consistent with its emphasis on concentrating on its strategic business sectors.

Pernod-Ricard

Pernod, a French family company, is a leading wines and spirits producer which owns the world's third largest selling spirits brand. Its net profit margin on sales of FFr12.5 billion (approximately $2 billion) was 5.7 percent in 1987. As Exhibit 22-10 shows, its French wines and spirits division is the largest contributor to profits. A breakdown of these profits shows that 75 percent came from the French market. These profits in turn are concentrated on a small number of alcoholic products. Overseas, despite aggressive promotion, the entire foreign non-alcoholic drinks and products division contributed a mere FFr12 million to operating profits.

The company's top selling brand in France is Ricard, with about 7.4 million cases a year, followed by Pastis 51 with annual sales of 2.4 million cases, and then the aperitif Suze, with 1.6 million cases per year. The vast majority of Pernod's profits comes from Pastis which is difficult to export because its aniseed flavor is not too palatable outside France itself. Yet there is not much room to expand in France because its Ricard and Pastis 51 brands have such enormous market shares.

EXHIBIT 22-10

Trading Profit of Pernod-Ricard by Sector

	1987	
	Ffr (million)	%
France		
Wines & Spirits	4.997	47%
Non-alcoholic Beverages & Products	3.035	28%
Exports and Abroad		
Wines & Spirits	1.787	17%
Non-alcoholic Beverages & Products	3.035	8%
Total	12.854	100%

Source: *Financial Times*, September 5, 1988.

The company has expanded in recent years through a number of French acquisitions. For instance, last year it bought the distillery that produces the champagne Carlton. However, it has also gone searching outside its traditional drinks sector, by spending FFr645 million on a 3 percent stake in the recently privatized banking and investment conglomerate, Compagnie Financiere de Suez. In addition, it spent a considerable sum on a stock buy-back plan, purchasing 5 percent of its equity.

Overseas, Pernod made a number of recent acquisitions. In the United States, it purchased Austin Nichols, with its subsidiary Boulevard Distilleries and the Wild Turkey bourbon label. It also owns the Scotch whiskey brand, Clan Campbell.

In the nonalcoholic market, Pernod licenses in France brands like Coca-Cola and Fanta, while it also sells its own brands such as Orangina and Pampryl. It bought the Yoo Hoo chocolate drink company in the United States and has made concerted efforts to expand sales of its soft drink Orangina. Pernod is at

EXHIBIT 22-11

A Comparison of Sales Revenue of Competing Firms

1987 Sales Revenue

Grand Met:	£705.5 million	£507.5 million
Pernod:	FFr12.5 billion	£1.2 billion
IDG:	I£229.8 million	£193.3 million

Source: Corporate Annual Reports.

present embroiled in a legal battle with Coca-Cola, where the latter is trying to get back its French concessions for its Coke, Fanta, Sprite and Finley brands.

Comparing Size

Using the average exchange rates in effect during the bidding process, May 1988 to September 1988: £1 = I£1.19 = FFr10.4 = $1.82, Exhibit 22-11 gives a comparison of the sales revenue of the three companies in this case.

Thus, Pernod is about twice as big as Grand Met, which in turn is about 30 times as big as IDG.

Government Intervention and the Bidding Contest

Events have moved at a fast and furious pace in the bidding war for IDG. In May 1988, Grand Met and Allied-Lyons, two of Britain's biggest drinks groups set up an Irish joint venture, GC & C Brands, specifically to take over IDG. GC & C was 50 percent owned by Gilbeys, an Irish subsidiary of Grand Met and 50 percent owned by C & C, which in turn was a subsidiary of Allied-Lyons. The Guinness Group, in turn, owned 49.6 percent of C & C. The make-up of this venture was unusual in that Grand Met and Allied-Lyons were rivals in the international drinks business. On May 30th, GC & C Brands made a bid of I315p per share in cash for IDG. The consortium's plan was that C & C would take over the marketing and distribution of the Bushmills, Powers and Tullamore Dew whiskey brands as well as Huzzar vodka and distribute them internationally through the Hiram Walker-Allied network. Gilbeys would concentrate on the Jameson and Paddy whiskey brands, as well as Cork Dry gin.

Because of the GC & C Brands bid, IDG shares closed Monday, May 30 at I340p per share, up from the previous Friday's close of I275p per share. The board of IDG immediately rejected the bid, asserting that the bid was "an attempt to break up the Irish whiskey industry whereby famous brands like Jameson, Powers, Paddy and Bushmills would end up in the hands of multinational companies, where they would be dominated by a wide variety of much larger brands."[4]

On June 30, IDG made a formal complaint to the European Commission stating that the bid contravened EC competition policy, specifically articles 85 and 86 of the Treaty of Rome. IDG called on the Commission to fine Grand Met, Guinness and Allied-Lyons a sum equal to 10 percent of their combined turnover or L1.2 billion. IDG's contention was that each of the bidders was on its own a potential acquirer of IDG. Hence, they argued "their concerted action prevents competition that might otherwise occur between independent companies seeking to strengthen their position through a corporate acquisition."[5]

What made this situation so intriguing was that it formed a nice backdrop to the haggling then going on in the EC regarding merger policy. At the time, the Commission's power

to take preemptive action had been restricted to cases of anti-competitive behavior. It could be argued that in this case, the GC & C consortium's breaking up IDG would in fact increase overall competition. Up to that point, the Commission could only take action against mergers after the fact. Clearly, for those angling for a greater Commission role in international mergers, the IDG saga provided a wonderful opportunity to set a precedent.

On July 6, the Irish Minister for Industry referred the consortium bid to the Irish Fair Trade Commission. This body had the right to prevent the takeover should it deem that permitting it would have a negative impact on competition or on employment in Ireland. One day later, IDG forecasted record profits, earnings and dividends for the year up to September. Not surprisingly, these figures were dismissed by the consortium as lacking credibility.

IDG decided to play a nationalist card. An advertisement campaign was mounted on billboards and newspapers with the slogan "Keep the Irish in Whiskey." The IDG board argued that the takeover process was about the future of Irish business and its ability to compete independently in the international marketplace. It warned that if the bid was successful IDG would be moved to England with severe implications for the Irish business community.

By July 19, acceptances had been received by GC & C for 20.21 percent of IDG shares. This included, the 20.02 percent owned by FII Fyffes. The same day, GC & C extended their bid by three weeks, namely to August 8. On July 29, the Commission ruled that the bid did indeed contravene EC competition rules. It stated that the three drinks companies had not competed with one another, thereby contravening the normal laws of competition by launching a joint bid through the consortium. It gave the consortium two weeks to answer its complaints and asked it to cease buying shares in IDG. At this stage, the second closing date for acceptance was Monday, August 8

[4] *Financial Times*, May 31, 1988.

[5] *Financial Times*, July 1, 1988.

and GC & C had only until the following Friday, August 12 to increase its bid. Shares dropped in the United Kingdom by 11p to 294p a share as a result of the ruling. On August 9, the number of acceptances were still at 20.34 percent, so the bid was extended until August 19.

Meanwhile, the U.K. Takeover Panel in London was also looking at the bid since IDG argued that it contravened its rules against collusion. On August 12, IDG confirmed that Pernod-Ricard had taken a less than 1 percent stake in IDG. On August 17, the European Commission forced the complete breakup of the consortium but it did allow each of the three companies the freedom to make independent bids. It also freed FII Fyffes from its commitment to sell its 20.02 percent to the consortium, thereby not giving any of the three consortium companies any advantage in a new bid. On the other hand, U.K. Takeover Panel rules stated that a bidder making an illegal bid cannot do so for 12 months. The EC agreed to a proposal from the consortium that Allied-Lyons and Guinness sell their stake in GC & C to Grand Met, which could then continue with the original bid. IDG had argued that since Grand Met was part of the consortium bid that was broken up, it therefore should not be allowed to bid again for another 12 months.

On August 19, the Takeover Panel allowed Grand Met to make a new bid. The rationale was that the shareholders of IDG had not really had an opportunity to consider the merits of the case. Nobody, except some Irish newspaper columnists, seemed to find it at all peculiar that a British government body was dictating what was in the best interests of the IDG shareholders, 80 percent of whom were citizens of another sovereign country, the Irish Republic. Grand Met, on that same day August 19, launched a new bid, 1400p per share in cash or guaranteed loan notes. Under the Takeover Panel rules, Grand Met was not allowed to extend the bid after September 12th or increase it unless a competing bid emerged

in the interim. The bid closing date was set for September 12. IDG shares closed that night at 1390p each, up 120p from the previous close.

It did not take IDG long to reject the new bid. On August 22, Mr. Joe McCabe, chairman of IDG stated that the Grand Met bid did not "adequately reflect the true worth of the company, its profitability and future potential."[6]

Pernod, meanwhile stated at this time that it was "not planning to bid for Irish Distillers nor considering becoming a minority shareholder."[7] When IDG announced a day later that it was examining a number of approaches, investors were puzzled given the Pernod announcement. Guinness, Allied-Lyon and Suntory were understood not to be in the running and Seagrams, which had a year before sold its stake in IDG had a distribution agreement with Grand Met allowing it access to its whiskey brands should they be acquired by Grand Met.

A day later the white knight emerged, lo and behold! none other than Pernod itself. It announced that it had an undisclosed stake in IDG, was having discussions with IDG management and would announce its intentions the following week. Clearly, IDG management welcomed a bid from Pernod since Grand Met planned to break up and perhaps sell the Bushmills, Power's, Tullamore Dew and Huzzar brands whereas Pernod promised to keep them together. IDG management was also keenly aware of Grand Met's reputation for running a lean operation and for cleaning house after a takeover.

On August 30, the Irish Minister for Industry and Commerce, expressing concern that there was no Irish representation on the London-based U.K. Takeover Panel, said he intended to ultimately make the decision on whether the bid should proceed. In addition, he referred the Grand Met bid to the Irish Fair Trade Commission. On August 31, IDG shares

---

[6]*Financial Times*, August 23, 1988.

[7]Ibid.

were pushed up 113p to 1420p per share. A day later Pernod announced that it had increased its stake to 2.8 percent from less than 1 percent. It had until Monday September 5 to launch a rival bid to that of Grand Met. On Thursday, September 2, Grand Met said it intended to fight any Pernod bid, an unusual step, apparently a warning that was aimed at FII Fyffes not to throw in its lot with Pernod.

At this stage, Pernod was understood to have increased its stake to 5 percent but was keen not to get into a long drawn-out fight with Grand Met. Grand Met's share in IDG was 6.5 percent. IDG said the Grand Met pledge to fight proved that Grand Met's bid was not high enough. Shares rose on September 2nd to 1430p per share.

On Saturday, September 4, Pernod was in negotiations with FI Fyffes and Irish Life. Nihal had received information from a "mole" that there was a verbal commitment between the parties. He found the description, "Hands were shaken on the deal and backs were slapped," amusing. However, the agreement would not be signed until Sunday at 4:00 PM. Nihal phoned FII Fyffes and got an undertaking that it would not agree to sell to Pernod if Grand Met would increase its bid to 1525p per share immediately, a whopping 1125p over its previous bid and 175p over Pernod's proposed bid. Nihal was told that Irish Life had already signed an agreement that conditional on Pernod getting at least 45 percent of the shares in irrevocable commitments it would sell its 9.8 percent share. Apparently, several smaller shareholders had also given irrevocable undertakings to Pernod on the basis of the proposed 1450p per share bid.

With these events forming a backdrop, Nihal had his bankers approach the U.K. Takeover Panel. They received the permission of the Executive Committee of the Takeover Panel to increase their bid, waiving Rule 35 of its Takeover Code, the Committee ruling that Pernod's approaches to the IDG should be treated as a competitive bid. The Executive Committee's view was that it was correct to treat the Pernod proposal of 1450p per share, under which they would have secured control of the company before launching a formal bid, as being a bid in all but name.

Legal and Business Ramifications

If Grand Met does bid 1525p per share, Nihal believes that Pernod will immediately take FII Fyffes to court in Ireland asking for a restraint on that company getting out of the verbal agreement to sell to Pernod at 1450p per share. Pernod's argument would be based on the severe financial loss suffered, should it not now be able to secure the FII Fyffes stake. The Irish High Court would then have to decide if FII Fyffes had entered into a binding agreement with Pernod. If so, should Grand Met begin to buy shares at 1525p each and be later forced to sell back to Pernod it stands to lose a considerable sum of money. At the moment, Grand Met owns 12.1 percent of IDG shares. Under Irish Law, a company needs acceptances from 80 percent of shareholders before it can apply for compulsory acquisition procedures. Should Grand Met increase its share to 20 percent, then it could block Pernod's bid.

Grand Met's lawyers have told Nihal that their company should complain to the European Commission that the arrangement between IDG and Pernod has as its objective the elimination of competition in the bidding process. As the GC & C consortium bid showed, the Commission is only too anxious to get involved in this case in order to stake out more clearly the limits of EC competition policy. Moreover, the commissioner in charge of EC competition is an Irishman, Mr. Peter Sutherland, with close links to the Irish business and political establishment. Grand Met will claim that the irrevocable undertakings between Pernod and the shareholders prevented all shareholders from being able to consider Grand Met's higher bid. EC competition rules outlaw any anti-competitive agreement, such as the earlier abortive consortium bid by GC & C.

The full U.K. Takeover Panel could either accept or reject an anticipated appeal by Pernod that Grand Met increase its bid to I525p per share, thereby pre-empting Pernod's I450p per share bid. The Executive Committee said that it had permission to do so because Pernod's bid was a bid in all but name. Yet, Grand Met's bid had been declared a final one at the request of the panel unless a competing bid emerged. Grand Met's argument would be that Pernod's maneuvering was in affect a bid. Also the U.K. Takeover Panel must decide if Pernod broke the U.K. Takeover Code by gaining irrevocable acceptances from FII Fyffes and another 18.8 percent from over 600 other shareholders.

The U.K. Takeover Panel, however, does not have the power to overrule the Irish High Court. Yet, if the Irish Court does uphold the binding nature of the agreement between FII Fyffes and Pernod, the U.K. Takeover Panel will be the one to decide whether the Takeover Code was broken—that is, were shareholders that weekend given enough time, information and advice before pledging their shares to Pernod? Of course, the Irish High Court could also rule that the code was breached but that the transgression was not serious enough that the shareholders should be released from their commitments.

The Irish Fair Trade Commission and Minister for Industry and Commerce must also approve the Pernod bid. Nihal's feeling is that they will allow the Pernod bid given its pledge regarding the maintenance of Irish employment. He believes the Irish Government has received a verbal commitment from Pernod that it will not dispose of any IDG Brands without the approval of the Minister.

Nihal is aware of Pernod's reputation. It has ambitions to play on the world stage but

EXHIBIT 22-12

Irish Distillers Group
Average Monthly Share Price

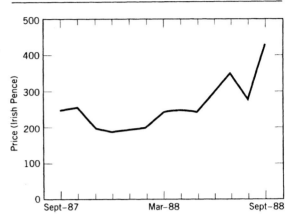

Source: *Financial Times*, September 6, 1988.

as he heard it put, "cannot summon up the nerve to pay the sort of price that ambition now requires."[8] Its dilly-dallying in the last few weeks about buying IDG suggested it was a company that had not yet made up its mind about its future. The company is not short of cash, and with its low debt level, some Ffr273 million of medium and long-term debt, analysts estimate it could provide around FFr8 billion at short notice. He knows that even if the IDG board is rooting for Pernod the French will have to show they have both the stomach and resolve to externally grow through acquisition. In Nihal's opinion, a substantially increased bid by Grand Met could shock Pernod out of this contest.

Another issue to be considered is that Grand Met has joint drinks-distribution arrangements in Japan, the United States and Brazil with Pernod. It wants to preserve these agreements so that if it loses to Pernod and ends up with, say, 30 percent of the shares it will have to sell, since Pernod has warned Grand Met

[8]*Financial Times*, September 5, 1988.

that it will find it hard to run IDG with Grand Met as a big minority shareholder.

Nihal takes one last look at his laptop (Exhibit 22-12) which shows movements in the IDG shares over the past year. Then he reaches for the telephone to phone Mr. Sheppard with his recommendation.

The Assignment

1. Should Nihal proceed with the bid? Explain why or why not.

2. If he decides to proceed, how much should he bid for IDG shares? What is the P/E ratio for comparable companies in the United Kingdom and the United States?

3. Show possible scenarios in the event that Nihal bids, and then Grand Met either takes over IDG, or is forced to divest by one of the courts.

4. Examine the feasibility of the bid for IDG in terms of the internal rate of return (IRR) model from Grand Met's perspective. Prepare a seven-year cash flow for IDG (by an extrapolation of the past couple of years). Do you think that Grand Met shareholders stand to lose if its I520p per share bid is not accepted?

5. How should Grand Met fund the proposed acquisition of IDG? Which source of funds is more attractive—internal funding, revolving Euronotes or Eurobonds? Explain your findings by citing actual data.

6. How do you feel about IDG management's role in the takeover proceedings? Whose welfare are they most concerned about? What is your opinion on the ethics of FII Fyffes actions?

7. In the EC of 1992, mergers and acquisitions are likely to become widespread. Survey the anti-competitive regulations in the EC and several major countries. Prepare a comparative analysis of these regulations. Determine how different is the national anti-competitive legislation from the EC model?

The Ginza Motor Corporation, Ltd.

Japanese Investment in the U.S. Motor Vehicle Parts Industry

HARVEY A. PONIACHEK

The U.S. Motor Vehicle Parts and Accessories Industry

An automobile is composed of over 20,000 parts and accessories, which are classified by the Department of Commerce, *U.S. Industrial Outlook 1989*, in terms of several Standard Industrial Classifications (SICs): automotive parts and accessories (SIC 3714); automotive stamping (SIC 3465); carburetors, pistons and rings (SIC 3592); vehicular lighting equipment (SIC 3647); storage batteries (SIC 3691); and engine electrical equipment (SIC 3694).

The main business of the motor vehicle parts and accessories industry is to supply original equipment manufacturers (OEM) and automakers parts and components. The industry also provides replacement parts to the aftermarket. The value of products and services sold by the U.S. motor vehicle parts industry reached approximately $90 billion in 1989, of which parts and accessories accounted for two-thirds.

The U.S. motor vehicle parts industry's performance is affected by several factors:

1. The health of the auto manufacturing industry, with which it has generally experienced similar business cycles.

2. The market share of the Big 3 U.S. automakers (i.e., GM, Ford, and Chrysler), which has declined in recent years. Most foreign car manufacturers in the United States do not use American-made original parts and accessories.

3. The Japanese output (capacity) share of the U.S. registered vehicles, which could reach 15 percent, or 2 million cars and light trucks, by the early 1990s. The increased Japanese auto manufacturing and assembly in the United States rely primarily on imports of the major components and original equipment from Japan. They are increasingly turning to Japanese manufacturers of parts in the United States,

4. Quality, cost, and delivery schedules are the critical considerations in auto parts competitiveness, whereas quality control continues to be a major issue confronting the industry. Also, U.S. Big 3 shifted some of the responsibility for product design, research and development onto parts producers.

Demand for auto parts is expected to advance in the medium and long term at 2 to 3 percent annually. Foreign competition for automotive parts will remain keen, especially in the Japanese aftermarket. The industry is in

431

the process of internationalization with major implications on output, prices and earnings. Foreign sourcing of parts will continue to exert pressure on the U.S. companies. Many U.S. companies are seeking business with Japanese auto manufacturers but with limited success. Japanese parts makers in the United States supply primarily Japanese vehicle makers in the United States, but they could attempt in the long run to challenge the traditional U.S. suppliers of the Big 3 auto manufacturers. (For further information on the Japanese auto-parts industry please see the following references: Yuzo Yamaguchi, "Japanese Firms Settle for 'Parts' of the U.S. Automotive Market," *Economic World*, August 1989, pp. 34–37; "Japanese Automobiles: Made in the U.S.A.," *Economic World*, August 1988, p. 21–26.)

Coming to America: Following the Customers

The sharp appreciation of the Japanese yen since 1985 raised significantly the cost of auto manufacturing and assembling in Japan, including the cost of parts manufacturing and procurement, labor and shipping cost. The Yen appreciation combined with an attempt to preempt the local content legislation, induced many Japanese companies to go abroad and locate near their markets as an alternative to manufacturing at home.

All the Japanese car makers are involved to some extent in manufacturing or assembling in the United States. As Japanese automakers shift their production facilities to the United States, Japanese auto-parts makers have begun to move with them.

There are currently more than 300 Japanese-owned plants producing automotive components in the United States, with an expected capacity to produce $8 billion worth of parts by the early 1990s. The influx into the United States of Japanese motor vehicle parts makers will induce domestic parts sourcing by

Japanese automakers in the United States, but to a lesser extent from traditional U.S. suppliers.

Unlike their American counterparts, Japanese auto companies in the United States buy all but the most crucial components of their vehicles from outside suppliers. They establish a "pyramid" of relationships with these companies, with the automakers at the top, a number of parts suppliers below, and the suppliers of raw materials on the next level below.

Japanese automakers frequently secure their relationship with component supplier companies by acquiring a share of their equity. Many car makers also set up an association of cooperative parts makers with selected suppliers, known as a *Kyoryokukai*. Most of the Japanese parts companies are members of the automotive association or family-like structure that characterizes the Japanese auto industry. These relationships are a major impediment to the ability of U.S. parts makers to sell to the Japanese auto manufacturers in Japan and in the United States.

These ties have drawn severe criticism in recent years from U.S. parts suppliers, who claim that these relationships constitute unfair competition. Therefore, the Japan Auto Parts Industries Association (JAPIA) recommended in 1987 that members establishing U.S. operations should attempt to do so through joint ventures with U.S. parts manufacturers, rather than under the auspices of a Japanese car maker. However, the JAPIA recommendation had relatively little impact. Some Japanese companies suggest that coming to America through a joint venture is very difficult because of different management styles, and perception about investment payoffs.

Some companies are establishing joint ventures in order to mitigate the U.S. allegation about pyramid car and parts-makers relationships. Benefits of a joint venture are technology exchanges and readily available markets and clients. Japanese auto makers have contracts with U.S. motor parts suppliers when they establish their manufacturing activities here, so new companies can become motor parts suppliers when the auto makers expand or add new models.

Japanese parts suppliers do substantial business with U.S. auto makers and fiercely compete with U.S. vendors. The Japanese auto makers are importing parts from the United States in order to satisfy government demand.

The Japanese Company

The Japanese company, Ginza Motors Company Ltd. (Ginza) of Tokyo, was established in 1920 and is primarily engaged in the manufacturing and sales of hydraulic equipment, shock absorbers, and special-purpose vehicles. The firm is a member of Toyota's part association in Japan, but they don't have any similar relationship with the Toyota company in the United States. Toyota's spokesperson suggested that associate relations, the pyramid of auto maker/supplier relationships do not hold in the United States, and that Toyota in Japan is also trying to broaden its suppliers base.

Ginza's sales in the year ended March 31, 1989 exceeded $998 million and total assets were $871 million. Financial data are available in Exhibit 23-1. The company is public and listed on Tokyo, Osaka, and Nagoya Stock Exchanges. Ginza has done business in the United States through its wholly-owned subsidiary, Ginza Corporation of America, Inc. (Ginza USA), a wholesale distributor of motor parts, which was incorporated in the early 1970s. Sales for the year ended on March 31, 1989 were almost $5 million and assets were $3.5 million. See Exhibit 23-2 for financial data. The firm has a well developed product line and a loyal customer base, particularly among Japanese automakers. Ginza USA is currently doing business with 110 parts suppliers, of which 50 percent are American companies, 32

EXHIBIT 23-1

Ginza Motors Corporation, Ltd., Tokyo
Consolidated Balance Sheet
(Year Ended March 31,
thousands of dollars)

ASSETS	1989	1988	1987
Cash	28,272	26,038	23,955
Marketable securities	8,556	6,344	5,836
Trade receivables	243,666	247,782	227,959
Inventories	186,464	200,017	184,016
Other current assets	30,600	29,895	27,503
Total Current Assets	497,558	510,075	469,269
Total property & equipment	481,944	487,579	448,573
Less accumulated deprec.	251,040	248,767	228,866
Net property & equipment	230,904	248,812	228,907
Investment & other assets	128,344	126,143	116,051
Foreign currency trans, adj.	15,008	21,912	20,159
Total Assets	871,814	896,942	825,186
Liabilities			
Short-term loans	277,820	291,957	268,600
Debt due	19,230	1,825	1,679
Notes & account payables	166,734	178,320	164,054
Accrued expenses	29,208	29,446	27,090
Accrued taxes	6,364	6,455	5,938
Other current liabilities	12,000	10,229	9,411
Total current liabilities	511,356	518,231	476,773
Long-term debt	193,924	192,158	176,785
Retirement benefits	29,560	31,545	29,021
Other long-term liabilities	15,526	12,038	11,075
Minority interest	6,030	6,113	5,624
Common stock	31,942	40,025	36,823
Capital surplus	54,348	61,036	56,153
Legal reserve	3,294	3,346	3,078
Retained earnings	25,834	32,451	29,855
Shareholders' equity	115,418	136,857	125,909
Total Liability & Stockholders' Equity	871,814	896,942	825,186

Consolidated Income Statement
(Year ended March 31, thousands of dollars)

	1989	1988	1987
Net sales	998,430	982,500	903,900
Cost of sales	748,430	724,767	666,786
Selling, general and administrative expenses	232,644	220,961	203,284
Operating income	29,432	36,773	33,831
Interest & dividend income	11,192	12,630	11,619
Interest expenses	27,560	27,399	25,207
Other expenses, net	4,140	4,045	3,722
Extraordinary charge	0	2,534	2,331
Income before taxes	8,924	15,425	14,191

(Continued)

ASSETS	1989	1988	1987
Income taxes	7,996	9,387	8,636
Minority interest	324	491	451
Foreign currency translation			
adjustment	15,448	6,549	6,025
Net Income	16,052	12,096	11,128
Previously retained earnings	12,474	24,280	22,338
Merger of consolidated			
subsidiaries	88	150	138
Cash dividends	2,946	2,306	2,122
Transfers	312	250	230
Bonuses	166	171	157
Foreign currency translation			
adjustment	820	1,047	963
Retained earnings	25,834	32,451	29,855

EXHIBIT 23-2

Ginza Corporation of America, Inc. Statement of Conditions (Year ended March 31, thousands of dollars)

ASSETS	1989	1988	1987
Cash	179	175	337
Mrktable securities	0	519	0
Receivables	721	584	559
Inventories	926	696	703
Raw materials	0	0	0
Work in progress	0	0	0
Finished goods	0	0	0
Notes receivable	0	0	0
Other current assets	71	117	79
Total current assets	1,898	2,091	1,677
Property, plant & equipment	2,358	1,473	1,232
Accumulated depreciation	783	648	552
Net property & equipment	1,575	825	680
Invest & adv to subs	0	0	0
Other non-cur assets	0	0	0
Deferred charges	0	0	0
Intangibles	65	58	0
Deposits & other assets	0	0	34
Total assets	3,538	2,974	2,392
LIABILITIES AND STOCKHOLDERS' EQUITY			
Notes payable	0	0	0
Accounts payable	544	172	191
Current-long-term debt	18	12	11
Current port cap leases	0	0	0
Accured expenses	71	35	135
Income taxes	24	196	0
Other current liability	62	58	0
Total current liability	719	472	338
Mortgages	0	0	0
Deferred charges / (income)	102	86	56
Convertible debt	0	0	0
Long-term debt	107	77	89
Non-current capital leases	0	0	0
Other long-term liability	0	0	0
Total liabilities	928	635	482
Minority interest (liabilities)	0	0	0
Preferred stock	0	0	0
Common stock net	117	116	115
Capital surplus	1,493	1,432	1,351
Retained earnings	1,049	824	444
Treasury stock	0	0	0
Other liabilities	(50)	(34)	0
Shareholder equity	2,610	2,339	1,910
Tot liability & net worth	3,538	2,974	2,392

Statement of Income and Expenses

Net sales	4,863	4,552	4,235
Cost of goods	3,294	2,956	2,636
Gross profit	1,569	1,597	1,599
R&D expenditures	228	230	275
Selling, general and			
administrative expenses	1,019	760	797
Income before depreciation			
and amortization	322	606	526
Depreciation & Amortization	0	0	0
Non-operating income	24	39	(119)
Interest expense	0	7	8
Income before tax	346	638	399
Provisions for income taxes	121	257	69
Minority interest / (income)	0	0	0
Invest gains / losses	0	0	0
Other income	0	0	0
Net income before			
extraordinary items	225	380	330
Extraordinary items			
& discontinued operations	0	0	0
Net income	225	380	330

percent are Japanese suppliers, and 18 percent are U.S.–Japanese joint ventures.

Because exporting from Japan to their U.S. clients has become increasingly difficult due to the yen/$ exchange rate in the past several years, Ginza USA seeks to follow its clients to the United States by establishing itself in a Midwestern or Southern state. The corporation considers a broad range of options, including a possible acquisition of a U.S. firm, a joint venture with a U.S. company—but with a Japanese majority ownership and an option of full ownership in a decade—or a de novo start up. The Japanese have not yet determined which corporate organization—that is, a branch or subsidiary—is the most suitable, and what are the tax implications of their strategy.

Funding of this venture will be available from internally generated sources, a Japanese pension fund, Japanese offshore banks and Japanese banks in the United States, as well as other relatively cheap sources. Some Japanese companies have entered into joint ventures in the United States to avoid a high investment for local production.

The U.S. Target Company

Ginza USA contracted the investment banking services of Merrill-Lynch for assistance in identifying and negotiating the acquisition, entirely or partially, of a suitable firm in the auto-parts manufacturing business. The investment bank provided Ginza information on the U.S. target companies, which is available in Exhibit 23-3.

The Assignment

1. Evaluate Ginza's most appropriate entry strategy into the United States. (Entry into the United States could occur through an expansion of Ginza USA, a joint venture or merger with one of the ten target companies, or an outright acquisition of one of the ten target firms, or some alternative form.)

2. Select the most suitable acquisition target among the 10 target companies. Assess the target in terms of the cost (assume a price of 25% above the market's P/E ratio or 2–3 times networth), the implications on Ginza's capital structure, and expected earnings. Assume that the acquired firm could enjoy over time a higher growth rate, and greater operating efficiency.

3. Propose an investment funding strategy.

EXHIBIT 23-3

Prospective Target Companies[a]

Company Name	State	Primary SIC	Total Assets ($000s)	Shareholder Equity ($000s)	Net Sales ($000s)	Income Bef-tax ($000s)	Price/ Earnings Ratio
MR Gasket Co.	OH	3714	85,214	− 10,396	71,200	− 23,181	NA
Defiance, Inc.	OH	3714	49,558	19,037	59,132	− 1,085	36.1
Lifetime Products, Inc.	TX	3714	27,169	33	45,155	6,660	− 5.5
Code Alarm, Inc.	MI	3714	25,439	15,439	43,572	− 872	− 22.3
Filtertek, Inc.	IL	3714	37,944	20,748	40,667	− 653	20.5
R & B, Inc.	PA	3714	28,856	20,310	40,597	5,782	NA
Sprague Devices, Inc.	IN	3714	22,079	7,744	40,236	1,738	NA
ABS Industries, Inc.	OH	3714	35,559	6,538	36,222	1,158	18.5
Duratek Corp.	MD	3714	9,669	3,115	32,820	− 1,560	− 12.5
Airsensors, Inc.	WA	3714	19,352	2,738	30,530	− 850	− 4.5
Gentex Corp.	MI	3714	37,231	28,195	26,893	2,660	67.6
Athey Products Corp.	NC	3711	31,554	26,618	23,418	− 3,848	− 7.0

[a]All data address the year 1991, except Airsensors, Inc. and Athey Products Corp. NA = Not Available.

Source: Disclosure (company data submitted to Security Exchange Commission), July 1992.

(Could the venture be funded entirely by debt? Is excessive debt financing prohibited in the United States? What are the implications of high leverage or excessive debt on U.S. corporate income taxes?)

4. Following Ginza's acquisition, what would the corporation's new dollar exchange translation and transaction exposure be? How can Ginza manage its exposure in the most effective manner?

Direct Foreign Investment in the United States

Direct foreign investment is defined as the movement of long-term capital to finance the establishment, acquisition, or expansion of an enterprise abroad with a controlling interest of at least 10%. Global direct foreign investment has reached an estimated book value of $750 to $850 billion, of which 75% is located in the industrial countries, and 25% in the less developed countries (LDCs). Despite the recent acceleration in Japanese and Western European investment activities, the United States remains the principal investor with an estimated $308 billion book value at the end of 1987, or 35% of total global investments, down from 51% in 1978. During the same period, the share of Western Europe investment went up from 36.6% to 50.4%, and Japan's from 6.5% to 10.7%.

Multinational companies (MNCs) account for a growing share of business activities. The largest 600 industrial companies in the world account for 20% to 25% of value added in global manufacturing, and 25% of trade in industrial products. The United States hosts about 22,000 foreign subsidiaries that have over $925 billion in assets, over $730 billion in sales and employ over 3.1 million people.

Direct foreign investment in the United States reached about $330 billion in 1988, up by 20% from the previous year. Investment inflows have expanded at 20% annually in the past five years. The largest investors in the United States are the EC (12), with over 59%

of the total. The United Kingdom has 31% of total direct foreign investment in the United States, the Netherlands, 15%, Japan, 16%, Canada, 8%, are the largest investors.

Japanese investment in the United States reached over $53 billion in 1988 and it experiences the fastest growth in the past five years, averaging 113% annually, thereby expanding their share of the U.S. direct foreign investment from under 8% in 1982 to over 16% at present. Investors from Germany were timid, expanding below the market's average, at 7.3%.

Most Japanese investment is in wholesale trade (34% of total), manufacturing (23%), and real estate (19%). However, new investment is increasingly directed toward manufacturing activities. In the manufacturing area, Japan is primarily concentrated in machinery (21%), and primary fabricated metals (21%).

In 1988, foreign investors' spending to acquire or establish U.S. business enterprises remained strong (at $30 billion in 1987, the last year for which data is available). The number of foreign acquisitions in 1987 was 220. The number of acquisitions of large U.S. firms increased substantially during the 1980s. The recent increase in foreign takeovers of U.S. firms is frequently attributed to Japan and Germany. However, the U.K. and Canada are the largest acquirers of U.S. firms, accounting for over 50% of the total number of acquisitions over the past decade. In 1987, of the 220 foreign acquisitions of U.S. companies, Japan accounted for 15 or about 7%, while in the past decade there were 1967 acquisitions, totaling $140 billion in asset, of which Japan accounted for 94 or less than 5%.

Japanese investment in the United States is financed by equity inflows (81% of total, compared with 65% for EC), retained earnings (which constitute a small fraction of 2%, compared with 17% for the EC), intercompany debt (17% for Japan, the same proportion as for the EC).

The return on equity (ROE) invested in the United States was 5.6% in 1988, however, there were substantial variations in the performance. The highest rate was reported for the United Kingdom, at 8% and among the lowest for the Japanese, at 3.3%. (Data for 1988 show that the rate of return on U.S. investment abroad averaged 15%.)

Several factors continued to attract foreign investors to the United States:

1. The decline in the dollar induced foreign firms to shift operations to the United States.
2. The fears of U.S. protectionist measures encouraged some foreign companies to produce, rather than export to this country,
3. A favorable economic environment in the United States.
4. Corporate restructuring in the United States provided acquisition opportunities for foreigners,
5. Large current account surpluses in several major industrial countries, notably in Japan and Germany, provided foreigners with the vast amount of funds for investment in the United States.

Foreign investment inflows into the United States are expected to continue at a somewhat lower rate than in the past five years. The expected moderation is attributed to the reversal in some of the favorable factors that induced it to date, primarily the foreign exchange rate.

Bibliography

1. HARVEY A. PONIACHEK, Direct Foreign Investment in the United States, Lexington Books, Lexington, MA 1986.
2. NED G. HOWENSTINE "U.S. Affiliates of Foreign Corporations, 1987 Benchmark Survey Results." U.S. Commerce Department, Survey of Current Business, July 1989.
3. U.S. DEPARTMENT OF COMMERCE, Survey of Current Business, U.S. "Direct Investment Abroad, Detailed Position and Balance of Payments Flows, 1988," August 1989.

Foreign Direct Investment in the United States: Detail for Position and Balance of Payments Flows, 1989

The following tables[1] contain BEA's country-by-industry estimates and estimates by detailed account of the position and related capital and income flows for foreign direct investment in the United States. They also contain estimates of the position, capital flows, and income for all countries and for all industries in which there was investment.[2]

Summary position and flow estimates and analyses of the estimates were published in the June 1990 Survey of Current Business in the articles "International Investment Position: Component Detail for 1989" and "U.S. Inter-

---

[1] Tables from Survey of Current Business, August 1990.

[2] The quarterly survey from which the annual estimates of foreign direct investment in the United States were derived was conducted by Gregory G. Fouch under the supervision of James L. Bomkamp, Chief, Foreign Direct Investment in the United States Branch. Nancy F. Halvorson, Tracy K. Leigh, Beverly E. Palmer, and Amy L. Ward assisted in preparing the estimates. Smith W. Allnutt III, Chief, Data Retrieval and Analysis Branch, designed the computer programs for data retrieval and tabular presentation.

national Transactions, First Quarter 1990." Two other articles on foreign direct investment in the United States—"U.S. Business Enterprises Acquired or Established by Foreign Direct Investors in 1989" and "U.S. Affiliates of Foreign Companies: Operations in 1988"—appeared in the May 1990 and July 1990 *Surveys*, respectively. A general description of BEA data on foreign direct investment in the United States was published in the February 1990 *Survey* in the article "A Guide to BEA Statistics on Foreign Direct Investment in the United States."

Table A23-1 FOREIGN DIRECT INVESTMENT POSITION IN THE UNITED STATES

| | Direct Investment Position | | | Change | | | |
| | Millions of Dollars | | | Millions of Dollars | | Percent | |
	1987	1988	1989	1988	1989	1988	1989
All areas	**271,788**	**328,850**	**400,817**	**57,062**	**71,967**	**21.0**	**21.9**
Petroleum	35,598	34,704	35,089	−894	384	−2.5	1.1
Manufacturing	94,745	121,434	160,216	26,690	38,782	28.2	31.9
Wholesale trade	39,754	50,160	54,549	10,406	4,389	26.2	8.8
Other	101,691	122,552	150,963	20,861	28,411	20.5	23.2
Canada	**24,013**	**27,361**	**31,538**	**3,348**	**4,177**	**13.9**	**15.3**
Petroleum	1,426	1,614	1,679	188	65	13.2	4.0
Manufacturing	7,636	9,391	11,586	1,755	2,195	23.0	23.4
Wholesale trade	2,264	2,548	2,338	284	−210	12.5	−8.3
Other	12,688	13,808	15,935	1,121	2,127	8.8	15.4
Europe	**186,076**	**216,418**	**262,011**	**30,341**	**45,593**	**16.3**	**21.1**
Petroleum	32,957	31,536	30,866	−1,421	−669	−4.3	−2.1
Manufacturing	73,981	91,932	121,633	17,952	29,701	24.3	32.3
Wholesale trade	20,202	24,825	26,961	4,624	2,136	22.9	8.6
Other	58,938	68,124	82,551	9,187	14,427	15.6	21.2
Of which:							
Netherlands	49,115	48,991	60,483	−124	11,492	−.3	23.5
Petroleum	D	D	10,660	D	D	D	D
Manufacturing	16,137	17,153	24,101	1,016	6,948	6.3	40.5
Wholesale trade	2,250	3,270	3,139	1,020	−131	45.3	−4.0
Other	D	D	22,583	D	D	D	D
United Kingdom	76,669	101,909	119,137	22,241	17,228	27.9	16.9
Petroleum	D	18,779	16,811	D	−1,969	D	−10.5
Manufacturing	27,061	37,021	50,704	9,960	13,683	36.8	37.0
Wholesale trade	8,200	10,049	11,318	1,849	1,270	22.6	12.6
Other	D	36,060	40,305	D	4,245	D	11.8
Japan	**35,151**	**53,354**	**69,699**	**18,2002**	**16,346**	**51.8**	**30.6**
Petroleum	−2	−79	68	−77	147	1	1
Manufacturing	5,345	12,222	17,255	6,877	5,033	128.7	41.2
Wholesale trade	15,352	18,390	20,486	3,038	2,096	19.8	11.4
Other	14,456	22,820	31,891	8,364	9,071	57.9	39.7

(*Continued*)

| | Direct Investment Position | | | Change | | | |
| | Millions of Dollars | | | Millions of Dollars | | Percent | |
	1987	1988	1989	1988	1989	1988	1989
Other	**26,547**	**31,718**	**37,568**	**5,171**	**5,851**	**19.5**	**18.4**
Petroleum	1,218	1,633	2,476	416	842	34.1	51.6
Manufacturing	7,783	7,890	9,742	107	1,853	1.4	23.5
Wholesale trade	1,936	4,396	4,764	2,460	368	127.1	8.4
Other	15,610	17,799	20,586	2,188	2,788	14.0	15.7

[D]Suppressed to avoid disclosure of data of individual companies.

[1]Percent change is not defined because the position is negative in 1 of the 2 years.

Table 23-2 FOREIGN DIRECT INVESTMENT POSITION IN THE UNITED STATES BY ACCOUNT (millions of dollars)

	1988					1989				
				Intercompany Debt					Intercompany Debt	
				U.S. Affiliates'	U.S. Affiliates'				U.S. Affiliates'	U.S. Affiliates'
	Total	Equity[1]	Net	Payables	Receivables	Total	Equity[1]	Net	Payables	Receivables
All areas	**328,850**	**244,248**	**84,602**	**115,285**	**30,683**	**400,817**	**290,566**	**110,251**	**144,456**	**34,205**
Petroleum	34,704	24,520	10,184	11,246	1,062	35,089	24,574	10,515	11,564	1,049
Manufacturing	121,434	85,508	35,927	40,101	4,174	160,216	112,215	48,001	53,492	5,491
Wholesale trade	50,160	33,093	17,067	22,709	5,642	54,549	35,822	18,727	25,602	6,876
Other	122,552	101,128	21,424	41,230	19,806	150,963	117,955	33,009	53,798	20,789
Canada	**27,361**	**20,970**	**6,391**	**7,668**	**1,277**	**31,538**	**23,759**	**7,779**	**9,804**	**2,025**
Petroleum	1,614	905	709	878	170	1,679	D	D	877	D
Manufacturing	9,391	7,999	1,392	1,949	557	11,586	9,547	2,039	2,837	798
Wholesale trade	2,548	1,412	1,136	1,311	175	2,338	1,438	900	1,392	492
Other	13,808	10,654	3,155	3,530	375	15,935	D	D	4,698	D
Europe	**216,418**	**154,972**	**61,446**	**77,171**	**15,726**	**262,011**	**183,968**	**78,043**	**96,169**	**18,125**
Petroleum	31,536	22,615	8,920	9,516	596	30,866	22,279	8,587	9,231	643
Manufacturing	91,932	63,070	28,862	31,572	2,710	121,633	82,679	38,954	42,339	3,385
Wholesale trade	24,825	14,681	10,144	11,879	1,734	26,961	16,141	10,820	12,449	1,629
Other	68,124	54,606	13,519	24,204	10,685	82,551	62,869	19,682	32,150	12,468

Of which:

	Total	Equity[1]	Net	Payables	Receivables	Total	Equity[1]	Net	Payables	Receivables
Netherlands	48,991	31,841	17,150	17,894	744	60,483	36,782	23,701	24,560	858
Petroleum	D	D	358	386	28	10,660	D	D	D	47
Manufacturing	17,153	9,865	7,288	7,446	157	24,101	13,069	11,032	11,290	258
Wholesale trade	3,270	1,770	1,500	1,843	343	3,139	1,567	1,573	1,898	325
Other	D	D	8,004	8,219	215	22,583	D	D	D	228
United Kingdom	101,909	68,778	33,131	39,870	6,738	119,137	79,916	39,222	47,362	8,140
Petroleum	18,779	D	D	D	285	16,811	8,635	8,176	8,447	271
Manufacturing	37,021	25,160	11,861	13,314	1,453	50,704	33,860	16,844	18,504	1,661
Wholesale trade	10,049	5,370	4,679	5,423	743	11,318	6,329	4,989	5,562	572
Other	36,060	D	D	D	4,257	40,305	31,092	9,213	14,849	5,636

(Continued)

	1988					1989				
				Intercompany Debt					Intercompany Debt	
	Total	Equity[1]	Net	U.S. Affiliates' Payables	U.S. Affiliates' Receivables	Total	Equity[1]	Net	U.S. Affiliates' Payables	U.S. Affiliates' Receivables
Japan	53,354	40,296	13,057	18,983	5,926	69,699	50,756	18,943	24,324	5,381
Petroleum	−79	20	−99	112	211	68	63	5	154	149
Manufacturing	12,222	9,882	2,339	2,648	308	17,255	13,331	3,923	4,312	388
Wholesale trade	18,390	13,974	4,416	7,286	2,869	20,486	14,951	5,535	8,740	3,205
Other	22,820	16,420	6,401	8,938	2,537	31,891	22,410	9,481	11,119	1,639
Other	31,718	28,010	3,708	11,462	7,755	37,568	32,083	5,486	14,159	8,673
Petroleum	1,633	980	654	739	85	2,476	D	D	1,302	D
Manufacturing	7,890	4,556	3,334	3,932	598	9,742	6,658	3,085	4,005	920
Wholesale trade	4,396	3,026	1,370	2,233	863	4,764	3,292	1,472	3,021	1,549
Other	17,799	19,449	−1,650	4,558	6,208	20,586	D	D	5,831	D

[D] Suppressed to avoid disclosure of data of individual companies.

[1] Includes capital stock, additional paid-in capital, and retained earnings.

Table A23-3   CHANGE IN THE FOREIGN DIRECT INVESTMENT POSITION IN THE UNITED STATES BY ACCOUNT (millions of dollars)

		Capital Inflows								
		Equity Capital					Intercompany Debt			
	Total	Total	Net	Increases	Decreases	Reinvested Earnings	Net	Increases in U.S. Affiliates' Payables	Increases in U.S. Affiliates' Receivables[1]	Valuation Adjustments
1988										
All areas	57,062	58,435	40,362	43,644	3,282	6,560	11,513	17,747	6,234	−1,373
Petroleum	−894	−863	866	D	D	696	−2,426	−2,438	−12	−31
Manufacturing	26,690	28,232	17,573	18,407	834	4,030	6,629	6,684	55	−1,542
Wholesale trade	10,406	10,390	5,765	5,887	122	1,353	3,272	4,173	902	16
Other	20,861	20,677	16,158	D	D	480	4,038	9,328	5,290	184
Canada	3,348	2,847	2,184	2,799	615	−183	845	1,174	329	501
Petroleum	188	188	D	D	1	57	D	47	D	0
Manufacturing	1,755	1,417	1,093	1,099	6	395	−71	120	190	338
Wholesale trade	284	286	60	D	D	−141	367	380	13	−3
Other	1,121	955	D	1,399	D	−494	D	627	D	166
Europe	30,341	29,824	20,369	21,974	1,605	5,916	3,539	8,030	4,492	517
Petroleum	−1,421	−1,390	650	D	D	642	−2,683	−2,839	−157	−31
Manufacturing	17,952	17,414	9,909	10,310	401	3,429	4,076	3,777	−299	538
Wholesale trade	4,624	4,349	1,948	1,957	8	579	1,822	2,126	304	274
Other	9,187	9,452	7,862	D	D	1,266	324	4,967	4,643	−265
Of which:										
Netherlands	−124	4,766	1,535	2,066	531	867	2,365	2,771	406	−4,890
Petroleum	D	D	14	D	D	539	D	−187	D	−4,079
Manufacturing	1,016	2,074	452	D	D	301	1,322	1,397	75	−1,058
Wholesale trade	1,020	746	D	D	1	−47	D	572	D	274
Other	D	D	D	865	293	74	945	988	44	−27

(Continued)

	Capital Inflows									
	Equity Capital						Intercompany Debt			
	Total	Total	Net	Increases	Decreases	Rein-vested Earnings	Net	Increases in U.S. Affiliates' Payables	Increases in U.S. Affiliates' Receivables[1]	Valuation Adjust-ments
United Kingdom	22,241	18,774	11,608	11,997	389	3,337	3,829	4,443	615	3,467
Petroleum	D	D	D	D	0	−97	−2,466	D	D	4,051
Manufacturing	9,960	9,873	5,400	5,528	129	2,092	2,382	1,888	−494	87
Wholesale trade	1,849	1,849	441	441	*	314	1,094	1,263	170	1
Other	D	D	D	D	260	1,028	2,819	D	D	−672
Japan	18,202	17,838	14,472	14,507	35	364	3,001	4,384	1,383	365
Petroleum	−77	−77	15	15	0	−72	−20	61	82	0
Manufacturing	6,877	6,782	6,209	6,213	4	−120	692	879	187	95
Wholesale trade	3,038	3,025	1,837	1,837	*	835	352	928	575	13
Other	8,364	8,108	6,410	6,440	30	−279	1,977	2,516	539	256
Other	5,171	7,927	3,337	4,364	1,028	462	4,128	4,158	30	−2,756
Petroleum	416	416	D	D	0	69	D	293	D	0
Manufacturing	107	2,620	362	785	423	326	1,932	1,908	−23	−2,513
Wholesale trade	2,460	2,729	1,919	D	D	80	730	740	9	−269
Other	2,188	2,162	D	D	D	−12	D	1,217	D	26

1989

All areas	71,967	72,244	46,683	49,527	2,844	−88	25,649	29,171	3,521	−277
Petroleum	384	568	698	D	D	−461	331	318	−13	−184
Manufacturing	38,782	38,882	25,405	25,621	216	1,403	12,074	13,392	1,318	−100
Wholesale trade	4,389	4,371	2,879	3,093	214	−168	1,660	2,893	1,233	18
Other	28,411	28,423	17,700	D	D	−862	11,585	12,568	983	−11
Canada	4,177	2,736	1,498	3,046	1,548	−150	1,388	2,136	748	1,441
Petroleum	65	158	D	D	*	118	D	−1	D	−93
Manufacturing	2,195	2,046	1,016	D	D	382	647	888	241	150
Wholesale trade	−210	−210	23	23	0	3	−236	81	317	0
Other	2,127	742	D	1,943	D	−653	D	1,168	D	1,384
Europe	45,593	47,368	29,876	30,588	712	895	16,597	18,997	2,400	−1,775
Petroleum	−669	−487	460	460	*	−613	−333	−286	47	−183
Manufacturing	29,701	30,263	18,719	D	D	1,452	10,092	10,767	675	−562
Wholesale trade	2,136	2,206	1,797	2,009	212	−266	676	571	−105	−70
Other	14,427	15,386	8,900	D	D	323	6,163	7,945	1,782	−960

Of which:

Netherlands	11,492	9,826	2,897	2,959	62	378	6,552	6,666	114	1,666
Petroleum	D	D	D	D	0	697	66	85	19	−12
Manufacturing	6,948	5,459	1,336	1,336	0	379	3,743	3,844	101	1,489
Wholesale trade	−131	−141	24	D	D	−238	73	55	−18	10
Other	D	D	D	1,392	D	−461	2,670	2,682	12	179
United Kingdom	17,228	20,235	14,192	14,387	195	−48	6,090	7,492	1,402	−3,006
Petroleum	−1,969	−1,890	D	D	*	−1,534			−14	−79
Manufacturing	13,683	15,790	10,018	10,022	4	789	4,982	5,190	208	−2,107
Wholesale trade	1,270	1,328	1,039	D	D	−22	310	139	−171	−58
Other	4,245	5,007	D	3,096	D	718	D	D	1,379	−762
Japan	16,346	17,269	11,684	11,770	86	−301	5,886	5,341	−545	−923
Petroleum	147	147	73	73	0	−30	104	42	−62	*
Manufacturing	5,033	5,040	3,948	3,954	6	−492	1,584	1,664	80	−7
Wholesale trade	2,096	2,005	659	660	1	228	1,118	1,454	335	91
Other	9,071	10,077	7,005	7,084	79	−8	3,080	2,181	−898	−1,007

(Continued)

| | | Capital Inflows | | | | | | | | |
| | | Equity Capital | | | | Rein-vested Earnings | Intercompany Debt | | | Valuation Adjust-ments |
	Total	Total	Net	Increases	Decreases		Net	Increases in U.S. Affiliates' Payables	Increases in U.S. Affiliates' Receivables[1]	
Other	**5,851**	**4,871**	**3,625**[D]	**4,122**	**498**[D]	**−532**	**1,778**[D]	**2,697**	**919**[D]	**980**
Petroleum	842	751	[D]	174	[D]	64	[D]	563	[D]	92
Manufacturing	1,853	1,533	1,721	1,721	*	61	−249	73	322	320
Wholesale trade	368	370	401	402	1	−133	102	788	686	−2
Other	2,788	2,217	[D]	1,826	[D]	−525	[D]	1,273	[D]	571

*Less than $500,000 (±).

[D]Suppressed to avoid disclosure of data of individual companies.

[1]An increase in U.S. affiliates' receivables is a decrease in intercompany debt and, thus, a capital outflow.

Table A23-4 FOREIGN DIRECT INVESTMENT IN THE UNITED STATES: EARNINGS AND REINVESTMENT RATIOS (millions of dollars or ratio)

| | 1988 | | | | 1989 | | | | 1988–89 Change in Earnings | | |
| | Earnings | | | Reinvest-ment Ratio[1] | Earnings | | | Reinvest-ment Ratio[1] | | | |
	Total	Distributed	Rein-vested		Total	Distributed	Rein-vested		Total	Distributed	Rein-vested
All areas	**12,061**	**5,501**	**6,560**	**.54**	**6,754**	**6,842**	**−88**	[2]	**−5,307**	**1,341**	**−6,648**
Petroleum	2,155	1,459	696	.32	[D]	[D]	−461	[D]	[D]	[D]	−1,157
Manufacturing	5,253	1,223	4,030	.77	2,336	933	1,403	.60	−2,917	−290	−2,627
Wholesale trade	2,167	814	1,353	.62	792	960	−168	[2]	−1,375	146	−1,521
Other	2,485	2,005	480	.19	[D]	[D]	−862	[2]	[D]	[D]	−1,343
Canada	**842**	**1,025**	**−183**	[2]	**501**	**651**	**150**	[2]	**−341**	**−374**	**33**
Petroleum	128	70	57	.45	183	65	118	.65	55	−5	61
Manufacturing	427	32	395	.93	391	9	382	.98	−36	−23	−13
Wholesale trade	[D]	[D]	−141	[2]	[D]	[D]	3	[D]	−61	−205	144
Other	[D]	[D]	−494	[2]	[D]	[D]	−653	[2]	−300	−141	−159
Europe	**9,505**	**3,589**	**5,916**	**.62**	**5,934**	**5,039**	**895**	**.15**	**−3,571**	**1,450**	**−5,021**
Petroleum	[D]	[D]	642	[D]	[D]	[D]	−613	[2]	−26	1,230	−1,256
Manufacturing	4,563	1,134	3,429	.75	2,299	847	1,452	.63	−2,265	−287	−1,977
Wholesale trade	943	364	579	.61	475	741	−266	[2]	−468	377	−845
Other	[D]	[D]	1,266	[D]	[D]	[D]	323	[D]	−812	130	−943
Of which:											
Netherlands	1,608	741	867	.54	583	205	378	.65	−1,025	−536	−489
Petroleum	[D]	[D]	539	[D]	697	0	697	1.00	[D]	[D]	158
Manufacturing	[D]	[D]	301	[D]	398	19	379	.95	[D]	79	
Wholesale trade	[D]	[D]	−47	[2]	−198	46	−238	[2]	[D]	[D]	−191
Other	201	127	74	.37	−320	141	−461	[2]	−521	14	−535
United Kingdom	5,099	1,762	3,337	.65	3,415	3,462	−48	[2]	−1,684	1,701	−3,385
Petroleum	[D]	[D]	−97	[2]	[D]	[D]	−1,534	[2]	−215	1,222	−1,437
Manufacturing	2,265	173	2,092	.92	991	202	789	.80	−1,273	.29	−1,303
Wholesale trade	382	68	314	.82	[D]	[D]	−22	[2]	[D]	[D]	−336
Other	[D]	[D]	1,028	[D]	1,109	390	718	.65	[D]	[D]	−310

(Continued)

	1988 Earnings Total	Distributed	Reinvested	1988 Reinvestment Ratio¹	1989 Earnings Total	Distributed	Reinvested	1989 Reinvestment Ratio¹	1988–89 Change in Earnings Total	Distributed	Reinvested
Japan	1,026	662	364	.35	596	897	−301	²	−430	235	−665
Petroleum	−72	1	−72	²	−29	*	−30	²	43	*	43
Manufacturing	−87	33	−120	²	−452	40	−492	²	−365	7	−372
Wholesale trade	945	110	835	.88	342	114	228	.67	−603	4	−607
Other	240	518	−279	²	735	743	−8	²	496	225	271
Other	688	226	462	.67	−277	255	−532	²	−965	29	−994
Petroleum	D	D	69	D	107	43	64	.60	D	D	−5
Manufacturing	350	24	326	.93	98	37	61	.62	−252	13	−265
Wholesale trade	D	D	80	D	D	D	−133	²	−242	−30	−212
Other	130	142	−12	²	D	D	−525	²	D	D	−512

*Less than $500,000 (±).

ᴰSuppressed to avoid disclosure of data of individual companies.

[1]Reinvested earnings divided by earnings.

[2]Reinvestment ratio is not defined because reinvested earnings are negative.

Table A23-5   FOREIGN DIRECT INVESTMENT IN THE UNITED STATES: INCOME (millions of dollars)

	Income 1987	Income 1988	Income 1989	Change 1988	Change 1989
All areas	9,500	16,748	14,004	7,248	−2,744
Petroleum	2,345	2,929	2,991	583	621
Manufacturing	3,864	7,172	5,752	3,308	−1,420
Wholesale trade	2,051	2,627	1,562	576	−1,065
Other	1,240	4,020	3,700	2,780	−321
Canada	943	1,082	894	139	−188
Petroleum	7	126	200	119	74
Manufacturing	186	451	447	265	−4
Wholesale trade	661	178	128	−483	−50
Other	88	327	119	239	−208
Europe	8,465	13,370	11,788	4,905	−1,581
Petroleum	2,410	2,774	2,690	364	−84
Manufacturing	3,841	6,288	5,373	2,447	−916
Wholesale trade	701	1,383	1,083	681	−299
Other	1,513	2,925	2,643	1,412	−283
Of which:					
Netherlands	2,240	2,869	2,464	629	−405
Petroleum	D	623	726	D	103
Manufacturing	1,035	1,267	1,347	233	80
Wholesale trade	146	159	−29	12	−188
Other	D	820	420	D	−400

(*Continued*)

	Income			Change	
	1987	1988	1989	1988	1989
United Kingdom	4,520	7,259	6,778	2,739	−481
Petroleum	1,192	1,867	1,597	675	−271
Manufacturing	1,774	2,960	2,428	1,185	−532
Wholesale trade	526	568	719	42	151
Other	1,027	1,864	2,034	837	170
Japan	**846**	**1,478**	**1,277**	**632**	**−201**
Petroleum	−73	−70	−24	3	46
Manufacturing	−26	−40	−353	−14	−313
Wholesale trade	641	962	360	321	−602
Other	304	626	1,294	322	668
Other	**−754**	**818**	**45**	**1,572**	**−773**
Petroleum	1	99	125	98	26
Manufacturing	−137	473	286	610	−187
Wholesale trade	47	104	−10	57	−114
Other	−666	141	−356	807	−498

[D]Suppressed to avoid disclosure of data of individual companies.

Table A23-6 SOURCE AND RELATIONSHIP OF INCOME AND ITS COMPONENTS (millions of dollars)

Line		1989 Amount	Source and Relationship
1	Earnings	6,754	2 + 3
2	Capital gains/losses	2,567	Reported[1]
3	Earnings before capital gains/losses	4,187	Extrapolated[2]
4	Distributed earnings	6,842	6 + 11
5	Reinvested earnings	−88	1 − 4
6	Withholding taxes on distributed earnings	220	Extrapolated[2]
7	Interest (net of withholding taxes)	7,471	Extrapolated[2]
8	Income	14,004	1 − 6 + 7
9	Income before capital gains/losses	11,437	8 − 2
10	Earnings (net of withholding taxes)	6,533	1 − 6
11	Distributed earnings (net of withholding taxes)	6,621	Extrapolated[2]

[1]Data are as reported by the sample; no estimate for nonreporting affiliates is made.

[2]Universe estimates are calculated by extrapolating forward data from the 1980 benchmark survey, based on the movement of reported sample data in subsequent years.

Table A23-7 FOREIGN DIRECT INVESTMENT IN THE UNITED STATES: INCOME AND RATE OF RETURN
(millions of dollars or percent)

	1988 Income									1989 Income								
	Total (=Col. 2 Less Col. 5 Plus Col. 6) (1)	Earnings — Total (2)	Earnings — Before Capital Gains/Losses (3)	Earnings — Capital Gains/Losses (4)	With-holding Taxes on Distributed Earnings (5)	Interest (Net of Withholding Taxes) — Net (6)	Interest — U.S. Affiliates' Payments (7)	Interest — U.S. Affiliates' Receipts (8)	Rate of Return[1] (9)	Total (=Col. 11 Less Col. 14 plus Col. 15) (10)	Earnings — Total (11)	Earnings — Before Capital Gains/Losses (12)	Earnings — Capital Gains/Losses (13)	With-Holding Taxes on Distributed Earnings (14)	Interest (Net of Withholding Taxes) — Net (15)	Interest — U.S. Affiliates' Payments (16)	Interest — U.S. Affiliates' Receipts (17)	Rate of Return[1] (18)
All areas	16,748	12,061	11,195	866	232	4,918	6,240	1,321	5.6	14,004	6,754	4,187	2,567	220	7,471	9,343	1,872	3.8
Petroleum	2,929	2,155	2,227	-72	77	850	886	35	8.3	2,991	2,189	2,189	D	D	841	867	26	8.6
Manufacturing	7,172	5,253	4,043	1,211	70	1,989	2,149	160	6.6	5,752	2,336	1,889	447	50	3,466	3,712	246	4.1
Wholesale trade	2,627	2,167	2,047	120	32	492	676	184	5.8	1,562	792	588	204	23	793	999	206	3.0
Other	4,020	2,485	2,879	-393	53	1,588	2,529	942	3.6	3,700	D	-479	D	D	2,371	3,766	1,395	2.7
Canada	1,082	842	1,414	-572	15	255	268	13	4.2	894	501	374	127	8	401	424	23	3.0
Petroleum	126	128	128	D	5	5	6	1	8.3	200	183	179	4	6	23	24	1	12.2
Manufacturing	451	427	303	124	4	29	36	7	5.3	447	391	404	-13	1	56	68	12	4.3
Wholesale trade	178	163	165	-2	1	16	18	2	7.4	128	D	37	D	D	26	27	*	5.2
Other	327	125	125	D	3	205	208	3	2.5	119	D	-245	D	D	295	306	10	.8
Europe	13,370	9,505	8,344	1,160	173	4,039	4,907	869	6.6	11,788	5,934	4,381	1,553	161	6,016	7,292	1,276	4.9
Petroleum	2,774	2,007	2,086	-79	67	834	867	337	8.6	2,690	D	1,934	D	D	794	818	24	8.6
Manufacturing	6,288	4,563	3,506	1,058	60	1,785	1,917	132	7.6	5,373	2,299	2,107	192	43	3,117	3,317	200	5.0
Wholesale trade	1,383	943	831	112	17	457	504	47	6.1	1,083	475	398	77	11	620	734	114	4.2
Other	2,925	1,991	1,922	69	29	963	1,620	656	4.6	2,643	D	-58	D	D	1,486	2,423	937	3.5
Of which:																		
Netherlands	2,869	1,608	1,763	-154	41	1,302	1,317	15	5.8	2,464	583	469	114	9	1,890	1,922	32	4.5
Petroleum	623	584	D	D	D	D	1	1	D	726	697	D	D	0	29	31	2	D
Manufacturing	1,267	809	814	-5	26	484	491	6	7.6	1,347	398	318	80	1	950	970	20	6.5
Wholesale trade	159	14	8	6	3	147	149	2	5.7	-29	-192	-197	5	2	164	168	3	-.9
Other	820	201	D	D	D	D	D	6	D	420	-320	D	D	7	747	755	8	D
United Kingdom	7,259	5,099	4,114	984	91	2,251	2,629	377	8.0	6,778	3,415	2,769	645	100	3,464	4,105	642	6.1
Petroleum	1,867	1,123	1,166	-43	D	706	800	94	10.4	1,597	D	886	D	D	1,444	1,560	116	9.0
Manufacturing	2,960	2,265	1,339	925	11	190	226	36	9.2	2,428	991	941	50	D	315	391	76	5.5
Wholesale trade	568	382	396	-14	3	D	D	D	6.2	719	D	392	D	D	D	448	448	6.7
Other	1,864	1,330	1,213	117	D	D	D	D	5.9	2,034	1,109	550	559	D	D	D	2	5.3
Japan	1,478	1,026	1,033	-7	25	477	585	108	3.3	1,277	596	337	259	28	710	864	154	2.1[2]
Petroleum	-40	-87	-79	-8	3	49	57	8	-.5	-24	-29	-29	*	*	*	*	*	[2]
Manufacturing	962	945	940	5	11	28	32	4	5.7	-353	-452	-465	13	3	101	103	0	[2]
Wholesale trade	626	240	D	D	12	398	409	10	3.4	360	342	286	56	11	30	103	73	4.7
Other	-70	-72	D	D	*	2	D	D	[2]	1,294	735	545	190	14	573	D	D	.1
Other	818	688	404	284	18	148	480	332	2.8	45	D	-906	D	22	344	763	418	.1
Petroleum	99	92	94	-2	3	10	13	D	6.9	125	107	105	3	4	19	20	1	6.1
Manufacturing	473	350	313	37	3	126	139	13	6.0	286	D	-157	D	D	192	D	4	3.2
Wholesale trade	104	117	111	6	3	-10	D	D	3.3	-10	D	-132	D	D	117	135	D	-.2
Other	141	130	-114	244	9	21	293	272	.8	-356	D	-721	D	D	16	D	18	-1.9

*Less than $500,000 (±).

ᵇSuppressed to avoid disclosure of data of individual companies.

[1]Income divided by the average of the beginning- and end-of-year direct investment position.

[2]Rate of return is not defined because the average position for the year is negative.

445

Table A23-8 FOREIGN DIRECT INVESTMENT IN THE UNITED STATES: ROYALTIES AND LICENSE FEES AND CHARGES FOR OTHER SERVICES (millions of dollars)

| | 1988 | | | | | | 1989 | | | | | |
| | Royalties and License Fees | | | Charges for Other Services[1] | | | Royalties and License Fees | | | Charges for Other Services[1] | | |
	Net	U.S. Affiliates' Payments	U.S. Affiliates' Receipts	Net	U.S. Affiliates' Payments	U.S. Affiliates' Receipts	Net	U.S. Affiliates' Payments	U.S. Affiliates' Receipts	Net	U.S. Affiliates' Payments	U.S. Affiliates' Receipts
All areas	**968**	**1,205**	**238**	**-694**	**2,334**	**3,028**	**1,374**	**1,725**	**352**	**-581**	**2,918**	**3,498**
Petroleum	10	11	1	-211	114	325	13	14	1	-113	210	323
Manufacturing	598	750	152	40	807	766	890	1,085	196	232	1,243	1,011
Wholesale trade	321	360	39	-343	304	647	406	431	25	-500	319	819
Other	38	84	46	-179	1,110	1,289	65	195	130	-200	1,145	1,345
Canada	**-1**	**24**	**24**	**307**	**714**	**407**	**-53**	**23**	**76**	**366**	**921**	**555**
Petroleum	0	0	0	-96	26	122	0	0	0	-72	80	152
Manufacturing	5	13	8	53	103	50	-21	14	34	299	378	79
Wholesale trade	*	2	2	44	63	19	-1	2	3	26	59	33
Other	-6	9	15	306	522	215	-31	8	39	112	404	292
Europe	**741**	**889**	**148**	**-243**	**1,176**	**1,420**	**1,140**	**1,309**	**169**	**-263**	**1,400**	**1,663**
Petroleum	10	11	1	-100	81	181	13	14	1	-18	127	145
Manufacturing	569	678	109	-45	550	595	860	965	105	-152	663	815
Wholesale trade	112	138	27	-121	105	226	156	168	11	-170	111	280
Other	50	61	11	22	441	418	111	163	52	77	500	423
Of which:												
Netherlands	24	42	18	38 D	130 D	92 D	101	107	5	218	278	60
Petroleum	0	0	0	-3	2	5	0	0	0	-21	1	22
Manufacturing	26 D	28	2	47 D	60 D	13 D	48	49	2	129	144	15
Wholesale trade	D	9	D	26	42	16	43	44	1	16	23	7
Other	D	5	D	D	D	D	11	13	2	94	110	16
United Kingdom	196	266 D	70	-229 D	301 D	530 D	343	427	83	-233 D	412 D	645 D
Petroleum	D	0	0	D	D	D	9	9	0	D	D	0 D
Manufacturing	173	229	56	-137	119	255	313	374	62	-272	114	386 D
Wholesale trade	8 D	17 D	9	-36 D	29 D	65 D	20	35	15	-27 D	35 D	62 D
Other	D	D	5	D	D	D	D	9	D	D	D	D
Japan	**249**	**273**	**24**	**-406**	**194**	**600**	**328**	**359**	**32**	**-497 D**	**309**	**807 D**
Petroleum	*	*	0 D	-3	2	5	*	*	*	1	1	D
Manufacturing	D	51	7 D	62	97	35	77	98	21	85	126	41
Wholesale trade	204	211	D	-262	46	308	244	252	8	-294 D	93	386 D
Other	D	11	D	-204	49	252	6	9	3	D	89	D
Other	**-21**	**20**	**41**	**-351**	**250**	**601**	**-41**	**33**	**74**	**-186 D**	**287**	**474 D**
Petroleum	D	0	0	-13	5	18	0	0	0	0	2	18
Manufacturing	D	8	D	-30	57	86	-27	9	36	-27	76	76
Wholesale trade	6 D	9	3 D	-4	90	94	7	9	2	-63 D	56	D
Other	D	3	D	-305	99	403	-21	15	36	D	152	119 D

*Less than $500,000 (±).

D Suppressed to avoid disclosure of data of individual companies.

[1] Consists of service charges, rentals for the use of tangible property, and film and television tape rentals. In 1989, U.S. affiliates' payments of service charges were $2,692 million, payments of rentals for the use of tangible property were $224 million, and payments of film and television tape rentals were $1 million; U.S. affiliates' receipts were $3,334 million, $164 million, and less than $500 thousand, respectively.

Table A23-9 FOREIGN DIRECT INVESTMENT IN THE UNITED STATES: POSITION AND BALANCE OF PAYMENTS FLOWS, 1980–89
(millions of dollars)

	1980	1981	1982	1983	1984	1985	1986	1987	1988	1989
Direct investment position	83,046	108,714	124,677	137,061	164,583	184,615	220,414	271,788	328,850	400,817
Capital inflows (outflows(−))	16,918	25,195	13,792	11,946	25,359	19,022	34,091	46,894	58,435	72,244
Equity capital	9,027	14,795	9,723	8,699	15,044	15,214	25,086	30,621	40,362	46,683
Reinvested earnings	5,177	2,945	−2,379	89	2,896	−1,378	−2,293	1,481	6,560	−88
Intercompany debt	2,713	7,455	6,448	3,159	7,418	5,186	11,298	14,792	11,513	25,649
Income	8,635	6,898	3,155	5,598	9,229	6,079	5,379	9,500	16,748	14,004
Royalties and license fees, net payments	378	413	325	405	597	466	602	843	968	1,374
Charges for other services, net payments[1]	50	−52	−403	−471	−478	−696	−1,284	−616	−694	−581

[1]Consists of service charges, rentals for the use of tangible property, and film and television tape rentals.

Table A23-10 FOREIGN DIRECT INVESTMENT POSITION IN THE UNITED STATES, 1988 (millions of dollars)

	All Industries	Mining	Petroleum	Manufacturing Total	Food and Kindred Products	Chemicals and Allied Products	Primary and Fabricated Metals	Machinery	Other Manufacturing	Wholesale Trade	Retail Trade	Banking	Finance, (Except Banking)	Insurance	Real Estate	Other Industries
All countries	328,850	6,390	34,704	121,434	16,437	34,146	12,541	19,281	39,030	50,160	14,770	17,453	2,124	20,252	31,929	29,635
Canada	27,361	900	1,614	9,391	531	623	3,414	2,346	2,477	2,548	965	1,458	600	2,993	4,169	2,724
Europe	216,418	1,843	31,536	91,932	14,916	31,832	5,324	13,874	25,985	24,825	11,884	9,099	2,417	15,812	10,532	16,537
European Communities (12)	193,912	1,751	31,169	79,525	12,424	28,173	4,318	10,347	24,264	21,040	11,858	8,804	1,745	13,535	10,016	14,469
Belgium	4,024	D	D	989	D	594	D	-67	258	523	172	34	56	*	12	-5
France	11,364	D	D	9,908	455	4,549	852	592	3,459	505	15	687	-764	139	95	604
Germany, Federal Republic of	23,845	319	172	13,268	633	7,537	457	2,483	2,159	5,677	1,174	293	-626	1,776	1,079	715
Italy	667	D	D	107	D	-15	D	-59	155	520	-5	446	D	D	D	104
Luxembourg	525	5	D	346	0	0	D	4	60	92	D	12	15	0	10	41
Netherlands	48,991	311	D	17,153	5,852	4,964	921	1,972	3,443	3,270	1,883	2,729	3,190	4,685	3,340	D
United Kingdom	101,909	563	18,779	37,021	5,204	10,534	1,688	5,370	14,224	10,049	8,598	3,669	870	6,863	5,323	10,174
Other EC	2,587	0	D	733	D	10	D	52	504	404	D	935	D	D	D	D
Other Europe	22,505	92	367	12,407	2,493	3,659	1,006	3,528	1,721	3,785	26	295	671	2,277	517	2,068
Sweden	5,263	D	395	3,618	-2	421	270	2,348	580	1,479	3	D	D	D	13	171
Switzerland	15,896	D	92	8,072	D	3,142	D	1,123	1,051	2,060	23	D	1,411	1,935	388	1,825
Other	1,347	0	-120	717	D	96	D	56	90	247	D	181	D	D	116	72
Japan	53,354	D	-79	12,222	302	1,137	2,323	2,542	5,917	18,390	346	3,895	2,863	D	10,017	5,374
Australia, New Zealand, and South Africa	5,624	D	287	2,279	208	-103	803	10	1,361	330	88	11	-838	D	416	276
Latin America and Other Western Hemisphere	17,019	723	898	4,221	60	539	276	404	2,940	2,589	1,344	1,942	-3,108	1,150	5,217	2,043
South and Central America	4,978	0	446	406	20	162	D	D	19	262	64	1,845	47	D	338	D
Panama	2,747	0	6	501	D	D	D	-16	25	140	69	D	46	D	216	77
Other	2,232	0	440	-95	D	-2	-2	D	-6	122	-5	D	1	D	122	D
Other Western Hemisphere	12,040	723	452	3,815	41	378	*	D	2,921	2,327	1,281	97	-3,154	D	4,878	D
Bermuda	1,680	0	107	328	D	4	D	D	321	588	D	D	D	-113	242	99
Netherlands Antilles	10,591	D	264	3,118	D	268	D	420	2,407	1,589	494	83	153	D	3,190	1,454
U.K. Islands, Caribbean	-1,104	D	D	355	6	D	D	50	188	120	80	14	-3,658	1	1,354	D
Other	873	0	D	13	0	D	-28	D	5	30	D	*	D	2	92	47
Middle East	5,831	0	D	281	1	2	D	D	-10	907	3	657	216	0	923	D
Israel	519	0	0	D	1	4	D	D	-9	D	0	433	D	0	1	D
Other	5,312	D	D	D	0	-2	D	14	-1	D	3	224	D	0	922	-7
Other Africa, Asia, and Pacific	3,243	D	D	1,109	418	114	D	D	359	570	139	390	-26	8	655	D
Addendum—OPEC[1]	6,221	D	745	571	D	-10	D	-16	-1	D	3	363	26	0	879	D

*Less than $500,000 (±).

D Suppressed to avoid disclosure of data of individual companies.

[1] OPEC is the Organization of Petroleum Exporting Countries. Its members are Algeria, Ecuador, Gabon, Indonesia, Iran, Iraq, Kuwait, Libya, Nigeria, Qatar, Saudi Arabia, the United Arab Emirates, and Venezuela.

Table A23-11 FOREIGN DIRECT INVESTMENT POSITION IN THE UNITED STATES, 1989
(millions of dollars)

	All Industries	Mining	Petroleum	Manufacturing						Wholesale Trade	Retail Trade	Banking	Finance, (Except Banking)	Insurance	Real Estate	Other Industries
				Total	Food and Kindred Products	Chemicals and Allied Products	Primary and Fabricated Metals	Machinery	Other Manufacturing							
All countries	400,817	7,179	35,089	160,216	23,927	46,268	18,569	26,472	44,981	54,549	16,802	19,581	11,403	22,713	35,853	37,432
Canada	31,538	1,077	1,679	11,586	895	546	3,900	2,789	3,457	2,338	852	1,493	876	3,483	3,921	4,233
Europe	262,011	2,179	30,866	121,633	21,597	42,470	9,738	17,976	29,852	26,961	13,510	10,639	6,316	17,459	11,330	21,119
European Communities (12)	234,794	2,080	30,244	106,411	19,109	38,700	6,947	14,173	27,482	23,015	13,532	10,420	4,903	14,787	10,586	18,815
Belgium	4,535	D	D	1,205	D	733	D	38	249	639	233	35	26	*	28	49
France	16,375	D	D	13,916	780	5,821	2,389	1,040	3,885	762	1	870	-468	134	73	864
Germany, Federal Republic of	28,223	293	250	15,232	583	9,117	507	2,413	2,613	6,218	1,175	699	-351	2,089	1,173	1,144
Italy	1,586	D	D	264	D	-68	D	140	198	496	-2	506	D	D	-53	-1
Luxembourg	935	D	D	94	0	0	D	4	61	60	29	8	198	0	512	55
Netherlands	60,483	364	10,660	24,101	6,551	6,828	1,706	4,751	4,264	3,139	2,410	3,148	4,507	5,266	3,410	3,478
United Kingdom	119,137	859	16,811	50,704	10,881	16,248	2,226	5,733	15,616	11,318	9,695	3,748	822	7,222	5,234	12,724
Other EC	3,519	0	73	896	229	21	-4	54	595	382	-9	1,405	D	D	209	202
Other Europe	27,217	99	622	15,221	2,488	3,770	2,791	3,803	2,369	3,946	-23	220	1,412	2,671	745	2,303
Sweden	4,925	D	439	3,557	-3	484	218	1,959	898	1,585	2	D	2	D	79	184
Switzerland	19,329	D	105	10,107	D	3,169	D	1,516	1,172	2,099	-16	D	2,345	2,279	370	1,961
Other	2,963	D	79	1,557	D	117	D	328	299	262	-9	137	D	D	295	158
Japan	69,699	D	68	17,255	397	2,420	3,304	4,960	6,173	20,486	519	4,441	5,830	D	14,294	6,397
Australia, New Zealand, and South Africa	6,532	D	425	3,396	380	-223	956	4	2,279	503	D	-90	-1,497	D	379	300
Latin America and Other Western Hemisphere	20,348	715	1,473	4,230	115	501	219	606	2,789	2,838	1,604	2,026	-532	1,387	4,223	2,384
South and Central America	5,915	0	968	541	19	129	D	D	120	173	79	1,888	183	D	308	D
Panama	2,961	0	29	545	D	D	D	-24	67	72	82	D	121	D	204	55
Other	2,955	0	939	-4	D	D	-4	D	53	101	-3	D	62	D	105	D
Other Western Hemisphere	14,432	715	506	3,689	96	372	D	D	2,669	2,665	1,525	138	-715	-133	3,915	98
Bermuda	1,936	0	113	278	D	-4	-28	D	D	1,028	594	D	D	D	218	1,517
Netherlands Antilles	10,570	D	321	2,786	D	264	168	422	2,094	1,535	148	86	223	3	3,239	D
U.K. Islands, Caribbean	1,128	D	D	800	D	D	D	174	304	71	86	21	-1,299	3	481	53
Other	798	0	D	-176	0	D	D	D	D	30	21	D	D	D	-24	D
Middle East	6,425	0	D	416	1	5	D	D	-16	1,133	D	670	194	0	936	D
Israel	422	0	0	D	1	D	0	3	-16	D	0	460	D	0	1	7
Other	6,003	0	0	D	0	D	0	D	*	D	0	210	D	0	935	D
Other Africa, Asia, and Pacific	4,263	D	D	1,701	543	549	D	D	446	290	235	402	216	11	770	D
Addendum—OPEC[1]	7,462	D	1,202	D	D	-3	D	-3	-2	D	4	372	26	0	883	D

*Less than $500,000 (±).

D Suppressed to avoid disclosure of data of individual companies.

[1] OPEC is the Organization of Petroleum Exporting Countries. Its members are Algeria, Ecuador, Gabon, Indonesia, Iran, Iraq, Kuwait, Libya, Nigeria, Qatar, Saudi Arabia, the United Arab Emirates, and Venezuela.

Table A23-12 FOREIGN DIRECT INVESTMENT IN THE UNITED STATES: CAPITAL INFLOWS, 1988
(millions of dollars; outflows (−))

	All Industries	Mining	Petroleum	Manufacturing						Wholesale Trade	Retail Trade	Banking	Finance, (Except Banking)	Insurance	Real Estate	Other Industries
				Total	Food and Kindred Products	Chemicals and Allied Products	Primary and Fabricated Metals	Machinery	Other Manufacturing							
All countries	**58,435**	**644**	**−863**	**28,232**	**1,895**	**4,515**	**3,492**	**3,222**	**15,108**	**10,390**	**3,863**	**2,887**	**−935**	**2,826**	**4,532**	**6,860**
Canada	**2,847**	**94**	**188**	**1,417**	**128**	**236**	**345**	**457**	**251**	**286**	**−401**	**105**	**120**	**405**	**−287**	**919**
Europe	**29,824**	**201**	**−1,390**	**17,414**	**1,265**	**3,764**	**1,596**	**1,559**	**9,230**	**4,349**	**3,826**	**2,231**	**−2,233**	**2,106**	**151**	**3,171**
European Communities (12)	28,365	169	−1,405	16,942	D	3,315	D	1,021	8,982	3,654	3,865	2,108	−1,720	1,738	165	2,851
Belgium	1,387	D	288	288	D	146	D	−81	195	256	27	2	D	*	−1	−8
France	962	D	D	1,399	63	182	101	−469	1,523	160	−640	40	−103	15	38	24
Germany, Federal Republic of	2,306	−30	23	2,800	579	1,547	186	221	266	589	123	−75	−1,281	146	−5	66
Italy	−1,039	D	D	−138	D	−19	D	−95	−7	34	−1	18	D	D	D	98
Luxembourg	360	51	D	264	D	0	D	*	8	21	D	6	30	0	−6	−6
Netherlands	4,766	−32	D	2,074	489	6	267	209	1,103	746	44	178	605	824	26	D
United Kingdom	18,774	135	D	9,873	1,037	1,450	503	1,201	5,682	1,849	4,332	1,570	D	723	175	2,643
Other EC	850	0	D	381	D	3	D	35	212	−1	D	369	D	D	D	D
Other Europe	1,459	32	15	472	D	449	D	537	249	695	−39	123	−513	368	−13	319
Sweden	310	D	44	497	*	64	−39	430	42	258	1	D	D	D	6	9
Switzerland	813	D	−108	−290	D	371	D	109	164	426	−35	D	186	317	−4	335
Other	336	D	78	266	D	14	D	−1	43	12	−6	98	D	D	−15	−24
Japan	**17,838**	**D**	**−77**	**6,782**	**139**	**563**	**1,724**	**1,008**	**3,348**	**3,025**	**21**	**381**	**745**	**D**	**3,920**	**2,980**
Australia, New Zealand, and South Africa	**289**	**D**	**192**	**394**	**D**	**−197**	**D**	**2**	**578**	**200**	**18**	**−17**	**−747**	**D**	**87**	**−86**
Latin America and Other Western Hemisphere	**5,899**	**25**	**150**	**1,938**	**16**	**154**	**−179**	**179**	**1,768**	**1,291**	**482**	**135**	**1,026**	**219**	**573**	**60**
South and Central America	584	0	203	−75	3	−52	D	D	1	38	4	140	−5	D	54	D
Panama	366	0	D	−38	D	D	D	−5	2	29	7	D	5	D	66	D
Other	218	0	D	−37	D	D	−5	D	−1	10	−3	D	−10	D	−12	−3
Other Western Hemisphere	5,314	25	−54	2,013	13	207	D	D	1,767	1,253	478	−4	1,031	D	519	D
Bermuda	17	D	−131	111	D	7	D	D	51	23	25	*	D	D	−8	21
Netherlands Antilles	2,806	D	74	2,031	D	195	D	D	1,825	1,214	12	D	−62	2	−396	−92
U.K. Islands, Caribbean	1,970	D	D	−108	4	D	D	−1	−108	13	D	D	1,103	2	847	D
Other	521	D	D	−20	0	D	−24	D	−1	3	D	*	D	0	76	D
Middle East	**818**	**D**	**D**	**19**	**D**	**1**	**D**	**D**	**−55**	**832**	**−1**	**47**	**11**	**0**	**54**	**9**
Israel	5	0	0	D	D	1	0	D	D	D	0	29	D	0	0	D
Other	813	D	D	D	0	*	D	3	D	D	−1	18	D	0	54	2
Other Africa, Asia, and Pacific	**921**	**D**	**D**	**268**	**D**	**−6**	**D**	**D**	**−12**	**406**	**−81**	**6**	**142**	**−2**	**34**	**D**
Addendum—OPEC[1]	**1,309**	**D**	**D**	**392**	**D**	**−5**	**D**	**4**	*****	**D**	**−1**	**7**	*****	**0**	**42**	**D**

*Less than $500,000 (±).

D Suppressed to avoid disclosure of data of individual companies.

[1] See footnote 1, Table A23-10.

Table A23-13 FOREIGN DIRECT INVESTMENT IN THE UNITED STATES: CAPITAL INFLOWS, 1989
(millions of dollars; outflows (−))

	All Industries	Mining	Petroleum	Manufacturing						Wholesale Trade	Retail Trade	Banking	Finance, (Except Banking)	Insurance	Real Estate	Other Industries
				Total	Food and Kindred Products	Chemicals and Allied Products	Primary and Fabricated Metals	Machinery	Other Manufacturing							
All countries	72,244	903	568	38,882	7,382	12,033	5,854	6,681	6,931	4,371	1,720	2,123	8,851	2,550	3,935	8,341
Canada	2,736	262	158	2,046	363	-77	468	291	1,000	-210	-216	35	276	370	-264	280
Europe	47,368	364	-487	30,263	6,633	10,651	4,305	3,749	4,925	2,206	1,600	1,540	3,713	1,879	884	5,406
European Communities (12)	42,486	358	-742	27,455	6,637	10,541	2,462	3,462	4,353	2,049	1,649	1,616	3,002	1,484	653	4,962
Belgium	345	D	50	50	D	21	D	57	-8	116	61	1	-30	*	16	54
France	5,299	D	D	3,985	325	1,249	1,537	449	426	251	-40	183	300	-6	-22	572
Germany, Federal Republic of	4,229	3	79	1,894	-50	1,514	50	-68	448	572	1	407	163	287	94	730
Italy	987	D	D	167	D	-53	D	200	43	-24	3	60	D	D	D	-45
Luxembourg	610	D	D	-50	D	0	D	*	1	-30	D	-4	183	0	498	13
Netherlands	9,826	53	D	5,459	550	2,052	427	1,591	838	-141	527	419	1,295	367	65	D
United Kingdom	20,235	296	-1,890	15,790	5,778	5,747	516	1,232	2,517	1,328	1,097	79	-57	832	4	2,755
Other EC	955	0	D	161	D	11	D	2	89	-22	D	471	D	D	D	D
Other Europe	4,882	7	255	2,807	-5	111	1,842	287	573	157	-49	-76	711	394	231	444
Sweden	-357	D	44	-88	-1	62	5	-392	238	106	-1	D	D	D	66	21
Switzerland	3,586	D	13	2,035	D	27	D	393	121	35	-38	D	919	344	-17	308
Other	1,653	0	199	860	D	21	D	287	213	15	-9	-43	D	D	182	115
Japan	17,269	D	147	5,040	95	1,180	981	2,546	239	2,005	174	541	3,019	D	4,296	1,963
Australia, New Zealand, and South Africa	839	D	138	977	172	-121	153	-6	778	173	D	-100	-659	D	34	23
Latin America and Other Western Hemisphere	2,494	-8	518	-128	55	-39	-104	61	-101	251	75	83	2,281	215	-1,143	351
South and Central America	910	0	496	135	*	-32	D	D	101	-88	9	49	136	D	-30	D
Panama	187	0	-2	44	D	D	D	-8	42	-68	6	D	76	D	-13	-24
Other	723	0	498	91	55	D	-2	D	59	-20	3	D	61	D	-17	D
Other Western Hemisphere	1,585	-8	21	-263	D	-6	-28	D	-202	339	66	34	2,144	D	-1,113	D
Bermuda	355	0	6	41	D	-8	D	2	D	442	100	D	D	-20	-24	*
Netherlands Antilles	-144	D	27	-332	D	-4	D	-9	-313	-54	-110	3	86	2	-71	75
U.K. Islands, Caribbean	1,471	D	D	216	0	D	D	D	68	-50	D	*	2,041	D	-903	D
Other	-97	0	D	-189	D	D	D	D	D	1	D	D	D	D	-116	6
Middle East	594	0	D	135	3	3	D	D	-6	225	0	13	-22	0	13	D
Israel	-97	0	0	D	*	*	0	D	-8	D	D	27	D	0	13	-1
Other	691	0	D	D	0	D	D	D	1	D	D	-14	D	0	0	D
Other Africa, Asia, and Pacific	944	D	D	550	66	435	D	D	97	-279	96	12	243	3	115	D
Addendum—OPEC[1]	1,240	D	457	D	D	7	D	14	-1	D	1	9	*	0	5	D

*Less than $500,000 (±).

D Suppressed to avoid disclosure of data of individual companies.

[1] See footnote 1, Table A23-10.

451

Table A23-14 FOREIGN DIRECT INVESTMENT IN THE UNITED STATES: EQUITY CAPITAL INFLOWS, 1988
(millions of dollars; outflows (−))

	All Industries	Mining	Petroleum	Manufacturing						Wholesale Trade	Retail Trade	Banking	Finance, (Except Banking)	Insurance	Real Estate	Other Industries
				Total	Food and Kindred Products	Chemicals and Allied Products	Primary and Fabricated Metals	Machinery	Other Manufacturing							
All countries	40,362	438	866	17,573	1,322	1,491	2,257	3,710	8,793	5,765	468	2,707	2,324	1,260	2,737	6,225
Canada	2,184	D	D	1,093	D	D	1	D	297	60	-18	106	D	293	13	386
Europe	20,369	179	650	9,909	782	810	619	2,198	5,500	1,948	498	1,786	1,369	892	500	2,638
European Communities (12)	18,526	D	D	9,435	782	626	500	2,110	5,418	1,090	496	1,704	1,370	D	464	2,345
Belgium	820	0	D	D	D	*	0	0	D	0	0	D	D	*	0	*
France	1,822	0	1	1,741	D	160	*	D	1,443	17	D	39	D	4	45	94
Germany, Federal Republic of	1,730	D	5	1,184	5	D	D	475	143	120	D	16	D	44	6	D
Italy	147	0	0	35	0	0	D	0	D	1	0	D	0	0	0	D
Luxembourg	219	0	0	D	0	0	D	0	0	0	0	6	0	D	*	D
Netherlands	1,535	0	14	452	341	D	D	186	-48	60	60	-73	41	D	161	86
United Kingdom	11,608	182	D	5,400	D	D	D	1,316	3,603	441	729	1,375	D	D	252	1,877
Other EC	647	0	0	239	D	0	0	D	D	D	0	340	0	D	0	D
Other Europe	1,843	D	D	474	1	184	119	89	82	859	2	82	-1	D	36	293
Sweden	195	D	0	115	0	D	0	78	D	D	0	0	0	*	D	D
Switzerland	1,396	0	0	207	0	D	D	6	44	D	2	16	*	D	D	293
Other	252	0	D	152	1	0	D	5	D	D	D	67	-1	-1	24	0
Japan	14,472	0	15	6,209	85	666	1,696	860	2,902	1,837	D	782	724	D	1,833	3,050
Australia, New Zealand, and South Africa	604	D	D	D	*	D	D	0	D	D	0	-6	D	D	D	-101
Latin America and Other Western Hemisphere	1,551	0	0	-125	1	*	D	D	-105	D	91	-29	D	0	256	D
South and Central America	-1	0	0	1	1	0	0	0	0	9	0	-31	D	0	12	D
Panama	24	0	0	1	1	0	0	0	0	9	0	3	D	0	D	0
Other	-25	0	0	0	0	0	0	0	*	*	0	-33	0	0	D	0
Other Western Hemisphere	1,552	0	0	-126	0	*	D	D	-105	D	91	2	*	0	244	D
Bermuda	17	0	0	0	0	0	D	0	0	2	3	2	0	0	1	11
Netherlands Antilles	1,437	0	0	-22	0	0	D	0	-1	D	D	2	0	0	181	D
U.K. Islands, Caribbean	94	0	0	-104	0	0	0	0	-104	6	D	0	*	0	60	D
Other	3	0	D	D	0	0	0	0	0	1	0	0	0	0	1	1
Middle East	746	0	0	0	0	0	0	0	0	D	0	17	D	0	D	D
Israel	-8	0	D	0	0	0	0	0	0	0	0	D	0	0	1	D
Other	753	0	D	D	0	0	0	0	0	D	0	D	0	0	D	D
Other Africa, Asia, and Pacific	437	D	D	282	D	0	D	-56	D	47	D	50	1	0	36	D
Addendum—OPEC[1]	1,034	0	D	D	D	0	D	0	0	D	0	-13	0	0	D	D

*Less than $500,000 (±).

D Suppressed to avoid disclosure of data of individual companies.

[1] See footnote 1, Table A23-10.

Table A23-15 FOREIGN DIRECT INVESTMENT IN THE UNITED STATES: EQUITY CAPITAL INFLOWS, 1989
(millions of dollars; outflows (−))

	All Industries	Mining	Petroleum	Manufacturing — Total	Food and Kindred Products	Chemicals and Allied Products	Primary and Fabricated Metals	Machinery	Other Manufacturing	Wholesale Trade	Retail Trade	Banking	Finance, (Except Banking)	Insurance	Real Estate	Other Industries
All countries	46,683	547	698	25,405	1,692	9,154	4,345	3,587	6,626	2,879	231	3,025	4,203	588	3,938	5,168
Canada	1,498	D	D	1,016	D	D	D	136	711	23	D	161	D	-61	222	-321
Europe	29,876	D	460	18,719	1,410	7,693	3,408	2,028	4,181	1,797	D	2,113	1,712	631	927	3,241
European Communities (12)	25,596	D	460	16,536	D	7,857	D	1,798	3,703	1,606	D	1,979	926	209	836	2,775
Belgium	208	0	D	D	0	D	0	0	0	0	4	D	0	0	D	D
France	4,686	0	D	3,591	256	D	0	555	D	66	D	199	360	0	1	D
Germany, Federal Republic of	2,696	D	D	1,263	D	751	D	286	D	476	0	450	212	96	129	30
Italy	329	0	0	251	D	0	-1	D	D	0	0	62	0	0	D	D
Luxembourg	53	0	0	1	0	0	D	0	1	0	0	-1	D	0	D	D
Netherlands	2,897	0	D	1,336	20	D	D	D	653	24	43	D	D	D	397	310
United Kingdom	14,192	0	D	10,018	D	0	D	410	2,508	1,039	D	438	0	23	232	D
Other EC	534	0	0	534	D	0	0	3	D	0	5	D	0	0	D	3
Other Europe	4,280	0	0	2,183	D	-164	D	229	479	191	6	134	786	422	91	467
Sweden	433	0	0	247	0	D	*	D	201	D	6	1	D	D	78	D
Switzerland	2,987	0	0	D	0	D	D	D	D	D	6	21	556	D	6	361
Other	860	0	0	D	D	D	D	130	D	7	0	112	D	D	7	D
Japan	11,684	0	73	3,948	45	1,066	689	1,283	865	659	D	458	2,089	D	2,489	1,757
Australia, New Zealand, and South Africa	1,253	D	0	D	0	0	D	0	D	D	0	42	D	4	*	8
Latin America and Other Western Hemisphere	1,122	0	D	291	D	D	D	4	109	8	-14	190	24	D	228	290
South and Central America	494	0	D	96	0	0	0	0	96	*	0	184	D	0	4	0
Panama	65	0	0	D	0	0	0	0	D	*	0	*	D	0	4	0
Other	428	0	D	D	0	0	0	0	D	0	0	185	D	0	0	0
Other Western Hemisphere	629	0	D	195	0	D	D	4	13	8	-14	6	D	D	224	290
Bermuda	D	0	0	D	0	0	0	0	D	0	0	6	0	0	1	D
Netherlands Antilles	363	0	0	D	0	0	0	0	D	0	81	6	0	0	195	200
U.K. Islands, Caribbean	283	0	0	175	0	0	0	4	8	D	-94	*	0	1	28	
Other	D	0	0	D	0	0	0	0	0	D	0	0	0	0	D	0
Middle East	107	0	0	0	0	0	0	0	0	0	0	8	0	0	D	1
Israel	5	0	0	0	0	0	D	0	0	0	0	5	0	0	0	0
Other	102	0	D	D	0	0	D	0	0	0	0	3	0	0	0	1
Other Africa, Asia, and Pacific	1,143	0	D	563	3	376	D	136	D	D	0	54	D	0	D	191
Addendum—OPEC[1]	266	0	D	D	0	0	D	0	0	0	0	22	0	0	D	1

*Less than $500,000 (±).

D Suppressed to avoid disclosure of data of individual companies.

[1] See footnote 1, Table A23-10.

Table A23-16 FOREIGN DIRECT INVESTMENT IN THE UNITED STATES: REINVESTED EARNINGS, 1988 (millions of dollars)

	All Industries	Mining	Petroleum	Manufacturing						Wholesale Trade	Retail Trade	Banking	Finance, (Except Banking)	Insurance	Real Estate	Other Industries
				Total	Food and Kindred Products	Chemicals and Allied Products	Primary and Fabricated Metals	Machinery	Other Manufacturing							
All countries	6,560	128	696	4,030	711	2,213	610	-221	718	1,353	65	581	197	1,136	-1,428	-198
Canada	-183	-5	57	395	16	154	227	55	-57	-141	-430	-10	29	181	-281	21
Europe	5,916	24	642	3,429	685	1,803	330	-215	826	579	522	431	29	711	-538	87
European Communities (12)	4,817	18	560	2,845	771	1,437	174	-328	791	419	525	471	-95	496	-494	73
Belgium	273	4	D	174	-5	D	7	*	D	-18	D	-2	1	*	-1	-9
France	*	-7	-3	74	8	48	12	-72	78	-8	-8	1	-41	11	-5	-15
Germany, Federal Republic of	253	-1	25	191	-1	282	42	-316	183	139	48	-91	-86	113	-28	-57
Italy	-79	D	-16	-125	-5	3	3	-113	-13	43	-2	7	D	4	D	-2
Luxembourg	27	D	-1	10	-2	0	4		8	14	*	-1	1	0	D	8
Netherlands	867	-24	539	301	-19	269	62	33	-43	-47	33	332	62	91	-258	-162
United Kingdom	3,337	22	-97	2,092	791	672	46	138	445	314	448	195	-29	278	-182	297
Other EC	140	0	D	129	4	D	-2	2	-18	-18	D	30	D	-2	*	13
Other Europe	1,099	6	82	584	-86	366	156	113	36	160	-2	-40	124	215	-44	14
Sweden	379	D	32	185	*	D	D	125	-3	63	*	D	D	D	1	7
Switzerland	764	D	35	365	D	297	D	5	41	101	4	D	125	161	-8	9
Other	-44	0	15	34	D	D	54	-17	-3	-4	-6	-49	D	D	-38	-3
Japan	364	D	-72	-120	20	78	40	-37	-220	835	-26	12	-54	19	-184	D
Australia, New Zealand, and South Africa	148	D	-14	17	-1	2	19	*	-3	9	D	-11	8	2	44	21
Latin America and Other Western Hemisphere	620	25	78	334	-4	177	-2	4	159	84	-27	169	171	222	-439	3
South and Central America	444	0	D	-4	1	1	1	-9	2	12	7	175	-2	D	-27	19
Panama	242	0	1	1	1	1	2	-5	2	*	7	D	-3	D	-17	-3
Other	202	0	D	-5	*	0	-1	-4	0	12	*	D	*	4	-10	22
Other Western Hemisphere	176	25	D	339	-5	177	-2	13	157	72	-34	-6	173	D	-412	-17
Bermuda	85	D	D	103	-2	0	-1	*	106	22	-5	D	1	D	-1	8
Netherlands Antilles	-58	0	74	227	-2	172	-1	16	41	44	-32	-5	-4	D	-356	-30
U.K. Islands, Caribbean	105	*	D	3	-2	*	-1	-3	9	4	D	-1	168	2	-57	*
Other	44	D	D	6	0	5	D	*	*	3	D	*	7	0	3	6
Middle East	-183	-5	5	28	*	D	D	4	D	-2	D	34	13	0	5	D
Israel	43	0	0	D	*	0	0	*	D	-1	D	41	D	0	0	1
Other	-226	-5	5	D	0	D	D	4	0	-1	D	-7	D	0	5	D
Other Africa, Asia, and Pacific	-123	*	0	-53	-5	D	D	-33	D	-12	17	-44	1	*	-34	2
Addendum—OPEC[1]	-123	-5	D	D	*	*	D	*	0	-1	0	24	1	0	-3	D

*Less than $500,000 (±).

Suppressed to avoid disclosure of data of individual companies.

[1]See footnote 1, Table A23-10.

Table A23-17 FOREIGN DIRECT INVESTMENT IN THE UNITED STATES: REINVESTED EARNINGS, 1989
(millions of dollars)

	All Industries	Mining	Petroleum	Manufacturing — Total	Food and Kindred Products	Chemicals and Allied Products	Primary and Fabricated Metals	Machinery	Other Manufacturing	Wholesale Trade	Retail Trade	Banking	Finance, (Except Banking)	Insurance	Real Estate	Other Industries
All countries	−88	208	−461	1,403	109	1,199	591	−807	311	−168	33	−762	16	1,825	−2,341	158
Canada	−150	82	118	382	−33	21	216	149	30	3	−447	−118	41	276	−537	49
Europe	895	23	−613	1,452	176	1,066	302	−753	660	−266	572	−418	−343	1,272	−847	63
European Communities (12)	307	17	−713	1,031	119	785	299	−755	584	−250	576	−294	−317	960	−769	66
Belgium	193	D	D	63	2	45	3	7	6	−23	D	11	D	0	D	−8
France	−493	−6	−1	−302	−19	−366	121	−88	51	−23	−10	−16	−170	10	−8	33
Germany, Federal Republic of	286	−2	17	92	−2	408	9	−426	103	43	−18	−44	52	174	−37	10
Italy	−91	D	−20	−57	−15	3	*	−24	−21	2	−2	−2	D	5	D	−5
Luxembourg	−30	1	−1	7	−2	0	9	*	*	5	−1	−3	1	0	−11	−29
Netherlands	378	−32	697	379	349	233	49	−274	22	−238	15	83	−196	119	−430	−20
United Kingdom	−48	45	−1,534	789	−185	459	110	48	357	−22	540	−352	16	654	−259	73
Other EC	111	0	D	60	−8	3	−2	2	65	5	D	28	D	−2	*	12
Other Europe	588	6	99	421	57	282	3	3	76	−16	−3	−124	−25	311	−78	−3
Sweden	134	D	33	112	−1	40	3	38	29	−9	D	2	D	−15	−8	18
Switzerland	546	D	52	237	D	D	6	4	62	15	6	−41	D	319	−24	−14
Other	−91	0	15	71	D	D	−13	−39	−14	−21	D	−84	D	7	−47	−7
Japan	−301	D	−30	−492	9	28	15	−66	−478	228	−47	91	103	29	−176	−28
Australia, New Zealand, and South Africa	−77	50	D	15	−9	D	53	D	−30	D	D	−142	11	6	19	D
Latin America and Other Western Hemisphere	−369	13	74	123	−17	53	D	D	93	1	−65	−142	194	239	−732	−73
South and Central America	148	0	D	15	−1	−7	D	D	*	7	4	−139	D	D	−34	−17
Panama	188	0	5	19	−2	−7	D	D	*	−9	5	D	D	D	−17	−22
Other	−40	0	D	−4	*	0	−1	−3	0	15	−1	D	*	3	−17	5
Other Western Hemisphere	−516	13	D	108	−15	60	−23	−8	94	−6	−70	−3	D	D	−698	−56
Bermuda	−22	0	−5	−12	−3	0	D	D	18	19	−54	1	2	−10	31	7
Netherlands Antilles	−460	D	58	80	−4	D	D	5	27	25	D	−4	7	D	−596	−44
U.K. Islands, Caribbean	−51	D	D	31	−9	*	3	−13	51	D	−10	*	3	*	−130	−16
Other	16	0	7	9	0	D	5	D	−3	D	D	*	3	*	−3	−2
Middle East	243	0	−6	D	D	D	D	3	−8	D	D	9	9	0	−7	D
Israel	32	0	0	−7	*	0	0	*	−8	7	D	26	10	0	0	−3
Other	211	D	−6	D	0	*	D	2	0	D	D	−17	−1	0	−7	D
Other Africa, Asia, and Pacific	−329	*	D	D	−18	D	−40	−121	43	−126	7	−42	*	3	−60	−12
Addendum—OPEC[1]	252	D	D	*	*	*	D	*	0	D	0	−13	−1	0	−15	D

*Less than $500,000 (±).

DSuppressed to avoid disclosure of data of individual companies.

[1]See footnote 1, Table A23-10.

455

Table A23-18 FOREIGN DIRECT INVESTMENT IN THE UNITED STATES: INTERCOMPANY DEBT INFLOWS, 1988 (millions of dollars; outflows (−))

	All Industries	Mining	Petroleum	Manufacturing Total	Food and Kindred Products	Chemicals and Allied Products	Primary and Fabricated Metals	Machinery	Other Manufacturing	Wholesale Trade	Retail Trade	Banking	Finance, (Except Banking)	Insurance	Real Estate	Other Industries
All countries	11,513	77	-2,426	6,629	-138	811	626	-267	5,597	3,272	3,330	-400	-3,455	431	3,223	833
Canada	845	D	D	D	D	D	116	D	11	367	47	8	D	-70	-19	513
Europe	3,539	-2	-2,683	4,076	-202	1,151	647	-425	2,904	1,822	2,806	14	-3,631	503	189	446
European Communities (12)	5,022	D	D	4,662	D	1,251	D	-760	2,773	2,145	2,844	-67	-2,995	D	194	433
Belgium	294	D	69	D	-1	D	D	-81	7	274	D	D	10	*	0	1
France	-860	D	D	-415	D	-26	89	D	2	151	D	0	D	*	-2	-56
Germany, Federal Republic of	323	D	-7	1,425	575	D	D	61	-60	330	D	0	D	-11	-34	D
Italy	-1,107	-2	-49	-49	D	-21	D	*	D	-10	1	D	-1,031	D	0	D
Luxembourg	114	D	D	D	D	0	57	*	0	7	D	0	29	0	0	D
Netherlands	2,365	-9	D	1,322	167	D	D	-9	1,195	D	-48	-81	502	D	124	D
United Kingdom	3,829	-69	-2,466	2,382	D	D	D	-252	1,633	1,094	3,155	1	D	D	105	469
Other EC	63	D	0	13	-1	D	D	D	D	D	D	0	-3	D	D	50
Other Europe	-1,483	D	D	-586	D	-101	D	336	131	-323	-39	81	-636	0	-5	12
Sweden	-264	1	12	196	1	-23	D	227	D	D	1	0	-620	*	D	1
Switzerland	-1,346	*	-143	-862	D	D	-18	98	79	D	-40	0	60	-1	D	33
Other	128	D	79	79	1	D	56	11	D	D	*	81	-77	-1	-1	-22
Japan	3,001	0	-20	692	33	-181	-11	185	666	352	D	-413	76	6	2,272	D
Australia, New Zealand, and South Africa	-463	*	D	D	D	D	D	2	D	D	D	0	D	-3	D	-6
Latin America and Other Western Hemisphere	3,728	*	72	1,729	19	-23	D	D	1,714	D	418	-5	D	-3	755	D
South and Central America	141	0	D	-72	*	-53	D	D	-1	17	-4	-5	D	*	69	-19
Panama	100	0	D	-40	D	D	D	*	0	19	-1	0	D	D	D	-1
Other	41	0	114	-32	D	D	-4	D	-1	-2	-3	-5	-10	D	D	-18
Other Western Hemisphere	3,587	*	D	1,801	19	30	-24	61	1,715	421	D	-1	858	-3	686	D
Bermuda	-85	D	D	8	D	7	D	D	-55	-1	D	0	D	1	-8	2
Netherlands Antilles	1,428	*	0	1,826	D	23	0	D	1,784	D	D	D	-58	-6	-221	D
U.K. Islands, Caribbean	1,770	D	*	-7	5	D	0	2	-13	3	0	D	935	-6	844	-4
Other	474	0	-26	-26	0	D	-24	D	-1	*	442	0	D	2	71	2
Middle East	255	D	-10	D	D	D	-15	D	D	D	D	-4	-2	0	D	13
Israel	-30	0	0	-42	D	1	0	D	-44	0	0	D	-6	0	D	D
Other	285	D	-10	D	0	D	-15	-1	D	262	D	D	4	0	D	D
Other Africa, Asia, and Pacific	608	5	56	39	-11	D	-2	D	-45	371	D	0	140	-3	31	D
Addendum—OPEC[1]	398	D	99	-12	0	-4	-12	4	*	275	-1	-5	-1	0	D	12

*Less than $500,000 (±).

D Suppressed to avoid disclosure of data of individual companies.

[1] See footnote 1, Table A23-10.

Table A23-19 FOREIGN DIRECT INVESTMENT IN THE UNITED STATES: INTERCOMPANY DEBT INFLOWS, 1989 (millions of dollars; outflows (−))

	All Industries	Mining	Petroleum	Manufacturing						Wholesale Trade	Retail Trade	Banking	Finance, (Except Banking)	Insurance	Real Estate	Other Industries
				Total	Food and Kindred Products	Chemicals and Allied Products	Primary and Fabricated Metals	Machinery	Other Manufacturing							
All countries	25,649	147	331	12,074	5,581	1,679	918	3,901	-5	1,660	1,456	-140	4,631	137	2,338	3,015
Canada	1,388	D	D	647	D	D	D	7	259	-236	D	-8	D	155	50	551
Europe	16,597	D	-333	10,092	5,047	1,892	595	2,474	84	676	-155	-155	2,343	-24	804	2,101
European Communities (12)	16,584	D	-489	9,888	D	1,899	D	2,419	66	694	D	-69	2,393	315	586	2,121
Belgium	-56	*	-193	D	D	-56	D	50	-15	139	D	D	D	*	D	D
France	1,106	D	38	696	88	D	D	-18	D	208	D	0	110	D	-16	D
Germany, Federal Republic of	1,247	D	D	539	-48	355	D	71	D	53	20	0	-101	17	2	690
Italy	748	-1	D	-26	2	-56	D	D	D	-26	5	0	849	D	0	D
Luxembourg	587	D	D	-57	D	0	D	*	0	-35	D	0	182	0	98	D
Netherlands	6,552	85	66	3,743	181	D	D	774	163	73	469	D	D	D	31	D
United Kingdom	6,090	D	D	4,982	D	D	D	-4	-349	310	*	5	293	154	0	D
Other EC	309	0	*	D	21	8	D	55	D	-27	D	D	-50	D	D	D
Other Europe	14	*	156	204	D	-7	-1	D	18	-19	-51	-86	-50	-339	218	-20
Sweden	-924	0	11	-447	-1	D	D	D	9	D	D	D	-525	D	-4	D
Switzerland	54	*	-39	D	D	D	D	D	D	D	-50	D	D	D	0	-39
Other	884	0	185	D	3	*	191	195	D	30	D	-71	D	1	222	D
Japan	5,886	-12	104	1,584	41	85	277	1,329	-149	1,118	D	-8	827	-1	1,984	D
Australia, New Zealand, and South Africa	-337	-9	D	D	180	D	D	D	D	2	-23	0	D	D	15	43
Latin America and Other Western Hemisphere	1,741	-22	D	-542	D	D	-198	D	-303	242	154	35	2,062	D	-639	135
South and Central America	269	0	D	24	1	-25	*	43	5	-95	4	3	1	D	1	D
Panama	-66	0	-7	D	D	D	2	D	D	-59	*	0	15	D	1	-2
Other	335	0	D	D	D	D	-1	D	D	-36	4	3	D	D	*	D
Other Western Hemisphere	1,472	-22	4	-566	D	D	-198	D	-308	337	150	31	D	-8	-640	D
Bermuda	-48	0	11	D	D	-8	D	D	22	423	D	D	78	-10	-56	D
Netherlands Antilles	D	4	D	D	D	-73	0	-3	D	-79	D	1	1,932	D	331	D
U.K. Islands, Caribbean	1,239	-25	*	11	D	D	0	0	9	-6	-5	0	D	D	-800	D
Other	D	0	D	-198	0	-1	0	*	D	-2	171	D	D	1	-114	8
Middle East	245	21	7	D	0	3	0	D	2	D	1	-4	-30	0	0	22
Israel	-134	0	0	D	0	0	0	D	*	D	0	-4	D	0	0	2
Other	378	21	7	3	0	0	0	D	1	355	1	0	D	0	D	20
Other Africa, Asia, and Pacific	130	D	90	D	80	D	-74	D	D	D	89	0	D	1	D	D
Addendum—OPEC[1]	722	21	314	19	D	7	D	14	-1	348	1	0	1	0	D	D

*Less than $500,000 (±).

D Suppressed to avoid disclosure of data of individual companies.

[1] See footnote 1, Table A23-10.

Table A23-20 FOREIGN DIRECT INVESTMENT IN THE UNITED STATES: INCOME, 1988
(millions of dollars)

	All Industries	Mining	Petroleum	Manufacturing Total	Food and Kindred Products	Chemicals and Allied Products	Primary and Fabricated Metals	Machinery	Other Manufacturing	Wholesale Trade	Retail Trade	Banking	Finance, (Except Banking)	Insurance	Real Estate	Other Industries
All countries	16,748	195	2,929	7,172	1,706	2,985	1,005	11	1,465	2,627	587	1,724	-232	1,430	-118	433
Canada	1,082	9	126	451	20	156	237	57	-20	178	-400	302	37	246	-16	149
Europe	13,370	69	2,774	6,288	1,663	2,547	678	-2	1,401	1,383	955	738	-257	950	-46	516
European Communities (12)	11,657	61	2,710	5,301	1,565	2,139	515	-226	1,309	1,050	947	692	-269	712	-21	475
Belgium	405	5	D	183	3	D	8	-1	D	-6	12	1	*	-1	-8	
France	414	-7	-3	466	19	134	272	-60	102	5	8	47	-102	12	-5	-8
Germany, Federal Republic of	589	1	32	391	56	389	50	-312	208	269	52	-51	-169	118	-14	-47
Italy	-83	D	-8	-122	-5	2	4	-113	-10	46	-2	24	D	4	D	-2
Luxembourg	23	D	-1	14	-2	0	7	1	8	15	*	-1	-9	0	D	8
Netherlands	2,869	13	623	1,267	498	454	92	58	166	159	154	349	195	215	-18	-89
United Kingdom	7,259	26	1,867	2,960	992	993	84	200	692	568	710	269	-146	365	36	604
Other EC	181	0	D	141	4	D	-2	2	D	-6	D	43	D	-1	*	16
Other Europe	1,712	8	64	987	99	409	164	224	92	333	8	47	12	238	-25	41
Sweden	381	D	33	260	*	D	D	172	12	121	*	D	D	2	2	10
Switzerland	1,359	D	36	688	D	334	D	68	79	213	14	D	154	178	-2	33
Other	-28	0	-6	40	D	D	57	-17	1	*	-6	-40	D	D	-26	-2
Japan	1,478	D	-70	-40	24	83	53	-21	179	962	-25	461	25	20	137	D
Australia, New Zealand, and South Africa	130	D	-11	33	2	-6	29	*	9	10	D	-5	-46	2	46	22
Latin America and Other Western Hemisphere	893	25	105	433	*	194	1	3	235	123	21	197	5	211	-251	24
South and Central America	517	0	D	-3	2	1	3	-11	2	10	7	203	-2	D	-9	24
Panama	275	0	1	4	1	1	5	-5	2	-2	7	D	-2	D	-1	-3
Other	243	0	D	-6	1	*	-1	-5	0	12	*	D	*	4	-9	26
Other Western Hemisphere	376	25	D	435	-2	193	-2	13	232	113	14	-6	7	D	-242	1
Bermuda	95	0	D	104	1	0	-1	-1	106	33	-3	*	3	D	7	9
Netherlands Antilles	235	D	83	319	-2	188	*	18	115	73	-29	-5	-3	2	-211	-16
U.K. Islands, Caribbean	-51	*	D	7	*	*	-1	-3	12	4	D	-1	-1	0	-49	1
Other	96	D	D	6	0	5	*	*	D	3	D	*	7	0	10	6
Middle East	-154	-2	5	28	*	D	D	4	D	-5	D	40	16	0	28	D
Israel	43	0	0	D	*	0	0	4	D	-4	0	45	D	0	0	-1
Other	-197	-2	5	D	0	D	0	4	0	-1	D	-6	D	0	28	D
Other Africa, Asia, and Pacific	-51	*	*	-21	-4	D	D	-31	D	-24	26	-8	-12	*	-16	
Addendum—OPEC[1]	-78	-2	D	D	*	*	D	-1	0	-1	*	25	2	0	20	D

*Less than $500,000 (±).

D Suppressed to avoid disclosure of data of individual companies.

[1] See footnote 1, Table A23-10.

Table A23-21 FOREIGN DIRECT INVESTMENT IN THE UNITED STATES: INCOME, 1989

(millions of dollars)

	All Industries	Mining	Petroleum	Manufacturing Total	Food and Kindred Products	Chemicals and Allied Products	Primary and Fabricated Metals	Machinery	Other Manufacturing	Wholesale Trade	Retail Trade	Banking	Finance (Except Banking)	Insurance	Real Estate	Other Industries
All countries	**14,004**	**300**	**2,991**	**5,752**	**1,403**	**2,351**	**940**	**-412**	**1,469**	**1,562**	**830**	**715**	**-396**	**2,165**	**-975**	**1,061**
Canada	**894**	**87**	**200**	**447**	**-18**	**23**	**238**	**153**	**51**	**128**	**-399**	**236**	**53**	**317**	**-444**	**270**
Europe	**11,788**	**99**	**2,690**	**5,373**	**1,412**	**2,206**	**573**	**-390**	**1,571**	**1,083**	**1,212**	**-37**	**-550**	**1,577**	**-284**	**626**
European Communities (12)	10,052	90	2,604	4,171	1,141	1,652	504	-547	1,421	900	1,197	-1	-523	1,248	-228	593
Belgium	378	D	D	20	-1	-8	D	4	1	-22	D	23	D	0	D	-8
France	-198	-6	3	-56	20	-294	206	-93	104	7	-10	33	-217	12	-8	45
Germany, Federal Republic of	627	-1	23	352	52	576	18	-432	138	199	-4	-25	-107	179	-18	30
Italy	-140	D	-12	-59	-15	-4	*	-24	-17	5	-2	16	D	5	D	-5
Luxembourg	-28	1	-1	12	-2	0	14	*	*	6	-1	-3	-2	0	-11	-29
Netherlands	2,464	23	726	1,347	476	514	102	-182	436	-29	122	120	10	293	-208	60
United Kingdom	6,778	62	1,597	2,428	610	802	162	176	677	719	1,030	-208	-129	762	41	477
Other EC	171	0	D	74	-8	3	-2	2	79	15	D	43	D	-2	*	23
Other Europe	1,736	9	85	1,202	271	554	69	157	151	183	14	-36	-27	329	-56	33
Sweden	291	D	34	264	-1	82	11	118	53	57	D	2	D	-5	-8	21
Switzerland	1,470	D	52	836	D	D	41	57	107	141	24	35	D	327	-17	18
Other	-25	0	*	103	D	D	17	-18	-10	-15	D	-74	D	7	-31	-6
Japan	**1,277**	**52**	**-24**	**-353**	**16**	**D**	**67**	**-47**	**-394**	**360**	**-44**	**741**	**218**	**29**	**278**	**D**
Australia, New Zealand, and South Africa	**-189**		**D**	**64**	**19**	**D**	**D**	**D**	**-9**	**D**	**D**	**-140**	**-175**	**7**	**22**	**-26**
Latin American and Other Western Hemisphere	**73**	**11**	**120**	**272**	**-13**	**60**	**D**	**D**	**214**	**29**	**32**	**-118**	**61**	**233**	**-534**	**34**
South and Central America	239	0	D	20	-1	-8	D	D	1	5	4	-115	D	D	-21	-14
Panama	220	0	5	24	-2	-7	-1	D	1	-11	5	D	*	D	-6	-22
Other	18	0	D	-4	*	*	-13	-3	0	16	-1	D	D	3	-16	8
Other Western Hemisphere	-166	11	D	252	-11	67	D	-3	213	24	28	-3	6	D	-513	-20
Bermuda	-11	D	-5	-7	*	0	D	D	18	21	-52	1	8	-24	41	8
Netherlands Antilles	-116	D	65	207	-4	D	9	7	145	52	1	-4	D	*	-441	-21
U.K. Islands, Caribbean	-173	D	D	40	-8	D	9	-13	52	D	-10	*	9	D	-121	-10
Other	135	0	7	12	0	D	D	D	-3	D	D	1	10	*	7	3
Middle East	**331**	**0**	**-5**	**-7**	*****	**D**	**0**	**3**	**-8**	**3**	**0**	**16**	**10**	**0**	**17**	**3**
Israel	33	0	0	D	*	0	D	*	-8	D	D	31	10	0	0	D
Other	298	D	-5	D	0	*	D	2	0	D	D	-15	*	0	17	D
Other Africa, Asia, and Pacific	**-170**	*****	**D**	**D**	**-14**	**D**	**-39**	**-116**	**44**	**-83**	**16**	**17**	**-13**	**3**	**-30**	**8**
Addendum—OPEC[1]	378	D	D	D	*	*	D	*	0	D	*	-11	-1	0	9	D

*Less than $500,000 (±).

D Suppressed to avoid disclosure of data of individual companies.

[1] See footnote 1, Table A23-10.

459

Table A23-22 FOREIGN DIRECT INVESTMENT IN THE UNITED STATES: COUNTRY DETAIL FOR SELECTED ITEMS (millions of dollars)

Line		Direct Investment Position					Capital Inflows (Outflows (−))					Income				
		1985	1986	1987	1988	1989	1985	1986	1987	1988	1989	1985	1986	1987	1988	1989
1	All countries	184,615	220,414	271,788	328,850	400,817	19,022	34,091	46,894	58,435	72,244	6,079	5,379	9,500	16,748	14,004
2	Canada	17,131	20,318	24,013	27,361	31,538	911	2,547	1,614	2,847	2,736	348	390	943	1,082	894
3	Europe	121,413	144,181	186,076	216,418	262,011	12,794	21,730	40,436	29,824	47,368	5,240	5,701	8,465	13,370	11,788
4	European Communities (10)	107,105	126,853	164,969	193,301	234,120	9,823	19,000	36,096	28,215	42,425	4,801	4,846	7,021	11,610	10,028
5	Belgium	2,291	2,487	2,638	4,024	4,535	-171	597	115	1,387	345	80	-23	339	405	378
6	France	6,670	7,709	10,119	11,364	16,375	30	1,017	2,471	962	5,299	-157	54	56	414	-198
7	Germany, Federal Republic of	14,816	17,250	20,315	23,845	28,223	2,292	1,982	3,150	2,306	4,229	605	-23	-172	589	627
8	Italy	1,237	1,323	1,707	667	1,586	-5	114	-334	-1,039	987	-115	18	-53	-83	-149
9	Luxembourg	345	263	133	525	935	-176	-45	-147	360	610	61	3	7	23	-28
10	Netherlands	37,056	40,717	49,115	49,991	60,483	2,776	4,374	8,293	4,766	9,826	2,131	2,179	2,240	2,869	2,464
11	United Kingdom	43,555	55,935	79,669	101,909	119,137	4,665	10,827	22,444	18,774	20,235	2,127	2,611	4,520	7,259	6,778
12	Denmark, Greece, and Ireland	1,135	1,168	1,274	1,976	2,845	413	134	104	700	893	69	27	85	134	147
13	Denmark	577	552	532	594	601	230	57	-18	63	49	27	-52	-28	-8	-7
14	Greece	D	256	268	278	277	D	D	13	8	-1	8	D	D	D	-3
15	Ireland	D	360	474	1,103	1,967	D	D	109	630	845	35	D	133	157	157
16	Other Europe	14,308	17,328	21,107	23,116	27,891	2,970	2,729	4,340	1,609	4,944	439	855	1,444	1,760	1,761
17	Sweden	2,357	3,963	4,953	5,263	4,925	236	1,395	973	310	-357	175	164	399	381	291
18	Switzerland	10,568	12,058	14,686	15,896	19,329	2,722	1,414	3,210	813	3,586	625	864	1,052	1,359	1,470
19	Other	1,382	1,308	1,468	1,958	3,638	13	-80	156	486	1,715	-360	-173	-7	19	-1
20	Andorra	1	3	1	1	1	*	2	-2	0	1	0		0	*	*
21	Austria	127	118	131	174	372	-293	-11	13	43	213	-377	-209	-26	-46	-87
22	Bulgaria	D	D	D	D	D	D	0	0	0	D	0	0	0	0	0
23	Cyprus	D	D	D	D	D	D	D	0	D	0	0	0	0	0	0
24	Czechoslovakia	1	1	1	1	1	0	0	0	0	0	-1	0	0	0	0
25	Finland	220	195	228	377	1,466	113	-25	29	149	1,074	0		0	-22	91
26	Gibraltar	3	3	3	3	9	0	0	0	0	6	4	0	0	*	*
27	Hungary	8	9	9	8	7	-1	1	*	-1	-D			0	-5	*
28	Iceland	D	D	D	D	D	D	D	D	D	D			*	-1	
29	Liechtenstein	221	230	229	261	275	-5	*	14	32	13	-10	3	3	0	2
30	Malta	*	3	*	*	2	*	*	0	0	2		0	*		13
31	Norway	396	241	271	382	686	121	-160	27	111	338	-10	-6	-11	36	-50
32	Poland	29	30	30	33	33	1	2	-1	4	*	2	1	1	1	0
33	Portugal	*	18	21	23	22	4	18	-1	1	-1			1	3	1
34	Spain	273	350	436	588	653	64	77	79	148	62	33	31	18	45	23
35	Turkey	1	1	2	3	*	*	-1	2	1	1	*	*	4	5	6
36	Union of Soviet Socialist Republics	12	12	11	11	8	-1	-1	-1	-1	-3	-1	-1	*	*	*
37	Yugoslavia	39	60	40	40	48	-4	21	-19	*	8	-1	-1	3	4	*
38	Japan	19,313	26,824	35,151	53,354	69,699	3,394	7,268	7,504	17,838	17,269	1,561	1,009	846	1,478	1,277
39	Australia, New Zealand, and South Africa	3,324	5,634	6,552	5,624	6,532	1,235	2,719	793	289	839	27	28	-183	130	-189
40	Australia	3,264	5,466	6,015	5,330	6,236	1,209	2,606	469	532	837	22	39	-174	120	-173
41	New Zealand	72	97	272	213	237	20	29	130	-59	23	2	-11	-13	8	-17
42	South Africa	-12	72	265	81	59	6	84	194	-184	-22	3	1	4	2	1
43	Latin America and Other Western Hemisphere	16,826	16,763	12,671	17,019	20,348	719	-332	-4,200	5,899	2,494	-693	-1,395	-247	893	73
44	South and Central America	3,491	4,190	4,394	4,978	5,915	424	826	108	584	910	-6	241	102	517	239
45	Panama	2,204	2,202	2,319	2,747	2,961	73	57	54	366	187	-103	128	6	275	220
46	Other	1,287	1,988	2,075	2,232	2,955	350	769	54	218	723	97	113	97	243	18
47	Argentina	280	292	339	324	384	43	12	24	-14	59	35	25	9	22	17

(Continued)

No.	Country	1	2	3	4	5	6	7	8	9	10	11	12	13	14
48	Belize	D	D	*	*	-1	D	D	0	0	0	0	0	0	D
49	Bolivia	0	0	0	0	5	2	0	0	0	0	0	0	0	D
50	Brazil	201	182	249	279	334	42	-13	58	28	20	15	16	47	64
51	Chile	16	14	26	29	16	21	-1	11	3	2	2	2	1	1
52	Colombia	75	78	75	73	58	6	3	-3	-2	2	12	-4	2	*
53	Costa Rica	-3	D	-1	-1	*	*	-1	-1	*	*	*	*	*	*
54	Ecuador	41	45	4	4	3	7	4	-1	1	4	4	4	1	1
55	El Salvador	D	D	D	1	2	D	D	2	1	D	2	4	1	*
56	Guatemala	8	8	6	7	3	7	-2	1	1	*	*	1	1	1
57	Honduras	6	6	5	5	5	D	*	*	1	1	1	*	*	*
58	Mexico	533	847	903	858	958	222	315	26	18	-1	-21	-11	36	-133
59	Nicaragua	-7	1	2	2	3	1	*	1	1	-5	1	*	*	1
60	Paraguay	-7	1	1	1	4	-5	-2	1	1	-5	1	1	1	D
61	Peru	4	D	6	7	8	1	D	*	-2	*	*	1	1	0
62	Suriname	0	0	*	-2	-2	D	0	0	-9	0	-1	0	0	0
63	Uruguay	2	2	1	-8	4	D	-1	-1	-2	0	74	30	-1	0
64	Venezuela	103	476	456	649	1,170	55	444	-23	193	30	74	81	133	81
65	Other Western Hemisphere	13,335	12,573	8,277	12,040	14,432	296	-1,157	-4,308	5,314	-687	-1,636	-349	376	-166
66	Bermuda	1,691	2,002	1,712	1,680	1,936	333	19	-149	17	-255	193	140	95	-11
67	Netherlands Antilles	10,443	9,685	9,317	10,591	10,570	-224	-750	-459	2,806	-462	-1,742	-286	235	-116
68	United Kingdom Islands, Caribbean	1,028	560	-3,148	-1,104	1,128	170	-554	-3,753	1,970	51	-122	-247	-51	-173
69	Other	172	326	396	873	798	18	127	53	521	-20	35	44	96	135
70	Bahamas	154	309	201	157	D	13	129	-124	1	-20	32	37	47	3D
71	Barbados	D	D	41	D	5	2	D	D	D	2	3	5	D	3D
72	Dominican Republic	-2	-2	*	0	0	-2	*	*	*	-2	0	*	0	0
73	French Islands, Caribbean														
74	Haiti	1	1	1	1	1	0	*	0	0	0	0	0	0	0
75	Jamaica	5	1	154	D	D	5	-5	154	D	0	0	2	D	0D
76	St. Kitts and Nevis	*	D	*	*	0	0	D	D	0	0	0	0	0	0
77	*	-1	-1	*	-1	1	0	-1	1	-1	0	0	0	0	0
78	Middle East	4,954	4,870	4,998	5,831	6,425	-370	-68	117	818	-396	-389	-352	-154	331
79	Israel	494	567	514	519	422	-28	49	-61	5	13	1	11	43	33
80	Other	4,460	4,303	4,484	5,312	6,003	-342	-117	178	813	-409	-390	-363	-197	298
81	Bahrain	-3	23	40	40	16	6	27	13	8	-2	-3	-2	1	-1
82	Iran	16	14	14	13	11	-1	-2	*	-2	-1	-2	-2	-1	-2
83	Iraq-Saudi Arabia Neutral Zone	0	0	0	0	0	0	0	0	0	0	0	0	0	0
84	Iraq	0	*	*	*	*	*	*	*	*	*	*	*	*	*
85	Jordan	-3	*	-2	2	-1	6	3	-3	5	2	3	4	5	5
86	Kuwait	3,968	3,771	3,919	3,852	4,197	-352	-154	163	-67	-403	-391	-355	-196	266
87	Lebanon	40	49	56	64	70	9	6	10	8	5	8	D	8	5
88	Oman	-1	*	*	D	D	2	1	0	0	0	0	0	0	0
89	Qatar	3	3	3	6	*	1	-1	-1	4	*	D	*	*	*
90	Saudi Arabia	420	436	438	1,280	1,638	-10	16	-2	826	-5	10	-9	-3	41
91	United Arab Emirates	19	4	16	55	53	-1	-15	-2	39	-3	-16	-10	-11	-17
92	Other Africa, Asia, and Pacific	1,654	1,823	2,325	3,243	4,263	339	228	630	921	-9	34	27	-51	-170
93	Afghanistan	2	D	D	D	D	D	D	D	D	0	D	0	0	0
94	Algeria	D	D	0	0	0	D	0	D	0	0	-2	-1	-1	0
95	Bangladesh	0	0	*	*	0	0	0	0	*	0	0	0	0	0
96	Brunei	0	0	0	0	0	1	0	*	0	0	0	0	0	0
97	Cameroon	*	*	-1	-1	-1	1	1	1	-1	*	-1	-3	-3	0
98	China	8	10	12	34	83	1	16	21	21	2	10	-9	-11	41
99	Congo	*	4	*	*	*	*	-15	0	*	0	-16	-10	-51	-17
100	Egypt	4	9	12	11	5	D	3	4	-1	0	34	27	0	-170
101	Fiji	*	*	*	*	*	*	0	0	0	0	0	0	0	0
102	French Islands, Indian Ocean	0	0	0	0	0	0	0	0	0	0	0	0	0	0
103	French Islands, Pacific	0	2	2	2	2	2	1	0	2	0	1	0	0	0
104	Gabon	*	0	0	-2	*	*	0	0	2	0	0	0	0	0

(Continued)

461

Line		Direct Investment Position					Capital Inflows (Outflows (−))					Income				
		1985	1986	1987	1988	1989	1985	1986	1987	1988	1989	1985	1986	1987	1988	1989
105	Ghana	0	1	3	3	3	0	1	2	*	0	0	0	0	0	0
106	Guinea-Bissau	0	*	*	3	3	0	*	*	0	0	0	0	0	0	0
107	Hong Kong	640	605	944	892	1,198	2	41	509	−48	246	34	83	17	−41	−139
108	India	19	18	19	19	25	3	−1	1	D	5	*	−3	1	2	1
109	Indonesia	49	37	43	D	377	33	−11	6	D	D	*	−7	*	−4	5
110	Ivory Coast	1	1	2	2	2	*	*	*	*	*	*	*	*	*	*
111	Kampuchea	0	0	0	0	−3	0	0	0	0	−3	0	0	0	0	0
112	Kenya	−1	−4	−4	8	D	*	−3	*	12	D	*	*	*	*	*
113	Loas	−3	−4	−5	D	D	−1	−1	−1	D	D	0	0	0	0	0
114	Liberia	361	87	139	216	500	233	−273	19	77	210	−1	−1	−1	−1	−1
115	Libya	0	2	2	2	2	0	0	D	D	D	−2	−35	14	−21	−6
116	Madagascar	0	2	D	0	0	0	2	0	−1	*	0	0	0	0	*
117	Malawi	0	0	0	−1	−1	−5	0	0	75	−34	0	0	0	0	0
118	Malaysia	16	39	9	84	50	0	23	−30	75	−34	−1	−4	−2	−1	D
119	Maldives	0	0	0	0	0	*	0	0	0	0	0	0	0	0	0
120	Morocco	1	1	1	1	1	1	*	*	*	*	*	*	−2	*	*
121	Namibia	D	D	D	D	D	D	D	D	D	D	*	*	−1	0	−2
122	Nauru	−8	6	1	3	2	1	14	−5	2	3	0	0	−1	4	1
123	Nigeria	15	19	19	18	21	−2	4	−1	*	*	0	3	3	2	3
124	Pakistan	15	19	19	18	21	−3	−5	9	19	3	−1	3	8	3	7
125	Philippines	118	113	121	140	158	34	−73	0	0	19	3	5	0	14	12
126	Senegal	0	0	0	0	0	−3	0	0	0	0	0	0	0	0	0
127	Singapore	242	169	398	475	1,216	6	−73	229	79	741	6	5	−1	9	67
128	South Korea	−101	383	192	456	−216	−53	474	−199	264	−672	−53	−17	−54	−34	−55
129	Sri Lanka	*	0	0	0	0	*	0	30	0	0	0	0	0	0	0
130	Taiwan	107	177	207	329	620	37	71	30	121	341	*	10	45	30	22
131	Tanzania	1	1	0	1	1	1	0	0	0	0	1	−3	1	1	1
132	Thailand	13	14	60	55	71	−5	−8	47	−6	16	−3	−3	−3	1	D
133	Togo	*	*	*	0	0	0	0	0	0	0	0	0	0	0	0
134	Tunisia	0	*	0	0	*	−1	*	−1	)	*	−1	*	*	0	0
135	United Kingdom Islands, Atlantic (Africa)	0	0	0	0	*	0	0	0	0	*	0	0	0	0	0
136	United Kingdom Islands, Pacific	0	0	0	0	*	0	0	0	0	0	0	0	0	0	0
137	Vanuatu	0	0	0	5	5	0	0	0	5	0	0	*	0	*	0
138	Zaire	D	D	D	D	D	D	D	D	D	−1	*	*	D	*	−1
139	Zambia	*	*	*	D	D	D	0	D	D	D	*	*	0	1	−1
140	Zimbabwe	0	*	D	0	0	0	*	D	0	0	0	0	0	0	0
	Addenda:															
141	OPEC	4,607	4,787	4,897	6,221	7,462	−277	294	147	1,309	1,240	−380	−329	−291	−78	378
142	European Communities (12)[2]		127,221	165,427	193,312	234,794		19,095	36,174	28,365	42,486		4,878	7,040	11,657	10,052

*Less than $500,000 (±).

bSuppressed to avoid disclosure of data of individual companies.

[1] See footnote 1, Table A23-10.

[2] In 1986, Portugal and Spain joined the European Communities; prior to 1986, data for Portugal and Spain were included in "Other Europe."

Table A23-23 FOREIGN DIRECT INVESTMENT IN THE UNITED STATES: INDUSTRY DETAIL FOR SELECTED ITEMS (Millions of dollars)

Line		Direct Investment Position					Capital Inflows (Outflows(−))					Income				
		1985	1986	1987	1988	1989	1985	1986	1987	1988	1989	1985	1986	1987	1988	1989
1	All industries	184,615	220,414	271,788	328,850	400,817	19,022	34,091	46,894	58,435	72,244	6,079	5,379	9,500	16,748	14,004
2	Mining	4,039	5,080	5,718	6,390	7,179	−57	962	515	644	903	−501	−140	134	195	300
3	Metal mining	753	1,099	1,738	1,989	2,217	−95	346	614	251	312	−209	27	77	75	162
4	Iron ores	D	D	D	D	D	D	D	D	D	D	D	D	D	D	D
5	Copper, lead, zinc, gold, and silver ores	348	656	1,265	1,459	1,615	D	308	594	194	240	−189	37	53	42	114
6	Bauxite and other aluminum ores	0	0	0	0	0	0	0	0	0	0	0	0	0	0	0
7	Other metallic ores	276	292	309	349	401	40	16	17	40	52	14	19	15	12	24
8	Metal mining services	−1	D	D	D	D	−1	D	D	D	D	−1	D	D	D	D
9	Coal	2,871	3,480	3,223	3,459	3,617	56	543	−355	208	186	−331	−227	−8	68	53
10	Nonmetallic minerals, except fuels	415	500	757	942	1,346	−18	73	257	184	404	39	59	65	52	85
11	Petroleum	28,270	29,094	35,598	34,704	35,089	3,147	662	6,619	−863	568	2,153	302	2,345	2,929	2,991
12	Oil and gas extraction	2,839	2,392	2,279	3,050	3,341	424	−405	−168	798	468	−50	−462	−49	−43	129
13	Crude petroleum (no refining) and natural gas	2,163	1,849	1,727	2,458	2,752	450	−271	−178	759	349	−34	−343	−45	−73	80
14	Oil and gas field services	676	542	552	592	679	−27	−134	10	40	119	−16	−118	−4	30	49
15	Petroleum and coal products manufacturing	22,163	22,434	30,779	29,361	29,004	1,902	−2,909	7,227	−1,418	−357	1,957	515	2,275	2,774	2,597
16	Integrated petroleum refining and extraction	22,142	22,376	30,666	29,184	28,127	1,909	−220	7,172	−1,482	−1,056	1,964	517	2,249	2,708	2,535
17	Petroleum refining without extraction	D	7	60	108	D	−8	D	52	49	D	−8	−5	D	D	D
18	Petroleum and coal products, nec	D	51	54	69	D	1	D	3	15	D	D	3	D	D	D
19	Petroleum wholesale trade	2,767	3,734	1,658	1,351	1,674	835	1,243	−794	−304	420	146	159	−4	98	175
20	Other	501	534	882	942	980	−14	33	354	61	38	100	90	124	100	90
21	Petroleum tanker operations	313	296	371	368	388	13	3	D	D	D	81	79	67	D	50
22	Pipelines, petroleum and natural gas	125	115	114	120	127	−19	−18	75	−3	20	14	8	16	D	D
23	Petroleum storage for hire	D	D	D	D	D	−10	−10	6	5	7	3	8	D	0	D
24	Gasoline service stations						2	D	D	D	D	2	D	D	D	0
25	Manufacturing	59,584	71,963	94,745	121,434	160,216	8,049	11,865	23,372	28,232	38,882	200	75	3,864	7,172	5,752
26	Food and kindred products	10,710	12,147	15,638	16,437	23,927	2,538	1,337	3,491	1,895	7,382	441	797	772	1,709	1,403
27	Grain mill and bakery products	684	1,054	1,207	1,420	1,845	143	316	260	213	424	54	96	95	132	53
28	Grain mill products	223	258	505	605	815	30	34	251	100	210	19	D	D	54	81
29	Bakery products	461	796	702	815	1,030	113	281	9	113	215	34	D	D	78	−29
30	Beverages	6,135	6,448	8,984	7,425	14,459	600	218	2,492	−478	6,975	380	434	458	1,260	879
31	Other	3,891	4,645	5,448	7,592	7,623	1,794	803	738	2,159	−17	7	266	219	314	472
32	Meat products	144	162	183	195	232	127	8	9	12	37	−17	−3	4	6	9
33	Dairy products	303	443	470	702	977	19	199	27	233	275	19	33	23	25	8
34	Preserved fruits and vegetables	D	34	41	51	62	D	D	7	10	11	3	4	2	6	3
35	Other food and kindred products	D	D	4,754	6,643	6,351	1	D	696	1,905	−341	1	232	189	276	451
36	Chemicals and allied products	18,836	22,954	29,943	34,146	46,268	1,945	4,106	7,859	4,515	12,033	488	518	2,049	2,985	2,351
37	Industrial chemicals and synthetics	12,844	16,196	19,833	21,695	25,316	1,973	3,216	4,416	2,499	3,602	336	176	1,109	1,864	1,241
38	Drugs	2,428	3,339	3,750	4,433	10,825	104	1,022	435	619	6,358	131	257	475	555	443
39	Soap, cleaners, and toilet goods	1,815	2,036	4,294	5,403	6,476	−371	220	2,258	1,085	1,074	10	56	323	431	486
40	Agricultural chemicals	989	454	525	613	626	−33	−496	72	88	13	1	3	59	73	62
41	Other	760	929	1,541	2,002	3,024	272	144	677	223	986	9	26	83	61	120
42	Paints and allied products	−5	−2	3	7	13	−1	3	4	4	6	9	5	6	6	7
43	Chemical products, nec	765	931	1,539	1,995	3,011	273	141	673	219	980	7	21	77	55	112

(Continued)

Line		Direct Investment Position					Capital Inflows (Outflows (−))					Income				
		1985	1986	1987	1988	1989	1985	1986	1987	1988	1989	1985	1986	1987	1988	1989
44	Primary and fabricated results	6,952	7,282	8,967	12,541	18,569	1,089	448	1,679	3,492	5,954	-408	31	384	1,005	940
45	Primary and fabricated metals	6,952	7,282	8,967	12,541	18,569	1,089	448	1,679	3,492	5,854	-408	31	384	1,005	940
45	Primary metal industries	5,296	5,342	6,065	7,484	10,833	892	170	727	1,343	3,175	-496	-98	215	795	757
46	Ferrous	1,454	1,618	1,773	2,360	2,927	-289	208	115	487	559	-305	-74	-70	212	166
47	Nonferrous	3,842	3,724	4,292	5,124	7,906	1,180	-38	611	856	2,617	-190	-24	285	583	591
48	Fabricated metal products	1,656	1,940	2,903	5,057	7,736	198	278	952	2,149	2,679	88	129	169	210	184
49	Metal cans and shipping containers	-7	D	*	13	43	-2	D	D	13	30	-2	-2	-1	-1	*
50	Cutlery, hand tools, and hardware	64	82	90	648	692	20	18	8	557	44	3	3	6	13	-7
51	Plumbing fixtures and heating equipment ex. electric 6	D 161	D	D	-3	D	D	D	D	-3	8	9	7	6		
52	Fabricated structural metal products	508	572	1,008	990	2,752	37	63	427	-22	1,762	30	44	86	78	72
53	Screw machine products, bolts, etc.	5	5	6	6	6	-3	-1	1	*	*	-3	-1	1	2	1
54	Metal forgings and stampings	77	110	161	D	D	8	31	51	D	D	5	2	-5	-1	-14
55	Fabricated metal products, nec, ordnance, and services 1,003	1,019	1,477	1,876	2,735	142	12	459	399	859	58	74	72	113	125	
56	Machinery	9,234	11,547	15,983	18,281	26,472	-357	1,695	4,477	3,222	6,681	-836	-2,257	-607	11	-412
57	Machinery, except electrical	3,916	4,349	5,965	7,992	10,213	230	312	1,611	2,008	2,077	-206	-288	-202	155	-39
58	Construction, mining, and materials handling machinery	1,089	1,133	1,159	1,898	2,449	160	-33	-38	739	383	-102	-79	-167	76	69
59	Special industry machinery	512	640	802	1,098	1,056	-36	107	172	297	-72	-25	-14	8	6	-86
60	Office and computing machines	1,025	1,126	2,491	2,701	4,048	-120	74	1,448	210	1,305	-44	-42	128	156	*
61	Other	1,291	1,450	1,513	2,295	2,661	226	164	29	762	461	-35	-154	-170	-83	-22
62	Engines and turbines	218	430	361	375	435	92	212	-69	14	67	-28	-30	D	-21	-68
63	Farm and garden machinery	70	-57	-54	63	53	-44	-127	3	117	-10	-19	-36	-63	-105	-5
64	Metalworking machinery	332	318	340	462	679	18	-10	14	121	305	-2	-53	6	12	39
65	General industry machinery	406	543	616	1,076	1,168	33	131	71	458	92	-1	-2	40	29	24
66	Refrigeration and service industry machinery	67	69	66	118	80	36	9	-17	52	-38	35	-5	D	1	-6
67	Machinery, except electrical, nec	197	148	184	201	245	92	-50	27	-1	45	-10	-28	9	*	-7
68	Electric and electronic equipment	5,318	7,198	10,018	11,288	16,259	-587	1,384	2,867	1,214	4,604	-630	-1,968	-405	-145	-373
69	Radio, television, and communication equipment	1,969	3,544	5,167	4,598	5,209	-23	1,057	1,637	-581	664	92	D	-90	-189	-5
70	Electronic components and accessories	2,172	2,059	2,792	3,052	6,929	-562	-1,068	1,083	915	3,458	-721	D	-367	-50	-418
71	Other	1,177	2,643	D	3,639	4,121	-2	1,394	146	880	482	-2	13	51	94	50
72	Household appliances	441	D	D	D	D	77	-332	59	-147	157	D	D	D	149	92
73	Electric lighting and wiring equipment	23	26	35	25	93	D	2	7	-10	68	D	D	D	-8	-22
74	Electrical machinery, nec	712	D	D	D	D	-2	2	D	D	D	-71	-84	-90	-47	-21
75	Other manufacturing	13,852	18,033	24,213	39,030	44,981	2,834	4,278	5,867	15,108	6,931	515	987	1,265	1,465	1,469
76	Textile products and apparel	440	747	1,053	1,424	1,757	-4	270	256	365	322	36	62	142	73	51
77	Textile mill products	172	267	418	632	896	40	95	102	213	253	12	28	57	25	23
78	Apparel and other textile products	269	480	635	792	861	77	174	155	151	69	25	34	85	49	28
79	Lumber, wood, furniture, and fixtures	1,170	829	893	771	777						-17	-11	89	117	116
80	Lumber and wood products	D	575	644	419	576						-16	-20	75	84	105
81	Furniture and fixtures	D	254	249	352	201						-2	10	14	33	12
82	Paper and allied products	1,141	1,292	1,743	2,003	2,530	611	151	424	261	527	82	131	189	333	293
83	Pulp, paper, and board mills	513	567	747	773	1,152	484	54	169	26	379	5	19	47	88	91
84	Miscellaneous converted paper products	467	556	657	720	736	105	89	101	62	16	61	71	56	59	51

(Continued)

Line		Direct Investment Position					Capital Inflows (Outflows (-))					Income				
		1985	1986	1987	1988	1989	1985	1986	1987	1988	1989	1985	1986	1987	1988	1989
85	Paperboard containers and boxes	161	169	338	510	642	21	8	154	173	132	16	40	87	187	150
86	Printing and publishing	3,326	4,978	6,019	12,816	12,971	872	1,844	995	6,797	465	208	227	-125	120	335
87	Rubber and plastics products	774	1,353	2,210	5,588	5,885	46	432	987	3,411	338	3	88	168	53	-105
88	Rubber products	258	251	666	2,467	2,531	-24	13	733	1,800	64	11	19	-18	-47	-246
89	Miscellaneous plastics products	517	1,103	1,543	3,122	3,354	70	419	254	1,611	274	-8	70	185	100	141
90	Stone, clay, and glass products	3,275	3,347	4,332	6,915	6,963	662	-45	826	2,631	36	251	442	276	474	420
91	Glass products	D	293	312	606	752	D	D	19	294	146	44	20	-11	17	47
92	Stone, clay, concrete, gypsum, etc	D	3,054	4,020	6,309	6,210	D	D	807	2,337	-110	207	422	287	447	373
93	Transportation equipment	2,142	2,358	2,500	2,898	4,828	296	217	345	347	2,593	-145	-201	120	-111	-222
94	Motor vehicles and equipment	1,537	1,899	1,891	2,383	3,912	235	362	189	473	2,191	-163	-115	94	-64	-243
95	Other transportation equipment, nec	605	459	609	514	916	61	-145	157	-126	402	18	-86	26	-46	21
96	Instruments and related products	1,049	1,981	3,661	4,557	5,985	323	1,222	1,329	883	1,410	124	110	215	153	186
97	Scientific and measuring instruments	191	453	233	702	1,066	21	472	27	456	364	1	14	19	18	23
98	Optical and opthalmic goods	245	287	343	377	471	D	42	56	34	93	36	32	63	53	64
99	Medical instruments and supplies	312	702	1,923	2,279	2,870	101	370	719	357	591	29	31	113	52	32
100	Photographic equipment and supplies	192	494	D	1,077	1,423	24	303	D	D	329	13	17	7	15	24
101	Watches, clocks, and watches	109	144	D	121	155	D	34	D	D	34	45	16	13	15	43
102	Other	535	1,147	1,802	2,057	3,284	-89	521	648	457	1,184	-27	138	191	262	396
103	Tobacco manufactures	0	0	0	0	0	1	0	0	0	0	-1	0	0	0	0
104	Leather and leather products	208	D	D	D	D	D	D	D	D	D	D	D	D	D	D
105	Miscellaneous manufacturing industries	326	D	D	D	D	D	D	D	D	D	D	D	D	D	D
106	**Wholesale trade**	**29,051**	**33,997**	**39,754**	**50,160**	**43,549**	**3,882**	**4,679**	**5,212**	**10,390**	**4,371**	**2,412**	**1,491**	**2,051**	**2,627**	**1,562**
107	Motor vehicles and equipment	11,043	12,349	13,735	15,506	16,380	2,218	1,215	1,265	1,771	809	2,060	1,377	694	953	209
108	Metals and minerals, except petroleum	3,491	3,583	3,565	3,593	4,354	-224	47	-376	16	761	-58	15	238	157	249
109	Other durable goods	9,431	11,705	13,672	20,148	22,623	1,141	2,303	1,630	6,484	2,323	99	123	77	813	826
110	Lumber and other construction materials	601	747	800	823	1,009	237	146	56	22	186	3	24	54	65	46
111	Farm and garden machinery, equipment, and supplies	103	204	183	331	315	-40	95	-151	152	-16	5	11	26	12	-26
112	Electrical goods	3,219	4,243	4,887	7,415	8,995	477	976	592	2,528	1,554	-111	-49	-107	296	286
113	Hardware, plumbing, and heating equipment and supplies	120	130	226	544	675	22	11	11	318	4	10	8	16	46	84
114	Machinery, equipment, and supplies, nec	3,191	3,714	4,741	7,718	8,071	15	447	937	2,982	354	24	110	106	356	282
115	Durable goods, nec	2,198	2,666	2,835	3,317	3,559	430	628	184	482	242	168	20	-18	38	155
116	Farm product raw materials	1,049	1,357	1,741	2,117	1,591	178	257	399	374	-532	-58	77	114	203	-46
117	Other nondurable goods	4,036	5,003	7,040	8,795	9,601	568	857	2,294	1,745	1,011	297	-94	927	501	323
118	Paper and paper products	191	342	582	742	1,076	96	119	240	151	334	2	16	31	62	21
119	Drugs, proprietaries, and sundries	298	492	475	518	532	68	104	-17	44	14	70	85	124	114	58
120	Apparel, piece goods, and notions	191	124	160	300	236	101	-67	27	140	-36	12	-50	-11	3	-82
121	Groceries and related products	1,182	2,190	2,723	3,272	2,790	104	1,002	439	548	-294	78	102	142	115	101
122	Nondurablegoods, nec	2,174	1,855	3,100	3,963	4,967	200	-301	1,605	863	992	135	-247	641	207	224
123	**Retail trade**	**6,822**	**8,923**	**10,255**	**14,770**	**16,802**	**-21**	**1,759**	**1,251**	**3,863**	**1,720**	**249**	**818**	**591**	**587**	**830**
124	Food stores and eating and drinking place	2,886	3,619	4,018	3,739	4,308	72	663	244	-628	319	66	284	252	193	228
125	Retail trade, nec	3,937	5,304	6,236	11,031	13,494	-94	1,096	1,007	4,492	1,410	182	534	340	394	601
126	**Banking**	**11,377**	**12,394**	**14,455**	**17,453**	**19,581**	**1,445**	**1,757**	**886**	**2,887**	**2,123**	**1,379**	**1,448**	**216**	**1,724**	**715**

(Continued)

465

Line		Direct Investment Position					Capital Inflows (Outflows(-))					Income				
		1985	1986	1987	1988	1989	1985	1986	1987	1988	1989	1985	1986	1987	1988	1989
127	Finance, except banking	4,246	7,239	3,828	2,124	11,403	-1,530	1,896	-3,564	-935	8,851	-50	74	-108	-232	-396
128	Franchising business—selling or licensing	55	D	D	32	45	D	D	D	D	13	2	3	-4	*	-1
129	Holding companies	3,793	3,560	4,610	5,014	6,630	-162	441	1,016	711	1,522	-63	25	221	256	-185
130	Other finance	398	D	D	-2,922	4,728	D	D	D	D	7,316	11	46	-325	-488	-210
131	Insurance	11,806	14,345	17,392	20,252	22,713	2,250	3,702	396	2,826	2,550	892	1,698	992	1,430	2,165
132	Life insurance	7,260	9,363	10,898	12,284	13,596	1,229	2,653	-123	1,383	1,194	567	1,049	517	827	1,072
133	Accident and health insurance	D	D	D	D	D	261	D	D	D	D	D	D	D	D	D
134	Other insurance	D	D	D	D	D	759	D	D	D	D	D	D	D	D	D
135	Real estate	19,402	22,512	27,516	31,929	35,853	1,574	3,099	3,797	4,532	3,935	29	73	-180	-118	-975
136	Lessors of agricultural and forestry real estate	493	474	445	404	328	-27	-27	-28	-41	-77	-17	-23	-27	-40	-71
137	Real estate, nec	18,909	22,038	27,071	31,524	35,525	1,601	3,127	3,824	4,573	4,011	46	97	-153	-78	-904
138	Other industries	10,019	13,868	22,527	29,635	37,432	285	3,710	8,409	6,860	8,341	-684	-461	-405	433	1,061
139	Agriculture	952	1,068	1,398	1,525	1,759	-29	111	233	132	192	-44	-6	3	58	2
140	Agricultural production—crops	647	664	806	807	1,036	-31	26	98	1	186	-49	7	3	33	3
141	Agricultural production—livestock, ex. beef cattle idlt 266	320	365	502	507	27	38	45	142	5	7	-7	8	30	*	
142	Agricultural production—beef cattle feedlots	D	D	D	D	133	D	D	86	-2	2	-1	-1	-3	-2	-1
143	Agricultural services	D	47	133	131	84	D	D	4	-9	-1	-1	-5	-6	-3	*
144	Forestry and fishing	154	182	263	208	216	3	28	81	-55	12	-2	-1	2	-45	6
145	Forestry	145	169	194	136	147	2	24	24	-58	11	-3	-4	1	-38	13
146	Fishing, hunting, and trapping	9	13	69	73	69	1	4	56	3	1	2	2	1	-7	-7
147	Construction	4,037	3,602	2,542	3,397	3,877	-334	-402	-45	-145	494	-505	-529	-424	-330	305
148	Transportation	1,459	1,797	3,096	4,158	3,927	189	370	1,204	1,062	-72	33	21	101	218	70
149	Railroads	666	632	625	1,015	995	35	-35	-7	390	-20	8	-34	10	20	4
150	Water transportation	190	386	1,192	1,225	890	23	228	721	32	-335	12	15	60	63	41
151	Transportation by air	153	191	523	5121	703	18	38	345	-10	191	2	-5	12	59	42
152	Pipelines, except petroleum and natural gas	1	1	2	2	2	*	*	*	*	*	*	*	*	*	*
153	Travel agents	12	15	33	437	235	24	3	18	403	-43	7	7	*	22	17

(Continued)

Line		Direct Investment Position					Capital Inflows (Outflows(−))					Income				
		1985	1986	1987	1988	1989	1985	1986	1987	1988	1989	1985	1986	1987	1988	1989
154	Transportation and related services, nec	437	572	721	968	1,102	89	135	126	247	134	5	38	20	54	−34
155	Communication and public utilities	475	495	592	528	512	−34	140	83	−102	−1,186	−83	−26	−29	64	21
156	Communication	383	397	480	372	335	D	134	69	−145	−1,208	−75	20	−28	66	7
157	Electric, gas, and sanitary services	91	98	112	156	177	D	7	14	44	22	−8	−6	−1	−2	14
158	Services	2,943	6,724	13,637	19,819	27,141	490	3,461	6,853	5,967	8,902	−83	81	−57	468	657
159	Hotels and other lodging places	629	1,082	3,283	6,834	8,016	39	421	2,198	3,618	2,269	−8	130	−55	77	205
160	Business services	1,204	2,591	5,900	6,858	10,319	103	1,154	3,338	396	4,214	−94	−50	−141	37	−161
161	Advertising	D	602	816	910	984	−17	D	D	94	74	1	38	56	D	38
162	Research and development, and commercial testing lbs	83	134	D	D	D	3	50	6	D	D	6	3	−45	−55	−43
163	Management, consulting, and public relations	354	484	790	516	598	−2	102	329	−273	253	−110	−106	−111	−119	−135
164	Equipment rental and leasing, exc. autos & computers	135	413	641	1,116	1,473	−6	278	212	222	668	2	−10	−14	26	12
165	Employment agencies and temporary help supply	D	43	D	D	D	−3	D	D	D	D	−3	3	3	D	−5
166	Computer and data processing service	257	386	819	813	2,277	70	122	511	−7	1,409	30	16	−43	24	−6
167	Business services, nec	304	528	1,241	1,466	2,948	58	255	708	188	1,527	−19	5	13	33	−22
168	Motion pictures, including television tape and film	84	D	D	2,138	2,560	83	855	D	D	423	11	−35	−35	176	94
169	Engineering, architectural, and surveying services	200	D	D	238	814	26	47	D	D	589	−18	−15	*	7	26
170	Other services	827	1,801	3,069	4,025	5,431	240	985	1,253	956	1,408	25	51	173	172	493
171	Accounting, auditing, and bookkeeping services	D	D	D	D	D	D	D	D	D	D	1	1	2	2	2
172	Automotive rental and leasing, without drivers	13	D	D	D	233	D	D	D	D	D	0	−3	−2	−1	D
173	Health services	D	250	280	265	324	31	D	30	−16	59	13	17	22	14	D
174	Legal services	0	0	0	0	D	0	0	0	0	0	0	0	0	0	0
175	Educational services	0	0	0	*	D	0	0	0	*	D	0	0	0	0	*
176	Services, nec. provided on a commercial basis	584	1,516	2,748	3,685	4,846	196	943	1,217	926	1,162	11	35	152	157	433

*Less than $500,000 (±).

[b]Suppressed to avoid disclosure of data of individual companies.

Japanese Investment Abroad

JAPANESE FOREIGN INVESTMENT BY SECTORS AS OF END-FY 1988[a]
(US$ millions)

	FY1988	Cumulative FY1951–88		FY1988	Cumulative FY1951–88
North America					
Manufacturing	9,191	23,944	**Nonmanufacturing**	5,427	26,794
Others	3,542	4,684	Real estate	1,714	3,218
Electrical machinery	1,501	5,952	Finance/insurance	1,431	3,518
Iron/nonferrous metals	903	2,553	Services	869	4,697
Machinery	894	2,610	Commerce	544	2,827
Chemicals	812	2,311			
Transport equipment	809	3,030	**Latin America**		
Nonmanufacturing	13,096	49,949	**Manufacturing**	443	5,437
Real estate	5,652	15,782	Iron/nonferrous metals	169	1,933
Finance/insurance	3,221	12,370	Electrical machinery	125	491
Commerce	1,966	11,693	Transport equipment	55	1,050
Services	1,695	4,859	**Nonmanufacturing**	5,985	26,111
			Finance/insurance	4,077	10,990
			Transportation	1,545	9,235
Europe			Commerce	111	1,508
Manufacturing	1,547	4,857			
Electrical machinery	557	1,261	**Middle East**		
Machinery	261	626			
Chemical	247	594	**Manufacturing**	13	1,273
Transport equipment	116	913	Iron/nonferrous metals	7	66
Nonmanufacturing	7,304	24,098	Chemicals	4	1,128
Finance/insurance	4,345	14,853	**Nonmanufacturing**	225	673
Real estate	1,118	1,386	Mining	194	393
Services	1,030	1,570	Finance/insurance	30	123
Commerce	581	3,955			
Asia / Pacific			**Africa**		
Manufacturing	2,610	14,106	**Manufacturing**	1	226
Electrical machinery	855	2,470	Chemicals	1	20
Transport equipment	301	1,942	**Nonmanufacturing**	652	4,374
Others	292	1,505	Transportation	547	2,079
Machinery	259	1,090	Real estate	69	69
Iron/nonferrous metals	235	2,663			

[a]Ended March 31, 1989.

Source: Business International, October 16, 1989, p. 316.

The Teleport Project in St. Petersburg and Moscow

A Telecommunications Joint Venture in Russia

PAUL DYSENCHUK

ASSISTED BY HARVEY A. PONIACHEK

The needs of the former Union of Soviet Socialist Republics are enormous. One of the most important vehicles in transforming a country to an industrialized market-oriented economy is the telecommunications sector. AMRU International Corporation is proceeding to establish a joint telecommunications venture in Russia between the Russian Ministry of Communications and western partners, which it seeks to find. Capitalizing on the former Soviets advanced space program and technology, AMRU knew that using a satellite link to an earth station could greatly increase the amount of international phone lines between the United States and St. Petersburg (formerly called Leningrad under the USSR) and Moscow in the Russian Federation.

In analyzing the feasibility of this joint venture, AMRU anticipated to earn "hard currency" and rubles. By charging foreign businesses dollars, AMRU assumed that the revenue generated in international calls would quickly cover the cost of the project. Rubles denominated earnings would be used to defray expenses incurred by the Russian joint-venture partner.

This case presents the Teleport Project proposal formulated by AMRU International Corporation as well as background on the Russian economy in mid-1992. The reader is required to determine the feasibility of the project in light of the financial data and the economic and political circumstances of the country.

Highlights of the Economy

The Government of Boris Yeltsin, until only recently the feared "evil empire," told the International Monetary Fund in February 1992 that "the economy was in a state of acute crisis, marked by declining output, accelerating inflation, obsolescent capital stock, pervasive distortions in the relative price structure, serious structural imbalances, and severe ecological problems." The near term problems the government assumed would make this statement seem tame: a drop in the former Soviet Union's measured gross national product of 4 percent in 1990 and 13 percent in 1991, a decline in 1990 and 1991's oil production, which accounted for much of its hard currency earnings, a sharp reduction in gold reserves held by the Central Authorities, virtually no foreign exchange reserves and an external debt of over $80 billion, average wage rate up by over 20 percent between 1987 and 1990 and projected to double in 1991, a budget deficit for the Union/CIS of 20 percent of GDP in 1991, a currency system that knows little coordination among the remaining republics, a breakdown of supply and demand of goods among the enterprises, a collapsing infrastructure, and pollution so bad that it has shortened the life expectancy of most of its citizens.

Certain Risk Factors

Stability, consistency, convertability, military: these are just some of the words that come to mind when considering the risks of doing business in the former Soviet Union and some of the problems AMRU faced as it tried to complete the Teleport Project. The stability of the USSR was maintained by an ironhand from the Politburo of the Communist Party based in Moscow. This "stability" often extended beyond Moscow's borders and usually involved the use of force by the Soviet Army. As Mikhail Gorbachev rose to power, he saw that this method of control was a political and financial liability. He sought to loosen the ties with the former Eastern Bloc countries and achieve a "peace with honor" solution for the crisis in Afghanistan. The "evil empire" of communism was quickly disintegrating.

The army generals, *apparatchiks* and *nomenklatura* saw their position, power and prestige vanish before their eyes. In August 1991 while Gorbachev and his family were vacationing at their summer *dacha*, a coup was taking place in Moscow by certain members of this disenfranchised group. "The vodka *putsch*" was what it became known as due to the condition of some of its "leaders." This *coup de état* failed miserably and with it came the fall of Mikhail Gorbachev and the *peaceful* transition of power to Boris Yeltsin.

Boris Yeltsin has lasted longer than many people thought. He has stated that he will not seek another term in office at the end of his current five-year term. Whether the nationalistic and emotional outbursts of the masses will allow him to accomplish this remains to be seen.

AMRU is facing considerable problems with the constantly changing laws regarding ownership, taxation and investment. The question of privatization and ownership is of utmost importance. How do you go from a system where all means of production are controlled and owned by the state to one where private ownership is paramount? Many of these state-owned enterprises employ well over 100,000 people. What are the labor and social implications when such an enterprise is reorganized or placed in the Russian version of Chapter 11. Remember this was a society that literally used to be taken care of from "cradle to grave." AMRU believed that it had all the necessary legal approvals and signatures from the Space and Telecommunications Ministries of the Russian Federation for the Teleport Project to proceed smoothly.

The Russian Federation has recently joined the World Bank. One of the branches of the Bank is the Multilateral Investment Guarantee Agency (MIGA). This branch was established to promote private investment for economic development by insuring against noncommercial risk and providing promotional and advisory services to help member countries create an attractive investment climate. Russia is expected to join MIGA, which would lend a measure of comfortability to any and all companies investing here. The United States Governments Overseas Private Investment Corporation (OPIC) is also starting to insure certain projects that are taking place in Russia and other countries in the Commonwealth of Independent States. Bilateral investment treaties are being signed between governments and even Russian and western style insurance companies are starting to make their presence known and services available for the foreign investor.

The infrastructure is one of the problems that many companies face when investing in Russia. Before the break-up of the USSR, the Soviet Union had one of the best transportation systems. Now everything is in disarray and if your project needs to move raw materials to your plant or if you have to export your product quickly you should consider what means of transportation you will use to achieve this objective. With 13 telephones per 100 people, Russia is only slightly above most developing countries. AMRU knows that this part of the infrastructure needs improvement and can be profitable for the right company.

Repatriation of profits are allowed from Russia, but legislation and regulations keep constantly changing, which leaves the foreign investor totally confused. Even if you wanted to purchase and export certain products, an export tax of 20 percent is usually required, which may make any transaction prohibitive. Repatriation of hard currency by the investor is allowed, but again an absurd tax is placed on any amount over a certain value. The Russian ruble is convertible but fluctuates wildly and no major bank is willing to trade in them.

Any large transnational corporation cannot ignore Russia as it is a huge market. For a company with patience and perseverance— and one that is not looking at the next quarter's "bottom line"—the potential for profit can be enormous. The risks may be just as large, but AMRU believes that the Teleport Project will create meaningful jobs, generate hard currency and afford a transfer of technology to all elements that will diminish the risk of political intervention and lead to a successful and profitable project. Investment anywhere is a risk-taking proposition. In Russia it may be even more so, but for that country and the rest of the Commonwealth of Independent States there is no going back to the system that once was.

What Is a Teleport?[1]

As railway depots and seaports were the economic centers of the Industrial Age, so teleports are becoming the economic centers of the Information Age. And as modern highways and airports revolutionized transportation following the Second World War, so teleports are revolutionizing domestic and international telecommunications worldwide.

What is a teleport? The World Teleport Association defines a teleport as "an access facility to satellite or other long-haul telecommunications media incorporating a distribution network serving the greater regional community and often associated with a related real estate or other economic development."

Concentrating Information

The best way to understand the teleport concept is to compare it to today's airports. Airports are placed where traffic is concentrated, sorted and dispatched to other locations. And what is the point of this concentration? It permits facilities such as towers, terminals, runways, radar, and other equipment—which would be prohibitively expensive and needlessly redundant for individual airlines to build—to be shared by many air carriers. It also provides travelers with a single, convenient point of access to multiple carriers, as well as a concentration of ground transportation to move passengers to and from the airport. And not surprisingly, airports have also become natural office and warehouse locations

[1]Excerpts from AMRU Business Plan, 1992.

for companies that specialize in moving people and cargo by air.

A teleport is to information what an airport is to air passengers and cargo. A teleport consists of a telecommunications facility providing access to satellites, to microwave or fiber-optic networks serving individual locations or entire regions, and usually to telephone carriers as well. The teleports's customers enjoy single-source, shared access to these sophisticated telecommunications facilities without incurring directly the enormous expense of their construction.

Teleport Customers

Currently, two industries rank first among the customers of teleports: television and radio production and distribution companies (including cable TV), and the financial services industry, where the growth of 24-hour, round-the-world banking and trading have made investment in international telecommunications a basic prerequisite. But, while these two industries currently account for the bulk of world teleport traffic, all forms of business are now investing in telecommunications as never before in history.

International trade is one engine powering this boom in telecommunications. The immense growth of international trade has been the success story of the post-war decades. For large and small companies operating in dozens of fast-changing markets around the world, advanced global telecommunications is becoming a necessity of doing business. And as a company's telecommunications traffic grows and its needs become more sophisticated, teleports become a natural solution to high cost and complexity.

Computers are the other engine driving teleport development. The national and international expansion of business in the age of the computer has led to the need to send immense streams of data between distant locations. And because computer data is less for-

giving of error than voice transmissions, the demand for expensive, high-quality circuits has sky-rocketed. Here again, the teleport has proven to be the answer by providing sophisticated, high-quality facilities and services at a shared cost.

Office Space for Information Specialists

In the most cases, however, a teleport is more than a telecommunications facility. Typically, it is associated with a real estate development —"associated" meaning that the real estate project is most often launched not by the telecommunications provider but by a real estate developer or economic development agency working in formal or informal partnership. And it is from this association that significant benefits of the teleport concept can spring.

Ideally, the companies occupying the teleport office park are those which will benefit directly from close proximity to advanced telecommunications. Many teleport office parks, for example, will soon house the data processing centers of international corporations. The data centers receive information streams (financial transactions, orders, inventory levels) from offices around the world for processing and send the processed information (transaction confirmations, shipping data, profit-and-loss statements) back "downstream" to the remote offices as well as to headquarters for management overview. Teleports are already landlords for TV and radio broadcasters, cable TV distributors, publishers, and news organizations, in addition to providing telecommunications services to companies in these industries that are not tenants.

The combination of telecommunications and real estate development can have an impact on entire regions. Indeed, most developers of full-service teleports speak of "regional economic development"—the preservation and creation of jobs, business income and tax revenue—as a major goal. As business worldwide becomes ever more dependent on telecommunications, regions that cannot offer businesses attractive locations backed by advanced telecommunications are likely to fall behind economically.

Variations in Form

In practice, teleport development has proceeded differently in different regions of the world. In the United States, teleport development has been a largely private affair. It arose first from the needs of the television industry, particularly cable TV, for satellite distribution services; and the first U.S. teleports were telecommunication-only, satellite-only facilities. By the mid-1980's, however, several teleports combining satellite and terrestrial telecommunications with real estate developments had sprung up. One impetus to the development of these more diversified operations was the deregulation of the telephone market. One of the leading services sold by these teleports was alternate access to long-distance telephone carriers, particularly for data communication, bypassing the more costly local exchange.

In Canada, all teleport development has been undertaken by a government-chartered company, Telesat Canada. Concentrating almost exclusively on satellite service (and occasionally bypassing telephone circuits), this company has developed a nationwide network of facilities, including several operating teleports (one of which has an associated office park) and several more under development.

In Europe, the development of teleports has been spearheaded primarily by government and quasi-government agencies. A city government, port authority or other agency typically promotes the real estate development and provides incentive for private companies to build or occupy government-built premises. Telecommunications services —including satellite, microwave and fiber-optic networks, and telephonic system interconnection—are provided by the national telecommunications monopoly provider (PTT). It is worth nothing that, in the United Kingdom, the government has permitted two companies to compete in telecommunications services; each has constructed a teleport in London and operates nationwide terrestrial networks.

Government has an equally active involvement in Asia. The exact nature of this involvement varies from nation to nation. In several Asian nations, including South Korea and Hong Kong, the government-chartered monopoly carrier provides the services of a teleport without the actual construction of discrete facilities or a specific real estate development. In Japan, however, teleport development has proceeded along lines that resemble both the European and U.S. approaches. Like the governments of Europe, Japan's government has been heavily involved, and has developed a "Teletopia" plan, backed by strong tax and other incentives, designed to make telecommunications a means for catapulting Japan into the 21st Century. Individual cities selected as "Model Cities" under the plan are now proceeding with the development of no less than five teleport real estate complexes, and up to 60 more initiatives are expected in the future. Nippon Telegraph & Telephone (NTT) has also completed fiber-optic trunk cable extending the length of Japan.

But Japan has also been the first Asian nation to deregulate its telecommunications market, throwing open equipment supply and both domestic and international service to competition. The development of teleports will, therefore, take place in an environment of telecommunications competition more nearly resembling that of the United States than of Europe.

Outside these regions, teleport development is sparse, and the efforts of teleport developers are therefore all the more remarkable, given the usual lack of an existing "high-tech" industrial infrastructure.

The "Intelligent City"

The role which government is playing around the world in promoting teleport development is giving rise to an extension of the teleport concept. Increasingly, governments and public–private developers involved in telecommunications speak of creating "the advanced information society" or "the intelligent city" of the future. In this scenario, the benefits that data processing and telecommunications have brought to business—to the "intelligent office"—will be extended to the population of an entire city or region. By digitizing telephone service through implementation of the complex Integrated Systems Digital Network (ISDN), public carriers plan to give the public network the ability to offer the specialized services that currently require separate, often leased circuits. Each telephone will become a combination telephone, telefax machine and data terminal capable of communicating universally. It remains to be seen what impact ISDN, which is undergoing preliminary tests in several nations, will have on the emerging teleport industry.

The World Teleport Association

The World Teleport Association (WTA) was founded in 1985 in New York City to encourage mutual assistance and cooperation among its members in promoting the development of teleports, advanced telecommunications, and regional economic development projects around the world. Its primary goal is to encourage the development of new teleports and advanced telecommunications, to assist existing teleports, and to promote the teleport concept and the standardization of telecommunications worldwide.

The WTA's membership includes operating teleports, teleports under development, telecommunications carriers, telecommunications equipment manufacturers and suppliers, and others related to the field. In 1990, AMRU became the 19th member of the World Teleport Association.

The WTA is a non-profit organization governed by an international board of directors elected by the membership. In addition to the board, the membership has regional representation through regional committees, including:

- WTA-Asia
- WTA-Europe
- WTA-North America
- WTA-Latin America
- WTA-Africa/Middle East

Members also serve on general committees including teleport applications, real estate and economic development, membership, emerging role of teleports, and teleport development.

The Association provides its members and other interested parties with technical and marketing assistance, legal advice, industry education and seminars, general and regional committee participation, a quarterly newsletter, and annual general assemblies.

The Project Description[2]

Background

This plan outlines a global telecommunications business utilizing the St. Petersburg gateway and earth station in combination with American built and currently deployed satellite systems to provide a public network for voice (telephone and fax), data and video links between business customers and individuals, largely tourists, in the Russian Federation and in the United States.

[2]Excerpts from AMRU Business Plan, 1992.

CURRENT LACK OF LONG DISTANCE CAPACITY IN RUSSIA

With the dramatic increase of internal Russian and foreign investment activity there following the changes of the last 18 months or so, the number of foreign tourists and business visitors has more than doubled. The resulting demand to place incoming and outgoing international telephone calls has more than matched this growth. However, due to outdated and inadequate public telephone switching equipment there has been a severe lack of telecommunications capacity. Ratios of international calls being connected are reported to range from 1 to 30 and 1 to 300 attempts. Moscow's switches are especially overloaded. Along with the frustrations of delays, lost time and business there has been a major loss of revenue opportunity to the Russians and to prospective international long-distance carrier and business venture partners. Pent-up unfulfilled demand from domestic Russian telephone callers, while difficult to estimate, extends this opportunity further.

COMPETITOR TELECOM VENTURES IN RUSSIA

Many of the international telecommunication equipment and services vendors were at various stages of negotiations with first the USSR and now with individual republics' ministries of communications to offer additional capacity and more modern equipment. The main focus has been on the Moscow and St. Petersburg gateways.

Several joint ventures have been announced including cellular, microwave to satellite, and in sparsely populated Armenia, digitally switched direct dialing international service. Due to the enormous expense and time that will be required to modernize switching equipment and to install fiber-optic cables internally, communication by satellites has been emerging as both a near term and longer term answer for international calls, fax, data and video transmission. Domestic connectivity in this vast confederation of republics will follow.

RUSSIAN

AMRU International Trading Corporation is an international trading, consulting and project management firm with corporate headquarters in New York and an office in Moscow. It has traded extensively for the past 20 years with Russian companies, gaining in addition to local know-how a position of confidence, friendship and respect shared by relatively few outsiders. Due to this strong relationship with senior government and business leaders in the Russian Confederation, AMRU was asked two years ago by the heads of the then Ministry of General Machine Building and their sub department, GLAVCOSMOS (the Russian Space Agency) to develop and manage a joint venture in satellite communications.

MOSCOW TELEPORT—ORIGINAL PROJECT

The initial plan was to combine Russian satellite capability, generally viewed as second to none, and equipment on a teleport site which they were awarded by the City of Moscow with AMRU project development and management skills, finance and skilled personnel sourcing and established relationships with the major long-distance carriers. Russian earth station equipment and small network switches were to be used with one or two Russian satellites and correcting Russian earth stations, one at the Moscow teleport site and one in the United States. This would bypass the large gateway switch that is needed eventually.

Exploratory discussions were held with several major long-distance carriers with varying strategies, some influenced by equipment sales priorities, but all with interest in participating in this well-recognized, high-profile growth opportunity.

The Moscow teleport permits were awarded in 1991, first by the central government and later by the Russian Republic Ministry of Communications and the City of Moscow. A teleport site and building complex development plan with self-contained office/industrial park was prepared, prospective tenants secured and first stage project financing in place.

St. Petersburg Teleport New First Priority

Due to the greater immediate attraction of a recent request from the City of St. Petersburg and its location as the oldest international gateway, the Moscow teleport project has been re-evaluated and judged to be a more logical second project in sequence. That project is temporarily on hold but ready to activate after the St. Petersburg Teleport.

When AMRU was diverted by its Russian partners at the two ministries to develop the St. Petersburg teleport project, it was with Russian satellites and earth stations in mind. This still can be done but may not be the optimum or most efficient way to do this. Due to the overload on existing telecom switches and the intense competition for a limited number of ports in satellites now aloft— HORIZONT I & II and SALUCH—there is uncertainty in securing adequate capacity even when negotiated. Thus a longer term solution may be preferable subject to a greater amount of project finance to be secured.

Gateway Switch—Larger Term Alternative

The longer term alternative is to purchase and install a state-of-the-art gateway switch with 1000 to 20,000 lines adequate to absorb and service the most explosive current and future growth for some years. This has the second key advantage of expediting the whole process of setting up and installing the teleport and earth station, training a local Russian team and avoiding the often time consuming process of obtaining U.S. government permit for Russian earth station installation in the United States. Therefore it was also decided to start out in St. Petersburg with INTELSAT and U.S. earth stations at both ends. Flexibility can be built into this configuration to also be able to use Russian satellites and earth station and equipment in due course.

The Business Opportunity

Primary Long-Distance Service through St. Petersburg Gateway

The core business will be to establish an international communications teleport to provide by satellite, initially between the Russian republics through the St. Petersburg gateway and points in the United States. This will be a Russian–American joint venture utilizing existing satellites, permits, land and sponsorship by the Russian Ministries of General Machine Building and Communications and local authorities. In competitive terms this is expected to be the primary long-distance service through St. Petersburg. Long-distance calls from other points such as in Europe and Asia can be linked through separate transactions with the long-distance carriers from those respective countries.

Critically Public Network Capacity

This will be a public network and will offer outbound international communications service to private individuals and businesses, especially international corporations positioned within the Russian Federation. It will also service tourists and foreign business visitors in Russia to supplement the under-capacity existing in public communications services and the handful of new private networks when overburdened.

Russian Originating Calls Generating Hard Currency

This important expansion in the volume of international phone calls originating from the Russian Federation will generate critically needed hard currency which can be applied toward financing this venture and toward prospective teleport facilities in other cities in the Russian Federation.

WORLDWIDE LONG-DISTANCE SERVICE THROUGH ST. PETERSBURG

Access to this worldwide system will be provided by AMRU in conjunction with the selected long-distance carrier through separate, individual agreements with telecommunications companies in other countries.

The system will provide immediate worldwide coverage through three major segments:

- Atlantic—serving business markets in the United States and Europe,
- Pacific—serving the Pacific region, and
- Russian Federation—serving private and business customers.

Both the Atlantic and Pacific segments are expected to attract mainly non-Russian business customers with activities within the Russian Federation. The domestic segment will serve both Russian and non-Russian business customers by providing immediate fax and data transfer to world markets from remote locations inside the Russian Foundation.

PROJECTED EXPLOSION IN LONG-DISTANCE VOLUME

The greater volume of telephone, fax and data traffic and revenues is anticipated from communications placed from outside coming through the St. Petersburg gateway teleport to receivers within the Russian Confederation. This volume of telephone, fax, data and video traffic is difficult to estimate. Initially these services are expected to be most attractive to international and emerging Russian business corporations with major growth potential.

Traffic revenues from other than voice communications are thought to be incremental at first and are not included (or broken down) in the attached projections of U.S. and Russian

originating telephone traffic shown in Exhibit 24-1. These estimates in our opinion are understated as are those of Russian originating calls then taking into account the approximately five million tourists in 1991 who are calculated to place international calls of an average ten minutes.

ADDITIONAL TELEPORT OPPORTUNITIES IN RUSSIAN FEDERATION

In addition to being designated the primary long-distance carrier through the St. Petersburg gateway, additional teleport opportunities are anticipated in other major Russian Federation cities with the Moscow teleport project already well-advanced and on hold until St. Petersburg is on line. Russian satellite ports have been awarded by the Russian government for Moscow and future teleports.

Moscow earth station personnel will be trained in St. Petersburg and operating, accounting and partnership growing lessons and remedies will be applied. As mentioned earlier, Russian satellites and earth station equipment are also anticipated.

St. Petersburg Teleport Facility, Equipment and Ownership

Tourist Venture Participants and Roles/Responsibilities

AMRU's MANAGING PARTNER AND PROJECT MANAGER

AMRU International Trading Company was described briefly earlier. As managing partner of the joint venture AMRU International has developed the business plan to guide the Russian partners in the Board organization and permits to obtain as well as in the financial management of the joint venture.

AMRU will also be the project manager and will be the long-distance carrier, the earth sta-

EXHIBIT 24-1

Russian Volume Projection and Base Assumptions
for Telecommunications Traffic

		St. Petersburg	Moscow	Total
Market (in millions of minutes)				
U.S.–St. Petersburg		3.5	6.0	9.5
Beyond U.S.–St. Petersburg		4.1	7.0	11.1
St. Petersburg–U.S. beyond		4.1	7.0	11.1
St. Petersburg–U.S.		3.4	5.8	9.2
Total		15.1	25.8	40.9
General Market Share (%)				
U.S.–St. Petersburg	15%	0.5	0.9	1.4
Beyond U.S.–St. Petersburg	10%	0.4	0.7	1.1
St. Petersburg–U.S. beyond	10%	0.4	0.7	1.1
St. Petersburg–U.S.	10%	0.3	0.6	0.9
		1.6	2.9	4.5

Capacity @ 24 Channels		*Net Revenue per Minute*	
Gross Minutes	12.6	U.S.–St. Petersburg	$1.20
Utilization factor	75%	Beyond U.S.–St. Petersburg	$0.69
Minutes Available	9.5	St. Petersburg–U.S. beyond	$1.70
Competitor factor	50%	St. Petersburg–U.S.	$2.30
Annual Growth Rate	20%		

Source: MCI International.

tion operators and gateway switch, vendors along with arranging the capital structure.

The joint venture being organized and managed by AMRU entails a number of diverse functions:

- Negotiating with the Russian partners terms of the joint venture.
- Advising the Russian partners on technical and business measures, strategy and objectives in the local permit process.
- Arranging the financing.
- Negotiating purchase of a gateway switch.
- Selecting an earth station vendor.
- Assembling an earth station operation team, and

- Selecting and negotiating an operating contract with an international long-distance carrier and support services to be provided by them in engineering, accounting, maintenance and other key areas.

AMRU: MARKETING AND ON-GOING CONDITIONS ROLE

Once the teleport venture is negotiated and financed but prior to activation, AMRU will direct and carry out the marketing of the teleport's long-distance services in Russia to hotels, international corporations and other institutions. AMRU will also oversee the ongoing operations and coordinate between the Russian partners and the long-distance carrier, gateway switch and earth station operatives in on-going operations.

VENTURE PARTICIPANTS IN RUSSIA— THE ST. PETERSBURG TELEPORT COMPANY

The Russian partners, the St. Petersburg Teleport Company, are a consortium of several private and public participants. They provide the land, the gateway access, local permits and personnel, in addition to technical support and the contribution of satellites and earth station equipment. The partners are:

- Galactica Company—presided over by Oleg Antufyev, president of AMRU-STAR, 60 plants, 180,000 workers,
- Mercury Company—presided over by S. Reshetnyev, 40 plants, 60,000 workers,
- The office of the mayor of St. Petersburg,
- Town of Pushkin Development Authority,
- Bank of St. Petersburg, and
- AMRU-STAR—2% interest.

This will be in local partnership with the Russian Ministry of Communications. This Russian group brings to the proposed joint venture officially approved rights of access to the St. Petersburg gateway as the primary service provider of satellite communications and with the gateway switch of long-distance service. Also they have been ceded a teleport site in the St. Petersburg area of 480 hectares (over 960 acres). If electing as had been done originally to operate with a Russian satellite and earth station, they also have been awarded by the Ministry of Communications in an official written document, 24 ports in the Russian gateway of St. Petersburg which may be used now or later.

SWITCHING EQUIPMENT VENDOR

The gateway switch vendor will provide systems installation and network hook-up plus follow on engineering, maintenance and operation services. They will implement a detailed planning system to ensure that project schedules are met on time and according to specifications.

LONG-DISTANCE CARRIER

The long-distance carrier will provide complementary engineering services and will install and operate accounting systems embracing direct dial billing and collection.

EARTH STATION VENDOR AND OPERATOR

The earth station vendor and operator will have a track record of success and experience with Intelsat. Experience in installation and operation of earth stations in other parts of the world will be our advantage as will the working relationship with the long-distance carrier and switching equipment vendor to be selected.

Non-Russian Financing and Partnership Options

AMRU will raise finance independently in two parts and own 50 percent equity in the joint venture with the Russian partners owning the other 50 percent. Funds will be used as follows:

1. $1 million for purchase of an earth station to be placed in St. Petersburg including multiplexer. More than half of this amount is to cover installation, testing and start-up costs. If the selected long-distance carrier does not own or have access to a U.S. earth station, additional funding will be required.

2. $12 to 13 million for payment on a gateway switch, varying with the negotiated purchase price. The vendor will be expected to provide highly competitive credit terms, guarantees and/or the balance.

AMRU will obtain financial credits from the St. Petersburg Teleport Company through the

EXHIBIT 24-2

Earth Station: First Year Cash-Flow Projections

Item	St. Petersburg	Moscow	Total
	(Thousands of Dollars)		
Revenue			
U.S.–St. Petersburg	600	1,080	1,680
Beyond U.S.–St. Petersburg	275	483	758
St. Petersburg–U.S. beyond	680	1,190	1,870
St. Petersburg–U.S.	690	1,380	2,070
Total:	2,245	4,133	6,378
Costs			
Earth Station operator	192	348	540
Billing	192	348	540
Agency	250	466	716
Office	50	50	100
Bad debt (3%)	67	124	191
Satellite	600	300	900
Switch fee	320	580	900
Total:	1,671	2,216	3,887
Net cash flow	574	1,917	2,491
Debt service for component	200	100	300
Net profit before taxes	374	1,817	2,191
Venture interest	80%	80%	80%
Venture pretax profit	299	1,454	1,753

purchase and sale of high-demand Russian export products—probably commodities such as oil in the amount needed to purchase the gateway switch and earth station and services.

AMRU will seek a non-Russian investment partner, ideally a telecommunications company who also would provide operating know-how and possibly equipment or carrier services. This partner would gain synergistic operating and business growth benefits such as greater critical mass, favorable publicity from such a high-profile venture and lead market position—in addition to a highly attractive return on investment accelerating quickly. Joint venture profitability is projected in Exhibit 24-2 and joint-venture cash flow in Exhibit 24-3.

Conclusion

The AMRU–St. Petersburg Teleport Company joint venture with effective marketing should be a keystone in the Russian Confederation's progress toward a market economy. It will improve dramatically the quality, consistency and volume of incoming and outgoing international phone calls. This, in turn, will enhance inter-business, tourist and Russian citizen communication capability bringing

EXHIBIT 24-3

First Year Cash Flow Projection—Switches

	(Thousands of Dollars)		
	St. Petersburg	Moscow	Total
Revenue			
Non-venture international traffic	1,340	1,520	2,860
Venture international traffic	320	580	900
	1,660	2,100	3,760
Costs			
Operations @ 5%	83	105	188
Maintenance @ 10%	166	210	376
	249	315	554
Gross cash flow	1,411	1,785	3,196
Debt service	1,300	1,300	2,600
Net cash flow to venture	111	485	596

peoples closer together through greater contact. It will also enhance St. Petersburg's position as Russia's leading international gateway and pave the way to teleports in other Russian cities with attractive returns to its partners.

The Assignment

Assume that you are the consultant to the foreign investor that is considering investing in this project. Please assist the investor in determining the following:

1. The feasibility of the project. In determining the cost of capital necessary for analysis, you may assume that the investor is any U.S. telecommunications company.
2. Are the methods of raising the financing realistic?
3. Discuss the currency risk and how to hedge against it.
4. Does it make a difference if the investor is from the United States or another country (i.e., in respect to technology transfer, political interference, etc.)?
5. Since a teleport is a "greater regional community often associated with a related real estate or other economic development" project, would you recommend such a project for Russia? If yes, would it be before, during, or after the Teleport Project?

In addressing the assignment consult Appendices 24-1 and 24-2 and dated material on the Russian economy and political situation from: International Monetary Fund/World Bank, Economist Intelligence Unit Country Reports, OECD, *Business Eastern Europe, East European Markets, Business International's Investing Licensing, and Trading Conditions Abroad*.

The Project Proposal: Assumptions and Financial Data

Excerpts from AMRU Plan, 1992.

RUSSIAN TELEPORT VENTURE

- Borrowing entity: Joint venture named "Teleport."
- Partners in the joint venture: Russian—St. Petersburg Teleport Russian Ministry of Communications.
  Western—AMRU International Corporation.
- Purpose: Stimulate economic development and attract foreign investment by building a teleport that will provide Western-style accommodations and international telecommunications capability in St. Petersburg and Moscow.
- Project description: Both the Moscow and St. Petersburg teleports are essentially the same with minor variations to allow for differing sites. Each Teleport consists of two major components:
- *Telecommunications*: Install an earth station that will provide satellite link to the U.S.A. Initially, 24 channels have been allocated into the existing but overloaded gateway switch. International telecommunications are transacted in hard currency and settlements can be hypothecated to service debt. The 24 channels will be used to transit calls from the U.S. to Russia as well as from Russia to the U.S. and beyond. Preliminary commitments are in place to be confirmed upon realization of signaling which will provide hard currency hook-ups to the earth station from hotels in St. Petersburg. This will be accomplished through the use of an operator center which the joint venture will install. An earth station operator is expected to have an investment and equity position in this phase of the project. Initially, an Intelsat earth station utilizing Intelsat satellites will be installed to provide service. As soon as possible, based on licensing in the U.S., a Russian earth station utilizing Russian satellites will be installed, which will reduce operating costs. The Russian equipment is already authorized and constitutes a portion of the Russians' capital contribution. The Intelsat equipment can be moved to the next site or be utilized further in St. Petersburg depending on traffic demands. Revenues are based on minutes of service connected.

CAPITAL EXPENDITURES SUMMARY: RUSSIAN TELEPORT VENTURE
(estimated costs, amounts in millions of dollars)

Item	St. Petersburg	Moscow	Total
Telecommunications			
Install Intelsat			
earth station	2.0	1.0[a]	3.0
Purchase and Install			
gateway switch	13.0	13.0	26.0
	15.0	14.0	29.0

Initial working capital requirement will be provided by the equity investors.

[a]Moscow will be comprised entirely of Russian earth station components which are cheaper than U.S. components. Cost of erection in Moscow includes extra transportation cost to Moscow from Port St. Petersburg.

ST. PETERSBURG: 10-YEAR CASH FLOW[a]

	1	2	3	4	5	6	7	8	9	10	
Earth Stations											
Gross revenues	2,245	2,694	3,232	3,878	4,653	5,583	6,699	6,699	6,699	6,699	
Costs	1,671	2,005	2,406	2,887	3,464	4,157	4,988	4,988	4,988	4,988	
Gross profit	574	689	826	991	1,189	1,426	1,711	1,711	1,711	1,711	
Debt service	200	200	200	200	200	200	200	200	200	200	2,000
Cash flow to venture	299	391	500	632	791	980	1,208	1,208	1,208	1,208	
Switch											
Gross revenues	1,660	1,992	2,390	2,868	3,441	4,129	4,954	5,944	7,132	8558	
Costs	249	299	359	431	517	620	744	893	1,072	1,286	
Gross profit	1,411	1,693	2,031	2,437	2,924	3,509	4,210	5,051	6,060	7,272	
Debt service	1,300	1,300	1,300	1,300	1,300	1,300	1,300	1,300	1,300	1,300	13,000
Cash flow to venture	111	393	731	1,137	1,624	2,209	2,910	3,751	4,760	5,972	
Total											
Cash flow to venture:	410	784	1,231	1,769	2,415	3,189	4,118	4,959	5,968	7,180	

[a]All figures are expressed in thousands of dollars. Capital expenditures of $15 million are amortized over 10 years.

MOSCOW: 10-YEAR CASH FLOW[a]

	1	2	3	4	5	6	7	8	9	10	
Earth Stations											
Gross revenues	4,133	4,959	5,950	7,140	8,568	10,281	12,337	12,337	12,337	12,337	
Costs	2,216	2,659	3,191	3,829	4,595	5,514	6,617	7,940	7,940	7,940	
Gross profit	1,917	2,300	2,759	3,311	3,973	4,767	5,720	4,397	4,397	4,397	
Debt service	100	100	100	100	100	100	100	100	100	100	1,000
Cash flow to venture	1,453	1,760	2,127	2,568	3,098	3,733	4,496	3,437	3,437	3,437	
Switch											
Gross revenues	2,100	2,520	3,024	3,628	4,354	5,225	6,270	7,524	9,029	10,835	
Costs	315	378	454	545	654	785	942	1,130	1,356	1,628	
Gross profit	1,785	2,142	2,570	3,083	3,700	4,440	5,328	6,394	7,673	9,207	
Debt service	1,300	1,300	1,300	1,300	1,300	1,300	1,300	1,300	1,300	1,300	13,000
Cash flow to venture	485	842	1,270	1,783	2,400	3,140	4,028	5,094	6,373	7,907	

(Continued)

	1	2	3	4	5	6	7	8	9	10
Total										
Cash flow to venture:	1,938	2,602	3,397	4,351	5,498	6,873	8,524	8,531	9,810	11,344

[a]All figures are expressed in thousands of dollars. Capital expenditures of $14 million are amortized over 10 years.

APPENDIX **24-2**

AMRU's "Track Record" in Russia

AMRU is a small privately held company that has been doing business with the former Union of Soviet Socialist Republics for 20 years. Its first venture was the purchase of fur skins for coats that were later manufactured in the United States. Through transporting the very valuable fur skins, AMRU developed an excellent working relation with the Ministry of transportation. When Mikhail Gorbachev ascended to power, AMRU knew that things were about to change. During a long evening of celebrating a successful purchase and delivery of skins, the people at AMRU wanted to know who owned the rights to advertise on the then Soviet Union's transportation system. "Advertise" on buses, subways, and kiosks? The concept itself was unknown in the former USSR. The Transportation Ministry said the right to advertise was AMRU's for most of the major cities, a handshake and toasts solidified the deal, and official papers were later signed.

Transportation Displays Incorporated (TDI) of New York is the largest outdoor advertiser on buses and bus kiosks in the United States. It is a privately held company. One of AMRU's partners knew people in this company and approached them with their idea of advertising in the Soviet Union. TDI knew this to be a unique opportunity and eagerly expressed interest. A potential market of 280 million was something no one from Madison Avenue could pass up. AMRU then formed the joint-venture AMRU-STAR in Moscow to have the advertisements printed in Russian and to have them placed on the buses, subways, and kiosks. Due to the "opening up" of the former USSR and TDI's established relationship with numerous U.S. companies, ads for PepsiCo, Procter & Gamble, Colgate-Palmolive, Philip Morris, and RJR Nabisco products soon began to appear on the buses, subways, and kiosks in Moscow, Kiev, and St. Petersburg (Leningrad). (It should be noted that when the aborted coup took place in August 1991, many of these same buses with American advertising were seen "protecting" the Russian White House as well as other strategic places in Moscow.)

Harvey Pharmaceutical Corporation, Inc.

International Intercompany Transfer Pricing Determination

HARVEY A. PONIACHEK

Introduction

This case study concerns Harvey Pharmaceutical Corporation, Inc. (HPC), a U.S. multinational corporation with extensive international business, including a manufacturing affiliate in Montreal, a research and development center in Dublin, and a marketing network in Vienna. HPC conducts intercompany business transactions with its affiliates abroad, and determining the arm's length prices of these transactions is of utmost significance.

The arm's length intercompany transfer prices for tangible transactions, the royalty rates for intangible property, and compensation for intercompany services could tremendously affect the corporate worldwide profit and tax liabilities, and affect the performance of the parent company and its foreign affiliates.

Internal Revenue Code (IRC) Section 482 regulations require the establishment of arm's length pricing for international intercompany transactions—that is, price determination (and income distribution) between affiliated parties should occur in the same manner that would

be set in the marketplace between unrelated parties under similar circumstances.

The reader's task is to examine the facts related to the case and select the arm's length transfer prices. The case study requires knowledge of the various pricing methods and analytical techniques designed to approximate the transfer prices and/or charges according to the Internal Revenue Service Section 482 regulation. Appendix 25-1, "Transfer Pricing Determination: Theories, Practices, and IRS Regulations," provides a write-up and references on the various approaches for transfer pricing analysis.

The Facts

The Corporation

Harvey Pharmaceutical Corporation, Inc. of Chicago is a multinational pharmaceutical corporation with $500 million in sales and total assets of over $650 million. The corporation is engaged in research and development, manufacturing, and marketing of pharmaceutical products, including cardiovascular products, infectious-disease drugs and drugs for the treatment of metabolic disorders, and a line of several generic drugs. HPC was founded in 1953, and in the 1960s went through a series of successful mergers and acquisitions that positioned it competitively in the industry. In the late 1980s, HPC survived an unfriendly takeover attempt, which resulted in the divestiture of several unrelated business affiliates and the buy-back of some 10 percent of the outstanding common shares.

HPC's long-term corporate strategic plan (formulated in 1989 with the assistance of a major consulting firm) identified several areas around the world with highly attractive opportunities over the next decade. These opportunities required expansion of manufacturing capacity, additional research and development (R & D) capabilities, and enhanced marketing and distribution.

One promising area for pharmaceutical products was identified in North America thanks to the evolving U.S.–Canadian free trade, and the growing likelihood for the creation of a common North American Market, which would encompass Mexico. Another attractive market was the EC, primarily because of the 1992 enhancement of the European Community market. Western Europe has become an attractive market for pharmaceutical research because of its relatively cheap and large pool of scientists and university graduates. A third attractive market was identified in Eastern Europe where the collapse of Communism opened up attractive opportunities for the marketing of pharmaceuticals. HPC's strategic plan called for the expansion of manufacturing capacity in North America, establishment of an R & D center in Western Europe, and the creation of a distribution network to service the emerging Eastern European democracies.

Operation in Canada

Following an intensive fact-finding and feasibility analysis, which included the examination of several competing projects in the United States, Canada, and Mexico, Canada was selected as the ideal location for the manufacturing of two cardiovascular products and marketing HPC's entire product line in Canada, including drugs for infectious and cardiovascular diseases and metabolic disorders. Canada was selected because of its large domestic market, its proximity to the major U.S. markets, stability, high productivity, and attractive financing that was offered by the Government of the Province of Quebec.

In early 1990, HPC Corporation entered the market in Canada through a newly formed wholly-owned subsidiary, HPCCAN, to manufacture two cardiovascular products and market in Canada the full range of HPC's products. The entity was capitalized at $30 million through an injection of equity capital.

HPCCAN was provided with the necessary patents and technical know-how to manufacture the two cardiovascular products, and was given the marketing rights to distribute these products in Canada and the rest of the world, except the United States.

The Canadian entity was headed by an American chief executive officer (CEO), who was formerly vice president of manufacturing in the corporation's Ohio subsidiary, and a chief financial officer (CFO), who came from HPC's headquarters finance department.

The Canadian entity began operations in February 1990, where its entire output was sold to HPC in Chicago. In the second year of operation, because of weak demand in the United States, HPCCAN sold 25 percent of its output to an unrelated Canadian firm and shipped the balance to HPC in Chicago.

The agreement between HPC and HPCCAN did not assure the latter that all its output would be purchased by HPC Chicago. HPCCAN could sell its product directly to unaffiliated companies in Canada, and market its products outside North America through HPC's marketing network around the world or independently.

HPCCAN was required to pay HPC a royalty for the transfer of the technology and know-how and for the marketing rights. However, the royalties rate would be reviewed periodically to determine whether they were appropriate. The financial statements of HPC-CAN are shown in Exhibit 25-1.

Operation in Ireland

HPC's R&D activities center in Chicago, but several additional research centers—organized as wholly-owned subsidiaries—operate in California, New York, and Boston. The R&D centers outside Chicago are in some respect independent entities, with profit and loss (P&L) responsibilities, but their functions and activities are largely affected by HPC's strategic plan and budget allocation. The R&D subsidiaries often engage in contracts for outside entities for which they are compensated at the going market rate.

HPC incorporated a R&D center—HPCIRE—in 1990 under the laws of the Republic of Ireland, with its principal place of business in Dublin. Ireland provided several incentives for the establishment of this facility there, including the relatively cheap pool of trained scientists and college trained graduates, and generous fiscal incentives.

The Industrial Development Authority of Ireland (IDA) is responsible for promoting industrial development in Ireland. Following a fact-finding trip to Ireland in 1989, the HPC finance department engaged in a feasibility assessment designed to determine the most attractive location of the R&D center. Several competing sites were considered, including Paris, Madrid, and Cambridge, England. The project assessment applied a standard budgetary analysis based on Net Present Value and Internal Rate of Return.

In assessing the feasibility of locating in Dublin, the fiscal incentives provided by the Irish authorities played a significant role in affecting the project's projected cash flows. The IDA and Irish government offered an attractive financial package, which included capital grants of 30 percent of the required capital

investment, low-cost lease financing on 30 percent of the total investment, trained grants to cover the cost of training employees, subsidized local bank loans, and a tax holiday on export earnings for 10 years.

The entity was capitalized by $10 million, of which the bulk of the investment was obtained through concessionary finance and grants from IDA and local banks.

HPC personnel were sent to Ireland to set up the research center, hire the personnel, and commence operation. The entity was staffed by some 150 people, including Ph.D. biologists, pharmacologists, biochemists, and medical doctors, rendering it one of HPC's largest R&D centers.

The Irish R&D center commenced operation in 1990, where its tasks were established by HPC R&D corporate plan. HPCIRE operated as a contract R&D entity—that is, all its activities were ordered and approved by HPC chief scientists and all its expenses were underwritten by HPC. Exhibit 25-2 provides the financial data for HPCIRE.

Austrian Distribution Network

In light of the enhanced business potential, HPC has set up a sales commission network in Eastern Europe, HPC Trade, Ltd., with headquarters in Vienna. The commission sales agents in the various countries rely on back office services provided to them through the regional distribution center in Austria.

The task of the commission sales agents is limited to sales and the generation of leads, for which they are compensated by a commission. The sales commissioners' are incurring no inventory or credit risk. Inventory is maintained at the regional distribution office in Vienna, which fills the orders issued through the commission sales offices, ships the goods and issues invoices. Exhibit 25-3 provides the financial statement of comparable sales commissioners.

EXHIBIT 25-1

Harvey Pharmaceuticals Corporation Canada, Inc. (HPCCAN)

	1990	1991	1992	1993
Assets ($,000)				
Cash	3,346	3,747	4,159	4,617
Marketable securities	1,495	1,674	1,859	2,063
Receivables	26,347	29,508	32,754	36,357
Inventories	23,600	26,432	29,340	32,567
Other current assets	4,450	4,984	5,532	6,141
Total current assets	59,238	66,346	73,644	81,745
Property, plant & equipment	28,977	32,455	36,025	39,987
Accumulated Depreciation	NA[a]	NA	NA	NA
Net property & equipment	28,977	32,455	36,025	39,987
Investment & advances to subsidiaries	1,833	2,053	2,279	2,530
Other non-current assets	0	0	0	0
Intangibles	29,939	33,532	37,220	41,315
Deposits & other assets	32,751	36,681	40,716	45,195
Total assets	152,739	171,067	189,885	210,772
Liabilities ($,000)				
Notes payable	11,139	12,475	13,847	15,371
Account payable	10,804	12,101	13,432	14,909
Current long-term debt	6,666	7,465	8,287	9,198
Other current liabilities	0	0	0	0
Accrued expenses	15,428	17,279	19,180	21,289
Total current liabilities	44,036	49,320	54,746	60,768
Deferred charges	ERR	ERR	ERR	ERR
Convertible debt	20,684	23,166	25,715	28,543
Long-term debt	55,518	62,181	69,020	76,613
Total liabilities	120,239	134,667	149,481	165,924
Total equity	32,500	36,400	40,404	44,848
Total liabilities and networth	152,739	171,067	189,885	210,772
Annual Income ($,000)				
Net sales	57,369	65,400	73,248	82,771
Cost of goods sold	25,655	29,247	32,757	37,015
Gross profit	31,713	36,153	40,491	45,755
R&D expenditures	1,065	1,214	1,360	1,536
Selling, general & administrative expenditures	22,818	26,013	29,135	32,922
Income before depreciation and amortization	7,830	8,926	9,997	11,297
Depreciation and amortization	0	0	0	0
Non-operating income	2,215	2,525	2,828	3,195
Interest expense	6,148	7,008	7,849	8,870
Income before tax	3,897	4,443	4,976	5,623
Provision for income tax	1,442	1,644	1,841	2,080
Net income	2,455	2,799	3,135	3,542

[a]NA = not available.

EXHIBIT 25-2

Harvey Pharmaceuticals Corporation Ireland, Inc. (HPCIRE)

	1990	1991	1992	1993
Assets ($,000)				
Cash	7,439	7,811	8,436	9,448
Marketable securities	8,517	8,942	9,658	10,817
Receivables	3,263	3,426	3,700	4,144
Inventories	1,580	1,659	1,791	2,006
Other current assets	693	727	786	880
Total current assets	21,491	22,565	24,371	27,295
Property, plant & equipment	22,674	23,808	25,713	28,798
Accumulated depreciation	3,418	3,589	3,876	4,341
Net property & equipment	19,256	20,219	21,836	24,457
Investment & advances to subsidiaries	0	0	0	0
Other non-current assets	0	0	0	0
Intangibles	0	0	0	0
Deposits & other assets	1,485	1,560	1,684	1,887
Total assets	42,232	44,344	47,891	53,638
Liabilities ($,000)				
Notes payable	0	0	0	0
Account payable	845	888	959	1,074
Current long-term debt	18	19	21	23
Other current liabilities	0	0	0	0
Accrued expenses	1,546	1,623	1,753	1,963
Total current liabilities	2,409	2,530	2,732	3,060
Deferred charges	0	0	0	0
Convertible debt	10,981	11,530	12,452	14,947
Long-term debt	16,094	17,398	19,532	22,981
Total liabilities	29,484	31,458	34,717	39,987
Total equity	12,749	12,886	13,175	13,651
Total liabilities and networth	42,232	44,344	47,891	53,638
Annual Income ($,000)				
Net sales	13,571	14,249	15,674	18,025
Cost of goods sold	2,240	2,352	2,588	2,976
Gross profit	11,330	11,897	13,086	15,049
R&D expenditures	4,745	4,983	5,481	6,303
Selling, general & administrative expenditures	1,803	1,894	2,083	2,395
Income before depreciation and amortization	4,782	5,021	5,523	6,351
Depreciation & amortization	NA	NA	NA	NA
Non-operating income	NA	NA	NA	NA
Interest expense	425	446	491	565
Income before tax	4,356	4,574	5,032	5,786
Provision for income tax	1,608	1,688	1,857	2,135
Net income	2,749	2,886	3,175	3,651

[a]NA = not available.

EXHIBIT 25-3

Comparable Commissioners, Austria

Annual Income (Percent of Sales)	1990
Net sales	100.0
Cost of goods sold	82.0
Gross profit	18.0
Selling, general & administrative expenditures	16.5
Income before dep. & amor.	1.5
Other expense	0.5
Income before tax	1.0
Provision for income tax	0.3
Net income	0.8

The Assignment

1. Determine the royalty rate HPC should charge its Canadian affiliate for the intangible property transferred to it. What price should HPCCAN charge HPC for its two cardiovascular products?
2. How should HPC compensate HPCIRE for R&D services?
3. Design a commission rate for the sales commission agents in Eastern Europe.

Transfer Pricing Determination: Theories, Practices, and IRS Regulations

What Is Transfer Pricing?

The internationalization of corporate America over the past 25 years—primarily through rapid growth of direct foreign investment and international trade—has sharply expanded intercompany international transactions.[1] Appendix 25-2 provides details on the magnitude of U.S. international intercompany transactions. The task of determining appropriate transfer prices for these transactions confronts all the companies that conduct business with their foreign affiliates.

Essentially, all intercompany cost allocation is a form of transfer pricing. However, the term is more commonly associated with the price charges by one entity of a corporation for a product, service, or intangible sold or licensed to another entity of the same company.[2]

In Exhibit A25-1 Company A (United States) sells an intermediate product X to Company B (United Kingdom), its wholly-owned subsidiary. The latter, in turn, resells product X to unrelated third parties in Eastern Europe, and/or processes it into product Y and then sells it to unrelated parties in Western Europe. Company A may (or may not) sell product X to unrelated third parties in Western Europe. Company A transfers patents and manufacturing know-how to Company C, its subsidiary in Canada, and Company A provides technical

---

[1]For the scope of U.S. multinational companies' international intercompany business see various issues of the U.S. Department of Commerce, *Survey of Current Business.*

[2]Charles T. Horngren and George Foster, *Cost Accounting*, 6th ed., Prentice Hall, Englewood Cliffs, NJ, 1987, p. 836. Allen M. Rugman and Lorraine Eden, (eds.) *Multinationals and Transfer Pricing*, St. Martin's Press, New York, 1985, p. 1.

EXHIBIT A25-1

International Intercompany Transactions and Transfer Pricing Determination

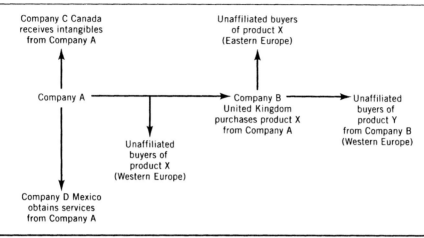

Notes: Company A is the parent company located in the United States. Company B is a subsidiary of Company A located in the United Kingdom. Company C is a wholly-owned subsidiary of Company A, and Company D is a wholly-owned subsidiary of Company A. Wholly-owned subsidiaries are referred to as affiliates. Non-affiliated companies are referred to as unaffiliates.

and managerial services to Company D, its subsidiary in Mexico.

The issues raised in this example and as demonstrated in Exhibit A25-1 are: At what level are the transfer prices set for tangibles, intangibles, and services? Could the transfer prices differ from the external market prices? How are the transfer prices determined under different circumstances of market structure, corporate organization, and type of business? What is the transfer pricing effects on the income taxes of each division and the entire corporation?

Transfer Pricing Theories and Practices

Transfer pricing determination can be considered as a process—in the context of a comprehensive corporate management control system—which seeks to establish congruent goals and facilitate performance evaluation throughout the corporation,[3] and to satisfy Internal Revenue Service Section 482.

Intercompany pricing can be affected by a host of internal and external circumstances. Transfer pricing could occasionally result in considerable ambiguity and controversy, because of its impact on income taxes and performance of the entities involved. The appropriateness of the international transfer pricing is subject to IRS audit and adjustment. Due to its enormous significance, transfer prices in centralized companies are established by the chief financial officer, and/or the vice president of finance, and/or the comptroller. In decentralized companies, transfer prices are usually formulated by division managers, but headquarters remain involved if problems arise.

There is a variety of transfer pricing methods that a company can utilize. Selection of a

[3]Ralph L. Benke, Jr. and James Don Edwards, *Transfer Pricing: Techniques and Uses*, National Association of Accountants, New York, 1980, p. 135.

EXHIBIT A25-2

Transfer Pricing Techniques

Division/Entity	Pricing Techniques
Profit Center	Market-based
	Prevailing market prices
	Adjusted market prices
	Negotiated prices
	Cost-based
	Opportunity cost
	Marginal cost
	Cost plus .
	Standard full cost
	Actual cost
	Resale method
	Contributing margin[a]
Cost Centers[b]	Cost-based
	Actual cost
	Variable
	Full
	Standard cost
	Variable
	Full

[a]Appendix 25-2 provides a description of the contributing margin approach.

[b]Cost-based techniques are based on accounting and economic cost concepts. The common cost concepts are: (1) cost plus, which is based on accounting cost; (2) opportunity cost; and (3) marginal cost. The last two are microeconomic concepts. Corporate accounting systems provide a reliable information basis upon which to make pricing determination—while the economic cost measures are not readily available. Many corporations use cost-based methods to derive transfer prices because they are simple and administratively convenient. The outcome, however, depends on the cost benchmark and magnitude of the markup.

Source: Adapted from Ralph L. Benke, Jr. and James Don Edwards, *Transfer Pricing: Techniques and Uses*, National Association of Accountants, New York, 1980, p. 30.

pricing method should adhere to Section 482 requirements, and satisfy other corporate objectives. The large number of transfer pricing approaches can generally be classified in terms of the following categories:

1. The *theoretical characterization* of transfer pricing determination and interpretation:

EXHIBIT A25-3

Transfer Pricing Methods Used in Practice

Methods	Used by Companies	%[a]
Cost-based Methods	46.8	46.0
Standard variable cost	2.9	
Actual variable cost	1.7	
Standard full cost	12.5	
Actual full cost	13.0	
Full cost plus profit markup based on corporate ROS	2.9	
Full cost plus profit markup based on corporate ROI	2.9	
Full cost plus some other defined profit	10.9	
Market-based Methods	53.2	49.0
Competitor's price	11.7	
Company's list price	17.2	
Most recent bid price received	2.1	
Negotiation	22.2	14.0
Other		5.0

[a]Data in the middle column is from Eccles, and data in the right column is from Tang et al.

Sources: Robert G. Eccles, *Transfer Pricing: A Theory for Practice*, Lexington Books, Boston, MA 1985, p. 41. Based on an survey of 239 conducted in 1978. R. Tang, C. Ealter, and R. Raymond, "Transfer Pricing—Japanese vs. American Style," *Management Accounting*, January 1979, pp. 12–16.

that is, based on microeconomics or marginal analysis, mathematical/linear programming determination of transfer pricing, accounting theory driven transfer pricing, or transfer pricing based on managerial theory.[4]

[4]Robert G. Eccles, *The Transfer Pricing Problem: A Theory for Practice*, Lexington Books, Lexington, MA, 1985, p. 48.

2. The *pricing basis*: that is, being *market-based* transfer pricing, *cost-based* transfer pricing or *negotiated prices*.[5]

3. The *type of corporate organization*: that is, in terms of profit and cost centers. Transfer prices for profit centers can be: (1) dictated prices based on full cost, (2) dictated prices based on marginal cost, (3) dictated prices based on market price quotation, and (4) market-based negotiated prices.[6]

Surveys of corporate transfer pricing practices[7] suggest an approximately equal use of (1) market-based pricing—that is determined by supply and demand in the free marketplace—and (2) cost-based methods—that are determined by each firm using its own discretion. These transfer pricing techniques are shown in Exhibits A25-2 and A25-3.

Transfer Pricing Methods Required by the IRS Regulations

Sales of Tangible Property, Reg. §1.482-2(e)(1)

A member of a group of controlled entities selling tangible property to another member of such group should charge an arm's length price for such sale. An arm's length price is the price that an unrelated party would have paid under the same circumstances for the property involved in the controlled sale. Since unrelated parties normally sell products at a profit, an arm's length price normally involves a profit to the seller.

The regulation specifies four methods of determining an arm's length price—that must be applied in the order listed—including the comparable uncontrolled, the resale price method, the cost plus method and the fourth methods.

Under the comparable uncontrolled pricing method the arm's length price of a controlled sale is equal to the price paid in comparable uncontrolled sales, adjusted as specified by the regulation. Uncontrolled sales are sales in which the seller and the buyers are not members of the same controlled group.

Resale Price Method, Reg. §1.482-2(e)(3)

Under the resale price method the arm's length price of a controlled sale is equal to the applicable resale price reduced by an appropriate markup, and adjusted as provided by the regulations. An appropriate markup is computed by multiplying the applicable resale price by the appropriate markup percent.

The Cost Plus Method, Reg. §1.482-2(e)(4)

Under the cost-plus method, the arm's length price of a controlled sale is computed by adding to the cost of producing such property an amount which is equal to such cost multiplied by the appropriate gross profit percentage, plus or minus any adjustments as required.

Fourth Methods Rate of Return

The fourth methods are based on various contemporary economic and financial theories and empirical methods designed to approximate arm's length transfer pricing. The upcoming section on Reg. §1.482.2(b) provides a detailed discussion of the approach.

Transfer of Intangible Property, Reg. §1.482-2(d)(1)

Intangible property transferred, sold, assigned, or otherwise made available in any manner by one member of a controlled group of con-

---

[5] Horngren and Foster, op.cit.

[6] Gordon Shillinglaw, *Managerial Cost Accounting*, 5th ed., Richard D. Irwin, Homewood, IL, 1982, p. 821.

[7] Reported in Benke and Edwards op cit., and in Eccles, op. cit.

trolled entities to another member of the group should be at arm's length consideration. Arm's length consideration should be in the form which is consistent with the form which would be adopted in transactions between unrelated parties under the same circumstances. In determining the amount of an arm's length consideration, the standard to be applied is the amount that would have been paid by an unrelated party for the same intangible under the same circumstances. An arm's length consideration may take any one or more of the following forms: (1) a royalty based on the transferee's output, sales, profits, or any other measure, (2) lump-sum payments, or (3) any other form.

Performance of Services for Another, Reg. §1.482-2(b)

When one member of a group of controlled entities performs marketing, managerial, technical, or other services for the benefit of, or on behalf of, another member of the group, the charge should be at arm's length. Arm's length charge is the charge that is charged for the same services in independent transactions with or between unrelated parties under similar circumstances. However, except in the case of services that are an integral part of the business of either entity, the arm's length charge will be deemed equal to the cost of rendering such services.

The IRS transfer price methods are shown in Exhibits A25-4, A25-5, and A25-6.

IRS PROPOSED NEW REGULATIONS FOR TRANSFER PRICING

The IRS issued proposed new regulations for transfer pricing in January 1992. These regulations adopted several innovative concepts in assessing the arm's length transfer pricing, and are expected to become effective in early 1993. Appendix 25-5 discusses the main principles of

EXHIBIT A25-4

Transfer Pricing Methods

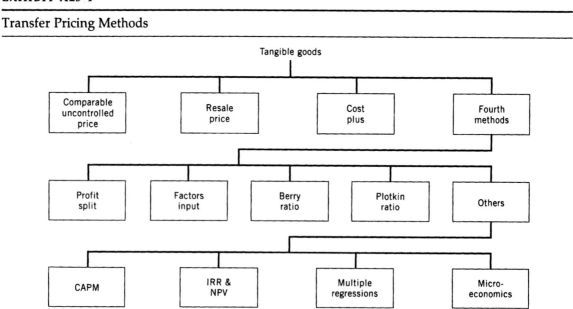

Notes: CAPM = Capital assets pricing model; IRR = Internal rate of return; NPV = Net present value.

EXHIBIT A25-5

Transfer Pricing Methods

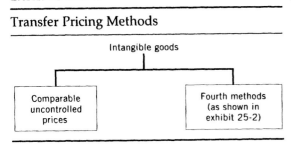

EXHIBIT A25-6

Transfer Pricing Methods

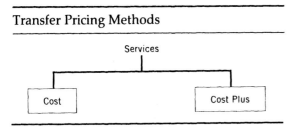

the proposal that are related to tangible and intangible property.

Further Analysis of Transfer Pricing of Tangible Property

Resale Price Method

Resellers (distributors, wholesalers, and retailers) may consider as their cost the cost of the product they purchase for resale, to which they add a profit margin or markup, sufficiently large to offset their operating cost and yield an acceptable rate of return on their activities. This approach establishes an arm's length price by measuring the value of the marketing function of an entity that acquires goods from a related party and resells it to an unaffiliated buyer. An arm's length price is calculated by adjusting for the percentage markup (or gross profit margin on the resale price, which is denoted by "% Markup") that applies to the resale according to the following formula:

THE RESALE PRICE FORMULA

> Arm's Length Price
> = Resale Price
> − % Markup × Resale Price
> Arm's Length Price
> = Resale Price (1 − % Markup)

The intercompany transfer price is determined at a level that results in the same gross profit markup percentage that is achieved by the independent reseller—that is, an arm's length intercompany price is determined by utilizing the gross markup on sales experienced by independent distributors performing similar functions to those of the integrated firm (i.e., comparable distributors). The gross profit markup of comparable distributors is considered the arm's length standard. The gross profit markup compensates the reseller for his cost and provides him with an appropriate operating profit on sales, investment and risk assumed. The validity of this approach depends on the functional and economic comparability of the markup estimated for independent distributors. If significant differences prevail, then appropriate adjustments are necessary.

Cost-plus Pricing Method

The cost-plus transfer price approximation formula is as follows:

THE COST-PLUS FORMULA

> Transfer Price = Cost
> + % Markup × Cost
> Transfer Price = Cost (1 + % Markup)

$$\text{Optimal \% Markup} = 1/1 + \left(\cfrac{1}{1 + \cfrac{1}{\varepsilon_p}} \right) - 1$$

The notations in this formula are: % Markup is the percentage profit markup on cost; ε_p is price elasticity of the demand for the product; Optimal % Markup suggests the maximum markup on cost given the market's price elasticities of demand.

There are various cost benchmarks that can be used, including actual full or variable costs incurred, or standard full or variable costs. Standard cost is the estimated or budgeted cost for a given level of output, which indicates what it should cost to manufacture a product given a set of assumptions (e.g., concerning the volume of output, capacity utilization). Standard costs are more viable than actual costs because they avoid the tendency to cost overload the transfer price. The disadvantages of using standard cost are their conjectural nature, and possible variance from the actual. A survey has shown that none of the companies used variable costs, and all used fully-loaded cost.[8]

The percentage markup on cost depends on the market's price elasticities, which are defined as the percent change in the quantity demand in response to a percent change in the price of the product. When this ratio is larger than 1 in absolute terms, the demand is considered elastic, and when it is smaller than 1, demand is considered inelastic—that is, the more price elastic the demand is for the product, the less is the percent markup and vice versa for less price elastic products.[9] This approach can be utilized to verify exact and inexact markets. Cross price and income elasticities could indicate whether products are exactly the same or—in microeconomic terms —if the products are substitutes, complements, or neutral.

The cost-plus approach is most suitable where a manufacturer or assembler has added significant value. An arm's length price is de-

rived by adding to the manufacturer's cost of production an appropriate profit margin that is earned by comparable uncontrolled manufacturers of similar goods under general comparable circumstances.

The cost oriented pricing methods are relatively simple and administratively convenient, but somewhat lacking because, first, the cost data might not be accurate and, second, demand conditions and competitors reaction are ignored.

Transfer pricing on the basis of standard variable cost requires a separate lump-sum periodic charge for fixed costs and profit. When intercompany pricing is subject to average variable cost, the entities are entitled to share the difference between the market price and total average cost—defined as the contributing margin—on a prorated overall contribution based on their relative share of average variable cost times the overall contribution.[10] Cost savings, thanks to internal transactions, may be split between the parties involved through negotiation or in some more rigorous manner (e.g., the contributing margin, or relative cost of both parties, etc).

The cost-plus method does not suggest whether higher pricing could be accepted by the market or whether lower prices are necessary. The market price typically established by the cost-plus method is the ceiling for transfer pricing, but under some circumstances lower prices may be justified to account for cost savings incurred in intercompany transactions.[11]

The Fourth Methods of Transfer Pricing Determination

In the absence of uncontrolled comparable prices, and if the resale and cost-plus transfer pricing methods are not applicable, unspeci-

---

[8] Benke and Edwards, op. cit., p. 49.

[9] Ibid., p. 30.

[10] Horngren and Foster, op. cit., p. 844.

[11] Ibid., p. 840.

fied "Fourth Methods" could be applied to approximate arm's length prices. The fourth methods are based on various contemporary economic and financial theories and empirical methods, which can be listed under the following headings:

1. Rate of return on sales and/or assets and/or the rate of return on capital (Plotkin's Ratio)
2. Income to Expenses Ratio (Berry's Ratio)
3. Capital Assets Pricing Model (CAPM)
4. Corporate capital budgeting methods, including the Internal Rate of Return (IRR) and/or the Net Present Value (NPV)
5. Econometric Analysis
6. Mathematical Modeling
7. Microeconomic or Marginal Pricing

The following are several select *transfer pricing approximation methods* that are classified under the fourth methods.

RATE OF RETURN ON EQUITY OR INVESTMENT (PLOTKIN'S RATIO)

The rate of return on equity or investment is a subset of the arm's length rate of return on assets.

Various rate of return or profitability performance indicators could be used to approximate and verify transfer prices. Of these indicators, the rate of return on equity (ROE) and the rate of return on investment (ROI) are most useful. The ROE or the ROI transfer pricing approach is also known in the transfer pricing literature as the Plotkin Approach.

The ROE/ROI approach is based on the premise that when intercompany transactions are set at arm's length, the parties involved will experience comparable risk-adjusted return on equity or investment. However, if these returns differ from the rates experienced by uncontrolled comparable parties or by the industry, the transfer prices are probably inadequate (i.e., not at arm's length).

In essence, the ROE or ROI pricing method maintains that the transfer price should reflect the average cost plus the rate of return on capital or equity employed. This transfer pricing method can be stated in the following formula:

ROE OR ROI TRANSFER PRICING

$$\text{Transfer Price} = AVC + \frac{TFC}{S} + r \times \frac{I}{S}$$

The transfer price is expressed in price per unit sold, AVC is average variable cost, TFC is total fixed cost, S is units of output or sales, TFC/S is average fixed costs, r is the arm's length ROE or ROI, and I is the equity or investment employed.

As stated in the formula, the transfer price is determined on the basis of costs, the output level, the level of equity or investment, and the actual or standard or desired rate of return on equity or investment. This information can be applied in the formula to obtain the transfer price that yields the arm's length transfer price. If the transfer price turns out to be inappropriate, the formula shows that adjustments can occur in several variables, namely in cost, output, equity, or investment, and in the ROE or ROI.

In the ROI approach, we determine the arm's length intercompany price on the basis of costs, the output level, the amount of investment, and the desired rate of return on investment. Corporate management knows the approximate manufacturing cost, output, price range, and required investment of a product. The marketing departure can provide projections on what quantities could be sold at different price levels, whereas the production, accounting, and purchasing departments will provide cost and investment estimates that correspond to various output levels. This information can then be simulated in the equation to obtain the corresponding transfer price that yields the desired rate of return. The same approach to transfer prices can be applied to obtain a desired rate of return on equity (ROE), rate of return on assets (ROA), rate of return on sales (ROS), or break-even-point (BEP).

The *theory of capital employed*[12] has been suggested as a "fourth" method of Section 482 transfer pricing determination. This approach considers capital as the firm's scarce resource, of which the allocation requires similar returns at the margin throughout the corporation—that is, marginal cost of capital needs to equal the corporation's internal rate of return. It assigns capital to the various activities and expects appropriate transfer pricing to yield satisfactory IRR. The utilization of the return on capital ratio allows the firm to *risk-adjust* the returns and strategically price appropriately to maintain desired rates of return on equity or capital employed. The theory of capital employed expects appropriate transfer pricing to yield satisfactory internal rate of return. This approach has been employed by Plotkin's famous rate of return on capital methods.[13]

Recent literature on international transfer pricing advocates use of time weighted investment measures to establish transfer prices to allocate global income.[14] While the principle of cost plus is maintained, the profit margin is determined on the basis of profit split between the parties on the basis of the relative capital employed by both. This approach is equivalent to splitting profit on the basis of employed assets for a given leverage level.

---

[12] Harlow N. Hoginbotham et al., "Effective Applications of the Section 482 Transfer Pricing Regulations," *The Law Review*, vol. 42, no. 2, Winter 1987.

[13] See Treasury Department, "A Study of Intercompany Pricing" (*The White Paper*), October 18, 1988, Ch. 5 and the references therein.

[14] Hoginbotham, op. cit.

INCOME TO EXPENSES RATIO (BERRY'S RATIO)

Charles Berry's Ratio has been hailed as an important contribution to transfer pricing analysis.[15] Berry's Ratio is defined as a gross income to expenses ratio which examines the structure of the income statement to approximate the transfer price. Berry's approach utilizes accounting systems reporting and its major analytical aspect is the comparison of actual and comparable company(ies) or industry standard revenue/cost ratios. To the extent that there are substantial variances, it could be evident of inappropriate pricing that warrant an adjustment. Berry's approach could be substituted for the arm's length rate of return on assets when firms have similar balance sheet structures.

Berry's Ratio is expressed mathematically in the equation below as a simple application of linear fully-loaded operating cost and gross profit (in accounting terms) based on accounting systems reporting. Berry's Ratio can be described in the following formula:

1. Net Sales $= Pm \times Q$

2. Cost of Goods Sold $= Pt \times Q$

3. Gross Profit $= Pm \times Q - Pt \times Q$

4. Berry's Ratio $= \dfrac{Q \times (Pm - Pt)}{\text{Op. Exp.}}$

Equation 1 states that net sales of the foreign affiliate equal the market price, Pm, times the quantity sold, Q. Equation 2 states that the cost of goods sold equals the transfer price, Pt, times the quantity sold, Q. Equation 3 defines the gross profit in terms of the difference in the net sales and cost of goods sold. Equation 4 defines the Berry's Ratio as gross profit to operating expenses, Op. Exp.

---

[15] Treasury Department, op. cit.

Equation 4 can be solved for the transfer price, *Pt*, given the Berry's Ratio that prevails for comparable firms in the industry or for the industry average; and for the foreign affiliate data on market prices, quantity sold, and operating expenses, Op. Exp.

MICROECONOMIC OR MARGINAL PRICING

Microeconomic theory, or marginal cost pricing, provides an important analytical approach to transfer price analysis and approximation. Microeconomic theory establishes profit maximization behavior or guidelines for the firm that simultaneously determines output levels and prices, where marginal revenue (MR) equals marginal cost (MC). Microeconomics or marginal cost transfer pricing has been established in the economic literature as the theoretically correct transfer price in vertically integrated entities.

Marginal analysis provides a powerful conceptual framework for price determination when accounting data are substituted for average cost and average revenue, and linearized cost revenue relationships are assumed.

The following example demonstrates how microeconomics can be used in a multinational corporation that is vertically integrated.

Two vertically integrated divisions—one is a manufacturer of a product and the other is a distributor of the product—could establish the market price as an appropriate transfer price when the product is traded in a perfect competition market.

If no external market exists for the product, or the external market is imperfect, the marginal cost of the manufacturing division will be the transfer price. The product will be priced by the selling entity at its MC = MR. The price derived by each division is thus determined by their marginal cost and demand circumstances.

When an imperfect external market exists for the product (e.g., competitive monopolies or oligopolies), the transfer price is set where the marginal cost of manufacturing the product equals the aggregate marginal revenue of both entities. The transfer price is set below the external market price for the product, while the price of the final product is set above both prices, depending on the firms demand curve for the final product.

The Case Law: Recent Court Cases

The court case involving Bausch & Lomb v. the IRS provides interesting insight into issues concerning the determination of royalty rates for intangible property between affiliated entities. Appendix 25-5 provides details on this case. Several additional court cases were decided in the past several years with important implications for IRC Section 482 intercompany pricing.

Bibliography

1. RALPH L. BENKE, JR. AND JAMES DON EDWARDS, *Transfer Pricing: Techniques and Uses*, National Association of Accountants, New York, 1980.
2. ROBERT G. ECCLES, *The Transfer Pricing Problem: A Theory for Practice*, Lexington Books, Lexington, MA, 1985, p. 15.
3. JACK HIRSHLEIFER, "On the Economics of Transfer Pricing," *Journal of Business*, 29, pp. 172–184, 1956; and "Economics of Divisionalized Firm," *Journal of Business*, 30, pp. 96–108, 1957.
4. HARLOW, N. HOGINBOTHAM et al., "Effective Application of the Section 482 Transfer Pricing Regulations," *The Law Review*, vol. 42, no. 2, Winter 1987.
5. JAMES L. PAPPAS AND MARK HIRSCHEY, *Managerial Economics*, 5th ed., Dryden Press, Chicago, 1987.
6. ROBERT S. PINDYCK AND DANIEL L. RUBINFELD, *Microeconomics*, Macmillan, New York, 1989, Chs. 2 and 4. Edwin Mansfield, *Microeconomics: Theory and Applications*, 6th ed., W. W. Norton, New York, 1988, Ch. 5.
7. THOMAS T. NAGLE, *The Strategy and Tactics of Pricing: A Guide to Profitable Decision Making*, Prentice Hall, Englewood Cliffs, NJ, 1987.

8. Alan M. Rugman and Lorraine Eden, (eds.) *Multinationals and Transfer Pricing*, St. Martin's Press, New York, 1985.

9. K. K. Seo, *Managerial Economics: Text, Problems and Short Cases*, 6th ed., Richard D. Irwin, Homewood, IL, 1984.

10. U.S. Treasury Department, "A Study of Intercompany Pricing" (*The White Paper*), October 18, 1988.

11. Donald S. Watson (ed.), *Price Theory in Action: A Book of Readings*, 3rd ed., Houghton Mifflin, Boston, MA, 1973.

12. E. Jerome McCarthy, *Basic Marketing: A Managerial Approach*, 4th ed., Richard D. Irwin, Homewood, IL, 1971.

13. William J. Baumol, *Economic Theory and Operations Analysis*, 3rd ed., Prentice Hall, Englewood Cliffs, NJ, 1972.

APPENDIX 25-2

The Scope of U.S. International Intercompany Transactions

U.S. MNCS INTERNATIONAL TRANSACTIONS WITH FOREIGN AFFILIATES[a]

	$, Billions	% of U.S.
Inflows		
Exports	68	30
Royalties, licenses	7	77
Services	3	18
	78	26
Outflows		
Imports	66	18
Royalties, licenses	1	57
Services	1	10
	68	13
Grand total	146	29

[a]There are some 18,000 affiliates abroad.

Source: U.S. Dept. of Commerce, 1988, and estimates by Harvey Poniachek, December 1988.

Contributing Margin Approach

The contributing margin transfer pricing method is a derivative of the traditional cost-plus pricing technique.[1] It involves allocating the contributing margin—defined as sales price less all the variable costs—between the manufacturing division and the purchasing division. The contributing margin of each division is determined on the basis of their actual or standard variable cost, or actual or standard full cost. The transfer price between two divisions is determined on the basis of these costs plus the contributing margin of the supplying division.

The contributing margin can essentially be considered a value-added technique of determining the transfer price, where each division receives a fraction of the total contribution based on the variable cost.[2]

Exhibit A25-7 shows a transaction between two divisions of the same company across national borders.

Definitions of the Variables

T/P is the transfer price, V/Ca is the variable cost of Division A, V/Cb is the variable cost of Division B, M/P is the market price, C/Ma and C/Mb are the contributing margins of Division A and B respectively, and C/M is the contributing margin of the entire corporation.

The contributing margin of each division can be determined in the following manner:

$$\frac{V/Ca}{V/Ca + V/Cb} \times C/M$$

[1]Ralph L. Benke, Jr. and James Don Edwards, *Transfer Pricing: Techniques and Uses*, National Association of Accountants, New York, 1980.

[2]Ibid.

EXHIBIT A25-7

Contributing Margin Transfer Pricing Methods

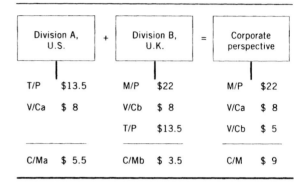

Division A, U.S.	+	Division B, U.K.	=	Corporate perspective
T/P $13.5		M/P $22		M/P $22
V/Ca $ 8		V/Cb $ 8		V/Ca $ 8
		T/P $13.5		V/Cb $ 5
C/Ma $ 5.5		C/Mb $ 3.5		C/M $ 9

Substituting the data for Division A, gives the following results.

$$\frac{\$8}{\$8 + \$5} \times \$9 = \$5.5$$

The transfer Price for Division A is determined as follows:

$$T/P = V/Ca + C/Ma$$

$$T/P = \$8 + \$5.5 = \$13.5$$

Hence, knowing the external market price for the product, and the variable cost of each division, one can determine the contributing margin of the entire corporation, calculate the share therein of the supplying division, and determine the transfer price. One can use various other benchmarks, such as full cost.

This approach provides sufficient room for arbitrary cost overloading and income shifting between geographic locations and entities. In the above example, if Division A's variable cost is changed from $8 to $10, its contributing margin goes up and the new transfer price is $14.7, up from $13.5, while Division B's contributing margin (and profit) per unit declines. This method of transfer pricing was popular among many companies surveyed.

APPENDIX 25-4

Target Transfer Pricing

Target pricing for corporate objectives could be considered as a sub-category of the corporate pricing practices listed under cost-based methods.

Competitiveness and financial performance remain the overriding concerns of corporations, and intercompany pricing policies is a significant vehicle to accomplish these objectives. The literature on corporate pricing (not necessarily on transfer pricing) identifies general implicit or explicit objectives to be accomplished through pricing policies.

There is some explicit evidence in the literature of international transfer pricing that target pricing is pursued. However, various corporate performance indicators of entities involved in intercompany transactions have become popular criteria for verifying whether transfer pricing truly approximates what should have been uncontrolled market prices. The IRS auditing, court decisions, and particularly *The White Paper* assert that when intercompany transactions are set at arm's length, the parties involved will experience acceptable risk-adjusted rates of return on capital, assets and sales. If these returns are below that of uncontrolled partied or industry averages, then the transfer price is apparently inadequate.

Target pricing for corporate objectives could be formulated according to the following criteria:

1. Pricing for a target rate of return on investment (ROI), or a target rate of return on equity (ROE), or rate of return on assets (ROA), or rate of return on sales (ROS), or break-even point (BEP) pricing.

2. Profit maximization pricing in the microeconomic sense.

3. Sales/marketing orientation pricing to increase or maintain dollar or unit sales volume in a targeted market; pricing to maintain, or capture, a market share, or preempt competition; skimming pricing, or full-line pricing.

4. Price leadership or discrimination à la oligopolist (i.e., pricing at various levels in various markets).

5. Pricing to position funds geographically, or to minimize taxes or custom duties. These pricing methods often contradict Section 482 regulation calling for arm's length transactions.

Bibliography

1. Robert S. Pindyck and Daniel L. Rubinfeld, *Microeconomics*, Macmillan Publishing Company, New York, 1989.

2. Edwin Mansfield, *Microeconomics: Theory and Applications*, 6th ed., W. W. Norton, New York, 1988.

Bausch & Lomb Inc. v. Commissioner of Internal Revenue: The Issues, the Economic Arguments, and Their Merit, and How to Improve the Economic Analysis

The Case & the Issues

Bausch & Lomb Inc. of Rochester, New York, (B&L Inc., Petitioner)—a prominent manufacturer of soft contact lenses in the United States, with a market share of over 40%—established in 1980 a foreign manufacturing subsidiary, Bausch & Lomb Ireland (B&L Ireland), for the production and marketing of soft contact lenses. The investment of some $10 million was largely funded through various government of Ireland subsidy programs, although with several strings attached. The parent company transferred to B&L Ireland all the necessary patents and know-how to commence operation; and provided it with a captive market in the United States and abroad—without a formal marketing agreement—through B&L Inc. and its foreign affiliates purchases. The royalty rate was fixed at 5% of sales, which was the standard rate in the industry, and the intracompany price was applied at $7.50.

The Commissioner of Internal Revenue Service (the Respondent) issued on December 30, 1985 a Statutory Notice of Deficiency under Section 482 allocating gross income from B&L Ireland to B&L Inc. for 1981 and 1982 of $2.8 million and $19.8 million. This adjustment represents more than 71% and 92% of B&L Ireland's net income before royalties. Respondent adjustment also eliminated royalty income paid to B&L Inc. for transfer of intangibles in the amount of $0.4 million and $1.4 million.

The rationale for that adjustment was the Commissioner's characterization of B&L Ireland as a mere "contract manufacturer" that bore no risk related to its manufacturing and sales activities. Therefore, it was not entitled to earn profits greater than similar contract manufacturers under similar circumstances. Stated alternatively, the Commissioner alleged that the royalty rate was too low and the intracompany price was too high, and that B&L Inc. would not have done such a deal with an unrelated company. Hence, the government ignored the bona fide business transaction between the entities. Expert economists for the Commissioner alleged that a more appropriate royalty rate is 27–33% of the average realized price (ARP)—obtained from the resale to unaffiliated parties, and an intracompany price of $2.25–3.00.

While the economists for the Petitioner and Respondent labor hard to back their respective clients, they fail to realize that an interim solution is more reasonable on theoretical and empirical grounds. The case provides significant analytical implications that could be utilized in addressing IRC Section 482 issues.

The Product and Industry

In the 1950s and 1960s, Dr. Otto Wichterle of Czechoslovakia pioneered development of the soft contact lens and its special material, for which he and his associates registered patents around the world in December 1961 and subsequently. In 1962, Dr. Wichterle filed an application for a patent with respect to the manufacture of soft contact lenses using the spin cast process (which B&L Inc. and B&L Ireland employed in subsequent years).

Many of the innovations and developments in the industry that occurred in the 1970s and early 1980s were made by individuals and small firms. Large companies, including B&L Inc., typically acquired new products of manufacturing process capabilities through licensing agreements.

On October 6, 1966, the National Patent Development Corporation (NPDC) and B&L Inc. entered into an agreement granting the latter an exclusive right to manufacture, use, sell, and distribute soft contact lenses under Dr. Wichterle's patents in the Western Hemisphere. B&L Inc. agreed to pay a royalty of 50% of net profit per lens (by applying a complicated and difficult to verify formula to determine the net profit). In 1973, following litigation between the parties, NPDC granted B&L Inc. nonexclusive, nonassignable, and nontransferable licenses for the manufacturing, use, selling, and distribution of lenses under the subject patents in the United Kingdom and 18 other European countries. B&L Inc. was required to pay a royalty of 6% of net sales in the United Kingdom and 5% in other countries.

B&L Inc. entered the soft contact lenses industry in the United States during 1971 and virtually established a monopolistic position. However, high profitability and the consequent entrance of some 30 new manufacturers into the industry by the early 1980s, combined with B&L Inc.'s inability to acquire the extended wear lenses, reduced its market share from 53% in 1980 to 48% in 1981 and 41% in 1982.

Soft contact lens products accounted for some 40% of B&L Inc. worldwide sales, or for some $200 million, during each year. In the early 1980s, companies in the United States employed various processes, but their products were essentially equivalent in price and use. For instance, in 1981 NPDC's standard cost of manufacturing soft contact lenses using the cast molding process was $3.33 per lens, of which $1.54 was overhead (the volume was over 41,000).

Manufacturing Abroad

Manufacturing abroad was a reasonable business decision in light of the circumstances and numerous advantages. B&L Inc. projected very high global growth for soft contact lenses at 20–25% annually, but confronted emerging capacity constraint at its Rochester facility. These conditions, combined with the need to service foreign clients more effectively, affected the company's decision to manufacture abroad.

Ireland offered a strategic location advantage vis-à-vis the EEC market, and a package of most attractive financial incentives through the Industrial Development Authority (IDA). These incentives included a capital grant of 45% of total investment, low-cost lease financing on 35% of the total investment, training grants, a tax holiday on export earnings through 1990, and low-cost commercial loans. The IDA capital grant stipulated that the royalty for intangibles should not exceed 5% of net export sales.

B&L Ireland and its manufacturing facility were incorporated in February 1980. With its establishment, B&L Inc. licensed to B&L Ireland certain intangibles for the manufacture of soft contact lenses, and assisted in its setting up operation (the patent transferred to Ireland was not protected there).

During 1981 and 1982, B&L Ireland engaged in the manufacturing and sales of soft contact lenses, with all the manufacturing activities conducted at Waterford, Ireland. In 1981 and 1982, B&L Ireland produced approximately 1.3 million and 4.0 million lenses, while the U.S. facility functioned as a swing plant by reducing its capacity utilization according to market conditions. During the two subject years, B&L Ireland sold its output to its parent (61% and 56% of total) and its foreign affiliates (39%, 44%). Initially, purchase orders were routed through B&L Inc., but eventually foreign affiliates ordered from Ireland directly, although B&L Inc. and B&L Ireland did not enter into a formal distribution.

Significant intangibles that B&L Inc. licensed to B&L Ireland were the low-cost Spin Cast manufacturing processes, including various technical know-how associated with it. In 1981, this process yielded a savings per lens ranging from $1.15–3.90, and perhaps of $2.00–3.50, compared with the lowest cost manufacturer. The licensing agreement called for a royalty of 5% of net sales of all licensed products, which was the standard royalty in the industry in the mid-1960s through the early 1980s, although in some cases an 8% rate was reported.

B&L Inc. established in 1979 a single uniform transfer price of $7.50 per soft contact lens for all sales to foreign affiliates. In 1981 and 1982, B&L Ireland sold its output to its parent and its foreign affiliates at this price on a C.I.F. basis. Unrelated parties transacted private labels of the same type produced by B&L Ireland at various list prices; of $16–18 and $7.50–12.50, and $8.45–14.00. Manfuacturers sold comparable soft contact lenses with a recognized trade name to unrelated distributors at a discount of 25–30% off the list price, whereas B&L Ireland offered 50–71% discount from the domestic average realized price (ARP) resold to an unrelated party.

Economic Arguments

Dr. Irving H. Plotkin, a prominent economist in the area of Section 482, testified for B&L

Inc. by conducting an analysis of uncontrolled comparables, cost savings shared by the parties, and risk-return. He essentially maintained that the transaction between the parties was at arm's length.

Accordingly, the $7.50 per lens paid by B&L Inc. to B&L Ireland was reasonable and arm's length, priced below the market for comparable private label products; there was no basis for reducing them. At this price, Dr. Plotkin alleged B&L Ireland did not capture any of the benefits of any marketing or other intangibles that may be attributable to B&L Inc. Therefore, B&L Inc. was not entitled to any additional compensation beyond that which was agreed upon between the parties. (Because their goods were selling at steep discount, he assumed that they could have been sold to unrelated parties instead.) Thus, B&L Ireland actually received less than other manufacturers received for their comparable lenses in the U.S. and there was no need to reduce their prices.

There were numerous comparable licensing transactions which indicated that a royalty of 5% of net sales was adequate and consistent with the industry's standard. Thus, a 5% rate was arm's length. Dr. Plotkin suggested that a royalty of 5% of net sales based on ARP was an appropriate arm's length royalty. This, however, constituted a considerable modification of the original royalty agreement by suggesting that the appropriate price for a parent subsidiary is the ARP, rather than the transfer price.

Dr. Plotkin asserted that the only intangible asset enjoyed by B&L Ireland was low cost advantage attributable to the manufacturing intangibles licensed by B&L Inc. to B&L Ireland. He suggested splitting the cost savings at 25% for B&L Inc. and 75% for B&L Ireland, since this apportionment was consistent with his experience in licensing. Based on B&L Ireland manufacturing cost savings (of $1.15–3.90 and possibly averaging $2.40), and its average realized price (ARP of $16.51), the royalty of 5% on ARP yielded $0.83 or 50% of the cost savings. However, it could be somewhat lower, perhaps 34% based on a cost savings of $2.4 per lens.

Hence, Dr. Plotkin concluded that a 5% royalty provided B&L Inc. with a more than generous share of the cost savings, which he asserted to have been the only benefit from the intangibles transferred. This level is consistent with the industry practice, and it is competitive with alternative available licenses, since it shares cost savings appropriately between the licensee and licensor at a level indicated above general economic theory (which he did not cite, but might be referred to as the risk–reward relationship).

Given the $7.50 per lens and the 5% royalty based on the ARP, the relative rate of return on operating assets enjoyed by B&L Ireland and B&L Inc. were appropriate, according to Dr. Plotkin. He discussed the rate of return and risk of the entities involved, but no information on the definition or its measurement was provided. He suggested, however, that the allocation by the Commissioner produced a rate of return on assets of 7–8%, while during this period government of Ireland securities yielded 18%. He maintained that B&L Inc. performed a reselling (distribution) function for B&L Ireland and obtained royalty income —two activities for which they were compensated adequately.

Dr. Plotkin argued that B&L Ireland maintained the bulk of the assets and it was most exposed to adverse scenarios, whereas B&L Business Unit (an analytically created entity by Dr. Plotkin to illustrate his point) performed the distribution of B&L Ireland products and transferred the intangibles to it. Ireland thus had greater financial responsibility than B&L Business Unit. Dr. Plotkin estimated the rate of return on operating assets for B&L Ireland at 106% and B&L Business Unit at 75%, which he considered to be commensurate with the relative risk incurred by both parties.

Dr. David Bradford, an economist who testified for the Commissioner, asserted a priori a contract manufacturer framework and suggested a cost-plus adjustment. He maintained that the transaction between the entities could have been structured in a number of ways, but sharing the profit should be the same. (This is indeed the case for multinational companies that consolidate their global operation and allocate resources to maximize stockholders' wealth.) While implicitly assuming that the transfer price of $7.50 was appropriate, he maintained that unrelated parties would not have established a compensation structure—as in the subject case—that would cause asymmetrical distribution of cost and benefit. An adjustment should therefore be made to reflect appropriate compensation for B&L Ireland's use of the intangibles. The amount of the adjustment could be determined by a mark-up percentage of B&L Ireland production cost.

Dr. Bradford reviewed the profit margins of three firms and concluded that there should be an allocation from B&L Ireland to the parent company for 1981 between $4.6–5.4 million and for 1982 between $15.0–17.8 million. These allocations are equal to a royalty on an ARP basis of 30–35%, and 55–65% on a net sales basis.

Dr. Clark J. Chandler, an economist, testified on behalf of the government. He sought to determine whether a 5% royalty was reasonably equivalent to an arm's length payment. He estimated the cost savings to B&L Ireland at $3.30–3.50, which he claimed belonged entirely to B&L Inc. since it was attributable to the intangibles provided by it. Dr. Chandler translated that sum into a royalty equivalent of 19–22% on net sales based on ARP.

He further argued that B&L Ireland had access to trademarks and other marketing intangibles worth approximately 3–5% of ARP. Dr. Chandler concluded that the royalty rate for use of patents and know-how should have been 4–8%, and 1% for FDA clearance of B&L Ireland. Dr. Chandler finally concluded that a 27–33% royalty on the basis of ARP was appropriate to qualify for arm's length transaction.

How to Improve the Economic Analysis

B&L Inc. established the Irish subsidiary as a bona fide entity, but its decision was considerably assisted by the generous incentives provided by the government of Ireland, including a decade-long tax holiday. The evidence (and the expert economists) failed to draw the similarity between the subject firm and hundreds of U.S. multinational companies that pursued a similar posture abroad during that era. This would have given B&L Inc.'s foreign investment decision in Ireland greater business validity.

Since uncontrolled comparables were identified for the intangibles and tangibles by the Petitioner, the strategy pursued by the economic experts was to demonstrate arm's length behavior by the entities involved. The Commissioner's experts implicitly assumed a contract manufacturing and, therefore, sought higher royalties and lower intracompany prices.

The arguments that were presented by Dr. Plotkin, B&L's expert economic witness, were made in the traditional context of Section 482, but they were lacking in several areas:

1. While the soft contact lenses were considered comparable throughout the industry, the intangibles that were transferred were rather inexact.

2. To establish his arguments, Dr. Plotkin elected to ignore the significance of the readily available markets for B&L Ireland products via B&L Inc. and its foreign affiliates. He assumed that at below market price, B&L Ireland could have sold its output to unrelated parties, as the theoretical model suggests; but he ignored the marketing cost and risk of failing to do so, as well as the time value of money. This is a significant intangible for which no compensation was offered.

3. The examination of risk is erroneous and misleading since it was not conducted in either the context of the Capital Asset Pricing Model (CAPM) or another acceptable fashion.

4. Sharing of cost savings derived from the cheap manufacturing process of the licensed intangibles is proposed at 25% and 75% in favor of Ireland without any convincing (theoretical or empirical) justification for doing so. The economists testifying for the government asserted that the entire savings belonged to the licensor. Indeed, in an integrated corporation, the theoretical model suggests a splitting of savings more like the Commissioner's economists' position.

5. Dr. Plotkin's rate of return analysis is rather innovative—and most common in competitive analysis of somewhat heterogeneous entities—but it introduced several assumptions that could be disputed. Plotkin does not examine, however, whether B&L Ireland earned an excessive profit in comparison to other firms in the industry.

6. Dr. Plotkin introduced the ARP concept, which explicitly suggested that the 5% royalty on sales needed an upward revision when intracompany transactions are concerned.

7. Dr. Plotkin did not refute effectively and convincingly the government's allegation that B&L Ireland was a contract manufacturer. He admitted, however, that the transaction could have been structured in various other forms.

The government economists—who pursued an approach that a priori assumed a contract manufacturer framework—provided cost-plus, rate of return, and profit-splitting analyses. However, they did not convincingly refute the Petitioner's approach.

An alternative approach along the following lines by B&L expert economist could have produced a more defensible position:

1. B&L could have benefited from a more thorough analysis of its risk and return in the context of a formal Capital Assets Pricing Model.

2. The location savings factor could have been advanced to warrant additional profit for B&L Ireland.

3. The government of Ireland's subsidies might have contributed, to some extent, to very high profitability performance, thus justifying lower compensation for the transferred intangibles.

4. Formal analysis of B&L Inc. and B&L Ireland in the context of an integrated firm, including the adjustments for subsidies and perhaps location savings, could have been quite revealing.

Finally, the materials reviewed (Brief for Petitioners and Reply Brief for Petitioners) presented incomplete information and testimonies. While the case was still pending in court in April 1988, a verdict calling for a profit split was ruled in the similar case of C. D. Searle & Company. Bausch & Lomb Inc. could have avoided expensive litigation if the economic advisor(s) pursued a more reasonable approach in recognizing the marketing intangibles and in determining the more appropriate intracompany compensation following the initial audit.

The Tax Court Decision

In the Section 482 case of Bausch & Lomb Incorporated v. the Commissioner of Internal Revenue Service concerning the alleged underpricing of soft contact lenses shipped from the corporate wholly-owned subsidiary in Ireland during 1981 and 1982, and the alleged too-low royalty rate for the transfer of intangibles upon the establishment of the entity in Ireland, the Court ruled as follows:

Based on comparable uncontrolled products' prices, the Court has accepted the transfer price as the appropriate arm's length price for the subject transaction.

The Court has rejected the Commissioner's assertion of a contract manufacturer and recognized that the creation of the subsidiary was for valid business reasons.

The Court did not accept the evidence concerning the comparability of the subject intangibles with transactions in similar technology that were conducted between unrelated entities.

The royalty rate of 5% was declared inappropriate, not at arm's length, and not commensurate with the uniqueness of the intangibles transferred upon the establishment of the subsidiary. The Court thus ignored the agreement between B&L Ireland and Ireland's Industrial Development Authority (IDA), which required that the company's royalties not exceed 5% of net sales.

Due to the significance of the intangibles concerned, the Court ruled that a profit split of 50%/50% between the parent and the subsidiary be instituted and reflected in the royalty rate.

In assessing the justification of the royalty rate the Court resorted to the Capital Budgeting Model, and has found though trial and error that a royalty rate of 20% of net sales constitutes an effective profit split as suggested above, and provides ample incentives to have undertaken the investment in Ireland.

The Court rejected a too-high royalty level advocated by the Commissioner's economists as rendering the investment unfeasible if unrelated parties would have negotiated it.

Implicitly, in determining the royalty level, the philosophy pursued by the Court could be interpreted in the context of a rate-of-return approach cum profit split. After satisfying the investor, the residual is split between the parties. (Since the parent is the stockholder, the implications for the consolidated company is only on the tax liabilities, and thus on post-taxable earning.)

The Royalty Determination: Some Technical Issues

Since the royalty rate of 5% of net sales was deemed too low and inappropriate, the Court constructed an arm's length royalty rate through the following procedure.

The Court rejected the use of ARP (average realized price) as an appropriate base for royalty payments.

Based on B&L's 1980 10-year project feasibility study, the Court determined the expected (prospective) profit to be generated from the establishment of a subsidiary in Ireland. However, to insert greater reality into the forecast, the Court diminished B&L's expected profit by assuming a steady erosion in demand, eventually falling as low as 20% of capacity by 1989, and an annual decline in the price per soft contact lens by $0.50.

The Court applied the Capital Budgeting Model in assessing the appropriate royalty level, although in a somewhat simplified manner. This framework is commonly utilized by the corporate sector to assess investment projects feasibility. The most common versions of this model are the Net Present Value (NPV) and the Internal Rate of Return (IRR). (The former is theoretically more appropriate, but the latter is very popular.)

The Court then simulated the implications of various royalty rates on B&L Ireland's Court constructed profit over a 10-year period. By utilizing the IRR Model and several royalty rates, the Court determined the internal rate of return, which equalizes the net present value of future earnings and the cost of investment in B&L Ireland.

By assuming a 50%–50% profit split on expected profit between the licensor and licensee, and by the determining the royalty equivalent on a net sales basis, the Court determined that a 20% royalty on B&L Ireland sales price is appropriate. This royalty level is consistent with a 27% return on investment (IRR), which in the Court' opinion provides a 15% risk premium and a (risk adjusted) return of 12%.

Implications for Taxpayers

The information utilized by the Court—that is, the project's feasibility study—is commonly available in all companies that undertake investment abroad. Therefore, in assessing appropriate levels of royalties on intangibles, we can benefit from already existing data.

The application of the Capital Budgeting Model by the Court raises a number of problems which could set the stage for an appeal:

1. The reconstruction of projected profit relies on several sensitive assumptions related to market demand and product prices, which depress the outlook and diminish the assessment of the royalty rate.

2. The discount rate might have been set at an excessively high level. Consequently, the present value of the expected profit from B&L Ireland was reduced. A substantially lower discount rate would have suggested room for a higher royalty level.

3. The theory of investment suggests that the discount rate should be the weighted cost of capital for B&L Ireland adjusted for risk (which was probably lower than the discount rate that the Court used, thanks to the generous subsidies).

In setting the royalty level, the Court has not necessarily used the super-royalty concept since it has based its analysis on historical rates rather than on actual outcome.

The Court has not considered the marketing arrangement as a transfer of intangibles because no formal buy-back arrangements existed between the parties.

The Court has implied that the intangibles have a finite life span, whereby their benefits rise and then fall rapidly. The lifetime was somewhat arbitrarily determined—on the basis of the company's feasibility study. Obviously, different time spans produce different cash flows and different rates of returns and royalty levels.

The Implications for Transfer Pricing Analysis

A number of concepts that were introduced by the *White Paper* have been proposed in the subject case.

1. The concept of exact and inexact comparables has been applied particularly for the intangibles. The Court has distinguished between the mere selling of know-how and the selling plus the commercial experience that accompanies it.

2. The Court's determination of the royalty could be deemed as commensurate with income (i.e., super royalty). While the Court could have resorted to actual data in figuring it out, as the *White Paper* proposes, it instead selected to replicate a real negotiation between unrelated parties and based on their expectations at the time. Hence, a far cry from setting a royalty on the basis of actual performance.

APPENDIX 25-6

IRS 1992 Proposed Intercompany Pricing

The Internal Revenue Service issued proposed Section 482 intercompany transfer pricing regulations on January 27, 1992. The proposed regulations, which might go into effect in early 1993, introduced several innovative concepts, the comparable profit interval (CPI), and sophis-ticated statistical methods, to determine whether arm's length pricing prevails.

Section 1.482-2(e) states the rules applicable to determine intercompany prices of transactions in tangible property. These rules include the comparable uncontrolled price (CUP), the resale price method (RPM), the cost-plus method (CPM), and the fourth methods. The regulations require that the last three methods be verified for reasonableness by applying the CPI criterion to determine whether the approximated arm's length intercompany price yields comparable rate(s) of return. If the CPI verification is satisfied, the transfer pricing is considered arm's length.

The new regulations modify the pricing priority that existed under the previous regulations. While the CUP method retains first priority, second priority is given to either the resale price method or the cost-plus method, depending on which approach yields the most accurate arm's length price under the circumstances of the transaction.

Exhibit A25-7 summarizes the proposed regulations for tangible property.

Section 1.482-2(f) describes the construction and application of the comparable profit interval (CPI). Exhibits A25-8 and A25-9 detail how the CPI is constructed and applied.

EXHIBIT A25-7

Proposed SEC 482 Regulations: Tangible Property 1.482-2(e)

PROPOSED REGULATIONS	CURRENT REGULATIONS
1. Comparable uncontrolled price (CUP)	Unchanged
2. Resale price method (RPM): Appropriate when a manufacturer sells to a controlled distributor which neither employs significant intangibles nor adds significant value added.	2nd priority
or	
Cost plus method (CPM): Appropriate when a manufacturer sells products to a controlled taxpayer which have considerable intangibles and/or adds substantial value added.	3rd Priority
CPM and RPM have equal priority.	
Validation of reasonableness by comparable profit interval (CPI) to confirm appropriateness of operating income (OI)	Informal validation
3. Other methods (Fourth methods): Various PLIs (e.g., rate of return analysis, various ratios/PLIs defined under the CPI), internal rate of return, functional analysis? Profit split, aggregate industry analysis? Customs representation?	Fourth methods
Required validation by the comparable profit interval (CPI)	

Section 1.482-2(d) contains the new regulations designed to determine the intercompany price of intercompany transactions in intangible property. Highest priority is given to the matching transaction method (MTM), which is an exact uncontrolled comparable—i.e., same intangible under the same or similar economic conditions and contractual terms. Second priority is afforded to the comparable adjustable transaction method (CAT), which is a comparable transaction that warrants some adjustments for quantifiable differences.

In the absence of the MTM or CAT, the comparable profit method (CPM), which is the rate of return analysis, is applicable. This approach must be verified for reasonableness by the application of the CPI analysis.

Exhibit A25-10 summarizes the proposed new regulations for intercompany transactions in intangible property.

EXHIBIT A25-8

Comparable Profit Interval (CPI) 1.482-2(f)

SIX STEPS TO CONSTRUCT
AND APPLY THE CPI

1. SELECT THE PARTY (TESTED PARTY) TO A CONTROLLED TRANSACTION TO BE TESTED. It is not necessarily the party under audit. Usually, the tested party will be wholesale distributor or manufacturer for tangibles property, and the transferee in case of intangibles.

2. DETERMINE THE APPLICABLE BUSINESS CLASSIFICATION (ABC) OF THE TESTED PARTY. E.g., SIC code and/or description of business, similar products, and/or functions. The tested party operations are matched the operation as closely as possible to similar operations of the uncontrolled taxpayers.

(Continued)

3. COMPUTE CONSTRUCTIVE OPERATING IN-COMES (COIs).

    a. Select uncontrolled taxpayer(s) within the same business.

    b. Select profit level indicators (PLIs) that provide a reliable basis for comparing profits.

    c. Calculate the PLIs for comparable companies.

    d. Calculate the constructive operating incomes (COIs).

4. DETERMINE THE CPI FROM A SET OF CONSTRUCTED OPERATING INCOMES THAT CONVERGE. The CPI derivation will be based on a three-year period, including the taxable year, the preceding and following year. Two types of convergence should be considered in constructing the CPI:

    a. Convergence of COIs of the tested party derived from several PLIs of a single uncontrolled taxpayer.

    b. COIs derived from one or more PLIs obtained from multiple uncontrolled taxpayers.

5. WHEN NECESSARY, DETERMINE THE MOST APPROPRIATE POINT IN THE CPI. Statistical methods: Apply measures of central tendency to determine the CPI. Determine the CPI analytically/judgmentally by comparability criteria of similarity of products, functions, and markets.

6. Determine the transfer price for the controlled transaction.

EXHIBIT A25-9

Comparable Profit Interval (CPI) 1.482-2(f)

HOW TO COMPUTE CONSTRUCTIVE OPERATING INCOMES (COIs)

1. Select uncontrolled taxpayer(s) within the same business.

2. Select profit level indicators (PLIs) that provide a reliable basis for comparing profits. Select PLIs that provide the most effective basis for comparison under the particular circumstances (e.g., the rate of return on assets, the ratio of operating income to sales, the ratio of gross income to operating expenses (Berry Ratio), and other ratios, including the ratio of operating income to labor cost, ratio of operating income to cost, excluding COG). Comparable profit splits (residual or overall approach). Residual: Allow a rate of return on assets prior to splitting the sums. Overall profit split without allowing a prior return on assets.

3. Calculate the PLIs for comparable companies.

4. Calculate the constructive operating incomes (COIs) levels. (i.e., apply the PLIs of the comparable companies to the tested party.) Adjust the PLIs for significant differences between the tested party and the uncontrolled taxpayer (e.g., if the comparable ROS is 5% then the OI required to provide the tested party a 5% ROS is the constructive OI).

EXHIBIT A25-10

Intangible property 1.482-2(d)

PROPOSED REGULATION

                                                            CURRENT REGULATION

1. MATCHING TRANSACTION METHOD (MTM). Exact intangible   CUP
and same or similar economic and contractual conditions.

2. COMPARABLE ADJUSTABLE TRANSACTION METHOD (CAT).   CUP
Inexact comparable. The same or similar intangible under adjustable procedures. Economic and contractual circumstances are

(Continued)

considered adjustable if they are sufficiently similar. Adjustments
are allowed for a limited number of differences. Requires validation
by the CPI (through comparison of OEs).

3. COMPARABLE PROFIT METHOD. Requires validation by the CPI   Fourth methods
   through comparison of OEs. Price is at arm's length if IO falls——
   within the CPI. If outside the CPI, transfer price may be adjusted to
   yield OI that is at the most appropriate point in the CPI.

Notes: Arm's length pricing must be commensurate with income.

Look-back Rule: Review the terms of multi-year controlled transactions in light of actual performance, but
the proposed regulations provide three exceptions (remain in CPI, 10 years at arm's length, new circumstances beyond control and fixed contracts).

Irving Oil versus the Queen

A Case Study in Transfer Pricing

ALAN M. RUGMAN

ALAIN VERBEKE

Executive Summary

This case study deals with Irving Oil and its use of transfer pricing. An appropriate system had to be designed that could incorporate all tax, legal, and operational considerations. In terms of income tax, the multinational enterprise (MNE) will try to minimize taxable income in high rate countries. This is done through transfer pricing, which is justified by internalization theory and its concern for efficiency. The overall goal is to maximize the firm's value from the parent's point of view. This must be achieved in the face of opinion to the effect that transfer pricing allows the MNE to be manipulative and to earn excessively high profits, when in reality transfer pricing reflects efficient managerial behavior.

Copyright (©) 1990. Alan M. Rugman is Professor of International Business and Research Director of the Ontario Centre for International Business at the University of Toronto. Alain Verbeke is Assistant Professor of International Business at the University of Toronto. Research assistance by David Heasman, Kelly Williams, and George Zakem at the Dalhousie University Centre for International Business Studies, Dalhousie University, and by Tom Boddez at the Ontario Centre for International Business, University of Toronto, is gratefully acknowledged.

In the Irving Case, the firm created a strategic subsidiary in Bermuda (Irvcal). Social, from whom Irving purchased oil, would direct it through Irvcal, who would then sell it at a higher price to parent Irving. In this way, profits were realized in tax-free Bermuda. Irvcal's profits were then returned to Irving in the form of dividends, equally divided between Socal and the Irving Family. This was desirable because dividend payments are taxed at a lower rate than are corporate profits.

The Canadian Federal Government alleged that the establishment of Irvcal was a sham, and that the profits of Irvcal were in essence Irving's profits, subject to taxation. The Federal Court of Canada disagreed, ruling in favor of Irving. This reaffirmed that the actions of Irving were rational and efficiency-driven, and that popular conceptions about MNEs earning abnormal profits and evading taxes were completely unfounded.

In this case study Canadian-owned Irving Oil provides the basis for a discussion of transfer pricing by multinational enterprises. Designing transfer pricing systems is complicated by considerations such as profit and dividend repatriation, domestic and foreign tax considerations, and legal and governmental implications. Irving Oil's response to these issues, and the governmental opposition to this response, are outlined in detail.

Introduction: Transfer Pricing and the Theory of Internalization

This case study of Irving Oil (a Canadian-owned company) aims to provide the basis for a conceptual discussion on the issue of transfer pricing by multinational enterprises (MNEs). Transfer pricing is the pricing of goods or services traded between divisions or subsidiaries of a company. Designing an appropriate transfer-pricing system within an MNE is a complex task because of the tax, legal and operational implications inherent in a transfer-pricing system.

In designing a transfer-pricing system for an MNE a number of important considerations must be made. Among these are: the international competitive position of the firm; constraints on repatriating profits and dividends; domestic and foreign tax considerations; and other legal and governmental implications.

A major consideration in setting a transfer price is the income tax effect. Profits may be influenced by setting transfer prices to minimize taxable income in any country with a high income tax rate. Tax haven affiliates have been used as trade intermediaries to drain off the income from transactions between related affiliates.

In the absence of government interference, the firm would prefer to pay higher prices to its selling affiliates in low tax countries. A variety of regulations and court cases exist on the reasonableness of transfer prices, including fees and royalties as well as prices set for physical merchandise. If a government taxing authority does not accept a transfer price, taxes will be increased or, as in the case of the Irving Oil dispute, taxes will be reassessed and the corporation will be forced to pay back taxes. An even greater danger from the corporate point of view is that two or more governments will try to protect their respective tax bases by contradictory policies that might sub-

ject the business to double taxation on the same income.

In choosing a transfer pricing system an MNE must be conscious of legislation requiring the "arm's length" pricing of intracompany transactions. An "arm's length" price is defined as the price which an unrelated party would have paid under the same circumstances for similar property. In other words, it is a price determined through arm's length bargaining.

Guidelines created by the tax authorities in the United States, Canada, and other members of the Organization for Economic Cooperation and Development (OECD) essentially stipulate the use of an "arm's length" intracompany pricing system. Three methods used by the OECD to determine an arm's length price are briefly outlined as follows.

1. *Comparable uncontrolled price method.* This method uses the price recently derived between two unrelated parties as a reference price in determining an arm's length transfer.

2. *Resale price method.* Here the reference price is calculated based on the price offered by a similar seller to an "independent purchaser."

3. *Cost-plus method.* This price is based on a supplier's cost plus an appropriate percentage markup derived by examining the markups associated with sales to other unrelated parties or by other sellers.

In contrast, Rugman[1] (1985) argues that transfer pricing can be explained and justified by the internalization theory of the MNE. Internalization theory is concerned with the efficiency aspects of the organization and

---

[1]Alan M. Rugman, "Transfer Pricing in the Canadian Petroleum Industry," in Alan M. Rugman and Lorraine Eden, eds., *Multinationals and Transfer Pricing*, New York: St. Martin's Press, and London: Croom Helm, 1985, pp. 173–192.

administration of internal markets. Internal markets are used by the MNE when regular markets fail or are inefficient. For example, internal markets are required when regular market costs are excessive or when the market fails to recognize the value of intangibles like knowledge. The MNE uses its internal market to maximize the value of its firm-specific advantages. The actions of the oil MNEs, such as Irving Oil, are no different. In this case, the behaviour of Irving Oil merely results from the existence of government-induced market imperfections (i.e., different income tax rates in different countries). Transfer pricing then is nothing more than an efficient strategic reaction to such imperfections.

It could be argued, in the spirit of Rugman (1985), that transfer pricing does not reflect excessive economic power held by MNEs, since:

1. MNEs provide social benefits by paying taxes and creating employment and spillover benefits in the host nations rather than the home nations.
2. The sovereign power of the nation state is ultimately greater than that of any corporation, since only the state can impose taxes and regulations, while MNEs can only respond to such measures.

Transfer pricing only means that if tax rate differentials or repatriation controls exist in the countries where the MNE operates, the MNE can efficiently respond by developing a transfer pricing policy that will maximize the firm's value from the parent's point of view.

Conceptually, there aren't any problems with internalization theory's view of transfer prices. However, the problem of sovereignty arises when the theory is put into practice internationally. The home nation, for example Canada, interprets efficiency and distributional elements differently. From an efficiency point of view, MNEs increase capital investment in a country, provide employment, increase exports, transfer technology and pay

taxes. The problem occurs when distributional elements are considered such as the perception that:

1. The MNE does not contribute enough to the welfare of the country, and is only interested in profits.
2. The payment of taxes can be avoided through "manipulations" available only to the MNE.

In this context, it is widely believed by the general public, many academics, and even some legislators, that profits of multinational corporations have been, and continue to be, excessively high. This view is simplistic and factually incorrect, which has been demonstrated at an aggregate level by Rugman, et al. (1985). Problems do arise, however, when such perceptions lead public policy makers, such as national tax authorities, to punish MNEs for engaging in transfer pricing, when in reality this merely reflects efficient managerial behaviour, respecting the constraints imposed by national laws.

Irving Oil versus the Queen

In 1978, Revenue Canada (the Canadian tax administration) reassessed the tax returns of Irving Oil Ltd. (Irving Oil). The Government disallowed nearly Can$142 million in crude oil costs Irving claimed it had paid to its wholly-owned subsidiary, Irving California Oil Company Limited (Irvcal). Questioned by Revenue Canada were the business relationships and the ensuing transactions between Irving, the Standard Oil Company of California Limited (Socal, now Chevron) and Irvcal.

Socal and the Irving family were the major shareholders of Irving Oil. Socal owned 49 percent and the Irving family the other 51 percent of Irving Oil since August 1957. In addition, a refining company existed of which Socal owned 51 percent and the Irving family the other 49 percent. Both Irving Oil and

EXHIBIT 26-1

Structure of Ownership

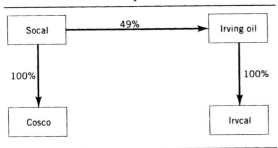

Irving Refining were held by a 50–50 voting position. The ownership structure between Irving Oil, Socal and their respective subsidiaries appears in Exhibit 26-1.

Irving Oil had established a contract to purchase crude oil from Socal in 1957. A long-term agreement was reached and the deal solidified the future business relationship between the two companies. Irving Oil was a dealer in finished petroleum products such as gasoline. In 1957, Irving had no facilities to handle crude oil and no refining capacity. However, given the long-term nature of the oil supply contract entered into with Socal, Irving agreed to build a refinery, with the financial assistance of Socal. The ownership structure of Irving Oil and Irving Refining remained unchanged from 1957 to 1973.

In the late 1960s, the increased demand for petroleum products and the construction of a modern oil terminal in Saint John (Canada) allowed Socal to achieve substantial cost savings. These included transportation cost savings through the use of very large crude carriers. From 1968 on, tough negotiations began between Irving and Socal, as the former aimed at partaking in the benefit accruing to the latter (the initial 1957 contract included a price reopening provision for review after 10 years).

At the initiative of Socal's tax department, a scheme was then proposed in 1971, whereby Irving Oil would benefit from Socal's produc-

tion and transportation savings. A strategic plan was designed "to effect savings, even substantial savings, in order to enhance commercial profitability." Socal, however, refused to sell crude oil in Canada at a price less than a fair market price. Socal refused to do so because any price below market price would subject its production and transportation profits to Canadian income tax. This income had already been highly taxed by foreign jurisdictions, namely in Saudi Arabia and Iran. The new scheme involved the eventual creation of a wholly-owned Irving subsidiary in Bermuda.

In the same year, Irving purchased the incorporated company Bomag in Bermuda and in 1972 renamed it Irving California Oil Company Ltd. (Irvcal). The strategic creation of this subsidiary enabled Irving (and Socal through its 49 percent ownership of Irving) to benefit from production and transportation savings realized by Socal as a result of the tax free nature of Bermuda.

The scheme devised by Socal's tax department worked as follows. Irvcal would buy oil from Socal's 100 percent owned subsidiary Cosco (Chevron Oil Sales Company) at a price of US $2.10 per barrel for the first two million barrels and $2.24 per barrel after that. These prices were approximately equal to Socal's production and transportation costs. Irvcal would then resell the oil to Irving Oil at US $2.90 per barrel, to effectively generate a profit. The paper flow of oil is depicted in Exhibit 26-2.

With respect to pricing, the price charged to Irving was an arm's length price (i.e., that price which would be charged in an independent transaction between unrelated parties). The US $0.80 or $0.66 difference in this transaction represented non-Canadian income, in the sense that it was income derived from the production of crude oil in Saudi Arabia and Iran and the transportation of oil from the Middle East to Canada. Irvcal's profits, which in essence represented Irving's non-Canadian

EXHIBIT 26-2

Flow of Oil

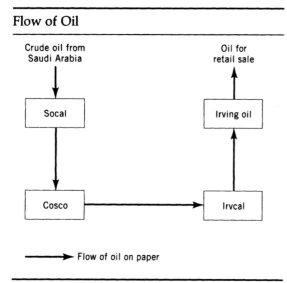

Crude oil from Saudi Arabia → Socal → Cosco → Irvcal

Oil for retail sale ← Irving oil

———→ Flow of oil on paper

EXHIBIT 26-3

Funds Flow

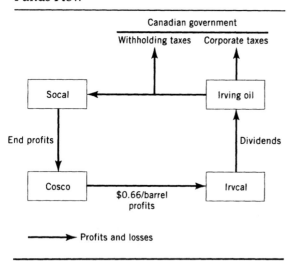

Canadian government

Withholding taxes   Corporate taxes

Socal ← Irving oil

End profits   Dividends

Cosco → Irvcal $0.66/barrel profits

———→ Profits and losses

income, were returned to Irving in the form of dividends which were then divided equally between Socal and the Irving family.

Dividend payments are subject to a lower tax rate than corporate income, thus the reason for the creation of the subsidiary. Socal

was entitled to 50 percent of these dividends, which when repatriated would be subject to a Canadian withholding tax. Exhibit 26-3 shows the funds flow graphically.

In May 1987, Irving brought suit against the Federal Government in an attempt to regain the taxes Irving stated had been wrongly assessed against them in 1978. Some of the main assumptions presented by the Revenue Minister in this law suit are listed below:

1. At all times Socal (and its associated companies) supplied the crude oil needs of Irving Oil.

2. The creation of Irvcal was not for a "bona fide business purpose" but in fact was a "sham." Essentially Socal sold the oil directly to Irving Oil.

3. Profits accrued by Irvcal were in substance those of Irving Oil. Irvcal's profits were earned by charging Irving an "inflated" price for oil.

4. Irvcal was in fact only a "paper routing intermediary" between Irving Oil and Socal.

5. Expenses incurred by Irving were not for the purposes of earning income as defined by the Income Tax Act. This act essentially states that in computing taxable income, eligible expenses are those incurred "for the purpose of gaining or producing income from the business."

6. The expenses incurred were not made under "reasonable circumstances."

7. If expenses stated by Irving were allowed, these would "artificially or unduly" reduce Irving's taxable income.

On March 4, 1988 the Federal Court, Trial Division ruled in favour of the plaintiff, Irving Oil. The statement below is taken from the "general conclusion" of this case:

The ultimate, if not precisely the bottom line in this case, in so far as the Trial Division is concerned, is that the plaintiff's expenses or outlays for the crude oil it acquired from Irvcal during the material times are properly allowable deductions and did not unduly, or artificially reduce the plaintiff's income.

As the court ruled in Irving's favor, the Government was ordered to return Can$142 million to Irving in taxes and interest. This case represents probably one of the most important judgments ever made against the Canadian Federal Government.

That same day, a member of the Irving family said to one of his friends:

There is justice in this country. We have been able to convince the Federal Court that our actions were efficiency driven and by no means aimed at taking away from the Canadian tax authorities what was rightfully theirs.

He then reflected on the elements of this case which had brought the court to rule in Irving Oil's favor. He wished to analyze and list all the factors involved in developing a successful strategy to win the case.

Conclusion

The Government's accusations regarding the legality of Irving's transfer pricing system are not as uncommon as one might suspect. As Rugman asserts, the attitude persists that there is something abnormal and even immoral about the profits earned by, and the general financial operations of, MNEs.[2]

A frequent argument made against the MNE is that, since it operates internationally, it is uniquely well endowed to engage in transfer pricing; that is, to manipulate intrafirm input prices between subsidiary and parent. The MNE is alleged to have the power to avoid payment of full local taxes, thus depriving host or home nation of some of its legitimate tax revenue.

The existing academic literature on foreign investment, the role of the MNE, and MNE related tax revenues, however, does not support the popular view that MNEs avoid taxa-

tion or fail to contribute to a nation's economic growth.[3]

Transfer prices and tax rates are intimately related. More specifically, the international tax rate differential on an input for the MNE enters into its production process as a cost item along with the normal costs of factors such as labor and capital. If international tax rates were uniform there would be no incentive for transfer pricing.

Analysis of the Irving Oil case then leads to the conclusion that Irving Oil established a wholly-owned subsidiary in Bermuda in order to increase profits within the constraints imposed by the Canadian tax laws. In this context, it should be remembered that tax laws prevail over equity considerations for tax authorities.

The Assignment

1. How can Irving Oil challenge the assumption by the Canadian tax ministry that crude oil is bought directly from Irvcal and indirectly from Socal?

2. How can Irving challenge the assumption that the creation of Irvcal is a "sham"? Does Socal charge Irving a competitive market price, or not? Did Irvcal perform the functions it was established to perform? How do the three parties minimize tax payments? What is the significance of Irvcal's premises in Bermuda?

3. Are Irvcal's profits inflated because Irving pays an "unfair" price for crude oil?

4. Is Irvcal an independent business entity, or not?

5. Does Irving pay an "arm's length" price to Irvcal, or not?

6. Are Irving Oil's expense "reasonable in the circumstances," or not?

7. Should Irvcal's profits be taxed inside or outside of Canada?

[2]Alan M. Rugman, *International Diversification and the Multinational Enterprise*, Lexington: D. C. Heath, 1979.

[3]Alan M. Rugman, Donald J. Lecraw and Laurence D. Booth, *International Business: Firm and Environment*, Toronto: McGraw-Hill, 1985.

CASE 27

Mobil Corporation

International Taxation and the Implications of Foreign Tax Credit

HARVEY A. PONIACHEK

Mobil Corporation is one of the largest integrated oil companies in the world, with 1989 revenue of $56.2 billion. Mobil paid $14.5 billion in taxes in 1989, of which $12.6 billion were excise and state gasoline taxes, import duties and property, production, payroll and other taxes paid primarily to foreign governments, and approximately $2.0 billion were income taxes, of which $258 million was paid to the U.S. Treasury and $1.7 billion was paid to foreign governments. For details see Appendex 27-1 for Mobil's financial and tax data.

The corporation's geographic distribution of earnings shows that in 1989 the United States accounted for $809 million and foreign operations for $1,614 million, or approximately one-third U.S. and two-thirds foreign. The geographic distribution of assets show that $16,592 million were in the United States and $19,972 million were located abroad.

The Assignment

Examine Appendix 27-1, "Mobil Corporation selected financial and tax data," review Appendix 27-3, "An Introductory Discussion on Foreign Tax Credit," and address the following questions:

1. Why is Mobil's geographic distribution of income, assets, and taxes extremely asymmetrical?

2. Could foreign tax credits explain the earnings-cum-tax asymmetry?

3. Is Mobil paying excessive taxes abroad? How could tax payments be more evenly distributed to correspond to the pre-tax earnings distribution?

4. We seek to determine whether the tax position of petroleum companies is unique. Compare the tax position of Ford Motor Company, shown in Appendix 27-2, "Ford Motor Company selected financial and tax data," with Mobil's as shown in Appendix 27-1. Address particularly the implications of the foreign tax credit of both corporations. For an introductory discussion of foreign tax credit, see Appendix 27-3. (If you wish to review additional information on Ford beyond what is provided here, consult Case 21.)

Mobil Corporation Selected Financial and Tax Data Excerpts from Annual Report 1989

FIVE-YEAR FINANCIAL SUMMARY

(IN MILLIONS OF DOLLARS EXCEPT FOR PER-SHARE AMOUNTS)	1989	1988	1987	1986	1985
REVENUES	**$56,188**	$54,361	$51,387	$44,792	$54,466
INCOME FROM CONTINUING OPERATIONS[a]	**$ 1,809**	$ 2,031	$ 1,218	$ 2,058[b]	$ 1,506
Per common share (based on average shares outstanding)	**$ 4.40**	$ 4.93	$ 2.96	$ 5.04	$ 3.69
NET INCOME, EXCLUDING THE EFFECT UNDER FAS 96 OF U.S AND SIGNIFICANT FOREIGN INCOME TAX RATE CHANGES	**$ 1,809**	$ 1,893	$ 1,448	$ 1,612[b, c]	$ 1,040[d]
NET INCOME (LOSS)[a]	**$ 1,809**	$ 2,087	$ 1,348	$ (354)[b, e]	$ 1,040[d]
Per common share (based on average shares outstanding)	**$ 4.40**	$ 5.07	$ 3.28	$ (.87)	$ 2.55
SEGMENT EARNINGS					
Petroleum Operations					
Exploration and Producing					
U.S.	**$ 147**	$ 100	$ 484	$ 88	$ 716
International	**971**	795	1,077	881	1,082
Total Exploration and Producing	**1,118**	895	1,561	969	1,798
Marketing and Refining					
U.S.	**350**	553	123	365	157
International	**380**	453	109	997	176
Total Marketing and Refining	**730**	1,006	232	1,362	333
Total Petroleum	**1,848**	1,901	1,793	2,331	2,131
Chemical	**575**	613	300	140	53
Corporate and Other	**(184)**	(206)	(180)	(228)	(26)
Net Financing Expense	**(430)**	(471)	(595)	(587)	(652)
Loss on Sale of Container Corporation of America	—	—	—	(150)	—
Effect under FAS 96 of U.S. and Significant Foreign Income Tax Rate Changes	—	194	(100)	552	—
Income from Continuing Operations	**1,809**	2,031	1,218	2,058	1,506
Discontinued Operations—Montgomery Ward	—	56	130	106	(466)[d]

(Continued)

(IN MILLIONS OF DOLLARS EXCEPT FOR PER-SHARE AMOUNTS)	1989	1988	1987	1986	1985
Income before Cumulative Effect of Change in Accounting Principle	**1,809**	2,087	1,348	2,164	1,040
Cumulative Effect of Change in Accounting Principle (FAS 96)	—	—	—	(2,518)	—
Net Income (Loss)	**$ 1,809**	$ 2,087	$ 1,348	$ (354)	$ 1,040
NET INCOME (LOSS) AS PERCENT OF—					
Average shareholders' equity	**11.3%**	13.6%	9.5%	(2.8)%	7.5%
Average capital employed[f]	**10.0%**	11.4%	8.5%	1.2%	6.8%
Revenues	**3.2%**	3.8%	2.6%	(0.8)%	1.9%
NET CASH FROM OPERATING ACTIVITIES	**$ 4,652**	$ 4,029	$ 3,013	$ 4,546	$ 4,801
CAPITAL AND EXPLORATION EXPENDITURES	**$ 3,393**	$ 3,915	$ 2,798	$2,890	$ 3,330
BALANCE SHEET POSITION AT YEAR-END					
Current assets	**$11,920**	$11,178	$11,097	$10,193	$12,193
Net properties, plants, and equipment	**$23,446**	$23,848	$24,071	$23,439	$24,533
Total assets	**$39,080**	$38,820	$40,272	$38,173	$40,668
Current liabilities	**11,216**	10,255	10,730	10,075	11,911
Long-term debt	**5,317**	6,498	7,143	7,939	9,323
Shareholders' equity	**$16,274**	$15,686	$15,000	$13,430	$14,089
Per common share	**$ 39.84**	$ 38.19	$ 36.46	$ 32.86	$ 34.50
DEBT-TO-CAPITALIZATION RATIO	**30%**	32%	37%	41%	45%
NUMBER OF COMMON SHARES OUTSTANDING (thousands of shares, year-end)	**408,515**	410,730	411,359	408,732	408,351
COMMON STOCK CASH DIVIDENDS	**$ 1,045**	$ 968	$ 903	$ 898	$ 898
As percent of net income	**58%**	46%	67%	41%[c]	86%
Per share	**$ 2.55**	$ 2.35	$ 2.20	$ 2.20	$ 2.20
YEAR-END MARKET PRICE PER COMMON SHARE	**$ 62⅝**	$ 45½	$ 39⅛	$ 40⅛	$ 30¼

[a]Income from continuing operations and net income (loss) include the effect under FAS 96. Accounting for income Taxes, of U.S. and significant foreign income tax rate changes. These income effects were $194 million in 1988, $(100) million in 1987, and $552 million in 1986.

[b]Includes the $150 million loss on sale of Container Corporation of America.

[c]Excludes $2,518 million cumulative charge through December 31, 1985, from adopting FAS 96. Accounting for Income Taxes.

[d]Includes the $508 million provision for restructuring Montgomery Ward.

[e]Includes $2,518 million cumulative charge through December 31, 1985, from adopting FAS 96, Accounting for Income Taxes.

[f]Net income plus income applicable to minority interests plus interest expense net of tax divided by the sum of average shareholders' equity, minority interests, and debt.

OPERATING HIGHLIGHTS

	1989	1988	1987	1986	1985
PETROLEUM PRODUCT SALES (thousands of barrels daily)					
United States	939	927	865	841	789
Europe	811	782	720	721	670
Far East and Australasia	567	492	465	448	429
Other Foreign	278	324	312	264	266
Worldwide	2,595	2,525	2,362	2,274	2,154
PETROLEUM PRODUCT SALES (millions of dollars)					
United States	$ 9,233	$ 8,074	$ 7,885	$ 6,965	$ 9,748
Europe	13,644	12,194	11,309	10,105	11,276
Far East and Australasia	7,030	6,720	6,484	6,088	6,683
Other Foreign	3,819	3,947	4,011	3,164	3,883
Worldwide	$33,726	$30,935	$29,689	$26,322	$31,590
AVERAGE UNITED STATES PRODUCT PRICE (per gallon)	64.5¢	56.9¢	58.6¢	53.5¢	79.8¢
REFINERY RUNS FOR MOBIL (thousands of barrels daily)					
United States	722	650	645	643	647
Europe	459	453	403	457	496
Far East and Australasia	402	375	330	308	331
Other Foreign	174	175	185	137	116
Worldwide	1,757	1,653	1,563	1,545	1,590
MILES OF PIPELINE[a] (including partly owned; year-end)					
United States	25,828	25,702	26,337	27,597	28,044
Foreign	11,234	11,152	11,099	11,195	11,116
Worldwide	37,062	36,854	37,436	38,792	39,160
CHEMICAL SALES BY PRODUCT CATEGORY (millions of dollars)					
Petrochemicals	$ 1,978	$ 2,179	$ 1,239	$ 990	$ 932
Plastics	1,795	1,711	1,514	1,274	1,184
Other	26	32	25	26	45
Net Sales to Trade	$ 3,799	$ 3,922	$ 2,778	$ 2,290	$ 2,161
NUMBER OF SHAREHOLDERS OF COMMON STOCK (year-end)	227,100	237,600	246,800	260,800	268,600

(Continued)

	1989	1988	1987	1986	1985
NUMBER OF EMPLOYEES (year-end)[b]					
Petroleum—United States	25,800	25,200	24,600	25,100	26,300
—Foreign	27,000	29,900	29,800	32,100	34,200
Chemical—United States	9,700	9,400	9,000	9,000	9,500
—Foreign	1,500	1,400	1,300	1,200	1,100
Other	3,900	3,700	3,500	3,700	23,900
Total	67,900	69,600	68,200	71,100	95,000

[a]Includes carbon dioxide line in United States.
[b]All years exclude Montgomery Ward.

DISTRIBUTION OF EARNINGS AND ASSETS

Segments (in millions)

	PETROLEUM OPERATIONS				
	EXPLORATION AND PRODUCING	MARKETING AND REFINING	CHEMICAL	ADJUSTMENTS AND ELIMINATIONS	TOTAL
YEAR ENDED DECEMBER 31, 1989					
REVENUES					
Nonaffiliated	$ 4,824	$46,615	$4,039	$ 710	$56,188
Intersegment	3,799	445	166	(4,410)	—
TOTAL REVENUES	$ 8,623	$47,060	$4,205	$(3,700)	$56,188
Pretax operating profit	$ 2,703	$ 1,130	$ 774	$ —	$ 4,607
Income taxes	(1,585)	(400)	(199)	—	(2,184)
SEGMENT EARNINGS	$ 1,118	$ 730	$ 575	$ —	$ 2,423
Corporate and other (net of income taxes)					(184)
Net financing expense (net of income taxes)					(430)

(Continued)

| | PETROLEUM OPERATIONS | | | | |
	EXPLORATION AND PRODUCING	MARKETING AND REFINING	CHEMICAL	ADJUSTMENTS AND ELIMINATIONS	TOTAL
NET INCOME					$ 1,809
Capital expenditures[a]	$ 1,258	$ 1,148	$ 199	$ —	$ 2,864
Depreciation, depletion, and amortization[b]	$ 1,811	$ 525	$ 128	$ —	$ 2,502
AT DECEMBER 31, 1989					
TOTAL SEGMENT ASSETS	$16,958	$17,178	$2,702	$ (387)	$36,451
Corporate and all other assets					2,629
TOTAL ASSETS					$39,080
YEAR ENDED DECEMBER 31, 1988					
REVENUES					
Nonaffiliated	$ 4,852	$44,567	$4,280	$ 662	$54,361
Intersegment	3,105	321	168	(3,594)	—
TOTAL REVENUES	$ 7,957	$44,888	$4,448	$(2,932)	$54,361
Pretax operating profit	$ 1,929	$ 1,596	$ 851	$ —	$ 4,376
Income taxes	(1,034)	(590)	(238)	—	(1,862)
SEGMENT EARNINGS	$ 895	$ 1,006	$ 613	$ —	$ 2,514
Corporate and other (net of income taxes)					(206)
Net financing expense (net of income taxes)					(471)
Effect under FAS 96 of U.S. and significant foreign income tax rate changes					194
INCOME FROM CONTINUING OPERATIONS					2,031
Discontinued operations— Montgomery Ward (net of income taxes)					56
NET INCOME					$ 2,087
Capital expenditures[a]	$ 1,198	$ 1,620	$ 219	$ —	$ 3,194
Depreciation, depletion, and amortization[b]	$ 2,016	$ 505	$ 129	$ —	$ 2,683
AT DECEMBER 31, 1988					
TOTAL SEGMENT ASSETS	$17,795	$16,141	$2,802	$ (314)	$36,424

(Continued)

| | PETROLEUM OPERATIONS | | | | |
	EXPLORATION AND PRODUCING	MARKETING AND REFINING	CHEMICAL	ADJUSTMENTS AND ELIMINATIONS	TOTAL
Corporate and all other assets					2,396
TOTAL ASSETS					$38,820

YEAR ENDED DECEMBER 31, 1987

	EXPLORATION AND PRODUCING	MARKETING AND REFINING	CHEMICAL	ADJUSTMENTS AND ELIMINATIONS	TOTAL
REVENUES					
Nonaffiliated	$ 4,868	$43,063	$2,926	$ 530	$51,387
Intersegment	3,705	266	164	(4,135)	—
TOTAL REVENUES	$ 8,573	$43,329	$3,090	$(3,605)	$51,387
Pretax operating profit	$ 3,103	$ 480	$ 433	$ —	$ 4,016
Income taxes	(1,542)	(248)	(133)	—	(1,923)
SEGMENT EARNINGS	$ 1,561	$ 232	$ 300	$ —	$ 2,093
Corporate and other (net of income taxes)					(180)
Net financing expense (net of income taxes)					(595)
Effect under FAS 96 of U.S. and significant foreign income tax rate changes					(100)
INCOME FROM CONTINUING OPERATIONS					1,218
Discontinued operations— Montgomery Ward (net of income taxes)					130
NET INCOME					$ 1,348
Capital expenditures[a]	$ 1,091	$ 957	$ 121	$ —	$ 2,287
Depreciation, depletion, and amortization[b]	$ 1,825	$ 474	$ 115	$ —	$ 2,457

AT DECEMBER 31, 1987

	EXPLORATION AND PRODUCING	MARKETING AND REFINING	CHEMICAL	ADJUSTMENTS AND ELIMINATIONS	TOTAL
TOTAL SEGMENT ASSETS	$18,820	$15,596	$2,456	$ (350)	$36,522
Corporate and other assets					2,211
Montgomery Ward net assets held for sale					1,539
TOTAL ASSETS					$40,272

[a] Total includes capital expenditures for corporate and all other assets of continuing operations.

[b] Total includes depreciation on corporate and all other assets of continuing operations.

Geographic (in millions)

	U.S.	FOREIGN CANADA	FOREIGN OTHER	FOREIGN TOTAL	ADJUSTMENTS AND ELIMINATIONS	TOTAL
YEAR ENDED DECEMBER 31, 1989						
REVENUES						
Nonaffiliated	$19,028	$ 993	$35,457	$36,450	710	$56,188
Intergeographic	163	65	997	1,062	(1,225)	—
TOTAL REVENUES	$19,191	$1,058	36,454	$37,512	$ (515)	$56,188
GEOGRAPHIC EARNINGS	$ 809	$ 95	$ 1,519	$ 1,614	$ —	$ 2,423
Corporate and other (net of income taxes)						(184)
Net financing expense (net of income taxes)						(430)
NET INCOME						$ 1,809
AT DECEMBER 31, 1989						
TOTAL GEOGRAPHIC ASSETS	$16,592	$2,936	$17,036	$19,972	$ (113)	$36,451
Corporate and all other assets						2,629
TOTAL ASSETS						$39,080
YEAR ENDED DECEMBER 31, 1988						
REVENUES						
Nonaffiliated	$17,298	$ 898	$35,503	$36,401	$ 662	$54,361
Intergeographic	113	144	769	913	(1,026)	—
TOTAL REVENUES	$17,411	$1,042	$36,272	$37,314	$ (364)	$54,361
GEOGRAPHIC EARNINGS	$ 997	$ 47	$ 1,470	$ 1,517	$ —	$ 2,514
Corporate and other (net of income taxes)						(206)
Net financing expense (net of income taxes)						(471)
Effect under FAS 96 of U.S. and significant foreign income tax rate changes						194
INCOME FROM CONTINUING OPERATIONS						2,031
Discontinued operations—						
Montgomery Ward (net of income taxes)						56

(*Continued*)

	U.S.	Foreign			Adjustments and Eliminations	Total
		Canada	Other	Total		
NET INCOME						$ 2,087
AT DECEMBER 31, 1988						
TOTAL GEOGRAPHIC ASSETS	$17,078	$3,060	$16,364	$19,424	$ (78)	$36,424
Corporate and all other assets						2,396
TOTAL ASSETS						$38,820
YEAR ENDED DECEMBER 31, 1987						
REVENUES						
Nonaffiliated	$16,189	$ 882	$33,786	$34,668	$ 530	$51,387
Intergeographic	116	260	777	1,037	(1,153)	—
TOTAL REVENUES	$16,305	$1,142	$34,563	$35,705	$ (623)	$51,387
GEOGRAPHIC EARNINGS	$ 788	$ 127	$ 1,178	$ 1,305	$ —	$ 2,093
Corporate and other (net of income taxes)						(180)
Net financing expense (net of income taxes)						(595)
Effect under FAS 96 of U.S. and significant foreign income tax rate changes						(100)
INCOME FROM CONTINUING OPERATIONS						1,218
Discontinued operations— Montgomery Ward (net of income taxes)						130
NET INCOME						$ 1,348
AT DECEMBER 31, 1987						
TOTAL GEOGRAPHIC ASSETS	$16,519	$3,073	$17,028	$20,101	$ (98)	$36,522
Corporate and other assets						2,211
Montgomery Ward net assets held for sale						1,539
TOTAL ASSETS						$40,272

Significant investments in companies owned 50% or less are accounted for on the equity method. The corporation's share of the net income of such companies is included in "Revenues."

Intersegment and intergeographic revenues are at estimated market prices.

Income taxes are allocated to segments and geographic areas on the basis of operating results, except for the effect under FAS 96 of U.S. and significant foreign income tax rate changes.

"Corporate and other" included Real Estate operations, Mining and Minerals, Corporate Administration, and other corporate items.

TAXES

TOTAL TAXES, YEAR ENDED DECEMBER 31 (IN MILLIONS)	1989			1988			1987		
	U.S.	FOREIGN	TOTAL	U.S.	FOREIGN	TOTAL	U.S.	FOREIGN	TOTAL
Excise and state gasoline	$1,765	$ 3,447	$ 5,212	$1,762	$ 3,362	$ 5,124	$1,430	$ 3,030	$ 4,460
Import duties[a]	—	6,795	6,795	—	6,633	6,633	—	5,738	5,738
Property, production, payroll, and other	441	188	629	398	225	623	437	189	626
Less discontinued operations	—	—	—	—	—	—	111	—	111
Total other than income taxes	2,206	10,430	12,636	2,160	10,220	12,380	1,756	8,957	10,713
Income taxes									
U.S. state and local income taxes	60	—	60	112	—	112	64	—	64
U.S. federal and foreign income taxes—current	248	1,615	1,863	489	1,247	1,736	96	1,420	1,516
—deferred	(50)	72	22	(354)	(85)	(439)	97	8	105
Less discontinued operations	—	—	—	(21)	—	(21)	88	—	88
Total income taxes	258	1,687	1,945	268	1,162	1,430	169	1,428	1,597
Total taxes	$2,464	$12,117	$14,581	$2,428	$11,382	$13,810	$1,925	$10,385	$12,310

[a]Excludes U.S. duties of $8 million in 1989, $7 million in 1988, $6 million in 1987 reported in cost of crude oil and products.

Income from continuing U.S. operations before income taxes was $1,273 million in 1989, $1,482 million in 1988, and $1,333 million in 1987. Income from foreign operations before income taxes for the same three years was $3,335 million, $2,894 million, and $2,683 million, respectively. The loss from Corporate and Other Net Financing Expense before income taxes for the same three years was $854 million, $915 million, and $1,201 million, respectively.

Deferred income taxes are provided for the temporary difference between the financial statement and tax bases of Mobil's assets and liabilities, and relate primarily to depreciation and intangible drilling costs.

Mobil does not provide deferred taxes for taxes that could result from the remittance of undistributed earnings since it is generally Mobil's intention to continue reinvesting these earnings indefinitely.

Mobil's share of the undistributed earnings of consolidated subsidiaries and companies accounted for on the equity method, which could be subject to additional income taxes if remitted, was approximately $2,800 million at December 31, 1989. It is not practicable to determine the unrecognized deferred tax liability applicable to the undistributed earnings, which, if remitted, would be subject to approximately $270 million of withholding taxes. If such amounts were remitted, foreign tax cred-

its available under present law would reduce the amount of U.S. taxes payable.

The following table reconciles the difference between the worldwide income tax provision for continuing operations and the application of the U.S. statutory income tax rate.

INCOME TAXES, YEAR ENDED DECEMBER 31 (IN MILLIONS)	1989		1988		1987	
	AMOUNT	%	AMOUNT	%	AMOUNT	%
Theoretical tax at U.S. rate	$1,276	34.0	$1,177	34.0	$1,126	40.0
Foreign taxes in excess of U.S. statutory rate	707	18.8	464	13.4	592	21.0
Investment tax credits	—	—	(3)	(.1)	(12)	(.4)
State and local income taxes	40	1.1	74	2.1	38	1.4
Effect under FAS 96 of U.S. and significant foreign income tax rate changes	—	—	(194)	(5.6)	100	3.5
Other items, net	(78)	(2.1)	(88)	(2.5)	(247)	(8.8)
Total	$1,945	51.8	$1,430	41.3	$1,597	56.7

APPENDIX 27-2

Ford Motor Company Selected Financial and Tax Data Excerpts from Annual Report 1987

CONSOLIDATED STATEMENT OF INCOME

For the Years Ended December 31, 1987, 1986, and 1985 (in millions)
Ford Motor Company and Consolidated Subsidiaries

	1987	1986	1985
SALES	$71,643.4	$62,715.8	$52,774.4
COSTS AND EXPENSES (NOTE 1)			
Costs, excluding items listed below	58,495.1	51,866.2	44,435.4
Depreciation	1,814.2	1,666.4	1,444.4
Amortization of special tools	1,353.2	1,293.2	948.4
Selling and administrative	3,281.4	3,122.1	2,525.2
Employee retirement plans (Note 2)	498.3	711.4	691.3

(Continued)

	1987	1986	1985
Total costs and expenses (Note 3)	65,442.2	58,659.3	50,044.7
OPERATING INCOME	6,201.2	4,056.5	2,729.7
Interest income			
Marketable securities and time deposits	647.4	550.2	569.8
Other	218.6	128.6	179.3
Interest expense	(440.6)	(482.9)	(446.6)
Net interest income	425.4	195.9	302.5
Equity in net income of unconsolidated subsidiaries and affiliates	753.4	816.9	598.1
INCOME BEFORE INCOME TAXES	7,380.0	5,069.3	3,630.3
Provision for income taxes (Note 4)	2,726.0	1,774.2	1,103.1
INCOME BEFORE MINORITY INTERESTS	4,654.0	3,295.1	2,527.2
Minority interests in net income of consolidated subsidiaries	28.8	10.0	11.8
NET INCOME	$ 4,625.2	$ 3,285.1	$2,515.4
Average number of shares of capital stock outstanding (Note 10)[a]	511.0	533.1	553.6
NET INCOME A SHARE (NOTES 5 AND 10)[a]	$9.05	$6.16	$4.54
NET INCOME A SHARE ASSUMING FULL DILUTION (NOTES 5 AND 10)[a]	$8.92	$6.05	$4.40
CASH DIVIDENDS A SHARE (NOTE 10)[a]	$1.58	$1.11	$0.80

[a]Adjusted to reflect the two-for-one stock split that was effective December 10, 1987.

Postretirement Health Care and Life Insurance Benefits

The company and certain of its subsidiaries provide selected health care and life insurance benefits for retired employees. Substantially all of the company's U.S. and Canadian employees may become eligible for those benefits if they reach retirement age while still working for the company. The estimated cost for postretirement life insurance benefits is accrued on an actuarially determined basis. The amounts accrued for such life insurance benefits are not funded in the U.S., but are reflected in the company's Consolidated Balance Sheet as an accrued liability. The cost for postretirement health care benefits is based on actual expenditures for the year. In 1987 and 1986, the cost for both U.S. and Canadian employees amounted to $341 million and $291 million, respectively, for postretirement health care benefits and $121 million and $111 million, respectively, for postretirement life insurance benefits.

For the company's subsidiaries outside the U.S., such benefits either are not provided, or may be provided by the subsidiary, by the subsidiary's pension plan, or by governmental agencies. The benefits provided may be in a substantially different form than those provided in the United States. The cost of such benefits at non-U.S. operations did not materially affect the company's results.

Note 3: Costs and Expenses

The costs and expenses included in the Consolidate Statement of Income have been reclassified, as shown below, to reflect as cost of sales those costs directly related to goods sold.

(in millions)	1987	1986	1985
Cost of sales	$61,960.0	$55,365.4	$47,362.4
Selling, administrative, and other expenses	3,482.2	3,293.9	2,682.3
Total costs and expenses	$65,442.2	$58.659.3	$50,044.7

Note 4: Income Taxes

The company's provision for income taxes was as follows:

(in millions)	1987	1986	1985
Currently payable			
U.S. Federal	$1,068.7	$ 809.3	$ 490.2
Foreign	572.2	653.0	184.1
State and local	131.3	63.9	51.3
Total currently payable	1,772.2	1,526.2	725.6
Deferred			
U.S. Federal	595.3	288.1	33.6
Foreign	358.5	(40.1)	343.9
Total deferred	953.8	248.0	377.5
Total provision	$2,726.0	$1,774.2	$1,103.1

The provision includes estimated taxes payable on that portion of retained earnings of foreign subsidiaries expected to be received by the company. No provision was made with respect to the balance of the retained earnings, approximately $3.8 billion at December 31, 1987. These retained earnings have been invested by the subsidiaries and have incurred foreign income taxes that would have the effect of reducing substantially tax liabilities that would result from their distribution. Deferred income taxes result from timing differences in the recognition of revenues and expenses between financial statements and tax returns. The principal sources of these differences and the related effect of each on the company's provision for income taxes were as follows (in millions): 1987–$582.6 for depreciation and amortization and $219.5 for employee benefit plans; 1986–$354.5 for depreciation and amortization, $164.8 for employee benefit plans, and $(203.6) for dealer and customer allowances and claims; 1985—$445.1 for depreciation and amortization and and $(218.9) for dealer and customer allowances and claims.

At December 31, 1987 and 1986, deferred tax assets totaling $390 million and $317.2 million, respectively, were included in other current assets in the Consolidated Balance Sheet.

The company's income before income taxes for its U.S. and foreign operations, excluding equity in net income of unconsolidated subsidiaries and affiliates, was as follows:

(in millions)	1987	1986	1985
United States	$4,536.8	$2,917.8	$2,057.3
Foreign	2,089.8	1,334.6	974.9
Total income before income taxes	$6,626.6	$4,252.4	$3,032.2

A reconciliation of the provision for income taxes compared with the amounts at the U.S. statutory tax rate is shown below:

(in millions)	1987	1986	1985
Tax provision at U.S. statutory rate (1987 at 40%, 1986 and 1985 at 46%)	$2,650.6	$1,956.1	$1,394.8

(Continued)

(in millions)	1987	1986	1985
Effect of:			
Credits utilized in			
determination of taxes	—	(104.6)	(345.5)
Foreign taxes over/(under)			
U.S. tax rate	94.8	(1.0)	79.5
Other	(19.4)	(76.3)	(25.7)
Provision for			
income taxes	$2,726.0	$1,774.2	$1,103.1
Effective Tax Rate	41.1%	41.7%	36.4%

Investment tax credits are accounted for by the flow-through method as a reduction of the provision for U.S. Federal income taxes in the year in which the tax credits can be utilized. Income taxes on earnings in the United States were offset partially by investment and other tax credits, some of which were carried forward from prior years.

In December 1987, the Financial Accounting Standards Board issued Statement of Financial Accounting Standards No. 96, "Accounting for Income Taxes" (SFAS No. 96). The company did not adopt SFAS No. 96 in 1987; adoption by 1989 is mandatory. When adopted, the standard, among other things, will result in the restatement of the company's worldwide deferred tax balances to the statutory tax rates in effect at the time these balances are expected to be payable. Because most of these deferred taxes were recorded at higher tax rates in prior years, net income will increase in the year SFAS No. 96 is adopted.

Note 12: Segment Information

INDUSTRY

The company and its consolidate subsidiaries comprise a vertically integrated business operating primarily in a single industry segment consisting of the manufacture, assembly, and sale of cars and trucks and related parts and accessories.

GEOGRAPHIC AREA

(in millions)	1987	1986	1985
Sales to Unaffiliated Customers			
United States	$47,688	$42,790	$36,779
Canada	3,942	3,158	2,901
Europe	15,731	12,481	8,745
Latin America	1,782	2,401	2,402
All other			
(primarily Asia-Pacific)	2,500	1,886	1,947
Total outside sales	$71,643	$62,716	$52,774
Intercompany Sales Among Geographic Areas			
United States	$7,614	$ 7,244	$ 6,747
Canada	6,057	6,624	6,172
Europe	1,471	1,128	821
Latin America	1,386	885	705
All other			
(primarily Asia-Pacific)	347	160	81
Total intercompany			
sales	$16,875	$16,041	$14,526
Total Sales Revenue			
United States	$55,302	$50,034	$43,526
Canada	9,999	9,782	9,073
Europe	17,202	13,609	9,566
Latin America	3,168	3,286	3,107
All other			
(primarily Asia-Pacific)	2,847	2,046	2,028
Elimination			
of intercompany sales	(16,875)	(16,041)	(14,526)
Total sales	$71,643	$62,716	$52,774
Net income (loss)			
United States	$ 3,441	$ 2,460	$ 1,988
Canada	143	167	148
Europe	1,079	559	326
Latin America	(95)	66	(57)
All other			
(primary Asia-Pacific)	57	33	110
Total net income	$ 4,625	$ 3,285	$ 2,515
Assets at December 31			
United States	$24,418	$22,701	$19,396
Canada	3,695	2,938	2,667

(Continued)

(in millions)	1987	1986	1985
Europe	15,270	11,179	9,107
Latin America	1,865	2,501	2,131
All other (primarily Asia-Pacific)	3,247	2,224	1,820
Elimination of intercompany receivables	(3,539)	(3,610)	(3,517)
Total assets	$44,956	$37,933	$31,604

Capital Expenditures (Facilities, Machinery and Equipment, and Tooling)

	1987	1986	1985
United States	$ 2,108	$ 1,966	$ 2,553
Canada	242	174	180
Europe	853	720	620
Latin America	124	295	256
All other (primarily Asia-Pacific)	285	198	128
Total capital expenditures	$ 3,612	$ 3,353	$ 3,737

Intercompany sales among geographic areas consist primarily of vehicles, parts, and components manufactured by affiliated companies and sold to other affiliated companies. Transfer prices between affiliated companies are established through negotiations between the affected parties. Generally, the buying affiliate incurs additional costs following the purchase and prior to the sale of a product to an unaffiliated customer.

An Introductory Discussion on Foreign Tax Credit

Introduction

A U.S. corporation receiving dividends (that were distributed from earnings and profits, E & P) from a foreign-owned subsidiary (in which it owns 10 percent or more of the voting shares) or subpart F inclusion is deemed to have paid a pro-rata share of the foreign taxes paid by their foreign subsidiary in the year that the dividend is received. The U.S. corporation may claim as a credit the income taxes paid by the foreign entity on the earnings and profits distributed to it. The amount of the deemed paid is determined by the following formula:

Foreign Taxes Deemed Paid

$$= \text{(Dividend/Post 1986 undistributed earnings)}$$
$$\times \text{Post 1986 Foreign Income Tax}$$

The Purpose of the indirect foreign tax credit is to equalize the tax burden of a U.S. shareholder of a foreign corporation with that of a foreign branch of a domestic corporation that is entitled to a direct foreign credit for the foreign taxes paid on the branch income. The foreign taxes deemed paid are addressed by Internal Revenue Code (IRC) Section 902 and 960.

This appendix addresses the circumstances under which a domestic U.S. corporation may claim a foreign tax credit for taxes paid by foreign subsidiaries, determines the earnings and profits out of which dividends are paid, and determines how foreign taxes paid are calculated.

Foreign Taxes Deemed Paid

The Tax Reform Act of 1986 (TRA) amended the regulations related to foreign taxes deemed paid by basing its determination on undistributed earnings, the amount of dividends distributed and the foreign income tax paid (as shown in the formula earlier).

Assume U.S. Corporation Y operates a branch in foreign country FC, which imposes an income tax of 25 percent. If the branch earns a profit of $100, Y's foreign income tax liability to country FC would be $25. Y's pre-credit income tax liability to the United States on the same income would be $46 (assuming a 46 percent tax rate) and Y's final income tax liability to the United States would be $21 because IRC §901(a) allows Y to credit against its U.S. tax liability the $25 foreign income tax that it paid to country FC. Y would pay a total of $46 in taxes; $25 to FC and $21 to the United States.

If there was no credit for foreign taxes deemed paid and Y Corporation was operating through a 100 percent owned foreign subsidiary (instead of a branch), then the subsidiary's profits available for distribution after taxes would be $75 and (upon distribution of the available earnings) the U.S. corporation would have a dividend of $75 and a U.S. tax liability of $34.50 on those earnings. Y's combined outlay for taxes (both foreign and domestic) on the subsidiary's income would be $59.50. This is $13.50 more than Y would have paid if it were operating a branch instead of a subsidiary in country FC. This inequity is remedied by IRC §902 and §78 which treat Y as if it had received a $100 dividend and paid foreign taxes of $25. As a result Y pays a total of $46 in taxes, $25 to FC and $21 to the United States, whether it operates through a branch or through a subsidiary.

This rule applies eventhough the distribution is out of earnings and profits of the foreign corporation accumulated several years prior to the year of receipt.

Post-1986 foreign taxes deemed paid from controlled foreign corporations (CFCs) will have to be determined on a basket-by-basket basis.

EXAMPLE 1

Assume that CFCs has the dollar as its functional currency with the following earnings and profits and taxes pools. Also assume that none of the earnings are subpart F income and that the stated earnings and profits are after reduction for foreign taxes.

| Year | General Limitation | | Shipping | |
	E & P	Taxes	E & P	Taxes
1987	100	20	100	40
1988	100	40	100	40
Totals	200	60	200	80

On 12/31/88 subsidiary S pays a $200 dividend to its sole U.S. shareholder, P. One-half of the dividend will be treated as out of general limitation E & P and one-half will be treated as out of shipping E & P under the IRC §904 dividend look-through rule. Foreign taxes deemed paid would be computed as follows:

General	$100/$200 × $60 = $30
Shipping	$100/$200 × $80 = $40

P would have the following income:

General		Shipping	
$100	Dividend	$100	Dividend
30	Gross-up	40	Gross-up
$130	Total	$140	Total

P's foreign taxes deemed paid would be $30 in the general basket and $40 in the shipping basket.

IRC §78 Gross-Up

A domestic corporation that: (1) receives a dividend from a foreign corporation; (2) includes Subpart F income in its gross income;

or (3) treats as a dividend a portion of the gain on the sale of stock in a foreign corporation under IRC §1248; is required to include in its income an amount equal to the foreign income taxes deemed paid by such corporation with respect to the dividend received or the subpart F income.

Foreign Corporation X had pre-tax earnings and profits in 1983 of $200 upon which it paid an income tax of $80 to its country of incorporation. In 1983 the corporation paid a dividend of $30 to Y, its U.S. parent.

The foreign taxes deemed paid applicable to the $30 dividend are $20 computed as follows:

$$\frac{\text{Dividend } 30}{\text{Earnings } 120} \times \text{Income } 80 = \begin{array}{l}\text{Foreign} \\ \text{Taxes Deemed} \\ \text{Paid } 20\end{array}$$
$$\text{\& Profits} \qquad \text{Tax}$$

The $30 dividend is grossed-up (i.e. increased) by the $20 of foreign taxes deemed paid. Therefore, Y reports a dividend of $50 in its return for 1983. This gross-up is generally computed in the same manner under the TRA of 1986. However, the computation is done basket-by-basket.

Foreign Taxes Deemed Paid for Second and Third Tier Foreign Corporations

A U.S. shareholder is also considered to have paid the foreign income taxes deemed paid by a first tier foreign corporation on distributions from a second tier foreign corporation and by such second tier foreign corporation on distributions from a third tier foreign corporation. In order to qualify for the credit the first tier foreign corporation must own at least 10 percent of the voting stock of the second tier corporation and such second tier corporation must own at least 10 percent of the voting stock of the third tier corporation. For this rule to apply the U.S. shareholder's percentage of voting in the first tier foreign corporation and between the first, second, and third tier foreign corporations when multiplied together must equal at least 5 percent. Both the 10 and 5 percent requirements must be met.

Foreign Currency Implications

For tax years beginning after December 31, 1986, the earnings and profits of a foreign corporation are to be determined in the corporation's functional currency under a profit and loss method. Earnings and profits so determined are translated (if necessary) into U.S. dollars at the current exchange rate on the date the distribution is included in the shareholder's income. Thus, unrealized exchange gains or losses will generally not be reflected in E & P, because no exchange gain or loss attributable to exchange rate fluctuations between the time the E & P arose and the time of distribution is separately recognized. However, special rules exist for translating E & P in certain hyperinflationary currencies.

Tax Planning Aspects of E & P Computations

When there is sufficient foreign source taxable income, one tax planning objective is to reduce the earnings and profits of certain foreign subsidiaries as much as possible. This reduction enables the U.S. shareholder to receive distributions from the foreign corporation wholly or partially tax free. In addition, the foreign withholding taxes on the distributions might be available to offset the U.S. tax due on other foreign source income if such taxes qualify as income taxes directly paid by a domestic corporation to a foreign country. This technique was feasible when the U.S. parent also received income subject to a low effective foreign tax rate, (e.g., interest and royalties). For post-1986, such income may be in different baskets and, therefore, the taxpayers ability to average high and low foreign effective rates may be limited. In addition, the reduction of earnings and profits could increase the effective rate of tax on those earnings and profits. For example:

	Before Decrease	After Decrease
Pre-tax earnings and profits	$1,000	$750
Less:		
Foreign income taxes	(500)	(500)
Current earnings and profits	$ 500	$250
Effective foreign tax rate	50%	66.6%

Conversely, if the U.S. shareholder's nondividend foreign source income (e.g., royalties income) is sufficient to offset the allocation of certain home office expenses against foreign source income, the tax planning objective is normally to increase a foreign corporation's earnings and profits in order to reduce the effective rate of the foreign income taxes.

The following example shows how an increase in earnings and profits can change the effective rate of the foreign income taxes.

	Before Decrease	After Decrease
Pre-tax earning and profits	$1,000	$1,500
Less:		
Foreign taxes	(500)	(500)
Current earnings and profits	$ 500	$1,000
Effective foreign tax rate	50%	33.3%

With respect to pre-1987 tax years, a single dollar of earnings and profits in a year is all that is needed for a U.S. shareholder to bring up the foreign taxes paid by the foreign corporation for that year. Thus, it is theoretically possible to receive 99 percent of a distribution from a foreign corporation tax-free as a return of capital and 1 percent of the distribution taxable as a dividend that would bring with it significant deemed paid foreign tax credits.

The EC-1992 Program

The Implications for U.S. Multinational Corporations

HARVEY A. PONIACHEK

Introduction

Europe is poised for an extraordinary period of economic change, and it could become the world's most dynamic growth region in the 1990s. The EC-1992 program, coupled with East Europe's democratization, has set the stage for a massive market-led restructuring of industries and economies.

The EC-1992 program is presenting U.S. multinational corporations (MNCs) with substantial opportunities and challenges. U.S. corporations have long viewed the continent as one economic region and they are well positioned to adjust to and prosper from the completion of market integration. Corporations exporting from the United States or with production facilities in Western Europe will find it easier to do business there as the existing maze of national technical standards is harmonized.

The EC's internal market integration is unlikely to result in a protectionist Europe, but it could have some negative implications for the United States. American companies can fully benefit from EC-1992 if market access for U.S. exporters is safeguarded and parity treatment of U.S.-based subsidiaries is afforded.

To position themselves more effectively to compete in the enlarged EC market, European and non-European firms sharply expanded their investment activities, including mergers and acquisitions. The widespread mergers and acquisitions since the adoption of the Single European Act signals the far-reaching changes that lie ahead.

This case study reviews background information about the EC and examines the implications for U.S. MNCs. The reader is required to analyze the effect of the EC-1992 on corporate management, particularly in the area of financial management and financial strategy.

The EC-1992: What Does It Mean?

In 1985, the EC published a *White Paper*—which identified physical, technical, and fiscal barriers to the free movement of goods, services, capital, and people—and issued some 279 legislative proposals to eliminate these barriers and create a unified market. To implement these proposals the EC adopted the Single European Act in July 1987, which revised the Treaty of Rome.

The 12 members of the EC are moving rapidly to create the world's largest market of 320 million people through the process known as EC-1992, which reflects the year-end target for the completion of the expansion and integration of the EC. This process intends to replicate the U.S. economic model in which goods, services, capital, and labor move freely within the United States. The EC members include Belgium, Denmark, France, Germany, Greece, Ireland, Italy, Luxembourg, the Netherlands, Portugal, Spain, and the United Kingdom.

The EC-1992 program has already altered the structure of the Community market, competitive conditions, and prospects for growth. Many European MNCs are already getting organized for the challenges of the expanded marketplace, which create opportunities for economies of scale, particularly in high-technology sectors where R&D expenses are usually very high. The likely economies of scale will make the EC-based companies more competitive in relation to their U.S. and Japanese rivals. However, the 1992 process could produce frictions within the Community and with other nations.

The EC-1992 will promote fierce competition through the concentration of commercial and economic powers in industrial giants that may enjoy advantages in developing, financing, and marketing leading-edge technologies. Much stronger European-based companies are emerging as formidable competitors on the Continent and globally. The U.S. position worldwide could diminish as European industrial and banking giants put renewed pressure on top U.S. firms.

Appendix 28-1 discusses the EC's integration objectives and process.

The European Monetary System, which was established in 1979, is a major building block in the EC long-term plan for monetary union and economic integration. The Community seeks to establish a single European currency, probably by late 1997, and a European system of center banks. The ECU could emerge in the future as an important international monetary asset rival to the dollar in international financial markets. The European Monetary Union has gained momentum with Britain's endorsement of the EC monetary aspirations.

The EC-1992 and U.S. MNCs

U.S. companies consider the EC-1992 program as a major market opportunity, especially if it becomes more dynamic and open. However, the enhanced economic integration of the Community could adversely affect trade and investment relations with the United States and raise major problems for U.S. exporters and MNCs.

The EC—the largest market for the U.S. export—purchases 24 percent of U.S. export, of which almost one-half is classified as high technology, including computers, aircrafts, semiconductors, and scientific instruments. The adverse trade impact on the United States could occur in industries that constitute a significant share of U.S. exports and in which the Europeans could ultimately enjoy significant economies of scale and enhanced competition.

The 1992 process could induce more protectionist European policies because there are several actual or potential obstacles for U.S. participation in the EC market which include:

1. The use of reciprocity,
2. Buy-European preferences,
3. Rules of origin, local content and government procurement policies,
4. Quotas and quantitative restrictions,
5. Enforcement of competition policy,
6. Participation in EC R&D consortia, and
7. Technical standards.

Emerging EC policies on such matters as local content requirements and rules of origin are designed to afford protection to certain sensitive industrial sectors. Because certain EC industrial sectors and companies still lack the scope and scale to compete they are likely to seek protection against non-EC companies to buy time to develop fully their competitive abilities. Industries likely to receive some protection include advanced materials, manufacturing processes, energy, ocean science, electronics, biotechnology, and telecommunications.

The EC has committed itself to ambitious high-technology research projects and adopted several protectionist policies to enhance its high-technology position, which include the following:

1. Protecting EC firms by maintaining external tariff barriers and by resisting common international technical standards.
2. Stalling the admission of foreign firms into European consortia.
3. Favoring European firms in public procurement of high-technology products.
4. Subordinating competition policy to strategic trade policy.

Appendix 28-2 provides additional information related to the implications of the EC 1992 on U.S. trade and industry.

U.S. MNC's Policies and Performance

U.S. multinationals are well positioned to benefit from the EC-1992 and they are expected to fare at least as well as their European competitors, and maybe somewhat better. U.S. companies with established production facilities in the Community can look forward to a sweeping relaxation of long-standing impediments to their efforts to compete in the 12 national markets of the EC.

Most major U.S. MNCs have since the early days of the Community established positions in the EC, with experience in producing and marketing there. The strong direct presence of the U.S. MNCs in Europe is illustrated by the fact that about 85 percent of the market for U.S. goods and services in the EC is transacted by the U.S. affiliates there. U.S. MNCs have $428 billion in assets and 2 million employees in Europe. The EC is a major location of U.S. direct investment, with approximately 40 percent of total U.S. direct investment abroad.

As suggested above, many U.S. MNCs are better positioned for the single European market than their European competitors in terms of organizational structure and product specialization. However, maintaining their position will be a major challenge in the face of the rising competition from Japanese and European firms.

There is a wide range of feasible strategies that U.S. MNCs could apply in the EC-1992 environment. To improve their position in the single EC market, U.S. MNCs are expected to pursue both reorganization strategies and an expansion of investment in existing entities and facilities. While many U.S. MNCs have achieved economies of scale in production, a realignment of their marketing and distribution functions could be necessary to move from a national to a regional orientation. Ultimately, suppliers will decide to produce in fewer places in Europe as European transportation systems become more unified after 1992, and as continent-wide distribution spreads to many products. Distribution of many products takes place on a continent-wide basis. Direct investment could play an important role for U.S. MNCs that seek to gain early footholds in fast-growing market segments.

In light of the EC-1992 program, some U.S. firms are reorganizing their treasury operations, their currency functions and pricing policies. Some corporations run their European business from their headquarters in Geneva or Brussels. Some U.S. MNCs are implementing an homogeneous pricing policy for the different markets, while allowing for some differences due to customs duty and other factors.

The Assignment

You, an enthusiastic, talented young manager with interest in international business and politics who has attended a summer program at a major French university while attending a northeast U.S. business school, have been appointed head of the corporate study team designated to address the implications of EC 1992 on your corporation. You have thoroughly reviewed the appendices and are ready to embark on the assignment. However, you realize that there is no single strategy applicable to every corporation. More intense competition within the Community will put a premium on the flexibility and timely deployment of corporate resources, will squeeze out inefficient corporations and operations, and will

EXHIBIT 28-1

The 1992 Analysis Matrix

Areas Affected[a]	Major Areas of the 1992 Process[b]							
	A	B	C	D	E	F	G	H
1. Suppliers Relations								
2. Manufacturing Scale Location								
3. Product R&D Products								
4. Marketing Sales Distribution Price								
5. Customer Service								
6. Organization								
7. Finance Funding Cash Management Investment Currency Management Taxation Control/Management								

[a] In rating the various factors listed in the left column, assign the following weights to each: Poor effect = 30%; medium effect = 70%; and good effect = 100%. For example, harmonized standards could have a good effect on manufacturing scale and location; hence assign each 100.

[b] A = Harmonization of standards; B = Open government procurement; C = Industry deregulation; D = Fiscal harmony; E = Community R&D policy; F = Reduction of fiscal barriers; G = Content, quota/tariff reform; H = Social dimension.

Source: Robert Williams, Mark Teagan and Jose Benyeto, *The World's Largest Market: A Business Guide to Europe 1992*, American Management Association, 1990, p. 64.

create important opportunities to specialize. These trends will attract new entrants into the market from both inside and outside Europe and lead to the proliferation of strategic economic alliances. The task remains for you to formulate responses to the opportunities and challenges posed by the EC-1992 program by applying the following planning process:

1. Assess your corporation's (or industry's) relative strengths and competitive position by applying the Analysis Matrix shown in Exhibit 28-1. (Pick a corporation from the *Fortune 500* list of companies, or an industrial sector either in manufacturing or services.)

2. Identify how EC-1992 would affect your financial management, funding, and currency hedging.

3. Generate specific action steps, particularly in the area of corporate finance.

Bibliography

1. Gary Cylde Hufbauer, (ed.), *Europe 1992: An American Perspective*, The Brookings Institute, Washington, D.C., 1990.

2. Europe 1992: Long-term Implications for the U.S. Economy, Hearing before the Joint Economic Committee Congress of the United States, One Hundred First Congress, First Session, April 26, 1989.

3. United Nations, *UNCTC Current Studies*, "Regional Economic Integration and Transnational Corporations in the 1990s: Europe 1992, North America, and Developing Countries," no. 15, Series A, July 1990.

4. The Center for Strategic and International Studies (CSIS), *Beyond 1992: U.S. Strategy toward the European Community*, September 1990, Washington, D.C.

5. Robert Williams, Mark Teagan and Jose Benyeto, *The World's Largest Market: A Business Guide to Europe 1992*, American Management Association, 1990.

6. The International Division of the Chamber of Commerce, Europe 1992, *A Practical Guide for American Business*, 1989.

7. Hearing before the Subcommittees on Europe and the Middle East, and on International Economic Policy and Trade of the Committee on Foreign Affairs House of Representatives, One Hundred First Congress, Second Session, February 20, 1990, Europe 1992: Administration Views.

8. Hearing before the Subcommittee on Trade of the Committee on Ways and Means, House of Representatives, One Hundred First Congress, First Session, March 20, 1989, Serial 101-4, Europe 1992.

EC-92 and U.S. Industry

Foreword

Over the past year, a new buzzword— EC-92—has sprung up in our vocabulary. EC-

Selected excerpts from testimonies by Honeywell, Inc.; the U.S. Semiconductor Industry Association (SIA); Motor & Equipment Manufacturers Association. Hearing before the Subcommittee on Trade of the Committee on Ways and Means House of Representatives, One Hundred First Congress, First session, March 20, 1989, Serial 101-4, Europe 1992.

92, of course, refers to the plans of the European Community to eliminate barriers to the completion of the E.C.-wide internal market by 1992. While the buzzword may be new, the work in the European Community to achieve this goal has been going on since 1985.

For U.S. manufacturers exporting to and operating in Europe, EC-92 is an extremely important issue. U.S. Exports to the EC amount to $80 billion and intra-EC sales of U.S. firms in Europe total $550 billion annually. Two-thirds of the non-communist world's GNP is accounted for by the economies of the E.C. and the United States. What goes on within the E.C. market, therefore, has an important bearing on the interests of the rest of the world.

While NAM has been following this issue since 1985, it was not clear to us exactly how the interests of the American manufacturing community were affected by EC-92, despite the rather extensive amount of recent press coverage. We decided, therefore, to conduct an extensive series of discussions and interviews with government and corporate officials on both sides of the Atlantic with the aim of producing a report on what EC-92 means to the American manufacturing community. Stephen Cooney, Director for International Investment and Finance at NAM, has been in charge of this work over the past six months and the results of his efforts follow.

This report is intended to help identify the important issues for American manufacturers in EC-92. It is designed as an information document and not as an NAM policy statement. Development of NAM policy positions on specific EC-92 issues will be coordinated by an NAM Task Force on EC-92, chaired by Glen J. Skovholt, Director, Policy and Strategy for Corporate Public Affairs, Honeywell Inc.

We would encourage any comments and analysis on this NAM report and we would be glad to answer questions or hear comments about how EC-92 affects American manufacturing interests.

Howard Lewis III
Vice President, International Economic Affairs
National Association of Manufacturers

EC-92 and U.S. Industry: Executive Summary

The plan to complete the opening of European Community internal market by 1992, known in shorthand as EC-92, promises to have major effects on U.S. industry. The overall view of U.S. industry is strongly positive.

NAM members emphasize the positive impact of strong and dynamic growth, in an increasingly deregulated market.

This report aims to provide guidance for NAM members on the changing European business environment. It focuses on the specific issues and proposals related to EC-92 that have been identified as being of most concern to U.S. industry, rather than the overall history, politics and economics of the E.C. internal market program. The report is based on extensive consultations by the author with NAM member firms in the United States and Europe, cooperating business associations, and information provided by representatives of the U.S. government, staff of the European Commission in Brussels and officials of E.C. member-state governments and private trade associations.

This report is divided into two parts:

Part I

Part I: Evolution of EC-92 and U.S. Industry is an overview of both the interests of U.S. industry in EC-92 and the development of the EC-92 program. The major subjects of this part of the report are as follows.

What Is at Stake for U.S. Industry?

As indicated in NAM's recent comprehensive trade report, the E.C. may be the strongest and most important market from the perspective of increasing U.S. exports. The fall in the dollar, improved E.C. growth rates and the relatively open E.C. market has led directly to a three-year boost in the level of U.S. exports. The 1988 level was $27 billion higher than in 1985. This has also meant reducing our trade deficit with the E.C. from $24 billion to $12 billion, accounting for over a third of the total $33 billion improvement in the U.S. trade deficit in 1988. Moreover, the E.C. is far and away the most important host for U.S.

manufacturing investment abroad—at $65 billion, more than half the worldwide total.

THE E.C. INTERNAL MARKET PROGRAM

The basis thrust of EC-92 is to *complete* the internal market established as a European objective by the Treaty of Rome over 30 years ago. As laid out in the E.C.'s 1985 "white paper," this involves the pragmatic elimination of three major types of barriers.

1. *Physical barriers* at the borders to the free flow of goods and persons.
2. *Technical barriers* that prevent goods produced or traded in one member state from being sold in others.
3. *Fiscal barriers* such as the red tape, delays and costs of different national tax systems which prevent cross-border trade.

Also associated with the elimination of these barriers are major initiatives in related areas, including competition policy, encouragement of research and development, establishment of coordinated monetary policies with possible monetary union, and decisions on common social policies.

PROSPECTS FOR COMPLETING EC-92 AND THE PROCESS OF ADOPTING EC-92 POLICIES

The first part of the report reviews the major issues involved in the completion of the ambitious EC-92 program. It notes that whatever the outcome of these politically sensitive questions, which could prevent the goals of the 1985 White Paper from being fully achieved, many directives and policies related to 1992 will go into effect as they are approved by the E.C. The reappointment of President Jacques Delors for a second term as President of the European Commission, beginning in January 1989, indicates the strong commitment of E.C. member states to achievement of the internal market goal. During the term of the new commission, which ends on December 31, 1992,

the conditions for U.S. companies of doing business in the E.C. will be changed in a major and irrevocable way.

The first part of the paper concludes with an analysis of how EC-92 policies are developed and adopted within the E.C. institutional framework. It also summarizes the ways in which U.S. companies can seek access to provide and receive information on how the process may affect their interests.

Part II

Part II: Major Issues for U.S. Companies in EC-92 reviews the major issues that could either enhance or reduce the opportunities for U.S. companies as investors in or exporters to the E.C. These major issues represent the subsections of Part II of the report. Within each subsection, the report analyzes the principal relevant proposals of the EC-92 program that have been adopted or considered to date.

1. *Technical and Environmental Standards.* The harmonization of technical standards, a major part of EC-92, can have a major impact on current and future access of goods produced by U.S. companies for the E.C. market. The expedited adoption of common E.C. standards is widely seen by U.S. companies as a major benefit. However, there are serious concerns regarding timely and adequate access to standards information through the voluntary E.C. "CEN/CENELEC" standards-setting process. Also, U.S. companies have concerns regarding the implementation of E.C. certification and testing recognition procedures.

2. *Public Procurement.* The enhancement of existing E.C. rules on the opening of member government procurement and the extension of E.C. rules to the sectors presently excluded from GATT or E.C. discipline are designed to increase dramati-

cally cross-border procurement within the E.C. The new rules, at least in the previously excluded sectors, will not necessarily apply to non-E.C. source products. But the E.C. has indicated a willingness to consider open access on a reciprocal basis, either bilaterally or multilaterally.

NAM members have indicated concern with the new local content rules included in the proposals regarding procurement in the presently excluded sectors, but are encouraged by the principle of opening these markets within the E.C. and the commitment to negotiating opening of these sectors to other signatories of the GATT procurement code.

3. *Reciprocity.* The controversial stated E.C. policy of extending intra-E.C. market opening initiatives to non-E.C. producers only insofar as E.C. trading partners provide equivalent access to their markets for E.C. producers has led to great public concern with the emergence of a "Fortress Europe" in world trade. The October 1988 Commission statement on the definition of reciprocity has alleviated some U.S. industry concerns regarding this subject.

4. *Sectoral Trade Issues.* This report particularly focuses on the future development of E.C. wide common commercial policies and other sectoral initiatives regarding automobiles, telecommunications and information technology, because of the broader implications of policies in these areas.

5. *Rules of Origin and Local Content.* U.S. industry is strongly concerned with the development of E.C. rules that determine whether goods are of E.C. origin, not only for the application of specific trade benefits or penalties, but also on a more general basis regarding the treatment and access of foreign companies or producers in the E.C. market.

6. *Intellectual Property.* Enhancement and completion of a Europe-wide system of protection of trademarks, patents and copyrights is a process that pre-dates EC-92. But it has been stimulated by plans to create a more integrated market. Generally, U.S. companies are supportive of proposals to allow registration in one member country to be valid for the whole Community, as well as to broaden the products that are covered by E.C.-wide copyright rules. There are concerns, however, with some proposed reform procedures.

7. *Social Dimension.* The increase in unemployment in the E.C. between the early 1970s and the 1980s has been a major stimulus for the acceptance of the EC-92 program. The "social dimension" of EC-92 includes new initiatives in employment and social affairs related to the creation of a more integrated E.C. market. Both U.S. companies and E.C. industry generally have been supportive of proposals aimed at establishing E.C.-wide safety standards, reducing regional disparities, improving worker training and enhancing labor mobility. Concerns have been expressed over other initiatives, that would have the effect of establishing more rigid E.C.-wide industrial relations policies and practices.

8. *Competition Policy.* Establishment of E.C.-level control over mergers and acquisitions, particularly large-scale multinational combinations, is seen by U.S. companies as potentially providing an expedited means of increasing E.C.-wide competition, while producing substantial gains for the E.C. through improved economies of scale.

9. *Monetary Policy.* The E.C. has already agreed on the elimination of all controls on capital movements within the E.C. Currently under consideration are the establishment of mandatory coordination of monetary policies and possible creation of a single E.C. central bank and currency. These policies not only enhance the ability of U.S. companies to operate within the

E.C. framework, but may also have a major impact on the E.C.'s international competitive status.

10. *Potential Issues.* The report concludes by noting two other issues not now included in the EC-92 program, but which may have a major effect on U.S. companies when they are considered by the E.C. in the future. These are future rules regarding the opening of defense procurement within the E.C. and the adoption of common E.C.-wide export control policies.

Introduction

There is no hotter subject among U.S. business leaders than the proposal to eliminate the European Community's remaining internal market barriers by 1992. Virtually every U.S. industry and major company now is trying to understand what "EC-92" means for them and for their world marketing strategies.

At this point, U.S. companies almost uniformly emphasize that EC-92 represents a major market opportunity. They see the proposed package as contributing both to a rapid expansion of the E.C. market and, in practice, to a deregulation of that market which will increase opportunities for competitive producers. Within this overall positive outlook, however, there are a series of major policy issues, the outcome of which could either enhance or reduce business opportunities for U.S.-based exporters or U.S.-owned companies already established within the E.C.

This report aims to provide guidance for NAM members on the changing European business environment. It focuses on the specific issues and proposals related to EC-92 that have been identified as being of most concern to U.S. industry, rather than the overall history, politics and economics of the E.C. internal market program. The report is based on extensive consultations by the author with

NAM member firms in the United States and Europe, as well as cooperating business associations. The firms consulted in Europe include European as well as American-owned enterprises. The report is also based on information provided by representatives of the U.S. government, staff of the European Commission in Brussels and officials of E.C. member-state governments and private trade associations. The report is not a formal NAM policy statement on EC-92 issues, though it may indicate those issues in EC-92 on which NAM policy may later be developed.

The following issues are those that have been identified as being of greatest importance to American industrial exporters and investors doing business in the E.C. Each is given a separate detailed section in Part II of the report, where the most critical specific proposals and policy choices are discussed.

1. Technical and Environmental Standards
2. Public Procurement
3. Reciprocity
4. Sectoral Issues
5. Rules of Origin and Local Content
6. Intellectual Property
7. Social Dimension
8. Competition Policy
9. Monetary Policy
10. Other Potential Issues

This report refers to many texts of specific documents and policy proposals related to these issues. Precise references are provided in the report for the use of members who wish to follow up on issues in more detail. In many cases these proposals will evolve as they move through the E.C. policy process. Listed at the end of the report are some contacts in the United States and Europe which are good sources of information for U.S. companies as they seek information on the issues of most importance to them.

Organization of this Report

This report is written in two parts. The first part is a general orientation for the business reader. It summarizes the importance of the E.C. market for U.S. business, then briefly describes the development of the EC-92 proposal and the policy processes of the European Community as amended by the Single European Act of 1987 (SEA). This latter constitutional change is so named because the E.C. member states used one negotiated instrument to amend the basic European Coal and Steel Community and Euratom treaties, as well as the Treaty of Rome that established the Common Market.

The second part of the report is based on a "watch list" of major EC-92 policy issues, whose development will be critical for the future role of U.S. business in Europe. These are not necessarily the most important or visible EC-92 issues from the member states' own political and economic perspectives, but may be the ones with the most impact on U.S. business and manufacturing interests. Accordingly, this is the range of issues which will receive most attention from NAM during the evolution of EC-92.

The Evolution of EC-92 and U.S. Industry

What Is at Stake for U.S. Industry?

Many commentators in recent years have criticized U.S. business for being too "Eurocentric," too focused on traditional and slow-growing markets in western Europe. We have been told that the future, high-growth markets are in such areas as the Pacific Basin, Latin America and other less-developed economic regions, or even the major Communist countries. These analyses underestimate the dynamism, openness and growth possibilities that remain in Europe. While U.S. exporters should seek markets wherever they can find them, for the foreseeable future the E.C. may remain the key growth market overseas for U.S. industrial companies.

Europe is our most important regional export market, and will remain so indefinitely. The value of U.S. exports to the European Community is about a quarter of total exports, a little higher than the share going to Canada. But a quarter of all U.S. exports to Canada are cars and parts involved in the two-way auto trade agreement. As for other countries and regions, Japan takes only 8 percent of our exports and the rest of East Asia another 13 percent. All of Latin America takes only 13 percent. And most importantly, no other regional market approaches the level of economic integration found in Europe today, much less what is being contemplated by 1992.

The E.C. is a critical market for many specific U.S. exports. In 1988, 46 percent of all U.S. exports of computers and parts have gone to the E.C.—that's a projected total of over $10 billion in exports of that product to the European Community. The E.C. is also the largest market for U.S. electrical machinery and parts, a category that includes semiconductors. Total U.S. exports to the E.C. in 1988 may have hit $4.5 billion. The E.C. takes about a third of U.S. aircraft exports, with sales this year running over $6 billion at an annual rate. And in scientific and controlling instruments, where U.S. manufacturers maintain a strong trade surplus, 35 percent of all exports in 1988 went to the E.C.

The E.C. market has been the most important one so far in turning around the U.S. trade deficit. The fall of the dollar has had a bigger and faster impact on growth in exports to Europe than any other region. U.S. export growth to Europe has been near or above double figures since 1985 and has been accelerating—9 percent in 1986, 14 percent in 1987 and an incredible 25 percent in 1988. Since 1985 the *increase* in our exports to the E.C. from $49 billion to $76 billion in 1988, has been roughly equal to our *total* exports to Japan in 1987. It's as if we have suddenly found a new export market out there the size of Japan. This export growth in 1988 cut the annual rate of the bilateral U.S. trade deficit with the E.C. in half: from $24 billion in 1987, to $12 billion in 1988. That change alone accounted for more than a third of the total improvement of the U.S. trade deficit in 1988.

Finally, let's look at investment. *The total U.S. direct investment stake in the European Community is nearly $125 billion, according to official statistics.* In manufacturing investment alone, total U.S. holdings in the E.C. were valued at $65 billion at the end of 1987—more than half the total value of U.S. companies' manufacturing investment abroad. It is more than double the amount in Canada, almost ten times the amount in Japan, four times the total for all Latin America and twelve times the total for all Asia outside Japan.

The E.C. Internal Market Program

Anything that affects U.S. economic interests on this scale is obviously of critical importance to U.S. industry and to the U.S. economy more generally. The E.C. internal market proposal —the goal of completing the internal E.C. market and removing all intra-E.C. trade barriers by 1992—is probably the most important policy initiative taken within the European Community since the founding of the Common Market in 1957. This explains the extraordinary interest of U.S. business in this initiative.

It is the very failure to complete the common market as originally envisioned that has led to the development of EC-92. For example, as one American executive with extensive experience in the E.C. has explained. "On January 1, 1958, the original six members of the Common Market took down their signs at the

internal borders that said 'Customs.' Then they put up new signs that said 'Taxes.'"

What he means is that differences in internal regulations—and not just taxes, but in other areas like technical standards and public procurement policies—have circumscribed the benefits of a truly open and free market among the Common Market's members. As the European Community doubled in members, this problem has not become any simpler to resolve. Cross-border controls remain in place for a plethora of reasons. According to the European Commission's official study, summarized in the report *The European Challenge— 1992* by Paolo Cecchini, the resulting "cost of non-Europe" may equal 3 to 6 percent of Europe's gross domestic product, or a total of $250 billion annually.

These costs were tolerable in the 1950s and '60s as the European economies boomed. There was visible progress in the initial elimination of national tariff barriers within Europe. American companies contributed to this progress by investing heavily and by bringing in their expertise in operating across a wide range of regional markets. But the initial momentum and optimism faded in the 1970s, with the energy and unemployment crises in Europe, a major growth slowdown, stagflation and the European version of the U.S. "malaise" of the late 1970s: "Eurosclerosis."

The proposal to establish a fully open internal market by 1992 is designed to sweep away the de facto obstructions to free trade within Europe. To understand the genesis of the proposal, which dates from 1985, it is necessary to understand the failures of previous efforts to eliminate internal market barriers by harmonizing national product standards and other policies. There were efforts to define specific E.C.-wide codes for goods on a product-by-product basis—Euro-beer, Euro-bread, Euro-ice cream and so on. Progress was so slow, that it could not even keep pace with the development of new products in the dynamic European economy.

Finally, in a landmark decision the European Court of Justice declared that member governments could not use their national standards and regulations as a basis for keeping out goods that were legitimately sold and consumed in other member countries. This decision—the Cassis de Dijon decision—meant that E.C. member countries had to accept some expeditious means of developing E.C.-wide minimum product standards. The alternative would be goods sold in their national markets that were produced under conflicting standards or even no standard at all.

Another impetus behind EC-92 was world competitiveness. The goal of a "United States of Europe," going all the way back to Jean Monnet, the father of the European idea, was always outward-looking as well as inward-looking. Monnet wanted Europe to be a power in world economic and political affairs. By the early 1980s, it had become clear that market barriers within Europe were inhibiting the development of economies of scale sufficient to make European-based enterprises competitive in the world economy.

We also cannot forget the employment question as a major impetus for change. Unemployment rates in Europe mounted and remained stubbornly high in the early 1980s. From essentially full employment, or even "negative unemployment" in some E.C. member countries around 1970, the total estimated E.C. unemployment rate rose through the 1970s and reached double digits, 10.5 percent, in 1983. Since then, it has not appreciably fallen. It became increasingly clear to E.C. members that it was necessary to add a new structural dynamic at the Europe-wide level, and that addressing the unemployment problem solely at the national level of structural adjustment provided an insufficient solution to national unemployment problems.

The Cecchini report estimates that the total growth in E.C. GDP as a result of elimination of internal market barriers would directly create 1.8 million new jobs. This would not solve the E.C. unemployment problem, though it would at least reduce unemployment by an estimated 1.5 percent, allowing for some initial job losses due to restructuring. More importantly, as with world competitiveness, there was a perceived need to create a solution to the unemployment problem that was on a greater scale than provided within the individual member country economies. This need was compounded by the great disparities in regional development within the E.C., especially after the addition of the three lower-income Mediterranean countries in 1981–86.

In 1985 the recently-appointed European Commissioner for the Internal Market. Lord Cockfield of the United Kingdom, produced a remarkable new proposal which has revitalized the European Community. Backed by the recent decision of the European Court of Justice, the Cockfield "White Paper" proposed a target list of about 300 directives and other policy actions, aimed at eliminating effective barriers to the internal market. Taken together, these directives would:

- Eliminate all remaining physical barriers to the movement of persons and goods within the E.C.

- Eliminate differences in national technical standards as barriers to the free movement of goods.

- Eliminate national differences in indirect tax rates as a trade barrier.

Moreover, Lord Cockfield insisted that the package was a package. It had to be achieved by a date certain—1992—or the whole process would be blocked by each member-state picking the benefits they wanted, and dragging their feet on the rest. Cockfield's program was both encouraged and fully backed by the European Commission President, Jacques Delors, who has made EC-92 his top priority. In addition, the Single European Act (SEA), specifically approved to expedite completion of the internal market, established that most internal market directives would be adopted by qualified majorities. No one member government could block directives by withholding its consent.

Prospects for Completing EC-92

EC-92 is a moving target. But this is a good halfway point at which to assess developments. Nearly half of the proposed list of directives in the 1985 White Paper have already been adopted or advanced to the final stages of approval. Due to differences with Prime Minister Margaret Thatcher over the speed of certain aspects of EC-92, Lord Cockfield has not been re-nominated to the Commission by the British government. But reappointment of Delors as President, for the new term starting in 1989, signifies that the process will continue, with the support of the E.C. member states.

The most serious political obstacles to achievement of the EC-92 package do not necessarily involve the most salient operational issues for U.S. companies. This is important for NAM members to remember as they follow the progress of the EC-92 program. Perhaps the most difficult decisions that the E.C. will have to make on the EC-92 agenda involve U.S. interests and U.S.–E.C. economic relations only indirectly, insofar as U.S. companies and the U.S. economy as a whole have a major stake in the successful completion of the EC-92 program. Such issues include:

- Harmonization of VAT rates.
- Complete elimination of frontier controls on movement of persons within the E.C.
- Monetary policy harmonization, including the possible establishment of an E.C. central bank and single currency.

Whatever the outcome of these politically sensitive questions, which could prevent the goals of the 1985 White Paper from being fully achieved, other directives and policies related to 1992 will go into effect as they are approved by the E.C. In this sense, Lord Cockfield's admonition that EC-92 must be achieved as a complete package is misleading: those parts of the package that attain final approval will immediately begin to affect how business is done in Europe. Moreover, some European economists dispute the conclusions of the Cecchini study regarding patterns of growth. The study predicts some loss of economic growth due to restructuring problems as EC-92 begins to affect E.C. economies, followed by large gains in the mid-1990s. But other economists see more "front-loaded" growth due to new efficiencies as parts of the EC-92 package enter into effect.

On January 1, 1989, a new Commission took office in Brussels. President Delors was reappointed, but there were many important changes in the other portfolios. U.S. companies should at least anticipate that a large part of the total EC-92 package will be in place by the end of this Commission's mandate in four years. During this period, the conditions for U.S. companies of doing business in the E.C. will be changed in a major and irrevocable way.

The Process of Adopting EC-92 Policies

Before analyzing in detail the major issues of EC-92 for U.S. companies, it is important that the reader have a general familiarity with European Community terms and institutions. Moreover, the fundamental relationship of the member states and organs of the E.C. has been altered by adoption of the SEA in 1987, specifically to enhance completion of the internal market. General background knowledge of the institutional relationships within the E.C. is necessary for determining the most appropriate points in the process for U.S. companies to raise questions or concerns regarding specific EC-92 proposals.

Most of the Internal Market legislative work will be carried out by three E.C. institutions: the *European Commission*, the *Council of Ministers*, and the *European Parliament*. These three institutions are responsible for proposing, debating and adopting Community legislation. In addition, the *European Court of Justice* decides on the legality of challenged E.C. legislative measures.

The *Commission* is responsible for formulating and proposing legislation and providing for the administration of Community policies. The Commission is led by 17 Commissioners (two each from France, the Federal Republic of Germany, Italy, Spain, and the United Kingdom, and one from each of the other member states).

The Commissioners and their staff draft all Community legislative proposals and policy statements. Each Commissioner is responsible for one or more areas of Community policy, such as economic affairs, agriculture, environment and energy. The staff of the Commission are organized into *directorates-general* (DGs)—there are 22 DGs at present, and they do not correspond exactly to the portfolios held by individual commissioners. The Commissioner responsible for the Internal Market program in the new Commission is Martin Bangermann, formerly Economics Minister of Germany. DG III is the directorate responsible for many internal market policies, but other directorates also have relevant areas of authority.

Once E.C. legislation is adopted, the Commission is responsible for implementation. If legislation is adopted in the form of a *regulation*, it immediately becomes law in the member state. However, most EC-92 policies are cast in the form of *directives*, which means that each member government must pass or have previously established national legislation conforming to the general terms of the E.C. policy. The Commission is also the executive body responsible for negotiations with non-E.C. countries and organizations in areas where member states have ceded authority to the E.C.—notably trade policy. These contacts are handled primarily through DG I (External Relations), though other directorates are involved in some specific functional issues.

The *Council of Ministers* is the decision-making body of the Community and must approve all Community legislation. It is the only Community organization whose members act as representatives of the individual E.C. member state governments. Member governments are represented at Council meetings by the national minister who has responsibility for the subject under discussion. The presidency of the Council rotates every six months, in accordance with the "E.C. alphabet:" the alphabetical order of member state names in their respective national languages. Thus, Germany (*Deutschland*) and Greece (*Ellas*) chaired the Council in 1988, to be followed by Spain (*Espana*) and France in 1989. This rotation is quite important, because the national government's own priorities can heavily influence the Council agenda during its presidency.

Formerly, the Council could only take decisions on most important matters by unanimous agreement. The SEA has amended the Treaty of Rome to allow Council approval on most internal market proposals by "qualified majority" voting. This change may prove extremely important to U.S. companies, who will no longer be able to rely on one country to block changes that may disadvantage them and who correspondingly may be less concerned about individual countries that oppose favorable internal market reforms. Appendix II explains the qualified majority voting rules. Note that not even two large countries voting together or any combination of one large country and two small ones can block an internal market proposal. In certain areas, such as 1992 measures, the

Council must also formally consult with the European Parliament and the Economic and Social Committee.

The *European Parliament* (EP) is composed of 518 members, directly elected by the voters in each of the member states, roughly in proportion to the member state's population. The Members of the European Parliament (MEPs) sit in nine political party groupings, such as the Socialist Group or the European People's Party, rather than in national groups. At present, the Socialists have the largest single voting bloc within the EP, augmented by a substantial number of Communist MEPs and members of other left-wing groups. Since 1979, the EP has been directly elected by voters in the member states. The next EP election is set for this year.

The EP advises the Commission and the Council on legislative proposals before any legislation is adopted. It also exercises a measure of democratic control over the Commission and the Council through its right to amend or delay legislation. This power has been increased under the SEA, especially with regard to EC-92 issues. Specifically, the EP may amend Commission proposals, then re-approve their amended version by a two-thirds majority, if the Commission does not accept the EP amendments. The Council may subsequently only reject the EP version and replace it with its own through a unanimous vote. The EP also must approve the E.C. budget, and, importantly for U.S. interests, must ratify all E.C. treaties with non-member countries.

The *Court of Justice* (ECJ) is comprised of thirteen Judges and six Advocate-Generals, each appointed by agreement among the national governments for six-year terms. As the "Supreme Court" of the Community, the ECJ determines the validity and correct interpretation of challenged Community law provisions. A new Court of First Instance has also been established to relieve the backlog of cases awaiting decision by the ECJ.

The ECJ does not have a role in legislating individual 1992 laws as do the other three Community institutions described above. Through its legal decisions, however, it has been a driving force behind European integration generally and in several instances has forced the Member States to eliminate barriers to free trade within the Community, as noted above in the Cassis de Dijon decision, and confirmed by recent decisions regarding Italian pasta regulations, the German beer purity law and the Danish bottle law. Individuals and companies may challenge E.C. or member-state policies directly in the ECJ. This is different, for example, to the GATT, where only member governments may lodge complaints against each other.

The institutional structure of the E.C. provides U.S. companies with a number of points of access to voice their concerns and opinions on EC-92 proposals:

- Specialists within the relevant directorate of the European Commission.
- Member state trade and industry associations, as well as the E.C.-wide employers' association (UNICE), headquartered in Brussels.
- Functional ministries of national governments in sympathetic member states.
- Member states' permanent delegations to the E.C., who do most of the background work for the Council of Ministers' meetings through the Committee of Permanent Representatives (COREPER).
- Members of the European Parliament who may be sympathetic to the position of the U.S. company.
- National E.C. member state legislatures, which must enact all EC-92 directives into specific laws.

Also, it is very important that U.S. companies should remember contacts with relevant U.S. government representatives in Washington and Brussels.

Major Issues for U.S. Companies in EC-92

Technical and Environmental Standards

One of the major components of the internal market is the elimination of differences in technical standards, that serve as barriers to intra-E.C. trade. The issues associated with the elimination of technical standards barriers within the E.C. and the establishment of a new E.C.-wide standards process may affect more U.S. companies than any other EC-92 issue.

In view of the Cassis de Dijon decision and the Internal Market program, a wide range of technical "framework" standards are being negotiated. Community projects will put particular emphasis on certain sectors, including information technology and telecommunications, pharmaceuticals, chemicals, medical products, construction equipment and food products.

From the U.S. perspective, it should be understood from the outset that the reform of the technical standards process in the E.C. is not intended as a market-opening device with respect to non-E.C. trade partners. E.C. documents indicate that the E.C. will remain bound by existing GATT obligations related to technical standards. But the E.C. has undertaken no commitment to widen opportunities or to eliminate existing standards conformance problems for producers outside the E.C. as part of the 1992 process.

Nevertheless, the harmonization of technical standards can potentially create substantial benefits for U.S. companies—even those operating outside the E.C. itself. Under EC-92, U.S. companies at most will need to obtain certification from only one E.C. authority for the product to be considered as duly acceptable throughout the E.C. market. In some cases, the continuation or renewal of existing international mutual recognition agreements may even mean that normal U.S. certification procedures will also allow products to be certified for use or sale throughout the E.C. But typically such agreements only exist for a limited range of products, and it is unclear how rapidly mutual recognition agreements will be developed under the new E.C. system. And the negotiation of new standards for testing procedures allow scope for the "harmonizing up" of standards to a degree that U.S. producers consider unreasonable, unnecessary or even anti-competitive with regard to world market sales.

THE NEW E.C. APPROACH TO STANDARDIZATION

Beginning in 1983, the E.C. developed a new approach to product standardization and harmonization, which has been incorporated into the internal market concept. As succinctly summarized in Ernst & Whinney's August 1988 report *Europe 1992: The Single Market.* "Any product which can be sold in the member state in which it is produced will be freely marketable in other parts of the E.C., unimpeded by diverse national standards or testing and certification practices." The emphasis in this approach is on "mutual recognition and equivalence," as opposed to negotiation of detailed manufacturing and process standards. There are three main ways of introducing this new approach:

Public Procurement

One of the most far-reaching proposals in the 1985 internal market package dealt with public procurement. The Cecchini report on the economic cost of "non-Europe" calculates that public sector purchasing is equal to 15 percent of the Community's total gross domestic product, or a total of about $600 billion. Currently, just 0.14 percent of GDP, or less than $1 billion worth of goods and services, is purchased from E.C. companies outside the purchasing country's national territory. This shocking statistic lies behind the Commission's drive to open national public sector procurement markets to intra-E.C. competition.

While E.C. directives on public works and supply contracts are currently in force, these are generally perceived as weak and ineffective. Completing the internal market will require government procurement to be based on fair competition as opposed to national identity. This process is effectively to be completed in two steps:

1. *Improving existing directives on public works and public supply contracts.* The new public supply contracts directive was approved in final form by the Council of Ministers on March 22, 1988 (Directive 88/295/EEC). An amended proposed directive on public works contract procedures was submitted to the Council of Ministers on June 21, 1988, following receipt of proposed amendments from the EP. The Council has adopted a "common position" on this draft directive, indicating general agreement on substance, and the directive should be approved in final form within the next year.

   These two directives work in a similar way. The bidding process in each country must be made completely transparent, with the elimination of single-bid or no-bid contracts without adequate public notice. This will be achieved by changes in contract notification procedures. In addition, the legal powers of the Commission to nullify contract awards will be strengthened. It is anticipated that in most cases these powers will be used on an advisory basis with respect to member state governments, before actual contract awards are made.

2. *More controversy has been aroused by the other major initiative, the proposed extension of open public procurement rules to previously excluded sectors—telecommunications, water, energy and transport.* The Commission's formal proposals in this area have only recently been announced, in three documents issued on October 11, 1988:

Proposed directive on procurement procedures of entities providing water, energy and transport services.
Proposed directive on procurement procedures in the telecommunications sector.
Communication explaining the Commission's policy proposals in these two areas.

Reciprocity

No issue has been of greater concern to the U.S. public regarding EC-92 than the question of reciprocity and whether the E.C. is seeking to construct a "Fortress Europe." This subject has already been broached in the previous section on public procurement; in the fourth section we will look in more depth at trade reciprocity aspects of policies in specific sectors which are of particular commercial policy interest in the E.C. This section will look at the more general evolution of the reciprocity issue.

In recent months, the outgoing E.C. Trade Commissioner, Willy de Clerq, has stated several times that any opening of the E.C. market to foreign firms would have to be matched by reciprocity in their markets for E.C.-based companies. These remarks contributed to a high level of international concern that the internal market meant the E.C. was retreating into a "Fortress Europe." Foreign access would only be granted on the basis of specifically negotiated bilateral reciprocal agreements. Concern over such an evolution of E.C. policy has been openly expressed here by the Secretary of Commerce and high-level representatives of the State and Treasury Departments.

This concern is amplified because the United States and the E.C. are also participating in the Uruguay Round negotiations on changing the rules in the GATT, the multilateral international trading system. The current commitment is to complete the GATT negotiations by 1990. But it is hardly likely that the E.C., which negotiates as a unit in trade issues with the rest of the world, will make any GATT commitments that would run afoul of its own evolving EC-92 policies on, for example, state subsidies, public procurement, local content and sectoral trade issues.

Another key issue is the question of the rights of foreign-owned enterprises operating in the E.C., in view of the reciprocity policy and Article 58 of the Treaty of Rome. Article 58 provides that any company organized to do business within the EC—without any explicit statement as to ultimate parentage of the company—shall be considered as having the same rights under the treaty as a "natural person." The reciprocity approach—particularly as framed in the draft Second Banking Directive of June 1988—seemed to call into question retrospectively the rights of U.S. subsidiaries established in the E.C., if it were determined that their home government did not provide "comparable market access" to E.C.-based enterprises. Reports that the Commission's Legal Service was being asked to review the application of Article 58 to foreign investment within the E.C. added to these concerns, even though no final report on this issue has been produced.

In an important statement issued on October 19, 1988, the Commission sought to define more clearly its position on the general question of reciprocity and related specific issues. The Commission took the unusual step of publicly declaring the outcome of an internal "policy debate" with in the Commission itself in this statement, entitled *Europe 1992: Europe World Partner*. The statement sought to reassure trading partners that "1992 Europe will not be a fortress Europe but a partnership Europe."

Sectoral Issues

A major subject within the EC-92 program is the effect of internal market liberalization on E.C. trade and competitiveness in specific commercial sectors. Generally, the E.C. is moving toward a common commercial policy in such sectors, which means not only liberalization of the internal market, but a common external trade policy, including elimination of remaining national trade barriers against non-E.C. goods. The battle over reciprocity in particular may be mostly fought over such specific sectoral trade issues. All commercial sectors may be affected in varying degrees, but three sectors especially illustrate the broad scope of the policies and practices that will be changed due to the impact of the EC-92 program.

AUTOMOTIVE TRADE

The "globalization" of existing E.C. national quotas is perhaps the most politically explosive subject on the EC-92 agenda, both among member states and in trade relations with the rest of the world. A U.S. auto company executive in Europe explains why in the following estimate:

Without quotas and asumed politically motivated restraints in some countries, the overall Japanese share of the European new-car market could rise from the current 11 percent to as high as the 30 percent that we see in North America. That shift would threaten perhaps ten major assembly plants and as many as 300,000 jobs in Europe.

Some E.C. countries, such as Germany and the Benelux countries, maintain no quotas on Japanese car exports to their markets. The U.K. maintains only an informally negotiated industry-to-industry "gentlemen's agreement." This effectively holds down the level of imports to around 11 percent. Also, Japanese companies have been required to meet a local content standard if they are to receive regional aid, and if vehicles from factories in the U.K. are not to be counted against the voluntary restraint agreement. France uses its vehicle registration procedures to keep Japanese imports to 3 percent of the market, while Italy and Spain allow only a small, specified number of units, under quotas registered with the GATT. Thus, not only quota levels but the nature and implementation of the quotas vary significantly among the E.C. member states.

No decision has been taken regarding the harmonization of Japanese car quotas. The French government and automobile industry have pressed for an E.C.-wide quota, with an 80 percent local content standard to prevent Japanese evasion of the quota through assembly operations. Both the German government and car industry have opposed such a stringent quota and local content policy. At this point, only two principles appear relatively certain:

1. There will be some type of E.C.-level restraint.

2. In principle, any restraint will be temporary.

In 1988, The Brussels-based European carmakers association (CCMC—representing all major E.C.-owned companies) did adopt a common industry position. This position called for the stabilization of total Japanese exports to the E.C., at least until E.C. car exports to Japan reached half the level of Japanese exports to the E.C. CCMC called for establishment of an 80 percent E.C.-content standard to determine whether cars made by Japanese producers should count against the number of units included in the stabilization agreement. But under pressure from German companies this common position is currently being reassessed in view of the question of the impact on automotive trade with the United States.

The automotive quota issue is of major concern to U.S. interests for a number of reasons. The two largest U.S. car manufacturers have extensive operations in the E.C. and are among the six companies that hold roughly coequal leading shares of the mass market. At present neither company is actively supporting tough

E.C.-wide quotas on Japanese cars. In fact, there is serious concern in Europe that Ford and GM could potentially cooperate with Japanese companies in exporting U.S.-assembled "transplants" into the E.C., to take advantage of low dollar-based costs and avoid any E.C. quotas on vehicles shipped directly from Japan. There are strong disagreements within the E.C. car industry on how this issue should be handled. For its part, the U.S. government has not so far indicated that it would accept any E.C. effort to transfer national E.C. car quotas to a global quota, especially if such a quota were made to apply to goods shipped from the United States.

TELECOMMUNICATIONS

No issue in EC-92 is thornier than its application to the telecommunications sector. A more efficient, less nationally-oriented and more internationally competitive telecommunications services and equipment sector is viewed as perhaps the crucial link in creating a more integrated E.C. internal market. The Cecchini study reports estimates of telecommunications equipment costs across the E.C. as being 80–100 percent higher than in the United States, with costs of business customer services typically higher by a similar proportion.

The strategy of the Commission is set out in its basic document on telecommunications policy, the "Green Paper" of June 30, 1987. One year later, the Council of Ministers approved a resolution explicitly linking development of a common market for telecommunications services and equipment to the EC-92 program. The telecommunications policy for the Commission is developed within a self-contained telecommunications directorate, DG XIII.

The Green Paper in fact represents a compromise between the traditional European concept of publicly-owned basic telecommunications network services and the newer international trend of establishing a free (or at least freer) market in services using the basic network and the equipment that can be linked to it. Basic services, redefined in the Green Paper as the "reserved services," are those which will be provided by government-owned or government-licensed telecommunications monopolies, based primarily on the principle of universal access and availability. Traditionally, this has clearly included telephone and telex service.

"Competitive services" are defined as including not only the manipulation and processing of data carried on the basic network, (the so-called "value-added" services) but also providing "intelligent networks" that handle communications according to a customer's own needs, often on equipment that the customer may have purchased and installed from an independent vendor. Another key compromise in the Green Paper is that the national telecommunications administrations (PTTs) would be allowed to participate in the competitive services market, while retaining their regulatory and reserved services functions.

To implement this policy, which leaves the "integrity" of the national basic services network intact, while encouraging the competitive stimulus of alternative equipment and services providers, the E.C. has adopted or proposed a number of specific steps. The development of these specific policy initiatives will be crucial for U.S.-owned companies that hope to be competitive in the evolving E.C. telecommunications market for both services and equipment:

Opening of Telecommunications Procurement This issue was discussed in the previous section on public procurement. In addition to the comments above, it should be noted that the draft directive of October 1988 requires a compulsory public and international call for all works and supply contracts. This includes a compulsory annual information notice announcing all intended purchases for the year

ahead. Also, as with existing procurement directives, there is a requirement for full transparency of the purchasing behavior of the telecommunications entities in E.C. member states.

The E.C. policy does not initially address continued discrimination against non-E.C. source products and services. It does allow member countries at their discretion to entertain competitive non-E.C.-source bids. And, as mentioned earlier, it indicates that the E.C. intends to negotiate bilateral and multilateral market access agreements.

The policy apparently conflicts with the telecommunications reciprocity provisions of the U.S. Omnibus Trade Act. Section 1374 of the U.S. law provides for the citation by USTR of those foreign countries denying equivalent market access to *U.S. firms*. In an announcement of February 21, 1989, the USTR stated that this provision at present includes some E.C. countries. The draft E.C. procurement directive would in principle ameliorate the current situation by guaranteeing equal access for those *U.S. firms operating in the E.C., which provide products and services meeting the E.C. local content standard*. However, the U.S. Trade Act provisions are also concerned with improved markets for *U.S. exports*, which would not be enhanced by the provisions of the draft telecommunications procurement directive, unless E.C. member states decided to accept U.S.-source bids.

Accordingly, the Office of the USTR identified the E.C. (along with Korea) as a "priority country" for negotiations involving telecommunications market access, as provided by the Trade Act. This decision is directed at existing market barriers to U.S. products and services. The USTR announcement does indicate that the degree of access varies considerably within the E.C.

Provision of Terminal Equipment and Telecommunications Services In addition to the effort to open the public procurement market, the E.C.

has already adopted a directive requiring member countries to eliminate all exclusive and special rights to telecommunications entities for the importation, marketing, connection and maintenance of telecommunications terminal equipment. The terminal equipment directive entered into force on May 16, 1988. But France has challenged the validity of this directive before the Court of Justice, on grounds that the E.C. has overreached its treaty authority. Meanwhile, there is a similar draft directive under discussion that would require member countries to eliminate exclusive or special rights granted to telecommunications entities for the provision of "non-basic" telecommunications services.

European Telecommunications Standards Institute (ETSI)   In conjunction with CEN/CENELEC, this body will establish agreed European standards for telecommunications equipment and services. The significance of ETSI is that it removes this function from the exclusive control of the European Conference of Postal and Telecommunications Administrations (CEPT), a collaborative body consisting solely of PTTs. CEPT will participate in ETSI standard-setting, but ETSI will also include other equipment and services providers, and user groups. ETSI, located in the south of France, began functioning in April 1988. All E.C. member state telecommunications authorities are now required to use agreed European standards as the basis for type approval of telecommunications terminal equipment.

E.C.-sponsored Research on Common Standards in Advanced Technologies (RACE and ISDN)   The Council of Ministers in 1986 approved a nonbinding Recommendation on the coordinated introduction of an Integrated Services Digital Network. This will allow Europe-wide voice, video and data capabilities via the national telecommunications network. In December 1987, the E.C. also approved the "main phase" of the RACE project, RACE being an acronym for a program of pre-competitive R&D aimed

at creating common standards in Europe for integrated "broadband" voice, video text and graphics communication. The main phase of RACE (to be completed by 1992) is open to the European subsidiaries of U.S. companies.

Open Network Provisions (ONP)   The Commission is currently preparing a directive on the conditions of access to networks. An initial proposal was approved in December 1988.

INFORMATION TECHNOLOGY AND ADVANCED ELECTRONICS

The E.C.'s collective sense of inferiority regarding telecommunications equipment and services extends to information technologies more generally. While there are many excellent and world-class E.C.-based companies in this broad field, most observers believe that the E.C. lags behind both the United States and Japan in many key areas, and that the balkanization of the E.C. market has been a major cause of this lag.

On the other hand, the E.C. seems more committed as a matter of policy to ensure that it retains a competitive base in the information technologies and electronics products industries—across the board from chips to consumer products. There is a strong sense among many E.C. companies and other groups that the U.S. policy of opening its consumer electronics and telecommunications equipment markets to foreign producers, without adequate safeguards against import surges, dumped goods and predatory pricing, and without requiring reciprocal access, was a major mistake.

It would be wrong, however, to indicate that there is a complete consensus within the E.C. as to the policy measures needed to improve E.C. world competitiveness in the advanced electronics industries. In this report, we will focus on one particularly significant E.C.-sponsored research program—ESPRIT—both as a guide to the E.C.'s overall policy direction and to the relationship with U.S. interests.

ESPRIT is the acronym for the European Program for Research and Development in Information Technology. ESPRIT was established in 1984 to promote precompetitive intra-European technological research cooperation on information telecommunications projects with commercial applications. The program provides matching funds (on a 50–50 basis) for approved precompetitive research projects selected from corporate, academic and government research laboratory proposals.

The first phase of ESPRIT, with a total budget of 1.5 billion ECU's (nearly $2 billion), was completed by 1988. To quote from a recent article on ESPRIT by Jonathan Todd in the May 1988 issue of the E.C. Delegation magazine *Europe*, the program "concentrated on microelectronics, advanced information processing systems (including software) and application technologies, including computer-integrated manufacturing and office systems." The Council of Ministers was sufficiently impressed with the results of the program to double its budget for the period 1989–93.

U.S. companies in Europe have been concerned that the goals of ESPRIT may be more oriented to improving the competitiveness of *E.C. firms*, rather than *E.C.-based industry*. This is perceived by some companies as reducing the opportunities for participation by U.S. firms operating in Europe. For example, the Todd article, which summarizes numerous projects, fails to mention any non-E.C. firms, even though U.S. companies operating in Europe played important roles in some ESPRIT projects. Similarly, some U.S. companies operating in Europe, that have developed proposals relevant to ESPRIT and other E.C.-sponsored research programs, have been informally advised to allow E.C. companies to take the lead in proposing such projects to insure approval.

Heightening this concern over possible current "second-class status" for U.S. companies' participation in some E.C.-sponsored research programs is the fear, mentioned by at least one U.S. company, of an E.C. backlash against similar tendencies in U.S. government-supported programs in semiconductor and super-conductivity research. Sources in the Commission note that Sematech and MCC remain closed to E.C.-owned, U.S.-based companies. If this "model" is pursued, they argue, in combination with Defense Department research that remains mostly closed to E.C. companies, then questions of mutual levels of access will increase on the E.C. side.

The primary consequence of exclusion of U.S.-owned firms from such officially-sponsored E.C. research could be in the standards area. One example may be seen in the Todd article, which cites, "'Herode,' a highly successful ESPRIT project led by Siemens, [which] developed a new international standard for office documentation architecture (ODA), now officially adopted by the International Standards Organization (ISO 8613). Siemens has been joined by ICL, Olivetti and Bull on a new project to develop practical applications for ODA, which must compete on the market against IBM's DCA/DIA standard." But, in fairness to the E.C., it should be noted that there are many ambiguities regarding competition and cooperation in these evolving information technology fields. For example, the Commission cites the fact that IBM Germany does have a minority participation role in the ESPRIT II ODA continuation project.

The general development of E.C. standards in information technology is proceeding through the application of the principles of Open Standards Interconnection (OSI). All U.S. companies with an interest in the E.C. market should become familiar with the E.C.'s OSI process. With the support of the E.C., an informal European Workshop on Open Standards (EWOS) has been established for the purpose of coordinating input from standards bodies, user groups and manufacturing organizations to develop E.C. standards in the evolving information telecommunications field. EWOS is also to discuss standards issues with equivalent U.S. and Japanese groups. At the same time, OSI-based procedures for product testing and certification are also being established.

Rules of Origin and Local Content

The previous sections raise a number of general questions about local content policies in the E.C. and rules of origin. These will be important issues in the context of the overall development of the E.C.-92 program. At present, the E.C. does not maintain a general local content policy. And rules of origin for non-preferential trading partners, such as the United States and Japan, are based on a rule adopted in 1968. This states that origin is conferred in the country where the last substantial process or operation that was economically justified was performed, providing also that a new product was thus created, or at least a major new stage in the manufacturing process resulted. This rule is similar in nature to the "substantial transformation" test used by the United States.

Since then, the E.C. has considered and adopted criteria to determine the last substantial operation for a number of specific products, such as radios, televisions, tape recorders, textile products, ceramic products and roller bearings. Currently, decisions are being made regarding rules of origin for semiconductors and copiers. As the subjects of these "rules of origin" decisions become more numerous, the concern is increasing that a de facto local content policy will emerge.

LOCAL CONTENT RULE FOR ANTIDUMPING ENFORCEMENT

The E.C. does maintain percentage content rules in some specific cases. Perhaps the most important example of such rules is the 40-percent local content rule applied to companies found to be dumping or illegally subsidizing exports to the E.C. market. An E.C. regulation of July 1988 (EEC 2423/88) on application of antidumping or countervailing duties addresses the problem of "screwdriver" plants —that is, final assembly operations that may be established to circumvent E.C. anti-dumping penalties. This regulation provided that anti-dumping duties could be applied to products whose final assembly was in the E.C. The penalty can be applied to goods shipped under the following conditions:

- Assembly is carried out "by a party which is related or associated to any of the manufacturers whose exports of the like product are subject to a definitive anti-dumping duty..."
- The "value of parts and materials" produced in the country of exportation subject to the anti-dumping rule is more than 60 percent.
- The assembly operation is started or substantially increased after the anti-dumping investigation was opened.

This 40-percent rule can be ameliorated by the possibility of including costs of "research and development carried out in and the technology applied within the Community." According to Commission staff sources, the E.C. has in practice reached accommodations with related assembly companies in "virtually all anti-circumvention cases." At the current time, there are no duties being levied at the premises of assemblers in the E.C.

Intellectual Property

The adequate protection of intellectual property rights is a major concern of both NAM member companies and U.S. international economic policy. A quick glance at the official U.S. balance of payments statistics reveals why. In 1987—the last year for which complete data are available—U.S. companies reported earning over $9 billion from foreign sources in licensing fees and royalties, while paying foreigners only $1.3 billion. This $7:1$ ratio remains the most asymmetrically positive component of the U.S. current account balance. It explains the major national interest, for example, in achieving a provision on intellectual property rights as a major goal in the current GATT negotiating round.

E.C. companies and member states also have a strong interest in protecting intellectual property rights, both internationally and within the E.C. context. The effort to achieve an improved and harmonized system of intellectual property rights within Europe antedates the 1992 internal market program, though the effort remains incomplete and unfinished. For example, an E.C. Patent Convention was signed in 1975. However, as of late 1988, five of the smaller or newer member states (Denmark, Ireland, Spain, Portugal and Greece) still had not signed the convention. A European Patent Office, with membership extending to many non-E.C. European countries, has been established in Munich. Completing and improving a harmonized E.C. intellectual property rights system is seen as an important task if a more integrated internal market is to be achieved. It is also considered essential to the development of world-class competitive technologies across European national borders.

A summary of some of the major intellectual property initiatives and their present status follows. It is largely based on information provided in the latest *Business Guide to EC Initiatives*, published by the American Chamber of Commerce in Belgium (see appended guide to information sources).

- *Regulation on Counterfeit Goods* (adopted 1986 by Council of Ministers, entered into force January 1, 1988). This regulation established an E.C.-wide policy to allow the confiscation of counterfeit goods imported from third countries, thus preventing their circulation and sale anywhere within the E.C. The regulation, it should be noted, applies only to goods which infringe registered trademarks. The regulation could be enlarged to include

other intellectual property rights such as copyrights in 1991.

- *Regulation on Community Trademark and Community Trademark Office* (consolidated text including member state reservations before Council for final action). This could establish a central E.C. Trademark Office in Madrid, with a Board of Appeal in Luxembourg, the seat of the ECJ. It would eliminate the present need to register trademarks in each of the ten separate national jurisdictions (Benelux presently maintains a single system for those three countries)—though these national systems would not be eliminated.

Benefits for U.S. companies could include the elimination of national compulsory use rules, since once the trademark has been used in one member state, it would be valid throughout the E.C. Also, recognition of an infringement in one member state could also be extended to prevent use in all other E.C. markets.

Competition Policy

The E.C. actively and directly regulates competition in Europe, under authority assigned to it by Articles 85-86 of the Treaty of Rome. This means that the E.C. may establish regulations which have the force of law within the member states. DG IV is the competition policy directorate. Since the 1985 Cockfield White Paper was developed in DG III, it did not include any specific competition policy proposals. However, there is no doubt that major changes in competition policy within Europe must accompany the development of EC-92.

This is because member state governments also retain rights of regulating competition. The coexistence of E.C. and member state regulation creates a patchwork of rules regulating mergers and takeovers within the E.C. and results in companies in different E.C. countries playing by quite different rules. The assumption is that member state governments, through their own, competition and merger control policies, should not be able to frustrate cross-border mergers and acquisitions needed to create larger economies of scale and enhance E.C. international competitiveness. And because U.S. companies have typically expanded in Europe by acquiring existing E.C. firms or establishing joint venture arrangements with them, any major changes proposed in competition policy will have a major effect on the ability of U.S.-owned firms to cope with EC-92 market changes.

E.C. enforcement of competition policy has been restricted to company *practices*, and has not included direct control of mergers and acquisitions. Each country has its own policy in this latter area. The U.K. and Germany have the most aggressive national antitrust policies of the U.S. type, enforced through the Mergers and Monopolies Commission and the Bundeskartellamt, respectively. Other countries, such as France and Italy, do not have highly developed antitrust policies, but do control company actions and merger activities as a function of national industrial policies, tax laws, price controls and other policies. Among all the E.C. countries, only the U.K. allows hostile takeovers similar to the U.S. model. And some specifically discriminate against foreign acquisitions—the Netherlands, for example, allows only 20 percent of the voting shares of any publicly-owned Dutch company to be held by foreign persons.

Proposals to establish direct E.C. control over mergers and acquisitions have been debated in Community institutions for fifteen years, with little forward progress. But the imminence of the enhanced internal market has spurred progress toward achievement of a new E.C. regulation in this area. *The major proposal to emerge from DG IV, under the leadership of departing Commissioner Peter Sutherland, is the revised draft regulation to establish E.C. control over all mergers "having a Community dimension."* It was proposed by the Commission in May 1988, after considering EP amendments to earlier drafts. Several revised versions have subsequently been circulated.

This draft regulation would establish E.C. control over all proposed "concentrations" (mergers and acquisitions) of companies with an E.C. dimension. An E.C. dimension is defined as:

- Worldwide turnover greater than 1 billion ECUs for the companies combined.
- Aggregate E.C.-wide turnover of 100 million ECUs, with no more than 75 percent of the total in any one E.C. member state.

In a recent twelve-month period, the Commission counted 171 transactions that would have exceeded the turnover thresholds of the regulation, though only a relatively small share of these also met the distribution requirement. For such major cases, the Commission's intent is that it should become the sole regulating body. The preamble to the draft regulation states that, "In order to provide for a uniform system of control of concentrations having a Community dimension throughout the common market, the Member States must refrain from taking any measure which might undermine the full effect of decisions pursuant to this Regulation." (Paragraph 27, quoted from draft of July 25, 1988.)

Because the Treaty of Rome limits E.C. authority to the competition policy area, however, the very next paragraph establishes a major qualification: "...This principle does not prevent Member States from taking measures with a view to protecting legitimate interests other than competition..."

This qualification may critically affect the attitude of both E.C. companies and U.S.-owned companies active in Europe. There is strong acceptance of the concept of a Brussels-based competition policy authority, which could expedite the approval of mergers and acquisitions creating larger economies of scale in the E.C. On the other hand, both U.S. and many E.C. companies are concerned about the "double jeopardy" aspect of establishing a

Brussels-based merger authority, while continuing to maintain a veto authority in the national capitals over acquisitions.

There is also a further issue that affects U.S. interests and that also currently obstructs U.K. acceptance of the principle of an E.C. merger regulation. This is whether there should be a single E.C. policy on hostile takeovers. Britain, virtually alone in the E.C., currently allows hostile takeovers (witness the recent battle between Nestlé and Suchard, two Swiss confectionery companies, for the British company Rowntree Mackintosh, a firm with widespread activities and brand recognition throughout the E.C.). The U.K. government can stop takeovers, but principally on competition policy grounds. In the British view, it would be unfair to disarm the U.K. government's major defense against large takeovers that it views unfavorably, while permitting the effective ban on hostile takeovers in other E.C. countries.

This British view could force the E.C. and its members into a harmonization of takeover rules. Certainly it is interesting that the new British Conservative Commissioner, Sir Leon Brittan, who has been politically very close to Prime Minister Thatcher, has been selected to replace Sutherland as the competition policy commissioner. U.S. business readers should also recall the point noted earlier in discussing the Commission statement on reciprocity of October 19, 1988—that in applying any common takeover policy to non-E.C. firms, the Commission will consider the reciprocal rights of E.C. firms in the acquiring company's home market.

Monetary Policy

The commitment of the E.C. to closer monetary policy coordination will have a major impact on the way U.S. companies do business in Europe. At the same time, there are major issues in this area that will influence international monetary policy and exchange rate developments, and therefore the conditions of U.S. international trade.

In 1988, there were two critical developments:

1. *Full Liberalization of Capital Movements within the E.C.* On June 24, 1988, E.C. finance and economics ministers, meeting in the Council of Ministers, gave final approval to a directive providing for complete liberalization of capital movements within the E.C. This means the elimination of all foreign exchange controls. In addition, all domestic monetary regulations that have a specific impact on capital transactions with nonresidents are subject to a notification procedure.

   All E.C. member states must eliminate any remaining capital movements restrictions by July 1, 1990, except for Spain, Ireland, Greece and Portugal, who have a grace period through 1992. The Belgium–Luxembourg economic union must also eliminate its dual exchange rate by the end of 1992. The balance of payments safeguard provisions of the Treaty of Rome remain in effect, but the Commission will have supervisory authority over the implementation and maintenance of emergency exchange controls by members. U.S. companies operating in the E.C. can therefore look to essentially complete implementation of free capital movements within the E.C. between now and 1992.

2. *Monetary Union.* Agreement on the capital liberalization directive both cleared the way for and impelled the E.C. toward consideration of an economic and monetary union. The success of the European Monetary System (EMS) also encouraged a strategy of closer monetary policy cooperation. The Hanover E.C. summit of heads of government on June 27–28, 1988, therefore decided to establish a committee with the task of studying and proposing concrete stages leading toward such a union. The nature

and topic of study was the result of a compromise. Most E.C. governments would have been willing to include explicitly on the agenda the exploration of the questions of an E.C. central bank and a single E.C. currency, but such far-reaching measures were opposed by the British government, which has yet to join the EMS.

The importance of this subject to President Delors, formerly French finance minister, is indicated by the fact that he is personally chairing the study committee, and also holds the new Commission's monetary affairs portfolio. The leaders of E.C. central banks were also requested to join the committee in their "personal" capacities. The committee is to report its findings "in good time" before the scheduled heads of government summit in Madrid, in June 1989. Current plans call for release of a report in the spring, midway between the installation of the new Commission and the Madrid summit.

The report of the Delors committee will almost certainly make policy recommendations that go beyond the type of consultation and coordination of policies new existing within the EMS or the broader G-7 group of industrial countries. It is assumed that there would be some mandatory policy coordination features. Leaving aside the question of the British relationship to closer coordination, another essential issue is whether there should be a "once for all" major reevaluation of the Deutsche mark before implementation of some type of mandatory coordination system. Rates in the present EMS range keep other E.C. currencies, notably the French franc, closely aligned with the DM, and therefore effectively overvalued with respect to industrial competitiveness in third country markets. But the effect of a close EMS relationship with a strong DM has also had the salutary effect of sharply reducing inflation rates throughout the E.C.

The outcome of these discussions and decisions will have a major impact on U.S. international industrial competitiveness. The movement of the DM within the EMS will affect both dollar-rate production costs within the E.C. and the competitive prices of German and other E.C. manufactured goods on world markets. Of equal significance to U.S. companies, in combination with the complete liberalization of capital movements planned by 1990–92, will be the impact on production location decisions within the E.C. itself.

Europe 1992: The Implications for U.S. Trade and Industry

Testimony of Glen J. Skovholt, Honeywell, Inc.[1]

Mr. Chairman, I am Glen J. Skovholt, Director for Policy and Strategy in Corporate Public Affairs, Honeywell, Inc. Honeywell is a U.S. corporation offering a diversified line of electronic-based products and services to worldwide markets. We do business in over 90 countries worldwide, with almost $1.5 billion in international sales last year.

Honeywell has strong interests in the European Community both as a U.S. exporter to the E.C. market and as a company which has long had a substantial presence in Europe in all phases of our manufacturing and service activities. In 1988 more than two-thirds of our total sales outside the United States were in Europe, where we have 15 factories and employ 11,000 people.

For this reason, I was pleased to work with the National Association of Manufacturers as chairman of a task force which it recently formed on the European Community's Internal Market program, known in shorthand as "EC-92." Over 150 companies and cooperating

industry associations have worked with us in this group. This task force is presently focusing on some of the priority issues that have been identified in the NAM report, *EC-92 and U.S. Industry*, which was released earlier this month. I would like to submit a copy of this report to the subcommittee today, in addition to my prepared testimony. My comments will focus on some of the major issues in this report, which are of concern both in terms of the broad interests of NAM's members and the general international economic interests of the United States.

The EC-92 Market Opportunity

My major overall point is that U.S. companies almost uniformly emphasize that EC-92 represents a major market opportunity. We see the proposed package as contributing both to a rapid expansion of the E.C. market and, in practice, a deregulation of that market which will increase opportunities for competitive producers. Within this overall positive outlook, however, there are a series of major policy issues, the outcome of which could either enhance or reduce business opportunities for U.S.-based exporters or U.S.-owned companies already established within the E.C.

Let's first look at the scale of the market opportunity. By the European Commission's calculations, enactment of the full 1992 program can give a one-time boost of 5 percent or more to the total E.C. domestic product. While U.S. exporters should seek markets wherever they can find them, for the foreseeable future the E.C. may remain the key growth market overseas for U.S. Industrial companies, especially if it becomes more dynamic and open.

Selected excerpts from testimonies by Honeywell, Inc.; the U.S. Semiconductor Industry Association (SIA); Motor & Equipment Manufacturers Association. Hearing before the Subcommittee on Trade of the Committee on Ways and Means House of Representatives, One Hundred First Congress, First session, March 20, 1989, Serial 101-4, Europe 1992.

[1]Glen J. Skovholt, Director, Policy and Strategy Corporate Public Affairs Honeywell, Inc. and Chairman, Task force on the European Community Internal Market Program National Association of Manufacturers.

Europe is our most important regional export market, and will probably remain so indefinitely. Today about a quarter of total U.S. exports go to the European Community, which has just overtaken Canada as the largest regional or national market. As for other countries and regions, Japan takes only 8 percent of our exports and the rest of East Asia another 13 percent. All of Latin America takes only 13 percent. And most importantly, no other regional market approaches the level of economic integration found in Europe today, much less what is being contemplated by 1992.

The E.C. market has market has been the most important one so far in turning around the U.S. trade deficit. As noted in NAM's recently released comprehensive trade report, the fall of the dollar has had a bigger and faster impact on growth in exports to Europe than any other region. U.S. export growth to Europe has been near or above double figures since 1985 and has been accelerating—9 percent in 1986, 14 percent in 1987 and 25 percent in 1988. And this export growth in 1988 has cut the bilateral U.S. trade deficit with the E.C. in half: from $25 billion in 1987, to $12 billion in 1988. That improvement alone accounted for more than a third of the total improvement of the U.S. trade deficit in the first half of 1988.

Finally, let's look at the relationship between trade and investment. I've already noted that Honeywell has a major investment and manufacturing presence in Europe. For all U.S. manufacturers, total holdings in the E.C. were officially valued at $65 billion at the end of 1987. That's more than half the total value of all U.S. companies' manufacturing investment abroad.

Although most major U.S. investors in the E.C. produce a large proportion of their locally sold products in Europe, it is important to recognize that most, like Honeywell, are also significant exporters to Europe. In fact, about 30 percent of total U.S. exports to the E.C. is shipped directly to U.S. affiliates there.

I would conclude, therefore, that there is not a major difference in interest between U.S. companies with investments in the E.C. and those that service the market primarily through exporting. Many U.S. exporters directly or indirectly sell their products to or through large U.S. investing firms. Most U.S. investors do some significant exporting to the E.C. market. And in both types of activities, it is critically important to maintain close and positive relations with customers, distributors and joint venture partners that may be E.C.-headquartered companies. Finally, as Richard Heckert of Du Pont, the current chairman of NAM, testified in another Congressional forum, over the long term it is difficult to maintain a major presence in important overseas markets solely through exporting. Most companies must consider some type of investment eventually.

The 1992 Internal Market Program

The basic thrust of the 1992 program is to *complete* the internal market established as a European objective by the Treaty of Rome over 30 years ago. As laid out in the E.C.'s 1985 "white paper," this involves the pragmatic elimination of three major types of barriers.

- *Physical barriers* at the borders to the free flow of goods and persons
- *Technical barriers* that prevent good produced or traded in one member state from being sold in others
- *Fiscal barriers* such as the red tape, delays and costs of different national tax systems which prevent cross-border trade.

Also associated with the elimination of these barriers are major initiatives in competition policy, encouragement of research and development, establishment of coordinated monetary policies with possible monetary union, and decisions on common social policies.

On the whole, NAM's members view this program as a positive set of proposals that will have the effect of loosening many of the internal protectionist measures that remain within the E.C. and prevent its realization of a true common market. Both exporting and investing companies see the result as a more open and competitive environment, in which the major ultimate beneficiary is the individual E.C. citizen and consumer.

In studying this program with other NAM members, we have concluded that three aspects of the overall package stand out from the point of view of U.S. business:

1. EC-92 IS NOT DESIGNED, IN ITSELF, TO PROMOTE TRADE WITH NON-EC PARTNERS. It may have that effect, as European companies seek competitive products and commercial allies outside Europe as well as within. But as former European Commissioner Lord Cockfield, the primary architect of this program, emphasized in a meeting at NAM three years ago, "This program is not primarily for the benefit of our trading partners." I should also emphasize, however, that the E.C. has also maintained that it will respect all existing international obligations in developing and implementing EC-92. It will be very important that we keep this in mind—and remind the E.C. of their own pledge.

2. EC-92 IS BEING IMPLEMENTED TODAY. EC-92, which includes a list of 300 directives and other policy actions, is not like our recent Free Trade Agreement with Canada, that went into effect on a date certain—January 1, 1989. The EC-92 program is going into effect continuously, as directives and regulations are enacted, with conforming actions by national legislatures, governments and standard-setting bodies.

3. THE ECONOMIC IMPACT MAY BE FRONT-LOADED. Companies in the E.C. have made and are making decisions right now regarding cross-border alliances and rationalization of production. This includes U.S. companies operating in the E.C. Therefore, some observers believe that the European Commission's economic analysis is misleading, when it predicts maximum benefit only in the mid-1990s after a period of initial restructuring and lost output. Major positive benefits may be felt earlier than expected. Both U.S. business and the U.S. government must be prepared to deal with the early impact of change.

A "Watch List" of Issues

As I emphasize above, NAM's members generally view EC-92 as a positive development, that may already be revitalizing the European market. But there are specific developments and proposals that create some concern. These are the EC-92 policy areas where U.S. companies believe that specific decisions may enhance or reduce their opportunities to compete in a more open E.C. market. In the remainder of this testimony, I want to turn to the concerns on a "watch list" of such issues that has been developed by NAM.

TECHNICAL STANDARDS

The harmonization of technical standards, a key goal of EC-92, can have a major impact on current and future access of U.S. goods to the E.C. market. *In principle, the adoption of common standards is widely seen by U.S. companies in Europe as a major benefit.* U.S. companies with production facilities in Europe believe that they will be able to rationalize production across national frontiers to a much greater degree than at present. U.S. exporters may achieve comparable benefits. Whatever standard is adopted for a product, the potential U.S. exporter will be assured that complying with this standard provides access to the entire E.C. market.

But there are concerns among U.S. companies over the improved and expedited European standard-setting process. To allay some of these concerns, E.C. standards setting bodies have promised improved transparency and access to information as new standards are developed. NAM has discussed with the Commerce Department the concerns of its members, and asked that Secretary Mosbacher take the initiative in encouraging an improved dialogue between U.S. and E.C. broad-based standards setting bodies.

Public Procurement

EC-92 includes proposals to enhance existing E.C. rules on the opening of member government procurement and to extend E.C. rules to the sectors presently excluded from GATT or E.C. discipline. The opening of such procurement within the E.C. is a promising step, and could lead to a significant expansion of liberalization among present signatories of the GATT procurement code. On the negative side, the procurement directives for the four presently excluded sectors (water, energy, transport and telecommunications), include specific local content rules that favor E.C.-source products and services, unless trading partners liberalize their own procurement rules in an equivalent manner.

Reciprocity

The E.C. has adopted a controversial policy of extending intra-E.C. market opening initiatives to non-E.C. producers only insofar as E.C. trading partners provide equivalent access to their markets for E.C.-based producers and E.C. products. As far as industrial companies are concerned, there are some important qualifications on this approach, as elaborated in the European Commission statement of October 1988. This includes continued acceptance of the full citizenship rights of foreign-owned companies established in the E.C. as provided under Article 58 of the Treaty of Rome. And the E.C. has stated that the interpretation of treatment will be based on concepts of "equivalent" and "non-discriminatory" access, rather than a requirement that rules of access be exactly the same for foreign participants in the E.C. and E.C.-based companies in non-E.C. markets.

Another important point here is that the E.C. has stressed that reciprocity can be developed through either bilateral or multilateral negotiations. At NAM, we would particularly hope that this means that the current GATT negotiations will continue with full and active E.C. participation.

- *Sectoral Trade Issues.* NAM has particularly focused on the future development of E.C.-wide common commercial policies and other sectoral initiatives regarding automobiles, telecommunications and information technology, because of the broad implications of policies in these areas.

- *Rules of Origin and Local Content.* The development of E.C. rules that determine whether goods are of E.C. origin, for the application of regular or penalty tariffs, is not specifically related to the EC-92 program. At present, there is no general local content policy planned, although such provisions have appeared in specific directives. There are U.S. industrial concerns that these piecemeal approaches will eventually merge into a general E.C. pattern.

- *Intellectual Property Rights.* Enhancement and completion of a Europe-wide system of protection of trademarks, patents and copyrights is an important component of completing the internal market. In general, the E.C. appears to be adopting policies that are compatible with U.S. policy approaches. On the other hand, we should mention that the E.C. attack in the GATT on Section 337 of the U.S. Trade Law poses the possibility of a serious trade policy confrontation in this field.

- *Social Dimension.* U.S. companies with production facilities and large numbers of employees in Europe, like ourselves, are especially interested in this issue. The question is whether EC-92 should be accompanied by new initiatives in employment and social affairs, and what type of initiatives would be most effective under the EC-92 program.

- *Competition Policy.* Establishment of E.C.-level control over mergers and acquisitions involving large-scale multinational combinations, as proposed in a regulation drafted last year, is potentially of major importance for U.S. businesses in the E.C. Such a policy, if it allows for a quick and exclusive ruling by the E.C. on proposed mergers, can reduce the obstructive or delaying effect of approvals by multiple national jurisdictions.

- *Monetary Policy.* Elimination of all controls on capital movements within the E.C. has already been agreed. Establishment of mandatory coordination of monetary policies and possible creation of a single E.C. central bank and currency are currently being considered in a committee headed by European Commission President Delors. Such developments would expedite the ability of U.S. companies—as both exporters and investors—to operate across national boundaries. But there may also be a larger trade-related effect on the relationship of the dollar to the broad range of E.C. currencies.

- *Potential Issues.* NAM's members have identified two other areas where there are no formal proposals, but where future decisions will probably have a strong impact on U.S. business interests. One is the probable development of a single E.C.-wide export control system, as a result of EC-92. The other is the planned extension of tight E.C. government procurement rules to the generally excluded sector of defense procurement.

These are the major issues that have been identified as being of most direct interest and concern to the broad range of NAM's membership. These issues are identified and discussed in more detail in the report which I have presented to the subcommittee. In the near future, the NAM EC-92 Task Force will work to identify and develop specific policy positions and proposals related to some of these issues. In the meantime, I would be pleased to answer any questions that this subcommittee may have today, or to provide more detailed comments in writing.

Statement of the U.S. Semiconductor Industry Association

The Semiconductor Industry Association (SIA) is pleased to have the opportunity to testify at this hearing on "Europe 1992." My name is Michael Maibach, and I am the Director of Government Affairs for Intel Corporation.

The Semiconductor Industry Association, which represents U.S.-based semiconductor manufacturers, was created in 1977 to coordinate industry energies in solving international trade problems. In particular, SIA has focused on finding solutions to problems involving unfair trade practices and unequal access for American semiconductor products in world markets. SIA's main concern continues to be public policy issues that affect the industry's ability to remain competitive internationally. However, the range of SIA activities has expanded to include a broad spectrum of industry topics, such as occupational health, safety, and environment; industry statistics; public communications; and industry-oriented publications. The industry's interest in fostering competitiveness through cooperative ventures has led to the creation of a basic research consortium, the Semiconductor Research Corporation (SRC), and the formation of SEMA-TECH. SIA's most recent initiative is an exploration of ways to stimulate reentry by U.S. manufacturers into production of dynamic random access memory semiconductors (DRAMs), a critical sector in which the U.S.

industry has been decimated, due in large part to unfair Japanese trade practices.

SIA member firms represent over 90 percent of the U.S. industry. A list of member companies is attached.

In response to the Subcommittee's request, my testimony will address some of SIA's concerns with regard to the 1992 "single market" effort in Europe. I would emphasize that this is a very preliminary assessment; we don't know enough yet about the policy directions that Europe appears to be taking to reach any firm conclusions as to what the ultimate effects of the 1992 effort will be on U.S. companies operating in Europe. However, there have been a number of recent actions taken in Europe which have had negative repercussions for U.S. companies, and these events have caused us to take a closer look at what is happening in Europe and to be concerned about some of the signals that the Community appears to be sending in the electronics area.

Let me begin by pointing out that the European market is a very important market for U.S. semiconductor and electronics producers. Europe as a whole is one of the world's largest markets for semiconductors. Total semiconductor consumption in Europe in 1988 amounted to $8.253 billion. U.S.-based semiconductor producers were the largest suppliers to the European market, with sales of $3.697 billion (44.8% of the total European market). This compares with U.S. sales in 1988 of only $1.934 billion in the Japan market, which is now the world's largest semiconductor market (Japan's consumption of semiconductors was $18.108 billion in 1988, of which the U.S. share was 10.68%). Clearly, the United States industry has a strong interest in maintaining access to the European market, our largest export market, and we would be very concerned if we thought that the Community was trying to emulate the Japanese "closed market" model.

As you are aware, the much-heralded 1992 "single market" effort is an enormous legislative undertaking which is being implemented through increased centralization of authority in the hands of the EC Commission. Almost 300 directives will be considered as part of the EC effort to create a unified internal market of 320 million consumers. To date, I understand that the Commission has enacted some 100 directives. Among the objectives of the 1992 effort are to improve the competitiveness of EC firms, particularly in strategic sectors such as electronics; and to promote job creation through increased investment in Europe.

The creation of a single EC market certainly has the potential for many positive gains. However, the 1992 effort has also raised concerns as to whether the political and economic tradeoffs involved in that effort may result in increased barriers to non-EC companies' access to that market and/or increased pressures on non-EC companies to shift jobs, investment and technology to Europe to maintain their market presence.

One objective of the 1992 effort—to improve the competitiveness of EC firms—is nothing new in the electronics area. The EC has a long history of protection and promotion of EC electronics production. Concerns about the European industry's international competitiveness and EC dependence on foreign suppliers in critical information technologies have led to the use of policy tools which have been quite effective in increasing the competitive strength of EC producers. We estimate that over $1 billion/year is spent by the Community on government-subsidized microelectronics research and development and joint manufacturing efforts. These efforts have resulted in, among other accomplishments, a European 1-megabit DRAM capability. These same concerns have also led to European calls for a better "balance" in areas such as semiconductors, as European producers continue to lag foreign producers in share of their own market. The European Electronic Component Manufacturers Association (EECA) has been forthright in calling for subsidies, maintenance of the current tariff level on integrated circuits (ICs), "realistic" duty suspension procedures, "equitable" European origin rules, and similar policy measures aimed at improving the competitive position of European ICs vis-à-vis foreign chips.

In furtherance of its efforts to promote European electronics production, the European Community has erected a number of barriers —both tariff and nontariff—to imports. The EC has high tariffs on electronics products compared with the other major electronics-producing nations. For example, while the United States and Japan have eliminated duties on semiconductors and computer parts, the EC maintains tariffs on both—14% in the case of semiconductors.

More worrisome than tariffs—which, although they are a trade barrier, are at least transparent and less distortive than most other forms of protection—are nontariff barriers. Most of SIA's concerns in connection with 1992 have to do with what appears to be a trend toward increased use by the EC of non-transparent, non-tariff means to achieve policy objectives related to protection and promotion of European electronics industries.

This apparent trend has begun to manifest itself recently in the form of a number of initiatives which on their face may not seem to be objectionable—many can be justified for non-protectionist reasons—but which in their operation, or in their *interaction with other measures*, have had the effect (intended or not) of imposing competitive disadvantages of non-EC companies.

For example, on February 2, the EC adopted a new rule of origin for integrated circuits (ICs) under which the origin of the semiconductor is to be determined by the location of "diffusion" operations (wafer fabrication). Therefore, to obtain EC origin, a semiconductor will now have to contain a die (the silicon "chip" itself) fabricated in the EC. Prior to this change, assembly operations in the EC sufficed to bestow EC status on ICs. This change

in the EC's rule of origin for integrated circuits makes it more difficult for foreign-based companies to obtain EC origin for their products. Other restrictions require (or are interpreted, correctly or incorrectly, to require) a specified percentage of "EC content," the effect of which is to create disincentives to buy semiconductor components from non-EC suppliers—unless they have sufficient investment in the EC to achieve EC origin for their products.

Of particular concern are situations where restrictive measures (e.g., local content rules imposed in connection with quotas, procurement preferences, etc.) are applied to end products containing semiconductors. Such rules may appear innocuous in isolation, but *in combination*, they can and so operate to create incentives for downstream product manufacturers to buy European, rather than non-EC origin, components. A number of such restrictions currently exist, both at the national level and at the Community level. At the national level, examples of such restrictions include quotas imposed by several countries, including Italy and France, on imports of Japanese automobiles that contain more than a certain percentage of foreign content. There are reports that such quotas may also be imposed at the Community level. The fact that these quotas are being administered to require certain minimum levels of EC content (80% in France) to escape the quotas has an impact on U.S. suppliers of semiconductors, for whom the rapidly growing automobile end-use market is a very important market. The automotive semiconductor market in Europe was about $591 million—approximately 7% of the total European semiconductor market—in 1988. Clearly, restrictions that create incentives for manufacturers to purchase European semiconductors in place of U.S. semiconductors to avoid automobile quotas put U.S. companies at a competitive disadvantage.

At the Community level, such restrictions include special origin rules for a number of consumer electronics products which require a minimum percentage of EC content for the product to obtain EC origin (e.g., 45% for radio and TV receivers and tape recorders). Similar rules are being considered for VCRs and photocopiers. These EC content rules become important when combined with quotas, high tariffs, screwdriver assembly dumping duties or other restrictions on these downstream products, because a manufacturer can escape such restrictions by adding more EC content to its product. Again, this creates incentives for producers of these goods to replace U.S. components with EC-origin parts.

We have received reports that an EC content requirement is effectively being applied in certain dumping cases involving assembly in Europe through the EC's "screwdriver assembly" regulation. The purpose of the screwdriver assembly regulation is to avoid circumvention of antidumping duties through establishment of low-value-added assembly operations in the Community. However, problems have arisen with the way the rule apparently is being applied in combination with other EC content requirements on subassemblies to create pressure to include certain minimum amounts of EC content in the EC-assembled product. This result is not required by the screwdriver assembly rule itself and is contrary to GATT principles. The practical result, however, is that several U.S. companies have already been dropped by Japanese customers in favor or EC sources. Semiconductor vendors are also now being asked to disclose the location of diffusion operations in sales proposals, as well as to indicate what their future plans are to "Europeanize" their product lines.

A recent example will illustrate the problem. A Japanese printer manufacturer told its U.S. supplier that to avoid dumping duties on its printers assembled in Europe under the EC's "screwdriver assembly" regulation, it must "design out" U.S. semiconductors so that boards going into its printers will count as EC-origin rather than Japanese manufacturers are apparently being told that there must be at least 45% European content in the boards. By replacing U.S. chips with European chips, the European content of the boards can be raised to 45%, and the Japanese manufacturer thereby increases its total non-Japanese content in the finished product to over 40% and avoids the "screwdriver" dumping duty. (See example attached.) Note that this is accomplished without actually reducing the number of Japanese parts—Japanese content levels are maintained as U.S. chips are replaced with European chips. The loser in this equation, obviously, is the U.S. supplier.

We are concerned that there will be an increasing number of restrictions such as those I have described, with adverse consequences for U.S. exports, in connection with the entire "Europe 1992" initiative. There is a proposed EC directive on telecommunications procurement which would establish preferences for products containing 50% or more EC content (and permit discrimination against products that do not). Furthermore, there are various other EC initiatives that appear to be shaping up more as "industrial policy" measures (i.e., measures intended to force investment in Europe or promote EC industry at the expense of non-EC companies) than market-liberalizing measures.

In conclusion, what many U.S. companies see occurring—and sales have already been lost—as a result of these recent initiatives, is the prospect of a domestic content/manufacturing requirement for electronics products sold in Europe. A domestic content policy—which both the EC Commission and the U.S. government are on record as opposing—would put pressure on U.S. companies to increase significantly their manufacturing investments and technology transfers to the EC, regardless of whether competitive considerations would support such decisions, in the face of discrimination against their products if they do not. U.S. companies would feel forced to respond by transferring jobs, technology and investments to Europe. Those decisions would have important adverse implications for the U.S. economy and the U.S. industry's global competitiveness.

While it may be premature at this juncture to conclude that a "Fortress Europe" is being built in the electronics sector, the trend is not promising—we cannot afford to let it happen. Close scrutiny and further analysis of these developments is clearly warranted. We intend to keep a watchful eye on regulatory developments in Europe and urge you to Congress to do the same.

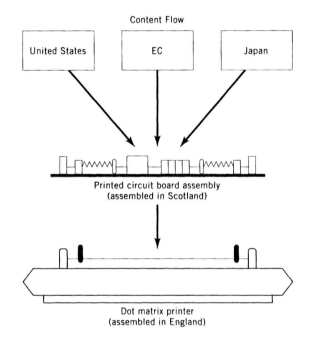

Content Flow

Printed circuit board assembly
(assembled in Scotland)

Dot matrix printer
(assembled in England)

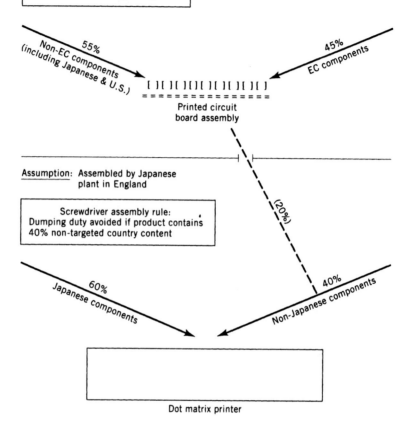

Assumption: Assembled by subcontract vendor in
Scotland engaged by Japanese company

Community safeguard rule:
If product contains 45% EC content,
it is considered EC originating

55%
Non-EC components
(including Japanese & U.S.)

45%
EC components

[ ][ ][ ][ ][ ][ ][ ][ ][ ]
= = = = = = = = = = = = = = = =
Printed circuit
board assembly

Assumption: Assembled by Japanese
plant in England

Screwdriver assembly rule:
Dumping duty avoided if product contains
40% non-targeted country content

(20%)

60%
Japanese components

40%
Non-Japanese components

Dot matrix printer

U.S. Case Study

Japanese Board

	Japan	EC	United States
Content:	55	15	30

Impact of EC
"screwdriver" rule

United States
loss of sale

EC Board

	Japan	EC	United States
Content:	55	15	0

45% EC content

DIFFERENCES IN U.S. AND EC TARIFF TREATMENT OF ELECTRONICS PRODUCTS

Tariffs	United States	EC
Components:		
Semiconductors	Duty-free	14% (Duty suspensions)
Wafers	Duty-free	9%
S/C parts	Duty-free	5.8%
Computer parts	Duty-free	4%
Completed peripherals:	3.7%	4% or 4.9%
Computers:	3.9%	4.9%

FORTY-TWO YEARS AFTER GATT WAS SIGNED: WORLDWIDE TARIFFS ON INTEGRATED CIRCUITS—1989

Country	Official IC Tariff	Comments
Argentina	5% (hybrids: 43–65%)	VAT 15% Misc. taxes = 6%
Australia	2%	
Austria		
Brazil	40–55%	
Canada	0% (considering 9% VAT)	US–Japan–Canada IC Pact
Chile	15%	
China	6% (LSI) 20% (others)	
Columbia		
EC	14%	plus 6% VAT
Finland		
Hong Kong	0%	
India	100% (150% on electronic parts)	
Indonesia	0%	10% VAT
Israel	0%	US–Israel Free-Trade Pact
Japan	0% 3% VAT	US–Japan–Canada IC Pact
Malaysia	2% on ICs—5% on IC parts	
Mexico	5–15% (hybrids: 10–40%)	
New Zealand	5%	
Norway	1 KRONER/IC	20% VAT
Philippines	10–30%	10% VAT
Singapore	0%	
South Africa	0–5%	
South Korea	20% (temporary rate: 10%)	
Spain	19.9%	Goes to EC Level 1993
Sweden	2.5%	23.5% VAT
Switzerland	50 Francs/100 KG. Gross	
Taiwan	20%	
Thailand	25–35%	
Turkey		
USA	0%	US–Japan–Canada IC Pact
Venezuela	1% w/5% surcharge on ICs	

Source: U.S. Department of Commerce.

Motor & Equipment Manufacturers Association: Prepared Statement Regarding the Impact of "Europe 1992" on the Motor Vehicle Parts Manufacturing Industry

The Motor and Equipment Manufacturers Association (MEMA) appreciates the opportunity to present its views to the House Subcommittee on Trade regarding the impact of "Europe 1992" on the motor vehicle parts manufacturing industry.

Founded in 1904, MEMA is the oldest trade association in the U.S. automotive industry. It is the only association devoted exclusively to representing and serving the needs of U.S. manufacturers of motor vehicle parts, accessories, and allied products.

The European Community (EC) is the third largest U.S. export market for motor vehicle parts after Canada and Mexico, with purchases rising from $.9 billion in 1987 to $1.4 billion last year. The percentage increase in U.S. exports to every EC country except Greece and Italy was greater than the 20% gain in total U.S. exports of motor vehicle parts from 1987 to 1988.

The United States, however, continues to run a $2 billion deficit with the EC in motor vehicle parts trade, although there was a slight decline in this deficit last year. U.S. parts imports from the EC reached $3.6 billion in 1988, up from $3.3 billion in 1987. Thus, two-way U.S.–EC trade in motor vehicle parts is substantial, and the trend has begun to reflect the growing competiveness of U.S. exporters due in part to favorable exchange rate shifts.

U.S. parts makers also have a large and growing direct investment position in Europe. Reliable data on the total book value of such investments is not available. However, survey data from the International Trade Commission's 1987 study of the industry show that annual capital expenditures by subsidiaries and affiliates of U.S. parts manufacturers in the 4 largest EC countries increased from $84 million in 1982 to over $200 million in 1986.

As these data show, our industry has a very important stake in ensuring that Europe remains a healthy market for U.S. exports, and that new trade or investment barriers are not erected.

U.S. parts manufacturers have somewhat mixed views on the implications of "Europe 1992" for their businesses. Most firms with experience as exporters or producers in Europe are guardedly optimistic that further EC market integration will promote a healthier European economy and lead to new market opportunities. This view is often not shared by companies which lack manufacturing operations or a strong distribution and sales network in the EC.

There is widespread concern that U.S. parts exporters will encounter greater difficulties in selling to the EC in the 1990s. These concerns are based on:

1. Expectations that EC auto policy, while aimed at restricting market penetration by Japanese producers and their local affiliates, will indirectly harm U.S. export interests.

2. The belief that harmonization of EC industrial standards and testing/certification policies will facilitate internal EC trade, but discourage imports from non-member countries such as the United States.

3. The likelihood that European parts manufacturers will become vastly more competitive regionally, as well as internationally, due to the "Europe 1992" process.

There are several areas of EC regulation or policy which our industry is now monitoring closely as part of their strategic planning activities. These include: EC auto industry trade policy; EC technical standardization, testing and certification policies; customs and other border regulations; and competition (antitrust, merger and acquisition, and product liability) policies. The balance of this testimony focuses on the first two, which have proven to be most controversial.

EC Auto Industry Trade Policy

While the specific terms of future auto industry trade policy are still under discussion, the general direction of this policy is clear.

- The EC will negotiate a regional export restraint agreement with Japan to replace current national arrangements. These EC-wide restraints will not be removed until EC auto exports to Japan increase to roughly half the level of Japanese exports to the EC.
- To ensure Japanese assemblers entering Europe make substantial use of local suppliers, the EC will establish stringent rules of origin as a condition for free trade in finished vehicles among member countries.

These policies, if implemented as expected, will put pressure on U.S. as well as Japanese suppliers of original equipment parts to establish or expand their manufacturing presence in Europe, whether directly or through strategic alliances with locally-based manufacturers. A number of large and mid-size U.S. parts makers already have taken such steps to avoid "Fortress Europe" and take advantage of expected growth in regional demand due to internal market liberalization.

On the positive side, new opportunities may emerge for European operations of U.S. companies with experience in selling to Japanese customers in North America. While Japanese vehicle assembly capacity in Europe lags far behind that in North America, a more aggressive Japanese push into Europe can be expected by 1990. Assembly capacity for Japanese-design cars in the EC should reach 500,000 units or more by the early 1990s.

On the negative side, EC automotive trade policy could result in:

1. Diversion of some Japanese vehicle exports to non-EC markets, including the United States;
2. Discouragement of large-scale imports of U.S.-built, Japanese-design vehicles; and/or
3. Reduced opportunities for exports of original equipment parts if EC rule of origin requirements are set at an excessive level (a minimum of up to 80% is under discussion).

Although the EC is not proposing to raise its external tariff on imports from non-member countries, EC tariffs on both vehicles and parts are significant, and are higher on average than U.S. or Japanese tariffs. In conjunction with more stringent rules of origin for automotive products, therefore, such tariffs are likely to discourage imports from the U.S. and other non-EC countries to a greater degree than in the past.

U.S. exports of replacement parts to Europe should not be affected as immediately as exports of original equipment parts by a more stringent EC rule of origin or vehicle import restraint arrangement with Japan. However, since replacement parts sales in Europe are more closely tied to vehicle producers and their original equipment suppliers, some adverse longer term affects could be felt.

Harmonization of EC Standards and Testing/Certification Policies

Through regional standards bodies (CEN/CENELEC), the EC is seeking to harmonize member country standards for industrial products based on a new concept of "essential requirements," rather than detailed design standards. The EC has pledged to rely upon existing international standards (ISO/IEC) in developing these standards, where feasible. EC members would then be required to accept products exported to them by other member countries which meet these newly defined "essential requirements."

CEN/CENELEC also is drafting a proposal to establish an EC-wide product testing and certification system. The intent is to develop a system of lab accreditation and third-party testing as a complement to manufacturers' own internal quality assurance and testing/ self certification programs.

This approach offers the potential for additional EC regulation of products produced within the Community as well as those exported to it. Moreover, non-EC manufacturers do not have adequate access to the EC standards development process, which is far less open and transparent than those used by ANSI, ASTM, and SAE in the United States. Finally, because the "mutual recognition" concept does not appear to included products made outside the EC, U.S. exporters may derive few if any benefits from the new harmonization approach.

For these reasons, MEMA is now working in cooperation with the Commerce Department and other private sector groups to improve U.S. industry's access to the EC standards development process. MEMA is encouraged by recent statements by the directors of CEN and CENELEC regarding their willingness to engage in a constructive dialogue on this issue with experts from the U.S. standards community. Commerce Secretary Mosbacher's announced support for this type of initiative also is a welcome development.

MEMA Activities Regarding "Europe 1992"

Since last year, MEMA has taken an active interest in monitoring the progress of "Europe 1992," analyzing key developments, and reporting findings to members on a regular basis. Analysis of "Europe 1992" issues and related outreach to the U.S. parts manufacturing industry will remain a focal point of MEMA's international program activities in the foreseeable future.

To date MEMA activities in this area have included:

1. close collaboration with the Commerce Department in obtaining and analyzing new Directives of Interest to members as they are issued;
2. participation in and information exchanges with various industry standards groups and broad private sector task forces considering the impact of "Europe 1992;" and
3. extensive outreach to U.S. auto parts manufacturers through participation in several industry conferences and direct reports to members.

A growing number of manufacturers in our industry are looking carefully at how "Europe 1992" will affect their market position in Europe. For exporters in particular, however, there are no clear answers regarding appropriate strategies at this stage.

EC implementation of new and planned Directives may vary significantly from stated intent and thus will require careful monitoring by both industry and government. MEMA believes sustained U.S. surveillance of the "Europe 1992" process is therefore essential to protect U.S. interests, particularly with regard to exports.

The Chip War

United States – Japan Trade Conflict in Semiconductors

RICHARD W. MOXON

Representatives of the U.S. government faced difficult choices in early April 1986 as they reassessed the progress of negotiations with the Japanese government on the semiconductor trade situation. The talks had just been suspended after reaching an impasse on the two major issues being discussed—access of U.S. firms to the Japanese market, and the pricing practices of Japanese firms in the U.S. The negotiating teams had hoped to reach an agreement before Prime Miniser Yasuhiro Nakasone's visit to the United States beginning April 12, but the prospects now appeared bleak. The issues separating the two countries were serious ones, and disagreements within the U.S. team complicated the prospects for quick compromise.

The Section 301 "unfair trade practices" complaint brought before the U.S. Trade Representative by the Semiconductor Industry Association, together with a series of dumping and other cases, had brought to a boil a controversy that had been heating up for several years. The stakes in the case were enormous, and the outcome could set the tone for U.S.–Japan trade relations in high technology for years to come. Economically, the case in-

volved an industry at the heart of modern electronics, a bedrock of U.S. industrial competitiveness and at the same time one of Japan's strategically targeted sectors. Politically, the case pitted powerful forces for "fair trade" against the "free trade" principles of the Reagan administration.

This case deals with issues concerning U.S. firms access to Japanese markets and pricing practices of Japanese firms on the U.S. markets. The case contains three parts. Part A addresses the semiconductor industry, Part B deals with the trade policy of the U.S. semiconductor industry and the government, and Part C addresses the U.S.–Japan agreement to settle semiconductor trade. The case study is accompanied by four assignments each of which can be assigned to a separate group of students.

Part A: The Semiconductor Industry

Products and Markets

The semiconductor industry produced electronics components for use in a wide variety of electronic and other equipment. Semiconductors were often considered to be the basic raw material of electronics equipment, since they were the "brains" of consumer, com-

Prepared by Professor Richard W. Moxon, University of Washington, Graduate School of Business, © 1987, as a basis for class discussion.

puter, telecommunications and military electronics devices. Semiconductor products were based on tiny chips of semiconducting materials, the most common being silicon, into which impurities were introduced to form electronic circuits. Semiconductor products were classified into two major groups:

1. *Discrete semiconductors:*—Devices containing only one active electronic element, or switch, on a chip. Diodes and transistors were the most important discrete devices.

2. *Integrated circuits:*—Devices containing many active electronic elements on a chip.

Integrated circuits, or ICs, were by far the most important semiconductor devices, and were produced using a variety of technologies for a wide range of product applications. Industry sources classified ICs by technology, function, circuit density, and degree of standardization:

1. *Technology.* The most basic distinction was between linear and digital devices. Linear devices worked with electrical signals in continuous linear form, while digital devices worked with signals having discrete values, or an "on–off" form. Some linear devices transformed signals between linear and digital forms. Another technological distinction was in the basic physics of building the desired electronic function into a semiconducting material. The two main alternatives here were bipolar and metal-oxide-silicon, or MOS, technology.

2. *Function.* The most important uses of ICs were as logic and memory devices. Logic devices ranged from simple products to microprocessors incorporating a computer processing unit on a chip, and to microcomputer chips having both processing and memory capabilities. Memory devices included random-access memories (RAMs) and read-only memories (ROMs). RAMs were used for applications requiring both reading from and writing into memory. RAMs were either dynamic (DRAMs), requiring constant voltge pulses to refresh their storage capabilities, or static (SRAMs), which maintained information as long as power was supplied. ROMs were used to store permanent information, often a hardware manufacturer's proprietary software, which was maintained even with loss of electrical power. Information was written into ROMs during manufacture, but new erasable and electrically-erasable programmable ROMs (EPROMs and EEPROMs) allowed programming and changes to the information after manufacture.

3. *Circuit density.* Density was measured by the approximate number of electronics elements on a chip. Small scale integration (SSI) referred to devices with about 10 elements per chip, medium scale (MSI) chips had about 100 elements, large scale (LSI) chips had about 1000 to 10,000, very large scale (VLSI) chips had about 100,000, and ultra large scale (ULSI) chips had on the order of a million electronic elements.

4. *Standardization.* Most semiconductor devices were produced in versatile standard designs, and in fact rival manufacturers competed to win acceptance for their products as industry standards. But increasingly users demanded custom designs tailored to their applications and allowing them to differentiate their equipment. Custom and semi-custom ICs were a rapidly growing product category.

Exhibits 29-1 through 29-3 provide breakdowns of world semiconductor sales and production by product type and geographic area. For a number of reasons the sales and production statistics for the industry were often confusing and contradictory. First, the proliferation of products meant that the statistics were reported in many different ways, and not all sources used the same definition of the industry. Second, production statistics were usually reported by headquarters location of the manufacturer. For example, production in the U.S. by a Japanese manufacturer was often reported as Japanese production. Finally, the output and use of semiconductors by so-called "captive producers," companies mainly producing semiconductors for their own use in electronics equipment, were sometimes included and sometimes excluded from industry statistics.

The United States and Japan were by far the most important markets. The mix of products sold in each country was quite different, however, reflecting the relative strengths of their end-use industries. Though this was changing, Japan's semiconductor market had traditionally been dominated by consumer electronics applications, while the U.S. market was predominantly in computers, military and industrial equipment.

Exhbit 29-4 shows estimated world semiconductor production over time. While growth had been phenomenal, the industry had suffered several times from market slowdowns generated by fluctuations in end-use markets. Such slowdowns had led at times to severe

EXHIBIT 29-1

World Semiconductor Market, 1985[a]
(estimated figures in millions of dollars)

	Discrete Devices	Integrated Circuits	Total
United States	1,750	7,400	9,150
Europe	1,275	3,675	4,950
Japan	2,200	5,800	8,000
Rest of world	450	1,000	1,450
Total	5,675	17,875	23,550

[a]Not including U.S. captive production.

Source: *Status 1986: A Report on the Integrated Circuit Industry*, Integrated Circuit Engineering Corporation, 1986.

EXHIBIT 29-2

Semiconductor Market in the United States and Japan, by Product Type, 1985
(in millions of dollars)

	United States	Japan
Discrete devices	1,460	2,584
Optoelectronic devices	271	1,212
Integrated circuits	8,665	8,074
Linear	1,192	2,108
Digital	7,473	5,966
Memories	1,946	1,668
RAMs	1,143	1,153
ROMs	788	515
Standard logic	1,780	1,218
Microprocessors & microcomputer chips	1,504	1,178
Other	2,243	1,902
Total[a]	10,396	11,870

[a]Totals don't always add up, as minor product categories sometimes omitted.

Source: *Electronics*, January 8, 1987 and January 22, 1987.

EXHIBIT 29-3

World Semiconductor Production by Geographic Headquarters Location, 1985
(millions of dollars)

	Discrete Devices	Integrated Circuits	Total
United States			
Merchant producers	1,700	9,300	11,000
Captive producers[a]	460	4,800	5,260
Total	2,160	14,100	16,260
Europe	1,175	1,460	2,635
Japan	2,380	7,050	9.430
Rest of world[b]	250	400	650
Total	5,965	23,010	28,975

[a]Companies producing mainly for their own needs.

[b]Excludes Soviet Bloc but includes People's Republic of China.

Source: *Status 1987: A Report on the Integrated Circuit Industry*, Integrated Circuit Engineering Corporation, 1987.

EXHIBIT 29-4

World Semiconductor Production and Growth Rate, 1974–1985 (millions of dollars)

Segment	1974	1975	1976	1977	1978	1979	1980	1981	1982	1983	1984	1985
North America	1,900	1,570	2,170	2,590	3,420	4,670	6,360	6,050	6,205	7,850	12,250	9,300
Europe	290	250	275	400	455	600	710	790	835	1,040	1,545	1,480
Japan	375	350	595	595	1,220	1,555	2,290	2,815	2,990	4,420	7,800	7,050
Row	40	30	40	50	65	90	130	160	165	230	370	400
Total Merchant IC	2,605	2,200	3,080	3,735	4,980	6,915	9,490	9,815	10,195	13,540	21,965	18,210
Captive ICs	400	440	675	1,050	1,300	2,010	2,695	2,900	3,160	3,625	4,280	4,800
Total WW Discrete[a]	2,900	2,250	2,900	3,150	3,700	4,000	4,460	4,730	4,450	5,070	6,650	5,965
Total WW Semiconductor	5,905	4,890	6,655	7,935	9,980	13,015	16,645	17,445	17,805	22,235	32,895	28,975

[a] Includes captive.

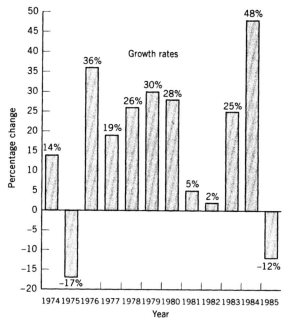

Source: *Status 1987: A Report on the Integrated Circuit Industry*, Integrated Circuit Engineering Corporation, 1987.

overcapacity in the industry. In late 1984 the industry entered the worst recession in its history, with sales in the United States falling especially fast due to a decline in computer demand. Prices dropped spectacularly for commodity-type memory products, as shown in Exhibit 29-5, causing some companies to stop production or forego market entry. Despite the recession, however, industry observers expected the worldwide semiconductor market to more than double over the next five years.

EXHIBIT 29-5

Price Decline for 256K Dram Chips

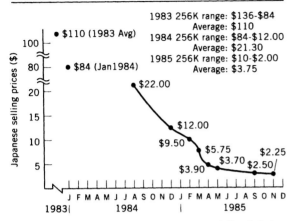

1983 256K range: $136-$84
            Average: $110
1984 256K range: $84-$12.00
            Average: $21.30
1985 256K range: $10-$2.00
            Average: $3.75

Source: *Status 1986: A Survey of the Integrated Circuit Industry*, Integrated Circuit Engineering Corporation, 1986.

Technology and Costs

The semiconductor industry was technology driven. Rapid technological progress had resulted in new products and applications that reduced costs and prices dramatically. Technology advances allowed packing more electronic elements on a chip, and accumulated experience allowed achievement of lower costs in the complex manufacturing process. Declining prices created new product applications that were previously uneconomical. Exhibit 29-6 shows the trend to increased circuit density and the declining prices of memory chips over time. Product life cycles were short, with peak sales of successive generations of memory devices only about 3 years apart.

Semiconductor manufacturing was thought to be the most complex manufacturing process used in any industry. It consisted of four major stages—the production of circuit photomasks, wafer fabrication and testing, assembly, and final testing and sorting.

Manufacturing began with a drawing, or series of drawings, of the circuit at several hundred times the final size. The drawings

EXHIBIT 29-6

Declining Prices and Increasing Circuit Density for Memory Chips

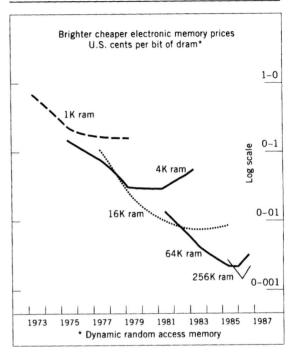

Source: "The High-tech Commodity," *The Economist*, November 22, 1986.

were reduced and used to make photomasks, which were used to transfer the circuit design to highly polished slices, or wafers, of pure silicon.

Wafer fabrication was the key step in semiconductor manufacturing. High-intensity light was beamed through the mask onto a silicon wafer coated with a light sensitive emulsion, thereby transferring the circuit pattern to the wafer. This pattern defined the regions into which impurities were introduced via a diffusion process in high temperature furnaces. This masking–diffusion sequence was repeated several times for complex circuits. A layer of aluminum was added and etched after final diffusion to form interconnections on the wafer. Throughout fabrication the wafers were tested many times. After the final fabrication step individual chips were tested in the high speed computer-controlled "wafer probe" process. The wafers were then cut into individual chips and defective devices were discarded. Wafer fabrication was capital intensive and technologically demanding, requiring the use of ultra-clean facilities, and the monitoring and control by a team of engineers and other technical personnel.

The assembly process consisted of bonding the chip to a base, connecting the chip via very fine wires to a package that could be inserted in a printed circuit board in a computer or other equipment, and sealing the package. Assembly was typically a labor-intensive operation, although it was increasingly computer-assisted, and automation was used by some manufacturers for high volume standard products. After assembly, the devices were tested and sorted according to their electronic properties. Testing was capital intensive, usually using computer-controlled equipment.

Exhibit 29-7 summarizes the manufacturing process, and shows a cost breakdown for a typical product. A very important determinant of the manufacturing cost of semiconductors was process yield. Due to the complexity of the manufacturing process, only a fraction of the chips that started the process emerged as usable devices. The fraction that survived, or yield, could vary from 5 percent for complex new circuits to 80 percent for simple devices of mature technology. Yields were typically 90 percent or more in assembly, but much lower in fabrication. Yields depended on chip complexity and on the manufacturer's process experience. Complex chips with finer features required more processing steps and a heavier investment in plant and equipment. When such a chip was first introduced, yields were typically low, but increased rapidly as experience was accumulated. A rough rule of thumb

was that cost decreased by 25 to 30 percent with each doubling of production volume of a type of device. So important was the role of learning economies, that chip pricing was often based on anticipated cost declines. By pricing low, sometimes below current cost levels, a firm hoped to gain a large share of market volume, thereby rapidly accumulating experience and reducing costs to a level where it could later achieve a high profit margin while still quoting competitive prices.

An overall breakdown of the cost structure of the industry is shown in Exhibit 29-8. Research and development spending was among the highest of any industry. Development costs for new ICs had increased greatly with rising circuit complexity, and were on the order of $100 million for an advanced microprocessor. Capital intensity had also increased. There was a significant increase in the capital/output ratio for the industry over the last few years, and a production facility for an advanced IC could cost $100 million or more. The industry's research and capital intensity meant that fixed costs accounted for a very high percentage of total costs for most products.

Competitors and Industry Structure

The major consumers of semiconductors were also the major producers, with the United States and Japan dominating the industry. The U.S. industry contained two important classes of semiconductor producers, the captive producers and the merchant producers. The captives, the most important of which were IBM and AT&T, produced chips primarily or exclusively for their own use as equipment components, and accounted for about 30 pecent of U.S. semiconductor output. The merchant producers manufactured chips primarily for outside customers, and semiconductors typically accounted for a very high percentage of their total sales. Many of these companies had been entrepreneurial ventures started by individuals or by small companies in other industries,

EXHIBIT 29-7

Manufacturing Steps, Yields and Cost Estimates for a Typical IC

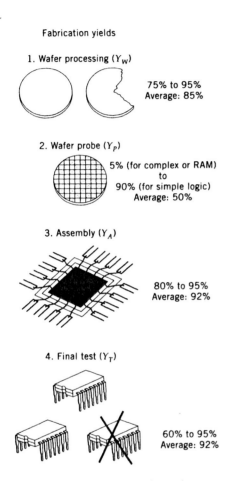

Fabrication yields

1. Wafer processing (Y_W)

75% to 95%
Average: 85%

2. Wafer probe (Y_P)

5% (for complex or RAM)
to
90% (for simple logic)
Average: 50%

3. Assembly (Y_A)

80% to 95%
Average: 92%

4. Final test (Y_T)

60% to 95%
Average: 92%

ESTIMATE OF 256K DRAM MANUFACTURING COSTS	
Cost Factors	Late 85, HMOS
Wafer size (m)	150
Wafer cost	$25.00
Wafer process cost	$150.00
Wafer processing yield	95%
Yielded whole wafer cost	$167.90
Die size (Mils^2)	50,625
Total die available	486
Wafer probe cost	$28.82
Tested wafer cost	$186.52
Probe yield	60%
Number of good dice	293
Cost per good die	$0.54
Packaging cost (plastic)	$0,10
Assembly yield	92%
Yielded assembly cost	$0.80
Burn-in cost	$0.10
Final test cost	$0.20
Final test yield	85%
Factory cost	$1.29
Gross margin	50%
Minimum profitable selling price	$2.58

Total Yield = (Y_W) (Y_P) (Y_A) (Y_T) = 29% (Average)

Source: Status 1986: A Report of the Integrated Circuit Industry, Integrated Circuit Engineering Corporation, 1986.

rather than by major existing electronics companies.

The Japanese industry was quite different from that of the United States, being based on a few large vertically-integrated and diversified electronics companies, with semiconductors typically representing less than 20 percent of sales. Five firms accounted for 70 percent or more of Japanese output for most kinds of semiconductors. These firms produced both for their own use and for sale to others, with internal sales averaging 35 percent of output.

The European industry, like that of Japan, was based on large vertically-integrated com-

EXHIBIT 29-8

Estimated Breakdown of World Semiconductor Production Value
(1986 estimates in billions of dollars)

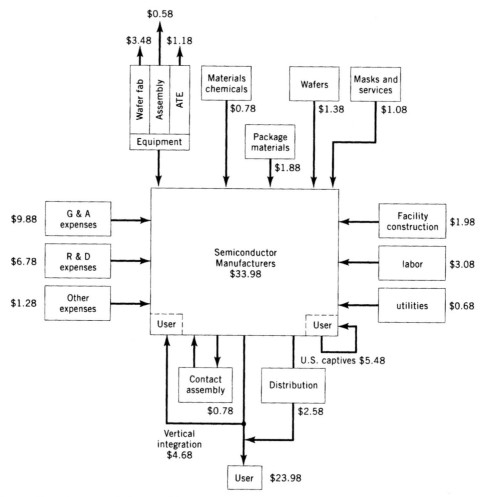

Source: *Status 1987: A Report on the Integrated Circuit Industry,* Integrated Circuit Engineering
Corporation, 1987.

panies. Unlike Japan's industry, however, the European industry was relatively weak. Government attempts to build national semiconductor companies had resulted in a fragmentation of the European market, and European firms had lagged in technology.

The industry in the rest of the world was very small outside the assembly facilities. New entrants were beginning to emerge in the developing countries, however, with the Koreans leading the way. Korean companies had acquired technology and invested heavily in fabrication facilities, and by 1986 were producing VLSI memory chips.

Exhibit 29-9 lists the most important competitors in the world semiconductor industry as of 1986. Membership and rank in this list had changed substantially from 10 years earlier, due to a wave of acquisitions, the rise of the Japanese firms to a position of prominence, and the decline or demise of other companies. The Japanese had only in the last few years risen to the top of the list. Many observers expected these trends to continue.

As chips became more complex, their function was becoming more that of "systems" than of "components," with the result that the proprietary core of much electronic equipment was imbedded in the chips. This encouraged equipment manufacturers to integrate backwards into chip production, and chip manufacturers to integrate forward into electronic systems. Magnifying this trend was the increasing capital intensity of the industry, making it difficult for the small merchant firms to survive. Some observers argued that this was a symptom of a maturing of the industry, and over time it could be expected that technology would become less important to a firm's success, while manufacturing volume and distribution strength would be needed to achieve low costs. Others disputed this analysis, noting the numerous new firms being started up, many to supply the booming custom chip market. Many of these companies specialized in quick design to customer specifications, and flexible manufacturing to allow rapid delivery. Some companies subcontracted the manufacturing of these chips to other companies, limiting themselves to the design and marketing functions and avoiding large manufacturing investments.

International Trade and Investment

The pattern of international trade reflected the structure of the industry, but also the characteristics of the production process, with a large

EXHIBIT 29-9

Worldwide Top 10 Semiconductors Firms

1985 Rank	1986 (EST) Rank	Company	1985 Production ($M)	Estimated 1985 Production ($M)
1	1	NEC	2,070	2,825
4	2	Hitachi	1,675	2,045
5	3	Toshiba	1,460	2,005
3	4	Motorola[a]	1,800	2,000
2	5	TI	1,830	1,830
6	6	Fujitsu	1,055	1,550
7	7	Philips[b]	1,010	1,215
10	8	Matsushita	855	1,165
9	9	National	950	970
—	10	Mitsubishi	660	910

[a] Includes a $150M of non-Semiconductor Sector packaging (non-hybrid).

[b] Including Signetics.

Source: Status 1987: A Report on the Integrated Circuit Industry, Integrated Circuit Engineering Corporation, 1987.

proportion of the labor-intensive assembly peformed in less-developed countries. Light weight made air transportation feasible, and encouraged international trade. National industries were also tied together by a web of international investments. Exhibit 29-10 shows in summary form the pattern of international trade in the industry.

The United States was both a big exporter and big importer of semiconductors. Europe and Japan were important export markets, while Japan was the major source of imports. U.S. trade with the developing countries consisted in large part of the export of chips to the developing countries for assembly and testing, and either re-export to the United States or export to other markets. U.S. firms had also invested in manufacturing subsidiaries in all regions. In Europe, these were both assembly and wafer fabrication plants, and U.S.-owned plants accounted for a large percentage of European production. The rationale for these plants was to overcome tariff barriers and to cultivate local customers and governments. In Japan, entry by U.S. firms was much slower, due in large part to Japanese government policies. Texas Instruments was the only merchant firm to have a Japanese manufacturing facility until 1980, and U.S. semiconductor investment in Japan was still very low in 1986. Liberalization of foreign in-

vestment regulations, and the need to be close to major customers, encouraged several U.S. firms to aggressively expand investments in Japan, and by 1986 several firms had established, or were in the process of establishing, assembly and wafer fabrication plants in Japan. Many U.S. firms were heavily engaged in investment in assembly operations in developing countries, with most plants concentrated

EXHIBIT 29-10

Overview of International Trade in Semiconductors, 1985 (billions of dollars)

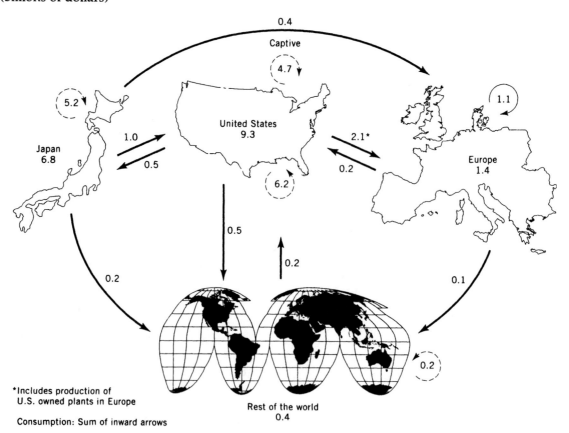

*Includes production of U.S. owned plants in Europe

Consumption: Sum of inward arrows

Rest of the world 0.4

Source: Status 1987: A Report of the Integrated Circuit Industry, Integrated Circuit Engineering Corporation, 1987.

in Southeast Asia. These operations benefitted from a provision of U.S. tariff law allowing import duties to be assessed only on the value added abroad. IBM was an exception to this pattern, favoring more automated assembly in the United States.

Japanese exports of semiconductors only began increasing rapidly in the mid-1970s, but by the mid-1980s Japan enjoyed a substantial trade surplus in semiconductors. Exhibit 29-11 shows the trend of U.S.–Japan semiconductor trade. In recent years Japanese firms had begun investing in the United States and Europe in both assembly and wafer fabrication facilities. Japanese acquisitions in the United States had been minor, the largest being NEC's acquisition of Electronic Arrays in 1978. Unlike U.S. firms, Japanese investment in assembly plants for semiconductors in developing countries was modest, reflecting their tendency to automate assembly rather then rely on labor intensive operations.

Most European production was for the European market, and the major firms were not major players in export markets. In an attempt to overcome technological and market limits,

EXHIBIT 29-11

U.S.–Japan Trade in Integrated Circuits, 1975–1985

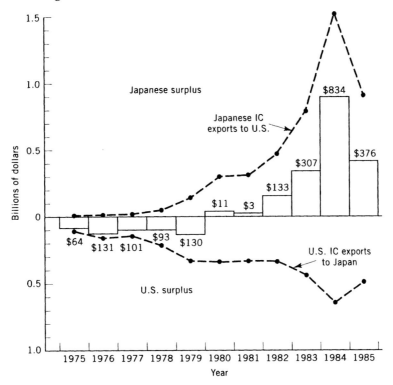

Source: *Status 1987: A Report on the Integrated Circuit Industry*, Integrated Circuit Engineering, 1987.

however, European companies had acquired a number of U.S. producers, a trend that peaked in the late 1970s with the acquisitions of Signetics by Philips, and of Fairchild by Schlumberger.

Government Policies

The semiconductor industry was seen as strategic by many governments, due to its technological connections with other industries and its defense implications, and government policies designed to maintain or improve the capabilities of local companies were pervasive. Since governments owned some of the important customers, especially the telecommunications monopolies in many countries, they had easy points of leverage. Government policy had a major impact on the competitiveness of national industries.

From the invention of the transistor in 1948 until the mid-1960s, the U.S. government played an important role in stimulating the development of the semiconductor industry. Military requirements and R&D programs, emphasizing miniaturization, reliability and high performance in combat conditions, set the direction for product design, and defense and space procurement provided important early markets on which the U.S. industry accumulated design and manufacturing experience. Government demand provided the base for commercial development and competitiveness. Also critical was government policy with respect to Bell Laboratories, the AT&T subsidiary that did much of the early basic semiconductor research work. Under an antitrust consent decree in 1956, Bell Labs technology was allowed to diffuse cheaply to small new firms which then commercialized it.

After these early years, the government influence on the industry waned. Circuit development was largely based on the evolving needs of the computer industry, which set the direction for design and provided the volume orders. In the mid-1970s, with the develop-

ment of the microprocessor and semiconductor memories, the end-use markets broadened into consumer, telecommunications and other products. Government sponsorship of semiconductor R&D also had a relatively minor effect on commercial competitiveness. The military became increasingly concerned with the slow pace at which commerical technology was transferred to military uses, resulting finally in a DOD-sponsored very-high-speed-integrated-circuit project designed to overcome this problem.

In Japan, government policy had different objectives and used different methods. Whereas the U.S. industry was the leader, Japan was a follower, and government policy attempted to help the industry to catch up. Government policy focused on overcoming the technology gap with U.S. firms, and on providing a protected home market in which Japanese companies could build experience and reach competitive volumes and costs.

Limits on the entry of foreign companies, and the aggressive licensing of foreign technology, were important in the early development of the industry. Both imports and incoming foreign investment were tightly controlled. High tariffs and restrictive quotas limited market penetration by foreign firms, and the government consistently rejected foreign bids to establish manufacturing facilities or acquire Japanese firms. The price to U.S. firms for limited access to the Japanese market was the licensing to Japanese companies of advanced technology. Texas Instruments was the most aggressive entrant, but its intent to establish a wholly-owned subsidiary in Japan was strongly resisted by Japanese producers. It was finally allowed to establish a joint venture with Sony (later converted to a wholly-owned subsidiary) after agreeing to license key elements of its IC technology to Japanese firms and agreeing to limit its market share in Japan. The early 1980s saw an easing of access of the Japanese market, and in fact in 1985 all tariffs were removed. But U.S. firms contended that both government policy and the policies of Japanese companies made market penetration by foreign firms very difficult.

The other major policy of the Japanese government was the encouragement of joint development of technology. Programs such as the VLSI project in the 1970s brought together the major industry competitors in developing basic technologies, and in refining manufacturing techniques. These technologies were then commercialized by individual firms, often with government help through low-cost financing and premium-price government procurement. The government support of technology development and acquisition, together with protection from foreign competition in its formative years, allowed Japanese competitors to catch up and become world competitors.

European policies also aimed to catch up to the United States, but were different from those of Japan in many respects. While the European Community maintained a relatively high tariff, and non-tariff barriers existed in many countries, U.S. firms were successful in establishing local manufacturing facilities, thereby absorbing much of the market growth and denying local competitors the volume of production needed to accumulate experience. Several governments were anxious to maintain "national champions," but the small size of national markets made this a costly policy. Attempts to form European research and manufacturing consortia floundered in the face of national pressures, with the result that the "European" industry was by the 1980s made up largely of relatively weak national producers and the European subsidiaries of U.S. companies.

Part B: The Trade Conflict

Early Developments

The U.S. industry's concern with Japanese competition began with the Japanese invasion of the 16K DRAM market in the late 1970s. The Japanese competitors gained a foothold in the U.S. market during a period of booming demand in 1978 and 1979. U.S. production shortages of these new chips, caused in part by a cutback in investment by U.S. competitors during the recession of the mid-1970s, allowed the Japanese firms to attract U.S. customers. As they gained a reputation for quality and reliable delivery, they quickly took over 40 percent of the 16K merchant market by 1979. As new U.S. capacity came into production, and the market began to soften, prices declined steeply, and producers recorded substantial losses in this product line.

The competition in the next major memory market product, the 64K DRAM, was quite different, with the Japanese transformed into market leaders. Fujitsu was the first to market a 64K chip, but was closely followed by its U.S. and Japanese competitors. The U.S. firms experienced considerable difficulty in producing these chips in commercial quantities. By late 1981 only Motorola and Texas Instruments were producing in large amounts, and against them were arrayed six Japanese firms, who managed to capture about 70 percent of the world merchant market for the product in 1982. Relatively slow development of the market allowed other U.S. firms to enter, but continued aggressive capital investment and pricing by the Japanese allowed them to maintain their market share.

As part of a lobbying campaign asking for a broad range of reforms in U.S. government tax, R&D and trade policies, the Semiconductor Industry Association (SIA) had consistently taken the lead in U.S. complaints about Japanese competitive practices. Its complaints about alleged Japanese dumping of 16K and 64K chips were thought to have influenced the Japanese firms to alter their pricing behavior. It also initiated a series of studies and lobbying efforts attacking Japanese government protection and subsidization of the semiconductor industry. By 1982 the SIA had encouraged the U.S. government to begin a series of negotiations with the Japanese government to identify and address sources of trade friction in semiconductors. Intensive discussions were held in this so-called U.S.–Japan High Technology Working Group. In 1983 this group produced a series of recommendations, later endoresed by the two governments, which were aimed to eliminate barriers to market access. The Japanese government agreed to encourage major Japanese semiconductor users to buy U.S. products, and U.S. companies stepped up their sales efforts in Japan.

Although initial indicators were encouraging, by 1985 the SIA was clearly disappointed with the lack of progress in increasing sales in the Japanese market. In that year it produced a report, *The Impact of Japanese Market Barriers in Microelectronics*, detailing its complaints about continued Japanese government barriers to imports and foreign investment, asserting the importance of the U.S. semiconductor industry for the U.S. economy, and calling for increased U.S. government efforts to open the Japanese market. The recession in the computer industry, and the consequent reduction in sales in semiconductors, made the situation even more pressing in the SIA's eyes.

Despite increasing agitation in the U.S. indusry about Japanese competition, progress seemed to be made in discussions between the two governments through early 1985. So-called market-oriented sector-selective (MOSS) talks for semiconductors were initiated between the two governments in early 1985. In April the two countries agreed to eliminate tariffs on semiconductor imports, and in May the Japanese government enacted a U.S.-requested law aiding the protection of proprietary semiconductor designs. And while the SIA continued its intensive lobby efforts, neither it nor U.S. companies had formally filed dumping or unfair practices complaints. Some observers noted that the SIA was dissuaded from taking this final plunge because of dis-

agreement among its members. Representing both major producers and users of semiconductors, it was difficult for the group to find a consensus on just what U.S. policy should be.

In June 1985, however, both dumping and unfair trade practices actions were filed against the Japanese. These were followed later in the year by antitrust and patent infringement suits. The following sections summarize the issues in the dumping and unfair trade practices cases.

The Dumping Cases

Three dumping suits were filed against Japanese semiconductor firms in 1985, claiming that the U.S. industry was injured by reason of Japanese pricing at less than fair value. The first suit, filed by Micron Technology, a small U.S. firm, concerned 64K DRAMs. The second concerned EPROMs, and was filed by Intel, National Semiconductor and Advanced Micro Devices. The third was filed by the U.S. government, and involved 256K and larger DRAMs. Government-initiated dumping cases were very unusual, and the fact that it included products that were not even being produced or imported in commercial quantities seemed to illustrate an attempt to deal with the criticism that the anti-dumping laws were often "too little and too late."

The dumping suits followed a standard procedure prescribed in U.S. trade law. The U.S. International Trade Commission (ITC) investigates the claim of injury, while the Department of Commerce (DOC) simultaneously investigates the claim of dumping. Each issues both a preliminary finding and a final determination. If the preliminary findings indicate that both injury and dumping exist, a bond equal in value to the preliminary dumping margin —the percentage by which fair market value exceeds the actual prices—must be posted for all imports brought into the United States after the preliminary finding. Dumping margins may vary from exporter to exporter. If the final determinations are that dumping and injury exist, duties equal to the final dumping margin are collected on all subsequent imports, and duties are also collected on imports occurring after the preliminary finding, up to the amount of the posted bond. The DOC must review the dumping ruling at least once a year, and the duties can be reduced or eliminated if the dumping margins are found to have changed.

The anti-dumping law specifies that a comparison between the export price (in this case the price quoted by the Japanese for export to the U.S.) and the price in the foreign market (in this case the price in Japan) is the preferred method of determining dumping. But if the export price is below the foreign cost of production, then a so-called "constructed value" is substituted for the foreign market price. The constructed value includes the costs of materials, labor and other manufacturing costs, plus general selling and administrative costs (which must equal to at least 10 percent of the first group of costs), plus a profit margin (which must equal at least 8 percent of all the costs above), plus packing and distribution costs. The DOC prefers to obtain such data from the foreign firms, but if this is not possible it uses the best available data. If the foreign firms submit data, the DOC discusses the data with the firms and attempts to verify its accuracy and compatibility with U.S. definitions of costs. Adjustments are often needed in the allocation of overheads to reflect fully allocated average costs.

The three dumping suits involved similar issues, so for simplicity only the EPROM case will be described in detail. The petitioners alleged first that Japanese firms were selling EPROMs in the United States at less than fair value. They further stated that since Japanese prices also were less than production costs, that the comparison had to be based on "constructed value." The petitioners provided cost estimates for Japanese producers based on a model of the costs of Hitachi, the largest

Japanese EPROM producer. The cost estimates were based on estimates of input costs, of the yields of usable chips in the manufacturing process, and of reasonable allocations of R&D and other costs. Dumping margins of from 135 to 227 percent at the distributor level, and 76 to 145 percent at the end-user level were found. The petitioners said that they based their estimates on the best available data, but suggested that the DOC should ask for actual data on Japanese yields in order to generate better estimates.

With regard to the question of injury, the petitioners alleged that the Japanese were trying to drive U.S. manufacturers out of the EPROM business, and that the evidence suggested that they were succeeding. Instead of cutting production, these firms were said to drop prices way below the costs that would be expected using a normal learning curve. In this way the Japanese kept accumulating experience and lowering their costs, while the Americans were prevented from recouping their investments in R&D and facilities, making it difficult to make needed investments in the next generation of technology. The Japanese market share in the United States was estimated to be 60 percent of the 64K and 128K EPROMs, and 20 percent in 256K. This resulted in an estimated loss of revenue of $45 million over the latest one year period. Furthermore, excess Japanese capacity offered no hope for more reasonable pricing in the future. Key to the argument was a Hitachi memo to its U.S. distributors stating "Win with the 10% rule. Find AMD and Intel sockets; quote 10% below their price; if they requote, go 10% again; don't quit until you win!" Hitachi claimed that the memo did not reflect official company policy; though it admitted that it originated in a Hitachi office.

In conducting their investigations, the DOC sent questionnaires to the Japanese firms requesting cost information, and the ITC held a hearing and accepted written submissions from interested parties. In the EPROM case, despite complaints about the amount of information required and worries about confidentiality, three of four Japanese firms submitted cost information.

Several Japanese firms also submitted testimony to the ITC. They argued that the petitioners lacked standing to submit such a petition, as they did not produce the product in the United States. This argument was based on the fact that all the petitioners fabricated EPROM chips in the United States, but performed final assembly offshore. This argument reflected the complex pattern of trade and investment relationships in the industry. While U.S. firms assembled offshore in developing countries, Fujitsu assembled in the United States and could thus be considered a U.S. producer. Likewise, Texas Instruments and Motorola declined to join in the petition, as both produced EPROMs in Japan, and imported them to the United States. The Japanese firms also argued that in evaluating injury, the ITC should consider the health of both captive and merchant producers. They argued that no evidence of injury existed, and that if any injury could be found, it was fully attributable to other causes, especially the decline in demand by the personal computer industry. No causal nexus existed between imports and injury, as it was impossible to determine who was pricing more aggressively, and the Japanese had a smaller market share than what was alleged.

Preliminary findings of dumping and injury were issued by the DOC and ITC in all three cases in late 1985 and early 1986. The dumping margins ranged from 9 percent to 188 percent, varying by product and manufacturer. Appendix 29-1 is a copy of the DOC finding in the EPROM case, and illustrates how it calculated fair value. In this same case, the ITC rejected the argument that the petitioners lacked standing, arguing that EPROM chips were substantially the same product as finished EPROMs. The ITC found that injury existed, basing its determination on falling prices, profits, wages and capacity utilization, and on rising inventories. It also found that imported products contributed to injury through lost sales and reduced prices by domestic manufacturers. Final rulings of dumping and injury in these cases were expected over the period of April to July.

The Section 301 Unfair Trade Practices Case

In June 1985, the Semiconductor Industry Association (SIA) filed a petition asking the U.S. government to investigate under Section 301 of the 1974 Trade Act alleged unfair trade practices by the Japanese government. Section 301 gave the government broad powers to investigate allegations of unfair trade practices by foreign governments and to seek remedies. Section 301 was amended in 1984 to include restrictions on foreign market access as a basis of complaint and action. Petitions were brought to the U.S. Trade Representative (USTR), which determined if the petition had any merit and then began an investigation. Under Section 301, the USTR simultaneously investigated the case and began negotiations with the foreign government. It had one year to resolve the case or to submit its recommendation to the President. The President then had 21 days in which to decide on action. Section 301 cases provided considerable discretion to the executive branch on the handling of the case, and required a less strict standard of proof than dumping and other trade actions.

The SIA petition alleged that U.S. semiconductor firms faced severe barriers to access to the Japanese market. While barriers to trade and investment had been "liberalized", the effects of past barriers were still being felt. Furthermore, the Japanese government was alleged to tolerate a market structure conducive to collusion and that effectively excluded outsiders. Japanese government support for the industry led to capacity expansion races that led to periodic overcapacity of the industry and dumping of semiconductors in the U.S. market.

The SIA offered as evidence of market barriers the fact that the U.S. firms' share of the Japanese market had remained at a level of approximately 10 percent since the early 1970s, a share much lower than in any other national or regional market. The SIA contrasted this with the growing share of the Japanese in the U.S. market, which by 1984 was alleged to be 17 percent. The SIA argued that although foreign entry had been liberalized since the mid-1970s, a series of countermeasures were used by the government to offset the effects of liberalization. These included restrictions on entry to the industry and encouragement for each Japanese firm to specialize in certain devices, creating scale economies and an incentive to firms to buy from one another. The government was also said to encourage cooperative R&D, production and sales, and provided subsidies to research programs with clear commercial objectives. The SIA contended that the government tolerated this market structure rather than investigating violations of the country's antitrust laws. In addition, the SIA argued that the Japanese government had failed to adhere to the agreement reached under the U.S.–Japan High Technology Working Group. While some semiconductors were purchased from U.S. firms, they were seen as residual suppliers, to be used only when a product could not be obtained from a Japanese firm.

The SIA claimed that the unfair practices had substantially injured the industry and U.S. national interests. Denial of access to the Japanese market, as well as Japanese dumping had reduced the revenues of U.S. firms, and constrained amounts available for investment in R&D and equipment. Some manufacturers

had been forced out of certain product lines, and a lower level of sales limited their ability to achieve learning economies. The SIA alleged that allowing Japanese producers to take over the industry would put U.S. equipment producers at the mercy of future Japanese pricing and supply policies, when these same Japanese firms competed with the United States in electronics equipment.

The SIA requested that the U.S. government seek relief in several ways, the most important of which were (1) that the Japanese government effectively encourage its firms to purchase from U.S. firms, and that this effectiveness be judged by results, specifically U.S. market share in Japan, (2) that the U.S. government implement a system for gathering data on Japanese costs and for monitoring Japanese export prices so as to swiftly act against dumping, and (3) that the U.S. government seek to encourage an investigation by the Japan Fair Trade Commission of possible violations of Japanese antitrust laws.

The Electronics Industry Association of Japan (EIAJ) responded formally to the SIA petition by filing an extensive brief with the USTR. The EIAJ maintained that the announcement of so-called "countermeasures" was necessary to gain political support for liberalization, but that they were never effectively enforced. Specifically, there was no government-mandated division of production, no prohibition on entry to the industry, and no excessive concentration. The only effective measure was the government support of cooperative R&D, a domestic subsidy of a type permitted by GATT, and used by the U.S. government to support defense-related R&D. The EIAJ contended that there was nothing illegal about the Japanese industry structure of practices, that there was no evidence of collusion, and that any specialization that existed was due to competition and the need to reduce costs. It also noted the existence of large vertically-integrated producers in the United

States, and argued that the failure of firms like GE and RCA to achieve success in the merchant chip market indicated that size was not a guarantee of success.

The EIAJ presented several reasons for the U.S. failure to gain a larger market share in Japan, including the strong dollar, low product quality, less reliable delivery, poorer technical support and service, an unwillingness to modify designs, the lack of products suitable to the consumer electronics users that dominated Japanese demand, and the lack of local manufacturing facilities, especially as compared to the case in Europe. The more successful firms in Japan, Texas Instruments and Motorola, had overcome many of these problems. In short, the EIAJ contended that while restrictions had existed in the past, the Japanese market was now open, and that the Japanese government could not be expected to force Japanese private firms to buy inferior U.S. products.

The EIAJ disputed the SIA market share estimates for the United States and Japan. It contended that the SIA's failure to include production of U.S. captive producers resulted in overstating the Japanese share in the United States, and the U.S. market share in Japan was said to be understated. The EIAJ alleged that the U.S. market share in ICs in Japan was 19 percent, while the share of the Japanese in the United States was less than 10 percent. The EIAJ had trouble supporting its figures, however, and the SIA figures were generally viewed to be more reliable. The EIAJ noted that there was no apparent injury to U.S. firms, that the industry was still strong and profitable, and that any injury was largely the result of a slowdown in the U.S. market.

The EIAJ denied the charge of dumping, and while recognizing the tendency of Japanese firms to take a longer term view and continue investments during a slump in demand, noted that they had reduced investments recently in response to industry conditions. In addition, it seemed unreasonable to file a dumping charge in an industry known for its "learning curve pricing."

The remedies requested by the SIA were strongly contested by the EIAJ. The SIA seemed to be asking for a guaranteed share of the Japanese market, rather than equal market opportunities, a clear violation of GATT principles. The requested cost and price monitoring system was alleged by the EIAJ to be unworkable and extremely costly, given the dynamic technological and cost changes in this industry. Finally, the EIAJ noted that the SIA seemed to be suggesting a radical restructuring of the Japanese industry, a remedy that was unwarranted given the increasing tendency toward vertical integration in the United States and the obvious pro-competitive nature of the Japanese industry.

The USTR began pursuing negotiations with the Japanese government regarding these issues in August 1985, and removed these issues from the MOSS talks. The government worked very closely with representatives of the U.S. industry, briefing them in detail before and after meetings with the Japanese negotiators. U.S. industry officials had also reportedly met privately with Japanese representatives in an attempt to settle the case. The Japanese government proposed a floor price mechanism as a simple way to prevent low-priced imports to the United States. The U.S. government countered that such a plan would allow high-cost firms to continue dumping while low-cost firms might achieve excessive profits. It supported instead a company-by-company cost–price monitoring system. Regarding market access, the U.S. government asked for a commitment that U.S. firms achieve a substantial and growing share of the Japanese market, but refrained from a request for any specific figure. The Japanese government suggested only that it commit to efforts resulting in a gradual increase in the U.S. share. It also argued that any agreement should include ending the dumping suits. The U.S. government wanted only to suspend them, leaving it free to resume them later if the agreement was not working.

Discussions continued in late 1985 and early 1986, but little progress was made in narrowing the differences separating the two sides. A particularly tense exchange resulted when the U.S. government filed its 256K dumping case in December 1985, leading to a temporary Japanese walkout. The latest meeting, late in March 1986, ended in little if any progress toward an agreement. The U.S. team was obviously frustrated, and scheduled a meeting among the various agencies to reassess the U.S. position.

Economic and Political Pressures

The U.S. inter-agency group involved in the negotiations had been subject to conflicting pressures in attempting to forge an agreement with the Japanese government, and was far from united in its thinking and approach. While the USTR and the Department of Commerce were mostly concerned with the health of the domestic industry, the Department of State and the National Security Council representatives were more responsive to international political and security issues. Others like the Office of Management and the Budget were exponents of a free-market approach, and were skeptical of any kind of governmental intervention.

Similar pressures were thought to exist in Japan within the government, and between the government and the industry. The Ministry of Industry and Trade (MITI) was thought to recognize the seriousness of the problem with the United States, but could not be seen to be caving in to U.S. pressure. The Ministry of Foreign Affairs was naturally more concerned with smoothing relations with the Americans. The industry seemed to be following a hard line, and although MITI appeared

to be in full control of the negotiations, it was unclear how much leverage they had with the companies.

While the Reagan administration was committed to free trade, and had successfully resisted some of the most protectionist legislative proposals, it had shown a willingness to bend in several cases. And proponents of government intervention were becoming more sophisticated in their arguments. In fact some of the newest theories of international trade, emphasizing the role of scale economies and technology, seemed to offer a powerful justification for a "strategic" use of trade controls. With the semiconductor industry's defense and technological importance, and its historically strong support for free trade, the government certainly could not sit by and let the industry "go down the tubes." On the other hand, trade controls could hurt the U.S. consumers of semiconductors, and take the pressure off the industry to improve competitiveness on its own. And not everyone thought the industry was in a desperate situation, as is illustrated by the press report in Appendix 29-2.

Political pressures for a more activist trade policy were particularly powerful in the spring of 1986. A host of protectionist trade bills were still under consideration in Congress, and it was possible that a bill could make it to the floor in the early fall, just before the elections. Congress wanted something done about the mounting trade deficit, and even some of the more level-headed representatives and senators were prone to blame the situation on the Japanese. With a new round of GATT trade negotiations in the planning stage, the administration would have to go to Congress soon to ask for negotiating authority. The administration would need to show its toughness if it was to get congressional cooperation.

All these considerations were in the minds of group members as they considered once again what sort of an agreement with the

Japanese, if any, might make sense, and how it could be implemented.

Part C: Agreement and Aftermath

The Agreement

On August 1, 1986, the United States and Japan announced a five-year agreement to settle their dispute regarding semiconductor trade. The U.S. government agreed to suspend the semiconductor dumping suits in exchange for Japanese government agreement to prevent the dumping of semiconductors in the United States and third country markets and to open the Japanese market to sales of foreign semiconductors. The U.S. Department of Commerce was to set periodically the minimum prices at which each Japanese producer could sell in the United States, based on estimates of each company's costs. The Japanese governemnt was to police the agreement by monitoring the costs and prices of Japanese chip makers. There was also an implicit understanding that the government would monitor investment in chipmaking capacity, since overcapacity was seen as the root of the problem. The Japanese government also agreed to establish an organization to help foreign chip manufacturers sell in Japan. While the agreement specified no target percentage for the market share of U.S. chip makers in Japan, it was reported that the two governments had informally agreed to a 20 percent target share by 1990. The governments were to meet every six months to review the implementation of the agreement.

Complaints

Less than two months after the signing, the SIA asked the U.S. government to investigate violations of the agreement. The complaint noted continued serious dumping in third country markets, and insufficient efforts to open the Japanese market. The restraints on exports to the United States had caused a glut in the Japanese market, resulting in price declines in Japan and in Asian export markets. A gray market developed rapidly, in which cheap chips were bought in Asia and then imported to the United States outside Japanese government monitoring. There was also a tremendous temptation for the Japanese producers to sell chips cheaply to other Asian markets, where they could be assembled into printed circuit boards or finished products for export to the United States. The Japanese market glut also made it difficult for American producers to increase their market share in Japan.

The Japanese government had issued voluntary export controls and had been monitoring chip exports and prices, but as U.S. complaints intensified it tightened its controls. Guidelines on production quantities were announced, and while these did not have the force of law, they were believed to be generally followed. It also began policing third country exports more closely, and using its control of export licenses to limit the gray market. But its response was too little and too late to satisfy the United States.

Retaliation

As the two governments met in early 1987 to review U.S. complaints about implementation of the agreement, discussions became very heated, with threats and counterthreats filling the press reports. The Reagan Administration was under heavy pressure to retaliate against what was billed as Japanese failure to live up to the agreement, but at the same time was reluctant to take action that would hurt U.S. chip users or other companies. Its options included abrogating the agreement, retaliating against chip imports, or retaliating against other Japanese imports.

On April 17, 1987 the U.S. government imposed 100 percent penalty tariffs on selected Japanese products—certain portable and desktop computers, some color TV models, and selected power tools. These products were selected to have an impact on the Japanese companies exporting chips to the United States, but at the same time not to harm U.S. consumers and chip users. Retaliation was not in the form of limits on chip imports, as this might have resulted in U.S. chip users being put at a disadvantge with respect to foreign competitors. And the products selected had ready substitutes from other sources, limiting the impact on consumers. A portion of the sanctions was targeted specifically at the third country dumping, while another portion at the failure to open the Japanese market.

The portion of the retaliatory tariffs directed at third country dumping, those on televisions and power tools, was lifted in November 1987, but the portion directed at the opening of the Japanese market was left in place. Talks continued into 1988, both between the two governments and between chip makers from the two countries. Dumping was no longer seen to be a problem, but some U.S. firms continued to be unhappy about their inability to penetrate the Japanese market. In late 1987 U.S. exports reportedly accounted for 12.3 percent of the Japanese market, down from 12.6 percent six months earlier, but up from 10.3 percent in early 1986. With a growing total market in Japan, U.S. exports had increased substantially, but some U.S. companies complained that the declining market share was clear evidence of insufficient Japanese commitment to buy foreign chips. Japanese negotiators countered that there was no guaranteed U.S. market share in Japan, and that U.S. firms were making insufficient efforts to penetrate the market. Customers in Japan complained that U.S. firms were unwilling to develop the types of chips they needed, and that delivery schedules were too long. Some U.S. firms with operations in Japan, particu-

larly Texas Instruments and Motorola, however, expressed satisfaction with their efforts to sell in Japan. But by summer 1988 pressure was building again for increased U.S. action against Japan.

Chip Prices

The two years after the agreement saw a strong recovery of memory chip prices. The new one megabit DRAMs were in particularly short supply, but 256K DRAMs were also affected. Prices for 256K chips were approximately $6 in early 1988, three times the levels of two years earlier. Some computer makers were forced to delay shipments due to inability to obtain sufficient chips, and memory-intensive software development was being held up due to the cost of memory. Even IBM was affected, though its in-house chip production increasingly insulated it from these outside developments.

The remaining U.S. DRAM producers, giant Texas Instruments and little Micron Technology, were booming. Micron saw sales go from $20.1 million in the quarter ending March 1987 to $58.3 one year later, and moved from a loss of $10.9 to a profit of $16.9. The profits of Japanese producers were also way up. Other U.S. companies had not jumped back into DRAM production, but Motorola announced in late 1987 that it would reenter with production of one and four megabit chips using technology obtained in an agreement with Toshiba. Computer hardware and software producers were unhappy with the rising prices, and some blamed the chip agreement. One computer maker, Atari, even sued Micron for breach of contract, alleging that Micron had broken an agreement to sell chips at a given price, and had insisted on a higher price. Other observers, however, blamed the rising prices on the booming market and on difficulties some companies were having in increasing production of one megabit chips, and saw the agreement as having little impact.

Other Reactions to the Agreement

Japanese chip makers increasingly looked to the United States as a source of production, though their investment in U.S. manufacturing was in most cases cautious. NEC was the only company with a commercial production operation in the United States as of 1987, but Hitachi announced that it intended to begin production of memory chips in the United States in 1988, and others were expected to make similar moves. The dramatic rise of the yen made such investments increasingly attractive.

The most dramatic Japanese move to establish a U.S. chip manufacturing presence was Fujitsu's attempted acquisition of Fairchild. Fairchild was one of the U.S. chip pioneers, but as its fortunes declined it was acquired in 1979 by the French company Schlumberger. It was generally seen as having a weak competitive position, and had been losing money heavily. Fujitsu's planned acquisition, announced in late 1986 at a price of over $200 million, caused immediate complaints by other U.S. chip makers, who complained that the acquisition violated U.S. antitrust laws and would make the U.S. defense industry too dependent on foreign-made chips. In early 1987 Fujitsu, citing political tensions between the United States and Japan, dropped its acquisition plan, and instead agreed with Fairchild to pursue technological cooperation. Later Fujitsu announced plans to build its own factory in the United States, and National Semiconductor acquired Fairchild for $122 million.

The Europeans were unhappy about the chip agreement, fearing that they would be hurt. The European Community filed a complaint with GATT in late 1986 alleging that Japanese government monitoring of export prices, and licensing of exports, violated GATT guidelines and harmed European chip customers by raising prices. It also alleged that the opening of the Japanese market was biased in favor of U.S. firms. The Japanese government denied these allegations. In early 1988 the GATT investigative panel agreed with the Europeans on the complaint against export price controls, but did not find the agreement biased against European exporters in Japan. The Japanese government was expected to be able to modify its monitoring of exports to conform to GATT guidelines and still satisfy the requirements of the chips agreement.

The Koreans, on the other hand, were happy with the chip accord. As Korean companies increased capacity in 256K memories, and invested in one megabit and four megabit development, the agreement helped provide a price umbrella. Korean productivity and prices were seen to be reaching Japanese levels for these basic commodity memory products.

The SIA continued to press aggressively for government attention to the competitive problems of the semiconductor industry. As the chairman of the SIA put it: "We can continue to sit back and watch the Japanese assult yet another critical American industry, or we can do what is necessary to repel this attack." It wanted government subsidies and incentives for semiconductor R&D and manufacturing. The group in early 1987 announced formation of a consortium of chip manufacturers, SEMATECH, with government backing to share development of new manufacturing processes. This effort was controversial, however, with some doubting the ability to coordinate the efforts of the partners, and some small chip makers seeing it as a government subsidy for the big commodity chip manufacturers.

Future Competition in the Semiconductor Industry

Chip competition was changing rapidly. International and domestic alliances were increasingly common. In the United States, Texas Instruments and Intel announced an agreement to jointly develop a line of semi-custom chips. Motorola and Toshiba agreed to a significant exchange of technology, as well as a joint venture in Japan, and many other alliances had been signed both among large manufacturers and between small and large companies on both sides of the Pacific. Many observers saw the semiconductor market moving increasingly to custom or semicustom chips. ASICs (application specific integrated circuits) were a booming market, and both large and small U.S. and Asian competitors were trying to establish their positions. Over 100 new chip companies had been established in the United States in the 10 years up to 1988, most in this custom chip market. Many of these specialized in design, while contracting out production to other firms in the United States, Japan, Korea and Taiwan. Some observers saw this as proof of the dynamism and health of the U.S. industry, while others predicted that even this custom market would ultimately be dominated by large integrated firms, and that the U.S. success would be short-lived. But the U.S. firms continued to dominate the huge microprocessor market, and some even saw hope for the United States to reconquer the memory market. The development of new technology such as "flash memory," had the potential to make most DRAMs obsolete, and the U.S. firms were reported to have the lead in this field.

Group Assignments: The Chip War Case[1]

The time frame of the first four assignments is April 1986.

GROUP 1

Your assignment is to examine the factors that determine the competitive performance of semicon-

[1] The assignments were composed by Professor Tom Pugel of New York University, Stern School of Business.

ductor producers home-based in different countries. First, in the absence of any specific national government policies toward the industry, what are the fundamental economic and other factors that would determine this performance? In the absence of government policies, would we expect U.S.-based firms to be of major importance in the industry? Are we surprised that Japanese firms have become of major importance? Would we expect European-based firms or firms based in developing countries to be of major importance? Second, in what ways have government policies influenced or altered the relative competitive performance of suppliers home-based in different countries?

GROUP 2

Your assignment is to evaluate the allegations of Japanese dumping of chips in the United States. What is dumping? Was there dumping? What are the possible causes or reasons for this dumping? Which of these seem to explain this particular instance of alleged dumping? What are the advantages and disadvantages for the United States of imposing anti-dumping duties?

GROUP 3

Your assignment is to evaluate the allegations of unfair trade practices by the Japanese government, being investigated under Section 301 of the U.S. Trade Act of 1974. You can focus on the complaints about barriers to U.S. access to the Japanese market for semiconductors. A major piece of evidence is a U.S. share of the Japanese semiconductor market of about 10 percent, which the United States views as unacceptably low (as well as surprisingly stable). What are the possible explanations for this low U.S. share? What do you think explains the low U.S. share? Are Japanese government policies and practices in violation of Section 301?

GROUP 4

You are the President of the United States. The deadlines for deciding the various trade actions are approaching soon. The two governments have been talking in an effort to reach a negotiated resolution. Progress so far has been slow, but the Japanese are likely to prefer a negotiated solution rather than unilateral decisions by the United States. What are your main options, in terms of both negotiating process and changes in government policies, for attempting to resolve the friction? Define and defend what you conclude would be a desirable and realistic solution to the issues, desirable from the viewpoint of the U.S. national interest (or some balancing of the various particular interests of the United States), and realistic in terms of the probable willingness of the Japanese government negotiators to accept such a solution.

GROUP 5

The time frame of the following assignment is January 1989.

Assess the August 1, 1986 U.S.–Japan Five-Year Agreement related to the semiconductor trade. Examine particularly whether the agreement afforded U.S. companies a level playing field. Why were U.S. manufacturers of chips dissatisfied with the agreement, and what are the long-term implications of the agreement for the U.S. semiconductor industry?

APPENDIX 29-1

Department of Commerce Dumping Finding in the EPROM Case

Summary: We have preliminarily determined that EPROMs from Japan are being, or are likely to be, sold in the United States at less than fair value, and have notified the U.S. International Trade Commission (ITC) of our determination. We have also directed the U.S. Customs Service to suspend the liquidation of all entries of EPROMs from Japan that are entered, or withdrawn from warehouse, for consumption, on or after the date of publication of this notice, and to require a cash deposit or bond for each entry in an amount equal to the estimated dumping margins as described in the "Suspension of Liquidation" section of this notice.

If this investigation proceeds normally, we will make our final determination by May 27, 1988.
Effective Date: March 17, 1988.
For Further Information Contact: David Mueller, William Kane, or Raymond Busen,

Source: Federal Register, vol. 51, no. 51, Monday, 17, 1986, Notices.

Office of Investigations, Import Administration, International Trade Administration, U.S. Department of Commerce, 14th Street and Constitution Avenue, N.W., Washington, DC 20230; telephone (202) 377-2923, 377-1766, or 377-3464.

Preliminary Determination

We have preliminarily determined that EPROMs from Japan are being, or are likely to be, sold in the United States at less than fair value, as provided in section 733(b) of the Tariff Act of 1930, as amended (19 U.S.C. 1673(b)) (the Act). Except in the instances where we used the best information available, we made fair value comparisons on virtually all sales of the class or kind of merchandise to the United States by the respondents during the period of investigation, April 1 through September 30, 1985. The weighted-average margins are shown in the "Suspension of Liquidation" section of this notice.

Case History

On September 30, 1985, we received a petition from Intel Corporation, Advanced Micro Devices, Inc., and National Semiconductor Corporation on behalf of the domestic manufacturers of EPROMs. In compliance with the filing requirements of §353.36 of the Commerce Regulations (19 CFR 353.36), the petition alleged that the imports of EPROMs from Japan are being, or are likely to be sold in the United States at less than fair value within the meaning of section 731 of the Act, and that these imports are materially injuring, or are threatening material injury to, a United States industry. The petition also alleged that sales of the subject merchandise were being made at less than the cost of production. After reviewing the petition, we determined that it contained sufficient grounds upon which to initiate an antidumping duty investigation. We notified the ITC of our action and initiated such an investigation on October 21, 1985 (50 FR43603). On November 14, 1985, the ITC determined that there is reasonable indication that imports of EPROMs from Japan are materially injuring, or are threatening material injury to, a U.S. industry (50 FR 47852).

On December 2, 1985, we presented antidumping duty questionnaires to Hitachi Ltd. (Hitachi), Fujitsu Limited (Fujitsu), Toshiba Corporation (Toshiba), and NEC Corporation (NEC). Respondents were requested to answer the questionaire in 30 days. However, at the request of Hitachi, Fujitsu, Toshiba, and the Japanese Ministry of International Trade and Industry, we granted an extension to January 17, 1986. On January 17, 1986, we received incomplete responses from Hitachi, Fujitsu, and Toshiba, and a letter from NEC stating that it would not respond to our questionnaire. In letters dated February 3, 1986, the Department requested supplemental information from each of the three respondents. Additional information was submitted by these respondents on February 18, 1986.

Products Under Investigation

The products covered by this investigation are erasable programmable read only memories (EPROMs), which are a type of memory integrated circuit thatis manufactured using variations of Metal Oxide-Semiconductor (MOS) process technology, including both Complementary (CMOS) and N-Channel (NMOS). The products include processed wafers, dice and assembled EPROMs produced in Japan and imported into the United States from Japan.

Finished EPROMs are currently provided for in the Tariff Schedules of the United States Annotated (TSUSA) under item 687.7445. Unassembled EPROMs, including unmounted chips, wafers, and dice, are provided for under TSUSA item 687.7405.

In the notice of initiation in this case we tentatively included in the scope of this investigation processed wafers and dice produced in Japan and assembled into finished EPROMs in another country prior to importation into the United States from the other country. Based on the responses received, there are currently no such third-country assembly/imports. We have preliminarily determined that the question as to whether we have authority to include these third country imports is dependent, in part, on certain factual considerations. Thus, we can make such a determination in the abstract, absent information as to what might actually occur in the third country. Should we receive evidence at some future date that these third-country assembly/imports are occurring, we will determine whether to include them in the scope of the proceeding at that time.

Fair Value Comparisons

For the three responding firms, to determine whether sales of the subject merchandise in the United States were made at less than fair value, we compared the United States price with foreign market value as specified below. For NEC, we made our fair value comparison using the best information available for both United States price and foreign market value, as NEC did not respond to our questionnaire. The best information available was the United States price and foreign market value developed in the petition.

For purposes of this preliminary determination, we used the date of shipment as the date of sale in both the U.S. and home markets. We will continue to evaluate whether these are the appropriate dates at verification and for the final determination.

United States Price

As provided in section 772(c) of the Act, we used exporter's sale price (ESP) to represent United States price, as the merchandise was sold to unrelated purchasers after the date of importation. A small number of Hitachi's sales were made to unrelated purchasers prior to importation, but no calculations were performed on these sales.

We calculated ESP based on the packed, duty paid. C.I.F. delivered price to unrelated purchasers in the United States. Where appropriate, we made deductions for brokerage charges in Japan and the U.S. foreign inland freight and insurance, freight and insurance, U.S. duty, U.S. freight and insurance, commissions to unrelted parties. U.S. selling expenses incurred in Japan and the U.S. credit expenses, warranties, technical services, advertising, discounts, and rebates in the U.S. market. The cost of additional packing performed in the U.S. was deducted. For Fujitsu, the cost of further processing in the U.S. was also deducted.

Foreign Market Value

The petitioner alleged that sales in the home market by all the respondents were at prices below the cost of producing the merchandise.

In accordance with section 773(a) of the Act, we calculated foreign market value based on home market prices where there were sufficient home market sales at or above the cost of production to determine foreign market value. We used constructed value as the basis for calculating foreign market value where there were no sales of such or similar merchandise in the home market or where there were not sufficient sales above the cost of production, as defined in section 733(b) of the Act.

Where foreign market value was based on home market prices, we calculated a foreign market value for each product for each month of the period of investigation, due to sharp declines in monthly prices. Where foreign market value was based on constructed value we used a monthly constructed value for each product.

Cost of Production

The Department analyzed the unverified cost submissions of the respondents to determine the sufficiency of such data for the purposes of calculating the cost of production for the preliminary determination. Where the Department determined that a submission was substantially complete and sufficient, it used the submission for the preliminary determination. However, adjustments to the respondents' data were made when it appeared from the explanation provided in the response that certain costs necessary for the production of EPROMs were not included or were not appropriately quantified or valued.

Some adjustments were made to the cost of production of all the respondents. These were:

1. Matching the sales to cost of production incurred two months prior to the sales.
2. Including the expense of sales credit for the home market sales.
3. Including interest expense equal to the percentage of interest expense to the cost of

sales, based on the consolidated operations of the company.

For Fujitsu, the product specific R&D was revised because the cost of production did not include historic R&D costs.

For Toshiba, the depreciation expense was revised because Toshiba based such expenses on a useful life of three years for its equipment; the product-specific R&D was revised because a clearer explanation of the allocation method was not presented.

For Hitachi, general, administrative and selling expenses were revised because of the apparent omission of certain general costs.

Price to Price Comparisons

For each company examined, we found sufficient sales above the cost of production for certain products to allow use of home market prices in accordance with section 773(a)(1)(A) of the Act to determine foreign market value. Where we used home market prices as the basis for foreign market value, we calculated the home market price on the basis of the delivered price to unrelated purchasers. We made deductions, where appropriate, for foreign freight and insurance, discounts, rebates, and commissions to unrelated parties in the home market. We also made deductions, where appropriate, for differences in circumstances of sale for credit terms, technical services, and warranty, in accordance with §353.15 of our regulations. We deducted home market packing costs and added U.S. packing costs. Where appropriate, we offset commissions paid on U.S. sales with indirect selling expenses in the home market, in accordance with §353.15(c) of our regulations. We also used indirect selling expenses to offset United States selling expenses, in accordance with §353.15(c) of our regulations.

On March 6, 1988, Fujitsu submitted a revised listing of home market sales reflecting a recalculation of credit expenses and discounts.

We did not receive this new information in sufficient time to evaluate and incorporate it in our calculations. We will consider that information prior to our final determination.

Constructed Value

In accordance with section 773(e) of the Act we calculated foreign market value based on constructed value when there were insufficient home market sales of such or similar merchandise above the cost of production for comparison. For constructed value, the Department used the materials, fabrication, and general expenses, based on the respondents submissions revised as detailed under the "Foreign Market Value—Cost of Production" section of this notice. The actual general expenses were used, since in all cases, such expenses exceeded the statutory minimum of 10 percent of materials and fabrication. "Since all of the respondents' submissions indicated that the actual profit for merchandise of the same general class or kind was less than 8 percent, the Department used the 8 percent statutory minimum for profit. We made adjustments under §353.15 of the regulations for differences in circumstances of sale between the two markets.

Currency Conversion

For ESP comparisons, we used the official exchange rate for the date of purchase since the use of that exchange rate is consistent with section 615 of the Tariff and Trade Act of 1984 (1984 Act). We followed section 615 of the 1984 Act rather than §353.56(a)(2) of our regulations because the later supersedes that section of the regulations.

Verification

We will verify all the information used in making our final determination in accordance with section 776(a) of the Act. We will use standard verification procedures, including examination of relevant sales and financial records of the company.

APPENDIX 29-2

Excerpt from Article on U.S.– Japan High-Technology Competition[1]

Chips with Everything

Gone are the days when American semiconductor firms short-sightedly sold their licenses and know how to Japanese microchip makers. America's electronics firms have maintained their global leadership in all branches of their business save one. They kissed goodbye consumer electronics (television, hi-fi, video recorders, etc.) as customers across the country voted with their pockets for shiny boxes with flashing lights and labels like Panasonic, Technics, JVC and Sony.

The American electronics industry came close to allowing much the same to happen in microchips. In 1982, Silicon Valley took a caning when the Japanese started flooding the market with cheap 64K RAMs (random-access memory chips capable of storing over 64,000 bits of computer data). Most beat a hasty retreat up or out of the market.

From having a dozen mass producers of dynamic-RAMs in 1980, only five American chip makers were still in the high-volume-memory business by 1983. Today, there are effectively only two or three with the capacity to produce the latest generation of memory chips (1 megabit RAMs) in anything like economic volumes. Meanwhile, the six Japanese firms that plunged into the memory-chip business back in the early 1970s are still

around—and now have a 70% share of the dynamic-RAM market in America.

Microchips have been the engine powering Japan's drive into high-tech generally. But before it could join the microchip generation, Japan had to find a way of disseminating this vital American technology throughout its fledgling semiconductor industry. The trick adopted was, first, to protect the home market, and then to bully abler firms into joining government-sponsored research schemes—one run by the Japanese telephone authority NTT and the other by the Ministry of International Trade and Industry—to develop the know-how for making their own very large-scale integrated (VLSI) circuits.

Next, by "blessing" VLSI as the wave of the future and crucial to Japan's survival, the government triggered a scramble among the country's electronics firms (encouraged by their long-term investment banks) to build VLSI plants. The net result was massive overcapacity (first in 64K RAMs and then in 256K versions), abundant local supply for the domestic consumer electronics makers and an impelling urgency to export (or dump) surplus microchips abroad.

This targeting ploy had been tried before. Japanese manufacturers found it worked moderately well with steel, much better with motorcycles, better still with consumer electronics and best of all with semiconductors. The only requirement was a steeply falling "learning curve" (that is, rapidly reducing unit costs as production volume builds up and manufactur-

[1]Article from *The Economist*, August 23, 1986.

ers learn how to squeeze waste out of the process).

The trick was simply to devise a forward-pricing strategy that allowed Japanese manufacturers to capture all the new growth that their below-cost pricing created in export markets, while underwriting the negative cash-flow by cross-subsidies and higher prices back home.

The Americans finally lost their patience when the Japanese tried to do a repeat performance with pricier memory chips called EPROMs. The price fell from $17 each when the Japanese first entered the American market with their EPROM chps early in 1985 to less than $4 six months later. Intel, National Semiconductor and Advanced Micro Devices promptly filed a joint petition, accusing the Japanese of dumping EPROMs on the American market at below their manufacturing costs in Japan (then estimated to be $6.30 apeice). The issue is currently being used by Washington as a battering ram to breach the wall Japan has erected around its own $8 billion semiconductor market back home.

For America, this get-tough policy has come only just in time. Japan now enjoys a 27% share (to America's 64%) of the world's $42 billion semiconductor market. And while cut-throat competition may make memory chips a loss-leader, acquiring the technology for producing RAMs has given Japan's microcircuit makers a leg-up in getting to grips with more complex semiconductors used in computer graphics, communications and video equipment.

So far, however, it has not helped Japanese chip makers to loosen the stranglehold that American semiconductor firms have on the lucrative microprocessor business. Where 256K RAMs have become commodity products that sell wholesale for $1 or so each, 32-bit microprocessors from the likes of Motorola, Intel, National Semiconductor, Texas Instruments, AT&T and Zilog cost hundreds of dollars apiece. Betwen them, these six American chip makers control 90% of the world market for the latest generation of microprocessors, leaving just 10% for the rest of the American semiconductor industry, Europe and Japan.

Fortunately for the Americans, microprocessors are not like memory chips. Being literally a "computer-on-a-chip," they are vastly more complex and cannot be designed in any routine manner. Sweat, insight and inspiration are needed every step of the way. And they have to be designed with their software applications in mind. Americans have been doing this longer, and are better at it, than anyone else.

More to the point, American firms are not parting with their patents as readily as they did in the past. Hitachi has been trying (with little luck) to persuade Motorola to sell it a licence for making its advanced 68020 microprocessor. Meanwhile, Japan's leading electronics firm, NEC, is having to defend itself in the American courts for infringing one of Intel's microprocessor patents.

With America's new, stricter copyright laws making it difficult to imitate American designs, Japanese chip makers are being shut out of all the major markets for microprocessors. Fujitsu, Matsushita, Mitsubishi and Toshiba are all gambling on a microprocessor design called TRON developed at the University of Tokyo. But nobody, least of all NEC or Hitachi, holds out much hope for the TRON design winning a big enough share of the market in its own right to be economic—at least, not until the mid-1990s. And, by then, Silicon Valley will have upped the technological stakes again.

When, late at night, the conversation gets down to *honne* (brass tacks), even Japan's ablest microchip wizards despair at ever matching Silicon Valley's mix of entrepreneurial and innovative flair. "Japan is powerful in only one sub-field of a single application of semiconductors tied to a specific line of products," bemoans Mr. Atsushi Asada of Sharp Corporation.

Country Risk Associates

Assessing Quantitatively Country Risk and Default

HARVEY A. PONIACHEK

The expansion of international business has made the analysis of country risk essential. This case study defines country risk and examines several of its theoretical interpretations. A checklist risk rating model based on international cash flow of the balance of payments is formulated. The reader is required to apply the checklist model by obtaining country data, to derive the ratings, and to provide an interpretation.

Definitions

Generally, risk indicators could measure either creditworthiness or the likelihood of default. Country risk measures a country's ability to provide its resident corporations and government entities with sufficient foreign exchange to service international obligations denominated in foreign currency. This ability is referred to as convertibility—from local to foreign currency—or transfer risk—the ability to facilitate a transfer payment abroad or credit-worthiness.[1] High country risk, high transfer risk, or low creditworthiness could reduce the ability, for example, of a creditworthy corporation located abroad, or of a foreign subsidiary of a U.S. corporation, to purchase from the local commercial banks or monetary authorities sufficient foreign exchange to service foreign obligations. An alternative country risk rating could measure the probability of external debt servicing difficulties or default. Country risk is often erroneously interchanged with sovereign risk and political risk.

Country risk affects a wide variety of international transactions and assets, including lending, extension of credit, currency transactions and payments clearing, export credit, remittances of dividends, repatriation of capital, and foreign direct investment. Country risk applies to assets but not to liabilities; however, it affects various exposed assets differently. The risk of foreign lending, or extension of international credit, is defined as country risk, transfer risk, or sovereign risk.

Sovereign risk concerns loans extended to, or guaranteed by, foreign governments or their public entities. It measures ability to service

[1]M. G. Martinson and J. V. Huopt, "Transfer Risk in U.S. Banks," *Federal Reserve Bulletin*, April 1989.

foreign currency denominated obligations, or the probability of default on foreign currency denominated external debt, by a government or public entity, on foreign loans guaranteed by the government. Default could be an outright repudiation of international debt or a rescheduling with the latter being the most common occurrence.

Political risk measures the risk due to political instability, expropriation, nationalization, revolution, and war. The risk to direct investment abroad is referred to as political risk, since it is often primarily attributed to adverse political development.

Country risk is affected by adverse economic, social, or political developments in a country that were caused by corporate and government policies, or due to changes in the international environment. The degree of risk —whether country, sovereign, or political—is affected by the sensitivity of risk to various events giving rise to risk. In addition, the degree of risk is affected by the time horizon of the exposure, the amount and type of exposed assets, and the available means to hedge risk and risk management capabilities.

The Models and Interpretations

Economic, financial, political, and social events can lead to country risk. Country risk assessment seeks to evaluate these events and their effect on the country's capabilities of servicing foreign obligation, or to assess the probability of external debt servicing difficulties.

There are a variety of theoretical interpretations and models for country risk assessment, but there is no consensus on which theory or model is best. Empirical or quantitative country risk assessment is affected by the type of model used, the quality of the data applied, and the interpretation of the results. Country risk assessment theory often relies on an international cash flow approach based on the bal-

ance of payments (BOP). The cash flow or the balance of payments approach to country risk assessment analyzes the external debt problem of a country analogously to a corporation that faces a cash flow or liquidity difficulty.

The cash flow theory recognizes that external debt is serviced out of foreign exchange receipts that are generated through the export of goods, services, transfers, and capital inflows. Some (or often most or all) of these receipts pay for imports of goods, services, transfers, and service external debt obligations. When the current account of the BOP—one of the most significant accounts of the BOP—is in continuous deficit, external debt commonly expands and debt service (i.e., payments of interest and amortization of the principal) becomes difficult. Under such circumstances, unless additional foreign capital becomes available through new foreign loans, or the inflow of non-debt capital (direct foreign investment, or portfolio investment, etc.), servicing foreign debt could become difficult or impossible. Occasionally, when balance of payments difficulties arise and shortages in foreign exchange occur, governments institute foreign exchange controls to ration scarce foreign exchange resources to sectors that are most viable for the economy.

In the context of the international cash flow analysis, country risk arises from the economic, social and political environment of the country and their effect on the BOP. More specifically, the BOP and, in turn, the ability to service foreign obligations are affected by macroeconomic and financial conditions (e.g., GNP growth rate, inflation, and international competitiveness) and by the structural characteristics of the economy (i.e., high-tech industry, availability of natural resources, etc.). Hence, the BOP performance and its outlook are crucial in determining a country's ability to service its foreign debt. However, because it is very difficult to forecast the evolution of the balance of payments, we employ various ratios or proxies that describe the relationship between the BOP and country risk.

Applications

The application of models and empirical methods for country risk assessment ensures the comparability of country risk ratings of different countries. A country risk rating could be based on historic data or on short-, medium- or long-term projections. Most of the information required for country risk analysis is published, but for many developing countries data is usually available after a considerable time lag.

The Checklist Method

The checklist method consists of several variables—related to the international cash flows or the balance of payments approach—that are weighted according to their impact on debt servicing ability, with the weights ranging from 0 to 100. The weights or coefficients assigned to the various variables can be determined on the basis of experience, as we have done in the model shown in Exhibit 30-1, or derived empirically by applying econometric methods[2], or by using multiple discriminate analysis.

Each variable in the model is weighted or multiplied by a fixed weight, or coefficient, and the results are aggregated to form the index or composite score. Factors that adversely affect the country's ability to service foreign debt, or creditworthiness, have negative coefficients. The indexes of the various countries, or the indexes of the same country over a period of time, should be standardized. The higher the score, the better off the country, while the lower the score, the higher the likelihood of default.[3]

[2]Harvey A. Poniachek, (ed.), *International Corporate Finance*, Unwin & Hayman, 1989.
[3]One can derive the risk of default index from the country risk index. For example, we may assume that a country with a risk rating of 75% has a default risk of 25% (i.e., 100% − 75% = 25%).

EXHIBIT 30-1

Country Risk Rating: The Checklist Method
An example of how to apply the checklist method:

Variables	(a) Weights[1]	(b) Country I	(a) × (b)
Domestic			
GNP Growth, %	5	0.05	0.25
GNP/Population[2]	10	30.00	3.00
Inflation, %	−5	0.15	−0.75
International			
Reserves/Imports[3]	10	75.00	7.50
Current Account/GNP	15	−15.00	2.25
Debt Service Ratio	−25	0.25	−6.25
Debt/GNP	−15	0.30	−5.25
Political			
Political Stability[4]	15	0.50	7.50
	100%		7.75[5]

Notes:

[1]Total weights (in absolute value) equal 100%. However, in applying the weights the negative sign needs to be observed.

[2]The GNP/Population is usually calculated in dollars, but we ranked it vis-à-vis a sample of some 100 countries. In this case GNP/Population for Country I is ranked 70th, which corresponds to a rate of (100 − 70)/100 = 30/100 = 0.30.

[3]Reserves/Imports measures the monthly import levels that can be financed out of reserves, ranked as shown in note 2.

[4]Political stability is considered on a scale of 0 to 1, with 1 being most stable, and 0 being least stable.

[5]The 7.75 score needs to be standardized. If the country with the highest score is 48.85, then the scaling is performed as follows: (7.75/48.85) × 100 = 15.86, which is the country risk rating of Country I on a scale of 0 to 100.

The checklist approach yields a risk rating on a scale of 0 to 100, to which a letter classification can then be assigned.

The checklist model has several shortcomings, however, which include the somewhat discretionary/arbitrary selection of the variables, and the often discretionary assignment of weights to the variables. In addition, the adequacy of the variables and their relative significance could vary over time and between the industrial and developing countries. If, however, structural relationships in the country change substantially and frequently, the model might be deemed unstable and incapable of providing an accurate prediction of country risk.

In practice, the application of the model, shown in Exhibit 31-1, should follow the following algorithm.

1. Select the variables.
2. Assign weights (or coefficients) to each variable, where the total weight should be 100 percent (in absolute terms).
3. Obtain the data for the variables.
4. Multiply the weights column by the data column for the country.
5. Add the product to obtain the summary index.
6. Standardize the summary index.

The model can be constructed, maintained and updated by utilizing a Lotus 1-2-3 spreadsheet or by applying an alternative spreadsheet software program. The model's variables must be measured consistently and the variable weights must be applied consistently over time and for different countries.

The Assignment

As a summer intern at Country Risk Associates you joined a research team that was requested to apply the checklist model of country risk assessment previously discussed and specified in Exhibit 30-1, by pursuing the following assignment:

1. Gather data for the independent and the dependent variables from publicly available sources, such as the International Monetary Fund, *International Financial Statistics*; OECD; U.N.; U.S. Commerce Department; and Business International.
2. Estimate by multiple regression analysis, or judgmentally, the coefficients or weights for the independent or explanatory variables.
3. Assess the country risk rating of an industrial and developing country in 1989. (You may utilize the coefficients that you estimated or use those in Exhibit 30-1.)
4. Compare your ratings with those provided by *Institutional Investor*, *Euromoney*, or *Bankers' Magazine*.
5. Examine the sensitivity of your ratings through simulations. Is the model sufficiently sensitive to a possible improvement in the current account by 25 percent and a reduction in the debt service ration by 20 percent?
6. Explain the reasonableness of your model specification and empirical capabilities (i.e., by applying it to two countries that defaulted on their international debt or required rescheduling). Determine if the model is capable of identifying countries (of your choice) that have either defaulted on their international obligations, required rescheduling, or needed other external debt relief (sometime during 1985 to 1990). (Hint: Examine the IMF *Annual Report* for data on which countries have rescheduled or requested financial assistance.)

The World Commercial Aircraft Industry

Booming into the 1990s

THOMAS N. GLADWIN

The Industry in Quotes

On Economics[1]

It's high stakes poker.... the world just might not be big enough for McDonnell Douglas, Airbus and Boeing. (Morten Beyer, president of Avmark, an airline consulting firm, February 1987)

It's the famous boom-or-bust syndrome. (Reinder J. van Duinen, acting chairman of N.V. Fokker, April 1989)

Building and selling civil jets is a business of modest returns and immodest risks. (*Forbes*, February 1987)

On Competition[2]

It's war. (Pierre G. Pailleret, senior vice president for marketing of Airbus, September 1985)

You don't succeed in this business by being cautious. (Frank Shrontz, chairman of Boeing, July 1989)

We are up against one tough competitor that has more than half the world market, and another

that's subsidized.... there's a major problem as to how we become successful in that market. (John F. McDonnell, chairman of McDonnell Douglas, March, 1988)

On Cooperation[3]

I don't think there's a major airframe or engine program undertaking now that is not international in some way. (Edward C. Bursk, chairman of the Aerospace Industry Association International Council, 1988)

What you can be sure of is everyone in aerospace is talking to everyone else in aerospace. (Ian Wild, analyst with Barclays' de Zoete Weld, March 1989)

How do you marry someone you are trying to kill? (Airbus executive discussing possible partnership with McDonnell Douglas, March 1988)

On Performance[4]

We're not being treated as a poor relation or an upstart anymore... we're being treated as a member of the family. (Alan Boyd, chairman of Airbus' North American operations, July 1989)

This case was prepared by Thomas N. Gladwin, Professor of Management and International Business, Leonard N. Stern School of Business, New York University, copyright © 1989.

[1] *The New York Times*, February 22, 1987; *The New York Times*, April 25, 1989; and *Forbes*, February 23, 1987.

[2] *Business Week*, September 23, 1985; and *Fortune*, July 17, 1989.

[3] "The Jet Age," Air & Space Smithsonian Institution, 1988; *Financial Times*, March 22, 1989; and *Business Week*, March 21, 1988.

[4] *The New York Times*, July 5, 1989; *Business Week*, March 13, 1989; and "The Jetliner Business," The First Boston Corp. October 5, 1984.

Is something wrong with Boeing? (*Business Week*, March 1989)

Economic failure is the norm in the civil aircraft business. (First Boston Corporation analysts, October 1984)

On the Future[5]

World airlines will buy 8417 new jet aircraft of all types from all manufacturers between now and the year 2005. (Jack Howard, Boeing director of market research, March 1989)

In a growing number of aviation related areas, foreign technical capabilities are now comparable, if not superior, to those of the United States. (U.S. Office of Science and Technology, March 1985)

It's no secret the Japanese are trying to develop a healthy aerospace industry, but they're not going to be a competitor in the market tomorrow. (Jack Gamble, Boeing spokesperson, March 1986)

Structure of the Industry

As displayed in Exhibit 31-1 the aircraft industry has the structure of a pyramid, with a few prime contractors (the airframe integrators) orchestrating the work of thousands of subcontractors, both domestic and foreign. The airframe manufacturers design the aircraft, integrate all its systems, manage the vast network of suppliers and subcontractors, complete the final assembly, market the airplane and provide customer support for the 20 to 30 years of its life. Engine manufacturers design and build propulsion systems in close association with the airframe manufacturers and maintain their own marketing and customer support networks. Risk-sharing subcontractors do detailed design and use their own tooling to assemble major subsections of new trans-

ports. Finally, layers of suppliers develop systems and equipment for aircraft, including cockpit displays, computers, hydraulics, seats, and galleys, and they rely in turn on a wide range of component manufacturers.[6] (*Note:* Throughout this case we will be dealing only with large commercial transports produced in western nations, thus excluding smaller general aviation, helicopters and military aircraft.)

Airframe Integrators

The number of civilian aircraft manufacturers numbered 25 in the 1940s, 17 in 1960, and today, only five remain:

Boeing

Boeing, based in Seattle, Washington, is the world's number-one plane maker, accounting for 62 percent of the total value of delivered commercial airliners in 1988. One competitor describes it as the "original 800 lb. gorilla."[7] Two-thirds of its revenues of $16,962 million in 1988, and 70 percent of its 1988 profits of $614 million came from building commercial airliners, with the rest flowing from space and military work. Seventy-five percent of its 1989 revenues were expected to derive from its commercial plane business.

The company employed 147,300 as of year end 1988, and had assets of $12,608 million, a cash flow of $1,155 million and a market value of $10,192 million in that year. It's exports in 1988 were $7,849 million, making it America's third leading exporter after GM and Ford. Boeing spent $824 million on R&D in 1987, equivalent to 5.4 percent of its sales. (The aerospace industry in general spent 4.4%, while all of American industry averaged 3.4% on R&D.)

---

[5]*Financial Times*, March 13, 1989; Office of Science and Technology Policy, "National Aeronautical R&D Goals: Technology for American Future," Washington, D.C., March 1985; and *The New York Times*, March 7, 1986.

[6]Michael L. Dertouzus, et al., *Made in America: Regaining the Productive Edge* (Cambridge: MIT Press, 1989), p. 202.

[7]*The Economist*, September 3, 1988.

EXHIBIT 31-1

The Aircraft Industry Pyramid

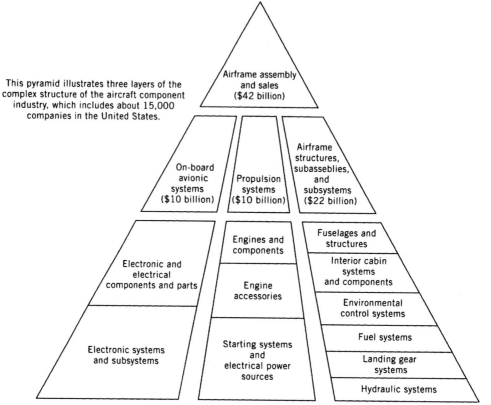

This pyramid illustrates three layers of the complex structure of the aircraft component industry, which includes about 15,000 companies in the United States.

Airframe assembly and sales ($42 billion)

On-board avionic systems ($10 billion)

Propulsion systems ($10 billion)

Airframe structures, subasseblies, and subsystems ($22 billion)

Electronic and electrical components and parts

Engines and components

Fuselages and structures

Interior cabin systems and components

Engine accessories

Environmental control systems

Fuel systems

Electronic systems and subsystems

Starting systems and electrical power sources

Landing gear systems

Hydraulic systems

Source: SRI International, "Changing Markets for Aircraft Products," Report 740, Fall 1986, Gerald W. Bernstein.

Founded in 1916, the firm has gone on to sell over 9000 jetliners, more than all the other manufacturers in the western world put together; it makes the best selling small jet, the best selling medium-size jet and the only jumbo jet. Much of its success can be traced to the experience gained during WWII producing the renowned B-17 Flying Fortress and the B-29 Super Fortress. It has long enjoyed a reputation for superlative quality; the *Fortune* 1988 Annual Survey found it to be America's eighth most admired corporation. Seeing itself "in the high technology transportation business,"[8] Boeing in mid-1989 had $4 billion of cash on hand, practically no debt on its balance sheet, and a phenomenal $80 billion order backlog.

AIRBUS INDUSTRIES

Airbus Industries, headquartered in Toulouse, France, is a partnership made up of Europe's

[8]*Business Week*, September 23, 1985.

EXHIBIT 31-2

The Structure of Airbus Industrie

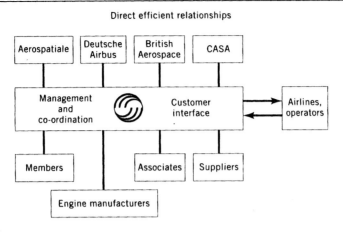

Direct efficient relationships

Source: Airbus Industrie.

four leading aerospace manufacturers, with equity ownership broken down as follows:

- 37.9 percent by Aerospatiale, the French government-owned company created by the rationalization of Nord and Sud Aviation in 1970.
- 37.9 percent by Deutsche Airbus, a wholly-owned subsidiary of Messerschmitt-Boelkow-Blohm, (MBB), as of mid-1989, soon to be majority acquired by Daimler-Benz.
- 20 percent by British Aerospace, formed by the amalgamation of British Aircraft, Hawker Siddeley and Scottish Aviation in 1977 and collectively privatized by the British government between 1980 and 1985.
- 4.2 percent by Construcciones Aeronauticas (CASA), a 72 percent government-owned aircraft manufacturer in Spain.

Founded in 1970, the partnership has the status of a *Groupement d'Interet Economique* (GIE, or "pooling of common interests") whose purpose is to expand its shareholders' interests, but not to make a profit for itself. This structure permits individual partner compa-

nies to act as subcontractors, developing and manufacturing aircraft subassemblies (e.g., tailplanes by CASA, fuselages by MBB, wings by British Aerospace, flight systems and fuselage sections by Aerospatiale), which are shipped to Toulouse for final assembly.

As shown in Exhibit 31-2 the chief roles of Airbus Industrie are customer interface (sales and product support) and management of relationships with outside suppliers, engine producers, and associate members (e.g., Fokker of the Netherlands, Belairbus of Belgium). Airbus must also coordinate its partners' design, development and production activities.

During the 1970s, Airbus was sneered at as a government-funded make-work project and a nuisance in the marketplace. But by 1987 it accounted for 23 percent of all new orders and in 1988 accounted for 18 percent of actual deliveries. As detailed later in this case, this was made possible, in part, by an estimated $15 billion in direct and indirect subsidies from the parent governments of its members, along with aggressive high-technology and marketing strategies. Its finances have always been shrouded in secrecy, since the GIE status does not require it to publish any accounts (its income and expenses disappear into the labyrinth of each partner's financial statements). Airbus proclaims that its objective is to achieve a 30 percent share of the global market by the mid-1990s and to become self-sustaining (i.e., profitable) at that time. With these objectives in mind, and after a year of difficult negotiations, the consortium announced a restructuring plan in March 1989 designed to streamline its management structure, tighten its financial controls and make its subcontracting more competitive.

McDONNELL DOUGLAS

The commercial airframe division of McDonnell Douglas, based in Long Beach, California, accounted for 17 percent of the total value of delivered commercial airliners in 1988. The division accounted for only 20 percent of its parent's sales in 1987, with military aircraft representing 55 percent of McDonnell Douglas' sales, and the remainder coming from missiles, computers and space equipment. The commercial division (then the Douglas Aircraft Company) was preeminent in the piston era in the 1930–40s with its DC-3 and DC-7 series.

It was also a powerhouse in the early years of the jet age. In 1968, for example, the year after Douglas was acquired by the McDonnell Aircraft Corporation of St. Louis, the company delivered 300 airliners to customers. But its DC-10 widebody jet got into a debilitating market battle with Lockheed Corporation's L-1011 (which drove Lockheed to quit the civilian market in 1981 after it lost $2.5 billion). The epic struggle, which nearly bankrupted McDonnell Douglas, along with the economic recession of the early 1980s, reduced Douglas' fortunes, such that it only delivered 50 commercial jets in 1982, and its parent seriously considered closing down its transport aircraft business.

But a willingness to take risks when the situation looked the bleakest, along with ag-gressive financing/leasing strategies, allowed the niche player (selling only derivatives of its DC-9 and DC-10 models) to survive. Douglas booked firm orders for 138 planes in 1987 and 246 in 1988. In 1988 the parent McDonnell Douglas had sales of $15,072 million, profits of $350 million, assets of $11,885 million, a cash flow of $983 million, a market value of $3,437.1 million, employees numbering 121,421, and exports of $3,471 million, making it America's eighth leading exporter.

N.V. FOKKER AND BRITISH AEROSPACE

The remaining 6 percent of world market share in 1988 (based on deliveries) was split equally by N.V. Fokker of the Netherlands and British Aerospace, both building smaller short-range transports. British Aerospace, a member of Airbus as well as an independent producer, had 1988 sales of $8,836 million, profits of $244 million, assets of $10,175 million and a return on equity of 7.5 percent. Fokker, during 1987 and early 1988 experienced massive cost overruns, a cash crisis, a management shake-up and a Dutch government rescue from near bankruptcy. A $3.1 billion order from American Airlines for 150 of Fokker's F-100s (a two-engine fanjet that seats 100 passengers and has a range of 1,400 miles) in the Spring of 1989, however, revived the firm.[9]

Development and Production Economics

"If you're a beginner, let me strongly suggest the stakes are too high and the risks too great," warns the president of United Technologies (parent of engine producer Pratt & Whitney).[10] It's an industry truism that because of the huge capital investments required, a company

---

[9]*The New York Times*, April 25, 1989.

[10]*The Economist*, May 28, 1983.

in effect "bets the company" in a Las Vegas-type "Sporty Game,"[11] every time it brings out a major new commercial aircraft design. Boeing's 747 cost $1 billion to develop in the late 1960s and nearly bankrupted the firm. Tex Boullioun, the president of Boeing's aircraft subsidiary at the time admitted in the early 1970s that the company "came within a gnat's whisker of not making it."[12] In the late 1970s Boeing committed more than the entire net worth of the company to launch the 757 and 767. Airbus spent $1.7 billion launching the A320 in the early 1980s and launch costs for its A330/A340 series exceeded $4 billion. Even for McDonnell Douglas to launch its MD-11, just an enlarged derivative of its old DC-10, entailed development costs of over $1 billion.

Moving into the 1990s, it now costs $3 to 4 billion to bring a new type of commercial aircraft to the market. Exhibit 31-3 displays the typical pre-tax cash flow pattern associated with a large commercial transport program. The new airframe will absorb around $1.5 billion in non-recurring costs such as design, tooling, development and certification over a period of about 4 years. When recurring costs (e.g., wages and the maintenance of facilities) are added in, peak investment in an aircraft will reach the $3 to 4 billion level 5 to 6 years after the decision to launch the program, excluding interest. Depending on the rate of sales, the project may manage to recover its costs 8 years after the first aircraft is delivered.

In the absence of governmental funding or diversification, enduring long periods of negative cash flow requires a firm to have multiple models with overlapping product life cycles competing in different market segments. The fact that most producers (Boeing the exception) have not enjoyed this cushion led one observer to conclude in 1987 that "commercial

aviation is a business in which normally sensible people lose all touch with reality when it comes to investing in new planes... the basic problem in this industry is that it is grotesquely undercapitalized in relation to the size of the investments that have to be made.[13]

Achieving breakeven 12 years after the decision to launch assumes sales of a small airliner, such as the A320, of about 600 in its first 7 or 8 years of production; for a larger airliner the number would be smaller (i.e., about 400). Sales of approximately 700 are needed for a new aircraft to earn a return comparable with other investments. As of the late 1980s, only a few planes had been able to accomplish this (e.g., Boeing 707, 727, 747, 737-300, and possibly the MD-80). Of the 11 American and 12 European airliners that entered services in various presentations since the jet age began in 1952, only half a dozen have recovered their investment. Aerospace analysts estimated that from 1952 to 1984, jet transports lost their manufacturers some $40 billion on revenues of $180 billion; at this time, Boeing had not even cumulatively broken even.[14]

The importance of achieving volume highlights another rule of thumb in the industry: "two competitors in a market segment means at least one will lose and three competitors in a segment guarantees none will make money."[15] This rule guided industry and Wall Street logic throughout much of the 1980s and explained incentives for competitors to collaborate; the massive order boom of the 1988 and 1989 may test the validity of this "Three's a Crowd" rule.

Volume also matters because of the steep learning curves (i.e., manufacturing costs falling sharply as more units are produced) which dominate the economics of building aircraft. As shown in Exhibit 31-4, long pro-

---

[11]John Newhouse, *The Sporty Game* (New York: Alfred A. Knopf, 1985).

[12]"The Jet Set," op. cit.

[13]*The New York Times*, February 22, 1987.

[14]"The Jetliner Business," op. cit.

[15]*Forbes*, February 23, 1987.

EXHIBIT 31-3

Cash Flow Patterns in Commercial Aircraft

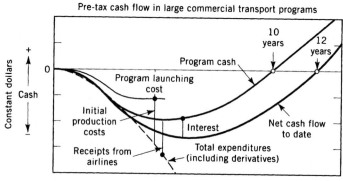

Pre-tax cash flow in large commercial transport programs

Source: Aerospace Industries Association.

EXHIBIT 31-4

The Learning Effect in Aircraft Production

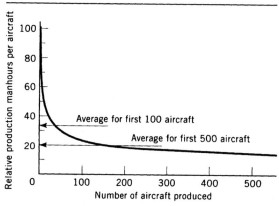

Source: Airbus Industrie.

duction runs allow the spreading of fixed development costs and the lowering of variable costs through accumulation of manufacturing experience. Boeing reckons that by the time it produces the 500th aircraft, the number of man hours per unit is only a quarter of the amount needed at the start of production. The advantages of high volume can be enormous. Aerospace analyst Wolfgang Demisch estimated in December 1985, for example, that

"Boeing's total production costs, including the upfront design, engineering and tooling, may soon fall below Airbus' costs for labor and materials alone."[16]

In sum, "making airlines will always be risky: the business is one of high investment, sophisticated technology, long lead times and low volumes... the trick is to limit the risk; the danger is that this will surrender the market to a macho rival who takes the risks and wins... the trick for the manufacturers is not to clash head on with identical products—the trick for the airlines, ever anxious to drive down the prices, is to ensure that they do."[17]

Aircraft Industry Suppliers

Boeing, McDonnell Douglas and Airbus "have become essentially assemblers of parts produced around the world," according to Alan Boyd, chairman of Airbus Industrie of North America.[18] Thousands of subcontractors fabri-

[16] *Fortune*, December 23, 1985.

[17] *The Economist*, June 1, 1985.

[18] "The Jet Set," op. cit.

cate between 60 and 70 percent of the value of American airframes (the percentages are lower for Airbus). The new 747-400, for example, which has 175 miles of wires and a few million parts, draws on 3000 subcontractors scattered around the world.

Exhibit 31-5 provides a rundown of the main subcontractors for McDonnell Douglas' MD-11, showing suppliers from South Korea, Britain, Spain, Canada, France, Italy, Austria, Brazil, Japan and the United States. The company's MD-80 draws upon suppliers in those nations as well as others, including Australia, Sweden, Switzerland and China. The American content of Airbus planes can be as high as 30 percent, with power plants from General Electric or Pratt & Whitney, auxiliary power

units from Garett, navigation and communication equipment from Sperry, and tires, wheels and brakes from Goodyear and Bendix. (Airbus estimates it bought approximately $3.5 billion worth of U.S.-manufactured components from 1978 through 1987.) Up to 29 percent of the new Boeing 747-400 can be non-American if it has a Rolls-Royce engine. In 1987, Boeing spent about $1.7 billion, or 11 percent of its turnover on goods and services supplied by companies outside America.

The internationalization of airplane content has accelerated in recent years, for both marketing and production reasons. Subcontracting has extended throughout the world, partly at the insistence of overseas customers or their governments. Airframe manufacturers, in or-

EXHIBIT 31-5

Global Sourcing on the MD-11

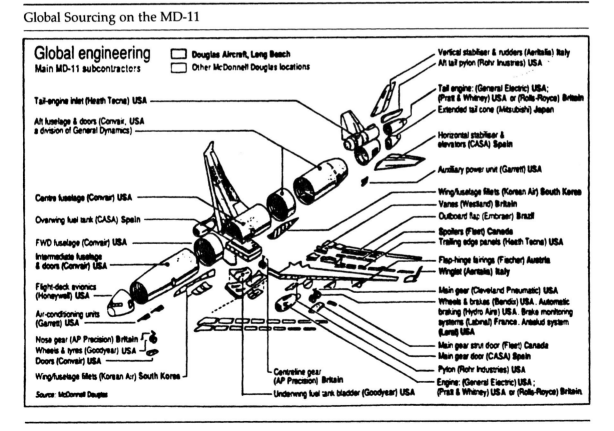

der to sell airplanes in many countries, have had to accept offset agreements that give a share of production to firms in those countries. In addition to its role as a marketing ploy, global subcontracting has been employed to reduce costs and risks. Boeing, for example, uses Aeritalia in Italy and a consortium of Japanese partners called the Civil Transport Development Corporation as risk-sharing subcontractors in the production of its 767 jet. Under this agreement with the Japanese, they were assigned to produce 15 percent of the airframe, in return for putting up some of the initial investment (half came from MITI) and assuming some of the market risk (if 8 planes a month and over 500 planes cumulatively were not sold, both Boeing and the Japanese enterprises would get lower returns to their investments—which in fact was the case in the early years of 767 production).

Engines represent 20–30 percent of the initial cost of a huge aircraft. Over the lifetime of an airplane, the cumulative cost of its replacement engines and their spare parts often equals the purchase price of the plane. (New engines and parts are the most profitable part of the business.) Engine producers, namely General Electric (the world's biggest and lowest-cost engine producer as of 1989), Pratt & Whitney (a division of United Technologies) and Rolls-Royce Ltd., confront high-risk economics similar to the airframe integrators. The costs of developing a new jet engine from scratch range from $1–2 billion, and it usually takes longer to develop and certify engines than new aircraft. The engine manufacturers work closely with the airframe companies in specifying power plant performance (engines typically represent the principal "pacing technology" for new generation aircraft), and they market their products to both the airframe builders and the airline customers. "Airframe and engine makers live in each other's pockets; they can make money only if they cooperate, and they know that a bad engine can ruin

a good airframe and vice versa."[19] Cooperation, however, is mitigated by the fact that most airframes are now offered with a choice of engines, thereby intensifying competition among engine producers. The new Boeing 747-400, for example, was certified for engines of all three major producers.

Along with high development costs and long lead times, the engine producers also share with integrators such economic realities as steep learning curves, gut wrenching risks, high breakeven points (in the words of a GE worker, "Fewer than 2000 engines sold is a disaster; 4000 is a great success"[20], need for multiple overlapping product cycles to buffer negative cash flow periods, and huge penalties for splitting or misjudging the market—hence the appeal of risk-minimizing collaboration.

The high costs and risks, along with the need to gain market access, have already moved the aircraft engine industry in the direction of a duopoly.[21] GE joined with SNECMA (the French state-run engine corporation) in 1971, and today this development, and manufacturing partnership, called CFM International, dominates engine markets with its CFM-56 series of medium jet engines in such highly successful aircraft as the Boeing 737-300, 400 and 500 series, and the European A-320 Airbus. The success of CFM stimulated the creation of the International Aero Engines consortium in March 1983, consisting of Rolls-Royce, Pratt & Whitney, Japan Aero Engines (i.e., Kawasaki, Mitsubishi Heavy Industries and Ishikawajima-Harima), Motoren & Turbinen Union of West Germany, and Fiat Aviazione of Italy. The consortium pumped more than $1 billion into developing its V2500 engine (designed for 150-seat airplanes) and

[19] The Economist, June 1, 1985.

[20] The Economist, June 1, 1985.

[21] Financial Times, October 17, 1988.

plans to spend an additional $1 billion producing the first 300 of these engines. Needless to say, the consortium is years from profitability.

Aircraft Industry Customers

"It's a business of putting bums on seats" is how a boss of Eastern Airlines once described his industry.[22] The 10 largest bum-transporters around the world in 1988 (as measured in billions of revenue passenger miles, i.e., one paying passenger flown one mile) were Aeroflot (136.6), United (69.1), American (64.7), Delta (51.7), Continental (40.7), Northwest (40.6), British Airways, (35.5), TWA (34.8), Japan Airlines (30.1), and Pan Am (29.6).[23] As the names reflect, the U.S. market is still the world's largest, accounting for about 40 percent of world revenue passenger miles in 1988 and about half of new world aircraft orders in that year.

Unlike the United States, most foreign carriers are still owned or operated by their governments. These governments naturally take an active role in aircraft purchase negotiations —often setting such conditions of purchase as liberal export financing from the aircraft producer's home government (e.g., EXIM bank in the United States) as well as offset and co-production agreements of the kind mentioned above. Much of Airbus' sales have been found in this governmental sector. From 1978 to 1985, 65 percent of Airbus sales (213 A300/A310s) went to government-owned or controlled airlines, whereas only 20 percent of Boeing's sales were in this market niche (67 575/767s).

Impact of Deregulation

From 1938 to 1978 the U.S. Civil Aeronautics Board (CAB) created markets and stimulated demand for advanced technology by controlling entry, pricing and route structure—thus preventing price competition and encouraging service-based competition. The regulated airlines were guaranteed fares high enough to pay for large engineering staffs and for rapid shifts to more sophisticated aircraft. The engineering staffs worked closely with the manufacturers, pushing them for advances in speed, payload and range that might provide an edge in service-based performance, knowing that the costs of such advances could easily be passed on to end-customers via CAB approved fare increases. Relationships between the technologically-sophisticated airlines and the manufacturers were intimate and relatively stable. "Launch customers" would often provide producers launch payments that met 20–30 percent of the producer's working capital needs.

The Airline Deregulation Act of 1978, initiated by Jimmy Carter's CAB chairman, economist Alfred Kahn, changed much of this. On the theory that airlines were not really natural monopolies, but were really naturally competitive, "economists predicted that new airline companies with lower costs and closer-to-the market pricing strategies would drive down fares, and that monopoly pricing and inefficient labor and management practices would be competed away."[24] This appeared to be happening in the early and mid-1980s. A swarm of new airlines forced the established carriers to compete on fares. Traffic skyrocketed, but U.S. airlines began flying more but earning less—experiencing collective operating losses in 1980–82, and low or nonexistent profits for most carriers through 1986. A $7 billion frenzy of "buy-or-be-bought" set in as a shakeout device in the mid-1980s. Airlines eliminated or reduced their engineering staffs

[22]*The Economist*, June 1, 1985.

[23]*The New York Times*, May 7, 1989.

[24]Robert Kuttner, "Plane Truth," *The New Republic*, July 17 & July 24, 1989.

to cut costs, especially in the United States. Purchase decisions began to be dominated by financial and marketing types. Airlines sought to shift the risks of development on to the manufacturers, thus drying up sources of launch capital. Close technically-oriented customer relations became arms-length negotiating relationships. Deregulation, in short, raised cost-consciousness and shifted the basis of competition from performance to price.

The picture shifted a bit in the late 1980s with the re-emergence of an airline cartel. As noted by Robert Kuttner in July 1989: "Something has gone disastrously wrong with airline deregulation. Fares have been rising far faster than inflation. Most of the small, upstart airline companies launched in the early 1980s have gone broke or been gobbled up by the big carriers. The top five airlines control more of the market (71 percent) than they did in 1977, the last year of the fully regulated regime."[25] Profits are back (e.g., industry operating profits were projected to be about $3 billion in 1989, the same as in 1988) as the give-away fares disappeared—and airlines naturally order more new airplanes when they make profits and fewer when they make losses.

Europe may go through some of the same cycle of free market turbulence in the airline industry after the EEC abolishes many restrictions in air travel markets after 1992. This should provide great opportunities for efficient carriers (such as British Airways) and should eventually lead to a reduction in the number of carriers overall if the same U.S. shakeout pattern manifests itself. The international trend to more open skies may bring about an industry dominated by 20 or fewer global airlines, or global alliances of carriers (e.g., the British Airways and United Airlines joint marketing program that integrates their route networks, flight schedules, ticketing and baggage handling).

Airline Operating Costs and Challenges

The composition of operating costs confronted by airlines has changed radically over the past decade and a half. Back in 1973 the cost structure of a typical airline was as follows: crew, 21 percent; fuel and oil, 12 percent; landing and other fees, 19 percent; maintenance and overhaul, 12 percent; equipment, depreciation and rental, 9 percent; and administration, 27 percent. Fuel jumped to 20 percent of operating costs in 1976, 29 percent in 1981, and according to Boeing, 40 percent when oil and jet fuel prices were at their highest.[26] But these prices tumbled by about 60 percent from 1981 through 1987, with the result that in 1988 fuel accounted for only 16 percent of costs.

The dramatic decline in fuel costs has been matched by a dramatic increase in the costs of finance to acquire airliners, whether by leasing or purchase. The capital cost of aircraft, as a percent of operating costs was estimated to be 51 percent on average as of 1988.

Along with rising capital costs, which naturally shift buyer priorities from fuel economy to low acquisition cost, airlines are also concerned about their aging fleets. Attention to the problem of "geriatric jets" was amplified in late February of 1989 when a Boeing-built United Airlines 747 shed a substantial chunk of its fuselage at an altitude of 22,000 feet near Hawaii, sucking 9 passengers to their deaths. More than half of the world's air fleet is now more than 10 years old. (The average plane age in the U.S. in July 1988 was 12.67 years.) Some 1500 jets are near the usual retirement age of 20 years. Along with mounting concerns over the safety of such old planes, many in the industry expect that airports and governments will soon impose stricter noise regulations. Older aircraft, such as Boeing 727s,

---

[25] Ibid.

[26] *The Economist*, May 28, 1983; and *The Economist*, September 3, 1988.

737s or Douglas DC-9s, already do not meet the noise restrictions at a growing number of airports.

Still another concern of the airlines moving into the 1990s is increasing congestion of airways and airports. Sixteen major U.S. airports are seriously congested and plagued by enormous delays. By the year 2000, 42 others are projected to be in similarly dismal shape. Such congestion, combined with traffic growth, naturally pushes airlines toward an interest in higher capacity planes. The logic of flying more people in fewer planes makes sense, as bigger airplanes are cheaper to buy and operate per seat mile than smaller ones.

Airline Passenger Growth

Demand for air travel has traditionally been viewed as a function of two variables: real GNP growth and changes in ticket prices. McDonnell Douglas' formula in the mid-1980s was that revenue passenger miles grew at 1.8 times the rate of GNP. In times of high ticket demand, of course, the airlines cut out their cheap fare offers, thus raising their ticket prices and yield—and demand hence starts to fall.

Over one billion people traveled by air in 1988, and with continued projected growth in discretionary income (much of which goes to air travel, especially for leisure purposes), along with decreases in the real cost of air travel, that number will double by the year 2000. Exhibit 31-6 provides some highlights from Boeing's "Current Market Outlook" issued in 1989.[27] Based on assumptions of no economic recession and relatively stable aviation fuel prices, Boeing forecasts that over the next 15 years, a total of 8417 jet airliners of all types from all manufacturers will be delivered (up from the 6908 it was forecasting a year before). By value, purchases will total $516 billion, including the $96 billion of new jets already on order books. About 70 percent of

[27]*Financial Times*, June 7, 1989.

all the anticipated new aircraft will be bought to meet the growth in traffic, while most of the rest will be to meet the replacement market. Boeing sees 56 percent of sales from now until 2005 being made to non-U.S. airlines, with the Asia-Pacific region (where passenger travel has been growing around 20 percent) as the fastest growing market of the future. Europe, Africa and the Middle East are viewed as relatively declining markets.

The Current Order Boom

The highly cyclical nature of the aircraft industry, with violent swings in demand occurring every 5 to 7 years, is revealed in Exhibit 31-7 which provides data on commercial jet transport deliveries on a global basis from 1958 through 1986. Orders for western producers numbered 726, worth $39 billion in 1987. In 1988, airlines ordered 1047 new jets at a cost of $47.5 billion. The order frenzy to modernize fleets and meet growth plans continued through mid-1989, at which point the five western producers had a backlog of 3500 planes. Part of the hypersonic order boom may have been self-feeding as delivery times on popular models began to stretch out to 1992 and 1993. Customers may have been prompted to place even more orders to avoid having to wait until the end of the century to get new planes.

The boom of 1988–89 featured some new dimensions in aircraft purchasing as compared to former booms, namely bulk buying and leasing. In May 1988 the International Lease Finance Corporation (ILFC) of Beverly Hills, placed firm orders for 100 planes with $3.69 billion from Boeing (with an additional 24 options) and orders for 30 worth $1.35 billion from Airbus (with options for 16). The firm also ordered nearly $1 billion worth of aircraft engines from General Electric (about 70% of them), Pratt & Whitney and Rolls-Royce. International Lease played all sides against each

EXHIBIT 31-6

Boeing's Annual Market Forecast (1989)

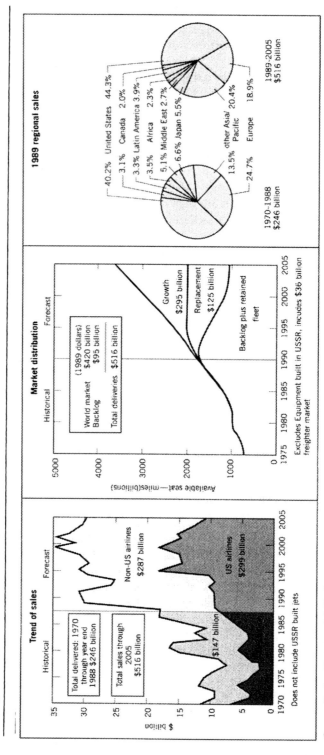

Source: Boeing Commercial Airplanes.

EXHIBIT 31-7

Commercial Jet Transport Aircraft Deliveries

	1958	'59	'60	'61	'62	'63	'64	'65	'66	'67	'68	'69	'70	'71	'72	'73	'74	'75	'76	'77	'78	'79	'80	'81	'82	'83	'84	'85	'86	Total
U.S. Manufacturers																														
707	8	77	91	80	68	34	38	61	83	118	111	59	19	10	4	11	21	7	9	8	13	6	3	2	8	8	8	3	4	972
727						6	95	111	135	155	160	115	54	33	41	92	91	91	61	67	118	136	131	94	26	11	8			1,831
737										4	105	114	37	29	22	23	55	51	41	25	40	77	92	108	95	82	67	115	141	1,323
747												4	92	69	30	30	22	21	27	20	32	67	73	53	25	23	16	24	35	663
757																									2	25	18	36	35	116
767																									20	55	29	25	27	156
DC-8		21	91	42	22	19	20	31	32	41	102	85	33	13	4															556
DC-9/MD-80								5	69	152	203	121	53	45	32	29	48	42	50	22	22	39	23	78	43	51	44	71	85	1,327
DC-10														13	52	57	47	43	19	14	18	36	40	25	11	12	10	11	17	425
L-1011															17	39	41	25	16	11	8	14	24	28	14	6	4	2		249
880/990			14	33	33	16	4	2																						102
Subtotal	8	98	196	155	123	75	157	210	319	470	681	498	288	212	202	281	325	280	223	167	251	375	386	388	244	273	204	287	344	7,720
European Manufacturers																														
Comet	7[a]	19	20	14	13	2	2	1		1																				112
Caravelle		18	39	39	35	23	22	18	18	20	15	11	9	4	5	3														279
Trident							12	10	11	1	11	9	2	11	8	2	8	8	8	8	8									117
VC-10							13	12	7	10	9	2	1																	54
BAC-11								34	46	20	26	40	22	12	10	7	2	2	6	3	2	1	1	1	1					236
F-28												10	11	12	13	19	9	20	17	13	11	13	13	12	10	16	17	12	11	239
Mercury																	6	4	1											11
A300																	4	9	13	16	15	24	39	38	46	19	19	16	10	268
S310																										17	29	26	18	90
BAe 146																										10	10	18	23	61
Concorde																		1	6	2	5									14
Subtotal	7[a]	37	59	53	48	25	49	75	82	52	61	72	45	39	36	31	27	44	45	44	33	37	60	52	58	63	77	71	64	1,481
USSR Manufacturers																														
TU-104																														200
TU-124																														150
TU-144																														4
YAK 40																														1,000
TU-134																														650
TU-154																														860
IL-76																														350
IL-86																														220
YAK 42																														150
Subtotal																														3,584
Total	15[a]	135	255	208	171	100	206	285	401	522	742	570	333	251	238	312	352	324	268	211	284	412	446	440	302	336	281	360	408	12,785

The USSR did not release information on its aircraft programs or deliveries. Program delivery totals are based on western estimates.

[a] Plus 33 Comets 1952–1957.
[b] Excluding USSR annual deliveries.

Source: Boeing Company.

other, with its president admitting that the firm was "trying to get a very attractive deal that locks up a lot of aircraft over a four year period."[28] This blockbuster deal was quickly followed by multibillion dollar orders by American, United Airlines, British Airways and Japan Air Line Corporation. In early April of 1989 the largest order on record was placed by GPA (Guinness Peat Aviation), the Irish Leasing company, for 308 aircraft valued at $16.8 billion (Boeing's share was $9.4 billion, Airbus $4.3 billion and McDonnell Douglas, $3.1 billion). *Financial Times* estimated that by buying in bulk, GPA gained discounts reaching 25 percent.[29] The largest individual order to one producer was made by United Airlines, 8 days after the GPA deal, when it ordered 370 aircraft, worth $15.74 billion from Boeing alone.

Many in the industry contend that these huge orders, especially from the lessors that have not yet been committed to airlines, "have turned the buying of commercial aircraft into a form of commodity speculation, which may have inflated the manufacturer's order books."[30] Analysts also worry that the growing dominance of the big leasing companies may force carriers who need planes to lease, even though they would rather buy.

GPA, however, explained in an ad in 1989 why it ordered 819 new aircraft worth $30 billion:

As the airline industry matures like other service businesses, there is increasing separation of ownership and operation. Leasing makes this possible. Nearly half the U.S. fleet, the largest in the world, is on lease. Worldwide, established airlines are improving their balance sheets through a better mix of owned and leased equipment. New carriers entering the industry with leased aircraft are expanding services to the public and demand for the manufacturers. GPA has defined the concept of the *operating*

lease for new aircraft. An operating lease enables an airline to acquire the use of an aircraft without having to finance its full cost. GPA thus provides airlines with access to a pool of aircraft at relatively short lead times and on flexible financing terms.[31]

Leasing, as a financial tool, allows the airlines to stay as liquid as possible, unburdened by high capital costs, yet able to change both the number and types of planes they fly in a highly competitive and quickly changing market. It also helps them shed aircraft and debt if serious economic downturns develop. In return, the airline, usually for a period of 5 to 7 years, pays a monthly lease rate slightly more than 1 percent of the aircraft's capital value. Thus the monthly rate payable on a standard Boeing 737 purchase priced at $25 million, would be $250,000. Frank Shrontz, Boeing's chairman, noted that "the leasing companies do bring something to the marketplace; they are able to finance airplanes to airlines that we would not be able to. But there is a concern that they could become a buffer between us and our customers. We have to work to see that doesn't happen."[32]

Global Product Wars

Boeing Strategy

According to MIT's Commission on Industrial Productivity, "The Boeing Commercial Airline Company established its hegemony by means of its technological leadership. It has maintained its position by having the right product ready for the market at the right time, by building a family of excellent airplanes that cover most payload and range segments of the market, by establishing an outstanding reputation for integrity and commitment to safety,

---

[28] *The Wall Street Journal*, May 2, 1988.

[29] *Financial Times*, April 19, 1989.

[30] *The New York Times*, April 11, 1989.

[31] *The Economist*, April 22, 1989.

[32] *The New York Times*, April 11, 1989.

and by offering unparalleled product support to its customers throughout the world."[33]

The virtual monopoly of American producers (Boeing, McDonnell Douglas and Lockheed) in commercial aviation from the end of WWII into the early 1980s has typically been linked to the technology stimulus provided by heavily regulated service-driven customers, to the large size of the U.S. market with its widely scattered cities (accounting at its height for as much as 80% of total passenger miles traveled), and to the side benefits of large military projects—namely, validation of new high-risk technologies, underwriting development of jet engines, and providing a legacy of production capacity, tooling and skills in project management and engineering.

Boeing capitalized on these "national" advantages to become the first global competitor in aircraft. As a "first-mover," it acquired scale and learning advantages that have ever since made competing with it difficult. Boeing chose to concentrate R & D and manufacturing (mostly near Seattle) in an effort to become the low-cost producer. It standardized basic product designs, marketing and service functions, recognizing the homogeneity that characterizes aircraft purchasing. It built a highly sophisticated and well-coordinated marketing team on a global basis, that enabled it to proactively and reactively develop sales prospects. Today, to advise its customers, the company stations a network of 198 field representatives in 109 cities in 55 nations. Boeing keeps 15 million spare parts in inventory (and ships one part every 45 seconds) at seven major parts centers in such capitals as Brussels and Singapore.[34] Manufacturers tend to make bigger profits from servicing and spare parts agreements than from aircraft sales themselves.

[33]*Made in America*, op. cit., p. 208.

[34]*Fortune*, July 17, 1989.

Two key elements of Boeing's product strategy are captured in the industry buzzwords of "family" and "commonality." Boeing, early on, chose to develop a full line of aircraft to meet the varied needs of the world's airlines. Each of its basic aircraft types (from the short range twin-engined 737, to the medium range twin-engined 757, the medium to long range twin-engined 767, and the long range 747) are currently available in a variety of squeezed or stretched versions, which means that Boeing can offer more than 20 different models to satisfy variations of seating and range configurations. Exhibit 31-8 shows the positioning of Boeing's stock models versus those of its competitors. The broad line strategy provides a range of economies and cushions ups and downs in any one model's demand pattern. It offers customers the efficiency of "one-stop shopping."

The other buzzword is "commonality," something that Boeing has also championed. The idea here is that of making different aircraft with many parts in common, such that scale economies enable each variant to be produced more cheaply. The benefits from the customer's point of view are lauded in Boeing's advertising, such as this text associated with a two full-page spread displaying a cockpit in *The Wall Street Journal*:

What in the world will Boeing think of next? One important use of high technology is to keep things simple. The cockpits for two Boeing advanced technology jetliners are a case in point. The jetliners are the Boeing 757 and the Boeing 767, close members of the same family. Together they offer airlines many options in airplane size and range. Boeing makes it simple to use the options. For example, even a Boeing test pilot would have to look twice to tell you whether this photo was taken in a 767 or a 757. The cockpits are the same. Even the windows are designed so pilots have the same perspective on takeoff and landing in either airplane. Because the two airplanes feel and fly alike, flight crew productivity is increased dramatically. Pilots trained in one of the airplanes can fly the other—and, after a few hours of additional training, be certified in both.

EXHIBIT 31-8

Range and Seating Capacity of Commercial Jet Aircraft

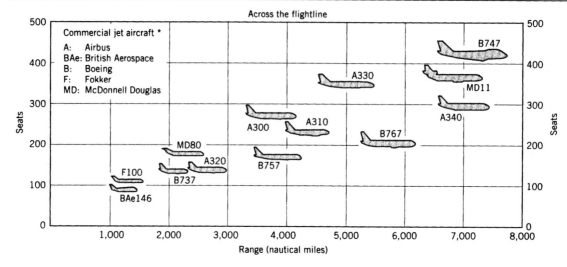

Across the flightline

Commercial jet aircraft *
A: Airbus
BAe: British Aerospace
B: Boeing
F: Fokker
MD: McDonnell Douglas

Seats (y-axis): 0, 100, 200, 300, 400, 500
Range (nautical miles) (x-axis): 1,000 2,000 3,000 4,000 5,000 6,000 7,000 8,000

Aircraft plotted: B747, A330, MD11, A310, A300, A340, B767, MD80, A320, B757, F100, B737, BAe146

Source: Company reports   * Positions may vary with different versions of the same aircraft

Source: Company reports.

Their added productivity helps airlines hold the line on your travel costs. Ground crews are more productive, too. Most avionics spare parts are the same for both airlines, so inventory costs are lower and maintenance procedures are simplified. Practical technology like this is just one more way we're helping to keep flying the best travel value available. It's also proof that when it comes to technology, you can count on the people at Boeing to do it right.[35]

Airbus Strategy

Confronted with extraordinary entry barriers, Airbus chose to enter the global market with a niche strategy by first developing fuel efficient mass transports in the 1970s suited for short to medium distances, with frequent landings and takeoffs—one of the very few segments left

[35] *The Wall Street Journal*, September 27, 1988.

unfilled by Boeing. Exhibit 31-8 shows these A300 and A310 widebody twin-engine models filling the 200 to 300 seat and 3000 to 5000 nautical mile range segments, generally local and regional in nature. Boeing later developed its B757 and B767 models to provide nearby segment competition.

To remain as a durable force in the industry, Airbus knew it had to broaden its "family" to cover a wide array of payload and range segments. So in a very short time (about a third of the time it took Boeing), with the aid of massive governmental launch assistance, Airbus developed the A320 (a twin-engined, 150-seater jet, selling for $35 to 38 million, which as of April 1989 had achieved sales of over 455 against fierce competition from versions of the Boeing 737 and McDonnell Douglas MD-80s series of jets). It then targeted the "long-thin" segments and launched the A330 (a twin-engined 320 seat jet that will debut in 1993 and sell for about $85–90 million) along with its sister A340 (a four-engined, long-distance widebody seating 290 passengers in a 3-class arrangement, costing about $95 million). The A330 and A340 will share about 80 percent of their parts, moving Airbus into the "commonality" game in a major way (as of July 1989, airlines had placed more than 300 orders and options for A330s and 340s). Finally, in May 1989, Airbus announced plans for an A321 (a stretched derivative of its hot selling A320) that would seat 186 to 200 and possibly enter into service by the end of 1994. So by the mid-1990s, Airbus will have a product line that will almost match Boeing nose to nose across the tarmac.

Advanced technology has been another key in Airbus' efforts to overcome enormous entry barriers. It has aggressively exploited advances in materials applications, systems for flight control and safety, and aerodynamics. Airbus adopted "fly-by-wire," a computerized steering system that is lighter, faster and easier to use than the decades old "stick and rudder" hydraulics that American producers still depend on. The technology push is emphasized in Airbus promotion. A recent ad reads as follows:

Saves Fuel for Airlines that Don't Have Money to Burn—Even at today's prices, fuel costs make up a major chunk of your operating costs. And burn up potential profits. But imagine an aircraft that will burn up to 24% less fuel per seat-mile than its closest competitors. Right away you're looking at a major improvement to an airline's bottom line. And you're looking at the Airbus A320. The most technologically advanced, fuel efficient aircraft in the world. Its sophisticated fly-by-wire controls and second-generation flight management system combine to optimize operating and fuel efficiencies. And a unique load alleviation system allows lighter wings to save still more fuel. Of course, you'll discover fuel-saving innovations throughout the full family of Airbus Industrie aircraft. Like major applications of composite materials to reduce weight. And wing-tip fences to reduce drag. Our A300-600R and A310-300 also feature a tailplane trim tank, to cut drag even further. Taken together, all these

Airbus Industrie innovations significantly lower your fuel burn. To improve your bottom line today. And to protect it if the price of fuel should rise tomorrow. Airbus Industrie. The certain choice for an uncertain world.[36]

Boeing calls much of Airbus' technology "bells and whistles."[37] But the razzle-dazzle does inspire comments such as the following: Morten Beyer, president of Avmark, an aviation consulting firm, noting that the A300 will probably have "the lowest seat cost of any aircraft" and is "at least ten years newer than the 767 in terms of the greater use of composite materials, wing design and computer driven controls."[38] Also consider the statement by G. Edward Bollinger, Northwest's vice president for purchasing after the airline placed orders for 100 A320s and 30 A330s and A340s: "The basic decision was made because of the technology of the A320 which is more advanced than what Boeing and McDonnell Douglas are producing."[39] (Note: Northwest was also able to make the smallest downpayment in history in this deal.)

The technological leaping of Airbus stands in great contrast to the incremental innovation product strategies of McDonnell Douglas and Boeing. Douglas has made no commitments to a new generation aircraft for over two decades; Boeing's last effort at radical innovation was its 757 and 767 programs of the late 1970s. The strategy, instead, has been that of developing "derivatives" (i.e., better, bigger or smaller versions of what is already on the production line—(the MD-80 as a retooled DC-9 and MD-11 as a revamped DC-10). The derivative strategy cuts lead times and development costs, thus driving down manufacturing costs and facilitating extensions of the product

---

[36] *Fortune,* Fall 1988.

[37] *The New York Times,* July 5, 1989.

[38] *Financial Times,* April 4, 1989.

[39] *The New York Times,* July 5, 1989.

"family." A Goldman Sachs analyst believes "the industry has proven that this is the way to go."[40] A Merrill Lynch analyst observes that "people want to make hay when the sun shines," they're opting "to build a satisfactory plane two years from now as opposed to the perfect plane six years from now."[41]

The derivative strategy, on the other hand, condemns a model range to aging technology (such as 1960s airframe technology) and runs the risk of not having a new aircraft ready in time if there is a major swing in the market, say toward fuel economy. Boeing, for example, shelved the development of a next generation, fuel efficient 7J7 airplane using advanced "propfan" technology in 1988 when it (and its Japanese partners) learned that potential customers were no longer strongly concerned about fuel prices and also couldn't agree on the right size of the plane. Shelving the risky $3 billion project permitted Boeing to divert an estimated $500 million in 1988 to the increasingly fierce marketing combat with Airbus.[42]

Global Deal Making Wars

The commercial aircraft industry is a brutally price competitive industry, especially during periods of flagrant overcapacity among the plane makers. Each maker is constantly complaining in bitter ways about the others' pricing and marketing tactics. McDonnell Douglas is blamed for pioneering creative pricing. Charles "Pete" Conrad, senior vice president for Marketing for McDonnell Douglas Commercial Aircraft, proclaimed in 1983 that "creative financing is the name of the game. Every-

body builds a good airliner these days."[43] McDonnell developed such successful plane selling ploys as cut rate leases (according to Boeing, "very substantially subsidized") and promises to deliver faster than Boeing. It has successfully exploited price to keep Boeing on its toes (e.g., by pricing its MD-80, a rival of the $31 million B737, at $25 million).

The two American producers accuse Airbus of pricing its planes at rates 10 to 20 percent below what is needed to allow them to break even. (Some estimates in 1988 showed Airbus losing as much as $8 million per plane.) In 1987, for example, McDonnell Douglas was selling its long range MD-11 for about $95 million, while Airbus was offering the A340 (a plane that cost three times as much to develop) for a mere $80 million—"They are pricing 15 percent below the MD-11 for a comparable plane," complained President John McDonnell.[44] Some of the harshest criticism from the Americans has been reserved for Airbus' political dealing in association with aircraft sales, with allegations of landing rights, concessionary export financing, preferential routes, military assistance, atomic power plants, petrochemical facilities, favorable import quotas, positive votes in international organizations, etc. being woven into the selling process with the aid of the French, German, British and Spanish governments.

As for Boeing, its president in 1987 admitted that it "used to sell 727s like you sell Mercedes. This one's nice and there's the price on the window, take it or leave it. But times have changed."[45] Since then, Boeing has not abstained from creative (i.e., often very sweet) dealing; for example, agreeing to take $700 million in convertible Allegis Corporation notes in payment for 747s sold to its United Airlines Division or providing AMR, parent of American Airlines, virtually risk-free "snap-

[40]*The Wall Street Journal*, May 31, 1989.

[41]*The Wall Street Journal*, May 31, 1989.

[42]*The Wall Street Journal*, September 2, 1987.

[43]*The Economist*, May 28, 1983.

[44]*Business Week*, July 6, 1987.

[45]*Time*, May 11, 1987.

back" leases by which the airline could return the planes with just 30 days notice in the event of an economic downturn. Beyond such enticements, the chief complaint against Boeing has been charges of "monopolistic pricing" tactics, chiefly padding the prices of its 747 series jets (where it has no competition) in order to cross-subsidize its shorter haul 737, 757 and 767 airlines that directly compete with Airbus and McDonnell Douglas models.

Airbus charges that Boeing and McDonnell Douglas have for years offered their planes in North America at low prices to try to keep Airbus from establishing itself in this lucrative market. After breaking into the American market with sales to Eastern Airlines in 1978, Airbus indeed struggled, failing to book another order there until it signed Pan Am in 1985. This was partly due to "buy American" traditions but also to real uncertainties as to whether Airbus could provide enough support in terms of spare parts and maintenance. But big breakthroughs came in 1988 and 1989, with big orders for Airbus planes coming from the likes of Northwest, TWA and Air Canada —in part because Boeing's order books became so backed up. In any case, current orders ensure that nearly 500 Airbus planes will be in service in North America by 1995, compared with just 34 in 1985. The Boeing backlog was also a saving grace for Fokker N.V., which in March 1989 received an American Airlines order for 75 F-100s (twin-engined short haul regional jets) and options for 75 others. American's senior vice president for finance admitted that "the U.S. manufacturers were pretty well sold out through 1993–94."[46] An alternative perspective on the successful penetration of North America is provided by Michael Donne, aerospace correspondent for *Financial Times*: "The European manufacturers... now have the right products at the right time and at the right price, and have now also devel-oped a maturer understanding or world markets."[47]

Global Trade Wars

As Airbus' global market share steadily rose during the 1980s, so too did American producer and government complaints that it is unfairly subsidized and thus "distorting" international trade and competition. Boeing, McDonnell Douglas and the U.S. trade representative in the White House mounted a vigorous lobbying campaign, charging that Airbus received governmental loans and subsidies totaling more than $15 billion, most of which were not likely to be repaid. The Commerce Department estimated that European governments provided one-fourth of Airbus Industrie's cash flow of $35 to 40 billion between 1974 and 1987.[48] Boeing's investigators concluded in 1987 that the governments were not just subsidizing nonrecurring costs of developing airplanes, but also were indirectly underwriting production costs by about $3 million per plane.[49] They calculated that Airbus had experienced a total negative cash flow of $10 to 12 billion as of 1984, which, with the launch of the A330/A340, would grow to $15 to 22 billion by 1994 (25 years after the start of the Airbus program). Given such magnitudes, any expectation of repayment was deemed absurd.

Along with the unfair political tactics (arm sales, landing rights, etc.) used to win orders, these subsidy claims led the United States to charge that these Airbus practices contravene key articles (primarily #4 and #6—see Exhibit 31-9) of the Agreement on Trade in Civil Aircraft concluded in 1979 under the General Agreement on Tariffs and Trade (GATT) and

[46]*The New York Times*, April 25, 1989.

[47]*Financial Times*, April 4, 1989.

[48]*Fortune*, July 17, 1989.

[49]*The Wall Street Journal*, September 2, 1987.

EXHIBIT 31-9

GATT Agreement on Trade in Civil Aircraft

ARTICLE 4

Government-directed Procurement, Mandatory Sub-Contracts and Inducements

- 4.1 Purchases of civil aircraft should be free to select suppliers on the basis of commercial and technological factors.

- 4.2 Signatories shall not require airlines, aircraft, manufacturers, or other entities engaged in the purchase of civil aircraft, nor exert unreasonable pressure on them, to procure civil aircraft from any particular source, which would create discrimination against suppliers from any Signatory.

- 4.3 Signatories agree that the purchase of products covered by this Agreement should be made only on a competitive price, quality and delivery basis. In conjunction with the approval or awarding of procurement contracts for products covered by this Agreement a Signatory may, however, require that its qualified firms be provided with access to business opportunities on a competitive basis and on terms no less favourable than those available to the qualified firms of other Signatories. (Use of the phrase "access to business opportunities ... on terms no less favourable ..." does not mean that the amount of contracts awarded to the qualified firms of one Signatory entitles the qualified firms of other Signatories to contracts of a similar amount.)

- 4.4 Signatories agree to avoid attaching inducements of any kind to the sale or purchase of civil aircraft from any particular source which would create discrimination against suppliers from any Signatory.

ARTICLE 6

Government Support, Export Credits, and Aircraft Marketing

- 6.1 Signatories note that the provisions of the Agreement on Interpretation and Application of Articles VI, XVI and XXIII of the General Agreement on Tariffs and Trade (Agreement on Subsidies and Countervailing Measures) apply to trade in civil aircraft. They affirm that in their participation in, or support of, civil aircraft programmes they shall seek to avoid adverse effects on trade in civil aircraft in the sense of Articles 8.3 and 8.4 of the Agreement on Subsidies and Countervailing Measures. They also shall take into account the special factors which apply in the aircraft sector, in particular the widespread governmental support in this area, their international economic interests, and the desire of producers of all Signatories to participate in the expansion of the world civil aircraft market.

- 6.2 Signatories agree that pricing of civil aircraft should be based on a reasonable expectation of recoupment of all costs, including non-recurring programme costs, identifiable and pro-rated costs of military research and development on aircraft, components, and systems that are subsequently applied to the production of such civil aircraft, average production costs, and financial costs.

Source: General Agreement on Tariffs and Trade Agreement on Trade in Civil Aircraft Geneva, 1985.

---

to which the governments participating in the consortium are party. Perhaps the key phrase is in Section 6.2, where the signatories agreed that "pricing of civil aircraft should be based on a reasonable expectation of recoupment of all costs ..."

As explained by Dean D. Thornton, president of Boeing Commercial Airlines in 1985, "we're dealing with a company that fixes prices without regard to costs and that builds planes without receiving an order."[50] The massive financial support for Airbus, according to the American producers, has also inoculated Airbus against the industry's feast-or-famine disease—Airbus is able to build aircraft inventories, which in turn allows for instant delivery and stable production rates. The support has also permitted Airbus to introduce new or derivative models irrespective of profit considerations or competitive offerings, and has also allowed it to introduce technical advances (e.g., "fly-by-wire") for

[50]*Business Week*, September 23, 1985.

which the costs involved cannot be recovered through justifiable price increases.

Airbus Industries, the four European governments involved, as well as the EEC, view the American complaints as sour grapes. Airbus has not received any subsidies, only loans and these will be repaid. The support is absolutely necessary to prevent Boeing from monopolizing the world industry. In any case, Europe is only doing what the U.S. government did many years ago. Even more recently, the United States has provided its own defense and space subsidies: about $23 billion, directly and indirectly, between 1978 and 1987 to Boeing and McDonnell Douglas, according to an EEC study. (The U.S. trade representative complained that the study was riddled with "false conclusions.") Furthermore, Boeing paid no corporate taxes from 1979 to 1984, even though profits totaled more than $2 billion. And if Airbus is "dumping" as the Americans allege, how come Boeing has done so well in Europe while Airbus has struggled to penetrate markets in America? Even the captive European flag carriers of the Airbus parent nations have bought more from Boeing than Airbus. The Europeans also emphasize the U.S. sourcing that goes into an Airbus, as well as plans in the near future to establish production facilities in the United States. In sum, according to Jean Pierson, president of Airbus, "The American competition is making claims against Airbus. But there is a better way for them to compete: drop costs, offer better management, develop better aircraft and stop complaining about the fact that the U.S. no longer holds a monopoly in this industry."[51]

Despite the friendly advice, the battle over unfair subsidies did not ease during 1988–89. The U.S. government filed a formal protest in November 1988 directed at the newest wrinkle in Airbus subsidies. The protest arose from the decision of the West German cabinet to ap-

prove a controversial plan to provide up to $2.3 billion in new subsidies for the German partner of Airbus. In order to persuade Daimler-Benz, West Germany's largest firm, to acquire a 30 percent stake (rising to 51% later on) in Messerschmitt-Boelkow-Blohm, Bonn was pressed by Daimler to shield it up to the year 2000 from losses on Airbus business caused by any movement in the dollar rate down to DM 1.60 (on a worst case basis estimated at $2.3 billion). West German officials justified the new subsidy on the grounds that aircraft sales are denominated in dollars, yet Airbus costs are mainly in European currencies. Unconvinced, the U.S. trade representative accused the West Germans of taking " unilateral action" that "will greatly increase tensions in the trade area," charging that it was "incongruous and indefensible" for West Germany, with a huge surplus, to subsidize a product intended for export and reminding the Germans that it is "an essential tenet of private enterprise that business firms absorb the risks associated with commercial ventures, including exchange rate risks."[52]

In May 1989 the EEC vigorously rejected the U.S. complaint that the West German government was violating the GATT with its exchange rate guarantees. McDonnell Douglas began urging the U.S. trade representative, Carla Hills, to start a formal trade action against the four partners of Airbus. "I don't see any resolution of our dispute as long as European governments are prepared to absorb Airbus' losses or risks," commented Lou Harrington, McDonnell Douglas vice president for the MD-11, while a U.S. government official stated: "We are looking for an agreement that disciplines subsidies and makes sure the aircraft industry is funded more in a commercial way," both in July 1989.[53] Carla Hills a bit earlier warned the Europeans that the

---

[51]*Time*, August 3, 1987.

[52]*The New York Times*, November 8, 1988.

[53]*The New York Times*, July 5, 1989.

United States has "some very strong unilateral tools that we can use in these sorts of circumstances, and we will seriously consider them if our bilateral negotiations do not succeed."[54]

Global Partnering Wars

Almost all of the factors that have normally been used to explain strategic alliances among former or current competitors—accelerating tempo of technology, rising capital intensity, escalating R&D costs, growing neoprotectionism, homogenization of consumer tastes, globalization of competition, etc.—are quite manifest in the aircraft industry. So it is not surprising that from early on, the industry has been a dynamic hotbed of offensive and defensive partnering, with no company working entirely alone. As one observer noted: "The big players in the aircraft industry always gang up to beat a rival or to spread their bets."[55] Such Machiavellian games began in full force with the "Battle of Britain" in the late 1970s when Boeing, McDonnell Douglas and Airbus all individually wined and dined British Aerospace in an effort to deny the flow of resources going to a rival. (Airbus, of course, won.) Similar courting dances have been done in Japan, with Boeing winning the favors of Mitsubishi Heavy Industries, Kawasaki Heavy Industries and Fuji Heavy Industries, first as risk sharing subcontractors on the B767, and then as 25 percent equity partners on the now-cancelled futuristic 7J7 propfan plane. Other examples of strategic partnering (for risk sharing, resource exchanging, market opening and competition eliminating purposes) have been previously dealt with, (e.g., Airbus Industrie, CFM International, and International Aero Engines).

Perhaps the most titillating effort to discover the logic of "competitive collaboration" is found in the six-year story of on-again, off-again discussions between McDonnell Douglas and Airbus. Exploratory talks about the logic of joining forces to go after Boeing began in the early 1980s. From the perspective of John McDonnell, president of McDonnell Douglas, "It would make sense long term for Airbus and us to do something together . . . we have a complementary product line and a dominant competitor."[56] From the perspective of Henri Matre, chairman of Aerospatiale, "Boeing's ambition is to have a complete monopoly, and the only way to counter that is for Airbus and McDonnell Douglas to cooperate."[57]

Really substantive talks began when McDonnell proposed collaboration on production of wide-body jets in the Spring of 1986. McDonnell reportedly suggested that Airbus embrace the MD-11 program and drop its A340, in return for McDonnell joining the A330 program, with Airbus retaining the lead role. The counter proposal of Airbus was for McDonnell to abandon its MD-11 or to offer it instead as the basis for a jointly developed new airplane that would compete with Boeing's cash cow, the 747.[58] Other proposals dealt with merging their efforts in the big 150-seat market. Talks broke off in September of 1986 when it became clear that both sides were committed to launching their own projects (particularly the MD-11 and A340).

Talks resumed in the Spring of 1987, after McDonnell Douglas revived discussions, both with individual Airbus partner companies and their governments (but not the top management of Airbus itself) regarding possible cooperation. Despite the head-to-head competition (analysts at this time were predicting a

---

[54] *Financial Times*, February 2, 1989.

[55] *The Economist*, June 1, 1985.

[56] *The New York Times*, February 22, 1987.

[57] *Business Week*, May 16, 1988.

[58] *The Wall Street Journal*, July 3, 1986.

"bloodbath" in the MD-11–A340 battle), McDonnell still felt it could work together with Airbus "on things that don't conflict."[59] Such projects might include a stretched version of the MD11 or a stretched version of the A320. But despite growing European government pressure on Airbus to link with Douglas, talks in 1987 were half-hearted, as "hawks" inside Airbus (apparently confident of launch aid for the A330/A340 program) decided "to go for the kill"—that is, to hurt McDonnell Douglas with its A340, even though it wouldn't be commercially successful.[60] Talks concentrated on whether McDonnell might agree to a U.S. production line for a stretched version of the A320 in the mid 1990s, but talks foundered when Airbus repeatedly demanded curtailment of McDonnell's plans for the MD94, a plane that would compete with the A340.

With the trade dispute on subsidies heating up, the European governments were much concerned in early 1988 with finding ways to cooling the issue down and averting threatened U.S. trade sanctions. In February 1988, John F. McDonnell made a secret swing around Western Europe in an effort to persuade European finance and trade ministers to pressure Airbus "into agreeing to an alliance with Douglas."[61] Partly as a result, the four nations that support Airbus ordered it on March 1, 1988 to try to cut a deal with McDonnell Douglas by June (at the same time they approved $3.5 billion of launch aid for the A330/A340 program). Talks began again in April, focusing mainly on the idea of a stretched version of the MD11 fuselage, fitted with Airbus A330 wings. The plane would have more than 500 seats and the range to do everything a Boeing 747 would do—but with three engines instead of four, thus making it a

cheaper airplane to fly. This AM300, dubbed the "McAirbus," could also be developed without the cost of going back to the drawing board to build an entirely new airplane.

Talks proceeded quite far on the AM300, but one negotiator admitted in May 1988 that there were an "unbelievable number of differences and drawbacks."[62] As might be expected, they broke down again in September 1988, with the parties saying *"au revoir* but not *adieu."*[63] The order boom, at least for awhile, reduced the urgency of linking up against Boeing. But the fundamental problem of figuring how to simultaneously compete and cooperate remained. As summed up by Alan Boyd, chairman of Airbus Industrie of North America, "It would be like U. S. Grant and Robert E. Lee being asked to share the same bed in a motel prior to Appomattox. I doubt that either of them would get a hell of a lot of sleep."[64]

Performance In and Out of the Industry

How have these competitive wars impacted the financial performance of the key players? Comparing 1988 with 1980 shares of the world commercial aircraft market shows Boeing moving from 80 to 62 percent, Airbus jumping from 7 to 18 percent, McDonnell improving from 7 to 17 percent, and others (i.e., Fokker, British Aerospace), falling from 6 to 3 percent.[65]

Airbus Industrie has yet to make money, and its stated goal of doing so by 1995 may be quite optimistic, if the estimates of negative cumulative cash flow presented earlier in the trade war section are correct. This is even

[59]*The Wall Street Journal*, March 9, 1987.

[60]*Business Week*, July 6, 1987.

[61]*Business Week*, March 21, 1988.

[62]*Business Week*, May 16, 1988.

[63]*Forbes* October 31, 1988.

[64]"The Jet Set," op. cit. (1988).

[65]*Made in America*, op. cit., p. 209.

more true if one considers the losses attributable to selling in dollar terms (as is the practice in the industry) yet paying for expenses in strong European currencies. But Airbus has gained market share, has penetrated the tough North American market, has rapidly expanded production and has substantially broadened its product line. In the July 1989 words of Wolfgang Demisch of UBS Securities, "They're now definitely part of the landscape...Airbus is a spectacular success in terms of what it was designed for—to manifest Europe's capabilities and to regain a leading role in the civil aerospace market worldwide."[66]

Airbus had clearly had another powerful effect, namely helping to cut Boeing's margins in half over the past ten years. Exhibit 31-10 provides profitability data for key U.S. players in the industry, along with comparisons of aerospace with other manufacturing industries. Boeing's profits as a percentage of sales were 9.4 percent in 1978, but only 3.6 percent in 1988. Boeing's return on stockholder's equity reached 30 percent during its 1979 order peak; as of 1988 it was 11.4 percent. As one analyst put it, "They're (Boeing) earning grocery store margins on a high tech product."[67] The key concern of many, including senior Boeing executives, is whether the subpar margins are adequate to finance the next decade's aircraft development.

Exhibit 31-10 shows McDonnell Douglas to be struggling even harder than Boeing. Its operating margin of 2.3 percent for 1988 was lower than Boeing's and lower than the median in practically every industry in America. In April 1989, McDonnell Douglas announced a startling $66 million operating loss for its commercial aircraft division in the first quarter of 1989. The aerospace giant's stock plummeted more than 8 points on the news. It reminded investors once again that since the dawn of the jet age, it has often been easier to make an excellent aircraft than to produce a decent profit.

Challenges of the 1990s

Bursting into the 1990s the entire commercial aircraft industry confronted significant risks and challenges. For the American producers, in particular for Boeing, the following five issues would surely be demanding attention:

Eroding Technological Edge?

Former U.S. astronaut Charles Conrad, a staff vice president at McDonnell Douglas in 1987, put it bluntly: "It galls me that the highest-technology commercial ship about to fly is the A320—and not a US-made plane. In this world technology sells airliners, and we have got to get off our butts fast."[68] Conrad's concerns are shared more widely by the U.S. Aerospace Industries Association that America's competitive and technological edge is eroding because the United States has been exploiting its technology reserves without replenishing them. As summarized by the MIT Commission on Industrial Productivity: "The products on which the current aerospace trade surplus is based draw on technologies developed from 10 to 25 years ago. The American government has since reduced its support of aeronautical research and development both as a percentage of GNP and as a percentage of the NASA budget. Technology validation, the longest and most expensive stage in new-technology development, has become the weakest link in the American R&D chain. With the military providing much less validation and NASA not filling the gap, commercial developers no longer have a solid foundation on which to

[66]*The New York Times*, July 5, 1989.

[67]*Business Week*, May 8, 1989.

[68]*Time*, August 3, 1987.

EXHIBIT 31-10

Profitability Data for Fortune 500 Manufacturing Industries

	1988 Profits as % of:			Total Return to Investors 1988 (%)[b]	Total Return to Investors 1978–88 Annual Average (%)
	Sales	Assets	Stockholders' Equity[a]		
Companies					
Boeing	3.6	4.9	11.4	68.4	15.2
McDonnell Douglas	2.3	2.9	11.0	31.5	11.7
General Electric	6.9	3.1	18.3	4.8	19.0
United Technologies	3.6	5.2	13.7	26.3	12.4
Industry Medians					
Aerospace	3.6	4.9	11.4	19.5	14.4
Apparel	4.3	6.1	17.5	24.1	22.8
Beverages	8.0	6.8	22.8	21.2	20.7
Building Materials	4.5	4.9	−3.3	24.9	12.7
Chemicals	6.9	7.5	16.8	11.0	18.3
Computers/Office Equipment	6.2	5.6	14.7	−11.5	11.9
Electronics	5.1	6.1	16.8	4.8	14.8
Food	2.8	6.7	15.7	24.9	26.4
Forest Products	8.7	8.4	19.8	12.0	17.4
Furniture	5.6	8.8	15.9	8.0	20.7
Industrial/Farm Equipment	4.3	5.4	12.7	20.3	11.3
Metal Products	4.6	5.8	12.7	9.9	16.9
Metals	6.2	8.2	18.4	16.0	11.6
Mining, Crude Oil Production	3.3	1.3	2.4	9.2	10.4
Motor Vehicles and Parts	3.5	3.9	14.5	22.2	17.7
Petroleum Refining	4.7	5.3	15.3	22.9	13.3
Pharmaceuticals	13.5	13.1	23.6	14.7	17.9
Publishing, Printing	7.1	7.3	17.7	8.6	22.1
Rubber Products	4.4	6.4	15.8	31.3	18.8
Scientific/Photo Equipment	5.0	4.9	12.1	1.6	11.2
Soaps, Cosmetics	5.3	8.9	18.5	15.0	17.2
Textiles	3.5	4.7	10.8	18.4	21.3
Tobacco	7.8	6.0	22.5	36.9	25.0
Transportation Equipment	3.1	5.4	13.4	39.2	22.3
Fortune 500 Median	5.5	6.8	16.2	14.1	17.5

[a]Stockholders' equity is the sum of capital stock, surplus, and retained earnings at the company's year end.

[b]Total return to investors includes both price appreciation and dividend yield to an investor in the company's stock.

Source: "The Fortune 500," *Fortune* (April 24, 1989).

apply new technologies, and there are fewer new technologies in the pipeline. The situation with regard to process technologies is even bleaker."[69]

Along with such emerging weaknesses in industry infrastructure, one must also add the points that the European and Japanese governments are spending more heavily than the United States on aviation research, that the demand pull for technology has diminished due to deregulation, that airline engineering has declined, that leasing intermediaries have weakened close customer relationships, and that proliferating strategic alliances have widely and rapidly diffused American technological competencies.

Limits on Radical Innovation?

Many wonder if new realities of American financial markets, including those for corporate control, are reducing the capacities of companies such as Boeing to take big risks and to think long term. We noted earlier the constraints of subpar margins and the risks of concentrating only on incremental derivatives versus substantial innovation. Is Boeing's traditional strategy of hoarding billions of cash to finance huge development projects increasingly running counter to the "gimme-it-now" attitude on Wall Street? What happens to an industry when decision-making moves out of the hands of engineers (or ex-pilots) into those of accountants and marketers? Is fear of the raider stifling innovation? In July 1987, T. Boone Pickens shocked Boeing by threatening to mount a takeover attempt. Boone was probably bluffing, but some airline executives think the Pickens scare contributed to Boeing's reluctance to commit $3 billion to its futuristic 7J7 project. More recent Wall Street reactions are even more telling. When brokers in June 1989 began predicting that Boeing would un-

veil plans for a new stretched version of its 767 at the Paris Air Show, Boeing's share price took a major nose dive on fears that earnings would be pinched by the $2.5 billion development costs attached to it.

Slipping of Quality?

Boeing experienced a lot of bad news during 1988 and 1989 regarding quality control problems.[70] In early 1988 Japan Airlines and British Airways complained about the quality of new planes they were receiving. British Airway's letter to Boeing, leaked to the press, claimed that the "underlying reason" for the wide variety of problems was that Boeing workers "are in general, inadequately trained, possess a low level of basic working skills, and of paramount concern, seem oblivious that they are building aircraft where any mistake not properly corrected, or hidden, represents a direct compromise with safety."[71] In April 1988, an Aloha 737 lost part of its roof in midair, creating concern about older Boeing aircraft. In August 1988 a wide variety of reports of misconnected wiring or fire system plumbing began to emerge. In the spring of 1989 a European governmental group called the Joint Airworthiness Requirements Committee raised concerns about the design of Boeing's new 747-400s, with the Netherlands even threatening to deny operating rights for the aircraft unless certain safety related changes were undertaken. In June 1989 airlines around the world acted to ground most of the worldwide fleet of Boeing 737-400s after three separate incidents involving aircraft flying for British Airways, including the January 1989 crash of the almost brand new British Midland Airways B737-400. This was the first time a Boeing fleet had ever been grounded.

---

[69]*Made in America*, op. cit., p. 214.

[70]*Business Week*, March 13, 1989.

[71]*The Wall Street Journal*, April 11, 1989.

Numerous observers added it all up to conclude that Boeing's reputation for quality had been badly tarnished. One industry expert commented: "Something is wrong...how can Boeing be going wrong this bad this quick."[72] The FAA's top man in Seattle said that Boeing's quality control program is "not as good as it used to be."[73] An American Airline spokesperson stated that "we're going to be vigilant about the kind of product we receive...," while British Airways' planning director summed it up this way: "Boeing has very, very, very, big problems, but we believe them when they say they are in the process of correcting them."[74]

Potential Cost Increases?

Boeing has long enjoyed the lowest production costs in the industry, but such a position does not guarantee a single sale when competing with the likes of Airbus. Boeing announced in May of 1989 that it was going to compensate airlines for 2 to 6-month-late deliveries of its 747-400 aircraft. This was the first time in 20 years that Boeing had missed a delivery schedule, and the company blamed it on late parts delivery, customer to customer variations in cabin configurations, an inexperienced work force, excessive overtime, and lengthy engine certification deliberations. Because of the penalties to be paid, as well as the extra costs of pushing production, analysts estimated that gross margins on the planes would fall to 20 percent, down from 30 percent on previous 747 levels.

Boeing's labor contracts with the International Association of Machinists and Aerospace Workers and with the Seattle Professional Engineering Employees Association, expired in the Fall of 1989. According to the general counsel for the engineers union, Boeing has "got a ton of money in the bank...now its time to share."[75] Boeing could ill-afford a strike in the fourth quarter of 1989, when it must deliver so many 747s.

The biggest challenge is that of greatly expanding production to meet the $80 billion order backlog while keeping costs down and quality up. With new production facilities coming on stream (e.g., a $300 million expansion of its Renton, Washington plant), with an influx of thousands of inexperienced workers, with massive overtime being paid, and with temporary workers being borrowed from Lockheed at bonus rates, the company may be hard pressed to meet its big backlog without letting costs get out of control.

Emergence of New Competitors?

Might new sources of competition be lurking around airports in the 1990s? Might Lockheed get back into the commercial transport business as a partner or subcontractor? Might another Airbus-type consortium emerge in a post 1992 "Fortress Europe" involving Fokker N.V. and other small producers? What about the ambitions of the Chinese and South Koreans? What can we expect from Daimler-Benz if it acquires MBB and becomes an aerospace, electronics and vehicle powerhouse? Will Airbus and McDonnell Douglas ever fall in love?

Most seriously, will the Japanese become an independent force in commercial aviation? The Japanese government has designated aerospace as one of three key technologies for the next century. The industry plays a central role in Japan's strategic vision of its future of sustainable export competitiveness. Yet the aviation business differs structurally from the type Japan has traditionally targeted and succeeded at, (e.g., cars and electronics). The domestic Japanese market for civil transports is

---

[72]*The New York Times*, February 25, 1989.

[73]*Business Week*, March 13, 1989.

[74]*Fortune*, July 17, 1989.

[75]*Business Week*, May 8, 1989.

small and will remain so. Production levels are highly variable, the start-up costs are huge, global competitors are already well entrenched, defense spending is limited, Europeans and Americans are still 10 years ahead in some key technologies, and the strong yen would make it difficult to become a low-cost producer any time soon. Japan's experience with the industry as an independent actor, so far, despite government support, has been disastrous. One example is the aircraft failures such as the YS-11 and Asuka, in the 1960s and 1970s. Another example is the more recent disappointments with the VT-2000 engine built by the IAE consortium in which Japanese companies hold a 30 percent interest—ANA, Japan's second largest airline, refused to buy the engine and chose GE instead.

On the other hand, the Japanese are developing advanced technology in the fields of materials processing, composites, ceramics, electronics and computers—all foundations for aerospace advance. They are already moving down the learning curve of western aerospace technology through their involvement as partners and subcontractors; Boeing buys parts from 200 Japanese firms. The firms are already producing world-class satellites, rockets, radar jamming equipment, fuselage parts and guided missiles. Government aid to jet engines by the early 1980s came close to equaling that given to computers; it exceeded that for telecommunications and energy.

Japan's market structure in aerospace is highly concentrated, with the top three companies producing aerospace products accounting for more than 70 percent of the market; as such, world-class capabilities could develop quickly. It is possible that an initial military emphasis (focusing on hypersonic and supersonic segments) could then be used to provide a foundation for commercial aviation. Perhaps John Harbison, vice president in Aerospace Practice of Booz Allen & Hamilton has it right: "The Japanese are seeking technology leadership rather than cost advantage and will emerge as a dominant force in certain segments of the market much faster than is generally expected."[76]

The Assignment

1. What are the primary determinants of industry demand and supply in this industry?

2. What are the key forces driving competition in this industry?

3. Considering major dimensions of competitive strategy, in what way were the strategies of Boeing, Airbus and McDonnell Douglas similar and different during the 1980s?

4. Should the U.S. government retaliate in some way against Airbus (or its parent firms or governments) if bilateral negotiations do not succeed, from the American point of view, in effectively halting or disciplining government subsidies to Airbus?

5. Does strategic collaboration between Airbus and McDonnell Douglas that is targeted against Boeing (say, co-development and production of a plane that competes with the B747) make sense? What's the probability that such collaboration will actually happen over the next six years?

6. What are the "key success factors" necessary for significant entry into this industry that can be learned from the Airbus experience? Can the Japanese significantly enter the industry by the year 2000?

7. Given the challenges that Boeing confronts moving into the 1990s, what key pieces of strategic advice (say 5 of them) can you offer the firm so as to improve its competitive and financial performance?

[76]*The New York Times*, June 25, 1989.

dom
td.